FIFTY YEARS OF THE DEUTSCHE MARK

Fifty years of the Deutsche Mark

Central Bank and the Currency in Germany since 1948

With contributions by

Ernst Baltensperger, Peter Bernholz,
Christoph Buchheim, Günter Franke,
Jacob A. Frenkel, Morris Goldstein,
Jürgen von Hagen, Carl-Ludwig Holtfrerich,
Harold James, Wolfgang Kitterer,
Manfred J. M. Neumann, Jochen Plassmann,
Rudolf Richter, Klaus Stern, Manfred E. Streit,
H. Jörg Thieme

with a Preface by Hans Tietmeyer
and a Foreword by Otmar Issing

Edited by the Deutsche Bundesbank

UNIVERSITY PRESS

OXFORD
UNIVERSITY PRESS

Great Clarendon Street, Oxford OX2 6DP

Oxford University Press is a department of the University of Oxford.
It furthers the University's objective of excellence in research, scholarship,
and education by publishing worldwide in

Oxford New York

Athens Auckland Bangkok Bogotá Buenos Aires Calcutta
Cape Town Chennai Dar es Salaam Delhi Florence Hong Kong Istanbul
Karachi Kuala Lumpur Madrid Melbourne Mexico City Mumbai
Nairobi Paris São Paulo Singapore Taipei Tokyo Toronto Warsaw

with associated companies in Berlin Ibadan

Oxford is a registered trade mark of Oxford University Press
in the UK and in certain other countries

Published in the United States
by Oxford University Press Inc., New York

© Oxford University Press 1999

First published 1999

The translation is based on the following German edition:
Fünfzig Jahre Deutsche Mark. Notenbank und Währung in Deutschland seit 1948,
Verlag C. H. Beck, Munich 1998

The articles have been translated from the German by
Andrew Watt (articles by Ernst Baltensperger, Carl-Ludwig Holtfrerich,
Manfred J. M. Neumann, Rudolf Richter, Jürgen von Hagen),
Fry & Bonthrone, Language Consultancy and Services (articles by
Peter Bernholz, Cristoph Buchheim, Günter Franke, Wolfgang Kitterer),
Andrew Sims (articles by Jochen Plassmann, Manfred E. Streit, H. Jörg Thieme),
and Neil Mussett (article by Klaus Stern)

With 41 tables and 45 figures in the text

British Library Cataloguing in Publication Data

Data available

Library of Congress Cataloging in Publication Data

Data available

ISBN 0–19–829254–6

3 5 7 9 10 8 6 4 2

Typeset in Garamond
by BookMan Services
Printed in Great Britain
on acid-free paper by
Biddles Ltd., Guildford and King's Lynn

Articles

Contents

Part Two
THE CENTRAL BANK IN THE
CONSTITUTIONAL AND FINANCIAL SET-UP
OF THE FEDERAL REPUBLIC OF GERMANY

Part Three
MONETARY POLICY IN THE
FEDERAL REPUBLIC OF GERMANY

Part Four
ASPECTS OF MONETARY POLICY
IN THE TWO GERMANYS

Part Five
THE INTERNATIONAL SCENE

ANNEX

Presidential Preface

20 June 1948 marks one of the most important dates in the history of German currency.

At that time—the circumstances could hardly have been less auspicious—the *First Act Restructuring the Monetary System (Currency Act)*, passed as part of the legislation of the Allied occupying powers, laid down the legal basis for the new currency. Now, the name Deutsche Mark is just as inseparably linked with reconstruction and prosperity as it is with the high degree of social stability our country enjoys. The present year has seen the fiftieth anniversary of the introduction of the D-mark.

The introduction of the D-mark as a new and the sole legal tender was preceded in March of the same year by the establishment of the Bank deutscher Länder; since 1957, its legal successor, the Deutsche Bundesbank, has been discharging the monetary policy making duties assigned to it by parliament.

The Deutsche Bundesbank, the central bank of the Federal Republic of Germany, is taking the opportunity presented by this anniversary to introduce this book, *Fifty Years of the Deutsche Mark. Central Bank and the Currency in Germany since 1948*, to the general public. The Bundesbank is thereby not merely continuing a tradition of marking such occasions, but is also accounting for its deeds and actions in the area of sovereign authority assigned to it in accordance with its conception of itself as an integral part of the overall constitutional order of a pluralistic and democratic community.

Such retrospection is probably especially appropriate at a time when the preparations for final entry into European economic and monetary union, as agreed upon in 1992 under the Maastricht Treaty, are at the forefront of current debate and upcoming decisions. Historical experience in the monetary sector, however much it may be conditioned by its own time, is still a major source of findings for the present and future as well.

This book is the outcome of joint efforts by many people; thanking them and paying tribute to their achievements is both a duty and a pleasure for me. This applies first and foremost to the authors, whose individual contributions enabled them to leave their specific mark on this book. The design and structure of the book, as well as the overall organization, were the special responsibility of Professor Otmar Issing, sometime Member of the Directorate of the Deutsche Bundesbank.

While the book was at the design stage, Professor Manfred J. M. Neumann tendered advice and Professor (emeritus) Knut Borchardt provided valuable ideas. In the Bundesbank, it was primarily Professor Dieter Lindenlaub, Mr Gerhard Ziebarth, Mr Günter Jost, and staff members of the Economics Department and the Library and Archives of the Deutsche Bundesbank who were involved in preparing this volume.

Last, but not least, my thanks go out to Oxford University Press, which published this volume with its usual care and precision.

It is my hope that the reader will benefit greatly from this volume.

Frankfurt am Main
December 1998

Hans Tietmeyer
President, Deutsche Bundesbank

Foreword

The primary purpose of this volume is to provide as objective and penetrating an overview as possible of half a century of German domestic and external monetary policy, with its various phases of commencement, continuity, and relative calm, as well as of upheaval and reorientation. The basic approach of the book was drawn up in the Bundesbank and thrashed out in a multi-stage process. It constitutes, so to speak, the overall framework for the individual articles, which were eventually commissioned from a distinguished range of eminently well-qualified economists.

As regards the content, the focus was not on a complete, chronological presentation of the different eras of monetary policy. Instead, under the compositional approach adopted here, the development of the economy of the Federal Republic of Germany forms the empirical backdrop to the scientific treatment of major historic and current issues raised by practical central bank policy and their critical assessment by independent experts.

This approach had to be implemented with respect to an exceptionally complex subject. Any such project calls for a certain measure of co-ordination, but at the same time determines the distribution of roles between the entities involved. In this context, the Bundesbank took upon itself the role of the presenter; by arrangement with the authors, this also included the offer to be a party to discussions.

We attached particular importance to not acting strictly along the lines of a purely sequential longitudinal-section survey. Instead, our main aim was, as far as possible, to interpret monetary policy, and the national and international environment shaping it, in a comprehensive sense, as a single, intimately interlinked, overall context.

It should be emphasized once again that the authors from whom these papers were commissioned composed their articles entirely on their own responsibility and in their own name. In the process, some diverging views on, and interpretations of, historical events and developments emerged and, in a number of articles, aspects of issues were examined from individual standpoints and by individual methods. This outcome is fully in line with the chosen approach of a book written by independent experts.

Notwithstanding this diversity, there was some common ground in the efforts to identify the scope for action and the motives behind the domestic and external monetary policy pursued in the past fifty years, to analyse the areas of tension and conflict, and, in particular, to highlight those conditions for success which account for the comparatively pronounced stability of the D-mark at home, and have made it a hard and internationally sought-after currency abroad. Moreover, the strong integrative effect of consistently good money, especially if it is accompanied by a firmly established free market system, under the conditions of a liberal and democratic basic constitutional order, was impressively demonstrated once again by the events surrounding German reunification.

To ensure the maximum transparency of developments and occurrences, the Bundesbank provided technical assistance whilst observing statutory provisions. To this end, it opened its Historical Archives and its document files for evaluation. The requirement of the maintenance of confidentiality with respect to the persons involved was met by arranging that, in accordance with the Federal Archives Act, the files were opened for unrestricted access only to documents that were over 30 years old.

Access was likewise granted to some documents of more recent date, but only on condition that neither names nor quotations from them be extracted and used. Work on the manuscripts was discontinued on 1 May 1997.

The Deutsche Bundesbank wishes the present volume a wide dissemination among the general public, policy makers, and economists. That wish is coupled with the hope that a contribution has been made to a deeper understanding of the opportunities presented by, as well as the limits set to, a domestic and external monetary policy consistent with price stability. May this wealth of past experience find a place in the stability culture of a common European monetary system.

Frankfurt am Main
December 1998

OTMAR ISSING
Sometime Member of the Directorate,
Deutsche Bundesbank

Part One

LEGACY AND FRESH START

I. The Reichsbank 1876–1945

By Harold James

1. Introduction

At the moment of its birth, the Reichsbank stood unambiguously for progress as the mid-nineteenth century conceived it. It was progress, most immediately in terms of new institutional monetary arrangements, which swept away a multiplicity of complicated and limiting regulations and special monetary standards, and created a fairly transparent monetary regime which provided an adequate basis for dynamic economic growth; progress, in commitment to internationalism, and to the gold standard as an international rule; but also progress in domestic politics, in which legislation could be shaped rationally by the participation of greater numbers of people in factual and apolitical debates about public policy. The creation of a German central bank came about as a coincidence of liberal pressure from the South German states, and from liberal leaders in the Reichstag, forcing concessions from a Prussian government initially opposed to the institutional innovation. Its realization in fact marks a high point in the legislative achievement of mid-nineteenth century German liberalism. The resulting institution would be rule-based and thus blind to particular pressures and interests, and not dependent on the personal preconceptions, or involvements, or whims of its managers.

2. Designing a central bank

In the 1860s and 1870s discussion of German monetary reform took place in the context of the drive to political union; but also in a broader setting of a new level of integration in a global economy. The German decision to adopt a gold currency in fact provided the decisive step in making the gold

The author would like to thank Professors Knut Borchardt, Gerald D. Feldman and Peter Kenen for their very helpful and detailed comments on a draft of this study.

standard the world currency system. An international move to the gold standard was well underway before the creation of a united Germany in 1871. In the 1860s, only two countries—Britain and Portugal—had followed a true gold standard, but the adoption of gold appeared attractive to many as the best and easiest way of facilitating international commerce through the creation of a genuine single world currency. The railway and the telegraph cable linked markets more effectively. The 1850s and 1860s were marked by an unprecedented drive for the internationalization of standards and norms, and by a new enthusiasm for international regulation. Money was a very obvious area where internationalization would provide major benefits. In 1866 a US Congressional Coinage Committee concluded that: 'the only interest of any nation that could possibly be injuriously affected by the establishment of this uniformity is that of the money-changers—an interest which contributes little to the public welfare.'[1]

The reasons for the new international enthusiasm for the adoption of gold were complex. Some economists at this time believed it impossible to operate a joint gold and silver standard (bimetallism, or as it was known in the nineteenth century, the 'double standard'): although a succession of very distinguished thinkers, from Leon Walras through Joseph Schumpeter to Milton Friedman, have argued that the bimetallic standard would have had substantial advantages in terms of securing international price stability. Many believed that gold, because it was more precious, would be a more convenient means for transactions. Large weights of money would not be needed; on the other hand, the same consideration made gold unsuitable for everyday transactions. The discovery of large gold deposits in California and South Africa at the end of the 1840s banished the possibility of a scarcity of metallic gold and hence of a deflationary pressure if gold became the world currency. Finally, gold also produced a bandwagon effect: once a critical mass of countries accepted it, further countries would find it irresistible as a means of integration in the newly dynamic world economy. Modern economists thus argue that its adoption was 'path dependent'. The German attitude was decisive for the rest of the world financial system—especially as it was rather predictable that a German choice for gold would place a great deal of silver on the world market and depress the price.[2]

In Germany, gold appeared as the choice of modernity and progress. At the International Monetary Conference of 1867, called by Emperor Napoleon III to urge the general adoption of gold, the Prussian delegate, Meinecke, had given a decisive opinion, which helped the delegates to move to a golden consensus. Though Prussia was on a silver standard, he said that

[1] Russell, 1898, p. 35.
[2] Cf. Gallarotti, 1993, pp. 39–42.

'it would be necessary to prepare the change from one standard to another by measures of transition'.[3] Germany's foremost monetary economist, Adolf Soetbeer, was the official reporter of the Fourth German Trade Assembly which met in Berlin in October 1868. It produced a recommendation for the adoption of a single standard, based on a gold coinage with a 25 franc piece and a gulden of 2.50 francs. The conclusion was that 'the speedy attainment of a practicable monetary unity in all German states is now, as formerly, regarded as exceedingly important and desirable'.[4]

The move to gold became increasingly urgent with the prospect of a general silver glut following the opening of the gigantic silver lode in the American state of Nevada. But there was a parallel political dynamic. The move to monetary unity in Germany at the same time became urgent because of the acceleration of the political process of unification. Institutionally the establishment of the 1867 North German Confederation, with a federal parliament, was a decisive step. The outstanding British monetary expert, Walter Bagehot, commented in 1869 that: 'Germany has a currency to choose; none of her many currencies which have descended from her divided states are fit to be her exclusive currency now that she is one. If things remain as now, she is sure to adopt the French currency; already there is a proposal in the Federal Parliament that she should take it.'[5]

Of course, things did not remain as they were. The Franco-Prussian war of 1870–1 turned events in a different direction. The coinage system adopted after 1871 was not the franc-based internationalist version recommended by Soetbeer and the Trade Assembly, but rather a Prussian-centred reform which corresponded better to the actual distribution of political power in the new Prusso-centric Empire. The political character of the new currency arrangements was underlined by the fact that the necessary gold reserves came in large part from the 5 billion gold franc indemnity paid by France under the terms of the Treaty of Frankfurt.

The critical legislation was the proclamation of 4 December 1871, on the minting of imperial gold coins, and the Coinage Act of 9 July 1873. The basic unit of account would be the Mark, worth one tenth of the 'Reich Gold Coin', and valued as M 1,395 for a pound of gold. The Thaler of the Prussian north was given a conveniently round figure of M 3, while the southern Gulden was valued at the arithmetically complicated level of M 1.71. Silver Thaler coins in fact continued to circulate until 1907, and it was technically only then that a full gold currency operated, although the

---

[3] U.S. Senate, 1879, p. 826.
[4] U.S. Senate, 1879, p. 728.
[5] Russell, 1898, pp. 90f.

remaining German note-issuing banks did not usually pay out silver on demand against their banknotes.[6]

On its own, currency reform was not enough. The introduction of a gold standard did not necessarily imply the establishment of a central bank. Many central banking functions could be handled quite adequately by existing, private banks. Even the business of selling silver in the transition to the new monetary regime was handled by the (private) Deutsche Bank, through its branches in Asia (the large quantities involved would have depressed prices on the London market, and led to losses for the Reich).[7] But the private banking world in general was in turmoil, and needed some sort of regulation.

Germany faced a general monetary and banking chaos. Some foundation for the simplification of coinage had already been given by the Dresden Coin Convention of 1838, but that had left the Thaler and Gulden as two rival systems. The 1857 Vienna Coin Treaty gave the Thaler some preeminence, with legal tender status throughout the Zollverein, but the coinage issue was still not solved. In the boom of the mid-century, as the demand for money rose with the general level of economic activity, note banks were created, mostly in the form of private banks licensed by the German states. They tried to make up for the shortage of circulating money, and provide a remedy for the complexity of a situation in which coins of different values and issued by different states were circulating in parallel. There were thus some forty different types of state-issued paper money, leading to obvious difficulties in detecting forgeries. Some micro-states, such as Anhalt-Bernburg and Anhalt-Köthen succumbed to the temptation to over-issue money.[8] The profits of the note banks depended on their success in issuing as many small denomination notes as possible, and keeping them in circulation. In 1851 there had been nine of these note banks, while by 1857 there were already 29.[9] By the beginning of the 1870s, there were thirty-three banks, issuing around one and a third billion Marks[10] (which represented around 8 per cent of the gross domestic product).

The multiplicity of banks made for instability, as in any potential panic it was clear that the note banks would be unable to pay out. If this proliferation of fundamentally unregulated banking had continued, German history might well have resembled the monetary history of the United States in the nineteenth century, with its periodic rounds of crises of confidence and bank failures, followed by outbursts of populist anger. As it was in Germany,

[6] Cf. Borchardt, 1976, pp. 8f.

[7] Cf. Barth, 1995, pp. 20f.

[8] Cf. Sommer, 1931, p. 57.

[9] Cf. Dierschke and Müller, 1926, vol. 1, p. 6.

[10] Cf. Born, 1991, p. 262.

there were widespread panics in 1857 and again in 1866. In 1866, if the Prussian armies had not defeated Austria at Königgrätz, there would have been a major financial collapse in Berlin.

One of the aims of the banking reform, according to its major author, was to ensure through a 'douce violence' that the note banks would give up their issuing activities.[11] While in the first years after unification, the central monetary problem had been the choice of a monetary standard, the debate thus shifted increasingly to the suitable institutional design of a mechanism for restraining speculative tendencies and banking abuses. This consideration became central after the boom and then the crash (*Gründerkrach*) of 1873. Many of the newly founded joint stock banks were created in order to launch industrial companies, and a speculative mania developed. In 1873, a number of banks failed, including one of the largest of the new banks, the Quistorpsche Vereinsbank.

The second major issue was a consequence of internationalization and the adoption of the gold standard. The international linkages created by gold required a new approach to monetary management. After 1874, a massive drain of gold from Germany began, with a loss of M 900–950 million (more than the total of Reich Gold Coins issued up to 1873).[12] The Reichstag discussion of whether a new central bank would be needed took place in the context of actual gold losses, and a fear of even greater outflows. A central bank would, it was argued, be the best mechanism to orchestrate an appropriate response to a flow of precious metal. The first President of the Reichsbank, Hermann von Dechend, who never became a convinced adherent of mono-metallism, later characteristically defined the institution's 'principal task' as 'providing for the currency and sustaining monetary circulation in the country'.[13] It was in the context of protecting German gold from flowing out that the phrase 'guardian of the currency' was first used.

The argument for a Reichsbank was put most powerfully in the 1870s not by the Reich or the Prussian government (the latter was actively opposed) but by a liberal deputy, Ludwig Bamberger, when a draft banking act not including a central bank was brought for debate to the Reichstag (16–18 November 1874). The course of the parliamentary discussion in fact proved to be a striking instance of institutional design being shaped by the legislature, and not—as a stereotype view of the *Kaiserreich* as an authoritarian system would suggest—from above, by Bismarck.

Bamberger argued that a central bank could control credit conditions (and

[11] Cf. Deutscher Reichstag, 1889–90, p. 619.
[12] Cf. Helfferich, 1898, p. 378.
[13] Deutscher Reichstag, 1889–90, p. 203.

so avoid speculative excess) through an appropriate use of its major policy tool: the purchase of bills from commercial banks. Without such support, the large flows of money across national boundaries that might result from the adoption of the gold standard, might threaten the structure of credit, and the Reichsbank would not be able to support private banks. The major function of a new central bank was thus not so much the provision of monetary stability—that was to be secured through the gold standard—but as a lender of last resort to stabilize the financial system.

The discussions in the Reichstag had decisively affected the outcome of the debate on the limits to be placed on note issue of the new institution. An obvious model to take would have been the English system. Many liberals liked to think of Britain as a general reservoir of enlightened institutional experience. The 1844 Peel Act fixed the note issue of the Bank of England as in part a fixed amount, based on confidence in the Bank (the 'fiduciary issue'); above this amount, notes could only be issued if they were fully backed by gold in the Bank of England's reserves. It was this constraint that terrified most Germans. A sharply defined limit, such as that provided by the Peel Act—it was feared—would cause business failures. Though it was possible for the British parliament to authorize a temporary suspension of the limits of the Act, this would be a clumsy, and noisy way of dealing with the crisis. Instead, the Reichsbank was permitted to issue notes 'according to the needs of its business', if one third were backed by current German money, Reich notes, or gold in bars or foreign coins. The rest of the note issue would be backed by discounted bills or checks.

The Reichsbank's role as a central bank was strikingly incomplete. While the Preußische Bank disappeared into the Reichsbank, the state banks of Bavaria, Saxony, and Württemberg continued to print notes. The Reichsbank could only issue notes of M 100 or more. Since this minimum sum corresponded to four times the monthly income of a textile worker, the general public would never be exposed to the Reichsbank's paper. Finally, the Reichsbank's note privilege was granted for a limited time only, and an intensive debate about the bank's policy took place when the law was renewed after 15 years.

The Reichsbank Act contained a mechanism to limit the tendency to issue currency. The first M 250 million of the note issue (in 1899 the sum was raised to M 450 million) would be free of tax; beyond that a tax would be levied on notes exceeding the one-third coverage requirement. This taxed issue of notes was intended to be exceptional, but the exception was not as spectacular as the operationally equivalent business of suspending the British Bank Act. As envisaged by the authors of the Reichsbank Act, the tax would create an incentive for the Reichsbank to avoid the costly losses entailed by an issue of notes not adequately covered by gold; and indeed for most of its pre-war history, the Reichsbank's notes were duly covered. Occasionally, however, the Reichsbank entered the 'note-tax area'.

The practical conduct of the Reichsbank was further shaped by its legal form. Much of the structure resembled that of the Preußische Bank, which it replaced. The Reichsbank was supervised by a Bank Curatorium, consisting of the Reich Chancellor as chairman, and four members, meeting quarterly, who represented the federal German states. The management of the bank consisted of a Reichsbank Directorate, under a President, following the general principles of conduct set by the Reich Chancellor. It could thus on occasion be subjected to direct political commands, as on the famous occasion in 1887 when, for foreign policy reasons, and at Bismarck's insistence, the Reichsbank forbade the *Lombardierung* (use as a security deposit against loans) of Russian bonds.[14] This was hardly the action of an independent central bank. Even entirely autonomous central banks, such as the Bank of England, however, at that time took political and especially foreign policy considerations into account.

Like the Preußische Bank, or the Bank of England, the Reichsbank was a privately owned institution, with annual meetings of shareholders, who would be represented in between meetings by a Central Committee of fifteen members, of whom at least nine would live in Berlin, which would meet on a monthly basis and receive reports from the management. The Central Committee would also approve the amount used to purchase commercial paper. Three deputies appointed by the Central Committee would participate in the meetings of the Directorate. Profits would be distributed to the owners in the shape of an ordinary dividend of 3.5 per cent; above this, one quarter went to the shareowners, and the rest to the Reich. In order to emphasize (and maximize) the practical character of the Reichsbank as a profit-oriented institution, officials of the bank were paid in part on the basis of profits in their particular area.

This semi-public and semi-private character of the Reichsbank may appear puzzling in historical retrospect. But in one of the final Reichstag debates on the Reichsbank, the balanced character was depicted as critical to the successful operation of the new institution. The balance was actually a neat expression of the new Empire—a mixture of private interest and a new public framework. Progress, in this period (and maybe in every age), meant using the private interests and adapting them to produce an outcome that corresponded to the public good. The commission that had drafted the legislation, whose rapporteur was Bamberger, explained that the capital of the bank would be safer if it were not owned or managed directly by the

---

[14] Cf. Holtfrerich, 1988, pp. 105–59.

state.[15] This calculation reflects the skilful character of the compromise of the early 1870s, when the task for public policy lay in stabilizing a volatile and immature financial system that shuddered quickly and spectacularly from boom to bust. If the bank had been managed by the state alone, there would be too great an inclination to bail out banks and businesses in a crisis of confidence; if the private interests were represented, there would be an incentive to limit support to as short-term a basis as possible.

This argument was made again and again, in particular by the political left, in the course of the next 50 years in defence of the Reichsbank's relative autonomy; and it was often given a distinct political edge. In other words, it was those groups excluded from power especially in the more authoritarian post-1879 Empire who saw in the Reichsbank's independence a desirable counterweight to the power of the Prussian-German state. The liberals pointed out that in progressive states central banks were controlled by private owners: 'that in no large civilized state, with the exception of Russia, is there a central bank owned by the state; rather they are all based on private capital'.[16] By the first decade of the twentieth century, the socialists too, who now played a much more central part in the political debates, elaborated this case.

The two predominant economic concerns of the Reichstag debates on the creation of the Reichsbank—the preservation of the gold stock and the appropriate response to financial distress—were fully reflected in the eventual behaviour of the new institution. Institutionally, the Reichsbank disliked the idea of gold movements. In the earlier years of the Reichsbank's activity, it used technical, and controversial, ways of limiting the activity of gold exporters: refusing, for instance, to provide gold at the shipping point of Hamburg, and insisting on Berlin. In addition, for a short time between 1879 and 1881, it bought gold at prices over the official gold price.[17] Most consistently, it used its discount policy and its bill portfolio as instruments in order to achieve a target in terms of its gold holdings.[18]

Secondly, until the experience of hyper-inflation and financial destabilization in the 1920s forced a rethinking, the Reichsbank was always prepared to act as lender of last resort to the German banking system, even when such support became increasingly problematical in the years preceding the First World War. 'The Reichsbank is the last support of the German home market', argued the commemorative volume published in 1900.[19]

[15] Cf. Deutscher Reichstag, 1874–5, p. 1356.
[16] Deutscher Reichstag, 1889–90, p. 193.
[17] Cf. The Reichsbank, 1910, p. 236.
[18] Cf. Giovannini, 1986.
[19] The Reichsbank, 1910, p. 41.

The legislative makeup of the Reichsbank had created a near perfect instrument for the management of a gold standard operating not on the basis of gold movements (specie flow) but through the regulation of domestic credit policy. The major reason for the Reichsbank to change the rate of interest on bill discounts lay in changes in the Reichsbank's liquidity: in particular the ratio of banknotes outstanding, and of short-term liabilities, to gold and silver. Thus if discounts by the Reichsbank rose—either because its rate was closer to the (generally lower) prime rate, or because interest rates abroad increased—it would be likely to increase the discount rate. If it lost gold it would respond similarly.[20] It is remarkable that an institutional arrangement could be found that obliged the rather unwilling managers of the bank to bend themselves to the golden rule. Von Dechend, in particular, had originally been so antagonistic to the proposed transition to gold that he took the highly unusual step of addressing a direct petition to the *Kaiser*, expressing the conviction that 'the planned Banking Act was in the highest degree dangerous to the welfare of the country'.[21] The manner in which von Dechend submitted to his new responsibilities is a striking (and encouraging) demonstration of the triumph of rules and laws over personal judgement.

As had been established in the initial debates through the rejection of a Peel Act type regulation, the Reichsbank would always be in a position to buy domestic bills. Bills became as a result a practical substitute for money. The cash value of commercial bills provided an absolutely secure basis for the expansion of German banking. This security provided a dramatic contrast with the uncertainty prevailing in most other banking systems. The German experts interviewed by the US National Monetary Commission stated that 'the great strength of our financial system in Germany is the Reichsbank. Under that system the question of our own cash reserve is of secondary importance, as we can at all times convert our holdings of commercial paper into cash at the Reichsbank.'[22]

There was an additional peculiarity, in that the Reichsbank did not only purchase bills from the banking system, but also used its own wide branch network. It bought bills directly from a wide range of customers. A total of 66,821 persons and firms were eligible to discount at the Reichsbank in 1910, of which only 2,361 were bankers.[23] Some of these customers were extremely small businesses, and the Reichsbank even thought of this

---

[20] Cf. Sommariva and Tullio, 1986, pp. 83–120.
[21] Sommer, 1931, p. 109.
[22] National Monetary Commission, 1910–11, pp. 373ff.
[23] Cf. The Reichsbank, 1910, pp. 154–7.

function as 'a certain social policy via the giving of credit'.[24] Some bills were as small as M 10. Since the discount rate at the Reichsbank was usually above the rate for prime bank bills, first class customers often chose to go to the commercial banks rather than to the Reichsbank. The reduced quality of the Reichsbank's bill portfolio inevitably led to occasional payment problems.

For an initial period, there were inevitably doubts and uncertainties as to whether financial panics could be avoided in this way. But when the system had been operating long enough for the credibility of the Reichsbank guarantee to be fully established, the result was a tremendous expansion of commercial banking after the 1890s, on a scale which largely threatened the Reichsbank's control of the German money supply. The Reichsbank was rapidly surpassed in size and importance by the large Berlin banks.[25] While the problem of the first 20 years of the Reichsbank's operations lay in establishing its credibility, after that its solidity led to a danger of a loss of control.

The crisis-minimizing quality of German monetary management in the pre-war period has attracted many plaudits. The Hamburg banker and monetary theorist Friedrich Bendixen in 1909 concluded: 'we Germans are so lucky to have an ideal solution to the problem of a central bank constitution, and intelligent observers abroad envy us.'[26] The institutional arrangements affected the course of German business development. A recent commentator, McGouldrick, has noted that 'German cycles were mild compared either to those in other countries at the time or in West Germany after 1950'. He comes to the conclusion that 'intentionally or not the Reichsbank thus reached a goal that has eluded modern central banks at different periods, namely, avoiding procyclical movements in its money liabilities'.[27] This type of point is likely to occur particularly to American analysts, because the contrast with the history of the United States (or of Latin America at this time) is very stark: there, the absence of a central bank, and the speculative character of banking, caused repeated failures of confidence, and gave economic development a much jerkier shape. Whether the absence of major financial crises increased the overall growth rate is debatable; but it certainly made growth smoother, and perhaps also less politically contentious for the moment.

[24] Eynern, 1928, p. 35.
[25] Cf. Eynern, 1928, p. 45.
[26] Bendixen, 1920, p. 137; cf. also The Statist, 12 Oct. 1901.
[27] McGouldrick, 1984, pp. 312, 319; cf. also Lewis, 1978, pp. 22f.

3. The practice of central banking

In its early years, the major activity of the Reichsbank lay in the attempt to build up the gold reserve. The bank bought large quantities of silver coin (2.9 million kg from 1876 to 1878) and sold it for gold on the London market. But the requirement of launching gold coins into circulation meant that the gold reserve fell dramatically. At the beginning of 1876, gold worth M 346 million had constituted 78 per cent of the Reichsbank's reserves; at the end of 1878, M 180 million of gold only amounted to 38 per cent of reserves.[28] The sale of silver was halted in May 1879, as the heavy volume of sales had helped to push down the world silver price, and made the gold purchase policy expensive. In the early 1880s, the Reichsbank lost reserves; but between 1885 and 1895 it was able to make major purchases of gold— even though the silver price continued its dramatic decline—and the reserve ratio rose (in some months it was even more than 100 per cent). This allowed the discount rate to stay at relatively low levels, sometimes as low as 3 per cent. The favourable reserve position, accompanied by low discount rates, helped to build confidence in the system.

The semi-autonomous character of the bank remained a source of controversy. The prolonged price deflation of the 1870s and 1880s, which was in part a consequence of the worldwide move to a gold standard led to a demand for a change in monetary policy. Debtors argued that a looser credit policy would stimulate business; and then called for greater government control of the banking system in order to promote a beneficent reflation. This push was a persistent theme of the political right. In the new century, a new wave of public criticism went along with a period of self-reflection and self-doubt in the Reichsbank. The most obvious problem was that maintaining the level of gold reserves had become again a very problematical task.

After the mid-1890s, credit conditions had changed dramatically. A very large expansion of commercial bank credit began, and at the same time new gold discoveries in Alaska and South Africa increased the international supply of metallic money. The rapid development of German banks produced a domestic monetary expansion, but one which generated apparently greater risks of a crisis of confidence. In 1901 the Reichsbank lived up to its task of lender of last resort. A series of bank runs brought down the Dresdner Kreditanstalt and the Leipziger Bank; and even the large Dresdner Bank lost M 60 million deposits because its name suggested a close association with Saxony.[29] The Reichsbank's success in halting the runs

---

[28] Cf. Borchardt, 1976, p. 34 and Bopp, 1953, p. 33.
[29] Cf. Eynern, 1928, pp. 40f.

rapidly produced a moral hazard problem: it had been *too good* as a lender of last resort.

The aftermath of the crisis encouraged German banks to expand lending and reduce their cash reserves and their deposits with the Reichsbank. If the Reichsbank were always prepared to discount bills, it was clear that bills could be treated as an immediate (and profit-bringing) reserve. From 1890 to 1910 the cash reserves of German joint stock banks fell as a proportion of liabilities in the year end reports from 15 to 7.6 per cent.[30] The Berlin big banks were able to use the Reichsbank's implicit guarantee of their bill business to extend their balance sheets quickly. As a consequence, their bill portfolio grew very much more quickly than that of the Reichsbank, which lost contact with the market—except in periods of crisis.

The dangers of over-confidence became evident in 1907, when an international monetary crisis originated in the United States. One result of 1907 was a new debate about what international action could be undertaken to prevent such worldwide crises of confidence—now made more simultaneous because of the transfer of news through the transatlantic telegraph cable. Some past crises had been overcome cooperatively. In 1907 the Banque de France gave an advance to the Bank of England and agreed to discount first class American bills in order to help the New York market.[31] But after 1907 Germans saw no possibility of similar actions: in part because of the magnitude and simultaneity of financial crises, but also in part because the deteriorating international political situation made foreign help look increasingly problematic. The 1911 crisis associated with Morocco was a telling example. In any case, Germany had played little part in the central bank cooperation of 1907, while at an early stage of the crisis even the Oesterreichische Nationalbank had stepped in to supply the Bank of England and the Banque de France with gold.[32]

The old demands of the right were repeated, but now in a different context. Though there was no longer a danger of deflation, they asked for the creation of 'a silver wall around our golden treasure'; and for measures to prevent the loss of reserves. Gold should be national, and should not be allowed to move in accordance with the need to make international payments. This discussion, polemical and politicized though it was, reflected a major economic problem that entered into theoretical reflections as well. The classical way of understanding the gold standard had been in terms of a price–specie flow, in which metal moved in response to price differentials

[30] Cf. Lumm, 1912, p. 182.
[31] Cf. 'Zur internationalen Börsenkrisis', in: Berliner Actionair, 813, 6 Nov. 1907 and 818, 23 Nov. 1907.
[32] Cf. Volkswirtschaftliche Wochenschrift, Vienna, 28 Mar. 1902.

that produced trade imbalances. The flow of gold compensated for the flow of goods. The conventional understanding was that Germany's trade deficit in the years before the First World War was a consequence of high population growth leading to increased imports.[33] By the 1900s, however, German economists increasingly argued that it was not the trade balance that was driving central bank policy as revealed in discount rates, but the discount policies of other countries: that the exchange rate could be viewed as an outcome of interest rate differentials, given that there was only a very remote probability of an alteration of exchange rate parities (i.e. an abandonment of gold) by one or more of the major central banks. The determinant of interest rates was now increasingly the pattern of international borrowing, and the capital account rather than the current account was driving German monetary developments.

Criticisms of the Reichsbank led to a change in its management. The President, Richard Koch, resigned on grounds of age (he was 73). The new President, appointed at the beginning of 1908, was a vigorous civil servant, Rudolf von Havenstein, who had been the head of the Preußische Staatsbank (Seehandlung) between 1900 and 1908, and was believed to possess a surer hand than his predecessor in deflecting and defusing agrarian criticisms of bank policy.

Havenstein's defence of the principle of central bank independence depended on the notion that the Reichsbank was not free in its discount policy. 'The Reichsbank—as has often been said—cannot set the discount rate but only follow the market, and has only limited influence.' It followed that the bank's monetary policy 'is not set by the financial needs of the state and is not influenced by the fiscal interests and wishes of the state or the even more undesirable interests of the government or the political parties'.[34]

The immediate response to the loss of reserves in the 1907 panic had been to try to extract gold from circulation by issuing new notes: in 1906, 20 and 50 Mark notes were issued; and the Reichsbank's notes at last became legal tender at the beginning of 1910. But a more general response of the Reichsbank lay in an attempt to curb the expansion of the commercial banks, to restrain what Havenstein, only three days after he came into office, called 'over-production and over-speculation'.[35] If interest rates were to fall, this could come about only if the big banks limited their credit policy and if the state cut back on the military expenditure consequent on the accelerating arms race.[36]

---

[33] Cf. Glasenapp memorandum of 10 Mar. 1922 (Bundesarchiv Koblenz and Berlin R 2501 [Reichsbank] 6430).

[34] Deutscher Reichstag, 1907–08, pp. 7072f.

[35] Deutscher Reichstag, 1907–08, p. 2414.

[36] Cf. Lumm, 1912, p. 180.

From the standpoint of the Reichsbank, the solution was to oblige banks to present bi-monthly balance sheets (which appeared after 1912). But such a solution hardly dealt with the immediate problem of what seemed dangerously low cash reserves. The Reichsbank's demand for limitations on the credit-giving of banks took an increasingly militant tone. The Reichsbank's problems stemmed from a theoretical framework that was increasingly inadequate to the task of monetary management. The theory that lay behind the Reichsbank's approach was the 'real bills doctrine', an approach advocated in the great theoretical debates of the early nineteenth century by the 'banking school' (in opposition to the 'currency school', whose views resembled more those of twentieth century quantity theorists). This vision of economic management saw value as being generated by trade and commerce; so that as long as credit was granted on the basis of trade, it could not destabilize or undermine the real economy. Its practitioners distinguished 'commercial bills' from speculative or 'finance bills', which should be avoided. According to the leading economic treatises and textbooks (Gerhart von Schulze-Gaevernitz, Felix Somary, Adolf Weber), banks did not create money, but only lent funds deposited with them.[37] As commercial banks discounted more and more bills, the central bank was no longer in a position to make the distinction between commercial and finance bills in normal times. And as international capital markets expanded, the financial bill became a standard form of international borrowing.

The dominance in Germany of the 'banking school' explains why the Reichsbank's management insisted so vehemently on their function as lender of last resort, and why they were so perplexed and so helpless in the face of the expansion of bank credit. This philosophy, however, was not simply a consequence of an abstract intellectual preference. It was the concrete product of the Reichsbank's origins in the unstable situation of the early 1870s, when financial panics and massive instability had seemed to challenge and undermine the political institutions of the new *Reich*. At that time, the Reichsbank's major *raison d'être* had been seen as the prevention of banking collapse (it was not needed for the operation of the gold standard, which could have run automatically). By the 1900s, the Reichsbank support had become so obviously effective that banks could use it as the basis for credit expansion, financed in part by borrowing from abroad, which corresponded to current account deficits and represented a constant threat to the Reichsbank's other major function, as keeper of Germany's gold.

The dilemma of the Reichsbank—whether to keep its gold reserve by raising interest rates or by disciplining banks to lend less—had an additional political element that became increasingly significant in discussions before

[37] Cf. Ellis, 1934, pp. 395f.

1914. The Reichsbank's gold reserve was a military asset that would permit Germany to fight a war. Havenstein was not just a banker—he was regarded as the vital mobilizer of resources for the state's military requirements.[38]

4. Inflation and hyper-inflation

The First World War brought to an end the era of liberal internationalism, with its free movement of capital and of goods (subject only to tariffs), and its monetary stability. In every country, old certainties were destroyed, and one casualty was the general expectation of monetary stability, which was universally deplored. The German inflation and hyper-inflation is one of the most notorious, and most studied, monetary catastrophes in human history. By November 1923, the Mark had sunk to $1/10^{12}$ of its pre-war value against the dollar. In the last months of the German inflation the central bank believed that it needed to respond to the real fall in the value of currency by producing more currency at faster rates. The Reichsbank boasted of the efficiency of its 30 paper factories and 29 plate factories producing 400,000 printing plates to be employed by the 7,500 workers in the Reichsbank's own printing works, as well as by 132 other printing firms temporarily working to satisfy the need for currency.[39]

The fundamental cause of the German inflation was the First World War, and the methods with which the military conflict and its aftermath were financed.

1. In July and August 1914, almost everyone expected a *short war*. The financial measures originally adopted were intended to deal with a short-term emergency, as a bank run developed in July 1914, as well as with meeting the immediate costs of war. The gold convertibility obligations of the Reichsbank Act were suspended, as were the limits on the discounting of treasury bills. In addition, loan bureaux were established to provide credit on the security of public sector paper, including that of the federal states and the communes. The notes of the loan bureaux could in turn be taken to the Reichsbank and used to obtain Reichsbank notes. By the end of 1918, M 10.1 billion of loan bureau notes were in circulation, as well as M 22.2 b of Reichsbank notes.[40] The result of the monetary expansion was that, by the end of 1918, there was five times as much cash in circulation as there had been at the end of 1913.

---

[38] Feldman, 1993, p. 32.
[39] Cf. Reichsbank, Verwaltungsbericht für das Jahr 1922, p. 14.
[40] Cf. Holtfrerich, 1986, pp. 50f.; Feldman, 1993, p. 35.

The note cover regulations were amended to allow note issues to be backed by state paper as well as by gold. Throughout the war, the Reichsbank maintained in consequence its increasingly fictional adherence to gold coverage. This provision was only lifted in 1922.

2. When it was clear that there would be no quick military decision, the German government—like other governments in continental Europe—rejected the possibility of financing military costs through *increased taxation*. For the first two years of war, the government successfully issued war bonds, whose purchase by the public was widely treated as a vote of confidence in the government and its military policy. A recent historian has written of the 'verve, skill and imagination' of the Reichsbank in promoting war bonds.[41] After 1916, however, the government could not place all the bonds with the public. At this stage, the public debt had to be financed increasingly by the banking system, and this meant in practice through the Reichsbank's discounts.

3. The end of the war brought *new expenditures*. The German government faced a large bill for the social costs of the war—payments to the crippled of the war, and to widows and orphans. But it also became involved in paying large amounts to keep the social peace in a political situation that hovered perilously on the brink of social revolution. Food supplies were subsidized. In 1920, 12 per cent of Reich expenditure went to finance deficits in the post and railroad systems, where employment was judged a social necessity. This proportion rose in subsequent years.[42] The government in effect adopted a full employment programme, for social policy reasons. At the same time, similar considerations guided tax policy. Weak coalition governments found raising taxes noticeably politically unappealing; and there was increasingly militant opposition from business interests to the idea of paying taxes.[43]

At the peace conference, the amount of Germany's reparations obligations was not fixed; it was only determined in May 1921 in the London ultimatum, when a total of 132 billion Gold Marks (GM) was specified. Debate about the problem of the budget focused increasingly on the payments imposed by the Versailles Treaty, rather than on domestic payments. To some extent, this emphasis is intelligible as an attempt to shift the blame for Germany's misfortunes away from the participants in the fragile but expensive post-revolutionary social compromise, and to find a convenient foreign whipping boy in the menacing shape of the reparation creditors. But it is also true that reparations themselves clearly posed a substantial potential

[41] Feldman, 1993, p. 654.
[42] Cf. Ferguson, 1995, p. 278.
[43] Cf. Ferguson, 1995, p. 369.

burden on the budget. The payments required under the Versailles Treaty now came to represent a major part of government expenditure: 32.4 per cent of the total in 1921, and 35.7 per cent in 1922.[44]

In consequence, and despite an attempt in 1920 to make cuts in expenditure and to impose a more realistic tax regime, the government budget remained unbalanced. It was financed increasingly through short-term (or floating) debt. The only major saving came from the effects of inflation in radically reducing the real costs of debt service.

4. The Reichsbank accommodated this public sector deficit by *discounting government bills*. The fall of the Mark on foreign exchange markets, which had already begun during the war, reflected the expectations about the extent to which government deficits would be financed by the central bank.[45] In the phase of gradual or creeping inflation, which lasted until the summer of 1922, not all the debt was refinanced in this way; foreigners in particular bought substantial numbers of German securities in the belief that there would be a recovery of the Mark. Such capital inflows, estimated at the time at between GM 7.6 and 8.7 billion and more recently at as much as GM 15 billion (or between 5 and 10 per cent of the net domestic product in 1919–22),[46] helped to keep the Mark rate up. The confidence about a potential recovery was revealed by a premium for the Mark on forward markets until 1922. After July 1922, however, when the government and political order were destabilized by the assassination of Foreign Minister Walther Rathenau, these expectations changed. The proportion of short-term debt held by the Reichsbank now rose dramatically.

5. During this period, the Reichsbank also continued to *discount private bills*, at negative real interest rates (i.e. rates well below the inflation level): the discount rate was held at an amazingly low 5 per cent until July 1922. This policy was highly controversial at the time and has remained so subsequently. Contemporary critics, including Walter Eucken and L. Albert Hahn as well as the Italian economist Costantino Bresciani-Turroni (a member of the Allied Reparation Commission) who wrote the first major study of the German inflation, thought that the discount policy represented an illegitimate subsidy to that part of the business community having access to the Reichsbank.

The defence offered by the Reichsbank, which has been repeated by subsequent analysts, was that an increase in the discount rate would not affect the demand for credit, either on the part of the government or from business. As far as the government is concerned, a rise in the discount rate would

[44] Cf. Webb, 1989, p. 37.
[45] Cf. Webb, 1989.
[46] Cf. Holtfrerich, 1986; cf. also Feldman, 1993, p. 598.

have radically increased the cost of financing the short-term debt, and thus (under a *ceteris paribus* assumption) also widened the government deficit. Both parts of the argument in support of the Reichsbank's discount policy contain logical fallacies, however. The argument about the government's increased costs ignores the way in which a realistic interest level would have forced the government to undertake more rapid adjustment, and perhaps would have made the brief-lived attempt in 1920 at fiscal stabilization more durable. The argument about the private demand for credit ignores the fact that persistently negative real interest rates for favoured sectors of the economy ('interest rate repression') create perverse incentives and are very harmful to economic growth if followed for substantial periods of time.[47]

The Reichsbank's discount policy was doubtless not the prime cause of the inflation—that lay in the government's fiscal policy—but it created incentives, and allowed power blocs and interest groups to form which helped to perpetuate the inflationary mechanism. In order to understand why the Reichsbank behaved in this way, it is necessary to consider the erroneous nature of the beliefs about monetary policy which fatefully gripped its decision makers. This dominance of dogma was characteristic of the Reichsbank both while it was part of the government structure (until 1922), and after its autonomy was guaranteed through a new law, imposed by the allies in 1922 as the price for a temporary reparations moratorium. Indeed the Reichsbank consistently argued that it had taken treasury bills by choice, to discharge its duty to the German economy, and not because it had been instructed to do so by the Reich Chancellor.[48]

The Reichsbank viewed the origins of the inflation as lying in the balance of payments as well as in the budget deficit. Neither of these interpretations was completely implausible.[49] But neither helped the Reichsbank pursue an appropriate monetary policy; since both involved blaming processes outside the Reichsbank for the course of monetary development. Both consequently led to an institutional passivity. The most striking feature of the Reichsbank's public pronouncements is that it consistently explained that it was simply responding to an increased demand for money. Especially in the earlier stages of the inflation, it even argued that its actions were required because of a falling velocity of circulation. During the war, new printing works were taken into operation, and in October 1918 the communes were encouraged to print emergency money (*Notgeld*). A law of 1922 regularized the status of these special issues.[50]

[47] Cf. World Bank, 1993, p. 237.
[48] Cf. Reichsbank, Verwaltungsbericht für das Jahr 1922, p. 10.
[49] Cf. Kindleberger, 1993, pp. 301–5.
[50] Cf. RGBl 1, p. 693.

This ineffectiveness on the part of the Reichsbank had an intellectual underpinning. It was the continued adherence to the real bills doctrine which resulted in an inability to guide monetary policy. In the last stages of the hyper-inflation, Havenstein used this theory as the major argument in a defence of the Reichsbank's actions given in a speech before the Reichsbank's Central Committee. 'It is not disputed that central bank credit increases the circulation of paper; but to the extent to which the central bank gives economically desirable and needed credits, which help production and the sale of goods, it does not create artificial purchasing power.'[51] There is no doubt that this view was widely shared, especially by those who benefited from Reichsbank credits (and they were heavily represented on the Central Committee); but toward the end of the inflation, on 2 August 1923, the Reichsbank Directorate overruled the Central Committee and went ahead with an increase in the discount rate. Only very late, then, did a learning process set in for the Reichsbank's leadership. At the beginning of 1923, it undertook a dramatic attempt at credit restriction, with very strict guidelines on the bills that would be eligible for Reichsbank discount; but the severe consequences for business and the protests were too great in a situation exacerbated by the French occupation of the Ruhr, and the Reichsbank soon abandoned the brief flirtation with credit stability.[52]

The Reichsbank in fact took from the pre-war world a concern for financing production—any kind of production. This approach fitted perfectly with the predominant tendency of viewing the inflation as originating with the balance of payments. According to this diagnosis of the German malaise, Germany needed to produce more in order to export more, and in this way help to tackle the balance of payments problem. This *Produktionspolitik* fitted perfectly with the social-psychological analysis that had been created by German elites in the aftermath of the Russian revolution: that producing and creating work was essential in order to preserve Germany's fragile political stability.

A central bank never likes to feel intellectually isolated. In defending its position, it is remarkable how much the Reichsbank relied on an argument that its policy was supported by an international consensus of central bankers—such as that represented in 1920 at the Brussels Financial Conference.

In the course of 1923, however, the attitude of the international financial community changed. Especially after the Reichsbank used a large part of its reserves in the spring of 1923 in an abortive attempt to 'lean against the

---

[51] Havenstein's Speech, in: Deutsche Allgemeine Zeitung, no. 392, 25 Aug. 1923.
[52] Cf. Eynern, 1928, pp. 81f.

wind' and beat the speculators by intervention on the foreign exchange markets, the Bank of England and the Federal Reserve Bank of New York became very critical of Havenstein's management, and the intellectual underpinning of Reichsbank policy became more controversial.[53]

In order to stop the inflation, a clear cut was needed. It is possible to imagine high levels of inflation continuing for lengthy periods of time (and this has been the experience of many Latin American economies for large parts of the post-1945 era); but a hyper-inflation calls for a more dramatic response. The German situation was radically transformed by the French occupation of the Ruhr (January 1923), and by the new expenditure involved in paying the workforce and the factories of the occupied areas not to work. By the autumn of 1923, as the hyper-inflation reached a peak, Germany nearly disintegrated in civil war.

By late 1923, there were few social groups (apart from the radical and undemocratic political parties) who continued to see any advantages to inflation, and as a result a consensus for stabilization emerged. The Stresemann government, formed on 14 August 1923, had broader, though fragile, support than its predecessors; and throughout the critical period to February 1924, the Reichstag was prepared to accept emergency legislation enacted under article 48 of the Weimar constitution as a way of tackling the urgent financial problems. A stabilization could be carried out only in cooperation with the foreign powers, however; and these played a crucial part not only in designing the new institutional structure of the Reichsbank, but also in promoting a change in management. Foreign bankers and central banks could be expected to play a less political and more 'expert' function, and German decision makers hoped that such outside intervention would help to depoliticize and desensitize the complicated issues that had developed as different political and social groupings in Germany had pushed their respective needs and interests.

Governor Montagu Norman of the Bank of England insisted that Havenstein should be removed. When Havenstein used the autonomy of the Reichsbank to refuse a resignation, the Stresemann government appointed Hjalmar Schacht as Currency Commissar. Schacht had criticized government and Reichsbank policies during the inflation, and was associated with the left-wing liberal party DDP.[54] Schacht's office would have taken over many of the functions of the Reichsbank had not Havenstein been removed by a heart attack one day after his energetic defence of the Reichsbank's autonomy. When Schacht was appointed as his successor, the

---

[53] Cf. Norman to Havenstein, 13 June 1923 and 20 June 1923 (BoE OV 34/71).
[54] Cf. Feldman, 1993, p. 696.

opposition of the Reichsbank Directorate to his appointment (and their advocacy of the candidature of the nationalist wartime Reich Treasury Secretary Karl Helfferich) helped to convince Montagu Norman and Benjamin Strong, Governor of the Federal Reserve Bank of New York, that the German government had really made a very wise choice.[55]

In part because of the position of Havenstein, who could not legally be dismissed because of the autonomy law, but more importantly because of the political discrediting of the Reichsbank as a consequence of the inflation, the stabilization of the currency involved not one but two attempts at central bank creation. The first was the Rentenbank, established by decree on 17 October 1923, which issued 'value constant' Rentenmark, equivalent in value to the gold-convertible pre-1914 Mark. The Rentenbank strictly limited credit to the government, and also (via the Reichsbank) to business; while the Reichsbank would correspondingly cease the financing of government debt. On 15 November 1923, five days before the death of Havenstein, the Reichsbank stopped discounting treasury bills (at this point there were M 192 trillion or M 192×10^{18} in circulation).

The immediate cause of inflation was removed; but the credibility, both international and domestic, of the Reichsbank required rebuilding. In April 1924, another central bank was established, the Golddiskontbank, with a capital of £10 millions, of which half was paid in by the Reichsbank using foreign (mostly British) credits. Its primary purpose was to give hard currency loans to German business, but its statute also gave it the right (which it never formally used) to issue banknotes. By mid-1924, there were then three parallel German central banks: the Reichsbank, issuing a paper money whose value it was attempting to hold steady; the Rentenbank which issued value constant notes which were not legal tender but were widely used; and the sterling-based Golddiskontbank, which never had its own notes, but whose gold loan was issued divided into coupons and in practice also circulated as money.[56]

The Reichsbank survived because its new leadership gave it a new level of international standing. Initially, Schacht's role was critical in the winter of 1923–4 in saving German monetary unity by mobilizing British financial assistance and blocking a French plan for a separate Rheinlandbank intended as a prelude to the political separation of the Rhineland from Germany.[57] This achievement rescued Germany's political and economic integrity, but on its own it was not sufficient to build a new confidence.

[55] Cf. Pierre Jay to D. R. Crissinger, 14 Sept. 1925 (FRBNY, Reparations file).
[56] Cf. Woodward and Butler, 1924, vol. 26, 1924, pp. 905–8.
[57] Cf. Habedank, 1981, pp. 103f.; Schötz, 1987, pp. 34ff.

5. Deflation and depression

Having abandoned an unrealistic doctrine and buried the man who had emerged as its major exponent, the new Reichsbank set out to follow not a doctrine but a rule: fundamentally, the rule of a fixed exchange rate regime. But the rule brought new problems. It led to an inability to control the money supply (this is a general consequence of the adoption of a fixed exchange rate). The difficulties were accentuated by the fact that the commercial banking system continued to behave as if the old supportive Reichsbank that followed the real bills doctrine was still operating. Finally, the situation was exacerbated by the general massive deflationary and confidence problems associated at the international level with the gold exchange standard of the 1920s. As a consequence, the Reichsbank's policy before and during the Great Depression became as controversial as it had been at the time of inflation.

The new Reichsbank, designed as part of the Dawes reparations plan, and created by the Banking Act of 30 August 1924, bore some obvious resemblances to its predecessor of 1875. The separate currrencies, such as the Rentenmark and the various issues of emergency money, were withdrawn from circulation. A gold rule was restored as the core of the Reichsbank's operation, with a commitment to exchange 1,392 Reichsmark (RM) for a pound of gold; and from October 1924 the new Reichsmark began to circulate. Forty per cent of the note issue had to be backed by gold and foreign exchange, of which foreign exchange should represent no more than one quarter. Although occasional operations with a lower rate were permitted in 'exceptional circumstances', there was then a minimum discount rate of 5 per cent. Furthermore the consent of a newly created General Council (which replaced the General Committee) was required for this operation. The observation of the reserve rule had the consequence that as the coverage neared the 40 per cent limit, a much more radical reduction in note issue was required (by 100/40, or 2.5 times) in order to maintain the legal ratio. Thus reserve losses of RM 100 million at such a time would necessitate a note issue reduced by a very deflationary RM 250 million. Loans to the government through Reichsbank discounting of treasury paper were limited, at first to RM 100 million (in 1926, the law was revised to permit a total of RM 400 million discounted or taken as Lombard security).

The first article of the new Banking Act stated emphatically the autonomy of the central bank: 'The Reichsbank is a bank independent of the Reich Government'. This autonomy was institutionally anchored. The 14 member General Council was half composed of foreign representatives; its consent was needed for the nomination of members of the Reichsbank Directorate and of the President. One of the foreign members of the General Council, the Commissar for Note Issue, could stop note issue if in his judgement the stability or gold convertibility of the currency were endangered. In addition, the foreign control of German finances was secured through the institution of an Agent-General for Reparations Payments, to supervise the collection and the transfer of reparations; and by foreign control of the administration of the Reich Railways, which was also a source of reparation payments. On the positive side, the new reparations plan was backed with a 800 million Gold Mark loan (the Dawes Loan) issued internationally, which signalled a return of international confidence in Germany.

Maintaining the gold parity after the large-scale destruction of capital during the German inflation required high levels of interest. These contributed decisively to the weak performance of the Weimar economy even during the so-called 'golden years'.[58] This diagnosis was fully shared by the Reichsbank, which noted that 'the continuing high interest rates cast a shadow on all of German economic life'.[59] However, it was difficult at the time and even now to see what realistic alternative there could have been in the aftermath of inflation. In part, the constraints were legal in character— the Dawes agreement embedded the Reichsbank Act in international treaties —but in part they were also an outcome of domestic German opinion.[60] There were still massive fears in the population about new inflations, and any attempt at alternative currency policies, such as floating or any kind of crawling peg, would have produced immediate confidence problems. The stabilization policy required the fixed exchange rate in order to provide an anchor for the currency. Once the pegged rate was chosen, relatively high interest rates (above the levels prevailing in the United Kingdom or the United States) were needed in its defence. Hjalmar Schacht saw this more quickly than other politicians, and rejected alternative domestic schemes discussed in 1923–4 for a currency backed by rent taxes or by commodities (for a time the political right favoured a rye currency). After the 1922 Genoa Monetary Conference, choosing an internationally credible currency meant adherence to gold.

Stabilization also required commitment to fiscal retrenchment. An extensive tax reform was introduced by the Tax Emergency Decree of 14 February 1924, imposing particular burdens on businesses and homeowners who had benefited from the debt reduction effects of the inflation. Would

---

[58] Cf. Diehl, 1932; cf. also Holtfrerich, 1984; Voth, 1995.

[59] 'Wie weit kann die Auslandsverschuldung Deutschlands fortgesetzt werden?' of 14 Jan. 1929 (Bundesarchiv Koblenz and Berlin R 2501 [Reichsbank] 6704); cf. also Reichsbank, Verwaltungsbericht für das Jahr 1928, p. 3.

[60] Cf. Borchardt, 1979, pp. 87–132.

attachment to the gold standard and advocacy of fiscal orthodoxy be enough? For much of the 1920s, the Reichsbank faced the problem of the inflationary consequences of capital inflows. For the first time in 1927, the Annual Report of the Reichsbank clearly set out an argument about the relationship between the quantity of money and price stability: 'a substantial increase in the circulation of money, even if fully backed by gold, must have harmful price effects'.[61]

Schacht brought a new, more authoritarian and less collegial, style to the management of the Reichsbank.[62] But he consistently recognized that his strength lay in his good contacts with the foreign central bankers, and his first Presidency (1924–30) may be seen as an early experiment in 'central bank cooperation'. His relationship with Montagu Norman was especially close. The two friends worked together in 1927 in successfully pressing for a cut in Federal Reserve rates in order to ease the monetary situation in Europe. Later, at the turn of 1928–9, when the pound was under pressure while inflows of funds were pushing up the Mark, Schacht was willing to agree to sell Marks for sterling in cooperation with the Bank of England.[63] In 1930 and 1931 Norman played a major, but ultimately unsuccessful, role in trying to ward off pressure on the Mark.

An essential component of the practice of central bank cooperation in the 1920s was not only the legal autonomy of central banks, but also their practical independence from national pressures, both political and commercial. Schacht dealt with the historical legacy of the Reichsbank by fierce criticism of those relationships which had brought so much trouble during the inflation—with public authorities, and with the banking system. At first, he directed most of his attention to the rationalization of public finance, and demanded that the Reich, as well as the postal and railroad systems, should deposit surplus funds with the Reichsbank. Later, as government expenditure increased from the austerity levels of the stabilization period, Schacht began to criticize public spending. He tried to control borrowing on foreign markets—from banks and through bond issues—by making bond issues subject to approval from an Advisory Office for External Credits, instituted in 1925. He made sure that his central bank colleagues in other countries heard about his criticism, since that would build up the credibility of the Reichsbank.

In the course of 1927, Schacht's relations with the government deteriorated sharply. In November 1927, in a speech give at Bochum, he lambasted

---

[61] Reichsbank, Verwaltungsbericht für das Jahr 1927, p. 7.

[62] Cf. Vocke, 1973, pp. 92f.

[63] Cf. Norman to Schacht, 15 Aug. 1928 and Schacht to Norman, 15 Dec. 1928 (BoE, G1/414).

the profligacy of German municipalities.[64] In 1929, the confrontations increased, as Schacht attacked the Reich government's handling of the reparations revision negotiations at the Hague conference. In December 1929, he issued a ferociously confrontational memorandum attacking government fiscal policies, and their consequences for the money and capital markets.[65]

Government finance was not the only cause of the Reichsbank's difficulties. The Reichsbank had lost control of the money supply, but for a different reason.[66] While Schacht felt that his constant campaign may have helped to curtail some of the public sector debt, his dealings with banks had been less successful.[67] After the stabilization in 1923–4, banks rebuilt their portfolios and started a competitive expansion of loans. Since the Reichsbank could not influence banks' policies directly at most times, it changed its handling of crises and started to use the restriction of Reichsbank credit as a major weapon of policy.

Schacht initially believed that he had saved the Mark stabilization in the spring of 1924 by imposing credit restraints, which sent domestic short-term interest rates to very high levels (an average of 45 per cent for April 1924).[68] On 11 May 1927 the Reichsbank took a new initiative in credit policy by announcing that it would ration discounts to banks according to their cash reserve and their Giro accounts in relation to their liabilities. Short-term money again leaped up to over 6 per cent.[69] The credit rationing was an attempt to curb speculation on the bourse in Germany, and to deter the inflow of foreign funds attracted by the appreciation of German shares. Schacht summoned the chairman of the Berlin bank cartel and told the banks to cut loans against securities as a condition for access to the Reichsbank.

The Reichsbank believed that it had little choice, in that discount rate changes would not work in the desired way because of the extent of short-term international capital movements. If the Reichsbank were to attempt to curb the economy or cut monetary expansion by a discount rate rise, the measure would only attract in foreign capital, and thus be counter-productive. This policy dilemma is typical for a central bank operating in a fixed exchange rate environment (in the 1960s, a similar situation led to the argument that fixed exchange rates provided a mechanism for importing inflation). So the Reichsbank came to believe that it had little choice except to apply the admittedly clumsy and discriminatory mechanism of credit

[64] Cf. Schacht, 1927, p. 22.
[65] Cf. Akten der Reichskanzlei, 1970, p. 1228.
[66] Cf. Hardach, 1976, pp. 71ff.
[67] Cf. Schacht to Norman, 15 Dec. 1928 (BoE G1/414).
[68] Cf. Ausschuß, 1929, p. 61.
[69] Cf. Ausschuß, 1929, p. 62.

rationing. Such measures, however, intended in the first place to stop monetary expansion, were seriously flawed when it came to dealing with an external drain and a loss of confidence.

The Reichsbank clearly followed the growth of both private and public foreign indebtedness with mounting concern, but it found it hard to gather adequate information about the emerging problem, and its surveys seriously under-estimated the extent of German debt. The last Reichsbank estimate before the outbreak of the debt crisis in 1931 gave RM 19.3 billion, of which 8 billion was short-term debt. In 1934 the German government produced a final figure for the July 1931 short-term level as RM 13.1 billion.[70]

The new willingness at the Reichsbank to ration access to its credit should have changed bank behaviour, but it did not. Whereas before the First World War, banks could confidently treat bills as a primary reserve asset and operate with very low reserves of cash and deposits at the central bank, in the light of 1924 and 1927, they should have been more cautious. In fact, they continued to have very low cash reserves, and were confident that either they could obtain credit on the foreign market if needed, or that in an emergency, the Reichsbank would not allow a major banking crisis to occur. Competitive pressure made holding an extensive cash reserve an apparently too expensive luxury. The extent to which this attitude was widespread is reflected in an internal Reichsbank memorandum of the Statistical Department in August 1930, just before the onset of the first major wave of panic. The paper appealed for higher bank reserves, and argued a case for a 5 per cent deposit of the banks at the Reichsbank to reduce the likelihood of bank panic. But it observed 'that one of the big banks or one of the large regional banks even in the case of a crisis will enjoy more confidence than a small or medium-sized bank, and is thus less likely to be exposed to a run'. And the report concluded with the calculation that in the last resort the Reichsbank would have to help. 'The smaller the buffer of a cash reserve is, the more suddenly will the demand for additional Reichsbank help be made. In no case could the Reichsbank withdraw from this responsibility. If the Reichsbank imposed a credit restriction in the light of other threats, for instance to the exchange rate, the unavoidable consequence would be a complete collapse of economic life.'[71] This statement about an absolutely unimaginable possibility in fact became a chillingly accurate forecast of the events of 1931.

A first sign of panic occurred during the 1929 reparations negotiations,

---

[70] Cf. Schacht, 1927; memorandum of 14 Jan. 1929 (Bundesarchiv Koblenz and Berlin R 2501 [Reichsbank] 6704); Schuker, 1988, p. 114.

[71] 'Das Problem der volkswirtschaftlichen Liquidität', memorandum of 21 Aug. 1930 (Bundesarchiv Koblenz and Berlin R 2501 [Reichsbank] 6484).

when the Reichsbank again restricted credit. But the final catastrophe occurred only after Schacht had left the Reichsbank. The long-standing confrontation with the government, and the criticism of the Young plan for reparations payments, had eventually led in March 1930 to Schacht's resignation. The government nominated in his place Hans Luther, a former Reich Chancellor who, as finance minister in 1923–4, had been one of the major architects of the fiscal side of the stabilization of the Mark. After leaving government office, Luther had focused his efforts on revising the fiscal balance between the Reich, the Länder, and the communes. He had no training as a central banker, and in 1930 almost immediately faced apparently insurmountable problems.

After May 1930, deposits in German banks contracted. The shrinking of deposits became much quicker after the Reichstag elections of September 1930 produced unexpectedly large gains for the NSDAP. A new panic occurred in May 1931, after the failure of the Vienna Creditanstalt.

In the subsequent reports of the Reichsbank, as well as in most textbooks and historical accounts these movements out of Mark deposits in 1930–1 have been interpreted as a withdrawal of foreign capital. But at the time, the Reichsbank, as well as many commentators in Germany, and the crucially important foreign central banks, interpreted the losses as German capital flight.[72] The Bank of England and the Federal Reserve Bank of New York believed in consequence that they should only help Germany if the Reichsbank were to take effective measures against capital flight.[73] This would mean restricting banks' access to foreign exchange by denying them credit facilities.

The loss of confidence produced a shrinking of Reichsbank reserves. While on 23 September 1930, before the Reichstag elections, the reserve ratio had stood at 69.6 per cent, and it was still at a high level on 23 May 1931, a rapid slide then occurred: on 30 June, the gold and foreign exchange reserves were at the perilous level of 40.1 per cent of note issue. The Reichsbank tried to raise its reserves by taking a US $100 million central bank credit, but was constantly told that the price for external assistance of this type was action to halt capital flight. A discount rate rise to 7 per cent on 13 June was not adequate to restore confidence or to penalize those who drew Marks in order to sell them on the foreign exchange market. In these circumstances, the Reichsbank for a final and fateful time rationed access to its discounts with effect from 22 June. Credit was limited to the amount outstanding on 19 June, and the additional instruction was given: 'in all

---

[72] Cf. Harrison telephone conversation with Norman, 2 July 1931 (FRBNY 3115.2).
[73] Cf. Committee of Treasury, 9 Aug. 1931 (BoE G8/60).

credit business, it is especially important to ensure that the Reichsbank's credit is not used for unjustified foreign exchange purchases'.[74] Banks could no longer rely on the Reichsbank for support; and a panic set in after big losses became evident at the DANAT bank. On 13 July 1931, after the failure of the DANAT, a general banking holiday was needed.

This crisis, which significantly worsened the German depression, was the outcome of the intertwining of two circumstances. First, there was the weakness and vulnerability of German banks in general, with doubts about the asset values of some major institutions (in particular the DANAT bank). Second, there were fears about the government's difficulties in balancing the budget and predictions that these might force Germany off the gold standard.[75] Either of these considerations might have prompted a crisis on its own. But the Reichsbank's attempt to deal with the second difficulty (waning confidence in Germany) by a restriction of discounts made the first problem much more acute and precipitated the final catastrophe. Luther was pushed into adopting this approach as a consequence of the reliance on foreign central bank support—the last vestige of the central bank cooperation of the 1920s. The absence of the support of the Reichsbank in turn made it hard for domestic banks to engage in rescue attempts after failures of other banks.

Banks not surprisingly blamed the Reichsbank for standing by and letting the banking crisis unfold. Hans Luther had concentrated all his energies on obtaining foreign assistance, even when the obvious panic of his aeroplane trip (a rarity at the time) to London, Paris and then on to the Bank for International Settlements in Basle increased nervousness on financial markets.

The Reichsbank in the crisis was constrained by the obligation to maintain the 1924 parity, and by the 40 per cent cover rule. After the banking crisis, its policy began to be more flexible:

1. The London conference in July 1931 recommended a freezing of German short-term debt. The Standstill Agreement, initialled on 19 August 1931, was initially in force for six months, but a more comprehensive arrangement was subsequently renegotiated annually as the German Credit Agreements (until the outbreak of the European War in 1939).

2. After the debt and banking crisis, the German government imposed exchange control.

3. Sheltered by the freezing of debts, and by exchange controls, the Reichsbank was free to pursue a more expansionary policy; although in public statements it took a rather harsh line because of the extent of public

---

[74] 'An sämtliche Reichsbankleitstellen', 21 June 1931 (Bundesarchiv Koblenz and Berlin R 28/49).

[75] Cf. Balderston, 1993; Hardach, 1976, pp. 126–31.

sensitivity about inflation.[76] But essentially the gold exchange standard constraint had ended on 13 July 1931, and after this, there was a dramatic relaxation in the quality of bills taken into the Reichsbank's portfolio. The Reichsbank now discounted substantial volumes of renewable medium term bills financing German exports to the USSR (thus in practice exceeding the 90 day requirement that had been a legal standard for the Reichsbank's operations under the 1875 and 1924 laws).

In September 1931, the Reichsbank participated in a conference organized by the Friedrich-List-Society to discuss anti-depression measures such as work creation, and their financing through the Reichsbank.[77] After the devaluation of the British pound provided a new shock to financial confidence, the Reichsbank avoided further public discussion. But it continued a secret or hidden expansion, and took bills from public sector institutions, the German Company for Public Works and the Bau- und Bodenbank, which financed construction, and in so doing began a practice which expanded in the NS dictatorship with the Metallurgical Research Company (Metallurgische Forschungsgesellschaft) playing an analogous role in the financing of rearmament. Finally, the Reichsbank created a subsidiary institution, the Akzept- und Garantiebank, to take frozen bank credits out of the portfolios of the commercial banks. The aftermath of the 1931 crisis removed many of the constraints that had limited the internationalized Reichsbank of the 1920s, and made it possible for it to build a much greater control over German financial markets.

6. The Reichsbank and the economics of control

After 1931, the Reichsbank was able to reassert itself in the German money market, but it did so as part of an increasingly regulated system, in which market signals were suppressed. In the development of economic policy and the move away from liberalism and toward control, the decisive break was 1931; and the political *caesura* of 1933 could do nothing but accelerate the development.

The crisis of 1931 and the imposition of exchange control severed the link between the Reichsmark and gold. After that, Reichsbank policy had no consistent guideline, although of course there were some policy priorities. At first, the Reichsbank tried to provide a stimulus to economic recovery, and it aimed at price stability later in the 1930s. But it never consciously

---

[76] Cf. Borchardt, 1985.
[77] Cf. Borchardt and Schötz, 1991.

adopted any operational equivalent of the gold standard rule, such as would have been represented for instance, by the adoption of a monetary target. Only such an impersonal rule could have served as a way of isolating its policy from political influences. After all, questions such as the best way to attain economic recovery, or what was meant by price and wage stability, could quite legitimately and plausibly be answered in a large number of ways, reflecting divergent political views and interests. Instead of a rule, the Reichsbank and its political masters saw matters in terms of the credibility attached to particular personalities.

The most striking financial personality was Hjalmar Schacht. His re-appointment as Reichsbank President in March 1933 was a vital move for Hitler, intended to build economic confidence in the new regime both internationally and domestically. He had consistently hammered away at an anti-inflationary theme, especially in the decisive years at the end of the Weimar Republic. The view that Schacht's personality was confidence-enhancing was widely shared. In the immediate aftermath of the banking crisis of 1931, leading bankers and industrialists had demanded the (legally impossible) dismissal of Luther and his replacement by Schacht. After the appointment of Hitler as Chancellor, Luther resigned; and, at Hitler's urging, the Reichsbank's General Council appointed Schacht as his successor. The incident demonstrates how even an apparently cast-iron legal autonomy of the central bank is not inevitably a guarantee against political intrusion.

If Hitler thought that the magic of Schacht's name would prevent panic or loss of confidence, Schacht in turn believed that the *'Führer's'* personality held the key to a new economic recovery. He had met Hitler for the first time on New Year's Day 1931, and had rapidly associated himself politically with National Socialism and its charismatic leader. But he never joined the party, and always remained more impressed by Hitler personally than by the movement or its ideology, and he intensely distrusted its populist rhetoric.

For a long time Schacht saw Hitler as a statesman of 'genius'. After 1945, he was still happy to state that 'I thought Hitler was a man with whom one could cooperate'.[78] Throughout the 1930s, even as he became increasingly disenchanted with National Socialism, Schacht treated Hitler obsequiously. From the beginning of his association with the new political movement, Schacht regarded it as his mission to harness Hitler's charisma, and to protect private ownership against the socialist claims of the NSDAP. His greatest success in this regard lay in turning the Bank Inquiry of 1933 into a relatively harmless opportunity for some of the more ideological National

[78] C. J. Hynning interrogation of Schacht, 20 July 1945 (IfZ ZS 135/2).

Socialists to appeal for a greater control of banking. The eventual outcome of the Enquete, the Banking Act of December 1934, reflected almost nothing of Nazi criticisms of finance capital. It laid out instead a regulatory framework which lasted into, and helped to shape, Germany's post-1945 experience. The size of loans to individual customers was limited. A Supervisory Office for Credit with the Reichsbank President as its chairman would determine the level of cash reserves and of first and second grade liquidity. Article 16 laid down that a cash reserve should be fixed at not more than 10 per cent of banks' liabilities. In this way, the law settled the old controversies about the Reichsbank's control over bank credit which had been fought out at least since the monetary crisis of 1907.

Further measures helped the Reichsbank control the money market. From October 1933, open market operations—the buying and selling of treasury bills with the purpose of supplying or absorbing excess liquidity—were permitted; although in practice they were not very substantial during the 1930s,[79] and this facility was less useful as an instrument of monetary control than it would have been during the 1920s, when the inflow of foreign funds had had major disruptive effects on bank liquidity. The amendments of the law effected in 1933 were fully compatible with the 1924 Act, since the Allies, now represented by the Bank for International Settlements, gave their consent. But the new law also abolished one of the key elements of the 1924 settlement, the controlling General Council.

With regard to the capital market, a major priority was the driving down of interest rates from the exceptionally high levels prevailing during the depression. Such a lowering would be crucial both for the stabilization of the economy, and for the satisfaction of the frequently indebted middle class clientele of the NSDAP. Rates would be lowered, not so much by the forced reduction contained in Brüning's emergency decree of December 1931, but rather more indirectly: through limitations on company dividends (law of 4 December 1934), and through a requirement that corporations obtain permission from the Reichsbank's Capital Market Committee (established in May 1933) to issue debt. In practice, there were few new issues in the 1930s, and the market remained the preserve of public sector borrowers. A large-scale debt conversion exercise in 1935 on bonds with over 6 per cent interest prepared the way for the issue of new government debt.

Such measures laid the basis for a large expansion of government expenditure. Schacht repeatedly explained that the reordering of the capital market was intended to finance large public projects. He always appeared in public statements to leave some doubt as to whether this meant a permanent move to statism. Many in the Reichsbank, as well as some outside observers,

[79] Cf. Stucken, 1953, pp. 104f., 139.

believed that the point of an expansion of state activity in the particular circumstances of the 1930s was simply a pump-priming to get out of depression, needed because of the virtual absence of private sector investment. (This ambiguity is reflected in the historical literature also. The consensus of most analysts is that National Socialist economics should not be viewed as an experiment in Keynesianism, although between 1933 and 1935 it may be possible to speak of a 'economically appropriate fiscal policy'.[80])

Schacht too emphasized employment creation and the building of roads as the most conspicuous goal of the early years of National Socialist economics, and the Reichsbank agreed to rediscount up to a billion Reichsmark bills to finance the first National Socialist work creation plan, the so-called Reinhardt programme. In addition, the bank's portfolio contained work creation bills from the Reich Railways and the *Autobahn* administration. In 1934, about half of the work creation bills were held by the Reichsbank.[81] But jobs were not the only issue at stake: Schacht also stated that the public use of the capital market was the prerequisite for effective German rearmament. At the end of 1934, he told the army that the law limiting dividends had been made 'in the interests of the rearmament policy'.

In addition to financing through borrowing, armaments were paid through the device of the Mefo-bill: a bill drawn by the munitions supplier on the Metallurgical Research Company (Mefo), accepted by the Mefo and paid through the Reichsbank's giro system. Since these were six month bills, they were ineligible for Reichsbank discounting in the first half of their life, but were taken by the Reichsbank's affiliate, the Golddiskontbank.[82] By August 1937, bills amounting to a total of RM 11,072 million had been issued. Half of the Mefo-bills issued were never presented to the Reichsbank or the Golddiskontbank for rediscount, but were held by the private sector.[83] The major intention of the device was to take some military expenditure off-budget. Though the Mefo-bills and the extent of their usage were kept secret, in fact they proved of little use in camouflaging German rearmament. It was quite possible for other countries to deduce what was happening in Germany. The Federal Reserve Bank of New York, for instance, knew exactly about not only the mechanism, but also the quantity of Mefo-bills outstanding (at the end of 1938, it estimated reasonably accurately at RM 12–15 billion).[84] After the end of 1937, the Reichsbank stopped the use of

[80] Cf. Erbe, 1958, p. 37; cf. also Bresciani-Turroni, 1950.

[81] Cf. Reichsbank to Reich finance ministry, 7 Oct. 1936 (Bundesarchiv Koblenz and Berlin R2/18701).

[82] Cf. Merkblatt 1936, sheet 4f. (Bundesarchiv Koblenz and Berlin R28/133).

[83] Cf. Schacht, 1955, pp. 317ff.

[84] Cf. Knoke and Despres, Notes on European Trip June 16–August 19, 1938 (FRBNY).

Mefo-bills, but a similar instrument (which could be submitted as security for Lombard credit) came into use, the 'treasury delivery note'.[85]

In practice, despite attempts to encourage cashless transactions as a way of slowing apparent monetary growth, during the peacetime years a new inflation had already begun. The government, obsessed by the damage that inflation might do to popular confidence, tried to use price controls as an anti-inflationary instrument. Hitler boasted: 'I had to show Schacht that the first cause of the stability of our currency is the concentration camp: the currency stays stable, when anyone who asks higher prices is arrested!'[86] In practice, the price controls brought unintended consequences, notably a steady deterioration of quality. And the official cost of living statistics undoubtedly understate the extent of German price inflation during the economic recovery.[87]

Schacht's position in the Reichsbank after August 1934 was peculiar with regard to the still existing legal requirement of bank autonomy. In that month, he added to his functions as President of the Reichsbank the commissary management of the Reich Economics Ministry (the appointment as acting minister came about because of the technicality that no serving minister was allowed to be on the Board of the Bank for International Settlements).[88] He was now a member of the government (indeed he remained as a minister without portfolio even after his dismissal as economics minister) and was thus directly involved in the major conflicts at the top of the National Socialist state. The double appointment of Schacht constituted a major breach of the Reichsbank Act, since it was clear that the President could not be independent any longer. The National Socialist approach, which saw economics as subordinate to political requirements, naturally had no room for such legal separation of functions. In May 1935 Schacht's formal power increased further with his appointment as General Plenipotentiary for the War Economy.

The tension implicit in these different roles grew greater as a result of Schacht's own political journey. Between 1934 and 1936, Schacht became disillusioned with the NSDAP party bosses, and after the war he claimed that he had begun to have doubts about Hitler in 1934.[89] The 1935 Annual Report of the Reichsbank, published in March 1936 as the unequal struggle between Reichsbank and government reached a preliminary climax, merely warned about the expansion of short-term government debt.

---

[85] Cf. Boelcke, 1992, p. 99.
[86] Cf. Jochmann, 1980, p. 88.
[87] Cf. Hachtmann, 1988, pp. 32–73.
[88] Cf. Simpson, 1969, p. 90.
[89] Cf. M. I. Gurfein interrogation of Schacht, 16 Oct. 1945 (NA).

Some part of Schacht's increasing disenchantment was a pragmatic, and probably not a deeply moral, consequence of the regime's anti-semitism. An elimination of Jews from business life would endanger the full employment programme. The attacks on Jews also clearly damaged Germany's external economic relations. However, Schacht's campaign was not based purely on calculations of economic benefits and losses. In May 1935, he presented Hitler personally with a strikingly and courageously worded memorandum 'On Exports', in which he attacked 'the harsh persecution of individual Jews instigated or assisted by the party, and the failure of state institutions to stop this persecution'.[90]

In 1935, while the Nuremberg racial laws were being prepared (they were promulgated during the party meeting in September), Schacht made some of these criticisms public during a speech at the Königsberg trade fair. His attack was particularly directed against 'spontaneous' anti-semitic actions, and the most powerful part of Schacht's argumentation contained an appeal for the rule of law. But Schacht dressed this criticism up in some compliments for National Socialism, and the speech also contained the statement: 'the Jews must come to terms with the fact that their influence here is finished once and for all'.[91]

Schacht usually treated the 'Jewish question' less as a general issue of principle than as a pragmatic problem. But he intervened personally on a number of occasions to help the German-Jewish banking elite—the Mendelssohns and Warburgs—and assisted them in the transfer of funds. In the winter of 1938–9, Schacht spent a considerable effort in promoting an (eventually fruitless) scheme allowing emigration to be financed through reduction of the German external debt.[92] These discussions produced in the Reichsbank one of the most staggeringly naive attempts to persuade the government of the economic desirability of higher Jewish emigration: a precisely worked out calculation of the costs of keeping Jews, who would now be economically inactive, in Germany. The Reichsbank envisaged that of the Jewish property registered in Germany in 1938 and worth RM 7.1 billion, RM 3.0 billion would be available after the payment of the tax on Jews levied after November 1938, and losses in selling off assets. This amount would be sufficient to pay for 10 years worth of existence (on the basis of a natural rate of death, and making the bizarre but revealing assumption that there would be no Jewish children). After this, maintaining the Jewish population would cost the Reich around RM 2.5 billion.[93] Such an

90 Fischer, 1995, pp. 154f.
91 Schacht, 1935, pp. 9–11.
92 Cf. Barkai, 1988, pp. 158–60; Fischer, 1995, pp. 216–20.
93 Cf. memorandum of 18 Jan. 1939 (Bundesarchiv Koblenz and Berlin R 2501 [Reichsbank] 6641).

appeal would be destined to fail, since National Socialism was ideologically opposed to the idea of treating racial policy on any sort of cost–benefit analysis, even the heartless one set out in the Reichsbank's calculation.

The issues that led to increasing hostility between the Reichsbank and the government were more financial and economic: the increased pace of rearmament, the expansion of the public sector, the growth of the public sector debt, and the orientation of German trade policy. It became increasingly clear that the expansion of the state-directed economy was not just an attempt at pump-priming a depressed market economy, but that it was developing a logic and a dynamic of its own. New elites in the party and also in business had an interest in its continuation. By emphasizing the limits on government spending, the Reichsbank kept any opposition fundamentally within its limited and technical sphere of responsibility: but it confronted the powerful interests of the new elites.

Throughout the first years of the National Socialist dictatorship, Schacht had repeatedly insisted on Germany's need to find export markets. In practice, however, he presided over an increasingly tight control of external trade. 'Schachtianism', as the system of blocked debts and politically managed trade was known abroad, came to be regarded as a new philosophy of economic management. The vigour of the economic recovery in 1933–4 endangered the last scarce German reserves, and prompted first a reintroduction of very radical exchange controls, and then, with the New Plan of September 1934, a move to bilateralization of foreign trade. Within the context of exchange control, different exchange rates were applied for different countries and products. Such controls were explained by Schacht as a counterpart to the refusal of creditor countries to write down German debt. In this way, Schacht and the Reichsbank were drawn into policies which made an export-based reintegration of Germany into the world economy ever harder. Nevertheless, Schacht struggled to resist further moves to autarky demanded by other parts of the state machinery: the Reich Agricultural Organization, the German Labour Front, and then, decisively, Hermann Göring.

In 1936, Schacht resisted the Four Year Plan; and responsibility for German rearmament was transferred to Göring and the Four Year Plan administration. In the following year, Schacht tried, but failed, to enlist the support of the Rhine–Ruhr steel elite in fighting Göring's plans for a state steel sector using very costly domestic ores (the Reichswerke Hermann Göring). Heavy industry abandoned Schacht's campaign against the government—as indeed it had in the very different circumstances of 1929–30, when Schacht had tried to launch a general political offensive against the Weimar's last fully parliamentary government.

An increasingly controversial issue raised by the discussion on rejoining the world economy was whether Germany should devalue the Mark and attempt to rejoin the international economy. In the aftermath of the 1931 crisis, devaluation was rejected because of legal constraints and of fears that it would be interpreted inside Germany as the beginning of a new inflation. In practice, the adoption of exchange control meant that Germany had left the world of gold standard orthodoxy. The Reichsmark was no longer freely convertible. After the US dollar left its gold parity in March 1933, the options for German currency policy appeared to increase. For the next three years, rumours about an impending parity alteration circulated constantly in Germany and created substantial political anxiety.[94] The Reichsbank set about attempting to limit this discussion, citing anti-inflation and anti-devaluation pronouncements by the National Socialist leaders. Until the summer of 1936, the Reichsbank remained resolutely opposed to any de-valuation. It repeated the widely believed argument about the dangers of inflation.

The end of the gold bloc and the devaluation of the French franc in October 1936 changed the calculation decisively. Schacht now began to see a devaluation as offering a way of reducing the costly and cumbersome control of exchange and trade. On 30 September 1936, with the devaluation of the franc imminent, Schacht told German press representatives that he was prepared to participate in international discussions of exchange rates.[95] This sign of unorthodoxy was enough to frighten the political leadership, for whom the argument about fear of inflation was always the prime consideration. Hitler and Goebbels in particular frequently stated that it was inflation which had destroyed the German Empire (during the First World War), as well as the republic of the 1920s. The Staatssekretär in the propaganda ministry, Walther R. Funk, when he heard of Schacht's willingness to devalue, 'went straight to the Führer and he intervened'. Funk's political master then concluded that Funk 'had prevented a German inflation'.[96]

This dispute was a preliminary to Schacht's dismissal as commissary economics minister, since Schacht no longer appeared to Hitler as the indispensable guarantor of currency stability: the role that had given Schacht (and the Reichsbank) their raison d'être in the early years of National Socialist economics. Instead, in late 1936 Hitler ordered an intensification

[94] Cf. Draft letter to the senior managers (Dr Nordhoff), 15 June 1934 (Bundesarchiv Koblenz and Berlin R 2501 [Reichsbank] 6510).

[95] Cf. 'Ausführungen des Herrn Präsidenten vor den Vertretern der Inlandspresse am 30. September 1936' (Bundesarchiv Koblenz and Berlin R 2501 [Reichsbank] 6994).

[96] Fröhlich, 1987, vol. 2, p. 689. The printed version makes the episode unintelligible because of a crucial transcription error. In the original diaries, Goebbels wrote 'Schacht wollte auch abwerten'. The Fröhlich edition incorrectly replaces abwerten (devalue) with abwarten (wait and see).

of price control with the appointment of Gauleiter Josef Wagner as Reich Price Commissar.

Criticism in public had to be presented as technical comments on subjects that lay in the Reichsbank's sphere of competence. There was no room for debate on general themes. Thus even Schacht's most daring public defiance, the 1935 Königsberg speech, closed with the lines: 'the listener will have concluded from my remarks that the financial execution of the great task of the Führer stands and falls with confidence in the security and strength of the Reich and its institutions.'[97]

The effect of Schacht's criticisms, which were well known and widely commented abroad, may not, in the end, have been very damaging to the National Socialist regime. Certainly, the Reichsbank was the most important internal German source of public criticism of government policy between 1935 and 1939, and in this way it played a quite remarkable role in the history of the dictatorship. But the appearance of debate and discussion was misleading. Schacht was both so well known internationally and so elegantly vociferous that his opposition was frequently, at least in the middle years of the decade, interpreted as a serious sign of disagreement within the German government. Or alternatively, it was read as an indication that after the creation of virtually full employment the German economic machine was losing its energy and that its financial resources were exhausted.[98] In fact neither of these widely believed interpretations had much truth. There was still plenty of scope for further economic expansion. The opposition of the Reichsbank's leadership did not in any way slow down the pace of rearmament in the late 1930s, nor was the final conflict which led to the dismissal of Schacht and the subordination of the Reichsbank anything more than an ephemeral embarrassment for Hitler.

In 1938 and 1939 the Reichsbank's conflict with the government reached a climax. The Reichsbank insisted that the volume of Mefo-bills outstanding should be reduced. But the state's financial needs were increasingly urgent. The fourth Reich loan of 1938 (for RM 1.5 billion) was the first dramatic failure of the government on the capital markets: a substantial part of the loan needed to be taken up by the underwriters.[99] In December 1938, the Reichsbank refused a request from the finance ministry for a special credit of RM 100 million, in a bid to press fiscal restraint.

On 7 January 1939, Schacht addressed a dramatic letter, signed by the entire Directorate, to Hitler, demanding a limitation of expenditure to the amount funded through taxation or long-term loans. The letter raised the

[97] Schacht, 1935, p. 17.
[98] Cf. Priester, 1936 and Balogh, 1938.
[99] Cf. James, 1995, pp. 329ff.

inflation theme again. It led to the dismissal, first of Schacht, Vice-President Friedrich Dreyse, and Ernst Hülse, and then of other members of the Directorate (Karl Blessing, Carl Ehrhardt, and Wilhelm Vocke).

On 15 June 1939, a new Reichsbank Act subordinated the bank directly to the 'Führer' and abolished the Central Committee. Instead, an Advisory Council composed of leading business figures, and divided into various sub-committees, was constituted. The 'Führer' was to determine the limit of the short-term credit that could be extended to the Reich, and the maximum volume of Reich Treasury Bills to be discounted. These measures in fact converted the Reichsbank back into a perfect machine for inflation: a role in which its officials felt most unhappy. The gold coverage rules, which were in any case wholly redundant at this stage, were abrogated. The application of the 'Führerprinzip' to the management of the Reichsbank meant the abolition of majority voting by the Directorate, and the vesting of sole responsibility for policy in the President (whose office was renamed: he was now no longer President of the Reichsbank Directorate but President of the German Reichsbank). Rather perversely, but quite characteristically for National Socialist politics, this apparent move toward an authoritarian principle meant little in practice. For the new President, unlike his predecessor, was a nonentity. Walther Funk had already been Schacht's successor as economics minister; and in fact he spent most of his working time at the ministry, not the bank. Schacht regarded Funk with a contempt that appears to have been widely shared by Reichsbank officials, and later told Allied interrogators, 'Mr. Funk is certainly stupid and in fact has no knowledge of finance.'[100]

Funk actually and surprisingly continued to preach about central bank independence, regardless of the politicized realities of rearmament and war. In an internal speech to Vorstandsbeamte given in 1940, he explained how undesirable it was for a central bank to be supervised and controlled by a finance ministry which borrowed and spent. How superior was the German model of a personal union, in which the Reichsbank President also happened to be economics minister! 'The Reichsbank always had the chance to object if any ministry came with improper demands, and in decisive issues could go straight to the Führer.'[101]

In fact, the practical management of the Reichsbank was in the hands of the Vice-Presidents, first Rudolf Brinkmann and then, after Brinkmann's mental collapse in 1939,[102] Emil Puhl, who managed the technical side of

[100] C. J. Hynning interrogation of Schacht, 11 July 1945 (IfZ 135/6).
[101] Funk speech, 2 Feb. 1940 (Bundesarchiv Koblenz and Berlin R 2501 [Reichsbank] 6363, sheet 79).
[102] Cf. Marsh, 1992, p. 129.

the Reichsbank's business, and Kurt Lange, who looked after the bank's political contacts. Puhl continued Schacht's tradition of more or less veiled critical remarks about the government in the presence of foreign experts.[103]

How did the ordinary staff of the Reichsbank react? At the beginning of the new era, in 1933, Schacht had issued an instruction to Reichsbank employees not to criticize National Socialism: 'if . . . there is no cheerful endorsement of the National Socialist spirit, I am not intending to impose any belief, but I expect in such a case silence'.[104] In the second half of 1938, as the conflict between the institution and the government neared its climax, two American visitors noted that: 'most of the Reichsbank officials who were trained in the doctrines of orthodox economic liberalism and who still retain serious doubts regarding the viability of a controlled economy . . . said that the system of exchange control, as indeed the whole system of control over Germany's economic life, was quite unworkable in the long run, although they saw no possibility of returning to a freer system unless fundamental changes occurred both in external economic conditions and in Germany's internal politics.'[105] In 1939, the economics ministry complained that 'the Reichsbank, in its current state, did not nearly satisfy the demands that are to be made of a National Socialist organization'.[106] The reordering of the Reichsbank after January 1939, however, did not change the attitudes of most Reichsbank officials, but it did limit their possibilities of acting even further. The Reichsbank, deprived of its role as 'guardian of the currency' in practice simply became one part of the mechanism for running the war economy.

7. The Second World War

Like the First World War, Hitler's war was fiscally ruinous. There were tax rises—beginning with the War Economy Degree of 4 September 1939— and in 1942 an effort to siphon off excess business profits; but tax revenues were barely sufficient to pay for the cost of the state's civilian expenditure. Military expenditure was not covered by revenue. While in the first year of war, 30.2 per cent of all public sector expenditure was met from normal income, by 1944–5 that proportion had fallen to 11.2 per cent.[107] There

---

[103] Jacobsson, Diary, 33, p. 101.
[104] Verfügungen, 29 Aug. 1933 (Bundesarchiv Koblenz and Berlin R 2501 [Reichsbank]).
[105] Knoke and Despres, Notes on European Trip June 16–August 19, 1938 (FRBNY).
[106] 'Betrifft Reichsbankgesetz', undated ('Special Archive' Moscow 1458-1-349, fol. 78).
[107] Cf. Boelcke, 1992, p. 109.

was little attempt to repeat the public issue of loans as in the First World War, or in the rearmament phase of the 1930s: because this might turn into an embarrassing sort of financial plebiscite, and because there were easier financing methods available. So the war was managed through the 'silent financing' of private savings channelled by the banks and savings banks into state paper, as they had been through the 1930s. Some part of the war was paid through impositions on occupied countries. But these sources were inadequate, and as the war progressed, its cost was increasingly met through the use of the printing press. With an increasing pace after 1943, the treasury bills and treasury certificates ended directly in the Reichsbank's portfolio. As a consequence, the currency in circulation rose from RM 11 billion at the outset of the war to RM 73 billion by the time of the German defeat.[108]

The extension of rationing, with price and incomes controls, rather than monetary limitation was the primary weapon against inflation. Official prices did not match the expansion of the Reichsbank's note issue: on the contrary, from 1939 to 1944, the official cost of living index rose by only 11.2 per cent.[109] Already on 27 August 1939, during the period of mobilization for war, a decree introduced rationing of essential goods. From an early stage, it was clear to the Reichsbank, at least as its officials could note in internal documents, that such mechanisms would in the longer run be inadequate to restrain inflation. If the duration of the war was to be longer, there would be the 'danger of a black market with uncontrolled prices'.[110] After the spring of 1941, the pace of money creation intensified, and the Reichsbank began to note price increases for some goods of up to 60 per cent. Its economists commented on the already widespread view 'that there are no major differences between the current situation and developments in the [First] World War, and that the inflationary screw has begun to turn'.[111] By 1944, Germany was close to a complete collapse of confidence in the currency. The 'cigarette currency' had already made its appearance in 1941, and after 1943 a large-scale black market developed, despite the efforts at control by a police state.

From the beginning of the war, the Reichsbank's economists had tried to refute some of the arguments made already in the previous war, according to which monetary policy had an insignificant role in wartime policy. They correctly reasoned that only monetary discipline, not more controls, could limit the damage done by the blossoming of the black market. Most of the

[108] Cf. Hansmeyer and Caesar, 1976, p. 417.

[109] Cf. Hansmeyer and Caesar, 1976, p. 414.

[110] Memorandum of 22 Feb. 1940 (Bundesarchiv Koblenz and Berlin R 2501 [Reichsbank] 7005, sheet 68–81 [quote from sheet 81]).

[111] Memorandum of 4 Oct. 1941 (Bundesarchiv Koblenz and Berlin R 2501 [Reichsbank] 7007, sheet 295–6).

German official mind did not share this view. In particular the economics ministry was claiming that 'the stability of the currency today depends in the first instance on price and wage policy, over which the Reichsbank has no control'.[112] But any self-assertion on the part of the Reichsbank's staff was frustrated by the bank's leaders.

Funk was at first blithely insouciant about the issue of war finance. Like the earlier wartime planners, he saw the problem as one that could be deferred until the (successful) outcome of the war. In the fall of 1941, while Operation Barbarossa was grinding to a halt outside Moscow, Funk told Hitler that the geopolitical reordering of Europe would solve the financial problem. With Hitler's larger economic area, 'Germany will have removed the entire finanical burden of the war within 10 years without destroying the purchasing power of our currency'.[113]

One of the major tasks of the Reichsbank in the early stages of the war lay in providing a blueprint for the New Europe. After the military successes of May and June 1940, with the United Kingdom left as Germany's only military opponent, Funk launched a major initiative. Funk ridiculed the idea of a gold-based currency as an American system: 'as a basis for European currency gold will in the future play no part, for currency is not dependent on the gold coverage but upon the value which the State, in this case the United States, gives it. . . . If one could take all the gold that is accumulated in the cellars in America and place it on an island and cause the island to disappear, the economic life of nations would not suffer in the least.' Instead the European economy would be tied together through long-term trade agreements, and a multilateralized clearing in place of the bilateral agreements which in the 1930s had restricted commercial development. 'By concluding long-term agreements with European countries, it is intended that the European economic systems shall adapt themselves to the German market by a system of production planned far into the future.'[114] The Reichsbank envisaged a return to a multilateral clearing system in which the Reichsbank would take the place previously occupied by the pound sterling.[115]

The European schemes developed in the Reichsbank have a very obvious interest to the present-day analyst, since they resemble both some aspects of the post-war international monetary order, as well as post-war plans for

---

[112] Memorandum of 27 Sept. 1940 (Bundesarchiv Koblenz and Berlin R 2501 [Reichsbank] 6428, sheet 105).

[113] Jochmann, 1980, p. 80.

[114] Funk, 1940, pp. 9, 11.

[115] Cf. Emil Puhl memorandum of 8 Apr. 1941 (Bundesarchiv Koblenz and Berlin R 2501 [Reichsbank] 7018, sheet 157ff.).

European economic and currency unions.[116] The spectacular propaganda initiatives with which the Funk plan was launched indeed played some part in pushing the United Kingdom and the United States to draw up their own currency plans for the post-war world. In this way, the 1940 plans stood at the origins of the Bretton Woods agreements of 1944. Aspects of the Bretton Woods system were then deliberately used in the late 1970s in the construction of a European Monetary System.

Such an intriguing historical retrospective may give greater significance to Funk's plan than existed at the time. These European currency schemes were a flash in the 1940 pan, which faded as it became clear that there would not be a short European war followed rapidly by a new peace settlement. As the war went on, the practical objections to the realization of the European currency union increased.

Even in 1940, the Reichsbank's economists were opposed to the most institutionally ambitious scheme, the Reich Economics Ministry's plan for the 'Europa-Bank'. They argued that it would be best to do without 'inter-state agreements' and 'rigid rules' and noted that: 'the more informal and unobtrusive is the monetary union, the greater the chances of success'. Instead, the Reichsbank envisaged a more modest multilateral clearing union for an 'inner European bloc' of countries under German influence, and including Bohemia-Moravia, Slovakia, the *Generalgouvernement* in Poland, Denmark, Norway, as well as Belgium, Luxembourg, and the Netherlands. For a wider area, including Bulgaria and Romania, there would be difficulties 'since for considerations of national prestige they are not prepared to let their balance of payments and their economy be guided so obviously by so visible a German influence'.[117]

The discussion of a currency area suffered from two apparently insoluble problems: the German unwillingness to let prices adjust; and a German reluctance to impose obvious economic humiliations on its trading area—which was also an area of political domination. In fact from the beginning of the expansion of German imperialism, political arguments had overridden any economic logic. In late February 1938, the Reichsbank had rapidly produced a plan for the currency union of Germany and Austria on the basis of an exchange rate of 2 schillings to RM 1, which corresponded to the Berlin market quotation. The Reichsbank's economists recognized that this rate did not reflect the higher purchasing power of the schilling, but saw in their suggestion a way of stimulating the Austrian economy.[118] Their view

---

[116] Cf. Marsh, 1992, pp. 132–5; cf. also Hoffmeyer, 1992, pp. 19f.

[117] Memorandum of 20 July 1940 (Bundesarchiv Koblenz and Berlin R 2501 [Reichsbank] 6428, pp. 9ff.).

[118] Cf. Memorandum of 26 Feb. 1938 (Bundesarchiv Koblenz and Berlin R 2501 [Reichsbank] 6673).

was supported by the Reich Economics Ministry, but eventually rejected on the grounds that it would be unpopular with the Austrians, who eventually thus received their Marks at the more favourable rate of 1.50 schillings. Exactly the same kinds of objection made the plans of 1940 irrelevant in the circumstances of the war. The large German clearing deficits formed an insuperable obstacle to the realization of a genuine clearing union that might prepare the way for German monetary integration.

The longer the war went on, the more illusory the clearing union became; hence it soon grew obvious that there was no possibility of implementing the plan. Not surprisingly, it gradually faded into oblivion. By 1943, German economists in the banks and in the Reichsbank were much more interested in the Allied schemes for the post-war order. The chief economist of the Bank for International Settlements, Per Jacobsson, even visited Berlin in June 1943 to explain the currency plans of John Maynard Keynes and Harry Dexter White.[119] When Funk gave another speech, in July 1944 (at the time of the Bretton Woods conference), he included in his polemic against the Allied schemes, entitled 'Economic Order Versus Currency Mechanism', an argument about why, from the German and European viewpoint, the British schemes would be more favourable than the 'plutocratic' American plan.[120]

In the large-scale business of German planning for a post-war monetary order, gold played an increasingly insignificant role. Funk again and again rejected 'the international rules of the game of gold automatism, because this system creates bondage'.[121] But in the day-to-day running of the war economy, gold still mattered greatly. It was used to pay for strategic imports, such as chrome and iron ores, that could not be obtained elsewhere. As a consequence, it became clear that gold 'will become the militarily most essential raw material'.[122] Gold no longer played a role as an international economic regulator: it reverted to its much earlier role as a strategic good, needed to keep armies in the field. Its management was handled at the highest political level. Funk explained that: 'in all discussions on the use of gold for trade-policy or political purposes, the Führer has therefore invariably consulted me personally'.[123]

This gold was sold to foreign central banks, mostly to the Schweizerische Nationalbank, which during the war bought Swiss francs 1,209.8 million. A total of RM 930 million of gold at the official exchange rate was sold in Switzerland; another RM 96 million was sold to Sweden, a vital source

---

[119] Cf. Jacobsson, 1979, pp. 178f.; cf. also James, 1994, pp. 205–18.
[120] Herbst, 1982, pp. 305–10.
[121] Funk, 1940, p. 22.
[122] Eysen, 1937, p. 1170.
[123] Funk to Körner, 14 July 1944 ('Special Archive' Moscow 700–1–86, fol. 3).

of raw materials including high grade iron ore, and RM 80 million directly to Romania. Although Switzerland provided some goods to Germany (including tank parts), her primary role was as a financial intermediary. The gold sold there was used to make payments on German account to countries which would not allow any bilateral clearing: Yugoslavia in 1940, and right up to the moment of the German invasion on 6 April 1941; Romania after 1942; and Spain and Portugal throughout the war. Portugal too was an intermediary for the vital trade in tungsten and industrial diamonds from South America. The last German sale of gold to the Schweizerische Nationalbank occurred as late as 6 April 1945, when s.f. 7.8 million (RM 4.4 million) was taken from Constance.[124]

Most of this gold had come into German hands as a result of German military action. Gold taken from occupied central banks amounted to RM 245 million from Austria and RM 64 million from Czechoslovakia (in which cases the transfer was recognized by the Bank for International Settlements); later on, RM 18 million in Czech gold coins and RM 3 million in Czech bullion were added, RM 560 million from Belgium, 340 million from the Netherlands, 198 million from Italy, 12 million from Luxembourg, 80 million from Hungary, and 10 from Gdansk.[125] The Belgian gold was particularly problematical. At the outset of the war, most of Belgium's gold reserves had been transferred to Britain and the United States; but part went to France, from where it was transported, after the German invasion, to Dakar. Vichy France moved this gold back across the Sahara, and the Banque de France, under pressure from Prime Minister Pierre Laval, agreed to its transfer to the Reichsbank. The Reichsbank tried to pay the Banque Nationale de Belgique in Marks, but that institution refused to sign the receipt which would have given the transfer at least a nominal legality.[126] Finally, the gold was seized in France, and taken to Berlin, where it was melted into new bars at the Prussian Mint and provided with certificates dated from the mid-1930s, 'since the provenance of the gold would otherwise have been obvious, and that would have led to difficulties on its sale'.[127] These bars were then sold to Switzerland.

The Bank for International Settlements, where Germans held crucial staff positions, including General Manager Paul Hechler, played a part in per-

---

[124] Cf. Golddepot des Reichsbankdirektoriums Berlin; Goldmünzdepot des Reichsbankdirektoriums Berlin (SNB Bern, 118, 119.8).

[125] Cf. memorandum 'Totalbetrag des nichtgeraubten Goldes, das den Deutschen während des Krieges zur Verfügung stand' of 5 Feb. 1946. NA RG59, 1945–49, Box 4206, 5 Feb. 1946 (SNB Bern, 0014, 1946); see also Smith, 1996, p. 163; Unabhängige Expertenkommission, 1997; Czech Republic, 1997; Bank of Italy, 1997.

[126] BNB (Governor: A. Goffin) to Reichsbank, 5 Aug. 1943 (SNB Bern 119.8).

[127] Memo, Aug. 1943 ('Special Archive' Moscow, 700–1–70, fol. 110).

petuating what the technocratic actors still referred to as 'central bank co-operation' in the odd and violent circumstances of wartime Europe.[128] The Schweizerische Nationalbank insisted on taking only gold that had been in legitimate German possession in 1939 and was thus not the 'plundered gold' against which the Western Allies warned. Puhl offered verbal assurances that the Reichsbank was shipping genuinely German gold; and the captured gold was melted down in Berlin and supplied with German certificates dated 1935.[129] In fact, at the beginning of the war, the Reichsbank's published gold reserve was only RM 70.8 million. Although the Swiss officials claimed that the inclusion of hidden reserves and the taking of Austrian and Czech gold made the real figure as high as RM 500 million, this was still substantially less than the volume of subsequent sales.[130] The Swiss officials were quite willing to let themselves be duped.

The Reichsbank also involved itself in the sinister and criminal business of taking and realizing gold from the victims of the concentration and annihilation camps. At least RM 6 million in gold in 76 consignments was transferred from camps in the Lublin district to the account of *SS-Hauptsturmführer* Bruno Melmer. When the main Reichsbank vault was evacuated at the beginning of 1945 to a salt mine at Thuringian Merkers, it contained not only 4,173 bags of gold bars, but also 207 containers of gold jewellery and silverware looted by the SS. Other looted goods were held in the local branches of the Reichsbank: the Regensburg office, for instance, had in its safe the tabernacle of a Russian orthodox church.[131] Altogether, the Reichsbank bought from the SS at least 1.28 tons of gold (worth RM 3.6 million), and channelled some of it (including gold tooth fillings), taken from victims of the National Socialist persecution and extermination policies, into international trade.[132]

The complicity of the Reichsbank and its officials in the criminal acts of the regime formed the basis of the indictments after 1945. Funk was sentenced at Nuremberg to life imprisonment; and Puhl to five years imprisonment at the subsequent 'Wilhelmstraße' trial. Schacht, who had been dismissed from the Reichsbank in January 1939, was acquitted of all charges at Nuremberg.

---

[128] Cf. Trepp, 1993.

[129] Cf. Report of 16 May 1945 (SNB Bern 105.7).

[130] Cf. Vogler, 1985, as well as 'Goldbestand am 1.9.1939' and 'Sonderdeviseneingang zwischen dem 1.9.1939 und dem 1.11.1944', both dated 28 Nov. 1944 ('Special Archive' Moscow 700–1–97).

[131] Cf. Exhibit 'A': Register of Shipments Received at Reichsbank Building Frankfurt (BoE C52/9).

[132] Cf. U.S. State Department, 1997.

8. Conclusion

The Reichsbank had forty good years, followed by thirty bad years. It followed, in short, the destiny of the German Empire. It also moulded that destiny. The monetary management of the *Kaiserreich* produced a more stable and less jerky economic development than that produced by the more chaotic monetary arrangements of the United States. But the doctrines evolved in the good years, the real bills doctrine, the Reichsbank's mission as saviour of the German banks, and its function as guardian and defender of the gold reserves, all directly produced the difficulties and troubles that followed once international circumstances changed with the World War and the collapse of the international gold standard.

The bad years eventually and very slowly prompted a learning experience, but that learning was itself painful. Central banks need as an operational asset a stock of credibility. Each of the failures, which necessitated a relearning, also constituted a dent in the Reichsbank's carapace of credibility. When the Reichsbank decided in the 1920s that it should not automatically act as lender of last resort to the banking system, it helped to produce the monetary collapse of 1930–1—in part because the banks did not fully expect the unaccommodating new behaviour of the Reichsbank. The lesson learnt in the inflation, that lending to the government and the public sector should be limited, also contributed to the crises of the late Weimar years; and after 1933, the new National Socialist masters were determined that—whatever the Reichsbank might think—they should not be limited in this manner. During the dictatorship, a rediscovery of the virtues of economic liberalism occurred as part of the 'expert' or 'technical' criticism of National Socialist economics; and this served as a valuable prelude to the post-war reordering of the economy.

In the longer term perspective, the events of the 1920s and 1930s were powerful negative models: the inflation, the monetary collapse and depression, and the National Socialist planned economy and its new inflation. These experiences challenged central bankers, and made economic analysis more central to their activity. But the apparently simple question asked proved much harder to answer: how could things have been managed differently and better?

The interwar Reichsbank had not learnt sufficiently from the bad experiences. The incompleteness of the criticism of government actions in the 1930s and 1940s was obviously in large part a consequence of the dangerous political circumstances, which ruled out a more extensive attack. But this was not the whole story. Schacht, who was clearly the most influential and charismatic figure in the second half of the Reichsbank's history, is a telling example of the incompleteness of institutional learning. While it was easy to discover what Schacht disliked—high foreign borrowing, unfunded government expenditures—it was much harder to find a positive economic principle or guideline that Schacht advocated or adopted as his own. Throughout his career in the Reichsbank, in fact he continued to assert variants of the real bills doctrine, and was suspicious of quantity theorists. The personal adulation for Hitler's charisma was the hallmark of a man who had lost his way, and who had no good explanation of what should be the guide to Reichsbank policy. Lack of theory prompted a reliance on personality. More generally, the experience of the Reichsbank as part of the mechanism of the National Socialist dictatorship also demonstrated quite clearly the limits of a purely 'technocratic' critique. Of National Socialist policies deserving criticism in the late 1930s, fiscal performance is really not the most obvious candidate.

Such political and even moral issues had actually been discussed at the time of the founding of the Reichsbank. One of the lessons of the 1870s, which had emerged during the long and productive debates about constitutional, economic, and political reordering was that the successful harnessing of private interests depends on the creation of a satisfactory overall legal and economic framework. It could not be achieved by a single institution alone. In economic terms, it also depended on the existence of a suitable international framework, the absence of which during the 1930s was a major cause of the difficulties of the Reichsbank in formulating any clear or attractive alternative to the economics of control.

9. Sources and bibliography

Sources

Archiv der Schweizer Nationalbank Bern (SNB)
Bank of England Archive (BoE)
Bundesarchiv Koblenz and Berlin
Central State Archive, Moscow ('Special Archive')
Federal Reserve Bank of New York Archive (FRBNY)
Institut für Zeitgeschichte (IfZ), Munich
National Archives, Washington (NA)
Universitätsbibliothek, Basel

Bibliography

Akten der Reichskanzlei (Weimarer Republik). Das Kabinett Müller II, 28. Juni 1928 bis 27. März 1930 (1970), vol. 2, ed. Karl D. Erdmann, Boppard am Rhein

Ausschuß zur Untersuchung der Erzeugungs- und Absatzbedingungen der deutschen Wirtschaft (Enquête-Ausschuß) (1929), Die Reichsbank, Berlin

Balderston, Theo (1993): The Banks and the Gold Standard in the German Financial Crisis of 1931, University of Manchester Working Papers in Economic and Social History 24

Balogh, Thomas (1938): The National Economy of Germany, in: Economic Journal 48, pp. 461–98

Bank of Italy (1997): The Story of the Gold Deposited at the Bank of Italy (1943–1958). Ein Beitrag zur Goldkonferenz in London, 2–4 December 1997, duplicated manuscript, n.p.

Barkai, Avraham (1988): Vom Boykott zur 'Entjudung': Der wirtschaftliche Existenzkampf der Juden im Dritten Reich, Frankfurt a.M.

Barth, Boris (1995): Die deutsche Hochfinanz und die Imperialismen: Banken und Außenpolitik vor 1914, Stuttgart

Bendixen, Felix (1920): Geld und Kapital: Gesammelte Aufsätze, Jena

Berger, Helge/Ritschl, Albrecht (1995): Germany and the Political Economy of the Marshall Plan 1947–52, in: Eichengreen, Barry (ed.): Europe's Post-War Recovery, Cambridge

Boelcke, Willi A. (1992): Die Finanzpolitik des Dritten Reiches, in: Bracher, Karl-Dietrich/ Funke, Manfred/Jacobsen, Hans-Adolf (eds.): Deutschland 1933–1945: Neue Studien zur nationalsozialistischen Herrschaft, Bonn

Bopp, Karl R. (1953): Reichsbank Operations 1876–1914, Federal Reserve Bank of Philadelphia

Borchardt, Knut (1976): Währung und Wirtschaft, in: Deutsche Bundesbank (ed.): Währung und Wirtschaft in Deutschland 1876–1975, Frankfurt a.M.

Borchardt, Knut (1979): Zwangslagen und Handlungsspielräume in der großen Wirtschaftskrise der frühen dreißiger Jahre: Zur Revision des überlieferten Geschichtsbildes, in: Jahrbuch 1979 der Bayerischen Akademie der Wissenschaften, Munich, pp. 87–132

Borchardt, Knut (1985): Das Gewicht der Inflationsangst in den wirtschaftspolitischen Entscheidungsprozessen während der Weltwirtschaftskrise, in: Feldman, Gerald D. (ed.): Die Nachwirkungen der Inflation auf die deutsche Geschichte 1924–1933, Munich, pp. 233–60

Borchardt, Knut/Schötz, Hans-Otto (1991): Wirtschaftspolitik in der Krise. Die (Geheim-) Konferenz der Friedrich-List-Gesellschaft im September 1931 über Möglichkeiten und Folgen einer Kreditausweitung, Baden-Baden

Born, Karl Erich (1967): Die deutsche Bankenkrise 1931: Finanzen und Politik, Munich

Born, Karl Erich (1991): Der Ausbau der Reichsinstitutionen und das Notenbankproblem: Die Herstellung der Währungseinheit und die Entstehung der Reichsbank, in: Kunisch, Johannes (ed.): Bismarck und seine Zeit, Berlin

Bresciani-Turroni, Costantino (1950): Economic Policy for the Thinking Man, London

Bresciani-Turroni, Costantino (1953): The Economics of Inflation: A Study of Currency Depreciation in Postwar Germany, London

Czech Republic (1997): Czechoslovak Gold Reserves and their Surrender to Nazi Germany. Ein Beitrag zur Goldkonferenz in London, 2–4 December 1997, duplicated manuscript, n.p.

Deutscher Reichstag (1874/75): Stenographische Berichte über die Verhandlungen des Deutschen Reichstages, vol. 35 (2. Legislaturperiode, II. Session)

Deutscher Reichstag (1889/90): Stenographische Berichte über die Verhandlungen des Deutschen Reichstages, vol. 111 (7. Legislaturperiode, V. Session)

Deutscher Reichstag (1907/08): Stenographische Berichte über die Verhandlungen des Deutschen Reichstages, vol. 229 (12. Legislaturperiode, I. Session)

Deutscher Reichstag (1909): Stenographische Berichte über die Verhandlungen des Deutschen Reichstages, vol. 235 (12. Legislaturperiode, I. Session)

Diehl, Karl (1932) (ed.): Wirkungen und Ursachen des hohen Zinsfußes in Deutschland, Jena

Dierschke, Karl/Müller, F. (1926): Die Notenbanken der Welt, Berlin

Ellis, Howard S. (1934): German Monetary Theory 1905–1933, Cambridge, Mass.

Erbe, René (1958): Die nationalsozialistische Wirtschaftspolitik 1933–1938 im Lichte der modernen Theorie, Zurich

Eucken, Walter (1923): Kritische Betrachtungen zum deutschen Geldproblem, Jena

Eynern, Gert von (1928): Die Reichsbank: Probleme des deutschen Zentralnoteninstituts in geschichtlicher Darstellung, Jena

Eysen, F. (1937): Wehrwirtschaftliche Grenzen der Selbstversorgung mit mineralischen Rohstoffen, in: Der deutsche Volkswirt 11, 24, pp. 1168–70

Feldman, Gerald D. (1993): The Great Disorder: Politics, Economics, and Society in the German Inflation 1914–1924, New York

Ferguson, Niall (1995): Paper and Iron: Hamburg Business and German Politics in the Era of Inflation 1897–1927, Cambridge

Fischer, Albert (1995): Hjalmar Schacht und Deutschlands 'Judenfrage': Der 'Wirtschafts-diktator' und die Vertreibung der Juden aus der deutschen Volkswirtschaft, Köln/Weimar/Wien

Forstmeier, Friedrich/Volkmann, Hans-Erich (1977) (eds.): Kriegswirtschaft und Rüstung 1939–1945, Düsseldorf

Fröhlich, Elke (1987) (ed.): Die Tagebücher von Joseph Goebbels: Sämtliche Fragmente, vol. 2, Munich

Funk, Walther (1940): The Economic Future of Europe, Berlin

Gallarotti, Giulio M. (1993): The Scramble for Gold: Monetary Regime Transformations in the 1870's, in: Bordo, Michael D./Capie, Forrest (eds.): Monetary Regimes in Transition, Cambridge

Giovannini, Alberto (1986): 'Rules of the Game' during the International Gold Standard: England and Germany, in: Journal of International Money and Finance 5, pp. 467–83

Habedank, Heinz (1981): Die Reichsbank in der Weimarer Republik: Zur Rolle der Zentral-bank in der Politik des deutschen Imperialismus, Berlin (East)

Hachtmann, Rüdiger (1988): Lebenshaltungskosten und Reallöhne während des 'Dritten Reiches', In: Vierteljahrsschrift für Sozial- und Wirtschaftsgeschichte 75, pp. 32–73

Hansmeyer, Karl-Heinrich/Caesar, Rolf (1976): Kriegswirtschaft und Inflation 1936–1948, in: Deutsche Bundesbank (ed.): Währung und Wirtschaft in Deutschland 1876–1975, Frankfurt a.M., pp. 367–429

Hardach, Gerd (1976): Weltmarktorientierung und relative Stagnation: Währungspolitik in Deutschland 1924–1931, Berlin

Helfferich, Karl (1898): Die Reform des deutschen Geldwesens nach der Gründung des Reiches, Leipzig

Herbst, Ludolf (1982): Der Totale Krieg und die Ordnung der Wirtschaft. Die Kriegs-wirtschaft im Spannungsfeld von Politik, Ideologie und Propaganda 1939–1945, Stuttgart

Hoffmeyer, Erik (1992): The International Monetary System: An Essay in Interpretation, Amsterdam *et al.*

Holtfrerich, Carl-Ludwig (1984): Zu hohe Löhne in der Weimarer Republik: Bemerkungen zur Borchardt-These, in: Geschichte und Gesellschaft 10, pp. 122–41

Holtfrerich, Carl-Ludwig (1986): The German Inflation 1914–1923, Berlin/New York

Holtfrerich, Carl-Ludwig (1988): Relations Between Monetary Authorities and Govern-mental Institutions: The Case of Germany from the 19th Century to the Present, in: Toniolo, Gianni (ed.): Central Banks' Independence in Historical Perspective, Berlin/New York, pp. 105–59

Holtfrerich, Carl-Ludwig (1993): Did Monetary Unification Precede or Follow Political Unification in the 19th Century?, in: European Economic Review 37, pp. 518–24

Jacobsson, Erin J. (1979): A Life for Sound Money: Per Jacobsson, His Biography, Oxford

James, Harold (1994): Post-War German Currency Plans, in: Buchheim, Christoph/Hutter, Michael/James, Harold (eds.): Zerrissene Zwischenkriegszeit: Wirtschaftshistorische Bei-träge, Knut Borchardt zum 65. Geburtstag, Baden-Baden, pp. 205–18

James, Harold (1995): Die Deutsche Bank und die Diktatur, in: Gall, Lothar *et al.*: Die Deutsche Bank 1870–1995, Munich, pp. 323–408

Jochmann, Werner (1980) (ed.): Adolf Hitlers Monologe im Führerhauptquartier 1941–1944: Die Aufzeichnungen Heinrich Heims, Hamburg

Kindleberger, Charles P. (1993): ²A Financial History of Western Europe, New York

Krowoth, Rudolf (1986): Die Finanzpolitik des Deutschen Reiches während der Reichs-kanzlerschaft Bethmann Hollwegs und die Geld- und Kapitalverhältnisse (1909–1913/14), Frankfurt a.M.

Lewis, William Arthur (1978): Growth and Fluctuations 1870–1913, London

Lumm, Karl (1912): Diskontpolitik, in: Bank-Archiv 11, pp. 129–36, 145–50, 162–7, 179–87

McGouldrick, Paul (1984): Operations of the German Central Bank and the Rules of the Game, 1879–1913, in: Bordo, Michael D./Schwartz, Anna J. (eds.): A Retrospective on the Classical Gold Standard 1821–1931, Chicago

Marsh, David (1992): The Bundesbank: The Bank that Rules Europe, London

National Monetary Commission (1910–11): Report on Banking and Central Banking, Gov-ernment Printing Office, Document 356, Washington D.C.

Neisser, Hans (1929): Der internationale Geldmarkt vor und nach dem Kriege, in: Weltwirt-schaftliches Archiv 29, pp. 171–226

Plenge, Johannes (1912): Von der Diskontpolitik zur Beherrschung des Geldmarktes, in: Bank-Archiv 11, pp. 219–26, 242–6, 251–61

Priester, Hans (1936): Das Deutsche Wirtschaftswunder, Amsterdam

Publications of the National Monetary Commission (1909), vol. 1, Interviews, Government Printing Office, Washington D.C.

Reddish, Angela (1993): The Latin Monetary Union and the Emergence of the International Gold Standard, in: Bordo, Michael D./Capie, Forrest (eds.): Monetary Regimes in Trans-ition, Cambridge, pp. 68–85

Reichsbank (various years): Verwaltungsberichte der Deutschen Reichsbank

The Reichsbank 1876–1900 (1910), Government Printing Office, Washington D.C.

Die Reichsbank 1876 bis 1910: Organisation und Geschäftsverkehr statistisch dargestellt (1912), Reichsdruckerei, Berlin

Russell, Henry B. (1898): International Monetary Conferences, New York

Schacht, Hjalmar (1927): Eigene oder geborgte Währung. Lecture, delivered on 18 November 1927, Leipzig

Schacht, Hjalmar (1932): Grundsätze deutscher Wirtschaftspolitik, Oldenburg

Schacht, Hjalmar (1935): Königsberger Rede. Rede des Reichbankpräsidenten und Beauf-tragten des Reichswirtschaftsministers Dr. Hjalmar Schacht auf der Deutschen Ostmesse Königsberg, on 18 August 1935, Berlin

Schacht, Hjalmar (1955): My First Seventy-Six Years, London

Schacht, Hjalmar (1957): Kleine Bekenntnisse aus 80 Jahren, Munich

Schötz, Hans-Otto (1987): Der Kampf um die Mark 1923/24. Die deutsche Währungs-stabilisierung unter dem Einfluß der nationalen Interessen Frankreichs, Großbritanniens und der USA, Veröffentlichungen der Historischen Kommission zu Berlin, vol. 68, Berlin

Schuker, Stephen A. (1988): American 'Reparations' to Germany 1919–1933: Implications for the Third World Debt Crisis, Princeton

Simpson, Amos E. (1969): Hjalmar Schacht in Perspective, The Hague

Smith, Arthur L. (1996): Hitler's Gold. The Story of the Nazi War Loot, Oxford

Sommariva, Andrea/Tullio, Giuseppe (1986): German Macroeconomic History 1880–1979: A Study of the Effects of Economic Policy on Inflation, Currency Depreciation, and Growth, Basingstoke

Sommer, Albrecht (1931): Die Reichsbank unter Hermann von Dechend, Berlin

Stucken, Rudolf (1953): ²Deutsche Geld- und Kreditpolitik 1914–1953, Tübingen

Trepp, Gian (1993): Bankgeschäfte mit dem Feind: Die Bank für Internationalen Zahlungsausgleich im Zweiten Weltkrieg. Von Hitlers Europabank zum Instrument des Marshallplans, Zurich

Turner, Henry Ashby (1985): Die Großunternehmer und der Aufstieg Hitlers, Berlin

Unabhängige Expertenkommission Schweiz—Zweiter Weltkrieg (1997): Goldtransaktionen im Zweiten Weltkrieg: kommentierte statistische Übersicht. Ein Beitrag zur Goldkonferenz in London, 2–4 December 1997, duplicated manuscript, Bern

U.S. Senate (1879), International Monetary Conference of 1878, 45th Congress, 3rd Session

U.S. State Department (1997): U.S. and Allied Efforts To Recover and Restore Gold and Other Assets Stolen or Hidden by Germany During World War II (Eizenstat Report), Co-ordinated by Stuart E. Eizenstat, May

Vocke, Wilhelm (1973): Memoiren, Stuttgart

Vogler, Robert (1985): Der Goldverkehr der Schweizerischen Nationalbank mit der Deut-schen Reichsbank 1939–1945, in: Geld, Währung und Konjunktur 3, 1, pp. 70–8

Voth, Hans-Joachim (1995): Did High Wages or High Interest Rates Bring Down the Weimar Republic? A Cointegration Model of Investment in Germany, in: Journal of Economic His-tory 55, pp. 801–21

Wagner, Adolph (1931): Die Handelskrisis von 1857 und ihre Veranlassungen: Sonderdruck aus: Preußisches Wochenblatt 1858, Reichsbank, Berlin

Webb, Steven B. (1989): Hyper-inflation and Stabilization in Weimar Germany, New York

Weber, Marie-Lise (1987): Ludwig Bamberger: Ideologie statt Realpolitik, Stuttgart

Woodward, Ernest L./Butler, Rohan D. (1947–) (eds.): Documents on British Foreign Policy, 1919–1939, 1st series, vol. 1–, Her Majesty's Stationery Office, London

World Bank (1993): East Asian Miracle, Washington D.C.

Ziegler, Dieter (1990): Das Korsett der 'Alten Dame': Die Geschäftspolitik der Bank of England 1844–1913, Frankfurt a.M.

Zilch, Reinhold (1987): Die Reichsbank und die finanzielle Kriegsvorbereitung 1907–1914, Berlin (East)

II. The Establishment of the Bank deutscher Länder and the West German Currency Reform

By Christoph Buchheim

1. Introduction

Although the currency reform is widely held to have been the trigger for the 'economic miracle' in western Germany, and the Deutsche Bundesbank is regarded as one of the most successful monetary institutions in the world, historians until the end of the 1980s largely ignored events leading up to the first, and the history of the second.[1] Only Eckhard Wandel analysed both in a single book, which failed to live up to the high expectations of its title. There have also been a few more recent essays on the currency reform or some of its aspects, for instance by Hans Möller, Heinz Sauermann, Ian Turner, and Albrecht Ritschl. The last of these was embedded in a controversy about the real economic importance of the currency reform. This emerged principally in a 1975 book by Werner Abelshauser, who tried to demonstrate that the currency reform played no more than a minor role in the growth that followed.[2] This heated debate has now run out of steam, and seems to have been decided in favour of Abelshauser's opponents.

The state of research into the currency reform is now much improved, reflecting the overall growth in interest in occupied Germany among historians. In 1993, Michael Brackmann published a study on the background to the currency reform, an expansive view which traced it back to the days of the Nazi regime. In the same year, a lengthy article by Christoph Buchheim appeared in the 'German Yearbook on Business History 1989–92', in which he summarized a variety of earlier publications. 1995 saw the publication of a book on the Allied Control Council by Gunther Mai, covering the Allied negotiations on a pan-German currency reform in great detail. This is complemented by an essay by Jochen Laufer on the Soviet Union's currency reform policy, in which Russian archive material is evaluated for the first

---

[1] Cf. Buchheim, 1988, p. 189.
[2] Cf. Buchheim, 1988, pp. 189f.; this article should also be seen as a contribution to this controversy.

time. In addition, Michael Wolff published a monograph in 1991 specifically dealing with the currency reform in Berlin.

However, the situation as regards the history of west German central bank organization is still very patchy. Theo Horstmann discusses the establishment of the Bank deutscher Länder in his book on Allied banking policy, a topic on which he had previously written two highly focused essays. Monika Dickhaus recently published a study of the role of the Bank deutscher Länder in the international monetary policy of West Germany and an article on the influence of the Allied Bank Commission on the Bank deutscher Länder. However, there is neither a comprehensive academic treatise on the overall history of the Bank deutscher Länder or the Deutsche Bundesbank, nor any more recent article on the early history of the central banking system in western Germany before the founding of the Bank deutscher Länder. The present article is an attempt to fill the latter gap.

It starts with a description of the overall economic situation in western Germany before the currency reform. The main focus is on the state of manufacturing industry and its incentive to produce, providing an explanation of the very low level of industrial output up to 1948. This is followed by a brief overview of the German banking system in the early post-war years. Section four then presents the Allied reforms of the central banking structures, including the establishment of the Land Central Banks. The final section centres around the currency reform itself, including an analysis of the Soviet position on the inter-allied negotiations, as reflected in Russian historical archives. It also shows that the reform did, indeed, act as a catalyst for rapid growth in western Germany.

2. The general economic situation in western Germany before the currency reform

The situation in western Germany at the close of the war was very grim. Allied bombing and shellfire had destroyed many towns and cities, the transport system was largely paralysed, and industrial production was at a standstill.

That many people were extremely pessimistic about Germany's economic future will come as no surprise. There were those, however, who were less easily deceived. One of them was Ludwig Erhard, who—shortly after the war had ended—was commissioned by the local military government to prepare a study on the problems of, and requirements for, economic reconstruction in Fürth. His impressions of the situation can be summarized as follows: 'in his view, the damage could be repaired quickly and was in any event not so grave as to seriously hamper any reconstruction. He knew that the workers had returned to their workplaces as soon as the war ended. In his talks with industrialists and businessmen, it had not escaped his notice that most plant and production facilities had remained undamaged, and that substantial stocks of raw materials were available almost everywhere.'[3] Elsewhere, other insiders were also optimistic. An analysis by Vereinigte Stahlwerke, for example, revealed that 12 out of 16 key plants could operate immediately at a minimum of 30 per cent capacity. Krupp, too, expected that the day after a production licence had been issued, it could produce 20 per cent of its maximum pig iron capacity, with 25 per cent for crude steel and almost 40 per cent for rolled steel products.[4]

a) The state of manufacturing industry

The conditions for resuming production in western Germany were actually very good. Despite the war dead, the influx of refugees and expellees saw a sharp rise in the general population. This phenomenon was also reflected in the expansion of the labour pool, which rose from 24.4 million people of employable age in 1939 to 25.7 million in 1946, and even 27.2 million in 1948.[5]

Overall, the skills structure of the workforce also showed an improvement over both the pre-war situation and the time of maximum production during the war. It was not merely that millions of German soldiers, including many skilled workers, returned home soon after the war. Another, equally important factor was that, during the war, the use of forced labour for less skilled activities had seen German workers rising to more demanding positions, acquiring the necessary know-how through special works training programmes as well as learning-by-doing.[6] In addition, many of the newcomers had been employed in industrial occupations and had the appropriate skills, although their settlement in rural areas meant that in the early days, they were unable to exercise them. This situation changed, however, as the towns and cities were rebuilt during the 1950s. The gradual absorption of the surplus of qualified workers into west German manufacturing industry when it was in a position to use their skills can also be viewed as a driving force of the 'economic miracle'.[7]

---

[3] Woller, 1986, p. 214.
[4] Cf. Henke, 1996, p. 544.
[5] Cf. Abelshauser, 1983, p. 23.
[6] See also Abelshauser, 1975, pp. 105f.
[7] Cf. Dumke, 1990, pp. 451ff.

The situation regarding industrial capacity was also relatively positive, as new investments during the war had far exceeded the plant and facilities destroyed. For this reason, west German industrial assets in 1945 were not only greater than before the war, but also more modern.[8] Although repair work was frequently necessary, particularly on buildings, the permanent employees at the factories started work on this as soon as the war was over. Industry was soon in a position to gear up production once again.[9]

If contemporary complaints are to be believed, continual shortages of raw materials hindered the growth in production. However, a certain degree of doubt must be cast on the substance of these claims. In the first instance, it was often possible to receive allocations from controlled stocks if corresponding orders had been received. These stocks were much sought-after because they were sold at the official—very low—prices. There is every reason to suspect that the requirements notified to the authorities were frequently inflated. Secondly, as Erhard had already observed, inventories generally appear to have been well filled at the end of the war. Together with safeguarding irreplaceable production facilities and keeping their core workforces intact, the accumulation of raw material reserves was part of the strategy adopted by companies as early as autumn 1944 to prepare for life after the war.[10]

The stockpiles were correspondingly large. The Thyssenhütte steelworks, for example, reports that it possessed 'handsome ore reserves' at the end of the war, and the Gutehoffnungshütte steelworks had sufficient stocks of ores, coke, scrap and limestone, as well as several tens of thousands of tonnes of pig iron and semi-finished products.[11] The situation at other companies was similar, if not better. This proves that many of the laments about shortages of raw materials were nothing more than a pretext.

The resources situation at the end of the war was thus surprisingly positive, and, contrary to all appearances, there were few barriers to rapid industrial recovery. The policy of the occupying powers, forced by the total occupation of Germany to assume government functions, was also marked by constructive pragmatism. The tone of the famous American Occupation Directive Joint Chiefs of Staff (JCS) 1067, which laid down guidelines for the conduct of military government in the initial phase following German capitulation—and still reflected in part the influence of the Morgenthau Plan—was very severe. However, it also incorporated a formula which allowed the military government to intervene to prevent famine, epidemics,

---

[8] Cf. Abelshauser, 1983, pp. 20ff.
[9] Cf. Henke, 1996, pp. 538f.
[10] Cf. Henke, 1996, p. 455.
[11] Cf. Henke, 1996, p. 543.

or unrest endangering the safety of the occupation troops. This formula was elastic, and came to be interpreted very flexibly by the members of the US Military Government, with the support of the War Department. The British had, in any case, rejected JCS 1067, as they believed that its implementation would ultimately harm the occupiers themselves.[12]

As events turned out, the military government took widespread steps to stabilize the economic situation and restart key industries as soon as the occupation took effect. Except for particularly sensitive sectors, including the steel industry, industrial enterprises received production licences in rapid succession. As early as mid-July, for example, most major plants in Cologne had been issued a licence.[13] Although many owners had been relieved of their functions as part of the denazification measures, they were replaced by trustees. Contrary to their poor reputation, the latter also looked after the interests of the companies in most cases, as many of them were relatives, senior executives, or other persons closely connected with the company.[14]

The effect of the highly publicized Level of Industry Plans and dismantling programmes on the revival of industrial production was practically zero. For a start, the former set the permitted production levels, for instance in the steel industry, so high that they were not actually achieved until 1950. The latter (i.e. the dismantling programmes) were never substantial in western Germany, and they mainly affected those sectors which had expanded most during the war. A recent study in this field points to the 'conspicuous discrepancy between the minimal economic impact of dismantlement in western Germany and the highly explosive political nature of the subject'.[15]

b) The lack of any serious incentive to produce

Given that the overall resources position was positive and that the policy of the occupying powers was generally constructive, the question arises of why the upturn in industrial production, and thus in economic growth in western Germany, was so restrained before mid-1948. According to official figures—the upward adjustments made by Abelshauser and Mathias Manz can now be regarded as groundless[16]—industrial production during this period amounted to around half of 1936 levels. But in most other west European countries which had suffered from the effects of the war, it had

---

[12] Cf. Henke, 1996, pp. 112ff.
[13] Cf. Schulz, 1996, p. 258 as well as Plumpe, 1987, pp. 84ff.
[14] Schulz, 1996, p. 259 as well as Woller, 1986, pp. 247ff.
[15] Kramer, 1991, pp. 445, 455.
[16] Cf. Ritschl, 1985, pp. 136ff.

practically regained (or even exceeded) pre-war levels as early as 1947.[17] Even in the Soviet Zone of Occupation it was higher than in West Germany.[18]

One reason for the low level of production was the drop in weekly working hours and the moderate labour productivity, which still hovered around 60 per cent of 1936 levels in the second quarter of 1948.[19] This was due in part to the poor nutrition situation, with rations for the average consumer at only around 1,000 to 1,500 kcal, at times even lower in urban centres such as the Ruhr.[20] A further factor, however, was that the official wages, which were more than sufficient to buy the scant rations available on the ration cards, provided no incentive whatsoever to work particularly hard; for on the black market, very high prices meant that the purchasing power of official wages was so low that mere wage-earners were more or less excluded from buying goods there.

This highlights the fundamental economic problem of the time: the massive excess liquidity which had arisen as a result of Third Reich financing of armaments and the general war effort, largely by borrowing from banks and the Reichsbank. This had seen the money supply grow out of all proportion. However, the resulting inflation was concealed by the price freeze imposed in 1936, a situation compounded by the extensive rationing of almost all goods at the beginning of the war. The military governments stuck to both the price freeze and the ration controls. But now the end of the disciplining war effort and the collapse of the totalitarian regime combined with the marked decline in the national product to reveal the all-too-obvious consequences of this suppressed inflation.

On the one hand, transactions where goods were sold against Reichs-marks at the official price were most unattractive to companies. Given the prevailing situation in general, they were nothing less than a reduction of assets. Sellers therefore tried to avoid such transactions unless they were linked to official allocations of raw materials. Enterprises switched to barter trade. This system of bartering goods against other goods eventually accounted for an estimated 50 per cent of all business transactions in the period before the currency reform.[21] The search for suitable barter partners, often requiring the organization of entire barter chains, increased trans-action costs sharply, which in itself must have been a disincentive to produce.

On the other hand, the terms at which barter transactions were concluded revealed that the structure of official prices was totally distorted. This meant that it was no longer possible to calculate company profits realistically using

[17] Cf. Mitchell, 1992, pp. 411f.
[18] Cf. Zank, 1987, pp. 192f.
[19] Cf., also on what follows: Buchheim, 1988, pp. 189ff. and Buchheim, 1993, pp. 85ff.
[20] Cf. Trittel, 1990, p. 216.
[21] Cf. Mendershausen, 1949, pp. 652ff.

these prices, even by multiplying them by a common factor to compensate for their excessively low overall levels. But as there was no currency other than the Reichsmark which could be used to form a suitable pricing structure, the profit motive was irrelevant in the period before the currency reform. This eliminated the principal incentive which normally motivates capitalist entrepreneurs to make every effort to produce goods and services and to sell them.[22]

Instead, they did everything they could to prepare their companies as well as possible for the time after the currency reform—which they were sure would happen—so as to be able to survive in the resurgent competitive environment. Achieving this goal meant repairing factory buildings and machinery, retaining their core workforce and regular customers, and stockpiling the largest possible inventories. It appears that companies were not so much interested in maintaining high levels of finished product inventories, but rather of semi-finished goods, and above all raw materials.[23] This policy was designed to retain a certain degree of flexibility. Above all, it afforded some protection against penalties in the event of official inspections, as they could always argue that the lack of specific materials prevented them from manufacturing finished products.

There are in fact some indications that contrary to the impression that they themselves tried to give in public—one which some authors seem over-eager to accept—companies hardly touched their wartime stocks of raw materials before the currency reform. Indeed, they even had some success in increasing them by falsifying their accounting for materials from controlled stocks, something which was almost impossible to check.[24]

The results of a study of one key enterprise in each of 14 industries by the Land Statistical Office of Hesse in early 1948 are interesting in this context, as the statisticians themselves assumed that these results were applicable across the board.[25] They showed that in 1945, the firms surveyed had raw materials inventories valued at RM 47 million, compared with only RM 18 million in 1936. These figures reveal the huge level of hoarded stocks which had been accumulated by the end of the war. Instead of inventories dropping as production was resumed, they rose further to reach a value of almost RM 60 million in 1946, a figure which remained constant in 1947. This means

[22] Cf. Walter Eucken's argument that production cannot be increased without the availability of a means for calculating as a control instrument; cf. the Minutes of the meeting on 6 Nov. 1947 (Institut für Zeitgeschichte [IfZ] Archive, Depositum Hans Möller, Sonderstelle Geld und Kredit).
[23] See also Plumpe, 1987, p. 184.
[24] Cf. Krumbein, 1989, pp. 160ff. as well as Drexler, 1985, p. 85.
[25] Betriebs- und finanzwirtschaftliche Probleme in 14 Unternehmen der hessischen Industrie (Bundesarchiv Koblenz Z 1/864).

that in 1947, the companies had stockpiled raw materials sufficient to cover twelve months' production requirements, whilst those in 1936 covered a mere two months. Despite this, most companies were still complaining about the scarcity of raw materials. In addition, finished goods inventories dropped from RM 15.9 to 14.9 million between 1945 and 1947, compared with an increase in semi-finished goods inventories from RM 20.4 to 22.6 million.

Similar trends are evident from other sources. For example, the Department for Economic Affairs estimated in mid-1947 that around 65,000 tonnes of semi-finished machine parts were stored at engineering works in the Bizone.[26] Günter Keiser, then head of the Special Economic Planning Department of the Economic Administration Office, recalled in 1972 that at the time of the currency reform, his office had been surprised by the 'larger reserves (at companies) than we had ever imagined'.[27]

Without exaggerating too much, a feasible conclusion is that, despite the overall favourable conditions as regards raw materials, west German industrial production displayed a strong trend towards stagnation from 1946 onwards simply because owners did not *want* to produce any more. The prevailing economic conditions—economic controls, rationing, and administrative price controls at a time of high liquidity—were such that entrepreneurs could no longer realize profits. Selling at the official prices meant an erosion of assets which endangered the economic survival of the companies.[28] The 1948 currency and economic reforms changed this situation at a stroke, and as we shall see, the comprehensive preparations made by the companies in the run-up to the reform proved their worth.

The low rate of industrial production in western Germany before the currency reform therefore was a consequence of a specific inconsistency in the reigning economic order. In view of the years of suppressed inflation, the attempts by the authorities to control production were incompatible with the notion of private ownership of enterprises, and thus failed in the vast majority of cases.

3. The German banking system in the early post-war years

As soon as Berlin had been occupied by the Russians, the local banks, including the head offices of all big banks, were forced to cease operating. Accounts were blocked, credit balances could no longer be withdrawn, and

---

[26] Abt. F I—Maschinenbau an Hauptabteilung B, 27.5.47 (Bundesarchiv Koblenz B 102/2371 H.1).

[27] Abelshauser, 1975, p. 150 Note 69.

[28] See also Plumpe, 1987, p. 179.

cash balances had to be transferred to the Berliner Stadtkontor. Apart from the savings bank, this was the only bank which was permitted to remain open, to ensure the supply of money in Berlin. It had emerged from the transformation of the Reichsbank head office and its Berlin branches. The closure of the other banks was announced as a 'temporary' measure, but in most cases it proved to be final. In July 1945, the Soviet Military Administration in Germany (SMAD) then issued an order on the 'Reorganization of German finance and credit institutions'. New Land and provincial banks were opened in the Soviet zone on the basis of this order, together with savings banks. Their initial funds came from public sector budgets. As a result of the break-up of the unified organization of the Reichsbank and the big banks, the banking system in the Soviet zone was thus not only decentralized, but also soon nationalized as well, as the banks were reorganized as public sector institutions.[29]

Developments in western Germany, on the other hand, took a completely different turn. The Anglo-American SHAEF[30] Handbook, with its comprehensive technical manuals,[31] which served as a guideline for members of the military governments during the occupation of Germany, laid down that the Allies should avail themselves of the existing financial and banking apparatus in Germany. However, it also stipulated that banks should remain closed until the military government was able to institute sufficient controls, that politically unacceptable employees should be dismissed, and that arrangements should be made to block particular accounts. The branches of the Reichsbank were to be used to transmit information and instructions from the military government to all affected credit institutions, as well as for banking supervision purposes.[32]

In fact, apart from brief interruptions, the banks in the western zones continued working after the end of the war. No particular restrictions were imposed upon them.[33] This was also the case with the branches of the Reichsbank. Although they had been robbed of their Berlin head office and—at least initially—of their mutual links, they still maintained a certain level of activity, for example cash inpayments and disbursements, and preserved the credit transfer system, at least at local level.

Now that the banks were unable to realize the Reich securities in their portfolios, the need to secure bank liquidity demanded the return to the

---

[29] Cf. Holtfrerich, 1995, pp. 435ff. and Bundesministerium für gesamtdeutsche Fragen, 1969, keyword: Banken.

[30] Supreme Headquarters Allied Expeditionary Forces.

[31] For greater details on the history of the Handbook and its—limited—significance, see Henke, 1996, pp. 100ff.

[32] Cf. Holtfrerich, 1995, p. 450 as well as Horstmann, 1991, pp. 21ff.

[33] Cf. Holtfrerich, 1995, p. 453.

banking system of the cash hoarded by the general public. To encourage this, the Reichsbank branch offices issued numerous appeals, together with calls to return to cashless payments. In response, cash deposits at banks reached substantial proportions soon after the occupation started, and the feared liquidity problems never arose.

A completely new area of activities for the Reichsbank branches was the implementation of military government law no. 52, which covered the blocking of the accounts of politically unacceptable persons and institutions, and no. 53, which governed the requirement to notify and surrender foreign currency holdings and other foreign assets. The Reichsbank branches' tasks were to transmit the instructions of the military government to the banks, decide difficult cases, process applications to release funds, and deal with extensive notification and reporting requirements—work which generally occupied a substantial proportion of the Reichsbank branch office staff.[34] The individual Reichsbank branches quickly re-established contact with each other by establishing their own courier service, replacing the crippled national postal service. This also restored the payment system between the branch sites.[35]

Finally, regional Reichsbank centres were established. Their function was to provide central accounting services for the branches and enable them to operate on a uniform basis. In July 1945, for example, a Reichsbank head office for Bavaria was set up at the central branch of the Reichsbank in Munich, quickly followed by a similar office in Stuttgart for Württemberg-Baden and in Frankfurt am Main for Hesse. In August 1945, the French Military Government made the Reichsbank branch office in Kaiserslautern the main branch for the northern part of the French zone, with the office in Freiburg taking responsibility for the southern half. In addition, a chief branch of the Reichsbank in the entire French zone was set up in Speyer in February 1946, headed by a directorate under the control of a French Reichsbank commissioner. In the British zone, a chief branch of the Reichsbank had already been established by a military government decree in November 1945.[36] Only in the US zone were there no efforts to organize Reichsbank branches formally at zonal level, although the central branch in

---

[34] Cf. Landeszentralbank von Württemberg-Baden, 1947, p. 3; Landeszentralbank von Bayern, 1947, pp. 14, 18; Landeszentralbank von Rheinland-Pfalz, 1947, p. 1; Reichsbank branch Hamburg, Economic Report no. 1, p. 8 (HA BBk B 330/4950); Reichsbank subbranch Worms, Economic Reports 1945 (HA BBk B 332/103 I).

[35] Cf. Chief Branch of the Reichsbank for the French zone to the Reichsbank Commissioner, 23 Jan. 1947 (HA BBk B 331–BW/53).

[36] Cf. Landeszentralbank von Bayern, 1947, pp. 18f.; Landeszentralbank von Rheinland-Pfalz, 1947, p. 1; Reichsbank branch Hamburg to all Reichsbank branches, 14 Dec. 1945 (HA BBk B 331–BW/53).

Munich apparently assumed some of the functions of such an organization for a time, at least informally.[37] At any rate, the accounts of the Reichsbank branch offices throughout the zone were coordinated there officially, and a zonal settlement agency was established in Frankfurt am Main.[38]

The restoration of a regional central bank structure as described above followed the tradition of the old Reichsbank, and also used its personnel. Reichsbank directors were appointed to key positions at the chief branches in Hamburg and Speyer, for instance, and practices at the head offices were also governed by the principle of continuity. This was explicitly stipulated for the chief branch of the Reichsbank in Hamburg in a corresponding decree, which stated that: 'the executive board will manage the business of the Reichsbank in the British zone in compliance with applicable German laws'. This meant that the constitution of the Reichsbank essentially formed the basis for the work of the chief branch.[39] In contrast, the applicable statute laid down that the activities of the chief branch of the Reichsbank in Speyer should only cover some of the functions of the former Reichsbank head office, including the organization of monetary movements and credit transfers, as well as monitoring the lending operations of the Reichsbank branches.[40] However, 'it inevitably had to assume further duties' very soon:

because in normal times the branches were required to obtain a decision from the Reichsbank Directorate in special cases, it was little wonder that they used the chief branch for this purpose once it had been set up. They increasingly turned to the chief branch for information and decisions in all areas. The chief branch therefore rapidly assumed responsibility for more comprehensive and executive functions, and the nature and extent of its activities turned it into a central administrative office covering all fields of activity of the Reichsbank.[41]

Partly with, partly without the involvement of the military government, the force of custom had reasserted itself, and in the British and French zones, the old German central bank structure had been resurrected to a large extent. There was also without doubt a similar trend in the American zone as well, but it did not gain general acceptance because the military government took

[37] Cf. meeting of the Banking Committee of the Länderrat of the American Zone of Occupation, 5 Jan. 1946 (Records of the Land Central Bank in Bavaria, HA BBk).
[38] Cf. Response to the letter of the Office of Military Government dated 1 Nov. 1945 (Records of the Land Central Bank in Bavaria, HA BBk).
[39] Cf. Reichsbank branch Hamburg to all Reichsbank branches, 14 Dec. 1945 (HA BBk B 331–BW/53); Monatsbericht der Reichsbankleitstelle Hamburg, Feb. 1948, p. 2 (HA BBk B 330/4950).
[40] Cf. Minutes of the meeting of Finance Officers and Reichsbank Directors on 14 Feb. 1946 in Tübingen (HA BBk B 331–BW/119).
[41] Die Tätigkeit der Leitstelle der Reichsbank für die französische Zone im Jahre 1946, pp. 1f. (HA BBk B 331–BW/53).

active steps to prevent it and, as we shall see, intended pushing through a fundamental reform.

Although the outer shell of a central bank organization had been largely re-established in western Germany, it was still missing the core components of a genuine central banking policy. For example, the Reichsbank organizations no longer actively regulated the currency in circulation. New banknotes were not issued, except to replace damaged notes withdrawn from circulation. In view of the tremendous excess liquidity, it is no surprise that there was little demand for credit from the private sector and commercial banks. Only the public sector raised new debt, often in large amounts, with the zone treasury department in the British occupation zone being the largest borrower. Owing to the substantial subsidies for coal mining and the iron and steel industry, the budget in this zone recorded a steady deficit, which had to be covered on a temporary basis by Reichsbank bridging loans.[42] In the French zone, the Office for External Trade of the Military Government (Oficomex), among others, needed Reichsbank loans to offset the negative zonal Reichsmark balance of external trade.[43] A mark of the lack of a true monetary policy was that, at 3.5 and 4.5 per cent respectively, the discount and Lombard rates in western Germany remained unchanged until 1948.

The work of the Reichsbank organization was correspondingly limited in the main to more technical areas. One important function of the Reichsbank central branches, for example, was the supervision of giro transactions within and between the zones. The money supply between individual regions was also evened out, with particular attention being paid to ensuring that the very scarce small notes and coins were distributed evenly. A centralized accounting system was established. They dealt with counterfeiting issues and tricky questions relating to military government laws no. 52 and no. 53, as well as maintaining comprehensive statistical data. The Reichsbank central branches also undertook bank supervision duties.[44] This was evidently all performed with relative efficiency, and one might have expected that the Reichsbank organization would also assume a monetary policy role following the planned currency reform. As it turned out, however, events would prove otherwise.

---

[42] Cf. Monatsbericht der Reichsbankleitstelle Hamburg, Feb. 1948, p. 3 (HA BBk B 330/4950).

[43] Cf. Minutes of the meeting of Finance Officers and Reichsbank Directors on 14 Feb. 1946 in Tübingen (HA BBk B 331–BW/119).

[44] Cf. Monatsbericht der Reichsbankleitstelle Hamburg, Feb. 1948, pp. 2ff. (HA BBk B 330/4950); Die Tätigkeit der Leitstelle der Reichsbank für die Französische Zone im Jahre 1945 (HA BBk B 331–BW/53).

4. Allied reforms of the central bank structures in western Germany

a) Inter-allied negotiations on the banking system

The policy of decentralization urged, for example, in US directive JCS 1067 was adopted in the Potsdam Agreement, in which it explicitly referred to economic life. During the ensuing period, the Americans in particular made it a major concern of their occupation policy, including their position on the banking system. Their policy was twofold. On the one hand, they wanted to curb the power of the private banks. Banks would therefore be prohibited from holding interests in industrial enterprises, and the big banks were to be broken up. On the other hand, the Americans wanted to prevent a unified national central bank organization for Germany. In its stead, a separate central bank and bank supervisory authority would be established in each Land. However, there was never any intention of granting the Land Central Banks the right to issue notes. In other words, this plan did not throw doubt on the intention to issue a new currency for all post-Potsdam Germany.[45] Overall, the American concepts were heavily inspired by the situation in the United States itself.

In autumn 1945, Joseph M. Dodge, General Lucius Clay's Finance Adviser, presented the part of the reorganization plans affecting the big banks for the first time to the Directorate of Finance of the Allied Control Authority, which immediately referred it to the Banking Committee.[46] Although the Russian and French representatives on this committee gave their approval, it ran into opposition from the British. They referred to the clause in the Potsdam Agreement which stipulated that Germany was to be treated as a single economic entity, arguing that this included the need to balance funds on a nationwide basis. This was an issue of particular interest to the British, not least because of the high borrowing requirements to balance their zonal budget. In their view, an efficiently functioning banking apparatus therefore took priority over the purely politically motivated reform plans of the other Allies, and in particular the Americans.

The Banking Committee was unable to resolve this conflict, and the matter was therefore returned undecided to the Directorate of Finance, where in April 1946, Dodge made a concession to the British position. He

[45] Cf. Horstmann, 1991, p. 84 as well as Holtfrerich, 1995, pp. 462ff.
[46] Cf., also on what follows: Horstmann, 1985, pp. 3ff.

proposed setting up a *Länder-Union-Bank*, which would control and coordinate the Land Central Banks, implement a common monetary policy, and balance the financial requirements of the national German economy. The American proposal to dissolve the Reichsbank and establish Land Central Banks was now itself an implicit subject for negotiation in the Control Council, albeit supplemented by the offer of a *Länder-Union-Bank*.

The British response was positive overall, but the French and Russian representatives in the Directorate of Finance now signalled their opposition to the new plan. For a time it appeared that the compromise proposed by the Americans to replace the *Länder-Union-Bank* with a less heavily institutionalized 'Laender Central Bank Commission', to be supervised by an 'Allied Banking Board', might be approved by all four occupying powers.[47] In the end, however, the Russians rejected this too, advancing their earlier position that any talk of establishing a central monetary authority was premature.

The higher-level talks in the Coordination Committee and the Control Council itself—which discussed the problem in October 1946—were also inconclusive. The military governors were then given a free hand to deal with the banking question in their own zones.

b) The Land Central Banks

In the Länder of the US zone, the Office of Military Government for Germany, United States (OMGUS) was now pushing for the enactment of Land Central Bank laws as quickly as possible. These had already been drafted by the Länder governments following initial pressure by the occupation authority. The laws were promulgated at the end of 1946 before the constitution of the Länder parliaments, which would normally have had to debate the bills, causing further delays.[48] In contrast to the Americans, the British clung to the centralized Reichsbank organization in their zone. In the French zone, the military government, which had previously allowed the reconstruction of the hierarchical Reichsbank structure, at least on a provisional basis, now made an about-turn. In a decree issued in February 1947, it too ordered the liquidation of the Reichsbank and the establishment of Land Central Banks. The French authorities claimed that this was in line with their programme of decentralization, a policy which they had strongly supported in the Control Council. Its implementation was oriented closely

---

[47] Cf. ACA DFIN Banking Committee, Elimination of Excessive Concentration of Economic Power in Banking, 21.6.1946 (HA BBk B 331–BW/341).
[48] Cf. Holtfrerich, 1995, pp. 470ff.; Horstmann, 1991, pp. 95ff.; Wandel, 1980, p. 61.

to the example of the American zone, evidently to prevent any potential consensus-based inter-allied reforms from being still-born.[49]

Similar institutions in the form of issuing and giro banks were set up in the Länder of the Soviet zone in the spring of that year, with the same functions in Berlin being performed by the Berliner Stadtkontor.[50] In theory at least, this kept alive the possibility of developing a common central banking system for the whole of post-Potsdam Germany. The exception was the special role of the British zone, but, as talks in the Control Council had shown, this was still very much open to negotiation.

Formally, the Land Central Banks were not the legal successors to the Reichsbank organization. In the Länder of the American and French zones, it was transferred to a trust agency to be administered and wound up. As a rule, however, the Land Central Banks not only took over the staff and buildings as well as the furniture and equipment of the Reichsbank branches in their region, but also their assets and liabilities, realizable claims and holdings of Reichsbank notes. The gaps between assets and the higher liabilities which appeared in the opening balance sheets were closed by granting a fictitious claim against the Reichsbank trust agencies. The capital stock, whose level was fixed by law for the individual Land Central Banks, was initially contributed by the Land. After a certain period, however, it was to be subscribed by local credit institutions.[51] This provision was later scrapped, and the Land Central Banks remained in the hands of the Länder.[52]

The governing bodies of the Land Central Banks were the Executive Board, which included the President or General Manager and his alternate, both of whom were nominated by the Land Prime Minister and could be recalled at any time for substantial reasons, and the Supervisory Board. The chairman of the Supervisory Board was also nominated by the Prime Minister. The *ex officio* deputy chairman was the President of the Land Central Bank. Further members included the head of the bank supervisory authority and representatives from agriculture, industry, and employees, to be nominated by the finance minister. The function of the Supervisory

---

[49] Cf. L'Administrateur Général Laffon à M. le Gouverneur de Bade, Objet: Création de Banques centrales, 3.2.47 (Ministère des Affaires Etrangères [MAE], Archives à Colmar, Service Français d'Occupation, c. 2156 p. 5a); Laffon à Oberpräsident de Bade, 24.1.47 (*ibid.*); Landeszentralbank von Rheinland-Pfalz, 1947, p. 1.

[50] Cf. Landeszentralbank von Württemberg-Baden, 1947, p. 4.

[51] Cf., also as an example for what follows: Landeszentralbank von Württemberg-Baden, 1947, pp. 4ff.; Landeszentralbank von Württemberg-Baden, 1948 and 1949, appendix 8 (Land Central Bank Law of 7 Dec. 1946); Landeszentralbank von Rheinland-Pfalz, 1947, pp. 1ff.; Landeszentralbank von Baden, 1947, pp. 12ff. (Land Decree on the Establishment of a Land Central Bank of 7 Apr. 1947).

[52] Cf. Gesetz zur Änderung der Gesetze über die Landeszentralbanken, BGBl. 1952 I, p. 729.

Board was to represent the interests of the various economic communities in the Land. Its task was to prepare principles governing the activities of the central bank, decide monetary policy, and supervise the management of the bank. There was no mention in the laws of direct, binding instructions from the government. However, the influence of the Länder governments was not insubstantial, as shown by the regulations covering the appointment of numerous officers and the institutionalized involvement of at least the head of the bank supervisory authority, in other words a representative of the government.[53]

The principal tasks of the Land Central Banks anchored in the laws were to manage the amount of money in circulation, assume the role of the commercial banks' bank, function as a state bank for the individual Länder, and manage payments within the Land and with areas outside the Land borders. To enable them to perform these duties, the Land Central Banks were given instruments, most of which had already been available to the Reichsbank. These instruments included discount and Lombard rate policies, the ability to conduct open market operations with particular fixed-income securities, permission to extend short-term cash advances to the public sector and involvement in the giro system. One innovation was a minimum reserve policy based on the American model. The Supervisory Board was charged with deciding the level of minimum reserves to be held with the Land Central Banks by the commercial banks as a proportion of their customers' deposits, as well as the level of interest rates applied by the central bank to its operations.

In contrast to the Reichsbank, the Land Central Banks could normally lend only to banks and the public sector, and not, for example, to industrial enterprises. This meant that they were no longer able to compete directly with other credit institutions. Even more important, however, was the fact that—as already envisaged in the Dodge Plan—the Land Central Banks were not granted the right to print and issue new banknotes. They thus lacked one of the main features of a central bank, which is normally synonymous with the idea of the 'central bank of issue'. This also saw them unable to fulfil their allotted task of managing the amount of currency in circulation, even in theory. It was thus clear that the system was still incomplete in this respect, and that further measures would be needed at the latest before the currency reform was instituted.

According to the Land Central Bank laws of the Länder in the American zone, a Banking Council was to be established, comprising representatives of the central banks. Its principal task was to coordinate their monetary policy, a function which had also been addressed in the Dodge Plan. The

---

[53] Cf. Horstmann, 1990, pp. 205f.

supervisory boards of the central banks were supposed to adhere to the recommendations issued by this Banking Council. However, the way in which this was worded was extremely vague.[54] In reality, the collaboration of the Land Central Banks in the American zone was relatively heavily institutionalized. In 1947, for example, a clearing house for intra-Länder payments was set up,[55] followed by an informal panel of Land Central Bank Presidents to agree on administrative issues[56] and a permanent Secretariat, whose duty was to implement the decisions of the Banking Council.[57]

An interesting insight is the support by the President of the Bavarian Land Central Bank for Munich as the seat of this Secretariat. In a letter dated May 1947, he wrote in this connection to the Bavarian State Chancellery that: 'I wish to emphasize that the Banking Council Secretariat is surely designed to be the cornerstone of the central management of banknote issue in Germany in the future, and that the importance to be attached to this establishment already goes far beyond the US zone'.[58]

The Banking Council can, in fact, be regarded as a smaller precursor of the Bank deutscher Länder[59] and its Secretariat corresponded essentially to the Board of Managers of the Bank deutscher Länder, as the author of this letter correctly recognized. Although the Secretariat did not appear anywhere in the law, it emerged spontaneously to meet the needs of the hour. The structure of the subsequent west German central bank organization was thus already taking shape in the American Zone of Occupation. It is also interesting to note that the sources do not contain pointers towards any departure in the policies of the individual Land Central Banks from the recommendations of the Banking Council, which were evidently regarded as binding.

A coordination authority similar to the Banking Council was not envisaged in the Land Central Bank laws in the Länder of the French zone. However, on the same day as the French Military Government issued its decree on the establishment of Land Central Banks, orders were also published concerning the establishment of a Coordinating Committee of these

---

[54] According to Hans A. Adler, Head of the OMGUS Banking Section, it was envisaged in the English document that the recommendations of the Banking Council would be binding on the Land Central Banks. Owing to a translation error, this was watered down in the decisive German text of the Land Central Bank laws. Cf. Adler, 1949, p. 328.

[55] Cf. Landeszentralbank von Württemberg-Baden, 1947, p. 9.

[56] Cf. Report on the meeting of the Land Central Bank Presidents on 22 May 1947 (HA BBk B 331–H/29).

[57] Cf. Minutes of the 3rd meeting of the Banking Council on 30 June 1947 (HA BBk B 331–H/29).

[58] Grassmann to Dr Pfeifer, Staatskanzlei, 9.5.47 (HA BBk B 330/11721).

[59] The same conclusion is reached in: Landeszentralbank von Württemberg-Baden, 1947, p. 6 and Adler, 1949, p. 328.

banks, and appointing a Commissioner from the occupying authority to control the new central banking system in the French zone.[60] As in the case of the Banking Council, representatives of the zonal Land Central Banks sat on the Coordinating Committee, whose prime function (of coordinating the monetary and credit policy of the Land Central Banks[61]) also mirrored that of the Banking Council. However, its members were agreed that, in contrast to the formal arrangements for the Banking Council, the decisions of the Coordinating Committee were binding on the Land Central Banks.[62] The Coordinating Committee also had a special office to prepare its meetings and implement the common tasks of the Land Central Banks, such as inter-Länder payments and the generation of statistical data.

There were thus great similarities between the institutional development of the new central banking system in the American and French zones. However, the fact cannot be overlooked that the Coordinating Committee was the direct successor to the chief branch of the Reichsbank in Speyer. The outward sign of this was that Speyer also became the venue for meetings of the Committee, and its office was located there. A degree of staff continuity was also retained, although some of the employees at the chief branch were reassigned to the Land Central Banks.[63] Finally, its duties and functions, particularly as regards monetary policy and clearing operations, were also relatively similar, supplemented by bank supervision in the French zone.[64] The greatest difference from the Reichsbank organization was evidently in the legal structure. Instead of a hierarchical institution with a central management, there were now several legally autonomous central banks. These collaborated in a joint body (the Coordinating Committee) on equal terms, with its decisions being binding on them.

The central banking system of the young Federal Republic had already started taking shape in 1947 in the French and American zones. As a clear continuity with the former Reichsbank organization is also evident, particularly in the French zone, one might conclude that the *de facto* differences between the two were not very significant. They were certainly not as great as the differences in the formal constitution. This also means that the overall strategy of decentralization of the central banking system pursued so vigor-

[60] Cf. Landeszentralbank von Rheinland-Pfalz, 1947, p. 1.
[61] Cf. Speech by Mr. Auboyneau, Director of Finance, during the 1st meeting of the Coordinating Committee on 21 Mar. 1947 (HA BBk B 331–RS/877).
[62] Cf. Provisional Minutes of the 1st meeting of the Coordinating Committee on 21 Mar. 1947 (HA BBk B 331–RS/877).
[63] Cf. Provisional Minutes of the preparatory meeting of the Coordinating Committee on 25 Feb. 1947 (HA BBk B 331–RS/877).
[64] Cf. Provisional Minutes of the 4th meeting of the Coordinating Committee on 23 July 1947 (HA BBk B 331–RS/877).

ously by the Americans was far less effective—even before the establishment of the Bank deutscher Länder—than might appear from a reading of the legislation. It was undoubtedly the case that the pragmatic arguments for a unified central bank organization advanced by the British were stronger than the reform plans which came off the political drawing board, and that inherent logic prevailed, more or less of its own accord. Moreover, the Board of Governors of the US Federal Reserve system, on which the American reforms of the central banking system in Germany were modelled, is itself a powerful institution which ultimately determines the course of national monetary policy. It is also independent of the individual Federal Reserve Banks.

Against this backdrop, it should come as no surprise that very close contact was maintained or forged between the central bank systems of the various western zones. The Land Central Banks in the French zone were explicitly encouraged to keep in touch with the Land Central Banks in the American zone and the chief branch of the Reichsbank in the British zone, without even involving the military government.[65] As an example, there were joint talks by the loan officers of the Land Central Banks in the American and French zones.[66] In December 1947, the chief branch of the Reichsbank in Hamburg and the office of the Coordinating Committee in Speyer joined up with the clearing house of the Land Central Banks in the American zone in Frankfurt am Main, opening the way for an efficient interzonal clearing system.[67]

Monetary policy in the individual zones also followed a similar path. The decision by the Banking Council to treat Reich securities as marketable for the Land Central Banks' lending policy was discussed in the Coordinating Committee, which supported the adoption of this principle in the French zone.[68] There were numerous debates in both the Banking Council and the Coordinating Committee on lowering the discount and Lombard rates. However, they repeatedly refrained from doing so, and the rates fixed in 1940 continued to apply in all the western zones, although lower rates to banks were permitted in some special cases.[69] The new instrument of the

[65] Cf. Minutes of the 5th Preliminary Discussions of the General Managers of the Land Central Banks on 22–3 Sept. 1947 (HA BBk B 331–RS/877).

[66] Cf. Memo no. 4 on the meeting of the General Managers of the Land Central Banks in the French zone on 22 Mar. 1948 (HA BBk B 331–RS/877).

[67] Cf. Landeszentralbank von Württemberg-Baden, 1947, p. 9.

[68] Cf. Provisional Minutes of the 8th meeting of the Coordinating Committee on 17 Feb. 1948 (HA BBk B 331–RS/877).

[69] Cf. Landeszentralbank von Württemberg-Baden, 1947, p. 7; Minutes of the extra-ordinary meeting of the Banking Council on 1 Aug. 1947 (HA BBk B 331–H/29); Provisional Minutes of the 2nd meeting of the Coordinating Committee on 13 June 1947 (HA BBk B 331–RS/877).

minimum reserve requirement was not applied by the Land Central Banks until after the currency reform, so that again there was no difference from the Reichsbank organization.[70] This common monetary policy was mirrored in the liberal payment system connecting the individual western zones, as shown by the high—and growing—net settlement balances between the central bank organizations, including across the zonal borders.[71]

c) The Bank deutscher Länder as the central bank of the Land Central Banks

The consequence of the decentralization of the central bank organization in the American and French zones was thus actually a return towards a degree of unification and centralization. This was also reflected in the negotiations held by the Americans and the British following the failure of the talks to this effect in the Allied Control Council. With the establishment of the Bizone, these discussions centred around a common banking structure in the two zones.[72] The Americans asked the British to dissolve the Reichsbank branches in their zone and establish Land Central Banks. Due not least to their financial dependence on the Americans, the British were unable to resist this request. In return, the British wanted to retain as many centralized elements as possible.

They insisted on a bizonal budget which would absorb the coal and steel subsidies, the establishment of a 'Reconstruction Loan Corporation' for long-term reconstruction finance including of the Ruhr industry (which subsequently became the Kreditanstalt für Wiederaufbau) and finally a bizonal central institution placed above the Land Central Banks. On this last point, OMGUS originally wanted to accept no more than a relatively weak Joint Banking Board. This would merely coordinate the policy of the Land Central Banks, which would remain the most important elements in the system. After General Clay had obtained backing in Washington, in the end it was agreed to establish a proper banking institution with its own apparatus and a Managing Board under a President, whose job was to implement the decisions of the Board of Directors. This was to be the supreme executive body of the bank, with its membership drawn primarily from the Land Central Bank Presidents.

[70] Cf. Landeszentralbank von Württemberg-Baden, 1947, p. 8; Landeszentralbank von Rheinland-Pfalz, 1947, p. 4.

[71] Cf. Landeszentralbank von Bayern, 1947, pp. 14ff.; Monatsbericht der Reichsbank-leitstelle Hamburg, May 1947, pp. 10f. (HA BBk B 330/4950).

[72] For what follows cf. Horstmann, 1991, pp. 134ff.; Horstmann, 1990, pp. 209ff.; Holtfrerich, 1995, pp. 487f.

In February 1948, a British Military Government decree came into force, establishing Land Central Banks in North-Rhine Westphalia, Lower Saxony, Schleswig-Holstein and Hamburg.[73] The Reichsbank central branch in Hamburg and its satellite branches in the zone were closed down at the end of March, the date which marks the definitive end of the Deutsche Reichsbank.[74]

Before this, on 1 March 1948, identical decrees on the establishment of the Bank deutscher Länder had taken effect in both the American and the British zones.[75] The Allied Bank Commission was constituted at almost the same time. One of its duties was to supervise the Bank deutscher Länder and its monetary policy. The result was the adoption of direct military government supervision of the central bank system in the Bizone, a situation which had previously existed only in the French zone. The Land Central Banks in the French zone were able to join the Bank deutscher Länder at the end of March,[76] creating the first trizonal German institution.[77] The structure of the Bank deutscher Länder was also designed in such a way that the integration of the issuing and giro banks in the Soviet zone would also have been possible.[78]

However, this was not to happen. The establishment of a Deutsche Emissions- und Girobank was mooted in the Soviet zone as a separate zonal central bank. It was set up at the end of May with a legal organization relatively similar to that of the Bank deutscher Länder. Following the separate currency reforms in West and East Germany, it was renamed the Deutsche Notenbank by a SMAD decree dated 20 July 1948, and was granted a monopoly to issue the new east German currency.[79]

The new central bank organization in western Germany had thus been completed in the spring of 1948. In particular, there was now an institution—the Bank deutscher Länder—which could bring a common currency into circulation, a key precondition for the planned currency reform. From the relatively complicated wording of article III of the Act establishing the Bank deutscher Länder (Gesetz über die Errichtung der Bank deutscher Länder), it was clear that the Bank deutscher Länder would receive these

---

[73] Cf. Emden Branch, Regulation no. 132 (HA BBk B 332/37).

[74] Cf. Monatsbericht der Reichsbankleitstelle Hamburg, Feb. 1948, p. 1 (HA BBk B 330/4950).

[75] Cf. Gesetz- und Verordnungsblatt des Wirtschaftsrates des Vereinigten Wirtschaftsgebietes no. 12, supplement no. 3; reprinted in Seidel, 1973, pp. 320ff.

[76] Cf. 3rd meeting of the Provisional Central Bank Council (ZBR) on 2 Apr. 1948 (HA BBk B 330/1); Bank deutscher Länder, 1948 and 1949, p. 52.

[77] Cf. Wandel, 1980, p. 73.

[78] Cf. Landeszentralbank von Württemberg-Baden, 1947, p. 4.

[79] Cf. various records (Bundesarchiv Koblenz and Berlin, Coswig Branch, DN 1 [alt]-405).

powers at the appropriate time, although the (geographical) area in which the new currency would apply was deliberately left open: 'in the event that the Allied authorities issue a corresponding directive, the Bank shall assume the character of a sole bank of issue, issuing banknotes and coins within its area of responsibility and bringing them into circulation in accordance with the aforementioned directive.'

In contrast to the Reichsbank organization, the new central bank system was two-tier, as both the Land Central Banks and the Bank deutscher Länder, whose capital stock was held by the Land Central Banks, were legally autonomous institutions. The Bank deutscher Länder functioned as the bank of the Land Central Banks, handling their settlement requirements. They obtained funds from it and were required to maintain minimum reserve balances with it. Otherwise, the Bank deutscher Länder was authorized to engage in foreign payments and conduct transactions with the Bizonal Economic Administration Office, subsequently replaced by the Federal Government. It was prohibited from dealings with other credit institutions, which were reserved for the Land Central Banks. However, the latter were tied to the monetary targets of the Bank deutscher Länder in this respect, as the Bank deutscher Länder Act expressly stipulated that: 'the Bank determines the common banking policy and ensures the greatest possible degree of unity in the banking policy of the individual Länder.'

In particular, this included setting the discount and Lombard rates, the rate for open market operations, and the level of minimum reserves which commercial banks were required to hold with the Land Central Banks. This saw the Land Central Banks essentially acting as executive agents of the Bank deutscher Länder. However, this centralist feature was offset by the policy making powers of the Board of Directors, whose members included all Land Central Bank Presidents. The most senior representatives of the Land Central Banks thus collectively passed resolutions by a simple majority of votes cast. These decisions were then binding on all the Land Central Banks—a specific blend of centralized and federalist elements.

Apart from the Land Central Bank Presidents, the only other members of the Board of Directors were the Chairman and the President of the Board of Managers, whom the Land Central Bank Presidents also elected. In stark contrast to the Land Central Banks, German government authorities therefore exercised no direct pressure on the management of the Bank deutscher Länder and were not represented in any of its executive bodies. As things stood though, no other arrangement was conceivable, if the Bank deutscher Länder was to remain open to other zones. This excluded the participation of German agencies in the Bizone.[80] Moreover, the independence of the

---

[80]	Cf. Horstmann, 1990, p. 216.

Bank deutscher Länder from any political authorities whatsoever (apart from the Allied Bank Commission) was firmly anchored in the law.

In 1951, there was a major political fuss about this provision when the Allied High Commission was revising the Occupation Statute. It offered to dispense with the powers of the Allied Bank Commission if these could be governed elsewhere by federal law.[81] The Ministry of Finance then drafted a bill in which the words 'Allied Bank Commission' were replaced by 'Federal Government' throughout the Bank deutscher Länder Act, in other words subordinating the Bank deutscher Länder in its entirety to the government. This met with strenuous protests from the bank and the general public.

The bill was withdrawn. The corresponding passage in the Transition Law which was then adopted and designed to remain in force until the Bundesbank Act envisaged in the Basic Law had been passed, read as follows: 'in the performance of its duties, the Bank deutscher Länder is obliged to observe and support the general economic policy of the Federal Government'. The provision included in the Bundesbank Act in 1957 was very similar. The much-vaunted central bank independence in the Federal Republic of Germany, a feature which remained untouched in the new law, is therefore based on an Allied requirement, which likewise applied to the independence of the Reichsbank in the Weimar Republic.

The Bank deutscher Länder assumed the functions of the Banking Council and the Coordinating Committee. The statistical office[82] and the clearing house[83] of the Land Central Banks in the American zone were also incorporated into the Bank deutscher Länder. The activities of the Board of Directors did not differ, at least initially, from those of the predecessor institutions. In view of the excess liquidity before the currency reform, it too was unable to institute any real monetary policy. The interest rates in the central banking system remained unchanged, and no minimum reserve requirements were set. At its meeting in mid-June 1948, however, it did discuss interest rates and minimum reserve ratios for the period after the currency reform, passing resolutions[84] which were then modified slightly by the Allied Bank Commission.[85] Overall, the central banking policy pursued before the establishment of the Bank deutscher Länder was continued to a large extent after its establishment. This situation only underwent

---

[81] Cf., also for what follows: Deutsche Bundesbank, 1988, pp. 101ff.

[82] Cf. 2nd Provisional Central Bank Council meeting held on 17 Mar. 1948 (HA BBk B 330/1).

[83] Cf. 1st Provisional Central Bank Council meeting held on 8 Mar. 1948 (HA BBk B 330/1).

[84] Cf. 10th Central Bank Council meeting held on 15/16 June 1948 (HA BBk B 330/2)

[85] Cf. Telegram from Laenderbank to various Land Central Banks on 21 June 1948 (HA BBk B 330/2).

radical change as a result of an essentially exogenous event—the currency reform.

A test case of the true strength of the decentralized elements of the new central bank system was the election of the Chairman of the Board of Directors and the President of the Board of Managers. At this point, it is worth taking a brief look at the background and experience of the Land Central Bank Presidents who made up the electoral college in the Board of Directors. Several of them were rooted strongly in the Reichsbank tradition. Eugen Hinckel, President of the Land Central Bank in Baden, had been a Reichsbank director in Freiburg, Ernst Hülse, President of the Land Central Bank in North-Rhine Westphalia, had even been a member of the Reichsbank Directorate and one of the directors of the chief branch of the Reichsbank in Hamburg. Max Sentz (Lower Saxony) had been on the Advisory Board of the Reichsbank, and Karl Mürdel (Württemberg-Hohenzollern) also came from the Reichsbank. Only in the American zone had only people with non-Reichsbank backgrounds been appointed Land Central Bank Presidents: Max Grasmann (Bavaria), Otto Pfleiderer (Württemberg-Baden), Otto Veit (Hesse) and Hermann Tepe (Bremen). In the other two zones, this applied only to Wilhelm Boden (Rhineland-Palatinate), Otto Burkhardt (Schleswig-Holstein) and Karl Klasen (Hamburg).[86] It is therefore inaccurate to suggest that the centralist Reichsbank tradition played no role in the membership of the Board of Directors, the federalist counterweight to the otherwise hierarchical relationship between the Bank deutscher Länder and the Land Central Banks. On the contrary, there were even decided critics of the new system on the Board of Directors.

Unsurprisingly, Otto Schniewind was elected Chairman of the Board of Directors by 8 votes to 3 in the first elections, and Hermann J. Abs was appointed President of the Board of Managers with a 7:4 majority. They both had a strong inclination towards centralization. This was also shown by a condition they placed on their acceptance of the vote. To allow them to fulfil their responsibility for ensuring the stability of the new currency, and to prevent them from being outvoted on lending policy issues by the Land Central Bank Presidents, whose institutions would benefit greatly from cheaper credit, they insisted that in the event of a consensus between them, they themselves could only be outvoted by a three-quarters majority. The Board of Directors agreed to this condition, which essentially weakened its own position. This in turn highlighted the attitude of the majority of its members to the concept of a decentralized central bank organization. However, the Allied Bank Commission rejected the election results, with the Americans in particular advancing political reservations against the winners.

---

[86] Cf. Dickhaus, 1996, pp. 60ff. and Horstmann, 1991, p. 111.

Karl Bernard was then elected Chairman of the Board of Directors, with Wilhelm Vocke appointed President of the Board of Managers and Wilhelm Könneker as his deputy. After some hesitation, all three accepted their appointments. It was no accident that the latter two had been Reichsbank employees. Indeed, Vocke had also been a member of the Directorate as well as one of the directors of the Reichsbank chief branch in Hamburg. As such, he was a very strong supporter of a centralized structure for the central bank system.[87]

The attitude of the President of the Board of Managers of the Bank deutscher Länder inevitably affected its management style and the public image of the bank. As its *de facto* head and the supreme representative of the central bank, Vocke increasingly moved into the limelight, and the Bank deutscher Länder outstripped the Land Central Banks in the eyes of the general public.[88] The decentralized elements and the formal two-tier arrangement gradually faded away. In addition to the weight of its top managers, this trend was reinforced by the sheer weight of the apparatus of the Bank deutscher Länder and the associated information advantage of the Board of Managers, something a mere executive board would normally never have been able to develop. Writing later, Wilhelm Könneker accurately described this situation as follows:

thanks to the pivotal position of the Bank deutscher Länder in developing principles for lending policy and operations, as well as to the extensive insight it gained from lending and banking statistics, audit activities, domestic and foreign payments, and dealings with the government and other public sector agencies, it [the Board of Managers; C. B.] provided the key inspiration for discussions and decisions by the Board of Directors. The activities and responsibilities of the Board of Managers thus extended not only to the institution under its control, but also to the entire system.[89]

In reality, the system functioned as a single-tier branch undertaking, a factor established in the explanatory memorandum to the Deutsche Bundesbank Act.[90] This was because it was impossible to institute monetary policy in a unified currency area in any other way. The Bundesbank Act recognized this by transforming the Land Central Banks into main offices of the Bundesbank, keeping their names but eliminating their autonomous legal status. This reversed the outward appearance of a two-tier central banking system in western Germany. One of the cornerstones of the Americans' efforts at decentralization had finally met with failure. Despite this, the

---

[87] Cf. Dickhaus, 1996, pp. 62f.; Horstmann, 1990, p. 214; Various meetings of the (Provisional) Central Bank Council (HA BBk B 330/1, B 330/2).
[88] Cf. Horstmann, 1990, p. 214 and Dickhaus, 1996, pp. 63f.
[89] Könneker, 1957, p. 797.
[90] Reprinted in: Seidel, 1973, pp. 335ff.

influence exerted by the occupying powers did produce two valuable results. First, it was an additional pillar of an anti-inflationary monetary policy and, in the form of the Allied Bank Commission, accelerated the creation of trust in the new currency, both at home and abroad. Secondly—and more importantly—it anchored the independence of the central bank from political influences so strongly that this principle could not be reversed at a later stage.

5. The currency reform

The Allies were responsible for the currency reform. This was inevitable because there was no responsible German authority which could have agreed on such a reform for the whole of Germany—the original intention. In their declaration of 5 June 1945, the occupying powers had explicitly assumed supreme governmental authority in Germany. This also applied to the currency reform, which was eventually restricted to the three western zones, because although there were German government institutions for the Bizone, none existed at the time of the currency reform for the 'Trizone'. The currency reform was accordingly introduced in western Germany through identical laws passed by the three military governments.

But the German authorities also declined any share of responsibility for the reform as it was implemented. The Currency Committee of the Bizonal Economic Council stated this quite explicitly from the outset to the members of the Conclave of Rothwesten, a body of German experts convened by the western Allies in April 1948 to draft concrete implementing regulations for the currency reform.[91] In a statement to the finance advisers of the three military governments at the close of the Conclave, these experts themselves declared that: 'the preparation of drafts does not mean that the key points of the measures provided for therein have been approved by the German experts. In their opinion, the special nature of the political, social and economic situation prevailing in Germany demanded a substantially different solution.'[92]

Some elements of the German position were undoubtedly motivated by tactical considerations. The Germans wanted the currency reform, which expropriated the bulk of financial assets, including those of many relatively small savers, to appear as something forced upon them by the occupying

[91] Cf. Möller, 1976, p. 446.
[92] Statement by the German Experts on the Participation in the Currency Reform, 8.6.48 (IfZ Archive, Depositum Hans Möller).

powers. In this way, they hoped to be able to divert all criticism and protests to those who were solely responsible—the Allies.[93] Indeed, it would have been impossible for a democratically elected German government to agree on a project for currency reform so radical, a factor on which its success depended heavily. This is shown by the experience in other countries. It is therefore an irony of history that simply because it was occupied, the best possible monetary conditions for subsequent growth were created in western Germany by a particularly drastic currency reform.[94] We have already seen that anchoring the principle of the political independence of the Bank deutscher Länder took a similar course.

a) German and American plans for currency reform

German influence on the details of the plan for currency reform was slight, in contrast to the subsequent—and in view of its success, quite understandable—tendency to paint it larger than it actually was. This latter view is also taken by a recently published interpretation,[95] which sees a direct link to semi-official German considerations during the war. Hans Möller, for example, who attended the Conclave and has published a selection of the host of German plans for currency reform[96] observes that all German opinions voiced on this topic 'met with a very muted response from the occupying powers', and that Allied contacts to the Special Bureau for Money and Credit of the Economic Council 'simply did not exist'.[97] Even if this is somewhat exaggerated, as there were indeed contacts, particularly at an informal level,[98] the fact that the 'Homburg Plan' devised by the Special Bureau differed fundamentally from the currency reform as it was ultimately implemented certainly supports this view. This plan[99] included the 'Draft law on the reorganization of the monetary system'. It was approved by the Currency Committee of the Economic Council and the members of the Conclave were instructed to do all they could to push it past the military governments.[100] There are thus good grounds for desig-

93 See also Brackmann, 1993, p. 268.
94 Clay's Finance Adviser advanced a similar argument; cf. Bennett to Coates, 15.12.47 (National Archives Washington [NA], RG 260 OMGUS, Office of Finance Adviser, Records relating to Specific Functional Policy Programs [Export-Import . . .], Box no. 119).
95 Cf. Brackmann, 1993.
96 Cf. Möller, 1961.
97 Möller, 1976, pp. 441f.
98 Cf. Brackmann, 1993, pp. 247f.
99 Reprinted in: Möller, 1961, pp. 477ff.
100 Cf. Möller, 1976, pp. 446f.

nating the Homburg Plan as a semi-official German project for currency reform.

The first fundamental difference relates to the treatment of excess liquidity itself. The currency reform simply eliminated it, i.e. it did not concede any claims exceeding the portion of Reichsmark balances converted into D-marks. In contrast, the Homburg plan provided for the allocation of Reichsmark liquidation certificates for the 80 per cent of the old credit balances which would not be converted into new money. This meant that there was no finality about the loss of financial assets, which—given the planned commutation of these 'Liquis'—could have led to political conflict and destabilization.

This was all the more likely because the equalization of burdens, also regulated in the Homburg Plan, was directly linked to the cut in the value of money, and thus to the Reichsmark liquidation certificates. This was principally to take the form of dividend payments on the Reichsmark liquidation certificates by an equalization fund to be established. Various asset levies were planned to finance these distributions, but most of them could also have been paid by surrendering the certificates. As calculations show, very little in the way of new money would have flowed into the equalization fund, and it certainly would have been impossible to redistribute tangible assets, as originally planned.[101] The equalization of burdens, or even a reasonable level of support from the equalization fund for those who had been impoverished by the war, would have been largely illusory.

As it turned out, there was a strict division between the equalization of burdens and the cut in the money supply. In the preamble to the Currency Act, however, it was mentioned as a task to be solved by the German legislature as a matter of great urgency. This commitment was met by the Immediate Assistance Act of August 1949 and the 1952 Equalization of Burdens Act itself, allowing compensation payments to be financed effectively. These made a decisive contribution to the integration of expellees and refugees, and thus to the maintenance of social harmony in the Federal Republic.

Another major difference between the Homburg Plan and the actual currency reform was that the former provided for a Currency Office reporting directly to the chairman of the bizonal Administrative Board, i.e. the later Federal Chancellor. It was designed to prepare the regulations needed to implement and supplement the currency reform, as well as 'monetary policy measures which appear to be urgently required'. Together with his status within the government, this very broadly worded function might

---

[101] Wolf, Zum Problem der Vermögensabgabe und des Lastenausgleichs, 25.3.48 (IfZ Archive, Depositum Hans Möller).

easily have made the President of the Currency Office a 'sort of superminister', as Hans Möller observes. He continues that it was 'understandable . . . with hindsight that the military governments did not accept this proposal, with its far-reaching interference in the way in which the German government functioned, and its curb on the independence of the central banking system'.[102] In its place, a currency department was established at the Bank deutscher Länder.

Other differences related to the arrangements for converting private debt. With the exception of short-term liabilities, this was to be converted at the general ratio of 1:1 under the Homburg Plan. As events turned out, it was actually converted at 10:1, which dispensed with the need for a large number of specific exemptions, and ensured that the inequity compared with the devaluation of savings deposits (10:0.65) was not too great. The Homburg Plan did not include any business quotas in the new currency for enterprises. Owing to the non-negotiability of Reich debt, the banks were granted equalization claims against the state to adjust their balance sheets following the currency reform. Nothing of this nature was required in the Homburg Plan because Reich debt remained essentially negotiable.

The Homburg Plan intended to organize the exchange of new for old money by paying out a *per capita* amount of RM 50 in new money at the rate of 1:1. In addition, 5 per cent of RM balances would be transferred to freely disposable accounts upon which the account owner could draw immediately, and 15 per cent to a blocked account. In contrast, the Allied plans called for a freely disposable amount of 10 per cent of RM balances, less a *per capita* amount of 25 Marks. The German experts argued against this, pleading the need to take account of social aspects. They took the line first that the non-deductible higher *per capita* amount was the simplest way to achieve a relative improvement in the position of large families and small owners of financial assets. Their second argument in favour of the lower freely disposable amount was that nobody knew the true need for money in the economy. If the initial money supply was set too low, it would be a simple matter to expand it, but the reverse was more or less impossible. In the end, the level of the *per capita* amount was the only point where the military governments made a slight concession to German wishes by stating their willingness to raise it to 50 Marks. However, they stuck to its deductibility and the 10 per cent freely disposable amount. The final arrangements described below were only adopted when it became obvious that the available banknotes would no longer be sufficient.[103]

This overview has shown that the Homburg Plan for currency reform

---

[102] Möller, 1976, p. 455.
[103] Cf. Buchheim, 1988, pp. 214f.

was largely irrelevant. In consequence, the influence of the German authorities on the fundamental principles of the reform can, to all intents and purposes, be ignored. Not that this was a bad thing, as the implementation of the Homburg Plan would most likely have had very dangerous repercussions. On the one hand, the tendency to postpone final decisions reflected in the plan would have awakened false hopes and resulted in a process of lengthy political bargaining, which in turn would have had an adverse impact on economic growth. The reason for this is that the best catalyst for growth is the elimination of an inflationary situation through immediate, conclusive regulatory action which abruptly and unconditionally refocuses the expectations of the economic actors on the new situation. On the other hand, the planned Currency Office was all too evidently tainted by the Third Reich tradition of creating special authorities, responsible practically to no one, outside the normal hierarchy of state institutions, to solve problems on an *ad hoc* basis. On top of this, it would have eroded the monetary policy independence vital for the stability of the new currency. The Homburg Plan is therefore ultimate proof of the contention made above that the currency reform was so successful because only the occupying powers were responsible for its implementation.

On 28 August 1946, General Clay introduced the Colm–Dodge–Goldsmith (CDG) Plan for currency reform in the Coordination Committee of the Control Authority. This 'Plan for the Liquidation of War Finance and the Financial Rehabilitation of Germany', named after its principal authors, the economists Gerhard Colm and Raymond W. Goldsmith (both of German descent), and Clay's Finance Adviser Joseph M. Dodge, was the result of a survey of the economic, financial, and monetary situation in Germany started in early 1946 at the instigation of OMGUS and resulting in numerous appendices.[104] The CDG Plan justified the need for a currency reform as follows: 'the real danger today is not a sudden collapse, but rather the creeping paralysis of the economic entity. Monetary and financial reform is not only—and not even primarily—necessary to prevent the collapse of price controls, but also to protect production and avoid economic chaos.'[105]

The analysis in the second section of this article has demonstrated that this diagnosis, dating from early 1946, was accurate. To actually put a stop to the negative developments, the reform had to be 'definitive', as the authors of the CDG Plan wrote.[106] This meant not just blocking the excess liquidity, but eliminating it. The chosen solution would also have to be too hard, rather than too lenient, so as to rule out the need for further reform.

[104] The CDG Plan is also reproduced in Möller, 1961, pp. 214ff.
[105] Möller, 1961, p. 225.
[106] Cf. Möller, 1961, p. 228.

The CDG Plan therefore proposed converting all monetary assets into the new currency unit at the rate of 10:1. In contrast, Reich debt would be cancelled in its entirety 'for ideological reasons'.[107] In its place, and in particular to ensure their continued solvency, financial institutions would receive certificates of newly created German public debt. The CDG Plan also envisaged setting up working parties of German experts to work out the implementing regulations for the currency reform.

The cut in the money supply was only the first phase in the overall reform project presented in the CDG Plan. A second stage provided for an equalization of burdens, to ensure the more equitable division of the losses caused by the war and financial reform. According to the Plan: 'any solution which runs counter to the sense of justice of a large proportion of the German population will have serious consequences for the young democratic government, in the same way that the clumsy solution of the inflation problems . . . jeopardized the existence of the Weimar government'.[108]

A war burdens equalization fund was to be set up which would issue certificates to those affected by losses. These would be redeemed within 20 years, perhaps in stages, depending on the type of losses and degree of need. The fund would be financed from the interest payments on, and redemption of, a 50 per cent compulsory mortgage to be levied on all tangible assets which remained intact. Debtor gains from the devaluation of the mortgages would be collected in advance in full, a concept which was actually implemented in the Mortgage Securing Act of September 1948 to support the equalization of burdens. In addition, the revenue from a capital levy on remaining net assets—with a strongly progressive scale—would also accrue to the fund. One of the reasons favouring this levy was that those who could pay more, should pay more. A feature of the arrangements for the equalization of burdens envisaged in the CDG Plan was that they were not linked to the currency reform proper. This boosted the chances of success of both measures, a sensible move because there was certainly much more to the overall plan than mere compensation for losses of financial assets.

b) Currency reform negotiations in the Control Council

Allied discussions of the currency reform issue were at first dilatory. Instead, the Control Council decided on 20 October 1945 to increase 'taxation in Germany as much as possible'. In the ensuing period, the rates for direct and indirect taxes were raised substantially, sometimes repeatedly. Key

---

[107] Möller, 1961, p. 234.
[108] Möller, 1961, p. 229.

stated objectives of this policy were to absorb excess liquidity and combat inflation. In fact, however, the bulk of the increased tax revenues was not immobilized, but used to finance the budgets, and thus the occupation costs. This meant that there was no question of any curb on inflation. On the contrary, it is quite likely that savings were also used to pay the taxes, thus having a reverse effect.[109]

General Clay had been presented with the CDG Plan as early as 20 May 1946.[110] The relatively long time-lag until its official submission to the Control Council at the end of August—although informal contacts meant that the other occupying powers had long been aware of its contents, and it initially appeared that a consensus could be reached relatively quickly[111]— was because Washington had misgivings, particularly about the broadness of the proposed equalization of burdens. US officials expressed both administrative and political reservations, the latter on the grounds of the substantial interference in the existing distribution of wealth and the massive growth in the economic power of the state. After repeated urging by General Clay however, the CDG Plan was finally accepted, at least as a basis for negotiations in the Control Council.[112]

The Coordination Committee referred the CDG Plan to the Directorate of Finance of the Control Authority for further deliberation. The British submitted a counter-proposal, the key elements of which were the realignment of unreal prices before the cut in the value of money, and a conversion rate of 2.5:1, with half of the converted amounts being paid out in new low-interest, non-redeemable government debt securities. This alternative suggestion was motivated on the one hand by the high drain on the budget of the British zone caused by high subsidy payments for coal mining, the cost of which had far outstripped official prices. The British expected that the adjustment to the price structure would result in an average increase of around 50 per cent in the overall price level. On the other hand, they regarded a 10:1 cut in the value of money as too steep. It could prevent prices and wages from being maintained at reasonable levels, possibly triggering off a deflationary spiral.

The British proposal was rejected. The majority view was that price alignments before the currency reform should be reserved only for the most blatant cases, and that these should not lead to a general increase in prices. A tentative agreement was eventually reached on the question of the con-

[109] Cf. Mai, 1995, pp. 257ff.
[110] Cf. Wandel, 1980, p. 99.
[111] Cf. Minutes of meeting, 19.6.46 (NA, RG 59, 1945–49, 862.51/6–846), and Möller, 1976, p. 443.
[112] Cf. Buchheim, 1988, p. 204; Brackmann, 1993, pp. 213ff.; Mai, 1995, p. 282.

version ratio, once the British had introduced the concept of a blockade on part of the excess liquidity instead of issuing government debt securities. 70 per cent of the currency in circulation would be eliminated, 20 per cent would be blocked and 10 per cent exchanged for new money.[113] In mid-December 1946, agreement was also reached in the Directorate of Finance that Reich debt would be annulled, and that the banks would be issued new government debt securities to replace it. Private debt—apart from mortgages —would be devalued at the rate of 10:1.[114]

During the same meeting, however, the representatives of the western Allies restated their position that they were not prepared to allow the new banknotes to be printed at a variety of locations. This very option had been demanded by the Soviet Union in October 1946 after an accord had been reached on all other technical aspects of banknote production in the Directorate of Finance. The Russians had vetoed the central production of banknotes in the Berlin Reich printing works, insisting that part of the production be relocated to Leipzig. Their justification was that as long as there was no Four-Power agreement on reparations and the creation of a central German administration, each occupying power must have the right to print the new currency in its own zone using the uniform design.[115] This was wholly in line with the Russian position during the negotiations on banking reform, where—as we have already seen—they rejected the establishment of a central monetary institution as premature.

The Russians clung to their stance on printing the new currency. In early 1947, the British and French were eventually ready to let them have their way, but not the Americans, who advanced security as the grounds for their refusal. An American analysis then came to the conclusion that the Russian approach was a reflection of their underlying delaying tactics, as the SMAD was not particularly interested in a successful currency reform because of the reorganization of the economic system in the Soviet zone. It proposed putting pressure on the Russians by starting to print the new banknotes in Berlin unilaterally.[116]

There certainly appear to have been voices on the Russian side expressing their fundamental lack of interest in currency reform. According to recent research based on Russian sources, however, the prime motive for the Soviet refusal to agree to the central production of banknotes and a single issuing

[113] Cf. Buchheim, 1988, pp. 204ff.; on the price policy of the Control Council cf. Mai, 1995, pp. 265ff.
[114] Cf. Memo by Bennet for Clay, 24.12.46 (IfZ Archive, MF 260, POLAD/459/9), as well as Brackmann, 1993, p. 233.
[115] Cf. CCG to C.O.G.A., 12.10.46 (Public Record Office London, FO 371/55418).
[116] Cf. Buchheim, 1988, pp. 206ff.; the analysis referred to is contained in Heath to Murphy, 15.5.47 (IfZ Archive, MF 260, POLAD/460/2).

agency for the new currency seems to have been much more obvious and simple. It also confirms the British suspicions that the Soviet Union was merely interested in ensuring that it could finance its occupation costs at all times.[117] The Soviet finance minister had told Molotov in March 1946 of his fundamental recognition of the need for currency reform in Germany, but at the same time had insisted that there must be clarity about 'the way in which our freedom to receive the funds needed to meet our costs (including reparations) will be ensured if the budget of the Soviet occupation zone records a deficit'.[118] This was because the Russian authorities suspected that the western Allies wanted to use the centralized issue of the new currency to control or even cut occupation and reparation costs in the Soviet zone,[119] a suspicion which could not be ruled out, given the massive interallied conflict on these points. Their insistence that the SMAD could hold an independent view on these questions was therefore quite understandable.

Apart from this point, the SMAD was evidently forced to wait in vain for a long time for detailed instructions from Moscow. This would also explain the volatility in their positions during inter-allied negotiations which caused confusion among the western Allies. There is certainly no evidence that the Russians were deliberately working towards the failure of a national German currency reform from the outset. However, they had been reckoning with the need for a separate reform in the Soviet zone since mid-1946 if the other occupying powers implemented one of their own.[120]

On the latter issue the Russian view was no different from that of their Allies. As early as July 1945, for example, the head of the department of finance in the British Military Government had pushed for work to start on a currency reform limited to the western zones, so that an option would be available if no agreement could be reached with the Soviet Union.[121] Following the flare-up of the controversy of where the banknotes would be printed and the establishment of the Bizone, the British and Americans intensified their deliberations on unilateral reform.[122] This went as far as the American decision in October 1947 to place an order for printing the new banknotes with the American Bank Note Company.[123] It was no different with the Russians. Around the turn of the year 1946–7, the SMAD

---

[117] Cf. Buchheim, 1988, p. 206.
[118] Zverev to Molotov, 21.3.46 (Foreign Policy Archive of the Russian Federation 082/30/130/32 p. 20); cited according to Laufer, 1998.
[119] Cf. Laufer, 1998.
[120] Cf. Laufer, 1998.
[121] Cf. Mai, 1995, p. 279.
[122] Cf. Mai, 1995, pp. 287f.
[123] Cf. Buchheim, 1988, p. 208.

presented proposals for printing separate banknotes for the Soviet zone and requested production of the necessary special paper.[124] During the course of 1947, coupons were printed which could be quickly glued onto the Reichsmark notes if a sudden currency reform was introduced in the western zones—a measure which was also contemplated at least by the Americans.[125] At the end of 1947, the Russians started giving thought to the idea of setting up a separate bank of issue in the Soviet zone.

Despite the preparations for a separate currency reform in west and east, the continued talks in the Control Council about a single currency reform in all four zones were more than mere window-dressing.[126] It was rather the case that each side was pursuing a two-pronged strategy, using their own plans to try to sound out the willingness of the other side to compromise. However, it was also increasingly clear that if the Four-Power negotiations were unsuccessful, they intended to shift the blame for deepening the partition of Germany, which would result from separate currency reforms, to the other side.[127]

Clay presented a final proposal for a common currency reform to the Control Council in January 1948. This was reduced to three key points: the exchange of old money at the rate of 10:1, cancellation of Reich debt and agreement that additional money could only be issued by the Control Council.[128] To the surprise of the western Allies, Marshall Vassily Sokolovsky, head of the SMAD, signalled his willingness to compromise. At long last, he agreed to the central manufacture of the new banknotes and proposed instructing the Directorate of Finance to come up with a plan for uniform currency reform within 60 days.[129] The Directorate did, in fact, start discussing this in great detail, and a consensus was apparently achieved on many issues. Whilst the French supported this and the British viewed it with mixed feelings,[130] it was now finally clear to the authorities in Washington that they did not want a common currency reform in all four zones because overall political developments had now taken a different course. Clay was correspondingly instructed to withdraw from the currency reform negotiations once the 60-day period was up.

With their withdrawal from the Control Council on 20 March, however, which they justified by the refusal of their Allies to inform them about the

[124] Cf., also for what follows: Laufer, 1998.
[125] Cf. Office Memo: Printing of a New German Mark Currency, 22.9.47 (NA, RG 59, 1945–49, 862.515/6–1247).
[126] According to Brackmann, 1993, pp. 231f.
[127] Cf. Mai, 1995, pp. 291ff. and Buchheim, 1988, p. 208.
[128] Cf., also for what follows: Buchheim, 1988, pp. 208ff. and Mai, 1995, pp. 299ff.
[129] Cf. Laufer, 1998.
[130] Cf. Turner, 1987, pp. 699f.

decisions of the London Conference in early 1948, the Russians pre-empted the Americans before they could put their intentions into practice, a move which would have made them responsible for the final partition of Germany in the eyes of the public. It is an open question whether—as Jochen Laufer suspects[131]—the unexpected success of the negotiations on a currency reform for the whole of Germany, something which neither the Russians nor the Americans now wanted, might also have played a role.

c) The currency reform in western Germany

The way was now open for a reform limited to western Germany only. This had long been the subject of talks between the Americans and the British in the Bipartite Board, the supreme Allied authority in the Bizone. A whole range of preconditions for currency reform had been realized by the end of March 1948. The Bank deutscher Länder had been established at the beginning of the month and was now ready to issue the new currency. A uniform exchange rate had been fixed at 30 US cents to the Mark. The price freeze had been officially repealed. Prices for industrial products had been raised to a level which covered costs, and wages had been increased by 15 per cent. This had seen the British pushing through one of their original demands, based on the justification that the price structure would be easier to adjust as long as there was an abundance of money.[132] The banknotes had also been printed and were being shipped to Germany.[133] For some time there had been informal talks about a separate currency reform with the French, who had evidently realized that their zone would have to participate in the western reform if the quadripartite currency reform were to fail.[134] This would also explain the accession of the Land Central Banks of the French zone to the Bank deutscher Länder at the end of March 1948.

The first official talks with the French about the principles for currency reform were held on 2 April 1948. General Pierre Koenig reported on this meeting that his American and British colleagues had proposed organizing the procedures basically in line with the CDG Plan, but incorporating the changes agreed in the Control Council. The Plan would also be presented to a small number of German experts in the near future. 'The primary purpose of these consultations was to give the Germans the feeling that they had not been excluded completely from preparatory work on financial

---

[131] Cf. Laufer, 1998.
[132] Cf. Buchheim, 1988, pp. 211f.
[133] Cf. Wandel, 1980, pp. 129f.
[134] Cf. Mai, 1995, pp. 292f.

reform. However, his colleagues were resolved not to allow any more major changes to their project.'[135]

This is exactly what happened. The Conclave of Rothwesten, which lasted from the end of April until 8 June, was forced to limit itself mainly to drafting laws, regulations, and notices as well as discussing organizational questions.[136] Despite a number of attempts, the French, too, were unable to achieve any substantial change. In fact the only area in which they prevailed concerned the tax reform linked to the cut in the volume of money. This was necessary so that the reduction in the exorbitant tax rates would increase the incentives to work harder and boost production. The French succeeded in reducing the extent of this tax reform. The dramatic negotiations on this point only culminated in a compromise on 17 June, just before the date chosen for the currency reform.[137]

The preparations for the logistics of the currency reform were running at the same time as the final negotiations. It had been decided that the ration book issuing offices would exchange the *per capita* amounts, as the records they held were best suited to avoiding double payments. The new money was transported by the military to the main and branch offices of the Land Central Banks, from where it was distributed to the savings banks in the catchment areas of the individual district food offices. The savings banks then delivered the appropriate amount of money to the ration book issuing offices, depending on the number of ration book holders registered with them. Families were supposed to receive the new money as a lump sum, i.e. large denomination notes would also be used because the number of smaller notes would otherwise have been insufficient. At the same time, the head of each household was to be issued a form for surrendering and registering the old money.[138]

Sunday 20 June 1948 was the big day, and the Issue and Currency Acts[139] came into force. The first of these implemented the intention announced in article III of the Bank deutscher Länder Act and assigned the Bank deutscher Länder the exclusive right to issue banknotes—and, until further notice, coins as well—in the currency area. Section 1 of the Currency Act set out that: 'the Deutsche Mark currency is valid with effect from 21 June 1948'. It also contained provisions relating to the *per capita* amount, which had now been fixed at DM 60 and was to be paid out in two instalments: of DM

[135] Objet: Réforme financière en Allemagne, 3.4.48 (MAE, Archives à Colmar, Groupe Français du Conseil de Contrôle) (Author's own translation).

[136] An—incomplete—overview of the work is contained in Möller, 1976, pp. 451f.

[137] Cf. Buchheim, 1988, pp. 215f.

[138] Betr.: Aufgaben der Kartenstellen im Falle einer Währungsumstellung, 29.5.48 (HA BBk B 332/37); Richtlinien für die Beamten der Landeszentralbanken (HA BBk B 332/37).

[139] These and other currency reform laws are reproduced in: Seidel, 1973.

40 and a further DM 20 within the next two months, the business quotas of DM 60 per employee, and the initial provision for public authorities. This Sunday has remained in the popular memory above all as the day when the first portion of the *per capita* amount was exchanged for RM 60. On the following day, the shop windows were filled with goods which had not been seen for many years. The psychological impact of this experience played a key role in the creation of the myth of the 'economic miracle', which soon fully eclipsed the fact that the cut in the money supply was essentially an expropriation of assets.

The radical nature of this cut in the money supply became clear in the Conversion Act of 27 June. The first part of this law governed the conversion of Reichsmark balances at banks, at which all Reichsmark cash holdings had to be paid in. The credit balances of banks, central, regional and local authorities, public sector enterprises, and Nazi organizations were cancelled. All other credit balances were converted into D-marks at the rate of 10:1 in line with the original Allied plan, after deduction of the *per capita* amounts and business quotas. However, the account owner could only freely dispose of half of the converted amount, after a review by the tax authorities if appropriate, with the other half out of reach in a blocked account for the time being. There was still talk of an additional entitlement, to be decided by the military governments, of one further D-mark for each 10 Reichsmarks for holders of old money (the so-called 'shadow quota'), but this never came to fruition. The Land Central Banks credited financial institutions with 15 per cent of their D-mark sight liabilities resulting from the conversion of their assets, and 7.5 per cent of their savings deposits. In cases where these funds and other assets remaining after the currency reform were insufficient to ensure the disclosure of adequate capital, they were to be allocated equalization claims against the government, as envisaged in the CDG Plan.

Part II of the Conversion Act covered debt, which was generally converted at the rate of 10:1. Exceptions to this were regularly recurring liabilities such as wages and salaries, rent, pensions, social security pensions, and taxes, which were to be paid in D-marks at the same rate as the former Reichsmark liabilities. This ensured a recurring link to the era before the currency reform. Reich debt was not converted. This meant that it could no longer be realized by creditors, which created the need for equalization claims.

Finally, a 'Fourth Law on the Reorganization of the Monetary System', the Blocked Accounts Act, came into force at the beginning of October 1948. This laid down that of the funds in blocked accounts, 70 per cent would be cancelled, 10 per cent would be credited to an investment account (until 1954) and 20 per cent would be released. The consequence of this was that the conversion ratio for substantial Reichsmark balances turned out to be not 10:1, but merely 100:6.5.

The Reichsmark balances registered by private individuals, companies other than banks, and public institutions amounted to around DM 145 billion. This was the basis for the sovereign creation of the new money, which totalled DM 4.4 billion by the end of June 1948, resulting from *per capita* amounts, business quotas, and the initial provisioning of public authorities and the occupying powers. By the end of December, it had grown to DM 12 billion, of which 5.3 billion were balances in freely disposable accounts. This last figure in particular highlights the radical nature of the cut in the money supply, as Reichsmark savings deposits alone had amounted to more than 70 billion, with a similar figure for call and time deposits.[140]

The heavy cut in even small savings must have shocked most savers, who had speculated with an exemption up to the last minute. The deduction in full of the *per capita* amounts from the deposits converted into D-marks also meant that many savers were left empty-handed after the conversion, because the *per capita* amounts of the members of their households were greater than one-tenth of their Reichsmark balances. The widespread feeling of expropriation which quickly arose was reinforced by the blocked accounts decision in October, resulting in a drop in confidence in the D-mark.

d) Currency reforms in the Soviet Zone of Occupation and West Berlin

As was only to be expected following the haggling in the Control Council, a separate currency reform was instituted in the Soviet zone in June 1948 by order of the SMAD. The first step was to glue the special coupons already prepared onto Reichsmark notes. This saw the so-called *Kuponmark* become the sole legal tender in East Germany. It was replaced at the end of July by a new currency, termed 'Deutsche Mark der Deutschen Notenbank'.[141] The separate currency reforms in the western zones and the Soviet Zone of Occupation finally sealed the partition of Germany.[142] This was highlighted by the Berlin Blockade, which started on 18 June 1948, the day the Currency Act was promulgated in western Germany, and which the Allies countered with their own blockade of the Soviet zone.

West Berlin had not been originally included in the west German currency

---

[140] Cf. Deutsche Bundesbank, 1976, p. 25.
[141] The relevant decrees are also reproduced in: Seidel, 1973; Zschaler, 1997.
[142] Cf. the appeal by the SMAD: An die Bevölkerung Deutschlands!, 19 June 48 (Bundesarchiv, Koblenz and Berlin, Coswig Branch, DN 6–5).

reform. In contrast, the SMAD unilaterally ordered the east German currency reform to be extended to the whole of Greater Berlin. Although the western powers would in principle have been willing to accept the east German Mark as the sole legal tender in their sectors of Berlin as well, they had no intention of bowing to a Soviet *diktat*. On 24 June 1948, one day after the announcement of the Soviet currency reform order, they issued their own order introducing the D-mark in West Berlin as well. The conversion rules were more favourable than in western Germany, as the DM 60 *per capita* amounts were not deducted, and balances were generally converted at the rate of 10:1 and released. The latter provision, however, only applied to deposits which had accrued since the end of the war. The 'pre-capitulation accounts' dating from before 9 May 1945 were not converted (at the rate of 20:1) until December 1949.

However, the east German Mark also remained in circulation. Indeed, vital goods and services such as food, rents, and public transport tariffs could be expressly paid in east German Marks instead of D-marks. The conversion rate was 1:1, although the free market rate soon settled down at around 4:1. Following the final political partition of Berlin into a western and an eastern sector, the D-mark was designated the sole legal tender on 20 March 1949, which meant that West Berlin was now a fully fledged member of the west German currency area. The east German Mark could still be used, but only at the prevailing market rate. A Berliner Zentralbank was now established. It assumed the duties of a Land Central Bank in West Berlin in all material respects, but formally at least was largely independent of the west German central banking system.[143]

e) Economic reform in western Germany

An economic reform was instituted in the Bizone at the same time as the currency reform. In contrast to the latter, it was driven primarily by German initiative.[144] Its principal promoter was Ludwig Erhard, then director of the Economic Administration Office of the United Economic Area. He was convinced that the currency reform would only meet with the desired success if free prices and markets could assume an allocational function at the same time. He was supported in this view by the majority of the Economic Advisory Council set up in his office at the beginning of 1948.[145]

---

[143] Cf. Bank deutscher Länder, 1948 and 1949, pp. 37ff. as well as Wolff, 1991; key regulations are also contained in Seidel, 1973.

[144] Cf., also for what follows: Buchheim, 1988, pp. 220ff.

[145] The discussion process on this subject is taken from: Nicholls, 1994.

Together with his colleague Leonhard Miksch, Erhard drafted the 'Law on the Principles of Economic Controls and Price Policy after the Currency Reform'. Following a fierce debate, it was adopted by the Economic Council two days before the currency reform, in the face of opposition from the SPD and others. To all intents and purposes, it was an enabling law. Its four articles authorized the director of the Economic Administration Office to institute wide-ranging measures in the area of economic and price controls. Of key importance was the appendix containing guidelines governing the actions of the director. The following two guidelines were crucial: 'The elimination of economic controls has priority over their retention', and 'The decontrol of prices has priority over their regulation by the authorities.'[146]

Although the consent of the military governments was still outstanding, Erhard announced the wide-ranging relaxation of economic controls and the abolition of price controls for the Monday following the currency reform.[147] On 25 June, he formally issued the 'Decree on Pricing and Price Controls following the Currency Reform' on the basis of his authorization under the 'Principles' law, under which the prices of almost all industrially produced finished goods were decontrolled. Most of the economic control regulations were not prolonged and lapsed automatically on 30 June as provided for by the Emergency Economic Controls Act of October 1947. The 'Principles' law was finally approved by the Bipartite Board on the same day. The American Military Government in particular supported the abolition of the majority of economic controls after the currency reform.

Although the market economy had been restored to large areas of the bizonal economy by the beginning of July 1948, full economic and price controls were retained in the French zone. They were relaxed later, but at a much slower pace. Despite a growing trend there to ignore the relevant regulations, transaction costs remained higher, and liquidity was scarcer than in the Bizone owing to the outflow of money. This had consequences for economic growth in that zone, as will be shown below.

f) *The consequences of currency and economic reform*

The currency and economic reforms resulted in the restoration of markets governed by free prices and the disappearance of barter trade, more or less from one day to the next. Money was in demand again, and the availability of goods and services rose accordingly, particularly as companies had only

---

[146] Gesetz- und Verordnungsblatt des Wirtschaftsrates des Vereinigten Wirtschaftsgebietes 1948, pp. 59f.
[147] Cf. Nicholls, 1994, p. 216.

been provided with a minimum of initial liquidity. But demand too was very high, with massive pent-up demand from consumers. Almost the entire *per capita* amounts and a substantial portion of the converted bank deposits flowed into consumption. This trend was even reinforced for a while because of the loss of confidence following the blocked accounts decision. This meant that the velocity of money in circulation was very high, leading to often massive price increases, although the money stock itself was relatively low in terms of national product, as the Bank deutscher Länder discovered.[148]

This fact alone shows that the Bank deutscher Länder was in no position to curb the initial inflationary trend, even if it had been capable of influencing the money stock.[149] Money creation was largely based on legislative actions, and the banks had high surplus reserves with a resulting substantial lending potential (owing to the generous initial provision of money to them), something they soon exploited. The result was that, in the initial stages, the central banking system was unable to regulate the provision of money to the economy effectively.[150] The price rises caused a great deal of unrest among the population and at times threatened the success of the currency reform. Only towards the end of the year did the combined effects of a number of factors start reversing the price trend.[151]

Together with the decision to fix a uniform exchange rate, the currency and economic reforms eliminated the chief obstacles to a far-reaching upturn in production. The price structure was realigned and business activities were once again governed by the profit motive. That saw a rapid increase in finished goods output, particularly as companies had stockpiled sufficient semi-finished goods and raw materials, retained their core workforces and repaired their plant and machinery. The preparations for Day X were now paying off. The official industrial production index in the Bizone grew by 26 per cent between June and August, and by a further 22 per cent by the end of the year. Industrial production grew in the French zone as well (by 23 per cent) in the first two months after the currency reform. This indicates that companies there had essentially behaved in the same way as those in the Bizone in the run-up to the reform. Industrial output had risen further by December, but, in contrast to the Bizone, growth was modest, at only 10 per cent.[152] This was most likely a direct effect of the delay in reforming economic controls in the French zone, which led to a relative liquidity

---

[148] Cf. for the entire preceding section: Bank deutscher Länder, 1948 and 1949, pp. 2ff.
[149] Cf. Gundlach, 1987, pp. 27f.
[150] Cf. Bank deutscher Länder, 1948 and 1949, pp. 5f.
[151] Cf. Borchardt and Buchheim, 1987, pp. 321ff.
[152] Cf. Ritschl, 1985, p. 164.

shortage and—according to contemporary observations—resulted in a rise in finished goods inventories at companies.[153]

Contrary to many expectations, the currency reform did not trigger a recession. Although there was a rise in officially registered unemployment, the number of people in employment also grew slightly. The average weekly working hours rose by 10 per cent and more. Capital spending also recorded heavy growth, more than doubling in the second half of 1948. However, it was not only input volumes which grew, there was also an appreciable long-term rise in productivity. In the brief period between June 1948 and March 1949, for example, labour productivity in the Bizone grew by more than 30 per cent.[154]

In conclusion, it must be said that despite an environment favouring reconstruction, industrial production in western Germany grew only slightly in the first few years after the war. This was because the prevailing economic system combined with the excess liquidity to form an effective blockade on production. The inability to reach an inter-allied consensus delayed the currency reform, regarded by many as vital to lift this blockade. When it was eventually implemented, the underlying conditions were practically ideal, particularly as regards the existing central bank system and the preparations by companies for the post-reform period. This allowed the currency and economic reforms to become a catalyst which succeeded in activating the massive growth potential, which in turn unleashed the 'economic miracle'.

6. Sources and bibliography

Unpublished sources

Bundesarchiv Koblenz and Berlin
Government Archive of the Russian Federation (GARF)
Historisches Archiv der Deutschen Bundesbank (HA BBk)
Institut für Zeitgeschichte (IfZ), Munich
Ministère des Affaires Etrangeres (MAE), Archives à Colmar
National Archives (NA), Washington
Public Record Office, London

---

[153] Cf. Buchheim, 1988, pp. 226f.
[154] Cf. Buchheim, 1988, pp. 223f.

Bibliography

Abelshauser, Werner (1975): Wirtschaft in Westdeutschland 1945–1948. Rekonstruktion und Wachstumsbedingungen in der amerikanischen und britischen Zone, Stuttgart
Abelshauser, Werner (1983): Wirtschaftsgeschichte der Bundesrepublik Deutschland (1945–1980), Frankfurt a.M.
Adler, Hans A. (1949): The Post-War Reorganization of the German Banking System, in: The Quarterly Journal of Economics 63, pp. 322–41
Bank deutscher Länder (1948 and 1949): Geschäftsbericht für die Jahre 1948 und 1949
Borchardt, Knut/Buchheim, Christoph (1987): Die Wirkung der Marshallplan-Hilfe in Schlüsselbranchen der deutschen Wirtschaft, in: Vierteljahrshefte für Zeitgeschichte 35, pp. 317–47
Brackmann, Michael (1993): Vom totalen Krieg zum Wirtschaftswunder. Die Vorgeschichte der westdeutschen Währungsreform 1948, Essen
Buchheim, Christoph (1988): Die Währungsreform 1948 in Westdeutschland, in: Vierteljahrshefte für Zeitgeschichte 36, pp. 189–231
Buchheim, Christoph (1993): The Currency Reform in West Germany in 1948, in: German Yearbook on Business History 1989–92, pp. 85–120
Bundesministerium für gesamtdeutsche Fragen (1969) (ed.): A bis Z. Ein Taschen- und Nachschlagebuch über den anderen Teil Deutschlands, Bonn
Deutsche Bundesbank (1976) (ed.): Deutsches Geld- und Bankwesen in Zahlen 1876–1975, Frankfurt a.M.
Deutsche Bundesbank (1988) (ed.): 30 Jahre Deutsche Bundesbank. Die Entstehung des Bundesbankgesetzes vom 26. Juli 1957. Dokumentation einer Ausstellung, Frankfurt a.M.
Dickhaus, Monika (1996): Die Bundesbank im westeuropäischen Wiederaufbau. Die internationale Währungspolitik der Bundesrepublik Deutschland 1948 bis 1958, Munich
Dickhaus, Monika (1997): The Foster-Mother of 'The Bank that rules Europe': the Bank deutscher Länder, the Bank of England and the Allied Banking Commission, in: Bance, Alan (ed.): The Cultural Legacy of the British Occupation in Germany, Stuttgart, pp. 294–324
Drexler, Alexander (1985): Planwirtschaft in Westdeutschland 1945–1948. Eine Fallstudie über die Textilbewirtschaftung in der britischen und Bizone, Stuttgart
Dumke, Rolf H. (1990): Reassessing the Wirtschaftswunder: Reconstruction and Postwar Growth in West Germany in an International Context, in: Oxford Bulletin of Economics and Statistics 52, pp. 451–91
Gesetz- und Verordnungsblatt des Wirtschaftsrates des Vereinigten Wirtschaftsgebiets 1948
Gundlach, Erich (1987): Währungsreform und wirtschaftliche Entwicklung: Westdeutschland 1948, Institut für Weltwirtschaft, Kieler Arbeitspapier no. 286, Kiel
Henke, Klaus-Dietmar (1996): Die amerikanische Besetzung Deutschlands, Munich
Holtfrerich, Carl-Ludwig (1995): Die Deutsche Bank vom Zweiten Weltkrieg über die Besatzungsherrschaft zur Rekonstruktion 1945–1957, in: Gall, Lothar et al.: Die Deutsche Bank 1870–1995, Munich, pp. 409–578
Horstmann, Theo (1985): Um 'das schlechteste Bankensystem der Welt'. Die interalliierten Auseinandersetzungen über amerikanische Pläne zur Reform des deutschen Bankwesens 1945/46, in: Bankhistorisches Archiv 11, pp. 3–27
Horstmann, Theo (1989): Kontinuität und Wandel im deutschen Notenbanksystem. Die Bank deutscher Länder als Ergebnis alliierter Besatzungspolitik nach dem Zweiten Weltkrieg, in: Pirker, Theo (ed.): Autonomie und Kontrolle. Beiträge zur Soziologie des Finanz- und Steuerstaates, Berlin, pp. 135–54
Horstmann, Theo (1990): Die Entstehung der Bank deutscher Länder als geldpolitische Lenkungsinstanz in der Bundesrepublik Deutschland, in: Riese, Hajo/Spahn, Heinz-Peter

(eds.): Geldpolitik und ökonomische Entwicklung. Ein Symposion, Regensburg, pp. 202–18

Horstmann, Theo (1991): Die Alliierten und die deutschen Großbanken. Bankenpolitik nach dem Zweiten Weltkrieg in Westdeutschland, Bonn

Könneker, Wilhelm (1957): Vom Zentralbanksystem zur Deutschen Bundesbank, in: Zeitschrift für das gesamte Kreditwesen 10, pp. 796–8

Kramer, Alan (1991): Die britische Demontagepolitik am Beispiel Hamburgs 1945–1950, Hamburg

Krumbein, Wolfgang (1989): Wirtschaftssteuerung in Westdeutschland 1945–1949. Organisationsformen und Steuerungsmethoden am Beispiel der Eisen- und Stahlindustrie in der britischen/Bi-Zone, Stuttgart

Landeszentralbank von Baden (1947): Verwaltungsbericht der Landeszentralbank von Baden für das Geschäftsjahr 1947

Landeszentralbank von Bayern (1947): Geschäftsbericht für das Jahr 1947

Landeszentralbank von Rheinland-Pfalz (1947): Geschäftsbericht für das Jahr 1947

Landeszentralbank von Württemberg-Baden (1947): Bericht über das erste Geschäftsjahr 1947

Landeszentralbank von Württemberg-Baden (1948 and 1949): Bericht über die Geschäftsjahre 1948 und 1949

Laufer, Jochen (1998): Die UdSSR und die deutsche Währungsfrage 1944–1948, in: Vierteljahrshefte für Zeitgeschichte 46, 5 455–85

Mai, Gunther (1995): Der alliierte Kontrollrat in Deutschland 1945–1948. Alliierte Einheit— deutsche Teilung?, Munich

Mendershausen, Horst (1949): Prices, Money and the Distribution of Goods in Postwar Germany, in: The American Economic Review 39, pp. 646–72

Mitchell, Brian R. (1992): International Historical Statistics. Europe 1750–1988, Basingstoke

Möller, Hans (1961) (ed.): Zur Vorgeschichte der Deutschen Mark. Die Währungsreformpläne 1945–1948, Basle

Möller, Hans (1976): Die westdeutsche Währungsreform von 1948, in: Deutsche Bundesbank (ed.): Währung und Wirtschaft in Deutschland 1876–1975, Frankfurt a.M., pp. 433–83

Nicholls, Anthony J. (1994): Freedom with Responsibility. The Social Market Economy in Germany 1918–1963, Oxford

Plumpe, Werner (1987): Vom Plan zum Markt. Wirtschaftsverwaltung und Unternehmerverbände in der britischen Zone, Düsseldorf

Ritschl, Albrecht (1985): Die Währungsreform von 1948 und der Wiederaufstieg der westdeutschen Industrie. Zu den Thesen von Mathias Manz und Werner Abelshauser über die Produktionswirkungen der Währungsreform, in: Vierteljahrshefte für Zeitgeschichte 33, pp. 136–65

Sauermann, Heinz (1979): On the Economic and Financial Rehabilitation of Western Germany (1945–1949), in: Zeitschrift für die gesamte Staatswissenschaft 135, pp. 301–19

Schulz, Günther (1996): Gläubiger und Schuldner: Die Kölner Unternehmer 1945, in: Dülffer, Jost (ed.): 'Wir haben schwere Zeiten hinter uns'. Die Kölner Region zwischen Krieg und Nachkriegszeit, Vierow, pp. 245–66

Seidel, Karl-Dieter (1973): Die deutsche Geldgesetzgebung seit 1871, Munich

Trittel, Günter J. (1990): Hunger und Politik. Die Ernährungskrise in der Bizone (1945–1949), Frankfurt a.M.

Turner, Ian (1987): Great Britain and the Post-War German Currency Reform, in: The Historical Journal 30, pp. 685–708

Wandel, Eckhard (1980): Die Entstehung der Bank deutscher Länder und die deutsche Währungsreform 1948. Die Rekonstruktion des westdeutschen Geld- und Währungssystems 1945–1949 unter Berücksichtigung der amerikanischen Besatzungspolitik, Frankfurt a.M.

Wolff, Michael W. (1991): Die Währungsreform in Berlin, Berlin

Woller, Hans (1986): Gesellschaft und Politik in der amerikanischen Besatzungszone. Die Region Ansbach und Fürth, Munich

Zank, Wolfgang (1987): Wirtschaft und Arbeit in Ostdeutschland 1945–1949. Probleme des Wiederaufbaus in der Sowjetischen Besatzungszone Deutschlands, Munich

Zschaler, Frank (1997): Die vergessene Währungsreform. Vorgeschichte, Durchführung und Ergebnisse der Geldumstellung in der SBZ 1948, in: Vierteljahrshefte für Zeitgeschichte 45, pp. 191–223

Part Two

THE CENTRAL BANK IN THE CONSTITUTIONAL AND FINANCIAL SET-UP OF THE FEDERAL REPUBLIC OF GERMANY

III. The Note-Issuing Bank within the State Structure

By Klaus Stern

1. Introduction

Writing about the position of the German note-issuing bank under state law shortly prior to the institution of a European note-issuing bank might create the impression of intending to take a more historical than a present-day view. Having said that, this impression is deceptive. Categorising the Bundesbank within the state structure as the central German note-issuing bank is also of primary importance for the European Central Bank since the status and the role of the Deutsche Bundesbank have in many ways become a model for Europe's common note-issuing bank, as reflected in article 105ff. of the Treaty Establishing the European Community in the version dated 7 February 1992. This discussion refers therefore not to a final balance sheet of the Bundesbank, but to the evaluation of a note-issuing bank in terms of state law, which in 1997—one year prior to the 50th Birthday of the D-mark—celebrated its 40th Anniversary and which enjoys worldwide respect, not only because of its wise monetary policy which is aimed to promote stability, but especially because of its legal and institutional structure. This means that its independence from political bodies as a fundamental precondition for monetary stability is one of the most significant achievements of the post-war period which is to be incorporated into the process of European Economic and Monetary Union.

If, like the Federal Constitutional Court, one regards the European Union as an 'association of states', the legal and institutional components which apply to the Bundesbank within the state structure of the Federal Republic of Germany should *mutatis mutandis* likewise be representative for the European Central Bank. The content of the 'Protocol on the Statute of the European System of Central Banks and of the European Central Bank', which was adopted in Maastricht in 1992, and is a part of the Treaty on European Union, allows no doubt as to this assessment. Consequently, a portrayal of the German note-issuing bank within the state structure is more than ever both worthwhile and future-oriented, not least because the topic of the independence of the note-issuing bank is also becoming attractive for states which do not grant this to their central banks. Wherever in recent times independence has been granted to a note-issuing bank, the German model has played an important role.

2. The constitutional status of the Bundesbank as a currency and note-issuing bank

a) The criteria set by constitutional law

In accordance with article 88 first sentence of the Basic Law (*Grundgesetz/ GG*), the Federal Government is to establish a note-issuing and currency bank in the form of a Federal Bank. Hence, this is the first time the German central bank has been anchored in a German constitution, and therefore in a constitutional setting. At the same time, this was a fundamental decision in relation to the structure of the economy of the Federal Republic of Germany.

In addition to the Federal Government's competence to establish the Bundesbank, along the lines of the model provided by earlier constitutions, the Basic Law confers further legislative responsibilities on the Federal Government in respect of 'currency, money and coinage' (article 73 no. 4), and also of 'banking' (article 74 no. 11). Article 73 no. 4 and article 74, no. 11 and article 88 first sentence *GG* complement each other: they refer to fields which, in conformity with the functional portrayal as 'note-issuing and currency bank' in article 88 first sentence *GG*, belong to the typical role of such an institution, and should preferably be carried out by the latter. One may not however infer from this that the Bundesbank occupies a monopoly position where it is the only administrative institution responsible for implementing the statutory regulations issued under article 73 no. 4 and article 74 no. 11 *GG*. That said, any substantial transfer of matters concerning the currency system to other bodies would probably be unconstitutional.

The allocation of competences in article 88 first sentence *GG* entitles and obliges the Federal Government to establish a note-issuing and currency bank in the sense of constituting, organizing, and allocating functions. Article 88 first sentence *GG* therefore contains a *constitutional mandate*. The specific addressee for the establishment is however not named. It has sometimes been inferred from this that establishment without a statute would be permissible because article 86 second sentence *GG* made the Federal Government the repository of organizational power insofar as the

(Basic) Law makes no other provision.[1] In practice, however, a statute is needed even if one takes this view: first, article 87 para. 3 first sentence *GG* requires legislation if the legal form selected is that of a new federal public corporation or institute. Secondly, a statute is needed if the Bundesbank is permitted to encroach upon the field of property and liberties. Finally, in a parliamentary, democratic state based on the rule of law it is parliament itself which has to lay the most important foundations of the organizational structure for organizational acts of the order of significance of the establishment of a note-issuing and currency bank. It is therefore parliament which is the addressee of the constitutional mandate to establish a note-issuing and currency bank.

Article 88 first sentence *GG* makes no provision for the participation of the Bundesrat in this establishment. Since the Bundesrat may only derive rights to participate from the Basic Law itself, no such right exists in relation to the establishment of the Bundesbank. Accordingly, the Federal Constitutional Court put it in the following succinct terms: 'if, without the consent of the Bundesrat, the Federal Government may establish a currency and note-issuing bank in the form of a Federal Bank in accordance with article 88, on the basis of the same provision, and also without the consent of the Bundesrat, it may, either by expressly amending and supplementing the Bundesbank Act (*Bundesbankgesetz*) or by means of a special Act such as the Banking Act (*Kreditwesengesetz*), assign further functions to the Bundesbank to the extent that these continue to fall within its sphere of operation as a currency and note-issuing bank.'[2]

Article 88 first sentence *GG* assigned to the Federal Government the establishment of the Bundesbank, and hence decided that the Bundesbank is a *Federal* and not a Länder institution.

Article 88 first sentence *GG* contains not only a constitutional mandate, but at the same time also a *constitutional guarantee of this institution*.[3] As a rule, problems are posed by determining the content of and the limits placed on such guarantees.[4] This applies to a particular extent to article 88 first sentence *GG*. Relatively little is gained by merely guaranteeing the existence of a Bundesbank. The emphasis is, rather, on distinguishing the protected field of operation of the central bank, which article 88 first sentence *GG* merely sketches with the terms 'currency and note-issuing bank'. The conclusion to be drawn from this is certainly that the constitution

---

[1] Cf. Klein, 1957, p. 1079.
[2] *BVerfGE* (*Entscheidungen des Bundesverfassungsgerichts*/Rulings of the Federal Constitutional Court) 14, p. 215.
[3] Cf. von Mangoldt and Klein, 1974, article 88, note II 3 and Hahn, 1982, pp. 70f.
[4] Cf. Stern, 1984, vol. 1, sections 11 and 12.

guarantees the existence of the institution as a 'bank' which essentially must be a 'currency and note-issuing' bank. This portrayal may not be called in question by parliament. What this includes in detail is however difficult to ascertain.[5]

In accordance with article 88 first sentence *GG* the Bundesbank has first and foremost to be a *bank*. This term has a character from the period prior to the creation of the constitution within the meaning of a credit institution which, in accordance with the so-called universal banking system which has become established in Germany, performs all customary banking transactions. These are now listed in section 1(1) second sentence of the Banking Act, and are thus guaranteed to the Bundesbank by its designation as a 'bank' in article 88 first sentence *GG*. Correspondingly, in accordance with sections 19 to 25 of the Bundesbank Act almost all banking transactions are permitted, even if in formal terms it is a question of an exhaustive list of permitted transactions within the meaning of a *numerus clausus*, and the permitted business operations with private non-banks and with the state are subjected to even tighter restrictions than those with commercial banks (cf. sections 20, 22, and 25 of the Bundesbank Act).

The Bundesbank must at the same time be a *currency bank*. 'Safeguarding the currency, the term "currency bank" also covers both supplying the general economy with funds and safeguarding the value of money.'[6] From a technical point of view, the Bundesbank thus performs the function of 'Bank of Banks' which, as a reserve bank and final source of refinancing for the credit institutions, guarantees the solvency of the entire German banking system.[7] Furthermore, article 88 first sentence *GG* protects the somewhat functional relationship to the currency in terms of ensuring its stability.[8] Both functions are conditional on the Bundesbank being equipped with the instruments required in order to fulfil its task. Both the Basic Law and the rulings of the highest courts are silent with regard to the question of which individual *monetary policy powers* fall under the constitutional guarantee. In the light of the short wording contained in the Basic Law, it is possible only to justify the guarantee of a 'monetary policy minimum' for exercising an effective influence on the currency, even if the trend is strong towards

---

[5] Höpker-Aschoff has already tried to make it clear in his letter to F. Klein concerning the latter's report that this is however where the actual difficulty lies; printed in: Höpker-Aschoff, 1956.

[6] *BVerwGE (Entscheidungen des Bundesverwaltungsgerichts*/Rulings of the Federal Administrative Court) 41, p. 349.

[7] This corresponds to the historical picture in accordance with section 12 of the 1875 Reichsbank Act (*Reichsbankgesetz*/RBG) and section 1 of the 1924 Reichsbank Act.

[8] As already stated in von Mangoldt (1953), *Grundgesetz*, article 88, note 2, in interpretation of the materials of the Parliamentary Council; since then the prevalent opinion, cf. Uhlenbruck, 1968, p. 25; Samm, 1967, p. 54, with further references.

regarding the existing instruments as a whole, which are considered to make sense from an overall economic point of view, as being guaranteed by the constitution. The Federal Administrative Court was correct to include minimum reserve policy in this (section 16 of the Bundesbank Act). Furthermore, discount policy should also belong here, as being the oldest means by which a note-issuing bank exercises control (section 15 of the Bundesbank Act). On the other hand, difficulties are posed by the classification of the relatively recent instrument of open market policy (section 15 of the Bundesbank Act). Open market operations in fixed-interest securities, with an agreement to buy them back, so-called securities repurchase transactions (repos), were not developed by the Bundesbank until 1979, but since mid-1985 have formed the basis of its management of the money market, and have long since displaced rediscount credit from its traditional number one position in the refinancing of credit institutions with the Bundesbank.[9] In the light of this development, this instrument should now also be covered by the guarantee contained in article 88 first sentence *GG*.

Article 88 first sentence *GG* guarantees the existence of a currency bank, but does not make this bank the sole repository of the currency system.[10] This emerges from article 74 no. 4, which defines competences, and from article 109 para. 2 *GG*, which generally imposes on the Federal Government and the Länder the duty to adhere to the requirements of overall economic equilibrium—and hence also of monetary stability.[11] Certainly, on the basis of the simultaneous allocation of functions to several bodies, a difficult competitive situation may arise in terms of a positive conflict of competences. This is alleviated in article 109 para. 2 *GG* by the fact that the role of safeguarding the currency, which is required in accordance with this provision, is to be carried out only within the restricted framework of the budget management of the Federal Government and the Länder. In accordance with article 88 first sentence *GG*, the general competence as 'guardian of the currency'[12] certainly remains the preserve of the Bundesbank.

Closely connected to the role of the Bundesbank as a currency bank is its task of being a *note-issuing bank*. As early as during its genesis, it was clear that it was to be afforded the sole right to issue banknotes.[13] This

---

[9] Cf. Deutsche Bundesbank, 1995, pp. 113ff.

[10] This was also the assumption made in the Government Draft of the Bundesbank Act, BT-Drucks. (Federal Parliament Publication) II/2781, p. 23; cf. also Lampe, 1971, p. 78; Beck, 1959, 2nd Book, section 3, K 54ff., pp. 149f.; Starke, 1957, p. 75.

[11] Cf. Stern *et al.*, 1972, article 109, note III 3 in conjunction with Stern *et al.*, 1972, Introduction A II 2 and section 1 of the Stability and Growth Act note III.

[12] This is the generally recognized wording, cf. von Spindler *et al.*, 1973, Part II, section 2, note 2, p. 169.

[13] Cf. Fögen, 1969, pp. 73f.; Püttner, 1969, p. 165; Samm, 1967, pp. 61f., 179; Schmidt-Bleibtreu and Klein, 1994, article 88, margin no. 4.

guarantee contained in article 88 first sentence *GG* is not contradicted, either, by the restriction contained in section 14 (1) fourth sentence of the Bundesbank Act, whereby the Bundesbank may only issue notes in denominations smaller than 10 D-mark by agreement with the Federal Cabinet. Since the Federal Government was granted only a very limited right of participation in this respect, but not a right of issue of its own, it is certainly not possible for additional central bank money to be issued *against* the will of the Bundesbank.

The situation however is different with the so-called prerogative of coinage. The Act on the Minting of Coins (*Gesetz über die Ausprägung von Scheidemünzen*) dated 8 July 17 1950 (BGBl. [Bundesgesetzblatt/Federal Law Gazette] Part I p. 323) in the version of the Act dated 10 December 1986 (BGBl. Part I p. 2414)—Coinage Act (*Münzgesetz*)—transfers to the Federal Government the most important powers regarding coins. The annual seigniorage and issuance are listed in the Federal budget.[14]

The role of the Bundesbank as *principal or commercial bank of the state*, now very much restricted, is not guaranteed by the constitution. Its role as the administrator of the monetary reserves—the Bundesbank is the sole agency in the Federal Republic of Germany which holds official monetary reserves, and hence guarantees the international liquidity of the state—is likewise not protected by article 88 first sentence *GG*.

b) Statutory allocation of functions

The constitution does not prohibit functions from being allocated to the Bundesbank by means of a statute associated with its role as a currency and note-issuing bank. This has frequently occurred in the fields of banking supervision, of legislation on foreign trade and payments, and in particular of restrictions on capital movements as well as on the basis of its position as principal bank of the state. Article 88 first sentence *GG*, however, requires that the role of currency and note-issuing bank is not to be placed at a disadvantage by means of such accidental functions.

c) Role of the Bundesbank as a constitutional body

The examination of the legal position of the Bundesbank, institutionalized within the state structure as it is by means of article 88 first sentence *GG*,

---

[14] Cf. Gramlich, 1988*a*, section 12 margin no. 1.

is frequently connected with the question of its role as a *constitutional body*.[15]

The question as to its role as a constitutional body can only be answered by the Basic Law itself. Constitutional bodies are those constituted by the constitution itself, whose competences emerge directly from the constitution, and which participate in the overall political structure of the state, in other words which therefore by their 'activities actually constitute the state and ensure its unity'.[16] These criteria do not apply to the Bundesbank.[17] The Bundesbank is guaranteed by the constitution itself in terms of its existence and in its functional nucleus, and it is possible to include a large number of its decision making powers as significant participation in terms of state policy in the decision making of the state. In the main, however, its functions and organization are governed by parliament itself. Even if the latter's room to manoeuvre is restricted by article 88 first sentence *GG*, the role of a constitutional body does not accrue to the institution which is guaranteed by means of this constitutional provision.

This does not however mean that the decision has yet been taken with regard to whether the Bundesbank may be an applicant or an opponent in a *dispute between highest Federal bodies relating to rights and duties (Organstreitverfahren)* before the Federal Constitutional Court in accordance with article 93 para. 1 no. 1 *GG* and section 13 no. 5 of the Act on the Federal Constitutional Court (*BVerfGE*). As a constitutional body, the Bundesbank would undoubtedly be able to be a party. Beyond the non-exhaustive list contained in section 63 of the Act on the Federal Constitutional Court, article 93 para. 1 no. 1 *GG* however satisfies itself with 'highest Federal bodies' or 'other parties', 'who have been vested with rights of their own by this Basic Law or by rules of procedure of a highest Federal body'. The Bundesbank may however derive rights neither from the Basic Law nor by rules of procedure of a highest Federal body, but only from ordinary Federal statutes, so that in this respect it is likewise unable to be a party to pursuing a dispute between the highest Federal bodies relating to rights and duties before the Federal Constitutional Court.[18]

---

[15] Cf. on this the references in von Mangoldt and Klein, 1974, article 88, FN 152; von Münch and Kunig, 1996, article 88, margin no. 3.

[16] Höpker-Aschoff, 1957, pp. 197f.; Stern, 1980, vol. 2, section 32 II 2 b.

[17] Cf. Dolzer and Vogel (n.d.), article 93, margin no. 100; Löwer, 1987, section 56, margin no. 18; Gramlich, 1988b, pp. 81f.; von Spindler *et al.*, 1973, Part II, section 2, note 1, p. 168.

[18] Ultimately also: von Münch and Kunig, 1996, article 88, margin no. 3; Faber, 1989, article 88, margin no. 35; von Spindler *et al.*, 1973, Part II, section 2, note 1, p. 168; Fögen, 1969, p. 661; Gramlich, 1980, p. 534.

d) Highest executive body of a special kind

Negating a role as a constitutional body and stating that the Bundesbank is unable to be a party in accordance with article 93 para. 1 no. 1 *GG* does not complete the picture as regards the position of the Bundesbank under state law. In accordance with the scheme of the three main state functions described in article 1 para. 3 and article 20 para. 2 *GG*, the Bundesbank is closest to the executive. In terms of its systematic position, article 88 *GG* is already a part of the regulatory context of the executive power, the 'Federal Administration', even if it is in many ways a special provision in Part VIII of the Basic Law: the activity of the Bundesbank is not, as has increasingly become the case for the administration, oriented towards implementing laws. Article 88 first sentence *GG* likewise does not speak of administration or of implementation of the statutes relating to the currency and banknotes system but, with the dual term 'currency and note-issuing bank', merely characterizes the scope of the role of the Bundesbank. Accordingly, article 88 first sentence *GG* regulates a *Federal executive competence of a special kind*, which differs both from the contents of the Federal Government's own administration, as contained in articles 86 to 87d *GG*, and is also an exception to the general provision contained in article 83 *GG* regulating competences.

This categorization as part of the executive area conforms to the classification of the Bundesbank in section 2 first sentence of the Bundesbank Act as a *Federal corporation under public law*. In the light of the role of the Bundesbank and of its freedom from instructions, however, its designation as an authority is applicable only to a very restricted extent:[19] the Bundesbank has its own legal capacity and its role primarily covers non-typical administrative activities. That has also indirectly been confirmed by parliament as the author of the Bundesbank Act, in that the latter saw fit to make express assignments under organizational law in order to bring about certain consequences under administrative law (sections 29 and 31 of the Bundesbank Act). Such provisions would otherwise be self-evident, and hence superfluous. In addition, section 29(1) first sentence of the Bundesbank Act grants only to the Central Bank Council and the Directorate of the Deutsche Bundesbank 'the status of supreme Federal authorities'. In the area of the executive, the Bundesbank therefore has a special status. It is comparable

---

[19] The Federal Administrative Court had already recognized difficulties in using the term 'authority' with regard to the predecessor of the Bundesbank, the Bank deutscher Länder, and had given the latter 'a unique status', comparable to that of a Federal Ministry, cf. *BVerwGE* 2, p. 218. *BVerwGE* 41, pp. 334ff., too, strictly avoided speaking of an administrative authority, an administrative act, and similar terms belonging to the administration.

not to a (Federal) administrative authority, but to a government body.[20] The consequence of this is that it is to be classified amongst the *highest executive state bodies.*

This allocation at the same time explains the problem of the Bundesbank's so-called *freedom from ministerial control.*[21] The control of all administrative activity by parliament is part and parcel of the system of parliamentary government. In order to achieve this aim, administrative activity is in principle supposed to lie at the door of a member of the government, who bears responsibility for this towards parliament. This is commonly used to derive the broad inadmissibility of so-called areas free of ministerial control. Article 88 *GG* does not yet grant freedom from ministerial control. Rather, this freedom emerges from the position of the Bundesbank, as governed by the Bundesbank Act, as a Federal corporation under public law which in the exercise of its powers in accordance with section 12 second sentence of the Bundesbank Act 'is independent of instructions from the Federal Cabinet'. If one makes the Bundesbank part of the system of administrative authorities, one must explain its freedom from ministerial control by means of a necessary case for its being excepted from the principle of allocation to a Ministry as permitted by the constitution, or for an 'important and relevant reason'.[22] If it is categorized as a highest state body with governmental features, freedom from ministerial control on the other hand becomes evident. There is, however, a need for compatibility with the principle of the democratic state based on the rule of law as defined in articles 20 and 28 *GG*. Hence, at the same time the cardinal question under state law of a note-issuing bank arises: independence from or control by the government and parliament.

3. The Bundesbank Act dated 1957 and its further legal development

a) The three fundamental decisions contained in the Bundesbank Act

In adopting the Act on the Deutsche Bundesbank dated 26 July 1957, parliament discharged its mandate under article 88 *GG* to establish a currency and note-issuing bank in the shape of a Federal Bank.

When, on 24 May 1949, the Basic Law entered into force, a decentralized

---

[20] As here: Fögen, 1969, p. 109; Samm, 1967, pp. 141f.; Samm, 1984, pp. 1–4; Studt, 1992, p. 92.

[21] Cf. on this *BVerfGE* 9, p. 282; Fichtmüller, 1966, pp. 297ff.

[22] Cf. von Mangoldt and Klein, 1974, article 88, note IV 3 b; Samm, 1967, pp. 89ff., 96f.

central bank system organized in two tiers which was not subject to the instructions of political bodies (from 1951 onwards this also applied in relation to the occupying powers) had already been established in the three west German zones of occupation. Article 88 *GG* did not set a date for the establishment of the Bundesbank in place of the central bank system set up under the law of the occupying powers. Nevertheless, for reasons of national sovereignty the law of the occupying powers had to be replaced by German law—at the latest since 5 May 1955. The discussions on the reform of the constitution of the German note-issuing bank started soon after the Basic Law had entered into force. However, it was not possible to conclude them until the end of the second legislative period of the German Bundestag. Involvement came primarily from the Federal Government, in particular the Federal Ministries of Finance and of Economics, from the Bundesrat, the political parties and the Bank deutscher Länder, all represented in the Bundestag Committee on Money and Credit, which debated the Act in 1953 and 1957.[23] Three contentious areas, with regard to which article 88 *GG* contained no (clear) instructions, were at the centre of the discussion: the organizational structure of the future Bundesbank (one-tier and centralized or two-tier and decentralized), its independence, in particular from the Federal Government, and its legal form.

Opinions with regard to these fundamental questions were so far apart that work on the Bundesbank Act was halted in the summer of 1953 at the end of the first legislative period and, because of the discontinuity of the legislative period, had to be broken off altogether. It was not until the end of 1955 that work was recommenced within the framework of the Second Deutscher Bundestag. In 1957, it was the particular achievement of the Chairman of the Bundestag Committee on Money and Credit, the CDU MP Hugo Scharnberg, to bring about a draft compromise which was acceptable to all sides. This was adopted by the Bundestag on 4 July 1957. On 19 July 1957, the Bundesrat gave the consent which it held to be necessary in accordance with article 84 para. 1 *GG*. Once it had been signed and promulgated by the Federal President, the Act on the Deutsche Bundesbank was notified on 30 July 1957, dated as at 26 July 1957, and entered into force on 1 August 1957.

The main bone of contention from the outset of the discussions was the organizational structure of the future Bundesbank. There were two opposing main opinions:[24] one view wished for a Bundesbank which would be organized in *two tiers and decentralized*, like the central bank system which

---

[23] For details on the genesis of the Act cf. Hentschel, 1988, pp. 3ff., 70ff.
[24] For details on this dispute cf. Beck, 1959, 1st book, E 117ff., pp. 87ff.; Deutsche Bundesbank, 1988, pp. 151ff. (overview of the various Draft Bills on p. 195); Becker, 1954, pp. 358ff., with further references.

had existed since 1948, that is with legally independent Land Central Banks, and where the highest decision making body would be constituted along federalist lines.[25] Another view, however, demanded a structure in line with the system of the Reichsbank of 1875–1945, which would be a *one-tier, centralized* structure with a central bank to which the Land Central Banks would be subject, and whose highest decision making body would be appointed largely by the Federal Government.[26]

The Basic Law made no stipulation with regard to this controversy. The term *Bundes*bank in article 88 *GG* does not prohibit the use of Länder institutions in the organizational structure, nor do the restrictions apply which are contained in article 87 para. 3 second sentence *GG* for the establishment of intermediate and lower federal authorities, since it is not a question of the establishment of 'new functions'. In this respect parliament was free to bring to fruition either the Land Central Bank system or the system of the Reichsbank.[27] The provision finally reached in the Bundesbank Act was a *compromise* between the two views: in accordance with section 1 of the Bundesbank Act, the existing Land Central Banks were amalgamated with the Bank deutscher Länder, and the latter was reformed to become the Deutsche Bundesbank. This therefore meant the dissolution of the Land Central Banks as independent legal entities. In accordance with section 8 of the Bundesbank Act, the designation Land Central Bank was retained, but these now hide Main Offices of the Bundesbank with restricted functional autonomy (section 8(2) of the Bundesbank Act) and a special federalist method of appointing the Presidents of the Land Central Bank (section 8(4) of the Bundesbank Act). In this way, only a remainder of the two-tiered structure and of decentralism is left. On the other hand, the Executive Boards of the Land Central Banks are at the same time governing bodies of the Bundesbank (section 5 of the Bundesbank Act) and the nine Presidents of the Land Central Banks are members of the Central Bank Council, which has a maximum of 17 members (section 6(2) of the Bundesbank Act). This construction is quite new, linking unitary and federalist or centralized and decentralized elements. Those who know the system acknowledge that it has proved itself.[28]

[25] Cf. BT-Drucks. I/4020 (Draft by Schaeffer); BT-Drucks. II/2832 (Draft by the Christian Social Union [CSU]); Deutsche Bundesbank, 1988, p. 179.

[26] Cf. BT-Drucks. II/2781 (Draft by Erhard); BT-Drucks. I/3929 (Draft by the Free Democratic Party [FDP]); Deutsche Bundesbank, 1988, p. 166.

[27] Cf. Klein, 1953; Deutsche Bundesbank, 1988, p. 160; a complaint of unconstitutionality on this by the Freie Demokratische Partei (FDP) dated 4 Feb. 1953 was rejected as inadmissible for procedural reasons by the Federal Constitutional Court by judgment dated 29 July 1953, cf. *BVerfGE* 3, p. 3, 12ff., so that no decision was taken on the merits.

[28] Cf. Veit, 1969, pp. 624ff.; Hahn, 1968, vol. 1, p. 150; Wagenhöfer, 1957, p. 8. Cf. also the contributions in: Deutsche Bundesbank, 1976.

Also, disagreement remained as to the question of the *independence* of the future Bundesbank in its relationship with the bodies of the leadership of the state, in particular with the Federal Government. Reservations existed against complete freedom of the Bundesbank from instructions, especially within the Federal Government. The Draft Bill of the Federal Ministry of Finance dated March 1950 accordingly provided for the institution of a Federal Committee for Currency and Economic Policy Decisions, which was to bring together both representatives of the Federal Government and of Central Bank Council, and whose decisions were to be binding on the Central Bank Council.[29] Federal Chancellor Konrad Adenauer also attacked the independence of the existing central bank system under the law of the occupying powers by openly criticizing the discount policy of the Central Bank Council of the Bank deutscher Länder which was pursued in the autumn of 1950 and between the summer of 1955 and the spring of 1956, which caused an economic downswing, but was oriented towards price stability. On the other hand, the Federal Minister of Economics, Ludwig Erhard, and the President of the Central Bank Council spoke out against any right of the Federal Government to issue instructions.[30] Sections 12 and 13 of the Bundesbank Act regulated the independence of the Bundesbank from instructions, with certain modifications.

The question of the *legal form* of the future Bundesbank was also left open in article 88 *GG* by the parliament which adopted the Basic Law. The ordinary legislators were therefore free to select a form of organization for the Bundesbank either under private law or under public law. It decided finally to establish a *Federal corporation under public law* (section 2 first sentence of the Bundesbank Act). This construction had already been selected for the Bank deutscher Länder. In the case of organization under private law, as had been assigned in part to the old Reichsbank in the light of its private shareholders,[31] state powers would have certainly had to be assigned to the Bundesbank, and hence it would have been assigned the status of a lender. In this respect, the decision for the legal form under public law was certainly sensible.

The designation chosen by parliament 'corporation under public law' leaves open the question of its nature as a corporation or institute. The Bank deutscher Länder had been expressly referred to as a corporation (article I no. 1 of Act no. 60), whereby certainly the original English text, which

---

[29] Excerpts printed in: Deutsche Bundesbank, 1988, p. 122.

[30] Repeat of the observations in: Deutsche Bundesbank, 1988, pp. 116, 125f.

[31] Cf. Laband, 1913, p. 142; Meyer and Anschütz, 1919, p. 832; contrasting, the prevalent opinion: RGZ 15, p. 236; RGZ 36, pp. 150f.; RGZ 45, p. 126; RGZ 53, p. 231; Breit, 1911, pp. 109f., with further references.

exceptionally was declared non-binding in accordance with article VIII no. 38 of Act no. 60, only refers to a 'juridical person under public law'. In contradistinction to this, the Government Draft of the Bundesbank Act used the terms 'institute'. It is evident that this problem, which was present during the history of the law on note-issuing banks, was held to be of a theoretical nature, and finally no decision was taken in the text of the Act. If one follows the classical criteria of the distinction between corporations and institutes, according to which, with the former, the emphasis is on the membership substrata and, with the latter, the content-related substrata is stressed, the Bundesbank is an institute. It has no members, mainly possesses the relevant administrative materials: gold, foreign currency, legal tender, securities, etc. Accordingly, the majority of the reference material qualifies the Bundesbank as an institute.[32] The lack of state supervision is not in opposition to the institutional nature. Such supervision would also not enable one to prove the character as a corporation since *both* institutions of the intermediary administration of the state in fact are only subject on principle to restricted or unrestricted state supervision. For the rest, sections 13 and 34 second and third sentences of the Bundesbank Act contain the rudiments of supervision.

By creating a separate legal personality for the Bundesbank, parliament opted for a construction as it was provided for in article 86 first sentence and article 87 para. 3 first sentence *GG*. The creation of a separate legal entity is more expedient for the nature of the powers which are to be exercised by the Bundesbank than incorporation into the apparatus of the state as an organizational complex with no autonomy. It is ideally adapted to the competences of the Bundesbank, and furthermore guarantees its independence.

b) The amendments made to the Bundesbank Act as a result of German reunification

As a result of the establishment of a Monetary, Economic, and Social Union between the Federal Republic of Germany and the German Democratic Republic by means of the State Treaty dated 18 May 1990, several supplements were initially added to the provisions of the Bundesbank Act. German

---

[32] Cf. von Mangoldt and Klein, 1974, article 88, p. 2418 (FN 130), with further references; Beck, 1959, 2nd Book, section 2 K 30, p. 139; von Spindler *et al.*, 1973, Part II, section 2 note 1, p. 168; Donner and Neumann, 1994, p. 153; Hahn, 1966, pp. 12f.; Schönle, 1976, section 33 II., p. 377; Waechter, 1994, p. 201, sees the Bundesbank as an 'untypical institute'.

reunification gave rise to major amendments, especially concerning the organizational structure of the Bundesbank.[33]

When, on 1 July 1990, the State Treaty entered into force, a uniform currency area was created between the two German States with the full monetary policy sovereignty of the Deutsche Bundesbank and with the D-mark as a common currency. The provisions of the Treaty created for the GDR a completely new foundation for monetary law, whereas the monetary statute for the Federal Republic of Germany remained unchanged. In accordance with article 3 of the Act on the State Treaty (*Gesetz zum Staatsvertrag*) dated 25 July 1990 a new 'Part 5a' (sections 25a–25d of the Bundesbank Act) was inserted into the Bundesbank Act as the legal basis for the establishment of the Bundesbank's own administrative organization in the GDR, as well as for the implementation of monetary policy in the newly included monetary area. In accordance with section 25a of the Bundesbank Act, the Bundesbank established a Provisional Administrative Agency in Berlin and 15 branches in the GDR, which were responsible for transactions with credit institutions in the GDR, as well as with the GDR, and with its public administration. From a technical, organizational, and personnel point of view, these branches were guided by the west German Land Central Banks, which to a certain extent acted as godparents of the various districts in the GDR. The Bundesbank was therefore able to exercise state powers on the territory of the GDR even prior to 3 October 1990 (appendix I article 14 para. 2 to the State Treaty).

A precondition for a well-functioning monetary policy by the Bundesbank in the extended currency area was the creation of an autonomous banking system in eastern Germany organized along market economy lines. The structure of the GDR's one-tier state bank system, where there were no private commercial banks at all, still reflected incorporation into the socialist state organized as a planned economy. The central institution was the state-controlled Staatsbank der DDR, which was both the note-issuing bank and performed the role of a commercial bank, and on whose instructions all other institutes of the credit sector with special functions depended (Deutsche Außenhandelsbank, Deutsche Handelsbank, Bank für Landwirtschaft und Nahrungsgüterwirtschaft, the savings banks, and the cooperative banks). The Bundesbank assumed the role of the Staatsbank as note-issuing bank, Bank of Banks, and principal bank of the state. In transforming the existing credit institutions into universal commercial banks the west German banks played a major role through joint ventures and with their own branches.

When the currency conversion took place, the credit institutions of the GDR were to be immediately incorporated into the interest and money

---

[33] Reprint of the Treaties on German reunification in Stern and Schmidt-Bleibtreu, 1990–1.

stock control of the Bundesbank, in particular into its refinancing and open market policy. However, at that time they had neither corresponding stocks of trade bills eligible for discount by the Bundesbank, nor securities which could be traded on the market within the meaning of sections 19(1) Nos. 1 to 3 and 21 of the Bundesbank Act. In accordance with section 25b(2) of the Bundesbank Act, the Bundesbank was empowered to temporarily grant special conditions to the credit institutions until such time as the refinancing conditions were adapted to western German circumstances. Thus, the Bundesbank enabled the credit institutions, within the context of fixed refinancing quotas, to have access to traditional rediscount and Lombard loans, initially via their own bank promissory notes which carry no further signatures.[34] The credit institutions were included in the minimum reserve requirement contained in section 16 of the Bundesbank Act from August 1990 onwards.

As a consequence of German reunification, the question arose of the definitive seat of the Bundesbank. Section 2 third sentence of the Bundesbank Act in fact created only a preliminary regulation: 'the Bank shall be domiciled at the seat of the Federal Government; as long as the latter is not in Berlin, the domicile of the Bank shall be Frankfurt am Main'. In order to avoid subsequently moving the Bundesbank to Berlin, this provision was amended by the Act dated 20 February 1991, and Frankfurt am Main was laid down as the definitive domicile.

The Unification Treaty dated 31 August 1990 (appendix I chapter IV subject area B section III no. 1) placed parliament under an obligation to adapt the Bundesbank Act to the new circumstances in the state within 12 months after the entry into force of accession on 3 October 1990. Because of considerable differences of opinion which arose between the Federal Government and the majority of the Länder, this obligation was not discharged until 1 November 1992 by the entry into force of the 'Fourth Act Amending the Act on the Deutsche Bundesbank dated 15 July 1992', one year late.

The Amending Act rescinded Part 5a of the Bundesbank Act, containing sections 25a–25d. This implied, at the same time, the dissolution of the Provisional Administrative Agency of the Bundesbank and of its 15 branches in the former GDR, effective as of 1 November 1992. The five new Länder were incorporated into the organizational structure of the Bundesbank. In this respect, the Amending Act was a compromise between the Federal Government, which was in favour of tightening up the organizational structure, and the Länder, the majority of which rejected this and, instead,

---

[34] For details cf. Deutsche Bundesbank, 1990, pp. 19f.; Deutsche Bundesbank, 1991, pp. 20f.; Weikart, 1993*b*, pp. 624f.

demanded expansion to 16 Land Central Banks.[35] In contrast to the previous rule, in accordance with which the Bundesbank kept a Main Office in each of the 11 old Länder, in accordance with section 8(1) of the Bundesbank Act there are now a total of nine Land Central Banks, five of which are responsible for two or three Länder each. In order to balance out the voting ratio in the Central Bank Council, the maximum number of members of the Directorate, as defined in section 7(2) first sentence of the Bundesbank Act, was reduced from 10 to eight. The rights of the Länder to participate in the Bundesbank, consisting in particular in participation in appointing the Presidents of the Land Central Banks, have on the whole not been reduced.

c) Changes to the rights and status of the Bundesbank through the legislation of the European Union

By the Act dated 8 July 1994—Fifth Act Amending the Bundesbank Act (*Fünftes Bundesbankänderungsgesetz*)—the Bundesbank Act was adapted to the *new provisions of the EC Treaty (ECT)* which entered into force as of 1 January 1994, which in turn was amended by the Treaty on European Union (TEU)—the so-called Maastricht Treaty—dated 7 February 1992.

Under the old law, the Bundesbank was empowered, in accordance with section 20(1) no. 1 of the Bundesbank Act, to grant to the Federal Government certain Federal special funds (the Federal Railways, the Federal Post Office, the 'Currency Conversion Equalization Fund', and the ERP Special Fund) as well as to the Länder, short-term loans in the shape of book credits and credits granted on treasury bills (cash advances). In accordance with section 20(1) no. 1(a)–(f) of the Bundesbank Act, the amount of the credits was limited by set ceilings. The granting of credits as such was at the discretion of the Bundesbank. On the basis of the priority of implementation of EU legislation before ordinary law, section 20(1) no. 1 of the Bundesbank Act has no longer been applicable since 1 January 1994 because of the opposing prohibition of the granting of credit to public institutions by the European Central Bank and national central banks in accordance with article 104 para. 1 in conjunction with article 109e para. 3 first sentence of the ECT, and was therefore deleted without a replacement. The credits granted by the Bundesbank to the Federal Government, the Special Funds, and the Länder were intended primarily to make it easier in technical terms

---

[35] Cf. BT-Drucks. XII/988 (Draft Bill by the Bundesrat) and BT-Drucks. XII/1869 (Draft Bill by the Federal Government); on the difference of opinion: cf. Deutsche Bundesbank, 1992*b*, pp. 49ff.; on the question of constitutionality: Häde and Hartmann, 1991, p. 407.

to carry out payment transactions, and not to finance state expenditure. With the deletion of section 20(1) no. 1 of the Bundesbank Act, the provision contained in its section 42(3) second sentence to the effect that liquidity paper issued by the Federal Government is not to be counted towards the credit ceiling specified in section 20(1) no. 1(a) of the Bundesbank Act became inapplicable, and was therefore deleted.

In connection with the deletion of section 20(1) no. 1 of the Bundesbank Act, parliament also made an obligation incumbent on the Federal Government, the Federal special funds, the Equalization Fund, and the ERP Special Fund, as well as on the Länder, under section 17 of the Bundesbank Act to deposit their liquid funds in giro accounts at the Bundesbank. In contrast to the situation under section 20(1) no. 1 of the Bundesbank Act, this amendment did not necessarily arise out of priority EU legislation, but was nevertheless carried out for reasons of common sense: if the central public budgets on the one hand were to be deprived of the privilege of using cash advances from the Bundesbank which were in principle interest-free, they should on the other hand also be released from the burden of making deposits, in other words be treated in this respect like other market players. The obligation to deposit was therefore rescinded at the start of Stage Two of monetary union by permitting deposits to be made elsewhere, in accordance with section 17 second sentence of the Bundesbank Act, first of all in fact, and then by statute, with the entry into force of the Amending Act as of 16 July 1994.[36] In the ensuing period, the public budgets distributed their liquid funds among a larger number of private and public law banks in order to avoid distortions of competition by affording preference to individual credit institutions.

As a consequence of the Treaty on European Union, which was signed on 7 February 1992 and entered into force on 1 November 1993, a far-reaching encroachment is due on the constitution of the German note-issuing and currency bank.[37] In accordance with the reworded articles 102a–109m of the ECT, the Treaty provides *inter alia* for the *creation of European Economic and Monetary Union* in three stages by 1 January 1999 at the latest. Whilst economic policy is coordinated in line with certain economic framework data, but should remain within the area of competence of the Member States, after a two-stage transitional period, monetary policy is to be fully transferred during a final stage to the European System of Central Banks (ESCB), which is to be established.

The most important institutional innovation in the area of monetary

---

[36] Highly critical on the actual abolition by the Deutsche Bundesbank: Gramlich, 1994, pp. 366f.

[37] On the details and the effects on the Deutsche Bundesbank: Galahn, 1996.

policy was the establishment of the *European Monetary Institute (EMI)* with its seat in Frankfurt am Main. In accordance with article 109f para. 1 first sentence of the ECT, the EMI has legal personality and 'shall enjoy in each of the Member States the most extensive legal capacity accorded to legal persons under their law' (article 14 of the Statute of the EMI). In accordance with article 1.2. of the Statute of the EMI, the *central banks of the Member States* are members of the EMI ('national central banks').

Immediately subsequent to the conclusion of the first or second assessments, with the decision on the time for the start of Stage Three, the Council and the governments of the participating Member States will take the steps necessary in accordance with article 109l para. 1 of the ECT for the *establishment of the ESCB and of the European Central Bank (ECB)*, which is to replace the EMI, in turn to be dissolved. The ESCB and the ECB will fully exercise their powers in line with the provisions of the EC Treaty and of the 'Protocol on the Statute of the European System of Central Banks and of the European Central Bank' (ESCB Statute) from the first day of the Stage Three. On this date, the Council, comprising the representatives of the governments of the participating Member States, will decide in accordance with article 109l para. 4 first sentence of the ECT, at the suggestion of the Commission, and after consulting the ECB, what the irrevocable, fixed exchange rates of the participating currencies are in relation to one another and to the European Currency Unit (ECU), which will replace them as the future common European currency.

The ESCB consists of the ECB and the national central banks. In accordance with article 106 para. 2 of the ECT, only the ECB has its own legal personality. The provisions contained in the EC Treaty and in the Statute of the ESCB regarding the role and organization of the ESCB agree to a great extent with the corresponding provisions contained in the Act on the Deutsche Bundesbank.

As a part of the ECB, the Deutsche Bundesbank will thus relinquish its competences to regulate in terms of its currency and monetary policy, and will lose its independence. It will remain able to take decisions in its own personnel and operational matters. There is still a need to clarify the question of the distribution of the executive competences between the ECB and the national central banks. Article 12.1 para. 3 of the Statute of the ECB grants considerable scope for manoeuvre here. Doubt remains as to the extent to which the subsidiarity principle contained in article 3b para. 2 of the ECT can be applied.[38]

The intention of the Draft Act Amending the Act on the Deutsche

---

[38] Cf. Jochimsen, 1994, p. 159; Lecheler, 1993, pp. 113ff.; Weber, 1994, pp. 59ff.

Bundesbank (Federal Parliament Publication [BT-Drucks.] XIII/7493) is for the implications to be drawn from the integration of the Deutsche Bundesbank into the European System of Central Banks. The Sixth Act Amending the Bundesbank Act was passed in December 1997. As from the day on which Germany accedes to the final stage of European monetary union, the Bundesbank will cease to determine monetary policy autonomously. That policy will be determined by the ECB, in the Governing Council of which the Bundesbank will participate in the person of its President. The Bundesbank will, however, remain the German central bank.

4. The organization of the Bundesbank

a) *The governing bodies of the Bundesbank*

In accordance with section 5 of the Bundesbank Act, the Bundesbank has *three governing bodies* assigned to it by law: the Central Bank Council, the Directorate, and the Executive Boards of the Land Central Banks. The Act makes no direct statement with regard to the relationship of these three governing bodies to one another, apart from that, in accordance with section 11 of the Bundesbank Act, the Directorate is called upon to represent the Deutsche Bundesbank in and out of court. In the area of a Land Central Bank or of a Branch (Branch Office) the power of representation also lies with their Executive Boards or Directors. However, the purpose of this trio of bodies becomes clear from their functions and staffing. The variety of the bodies continues to reflect the dispute between the one-tier, centralized or two-tier, decentralized structure. However, it is more important for a certain internal division of powers and control to be brought about. To this extent, the intention was for the Bundesbank to reflect the internal structure of the three functions of the state.

The *Central Bank Council* exercises legislative and executive powers. In accordance with section 6(1) of the Bundesbank Act, it determines the monetary and credit policy of the Bank. It draws up general guidelines governing the conduct of business and administration, and defines the responsibilities of the Directorate and the Executive Boards of the Land Central Banks in accordance with the provisions of this Act. In specific cases, it may also issue instructions to the Directorate and the Executive Boards of the Land Central Banks. The Central Bank Council therefore takes the Bank's fundamental and guiding decisions. This also emerges from further provisions relating to competences: sections 26(3) third sentence and 31 and 34 of the Bundesbank Act.

The Central Bank Council is a collegiate 'authority' (section 29 of the Bundesbank Act). In accordance with section 6(2) of the Bundesbank Act, it consists of the President and the Vice-President of the Deutsche Bundesbank, the other members of the Directorate, and of the Presidents of the nine Land Central Banks.

As a rule, the Central Bank Council meets every two weeks under the Chairmanship of the President or Vice-President of the Deutsche Bundesbank. It takes its decisions by a simple majority of the votes cast. The by-laws of the Bundesbank govern details (section 6(3) of the Bundesbank Act). In accordance with section 13(2) of the Bundesbank Act, members of the Federal Government are entitled to attend meetings and propose motions to the Central Bank Council. They may require a decision to be deferred for up to two weeks.

In accordance with section 7(1) of the Bundesbank Act, the *Directorate* is to implement the decisions of the Central Bank Council and to manage and administer the Bank, unless the Executive Boards of the Land Central Banks have competence. Certain transactions are expressly reserved for the Directorate in accordance with section 7(1) third sentence of the Bundesbank Act. This list is, however, not exhaustive, as is demonstrated by the words 'in particular' and by sections 11 and 26(3) first and third sentences, as well as section 38(5), of the Bundesbank Act. The Directorate is the central administrative body of the Bank. As is the case with the Central Bank Council, it is afforded the status of a supreme Federal authority (section 29(1) first sentence of the Bundesbank Act).

The Directorate is composed of the President and Vice-President of the Deutsche Bundesbank and up to six further members (section 7(2) of the Bundesbank Act). At the same time, they are also members of the Central Bank Council. The statutory maximum number of members was fully utilized, for the first time in the history of the Bundesbank, with effect from 1 March 1995. In accordance with section 7(2) second sentence of the Bundesbank Act, the members of the Directorate must have 'special professional qualifications'—a self-evident precondition which was obviously considered to be necessary because of the danger of 'politicizing' the Bank. They are appointed for eight years, or in exceptional cases, for a shorter term of office, but not for less than two years (section 7(3) third sentence of the Bundesbank Act) and are a special kind of office holder under public law (section 7(4) first sentence of the Bundesbank Act), similar to Federal Ministers (section 1 of the Act on Federal Ministers [BMinG]). Otherwise, their legal status relative to the Bundesbank, their salaries, etc.—in other words, the basic personal relationships—are regulated by contracts of employment under private law which are subject to the approval of the Federal Government (section 7(4) second and third sentences of the Bundesbank Act).

In the same way as the Central Bank Council, the Directorate holds its deliberations under the Chairmanship of the President or Vice-President of the Deutsche Bundesbank and decides by a simple majority of votes, unless other majorities are provided for in the by-laws. In the event of a tie, the Chairman has a casting vote (section 7(5) of the Bundesbank Act).

Another governing body is constituted by the respective *Executive Boards of the Land Central Banks*. The nine Land Central Banks are Main Offices of the Bundesbank, which are maintained in the Länder (section 8 of the Bundesbank Act) and the Länder Head Offices. The Executive Board of a Land Central Bank carries out the transactions and administrative duties pertaining to the area for which it is responsible. The Land Central Banks are solely responsible in particular transactions with the Land or the Länder, as well as with public authorities in the Land or in the Länder, and likewise transactions with credit institutions in their area, unless these are reserved for the Directorate in accordance with section 7(1) no. 2 of the Bundesbank Act.

The Executive Boards consist of the President and Vice-President of the Land Central Bank and, in the case of the two Land Central Banks which are responsible for three Länder (Bremen, Lower Saxony, and Saxony-Anhalt and Hamburg, Mecklenburg-Western Pomerania, and Schleswig-Holstein), one further member. Under the by-laws, it is also possible for up to two further members to be appointed. All Executive Board members must have a 'particular professional suitability' (section 8(3) of the Bundesbank Act). Their official position corresponds to that of the members of the Directorate (section 8(5) of the Bundesbank Act).

Although not expressly named in the Act as a governing body, because of section 7(5), section 8(4) third sentence, section 9(3), section 31(2), section 32 third sentence and section 41(4) of the Bundesbank Act, it is probably necessary to afford to the President of the Deutsche Bundesbank, too, the quality of a governing body in respect of the responsibilities specified in these provisions.

b) *The pluralism of the appointing institutions*

The members of the governing bodies of the Bundesbank are appointed by various state institutions. There is a *'pluralism of the appointing institutions'*.[39] This promotes the participation of parliamentary and executive, unitary and federal institutions in the staffing of the Bundesbank. Here lies an element of (personal) division of powers, and at the same time a guarantee of the independence of the Bank as is provided for in a similar form in the appointment of judges to the Federal Constitutional Court and other Federal Courts. In detail, provision is made for the following modalities:

- Once the Central Bank Council has been consulted, the President and the Vice-President and the other members of the Directorate are appointed by the Federal President, at the suggestion of the Federal Government (section 7(3) first and second sentences of the Bundesbank Act).
- The Presidents of the Land Central Banks are appointed by the Federal President at the suggestion of the Bundesrat (section 8(4) first and second sentences of the Bundesbank Act), which bases its selection on a proposal by the agency appropriate under Land law—as a rule the Land government—and after having consulted the Central Bank Council.
- The Vice-Presidents and the other members of the Executive Board are appointed by the President of the Deutsche Bundesbank at the suggestion of the Central Bank Council (section 8(4) third sentence of the Bundesbank Act).

c) Other agencies and employees of the Bundesbank

An *Advisory Board* is formed as an exclusive advisory body at each Land Central Bank, with not more than 14 members from banking, trade and industry, distribution, the insurance sector, the professions, agriculture, and from the ranks of wage and salary earners (section 9(2) of the Bundesbank Act). This Advisory Board is to confer with the President on questions concerning monetary and credit policy, and with the Executive Board of the Land Central Bank on other functions. It serves in particular to maintain continuous contact between the Bundesbank and the banking industry and/or industrial borrowers in the Länder. The competent Land Ministers may participate in the debates and may require the Advisory Board to be convened (section 9(4) second and third sentences of the Bundesbank Act). Proposed by the competent Land government, once the Executive Board of the Land Central Bank has been consulted by the President of the Bundes-

[39] Samm, 1967, p. 51 with further references; also Wagenhöfer, 1957, p. 114; Uhlenbruck, 1968, pp. 44ff.; Gaugenrieder, 1961, p. 123.

bank, the members of the Advisory Board are appointed for a period of three years (section 9(3) of the Bundesbank Act).

In accordance with section 10 of the Bundesbank Act, the Deutsche Bundesbank is entitled to maintain *Branch offices* (branches and sub-branches). Their existence was already provided for in section 37 of the 1875 Banking Act (*Bankgesetz*).[40] These are branches without legal capacity, and are managed by Directors who report to the respective Land Central Bank. The Bundesbank is hence represented by 'branches' in all significant bank places, which especially foster the currency supply and the handling of cashless transactions. As of 30 April 1997, 164 Branch Offices of the Deutsche Bundesbank still existed nationally, some of which are however to be closed over the next 10 years because of increasing computerization. In accordance with section 21 of the by-laws of the Deutsche Bundesbank dated 27 November 1958 (Federal Gazette no. 7 dated 13 January 1959 in the version of notification no. 1004/71, Federal Gazette no. 66 dated 1 April 1971), the Central Bank Council decides on the establishment and closure of sub-branches.

As is generally the case in the public service, the *staff members* of the Bundesbank are civil servants with life tenure (*Beamte*), civil servants without life tenure (*Angestellte*) and wage earners (*Arbeiter*) (section 31(1) of the Bundesbank Act). Although the Bundesbank is a corporation under public law, it has not been expressly granted the capacity to be an employer within the meaning of section 121 no. 2 of the Civil Service Framework Act (*Beamtenrechtsrahmengesetz BRRG*). Rather, the *Beamte* of the Deutsche Bundesbank are referred to as 'indirect Federal civil servants with life tenure' to whom the Federal Civil Service Act (*Bundesbeamtengesetz*) applies, with several modifications effected by the Bundesbank Act (section 31(3) of the Bundesbank Act). Accordingly, a special staffing statute (Federal Gazette no. 145 dated 30 July 1960, amended in accordance with Notification no. 2003/74 dated 9 January 1974, Federal Gazette 1974 no. 14) and its own provisions relating to previous education and career paths (Federal Gazette no. 81 dated 30 April 1971, in the version of Notification no. 2014/79 dated 28 December 1979, Federal Gazette 1980 no. 6, as last amended by notification no. 2005/94 dated 18 March 1994, Federal Gazette 1994 no. 65) were issued.[41] The supreme institutional authority is the President of the Deutsche Bundesbank (section 31(2) third sentence of the Bundesbank Act). All employees are subject to an increased duty of confidentiality.

---

[40] For more details cf. Breit, 1911, section 37.
[41] For more details cf. Gramlich, 1988a, section 31 margin nos. 18ff. and 35ff.

5. Duties, powers, and policy instruments of the Bundesbank

a) The statutory allocation of duties

Section 3 of the Bundesbank Act names as the *main duties* of the Bundesbank those of regulating the amount of money in circulation and of credit supplied to the economy with the aim of safeguarding the currency, as well as arranging for the execution of domestic and international payments.

This provision does not however contain an exhaustive list of the duties. The Act continues to describe the main duties elsewhere—partly by providing details, and partly by means of extension:

- to support the general economic policy of the Federal Government 'without prejudice to the performance of its duties' (section 12 first sentence);
- to advise the Federal Cabinet on monetary policy issues of major importance, and furnish it with information (section 13(1));
- to issue banknotes as legal tender and, where appropriate, call them in (section 14);
- to adopt by-laws (section 34);
- to conduct almost all banking transactions with credit institutions (section 19);
- to conduct the transactions specified in section 19(1) no. 4–9 with the Federal Government, Federal special funds, Länder governments, and other public authorities (section 20(1));
- to issue the debt securities of the Federal Government and its special funds as 'fiscal agent' (section 20(2));
- to conduct certain banking transactions with the general public (sections 22 and 19).

More detailed provisions relate to some kinds of activity (open market operations, certification of cheques, lending against and purchase of equalization claims) (sections 21, 23, and 24).

Furthermore, other duties are assigned to the Bundesbank in other Acts, for instance:

- within the framework of banking supervision, cooperation with the Federal Banking Supervisory Office—Bundesaufsichtsamt für das Kreditwesen (sections 7; 8(3) first sentence; 10; 11; 13; 16 second sentence; 25(3); 44(3); 44b of the Banking Act; details below at e);
- participation in the issuing of certain legal ordinances (sections 1(1) third sentence and 1(3) second sentence; 10(2) first sentence no. 3; 29(3) first

sentence; 31(1) first sentence; 47 and 48 of the Banking Act ['consultation']; sections 10a(6) eleventh sentence; 22 first sentence; 24(4) first
sentence; 25(4) first sentence of the Banking Act; sections 2(2) second
sentence and 27(1) fourth sentence of the Foreign Trade and Payments
Act [*Außenwirtschaftsgesetz—AWG*] ['involvement']);
- consent to establishing certain principles for the banking industry by the
Federal Banking Supervisory Office (sections 10(1) second sentence; 11
second sentence of the Banking Act);
- granting licences in accordance with section 12(2) first sentence; section
28(2) no. 1 in conjunction with section 2(2); sections 5–7; 22(1); 23; 24;
49(2) of the Foreign Trade and Payments Act in conjunction with section
3 of the Currency Act (*Währungsgesetz*);
- monitoring the deposit requirement in accordance with section 28a(1) in
conjunction with sections 6a and 44 of the Foreign Trade and Payments
Act;
- right of participation in the Stabilization Council for the Public Sector
and in the Fiscal Planning Council (section 18(4) of the 'Stability and
Growth Act' [*StabG*] and section 51(1) third sentence of the Act on
Budgetary Principles [*HGrG*]; details below at f);
- cooperation between the Bundesbank and Federal Government in issuing
instructions to the social insurance agencies, in accordance with section
1383b(2) of the Reich Insurance Code (RVO), section 110b(2) of the
Foreign Trade and Payments Act (section 30(1) of the Stability and
Growth Act) to maintain a part of their reserves in certain types of assets.

In the allocation of duties, however, it is necessary to always heed the main
duty, which must not be adversely affected, of being a currency and note-
issuing bank in accordance with article 88 *GG*, as is enshrined in the
constitution. This is not yet the case with the above-named duties, but it is
possible to recognize the boundaries.[42]

The Bundesbank is entitled to its independence only in accordance with
section 12 second sentence of the Bundesbank Act, and then only in the
exercise of its powers under the Bundesbank Act. Otherwise, it is generally
subject to instructions in accordance with article 86 *GG*.

Among the duties listed, the primary role is played by the monetary and
credit activity first designated in section 3 of the Bundesbank Act with the
aim of safeguarding the currency, for which the Bundesbank was mainly
established, as is the case with other currency and note-issuing banks. This
role gave rise to the designation which has frequently been used for the
Bundesbank as *'guardian of the currency'*—a term which had been coined

[42] Very generous: *BVerfGE* 14, pp. 215ff.

in earlier years.[43] This encapsulates its state, political, and economic significance. This is why the monetary and monetary policy powers of the Bundesbank are primarily placed at the service of discharging this main duty.[44]

b) Main aim: safeguarding the currency

With the aim of *safeguarding the currency*, the Bundesbank Act refrained from specifying the components of overall economic equilibrium, such as were later defined in section 1 of the Stability and Growth Act (*Gesetz zur Förderung der Stabilität und des Wachstums der Wirtschaft—StabG*) dated 8 June 1967: price stability, a high level of employment, external equilibrium, steady and adequate economic growth. The Bundesbank itself prefers to understand the aim as that of safeguarding price stability.

Only safeguarding the currency has been singled out from what are known as 'magic polygons'. This does not mean that the Bundesbank can be indifferent towards the other elements of overall economic equilibrium. They are also relevant to the Bundesbank via section 12 first sentence of the Bundesbank Act and section 13(3) of the Stability and Growth Act. That said, they are factors which may only play a role within the framework of its main aim, that of safeguarding the currency. They are subordinate to this aim.[45] Section 13(3) of the Stability and Growth Act is merely a 'recommended ruling', which is subject to the reservation of the respective allocation of duties. In addition, the Bundesbank Act should have priority as the more specific provision in cases of divergencies. In any conflicts of aims, the Bundesbank has clearly been given *one* aim which has *priority*,[46] whilst the other bodies of the Federal Government and of the Länder which are placed under an obligation in accordance with section 1 of the Stability and Growth Act are to bring about the four aims 'simultaneously'. As has already been explained, the Bundesbank is not the only institution under an obligation to safeguard the currency. Rather, the Federal Government and the Länder are called upon in their entirety. Thus, monetary stability is afforded a decisive value in economic policy—and rightly so in the light of the terrible experiences suffered by a state system in the case of the collapse of a currency.

---

[43] Cf. von Lumm, 1926, p. 8.

[44] Cf. Hahn, 1990, section 19 I 1, p. 269 margin no. 1.

[45] Cf. Coburger, 1987, pp. 43f.; Prost, 1974, p. 266; Fögen, 1969, p. 66. In this respect, I modify my view in Stern et al., 1972, section 13, note II. 4. From the time prior to the adoption of the Stability and Growth Act: Wagenhöfer, 1957, p. 8, who 'clearly [grants] priority to maintaining the value of money . . . over other economic aims'.

[46] Clear: Issing, 1993, p. 29; Coburger, 1987, p. 45; Woll and Vogl, 1976, p. 38.

In view of its monetary policy powers, the Federal Constitutional Court has certified that the Deutsche Bundesbank has 'a key position in the banking system of the Federal Republic' and/or a 'leading position at the vertex of the money economy and in the banking industry'.[47] It functions *inter alia* as a 'Bank of Banks' and also as the 'principal bank' for the Federal Government—now that sections 20(1) no. 1 and 17 of the Bundesbank Act have been deleted, this role is subject to severe restrictions. Furthermore, from a technical point of view, it ensures the execution of payments at home and abroad. The Bundesbank is the *central decision making body within the state in terms of monetary policy*. With the help of the monetary policy instruments which are available to it, the Bundesbank regulates the money stock by supplying legal tender, and by influencing its use. Via the interrelationship between granting loans and creating (deposit) money, it controls for instance the amount and price of credit offered, and hence the credit supply in the economy. At least in terms of quantity theory, the correct dosing of the money stock is decisive in order to achieve monetary equilibrium, whereby the extent to which the Bundesbank is actually able to control the money stock is however doubtful and the subject of dispute, as is the extent to which changes in the money stock have a causal effect on changes in the level of prices.[48] Certainly, the provision of money is not an end in itself, but always has to bear in mind the aim of safeguarding the currency. This means, to put it in a nutshell, protecting it from inflation or deflation, and in particular preserving the greatest possible stability of the internal value and (within certain limits) also of the external value of the currency in the sense of safeguarding its value and its purchasing power. While it is possible to put these aims into words succinctly and easily, it is mighty difficult to realize them. In this sense, the Act is able only to serve as a guideline. Its realization is the art of the policy of any note-issuing bank and needs a 'well-functioning banking system'.[49] A large portion of the good or bad luck of a note-issuing bank, and hence also of the prosperity of the state and of society, depends on this.

c) The monetary policy instruments and their legal qualification

In order enable it to perform its duties, the Bundesbank Act made available to the Bundesbank a wide variety of *instruments* which have developed over

---

[47] *BVerfGE* 14, pp. 212, 217.
[48] The Deutsche Bundesbank itself is quite convinced of this: Deutsche Bundesbank, 1993, pp. 104f. (Figure 10); Schlesinger, 1988, p. 3; Issing, 1994, pp. 682ff.
[49] *BVerfGE* 14, p. 217.

the 100 years which have passed since the establishment of the Reichsbank. In detail, they are based to an equal extent on theoretical considerations of economics, as well as on practical testing. More difficult than a description of its manner of functioning is the *legal qualification*. This was neglected by the parliament which established the Bundesbank, although it was inevitable on the basis of article 19 para. 4 *GG* that measures undertaken by the Bundesbank may also be subject to scrutiny by a court. The usual legal division of the measures undertaken by a corporation under public law, such as in accordance with the categories legislation, administrative act (general order), other measures under public law, and legal acts under private law, may for the Bundesbank alone not provide a complete explanation of the problem. It is only the effects of the individual instruments which are able to clarify their legal qualification. The only measures here which are of interest are those which have direct or indirect legal effects. In this context, the monetary policy instrument of so-called moral suasion, which had been applied with quite some success by the Bundesbank, but which is not enshrined in statute, is of no relevance:[50] this includes the calls by the Bundesbank, which are in principle non-binding, to credit institutions or non-banks (such as parties to collective bargaining agreements), by means of which the latter are called upon to conduct themselves within the meaning of the monetary policy aims, and to a certain extent are subjected to a kind of 'gentle persuasion'. The most important instrument to be named in this area is in particular the annual money stock target, which is announced in advance by the Bundesbank. Finally, also only those powers of the Bundesbank can be treated which are an integral element of the specific instruments of a note-issuing bank. There is no need to go into detail on the extent to which the Bundesbank carries out banking transactions like the other credit institutions. Only the specific monetary and currency policy instruments of the Bundesbank are decisive. These include:

– issuing banknotes,
– refinancing policy,
– open market policy,
– minimum reserve policy, and
– monetary policy.

Section 14(1) of the Bundesbank Act grants to the Bundesbank the sole

---

[50] Cf. Issing, 1993, pp. 127ff.; Hahn, 1990, section 20II, pp. 296f., margin no. 1; Weikart, 1992, pp. 105f.; Fröhlich, 1983, pp. 50ff.; Gramlich, 1988*a*, Intro., margin nos. 16ff.; fundamental description by Tuchtfeld, 1971, pp. 23f., more precisely p. 32; cf. also specifically on monetary policy the detailed investigation by Siegert, 1963; also Wilmer, 1975, pp. 340f.; Farthmann and Coehn, 1994, pp. 898f.

right to *issue banknotes*. Thus, its role as a note-issuing bank is made in reality in accordance with article 88 first sentence *GG*. The notes enjoy special protection under criminal law (section 35 of the Bundesbank Act, sections 146ff. of the Criminal Code [*StGB*]). D-mark notes—legal tender since 21 June 1948, and now the only unrestricted legal tender (section 14(1) of the Bundesbank Act)—are 'monetary tokens of a public law nature'; they are issued by force of the sovereignty of the state with regard to currency[51] and their value is intrinsic, in other words they are no longer linked to gold or similar cover.[52] Issuing notes is part of the central banks' money creation, or to put it more precisely: creation of 'notes and coin' in contrast to central bank deposits. It is an administrative act with no addressee to the extent that these notes are legal tender in their respective nominal value with an effect on and in relation to all. The same applies to withdrawal as an *actus contrarius*.[53]

The *refinancing policy* of the Bundesbank is oriented directly and exclusively towards the credit institutions. The latter obtain central bank money by means of refinancing, i.e. by borrowing from the Deutsche Bundesbank, by selling bills of exchange (rediscount credit), and by pledging securities (Lombard loans).

In accordance with section 15 of the Bundesbank Act the Bundesbank sets the respective *interest and discount rates* for these transactions. These are to be published in the Federal Gazette (section 33 of the Bundesbank Act). Assuming that the precondition contained in section 19(1) no. 1 and 2 of the Bundesbank Act is met, the price at which the Bundesbank is prepared to purchase, i.e. (re)discount, bills of exchange, cheques, and treasury bills is determined in accordance with the discount rate. Discount policy serves in particular the longer term supply of central bank money.

On the other hand, the Bundesbank grants Lombard loans to the credit institutions on principle for the purpose of short-term bridging of a temporary liquidity bottleneck.[54] In accordance with section 19(1) no. 3(a)–(f), Lombard loans are interest-bearing loans against a pledge with a maximum term of three months. As a rule, the interest rate for Lombard loans, the

[51] Cf. von Spindler *et al.*, 1973, Part II, section 14, note 1; Beck, 1959, 2nd Book, section 14, K 338; partly deviating Fögen, 1969, p. 74, who only recognizes such a 'state right' if it has been granted by statute.
[52] Cf. von Spindler *et al.*, 1973, Part II, section 14, note 2; Beck, 1959, 2nd Book, section 14, K 349.
[53] Cf. *BVerwGE* 94, pp. 295f.; observation on this by Häde, 1994, p. 924; Häde, 1991, pp. 50ff., 83, 96; Fögen, 1969, pp. 21, 23; von Spindler *et al.*, 1973, Part II, section 14, note 1 I. 4, pp. 283, note 4, p. 295; Pfennig, 1971, pp. 38, 55; for a differing view: Fröhlich, 1983, pp. 109ff., who sees legal standards in issuing and withdrawing banknotes.
[54] Cf. Deutsche Bundesbank, Geschäftsbericht 1989, p. 84 and Deutsche Bundesbank, Geschäftsbericht 1990, p. 101.

Lombard rate, which is set in accordance with section 15 of the Bundesbank Act, lies roughly 1–3 per cent above the discount rate, which emphasizes the exceptional nature of this form of refinancing.

Since the legal relations of the credit institutions with the Bundesbank, to the extent that it is a question of purchasing bills of exchange, etc., operate under private law, the setting of the rates of interest and discount, as well as the Lombard rates, is also frequently qualified as being under private law, mostly as a kind of General Terms of Business.[55] This view is contradicted by their being set by means of a unilateral order, by their binding nature, the duty to publish them, and the power which they have to guide the economy. Therefore, there is more in favour of placing it within the public law area, especially since the Federal Administrative Court has also ruled that public law applies to the setting of the minimum reserve ratios.[56]

The control of the money stock by means of discounting and Lombarding is, however, not restricted to the price components and the qualitative requirements placed on securities which can be traded with the Bundesbank. Rather, the Bundesbank may also *restrict the volume of refinancing* by setting special quantitative limits on the individual commercial banks.

In setting the individual rediscount contingents, the emphasis lies on regulating an individual case, so that it is to be categorized as an administrative act in accordance with section 35 first sentence of the Administrative Procedure Act (*VwVfG*).[57]

In accordance with section 15 of the Bundesbank Act, discount and Lombard policy serves the Deutsche Bundesbank 'to influence the amount of money in circulation and of credit granted'. By setting the interest rates and the quantitative refinancing ceilings, the Bundesbank is able to exercise a direct influence on the liquidity, and hence on the *policies of credit institutions*. Since the latter will not grant higher interest on the money market than they themselves would have to pay for short-term Lombard loans, the shorter term borrowing rate and credit interest of the credit institutions, in particular in transactions with non-banks, largely follow the movements of the discount and Lombard rates. In this respect, both interest rates retain their traditional role as macroeconomic 'official interest rates', in that they provide information regarding the bottom line of the Deutsche Bundesbank's monetary policy. The actual signalling effect for changes in interest rates in terms of monetary policy is however given by the open market

[55] Cf. Weiland, 1967, pp. 76ff.; Fögen, 1969, p. 76; Möschel, 1972, p. 105 with further references; also Prost, 1966, p. 808.

[56] Cf. *BVerwGE* 41, p. 351.

[57] In the same vein: Schönle, 1976, section 35 III 2, pp. 396f.; Coburger, 1987, p. 138; Kümpel, 1992, p. 9; perhaps also Fröhlich, 1983, p. 121.

policy of the Bundesbank, which has now assumed greater significance for credit institutions.[58]

As *an open market operation* within the meaning of section 15 of the Bundesbank Act, the purchase and sale of certain fixed-interest securities by the Bundesbank is referred to as being for its own account on the open market. The counterparts on the open market are primarily the credit institutions, but also public administrations and natural and legal entities operating under private law, i.e. in principle anyone. In accordance with section 21 in conjunction with sections 15, 19, 20, 22, and 42 of the Bundesbank Act, the Bundesbank may purchase the following securities 'in order to regulate the money market' but not for the purpose of making a profit: bills of exchange; treasury bills; bonds and Debt Register claims, the debtors in respect of which are the Federal Government, one of its special funds or a Land, as well as other bonds admitted to official trading on a stock exchange. Open market operations are to be carried out 'at market rates': in unilaterally determining the conditions, the Deutsche Bundesbank is therefore bound by the situation on the money market. Open market operations constitute purchase agreements under private law. The backbone of the open market policy of the Bundesbank is its so-called securities repos, open market operations under repurchase agreements, which it concludes exclusively with credit institutions which are under a duty to hold minimum reserves. The interest rates calculated in the case of securities repos serve as a signal for the interest expectations of the markets, and in this respect are also specifically used by the Bundesbank as an instrument of fine-tuning.

By entering into direct competition in open market operations with the range of investment opportunities offered by the credit institutions to non-banks, the Bundesbank also exercises a direct influence on the creditor interest rates of credit institutions.

In accordance with section 16(1) first sentence of the Bundesbank Act, the Bundesbank may require, in the context of its *minimum reserve policy*, credit institutions to maintain certain percentages of their liabilities in non-interest-bearing deposits in giro accounts at the Bank. It sets the percentages for the credit institutions' different reserve-carrying in the light of general considerations (third sentence). Depending on the nature of the liability, the reserve ratio—with the exception of the liabilities towards non-residents—is restricted to a maximum of 30 per cent (sight liabilities), 20 per cent (time liabilities), or 10 per cent (savings deposits) (second sentence).

If, originally, the minimum reserve policy served to ensure that the banks retained a reserve of liquidity, and hence to protect their creditors, today,

---

[58] Cf. Deutsche Bundesbank, 1993, p. 60; Geiger, 1988, pp. 136f.; Weikart, 1993*b*, pp. 629f.

in accordance with section 16(1) first sentence of the Bundesbank Act, the monetary policy control role 'to influence the amount of money in circulation and of credit granted' is in the foreground. The Bundesbank exercises a longer term influence on the liquidity of credit institutions, and hence on the granting of credit and on the currency in circulation.

Public law applies to the determination of minimum reserve ratios. The credit institutions are required by law to hold minimum reserves. The respective order relating to the minimum reserve is issued 'by means of a legal rule', whereby the Federal Administrative Court leaves it open as to whether this is 'a legal ordinance, an autonomous statute or a legal rule *sui generis*'.[59] This power to issue legal rules, as is granted by section 16 of the Bundesbank Act, is in accord with article 80 para. 1 second sentence *GG*, and is an expression of the autonomy of the Bundesbank in terms of its by-laws.

The obligation incumbent on the Deutsche Bundesbank to safeguard the currency also covers *safeguarding the external value of the D-mark* in relation to foreign currencies. On the German foreign exchange market, foreign currencies are traded at prices in D-marks. Within the framework of this *monetary policy*, one should fundamentally differentiate between two particularities of the foreign exchange market: freely 'floating' exchange rates and the system of fixed exchange rates.

Finally, several powers still need to be mentioned which fall within the area of exchange control and/or 'exchange prohibition'.[60] The statutory basis for *restrictions on the movement of capital* is the Foreign Trade and Payments Act dated 28 April 1961 (BGBl. Part I p. 481) in the version of the Act dated 9 August 1994 (BGBl. Part I p. 2068). The most important aspect here is the *cash deposit requirement* in accordance with section 6a(1) of the Foreign Trade and Payments Act (inserted by the Act dated 23 December 1971, BGBl. Part I p. 2124, and amended by the Act dated 23 February 1973, BGBl. Part I p. 109). Accordingly, the Federal Government is empowered to prescribe by means of a legal ordinance that residents are to hold a specific percentage in D-mark—in accordance with sub-section 4 second sentence a maximum of 100 per cent—of the credits obtained from loans raised from non-residents during a certain period of time in a non-interest-bearing account at the Bundesbank. The empowerment to determine the respective deposit ratio has been assigned to the Bundesbank in accordance

---

[59] *BVerwGE* 41, p. 351; for categorization as a legal ordinance: Maunz *et al.* (n.d.), article 88, margin nos. 26f.; Gramlich, 1988*a*, section 16, margin no. 74; Gramlich, 1989, p. 204; Gramlich, 1994, p. 374; Weiland, 1967, pp. 164ff.

[60] Term used in von Spindler *et al.*, 1973, Part I, section E IV 4, pp. 103f., who do not include it in the monetary policy powers of the Bundesbank, with the consequence that it is not covered by the guarantee of independence (Part II, section 16, notes 7b and d, pp. 351, 353f.).

with section 27(1) fifth sentence of the Foreign Trade and Payments Act. Because of the cash deposit requirement, the credits of those concerned become considerably more expensive. The intention is for them to be reduced by these means in order to (once more) afford greater effectiveness to the (other) measures taken in terms of credit policy. Thus, the cash deposit requirement, which applied between 1972 and 1974, was intended in particular to restrict enterprises' borrowing abroad since this cannot be directly controlled by means of the other instruments available to the Bundesbank. This is therefore a kind of variable exchange control whose legal effects on those concerned emerge directly from the ordinance. Only in cases of non-compliance does the Bundesbank issue corresponding administrative acts in accordance with section 28a of the Foreign Trade and Payments Act (for calling in) as well as implementing measures.[61] Objections to and appeals against such acts have no postponing effect (section 28a(2) of the Foreign Trade and Payments Act).

Additionally, in accordance with sections 2(1), 22, and 23 of the Foreign Trade and Payments Act, the possibility exists to submit exports and imports of money and capital to a general duty of approval, or even to prohibit them. The Deutsche Bundesbank has exclusive competence for issuing approval on the basis of the Foreign Trade and Payments Act in the area of the movement of capital and payments, as well as of transactions in foreign assets in accordance with section 28(2) no. 1 of the Foreign Trade and Payments Act. In order to monitor adherence to the law on foreign trade and payments, in accordance with section 44 of the Foreign Trade and Payments Act, the Deutsche Bundesbank has a right to receive information: it may demand that those subject to this obligation submit business documents, and may carry out investigations with regard to them.

d) Problems posed by legal protection against measures carried out by the Bundesbank

Determining the legal nature of the individual monetary policy instruments available to the Bundesbank is of importance with regard to the question of whether and to what extent *legal protection* exists for the credit institutions

---

[61] Cf. von Spindler *et al.*, 1973, Part II, section 16, note 7 d cc (pp. 353f.); Weiland, 1967, pp. 100ff., who views the instrument highly critically; further details in: Starck, 1973, pp. 1607ff.; Hübner, 1973, pp. 353ff. There have also been several rulings on the preconditions for holding a cash deposit, cf. Bundesverwaltungsgericht, 1977, pp. 1700f.; Bundesverwaltungsgericht, 1980, pp. 467ff.: a calling-in order had been issued in both cases; Bundesgerichtshof, 1977, pp. 2030ff.: claim for damage; Bundesgerichtshof, 1980, pp. 1572ff.: transactions for the purpose of evading a law.

and other parties *in respect of measures carried out by the Bundesbank.* Such measures in terms of monetary policy have as yet seldom been the subject of court disputes, so that little attention has been given to this question in the general reference material on constitutional and administrative law. On the basis of the allocation of the Bundesbank to the executive there can however be no doubt that sovereign activities of the Bundesbank are also subject to the guarantee of legal protection contained in article 19 para. 4 GG.[62] In principle, it is possible to derive from this the comprehensive judicial control of sovereign acts, both from a legal and a factual point of view.[63] Since, however, the courts are only able to rule in terms of the law, determination by a court that a breach of the law has taken place is conditional on the relevant dispute being a legal question at all. Particular difficulties are posed here by those decisions of the Bundesbank which are prognostic in nature.[64] Measures taken by the Bundesbank in terms of monetary policy are based less on the examinable investigation of the present monetary policy situation, but rather on the prognosis of future macroeconomic developments in particular, taking account of the effects of the instrument which is to be deployed. On the basis of its specific factual competence, the Bundesbank is a particularly predestined decision maker.[65] Judicial examination may therefore only restrict itself to the question of whether the Bundesbank used correct basic dimensions and scientifically defensible methods in the context of its decision making.[66] If it is to interpret *uncertain* legal terms of the Bundesbank Act of or other legal provisions, it therefore has only a restricted scope for discretion which can be examined.

It can be said in general terms that each measure carried out by the Bundesbank is limited by constitutional principles, in particular by the basic rights.[67] Furthermore, with regard to the existence of formal defects or procedural errors, or of the exceeding of discretionary rules and restrictions, it is necessary to adhere to the principles of administrative law.[68] The justiciability of measures carried out by the Bundesbank, and hence the proof of

---

[62] Cf. Siebelt, 1988, pp. 194f.; Gramlich, 1994, p. 381; Hahn, 1990, section 20 II, p. 305, margin no. 14. For the ECB cf. article 35 of the Statute of the ESCB; cf. for details on this Koenig, 1993, pp. 661ff.

[63] Cf. *BVerfGE* 31, p. 117; *BVerfGE* 35, p. 274; *BVerfGE* 51, p. 312; Maunz *et al.* (n.d.), article 19 IV margin no. 183; Stern, 1980, vol. 2, section 20 IV 5 f.

[64] Details in Coburger, 1987, pp. 116ff.

[65] Cf. Tettinger, 1982, p. 422; Tettinger, 1980, pp. 429ff.; Gramlich, 1994, p. 378.

[66] Cf. *BVerwG* (Federal Administrative Court), Urteil vom 26. März 1981, p. 980.

[67] Gramlich, 1994, p. 379, reports need for 'improvement' with regard to 'contours of the state based on the rule of law' and 'democratic legitimation' of the instruments available to the Bundesbank.

[68] Cf. Gramlich, 1994, p. 383; Coburger, 1987, pp. 113ff., 145ff.; restricted Hahn, 1990, section 20 II margin nos. 14ff.

a breach of the law, however, becomes more difficult for the party which calls on the court, the more it is a question of monetary policy. One should take particular account here of the fact that sufficient scope for discretion must be granted to the Bundesbank in order to fulfil its constitutional role of safeguarding the currency, and of protecting its independence. A breach of basic rights or of the powers defined in the Bundesbank Act will therefore only be determined in *special situations of self-evident misconduct*.

e) The participation of the Bundesbank in banking supervision

In accordance with the provisions of the Banking Act, the Bundesbank participates in *banking supervision*, where its functional area is affected by measures carried out by the other agencies participating in banking supervision (the Federal Banking Supervisory Office, the Federal Government, Federal Minister of Finance). In accordance with section 6(2) of the Banking Act, the aim of banking supervision is to ensure a well-functioning banking system for macroeconomic reasons. This aim is also in the interest of the Bundesbank since its major monetary policy instruments, those which serve to safeguard the currency, apply to the credit institutions, and therefore the success of its policy depends on a stable and well-functioning banking system.[69] Measures concerned with banking supervision may as a consequence develop major indirect interactions.

In accordance with section 7(1) first sentence of the Banking Act, the Bundesbank and the Federal Banking Supervisory Office are obliged to work together in terms of the Banking Act. They are to inform each other of observations and findings which may be significant for carrying out the functions of both (second sentence). Under section 7(2) of the Banking Act, the President of the Federal Banking Supervisory Office has the right to participate in the deliberations of the Central Bank Council of the Deutsche Bundesbank, whenever matters in this, his field of responsibility, are being discussed. He or she has no voting right there, but does have a right to file motions.

There is provision in the Banking Act for the participation of the Bundesbank in measures associated with banking supervision at three different levels of intensity:[70] the weakest form of participation is the 'consultation'

[69] Cf. *BVerfGE* 14, p. 212; Szagunn-Wohlschieß, 1986, section 7 *KWG*, margin no. 1; Humm, 1988, p. 115.

[70] Overview of all rights of participation in Szagunn-Wohlschieß, 1986, section 6 *KWG*, margin no. 27; Humm, 1988, pp. 118ff.; Reischauer and Kleinhans (n.d.), section 7 *KWG*, margin no. 2.

of the Bundesbank, which is to take place prior to the issuing of certain legal ordinances by the Federal Minister of Finance (sections 1(1) third sentence and (3) second sentence, 10(2) first sentence no. 3, 22 first sentence, 29(3) first sentence and 31(1) first sentence of the Banking Act) or by the Federal Government (sections 47(2) and 48(1) of the Banking Act) and prior to the appointment of the President of the Federal Banking Supervisory Office (section 5(2) of the Banking Act). A more detailed discussion of the reservations of the Bundesbank is necessary if in sections 10a(6) eleventh sentence, 24(4) first sentence and 25(4) first sentence of the Banking Act it is necessary to create an 'involvement' with the Bundesbank. The forms of participation of 'consultations' and of 'involvement' otherwise hardly vary since the supervisory authority is not bound by the observations of the Bundesbank in either case.[71] The situation is different, on the other hand, when establishing principles relating to equity capitalization or to the assessment of the liquidity of a credit institution in accordance with sections 10(1) second sentence and 11 second sentence of the Banking Act, in the case of which the Federal Banking Supervisory Office may act only in 'agreement' with the Bundesbank. In this case, the statement by the Bundesbank becomes binding, so that the Bundesbank may prevent the regulation intended by the Federal Banking Supervisory Office.

The functional areas of the Bundesbank also overlap with banking supervision in the area of information collection and evaluation. In accordance with section 7(1) third sentence of the Banking Act, the Bundesbank is to make available to the Federal Banking Supervisory Office, which as an autonomous higher Federal authority has no sub-structure of its own, its statistical data and information from the area of credit as well as their evaluations. For reasons of cost-effective administration, most reports from the credit institutions required under the Banking Act are to be submitted to the Bundesbank. The latter evaluates the data and only passes to the Federal Banking Supervisory Office those cases which are relevant to banking supervision, thus considerably reducing the burden on the Office.[72] In accordance with section 16(3) third sentence of the Bundesbank Act, the Bundesbank is also to inform the Federal Banking Supervisory Office if a financial institution considerably or repeatedly falls short of or exceeds the required minimum. In accordance with section 44(3) second sentence of the Banking Act, the Bundesbank may require from the credit institutions and the members of their governing bodies information regarding all business matters, as well as the submission of their books and publications with

---

[71] Cf. Humm, 1988, p. 119; Pohl, 1982, p. 53.
[72] Cf. Bähre and Schneider, 1986, section 50 *KWG*, note 2; Seeck and Steffens, 1979, pp. 37f.

regard to their duties to report. Such requests by the Bundesbank for information and submissions are probably an administrative act which can be challenged by means of general recourse to appeal.

f) The involvement of the Bundesbank in national and international economic, financial, and business cycle policy

The Deutsche Bundesbank is involved in taking decisions under economic, financial, and business cycle policy on a long-term basis at both national and international level: economic, financial, and business cycle policies are a prime duty of any government; irrespective of the participation of other state bodies, they are governmental responsibilities for obvious reasons,[73] and in the federal state are primarily assigned to the central bodies. The *Federal Government* therefore *advances* in this area to become the most important decision making body, which is nevertheless to avail itself of the support of expert institutions. These include the Bundesbank in particular. In accordance with section 13(3) of the Bundesbank Act, the Federal Government is to invite the President of the Deutsche Bundesbank to attend its deliberations on important monetary policy issues. This rule correlates with the entitlement of the members of the Federal Cabinet to attend meetings of the Central Bank Council in accordance with section 13(2) of the Bundesbank Act. In the view of the Bundesbank, it serves to 'establish closer relations between the Federal Government and the Bundesbank, and to enable the Bundesbank to remain abreast of the economic aims of the Federal Government'.[74] Section 13(3) of the Bundesbank Act is only a 'recommended' ruling. In the light of the large number of factors which are significant for monetary policy, it is however the rule for the President of the Bundesbank, or his representative, the Vice-President, (in accordance with sections 6(3) first sentence and 7(5) first sentence of the Bundesbank Act), to attend Cabinet meetings at which fundamental decisions are taken, even if it is at the discretion of the Federal Government to decide when items under discussion are 'matters of monetary policy significance', and an invitation to attend its meeting is issued in accordance with section 21(1) of the Standing Orders of the Federal Government (*GeschOBReg*). The Federal Chancellor has the final say, but under section 23(3) of the Standing Orders of the Federal Government, individual Ministers may also propose that the representative of the Bundesbank be invited.

The link between the Bundesbank and the Federal Government is

---

[73] Cf. Stern *et al.*, 1972, p. 72.
[74] Deutsche Bundesbank, Geschäftsbericht 1957, p. 7.

additionally strengthened by rights to participate on the part of the Bundesbank in the following *deliberation and coordination bodies* at government
level:

- On the basis of the Act concerning the Establishment of a Council of
  Economic Experts (Gesetz über die Bildung eines Sachverständigenrates)
  dated 14 August 1963, the *Council of Economic Experts* compiles an
  annual report assessing macroeconomic development, on the overall economic picture and its foreseeable developments, and submits it to the
  Federal Government. In particular, the five independent experts, the so-
  called five wise men, demonstrate the causes of present and potential
  tensions between macroeconomic demand and macroeconomic supply
  (section 2 of the Act). The Council of Economic Experts may consult the
  President of the Bundesbank on this, and conversely the latter may be
  allowed to submit his statement to the Council of Experts (section 5(1)
  and (2) of the Act).
- In accordance with section 18 of the Stability and Growth Act, since 1967
  the Federal Government has had the *Stabilization Council for the Public
  Secto*r. The Stabilization Council comprises the Federal Minister of
  Economics (as Chairman) and the Federal Minister of Finance, one representative of each the Länder and four representatives of the local authorities and of the local authority associations. Its role is to safeguard and
  coordinate the interests of the central, regional, and local authorities with
  regard to the Federal Government's business cycle policy. In accordance
  with section 18(2) second sentence of the Stability and Growth Act, the
  Stabilization Council is to be consulted, in particular, prior to measures
  undertaken by the Federal Government in accordance with sections 15,
  19, and 20 of the Stability and Growth Act (transfer of central, regional,
  and local authority funds to the anticyclical reserves, limitation of borrowing).[75] Beyond this, it advises on all business cycle policy measures
  necessary to achieve overall economic equilibrium and on the options
  available of satisfying the credit requirements of the public sector (section
  18(2) first sentence Nos. 1 and 2 of the Stability and Growth Act). Its
  decisions do not, however, have the force of law, but are only recommendations. In accordance with section 18(4) of the Stability and Growth
  Act, the Bundesbank—not a specific officeholder of one of the bodies of
  the Bundesbank—has the right to participate in the deliberations of the
  Stabilization Council at its own discretion.
- In accordance with section 18(3) of the Stability and Growth Act, the

---

[75] More details in Höfling, 1993, pp. 418ff.; Stern *et al.*, 1972, section 18; Wittman, 1977,
pp. 98f.; Wiesner, 1992, pp. 140f.

Committee for Public Sector Credit Issues was created in 1975. This Committee was born of a sub-committee of the Stabilization Council and is now a separate body for discussion. It is chaired by the Federal Minister of Finance. The committee investigates the situation on the capital market and the public sector's credit requirements. It is responsible for preparing any credit limitations which may become necessary in accordance with article 109 para. 4 *GG* and sections 19–22 of the Stability and Growth Act.[76] In accordance with section 1(1) third sentence of its rules of procedure, the Deutsche Bundesbank participates in the deliberations of the Committee as a permanent and active partner.

– In accordance with section 51 of the Act on Budgetary Principles, a further body for discussion and coordination on fiscal policy with the Federal Government is the *Fiscal Planning Council*, consisting of the Federal Minister of Finance (as Chairman) and the Federal Minister of Economics, the Ministers of the Länder who are responsible for finance, and four representatives of the local authorities and local authority associations. The Financial Planning Council gives non-binding recommendations for the coordination of the medium-term financial planning of the Federal Government with the planning of the Länder and local authorities, establishes a uniform system of financial planning, and determines macroeconomic and financial forecasts for financial planning, and points of emphasis for the fulfilment of public functions in accordance with the macroeconomic requirements. In doing so, it takes into account the measures which the Financial Planning Council considers to be necessary in order to achieve the aims of the Stability and Growth Act. In accordance with section 51(1) third sentence of the Act on Budgetary Principles, the Bundesbank may also attend the deliberations of the Financial Planning Council.

The Bundesbank's relationships with *international and supranational organizations and institutions* are based on differing legal foundations: in accordance with section 4 of the Bundesbank Act, the Bundesbank is entitled to participate in the Bank for International Settlements and, with the consent of the Federal Government, in other institutions which serve supranational monetary policy or international payments and credit. However, in most cases the Bundesbank is neither a contracting party to an international Convention itself, nor is it named as a public law enforcement agency in the agreements under international law.[77] In such cases, the obligations resulting from the relevant international agreements are to be adhered to by the

---

[76] Cf. Dickertmann and Siedenberg, 1984, p. 18; Höfling, 1993, pp. 421f.
[77] Cf. Gramlich, 1988*a*, section 4, margin nos. 12ff. and 32.

Federal Government; the Bundesbank is merely involved in implementation at national level. For this reason, the Bundesbank is involved internally by the Federal Government via section 13(3) of the Bundesbank Act in the preparatory work on such international agreements in the area of monetary policy. With regard to complying with the international agreements, in each case unpublished internal administrative agreements are concluded between the Bundesbank and the Federal Government.[78] Under EU law, however, the Bundesbank is included as such in certain institutions.

– In accordance with the provisions of the Maastricht Treaty, the Bundes-bank is directly involved in Stages Two and Three of *European economic and monetary union*. In accordance with article 106 para. 1 of the ECT, the Bundesbank is a part of the European System of Central Banks. In accordance with article 109f para. 1 of the ECT, the President of the Deutsche Bundesbank is a member of the Council of the European Monetary Institute during Stage Two. In the same way, once Stage Three has begun, in accordance with article 109a para. 1 of the ECT, he will be a member of the Governing Council of the European Central Bank. Finally, a representative of the Bundesbank is a member of the Monetary Committee with advisory status governed by article 109c of the ECT (at the beginning of Stage Three: Economic and Financial Committee).

– The *International Monetary Fund (IMF)* was established in 1945 subsequent to the Bretton Woods Conference, and the Federal Republic of Germany has been a member since 1952.[79] Its purpose is in particular to promote international monetary cooperation and exchange rate stability and the relaxation and abolition of exchange control.[80] The highest decision making body of the IMF is the Board of Governors: each member of the organization appoints one governor and one alternate for this purpose in a manner determined by the individual member (article XII section 2 a second sentence of the Articles of Agreement of the IMF). In accordance with international practice, the President of the Deutsche

---

[78] Details in Gramlich, 1988a, section 4, margin nos. 17ff.; Dickertmann and Siedenberg, 1984, p. 19; von Spindler *et al.*, 1973, Part II section 4, note 2, pp. 215f.; Hahn, 1990, section 15 I, p. 210, margin no. 2.

[79] Articles of Agreement of the International Monetary Fund dated 1/22 July 1944 in the new version dated 30 Apr. 1976; printed in Sartorius II; accession of the Federal Republic of Germany by the Act dated 28 July 1952 (BGBl. [Bundesgesetzblatt/Federal Law Gazette] Part II, pp. 637, 728), amended by the Acts dated 13 Aug. 1959 (BGBl. Part II, p. 930), 30 July 1965 (BGBl. Part II, p. 1089), 12 May 1966 (BGBl. Part II, p. 245), 23 Dec. 1968 (BGBl. Part II, p. 1225), 17 Dec. 1970 (BGBl. Part II, p. 1325), 9 Jan. 1978 (BGBl. Part II, p. 13) and 22 July 1991 (BGBl. Part II, p. 814).

[80] Deutsche Bundesbank, 1992a, pp. 1ff.; Hahn, 1990, sections 13 I and 15 I, pp. 174ff., 210ff.; Dickertmann and Siedenberg, 1984, pp. 21f.

Bundesbank has always exercised the office of the German governor; he or she acts in concert with the Federal Minister of Finance, who is the alternate governor.

– On 12 May 1930, the *Bank for International Settlements (BIS)* commenced operations in Basle, Switzerland.[81] Since it has fulfilled its original function, namely that of handling German reparations payments resulting from the First World War (the Young Plan), its role has consisted of promoting cooperation between central banks, creating new possibilities for international financial operations and acting as a Trustee in international payment transactions. The BIS has the legal form of a company limited by shares. With the exception of the state banks of Albania and of the CIS states, the shareholders are all the European note-issuing banks— therefore also including the Deutsche Bundesbank—and the note-issuing banks of Australia, Canada, Japan, South Africa, and the USA. The governing bodies of the BIS are the General Meeting and the Board of Governors, the latter being responsible for the management of the Bank. The President of the Bundesbank is a permanent member of the Board of Governors.

International monetary cooperation takes place not only within the context of formal international organizations, but also in various *informal bodies*, where groups of countries with comparable interests associate:

The *Group of Ten (G-10)* was founded in 1962 as an informal group of the 10 major industrialized countries, which agreed in a treaty with the IMF (General Arrangements to Borrow, GAB) to provide further credit as a source of refinancing for IMF members. The Deutsche Bundesbank is a direct contracting party to the GAB. Both the Ministers of Finance and the Governors of the central banks of the eleven member countries[82] attend the meetings of the G-10.

The most important body of informal monetary cooperation between the seven major industrialized countries of the world (Canada, France, Germany, Italy, Japan, the United Kingdom, and the USA) is the *Group of Seven (G-7)*. The nucleus of G-7 cooperation is constituted by the annual meetings of the heads of state and government, the so-called World Economic Summits. In addition, importance attaches to the joint meetings of

---

[81] Abkommen über die Bank für Internationalen Zahlungsausgleich vom 20. Januar 1930 with Constitutional Charter of the BIS and Statutes (RGBl. [Reichsgesetzblatt/Reich Law Gazette] Part II, p. 288); Bekanntmachung über Änderungen des Grundgesetzes und der Statuten vom 22. Juni 1970 (BGBl. Part II, p. 765); Bekanntmachung über Änderungen der Statuten der Bank für Internationalen Zahlungsausgleich, vom 6. November 1976 (BGBl. Part II, p. 1849).

[82] Switzerland has been the eleventh full member since 1983.

the Ministers of Finance and Governors of the central banks of the seven member countries, at which current global economic and monetary issues are discussed.

6. Independence and relations with national governing bodies as a constitutional basic issue facing central banks

a) *The constitutional and political significance of the problem*

The above observations have several times touched upon the constitutional basic issues facing every central and note-issuing bank, namely its categorization within the web of constitutional relationships between the national governing bodies, and in particular its independence, but have not yet provided an answer. Important phrases such as constitutionally guaranteed minimum, 'fourth power', being part of the executive, freedom from ministerial control, relations with the system of parliamentary government, support of the government's general economic policy and 'pluralism of the appointing institutions' demonstrate the *constitutional and political significance of the topic*. It is a matter of the central question of the position of the Deutsche Bundesbank in the free, democratic and social state based on the rule of law—a question which is significant, from a legal, and a political and economic point of view alike. A large number of monographs and essays have been devoted to this fundamental question.[83] I intend at this juncture to address only the relevant legal, preferably state law, aspects of the topic. The economic implications of the problem have been dealt with elsewhere. It is also impossible to tackle the 'massive interests and ideologies'[84] which have occasionally defined the contest over the Bundesbank. From a methodological point of view, the only conceivable approach to answering the question must be provided by the constitution itself or the legal system which was created on its basis.

b) *Independence in accordance with the Basic Law*

The Basic Law contains two provisions which play a role in defining the position of the Bundesbank in the constitutional system. One of these is

---

[83] Cf. the titles included in the list of references.
[84] Schmidt, 1973, p. 658.

article 88, which has already been mentioned several times, and the second is article 109 para. 4 first sentence no. 2, in accordance with which provisions may be issued through a federal statute relating to an obligation incumbent on the Federal Government and the Länder to hold non-interest-bearing deposits (anticyclical reserves) at the Deutsche Bundesbank. The latter provision is not very revealing as regards answering the fundamental question which has been asked. It assigns a role to the Bundesbank from a purely financial point of view in its capacity as (principal) bank of the state. Our investigations must therefore concentrate on *article 88 GG*.

Until article 88 second sentence *GG* entered into force on 25 December 1992, the old version of article 88 *GG* consisted merely of the sentence 'The Federal Government shall establish a note-issuing and currency bank as the Federal Bank (Bundesbank)'. This provision enabled one to infer the following content of the regulation:

- the Bundesbank is an institution of the executive;
- the Bundesbank is a currency and note-issuing bank;
- the existence of the Bundesbank as an institution is guaranteed, including a minimum standard of currency and note-issuing policy instruments.

There has been much controversy in discussions to date as to whether the old version of article 88 *GG*, now *article 88 first sentence*, also contains a *constitutional guarantee of the independence* of the Deutsche Bundesbank:

- Many commentators conclude that the old version of article 88 *GG* is in favour of the independence of the Deutsche Bundesbank—mostly on teleological or topical grounds, in other words because of the starting point constituted by a currency and note-issuing bank, as well as on the basis of historical argument. This interpretation is said to emerge both from the 'overall picture from the period prior to the creation of the constitution'[85] and from the duties of the Bundesbank associated with the collectively used terms 'currency and note-issuing bank', which from an academic point of view could only be discharged by an independent central bank. There is no need to repeat the arguments in detail here.[86]
- The rulings of the Federal Administrative Court[87] and the theory to date,

---

[85] The Federal Constitutional Court also recognizes a 'picture of the German currency and note-issuing bank from the period prior to the creation of the constitution' as an argumentative figure, *BVerfGE* 14, p. 216.

[86] More in Stern, 1980, vol. 2, section 35 V 2 a.

[87] Cf. *BVerwGE* 41, pp. 354ff.: 'it [independence] is however not guaranteed by article 88 *GG*. There is no confirmation of this either in the wording or in the meaning and purpose, nor in the genesis of article 88 *GG* . . . The fact that monetary policy can also be pursued when subject to instructions and parliamentary responsibility is demonstrated by the situation in other democratic states.'

on the other hand, have stated that the independence of the Deutsche Bundesbank is compatible with the old version of article 88 *GG*, but not such independence as is guaranteed by the constitution.[88] The argument mostly advanced is that no uniform overall picture emerges of the German central bank since 1875 from the period prior to the creation of the constitution, since it was only really independent between 1922 and 1937 and after 1945 in orders by the Allies and in the 1948 Act on the Establishment of the Bank deutscher Länder (*Gesetz zur Errichtung der Bank deutscher Länder*). In addition, the wording of the old version of article 88 *GG* was not able to give rise to a guarantee of independence: the difference was too obvious from wording in Articles 97 para. 1 and 114 para. 2 *GG*, which expressly guarantees the independence of judges, as well as of the members of the Federal Court of Auditors—in contrast to the old version of article 88 *GG*. The short wording of the old version of article 88 is also said not to allow any compelling conclusion to be drawn from the function as regards the status as an independent institution, even if this status would certainly be desirable from a monetary policy point of view.

However, the legal situation has changed decisively since the entry into force of the Amending Act to the Basic Law dated 21 December 1992 (BGBl. Part I pp. 2086f.). The inserted *article 88 second sentence GG* now specifies that the responsibilities and powers of the Deutsche Bundesbank within the framework of the European Union may only be transferred to a European Central Bank, 'which is independent and whose primary aim is to safeguard price stability'. Hence, for the first time it is expressly stated in article 88 *GG* that the aim of safeguarding the currency—at least at the European level—can be achieved only by an independent central bank. It is not evident why the constitutional principle established for the European Central Bank is not to apply to the national Bundesbank. On the basis of the conclusion drawn from article 88 second sentence *GG*, the first sentence of this article therefore now contains a *constitutional guarantee of the autonomy of the Bundesbank*.[89]

---

[88] Cf. Hettlage, 1956, p. 8; Schmidt, 1973, p. 671; Ketzel *et al.*, 1976, pp. 23ff.; Gramlich, 1980, p. 533; Gramlich, 1988*b*, p. 83; Hahn, 1990, section 18 III 1, margin nos. 18f.; Hahn, 1982, p. 35; Kaiser, 1980, p. 20. Faber, 1969, p. 14, doubts even the granting of independence under ordinary law.

[89] Also Studt, 1992, p. 87; perhaps also Pernice, 1995, p. 1068, FN 43; another view presented by: Papier, 1994, pp. 839ff., without justification: Weikart, 1993*a*, p. 840 and Weikart, 1993*b*, p. 644, with reference to BT-Drucks. XII/3896, p. 22, according to which the 'wording of article 88 second sentence *GG* has no effect on the present legal status of the Deutsche Bundesbank'; in the same vein Stober, 1996, section 14 I 2. Perhaps also the Special Committee on 'European Union (Maastricht Treaty)', BT-Drucks. XII/3896, p. 12, in stating, 'that the wording favoured in article 88 second sentence *GG* has no effect on the present legal status of the Deutsche Bundesbank'.

This interpretation is also supported by two more recent rulings by the Federal Constitutional Court: in the decision dated 3 November 1989, which is concerned with questions of internal German payment transactions, it says literally: 'the Deutsche Bundesbank, which, moreover, by reason of its constitutionally independent position is not subject to the supervision of other institutions of the executive, is hence able to a considerable extent to determine itself which criteria it is to take as a basis for its practice in granting approval.'[90] The following observation was made in the so-called Maastricht judgment of the Federal Constitutional Court: 'the addition to article 88 *GG*, made in the light of the European Union, permits powers to be transferred from the Bundesbank to a European Central Bank if the latter meet the "strict criteria of the Maastricht Treaty and of the Statute of the European System of Central Banks with regard to the independence of the central bank and to the priority of monetary stability" (decision/recommendation and report of the Special Commission on "European Union [Maastricht Treaty]" dated 1 December 1992, Federal Parliament Publication [BT-Drucks.] XII/3896 p. 21). The will of the parliament which amended the constitution is therefore evidently aimed at creating a constitutional basis for Monetary Union, as is provided for in the Union Treaty, but which however restricts to this case the granting of the associated powers and institutions made independent in the way which has been described. This modification of the principle of democracy in the service of safeguarding the trust in payment which is placed in a currency is justifiable because it takes account of the particularity which has been tested in the German legal order and has also proven itself from an academic point of view, that an independent central bank tends to safeguard the value of money, and hence the general economic basis for the state's budgetary policy, as well as for private planning and disposition in exercising free economic rights, better than sovereign bodies which, with regard to their ability and resources to act, are in turn largely dependent on the money stock and on the value of money, as well as on the short-term approval of political powers.'[91]

From a *historical* and *constitutional* point of view, the constitutionally protected independence of the Bundesbank corresponds to the aims of a free, democratic basic order, something which cannot be a matter of indifference, especially in relation to a cardinal question such as the stability of the currency, with which Germany has had some terrible experiences. Even if state-controlled central banks certainly exist in other states with

---

[90] *BVerfGE* 62, p. 183; different interpretation by Schmidt, 1990, section 8 II 2 b, p. 365 (fn 99).
[91] *BVerfGE* 89, pp. 208f.

parliamentary democracies,[92] historical experience and comparative analyses of the note-issuing bank systems of the world have as a rule demonstrated an independent note-issuing bank to be the better institution to maintain a stable currency than a central bank which is dependent on the government and on parliament. An independent note-issuing bank is an element in the idea of the existence of several 'restraining influences', each of which is quite differently constituted[93] on which a mixed constitution is based serving against parliaments and governments, the latter being subject to monetary policy temptations. This has nothing to do with 'myth',[94] 'Areopagus',[95] or lack of a plan.[96] It is, rather, a quite correct and accurate assessment of the political and economic realities with which the Federal Constitutional Court also concurred in the above Maastricht ruling. Never has the management of a central bank destroyed a currency on its own account. It was always the state which used currency depreciation as a means of financing budget deficits.[97] It is therefore correct for article 108 of the ECT in conjunction with article 109e para. 5 of the ECT to require all Member States of the European Union to grant independence to their national note-issuing banks at the latest on the establishment of the ESCB.

c) The corresponding structure of independence under the Bundesbank Act

In the Bundesbank Act, in accordance with the constitutional stipulations contained in article 88 *GG*, the *(ordinary) Federal Parliament* stipulated the position of the Bundesbank within the state structure, and in doing so confirmed its independence. Such finely woven material as the monetary system

---

[92] This applies in particular to the Bank of England: Klein, 1991, p. 71; Studt, 1992, pp. 112f.; Lück, 1994, pp. 312ff.; general: von Bonin, 1979, pp. 93ff.; Stoffers, 1974, pp. 113ff.; Lampe, 1971, pp. 54ff.; Prost, 1968, pp. 110f.; Veit, 1969, pp. 191ff.; Bernauer, 1960, pp. 77ff.; Schuppler, 1962, pp. 54ff.

[93] Thus Rittershausen, 1962, p. 52; cf. also Schiller, 1994, p. 133, who examines the role of the Bundesbank within the context of German reunification and comes to the following conclusion: 'on the whole, the Bundesbank has proven to be a refuge of common sense against much nonsense in a most turbulent society searching for an orientation. In a population which is sick of politics, or which is subject to daily persuasion that it should be, it embodies a solitary instance with authority. As an institution, it is evidently led by the concept of the common good . . .'

[94] Faber, 1969, p. 14.

[95] Schiller, 1967a, 10 May 1967, p. 4977.

[96] Cf. Arndt, 1963, pp. 286ff.

[97] Cf. Schuppler, 1962, p. 75, also p. 62; in the same vein Hahn, 1968, vol. 2, p. 36; agreement in Schmidt, 1973, p. 668.

as such requires a most prudent hand in order to treat this sensitive structure correctly. It comes as no surprise, therefore, if the genesis of the Act on the Deutsche Bundesbank dated 26 July 1957 took a considerable time, and that subsequently the official slogan for this monetary policy Basic Law was *'noli me tangere'*,[98] in spite of several challenges, such as in 1967 and 1973:

Although the constitutional principle did not yet exist at the time when the Bundesbank Act was created, the then parliament decided to create an independent Bundesbank—referring to the security of the currency, which can be freely manipulated, or rather, controlled: 'however, particularly because keeping our manipulated currency stable no longer depends on automatically functioning gold cover provisions, but largely on the decisions of the currency bank regarding the correct dosage of the money stock, these decisions may not be subject to instructions from any agency whatever which might be interested in a development of the money stock running counter to monetary policy, for whatever reasons. The security of the currency is more important than any oh so good reasons. It is the highest precondition for the retention of a market economy, and hence in the final analysis that of a free constitution for society and the state. Experience has shown that those who might be interested in a development in money stock running counter to monetary policy are all political bodies, all credit institutions, and all borrowers. Therefore, the note-issuing bank must be independent of these and subject only to the law.'[99] The solution finally found by parliament is based on the following elements of independence under formal law:

– own legal subjectivity (institutional independence) as a Federal corporation under public law;
– determination of material position in sections 12 and 13 of the Bundesbank Act, which whilst perhaps not brilliantly worded from a technical
   legal point of view are clear in terms of content, and which were allocated
   their own Part in the Act (functional independence);
– varied appointment instances for the members of the governing bodies of
   the Bundesbank (staff independence): Federal President, Federal Government, Bundesrat, Länder governments, Central Bank Council and the
   President of the Bundesbank;
– capital of DM 290 million held by the Federal Government (section 2

[98] Schiller, 1967*b*, 1 Sept. 1967, p. 184.
[99] Grounds for the Government Draft BT-Drucks. II/2781, p. 24; also printed in: Beck, 1959, M 404, p. 587; also, statement by the Bundesrat, Appendix 2 to BT-Drucks. II/2781, p. 49; also printed in: Beck, 1959, M 409, p. 594, and written report by the Chairman of the Committee for Money and Credit, H. Scharnberg, BT-Drucks. II/3603, p. 5; also printed in: Beck, 1959, p. 602.

second sentence of the Bundesbank Act) with distribution of profit determined by statute (section 27 of the Bundesbank Act), providing for this to be paid over to the Federal Government as a possibly remaining annual profit after allocation of certain reserves and claims (in other words no financial independence).

Hence, a sensible solution was found to the fundamental question arising under state law relating to the Bundesbank, which has proven itself, and which has made it possible over the 40 years of the existence of the Bundesbank for it to create a monetary policy which is respected by the populace as a whole, as well as worldwide.[100]

If one takes a closer look at the statutory solution, one will not find that the Bundesbank is independent *per se*, but rather that it is *independent in respect of certain functions*:

In accordance with section 12 second sentence of the Bundesbank Act, the note-issuing bank is *independent of instructions from the Federal Government* in the exercise of all of the powers to which it is entitled in accordance with the Bundesbank Act. This does not apply where it has been allocated functions in other statutes. Freedom from instructions from the Federal Government means exclusion of orders and supervision measures of all kind. The issuance of legal ordinances as a part of legislative activity is unlikely to be part of this.[101] However, the relevant statutes provide for the participation ('consultation', 'involvement', 'agreement') of the Bundesbank when the Federal Government issues such ordinances.

A not inconsiderable restriction of the independence under section 12 second sentence of the Bundesbank Act is comprised by the duty of the Bundesbank, as stipulated in section 12 first sentence of the Bundesbank Act, to support the general economic policy of the Federal Government, without prejudice to the performance of its duties. Furthermore, in the area of (foreign) monetary policy competences overlap between the Bundesbank and the Federal Government. Section 13 of the Bundesbank Act also provides for various forms of cooperation between the two governing bodies.

The Bundesbank is only independent as regards the Federal Government and its subordinate authorities, but *not* towards *parliament*. In accordance with article 20 para. 3 *GG*, the latter has priority since the executive power

---

[100] Cf. Steuer, 1970, pp. 292ff.; von Münch and Kunig, 1996, article 88, margin no. 26; Woll and Vogl, 1976, pp. 40, 143ff.; critical Könneker, 1973, pp. 89ff.; Faber, 1969, p. 14 ('Myth of Independence') with agreeing discussion by Hoffmann-Riem and Faber, 1971, p. 443; Tietmeyer, 1994, p. 4.

[101] Cf. von Spindler *et al.*, 1973, Part II section 12, note 3 III 2, p. 266.

is bound by the law. The consequence of this is however at the same time that other parliamentary decisions are not binding on the Bundesbank.[102]

The Bundesbank is also *not* independent of *court rulings*. The Bundesbank—as each executive body—has to respect these.

Independence is also restricted in terms of the *Federal Court of Auditors*. In accordance with section 26(4) of the Bundesbank Act, on the basis of the report of the auditor, the Court carries out its own examination of the annual financial statements of the Bundesbank. The report of the auditors, together with the comments of the Federal Court of Auditors in relation to it, are communicated to the Federal Ministry of Finance.

d) The Bundesbank and the Federal Government

In adopting the Bundesbank Act, parliament spoke out clearly in favour of the independence of the Bundesbank, whilst at the same time emphasizing that independence 'naturally (may) not be understood to mean that the currency bank becomes a state within the state'.[103] In this sense, the independence of the Bundesbank was restricted, in particular in its *relations with the Federal Government*:

In accordance with section 12 first sentence of the Bundesbank Act, the Bundesbank is obligated to support the general economic policy of the Federal Cabinet. Here too, however, the limits placed on the duty to provide support are to be adhered to. It is not the economic policy of the Federal Government as such which is to be supported, but the 'general' economic policy, i.e. not each individual measure, but only the basic line.[104] In addition, this duty incumbent on the Bundesbank to provide support exists only 'without prejudice to the performance of its duties', something which is aimed to safeguard the currency, as defined in section 3 of the Bundesbank Act. As has already been explained, this aim has priority. The Bundesbank is therefore only under an obligation to support such a general economic policy which does not run counter to its role, namely that of safeguarding the stability of the currency. In the light of the Stability and Growth Act, therefore, the following fact should once more be stressed: in its economic and financial policy, the Federal Government is legally obligated in terms

---

[102] Cf. Beck, 1959, 2nd Book, section 12, K 301; Samm, 1967, p. 37; Uhlenbruck, 1968, p. 36.

[103] Report by the Chairman of the Committee for Money and Credit, H. Scharnberg, BT-Drucks. II/3603, p. 5.

[104] Cf. Schmidt, 1973, p. 673; Gramlich, 1988a, section 12, margin no. 8; partly differing Schäfer, 1958, p. 246.

of the aims of the Stability and Growth Act, as they are defined in section 1. This includes price stability. If this aim is not respected by the Federal Government, its general economic policy is unlawful. At the same time, such a policy would also be likely to run counter to the role of the Bundesbank. If in its economic policy the Federal Government prefers to emphasize the other aims contained in section 1 of the Stability and Growth Act, without neglecting price stability, the Bundesbank is obliged to provide support only to the extent that this does not run counter to its own role of safeguarding the currency. In this sense, the wording contained in section 13(3) of the Stability and Growth Act 'within the scope of their responsibilities' and section 12 first sentence of the Bundesbank Act 'without prejudice to the performance of its duties' carry the same meaning. The Federal Government and the Bundesbank are therefore obliged by law to cooperate in terms of respecting the aims of both statutes.

The institutional configuration of the Bundesbank's functional independence, and of its duty to provide support with regard to general economic policy, is to be found in section 13 of the Bundesbank Act. On the one hand the ability to take part in the deliberations of the Central Bank Council, with no voting right, but with a right to file motions and a dilatory right of veto, open in theory to all members of the Federal Government, something which however applies in practice only to the Ministers of Finance or/and of Economics[105] (subs. 2); on the other hand the involvement of the President of the Deutsche Bundesbank in Cabinet deliberations relating to matters of monetary policy significance (subs. 3). In accordance with section 13(1) of the Bundesbank Act, the Bundesbank is also to advise the Federal Government in these matters and to provide it with information on request. Duties to give advice and provide information exist only with regard to the Federal Government in its totality, but not towards each individual Federal Minister.

Concurrent functions have been allocated between the Bundesbank and the Federal Government in the area of *foreign monetary policy*.[106] In international agreements in the area of monetary policy, as a rule it is not the Bundesbank but the Federal Government which is the contracting party; in terms of the internal relationship between the Federal Government and the

---

[105] In accordance with the standards of independence applied by the European Parliament, the right of the Federal Government to defer decisions of the Central Bank Council for up to two weeks constitutes an inadmissible encroachment on the functional independence of the Deutsche Bundesbank: Potacs, 1993a, p. 71; Galahn, 1996, p. 43.

[106] Cf. in contrast section 3(2) first sentence of the Government Draft of the Bundesbank Act, which did not become law: 'the responsibility of the Federal Government for safeguarding the currency shall remain unaffected', BT-Drucks. II/2781.

Bundesbank, the responsibilities and rights under the relevant international agreements are however transferred to the Bundesbank by internal administrative agreements. A different situation applies to a system of fixed exchange rates, for instance in the European Monetary System (EMS) or the original version of the Articles of Agreement of the IMF. Here, it is especially the changes in parity in respect of the currencies of other states which are not assigned to the Bundesbank,[107] but are ordered by the Federal Government.[108] This is not contradicted by the fact that for instance the first revaluation of the D-mark within the context of the Articles of Agreement of the IMF was made with fixed exchange rates and 'with the consent of the Bundesbank'.[109] The President of the Bundesbank is also involved in the decision making for changes in parity within the context of the European Monetary System. The final decision making power, however, lies with the Federal Government. By (re)defining exchange rate parities, it stipulates the framework for the monetary policy of the Bundesbank.

It is evident that the stability of a currency can be placed in danger by measures of foreign monetary policy. The question of role therefore also takes on a competence-related dimension. To put it another way: may the Federal Government, which is responsible for foreign monetary policy, erode the primary competence of the Bundesbank for safeguarding the currency by means of measures which lie within its area of competence? The problem cannot be solved solely by referring to the constitutional regulation of competences. If article 88 first sentence *GG* guarantees the existence of a currency bank, this then means at the same time that the task of 'safeguarding the currency' which is thereby imposed must also be respected by the other constitutional bodies within the framework of their constitutional competences. It emerges not only from article 109 para. 2 *GG* and section 1 of the Stability and Growth Act that the Federal Government and the Länder are also subject to a duty in this respect. The institutional guarantee contained in article 88 first sentence *GG* also guarantees an inviolable nucleus of functions which are assigned to the institution, since otherwise the institution which is the Bundesbank would be in danger of being only a constitutional decorum, and no longer an autonomous highest state body.

---

[107] Cf. Hoffmann, 1969, pp. 177f. with further references; Schmidt, 1973, p. 675; on changes in parity: Tomuschat, 1970; Hoffmann-Riem, 1969, pp. 1374ff.; Müller, 1971, pp. 726ff.; Caspers, 1961, pp. 343ff.; from the point of view of international law: Hahn, 1979, pp. 1ff.

[108] Cf. Fögen, 1969, pp. 62f.; von Spindler *et al.*, 1973, Part II, section 14, note 5, p. 298; Greitemann, 1968, pp. 245f.; Caspers, 1961, p. 343; different Tomuschat, 1970, pp. 38, 42; Müller, 1971, p. 729 (for Act); Hoffmann, 1969, pp. 146ff., 172f., 228f.; Hoffmann-Riem, 1969, p. 1376 (for Federal Chancellor and/or Federal Minister of Economics).

[109] Cf. Bekanntmachung über die neue Parität der D-Mark, vom 8. März 1961, p. 2.

The equally subtle and balanced regulation of the relationship between the Federal Government and the Bundesbank, which attempts to unite independence and cooperation, leaves open the procedure which is to be followed in cases of *conflict*. Apart from the already mentioned possibility of hindering decisions, something which is subject to strict time limits (section 13(2) third sentence of the Bundesbank Act), parliament has consciously refrained from taking institutional precautions against possible conflicts. If a conflict were to 'become dramatic', parliament's final recourse would be only to take a decision which would then either have to opt in general terms to retain or abolish the independence of the currency bank, or decide specifically on the statutory regulation of a specific individual question.[110] The conflict would therefore be carried out in public and under the control of public opinion. In particular, the solution opted for in the Oesterreichische Nationalbank Act (*Nationalbankgesetz*) has not been seized upon, in accordance with which a decision is to be taken by an arbitral tribunal consisting of two representatives each of the government and of the note-issuing bank, under the chairmanship of the neutral President of the Highest Court.[111] For this reason, sections 12 and 13 of the Bundesbank Act have been referred to as '*leges imperfectae*'.[112] This is only true insofar as neither provision as such offers a solution in case of a conflict. Then, however, the general regulations apply to deciding on a dispute. In accordance with these, the courts are called upon for this. Since the parties to the dispute are state bodies with competences governed by public law, the only recourse is to the constitutional courts or to the (general) administrative courts. A dispute belongs before the Federal Constitutional Court naturally only if it falls under one of that Court's listed competences. Furthermore, it is necessary for the interpretation and application of constitutional law to form the actual nucleus of the legal dispute, or for the contentious legal relationship to be decisively forged by constitutional law, and for those involved to be highest bodies as defined in article 93 para. 1 no. 1 *GG*. Neither of these scenarios applies in the case of conflicts between the Federal Government and the Bundesbank: such a dispute would be concerned with competences in accordance with the Bundesbank Act. Especially by calling

---

[110] Cf. report by H. Scharnberg MP (written report of the Committee on Money and Credit), regarding BT-Drucks. II/3603, p. 5; in the same vein also Hahn, 1982, p. 34; Gaugenrieder, 1961, pp. 171ff.

[111] Cf. section 41(3) and sections 4, 45, and 46 of the National Bank Act (*Nationalbankgesetz*) dated 8 Sept. 1955 (BGBl. no. 184); on further proposals cf. Beck, 1959, 2nd Book, section 12, K 309ff. The proposal to create a liaison committee between the Bundesbank and the Federal Government made by Starke, 1977, should be emphasized; on the whole topic Schuppler, 1962, pp. 73ff.

[112] Perhaps first by von Eynern, 1957, pp. 35f.

into play article 88 *GG*, it would also have a constitutional element, but this would not be its *nucleus*. Additionally, the Bundesbank is neither a constitutional body nor otherwise party to a dispute between highest Federal bodies relating to rights and duties. Hence, recourse would be available to the administrative courts for legal disputes between the Federal Government and the Bundesbank in accordance with section 40(1) of the Rules of Procedure of the Administrative Courts (VwGO). However, as has already been discussed, the courts may decide only in terms of the law. Conflicts relating to monetary policy between the Bundesbank and the Federal Government carried out before the administrative courts would however be neither expedient nor desirable.[113] An adequate court decision would in fact be all the more difficult the more it was a question of the modalities of monetary policy as such, and these were not individually regulated in statutes. Unless it is particularly evident that one party has acted incorrectly, as a rule the result will be that it will not be possible to restrict the party or parties carrying out the acts. The dispute will be shifted back to the 'political' level, perhaps with personal consequences.

e) The Bundesbank and parliament

Section 12 of the Bundesbank Act clarifies the position of the Bundesbank in the sense that its freedom from instructions is granted only in terms of the Federal Government. Its independence is therefore not 'absolute'. It has already been stated with regard to the provision on the position of the Bundesbank in terms of *parliament* that its position in the area free of ministerial control is justifiable in terms of its categorization with the highest bodies of the state, but that on the other hand the fact of its being bound by decisions taken by the Bundestag in the shape of statutes may not be questioned. The relationship between the two bodies cannot however simply be characterized by the succinct words of Reiner Schmidt: 'it [parliament] has merely to equip the Bank with a nucleus of monetary policy powers and with the right to issue banknotes.'[114] The problems are much more complicated. For this reason, it is surprising that *this* legal relationship has attracted much less attention in the reference material than the tensions with

---

[113] The Federal Government and the Bundesbank should on principle solve conflicts amongst themselves, i.e. without calling on the courts: Hasse, 1992, p. 29, constitutes a reminder by referring to Emminger, 1986, pp. 361f., to an exchange of letters between the two bodies in Nov. 1978, as a consequence of which the Bundesbank was granted the right by the Federal Government to discontinue exchange rate interventions in cases of conflict.

[114] Schmidt, 1973, p. 671.

the government.[115] The following characteristics can be identified in the light of the above observations:

The Bundesbank is not a 'fourth' power, but a part of the executive power. Hence, in accordance with article 20 para. 3 *GG*, it is bound by the law. This means for parliament that—primarily based on the definition of competences contained in article 73 no. 4 and article 74 no. 11 *GG*, as well as in article 88—it may issue legal rules relating to the activities, organization, and status of the Bundesbank. These must naturally be in accordance with the constitutional guarantee of the existence of the Bundesbank contained in article 88 *GG*, as well as with the other constitutional legal norms. In this respect, no particularity exists in comparison with other institutions of the executive, any more than it does in the lack of power to place under an obligation had by so-called simple parliamentary decisions taken on monetary issues.

The problems start however with the lack of subjection to the government, lying in independence, and with the consequent so-called parliamentary freedom of the Bundesbank, whereby this term is intended initially to stand as a cipher for a much more difficult relationship with the system of parliamentary government, and hence with the division of powers and functions as a whole, in other words with two fundamental structural principles of the constitutional order contained in the Basic Law which are declared inviolable by its article 79 para. 3 as an element of the democratic, parliamentary state based on the rule of law which is anchored in article 20. The reference material and rulings ultimately agree that the independence from the government granted to the Bundesbank, and the associated *exemption from parliamentary control*, are constitutional.[116] The justification in constitutional theory, however, varies considerably:

In some cases, reference is made to self-denial on the part of parliament, in some to the exceptional nature and to the existing system of factual and personal dependences—this is the view taken by the Federal Administrative Court[117]—in part to the special regulation contained in article 88 *GG*, and in other cases to the 'nature of the matter', as well as partly to the 'overall

---

[115] With regard to inclusion of the central bank in a parliamentary democracy, finally: Waechter, 1994, pp. 182ff., who sees the independent Bundesbank as a 'controlling body', on the basis of the principle of the division of powers, in relation to the legislative and the executive (pp. 197ff.).

[116] Prevailing opinion, cf. *BVerwGE* 41, pp. 356f.; von Münch and Kunig, 1996, article 88, margin nos. 24f.; Samm, 1967, pp. 148ff.; Schmidt, 1973, pp. 671ff., in each case with further references; reservations in Faber, 1969, p. 71; with agreeing discussion by Hoffmann-Riem and Faber, 1971, p. 445; Füsslein, 1970, pp. 338f.

[117] Cf. *BVerwGE* 41, p. 357.

picture prior to the existence of the statute'.[118] Even if there are correct elements in each justification, none seems convincing on its own: the self-denial could collide with the inviolability of the principles concerned; article 88 *GG* says nothing about the relationship with parliament, and its systematic position in Part VIII would even rather indicate parliamentary control; the nature of the matter and the overall picture prior to the existence of the statute are—as has already been indicated—not constitutional justifications which can be used, at least in relation to the Bundesbank. The most satisfactory idea appears to be to consider the exceptional situation which is permissible in terms of the constitution, which however requires additional support.

The starting point of freedom from parliamentary control must be the fact that the independence of the Bundesbank is not a 'myth', but that it is a principle which has been confirmed by historical experience, as well as by academic wisdom and knowledge of state policy, as being correct, sensible, and practicable for solving complicated tensions between the note-issuing bank and the state bodies which were established in order to provide political leadership. Both the Parliamentary Council and the parliament which adopted the Bundesbank Act were familiar with the fact that the stability of the currency was of necessity a matter of highest state policy. Safeguarding the currency could certainly be referred to as a constitutional mandate which initially was not expressly worded, but was immanent to the Basic Law. Article 109 para. 2 *GG* (overall economic equilibrium) made preservation of purchasing power an express element of constitutional status.[119] Now, article 88 second sentence *GG* also expressly stipulates that the role and powers of the Bundesbank may be transferred only to a European Central Bank 'whose primary aim is to safeguard price stability'. At the same time, however, the aim set out in the constitution also justifies taking the rational path towards the accomplishment of this role. The parliament which adopted the Bundesbank Act took its decision in the knowledge of the historical dangers posed to the German monetary system by 'steered' note-issuing banks. For this reason, it retained the note-issuing bank with special guarantees of independence, just as a historical parliament created the independent judiciary and the independent Court of Auditors.[120] Creating the latter did not create 'states within the state' any more than the former, since none of these three institutions have *plein pouvoir*, but have been

---

[118] Cf. on the individual arguments Stern, 1980, vol. 2, section 35 V 6 b; Samm, 1967, pp. 148ff.

[119] Cf. Schmidt-Preuß, 1977, p. 129.

[120] Cf. Geisler, 1953, pp. 157f.: 'independence of monetary policy from political influences is equally as important as the independence of the judiciary'.

assigned clearly defined functions. The independence of the Bundesbank challenges neither the principle of the affiliation of material governmental functions to the government in the organizational sense, nor that of parliament's power of control with regard to the government, but creates a body which is neutral towards the 'political' powers and which is highly functional in order to safeguard a high constitutional interest.[121] 'A democracy', as is correctly stated by Otmar Issing, 'is subject to the constant temptation to extend the political arena into all areas of life. This leads to an overburdening of the political area, the initial consequence of which is the disappointment of the people with regard to unmet expectations, and in connection with this a danger to democracy'.[122] A note-issuing bank which is independent from the government and distanced from parliamentary control and responsibility is not an 'illogical element of the constitutional system',[123] but a particularly rational institution, the selection of which demonstrates the wise moderation of those who could have acted differently, had they so wished. The free, democratic basic order in our state has demonstrably benefited from this decision. It has guaranteed a relatively stable German currency. Above all, however, the currency has largely remained outside parliamentary disputes, without on the other hand the system of parliamentary government having suffered. May the German model serve as the guiding principle for the European Central Bank!

7. Bibliography

Abkommen über die Bank für Internationalen Zahlungsausgleich, vom 20. Januar 1930 (1930), in: Reichsgesetzblatt, Part II, no. 7, pp. 288–327

Arndt, Hans-Joachim (1963): Politik und Sachverstand im Kreditwährungswesen, Berlin

Bähre, Inge Lore/Schneider, Manfred (1986): 3KWG-Kommentar, Munich

Beck, Heinz (1959): Gesetz über die Deutsche Bundesbank vom 20. Juli 1957, Kommentar, Mainz-Gonsenheim/Düsseldorf

Becker, Hans Joachim (1954): Grundgesetz und Bundesbank, in: Die öffentliche Verwaltung 7, pp. 358–60

Bekanntmachung über die neue Parität der D-Mark, vom 8. März 1961, in: Bundesanzeiger no. 48 dated 9 March 1961, p. 2

Bekanntmachung über Änderungen des Grundgesetzes und der Statuten der Bank für Internationalen Zahlungsausgleich, vom 22. Juni 1970, in: Bundesgesetzblatt, Part II, no. 40 (1970), pp. 765–87

---

[121] Cf. Schiller, 1994, p. 133; also Schmidt, 1990, section 8 II 2 b, pp. 364f.

[122] Issing, 1992, p. 7.

[123] Hüttl, 1972, p. 66.

Bekanntmachung über Änderungen der Statuten der Bank für Internationalen Zahlungsausgleich, vom 6. November 1976, in: Bundesgesetzblatt, Part II, no. 60 (1976), pp. 1849–51

Bernauer, Engelbert (1960): Staat und Notenbank, Freiburg i. Br.

Bonin, Konrad von (1979): Zentralbanken zwischen funktioneller Unabhängigkeit und politischer Autonomie, Baden-Baden

Breit, James (1911): Bankgesetz, Berlin

Bundesgerichtshof (1977): Anwendbarkeit des Außenwirtschaftsgesetzes auf ein Kreditgeschäft, Urteil vom 7. Juli 1977, in: Neue juristische Wochenschrift 30, pp. 2030–2

Bundesgerichtshof (1980): Scheingeschäft wegen Umgehung der Bardepotpflicht, Urteil vom 24. Januar 1980, in: Neue juristische Wochenschrift 33, pp. 1572–4

Bundesverwaltungsgericht (1977): Voraussetzungen für die Haltung eines sogenannten Bardepots, Urteil vom 3. Mai 1977, in: Neue juristische Wochenschrift 30, pp. 1700–01

Bundesverwaltungsgericht (1980): Voraussetzungen der Anordnung einer Depotpflicht, Urteil vom 12. Juli 1979, in: Neue juristische Wochenschrift 33, pp. 467–9

Bundesverwaltungsgericht (1981): Urteil vom 26. März 1981, in: Deutsches Verwaltungsblatt 96, pp. 975–83

Caspers, Hans-Friedrich (1961): Rechtliche Betrachtungen zur Aufwertung der Deutschen Mark, in: Der Betriebs-Berater 16, pp. 341–3

Coburger, Dieter (1987): Die währungspolitischen Befugnisse der Deutschen Bundesbank, Diss. Bochum

Deutsche Bundesbank (1976) (ed.): Währung und Wirtschaft in Deutschland 1876–1975, Frankfurt a.M.

Deutsche Bundesbank (1988): 30 Jahre Deutsche Bundesbank. Die Entstehung des Bundesbankgesetzes vom 26. Juli 1957. Dokumentation einer Ausstellung, Frankfurt a.M.

Deutsche Bundesbank (1990): Die Währungsunion mit der Deutschen Demokratischen Republik, in: Monatsbericht 42, 7, pp. 14–29

Deutsche Bundesbank (1991): Ein Jahr deutsche Währungs-, Wirtschafts- und Sozialunion, in: Monatsbericht 43, 7, pp. 18–30

Deutsche Bundesbank (1992a): ⁴Internationale Organisationen und Gremien im Bereich von Währung und Wirtschaft, Sonderdrucke der Deutschen Bundesbank no. 3, Frankfurt a.M.

Deutsche Bundesbank (1992b): Die Neuordnung der Bundesbankstruktur, in: Monatsbericht 44, 8, pp. 48–54

Die Deutsche Bundesbank (1993): ⁶Geldpolitische Aufgaben und Instrumente, Sonderdrucke der Deutschen Bundesbank no. 7, Frankfurt a.M.

Deutsche Bundesbank (1995): Die Geldpolitik der Bundesbank, Frankfurt a.M.

Deutsche Bundesbank (various years): Geschäftsberichte, Frankfurt a.M.

Dickertmann, Dietrich/Siedenberg, Axel (1984): ⁴Instrumentarium der Geldpolitik, Düsseldorf

Dolzer, Rudolf/Vogel, Klaus (n.d.) (eds.): Bonner Kommentar zum Grundgesetz, Heidelberg, loose-leaf edition

Donner, Hartwig/Neumann, Petra (1994): Die Auswirkungen der Europäischen Währungsunion auf die Unabhängigkeit der Deutschen Bundesbank, in: Bodin, Manfred/Hübl, Lothar (eds.): Banken in gesamtwirtschaftlicher Verantwortung, Stuttgart, pp. 151–64

Emminger, Otmar (1986): D-Mark, Dollar, Währungskrisen. Erinnerungen eines ehemaligen Bundesbankpräsidenten, Stuttgart

Eynern, Gert von (1957): Die Unabhängigkeit der Notenbank, Berlin

Faber, Heiko (1969): Wirtschaftsplanung und Bundesbankautonomie, Baden-Baden

Faber, Heiko (1989): Erläuterung von Art. 88 *GG*, in: ²Alternativ-Kommentar zum Grundgesetz für die Bundesrepublik Deutschland, Neuwied

Farthmann, Friedhelm/Coen, Martin (1994): § 19 Tarifautonomie, Unternehmensverfassung und Mitbestimmung, in: Benda, Ernst/Maihofer, Werner/Vogel, Hans-Jochen (eds.): Handbuch des Verfassungsrechts der Bundesrepublik Deutschland, Berlin/New York, pp. 851–960

Fichtmüller, Carl Peter (1966): Zulässigkeit ministerialfreien Raums in der Bundesverwaltung, in: Archiv des öffentlichen Rechts 91, pp. 297–355

Fögen, Hermann (1969): Geld- und Währungsrecht, Munich

Fröhlich, Wolfgang (1983): Die währungspolitischen Instrumente der Deutschen Bundesbank und ihre Einordnung in die Regelungskategorien des öffentlichen Rechts, Diss. Würzburg

Füsslein, Peter (1970): Ministerialfreie Verwaltung, Diss. Bonn

Galahn, Gunbritt (1996): Die Deutsche Bundesbank im Prozeß der europäischen Währungsintegration, Berlin

Gaugenrieder, Carl A. (1961): Die rechtliche Stellung der deutschen Zentralnotenbank im Staatsgefüge in Geschichte und Gegenwart, Diss. Würzburg

Geiger, Helmut (1988): Das Verhältnis von Refinanzierungs- und Offenmarktpolitik, in: Ehrlicher, Werner/Simmert, Diethard B. (eds.): Wandlungen des geldpolitischen Instrumentariums der Deutschen Bundesbank, Berlin, pp. 129–42

Geisler, Rudolf P. (1953): Notenbankverfassung und Notenbankentwicklung in USA und Westdeutschland, Berlin

Gramlich, Ludwig (1980): Abschied vom 'vorverfassungsmäßigen Gesamtbild', in: Deutsches Verwaltungsblatt 95, pp. 531–8

Gramlich, Ludwig (1988a): Bundesbankgesetz, Währungsgesetz, Münzgesetz—Kommentar, Cologne *et al.*

Gramlich, Ludwig (1988b): Die Deutsche Bundesbank im Verfassungsgefüge des Grundgesetzes, in: Juristische Schulung, pp. 81–4

Gramlich, Ludwig (1989): Streit um die Mindestreserve, in: Zeitschrift für Bankrecht und Bankwirtschaft 1, pp. 201–09

Gramlich, Ludwig (1994): Neu- oder Fehlentwicklungen im Währungs- und Bankrecht?, in: Die Verwaltung 27, pp. 361–89

Greitemann, Günter (1968): Die Verwaltung der Staatskassenmittel als Rechtsproblem im Schnittpunkt von Finanzrecht, Bankrecht und Recht der Währungspolitik, Munich

Häde, Ulrich (1991): Geldzeichen im Recht der Bundesrepublik Deutschland, Baden-Baden

Häde, Ulrich (1994): Ersatzpflicht der Bundesbank für gestohlene und beschädigte Banknoten—BVerwG, NJW 954, in: Juristische Schulung 34, 11, pp. 923–7

Häde, Ulrich/Hartmann, Uwe (1991): Der praktische Fall: Bundesbank und Europäische Zentralbank, in: Verwaltungsrundschau 37, pp. 404–12

Hahn, Hugo J. (1966): Rechtsfragen der Diskontsatzfestsetzung, Karlsruhe

Hahn, Hugo J. (1979): Aufwertung und Abwertung im internationalen Recht, in: Deutsche Gesellschaft für Völkerrecht (ed.): Fragen des Rechts der Auf- und Abwertung, Heidelberg/Karlsruhe, pp. 1–77

Hahn, Hugo J. (1982): Die Deutsche Bundesbank im Verfassungsrecht, in: Bayerische Verwaltungsblätter, pp. 33–7

Hahn, Hugo J. (1990): Währungsrecht, Munich

Hahn, Oswald (1968): Die Währungsbanken der Welt, 2 vols, Stuttgart

Hasse, Rolf H. (1992): Europäische Zentralbank—Europäische Währungsunion ante portas?, in: Aus Politik und Zeitgeschichte 42, pp. 23–32

Hentschel, Volker (1988): Die Entstehung des Bundesbankgesetzes 1949–1957, in: Bankhistorisches Archiv 14, pp. 3–31 (Part I), pp. 79–115 (Part II)

Hettlage, Karl M. (1956): Die Finanzverfassung im Rahmen der Staatsverfassung, Berlin, pp. 2–31

Hoffmann, Wolfgang P. (1969): Rechtsfragen der Währungsparität, Munich

Hoffmann-Riem, Wolfgang (1969): Rechtsprobleme der Aufwertung 1969, in: Der Betriebs-Berater 24, pp. 1374–82

Hoffmann-Riem, Wolfgang/Faber, Heiko (1971): Wirtschaftsplanung und Bundesbank-autonomie, in: Archiv des öffentlichen Rechts 96, pp. 443–6

Höfling, Wolfram (1993): Staatsschuldenrecht, Heidelberg

Höpker-Aschoff, Hermann (1956): Grundgesetz und Notenbank, Brief an Friedrich Klein zu dessen Rechtsgutachten, in: Wertpapier-Mitteilungen, Part IV 10, special supplement no. 7 to no. 37, pp. 12–17

Höpker-Aschoff, Hermann (1957): Bemerkungen des Bundesverfassungsgerichts zu dem Rechtsgutachten von Professor Richard Thoma, in: Jahrbuch des öffentlichen Rechts der Gegenwart 6, pp. 194–207

Hübner, Jürgen (1973): Ersatzansprüche bei rechtswidriger Heranziehung zum Bardepot?, in: Neue juristische Wochenschrift 26, pp. 353–7

Humm, Hubert (1988): Bankenaufsicht und Währungssicherung, Diss. Würzburg

Hüttl, Adolf (1972): Die Stellung der Deutschen Bundesbank im Verfassungsgefüge, in: Deutsches Verwaltungsblatt 87, pp. 64–6

Issing, Otmar (1975): Die Unabhängigkeit der Bundesbank, in: Klatt, Sigurd/Willms, Manfred (eds.): Strukturwandel und makroökonomische Steuerung, Festschrift für Fritz Voigt, Berlin, pp. 365–77

Issing, Otmar (1992): Unabhängigkeit der Notenbank und Geldwertstabilität, in: Deutsche Bundesbank: Auszüge aus Presseartikeln, no. 79, pp. 1–8

Issing, Otmar (1993): ⁵Einführung in die Geldpolitik, Munich

Issing, Otmar (1994): Geldmengensteuerung zur Sicherung des Geldwertes, in: WSI-Mitteilungen 47, pp. 682–690

Jochimsen, Reimut (1994): Perspektiven der europäischen Wirtschafts- und Währungsunion, Cologne

Kaiser, Rolf H. (1980): Bundesbankautonomie—Möglichkeiten und Grenzen einer unabhängigen Politik, Frankfurt a.M.

Ketzel, Eberhard/Köser, Reinhard/Pfisterer, Hans (1976): ²Die Notenbank, Stuttgart

Klein, Dietmar K. R. (1991): Die Bankensysteme der EG-Länder, Frankfurt a.M.

Klein, Friedrich (n.d. [around 1953]): Rechtsgutachten über die Vereinbarkeit sowohl der einstufig-zentralen als auch der zweistufig-dezentralen Konstruktion des Notenbank-systems mit dem Grundgesetz, Berlin

Klein, Friedrich (1957): Rechtsgutachten über die Frage, ob das Bundesnotenbankgesetz in der Fassung der Regierungsvorlage vom 18. Oktober 1956 der Zustimmung des Bundes-rates bedarf, in: Wertpapier-Mitteilungen, Part IV 11, pp. 1074–1088

Koenig, Christian (1993): Institutionelle Überlegungen zum Aufgabenzuwachs beim Euro-päischen Gerichtshof in der Währungsunion, in: Europäische Zeitschrift für Wirtschafts-recht 4, pp. 661–666

Könneker, Wilhelm (1973): ²Die Deutsche Bundesbank, Frankfurt a.M.

Kratzmann, Horst (1996): Über Anmaßung und Ohnmacht des Staates im Geldwesen, in: Der Staat 35, pp. 221–249

Kümpel, Siegfried (1992): Das währungspolitische Instrumentarium der Deutschen Bundes-bank aus rechtlicher Sicht, in: Wertpapier-Mitteilungen, Part IV 46, special supplement no. 1 to no. 3

Laband, Paul (1913): ⁵Das Staatsrecht des Deutschen Reiches, vol. 3, Tübingen

Lampe, Ortrun (1971): ²Die Unabhängigkeit der Deutschen Bundesbank, Munich

Lecheler, Helmut (1993): Das Subsidiaritätsprinzip, Berlin

Löwer, Wolfgang (1987): § 56 Zuständigkeiten und Verfahren des Bundesverfassungsgerichts, in: Isensee, Josef/Kirchhof, Paul (eds.): Handbuch des Staatsrechts, vol. 2, Heidelberg, pp. 737–848

Lück, Martin (1994): Die Politik der Bank of England: Whitehall entscheidet, in: Zeitschrift für das gesamte Kreditwesen 47, pp. 312–317

Lumm, Carl von (1926): Diskontpolitik, Berlin

Mangoldt, Hermann von (1953): Das Bonner Grundgesetz, Berlin/Frankfurt a.M.

Mangoldt, Hermann von/Klein, Friedrich (1974): ²Das Bonner Grundgesetz, vol. 3, Munich

Maunz, Theodor *et al.* (n.d.): Grundgesetz, Kommentar, Munich/Berlin, loose-leaf edition

Meyer, Georg/Anschütz, Gerhard (1919): ⁷Lehrbuch des Deutschen Staatsrechts, Third Part, Leipzig/Munich

Möschel, Wernhard (1972): Das Wirtschaftsrecht der Banken, Frankfurt a.M.

Müller, Klaus (1971): Die Änderung der Währungsparität als Problem der innerstaatlichen Kompetenzverteilung, in: Der Betriebs-Berater 26, pp. 726–729

Münch, Ingo von/Kunig, Philip (1996) (eds.): ³Grundgesetz-Kommentar, vol. 3, Munich

Papier, Hans-Jürgen (1994): § 18 Grundgesetz und Wirtschaftsordnung, in: Benda, Ernst/ Maihofer, Werner/Vogel, Hans-Jochen (eds.): ²Handbuch des Verfassungsrechts der Bundesrepublik Deutschland, Berlin/New York, pp. 799–850

Pernice, Ingolf (1995): Das Ende der währungspolitischen Souveränität nach dem Maastricht-Urteil des BVerfG, in: Due, Ole/Lutter, Marcus/Schwarze, Jürgen (eds.): Festschrift für Ulrich Everling, vol. 2, Baden-Baden, pp. 1057–1071

Pfennig, Gero (1971): Die Notenausgabe der Deutschen Bundesbank, Berlin

Pfleiderer, Otto (1967): Die Notenbank im Spannungsfeld von Wirtschafts- und Finanz-politik, in: Interdependenzen von Politik und Wirtschaft, Festgabe für Gert von Eynern, Berlin, pp. 563–575

Pfleiderer, Otto (1968): Die Notenbank im System der wirtschaftspolitischen Steuerung, in: Kaiser, Joseph H. (ed.): Mittel und Methoden planender Verwaltung, Baden-Baden, pp. 409–427

Pfleiderer, Otto (1976): Die Reichsbank in der Zeit der großen Inflation, die Stabilisierung der Mark und die Aufwertung von Kapitalforderungen, in: Deutsche Bundesbank (ed.): Währung und Wirtschaft in Deutschland 1876–1975, Frankfurt a.M., pp. 157–201

Pohl, Rudolf (1982): Die Deutsche Bundesbank und die Kreditaufsicht, Diss. Freiburg i. Br.

Potacs, Michael (1993*a*): Die Wirtschafts- und Währungsunion, in: Schwarze, Jürgen (ed.): Vom Binnenmarkt zur Europäischen Union, Baden-Baden 1993, pp. 71–82

Potacs, Michael (1993*b*): Nationale Zentralbanken in der Wirtschafts- und Währungsunion, in: Europarecht 28 (1993), pp. 23–40

Prost, Gerhard (1966): Die Diskontfestsetzung der Deutschen Bundesbank, in: Neue juristische Wochenschrift 19, pp. 806–810

Prost, Gerhard (1968): Die Deutsche Bundesbank im Spannungsbereich anderer unabhän-giger Organe und Institutionen, in: Büschgen, Hans E. (ed.): Geld, Kapital und Kredit, Festschrift Heinrich Rittershausen, Stuttgart, pp. 110–126

Prost, Gerhard (1972): Wandlungen im deutschen Notenbankwesen, Munich

Prost, Gerhard (1974): Die Unabhängigkeitsfrage, der zentrale und neuralgische Punkt der neueren deutschen Notenbankgesetzgebung, in: Österreichisches Bank-Archiv 22, pp. 259–270

Prost, Gerhard (1976): Rechtliche Betrachtungen zum 100-jährigen Bestehen des deutschen Zentralbankwesens, in: Juristenzeitung 31, pp. 263–268

Püttner, Günter (1969): Die öffentlichen Unternehmen, Bad Homburg v.d.H./Berlin/Zurich

Reichsbankgesetz, vom 14. März 1875, in: Reichsgesetzblatt no. 15 (1875), pp. 177–189 (Reichsbank Act)

Reichsbankgesetz, vom 30. August 1924, in: Reichsgesetzblatt Part II, no. 32 (1924), pp. 235–246 (Reichsbank Act)

Reischauer, Friedrich/Kleinhans, Joachim (n.d.): Kreditwesengesetz, Berlin, loose-leaf col-lection

Rittershausen, Heinrich (1962): Die Zentralnotenbank, Frankfurt a.M.

Samm, Carl-Theodor (1967): Die Stellung der Deutschen Bundesbank im Verfassungsgefüge, Diss. Munich

Samm, Carl-Theodor (1984): Verfassungsgarantierte Bundesbankautonomie, in: Wertpapier-Mitteilungen, Part IV 38, special supplement no. 5 to no. 27

Sartorius II, no. 44: Übereinkommen über den Internationalen Währungsfonds, Munich, loose-leaf edition

Schäfer, Hans (1958): Die bundeseigene Verwaltung, in: Die öffentliche Verwaltung 11, pp. 241–8

Schelling, Friedrich Wilhelm von (1975): Die Bundesbank in der Inflation, Frankfurt a.M.

Schiller, Karl (1967a) in: Verhandlungen des Deutschen Bundestages, Stenographische Berichte, 5. Wahlperiode, 108. Sitzung, Bonn, 10 May 1967, p. 184

Schiller, Karl (1967b) in: Verhandlungen des Deutschen Bundesrates, Stenographische Berichte, 313. Sitzung, Bonn, 1 September 1967, pp. 4977

Schiller, Karl (1994): Der schwierige Weg in die offene Gesellschaft, Berlin

Schlesinger, Helmut (1988): Das Konzept der Deutschen Bundesbank, in: Ehrlicher, Werner/ Simmert, Diethard B. (eds.): Wandlungen des geldpolitischen Instrumentariums der Deutschen Bundesbank, Berlin, pp. 3–20

Schmidt, Reiner (1973): Grundlagen und Grenzen der Unabhängigkeit der Deutschen Bundesbank, in: Caemmerer, Ernst von (ed.): Xenion: Festschrift für Pan. J. Zepos, vol. 2, Athen, pp. 655–80

Schmidt, Reiner (1990): Öffentliches Wirtschaftsrecht, Allgemeiner Teil, Berlin et al.

Schmidt-Bleibtreu, Bruno/Klein, Franz (1994): [8]Kommentar zum Grundgesetz, Neuwied, Kriftel/Berlin

Schmidt-Preuß, Matthias (1977): Verfassungsrechtliche Zentralfragen staatlicher Lohn- und Preisdirigismen, Baden-Baden

Schönle, Herbert (1976): [2]Bank- und Börsenrecht, Munich

Schreiner, Heinrich (1991): Bundesbankstruktur und Europäische Zentralbank, in: Zeitschrift für das gesamte Kreditwesen 44, pp. 612–14

Schuppler, Edith (1962): Die Unabhängigkeit der Notenbank, Vienna

Schuster, Leo (1967): Zentralbankpolitik und Bankenaufsicht in den EWG-Staaten, Cologne/ Opladen

Seeck, Horst/Steffens, Gernot (1979): [4]Die Deutsche Bundesbank, Düsseldorf

Siebelt, Johannes (1988): Der juristische Verhaltensspielraum der Zentralbank, Diss. Würzburg

Siegert, Werner (1963): Währungspolitik durch Seelenmassage? Frankfurt a.M.

Spindler, Joachim von/Becker, Willi/Starke, O.-Ernst (1973): [4]Die Deutsche Bundesbank, Grundzüge des Notenbankwesens und Kommentar zum Gesetz über die Deutsche Bundesbank, Stuttgart et al.

Starck, Christian (1973): Der Kreditbegriff und der Verhältnismäßigkeitsgrundsatz im Bardepotrecht, in: Der Betriebs-Berater 28, pp. 1607–12

Starke, O.-Ernst (1957): Die Stellung der Notenbank im Staatsgefüge, in: Wertpapier-Mitteilungen, Part IV 11, pp. 75–94

Starke, O.-Ernst (1977): Verfassungswidrigkeit der Aufgabenstellung der Bundesbank?, in: Wertpapier-Mitteilungen, Part IV 31, pp. 3–15

Stern, Klaus (1984/1980): Das Staatsrecht der Bundesrepublik Deutschland, [2]vol. 1 Munich, vol. 2 Munich

Stern, Klaus/Schmidt-Bleibtreu, Bruno (1990–1) (eds.): Verträge und Rechtsakte zur Deutschen Einheit, vols 1–3, Munich

Stern, Klaus/Münch, Paul/Hansmeyer, Karl-Heinrich (1972): [2]Gesetz zur Förderung der Stabilität und des Wachstums der Wirtschaft (Stabilitätsgesetz), Kommentar, Stuttgart et al.

Steuer, Werner (1970): Mehr Vollmacht für die Deutsche Bundesbank!, in: Wirtschaftsdienst 50, pp. 292–6

Stober, Rolf (1996): [10]Wirtschaftsverwaltungsrecht, Stuttgart et al.

Stoffers, Erich (1974): Die europäischen Notenbanken und die währungspolitische Zusammenarbeit in der Europäischen Gemeinschaft, in: Regul, Rudolf/Wolf, Herbert (eds.): Das Bankwesen im größeren Europa, Baden-Baden, pp. 105–12

Strickrodt, Georg (1952): Verfassungsgarantierte Währung, in: Zeitschrift für das gesamte Kreditwesen 5, pp. 533–6

Studt, Detlef (1992): Rechtsfragen einer europäischen Zentralbank, Diss. Erlangen, Nürnberg

Szagunn, Volkhard/Wohlschieß, Karl (1986): 4Gesetz über das Kreditwesen, Stuttgart *et al.*

Tettinger, Peter J. (1980): Rechtsanwendung und gerichtliche Kontrolle im Wirtschaftsverwaltungsrecht, Munich

Tettinger, Peter J. (1982): Überlegungen zu einem administrativen 'Prognosespielraum', in: Deutsches Verwaltungsblatt 97, pp. 421–33

Thomas, Karl (1991): Der Bund errichtet eine Währungs-Notenbank, in: Zeitschrift für das gesamte Kreditwesen 44, pp. 614–16

Tietmeyer, Hans (1994): Geldpolitik in europäischer Verantwortung, in: Deutsche Bundesbank: Auszüge aus Presseartikeln, no. 4, pp. 1–5

Tomuschat, Christian (1970): Die Aufwertung der Deutschen Mark, Cologne/Berlin

Tuchtfeldt, Egon (1971): Moral Suasion in der Wirtschaftspolitik, in: Hoppmann, Erich (ed.): Konzertierte Aktion, Frankfurt a.M., pp. 19–68

Uhlenbruck, Dirk (1968): Die verfassungsmäßige Unabhängigkeit der Deutschen Bundesbank und ihre Grenzen, Munich

Veit, Otto (1969): 3Grundriß der Währungspolitik, Frankfurt a.M.

Waechter, Kay (1994): Geminderte demokratische Legitimation, Berlin

Wagenhöfer, Carl (1957): Der Föderalismus und die Notenbankverfassung, in: Seidel, Hanns (ed.): Festschrift zum 70. Geburtstag von Dr. Hans Ehard, Munich, pp. 97–122

Weber, Albrecht (1994): Die Wirtschafts- und Währungsunion nach dem Maastricht-Urteil des BVerfG, in: Juristenzeitung 49, pp. 53–60

Weikart, Thomas (1992): Geldwert und Eigentumsgarantie, Baden-Baden

Weikart, Thomas (1993a): Die Änderung des Bundesbank-Artikels im Grundgesetz im Hinblick auf den Vertrag von Maastricht, in: Neue Zeitschrift für Verwaltungsrecht 12 (1993), pp. 834–41

Weikart, Thomas (1993b): Währungsrecht im Wandel—Die jüngsten Änderungen des Bundesbankgesetzes, in: Kredit und Kapital 26 (1993), pp. 608–46

Weiland, Gerd (1967): Regelungskompetenzen der Deutschen Bundesbank, Diss. Hamburg

Wiesner, Herbert (1992): 9Öffentliche Finanzwirtschaft, vol. 1, Heidelberg

Wilmer, Lothar (1975): Die Politik der 'Moral Suasion' der Deutschen Bundesbank, in: Staats- und Kommunal-Verwaltung 21, pp. 340–1

Wittmann, Walter (1977): 2Finanzwissenschaft, Fourth part, Stuttgart/New York

Woll, Artur/Vogl, Gerald (1976): Geldpolitik, Stuttgart

IV. Public Finance and the Central Bank

By Wolfgang Kitterer

1. Introduction

In a social market economy, the economic process is dominated by the autonomous activities of private households and enterprises. They react to price signals emanating from the market, which—if competition is perfect—ensures an optimum match between the supply of goods and services on the one hand, and demand, and thus the needs of the sovereign consumer, on the other.

Admittedly, the smooth functioning of such an economic system is not possible without an organizational and institutional framework, for which the state is largely responsible. It creates the environment (the rule of law, property rights, the liability principle, freedom of trade and of contract, regulation of competition, etc.) in which the economic process can develop efficiently with the minimum of disturbance. Over and above this more general function of the state, the task of the fiscal policy element of general economic policy is:

- to define the scope and structure of the services to be financed by the public sector budgets. One of the macroeconomic results of this is the government spending ratio, i.e. the ratio of public expenditure to gross domestic product (GDP), which may be regarded as the share of macroeconomic resources claimed for the state by the political executive;
- to adjust the distribution of the factor income resulting from the market process through taxes and public sector spending, so that it corresponds to socio-political notions of the equitable, or at least acceptable, distribution of income;
- to foster the stability of the economy in such a way that cyclical fluctuations in the degree of productive capacity utilization are avoided wherever possible, and economic growth is encouraged.

In practice, these problems cannot be solved in isolation by fiscal policy. Objectives may sometimes be mutually compatible or even beneficial, but in other cases they are contradictory. Other factors complicating the picture are that the results of government intervention in the workings of the

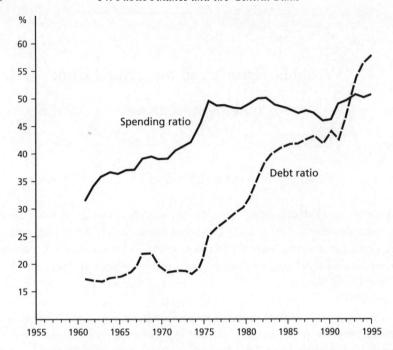

FIGURE 1: Government spending and debt ratios as a percentage of GDP
Source: Statistisches Bundesamt, Deutsche Bundesbank, Sachverständigenrat, Jahresgutachten, ongoing numbers.

economy and the operation of the instruments of fiscal policy cannot always be judged unequivocally, and that other public policy areas play a substantial role in meeting fiscal policy objectives. This is especially true for the central bank, whose main mission is to ensure monetary stability, and for the employers and trade unions who negotiate wages. The easier it is to distinguish between the tasks of the various economic policy actors, the clearer it becomes to identify who is responsible for what, making the crucial analysis of cause and effect more effective. On the other hand, allowance must also be made for the interdependencies between the various areas. There has been a change in public sector activities, although the limited scope of this essay means that only the broad outlines can be traced here. Against this backdrop, the essay will focus in particular on the relationship between fiscal policy and monetary policy, an issue which has frequently been the subject of varied and controversial analysis.

A review of the development of aggregate public sector budgets in recent decades highlights two particular aspects (shown quite clearly in Figure 1). On the one hand, the ratio of public spending (including that on social security) to GDP—the government spending ratio—rose sharply in the 1960s

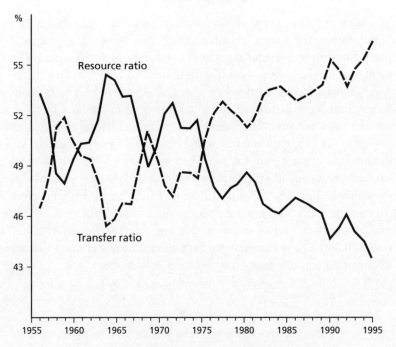

FIGURE 2: Public sector resource and transfer
ratios as a percentage of aggregate public sector spending

Source: Statistisches Bundesamt, Sachverständigenrat, Jahresgutachten, ongoing numbers.

and 1970s. The government spending ratio of the 1950s was still 30–35 per
cent. In contrast, it peaked at around 50 per cent in 1975 and 1982. In the
second half of the 1980s, it fell back to 46 per cent, but soon climbed above
the 50 per cent mark in the first half of the 1990s as a consequence of
the need to finance German unification. On the other hand, the rise in the
government debt ratio in the second half of the 1970s and the early 1980s,
as well as in the 1990s, was downright dramatic. Apart from an interim high
of around 22 per cent in 1967 and 1968, resulting from the Federal Republic's first economic crisis in 1966–7, the ratio of government debt to GDP
in the 1960s, and even in the early 1970s, was well under 20 per cent. It
then soared to over 40 per cent within a mere 10 years. In the second half
of the 1980s, strenuous efforts managed to consolidate the government debt
ratio at around 43 per cent, but the cost of German unification triggered a
massive climb to almost 60 per cent of GDP in only four years.

The development of aggregate public spending also highlights a structural
change (Figure 2). Until the mid-1970s, the ratio of public spending on
goods and services to overall public expenditure, i.e. the proportion denoting
the public sector's recourse to the resources of the economy (termed here

the 'resource ratio') hovered around a mean value of somewhat over 50 per cent, and hence the mean 'transfer ratio', the share of aggregate public spending flowing to private households and enterprises (including interest payments on public debt), was rather less than 50 per cent. But since 1975, the gap between the two ratios has widened appreciably. The transfer ratio has been climbing steadily, reaching 56 per cent in 1994. Over the same period, the resource ratio fell back to 44 per cent of total public spending.

It would be an exaggeration to suggest that these trends reflect the strength of fiscal policy management alone. They were due in part to a process of adjustment in response to critical economic and socio-political developments which frequently exposed the limits of the feasibility and credibility of government activity. There were phases of harmony—but more frequently of conflict—between what was desirable and what was actually achievable, not only while the government spending ratio and the debt ratio were rising, but also during the frequent consolidation processes.

2. Problems of budget surpluses in the 1950s

a) The fiscal policy environment

The 1950s were the era of the German 'economic miracle'. The government spending ratio was still relatively low. Economic debate revolved more around the underlying conditions needed for the social market economy, in particular the question of the liberalization of the movement of goods, services and capital, than around any adjustment to the market-driven distribution of income. Tax policy was geared towards cutting what were exorbitant tax rates by today's standards. In the 1953 'Minor' Tax Reform, for example, the top marginal income tax rate was cut from 95 per cent to 80 per cent, and the maximum average tax rate ('ceiling rate') from 80 to 70 per cent. The corporation tax levied on distributed profits was slashed from 60 to 30 per cent. In the 'Great' Tax Reform of 1954, the top marginal income tax rate was reduced to 63.45 per cent, the ceiling rate to 55 per cent, and the corporation tax rate charged on retained profits was lowered from 60 to 45 per cent.

The prime concerns of fiscal policy were to encourage enterprises to invest, to stimulate private households to accumulate assets, and to finance transport, education, and housing infrastructure. With the capital market of the day still underdeveloped, the only option open to enterprises was to rely on internal financing, i.e. to finance investments mainly from retained profits. This was therefore encouraged by tax breaks on retained profits and special depreciation charges. The risks inherent in this policy, however, were a lack of market control and a potential for misdirection of capital and disrupted growth, because enterprise decisions were too heavily oriented towards the tax concessions.[1] The tax privilege for retained profits was abolished as early as 1951.[2] The cut in the corporation tax rate for distributed profits to 30 per cent in the 'Minor' Tax Reform of 1953 was designed to encourage higher distributions and restrict internal financing. The 1958 tax reform reinforced this incentive. The corporation tax rate on retained earnings rose from 45 to 47 per cent, while the rate levied on distributed profits fell from 30 to 11 per cent. Increased company financing through borrowings (bonds) and equity financing (shares) was also designed to open up new investment opportunities to savers. On top of this, a stated aim of the government was to increase public sector investment financing through bond issues.[3] This was never achieved to the extent envisaged, however, first because of the need to nurse a capital market faced with an economic boom, and secondly because the strong rise in tax revenue rendered borrowing on a large scale superfluous.

At this stage, there was no attempt to operate an anticyclical fiscal policy —in the sense of Keynesian demand management—for a number of reasons. In the early 1950s, the theories of Keynesian economics were still largely unknown in West Germany, even among economists.[4] Moreover, the system of public finance and the budget legislation did not comply with the requirements of anticyclical fiscal policy. The division into an ordinary and an extraordinary budget allowed only 'project-oriented' credit financing 'for productive purposes' or for 'special needs', in other words solely for spending on investments. There was no provision for deficit spending for economic policy purposes, and this was even rejected out of hand by Fritz Schäffer, who headed the Federal Ministry of Finance between 1949 and 1957.[5] Neither was there essentially any real need for systematic, resolute demand management at the time. A global investment boom in the early 1950s bolstered the revival in the domestic economy. With growth rates

---

[1] Cf. Wissenschaftlicher Beirat beim Bundesministerium für Wirtschaft, 1973*a*.

[2] Cf. Bundesministerium der Finanzen, 1993, pp. 71f.

[3] Cf. Bundesministerium der Finanzen, 1994, p. 237.

[4] Cf. the recollections of Häuser, 1981, p. 2 and Timm, 1981, p. 21 on the impact of Fritz Neumark. Cf. also Schmölders, 1949, Schmölders, 1965, pp. 463–5, in particular refers to the precursors of fiscal policy in Germany.

[5] In his speech on the 1950 budget, Fritz Schäffer referred explicitly to the Basic Law: 'to use a modern term: "deficit spending" in German fiscal policy is prohibited by the Basic Law.' In his 1954 budget speech, he again protested against demands 'to adopt a policy of deficit spending, i.e. a policy of conscious disregard of the principle of a balanced budget'. Bundesministerium der Finanzen, 1992, pp. 81, 233.

high, incomes, savings, and capital spending rose largely in harmony. The state acted as a lender, particularly in the housing sector. Public sector budgets recorded overall financial surpluses. A famous example was the 'Julius Tower', the Federal budget surplus. Between 1953 and 1956, the Federal Minister of Finance deposited funds for building up the Bundeswehr in a special account at the Deutsche Bundesbank. These eventually reached DM 7 billion, but were quickly spent again in 1957 and 1958.

b) The 'Julius Tower' and monetary policy

In terms of fiscal policy, the 'Julius Tower' (named after the fortress in Spandau where the Prussian kings had stored their war treasures [translator's note]) was no success. On the contrary, it demonstrated a lack of coordination between fiscal planning and actual expenditure requirements. As unspent budget funds had to be carried along with the rest as 'unexpended budget balances' without being reappropriated, the management of public funds also became increasingly impenetrable. On the other hand, this budgetary policy did not clash seriously with monetary policy. In the 1950s, the central bank had its hands full coping with the conflict between external and domestic equilibrium. The rise in balance of payments surpluses had forced it to stabilize the D-mark exchange rate through heavy foreign currency buying. The result was a strong inflow of liquidity, which led to domestic inflationary symptoms, particularly during the cyclical upturn between the end of 1954 and early 1956. The Deutsche Bundesbank's attempt to use interest rate policy to stop the high level of liquidity overheating the domestic economy could not be a long-term success, because with lower interest rates abroad, rising German rates stimulated capital imports. In this situation, the liquidity skimmed off by the public sector budget surpluses actually supported the monetary objectives. Although the rapid dismantling of the 'Julius Tower' in 1957–8 led to an unwanted abundance of liquidity, it happened as the economy was slowing down.[6] Neither did the liquidation of government cash balances during the 1958/9 budget year have any expansionary impact on the domestic economy, as they were used primarily to settle foreign obligations.[7]

The creation of public sector budget surpluses and the expenditure of the budget funds deposited in the 'Julius Tower' were not motivated by economic policy considerations. In view of the balance of payments surpluses,

---

[6] Cf. Schlesinger, 1976, pp. 593f.

[7] Cf. Wissenschaftlicher Beirat beim Bundesministerium für Wirtschaft, 1973*d*, especially pp. 368f.

economic policy was driven more by tariff policy means. During the 1956 boom, several tariff reductions were implemented in rapid succession to take the strain off the domestic economy and bolster imports.[8] However, Schäffer's departure after the 1957 elections was followed by a reversal of fiscal policy. Franz Etzel, his successor at the Federal Ministry of Finance, was aware of the need for the public sector to orient itself more strongly to the economy as a whole. He was convinced that, by pursuing an active fiscal policy, the government would have a greater opportunity to safeguard overall economic equilibrium, and in particular to limit the extent and the impact of flagging economic activity.[9]

c) The failure of anticyclical fiscal policies during booms

The problem in the years that followed, however, was that of using surplus revenue to restrain an overheated economy and support the Bundesbank's efforts to stabilize the equilibrium of the domestic economy. The Economic Advisory Councils at the economics and finance ministries had already drafted recommendations on this point in 1956.[10] However, it proved impossible to harmonize monetary and fiscal policies, although this was urged publicly on several occasions by the Deutsche Bundesbank. In the summer of 1959, 'when it was quite evident that the economy was swinging towards a questionable boom', it had 'forcefully drawn attention to the need for an "anticyclical" policy, and in particular recommended measures to cool down the most "overheated" sector of the economy by cutting back public sector construction spending'.[11] Furthermore, it gave notice that its restrictive monetary measures in September 1959 should be interpreted as a warning signal to the public sector 'that it too should institute an anticyclical economic policy to help avoid any further substantial tightening of credit policy'.[12] Finally, the Central Bank Council passed a resolution in November 1959 urging fiscal policy makers to create revenue surpluses in this phase of high economic activity.[13] In September 1960, Bundesbank President Karl Blessing wrote to Federal Chancellor Konrad Adenauer, warning about inflationary trends and urging fiscal restraint during the election year 1961.[14]

[8] Cf. Bundesministerium der Finanzen, 1993, pp. 118, 121, 129.
[9] Cf. Bundesministerium der Finanzen, 1994, pp. 58f.
[10] Cf. Wissenschaftlicher Beirat beim Bundesministerium für Wirtschaft, 1973c, especially Section V: Fiscal Policy.
[11] Deutsche Bundesbank, Geschäftsbericht 1959, p. 2.
[12] Deutsche Bundesbank, Geschäftsbericht 1959, p. 35.
[13] Cf. Bundesministerium der Finanzen, 1993, p. 139.
[14] Cf. corresponding reference in: Bundesministerium der Finanzen, 1994, p. 32.

Despite these clear indications, the Federal Minister of Finance was unwilling to follow the proposals. A number of fiscal policy measures were instituted in July 1960 to check excess economic activity, with restrictions placed on declining-balance depreciation and the high depreciation allowances for residential property.[15] But in his 1961 budget speech in September 1960, Etzel was forced to admit that the large, fixed expenditure blocks meant that the degree of policy flexibility in the Federal budget was 'not very great. Calls to cut public sector spending in a boom, and at the same time to lodge additional tax revenue with the central bank as part of a deliberate policy of surplus accumulation, ignore the hard and immutable reality of the situation.'[16] In any case, he also ruled out any additional anticyclical immobilization of budget surpluses through tax increases.[17]

3. Changes and reforms in the 1960s

The 1960s saw many changes and reforms to the status of fiscal policy in the economy. Although the reasons for this had begun to emerge in the previous decade, they resulted in statutory and constitutional regulations only in the second half of the 1960s. The major fiscal policy reform projects in the 1960s included:

- the budget reform;
- the 'Great' Fiscal Reform;
- the statutory codification of anticyclical fiscal policy.

a) The road to budgetary reform

During the first 20 years after the Second World War, budget management by the Federal and Länder authorities was based mainly on the old 1922 Reich Budget Code. However, it soon emerged that this was unable to cope with the requirements of modern budgets. Merely appropriating budget items and classifying income and expenditure by administrative responsibil-

---

[15] Cf. Bundesministerium der Finanzen, 1993, p. 143.

[16] Bundesministerium der Finanzen, 1994, p. 217. The potential for an anticyclical fiscal policy was therefore viewed sceptically in the government's financial report for the 1961 budget. Cf. Bundesministerium der Finanzen, 1961.

[17] Bundesministerium der Finanzen, 1994, p. 249 and Bundesministerium der Finanzen, 1961, pp. 92f.

ities was neither adequate to ensure the clarity of political goals made necessary by the growing scope of public sector activities, nor could it in any
way satisfy the growing standards of interpretation required by economic
analysis, in particular for the implementation of an anticyclical fiscal policy.
The obscure administration of repeated carry-forwards of unexpended budget appropriations, which had reached more than DM 10 billion by 1959,[18]
undermined confidence in the government's ability to keep a grip on public
finance. Misuse of the division into ordinary and extraordinary budgets, a
practice which had become entirely arbitrary, contravened the need for
budget management transparency and made the prudent control of public
borrowing an impossible task.[19]

Public sector activities expanded into many areas of social policy and the
public sector accounted for an increasing share of the national product,
accompanied by a blurring of the boundaries of the revenue- and spending-
related activities at central, regional, and local levels. At the same time, there
was both a desire and a need to iron out fluctuations in the economy by en-
hancing the influence of anticyclical fiscal policy. The combination of these
factors served to highlight the lack of budgetary and fiscal coordination between Federal, Länder, and local authorities. In the final analysis, there was
no medium-range budgetary planning. This was a defect which could still
be tolerated during the surpluses of the 'economic miracle' era, but which
soon led to public finance taking a critical turn in the first half of the 1960s.
Despite certain structural crises, for instance in coal mining and the textile
industry,[20] economic growth was still high then, although running at a
slower rate than in the preceding years. The first signs of creeping inflation,
with prices edging up at 2–3 per cent, were registered with growing alarm.
But it proved to be increasingly difficult to steer the expansion in spending
on to a manageable course.[21] As Figure 1 illustrates, the government spending ratio rose appreciably. The Federal Social Assistance Act had been passed
in 1961, as had the rules instituting statutory continued payment of wages
during illness. These were followed by improved social security benefits,
as well as increases in child benefit, 'war victims' pensions and savings and
housing premiums.[22] The Federal Government instituted major structural
improvements to bring its financing of civil service pay into line with the

[18] Cf. Adami, 1970, pp. 61f.
[19] Cf. Dreißig, 1969, especially p. 16.
[20] Cf. Bundesministerium der Finanzen, 1995a, pp. 19, 152.
[21] Cf. the references by former Federal Finance Minister Dahlgrün to the increasing
narrowing of budgetary room for manoeuvre, Bundesministerium der Finanzen, 1995a, p.
225.
[22] Bundesministerium der Finanzen, 1995a, pp. 24–7.

changes already made by the Länder.[23] When the Federal Government was unexpectedly faced with additional expenditure for the Federal Railways, the coal mining industry and for foreign exchange offset requirements, coupled with shortfalls in tax receipts resulting from the 1964 and 1965 tax amendment laws and the improved social security benefits it had approved for election year 1965, it was forced to pass a 'Balanced Budget Act' at the end of 1965—three months after the national elections—which deferred spending already stipulated by law. But this was not enough to consolidate the budget. The sharp downturn in the economy which emerged in 1966 only exacerbated the budget crisis. When urgent retrenchment measures had to be taken in the autumn of 1966, but spending cuts and the reduction of tax concessions no longer appeared sufficient to keep the budget deficit within acceptable limits, the coalition partner FDP vehemently opposed tax increases to balance the budget and its ministers resigned. The Small Coalition ended one month later with the resignation of Chancellor Erhard. The Grand Coalition between the CDU/CSU and the SPD under Kurt Georg Kiesinger took office on 1 December. A few days later, on 8 December 1966, the Bundestag passed two further laws to consolidate the budget: the Financial Planning Act, which revised or deferred Federal subsidies for statutory pension schemes, transferred the maternity allowance to the unemployment insurance scheme, and reduced training allowances, and the Tax Amendment Act, which restricted the tax deductibility of journeys between home and workplace, cut savings promotion schemes, and increased mineral oil tax. Tobacco tax was increased in a second 1966 Tax Amendment Act. Although West Germany went through its first severe economic crisis in 1967 and the government instituted an expansionary, anticyclical fiscal policy (which will be analysed in greater detail below), it had to take further measures at the end of 1967 to balance the budget. The Bundestag passed the Second 1967 Tax Amendment Act in December. Tax concessions for the banking industry were reduced. For the first time, a 3 per cent surcharge on income and corporation tax was levied. The Finance Amendment Act adopted on the same day imposed overall spending limits and incorporated spending cuts in 36 laws to this end.[24]

Together with some constitutional amendments and the 1967 Stability and Growth Act, the 1969 budget reform created the key formal conditions for eliminating the weaknesses in the traditional public budget system,

[23] Cf. Bundesministerium der Finanzen, 1995a, pp. 137–9, 157. Despite the difficult budgetary situation, such structural improvements, i.e. 'a phased further increase of salaries and benefits and a substantial improvement in establishments' were agreed in 1965. Bundesministerium der Finanzen, 1995a, p. 253.

[24] Cf. Bundesministerium der Finanzen, 1993, p. 180.

improving the public sector's ability to exercise its function of helping shape economic and social policy.[25] The Budget Principles Act laid down common principles of budget law for the Federal Government and the Länder. Along lines similar to article 109 para. 2 of the Basic Law (the Federal German constitution) and article 1 of the Stability and Growth Act, it obliged the Federal and Länder authorities to 'have due regard to the requirements of overall economic equilibrium' when preparing and implementing their budgetary plans. The division into ordinary and extraordinary budgets was abolished and replaced by the provision of article 115 of the Basic Law, under which income from borrowings could not exceed the total spending on investments appropriated in the budget, with the concept of investment defined very narrowly.[26] The tiresome phenomenon of unexpended budget balances was eliminated by the introduction of the cash principle. Since then, expenditure can only be appropriated which will actually fall due and thus be expended in the respective budget year. Expenditure items no longer required expire, and must be reappropriated if necessary. The value of the economic and political information contained in the budget was enhanced by the introduction of a financing summary and an object classification system arranged by economic categories, as well as by a function classification plan arranged by functional areas. The Federal Government and the Länder were obliged to base their budgets on five-year plans. A Fiscal Planning Council was also established. Under the chairmanship of the Federal Minister of Finance, it draws up recommendations for the coordination of fiscal planning by all national, regional, and local authorities, and proposes the main objectives of public sector activities to meet the needs of the economy as a whole.

b) Fiscal reform: between unitarianism and federalism

Closer coordination of the public finance activities of public authorities at all levels also appeared necessary in other respects. In particular, this involved the fiscal equalization system, as originally envisaged in the Basic Law of the Federal Republic and already fundamentally revised in 1955. The division of functions originally set down in the Basic Law in a compromise between the unitary and the federal organization of the state appeared to be governed adequately and in sufficient detail. In contrast, the allocation of administrative responsibilities and (financing) burdens between the Federal

[25] Cf. on the budget law reforms of article 109 e.g. Piduch, 1996, Chap. 2: 'Verfassungsrechtliche Grundlagen', pp. 3–18.
[26] Cf. Friauf, 1990, pp. 342–5.

Government and the Länder was largely unregulated and uncertain. In the course of time, this situation produced a steadily expanding system of mixed financing—and chronic controversy because of the growing influence of the central government—even in those areas for which the Länder clearly enjoyed administrative and fiscal responsibility.[27] 'In this way, the first two decades governed by the Basic Law had seen the widespread proliferation of Federal Government financing of Länder functions.'[28]

The major fiscal reform in 1969 made allowance for the need to clarify these circumstances by anchoring a clear link between responsibility for functions and financing through the provision in article 104a para. 1 of the Basic Law: 'the Federation and the Länder shall separately meet the expenditure resulting from the discharge of their respective tasks'—the 'connexity principle'—and codified a catalogue of Länder functions which could be co-financed by the Federal Government—joint activities (Gemeinschaftsaufgaben), financial benefits legislation, financial support, war-induced burdens, and subsidies for social security burdens—as an explicit exception to the connexity principle. However, the *zeitgeist* which dominated this approach already contained an inherent inconsistency. On the one hand, the Länder were to retain their independence and responsibility for their own affairs—indeed, the constitutional reform was designed to restore to them what had previously been lost. On the other hand, the efforts to achieve a uniform standard of living and reinforce the influence of the national authorities were unmistakable.[29] It will therefore come as no surprise that, in the final analysis, the major fiscal reform did not limit the influence of the national government, and neither did it bring the Länder any closer to their goal of greater autonomy. Although the problems of growing interdependence in the system of 'cooperative federalism' were soon recognized,[30] it was not until the 1980s that more concrete measures were implemented to eliminate dual financing.[31]

c) *Conflicts between fiscal and monetary policy*

Politicians were very non-committal about anticyclical fiscal policy in the first half of the 1960s. One reason was that the expenditure policies they

---

[27] Cf. Pagenkopf, 1981, pp. 199–203.

[28] Vogel, 1990, p. 16.

[29] Cf. especially the report of the 'Troeger Committee', whose preliminary work had a major influence on the 1969 fiscal reform: Kommission für die Finanzreform, 1966.

[30] Hesse, 1978; Scharpf *et al.*, 1976, 1977.

[31] Cf. Frey, 1988, pp. 30–2; Wendt, 1990, pp. 1080–3.

imposed on the public sector were increasingly unmanageable, with spending cuts difficult to push through during an economic boom. The Federal Government certainly instituted measures to spread investments over longer periods, block construction spending and abandon the liquidation of unspent budget balances; it also tried to implement a budget to meet the needs of the business cycle.[32] But more far-reaching proposals by economists to issue a compulsory tax loan and freeze the liquid receipts[33] had no chance of being implemented, perhaps because the unhappy memories of the 'Julius Tower' in the 1950s made the politicians reluctant to create new surpluses.[34] However, other measures adopted by the government were hardly designed to support the economy. In June 1964, despite rising inflationary tensions, the Bundestag voted for enhanced depreciation allowances for buildings, followed in November by tax relief measures through changes to the income tax tariff to the tune of DM 3.5 billion.[35]

The government's procyclical behaviour proved to be a heavy burden on the economy in 1965. At almost 4 per cent, the rate of inflation reached a shocking high for the times (Figure 3). Because public sector receipts recorded only a slight rise owing to the tax relief measures, but spending rose disproportionately at the same time, there was a substantial increase in the public sector borrowing requirement (Figure 4). The Bundesbank's restrictive money and credit policy—an attempt to restrain the upward price movement—coupled with increasing public sector borrowing, and culminating in the imposition of a 25 per cent investment income tax on interest from fixed-income securities held by non-residents (coupon tax) in March 1965 (designed to curb inflation imported through balance of trade surpluses in the same way as the 1964 tariff cuts motivated by economic policy considerations) brought the capital market to the verge of collapse.[36] The market only calmed down after the Federal Government had brought together the key public agencies—the Federal ministries, the special funds and the municipalities—for round table talks in autumn 1965 at the urging of

[32] Cf. Federal Finance Minister Rolf Dahlgrün's 1965 budget speech, in: Bundesministerium der Finanzen, 1995a, p. 199; cf. also pp. 52, 73, 119, and 153.

[33] Cf. Wissenschaftlicher Beirat beim Bundesministerium der Finanzen, 1974a, b; Jahresgutachten 1967/8, p. 209.

[34] Cf. Bundesministerium der Finanzen, 1995a, p. 52.

[35] The Economic Advisory Council at the Federal Ministry of Finance explicitly urged postponing these tax cuts for cyclical reasons. Cf. Wissenschaftlicher Beirat beim Bundesministerium der Finanzen, 1974b.

[36] The German government regarded the restrictive discount policy of the Bundesbank as the cause of the disturbances on the capital market, while the Bundesbank held the heavy rise in public sector bonds responsible for the slump on the capital market. Cf. Bundesministerium der Finanzen, 1995a, p. 53 and Deutsche Bundesbank, Geschäftsbericht 1965, pp. 15f., 21f.

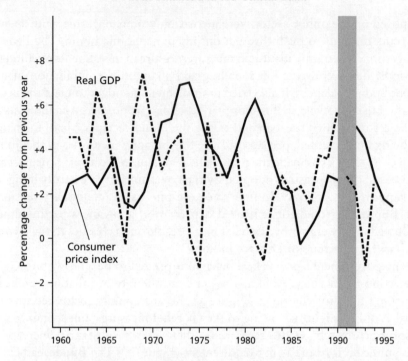

FIGURE 3: Inflation and economic growth

Note: Shaded area = enlargement of territory.

Source: Deutsche Bundesbank.

the Deutsche Bundesbank, and agreed to restrain and coordinate public sector borrowing demand.[37]

However, there was still no readiness to adopt a resolutely anticyclical fiscal policy. Finance Minister Rolf Dahlgrün's 1996 budget speech on 2 March 1966 is a perfect example of a verbose attempt to gloss over a politician's own powerlessness to act—or lack of will to coordinate stabilization policy—by pledging allegiance to certain fiscal policy principles, but as soon as the time came round for doing something concrete, passing the buck to other political authorities. In the preliminary skirmish about the points involved, the Minister of Finance started by emphasizing that the 'highest duty' of the Federal Government was 'to support the monetary efforts of the Deutsche Bundesbank through a *budgetary policy in line with the cyclical needs of the economy*',[38] and stated clearly that, among the 'pre-eminent

[37] Cf. Deutsche Bundesbank, Geschäftsbericht 1965, pp. 11f., 21f., 67f.
[38] This and the following quotes from the budget speech (including emphases) are quoted from: Bundesministerium der Finanzen, 1995a, pp. 238f.

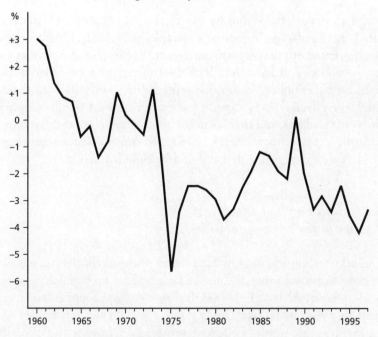

FIGURE 4: Public sector deficit ratio*

* Public sector financial balance as a percentage of GDP.

Source: Statistisches Bundesamt, Deutsche Bundesbank, Sachverständigenrat, Jahresgutach-ten, ongoing numbers.

guiding principles of the Federal Government's economic policy'—price stability and balanced economic growth—above all the goal of price stability had been harmed. Despite this, he shifted responsibility for overall economic stability to monetary policy: 'monetary imbalance always requires an excessive credit expansion. The aim must therefore be to restrict the scope for credit financing, which creates the basis for excessive demand. In the fight against general inflationary tendencies, this means that the emphasis must necessarily be on monetary and credit policy.' Covering all his flanks, he went on to remind the third partner in the domestic struggle for price stability of its duty by referring to a productivity-oriented wages policy, a topic much discussed at the time.[39] 'A policy of monetary and budgetary restriction would be ultimately futile if income growth in the economy did not remain within the limits set by productivity gains.'

[39] Cf. Wissenschaftlicher Beirat beim Bundesministerium für Wirtschaft, 1973*b*, *e*. The Advisory Council's opinions also contained a range of arguments against the application of a productivity-oriented wages policy, e.g. if the government spending ratio continued to rise.

In the face of such behaviour by the fiscal policy makers, it is understandable that the Deutsche Bundesbank complained of a lack of coordination and itself pointed out that despite the structure of its monetary policy instruments—which it regarded as 'modern'[40]—their limits are reached if they are opposed by fiscal policy: 'more than ever before, 1965 showed the degree to which the effectiveness of credit policy depends on the development of public sector budgets, and that it cannot compensate, let alone overcompensate, for the expansionary effect of high government deficits, reflected in a direct increase in aggregate demand and income formation.'[41]

d) The breakthrough of anticyclical fiscal policy in the 1966–7 recession

Anticyclical fiscal policy, unused until the mid-1960s for the reasons already given, rose to prominence during the first serious economic crisis in Germany in 1966–7. Although real GDP rose by 5.3 per cent in 1965 and 2.8 per cent in 1966, it fell back by 0.3 per cent in 1967 (cf. Figure 3). The unemployment rate trebled in 1967 from 0.7 to 2.1 per cent. Following the collapse of the Small Coalition between the CDU/CSU and the FDP in October 1966 owing to the efforts to balance the budget through tax increases, Kurt Schmücker, Minister of Finance in the CDU/CSU minority government, hinted at a potential reversal of budgetary policy by coming out in favour of a departure from the restrictive stance and a move towards increased spending on public sector investments, which he saw as a desirable economic policy move.[42] However, it was the Grand Coalition of CDU/CSU and SPD which quickly drafted a general 'Magna Carta' of anticyclical fiscal policy on the basis of the statutory groundwork for a stabilization policy prepared under Erhard's administration, although this had been largely oriented towards curbing the boom. Article 109 para. 2 was added to the constitution on 8 June 1967, stipulating that the Federal and Länder authorities must take account of the requirements of overall economic equilibrium in their budget management. It created the basis for the Stability and Growth Act, which obliges the Federal and Länder governments to implement their economic and fiscal measures 'in such a way that, within the framework of the market economy, they contribute concurrently to the stabilization of prices, to a high level of employment, and to external equilibrium with steady and adequate economic growth' (article 1).

[40] Cf. Deutsche Bundesbank, Geschäftsbericht 1965, p. 3.
[41] Deutsche Bundesbank, Geschäftsbericht 1965, p. 2.
[42] Cf. Bundesministerium der Finanzen, 1995a, pp. 279, 296.

Faced with growing indications of a cyclical downturn, the Federal Government approved in early 1967 special depreciation facilities for investment projects completed or ordered between 20 January and 31 October 1967, as well as a first cyclical investment programme (contingency budget) amounting to DM 2.5 billion. A second stimulus package (DM 5.3 billion) was approved in August 1967. The Deutsche Bundesbank announced its willingness to support the credit financing of the first stimulus package 'within the bounds of monetary feasibility' by further cutting the discount rate and the minimum reserve ratios.[43] Although the Council of Economic Experts advised the government in its 'March 1967 Special Report' to prepare a further contingency budget in addition to the capital budget already adopted,[44] the Deutsche Bundesbank expressed reservations in early 1967. In its view, the measures already instituted were sufficient to help the economy out of the recession, because combined with the stimulus package, the social security deficits and the high balance of payments surplus were also supporting economic activity.[45] It forcefully urged the need for a structural consolidation of the public sector budgets, i.e. a medium-term cutback in spending growth and in particular more restraint in government transfer payments.[46] Even its *de facto* support for the second stimulus package was tied to a condition that the revenue increases and spending cuts planned in the medium term would actually be achieved, preventing the deficits in 1967–8 from becoming a permanent feature.[47]

The final assessment of the success of anticyclical fiscal policy in the first major recession in the history of the Federal Republic certainly shows a mixed picture. In the opinion of the Economic Advisory Council at the Federal Ministry of Finance, the expansionary spending programmes and the resulting debt repayments corresponded 'largely to the governing principles of anticyclical fiscal policy'.[48] Looking back at the anticyclical fiscal policy of the period, Hansmeyer regarded it as perhaps 'the only successful phase to date of such a policy'.[49] In contrast, the assessment by the Council of Economic Experts in its Annual Report 1967/8 was critical. It argued that the overall impact of the public sector budgets was not expansionary,[50] and that the response of the Bundesbank's credit policy to the slowdown in

[43] Cf. Deutsche Bundesbank, Geschäftsbericht 1966, p. 17 and Deutsche Bundesbank, Geschäftsbericht 1967, pp. 5, 10.

[44] The Sondergutachten is reproduced in: Sachverständigenrat, Jahresgutachten 1967/8.

[45] Cf. Deutsche Bundesbank, Geschäftsbericht 1966, p. 18.

[46] Cf. Deutsche Bundesbank, Geschäftsbericht 1966, pp. 21f.

[47] Cf. Deutsche Bundesbank, Geschäftsbericht 1967, p. 19.

[48] Wissenschaftlicher Beirat beim Bundesministerium der Finanzen, 1984, p. 4.

[49] Hansmeyer, 1981, p. 21.

[50] Cf. Sachverständigenrat, Jahresgutachten 1967/8, para. 171.

the economy was 'too little, too late'.[51] In terms of the concept of concerted action as envisioned at the time by the Council of Economic Experts, the grounds for the recession lay 'in the lack of any methodical coordination of credit and fiscal policy, and in the lack of an effective concerted approach between government authorities on the one hand, and non-governmental on the other'.[52] The consequences of this unfavourable combination of circumstances essentially provoked political intervention in support of the economy, and thus enabled Keynesian economics to make a final breakthrough in the form of demand management.

Both the recession and its ramifications for public sector debt were soon surmounted. A cyclical upturn emerged at the end of 1967 and continued through 1968, with prices staying largely stable (cf. Figure 3). The government debt ratio, which had peaked at just on 22 per cent of GDP in 1967–8 (cf. Figure 1) returned to 1965 levels (around 18 per cent) in the following years. However, one legacy of the recession was a sharp increase in the government spending ratio. The government's share of GDP, which major efforts had stabilized at around 37 per cent in 1965–6, rose by about two percentage points during the course of the recession and never returned to its original level. Hence there were at the time already signs that the notion that the importance of the public sector is bound to increase in a recession because anticyclical fiscal policies use additional government spending to compensate for the drop in private-sector demand, but that spending levels can be restrained when there is a return to full employment to the extent that the original government spending ratio is regained, is unrealistic; In other words, there must be doubts about the claims for the 'allocative neutrality' of an anticyclical fiscal policy,[53] even in a phase in which it is regarded as successful.

---

[51] Sachverständigenrat, Jahresgutachten 1967/8, para. 232.

[52] Dürr, 1983, p. 32. Oberhauser, 1976, p. 628, also holds that the quicker application of monetary and fiscal policy instruments could have effectively weakened the recession. The government of the day conceded that it 'was not the objective economic factors which necessarily had to cause a recession, but to a large extent the subjective forces of the political mood, of the general climate'. Strauß, 1969, p. 30. However, it also believed that the Bundesbank had a major hand in the recession. Accompanying the deterioriation in the climate were 'the measures of the Bundesbank which weakened all economic activity. Their severity and duration had an objective and subjective impact, even if contrary effects would have been vital to cool the economy'. Oberhauser, 1976, pp. 30f.

[53] Cf. Hansmeyer, 1981, p. 28. Even convinced Keynesians believed that the tax ratio should not rise in a growing economy, and that the debt ratio should tend to fall. Cf. Schlieper, 1983, pp. 82f. The fiscal policy makers too evidently assumed that in the tensions between medium-term objectives and cyclical flexibility, 'merely the time when targets are to be achieved should be postponed or brought forward, depending on economic policy requirements, without any fundamental changes to the objectives and the established priorities themselves'. Strauß, 1969, p. 95.

4. Growth and inflation in the early 1970s

a) Growing collective needs of the affluent society

The upturn and the establishment of anticyclical fiscal policies in the second half of the 1960s did nothing to dispel the politicians' fears that they would have to submit to the 'primacy' of a cyclically oriented fiscal policy. This ran counter to the self-image and self-assurance of fiscal policy and its makers, which was growing in parallel with the expansion of its functions. Both the Minister of Finance of the CDU/CSU and SPD Grand Coalition, Franz Josef Strauß, and his counterpart in the SPD/FDP government, Helmut Schmidt, held the view that the social needs of the affluent society in the areas of infrastructure services, redistribution, and social policy should not take second place behind cyclical management.[54] With a view to increasing the investment component of public sector spending, fiscal politicians followed a widespread trend in the academic and political discussion in the 1960s, during which the benefits of public infrastructural spending, particularly in the field of education, were increasingly presented as crucial for increasing the prosperity of society and for economic growth.[55] At the time a number of academic experts voiced the opinion that a rise in the government spending ratio from 40 to 50 per cent, and an increase in the current government deficit ratio to just on 8 per cent of GNP, was advisable.[56] The Federal Government was evidently willing to support this viewpoint, at least in broad terms. In its first multiyear fiscal plan (1967 to 1971) for 1969, 1970 and 1971, it budgeted a total credit volume (net borrowing) of DM 3.8 billion, but in its second fiscal plan, for 1968 to 1972, the estimated borrowing requirement for the same period rose to DM 10.8 billion,[57] almost tripling the public sector borrowing requirement. The prevailing view at the time was apparently that drawing on private savings for public sector borrowing was less damaging than tax financing.[58] Even after government debt had ballooned dramatically in 1974–5, the government only saw

[54] Cf. Strauß, 1969, pp. 5f.; Schmidt, 1972, p. 1516.

[55] Cf. e.g. Stohler, 1965; Jochimsen, 1996; Jochimsen and Simonis, 1970; Frey, 1972.

[56] Cf. the report on the study by Prognos AG commissioned by the Federal Chancellery and completed in 1969: 'Gesellschaftspolitische Grundlagen der längerfristigen Sicherung des wirtschaftlichen Wachstums'; in: Schröder, 1970, especially pp. 439–43.

[57] Cf. Strauß, 1969, p. 96.

[58] Cf. Strauß, 1969, p. 96.

a limited need for consolidation. However, this was to be achieved not by spending cuts, but by tax increases.[59]

Against this background, it is hardly surprising that the government spending ratio continued to rise. It had already grown from 33 to 37 per cent in the first half of the 1960s, and climbed to 39 per cent of GDP during the stabilization crisis in 1966–7. By 1973, it had grown a further three percentage points to 42 per cent of GDP. The debt-to-GDP ratio during this period remained largely stable at around 18 per cent (cf. also Figure 1), but this result was attributable less to firm budgetary commitments than to the 'automatic stabilizers', in particular the abundant tax receipts and social security contributions. The 1968–9 boom was only interrupted by a mild downturn in 1970–1. In the following two years, the economy boomed again, accompanied by strong signs of overheating. The consequence was an upward price tendency never experienced in the Federal Republic either before or after this period. The average annual rate of inflation, still at just on 2 per cent in the boom year 1969, had shot up to almost 7 per cent by 1973 (cf. Figure 3).

b) The distribution struggle hots up

A number of factors were, of course, involved in this development. The battle over income distribution had grown more intense: actual wage rises often exceeded 10 per cent, far outstripping the increase in labour productivity. The public sector gave a strong boost to this trend by permitting high wage rises and simultaneously expanding the number of its established posts. In 1971, the rise in the staff expenses of central, regional, and local authorities was an explosive 19 per cent. Average earnings rose by 15 per cent, following a 13 per cent rise in the previous year (1970).[60] And in early 1974, the public sector employers were the first in the wage round to settle, setting a clear precedent for pay settlements throughout the year with wage rises of 12.5 per cent.[61] The Bundesbank's hands were tied by developments on the balance of payments front. Despite the revaluation of the D-mark in October 1969, the abrupt 'floating' of exchange rates and the realignment in 1971, as well as a number of restrictions imposed on capital movements in 1972, it was unable to ward off speculative currency inflows and the effects they had on the money supply by increasing liquidity.

---

[59] Cf. references of the former Chancellor Helmut Schmidt, 1977, p. 37 in his government policy statement, Dec. 1976.
[60] Cf. Deutsche Bundesbank, Geschäftsbericht 1971, pp. 8, 15.
[61] Cf. Deutsche Bundesbank, Geschäftsbericht 1974, p. 14.

It has already been suggested that fiscal policy makers also played a major role in reinforcing inflationary trends. It was inevitable that they would come into conflict with the goal of price stability, not only because of their stated intention of drawing on an even greater share of the national product. It was also because the government's stabilization policy was a failure for other reasons. It is clear that the Stability and Growth Act did not create a sufficiently reliable set of instruments to implement a restrictive fiscal policy. Although spending freezes were imposed, anticyclical reserves were set up, declining-balance depreciation was suspended and caps were placed on new borrowing by public authorities at all levels, the Stability and Growth Act failed to take account of the income distribution component, because measures to safeguard demand management through incomes policy were supposed to be dealt with by the 'Concerted Action'. But because this failed,[62] the stabilization policy was forced to carry the weight of income distribution burdens. For example, it was politically impossible to implement the symmetrically conceived linear tax increases for all income groups envisaged in the Stability and Growth Act. Instead, the government gave preference to measures outside the scope of the Stability and Growth Act which either appeared to be neutral in terms of income distribution, such as a stability bond, or which avoided a negative distribution impact on lower income groups, such as a stability levy with income limits.[63] In the final analysis, the government's stabilization policy was no more than half-hearted. Suffering from pressure to do more about income distribution, and clashing with the government's pursuit of a higher public spending ratio, it was far removed from the anticyclical approach demanded by events.[64]

5. Hopes of, and undue demands on, monetary and fiscal policies (1973–82)

a) Fiscal and monetary policy under a floating exchange-rate regime

In March 1973, six EC Member States (Belgium, Denmark, France, Germany, Luxembourg, and the Netherlands), plus Norway and Sweden, came

---

[62] Cf. Kloten, 1976, pp. 685f.
[63] Cf. Hansmeyer, 1981, especially pp. 38f.
[64] For a more detailed analysis of this phase, cf. Hansmeyer, 1981, and also e.g. Kloten, 1976, especially pp. 662–6, 672f., 684f.

together to form a block floating system. The floating of the exchange rate and the subsequent switch to monetary targeting saw a paradigm shift in monetary policy which also affected the anticyclical fiscal policy. Safeguarded against external influences, the Deutsche Bundesbank was in a position to use monetary policy to stabilize the domestic price level far more effectively than before. To define its field of responsibility more precisely and achieve a clearer distinction between monetary and fiscal policies, the Council of Economic Experts proposed defining

- 'monetary policy in terms of its responsibility for the supply of money to the economy, i.e. responsibility for the expansion of the monetary base,
- fiscal policy in terms of its responsibility for the volume and structure of public sector spending, and for public sector revenue arrangements'.[65]

Although this allocation of responsibilities appears self-evident at first glance, it concealed an assessment of the potential applications of both policies, within the framework of the stabilization policy, which differed substantially from conventional concepts. The Council of Economic Experts explicitly dismissed the illusion that 'the state can furnish and maintain a "guarantee" of full employment'.[66] Moreover, certain weaknesses in the concept of demand management induced the Council to relieve fiscal policy in full of its stabilization function, at least during a boom. It argued that, in the majority of cases, previous economic cycles had been associated with inflationary tendencies, and that more frequent, restrictive fiscal measures would have been necessary to cool down the economy. But it was precisely in these situations that policy makers usually failed. Relieved of a function it could not cope with, fiscal policy should be given an opportunity to fulfil its other public tasks with a greater degree of consistency.[67]

The Council of Economic Experts was only able to support this curb on fiscal policy because its estimate of the efficiency of monetary policy was vastly more optimistic, at least in the longer term. In its opinion, the central bank should, in principle, abandon any short-term anticyclical management of the monetary base. Instead, it should pursue a medium-term quantitative monetary policy which would be impervious to the inflationary behaviour of the government or autonomous groups. It was also aware of the limitation that monetary policy could impose conditions—which might be necessary, but would rarely be adequate—to bring about a cyclical upturn. But to avoid any confusion in an impact analysis, in the deployment of stabilization pol-

---

[65] Sachverständigenrat, Jahresgutachten 1974/5, para. 399.
[66] Sachverständigenrat, Jahresgutachten 1974/5, para. 369.
[67] Cf. Sachverständigenrat, Jahresgutachten 1974/5, para. 398.

icy instruments and the scope of the Bundesbank's responsibility, the task of the Bundesbank should be to integrate into the management of the monetary base not only its own influences on the supply of money to the economy, but also all partial monetary impulses associated with fiscal policy measures, in other words to compensate, sanction or reinforce, depending on the economic situation.

Shielded from external influences by floating exchange rates as the economy now was, the interaction between monetary and fiscal policy was first put to the test when the economy fell into a recession under the impact of the oil-price shock in 1973–4. What followed was a deliberately coordinated approach. While the Bundesbank initially strove to counter rising prices by limiting monetary expansion, fiscal policy was supposed to help avoid an undesirable impact on employment by adopting a moderately expansionary course.[68] As the signs of recession worsened and unemployment threatened to rise above the one million mark, for the first time since the mid-1950s, the Bundesbank switched to progressive interest-rate cuts and liquidity policy measures to stimulate monetary expansion, while the Federal Government instituted several programmes to encourage employment, investment and growth.

Things did not go completely smoothly, though. Despite the high level of liquidity in the banking system, there were disturbances in the capital market. The downward trend in interest rates was interrupted when, in mid-1975, supplementary Federal and Länder budgets gave the impression that the public sector would add to its already sharply increased deficits.[69] The scope for budgetary manoeuvre had become so narrow, and future burdens threatened to take on such a proportion, that the Federal Government was forced a few months later, still in the depths of the recession, to impose austerity measures by means of a Budget Structure Act. Numerous cash benefit rules were cut back, unemployment insurance contributions were increased and a rise in value-added tax, tobacco tax, and spirit duty was announced for 1 January 1977. Although such measures might appear to be counter-productive from the viewpoint of an academic primer on anticyclical demand management, they certainly helped strengthen confidence in the sustainability of fiscal policy. At any rate, the coordinated economic policy of the Federal Government and the Bundesbank can be deemed successful to the extent that the recession bottomed out in mid-1975 and the economy started recovering in 1976.

But the price was high. Unemployment persisted at more than 4 per cent,

[68] Cf. Deutsche Bundesbank, Geschäftsbericht 1974, pp. 1, 18 and Sachverständigenrat, Jahresgutachten 1974/5, para. 323.
[69] Cf. Deutsche Bundesbank, Geschäftsbericht 1975, pp. 17–22.

a high level at the time. And inflation also stayed high during the upturn, only falling back to an average annual rate of close on 3 per cent when the economy started cooling off again in 1977–8 (cf. Figure 3). There was no prospect of any cyclical cut in public sector deficits or a reduction in the cyclical expansion of public sector activities. The government debt ratio climbed sharply because of the enormous deficits (cf. Figure 4). In 1973, it had been somewhat over 18 per cent. By the end of 1976, government debt accounted for 26.5 per cent of GDP. The government spending ratio rose by more than six percentage points over the same period, to around 49 per cent (cf. Figure 1). Together with the Bundesbank, academics were already urging the consolidation of public sector budgets and a fundamental revision of public sector operations.[70]

b) The search for new solutions after the first oil crisis

The persistent problems of overall economic management, a concept which had initially been greeted with great enthusiasm—the high inflation rates at the end of the 1960s and in the first half of the 1970s, rising unemployment, growing government deficits, the unsolved adjustment problems in the light of structural changes in the global economy (in particular as a result of the oil crisis)—engendered a feeling of helplessness and triggered a search for new approaches in many areas of economic research, as well as among economic and social policy makers. The fact that a range of central banks came round to the monetarist concept of medium-term monetary targeting was an admission that the stabilization of the supply of money to the economy was necessary, owing among other reasons to the complexity of monetary transmission mechanisms and theoretical ignorance of the short-term development of economic interdependencies.[71] An OECD report by eight international experts on the problems of demand management in view of the 'deterioration of performance regarding growth, employment and prices'[72] did not identify any new answers and did little more than recommend the

[70] Cf. Wissenschaftlicher Beirat beim Bundesministerium der Finanzen, 1988; Deutsche Bundesbank, Geschäftsbericht 1975, pp. 27f.; Sachverständigenrat, Jahresgutachten 1975/6, paras. 333–59 and paras. 424–32; Sachverständigenrat, Jahresgutachten 1976/7, paras. 221–7 and paras. 338–48.

[71] Cf. Sachverständigenrat, Jahresgutachten 1974/5, para. 374; Mayer, 1978, pp. 50–4. Of course it is not merely the uncertainty itself, but rather the resulting serious errors which make monetarists warn against attempting economic fine-tuning. Cf. especially Milton Friedman's references to the uncertainty about the natural interest rate and the natural unemployment rate; in: Friedman, 1970, Chap. 5, Section I.

[72] McCracken *et al.*, 1977, p. 12.

stronger medium-term orientation of demand management.[73] In the report, Robert E. Lucas—later to win a Nobel prize—registered 'a tone of sad resignation'[74] and noted in this context: 'in 1966, it seemed to many that we had one theory which could quantitatively link fiscal policy to economic performance with sufficient accuracy that it could be responsibly applied to policymaking.[75] In 1977, we know we have none.'[76]

Uncertainty reigned in many other areas as well. The Federal Government established a committee to investigate the causes of economic and social change.[77] With the report by the economic research institutes on structural change, it created a new instrument for the analysis of structural change in the economy, and in particular of the structural and macroeconomic impact of government intervention.[78] The government also established the 'Commission of Inquiry into Transfer Payments', whose job was to examine the complexities of the tax transfer system and elaborate proposals for improvement.[79] Although the depth and range of information and analysis were on the increase, there was still a lack of any consistent theoretical approach which could explain social change. As a result, it proved to be very difficult to derive a convincing stance for economic and fiscal policy.

c) Demand management shows signs of strain

The fact that the problems were obviously known did not prevent politicians from overestimating their ability to control the financial aspects of the programmes they thought they had to implement in the interests of their voters. Although the government spending ratio stayed almost unchanged at a high level, as shown by Figure 1, the debt ratio rose by a further three percentage points within three years (1976–9) to almost 30 per cent. By the end of the 1970s, it was 10 percentage points higher than in the middle of the decade. An attempt to finance the expansion of public sector budgets through tax increases (if, indeed, it was ever taken seriously) collapsed in the face of taxpayer resistance and conflicts with cyclical and growth policies. The German economy slowed down again in 1977. At the same time, the

---

[73] Cf. McCracken *et al.*, 1977, p. 12.

[74] Lucas, 1981, p. 264.

[75] Meaning Keynesian theory.

[76] Lucas, 1981, p. 267.

[77] Cf. Kommission für wirtschaftlichen und sozialen Wandel, 1977.

[78] Cf. Schmidt, 1977 and Gahlen, 1982. Cf. also Markmann, 1977 and Gahlen, 1978, on the regulatory policy problems of investment control, much discussed at the time.

[79] Cf. Transfer-Enquête-Kommission, 1981.

'locomotive theory' was the subject of international debate. This held that the countries in a strong current account position (in particular Germany and Japan) should operate a policy of additional deficit spending so that the rise in their imports and the consequent multiplier effects would revive the global economy.[80] Against this backdrop, the Federal Republic changed tack towards an expansionary fiscal policy. Together with the 'Programme of Future Investments', with a volume of DM 16 billion in 1978–81,[81] a range of tax relief measures and a decision to adopt additional stimulative measures costing up to 1 per cent of GNP[82] to bolster demand and improve economic growth—which the Federal Government hoped would enable it to comply with the commitments it had given at the Bonn World Economic Summit in July 1978—were a heavy strain on future budgets, although there were no signs of any medium-term consolidation concept.

Neither did monetary policy stick firmly enough to its anti-inflationary course. It is true that the Bundesbank pursued the concept of monetary targeting, at least in principle. However, the goal of price stability was not achieved, despite a drop in inflation. One cause of this was that the monetary policy instruments used did not always match the concept of monetary targeting. Another was that—again at variance with this concept—monetary policy occasionally tended towards a short-term anticyclical reaction.[83] A more consistent, more heavily medium-term orientation of the supply of money would have been much more effective in curbing inflation.[84]

When the second jump in oil prices occurred in mid-1979, the current account went into the red, the D-mark depreciated heavily, average annual inflation approached the 5 per cent mark again (cf. Figure 3), interest rates worldwide reached unusually high levels, and unemployment went above two million for the first time in post-war history. The need to consolidate public sector finances was now so urgent that there was little that economic policy makers could do. The deficits rose wildly as spending grew and tax revenues slumped, and the government debt ratio went up by a further nine percentage points to 39 per cent of GDP (cf. Figures 4 and 1) within the space of two years (1980–2). However, economists and politicians viewed its macroeconomic impact in a negative light, because producers and consumers were disposed to show restraint in the light of increasingly uncertain future prospects about government strains on the capital market, doubts

[80] Cf. e.g. OECD, 1977.
[81] Cf. Bundesministerium der Finanzen, Finanzbericht 1978, pp.74–6.
[82] Cf. Bundesministerium der Finanzen, Finanzbericht 1979, p. 68.
[83] Cf. Sachverständigenrat, Jahresgutachten 1977/8, paras. 175f. and paras. 403–15; Sachverständigenrat, Jahresgutachten 1978/9, paras. 133–9.
[84] Cf. simulation study by Neumann, 1981.

about public sector financial discipline and general economic developments.[85]

As it was frequently called on to do in recessionary phases, after the second oil crisis fiscal policy had to solve the conflict between effective consolidation in the medium term and short-term expansion, and again it failed. From the outset, the Bundesbank had warned against trying to relieve the burdens of adjustment resulting from the second oil-price shock by expanding growth, because this would merely postpone the vital transfer of resources.[86] In particular, consumption-related demands on the national product by private and public sector budgets should be deferred, and necessary government spending should be met by higher taxes.[87] The unusually high public sector deficits and the heavy current account deficit coincided with a restrictive monetary policy in the United States, which led to a steep rise in interest rates and an improvement in the US current account balance. Together with the hopes evidently pinned on US economic policy after Ronald Reagan's election as President of the United States, this strengthened the dollar and weakened confidence in the D-mark. The gradual devaluation of the D-mark faced the Bundesbank with a dilemma. On the one hand, lower interest rates would have been desirable for the domestic economy to stimulate domestic investment activity. On the other, the Bundesbank was unable to distance itself from the high level of international interest rates, and was also afraid that devaluing the D-mark would accelerate imported inflation. It therefore pursued a more restrictive monetary policy than would have been necessary if it had been oriented exclusively to domestic requirements.

To sum up, monetary policy did not receive sufficient support from a determined policy of fiscal consolidation directly after the second oil-price shock (1979–81) to safeguard the goal of price stability. The adjustment pressure which it created through higher interest rates would have been lower if it had not been forced to help deal with the burdens of its own past stabilization policy as well—the inadequate measures to counter the inflation potential in the latter half of the 1970s and the subsequent delay in the switch to a more restrictive policy.[88]

---

[85] Cf. Sachverständigenrat, Jahresgutachten 1982/3; 1967 Sondergutachten, para. 58; but cf. also the dissenting opinion of Krupp; in: Sachverständigenrat, Jahresgutachten 1982/3; 1967 Sondergutachten, para. 59 and the Recommendations of the Fiscal Planning Council on consolidation in: Bundesministerium der Finanzen, Finanzbericht 1982, p. 97.

[86] Cf. Deutsche Bundesbank, Geschäftsbericht 1979, p. 48.

[87] Cf. Deutsche Bundesbank, Geschäftsbericht 1979, p. 43 and Deutsche Bundesbank, Geschäftsbericht 1980, pp. 18f.

[88] Cf. Sachverständigenrat, Jahresgutachten 1982/3; 1967 Sondergutachten, para. 11.

6. Consolidation and coordination in the 1980s

a) The changeover to supply-side economics

Fiscal policy in 1982 was marked by the budget crisis, with the economy as a whole suffering from a high level of stagflation. Between 1979 and 1982, the public sector financial deficit rose from DM 36 billion to DM 53 billion (cf. also Figure 4), without this debt expansion having any positive effects on the economy as a whole: in fact, the reverse happened. The government spending ratio also rose appreciably. In 1982, it topped the 50 per cent mark for the first time in the history of the Federal Republic (cf. Figure 1). In addition, the interest burdens on public sector budgets grew from DM 24 billion to DM 44 billion within the space of four years. A reversal of budgetary policy, urged so often, appeared more pressing than ever. A further complicating factor was the desperate economic position of the country, a situation which could no longer be mastered by the standard instruments of stabilization policy. Although the current account deficits resulting from the second oil crisis had been eliminated, the national product recorded minimum growth in real terms in 1981. It declined by 1 per cent in 1982, the year in which the consumer price index rose by 5.3 per cent (cf. Figure 3). The anticipated revival of investment activity had not materialized. On the contrary, capacity utilization fell back even further. At 7.2 per cent, the unemployment ratio reached its highest level since the war.

The budgetary and economic crisis ended in a government crisis. In September 1982, Federal Minister of Economics Otto Graf Lambsdorff (FDP) presented his 'Concept of a policy to overcome poor growth and combat unemployment' (the 'Lambsdorff Paper'), calling in particular for a more growth- and employment-oriented budgetary policy, cuts in the 'welfare net' and a more business-friendly policy.[89] This concept triggered the switch from the SPD/FDP government to the CDU/CSU and FDP coalition under Helmut Kohl in October 1982.

The supply-side shocks caused by the oil crises, simultaneous sluggish growth, and high inflation rates, as well as the failure of demand management despite a sharp rise in the public sector deficits, all combined to force the abandonment of economic management in favour of regulatory policy, and the re-evaluation of the functions of fiscal policy as a component of a

---

[89] Cf. on the proposals by Federal Economics Minister Graf Lambsdorff: Lambsdorff, 1982.

supply-side economic policy.[90] Its creed was Say's Law, which lays down that supply creates its own demand; its way of proceeding was to eliminate all disturbances and distortions which interfere with the motivation of the economic actors to work, the evolution of competition, and the efficiency, adaptability, and stimulative effects of the market economy system of relative prices. Within this framework, the goal of fiscal policy should be:

- to cut government debt and forgo discretionary fiscal policy measures using budget deficits in recessionary phases. This is because experience shows that the growth in government debt during a downturn is not cut back in subsequent upturns, and that tax increases or spending cuts are ultimately inevitable. To avoid a procyclical fiscal policy, however, cyclically induced deficits must be tolerated.
- to reduce the government spending ratio (quantitative consolidation) because it unduly narrows the scope for profitable private sector output, and because resistance to the associated tax burden grows ever stronger.
- to redesign the structure of public sector spending so that it encourages growth (qualitative consolidation). To this end, the portion of public sector spending expended on consumption should be curbed, but public sector spending on productive investment activities should rise. In addition, there should be a reduction in the diversity of transfer payments, through which the public sector distorts the incentive mechanisms.
- to create a situation where taxes boost capital spending and economic growth. To prevent any disproportionate rise in taxes, inflation and growth-related tax burdens arising from nominal and real incomes growth in a progressive tax system must be offset by a corresponding adjustment to the tax rates. But the existing high levels of taxation must be cut in addition to future levels. This reduces the incentives for tax avoidance and the migration of economic activities to the shadow economy, and reinforces the performance incentives of the individual economic unit.

The concept of supply-side policies met with a mixed reception, both in academic debate and among politicians. A particularly contentious point was where consolidation was supposed to start, how far it could go, and the

---

[90] The Council of Economic Experts had already outlined the concept of supply-side economic politics in the 1970s. Cf. Sachverständigenrat, Jahresgutachten 1976/7, chap. 3. In particular in the 1980s, it explained and developed it further in almost all of its reports. The Economic Advisory Councils at the Economics and Finance Ministries had also dealt with the subject in detail. Cf. Wissenschaftlicher Beirat beim Bundesministerium für Wirtschaft, 1981, 1983; Wissenschaftlicher Beirat beim Bundesministerium der Finanzen, 1984, in particular section 3.4.1. For US supply-side policies, cf. Kurz, 1993.

extent to which demand stimulation could and should really be abandoned. In fact, it was not at all easy to appreciate how one component of the public sector financial deficit could trigger a cyclical stimulus, while another, 'structural' component had to be cut back because it obstructed the restoration of macroeconomic stability,[91] all the more because it was assumed that a third component of the very same deficit—classed as 'cyclically induced'— did not stimulate the economy, but neither should it be curbed or else demand throughout the economy would shrink. Other critics of supply-side economics viewed the concept as fundamentally—i.e. also in the medium term—too one-sided, and the consolidation as too far-reaching.[92] There were also sporadic voices which drew a parallel between the consolidation of the public sector budget and Brüning's fatal austerity policy.[93]

b) Consolidation between demand risks and stimulated supply

From all the conceivable combinations of demand risks and supply-side incentives, fiscal policy makers in the 1980s had to seek out solutions that were politically feasible. In the first instance, this involved cutting back the high public sector financial deficits, which not only put a strain on the capital markets, but also substantially tightened the scope of budgetary policy because of the high interest servicing obligations. A sustained economic upturn made their task easier. However, the path towards fiscal stability was long and hard, and provided a painful reminder that if the initial level is high, reducing credit financing by no means guarantees any corresponding reduction in the government debt ratio. Although the public sector deficit of DM 54.2 billion in 1982 was reduced to less than half within a relatively short period—to only DM 21.1 billion in 1985 (cf. also Figure 4)—the debt ratio during the same period climbed by a further three percentage points to almost 42 per cent (cf. Figure 1). Any talk in this context of the 'successful consolidation' in the 1980s really means no more than that a further rise in the debt ratio was prevented (but neither was it reduced).

Much better results were achieved in other areas. The government spending ratio, still at 50 per cent in 1982, was cut to just on 46 per cent by 1989, its lowest level since 1975. Admittedly, it would have been preferable to have achieved the qualitative consolidation described above as well as this

---

[91] Cf. Krause-Junk, 1983.

[92] Cf. e.g. Gerfin, 1983, and the regular minority vote of one member of the Council of Economic Experts during the 1980s.

[93] Cf. Neumark, 1985, pp. 31f.; cf. also the criticism of such a view in Borchardt, 1985, pp. 51f.

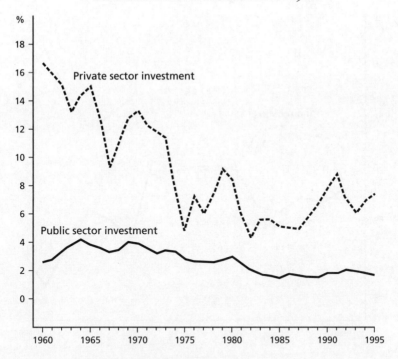

FIGURE 5: Private and public sector investment as a percentage of GDP
Source: Statistisches Bundesamt, Deutsche Bundesbank.

quantitative one, but this was not the case. As Figure 2 shows, the gap between the transfer and resources ratios in the national budget widened further. Following a slight drop in 1985 and 1986, the transfer ratio, i.e. the ratio of transfer payments to aggregate public sector spending, rose again in the second half of the 1980s. No appreciable change was evident in the area of public sector investments, which supply-side economics dictated would restrain the consumption-related component of public sector spending. Although the downward trend of the 1970s flattened out, the public sector investment ratio in the 1980s stabilized at a historically low level (Figure 5), in the same way as private sector investments did between 1982 and 1987.

At least some successes were recorded in terms of tax policy. The cut in the government spending ratio also saw a drop in the overall tax ratio. On the other hand, it proved to be much more difficult to restructure the tax system to stimulate growth by cutting consumer taxes. In 1982–3, there was a sporadic easing of corporate wealth tax and taxes on earnings and income. But as the recovery in the following years was driven primarily by exports

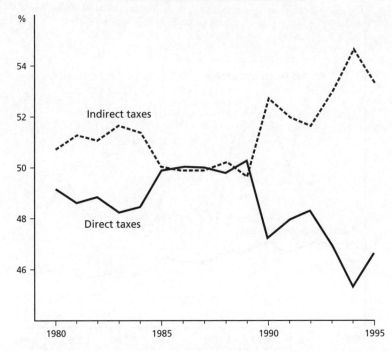

FIGURE 6: Direct and indirect taxes as a percentage of tax revenue
Source: Statistisches Bundesamt.

and—lagging behind—capital spending by enterprises, neither of which were subject to value-added tax, the share of indirect taxes actually fell, as shown in Figure 6.

Distribution and family policy objectives were the priority of the 1986/88 income tax reform, and only the 1990 Tax Reform Act brought a fundamental reform. The switch to a linear-progressive tax rate eliminated that component of the German income tax scale which imposed a steep progression in the middle-income bracket and was known as the 'middle-income bulge' because of the disproportionate rise in its marginal tax rate. The top marginal rate was cut from 56 to 53 per cent. The rate of corporation tax levied on retained profits was reduced from 56 to 50 per cent. Because a number of consumer taxes (mineral oil tax, tobacco tax, insurance tax, tax on natural and liquefied gas) had been increased in anticipation of the high volume of tax relief measures in 1989, a clear shift in the emphasis of the tax system towards indirect taxes was evident once the three-phase tax reform (1986/1988/1990) had been completed (cf. Figure 6). On the other hand, there had still been no far-reaching reform of corporate taxation.

c) The growing need for the international coordination of economic policy

Although the early 1980s were marked by a conflict between fiscal and monetary policy, the remainder of the decade saw largely harmonious co-ordination between the two policy areas. Fiscal and monetary policy makers instituted joint efforts to achieve consolidation. With its firm monetary targeting policy, the central bank contributed to a drop in the consumer price index, and price stability was actually achieved in 1986–7. However, the restoration of monetary stability was, to a large extent, a consequence of external influences. The revaluation of the D-mark intensified inter-national competitive pressure, and the falling prices of oil and other raw materials helped Germany to import stabilization.[94] When the Bundesbank switched to a more exchange-rate-oriented monetary policy in the second half of the 1980s and sanctioned an unreasonable expansion of the central bank money stock, the result was a growing inflation potential which drove up prices perceptibly in 1989–90.

The cause of the Bundesbank's external orientation was that, in contrast to the domestic coordination of monetary and fiscal policy, international coordination of economic policy in the 1980s was far less harmonious. After exchange rates had been floated in the 1970s, it emerged that the independence of individual countries' monetary and fiscal policies in a system of floating exchange rates was more heavily restricted than had at first been suspected. The reasons for this lay in part in the growing integration of the global economy and the increasing synchronization of cyclical trends, in part in the underestimated importance of exchange rate expectations and their impact on international capital movements. The result was massive fluctuations in real exchange rates, nominal exchange rate overshoots and 'J-curve effects' in the balance of trade. In the 1980s, a whole range of measures to coordinate monetary, exchange rate, and fiscal policy had therefore been proposed to enable a return to more stable exchange rates.[95]

A particular need for international cooperation resulted from the development of the US current account deficits and their repercussions for the dollar rate. During President Reagan's first period of office (1981–4), an expansionary fiscal and restrictive monetary policy initially proved successful for the US economy, reflected in a remarkable upward revaluation of the dollar.

[94] Cf. Sachverständigenrat, Jahresgutachten 1987/8, para. 236.
[95] An overview of these proposals and their assessment is contained in Willms, 1995, chap. 9; cf. also Sachverständigenrat, Jahresgutachten 1986/7, paras. 245–59; Sachverständigenrat, Jahresgutachten 1987/8, paras. 329–40.

But as the US budget and current account deficits grew steadily, and the rest of the world, and in particular Japan and Germany as well as the emerging Asian economies, recorded growing current account surpluses, and the sustained rise in the dollar rate became increasingly remote from the underlying negative economic data, the finance ministers and central bank governors of the top five industrialized nations forced a drop in the dollar rate through coordinated currency market operations.[96] The inevitable transition to consolidation in US economic policy at the start of Reagan's second administration (1985–9), coupled with the strongly expansionary but unsteady monetary policy of the Federal Reserve Board, sparked off massive uncertainty. On the one hand, confidence in the lasting success of US economic policy disappeared. This had seen the USA change from a traditionally major creditor country to the largest net debtor in the world. On the other hand, there were fears that a reversal of the high US budget and current account deficits would unleash a worldwide recession, and that excessive fluctuations of the US reserve currency could result in massive disruption of the currency and financial markets.

It was in such a situation that the USA called for stronger international coordination of economic policy.[97] To prevent recessionary trends in the global economy, it argued that countries running a surplus—in particular Germany and Japan—should pursue an expansionary monetary and fiscal policy. Additional external demand would accelerate the reduction in the US current account deficit and prevent the dollar from falling too heavily. At the same time, falling interest rates in the surplus countries could help the Federal Reserve Board adopt an expansionary course without having to fear a narrowing of international interest rate differentials in favour of the dollar; that is to say, adverse implications for the dollar were not to be feared.

Similar demands were placed on Germany in the European Monetary System (EMS). The weak external value of the D-mark resulting from the dollar revaluation had eased the tensions in the EMS in the first half of the 1980s. When the undervaluation of the D-mark was reduced as the dollar depreciated, pressure grew within the Exchange Rate Mechanism. The dominance of the D-mark, which had evolved into the *de facto* reserve currency of the EMS, meant that EMS participants had been forced to adopt a relatively restrictive policy in defence of the parities. Those countries with weak currencies therefore viewed the consolidation of the German national budget and the restrictive stance of the Bundesbank as an obstacle to their

---

[96] Cf. Deutsche Bundesbank, Geschäftsbericht 1985, pp. 66–70.

[97] Cf. e.g. the references in Oudiz and Sachs, 1984; Bergsten, 1987; Sachverständigenrat, Jahresgutachten 1987/8, paras. 4–7 and paras. 329–40; Wissenschaftlicher Beirat of the Bundesministerium für Wirtschaft, 1987.

own plans for expansion, as well as excessive (asymmetrical) participation on their part in the stability-driven adjustment burdens emanating from the Federal Republic. In consequence, they called on Germany to participate in a more expansionary monetary and fiscal policy.[98]

d) Limited cooperation in the interests of a stable currency

The appeals for stronger international coordination of economic policy met with a muted reception in Germany. Both the Federal Government and the Bundesbank certainly accepted the need for more effective cooperation at both European and global levels. The Federal Government signalled its 'fundamental' support for the concept of the Commission of the European Communities for a 'cooperative growth strategy for greater employment'[99] and for the efforts to stabilize exchange rates.[100] It used its scope for increased spending and tax cuts to such an extent that the consolidation of the national budget came to a standstill in 1987 and 1988 (cf. also Figures 1 and 4). The Bundesbank not only participated in international currency market operations to stabilize exchange rates, but even occasionally tolerated substantial overshooting of its monetary expansion targets between 1986 and 1988, so that it could support the economy with low interest rates and prevent any revaluation shock of the D-mark. However, Germany resisted any more far-reaching demand and exchange-rate-oriented integration of its national instruments of economic policy. This would also have been mistaken. The causes of the sharp fluctuations in real exchange rates lay mostly not in any lack of coordination, but in the changeable and contradictory stabilization policies of individual countries. In particular the high current account deficits in the USA were due not to any low level of demand, but to the massive public sector debt as well as the consequent low level of savings in that country.

In any event, the attempt to use monetary policy to stimulate real demand in the countries with surpluses would have failed in the long run. The total orientation of national monetary policy to the stabilization of exchange rates or corresponding target zones would have provoked problems similar to those faced by the Bretton Woods system. The central bank's responsibility for domestic price stability would have been suspended. Almost insurmountable adjustment problems would have arisen for fiscal policy. There was as

---

[98] Cf. Sachverständigenrat, Jahresgutachten 1987/8, para. 349; cf. on this problem also Wyplosz, 1988, p. 47 and Guth, 1996, pp. 413f.

[99] Kommission der Europäischen Gemeinschaften, 1985.

[100] Cf. Deutscher Bundestag, 1987, sections 38 and 39.

good as no theoretical or empirical justification for current account targets being defined by international agreement.[101] The stronger use of demand-oriented, expansionary fiscal policy measures by countries recording a surplus might have reduced their own current account surpluses and helped cut the US current account deficits more quickly. But for Germany, such an approach would have damaged the credibility of its medium-term stability and growth policy. The effect would have been similar if it had given in to the demands of the outflow countries in the EMS for a more expansionary monetary and fiscal policy. Ultimately, this would only have been possible by accepting even stronger domestic inflation, with a corresponding impact on the rest of the Community.

7. Double unification: Germany and Europe

German economic policies in the 1990s were confronted with a twofold historic challenge. In the first place, the collapse of the communist economic and social systems in Eastern Europe also extended to the GDR, and brought the Germans an unexpected unification. Secondly, the heads of state or government of the European Community meeting at the EC Summit in Maastricht in December 1991 decided to create a European Union and a single currency no later than 1 January 1999. The accomplishment of these two objectives has caused massive problems, in particular for fiscal policy, right up to the present.

a) Adjustment problems posed by the financing of German unification

The early days of the process of German unification were understandably accompanied by great euphoria.[102] But both the adjustment problems in eastern and western Germany and the financial burdens were underestimated. Ignorance of the real circumstances in the new Länder, in particular of the state of productive capital, was only one of the reasons. There was

---

[101] Cf. Issing, 1989; Issing and Masuch, 1989.

[102] The author has commented variously on the problems presented by financing German unification: Cf. Kitterer, 1993a, b, 1995. A certain degree of repetition is inevitable, but the repetitions need not be cited here in any great detail. Grossekettler, 1996–7, provides a detailed analysis of fiscal policy between 1990 and 1995.

also no adequate transformation theory for the conversion of communist planned economies into social market economies. Under the abstract conditions of perfect competition, one might have expected that when the borders were opened, capital would flow into the poorer region. Although no doubt a degree of pump-priming would be necessary, the economic renaissance in eastern Germany could almost have started under its own steam, because the lower capitalization levels there held out prospects of higher rates of return.[103] Such expectations were reflected in the revaluation of the D-mark and relatively high real interest rates in 1990. Admittedly, wages would have had to be adjusted to the still very low productivity levels to achieve this. But if employers and unions had actually settled on wages for eastern Germany at around one third or less of western German levels, there would certainly have been a mass migration to western Germany. To prevent this, the government had to subsidize the restructuring of eastern German enterprises at excessively high wage levels. A further complicating factor was that the 1:1 conversion of wages increased the gap between the prices obtainable on international markets and the production costs. On top of this, the eastern German enterprises lost their traditional markets in Eastern Europe.

All things considered, it became clear during 1991 at the latest that the transfer requirement for the reconstruction of eastern Germany would be far higher than originally expected. In fact, the eastern Länder benefited from transfers to the tune of DM 1,031 billion between 1990 and 1995 (Table 1). After deducting central government revenue from eastern Germany totalling around DM 190 billion, this still results in net transfers of DM 841 billion, around 4–5 per cent of the annual GDP of the western Länder.

Right from the start, there were warnings against wandering away from the path of budgetary rectitude to finance German unification, urging that the necessary funds should be raised through savings and reallocations.[104] Against its better judgement, however, the government initially stuck to its position that tax increases were not necessary. One reason was that politics dictated that errors of judgement could not be corrected before the first all-German elections. Another was that every time a new need was identified, there was a paralysing dispute about the distribution of the ensuing financial burden. The aura of a historical event soon dissipated and turned into

[103] As representative of the widespread optimism at the time, the reader may refer to the 'Überlegungen zur Wirtschaftspolitik' by the leading economic research institutes. Cf. Gemeinschaftsdiagnose Frühjahr 1990 der Forschungsinstitute, pp. 19–24.

[104] Cf. e.g. Deutsche Bundesbank, Geschäftsbericht 1989, pp. 25f.; Deutsche Bundesbank, Geschäftsbericht 1990, pp. 31f.; Sachverständigenrat, Jahresgutachten 1990/1, paras. 218–20.

TABLE 1: Public-sector transfers to the new Länder and East Berlin
(in billions of DM)

Transfer payments	1991	1992	1993	1994	1995	1991–5
Federal Government	75.7	95.9	117.8	120.4	156.5	566.3
Länder/local authorities (West)	5.0	5.0	10.0	14.0	17.0	51.0
'German Unity' Fund	35.0	33.9	35.2	34.6	9.5	148.2
European Union	4.0	5.0	5.0	6.0	7.0	27.0
Social security	30.2	50.8	56.4	49.8	51.5	238.7
Gross transfers[a]	149.9	190.6	224.4	224.8	241.5	1,031.2
Revenue from the new Länder	28.7	33.1	34.9	42.6	50.5	215
Net transfers	121.2	157.5	189.5	182.2	191.0	841.4
Memo item: as percentage of GDP West	3.8	4.5	4.6	4.2	5.0	

[a] not including multiple payments.

Source: Sachverständenrat, Jahresgutachten 1995/6, excerpt from Table 40 (final column added).

anxiety about financial burdens which were difficult to define, but for that very reason even more difficult to bear. There were politicians who expected solidarity from the taxpayers, but were themselves intent on ensuring as few cuts as possible in their own budgets. In 1990, the Unification Treaty suspended the system of horizontal fiscal equalization, which had been a heavy burden on the old Länder. Instead, the 'German Unity Fund' was established. It was designed as a transitional measure to meet the financing requirements of the new Länder until the end of 1994. This artifice benefited the western Länder to the detriment of central government and—paradoxically—favoured the financially strong Länder, as these would have had to bear the heaviest burdens under the system of horizontal fiscal equalization.[105] The Federal Government financed this itself in 1991 by increasing taxes which it alone collected (the 'solidarity surcharge', mineral oil tax, tobacco tax, insurance tax). Although the 'German Unity Fund' was supplemented in 1991 and 1992, it was foreseeable that these funds too would be inadequate. Other questions still unanswered were who should assume ultimate responsibility for the rapidly growing debts of the Debt to

[105] Cf. Wissenschaftlicher Beirat beim Bundesministerium der Finanzen, 1992, pp. 24–35.

Processing Fund, the Treuhand agency (Treuhandanstalt, i.e. the public agency entrusted with privatizing former state-owned enterprises in eastern Germany) and eastern German state-owned housing, and how the eastern German Länder and local authorities should be integrated into the fiscal equalization system after 1994. In consequence, both the extent and the nature of the funding burdens remained largely unclear. The 'Solidarity Pact' negotiations in early 1993 between the Federal Government, the heads of the major political parties and the minister-presidents of the Länder, culminating in the 'Federal Consolidation Programme', were held only after the 1992 unification-driven boom had turned into a cyclical downturn, the public sector deficits and the liabilities accumulated in the special funds had risen abruptly and it had become obvious that the transfer requirements for the new Länder and local authorities would climb even further.

b) The failure to consolidate public sector budgets

After long and agonizing discussions, the reorganization of the horizontal fiscal equalization between the Länder and the vertical fiscal equalization between the Federal Government and the Länder enabled the new Länder to plan their future financial position before the deadline specified in the Unification Treaty (end of 1994). However, the glaring fault in this programme was the nature of the consolidation. Because rows about distribution between the various authorities at all levels are simpler to solve if funding increases are redistributed, rather than through onslaughts on vested rights, the Federal Government and the Länder reached an agreement which damaged the interests of the third party involved: the taxpayer. Instead of cutting spending and reducing tax privileges, the main result of the agreement was tax increases. The Federal Consolidation Programme therefore provided a respite, but no genuine solution of the consolidation problem. It is certainly the case that the share of direct taxes was reduced, offset by an increase in indirect taxes (cf. Figure 6), and this must be judged a success in terms of supply-side economic policy. But the aggregate tax ratio rose in the first half of the 1990s to a record level of almost 44 per cent,[106] a situation which now constitutes a serious strain on the growth prospects and competitiveness of the German economy. The government spending ratio, which had been cut back to 46 per cent in the 1980s under favourable conditions, has climbed back to 50 per cent (Table 2). The gains have been few and far between: public sector debt has now grown to such proportions— by more than 15 percentage points to 58 per cent of GDP within the space

[106] Cf. Sachverständigenrat, Jahresgutachten 1996/7, Table 38*.

TABLE 2: Government spending, deficits, and debt

Year	Gross Domestic Product	Spending	Financial balance[a]	Debt
Billions of DM				
1980	1,472.04	721.88	−42.68	468.61
1990	2,426.00	1,118.12	−49.74	1,067.50
1991	2,853.60	1,395.04	−94.82	1,213.27
1992	3,075.60	1,526.72	−86.77	1,452.02
1993	3,158.10	1,598.74	−109.68	1,677.47
1994	3,320.40	1,662.11	−80.56	1,866.77
1995	3,457.40	1,751.10	−122.60	1,995.97
1996	3,554.00	1,796.50	−149.50 (−137.90[b])	2,061.90
1997	3,694.50	1,827.00	−122.50 (−105.00[b])	
As percentage of GDP				
1980		49.0	−2.9	31.8
1990		46.1	−2.1	44.0
1991		48.9	−3.3	42.5
1992		49.6	−2.8	47.2
1993		50.6	−3.5	53.1
1994		50.1	−2.4	56.2
1995		50.6	−3.5	57.7
1996		50.5	−4.2 (−3.9[b])	58.0
1997		49.4	−3.3 (−2.9[b])	

[a] As defined in the national accounts, but excluding the net borrowings of the Treuhand agency, which totalled DM 204 billion between 1990 and 1994.
[b] Data taken from: Deutscher Bundestag, 1997, p. 101.
Source: Sachverständigenrat, Jahresgutachten 1996/7.

of five years—that the public sector interest burden is now equivalent to 4 per cent of GDP.[107]

As is so often the case, fiscal policy makers now face the predicament of having to implement consolidation in a phase of slow growth. This will be

[107] This burden will continue to rise if, despite the high taxes, fiscal policy makers cannot keep the deficit ratio well under 3 per cent, as in the past (cf. Table 2). If the nominal growth rate of GDP actually turns out to be 4 per cent in the medium term, as the government assumes in its multiyear fiscal planning (cf. Bundesministerium der Finanzen, Finanzbericht 1997, p. 69), the sustainable consolidation of the debt ratio at 60 per cent of GDP could only be achieved if the average deficit ratio is less than 2.5 per cent of GDP.

no easy task. Spending cuts will not be enough: taxes must also be reduced. There is now a tremendous pent-up need for tax reform, not only because of the necessary tax breaks, but also because of fundamental structural deficits.

Structural improvements and tax breaks are necessary in the system of corporate taxation to safeguard the competitive position of the German economy. There have been calls for the abolition of trade tax for decades now, but there has been no movement because of the complicated repercussions on local authority finances. A fundamental income tax reform involving an appreciable reduction in marginal tax rates, the elimination of innumerable tax concessions and exemptions, and an expansion in the tax base itself— measures which have been discussed for many years—will demand sacrifices by many existing beneficiaries, but will still lead to tremendous shortfalls in tax revenue, with the means to balance them still uncertain. But if the authorities can succeed in implementing the 'Petersberg tax proposals' drafted by the tax reform committee,[108] they will have achieved a major reform for more growth and employment. However, it is equally important for the concept of a 'symmetrical public finance policy' presented by the government in 1995 to be put into practice. This aims at using strict spending limits to cut taxes and reduce the deficit in such a way that the government spending ratio will return to pre-unification levels (46 per cent) before the year 2000.[109]

c) Tensions in the European Monetary System

In contrast to the previous decade, the high public sector deficits in the first half of the 1990s saw a return to conflicting monetary and fiscal policies. The first problem facing the Bundesbank was how to avoid the risk of excess liquidity following German monetary union, because the question of how much of the converted balances in eastern Germany would affect demand, and how much would flow into financial and capital investments, was still unclear. Its relatively restrictive monetary targeting in 1991 came in for criticism at home.[110] However, the expansionary fiscal policy, the high wage settlements and rising inflation prompted the Bundesbank to stick to its domestic stability plans. These included relatively high interest rates, which

---

[108] Cf. Bundesministerium der Finanzen, 1997.
[109] Cf. Bundesministerium der Finanzen, 1996a.
[110] Cf. Sachverständigenrat, Jahresgutachten 1991/2, paras. 171–3; Gemeinschaftsdiagnose Frühjahr 1992 der Forschungsinstitute, p. 29 and the controversial discussion by Pohl *et al.*, 1991.

had repercussions for the other members of the Exchange Rate Mechanism, robbing them of their ability to pursue an independent monetary policy with low interest rates and alleviate the emerging cyclical downturn. In a reaction similar to what happened in 1985–7, this led to tensions within the EMS, and ultimately to the 1992–3 EMS crisis, as a result of which the fluctuation margins for bilateral central rates were widened to ±15 per cent. Again, the Bundesbank had to resist demands for a 'symmetrical' interest rate policy,[111] which would ultimately have demanded a relaxation in monetary policy driven by external considerations. Ignoring the fact that its monetary target had been exceeded substantially in 1992, and to a lesser extent in 1993, the Bundesbank rejected this approach on principle and emphasized the heavy responsibility shouldered by the anchor currency country for the future of the EMS.[112] It pointed out that the tensions in the EMS had their roots in the shortfalls in convergence which had arisen since 1987, in particular the widening price and cost differentials, and conflicts between domestic and external monetary policy orientation in specific countries.[113] It was also perfectly clear that the cause of the adverse German policy mix, i.e. huge deficits at a time of high interest rates, lay in the domestic economy. Together with public sector demands on the capital market, the need to finance German unification had also created the high borrowing requirements of the Treuhand agency, figures which were not disclosed in the public sector budgets (cf. Table 2). The controlling function of monetary policy was also handicapped by the fact that the signal effect of interest rates had been heavily curtailed for certain market participants. This was because the bulk of private sector investments in eastern Germany was supported by tax privileges and subsidies, and financed by low-interest loans, with the result that demand for credit was not restrained by the relatively high interest rates. Although its impact was felt throughout Europe, the roots of this monetary dilemma lay within the German economy, and it was there that the problem had to be solved.[114]

[111] Cf. Deutsche Bundesbank, Geschäftsbericht 1992, pp. 85f. and Kommission der Europäischen Gemeinschaften, 1993, p. 170.
[112] Cf. Kommission der Europäischen Gemeinschaften, 1993 and Deutsche Bundesbank, Geschäftsbericht 1993, p. 63.
[113] Cf. Deutsche Bundesbank, Geschäftsbericht 1992, pp. 81–4 and Deutsche Bundesbank, 1993, pp. 19f.
[114] Cf. Sachverständigenrat, Jahresgutachten 1992/3, para. 329. Cf. on the accusation that the high interest rates were a result of German unification e.g. Eichengreen and Wyplosz, 1993, p. 75. The Bundesbank held the view that the grounds for the high interest burdens in some partner countries were to be found in the countries themselves, cf. Deutsche Bundesbank, Geschäftsbericht 1992, p. 84.

d) *The fiscal convergence criteria of the Maastricht Treaty*

Although the more settled price situation means that there is currently no risk of further negative repercussions on price stability in Germany as a result of excessive deficits, experience shows that the relationship between monetary and fiscal policy, and in particular public sector credit financing, frequently emerges as the fault line in any stabilization policy, particularly where maintaining price stability is concerned. The Bundesbank has repeatedly stressed that the strain on monetary policy becomes unbearable if it has sole responsibility for ensuring price stability, and that the support of fiscal policy (including wages policy) is vital for avoiding inflation. This applies not only to Germany, but to an even greater extent to a range of other EMS members; in the past, with expansionary fiscal policies and rising inflation (or at least rising inflation differentials over more stable countries), they have tried to defend their exchange rate through extremely high interest rates. Such a policy mix overloads monetary policy, exposes the central bank to growing political pressure, and ultimately involves the risk of accelerating national and international inflationary tendencies. Fiscal discipline, meaning limits on public sector budget deficits, is therefore a crucial requirement for price stability in the European Union. To ensure that it is achieved, the Maastricht Treaty, signed in February 1992, contains the following common principles:

- The European Central Bank and national central banks are prohibited from financing public sector deficits through overdrafts or other credit facilities. This applies not only to central, regional, and local authorities, but also to all public corporations, other establishments governed by public law and public sector enterprises in the Member States. These public sector establishments are also prohibited from obtaining preferential access to financial institutions through specific measures.
- The Community is not liable for the public sector debt and liabilities of individual countries. Neither are countries liable for each other's debt and liabilities.
- The Member States are obliged to ensure the sustainable financial position of the public sector, i.e. to avoid any excessive government deficit. This rule is put into concrete form by two of the 'convergence criteria': the planned or actual budget deficit may not exceed 3 per cent of GDP at market prices, and total government debt may not exceed 60 per cent of GDP at market prices.

Although a degree of success in curbing inflation, cutting back interest rates and reaching stable exchange rates[115] has been achieved in the European Union in recent years, budgetary consolidation has not made the same progress. Since 1993, the average deficit ratio across all Member States has certainly been reduced, from over 6 to 4 per cent (1996). But the government debt ratio has risen over the same period from 66 to 73 per cent of GDP.[116] This means that the EU as a whole still has a long way to go to meet both the fiscal convergence criteria. In Germany, the government debt ratio has been climbing towards the 60 per cent limit, and at 3.5 per cent in 1995 and 4.2 per cent in 1996, the budget deficit substantially exceeded the reference value (cf. Table 2). But the Federal Government still hopes that it can reduce the deficit to 2.5 per cent in 1997.[117]

The need for the fiscal convergence criteria is controversial, as is their effectiveness. One of the views occasionally heard is that the coordination of fiscal policy is superfluous: the markets can ensure budgetary discipline by applying country-specific risk premiums.[118] In addition, if Stage Three of EMU actually happens and a single currency applies to all of the Member States of the European Union, they would no longer be able to pursue inflationary policies because they would not be able to create money themselves. Such views also hold that government debt criteria are in any event redundant, because countries which have cut their debt ratios through high inflation rates would come off relatively well.[119]

An objection to the last argument is that experience shows that the arduous task of consolidating government debt is primarily influenced by the level of debt and the resulting interest burdens; these restrict the scope for budgetary measures in the country concerned. The dynamic relationship between the deficit and the debt level must also be taken into consideration. As the German example of recent years shows, compliance with the deficit criteria in no way guarantees a constant or declining level of debt. At a somewhat higher level (of debt), this inverse relationship—a rising debt ratio and a simultaneously declining deficit ratio—also applies to the European Union average. In some cases, this means that consolidation of the high level of debt demands special efforts to reduce ongoing public sector credit financing.

There are also fears that the application of the fiscal convergence criteria is not sufficiently strict to impose a disciplined budgetary policy in the

---

[115] Cf. Kommission der Europäischen Gemeinschaften, 1996, pp. 39–48.
[116] Cf. Kommission der Europäischen Gemeinschaften, 1996, p. 26 and 1995, p. 25.
[117] Cf. Bundesministerium der Finanzen, 1996b, p. 24.
[118] Cf. Vaubel, 1980; Wissenschaftlicher Beirat beim Bundesministerium für Wirtschaft, 1989, pp. 22–5.
[119] Cf. Gemeinschaftsdiagnose Herbst 1995 der Forschungsinstitute, p. 31.

EU.[120] On the one hand, compliance with the criteria is subject to a variety of let-out clauses in the Maastricht Treaty, despite precise figures being specified. On the other, the potential sanctions if the rules are broken are weak and formulated in such a way as to encourage conflict. The incentive to run a higher level of debt may rise, because the devaluation risk for bad debtors disappears in a monetary union, and country-specific interest-rate hikes will be lower, owing in part to the larger capital market. The policy makers *could* tend towards interpreting the 3 per cent upper deficit ratio as the normal figure, viewing any overrun as justified in the event of even relatively minor economic crises. Although the liability exclusion is enshrined in the Treaty, it is not particularly credible because a financial crisis in one country could well damage its EMU partners. It is hardly likely that, in a union with a single currency, no support will be provided if there is a serious crisis. Finally, there is a risk that the development of particular compensation mechanisms in the European Union, such as the Cohesion Fund, will undermine the incentive of the recipient countries to observe budgetary discipline.

In the meantime, the Member States of the European Union have taken further steps to strengthen the monetary and fiscal stability of the Union. At the suggestion of the German Minister of Finance,[121] they reached agreement in December 1996 on a Stability and Growth Pact which contains a stricter interpretation of the fiscal convergence criteria.[122] The procedure for avoiding excessive deficits will be defined more closely and streamlined. The Member States have also undertaken not to exceed the 3 per cent upper limit for budget deficits during normal economic cycles, and to aim for a balanced budget or budget surplus in the medium term. Exceptions will only be allowed in emergencies (e.g. natural catastrophes) or severe recessions (e.g. if GDP falls by at least 2 per cent).

The continuing discussion about which Member States will meet the conditions for participating in Stage Three of EMU on 1 January 1999 have triggered further efforts in some countries to reduce government debt and public sector deficits. However, some of the methods practised demonstrate a questionable interpretation of the provisions of the Maastricht Treaty. In France, for example, a one-off payment of FRF 37.5 billion by France Télécom was added to the budget. This operation, based ultimately on advance payments for pension commitments and thus a purely financial

---

[120] Cf. Issing, 1993; Klein and Neumann, 1993; Wissenschaftlicher Beirat beim Bundesministerium für Wirtschaft, 1994, pp. 73–8; Sachverständigenrat, Jahresgutachten 1996/7, paras. 351–7.

[121] Cf. Bundesministerium der Finanzen, 1995*b*.

[122] Cf. Europäischer Rat in Dublin, 1997 and Deutscher Bundestag, 1997, Section E.

transaction, will reduce the government deficit in 1997 for accounting purposes, but will increase it *pro rata* in future years.[123] Italy has decided to
levy a 'Eurotax' in the form of a one-off income tax surcharge; it will be
repaid in part in 1999.[124] Belgium has switched to selling gold reserves and
making speculative currency purchases to cut its debt.[125] Even in the 'model
country' Germany, fiscal policy measures have been taken which will improve the picture of public finance only in the very short run. Such measures
include the postponement of payments to future budget years, the deferral
of repayments of the debts of the 'Redemption Fund for Inherited Liabilities' (*Erblastentilgungsfonds*), and the attempt to revalue the Bundesbank's
gold and foreign exchange reserves in 1997.[126] Such one-off measures are
not only an irresponsible manipulation of the facts, damaging political credibility. They also contradict the spirit of the Maastricht Treaty, which calls
for a financial situation which is sustainable in the long term as a condition
for Economic and Monetary Union.

e) *The risks of short-termism in debt management*

In Germany, the forced consolidation precipitated by compliance with the
fiscal convergence criteria has evidently seen the short-term prevention of
excessive deficits become the dominant goal of budgetary policy. Gross debt
and the government deficit are nudging the 60 and 3 per cent limits, so all
opportunities are being seized in order to restrict borrowing. With total
government debt running at around DM 2 trillion, interest payments rise
or fall by DM 20 billion every time interest rates go up or down by a single
percentage point. It is quite understandable for the public sector to use the
steadily sinking short-term interest rates, coupled with the steeper interest
rate structure towards the long end, to accumulate heavier short-term debts
and thus cut back its interest payments. As early as 1994, the Federal Government and its special funds started issuing one-year treasury discount and
financing paper.[127] Over the past year, the government has also issued treasury discount paper with maturities of less than one year ('Bubills') for the
first time to finance the budget. The maturities of borrower's notes have

[123] Cf. Statistisches Bundesamt, 1996.
[124] Cf. Bray and Sturani, 1996.
[125] Cf. Raphael, 1996, p. 15.
[126] Cf. Sachverständigenrat, Jahresgutachten 1997/8, para. 403; cf. also 'Selbst die nationale
Erbsenreserve wird überprüft, damit eine Null hinter dem Komma steht', in: Frankfurter
Allgemeine Zeitung, 3 July 1997.
[127] Cf. Deutsche Bundesbank, Geschäftsbericht 1994, p. 90.

also been cut. In particular the special funds, the 'Redemption Fund for Inherited Liabilities' and the 'German Unity Fund', have started issuing borrower's notes with maturities of less than one year.[128]

Gearing budgetary policy towards interest cost minimization may be justified for fiscal reasons. But if the structure of government debt changes in such a way that a substantial portion of it is held in short-term paper, the liquidity potential rises throughout the economy. This could cause a conflict with the central bank's objectives. Such situations involve more fundamental aspects of the relationship between government debt management and monetary policy, which also affect the potential impact of monetary policy in the European Economic and Monetary Union.

A growing trend towards short-term financing reinforces the dependence of the capital market, and ultimately of processes in the real economy as well, on the money market. On the supply and demand sides, the investment and financing terms vary more frequently, depending on the prevailing interest rate structure, with stronger price fluctuations arising particularly at the long end of the market. With capital project financing requirements and investors' lock-in periods increasingly mismatched, market volatility rises, reflected in high risk premiums, making it more difficult to control the money stock, and in particular to implement restrictive monetary policies. This is because, on the one hand, the overall liquidity potential grows when money can be made more quickly and with lower capital losses. On the other, the direct impact of its policy on the financing terms of capital projects might see the central bank coming under increasing political pressure. The Bundesbank therefore views the growing liquidity of the capital market over the past few years with some concern,[129] and has frequently voiced its fundamental misgivings about the cut in the maturity of government debt, and in particular about the issue by the public sector of debt securities with maturities of less one year.[130] It is afraid that the long-term orientation of the German financial sector, something it regards as a key asset in monetary policy and for the economy as a whole, is being undermined by the proliferation of short-term public debt instruments.[131] Such a development would also have a substantial negative impact on the stability of future European monetary policy. As the financing structure of the economy in other countries of the European Union is often much more short-term and closer to the money market, and a single European monetary policy will only be

[128] Cf. Deutsche Bundesbank, 1997, pp. 29f.
[129] Cf. e.g. Deutsche Bundesbank, 1995*b*.
[130] Cf. most recently Deutsche Bundesbank, 1997, pp. 29f.
[131] Cf. Deutsche Bundesbank, Geschäftsbericht 1992, p. 69; Deutsche Bundesbank, Geschäftsbericht 1994, pp. 91f.; Deutsche Bundesbank, 1995*a*, p. 48.

possible if the financial market structures and cultures in the Member States start to converge, it must also be in Germany's interest to promote a longer horizon in financial relations.[132] In this respect as well, monetary policy needs to be supported by fiscal policy, and especially by government debt management.

8. Bibliography

Adami, Nikolaus (1970): Die Haushaltspolitik des Bundes von 1955 bis 1965, Bonn
Arbeitsgemeinschaft deutscher wirtschaftswissenschaftlicher Forschungsinstitute (1990): Gemeinschaftsdiagnose: Die Lage der Weltwirtschaft und der deutschen Wirtschaft im Frühjahr 1990, Beurteilung der Wirtschaftslage durch die Mitglieder der Arbeitsgemeinschaft deutscher wirtschaftswissenschaftlicher Forschungsinstitute, Kiel
Arbeitsgemeinschaft deutscher wirtschaftswissenschaftlicher Forschungsinstitute (1992): Gemeinschaftsdiagnose: Die Lage der Weltwirtschaft und der deutschen Wirtschaft im Frühjahr 1992, Beurteilung der Wirtschaftslage durch die Mitglieder der Arbeitsgemeinschaft deutscher wirtschaftswissenschaftlicher Forschungsinstitute, Hamburg
Arbeitsgemeinschaft deutscher wirtschaftswissenschaftlicher Forschungsinstitute (1995): Gemeinschaftsdiagnose: Die Lage der Weltwirtschaft und der deutschen Wirtschaft im Frühjahr 1995, Beurteilung der Wirtschaftslage durch die Mitglieder der Arbeitsgemeinschaft deutscher wirtschaftswissenschaftlicher Forschungsinstitute, Halle (Saale)
Bergsten, Fred C. (1987): Resolving the Global Economic Crisis: After Wall Street. A Statement by thirty-three Economists from thirteen Countries, Institute for International Economics, Washington D.C.
Borchardt, Knut (1985): Können Gesellschaften aus Wirtschaftskrisen lernen?, in: Hemmer, Hans-Rimbert/Quandt, Siegfried (eds.): Deutsche Wirtschaft 1929/1983. Konjunkturen, Krisen, Perspektiven, Gießen, pp. 37–53
Bray, Nicholas/Sturani, Maria (1996): Surprise! Italy's 'Eurotax' Has a Give Back, in: Deutsche Bundesbank: Auszüge aus Presseartikeln, no. 73, p. 6
Bundesministerium der Finanzen (various years) (ed.): Finanzbericht, Bonn
Bundesministerium der Finanzen (1961): Möglichkeiten und Grenzen antizyklischer Finanzpolitik, in: Bundesministerium der Finanzen (ed.): Finanzbericht 1961, Bonn, pp. 85–93
Bundesministerium der Finanzen (1992) (ed.): Haushaltsreden—Die Ära Schäffer 1949 bis 1957, Dokumente—Hintergründe—Erläuterungen, Schriftenreihe zur Finanzgeschichte, vol. 1, Bonn
Bundesministerium der Finanzen (1993): Chronologie zur Finanzgeschichte 1945–1969, Daten und Erläuterungen, Schriftenreihe zur Finanzgeschichte, vol. 2, Bonn
Bundesministerium der Finanzen (1994) (ed.): Haushaltsreden—Franz Etzel 1957 bis 1961, Dokumente—Hintergründe—Erläuterungen, Schriftenreihe zur Finanzgeschichte, vol. 3, Bonn
Bundesministerium der Finanzen (1995a) (ed.): Haushaltsreden 1962–1966, Dokumente—Hintergründe—Erläuterungen, Schriftenreihe zur Finanzgeschichte, vol. 4, Bonn

---

[132] Cf. Tietmeyer, 1996, p. 437.

Bundesministerium der Finanzen (1995*b*): Stabilitätspakt für Europa—Finanzpolitik in der dritten Stufe der WWU, press release of 10 November

Bundesministerium der Finanzen (1996*a*): Finanzpolitik 2000. Neue Symmetrie zwischen einem leistungsfähigen Staat und einer wettbewerbsfähigen Wirtschaft, Schriftenreihe des Bundesministeriums der Finanzen, no. 58, Bonn

Bundesministerium der Finanzen (1996*b*): Deutsches Konvergenzprogramm, Bonn December

Bundesministerium der Finanzen (1997) (ed.): Reform der Einkommensbesteuerung—Vorschläge der Steuerreform-Kommission—vom 22. Januar 1997, 'Petersberger Steuervorschläge', Schriftenreihe des Bundesministeriums der Finanzen, no. 61, Bonn

Deutsche Bundesbank (various years): Geschäftsberichte, Frankfurt a.M.

Deutsche Bundesbank (1993): Die jüngsten geld- und währungspolitischen Beschlüsse und die Entwicklungen im Europäischen Währungssystem, in: Monatsbericht 45, 8, pp. 19–27

Deutsche Bundesbank (1995*a*): Die Geldpolitik der Bundesbank, Frankfurt a.M. 1995

Deutsche Bundesbank (1995*b*): Verbriefungstendenzen im deutschen Finanzsystem und ihre geldpolitische Bedeutung, in: Monatsbericht 47, 4, pp. 19–33

Deutsche Bundesbank (1997): Die Entwicklung der Staatsverschuldung seit der deutschen Vereinigung, in: Monatsbericht 49, 3, pp. 17–32

Deutscher Bundestag (1987): Jahreswirtschaftsbericht 1987 der Bundesregierung, Drucksache 10/6796, 15 January

Deutscher Bundestag (1997): Jahreswirtschaftsbericht 1997 der Bundesregierung, Drucksache 13/6800, 29 January

Dreißig, Wilhelmine (1969): Probleme des Haushaltsausgleichs, in: Haller, Heinz (ed.): Probleme der Haushalts- und Finanzplanung, Schriften des Vereins für Socialpolitik, N.F. vol. 52, Berlin, pp. 9–40

Dürr, Ernst (1983): Historische Erfahrungen über die Wirtschaftspolitik in der Bundesrepublik Deutschland, in: Siebert, Horst (ed.): Perspektiven der deutschen Wirtschaftspolitik, Stuttgart *et al.*, pp. 19–40

Eichengreen, Barry/Wyplosz Charles (1993): The Unstable EMS, in: Brookings Papers on Economic Activity 1, pp. 51–124

Europäischer Rat in Dublin (1997): Tagung der Staats- und Regierungschefs der Europäischen Union am 13. und 14. Dezember 1996, Schlußfolgerungen des Vorsitzes, in: Bulletin des Presse- und Informationsamtes der Bundesregierung, no. 19, 5 March, pp. 189–209

Frey, Dietrich (1988): Die Finanzverfassung der Bundesrepublik Deutschland, in: Arnold, Volker/Geske, Otto-Erich (eds.): Öffentliche Finanzwirtschaft, Munich, pp. 11–54

Frey, René L. (1972): Infrastruktur, Grundlagen der Planung öffentlicher Investitionen, 2nd, enlarged edition, Tübingen/Zurich

Friauf, Karl Heinrich (1990): Staatskredit, in: Isensee, Josef/Kirchhof, Paul (eds.): Handbuch des Staatsrechts der Bundesrepublik Deutschland, vol. 4, Finanzverfassung—Bundesstaatliche Ordnung, Heidelberg, pp. 321–355

Friedman, Milton (1970): Die optimale Geldmenge und andere Essays, Munich

Gahlen, Bernhard (1978): Strukturpolitik in der Marktwirtschaft, in: Wirtschaftsdienst 58, 1, pp. 22–7

Gahlen, Bernhard (1982) (ed.): Strukturberichterstattung der Wirtschaftsforschungsinstitute —Analyse und Diskussion—, Tübingen

Gerfin, Harald (1983): Ursachen der Arbeitslosigkeit, in: Siebert, Horst (ed.): Perspektiven der deutschen Wirtschaftspolitik, Stuttgart *et al.*, pp. 41–55

Grossekettler, Heinz (1996–7): Die ersten fünf Jahre. Ein Rückblick auf die gesamtdeutsche Finanzpolitik der Jahre 1990 bis 1995, in: Finanzarchiv N.F. 53, 2, pp. 194–303

Guth, Wilfried (1996): Vom EWS zur Europäischen Währungsunion, in: Bofinger, Peter/ Ketterer, Karl-Heinz (eds.): Neuere Entwicklungen in der Geldtheorie und Geldpolitik: Implikationen für die Europäische Währungsunion, Tübingen, pp. 409–29

Hansmeyer, Karl-Heinrich (1981): Ursachen des Wandels der Budgetpolitik, in: Häuser, Karl (ed.): Budgetpolitik im Wandel, Schriften des Vereins für Socialpolitik, N.F. vol. 149, Berlin, pp. 11–32

Häuser, Karl (1981): Ansprache eines Mitgliedes der früheren Fakultät, in: Finanzarchiv N.F. 39, pp. 1–10

Hesse, Joachim Jens (1978) (ed.): Politikverflechtung im föderativen Staat—Studien zum Planungs- und Finanzierungsverbund zwischen Bund, Ländern und Gemeinden, Baden-Baden

Issing, Otmar (1989): Leistungsbilanzungleichgewichte und Leistungsbilanzziele, in: Bub, Norbert/Duwendag, Dieter/Richter, Rudolf (eds.): Geldwertsicherung und Wirtschaftsstabilität, Frankfurt a.M., pp. 87–100

Issing, Otmar (1993): Disziplinierung der Finanzpolitik in der Europäischen Währungsunion?, in: Duwendag, Dieter/Siebke, Jürgen/Bofinger, Peter (eds.): Europa vor dem Eintritt in die Wirtschafts- und Währungsunion, Schriften des Vereins für Socialpolitik, N.F. vol. 220, Berlin, pp. 181–94

Issing, Otmar/Masuch, Klaus (1989): Zur Frage der normativen Interpretation von Leistungsbilanzsalden, in: Kredit und Kapital 22, 1, pp. 1–17

Jochimsen, Reimut (1966): Theorie der Infrastruktur—Grundlagen der marktwirtschaftlichen Entwicklung, Tübingen

Jochimsen, Reimut/Simonis, Udo E. (1970) (eds.): Theorie und Praxis der Infrastrukturpolitik, Schriften des Vereins für Socialpolitik, N.F. vol. 54, Berlin

Kitterer, Wolfgang (1993a): Rechtfertigung und Risiken einer Finanzierung der deutschen Einheit durch Staatsverschuldung, in: Hansmeyer, Karl-Heinrich (ed.): Finanzierungsprobleme der deutschen Einheit I, Schriften des Vereins für Socialpolitik, N.F. vol. 229/I, Berlin, pp. 39–76

Kitterer, Wolfgang (1993b): Staatsverschuldung und Haushaltskonsolidierung, in: Wirtschaftsdienst 73, pp. 633–8

Kitterer, Wolfgang (1995): Volkswirtschaftliche und finanzpolitische Aspekte einer Verbesserung der Rahmenbedingungen für die Entwicklung der neuen Bundesländer, in: Stern, Klaus (ed.): Vier Jahre Deutsche Einheit. Verbesserung der gesetzlichen, administrativen und finanzstrukturellen Rahmenbedingungen in der Bundesrepublik Deutschland, Munich, pp. 133–49

Klein, Martin/Neumann, Manfred J. M. (1993): Fiskalpolitische Regeln und Beitrittsbedingungen für die Europäische Währungsunion: Eine Analyse der Beschlüsse von Maastricht, in: Duwendag, Dieter/Siebke, Jürgen/Bofinger, Peter (eds.): Europa vor dem Eintritt in die Wirtschafts- und Währungsunion, Schriften des Vereins für Socialpolitik, N.F. vol. 220, Berlin, pp. 195–225

Kloten, Norbert (1976): Erfolg und Mißerfolg der Stabilisierungspolitik, in: Deutsche Bundesbank (ed.): Währung und Wirtschaft in Deutschland 1876–1975, Frankfurt a.M., pp. 643–90

Kommission der Europäischen Gemeinschaften (1985): Jahreswirtschaftsbericht 1985–1986. Eine kooperative Wachtumsstrategie für mehr Beschäftigung, in: Europäische Wirtschaft no. 26, pp. 5–85

Kommission der Europäischen Gemeinschaften (1993): Jahreswirtschaftsbericht 1993, in: Europäische Wirtschaft, no. 54

Kommission der Europäischen Gemeinschaften (1995): Jahreswirtschaftsbericht 1995, in: Europäische Wirtschaft, no. 59

Kommission der Europäischen Gemeinschaften (1996): Jahreswirtschaftsbericht 1996, in: Europäische Wirtschaft, no. 61

Kommission für die Finanzreform (1966): [2]Gutachten über die Finanzreform in der Bundesrepublik Deutschland, Stuttgart *et al.*

Kommission für wirtschaftlichen und sozialen Wandel (1977): Wirtschaftlicher und sozialer Wandel in der Bundesrepublik Deutschland, Göttingen

Krause-Junk, Gerold (1983): Zur Relevanz des sogenannten strukturellen Defizits, in: Finanzarchiv N.F. 41, pp. 52–9

Kurz, Rudi (1993): Angebotsorientierte Wirtschaftspolitik in den USA. Grundlagen, Praxis und Konsequenzen, Institut für Angewandte Wirtschaftsforschung Tübingen, Forschungsberichte, Serie A, no. 56, Tübingen

Lambsdorff, Otto Graf (1982): Lambsdorffs Vorschläge an den Kanzler: Drastische Sparmaßnahmen, Steueränderungen, höhere Investitionen, Liberalisierung, in: Deutsche Bundesbank: Auszüge aus Presseartikeln, no. 80, pp. 14–15

Lucas, Robert E. (1981): Studies in Business Cycle Theory, Oxford

McCracken, Paul *et al.* (1977): Towards Full Employment and Price Stability. A Report to the OECD by a Group of Independent Experts, Paris

Markmann, Heinz (1977): Strukturwandel und Investitionslenkung, in: Borgsdorf, U. *et al.* (eds.): Gewerkschaftliche Politik: Reform aus Solidarität. Zum 60. Geburtstag von Heinz O. Vetter, Cologne, pp. 427–47

Mayer, Thomas (1978): Die Struktur des Monetarismus, in: Ehrlicher, Werner/Becker, Wolf-Dieter (eds.): Die Monetarismus-Kontroverse, Supplement 4 of Kredit und Kapital, Berlin, pp. 9–55

Neumann, Manfred J. M. (1981): Der Beitrag der Geldpolitik zur konjunkturellen Entwicklung der Bundesrepublik Deutschland 1973–1980, in: Kyklos 34, pp. 405–31

Neumark, Fritz (1985): Historische Prozesse und wirtschaftspolitische Lösungsversuche 1929/1983, in: Hemmer, Hans-Rimbert/Quandt, Siegfried (eds.): Deutsche Wirtschaft 1929/1983. Konjunkturen, Krisen, Perspektiven, Gießen, pp. 21–35

Oberhauser, Alois (1976): Geld- und Kreditpolitik bei weitgehender Vollbeschäftigung und mäßigem Preisanstieg (1958–1968), in: Deutsche Bundesbank (ed.): Währung und Wirtschaft in Deutschland 1876–1975, Frankfurt a.M., pp. 609–42

OECD (1977): Economic Outlook 21, Paris

Oudiz, Gilles/Sachs, Jeffrey (1984): Macroeconomic Policy Coordination among the Industrial Economies, in: Brookings Papers on Economic Activity 1, pp. 1–75

Pagenkopf, Hans (1981): Der Finanzausgleich im Bundesstaat—Theorie und Praxis, Stuttgart *et al.*

Piduch, Erwin (1996): Bundeshaushaltsrecht, Stuttgart/Berlin/Cologne (loose-leaf edition)

Pohl, Rüdiger/Neumann, Manfred J. M./Reither, Franco (1991): Ist die Geldpolitik zu restriktiv?, in: Wirtschaftsdienst 71, 9, pp. 435–44

Raphael, Therese (1996): Lies, Damned Lies and Statistics, in: Deutsche Bundesbank: Auszüge aus Presseartikeln, no. 69, pp. 14–16

Sachverständigenrat zur Begutachtung der gesamtwirtschaftlichen Entwicklung (1967): Jahresgutachten 1967/8, Bundestagsdrucksache V/2310, Bonn, 4 December (including Sondergutachten März 1967)

Sachverständigenrat zur Begutachtung der gesamtwirtschaftlichen Entwicklung (1974/5–1997/8, ongoing issues): Jahresgutachten, Stuttgart

Scharpf, Fritz W./Reissert, Bernd/Schnabel, Fritz (1976): Politikverflechtung—Theorie und Praxis des kooperativen Föderalismus in der Bundesrepublik, Kronberg, Taunus

Scharpf, Fritz W./Reissert, Bernd/Schnabel, Fritz (1977): Politikverflechtung II—Kritik und Berichte aus der Praxis, Kronberg, Taunus

Schlesinger, Helmut (1976): Geldpolitik in der Phase des Wiederaufbaus (1950–1958), in: Deutsche Bundesbank (ed.): Währung und Wirtschaft in Deutschland 1876–1975, Frankfurt a.M., pp. 555–607

Schlieper, Ulrich (1983): Der Keynesianismus als wirtschaftspolitische Doktrin, in: Siebert, Horst (ed.): Perspektiven der deutschen Wirtschaftspolitik, Stuttgart *et al.*, pp. 79–84

Schmidt, Helmut (1972): Schwerpunkte der Finanz- und Wirtschaftspolitik, in: Bulletin des Presse- und Informationsamtes der Bundesregierung, no. 212, Bonn, 6 September, pp. 1514–6

Schmidt, Helmut (1977): Regierungserklärung des Bundeskanzlers vom 16. Dezember 1976, in: Verhandlungen des Deutschen Bundestages, 8. Wahlperiode, Stenographische Berichte, vol. 100, Plenarprotokolle 8/1—8/19, 14 December 1976—18 March 1977, Bonn, pp. 31–52

Schmölders, Günter (1949): Jüngste Entwicklung und Stand der Finanzwissenschaft in den Vereinigten Staaten, in: Zeitschrift für die gesamte Staatswissenschaft 105, pp. 751–7

Schmölders, Günter (1965): ²Finanzpolitik, Berlin/Heidelberg/New York

Schröder, Dieter (1970): Die Größenordnung der öffentlichen Ausgaben für die Infrastruktur in der Bundesrepublik Deutschland bis 1985, in: Jochimsen, Reimut/Simonis, Udo E. (eds.): Theorie und Praxis der Infrastrukturpolitik, Schriften des Vereins für Socialpolitik, N.F. vol. 54, Berlin, pp. 427–58

Statistisches Bundesamt (1996): Auskunft des Statistischen Bundesamtes an die Presse zum Fall France Télécom, in: Deutsche Bundesbank: Auszüge aus Presseartikeln, no. 69, p. 13

Stohler, Jacques (1965): Zur rationalen Planung der Infrastruktur, in: Konjunkturpolitik 11, pp. 279–308

Strauß, Franz Josef (1969): Finanzpolitik. Theorie und Wirklichkeit, Berlin/Frankfurt a.M.

Tietmeyer, Hans (1996): Auf dem Weg zur Währungsunion, in: Tietmeyer, Hans: Währungs-stabilität für Europa. Beiträge, Reden und Dokumente zur europäischen Währungsintegration aus vier Jahrzehnten, ed. Zentralbankrat der Deutschen Bundesbank, Baden-Baden, pp. 431–9

Timm, Herbert (1981): Fritz Neumark—Nestor und Mentor der deutschen Finanzwissen-schaft, in: Finanzarchiv N.F. 39, pp. 20–8

Transfer-Enquête-Kommission (1981): Das Transfersystem in der Bundesrepublik Deutsch-land. Bericht der Sachverständigenkommission zur Ermittlung des Einflusses staatlicher Transfereinkommen auf das verfügbare Einkommen der privaten Haushalte (Transfer-Enquête-Kommission), 6/1981, Stuttgart

Vaubel, Roland (1980): Internationale Absprachen oder Wettbewerb in der Konjunktur-politik? Tübingen

Vogel, Klaus (1990): Grundzüge des Finanzrechts des Grundgesetzes, in: Isensee, Josef/Kirchhof, Paul (eds.): Handbuch des Staatsrechts der Bundesrepublik Deutschland, vol. 4, Finanzverfassung—Bundesstaatliche Ordnung, Heidelberg, pp. 3–86

Wendt, Rudolf (1990): Finanzhoheit und Finanzausgleich, in: Isensee, Josef/Kirchhof, Paul (eds.): Handbuch des Staatsrechts der Bundesrepublik Deutschland, vol. 4, Finanz-verfassung—Bundesstaatliche Ordnung, Heidelberg, pp. 1021–89

Willms, Manfred (1995): ²Internationale Währungspolitik, Munich

Wissenschaftlicher Beirat beim Bundesministerium der Finanzen (1974a): Stellungnahme zu den Aufgaben und Möglichkeiten der Finanzpolitik angesichts der Gefahren konjunk-tureller Überhitzung vom 30. Januar 1960, cited after: Wissenschaftlicher Beirat beim Bundesministerium der Finanzen: Entschließungen, Stellungnahmen und Gutachten 1949–1973, ed. Bundesministerium der Finanzen, Tübingen, pp. 222–32

Wissenschaftlicher Beirat beim Bundesministerium der Finanzen (1974b): Stellungnahme betreffend Forderungen aus der konjunkturellen Lage für die Steuerpolitik vom 4. Juli 1964, cited after: Wissenschaftlicher Beirat beim Bundesministerium der Finanzen: Ent-schließungen, Stellungnahmen und Gutachten 1949–1973, ed. Bundesministerium der Finanzen, Tübingen, pp. 320–5

Wissenschaftlicher Beirat beim Bundesministerium der Finanzen (1984): Probleme einer Verringerung der öffentlichen Netto-Neuverschuldung, Schriftenreihe des Bundesminis-teriums der Finanzen, no. 34, Bonn

Wissenschaftlicher Beirat beim Bundesministerium der Finanzen (1988): Zur Lage und Entwicklung der Staatsfinanzen in der Bundesrepublik Deutschland, in: Bundesministerium der Finanzen (ed.): BMF-Dokumentation no. 15/75, Bonn, cited after: Wissenschaftlicher Beirat beim Bundesministerium der Finanzen: Gutachten und Stellungnahmen 1974–1987, ed. Bundesministerium der Finanzen, Tübingen, pp. 1–29

Wissenschaftlicher Beirat beim Bundesministerium der Finanzen (1992): Gutachten zum Länderfinanzausgleich in der Bundesrepublik Deutschland, Schriftenreihe des Bundesministeriums der Finanzen, no. 47, Bonn

Wissenschaftlicher Beirat beim Bundesministerium für Wirtschaft (1973*a*): Gutachten vom 10. Dezember 1950 zur 'Kapitalmarktpolitik und Investitionspolitik', cited after: Wissenschaftlicher Beirat beim Bundesministerium für Wirtschaft: Sammelband der Gutachten von 1948 bis 1972, ed. Bundesministerium für Wirtschaft, Göttingen, pp. 101–08

Wissenschaftlicher Beirat beim Bundesministerium für Wirtschaft (1973*b*): Gutachten vom 12. Juni 1955 über 'Probleme einer produktivitätsorientierten Lohnpolitik', cited after: Wissenschaftlicher Beirat beim Bundesministerium für Wirtschaft: Sammelband der Gutachten von 1948 bis 1972, ed. Bundesministerium für Wirtschaft, Göttingen, pp. 279–83

Wissenschaftlicher Beirat beim Bundesministerium für Wirtschaft (1973*c*): Gutachten vom 3. Juni 1956 und 8. Juli 1956 über: 'Instrumente der Konjunkturpolitik und ihre rechtliche Institutionalisierung', cited after: Wissenschaftlicher Beirat beim Bundesministerium für Wirtschaft: Sammelband der Gutachten von 1948 bis 1972, ed. Bundesministerium für Wirtschaft, Göttingen, pp. 291–320

Wissenschaftlicher Beirat beim Bundesministerium für Wirtschaft (1973*d*): Gutachten vom 14. April 1959 über die 'Konjunkturpolitische Situation der Bundesrepublik Deutschland im Frühjahr 1959', cited after: Wissenschaftlicher Beirat beim Bundesministerium für Wirtschaft: Sammelband der Gutachten von 1948 bis 1972, ed. Bundesministerium für Wirtschaft, Göttingen, pp. 367–70

Wissenschaftlicher Beirat beim Bundesministerium für Wirtschaft (1973*e*): Gutachten vom 21. Februar 1960 über 'Gegenwärtige Möglichkeiten und Grenzen einer konjunkturbewußten Lohnpolitik in der Bundesrepublik', cited after: Wissenschaftlicher Beirat beim Bundesministerium für Wirtschaft: Sammelband der Gutachten von 1948 bis 1972, ed. Bundesministerium für Wirtschaft, Göttingen, pp. 395–409

Wissenschaftlicher Beirat beim Bundesministerium für Wirtschaft (1981): Wirtschaftspolitik bei defizitärer Leistungsbilanz, Studien-Reihe 31, ed. Bundesministerium für Wirtschaft, Bonn

Wissenschaftlicher Beirat beim Bundesministerium für Wirtschaft (1983): Konjunkturpolitik —neu betrachtet, Studien-Reihe 38, ed. Bundesministerium für Wirtschaft, Bonn

Wissenschaftlicher Beirat beim Bundesministerium für Wirtschaft (1987): Gutachten vom 26./27. Februar 1988 über 'Wirtschaftspolitische Konsequenzen aus den außenwirtschaftlichen Ungleichgewichten der großen Industrieländer', Studienreihe des Bundesministers für Wirtschaft, no. 58, Bonn, cited after: Wissenschaftlicher Beirat beim Bundesministerium für Wirtschaft: Gutachten vom Dezember 1984 bis Dezember 1986, ed. Bundesministerium für Wirtschaft, vol. 13, Göttingen, pp. 1409–35

Wissenschaftlicher Beirat beim Bundesministerium für Wirtschaft (1989): Europäische Währungsordnung, Bonn

Wissenschaftlicher Beirat beim Bundesministerium für Wirtschaft (1994): Ordnungspolitische Orientierung für die Europäische Union, Dokumentation, no. 356, ed. Bundesministerium für Wirtschaft, Bonn

Wyplosz, Charles (1988): Discussion on Dornbusch, Rudiger: The European Monetary System, the dollar and the yen, in: Giavazzi, Francesco/Micossi, Stefano/Miller, Marcus H. (eds.): The European Monetary System, Cambridge, pp. 43–7

V. The Bundesbank and Financial Markets

By Günter Franke

1. Caught between safeguarding the value of money, financial market stability, and free competition

Article 3 of the Bundesbank Act stipulates that the Bundesbank regulates the amount of money in circulation and of credit supplied to the economy, and arranges for the execution of payment transactions. Its goal is to safeguard the currency, meaning to safeguard the value of money. This assignment does not answer the question of the extent to which the Bundesbank is supposed to exert its influence on the management of financial intermediaries and the regulation of financial markets. A restrictive interpretation limits the duties of the central bank to deploying its array of monetary policy instruments to safeguard the value of money, trusting in the forces of free competition. It is expected that such forces will induce financial intermediaries to manage their businesses prudently and effectively, inhibit trading in financial instruments which cause more harm than good, and encourage the development of financial instruments which are desirable for the economy as a whole, as well as the rules for trading them. The consequence is the evolution of efficient financial markets which guarantee fair financial contracts for all market participants.

Such a degree of trust in the forces of free competition is justified if largely transparent market processes meet with sound financial know-how in enterprises and private households, and free access to the market, in other words if financial markets are essentially friction-free. But there are well-founded doubts as to whether such a state of affairs actually exists. For example, individual market participants are able to take unfair advantage of others, or they put at risk the assets entrusted to them through reckless business policies. Moreover, if financial intermediaries collapse, they can destabilize the financial system, and thus an entire economy.

The potential, undesirable consequences of 'free' financial markets justify the regulation both of the financial markets and of the financial intermediaries. But all regulatory regimes exhibit inherent weaknesses because their instruments are imperfect, they restrict competition and regulators also pursue their own interests; therefore, regulation is always a controversial activity.

Central banks are often involved in the regulation of financial intermediaries, with the following justification being cited. To regulate the amount of money in circulation and the supply of credit to the economy, and ensure that the payment system functions smoothly, the central bank must rely on the collaboration of financial intermediaries, and above all of the credit institutions, as the mediators of its policies. This transmission mechanism can only function in the long run if the central bank can influence the business policies of the credit institutions, effectively pre-empting the systemic risks of the financial market arising from successive insolvencies of financial intermediaries. Because of its close cooperation with the credit institutions, the central bank has excellent information at its disposal, making it particularly suitable for participating in the regulation of the credit institutions. But that does not mean that the central bank is solely responsible for regulation. Because its prime obligation is to monetary stability—but not to free competition—it is to be expected that it will tolerate macroeconomically undesirable conduct by financial intermediaries that eases the task of safeguarding the value of money. This must therefore be counterbalanced by other institutions in the regulation process.

It is less easy to justify the involvement of the central bank in the regulation of financial instrument trading. This form of control relates to the instruments which may be traded and the rules for trading them. For example, if the central bank prohibits trading in instruments, this affects not just credit institutions, but other enterprises and private households as well. The argument that trading in these instruments jeopardizes the ability of the central bank to safeguard the value of money is only partially convincing. In the first instance, it is unclear if these instruments actually represent a risk. This can only be possible if such instruments are traded on a large scale. But large-scale trading indicates that these instruments bring substantial benefits. Secondly, the central bank should aim to improve its monetary policy instruments if new financial instruments blunt the effectiveness of its existing instruments.

In addition, a trading ban restricts competition on the financial markets, inhibiting innovative financial services and thus the development of efficient financial markets. This jeopardizes the existence of the domestic financial market, which must survive in an environment dominated by liberal foreign financial markets. However, it must be remembered that it is very difficult for the central bank at first to gauge the risks inherent in new financial instruments and more liberal trading rules, and that a restrained approach is therefore quite appropriate. A central bank committed to stability will therefore try to avoid risks, even if it gains a reputation for curbing the process of financial innovation.

These observations highlight the potential for conflicts in central bank policy. This essay, tracing developments since 1948, describes it in some detail. However, an overall verdict on the Bundesbank's policy presupposes an assessment of its various effects, something not intended here. It would also be unwarranted to judge decisions, many of which were taken a long time ago, on the basis of the better information available today.

2. The German banks

This section describes the banking system in Germany and outlines its importance for the economy, followed by an introduction to the development of new forms of financial intermediation.

a) *The banking system in Germany*

Universal banks with deposit-taking, lending and securities operations emerged in the latter half of the nineteenth century.[1] In Germany, there was never any division into banks which either accept deposits and grant credits, or operate a securities trading business. However, in addition to the universal banks there are also specialized banks which concentrate on particular fields of activity. The principal private specialized banks are mortgage banks, building and loan associations and investment companies, while the most important public specialized bank is the Kreditanstalt für Wiederaufbau (Reconstruction Loan Corporation).

The universal banks are divided into savings banks (*Sparkassen*) and *Landesbanken*, cooperative banks and commercial banks. The latter include the big banks (*Großbanken*), the regional banks, the small private banks (*Privatbanken*), and the German branches of foreign credit institutions. While most of the savings banks and *Landesbanken* are public sector institutions with a guarantor established under public law, this does not apply to the other universal banks.

Criticism of the universal banking system focuses on the conflicts of interest between the various operating activities.[2] For example, a credit institution can try to steer customer deposits towards low-interest savings accounts, instead of forms of investment saving offering a higher rate of interest. Or it can use information available to it as a lender for its securities trading operations (although this has been prohibited since 1994 by the

---

[1] Cf. Pohl, 1986, chap. II.1.e) and chap. III.
[2] Cf. Mühlhaupt, 1980, chap. 4.

Securities Trading Act). There are also fears that the universal banking system results in a concentration of power, impairing the efficiency of the capital market. The gist of this argument is that, because of their powerful position in the financial markets, the universal banks prevent the effective control of corporations, in contrast to the Anglo-American dual banking system.

But the disadvantages of the universal banking system are accompanied by many advantages. Customers can obtain all financial services from a single source, which can cut overall information and transaction costs. Especially since the early 1980s, the universal banks have employed 'one-stop' financial strategies to try and sell their customers comprehensive packages of financial services. A further advantage of the universal banking system lies in the risk diversification resulting from the large number of different activities—making solvency protection an easier task. In consequence, there is a trend in the UK, the USA and other English-speaking countries—as well as Japan—towards replacing the dual banking by a universal banking system.

b) The economic importance of the banks

The importance of the banks for the development of the German economy is evident from a number of indicators. Table 1 shows indicators for the period 1950 to 1995. In this data, published by the Bundesbank and the Federal Statistical Office, it should be noted that there have been changes over the years in the number of credit institutions included, and that eastern Germany has been included since 1991. Finally, the figures have not been adjusted for inflation. To highlight the relative significance of the figures given, gross national product (GNP) and the consumer price index are shown in the first two rows of the table.

Among other things, the importance of the banks is indicated by the volume of financial intermediation measured as total lendings by domestic credit institutions to domestic non-banks, and as the liabilities of domestic credit institutions to domestic non-banks. Table 1 shows that the ratio of the supply of credit by domestic credit institutions to domestic non-banks to GNP has grown over time. The same applies to deposits by domestic non-banks and borrowings from them. Neither of these trends is surprising, considering that, as a result of the war, lendings and deposits had dropped to very low levels by the time the D-mark was introduced in 1948. The accumulation of financial assets by private households and enterprises only started growing appreciably in the 1950s.

Deposit and lending operations are still the core business of the credit

Table 1: The banking industry: key indicators

Item	1950	1960	1970	1980	1990	1995
Gross National Product,[a] DM bn	98.6	303.0	675.7	1,477.4	2,448.6	3,445.6
Price index[b]	29.8	35.9	46.2	74.8	96.4	112.9
Loans by dom. credit institutions to dom. non-banks,[c] DM bn	28.2	167.7	513.1	1,462.0	2,875.0	4,436.9
Deposits and loans raised,[d] DM bn	21.3	148.0	439.5	1,155.7	2,334.5	3,021.1
Marketable bearer bonds of dom. credit institutions,[e] DM bn	1.8	29.6	118.7	413.6	900.3	1,596.5
Net interest income of dom. credit institutions, DM bn	n.a.	10.7[f]	14.0	40.2	80.5	133.5[g]
Net commission income of dom. credit institutions, DM bn	n.a.	1.5[f]	1.8	6.5	18.0	27.1[g]
Cross-border lendings of dom. credit institutions, US $ bn	n.a.	n.a.	48.7[h]	73.3	38.0	563.7
Cross-border borrowings of dom. credit institutions,[i] US $ bn	n.a.	n.a.	39.6[h]	74.2	22.5	539.2
Internat. lendings of German credit institutions, US $ bn	n.a.	n.a.	n.a.	133.9[j]	494.8	887.1
Internat. borrowings of German credit institutions,[i] US $ bn	n.a.	n.a.	n.a.	117.6[j]	349.8	859.2
Number of dom. credit institutions[k]	13,883[l]	13,234	8,549	5,355	4,180	3,487
thereof foreign-owned	n.a.	n.a.	n.a.	n.a.	117	129
Number of foreign branches of German credit institutions[m]	n.a.	n.a.	23[n]	74	128	181
Number of foreign subsidiaries of German credit institutions[o]	n.a.	n.a.	27[n]	52	96	117
Employees of dom. credit institutions,[p] thousands	n.a.	266	471	555	679	724[q]

[a] At current prices; 1995 incl. new Länder. [b] Consumer price index, 1991 = 100. [c] Including Treasury bills, securities and equalization claims. [d] Deposits by domestic non-banks and borrowings from them by domestic credit institutions, without debt securities of domestic credit institutions. [e] Including subordinate debt. [f] Value for 1968. [g] Provisional. [h] Value at end of 1977; the average official exchange rate for US $ in 1977 was 2.3217; 1980 1.8158, 1990 1.6161 and 1995 1.4338 DM/$. [i] International lendings and borrowings (= cross-border items plus local foreign currency items) of credit institutions in Germany and abroad whose parent is domiciled in Germany; intercompany items are not included. *Source:* BIS. [j] Value at end of 1983. [k] Number of credit institutions in Germany, not including postal giro and postal savings offices; until 1989 without building and loan associations. [l] Number at end of 1953. [m] Several branches in a country are counted as one. [n] Number at end of 1973. [o] Foreign credit institutions with a majority holding by German credit institutions. [p] Annual average. [q] Number at end of 1994. n.a. = not available.

Sources (unless otherwise stated): Federal Statistical Office, Deutsche Bundesbank.

institutions, but commission-related business has grown substantially in importance over the course of time. This relates above all to securities brokerage transactions for third-party accounts, e.g. the purchase and sale of securities and arranging securities issues, plus fees from guarantee commitments. To illustrate the relative shift in the sources of income, Table 1 shows domestic credit institutions' net interest income and net commissions received.

It is impossible to describe the activities of the credit institutions without including their international ties. There are two sorts of international interdependence: first, the cross-border lending and borrowing operations of domestic credit institutions, and secondly the cross-border lending and borrowing operations of domestic and foreign credit institutions whose parent is headquartered in Germany. The first type describes the international operations of credit institutions in Germany, regardless of where the parent company is headquartered. The second type describes the cross-border ties of German credit institutions, irrespective of whether they are operated by branches in or outside Germany. However, these figures, published by the Bank for International Settlements (BIS), do not go back to the early days of the D-mark. Table 1 shows the lendings and borrowings of both types in billions of US dollars. It should be noted that the figures published by the BIS for type 2 cover not only cross-border transactions, but also non-cross-border foreign currency positions.

These figures highlight the strong growth in international interdependence. Contributory factors to this trend include the growing presence of foreign credit institutions in Germany and of German credit institutions abroad, as shown by the number of domestic credit institutions in foreign ownership and the number of foreign branches and subsidiaries of German credit institutions.

Rationalization, growing competition, and the tightening of the capital adequacy standards for credit institutions have seen the number of credit institutions shrink over the passage of time. There have also been mergers, particularly of smaller institutions in the savings and cooperative banking sectors.

In contrast, the number of domestic banking outlets, i.e. of domestic credit institutions including their branches, rose for many years (not shown in Table 1). At 53,386, they reached their peak in 1992 as a consequence of German unification, since when they have been declining. The growing pressure to cut costs will continue to thin out the dense German branch network.

A final indicator of the economic importance of credit institutions is the number of persons employed in this sector. At present, around 2.5 per cent of those in employment work for credit institutions. A combination of the

rise in electronic banking services and the impact of rationalization programmes will see a drop in this number as well.

c) The emergence of new financial intermediaries

The financial intermediaries have always included the credit institutions—
including the specialized banks already mentioned—and in the broader
sense insurance companies as well, in particular life insurance companies,
which in Germany normally combine risk coverage with investment activities. Life insurance policies therefore contribute to pensions and other old
age provision in the same way as normal savings and investment saving with
banks. The result is considerable competition between the banks and the
insurance companies. Table 2 shows that the insurance companies have been
able to attract a growing share of financial asset accumulation by private
households. The investment portfolios of the insurance companies have
grown correspondingly.

Since 1956, credit institutions in particular have been running their investment business through investment companies. The credit institutions

TABLE 2: Financial asset accumulation of private households and
financial assets of insurance companies and investment funds (DM bn)

Year	1950	1960	1970	1980	1990	1994
Financial asset accumulation of private households	5,370[a]	28,610[a]	87,380	121,070	202,480	236,250
thereof invested with insurance companies	n.a.	n.a.	8,230	25,450	47,350	79,010
Financial assets portfolios of the insurance companies	4,024	24,222	84,238	278,752	713,812	1,011,395
Assets of domestic investment funds	n.a.	3,146	10,495	47,123	238,855	486,037

[a] Savings of private households shown in the Statistical Yearbook 1962. Cf. Statistisches
Bundesamt, 1962, p. 560.
n.a. = not available.

Sources: Deutsche Bundesbank, Federal Statistical Office.

sell the investment certificates, and the investment companies invest the funds. This profitable business has also become increasingly attractive to the banks in recent years because the commission rates in securities business have been coming under pressure from the growing number of direct banks. To date, the assets invested by insurance companies have been greater than those invested by investment companies.

A striking development in a universal banking system like that in Germany has been the emergence of new forms of financial intermediaries, because universal banks try to attract all financial operations for themselves. The new financial intermediaries include the credit card organizations, leasing companies, and the banking subsidiaries of the automobile companies, department stores, and of the mail-order trade. Leasing companies and credit card organizations do not run banking businesses as defined by the German Banking Act (*Kreditwesengesetz/KWG*). They are therefore not credit institutions, but financial institutions within the meaning of section 1(3) of the *KWG*. This means that they are also subject to various provisions of the *KWG* if the group includes a credit institution.

Credit card organizations offer a package of services, including electronic payments, payment guarantees for the recipients of payments and the granting of credits to the payer. Because these are also the classic functions of the credit institutions, the German banks established the German Eurocard Organization in 1976 after recognizing the market potential of credit cards. Employing aggressive marketing techniques, the credit institutions were able to achieve a rapid increase in the market share of their bank credit cards,[3] at just on 90 per cent at the end of 1996.[4]

Assuming that credit card transactions in Germany totalled DM 40 billion in 1994, dividing this by 12 (because of the monthly settlement procedure) gives a more modest figure. This indicates that so far, the reduction in the volume of banknotes in circulation (DM 236 billion at the end of 1994) due to credit cards has been insignificant.

A variety of new financial intermediaries specialize in financial services closely linked to non-financial transactions. For instance, in addition to financing various items, leasing companies also offer an assumption of responsibility for maintenance services and administrative functions, as well as cost-effective purchasing and realization of the item following the expiry of the contractual leasing period. The banking subsidiaries of the automobile manufacturers, department stores, and mail-order firms offer similar services.

[3] Cf. Gesellschaft für Zahlungssysteme, 1995.
[4] Cf. 'Der Markt für Kreditkarten wächst stärker als erwartet', in: Frankfurter Allgemeine Zeitung, 8 Feb. 1997, p. 21.

TABLE 3: Financing by leasing companies in Germany*

Year	1967	1977	1987	1990	1992	1994	1995
DM bn	0.2	7.2	28.4	41.1	56.5	56.2	58.1[a]

* Annual gross additions from new commitments.
[a] Estimated.
Sources: Bitz, 1989; Städtler, 1995.

TABLE 4: Lending by 'Automobile banks' in Germany*

Year	1989	1990	1991	1992	1993	1994	1995
DM bn	17.6	21.9	28.3	35.7	38.4	43.1	44[a]

* Loans to domestic non-banks; year-end figures.
[a] Estimated.
Source: Arbeitskreis der Banken und Leasinggesellschaften der Automobilwirtschaft, 1995. The figures relate to credit institutions which are members of the 'Arbeitskreis' (working party).

As with credit cards, the credit institutions were able to attract a substantial portion of the leasing business, often by establishing their own leasing companies. Table 3 shows the volume of leasing finance. In 1995, leasing accounted for around 11.5 per cent of total investments in Germany.

Table 4 shows the credits extended by 'automobile banks' to domestic non-banks. In 1995, total lendings by 'automobile banks' of DM 44 billion represented only just over 1 per cent of the volume of all credits extended by domestic credit institutions to domestic non-banks.

To sum up, it can be stated that in the past 20 years, the new financial intermediaries have built up their own markets and achieved above average growth rates, a trend which is likely to continue in future. Despite this, the classic credit institutions have no reason to fear these competitors. On the one hand, their lending volumes are modest, and on the other, the credit institutions have secured a strong position in the new markets.

The existence of the new financial intermediaries is of minor significance for the Bundesbank. Credit cards have had little impact on the demand for cash. The leasing companies provide no more than a relatively modest volume of finance. The banking subsidiaries of the department stores and mail-order firms are generally credit institutions subject to standard banking

supervision rules. This does not pose new challenges to either monetary policy or banking supervision.

3. The Bundesbank's services
for domestic credit institutions

As the 'banker's bank', the Bundesbank provides a variety of services for
credit institutions. These can be broken down into three areas: (1) the
provision of liquidity to credit institutions (refinancing), (2) the provision
of information, and (3) the provision of payment services.

a) Refinancing

One of the Bundesbank's functions is to regulate the supply of credit to the
economy and the amount of money in circulation, principally through the
involvement of domestic credit institutions. They can borrow funds from
the Bundesbank, but only against prime collateral such as bills and eligible
debt securities. The Bundesbank then provides the banks with central bank
balances in the amount of these credits. Part of these balances must be
deposited with the central bank as an interest-free minimum reserve.

The classic refinancing instruments are discount credits and Lombard
loans. The Bundesbank specifies a rediscount quota for each credit institution, within which it is willing to buy domestic and foreign bills meeting
particular quality standards. Utilization of these rediscount quotas is attractive to the credit institutions if the short-term money market rates
are higher than the discount rate at which the Bundesbank settles the bills.
When bought by the Bundesbank, the bills must fall due within at least 20,
and at most 90 days, whilst Lombard loans are used to bridge short-term
liquidity needs. To do this, the Bundesbank extends credit against the
collateral of eligible debt securities at a rate of interest known as the
'Lombard rate'.

The Lombard rate is always higher than the discount rate, on average by
one to two percentage points. As the Lombard rate is normally higher than
the day-to-day money rate, utilization of Lombard loans is usually low.

Since 1979, the Bundesbank has also offered credit institutions securities
repurchase transactions, under which it purchases securities eligible as collateral for Lombard loans from the credit institutions, which simultaneously
repurchase them forward. The Bundesbank charges the repurchase (or

TABLE 5: Refinancing of the banks by the Deutsche Bundesbank* (DM bn)

Year	1950	1960	1970	1980	1990	1995
Discount credits	4.24	1.43	17.41	43.68	84.91	61.8
Lombard loans	1.33	0.51	1.40	7.71	6.18	5.5
Securities repurchase transactions	—	—	—	6.16	117.43	145.8
Aggregate lending	5.57	1.94	18.81	57.55	208.52	213.1
Memo item: Deposits held with the Bundesbank	1.89	13.05	26.25	53.85	74.68	49.7

Sources: 1950: Bank deutscher Länder; 1960 ff.: Deusche Bundesbank.

'repo') rate on these transactions. As shown in Table 5, credits based on repurchase transactions now exceed discount credits and Lombard loans by a large margin. Since 1985, securities repurchase transactions have become the Bundesbank's primary fine-tuning instrument of monetary policy.

Domestic credit institutions are offered credit facilities by the Bundesbank, yet they also deposit money with the Bundesbank. The level of these deposits is principally governed by the minimum reserve regulations, with the minimum reserve ratios being cut substantially several times during the 1990s. At around DM 30 billion, the total deposits required by the credit institutions to settle payment transactions via the Bundesbank are currently less than the required minimum reserves of just on DM 40 billion.

b) Provision of information

Another of the Bundesbank's services is the provision of various information. According to article 18 of the Bundesbank Act, the Bundesbank is entitled to collect statistics in order to discharge its duties. In addition, the credit institutions file regulatory documents such as monthly reports, annual financial statements, and associated audit reports with the Bundesbank, as well as various reports under articles 13, 14, 16, and 24 of the *KWG*. These provide the Bundesbank with excellent information resources. The Bundesbank evaluates this information and publishes the results. The banking and capital market statistics, provided as supplements to the Bundesbank's monthly reports, deserve particular mention. The Bundesbank also publishes regular analyses of the annual financial statements of the credit institutions.

The Bundesbank also provides an important service as the credit register for *Millionenkredite*. All credit institutions are required to notify the names of all borrowers to the Bundesbank who have received a credit exceeding DM 1 million (from 1993 DM 3 million), as well as the loan amounts. On the basis of the reports received, the Bundesbank calculates the aggregate borrowings of each borrower and notifies the figure to the lending banks. A more far-reaching exchange of information between credit registers in several European countries has been developed in recent years.

c) Provision of payment services

The automation of the payment system

A large proportion of payments are cleared through the Bundesbank. This is one of the Bundesbank's functions, as a reliable, fast payment system is a precondition for a viable money and capital market. Because there is an imbalance between incoming and outgoing payments at the credit institutions, they must be able to even out sudden surpluses and deficits. Around 30 per cent of non-cash intercompany payments are processed by the Bundesbank.[5] It functions as a bridge between the giro networks of the savings banks, cooperative banks, big banks, and the Postbank, also offering settlement services to credit institutions which are not members of any of these networks.

There are three tasks in the organization of payment systems: (1) payment operations should be settled quickly and irrevocably in the interests of users; (2) the settlement costs and the necessary working balances (interest-free balances of credit institutions at the central bank for settling payments) should be kept to a minimum; (3) the risks of the payment system should be minimized. The Bundesbank has always committed itself to fulfilling these tasks.[6]

As early as 1950, the Land Central Banks and the Bank deutscher Länder endeavoured to institute a more rational system for clearing payments. In 1970, the banking system was able to handle automatic voucher processing. Since 1992, the Bundesbank offers the credit institutions an electronic payment system. The 'Electronic Clearing System with File Transfer' provides fully automatic clearing for domestic payments over DM 50,000 delivered in the standardized 'DTA' electronic payments format, as well as SWIFT domestic follow-up payments (worldwide electronic inter-bank payments).

---

[5] Cf. Deutsche Bundesbank, 1994c.
[6] Cf. Deutsche Bundesbank, 1994c.

TABLE 6: Payments handled by the Bundesbank in 1995

Item	Quantity (millions)	Volume (DM bn)
Bulk payments	2,272	4,700
thereof		
– MAOBE (optical character recognition) payments	115	267
– DTA-format payments	2,157	4,433
Large-value payments	35	189,407
Total	2,307	194,107

Source: Deutsche Bundesbank, Geschäftsbericht 1995, p. 125.

Credit institutions and other major customers can also execute real-time large-value payments via the Bundesbank. In addition, the Bundesbank has cut the routing times for credit transfers, direct debits, and cheques considerably, achieving a substantial reduction in the float. An interest-bearing float arises only if an amount is credited to the beneficiary with a value date later than the date when it is debited to the payer.

Until 1990, the Bundesbank cleared payments free of charge. In July 1990, the Central Bank Council decided to introduce compulsory charges. The lowest charges are for paperless payments. Table 6 provides an overview of payments handled by the Bundesbank in 1995. The dominance of low-cost payment instruments is clear.

Limiting payment risks

In addition to speed of settlement and the costs of payment, the systemic risk is another mark of the quality of a payment system. The risks of a payment system include the liquidity, the credit and the systemic risk. The liquidity risk is a consequence of the temporary illiquidity of a participant in the payment system; the credit risk is a result of permanent insolvency. A systemic risk arises if the failure of one participant to pay renders other participants insolvent and the whole payment system collapses (domino effect).

Another, albeit related risk arises if there is a time gap between payment and counter-payment, although both are supposed to occur simultaneously: the 'Herstatt risk'. Before the Herstatt Bank failed in 1974, D-mark amounts were irrevocably credited to it during the last business day before its closure.

However, payments of US dollars had not yet been executed, so the counter-parties suffered serious losses.

A payment system aims to exclude these risks as far as possible. Traditionally, the central banks used *net settlement systems*. In such systems, the payment orders arising during the course of a day are executed by the central bank, and credit institutions are required to square debit balances in the evening through money market operations or by raising loans against securities (Lombard loans). If these balances are not closed, the central bank reserves the right to cancel (reverse) payments which have already been executed, giving rise to liquidity, credit and systemic risks.

Such scenarios prompted the central banks to discuss improvements to the payment system. In 1990, the BIS published the Lamfalussy Report, which pinpointed a variety of ways to reduce risk.[7] This report also discussed *real-time gross settlement systems*, in which payments are executed immediately and finally by the central bank if the account of the ordering credit institution at the central bank has sufficient funds to cover the transaction.

The Bundesbank was involved in these talks and decided to test such a system. In 1995, it introduced alongside the net settlement system a second system for large-value payments which comes very close to a gross settlement system. The EAF 2 electronic clearing system is installed at the Land Central Bank in Frankfurt am Main. It is used for same-day payments between credit institutions, and with a daily volume of DM 600 billion, now accounts for more than 70 per cent of the volume of payments routed through the Bundesbank.[8]

With the EAF 2 clearing system, which processes payments in two phases, the Bundesbank has taken a major step forward. Most payment orders are settled finally within 20 minutes of receipt. This largely avoids inadvertent credit relations between credit institutions and their customers. In Phase I, undesirable high net payments by one bank to another are avoided by applying maximum sender amounts, but this protection no longer applies in the shorter Phase II. Because individual payments can only be reversed in Phase II, the systemic risk is low, compared with a net settlement system.

The risks arising from time differences in the settlement of payments and counter-obligations have not yet been satisfactorily resolved. In 1993, the BIS Nöell Report[9] made a number of suggestions as to how the central banks can reduce these time differences using their own systems.

[7] Cf. Bank für Internationalen Zahlungsausgleich, 1990.
[8] Cf. Deutsche Bundesbank, 1996a, p. 16.
[9] Bank für Internationalen Zahlungsausgleich, 1993.

4. The impact of the Bundesbank's interest rate policy on the financial markets

An array of instruments is available to the Bundesbank to safeguard the value of money. At the same time, the Bundesbank is subject to restrictions which prevent the free use of the instruments. Such restrictions become particularly evident when international agreements force the Bundesbank to intervene on the currency market to prevent the D-mark breaching its exchange rate bands. The inevitable negative consequences for monetary stability also harm the Bundesbank's long-term credibility. The next section will examine the question of the extent to which the Bundesbank actually influences the financial markets through its interest rate policy. Such influences will be evident in interest rate changes on the money and capital markets, share price, and exchange rate movements, as well as shifts in the volatility of interest rates, share prices, and exchange rates. If such effects exist, the actors on these markets will try to forecast them and make profits from them.

a) The Bundesbank's instruments of interest rate policy

The Bundesbank's interest rate policy instruments are its discount and Lombard policies, its securities repurchase transactions policy, and open market policy.[10] In addition, the Bundesbank can use its information policy, which since 1974 has included the announcement of a monetary target, to change the expectations of market participants and thus influence prices on the money and capital markets.

Discount and Lombard policies were outlined in section 3a, together with securities repurchase transactions. The Bundesbank operates its open market policy by buying and selling public debt instruments. However, the Bundesbank has used this policy on a large scale only 'sporadically'.[11] This is because it wants to avoid any suspicion that it is contributing to the financing of public sector budget deficits and exerting any predominant influence on long-term interest rates. Only the effects of the Bundesbank's discount and Lombard policies, as well as of its securities repurchase transactions, will therefore be examined below.

---

[10] The Bundesbank can also influence interest and exchange rates through its deposit policy (until 1994), its foreign exchange market policy and its minimum reserve policy.

[11] Deutsche Bundesbank, 1995a, p. 117.

b) Expected reactions in efficient financial markets

Any attempt to examine how the Bundesbank's interest rate policy affects the financial markets must distinguish between expected and unexpected interest rate policy measures. If the Bundesbank announces a closely defined measure for a particular time in the future, efficient financial markets respond immediately on the *announcement*. When the measure is subsequently implemented, there is no further response because no new information is linked to the implementation. But if measures are implemented unexpectedly, without any prior announcement, efficient financial markets react immediately on their *implementation*.

To distinguish between expected and unexpected interest rate policy measures, one can try to forecast the behaviour of the Bundesbank. Such behavioural forecasts are based on historical analysis, in which a link is established between interest rate policy measures, on the one hand, and macroeconomic indicators and financial market data, on the other. Such links can be used to forecast the Bundesbank's behaviour. The clearer the signals for particular measures are, the less surprising such measures are, the more muted should the financial market's reaction be. However, such measures still contain an information element, first as regards their extent, e.g. the amount of a rise in the discount rate, and secondly as regards their timing. As the Central Bank Council only changes the discount and Lombard rates relatively rarely, the financial markets are quite unsure about the timing of any change.

The element of surprise in a measure also depends on the purpose of the information which the Bundesbank intends the instrument in question to convey. Until the mid-1980s, discount and Lombard rates played the key role in signalling interest rate policy intentions. Since then, the Bundesbank has used securities repurchase transactions to fine-tune the money market. As these transactions are conducted on a weekly basis, in contrast to the rather rare changes in discount and Lombard rates, the Bundesbank primarily signals its interest rate policy nowadays in the rates for its securities repurchase transactions. Changes in the discount and Lombard rates are more of a retrospective nature and thus have a lower information content. It is therefore to be expected, that since the mid-1980s, the financial markets react less strongly to changes in the discount and Lombard rates.

The distinction between technical and non-technical interest rate policy measures has similar objectives. Technical measures merely follow developments on the financial markets and therefore have little information content. For example, the discount rate is normally lower than short-term money market rates. If the latter fall to, or below, the level of the discount rate, bill rediscounting is no longer an attractive option for the credit institutions. In such a situation, the Bundesbank therefore sees itself compelled to cut the discount rate. Such a cut comes as no surprise to the financial markets. These considerations show that the 'environment' must be taken into account when interpreting the reactions of the financial markets to the Bundesbank's interest rate policy measures.

c) Empirical findings

The shifting interest rate policy environment since 1948

As the background environment of the Bundesbank's interest rate policy has changed several times since 1948, the presentation of interest rate developments and policy in graphic form provides a clearer overview. Figure 1 shows the discount, Lombard and day-to-day money rates since 1949.

Interest rate movements during the era of German reconstruction from 1949 to 1960 were relatively calm. The average day-to-day money rate was always close to the discount rate. The period between 1960 and 1973 was initially marked by a sharp upsurge in prices towards the mid-1960s, which the Bundesbank tried to curb by raising the discount and Lombard rates. The end of the 1960s, as well as the period from January 1972 to March 1973, saw massive currency speculation under the Bretton Woods system, followed by its collapse. The Bundesbank was obliged to intervene on the currency market to support the US dollar. The Bundesbank tried to make liquidity in the D-mark money market more expensive through appreciable hikes in the discount and Lombard rates. However, these measures were instituted at a relatively late stage because the Bundesbank did not want to attract even more money from abroad by creating a high interest rate differential.

Overall, the Bundesbank was helpless in the face of the waves of international speculation, and resorted to using 'instruments of torture against the free movement of capital'.[12]

After the collapse of the Bretton Woods system in March 1973, the Bundesbank imposed massive increases in the discount and Lombard rates. For a time, it suspended Lombard loans in order to skim off D-mark liquidity, and the day-to-day money rate then rose to 36 per cent. From 1974 on, the money markets settled down, and the discount and Lombard rates were cut appreciably, a policy which also aimed to counter the serious recession in

---

[12] Schlesinger, 1988, p. 38.

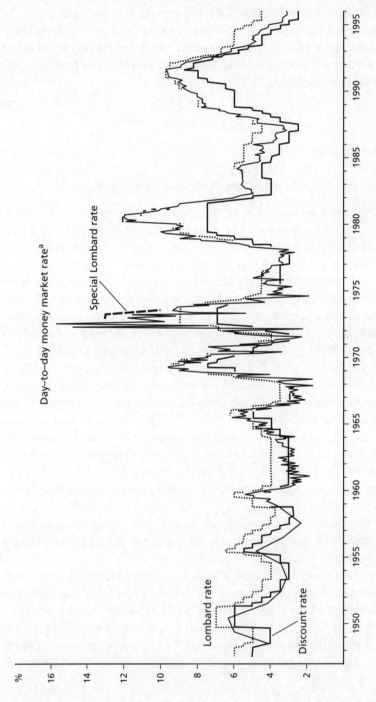

FIGURE 1: Monthly movement of selected central bank and money market rates, 1948–96

[a] Yearly from 1949 to 1959.

Source: Deutsche Bundesbank.

1975.[13] As a result of strict monetary targeting in the USA, interest rates climbed sharply in 1979 and 1980, followed by higher discount and Lombard rates. Interest rates fell back again significantly in 1982 and 1983 as inflation declined rapidly. At the end of the 1980s, the Bundesbank again countered inflation expectations by raising the discount and Lombard rates, a measure which proved to be significant when German unification triggered another boom. Money market, discount and Lombard rates only started falling fast when the economy cooled down in 1992; this trend in interest rates continued into 1996.

This overview shows that the environment for the Bundesbank's interest rate policy was subject to massive upheavals over the decades. Figure 1 also illustrates that, since the mid-1980s, the day-to-day money rate has almost always been floating between the discount and Lombard rates, a trend which emerged when the Bundesbank started using securities repurchase transactions for fine-tuning.

Reactions to changes in the discount and Lombard rates

A variety of empirical studies[14] has examined the changes in discount and Lombard policies. Between January 1961 and February 1995, the Central Bank Council met on 829 occasions, but the discount and/or Lombard rate was changed only 83 times. These changes were distributed equally across three phases:

– January 1961 to March 1973 (collapse of the Bretton Woods system),
– April 1973 to January 1985,
– February 1985 (intensive use of securities repurchase transactions starts) to February 1995.

The great differences between these periods are reflected in the discount and Lombard policies themselves. Their determinants can be analysed by linear regression.[15] In the first phase, changes in the discount and Lombard rates are easily explicable by the growth rates of real GNP in the preceding four quarters. High growth rates signalled an increase in the discount and Lombard rates, low growth rates signalled a drop. In the second phase, the 'growth rate' factor was joined by a second factor: 'change in the inflation rate in the most recent half-year compared with the preceding half-year'. A

[13] From November 1973 on, the Bundesbank also extended (for a limited period) special Lombard loans at higher special Lombard rates subject to change on a daily basis.

[14] Studies of how short-term lending rates react to changes in official interest rates can be found, for example, in: Deutsche Bundesbank, 1996*b*; Franke and Meyer, 1998; Hardy, 1996 and Borio and Fritz, 1995.

[15] Cf. Franke and Meyer, 1998.

rise in the inflation rate signals a rise in the discount and Lombard rates. In the third phase, on the other hand, changes in the discount and Lombard rates are easily explained solely by deviations in the average of the overnight and the one-month rate from the discount and Lombard rates. If the average of the overnight and the one-month rate nudges or exceeds the Lombard rate, an increase in the discount and Lombard rates is probable. Similarly, if the average drops close to or below the discount rate, a drop in the discount and Lombard rates is likely. This finding underscores the fact that, since February 1985, the rates for securities repurchase transactions have been the key signals of interest rate policy, and that discount and Lombard policies generally follow developments on the money market. It should correspondingly be expected that, since February 1985, the financial markets have reacted far less to changes in the discount and Lombard rates.

Figure 2 shows the relative changes in the overnight and one-month rate on the four days before, and six days after, a change in the discount and Lombard rates.[16] To isolate the effects more precisely, the change in the money market rate observed on day x is reduced by the change observed on day x of the most recent Central Bank Council meeting at which no interest rate policy decisions were taken. Day x is day $-4, -3, \ldots, 0, +1, \ldots,$ $+5$. The changes adjusted in this way are cumulated starting on day -4 and presented in graphical form in Figure 2. Bullets in the tables above the graphics mean that the adjusted relative changes on the days in question deviate significantly from zero.

In the first phase (1961–73), the one-month rate reacts in textbook fashion to changes in the discount and Lombard rates. Little happens before the announcement, but on the day after the announcement, the rate jumps up or down as expected and then persists at around the new level. The same applies to the second period (1973–85). In contrast, in the third phase (1985–95), the one-month rate rises before an increase or cut in the discount and Lombard rates; however, the rise is slight. On the day after the change is announced, the one-month rate reacts as expected, but returns over the next few days to the level prevailing before the announcement. Even if the picture in the third phase is diffuse, it can still be established that, in all the phases, the one-month rate reacts significantly—as expected—immediately after the announcement of the policy change.

This does not apply to the day-to-day money rate, which performs in textbook fashion only in the second phase. In the first phase, it rises immediately after the announcement of a rise in the discount and Lombard rates, but then falls back to below the initial level. The development in the

[16] Because both rates are normally changed in tandem, no distinction is made between a change of one rate only and a change in both rates.

third phase is unsystematic. This confirms the assumption that, since the use of securities repurchase transactions has intensified, discount and Lombard policies no longer have any significant, lasting influence on the day-to-day money and one-month rates.[17]

Figure 2 illustrates that, on average, the relative changes in the one-month fund rates are lower than those in the day-to-day money rates. The influence on the current yield on fixed-income securities is even less, as shown by Figure 3.[18]

In the second phase, the current yield reacts to changes in the discount and Lombard rates as expected, but there are already substantial changes in advance of the announcement. In the third phase, there are only minor, unsystematic changes in current yields. Overall, it can be seen that discount and Lombard policies affect the yield curve most in the shortest maturities, and in the long maturities hardly at all.[19] The influence is clearest until January 1985; thereafter, it tails off rapidly and is no longer evident after only a few days.

If discount and Lombard rates rise, share prices should *fall* (and vice versa), as higher interest rates hit the present value of dividends. In the first phase, the share prices react as expected immediately after the announcement of a change in the discount and Lombard rates, but the effect evaporates very quickly. The effects in the second and third phases are very slight.

The logical move is then to examine whether the reactions of the financial markets are more muted for *expected* discount and Lombard rate changes. Policy changes defined as expected are those with a high probability in line with the factors explaining policy changes, as shown in the analysis above. Unexpectedly, financial market reactions to expected discount and Lombard rate changes are not more muted.[20] A likely reason is that even with expected policy changes, there is a high degree of uncertainty as regards the timing and extent, and the change therefore contains important information.

These results also permit some conclusions as regards the question of whether the financial markets are efficient, in other words if they react without delay. The reactions immediately after an announcement of discount and Lombard rate changes are particularly significant, while there are practically no significant changes on subsequent days. This would support the

[17] Hardy, 1996, arrives at similar results for the two phases. However, he also observes significant reactions in the day-to-day money rate in the third phase.

[18] The Deutsche Bundesbank publishes the current yield of fixed-income securities every day. This statistical series has only been available since Mar. 1976. DAFOX is used for German share prices. This is a weighted index of German share prices calculated by the Karlsruher Kapitalmarktdatenbank (Karlsruhe capital market database).

[19] See also Deutsche Bundesbank, 1996b.

[20] Cf. Franke and Meyer, 1998. Hardy, 1996, finds weaker, but significant reactions.

	Day-to-day money market rate*											One-month fund rate*										
Day	−4	−3	−2	−1	0	+1	+2	+3	+4	+5		−4	−3	−2	−1	0	+1	+2	+3	+4	+5	Day
DL–A1					•											••						DL–A1
DL–A2				•		••										••						DL–A2
DL–A3		•	•	••									•	••		••						DL–A3
DL–S1	••				•••							•				•••						DL–S1
DL–S2					•••			•		•					•	•••						DL–S2
DL–S3					•••											•••						DL–S3

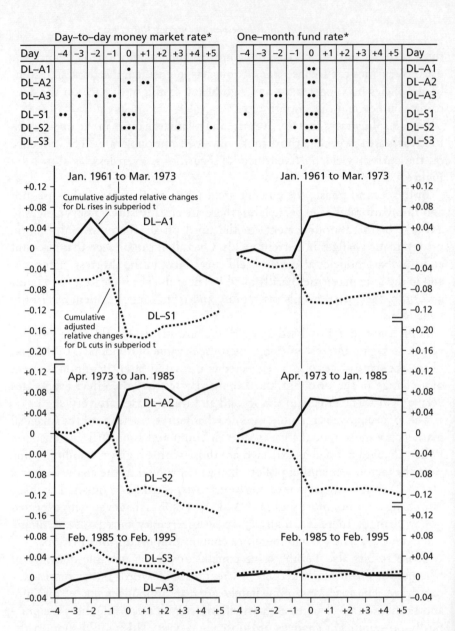

FIGURE 2: Reaction of day-to-day money market
and one-month fund rates to changes in key lending rates

* The vertical line denotes the time when the change in the discount or Lombard rate is announced. The dots in the tables indicate the significance level of the adjusted relative changes on a given day (• 10 per cent, •• 5 per cent, ••• 1 per cent).

Source: Franke and Meyer, 1998, p. 213. DL-A1,-A2,-A3: discount/Lombard rate increases in period 1 (January 1961 to March 1973), 2 (April 1973 to January 1985) and 3 (February 1985 to February 1995); DL-S1,-S2,-S3: discount/Lombard rate reductions in the respective periods.

Yield on bonds outstanding*										
Day	−4	−3	−2	−1	0	+1	+2	+3	+4	+5
DL–A2	••	•		•	•					
DL–A3										
DL–S2		••		••						
DL–S3				••						

Share prices*										
−4	−3	−2	−1	0	+1	+2	+3	+4	+5	Day
			•	••						DL–A1
										DL–A2
			••							DL–A3
••				•						DL–S1
										DL–S2
			••					•		DL–S3

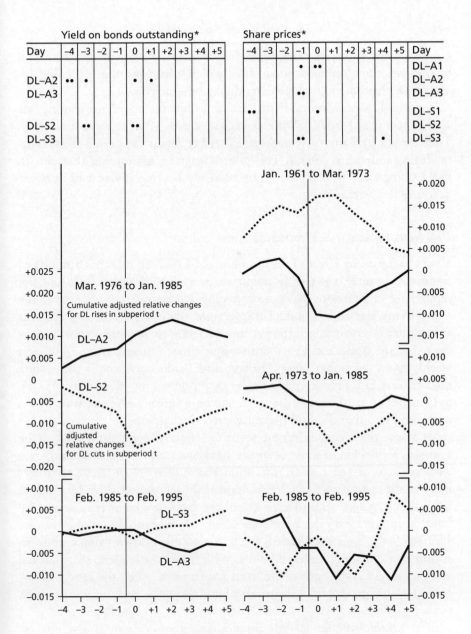

FIGURE 3: Reaction of the yield on bonds
outstanding and of share prices to changes in key lending rates

* The vertical line denotes the time when the change in the discount or Lombard rate is announced. The dots in the tables indicate the significance level of the adjusted relative changes on a given day (• 10 per cent, •• 5 per cent, ••• 1 per cent).

Source: Franke and Meyer, 1998, p. 214. DL-A1,-A2,-A3: discount/Lombard rate increases in period 1 (Jan. 1961 to Mar. 1973), 2 (Apr. 1973 to Jan. 1985) and 3 (Feb. 1985 to Feb. 1995); DL-S1,-S2,-S3: discount/Lombard rate reductions in the respective periods.

view that the financial markets are efficient. However, there are several further reactions on subsequent days which neutralize the preceding reactions, a phenomenon which casts doubt on efficiency.

Wasmund, Alexander and Feth[21] examine the influence of key lending rate changes on the D-mark/US dollar exchange rate between 1974 and 1994. They do not find any systematic effect, either across the period as a whole, or during individual phases. This contradicts the assumption that cuts in key lending rates weaken the home currency because investment at home becomes less attractive.

Reactions to securities repurchase transactions

Since the signalling effect of the discount and Lombard rates has diminished significantly since 1985, one might suspect that the rates for securities repurchase transactions have now assumed this function. In 1979, the Bundesbank started to conduct transactions under repurchase agreements at irregular intervals. Until the autumn of 1984, these were normally conducted at the beginning of a month—four times a month from 1988, and weekly from December 1993. On occasion, banks operating in the money market were also offered quick tenders with only a few days maturity. Up to October 1992, the maturities of repurchase agreements were four weeks or around two months, and thereafter two weeks.

To allow the signal effect of securities repurchase transactions to be assessed, a distinction must be made between variable-rate and fixed-rate tenders. In *fixed-rate tenders*, the Bundesbank offers to purchase securities from credit institutions which simultaneously repurchase them forward. If the volume of securities offered by all the banks together falls below the limit set internally by the Bundesbank, all bids submitted by the banks are allotted. If the limit is exceeded, the bids are scaled down using a uniform allotment ratio applying to all banks. With fixed-rate tenders, the financial markets receive two signals: the fixed interest rate when the tender is announced, and one day later, the total volume allotted as well as any allotment ratio.

In a *variable-rate tender*, the Bundesbank does not specify any interest rate; the banks state both the interest rate and the amount in their bids. Since September 1988, the Bundesbank has used the US-style auction method to set a marginal allotment rate: all bids with higher interest rates are allotted in full, and those with an interest rate equal to the marginal allotment rate can be scaled down. Variable-rate tenders give the financial markets several

---

[21] Cf. Wasmund *et al.*, 1996*b*.

information components: the marginal allotment rate, the major allotment rate (the rate spread within which the bulk of allotments were made), and the allotment volume.

A survey of securities repurchase transactions from 1979 until the beginning of March 1995 shows the following picture. In the case of fixed-rate tenders, the Bundesbank announces the fixed interest rate on the day of the tender. If this rate differs from the money market rate resulting from the extrapolation of a trend from the preceding days (equal to the expected money market rate), the difference can be interpreted as being unexpected. After the announcement of the fixed rate, the money market rate should correspondingly differ from the expected money market rate. This conjecture is confirmed by the data: for both day-to-day and one-month money, the unexpected rise (fall) after the announcement of the fixed interest rate is greater and more unexpected the more the fixed rate is above (below) the expected day-to-day money or one-month rate. The reaction of the day-to-day money rate to surprises is around twice as sensitive as the one-month rate.[22]

In the case of US-style variable-rate tenders, it emerges that deviations between the marginal allotment rate and the day-to-day money rate on the previous day result in approximately equivalent changes in the day-to-day money rate compared with the previous day. In contrast, no significant correlations are evident for the one-month rate.[23]

These findings show that the Bundesbank's fine-tuning measures using securities repurchase transactions affect the day-to-day money rate in particular, but less so the one-month rate. This leads to the question of whether the Bundesbank has tended to reduce or reinforce uncertainty about interest rate developments with its repo policy. It is quite possible that the Bundesbank's frequent fine-tuning measures increase uncertainty as regards short-term rates, but that they also contribute to the stabilization of medium and long-term rates. More detailed theoretical analysis of these correlations still needs to be done.

Some empirical findings are already available. These examine the volatility of interest rates, a measure of interest rate fluctuation calculated by the standard deviation of interest rate changes. Both the Bundesbank itself and Wasmund, Alexander and Ahrens[24] come to the conclusion that the volatility of the day-to-day money rate has probably increased with the more

---

[22] In contrast, Hardy, 1996, does not find any significant reactions by the day-to-day money and one-month rate.

[23] Hardy, 1996, finds a weak negative reaction by the day-to-day money rate, but a significantly positive reaction by the one-month rate.

[24] Cf. Deutsche Bundesbank, 1996*b* and Wasmund *et al.*, 1996*a*.

intensive use of securities repurchase transactions. However, Wasmund, Alexander and Ahrens also establish that the volatility of the one-month rate has declined. This means that the Bundesbank is apparently able to stabilize the development of the one-month rate, but at the cost of declining stability of the day-to-day money rate.

If fine-tuning the money market stabilizes the development of longer term interest rates, then the Bundesbank can count itself successful. This is because these interest rates affect enterprise and household plans. If fluctuations in these interest rates are reduced, planning is easier and economic development is encouraged.

5. The role of the Bundesbank in the liberalization of the financial markets

a) Liberalization: pro and contra

The liberalization of financial markets is a process in which there is permanent conflict between advocates and opponents. The greater the number of types of instruments which are traded and the lesser the trading in these instruments is regulated, the more liberal the financial market. From a liberal perspective, two persons should have the right to trade all conceivable financial instruments at terms they themselves have selected. This also encourages free competition. However, this principle is restricted for a number of reasons: (1) A typical feature of numerous financial contracts is that there are considerable periods between the settlement of an obligation and the counter-obligation. For this reason, there is a need for a legal system which ensures performance of the contracts at low transaction costs. (2) The effects of complicated financial instruments are not at all transparent. Legislators therefore see it as their duty to protect inadequately informed individuals from being taken advantage of. (3) In the same way, today's legislators try to prevent the exploitation of insider information in securities trading.

There are also macroeconomic arguments on top of these microeconomic ones: (1) Unrestricted trading of financial instruments in the domestic economy can make it more difficult for the central bank to safeguard the value of money. (2) Unrestricted trading can result in high losses at enterprises and thereby endanger the stability of the financial system. (3) Unrestricted trading can encourage undesirable changes in the behaviour of trading persons. For example, the Bundesbank is afraid that trading in short-term debt instruments will reinforce the short-term orientation of the trading persons.

Even if there is such a risk, the question of whether it is the Bundesbank's duty to influence this is still valid. These arguments may lead to a ban on individual financial instruments and to the regulation of trading, in other words to deliberalization.

The internationalization of the economy has given a strong impetus to liberalization. (1) Restrictions on the domestic trading of instruments stimulate the relocation of this trade abroad. This undermines the restrictions, and also exports jobs. (2) European integration has created a single European market which aims to guarantee the free movement of capital and services within the European Union. National regulations increasingly conflict with the principles of the free single market, and must therefore be adapted. (3) The liberalization of the financial market can also be employed as a political instrument. For instance, foreign credit institutions can be offered greater room for manoeuvre in Germany if there are reciprocal arrangements for German credit institutions abroad.

Developments in Germany since 1948 have been determined by two opposing tendencies. On the one hand, the variety of tradable instruments has increased dramatically in the past 50 years, but so has the number of statutory regulations governing trading. There can therefore be no talk of a general liberalization of the financial markets.

b) The actors involved in the liberalization process

The variety of arguments is reflected in the variety of actors working towards or against the liberalization of the financial markets. The first of these are the domestic credit institutions, who assume a key role on the financial markets as suppliers and brokers of financial services. If the credit institutions represented a homogeneous interest group, one might assume that they were against liberalization. This is because liberalization demolishes barriers to competition and therefore tends to cut the profits of the credit institutions. However, some banks try to use new financial instruments to open up new operating areas and attract new customers. The result is that innovative credit institutions in particular support liberalization.

Another interest group is that of enterprises and private households seeking financial services, although they do not appear as a homogeneous group as such. Court rulings often strengthen their position through restrictive interpretations of the statutory scope of the credit institutions. There must be doubts as to whether German legislators have any inherent interest in the liberalization of the financial markets. However, the Federal Government has always supported the creation of a single European market and the adoption of corresponding EC directives.

The final actors in the liberalization process are the Bundesbank and the Federal Banking Supervisory Office (Bundesaufsichtsamt für das Kreditwesen/BAKred). Even though neither institution can be termed an opponent of liberalization, their duties render a cautious stance desirable. Neither institution wants to prevent insolvencies at individual credit institutions (nor can they), but they do want to prevent risks to the financial system resulting from financial difficulties at numerous banks. As new financial instruments often create new risks for credit institutions, which still have to learn how to manage them, the Bundesbank and the BAKred are cautious about new instruments. At the Bundesbank, this caution is strengthened by worries that the new instruments might impair the effectiveness of its monetary policy. Overall, it must therefore be assumed that the Bundesbank and the BAKred do not prevent the liberalization of the financial markets, but certainly adopt a restrained stance.

The next section traces the role of the Bundesbank in the liberalization process up to 1996. The main focus is on the market for foreign D-mark debt securities, the new financial instruments and minimum reserve policy.

c) The liberalization of the market for foreign D-mark debt securities

The behaviour of the Bundesbank is highlighted in the development of the market for foreign D-mark debt securities. Until 1958, the D-mark was not convertible and thus unsuitable for international financial transactions. This changed on the introduction of convertibility. The D-mark gained a reputation as a stable currency with comparatively low interest rates, making it attractive to foreign debtors. This gave rise to the market for foreign D-mark debt securities.

In the narrower definition used here, foreign D-mark debt securities refer to all D-mark debt securities (bonds) issued *in Germany* by foreign debtors. These foreign debtors include public sector and private debtors domiciled abroad, but not the foreign subsidiaries of German companies.

The first foreign D-mark debt security was issued in 1958. This market segment remained relatively modest until the end of 1967, with the bonds reaching a volume outstanding of just on DM 5 billion, compared with DM 135 billion by domestic issuers.[25] This is surprising in view of the German coupon tax which was introduced in 1965, also at the urging of the Bundesbank. This was a withholding tax of 25 per cent on the interest income from domestic D-mark debt securities, payable by non-resident bondholders. The

---

[25] Deutsche Bundesbank, 1976, pp. 303, 306.

Bundesbank hoped to use this tax to keep foreign investors away from the German capital market at a time of high current account surpluses.

Issuing requests by foreign issuers jumped sharply in 1968. The Bundesbank was prompted to channel these issues. In February 1968, it therefore reached a gentleman's agreement with leading German credit institutions. This represented a 'voluntary agreement between the central bank and the credit institutions under which they undertook to conduct themselves in a particular way desired by the central bank in the interests of the economy as a whole for a particular period'.[26] The *anchoring principle* was agreed in this gentleman's agreement,[27] under which a German credit institution assumed the lead management of the issue of foreign D-mark debt securities in Germany, and at least the co-management of bonds with D-mark options. If this was not the case, German credit institutions were not involved in the issue.

The 'Sub-committee for foreign D-mark bonds' was also established in the Central Capital Market Committee in November 1968 to reconcile issue requests with the absorptive capacity of the domestic market. A member of the Bundesbank Directorate has also been a member of this committee since 1972. As there were fears that domestic issuers could be crowded out, the issue volume for foreign D-mark debt securities was limited to DM 300 million per month in January 1975.

The Bundesbank also attached importance to the informal *conversion and transfer clause*, under which the D-mark proceeds from issues had to be converted into foreign currency immediately and transferred abroad. In this way, the Bundesbank wanted to prevent large D-mark amounts migrating abroad, with the D-mark becoming an international reserve currency. The Bundesbank was afraid that this would disrupt its monetary policy, in particular in the event of currency speculation.

These agreements made it easier for the Bundesbank to stabilize recourse to the capital market. It also suited the German credit institutions, because they were shielded from competing foreign credit institutions and were thus able to achieve higher earnings in underwriting business.

To safeguard its policy, the Bundesbank had to prevent the issue of foreign D-mark debt securities abroad. It therefore intervened at foreign central banks and justified its approach on monetary policy grounds. The foreign central banks recognized this, and thus made the gentleman's agreement effective internationally.

---

[26] Issing, 1996, p. 136.
[27] Minutes of a meeting on 6 Feb. 1968 with representatives of credit institutions active in foreign underwriting business on recourse to the German credit markets by foreign issuers (HA BBk B 330/20665).

The gentleman's agreement was even extended in March 1980, when the credit institutions committed themselves not to issue Certificates of Deposit (CDs) denominated in D-mark or any variable-rate bonds. But it was repeatedly undermined in the ensuing years. It also became clearer that the Bundesbank's restrictive stance threatened to prevent the German financial market from keeping abreast of the variety of innovations at other financial centres. The risks from restricted competition were compounded by a gap in financial technology. The Bundesbank was aware that its image was that of hostility towards liberalization and innovation, and the gentleman's agreement was therefore lifted in April 1985.[28] From then on, German subsidiaries of foreign banks could assume the lead management of the issue of foreign D-mark debt securities. But the principle of anchoring D-mark issues in Germany remained.

The pressure to liberalize further grew in the early 1990s, particularly from the European Community. EC directives prepared the way for the Single European Market on 1 January 1993. The associated freedom of movement of capital and services was at odds with the Bundesbank's regulations. The Bundesbank was still unwilling to abandon the anchoring principle so that it could retain its influence on D-mark issues, and in particular on innovative forms; this protected Germany, as a financial centre, from the migration of underwriting business. Branches of foreign banks were therefore added to the list of permitted lead managers in August 1992, provided they had a sound syndication department in Germany.

d) The Bundesbank's stance on new financial instruments

In the 1970s, the futures exchanges in Chicago were able to develop a lively trade in futures and options. By securitizing classic and innovative forms of credit, the US investment banks attracted business from the commercial banks. By the end of the 1970s, this saw a wave of financial innovations which has lasted until today.

For the central banks, these financial innovations raised a number of questions (already addressed in section 5a). Until 1985, the Bundesbank viewed the risk of certain new financial instruments as very high, and correspondingly prevented their issuance in Germany.[29] In a draft on 'Capital investment offerings by German credit institutions on the international capital market' of December 1979, the Bundesbank noted that, for monetary policy

---

[28] Deutsche Bundesbank, 1985.
[29] This does not include the classic financial futures and options. Options started being traded again on German stock exchanges in 1970.

reasons, the attraction of the D-mark for foreigners should not be increased by offering CDs commonly traded on the international market. The availability of variable-rate credits also involved monetary risks because the debtors were exposed to a higher interest rate risk. The debtors would try to pass this on to others. The Bundesbank viewed this as a risk to monetary stability. A variable interest rate was also close to the indexing prohibited by article 3 of the Currency Act.

The Bundesbank only abandoned its resistance to CDs and variable-rate bonds in December 1985. By the end of June 1996, however, variable-rate bonds only accounted for 8.9 per cent of the volume of domestic D-mark debt securities, and 15.5 per cent of the volume of foreign D-mark securities.[30]

D-mark zero bonds whose yield is expressed in rises in the bond price were only admitted by the Bundesbank in April 1985. The Bundesbank's misgivings were directed towards the comparatively high price fluctuations in this paper when interest rates change, as well as towards the high one-off burden on the debtor at the redemption date. Overall, the German zero bonds market has experienced no more than sluggish growth. In the case of domestic D-mark debt securities, the volume outstanding had reached no more than 0.2 per cent by the end of June 1996, and that of D-mark zero bonds 2.3 per cent.[31] In June 1996, the Federal Ministry of Finance and the Bundesbank announced that from 1997, stripping will be allowed for particular long-term Federal bonds, with the coupons being traded separately.[32]

The Bundesbank also had objections to foreign D-mark debt securities linked to currency swaps, because their risks were insufficiently transparent. Again, the Bundesbank withdrew its objections in 1985.

The Bundesbank took a particularly critical view of short-term money market paper. It again feared that borrowers and lenders would become too short-termist, something which could damage the long-term stability of the D-mark. If more loans are securitized, mood swings are increasingly reflected in price fluctuations and heavy trading in the securitized loans.[33] These clear signals force the Bundesbank to counter the associated uncertainty. At the same time, it is more difficult for it to estimate the impact of its monetary policy. Secondly, the effectiveness of short-term funding of credit institutions by the Bundesbank can be impaired by the issue of short-term money market paper. Thirdly, the issue of short-term money market paper can make the funding of credit institutions—and thus loan finance to enterprises—

---

[30] Deutsche Bundesbank, 1996*d*, pp. 24, 41.
[31] Deutsche Bundesbank, 1996*d*, pp. 24, 41.
[32] Cf. Deutsche Bundesbank, press release, 12 June 1996.
[33] Cf. Deutsche Bundesbank, 1995*b*.

more expensive. This is because some of the savings deposits can be switched to money market paper offering a higher rate of interest, a development also observed in recent years.

However, the Bundesbank's principal concern related to safeguarding the minimum reserve system. Short-term money market paper opens up opportunities to bypass the minimum reserve requirements. For this reason, the Bundesbank's policy as regards money market paper will be discussed below together with the minimum reserve policy.

e) The Bundesbank's minimum reserve policy

The Bundesbank continues to emphasize that minimum reserves are an indispensable component of its policy. It is therefore trying to retain minimum reserves as an instrument in the European Monetary Union, although it is not in use in all Member States. The Euromarkets are exempt from minimum reserves.

Domestic credit institutions are required to maintain interest-free deposits at the Bundesbank for sight deposits, time deposits, and savings deposits (Minimum Reserves Order of the Bundesbank). The level of the minimum reserves is oriented towards the average amount of reserve-carrying liabilities, multiplied by the minimum reserve ratios for the various categories of liabilities.

Formerly, the minimum reserves were also viewed as a buffer for safeguarding the liquidity of credit institutions in a crisis. This function hardly applies any more, particularly as the minimum reserve ratios have been cut almost continuously since 1979. Since August 1995, the reserve ratio has been 2 per cent, and only 1.5 per cent for savings deposits. In 1977, the peak reserve ratio for sight deposits was still 14.9 per cent. Moreover, the function formerly attributed to the minimum reserves of curbing credit institutions' lending via the money-creation multiplier, is unconvincing in the light of the low level of reserve ratios. The Principles on Capital and Liquidity lay down much stricter limits.

Today, the minimum reserves help the Bundesbank fine-tune the money market. The minimum reserves guarantee demand by the credit institutions for central bank money. The Bundesbank also argues that the credit institutions' deposits with the central bank are an effective liquidity cushion, as the actual minimum reserves in any month are governed only by the average credit balance at the Bundesbank in the calendar month.[34] A credit institution can therefore draw on this buffer flexibly, depending on its needs. In addition, the Bundesbank can steer the money market precisely in the sec-

---

[34] Cf. Deutsche Bundesbank, 1994a.

ond half of the month using securities repurchase transactions, as it knows the extent to which the credit institutions require additional money to meet their minimum reserve obligations.

The strength of these arguments is increasingly under attack. This is because, with their strong international ties, the credit institutions can increasingly obtain and invest money internationally, albeit not central bank money. In addition, the Bundesbank can identify liquidity shortages on the money market from changes in the day-to-day money rate not running parallel with those in longer term money market rates.

The minimum reserve system was an important reason for the Bundesbank to slow down the liberalization of the German capital market. As debt securities with a contracted maturity of at least two years are not subject to minimum reserve requirements, the new financial instruments provide many opportunities for evading the minimum reserve requirements. For example, a credit institution can issue a variable-rate bond with a life of more than two years and apply for its listing on a securities exchange. Short-term depositors then buy such a bond for a short period, a procedure which bypasses the minimum reserve requirement. In addition, foreign subsidiaries of German credit institutions can sell short-term D-mark CDs to German investors (unless these are classified as foreign D-mark debt securities) without any minimum reserve requirement arising. This is also the case if investors extend credit directly to an enterprise, for example using commercial paper. It was therefore not unexpected that the Bundesbank abandoned its resistance to variable-rate bonds and CDs only in 1985 and 1986, respectively. The revision of the minimum reserve regulations in May 1986 also ensured that bank bonds and CDs with contracted maturities of less than two years are subject to minimum reserve requirements.

The Bundesbank made a further attempt to develop the D-mark money market following the currency turbulence in the European Monetary System in the autumn of 1992. The money stock had grown unexpectedly, and short-term paper was desirable to absorb liquidity. In addition, the minimum reserve requirement was forcing an increasing volume of deposits abroad. In February 1993, the Bundesbank therefore decided to cut the minimum reserve ratios appreciably and absorb the released liquidity by issuing 'Bulis' (*Bundesbank-Liquiditäts-U-Schätze*/Bundesbank liquidity paper). This discount paper with maturities of three, six, and nine months was auctioned. The Bundesbank's aim of attracting domestic non-banks in particular was a failure, as non-banks could only participate in the Buli auctions through banks. The Bundesbank therefore decided to discontinue the Buli issues in September 1994. At the same time, it continued to reject the issue by the public sector of paper with maturities of less than one year.

In 1988, the Land government of Lower Saxony introduced a bill amending the Investment Companies Act, which would have allowed structures similar to money market funds. Because investment funds are not subject to minimum reserve requirements, it was blocked by the Bundesbank. In 1993, the European Commission proposed an amendment to the UCITS Directive, under which money market funds authorized in one EU country could be automatically marketed in all other EU countries. In March 1994, the Bundesbank abandoned its opposition to money market funds. Its decision was made easier by the pronounced cut in minimum reserve ratios which had occurred in the meantime, as well as by the decision of the public sector not to issue short-term paper. Starting in September 1994, numerous banks established their own domestic money market funds. By June 1996, around DM 37.6 billion had been invested in these funds.[35]

To prevent the migration of larger investment amounts abroad, the Bundesbank decided in December 1996 to exempt deposits in the form of securities repurchase transactions from the minimum reserve requirement. Surprisingly, the Bundesbank also agreed to the issue of Bubills in 1996.[36] These are Federal discount paper running for six months; the total volume is not intended to exceed DM 20 billion.

f) The effects of the Bundesbank's policy on Germany as a financial centre

With a variety of factors influencing the business policy of credit institutions, it would be mistaken to fabricate any simple link between the Bundesbank's policy and the development of the German financial market. Despite this, a number of justified presumptions can still be made. The gentleman's agreement to issue foreign D-mark debt securities secured lead management for German credit institutions for many years, preventing any effective competition from foreign credit institutions. This ensured a lucrative business for German credit institutions. At the same time, these barriers to competition were an incentive to conduct business outside Germany, and German credit institutions repeatedly bypassed the gentleman's agreement through foreign branches or subsidiaries.

The minimum reserve requirement soon proved to be an incentive for large investors to invest in the exempt Euromarkets. German credit institutions are very active in Luxembourg and London. (The volume of business in Luxembourg in June 1996 was around DM 125 billion;[37] in the United Kingdom, particularly London, the volume was around DM 601 billion;

---

35 Cf. Deutsche Bundesbank, 1996d, p. 53.
36 Cf. Deutsche Bundesbank, press release, 12 June 1996.
37 Cf. Deutsche Bundesbank, 1996c, pp. 92, 94.

the total volume of business by German credit institutions abroad was around DM 1,247 billion.) Even though the minimum reserve ratios are now very low, the requirement still represents a tangible burden. As margins on international transactions have now shrunk to a few basis points, minimum reserve burdens of even one to two basis points are a considerable intrusion.

The restrictive stance of the Bundesbank on financial innovations has also contributed to the growth of financial centres like London and Luxembourg. Know-how about financial innovations developed in the UK and the USA in particular, but in Germany, it was not until the second half of the 1980s that the significance of these instruments was recognized.

The Bundesbank identified this problem at an early stage, but gave clear priority to safeguarding the value of money. In 1985, an internal Bundesbank paper reported that the existing regulations protected the privileged German banks from the 'cold winds' of international competition. This meant that the Bundesbank was supporting the 'monopoly profits' of the banking industry, and proven new financial instruments were only being used by residents in foreign financial centres. Since then, the Bundesbank has assumed a more competition-friendly attitude.

For example, it supported moves to strengthen the role of foreign banks in Germany on the basis of reciprocal agreements. In 1984, it recommended the abolition of the coupon tax to the Federal Minister of Finance. In 1985, it also advocated the abolition of the Securities Transfer Tax (although this only happened in 1991), because it feared an exodus of trading in variable-rate bonds to London. Finally, the Bundesbank supported the repeal of articles 795 and 808a of the German Civil Code, i.e. the provisions requiring government approval for the issue of debt securities. Nowadays, the German financial market can be regarded as largely liberalized as regards its tradable instruments. The Bundesbank now believes that new financial instruments cannot seriously endanger its monetary policy.[38]

6. The Bundesbank's role in banking supervision

a) The reasons for supervising credit institutions

Financial market liberalization and banking supervision cannot be analysed in isolation. Liberalization involves the admittance of financial instruments and the rules to be observed in their issuance and trading. Banking

---

[38] Cf. Deutsche Bundesbank, 1994*b*, 1995*b*.

supervision involves the rules to be observed in the establishment of banks and the conduct of banking operations. If the financial markets are liberalized, new business opportunities are available to the banks, which can increase their risk appreciably. If bank failures are to be prevented by banking supervision, then new risks demand new methods of banking supervision. It is therefore no surprise that the liberalization of the financial markets in the past two decades has been accompanied by a tightening of banking supervision.

Although there has been a Factory Inspectorate (*Gewerbeaufsicht*) in Germany for many years, this is not comparable with the supervision of credit institutions and insurance companies. These financial intermediaries are subject to particularly intensive—and not uncontroversial—supervision. The advocates of a pure market economy argue that any special banking supervision is redundant. They reason that banks not operating a sound business policy will be recognized as such, and will therefore find it extremely difficult to find business partners. However, this can only be expected if there are no deposit guarantee funds which render any prudence on the part of investors superfluous.

The proponents of banking supervision argue on both the micro- and the macro-level.[39] At the *micro-level*, the issue is the transaction costs of a business relationship. A saver wishing to deposit money with a bank must first obtain information about the credit standing of the bank. If the banking supervision authorities are able to dispense with the need for individual savers to assess the credit standing of the bank, transaction costs are saved. However, there are numerous examples where a banking supervision scheme has not prevented bank failures; all it can do is reduce their likelihood.

More convincing arguments for banking supervision are supplied by the *macro-level*. The banks have very close business links with each other. There is thus a risk that the collapse of one bank will cause the insolvency of others, causing a chain reaction. As the banks handle payments and much of the supply of credit to an economy, any disruption of these services can seriously damage economic activity. It is this key role which distinguishes the banking industry from other sectors of the economy. In all western industrialized nations, these considerations have led to elaborate banking supervision systems. The associated restrictions on competition are accepted. In Germany, this is evident in article 102 of the Act to Prevent Restriction of Competition, which explicitly permits anti-competitive conduct by credit institutions if this is approved or supervised by the BAKred and serves to promote the efficiency of the credit institutions.

---

[39] Cf. Dewatripont and Tirole, 1993, chap. 2.2.

From the viewpoint of the central bank, another factor in favour of banking supervision is that it is easier for it to implement its monetary policy the more heavily the banks are regulated.[40] This is because the banks transmit monetary policy.

Despite all these arguments in favour of banking supervision, its problems should not be ignored. In addition to the associated costs of administration, the disadvantages of restrictions on competition must also be remembered. Moreover, it must be expected that the banking supervisory actors pursue their own interests, which differ from those of society.[41] Finally, the implementation of banking supervision frequently demands the use of coarse instruments which may lead to undesirable evasive reactions by the banks.[42]

b) The allocation of banking supervision responsibilities

The basis of banking supervision in Germany is the Banking Act. After the Second World War, banking supervision was undertaken by the finance ministers of the Länder together with the Land Central Banks and the Bank deutscher Länder on the basis of the 1939 version of the Banking Act. In 1948, the Board of Directors of the Bank deutscher Länder started developing a banking supervision law[43] and examined the question of the allocation of banking supervision responsibilities. In August 1948, it adopted the guiding principle that the banking supervisory authorities of the Länder should supervise and ensure compliance with the directives issued by the Bank deutscher Länder.[44] This rigorous principle met with resistance from the Länder banking supervisory authorities, which feared the loss of their own sovereign powers.

In 1951, a working party composed of representatives of the central banking system and the banking supervisory authorities presented a draft banking act,[45] which met with resistance in the Board of Directors of the Bank deutscher Länder.[46] In January 1957, the Federal Cabinet unexpectedly

[40] Cf. Baltensperger, 1988.
[41] Cf. Boot and Thakor, 1993.
[42] Cf. Kim and Santomero, 1988.
[43] Cf. the Minutes of the 20th Meeting of the Board of Directors of the Bank deutscher Länder held on 19 Oct. 1948 (HA BBk B 330–006).
[44] Cf. the Minutes of the 15th Meeting of the Board of Directors of the Bank deutscher Länder held on 17 Aug. 1948 (HA BBk B 330–004).
[45] Cf. the Minutes of the 107th Meeting of the Board of Directors of the Bank deutscher Länder held on 7–8 Nov. 1951 (HA BBk B 330–049).
[46] Cf. the Minutes of the 112th Meeting of the Board of Directors of the Bank deutscher Länder held on 23–24 Jan. 1952 (HA BBk B 330–052).

agreed on a bill to establish a Federal Banking Supervisory Office. The Bank deutscher Länder was not even given an opportunity to submit an opinion.[47] This bill weakened the banking supervisory role of the central bank, and the Board of Directors consequently signalled its displeasure.[48] Meanwhile, the tug of war on the allocation of responsibilities continued between the Bundesbank, the Federal Minister of Finance and the Bundesrat.[49] A draft which the Central Bank Council found conditionally acceptable was finally presented in November 1958.[50] Under this draft, the BAKred assumed the sovereign functions, and the Bundesbank was responsible for implementing supervision in practice. Because the BAKred was not designed to have any regional offices, conflicts between it and the Bundesbank were minimized from the outset. The prolonged resistance of the Bundesrat meant that the law was not passed until 1961.

With the new Banking Act, the Bundesbank gained a strong position in banking supervision, in particular in its practical implementation. With the internationalization of the banking sector, its influence on the material aspects of banking supervision has now receded. Numerous banking law directives were issued by the European Community starting in the mid-1970s.

The Basle Committee on Banking Supervision has performed influential preparatory work, and continues to do so. The Basle Committee is composed of representatives of regulatory bodies and central banks of the G-10, plus Switzerland and Luxembourg. Although the Bundesbank can exert some influence here, the strong international presence means that such influence is necessarily moderate.

The following sections analyse the role of the Bundesbank in the regulation of lending and deposit rates, deposit protection, the internationalization of banking supervision and the definition of liable capital.

c) The regulation of lending and deposit rates

In many countries, the regulation of lending and deposit rates was viewed as a means of ensuring an adequate interest margin for the banks and a tool

---

[47] Cf. the Minutes of the 234th Meeting of the Board of Directors of the Bank deutscher Länder held on 9–10 Jan. 1957 (HA BBk B 330–099).

[48] Cf. the Minutes of the 234th Meeting of the Board of Directors of the Bank deutscher Länder held on 9–10 Jan. 1957 (HA BBk B 330–099).

[49] Cf. the Minutes of the 32nd Central Bank Council meeting held on 2 Oct. 1958 (HA BBk B 330–145).

[50] Cf. the Minutes of the 41st Central Bank Council meeting held on 19 Feb. 1959 (HA BBk B 330–150).

for the central banks to affect interest rate levels directly. Deposit rate caps were designed to prevent cut-throat competition between the banks, lending rate caps to protect smaller borrowers. In Germany, the central associations of the banking industry agreed common interest rates from 1931 after the banking crisis. After the Second World War, the Länder banking supervisory authorities assumed this role. However, 'grey' deposit rates were soon being paid without any penalties by the supervisory authorities.[51] Interest rate regulation was therefore a controversial subject in the Central Bank Council, but it did not advocate any interest rate decontrol, at least in its external communications.[52] The banking associations also attached great importance to interest rate regulation.[53] Finally, article 23 of the 1961 *KWG* stipulated that the Federal Minister of Economics can regulate interest rates in consultation with the Bundesbank. The minister delegated this right to the BAKred, which can take an active role after consulting the Bundesbank. On 1 March 1965, the first Interest Rates Order came into force. This linked maximum lending rates to the discount rate, and laid down fixed rates for maximum deposit rates.

But shortly after the Order came into force, the credit institutions issued medium-term notes, bypassing both the Interest Rates Order and the minimum reserve requirements.[54] Although the maximum deposit rates were subsequently adjusted to the market situation on numerous occasions, there were still many endeavours to circumvent the restrictions. Finally, the Federal Minister of Economics recommended the lifting of the Interest Rates Order in January 1967.[55] It expired at the end of March 1967 and was replaced by interest rate recommendations by the banking associations.

The failure of the Interest Rates Order highlighted the limits of banking supervision. Price controls collide with the principle of competition and are therefore difficult to enforce. If international alternatives appear, national regulations are at best relevant for 'small' bank customers, while the larger ones go elsewhere. In any attempt to control rates, the hands of the banking supervisory authorities are therefore tied.

[51] Cf. the Minutes of the 152nd Meeting of the Board of Directors of the Bank deutscher Länder held on 28 Oct. 1953 (HA BBk B 330–073).

[52] Cf. the Minutes of the 23rd Central Bank Council meeting held on 8–9 May 1958 (HA BBk B 330–140).

[53] Cf. Gesetzliche Regelung der Soll- und Habenzinsen der Kreditinstitute. Submission to the Central Bank Council on 16 May 1958 (HA BBk B 330–141).

[54] Cf. Umgehung der Zinsverordnung und der Mindestreserveregelung durch Ausgabe von Schuldverschreibungen und auf anderen Wegen. Submission to the Central Bank Council of 20 Apr. 1965 (HA BBk B 330–441).

[55] Cf. Letter from Federal Minster of Finance Karl Schiller to the President of the Deutsche Bundesbank, Karl Blessing, on 27 Jan. 1967 (HA BBk B 330–459).

d) Deposit protection

Another challenge for the Bundesbank arrived with the collapse of Bank-haus Herstatt in 1974. This bank had built up large forward exchange positions, and its final losses totalled DM 1.2 billion. A Bundesbank attempt to mount a rescue action failed, and the BAKred closed down the bank on 26 June 1974. The resulting crisis of confidence threatened to spill over into a liquidity crisis. Large amounts of deposits were withdrawn from the small private sector banks, with insurance companies and public-law institutions being particularly involved in these moves. The Bundesbank therefore extended its rediscount facilities and granted Lombard loans in unlimited amounts.

This case highlighted two particular problems. On the one hand, banks with an excellent credit standing were also affected by the loss of confidence, and the Bundesbank saw itself forced to support their liquidity as the lender of last resort. On the other hand, the guarantee fund established in 1969 by the Bundesverband deutscher Banken (German Banking Association) to guarantee deposits by natural persons up to a limit of DM 20,000 was insufficient to prevent a run. There was therefore a need for solutions to two problems: first to safeguard the liquidity of the banks, and secondly to prevent runs.

The Bundesbank developed the concept of a *liquidity consortium bank*, whose task was to extend liquidity assistance to banks of undoubted credit-worthiness which have run into liquidity problems by buying from them bills not eligible for discounting with the Bundesbank and converting them into eligible bills. This concept was implemented very quickly, with the Bundesbank taking a 30 per cent stake in the liquidity consortium bank.

Solving the problem of bank runs proved to be more difficult. The Federal Ministry of Finance presented a draft statutory regulation which met with little enthusiasm from both the banks and the BAKred. The Bundesbank met with an equal lack of success for its proposals in October 1974. Instead, the proposal by the Bundesverband deutscher Banken, which had been agreed with various Federal ministries, was adopted. A *deposit guarantee fund* was established, which all private sector banks meeting certain min-imum standards can join. The fund guarantees deposits up to 30 per cent of the bank's liable capital.

Although the members of the Central Bank Council did not regard this private sector solution as being ideal, it was adequate and could be im-plemented quickly. The public sector and cooperative banks had already created their own deposit protection schemes.

The problem involved in such a deposit protection scheme is that the individual bank is no longer required to convince its depositors of its credit-worthiness. The risks of any reckless business policy pursued by a bank are no longer borne, at least in part, by its depositors. However, these disadvantages of deposit protection are limited by the fact that deposits by other banks are not guaranteed, and a bank which wants to keep operating on the money market must therefore pay attention to its credit standing. In addition, member banks of the deposit guarantee fund can be audited by the audit association of private banks at any time.

e) Banking supervision beyond German borders

German banks have increasingly been drawn to the Euromarket since the 1960s, as large corporate customers have insisted on profiting from the more favourable Euromarket rates. Depositors took advantage of the stricter banking secrecy provisions in some foreign financial centres to escape German taxes. The Euromarket offered the banks other advantages, in addition to the lack of minimum reserve requirements: banking supervision was more relaxed. There was also much greater freedom as regards financial instruments, coupled with liberal company laws and tax privileges.

Because foreign subsidiaries were not subject to German banking supervision, but the parent companies in Germany were generally responsible for their subsidiaries' liabilities, the German regulatory authorities were handicapped. By shifting business abroad, the German banks could largely evade German banking supervision. Any tightening of supervision in Germany would have tended to exacerbate this problem. As early as 1977, the Central Bank Council therefore discussed options for eliminating this problem.

Attempts to cooperate with foreign supervisory authorities proved to be relatively unsuccessful. Although a subsequent gentleman's agreement provided the Bundesbank and the BAKred with audit reports on the Luxembourg subsidiaries of German banks, these were insufficiently detailed and were only provided once a year. The Central Bank Council therefore decided to ask the Federal Minister of Finance to amend the Banking Act. This amendment would have required the banks to submit consolidated monthly and annual financial statements including domestic and foreign participations in credit institutions (10 per cent interest and above). The regulations on capital adequacy and loan diversification would apply to the *banking group*.

The efforts to amend the Banking Act in 1981 were unsuccessful. The Bundesbank regarded the need as all the more urgent when some German banks concealed losses incurred in Germany by shifting them to foreign subsidiaries. In November 1983, these fears were confirmed when Bankhaus Schröder, Münchmeyer, Hengst & Co (SMH) collapsed and was only saved through concerted moves at the Bundesbank under the leadership of the President of the BAKred. SMH had extended considerable loans to a rapidly expanding group of companies not only from Germany, but above all via its Luxembourg subsidiary. This had resulted in the large exposure limit stipulated in the Banking Act being undermined by international transactions.

The Bundesbank also received support from Basle. The central bank governors of the Group of Ten and Switzerland had agreed the 'Basle Concordat', under which the banks were to be supervised on a cross-border basis using consolidated financial statements. Shortly thereafter, in June 1983, the European Community adopted the directive on the supervision of credit institutions on a consolidated basis. The Banking Act was then amended in 1984, and consolidated bank supervision became the law.

f) The dispute about 'liable capital'

The Bundesbank was less successful in the European dispute about defining 'liable capital'. This limits the activities of the banks, particularly as regards large exposures and other risks. The narrower the definition of liable capital, the lower the danger that risky transactions may result in a bank becoming insolvent. As with any other restraint, restricting a bank's freedom of choice causes costs, in particular in the form of profits forgone. When defining liable capital, two further criteria must be taken into account: competition must be fair (1) between the various banking groups within a country, and (2) between banks in different countries.

Note on (1): as early as 1963, the competitive strength of the cooperative banks—in contrast to the savings banks, which profited from their public guarantors' uncalled liability—had been reinforced by the addition of their members' uncalled liability to capital and reserves (Order on the determination of an addition for the calculation of the liable capital of credit institutions in the form of registered cooperatives). In the run-up to the amendment of the Banking Act in 1984, the savings bank organizations and umbrella associations of the local authorities lobbied for the addition of guarantors' uncalled liability to the liable capital of credit institutions established under public law as well. The Bundesbank opposed this move successfully, because it feared a fundamental weakening of the concept of capital. The uncalled members' liability component of the cooperative banks' liable capital was cut back at the same time.

Note on (2): at the international level, on the other hand, the Bundesbank had to yield. The Basle Committee on Banking Supervision (Cooke Committee) prepared a recommendation for calculating the capital adequacy of banks. Although the proposals of the Basle Committee need the approval of the central bank governors and the Bundesbank can thus make its influence felt, it could not prevent the Committee proposing a definition of liable capital which was much broader than the German concept. It stated that, in addition to the core capital of nominal equity and disclosed reserves, a supplementary tier of capital should be added. This would include revaluation reserves, i.e. unrealized gains from the appreciation of assets, as well as general provisions for bad debts. Although the capital ratio requirements were increased at the same time from 5.6 per cent to 8.0 per cent of risk assets, the final result was a weakening of the capital requirements.

The G-10 central bank governors approved the recommendation of the Cooke Committee in July 1988.[56] The Bundesbank's agreement was made easier by the fact that the recommendation forced numerous banks in the USA and Japan to increase their capital. A short while later, the European Community adopted this recommendation and issued the Own Funds Directive in April 1989. This was followed in December 1989 by the Solvency Ratio Directive, which laid down that liable capital must be at least 8 per cent of assets weighted by risk. At the same time, the Second Banking Coordination Directive was adopted, under which banking supervision by one EC country is recognized by the other EC countries. Banking activities licensed in the country of origin can be practised throughout the EC.

Nevertheless, the Central Bank Council decided in February 1990 to place greater emphasis on safeguarding the German banking system than on the creation of a level international playing field, and made a recommendation to the German government that revaluation reserves should not be admitted. But despite support from the BAKred, the Bundesbank failed to press home its argument. The January 1993 amendment of the Banking Act largely followed the recommendation of the Cooke Committee and allowed the limited inclusion of revaluation reserves, reserves for general bank risks and long-term liabilities as supplementary capital (article 10). In a further amendment of the Banking Act in 1997, 'tier three' capital (net profits and subordinated short-term liabilities with a contracted maturity of at least two years) was also included in the definition of capital adequacy.

In the 1990s, the influence of the Bundesbank on the development of prudential legislation has bowed to that of the European Union. The Basle Committee on Banking Supervision is also very influential. Although the Bundesbank has a potentially strong influence on this Committee (at least formally), this is also subject to political constraints.

---

[56] Cf. 'Basler Minimalkonsens', in: Börsenzeitung, 13 July 1988.

7. The strengths and weaknesses of the German financial market

There is no doubt that the Bundesbank's policies have had a considerable influence on the development of the German financial market. This concluding section therefore examines the strengths and weaknesses of that financial market in the light of Bundesbank policies.

The *strengths* of the German financial market include its stability. There have been comparatively few bank failures in Germany since 1948. Apart from the Herstatt Bank, there has not been a single insolvency which might have appreciably damaged the credit standing of German banks abroad. This outstanding record is due in part to the prudential arrangements in Germany, for which the Bundesbank has been responsible to a significant extent.

The stability of the German financial market is also supported by the deposit guarantee schemes of the various banking groups. These have largely eliminated the risk of bank runs, and there is no evidence that such systems have encouraged reckless behaviour by individual banks. One of the reasons could be that the systems are organized in the private sector, instead of being imposed by the state.

The German banks have also profited from the stability of the D-mark, a feature which has been decisive in the rise of the D-mark as a key international reserve currency. One consequence of this is that many cross-border credit and investment transactions have been—and continue to be—settled in D-marks. German banks have a natural home advantage in this business.

The German financial market has also benefited from the outstanding payment system, which is cost-effective, quick and low-risk because it has been largely automated. Again, the Bundesbank has played a key role here. The processing and settlement of trades in securities exchanges in Germany is also largely computerized.

These strengths of the German financial market are accompanied by a number of *weaknesses*. Although the Bundesbank has set aside its misgivings about the increasing short-termism of market participants, it has not relinquished them altogether. The problems posed by a short-term orientation are not merely that higher long-term income is sacrificed in favour of short-term gains. A policy which reduces short-term market value risks also increases long-term ones. The conflict between a short- and a long-term risk policy frequently goes unnoticed. Although this supports the Bundesbank's objections to a short-termist strategy, a valid question is still whether this justifies the Bundesbank's restrictive policy against short-dated paper until very recently.

The shortage of short-dated paper on the German financial market is to be seen in the context of a general perception that the share in the total volume of debt and equity securities in Germany accounted for by tradable securitized debt securities is very low. There are practically no longer any exchange-traded industrial bonds in Germany. In 1995, the market value of quoted German shares in Germany was around 27.0 per cent of gross domestic product. Contrast this with 93.0 per cent in the USA, 130.0 per cent in the United Kingdom and 74 per cent in Japan.[57]

Financial innovations are created mostly in the USA and the UK. Germany normally ends up imitating them, and financial innovation technology tends to appear in German banks after some delay. A major contributory factor was the Bundesbank's chronically restrictive stance on financial innovations up to 1985. At the same time, however, it must be said that German banks displayed little interest in financial innovations until the mid-1980s. One reason for this is probably the universal banking system itself. In a dual banking system, the investment banks put a great deal of effort into finding creative solutions enabling them to participate in credit and equity business using securitized debt instruments. In a universal banking system, there is no competition between commercial and investment banks, and thus little incentive to develop financial innovations.

The German banks still see the Bundesbank's minimum reserve requirement as a burden on the German financial market. Because the Bundesbank views the minimum reserve as a core element of its monetary policy, it is also trying to find ways to keep the minimum reserve requirement in the future European Monetary Union. These include exempting securities repurchase transactions and a willingness to reconsider the idea of an interest-bearing minimum reserve.

In view of the upcoming monetary union and the globalization of the financial markets, strengthening the competitiveness of the German financial market is becoming an increasingly important task. A distinction must be made between the competitive strength of the German financial market and that of the German banks. The large German banks have long been active in the leading international banking centres. By the end of 1995, German banks had 322 subsidiaries and 254 branches abroad.[58] Some German banks have also acquired foreign banks, particularly in the UK. The German banks now do a large portion of their business through their foreign offices. Table 7 shows first the international activities of credit institutions domiciled in a particular country, and secondly the international activities of credit

[57] Cf. Deutsches Aktieninstitut, 1996, p. FB–05–2–a.
[58] Cf. Deutsche Bundesbank, 1996c, p. 104. These figures are higher than those disclosed in Table 1, because participations of at least 50 per cent in credit institutions, factoring and leasing companies are included for the subsidiaries, and sub-branches for the branches.

TABLE 7: Cross-border lendings and borrowings of credit institutions*

Country	Credit institutions domiciled in the country in question[a]		Credit institutions with parent in the country in question[b]	
	Lendings	Borrowings	Lendings	Borrowings
Germany	563.7	539.2	887.1	859.2
France	614.8	612.9	653.3	716.4
United Kingdom	1,350.4	1,442.7	322.1	379.7
USA	600.7	870.2	338.5	450.8
Japan	1,217.9	738.3	1,181.8	925.8
Switzerland	437.6	366.6	337.6	380.8

* US $ billion; figures as at end of 1995.

[a] Cross-border lendings and borrowings of credit institutions domiciled in the country shown.

[b] Cross-border lendings and borrowings plus local foreign currency positions of credit institutions whose parent is domiciled in the country shown. Intracompany and intercompany positions are not included.

Source: Bank für Internationalen Zahlungsausgleich, 1996, Table 2A; Table 7 total position % related offices.

institutions whose parents are domiciled in a particular country. The figures in billions of US dollars relate to the end of 1995.

The first two columns of figures in Table 7 show that the cross-border assets (US $563.7 billion) and liabilities (US $539.2 billion) of credit institutions domiciled in Germany are comparatively modest. With the exception of Switzerland, all the other countries listed rank in front of Germany. This highlights the lack of appeal of Germany as a financial centre. However, German credit institutions have developed substantial activities through their domestic and foreign networks (third and fourth column) with international assets of US $887.1 billion and liabilities of US $859.2 billion, outperformed only by the Japanese banks. This means that German banks have a most respectable presence on the international scene.

Of the European financial centres, London clearly takes pole position.[59] The securities business in particular, with its wide variety of classic and innovative instruments, is much more extensive in London than Frankfurt. This is underlined by the decision by a number of big German banks to switch their securities business to London. And if the United Kingdom does

[59] Cf. London Business School, 1995, Section 10.

not become a member of any future monetary union, any regulation of the financial centres in the union will encourage business to move to London. This must also be remembered by the European Central Bank, one of whose aims must be to promote highly skilled jobs in the financial sector within the euro currency area. But the Bundesbank too will continue to play a key role in making Germany a more attractive financial centre.

8. Sources and bibliography

Unpublished sources

Historisches Archiv der Deutschen Bundesbank (HA BBk)

Bibliography

Arbeitskreis der Banken und Leasinggesellschaften der Automobilwirtschaft (1995): Finanzdienstleistungen für den Automobilmarkt 1995, press kit, Hamburg

Baltensperger, Ernst (1988): Die Regulierung des Bankensektors, in: Wirtschaftswissenschaftliches Studium 17, pp. 53–7

Bank für Internationalen Zahlungsausgleich (1990): Bericht des Ausschusses für Interbank-Netting-Systeme der Zentralbanken der Länder der Zehnergruppe, Basle

Bank für Internationalen Zahlungsausgleich (1993): Zahlungsverkehrsdienstleistungen der Zentralbanken für grenzüberschreitende und mehrere Währungen einbeziehende Transaktionen, Basle

Bank für Internationalen Zahlungsausgleich (1996): Entwicklung des Internationalen Bankgeschäfts und der Internationalen Finanzmärkte, Basle, August

Bitz, Michael (1989): Erscheinungsformen und Funktionen von Finanzintermediären, in: Wirtschaftswissenschaftliches Studium 18, pp. 430–6

Boot, Arnoud/Thakor, Anjan (1993): Self-Interested Bank Regulation, in: American Economic Review 83, pp. 206–12

Borio, Claudio/Fritz, Wilhelm (1995): The Response of Short-Term Bank Lending Rates to Policy Rates: A Cross-Country Perspective, BIS Working Paper 27, Basle

Deutsche Bundesbank (1976): Deutsches Geld- und Bankwesen in Zahlen 1876–1975, Frankfurt a.M.

Deutsche Bundesbank (1985): press release 12 April 1985, in: Auszüge aus Presseartikeln, no. 26

Deutsche Bundesbank (1993): ⁶Die Deutsche Bundesbank—Geldpolitische Aufgaben und Instrumente, Frankfurt a.M.

Deutsche Bundesbank (1994a): Zur Neugestaltung und Senkung der Mindestreserven, in: Monatsbericht 46, 2, pp. 13–17

Deutsche Bundesbank (1994b): Geldpolitische Implikationen der zunehmenden Verwendung derivativer Finanzinstrumente, in: Monatsbericht 46, 11, pp. 41–57

Deutsche Bundesbank (1994c): Neuere Entwicklungen im unbaren Zahlungsverkehr der Deutschen Bundesbank, in: Monatsbericht 46, 8, pp. 47–63

Deutsche Bundesbank (1995a): Die Geldpolitik der Bundesbank, Frankfurt a.M.

Deutsche Bundesbank (1995b): Verbriefungstendenzen im deutschen Finanzsystem und ihre geldpolitische Bedeutung, in: Monatsbericht 47, 4, pp. 19–33

Deutsche Bundesbank (1996a): Elektronische Abrechnung in Frankfurt am Main (EAF 2), in: Monatsbericht 48, 1, pp. 16–19

Deutsche Bundesbank (1996b): Reaktionen der Geldmarkt- und kurzfristigen Bankzinsen auf Änderungen der Notenbanksätze, in: Monatsbericht 48, 10, pp. 33–48

Deutsche Bundesbank (1996c): Bankenstatistik. Statistisches Beiheft zum Monatsbericht 1, October

Deutsche Bundesbank (1996d): Kapitalmarktstatistik, Statistisches Beiheft zum Monatsbericht 2, October

Deutsche Bundesbank (1996e): press release 12 Juni 1996, in: Auszüge aus Presseartikeln, no. 37

Deutsche Bundesbank (1996f): Geschäftsbericht 1995, Frankfurt a.M.

Deutsches Aktieninstitut (1996): DAI-Factbook 1996, Frankfurt a.M.

Dewatripont, Mathias/Tirole, Jean (1993): The Prudential Regulation of Banks, Cambridge, Mass.

Franke, Günter/Meyer, Bernd (1998): The Impact of German Discount and Lombard Policy on Financial Markets, in: Jaeger, Klaus/Koch, Karl-Josef (eds.): Trade, Growth, and Economic Policy in Open Economies—Essays in Honour of Hans-Jürgen Vosgerau, Heidelberg, pp. 193–217

Gesellschaft für Zahlungssysteme (1995): Entwicklung des Kreditkartenmarktes in Deutschland, Frankfurt a.M.

Hardy, Daniel (1996): Market Reaction to Changes in German Official Rates, Discussion paper 4, ed. Deutsche Bundesbank

Issing, Otmar (1996): 6Einführung in die Geldpolitik, München

Kim, Dacsik/Santomero, Anthony (1988): Risk in Banking and Capital Regulation, in: Journal of Finance 43, pp. 1219–33

London Business School (1995): The Competitive Position of London's Financial Services, Final Report, London March

Mühlhaupt, Ludwig (1980): 3Einführung in die Betriebswirtschaftslehre der Banken, Wiesbaden

Pohl, Manfred (1986): Entstehung und Entwicklung des Universalbankensystems, Frankfurt a.M.

Schlesinger, Helmut (1988): Die Rolle der Deutschen Bundesbank: Institutioneller Rahmen, Aufgaben und Politik, in: Kyongsang-nonch'ong, no. 6

Städtler, Arno (1995): Leasing in Deutschland: Immobilien weiter expansiv—Massengeschäft rückläufig, in: ifo-Schnelldienst 48, 1/2, pp. 8–15

Statistisches Bundesamt (1962): Statistisches Jahrbuch für die Bundesrepublik Deutschland 1962, Wiesbaden

Statistisches Bundesamt (1996): Statistisches Jahrbuch für die Bundesrepublik Deutschland 1996, Wiesbaden

Verband öffentlicher Banken (1996): 4Kreditwirtschaftlich wichtige Vorhaben der EU, Cologne

Wasmund, Jörn/Alexander, Volbert/Ahrens, Ralf (1996a): Zentralbankratssitzungen der Deutschen Bundesbank und die Volatilität von Geld- und Kapitalmarktzinsen, discussion paper, Giessen

Wasmund, Jörn/Alexander, Volbert/Feth, Christoph (1996b): Der Einfluß von Leitzinsänderungen in unterschiedlichen geldpolitischen Regimen auf Aktien- und Wechselkurse: empirische Evidenz für die BRD, discussion paper, Giessen

Part Three

MONETARY POLICY IN THE FEDERAL REPUBLIC OF GERMANY

'The cardinal monetary question is that of the independence of the central bank.'
Wilhelm Vocke, President of the Board of Directors of the Bank deutscher Länder

VI. Monetary Stability: Threat and Proven Response

By Manfred J. M. Neumann

1. Guaranteeing the value of money as an essential prerequisite of a market economy

The goal of ensuring the stability of the purchasing power of money can be justified ethically. The guiding 'ordo-liberal conception' of the market economy is that the economic activities of the population require a regulatory framework (*Ordnungsrahmen*) that offers them the greatest possible degree of individual freedom and self-fulfilment, with individual responsibility. This includes private property and open meritocratic competition. It also includes a currency whose purchasing power is stable. Only this sort of money is 'minted freedom'.[1] It is precisely because the state claims a monopoly of money creation that it is of central ethical importance that it offers citizens, in exchange for their services, a means of exchange whose purchasing power is stable.

The pre-eminence of the goal of monetary stability can also be derived from its importance for the effective functioning of the competitive system and, in the final analysis, for guaranteeing social security and social peace. Governments that treat monetary stability high-handedly are not honouring their obligations. If they supply money in an unstable and inflationary fashion, they prevent their citizens from fully exploiting the welfare potential of available resources. They induce citizens to take decisions that would be inefficient under a stable monetary system.

Persistent inflation reduces well-being in a number of ways. Let us merely recall here the most important economic and social costs. Inflation is harmful to the information and steering function of prices, because it makes it more difficult to distinguish between changes in relative prices and those in the general price level. Inflation leads to higher transaction costs, by creating

[1] Dostojevskij, 1971, p. 29.

an incentive to shorten the duration of contracts and to reduce cash balances to a level that is sub-optimal in macroeconomic terms. Inflation exerts an adverse effect on investment and saving because, given a progressive income tax, it raises marginal tax rates and the overall tax burden in real terms, and increases the uncertainty regarding the real rate of return that can be earned.

Overall, inflation is damaging to economic growth and thus restricts the scope for offering social security to those who, owing to personal handicaps or the barriers to labour market access, cannot support themselves. Moreover, inflation is detrimental to the position of the lower social strata to the extent that these sections of the population do not have the know-how to protect themselves from it. Thus they bear a disproportionate share of the burden of the inflation tax.[2]

2. The purchasing power of the Deutsche Mark—an international comparison

a) The facts

During the last 50 years the D-mark has gained a reputation for proverbial stability throughout the world. Yet in fact, the internal purchasing power of the D-mark, measured in terms of the consumer price index, has declined continuously. The only exceptions were the years 1950, 1952, 1953, and 1986. The D-mark's special reputation is due to the fact that the loss of purchasing power by other currencies has been far greater, and that the D-mark has consequently repeatedly been revalued since the end of the 1960s, in some cases dramatically.

Table 1 indicates average rates of inflation, as measured by consumer price indices. Between 1949 and 1996 the price level in Germany rose by an average of 2.8 per cent *per annum*; this was slightly less than in Switzerland (3.1 per cent), and far less than in all other industrialized countries. In the other large European countries, in particular France, the UK, and Italy, the cost of living has increased during the past half century at average rates of 6–7 per cent; more than double the German rate. Moreover, the standard deviations given in Table 1 indicate that price trends in Germany have generally been less volatile than in other countries.

In order to evaluate these results of German monetary policy, which are

---

[2] Tietmeyer terms this 'cold expropriation'. Cf. Tietmeyer, 1996, p. 38.

TABLE 1: Inflation rates from an international perspective, 1950–96. Price indices of the private cost of living: average inflation rate,[a] (standard deviation shown in brackets)

Periods	Gemany	Switzer-land	USA	Japan	France	United Kingdom	Italy
1949–96	2.8	3.1	4.1	4.4	5.9	6.6	7.0
	(2.3)	(2.4)	(3.1)	(4.7)	(4.3)	(5.0)	(5.8)
1949–59	1.1	1.1	2.1	2.9	6.2	4.3	2.7
	(3.3)	(1.8)	(2.2)	(5.8)	(6.1)	(2.8)	(2.8)
1960–72	2.9	3.7	2.8	5.6	4.4	4.5	3.8
	(1.2)	(1.5)	(1.6)	(1.3)	(1.4)	(2.1)	(2.1)
1973–9	4.9	4.7	8.2	10.1	10.2	14.7	15.5
	(1.5)	(3.4)	(2.1)	(6.0)	(1.8)	(5.0)	(2.9)
1980–96	2.8	3.2	4.7	2.0	5.2	6.1	8.6
	(1.7)	(1.8)	(2.9)	(1.9)	(4.1)	(4.0)	(5.5)
Memo item: Value of money end 1996 (1949=100)	27.3	23.8	15.2	13.3	6.7	5.3	4.2

[a] The average rates of inflation are calculated as geometric means.

Source: Deutsche Bundesbank; own calculations.

impressive by international standards, it has to be taken into account that the reported figures exaggerate the true scale of inflation. However, the degree to which inflation is exaggerated is unlikely to represent more than one percentage point. The widely held assumption that an official inflation rate of 2 per cent is equivalent to a true rate of zero must be called in question.[3]

A comparison of the results for specific periods shows that during the 1950s the Bundesbank and the Schweizerische Nationalbank managed to keep price inflation down to an annual average of around 1 per cent. Not until the 1970s did the inflationary trend get out of control; this occurred in all countries, although to varying degrees. This can largely be explained by the explosive rise in the US balance of payments deficits from 1970, a

[3] In a report for the Bundesfinanzhof (Federal Fiscal Court), the Bundesbank stated its position on this issue as follows: 'generally speaking, a rise in the consumer price index of perhaps 1 per cent *per annum* will not be considered a decline in the value of money . . ., and if the index rises by 1–2 per cent, this can be taken as a deterioration in the value of money only with reservations.' Cf. Deutsche Bundesbank, 1968, p. 12.

trend that initiated substantial intervention in support of the dollar, and
by the lack of caution exerted in cushioning the oil-price shock of 1973 by
monetary accommodation. Not until the 1980s did countries throughout
the world manage to bring the inflationary trend back down to the level
prevailing in the 1950s and 1960s. To this, the Bundesbank, which assumed
a leading role within the framework of the European Monetary System
(EMS), made a decisive contribution.

b) Shifts in the price level as a problem for monetary policy

The average price increase of 2.8 per cent during the last 50 years cannot
simply be equated with inflation. An analytical distinction can be made here
between an inflation component, which is caused by an excessive growth of
the money stock, and one-off changes in the price level, which can be caused,
for instance, by an increase in value-added tax rates or an upward shift in
the price of imported raw materials. Shifts in the price level reduce the purchasing power of money in precisely the same way as the inflation component, but this does not imply that it is the task of the central bank to prevent
any shift in the price level.

   The goal of price stability can be conceptualized in different ways. If price
stability were defined in the sense of maintaining absolute purchasing power,
the central bank would have to ensure that the price level did not deviate
lastingly from a constant target value. Shifts in the price level would call
for a restrictive response, in order to reverse them. An important argument
against such a conceptualization is that a surge in prices can lead to substantial structural adjustment problems and to a decline in output and employment. A restrictive response by the monetary authority would exacerbate
these trends.

   Alternatively, price stability can be defined in terms of avoiding inflation.
This means that the central bank has to orient the growth of the money
stock towards the medium-term growth of potential output. This would remove the most important reason for persistent losses of purchasing power
in the past. Such losses would still occur, however, owing to shifts in the
price level for non-monetary reasons.

   A superior conception of price stability brings together the goal of non-
inflationary growth of the money stock and that of reducing non-monetary
shifts in the price level: a shift in the price level is to be neither reversed nor
accepted; rather, attempts must be made to arrest it in such a way that it is
not taken as an occasion for higher wage settlements. The strategic goal is
that of preventing second-round effects.

   The Bundesbank has sought to act in accordance with this concept. The most important test came with the oil-price shock of the autumn of 1973. In March of that year, in the wake of the suspension of the exchange rate peg to the dollar, the Bundesbank had adopted an unprecedentedly restrictive monetary policy stance, with the aim of freeing the economy from the inflationary legacy of the Bretton Woods system. In 1972 the monetary base and M1 had been rising at rates of 13–16 per cent, and the inflation rate had risen to around 7 per cent at the start of 1973. Within the space of a few months the Bundesbank brought the growth of both monetary aggregates to a virtual standstill. It was in this situation that the bombshell of the quadrupling of oil prices struck in October 1973. It was evident that the decisive shift in factor price relations would exert an additional contractive effect on output and employment. A widespread passing-on of price increases, and an intensification of the domestic struggle over income distribution, had to be expected. In agreement with the governing social-democrat/liberal coalition, the Bundesbank opted for the goal of preventing, as far as possible, an even greater price surge. Consequently, in contrast to most other central banks, it retained its restrictive stance until well into the year 1974, and subsequently relaxed its position only gradually. By this means it proved possible to take the edge off the price surge and to limit inflation to 7 per cent in 1974. By contrast, the rate of inflation leapt up to 13 per cent in France, 16 per cent in the UK, 19 per cent in Italy, and to as much as 23 per cent in Japan. The price paid for the impressive success of the Bundesbank consisted of an exacerbation of the decline in output and employment.

Even in retrospect, it cannot be determined with any degree of certainty whether a less restrictive stance would have sufficed to restrict the oil-price-induced inflation to a sufficient extent, and remove the basis for exaggerated expectations regarding the scope for higher prices and wages. As far as the costs of fighting inflation are concerned, it must be borne in mind that the other industrialized countries also encountered output and employment crises of a similar order of magnitude. If the direct loss is calculated only in terms of the absolute decline in GDP, i.e. not the overall loss of economic growth, the losses in the UK and Italy amounted to 2.4 and 2.1 per cent, respectively, whereas in Germany and Japan it proved possible to keep them to just half this level (1.2 per cent). Even more impressive was the performance in the United States and France, whose output losses proved very minor, at 0.5 and 0.3 per cent, respectively.

In the final analysis, the Bundesbank's resolute position proved beneficial to the extent that it made it easier for it to fight inflation in the subsequent years. It managed to restrict the rate of inflation to under 3 per cent up to 1978, whereas the French rate fell only to 9 per cent. The figures given in Table 1 for the period 1973–9 show this clearly. While in Germany and Switzerland the average inflation rate was kept just under 5 per cent, the figure in Japan and France was around 10 per cent and in the UK and Italy around 15 per cent.

c) *Price stability: a drag on growth?*

As a consequence of post-Keynesian ideas, the erroneous view was propounded—in the academic sphere until the end of the 1960s and for long afterwards in the actual policy making of many countries—that the real rate of interest could be reduced with the help of an expansionary monetary policy (not merely temporarily, but permanently) and that, by this means, a higher growth path could be achieved.[4]

TABLE 2: Growth of real *per capita* GDP
(average rates of growth, standard deviation shown in brackets)

Periods	Germany	Switzer-land	USA	Japan	France	United Kingdom	Italy
1950–94	3.5	1.9	1.8	n.a.[b]	3.0	2.0	3.5
	(2.8)	(2.6)	(2.2)		(1.9)	(2.1)	(2.4)
1950–9	7.0	2.9	1.7	n.a.[b]	3.9	2.1	5.1
	(2.2)	(3.0)	(3.1)		(1.7)	(1.6)	(1.8)
1960–72	3.7	3.2	2.4	8.6	4.5	2.5	4.5
	(2.2)	(1.7)	(1.6)	(2.5)	(0.9)	(1.4)	(2.1)
1973–9	2.8	0.3	1.9	3.0	2.6	2.3	3.4
	(2.2)	(2.9)	(2.2)	(2.6)	(1.6)	(2.7)	(2.8)
1980–94	1.5	1.0	1.2	2.7	1.4	1.5	1.8
	(1.8)	(1.9)	(1.9)	(2.0)	(1.6)	(1.4)	(2.4)

[a] The average rates of growth are calculated as geometric means.
[b] Not available.

Source: Deutsche Bundesbank; own calculations.

Refined empirical methods are not required in order to appreciate that the alleged positive correlation between inflation and real growth does not exist. Table 2 comprises data on the growth of real GDP *per capita*. It is evident that, for example, the economy of an inflationary country such as Italy has grown substantially faster than the relatively price-stable Switzerland (3.5 compared with 1.9 per cent *per annum*), but not faster than the

---

[4] Cf. Tobin, 1965; for the opposing view, Friedman, 1968.

(West) German economy (3.5 per cent since end-1950). The UK, the country with the second-highest rate of inflation, achieved growth averaging just 2 per cent. Moreover, a comparison of sub-periods shows that, in all the countries under consideration, average real growth in the 1950s and 1960s, when inflation was low to moderate, was far higher than in later decades. Last but not least, developments since the start of the 1980s show that, in contrast to inflation rates, the real rates of economic growth have diverged only slightly between the countries.

Overall, the empirical evidence is clearly incompatible with the hypothesis that inflation stimulates growth. At the same time, the antithesis, i.e. that price stability is conducive to growth, cannot be confirmed with reference to this cross-national comparison either. In actual fact, detailed empirical models that allow explicitly for the most important growth factors would be required, in order to isolate the positive influence that a stable monetary order might have on growth. In this respect, the studies being conducted within the framework of the research programme on the new theory of endogenous growth are only in their infancy.

3. Characteristic features of the German monetary constitution

The periods of high inflation in the course of this century teach us that monetary stability cannot be maintained unless governments are prevented from gaining access to the country's money supply. For this reason, the monetarists proposed various monetary rules to which central banks should be subjected.[5] The alternative is to establish an independent central bank. This can be interpreted as a pre-commitment on the part of the government or the political system as a whole.[6] For a remarkably long time, monetary theorists did not recognize this solution, indeed rejected it.[7] Even today, the generally positive experiences of Germany and Switzerland are traced back

[5] Cf., for instance, Friedman, 1959, pp. 90ff. and Meltzer, 1984.

[6] Cf. Neumann, 1991, p. 99. In game-theory-oriented macroeconomics it is argued that it is impossible to offer an absolutely credible precommitment. Yet this overlooks the fact that the political costs of rescinding the legal guarantee of central bank independence can be prohibitively high.

[7] Cf. Friedman, 1962 and Brunner, 1983. Both emphasize the danger that independent central bank executives may use their scope for discretion for activities that are damaging to the economy. A historical case in point is the President of the German Reichsbank, Rudolf von Havenstein, who, although formally independent under the *Autonomiegesetz* (autonomy law), passed in May 1922 under the pressure of the Allied Reparation Commission, monetised the government's debts and thus opened the sluice-gates to hyper-inflation. He died on 20 Nov. 1923, the day the currency was stabilized.

less to the institutional guarantees of their central banks than to the existence of specific 'stability cultures'.[8]

The guiding thought behind this article is that Germany's success in terms of monetary stability has been decisively determined by the *de facto* far-reaching independence enjoyed by the Bundesbank. In the short run, the value of money is determined by myriad factors but, in the long run, exclusively by the rate of growth of the money stock. What is important, in the final analysis, is that the management of the central bank is in a position and is willing to exercise control over the money supply, against the specific interests of social groups, with the aim of monetary stability. This requires the independence of the central bank as an institution, and, equally importantly, the independence of the members of its executive organs.

a) The independence of the Bundesbank as an institution

The far-reaching independence of the Bundesbank as an institution is, at heart, rooted in its independence of instructions from the central government, as set out in the second sentence of section 12 of the Bundesbank Act. Although the Act was passed by the German parliament (in 1957), this provision owes much to the Allies, and in particular to US influence. Back in 1948, prior to the establishment of the Bundesbank, they stipulated, in the military law setting up the Bank deutscher Länder, that 'the bank is not subject to instructions from any political body or public office, with the exception of the courts'. That was a fundamental decision with an indelible effect.[9] It is true that the Allies had retained the option of themselves imposing restrictions on German monetary policy by decree, but no use was ever made of this possibility.

The Bundesbank's freedom from instruction applies to the powers listed in the Act. The most important of these are the issuing of currency; discount, credit and open market policy; minimum reserve policy; and the right to order statistical surveys in the banking and monetary sector. This freedom from instruction does not apply, on the other hand, to additional tasks as-

---

[8] On the importance of the stability culture see section 7 of this article.

[9] Accordingly, this provision remained unchanged when, in 1951, the Act was amended for the first time by the German parliament. Ludwig Erhard, the Minister of Economics, lent his support to this cause. A year earlier, however, at the meeting of the Central Bank Council on 22 Feb. 1950, he had declared that, if the Bank deutscher Länder refused to provide financing for a programme to fight unemployment, he was afraid 'that we will have a very hard time in the government and in the Bundestag in supporting the notion of an independent central bank.' Transcript of the 53rd Central Bank Council meeting held on 22–23 Feb. 1950, p. 1 (HA BBk B 330/23).

signed to the Bundesbank by law or other agreements. In principle, this constitutes a restriction on its independence. As far as safeguarding monetary stability is concerned, the most important case here is the assignment of the task of defending a given exchange-rate parity through intervention and other measures. It is inevitable that conflicts between the Federal Government and the Bundesbank arise over this important restriction of independence, one that implicitly poses a threat to the goal of maintaining monetary stability.[10]

The Act contains other provisions that influence the degree of independence of the Bundesbank as an institution. For instance, under section 13(2), members of the Federal Government have the right to participate in meetings of the Central Bank Council and to propose motions to it. Although they have no voting rights, they can require that a decision be postponed by up to two weeks. This suspensory veto does not constitute a decisive constraint on independence, provided it is not used extensively, although damage may be done in specific cases. In addition, under section 13(1) the Bundesbank is supposed to advise the Federal Government on monetary policy issues of major importance, and (under section 3 of the same article) the Government is expected to invite the President of the Bundesbank to attend its deliberations on important monetary policy issues. What is important is that the Bundesbank has consistently interpreted its duty to advise in a proactive way, as a right. It has taken the view that this advice is not 'tied to a corresponding request by the Federal Government. This means that the Bundesbank . . . can approach the Federal Government on its own initiative, and must [!] do so if it considers, in its duty-bound judgement, advice . . . to be called for'. If it were not to follow this interpretation, 'advice that might not be desired . . . could be thwarted, merely by not asking the Bundesbank for it'.[11]

The Act sets the Bundesbank only one goal: that of 'safeguarding the currency' (section 3). No other goals are to be pursued. Although the Bundesbank, according to the first sentence of section 12, is 'required to support the general economic policy of the Federal Government', it must only do so 'without prejudice to the performance of its duties'. This formulation is scarcely justiciable, and, in this sense, is of only declamatory importance.[12] Yet it opens up a grey area for attempts to exert pressure. In order to avoid this, the Bundesbank propounds an offensive interpretation of this provision, too. It, itself, must determine 'on its own duty-bound judgement' whether the conditions for a support of general economic policy are met.[13]

---

[10] This issue is dealt with in section 5 of this article.
[11] Deutsche Bundesbank, 1972, pp. 16f.
[12] Cf. Lindner, 1973, p. 345.
[13] Cf. Deutsche Bundesbank, 1972, p. 16.

The final element in the independence of the Bundesbank as an institution is that the public sector cannot draw on central bank credit as it sees fit. Up until the 1994 amendment to the Act, public bodies could obtain cash advances, but only within the framework of statutorily determined and tight ceilings.

b) Personal independence

A central bank may be relatively independent as an institution, but this will be of little value for the goal of monetary stability if the government is in a position to keep the members of the governing body, or at least a majority of them, on a relatively short rein. Whether or not this is the case is determined primarily by the nature of the nomination procedure, the distribution of nominations over time, and the duration of periods in office.[14]

The Central Bank Council consists of the members of the Directorate of the Bundesbank and the Presidents of the Land Central Banks. A condition of appointment is a 'particular professional suitability' ('*besondere fachliche Eignung*'). This has always been the case with the members of the Directorate, and is particularly true of the Presidents, who have come from the Bank or the Reichsbank, or from executive positions in the private sector and the Federal Ministry of Finance. Attention has usually also been paid to particular professional suitability in the case of the presidents of the Land Central Banks.[15]

The members of the Directorate are appointed after nomination by the Federal Government, the Presidents of the Land Central Banks after nomination by the Bundesrat, the second chamber of parliament representing the governments of the states. This pluralism of nomination procedures[16] is in accordance with the federal structure of Germany, and *a priori* restricts the influence of central government. Moreover, nominations are staggered over time, to prevent a large number of Central Bank Council members from being replaced in a single year, thus enabling political influence to be exerted. Over the period 1960–96 there were only four years in which four members were replaced; in all the other years fewer members were replaced, usually only one. Of particular interest is the political influence the govern-

---

[14] On the theoretical underpinning see Neumann, 1991.

[15] The Central Bank Council, which is to be consulted on every nomination, has raised objections in a number of cases, although on no occasion has this prevented an appointment. Cf. also Woll, 1988.

[16] For this, Germany has to thank the overwhelming influence exerted by the Americans on the military administration law governing the establishment of the Bank deutscher Länder.

ment of the day is able to exert on the composition of the Directorate, which, until the 1991 amendment to the Bundesbank Act, could consist of up to 10 members (since then: eight). During the above-mentioned period, there were a total of 20 new appointments. This means that, during a normal term of office of four years, the Federal Government was, on average, not able to nominate more than two new members.

Members of the Central Bank Council are appointed for eight years; in exceptional cases for shorter periods, but not for less than two years. This relatively long period in office, compared with that in other countries, is conducive to long-term thinking. Above all else, it promotes personal independence, the more so, the older the individuals nominated. The actual period in office that can be anticipated on entering the Central Bank Council is, in fact, substantially longer, because a renewed appointment for a further period of up to eight years is possible. This has been consistently practised in automatic fashion—that is, without regard to the individual concerned and his or her views—to the extent possible regarding individual age; the standard retirement age is between 65 and 68. If one looks at the 17 members of the Directorate who left between 1969 and 1993, and the 24 Land Central Bank Presidents leaving between 1972 and 1995 (in both cases excluding deceased members), it emerges that they were first appointed at an average age of 52 and remained on the Council for 14 years. This appointment practice is largely in accordance with an ideal-typical theoretical conception developed by the present author, in which entry age and period in office are to be combined in such a way that the position, on entering office, can be considered to be the last one occupied in the individual's working life, so that no incentive for political considerations is given (Thomas Becket effect).[17] The six Presidents of the Bundesbank were, on average, 60 years old on appointment.[18]

Certain theoretical considerations suggest that the behaviour of executive central bank staff can be influenced by their level of remuneration. However, the little information that is available on salaries does not suggest that it is particularly attractive to move from an executive function in the private banking sector, for instance, to the Central Bank Council. What is relevant

[17] Neumann, 1991, p. 103: 'the conditions of contract and of office would have to be set such that the appointee frees him- or herself from all former political ties or dependencies and accepts the central bank's objective of safeguarding the value of the currency as his or her professional leitmotif. We may call this a "Thomas Becket" effect.' The term for this desired effect goes back to the Chancellor of the English King Henry II who, as Chancellor, upheld the interests of the king against the Church, but after nomination as Archbishop of Canterbury represented the interests of the Church against the Crown. Cf. Issing, 1992.

[18] An exception was Karl Otto Pöhl, who was nominated Vice-President at the age of 47, and three years later took the post of President.

is that salary growth is in accordance with civil service agreements, and to this extent correlates positively with the inflation rate. In view of the impressive successes of the Bundesbank in achieving relative monetary stability, one is forced to the conclusion that the technocratic idea that inflation can only be prevented by reducing central bank salaries proportionally to the rate of inflation lacks an empirical basis.[19]

4. Areas of conflict

A stability-oriented monetary policy is permanently under a latent threat from special interests. What is vital in the final analysis is that the central bank is able to fight off such interests. For this reason we need to consider how the members of the Central Bank Council have fleshed out the monetary constitution in practice. The key question is whether the Central Bank Council is a 'politicized organ' that allows itself to be functionalized for the different political interests of central and Länder governments, or whether the alternative hypothesis of substantial personal independence, derived from the conditions of appointment and tenure, can be backed up with empirical evidence.

a) Support for electoral interests

The theory of the political business cycle, as set out by Nordhaus,[20] draws, from the government's interest in gaining re-election, the conclusion that a government will use the short-term trade-off between unemployment and inflation in order to bring down unemployment in an election year, by stimulating the economy. Empirical studies have not generated an unequivocal result on this question. Although evidence has been found of opportunistic behaviour in the interest of retaining power in some countries and in various phases, this has not been shown to be systematically the case.[21] If it is assumed that economic agents form rational expectations, even if they are bounded, the business cycle cannot be manipulated by the government or a dependent central bank by virtue of its control over monetary policy, because this will be anticipated and undermined by corresponding wage demands. It has, however, been suggested that attempted manipulation can

---

[19] See, for example, Vaubel, 1989 or Walsh, 1995.
[20] Cf. Nordhaus, 1975.
[21] Cf. Alesina, 1989 and Alesina and Roubini, 1992.

be detected in corresponding changes in the fiscal and monetary policy instruments.[22]

Applying this theory to the Bundesbank, if the Bundesbank is independent of the government, not only *de jure* but also *de facto*, the implications of the theory should not be confirmed empirically for Germany. An indirect, and thus very weak, test method consists of examining whether the Bundesbank has systematically accommodated the Federal Government's fiscal policy. Empirical investigations of this question have led to contradictory results.[23]

A direct implication of this theory is the hypothesis that the Bundesbank regularly cuts the discount rate in the run-up to elections, in support of the incumbent government. A simple evaluation of discount rate policy prior to all the general elections between 1953 and 1994 shows that this has not been systematically the case. While the discount rate was cut during the run-up to the elections in 1953, 1957, 1961, 1976, 1983, 1987, and 1994, these seven elections have to be seen against the background of the five elections in the run-up to which the discount rate was repeatedly raised: 1965, 1969, 1972, 1980, and 1990. Statistically, the ratio of 7 to 5 does not differ significantly from the null hypothesis of uniform distribution. Moreover, the interest-rate cuts may have been justified in economic terms. Consequently, Berger and Solveen examined, on the basis of reaction functions, whether the stricter hypothesis that the Bundesbank had reduced interest rates excessively could be justified. Their results are negative.[24]

Thus there is no confirmation of the hypothesis that the Bundesbank has attempted to promote the re-election of the incumbent Federal Government by pursuing a policy of cutting interest rates in the run-up to elections. This is evidence in favour of the *de facto* independence of the Bundesbank. Yet the finding is superficial. It does not tell us whether the members of the Central Bank Council were independent in their decisions, or whether they were, in fact, attempting to influence the electoral chances of the government and the opposition. The fact that the Council frequently took restrictive interest-rate-policy decisions prior to elections could, in theory, be explained by claiming that a majority of Council members were politically inclined towards the opposition, and thus attempted to improve its electoral chances by inducing, through monetary policy, a deterioration in the economic

[22] Cf. Rogoff and Sibert, 1988.
[23] According to Frey and Schneider, during the period 1957–77 the Bundesbank followed the fiscal policy stance of the Federal Government with a time-lag of half a year. Cf. Frey and Schneider, 1981. According to Berger, however, the hypothesis is falsified for the period 1950–71. Cf. Berger, 1996.
[24] Cf. Berger, 1996 and Solveen, 1996.

climate. Such voting patterns, with their unfavourable impact on the incumbent government, cannot be precluded *a priori*, because the government exerts an influence only on the appointment of members of the Directorate, and the staggering of appointments prevents all the members of the Directorate from being replaced in the course of a single session of parliament.

Vaubel was the first to examine whether the monetary policy pursued by the Bundesbank could be put down to the prevalence of certain party-political preferences on the Central Bank Council.[25] His initial hypothesis was that Council members who are or were members of a political party would place themselves at the service of the party, and, therefore, in the run-up to a general election, attempt to improve their party's election chances by setting the rates of monetary expansion at an appropriate rate. This implies that Council members considered to be supporters of the government would seek to ensure an expansionary monetary policy prior to elections, whereas those supportive of the opposition would be pulling in the opposite direction. Vaubel examined this strong hypothesis by comparing the rates of growth of M_1, the narrowly defined monetary aggregate, during the pre-election periods with the 'political majorities' he had identified on the Central Bank Council. He came to the conclusion that the hypothesis of a predominance of party-political preferences could not be rejected.[26]

If it were correct that the members of the Central Bank Council allowed themselves to be led by party-political considerations in taking their decisions, this should be reflected in their voting behaviour. This can be analysed here for the first time. The Central Bank Council votes on policy measures: specifically, on changes in interest rates, the minimum reserve ratios, and, since the end of 1974, the annual monetary targets. Decisions on interest rates are best suited to analysing voting behaviour. They enable a period stretching from 1952 to 1994 to be analysed, during which 12 parliamentary elections took place. Minimum reserve policy, on the other hand, has played no significant role since 1987, while the era of monetary targets is, at around 20 years, even shorter.

Table 3 indicates, for each parliamentary election, the political majority on the Central Bank Council prior to the election and the voting by the Council on changes in the discount and Lombard rates. Council members are marked with a 'C' if they can be counted to belong to the CDU/CSU or the liberal-conservative wing of the FDP; with an 'S' if they can be ascribed to the SPD or the social-liberal wing of the FDP; and with a '?' if they cannot be classified in either camp. These data were taken from Vaubel,

---

[25] Cf. Vaubel, 1993.
[26] Vaubel's results lack statistical significance, however. Cf. Neumann, 1993, pp. 82ff.

TABLE 3: Voting on interest-rate changes on the Central Bank Council

Year	Federal government C-led or S-led	Central Bank Council Political identity[a] C : S : ?	Measures Discount rate = D Lombard rate = L Increase = I Cut = C For: Against: Abstention
1952	C	5:5:3	
20.08.			C D+L 10:3:0
1953		5:5:1	
7.01.			C D+L 10:1:0
10.06.			C D+L 8:2:0
15.09.	Election		
1956	C	3:7:1	
5.09.			C D+L 9:2:0
1957		3:7:1	
9.01.			C D+L 8:3:0
15.09.	Election		
1960	C	7:9:4	
2.06.			I D+L 11:5:0
10.11.			C D+L Unanimous
1961		8:8:4	
19.01.			C D+L 18:1:0
4.05.			C D+L 15:2:0
17.09.	Election		
1964	C	10:7:3	No such measures
1965		10:8:2	
21.01.			I D+L 16:0:4
12.08.			I D+L 10:9:0
19.09.	Election		
1968	C–S coalition	11:7:2	No such measures
1969		11:7:2	
20.03.			I D+L
17.04.			I D+L
19.06.			I D+L
11.09.			I D+L
28.09.	Election		

TABLE 3: *(cont.)*

Year	Federal government C-led or S-led	Central Bank Council Political identity[a] C : S : ?	Measures Discount rate = D Lombard rate = L Increase = I Cut = C For: Against: Abstention
	Premature election		
1972	S	10:7:1	
6.10.			I D+L
2.11.			I D+L
19.11.	Election		
1975	S	9:9:1	
14.08.			C D+L
11.09.			C D+L
1976		10:9:1	No such measures
3.10.	Election		
1979	S		
12.07.		9:8:2	I D+L
31.10.		8:8:2	I D+L
1980		7:8:2	
28.02.			I D+L
30.04.			I D+L
18.09.			C L
5.10.	Election		
	Premature election		
1982	C	8:7:2	
21.10.			C D+L
2.12.			C D+L
1983		8:7:2	
6.03.	Election		
1986	C	8:7:2	
6.03.			C D
1987		8:7:2	
22.01.			C D+L
25.01.	Election		

TABLE 3: *(cont.)*

Year	Federal government C-led or S-led	Central Bank Council Political identity[a] C : S : ?	Measures Discount rate = D Lombard rate = L Increase = I Cut = C For: Against: Abstention
1989	C	8:7:2	
5.10.			I D+L
1990		10:6:2	
1.11.			I L
2.12.	Election		
1993	C	8:4:4	
1.07.			C D+L
29.07.			C L
9.09.		8:5:3	C D+L
21.10.		7:6:3	C D+L
1994		7:6:3	
14.04.			C D
14.05.			C D+L
11.06.			C D+L
16.07.	Election		

[a] C = CDU, CSU or FDP (excluding social-liberal wing). S = SPD or social-liberal wing of FDP.

Sources: Deutsche Bundesbank; author's findings.

and have been extended to cover the period 1991–94.[27] The figures on voting results were provided by the Bundesbank. Table 3 only publishes the results for the period 1952–65, because more recent voting results are subject to a closure period of 30 years. They were evaluated for the purpose of this study, however. In accordance with Vaubel's definition of the length of the pre-election period, decisions taken in the 15 months prior to regular parliamentary elections were considered. In the case of the two premature general elections (in 1972 and 1983), the pre-election period was reduced

[27] Cf. Vaubel, 1993. Vaubel's figures were corrected in two cases. One person classified by Vaubel as belonging to the S-group in the years 1964–8 was, in fact, not a party member; for 1990 Vaubel incorrectly classified one person who was also not a party member in the C-group.

to six months, because in both cases the votes of no confidence that led to the election occurred less than six months prior to it.

Vaubel's posited party-political voting behaviour can be formalized in the following hypotheses:

– *Re-election hypothesis*: members of the Central Bank Council from the same political camp as the incumbent Federal Government vote in favour of interest-rate cuts and against interest-rate hikes in the run-up to parliamentary elections.
– *De-selection hypothesis*: members sympathetic to the current opposition vote in favour of interest-rate hikes and against interest-rate cuts in the run-up to parliamentary elections.

Given that voting is anonymous, the hypotheses cannot be examined directly. An additional difficulty arises from the fact that in all periods some members of the Central Bank Council were not party members. The hypotheses say nothing about their voting behaviour.

If the evaluation of decisions on interest rate changes is based solely on whether, prior to elections, more Central Bank Council members belonged to the government or the opposition camp, one obtains the following results: the decisions prior to the elections of 1983, 1987, and 1994 are in accordance with the re-election hypothesis, but not those preceding the elections of 1965, 1980, and 1990. Decisions prior to the 1972 election are in line with the de-selection hypothesis, but not those prior to the 1957 election. The interest-rate-policy decisions taken in the run-up to the elections of 1953, 1961, 1969, and 1976 cannot be evaluated in these terms, either because neither political camp had a majority,[28] or, in the case of the 1969 election, because Germany was governed by a Grand Coalition. Overall, according to this test approach, which is in accordance with that taken by Vaubel, both hypotheses are to be rejected.

Yet such an approach is unsatisfactory in methodological terms, as the information on the voting patterns underlying the decisions remains unused. To the extent that the two hypotheses are correct, the majorities indicated in Table 3 ought to be directly reflected in corresponding voting results. This is a more stringent test, one that allows all the decisions to be evaluated. For example, in 1953 a C-led Federal Government was up for re-election. At the time, the Central Bank Council consisted of five C-members and five S-members, while one member did not belong to either camp. Depending on the decision taken by the last-mentioned member, both interest-rates cuts

---

[28] Although it could be taken into account that the President has a casting vote in the case of a split vote, no decision has ever been that close. On one occasion, however, the President was outvoted by a large majority.

TABLE 4: Voting on the Central Bank Council in the run-up to general elections*
(percentage)

Position	Composition of the CBC			Voting result		
	Political 'camp':					
	Govt.	Opposition	Neutral	For	Against	Abstention
a) 10 increases in the discount rate						
Mean	44.1	44.1	11.8	75.9	19.5	4.5
Standard (deviation)	(4.7)	(6.8)	(4.1)	(10.6)	(14.5)	(6.7)
b) 20 cuts in the discount rate						
Mean	42.8	42.4	14.8	85.8	12.2	1.9
Standard (deviation)	(6.4)	(8.8)	(5.8)	(11.0)	(11.1)	(3.6)

* The survey covered all decisions taken on interest rates in the 6 months prior to the premature elections of 1972 and 1973, and the 15 months prior to the remaining general elections between 1953 and 1994. The 1969 election was not considered (Grand Coalition).
Source: Deutsche Bundesbank; author's findings.

and hikes could be expected on the basis of the hypotheses. But the voting pattern would have to have been, in either case, 6:5:0 (for:against:abstention) if the Central Bank Council members had allowed themselves to be led by their party-political preferences. In fact, however, decisions to cut interest rates were taken on 7 January by 10:1:0 votes and on 10 June 1953 by 8:2:0 votes. Thus in the first case, at least four of the five members of the Central Bank Council coming from the S-opposition voted in favour of the interest-rate cut; in the second case so did at least two members. This is not in accordance with the hypothesis of party-political voting.

A cursory look at Table 3 is enough to show that Vaubel's party-political division of the Central Bank Council consistently failed to translate into corresponding voting patterns. In order to shed more light on this, decisions on the discount rate are brought together in Table 4.[29] All the parliamentary elections are considered, with the exception of the 1969 election: at that

[29] It is not necessary to evaluate the decisions on the Lombard rate separately as they seldom deviated.

time Germany was ruled by a Grand C-S Coalition, so that the hypotheses formulated above do not permit an unequivocal statement as to expected voting behaviour. During the remaining pre-election periods, a total of 20 decisions to cut the discount rate and 10 decisions to raise it were taken. Given that the size of the Central Bank Council changed over time, and that not all members were present for each decision, the composition of the Central Bank Council and the voting results given in Table 4 are expressed in percentages.

On the basis of the Table, the two hypotheses can be examined on the strength of average results. First, the average values for the composition of the Central Bank Council and the voting results show that all the decisions were supported, on average, by substantially more members of the Council than would be likely if the hypotheses were correct. The level of support for the proposals amounted to an average of around 76 per cent in the 10 cases of a rise in the discount rate and around 86 per cent in the 20 cases of a cut in the discount rate.

The re-election hypothesis posits that members of the government camp vote against discount-rate hikes. Panel A of Table 4 shows that, at 44 per cent, their votes were on average just as important as those of members of the opposition camp for such decisions. In other words, members of the government camp did in fact vote for increases in the discount rate. Even under the extreme assumption that all members of the opposition camp and all those independent of political parties voted for the decisions, members of the government camp accounted for at least 20 per cent of the votes in favour. This means that, on average, at least every second member of the government camp voted for the discount-rate increases. This result disproves the re-election hypothesis.

The de-selection hypothesis posits that members of the opposition camp vote against cuts in the discount rate. Such decisions were taken, on average, with the support of 86 per cent of the votes. Even under the extreme assumption that all members of the government camp and all the independents voted for the discount-rate cuts, members of the opposition camp supported the decisions to the extent of at least 28.2 per cent of the votes in favour. This means that at least two out of three members of the opposition camp also voted for discount-rate cuts. Thus the de-selection hypothesis has also been unequivocally disproved.

Particularly striking cases of disproof are the general elections of 1957 and 1965. Prior to the 1957 election there was a large majority of Central Bank Council members that belonged to the opposition SPD: together they accounted for around 64 per cent of the votes. They could therefore have raised the discount and Lombard rates, in line with the de-selection hypo-thesis, in order to reduce the re-election chances of the Adenauer government. Instead, a majority of them lent support to two cuts in interest rates. At the Council meeting of 5 September 1956, at least five of the seven voted for the cut in interest rates; at the meeting of 9 January 1957, at least four. In the run-up to the general election of 1965 that led to the reinstatement of the CDU-led government under Erhard, interest rates were increased twice, although the members of the government camp, which included the then President of the Bundesbank, could have prevented these decisions, as they held 10 out of 20 votes.

b) Selected cases of conflict

It is not possible, however, to conclude from the fact that the Central Bank Council has not allowed itself to be harnessed to the cart of electoral interests that monetary policy has been conducted in an entirely apolitical manner. Because monetary policy intervenes in the economic process and thus, in the final analysis, in people's lives, it cannot follow purely technocratic patterns. Monetary policy decisions cannot be taken with complete disregard for their implications for other policy areas. Provided the central bank sticks to the basic line of price stability, it can be perfectly justified in tolerating temporary infringements, for instance in view of the external position. On the other hand, it is inevitable that an independent central bank will repeatedly come into conflict with the interests of the national government and with those of the governments of important trading partners. Consequently, it must always expect political pressure to be exerted from outside and even attempts effectively to restrict its independence. If central bankers fail to maintain personal integrity in such a case, they will invariably be playing a losing game. Let me recall just two cases from the Bundesbank's rich history of conflicts.

Adenauer's 'guillotine speech'

Governments are seldom happy when the central bank adopts a more restrictive monetary policy stance in the interest of maintaining price stability. This is less to do with the fact that governments are not concerned about the goal of price stability, than with the fact that any slowdown in economic growth leads to reduced tax revenue and unpleasant adjustment constraints for government fiscal policy. As a result, the domestic political climate becomes more difficult. Although it is short-sighted for a government to seek to prevent the monetary authority from adopting a more restrictive stance (assuming that this is justified), as any postponement will require more drastic measures later, the political process is conducive to such short-termism.

It is therefore hardly surprising that both conservative and social-democrat-led governments have attempted, if not to prevent, then at least to delay the adoption of a more restrictive monetary policy stance.

The most striking attempt to dissuade the Bundesbank/Bank deutscher Länder from raising interest rates was made in 1956, by the then Chancellor Konrad Adenauer. The case is of special importance, both because on the one hand Adenauer did not hesitate to launch a public attack on the autonomy of the Bank and, on the other hand, because the Central Bank Council showed its ability to pursue an offensive political strategy in order to defend its independence. Back in October 1950, when the Central Bank Council wanted to raise the discount rate by two percentage points in the face of the drastic price rises initiated by the Korean crisis, Adenauer had attempted—in vain—to dissuade it. But at that time the Bank had still been under the protection of the law passed by the Allies in 1948. Five years later, when the Bank, following a long period of falling interest rates, wanted to raise the discount rate, this was no longer the case. Now, Adenauer was, in principle, able to change the law governing the policies of the Bank deutscher Länder; all he required was a parliamentary majority. Moreover, preparations had already begun with regard to passing the legislation regulating the establishment of the Bundesbank. This created the scope for exerting political pressure.

The Bank cautiously raised the discount and Lombard rates by half a percentage point in August 1955. This measure was, at bottom, too little too late, as the economy had been booming since mid-1954: within the space of a year, industrial output had grown by 15 per cent, employment had expanded by one million persons and the inflation rate had risen from zero to almost 3 per cent. The new monetary policy stance was none the less branded by industry as damaging to growth. Adenauer took up this criticism, and, on 7 November 1955, wrote to the President of the Board of Directors of the Bank deutscher Länder, Vocke: 'I would be grateful to you if the Bank deutscher Länder would not propose or implement incisive measures in the field of credit policy without prior consultation with the Federal Government.'[30] By return of post, Vocke put the ball back in Adenauer's court. On 8 November 1955 he responded equally unequivocally: '. . . may I point out that incisive credit policy measures are part of the responsibility of the Central Bank Council'.[31]

It was therefore inevitable that a trial of strength would occur as soon as interest rates had to be raised again. At the Central Bank Council meeting held on 7–8 March 1956, the two ministers present, Ludwig Erhard and

[30] Letter from Adenauer to Vocke, 7 Nov. 1955 (HA BBk B 330/2011).
[31] Letter from Vocke to Adenauer, 8 Nov. 1955 (HA BBk B 330/2011).

Fritz Schäffer, placed a suspensory veto against a renewed increase in interest rates, as they had been instructed to do.[32] The Central Bank Council nevertheless voted unanimously for an increase of one percentage point in the discount and Lombard rates. It argued that the suspensory veto was inadmissible, because the government's scope for postponing a decision had been practically exhausted: Schäffer had, on 22 February, asked by telephone for the postponement of any decision until Erhard had returned from a visit to England.[33]

What followed was a political inter-play between the Bank and the two ministers. A stabilization programme was drawn up, with which the ministers surprised the cabinet at its meeting on 17 May. The next day the Central Bank Council voted by eight votes to two, in the presence of the ministers, for a renewed increase in interest rates of one percentage point, and cut the rediscount quotas. These decisions received the support of the ministers. This meant that Adenauer had practically lost the trial of strength with the Bank. Yet he made defeat worse by committing a further error: on 23 May he distanced himself from the decision, and criticized the independence of the central bank in a speech to the employers' federation, the Bundesverband der Deutschen Industrie.

Amongst other things, he said that the Central Bank Council 'is of course responsible only unto itself; what we have here is an organ responsible to no one, neither to parliament nor to any government'. He went on: 'a heavy blow has been struck at the German economy, and it is the little ones who will suffer most . . . the guillotine falls on the man in the street, and that is what grieves me so much.'[34] The reactions in the German press were highly damaging to Adenauer. The media came out clearly in support of the Bank, which used the opportunity to make a public response in its next Monthly Report.[35]

The success of the Bank deutscher Länder in 1956, in its conflict with Adenauer over interest-rate policy, was of an importance that is difficult to

[32] Erhard, who argued for a rise in the discount rate, said: 'all I can do is fulfil this commission as I must do. I have, after all, stated my personal opinion on the question. I do not know whether the veto has already been exhausted or not.' Cf. Transcript of the 214th Central Bank Council meeting held on 7–8 Mar., p. 18 (HA BBk B 330/92).

[33] The argument that the government had already used up its suspensory veto by means of internal objections to interest-rate hikes that seemed to be in the offing has been used by the Bundesbank in subsequent cases of conflict. As a result there has since been no case in which the veto was formally lodged.

[34] Bank deutscher Länder, 1956*b*, p. 1.

[35] In which it dealt at length with the central arguments brought against its decisions and felt obliged to issue unusual admonishments such as '. . . it is one of the elementary economic principles . . .', or '. . . it would be ostrich-like behaviour if one were to ignore that . . .'. Bank deutscher Länder, 1956*a*, pp. 3ff.

overestimate for reinforcing the *de facto* independence of the central bank. Both the support given to the Bank by two key members of the government and the sharp attack made by the Chancellor proved auspicious; they led to public solidarity with the Bank, and this was to prove a driving force from then on. No federal chancellor since Adenauer has dared attack the Bundesbank in public in a similar fashion, and to call its independence into question. Although, at the start of 1979, under Chancellor Helmut Schmidt, open conflict broke out when *Staatssekretär* Manfred Lahnstein, after the Central Bank Council meeting of 18 January, surprisingly declared that a rise in the Lombard rate and minimum reserve ratios had come too early, he was wise enough to refrain from casting doubt on the independence of the Bundesbank.

The foundation of the Franco-German Finance and Economic Council

Given that the Bundesbank, following the establishment of the European Monetary System, had taken on the leading role in the fight against inflation in Europe, it was inevitable that it would gradually slip into the role of the leading central bank within the system. As the hardest currency, one that could be traded without restriction internationally, the D-mark became a stability anchor for the remaining member currencies. During the early years of the EMS, other member currencies, not least the second most important currency, the French franc, experienced repeated devaluations. Following the failure of François Mitterrand's Keynesian experiment to stimulate the French economy, from 1983 France adopted the stability constraints of the EMS as a positive challenge, in an unprecedented policy turnaround. Not withstanding this, efforts were made to step up the Bundesbank intervention financing, and these efforts bore fruit in September 1987 in the form of the Basle/Nyborg central bank agreement. Yet the all-but-hegemonic position of the D-mark was still regarded by some as a thorn in the flesh. France began to look for ways of participating in the leadership of the EMS. One far-out option was that of setting up a European Monetary Union, with a common central bank. More pragmatically, the attempt could be made to tie the Bundesbank into a Franco-German coordinating body.

This was the background to the astonishing proposal made at the Franco-German consultations held on 13 November 1987: in addition to a Franco-German Defence Council, an 'Economic and Monetary Council' was to be set up, consisting of the finance ministers and central bank governors of both countries. The Council was to be empowered to take 'decisions' on all issues coming under the responsibility of the finance ministers and the central bank governors of both countries. In particular, interest-rate policy was to be coordinated. If the proposal had been implemented, the independence of the Bundesbank would, to all intents and purposes, have been terminated.

The German government accepted the idea of a bilateral government agreement because of the close link between the establishment of the Defence Council and that of the Economic and Monetary Council. In the course of negotiations between the finance ministries of the two countries, the French proposal was toned down. The Council was extended to include the German Minister of Economics, and was renamed 'Finance and Economic Council'. More importantly still, as far as monetary policy was concerned, the only task of the Council was to be to 'discuss' monetary policies 'with a view to their convergence'. The Bundesbank was officially informed of the contents of the modified text on 13 January 1988. The Directorate raised objections. In response, on 14 January 1988, the German finance ministry sent an even more highly diluted text, under which the central bank governors would no longer be members of the Council, but would merely participate (as guests) at the meetings.

Not until 21 January 1988 was the Central Bank Council informed of the agreement, along with a request for its consent. The situation for the Bundesbank had once again grown more precarious. First, a more radical version had again been presented.[36] Once more the governors were to be members of the Council, and monetary policies were not to be discussed 'with a view to their convergence', but rather 'with the aim of as far-reaching a degree of coordination as possible'. Secondly, in line with French wishes, the text was not to be designed as a bilateral government agreement, but rather as a supplementary protocol, one requiring ratification, to the Franco-German Treaty of 1963. This meant that the agreement would be binding under international law, and would thus take precedence over the Bundesbank Act.

The voices raised during the debate on the Central Bank Council were almost unanimously negative in their appraisal. Although it was recognized that Germany's incorporation into the process of European integration, and monetary-policy cooperation with the USA and Japan would inevitably restrict the Bundesbank's *de facto* freedom of monetary-policy manoeuvre, this was no argument in favour of accepting a statutory restriction on the autonomy of the Bank. The German government had not even considered whether this was the case, it was argued. Although the Bundesbank was not a party to the Treaty, the President of the Bank would be forced to make concessions on the Finance and Economic Council. This would limit the relevance of the decisions taken by the Central Bank Council.

---

[36] The documents held in the Historisches Archiv der Deutschen Bundesbank shed no light on the question of why the relatively moderate version of 14 Jan. 1988 was not retained.

In the event, the Central Bank Council managed to extricate itself rather cleverly. It empowered its President to 'participate' in the Council, but it made its consent conditional on the caveat that the supplementary protocol would not substantively affect the independence of the Bundesbank, as summarized in section 3, section 6(1) and the second sentence of section 12 of the Bundesbank Act.

At the end of the day, it managed, owing to broad support from public opinion and parliament, to completely deflect the attempted high-jacking of the Bundesbank's competences during ratification of the protocol. The Federal Government issued a binding interpretation of the Treaty; a memorandum was added to the Bill and brought to the attention of the French government.[37] The memorandum made it clear that the Finance and Economic Council was a consultative body and not an executive organ; direct legal effects could not result from its consultations; the legal status of the Bundesbank was not affected by the protocol. Although the Finance and Economic Council continues to meet, it has never been heard of in public again.

5. Exchange-rate-policy considerations

The goal of domestic monetary stability cannot be reconciled with that of a stable nominal external value of the currency. This is clearly the case when the exchange rate is pegged to a currency the supply of which is being expanded at an inflationary rate. Yet it also applies when there are real disequilibria between economies. These necessitate adjustments in relative prices that are inevitably transposed into changes in nominal exchange rates, unless the domestic price levels of the economies concerned are permitted to shift to a sufficient extent.

The inherently conflicting relationship between the targets of domestic monetary stability and exchange-rate stability means that, within the framework of the monetary constitution of a country, a fundamental decision must be taken on the goal to which priority is to be given. In the case of Germany there can be no doubt that, since 1973 at the latest, the goal of domestic monetary stability has enjoyed priority. This is notwithstanding fact that, back in 1957, parliament avoided opting unambiguously for one or the other goal, formulating the policy target as 'safeguarding the cur-

---

[37] Cf. 'Unabhängigkeit der Bundesbank sicher. Denkschrift zum deutsch-französischen Finanz- und Wirtschaftsrat', in: Börsenzeitung, 3 Dec. 1988.

rency'.[38] At that time, most of those involved were only dimly aware of the inevitability of this conflict of goals. In 1957 Vocke declared succinctly: 'we don't want to revalue the currency, and we don't want to adopt the inflationary course taken by some countries.'[39] The major conflicts of goals were still to come, and inevitably they developed into conflicts between the Bundesbank and the government of the day, because it was not the central bank, but rather the government that was responsible for maintaining the sovereignty of the currency *vis-à-vis* the rest of the world.

This division of competences marks a fundamental limitation on the independence of the Bundesbank. The Federal Government, subject to the agreement of parliament, has the right to tie the D-mark into a system of fixed exchange rates. Any such system, depending on the specific rules of the game, imposes restrictions on the independence of the central bank, and thus exacerbates the problems posed by maintaining the domestic value of the currency. On the other hand, it is to be concluded from the logic of the long-accepted principle that domestic monetary stability is to be given priority that the government must not engage in exchange-rate commitments in such a way that it serves, *de facto*, to nullify the independence of the central bank. This means both that exchange-rate parities must be adjustable and, in order to guarantee this in practice, that no commitment to unlimited intervention must be given.

a) The problem of underpinning the external economic position

Looking back at the Bretton Woods era, it is striking to note the role reversal, prevailing up until the early 1970s, regarding the perception of the interrelationships between domestic and external stability. It was not the Bundesbank, but rather the Minister of Economics, Ludwig Erhard, who realized that revaluation of the D-mark could not be considered a taboo subject, if external economic disequilibrium, which began to increase in the mid-1950s, was to be reduced, and an acceleration of inflation avoided. The members of the Central Bank Council, by contrast, ignoring for a moment exceptions such as Otmar Emminger, were firmly opposed to any change

[38] In the justification of the draft bill put forward by the Federal Ministry of Economics on 28 Aug. 1956, it is stated that: 'the stability of domestic purchasing power is . . . of prime importance; nevertheless, the stability of external purchasing power . . . must not be left unconsidered.' Draft Bill on the Deutsche Bundesbank, 28 Aug. 1956, Bundestagsdrucksache 2781.
[39] Speech to the Banking Conference held on 23 May 1957, quoted from Marsh, 1992, pp. 240f.

in the D-mark/US dollar parity. Not only Vocke, but also his successor, the first President of the Bundesbank, Karl Blessing, considered the exchange-rate parity to be sacrosanct, just as if they were still living in the world of the gold standard. Thus it was that the first revaluation of the D-mark, in March 1961, occurred only after a long period of sustained Bundesbank opposition.

Yet the Bundesbank proved capable of learning from experience. Following the outbreak of a currency crisis in 1968, initiated by the French franc, a majority on the Central Bank Council—including Blessing—argued in favour of revaluation of the D-mark, whereas, under the influence of the banker Hermann Josef Abs, Chancellor Kurt Georg Kiesinger and Finance Minister Franz Josef Strauß were opposed. This was not at all true of Karl Schiller, however, the Federal Minister of Economics, and, from the autumn of 1969, also responsible for the Treasury. In subsequent years he repeatedly argued in favour of a general willingness to accept revaluations of the D-mark, and of group floating against the dollar. He did so in opposition to Blessing's successor as President of the Bundesbank, Karl Klasen, who was appointed in 1970. Klasen was resolutely opposed to revaluation, and all the more so to breaking the link between the D-mark and the dollar, i.e. to floating. Under his influence, in May 1971 a majority on the Central Bank Council opposed Schiller's proposal to allow the D-mark to float, and instead argued in favour of a ban on foreign curency imports, an option provided for under section 23 of the *Außenwirtschaftsgesetz* (foreign trade law). This scenario was repeated in June 1972. Whereas in 1971 Schiller had been able to push through provisional floating against the will of the Bundesbank, in 1972 he failed to gain the support of his cabinet colleagues.[40] Thus the Bundesbank helped to prolong the death throes of the Bretton Woods system for a further three-quarters of a year, to the detriment of the internal stability of the D-mark. Up until the end of support for the dollar on 2 March, and the start of European group floating on 18 March 1973, the Bundesbank was obliged to purchase additional foreign currency to the value of around DM 25 billion. This meant that the rate of monetary growth remained in two-digit figures and that the rate of inflation rose from just over 5 to 7 per cent.

It took the foreign-exchange 'flood' at the start of February 1973 and a historical coincidence[41] to bring about a change of heart in the Central Bank

[40] This led to Schiller's resignation. The rejection of floating was a factor, but the main reason was that Schiller was unable to get his way on fiscal policy. Cf. Emminger, 1986, p. 218.
[41] Vice-President Emminger chaired both the Board of Directors and the Central Bank Council, as President Klasen was unable to attend meetings between January and mid-March because of illness.

Council. But now it was Schiller's successor, Helmut Schmidt, who opposed floating for weeks on end. And once again a historical coincidence came to the rescue. On the decisive day, 1 March, Schmidt was absent owing to ill health. This enabled Emminger to intervene in the heat of the moment with Chancellor Willy Brandt, and ensure the closure of the foreign-exchange markets for the next day.[42]

Since the end of the Bretton Woods exchange-rate system, the majority on the Central Bank Council has never again suffered from the illusion that the Bundesbank must maintain exchange-rate parities at any price, and can, at the same time, fulfil its function of maintaining domestic monetary stability. As a result, when, at the end of the 1970s, the Federal Government confronted the Bundesbank with a new exchange-rate system, there was no doubt in the mind of those on the Central Bank Council that the German central bank would lose its independence and thus control over monetary expansion and domestic monetary stability, unless there were guarantees that exchange-rate parities could be changed.

b) The Bundesbank agrees to the setting-up of the European Monetary System

The major dollar crisis of 1978 led to a lively debate on ways in which to expand the European 'snake', which had contracted to the currencies of the so-called D-mark block. At the end of June 1978, the then Chancellor, Helmut Schmidt, indicated in an interview with *Business Week* that he was not thinking of an extension of the snake, but rather of something 'which goes *a little* beyond the present snake'.[43] At the meeting of the European Council at the start of June, the first blueprint for the EMS was duly presented, the aim being to develop a detailed proposal within six months.

This confronted the Bundesbank with two key questions. First, how should the EMS be designed in order to ensure that the door was not opened to an upward harmonization of national inflation rates; second, how could it be ensured in political terms that the EMS would not permanently prevent the Bundesbank from performing its task of safeguarding monetary stability. In preparation for the debate on the Central Bank Council, a discussion paper presented in September 1978 correctly pointed out that, for Germany, orienting the obligation to intervene on the foreign-exchange markets towards the EMS currency basket would impose a far greater burden of intervention and adjustment than a bilateral obligation based on the parity

[42] Cf. Emminger, 1986, pp. 240f.
[43] Deutsche Bundesbank, 1978, p. 2.

grid.[44] Moreover, the basket solution amounted to a stigmatization of any currency deviating from the 'convoy' of EMS currencies. In the discussion paper, rights of unilateral parity adjustment, and voluntary exit and suspension were mentioned as 'essentials'. Last but not least, a strict limit on mutual lending was considered desirable.

It emerged in subsequent weeks, during tough negotiations with the European partners, that most of the Bundesbank's positions did not enjoy majority support. It did, at least, manage to push through the parity grid as the frame of reference for bilateral intervention, thus reducing the importance of the deviation indicator. In view of the unsatisfactory outcome of the negotiations, the Central Bank Council was well aware that it was all the more important to receive reliable assurances from the Federal Government that it would vote only for those EMS rules that ensured the autonomy of the central bank, and, in particular, that it would ensure that the Bundesbank would not face excessive intervention obligations. In order to obtain these assurances, three 'principles' were formulated. The third principle was as follows:

The monetary-policy autonomy of the Bundesbank faces a particular threat, if, given substantial disequilibria, excessive obligations to intervene result in the future EMS posing a threat to domestic monetary stability. This would make it impossible for the Bundesbank to fulfil its statutory duties. The Bundesbank assumes, with reference to repeated oral assurances by the Chancellor and the Minister of Finance, that in such a case the Federal Government would rescue the Bundesbank from such a dilemma, either by adjusting the EMS parities, or, if necessary, by releasing the bank, temporarily at least, from the obligation to intervene.[45]

On 16 November 1978 the Central Bank Council gave its *placet* to the utilization of the basket of currencies as an indicator, to the provisional transfer of 20 per cent of gold and foreign-exchange reserves to the fund for monetary cooperation, and to expanding the short- and medium-term currency standby, conditional on the acceptance of these principles. On the same day, Bundesbank President Emminger wrote to the Chancellor to inform him of the decisions and the principles formulated by the Central Bank Council, and requested confirmation of complete agreement. The Bundesbank did not receive written confirmation of the third principle.

Chancellor Schmidt was, however, prepared to attend the next meeting of the Central Bank Council in order to present his view of things. He did

---

[44] The 'basket solution' implied that the D-mark, owing to its predominance in the currencies' weighting, could reach the permissible revaluation limit—and thus initiate Germany's obligation to intervene—without this implying that the remaining currencies would at the same time come up against their devaluation limit.

[45] Emminger, 1986, p. 361.

this in a very impressive and colourful way, dealing in detail with the under-lying motives (policy towards Europe) and Germany's specific political situ-ation and history. At the same time, he confirmed that he was in complete agreement with the Bundesbank with regard to the principles transmitted to him, and he emphasized that, for him, there could be no discussion of the independence of the Bundesbank.[46] For their part, the members of the Cent-ral Bank Council took advantage of the opportunity to register their concern about various points—among other things the deviation indicator as the in-itiator of measures, the credit mechanisms, and the settlement of balances—for the Chancellor to take with him to the final round of negotiations.

Any overall evaluation must recognize the fact that the Central Bank Council managed to push through its views concerning the design of the EMS only to a limited extent. There is some evidence for the belief that, in the final round of negotiations, the German government did not put enough weight behind these demands. For Chancellor Schmidt, currency policy was an instrument of foreign policy. He was aware of the risks associated with the EMS. In particular, as can be seen from his public statements, he was clear about the fact that the exchange-rate system could force a higher rate of monetary expansion on Germany. But he took the view that the risk must be taken for the sake of the goal of consolidating the European Community and strengthening its position *vis-à-vis* the USA.

On the other hand, it must also be concluded that the Central Bank Council was able to protect the independence of the central bank. It received a clear restatement of Bundesbank independence from the government, and —what has been worth more in the longer run—the concrete assurance of an emergency brake in the form of a suspension of the obligation to defend parities in the case of a threat to internal monetary stability. This assurance has proved extremely useful in the major crises that have hit the EMS.[47]

6. Strategic safeguarding by means of monetary targeting

For more than 20 years now, the Bundesbank has conducted its policy under the banner of public monetary growth targets. Following the transition to 'floating exchange rates' in 1973, the Bundesbank developed a concept of

---

[46] Marsh claims that the Chancellor had intimated that he would perhaps urge that restrictions be imposed on the independence of the Bundesbank by means of a change in the Bundesbank Act. This is incorrect and, moreover, would have been politically very unwise. Cf. Marsh, 1992, p. 258.

[47] The assurance was explicitly given only orally. A transcript was made, however, and retained by both sides.

money stock control and, at the end of 1974, decided for the first time to set a public monetary growth target for the following year.

The final 'straw' that tipped the scales in favour of monetary targeting was the 1974/5 Report by the Council of Economic Experts, which, as it were, rendered monetarist views on a policy of monetary management oriented towards the medium-term 'politically acceptable', without, however, mentioning the product by its brand name (paras. 312–16, 374–396).[48] Having said that, this intervention had been preceded by detailed debates on monetary policy within the Bundesbank and on the Central Bank Council, discussions that were conducted at a remarkably high level. Whereas back in 1968, a memorandum by Rolf Gocht, a member of the Directorate, entitled 'Heretical thoughts at night', which discussed some of Milton Friedman's views, had seemed strange, as early as mid-1970 the Central Bank Council was willing to consider the new school of thought in greater detail: this it did in the form of presentations by Gocht (pro) and Leonhard Gleske (contra) Friedman's monetary-policy proposals.[49] The view was increasingly accepted that the traditional strategy of orientating policy towards bank liquidity ought to be replaced by control of the monetary base or the central bank money stock.[50] Detailed discussions of the underlying strategy of money and credit policy and of the central bank's management instruments were held in the course of 1973. It was generally agreed that the buffer consisting of the free liquid reserves must be removed from the banking system, so that the Bundesbank was no longer merely a 'self-service shop' for the banks. Equally, it was quickly appreciated that the re-gaining of the initiative to create central bank money facilitated by the floating exchange rate between the D-mark and the dollar simultaneously required a more flexible steering of the money market, in order to avoid volatile fluctuations in interest rates that would have created uncertainty in the markets.

[48] Earlier Neumann had stated his view that the most important task was 'to stabilize the stabilization policy' and proposed a change 'from the cyclical orientation followed until now to a trend orientation'. Neumann, 1974a, p. 69. In addition, Neumann advised the Bundesbank to make greater efforts to publicize the change of course it adopted in the second half of 1974: 'in this the Bundesbank should state the limits that are in future to be imposed on monetary expansion.' Neumann, 1974b, p. 70.

[49] The remark made by Gleske was characteristic: 'the task of Herr Gocht, who has had here, in a sense, to act as Friedman's advocate, was certainly, from a psychological point of view, more difficult than mine; (for) Friedman's teachings . . . really do suggest that, in the final analysis, all of us sitting at this table are superfluous.' Quoted with the permission of Gleske.

[50] Cf. the presentations on this issue at the 1970 Konstanzer Seminar by Neumann, 1972, and Willms, 1972.

A central bank pursues two aims by announcing monetary targets. They serve the central bank as a yardstick that forces it to justify the appropriateness of individual measures and of any deviations from the target chosen. More important still is the information function for economic and political agents, both because this influences expectations of price trends, and because it makes it more difficult to exert pressure on the central bank for more rapid monetary expansion. The Central Bank Council was well aware of these two aspects when it took the decision on the first monetary growth target. The target itself, however, was formulated very nebulously: 'at the present juncture [!] a growth of the central bank money stock . . . of around 8 per cent may [!] appear reasonable.'[51]

As far as the derivation of the monetary target was concerned, during the 1970s the Bundesbank did not yet follow the recommendation for a medium-term orientation. This would have required that only expectations regarding the trend rate of growth of potential output and of the velocity of circulation be considered, while expectations regarding changes in the level of capacity utilization, or short-term deviations of the velocity of circulation from the secular trend, would have been excluded.[52] Not until the monetary target for 1983 was policy oriented towards the medium-term growth of potential output.[53]

In the course of the past two decades, the concept of monetary targeting has been repeatedly and critically discussed on the Central Bank Council. The concept was almost abandoned on two occasions: at the end of 1978 and the end of 1987. In both cases the target had been missed by a wide margin, 11 per cent instead of 8 per cent as the average for 1978, and 8 per cent instead of 3–6 per cent in the course of 1987. In both cases the reasons behind the overshooting of the target lay in the very substantial intervention on the foreign-exchange markets, in support of the dollar and the EMS currencies, respectively. In 1978 the increase in the net foreign asset position of the Bundesbank exceeded the expansion of the monetary base that year by 20 per cent, and in 1987 by as much as 70 per cent.

Not surprisingly, similar arguments were used on both occasions in the debate for and against the continuation of the concept of public monetary growth targets. Proponents of monetary targeting argued that abandoning the targets would be perceived by public opinion as resignation on the part of the Bundesbank, if not as a *carte blanche* for an expansionary monetary

---

[51] Deutsche Bundesbank, 1974, Author's emphases.

[52] For a critical analysis of the monetary targets set between 1979 and 1994, see Neumann, 1997.

[53] Indeed, that target was based only on the expected growth of potential output and the rate of inflation considered 'unavoidable'.

policy. This would be damaging to the credibility of the Bundesbank's orientation towards domestic monetary stability. The sceptics responded that, for external economic reasons, it would remain difficult to stick to the targets, and this would be damaging to the credibility of the central bank. For this reason it would be better to remove the binding character of the targets. Yet there was one important difference between 1978 and 1987: the position taken by the Federal Government. In 1978 the then Minister of Economics, Otto Graf Lambsdorff, lent his full support to the proponents of retaining monetary targets, arguing, amongst other things, that a signal must be sent to the partners in the newly founded EMS that the system was compatible with a stability policy, and that monetary control played a key role.[54] In 1987, by contrast, Lambsdorff's successor, Martin Bangemann, argued in favour of reducing the status of the monetary targets to that of an orientation variable, as this would avoid the problem of credibility and differences of opinion between the central bank and the government. In other words, in 1978 the Bundesbank was encouraged by the government to stick to its concept and to the monetary targets, whereas this did not occur in 1987.

Overall, the concept of public monetary growth targets, based on a money supply policy oriented towards the medium term, has proved its worth. Particularly noteworthy are the 'information function', which exerts a positive influence on price expectations, and the 'protective-shield function', which makes it easier for the central bank to withstand domestic and foreign pressure for a more expansionary monetary policy. The Bundesbank has proved that the money stock can be steered within sufficiently narrow limits, even if the target has been missed by a large margin in certain years. From a longer term perspective, the choice of the monetary aggregate to be targeted is of secondary importance. This is not so in the short term, however. To this extent the decision taken towards the end of 1987 to change from the central bank money stock to M3 was understandable.[55]

Finally, it is important to underline the fact that the policy strategy pursued by the Bundesbank does allow it to deviate from the envisaged growth rate in the short term, for instance in response to exchange-rate considerations. Studies of the reaction function of the Bundesbank have shown that it has pursued a moderate policy of leaning against the wind.[56] Such deviations must not be allowed to become entrenched, however: monetary growth must persistently be returned to the medium-term stability

---

[54] This is why von Hagen, in his contribution to this volume, calls the EMS the 'saviour' of monetary targeting.

[55] On this cf. Issing, 1995.

[56] Cf. Neumann and von Hagen, 1993, pp. 31ff. and Neumann, 1997, pp. 186ff.

trajectory if the credibility of the stability orientation is not to be put at risk. The Bundesbank has consistently faced up to this difficult task, even when the external parameters have been unfavourable. It is not least on this fact that its high international reputation rests.

7. Stability culture

The independence of the central bank is a necessary, but not a sufficient condition for maintaining monetary stability. In the final analysis, the central bank can only pursue such a policy if the centrality of the goal is accepted by the population. Notwithstanding the famous saying by Helmut Schmidt, in 1972, according to which 5 per cent inflation is to be preferred to 5 per cent unemployment, German public opinion has never seriously doubted that maintaining monetary stability is desirable, and, moreover, that price stability constitutes a vital parameter for the market economy and the maintenance of social peace. Helmut Schlesinger coined the term 'stability culture' (*Stabilitätskultur*) to describe this phenomenon, and this has led some foreign observers to the belief that Germany's success in terms of monetary stability owes less to the institution of the Bundesbank, than to the horrors experienced by the German population during the hyper-inflation of 1921 to 1923 and the pent-up inflation between 1936 and 1948. It is because of these experiences, the argument runs, that a specifically German preference for monetary stability has crystallized out within the German population.

What is correct about this view is that monetary stability cannot be maintained in the absence of a stability culture, that is, if a keen awareness of the importance of maintaining the value of money for individual welfare is lacking among broad sections of the population. In such a case, what is lacking, at bottom, is the legitimacy of the institution of central bank independence; a stability-oriented monetary policy would be branded as a job-killer, and, consequently, institutionalized independence would be removed through the democratic process.

Yet stability culture has not been a constant feature of German history. As with any form of culture, it is fragile and vulnerable to the decay of the knowledge that underpins it. It is here that the statutory institutionalization of the independence of the central bank has proved to be the vital foundation, on the basis of which such culture can be maintained. Decision makers at the central bank can only defend their specific power position against special political interests by tirelessly promoting the goal of monetary stability in the public domain, and explaining why, in order to achieve this goal, independence needs to be enshrined in law.[57] They are the bearers of this culture, in their own interest. From the very outset, the Bundesbank has given publicity work a level of attention unlike that of any other central bank. This includes the publication of the detailed Annual and Monthly Reports and the Statistical Supplements, monthly data made available on magnetic tape, and excerpts from press articles. It also includes the countless speeches given by members of the Central Bank Council on a whole variety of occasions, and, not least, systematic press work. If inflation is unpopular in Germany, then it is not because a substantial proportion of the population has experienced galloping inflation, but rather because those responsible at the central bank have never tired of explaining its adverse effects and incessantly sought to justify the particular importance of the goal of price stability and the independence of the central bank, that this priority, alone, can justify.

8. Sources and bibliography

Unpublished sources

Historisches Archiv der Deutschen Bundesbank (HA BBk)

Bibliography

Alesina, Alberto (1989): Comment on Nordhaus, in: Brookings Papers on Economic Activity 2, pp. 50–6
Alesina, Alberto/Roubini, Nouriel (1992): Political Cycles in the OECD Economies, in: Review of Economic Studies 59, pp. 663–88
Bank deutscher Länder (1956a): Neue kreditpolitische Maßnahmen, in: Monatsbericht, May, pp. 3–12
Bank deutscher Länder (1956b): Rede von Bundeskanzler Dr. Adenauer am 23. Mai 1956 in Köln vor dem Bundesverband der Deutschen Industrie, reproduced in: Auszüge aus Presseartikeln, no. 58, pp. 1–2
Berger, Helge (1996): The Bundesbank's Path to Independence. Evidence from the 1950s, Münchner Wirtschaftswissenschaftliche Beiträge, no. 96–09, Munich
Brunner, Karl (1983): The Pragmatic and Intellectual Tradition of Monetary Policy Making and the International Monetary Order, in: Ehrlicher, Werner/Richter, Rudolf (eds.): Geld und Währungsordnung, Berlin, pp. 97–141
Deutsche Bundesbank (1968): Das Ausmaß der Geldentwertung seit 1950 und die weitere Entwicklung des Geldwertes, in: Monatsbericht 24, 3, pp. 3–19

---

[57] In this case they need not fear the 'independence of parliament', but can count on public support, as the case of the conflict concerning the revaluation of the Bundesbank's gold and foreign exchange reserves in mid-1997 has recently shown.

Deutsche Bundesbank (1972): Bundesregierung und Bundesbank, in: Monatsbericht 20, 8, pp. 15–17

Deutsche Bundesbank (1974): press statement, 5 December, in: Auszüge aus Presseartikeln, no. 77/1974, p. 1

Deutsche Bundesbank (1978): What Germany will seek at the summit. Interview with Helmut Schmidt by G. Thomas Gibson and Robert F. Ingersoll, in: Auszüge aus Presseartikeln, no. 47, pp. 1–3

Dostojevskij, Fedor M. (1971): Aufzeichnungen aus einem Totenhause, Frankfurt a.M.

Emminger, Otmar (1986): D-Mark, Dollar, Währungskrisen. Erinnerungen eines ehemaligen Bundesbankpräsidenten, Stuttgart

Frey, Bruno S./Schneider, Friedrich (1981): Central Bank Behaviour. A Positive Empirical Analysis, in: Journal of Monetary Economics 7, pp. 291–315

Friedman, Milton (1959): A Program for Monetary Stability, New York

Friedman, Milton (1962): Should There Be an Independent Monetary Authority?, in: Yeager, Leland B. (ed.): In Search of a Monetary Constitution, Cambridge, Mass., pp. 219–43

Friedman, Milton (1968): The Role of Monetary Policy, in: American Economic Review 58, pp. 1–17

Issing, Otmar (1992): Perspektiven der Europäischen Währungsunion, in: Deutsche Bundesbank: Auszüge aus Presseartikeln, no. 18, pp. 1–6

Issing, Otmar (1995): Stability of Monetary Policy—Stability of the Monetary System, in: Deutsche Bundesbank: Auszüge aus Presseartikeln, no. 22, pp. 4–9

Lindner, Gudrun (1973): Die Krise als Steuerungsmittel. Eine Analyse der Bundesbankpolitik in den Jahren 1964–66/67, in: Leviathan 1, pp. 342–81

Marsh, David (1992): Die Bundesbank. Geschäfte mit der Macht, Gütersloh

Meltzer, Alan H. (1984): Overview, in: Federal Reserve Bank of Kansas City (ed.): Price Stability and Public Policy, Kansas City, pp. 209–22

Neumann, Manfred J. M. (1972): Bank Liquidity and the Extended Monetary Base as Indicators of German Monetary Policy, in: Brunner, Karl (ed.): Proceedings of the First Konstanzer Seminar on Monetary Theory and Monetary Policy, Supplement 1 of Kredit und Kapital, Berlin, pp. 165–217

Neumann, Manfred J. M. (1974a): Stabilisierungspolitik stabilisieren, in: Wirtschaftswoche 28, 25, pp. 69–74

Neumann, Manfred J. M. (1974b): Auf leisen Sohlen, in: Wirtschaftswoche 28, 44, p. 70

Neumann, Manfred J. M. (1991): Precommitment by Central Bank Independence, in: Open Economies Review 2, pp. 95–112

Neumann, Manfred J. M. (1993): Die Deutsche Bundesbank als ein Modell für die Europäische Zentralbank?, in: Duwendag, Dieter/Siebke, Jürgen/Bofinger, Peter (eds.): Europa vor dem Eintritt in die Wirtschafts- und Währungsunion, Schriften des Vereins für Socialpolitik, N.F. vol. 220, Berlin, pp. 81–96

Neumann, Manfred J. M. (1997): Monetary Targeting in Germany, in: Kuroda, Iwao (ed.): Towards More Effective Monetary Policy, Hampshire, pp. 176–98

Neumann, Manfred J. M./Hagen, Jürgen von (1993): Germany, in: Fratianni, Michele U./Salvatore, Dominick (eds.): Monetary Policy in Developed Economies, Westport, CT/London, pp. 299–334

Nordhaus, William D. (1975): The Political Business Cycle, in: Review of Economic Studies 42, pp. 169–90

Rogoff, Kenneth S./Sibert, Anne C. (1988): Elections and Macroeconomic Policy Cycles, in: Review of Economic Studies 55, pp. 1–16

Solveen, Ralph (1996): Verhindert die Unabhängigkeit der Zentralbank politische Konjunkturzyklen?, Kieler Arbeitspapier no. 747, Kiel

Tietmeyer, Hans (1996): The Value of Monetary Stability in the World Today, Von Hügel Lecture, in: Tietmeyer, Hans: Währungsstabilität für Europa. Beiträge, Reden und Dokumente zur europäischen Währungsintegration aus vier Jahrzehnten, ed. Zentralbankrat der Deutschen Bundesbank, Baden-Baden, pp. 29–43

Tobin, James (1965): Money and Economic Growth, in: Econometrica 33, pp. 671–84

Vaubel, Roland (1989): Überholte Glaubenssätze, in: Wirtschaftsdienst 69, pp. 276–9

Vaubel, Roland (1993): Eine Public-Choice-Analyse der Deutschen Bundesbank und ihre Implikationen für die Europäische Währungsunion, in: Duwendag, Dieter/Siebke, Jürgen/ Bofinger, Peter (eds.): Europa vor dem Eintritt in die Wirtschafts- und Währungsunion, Schriften des Vereins für Socialpolitik, N.F. vol. 220, Berlin, pp. 23–80

Walsh, Carl E. (1995): Optimal Contracts for Central Bankers, in: American Economic Review 85, pp. 150–67

Willms, Manfred (1972): An Evaluation of Monetary Indicators in Germany, in: Brunner, Karl (ed.): Proceedings of the First Konstanzer Seminar on Monetary Theory and Monetary Policy, Supplement 1 of Kredit und Kapital, Berlin, pp. 219–42

Woll, Arthur (1988): Zur Unabhängigkeit der Deutschen Bundesbank—Unzeitgemäße Betrachtungen zu einem aktuellen Problem, in: Nienhaus, Volker/Suntum, Ulrich van (eds.): Grundlagen und Erneuerung der Marktwirtschaft, Baden-Baden, pp. 185–97

VII. Monetary Policy under Fixed Exchange Rates
(1948–70)

By Carl-Ludwig Holtfrerich

1. Initial hypothesis

On the basis of a theoretical model, Robert Mundell has shown that the effectiveness of monetary policy in an open economy depends on the nature of the exchange-rate system and on the freedom of, or restrictions on, international capital movements.[1] He has shown that, in a situation of free capital movements and fixed exchange rates, monetary policy has less impact on domestic growth and employment than on the external position: the capital and the current account. Fiscal policy, on the other hand, is relatively effective in stabilizing the domestic business cycle. He concluded from this that, given fixed exchange rates, monetary policy should concentrate exclusively on establishing external equilibrium—or another desired balance of payments situation—while fiscal policy should focus on ensuring domestic equilibrium.[2] In the case of 'floating exchange rates', he identified precisely the reverse impacts for the two policy areas, and thus proposed a mirror-image division of tasks for them.[3]

If Mundell's hypothesis were correct, this present study should reveal that, following the move to the *de facto* convertibility of the D-mark as early as the mid-1950s, a restrictive monetary policy by the Bank deutscher Länder/Bundesbank to counter signs of cyclical overheating was regularly doomed to failure as regards the domestic economy unless such measures

---

[1] Cf. Mundell, 1960, 1962, 1963.

[2] The same result was obtained by Swoboda, 1973.

[3] Of the four standard goals of economic policy, Mundell neglected price stability, and of the three most important fields of economic policy, that of incomes policy. The most plausible explanation for this is that he considered, in a liberalized world economy, price trends for tradable goods to be determined by international price relations and, as a Keynesian, price trends for non-tradable goods to be more heavily dependent on incomes policy than on monetary policy. This view was also taken by the Bank deutscher Länder/Bundesbank until the early 1970s, as reflected in its repeated appeals to collective bargaining partners for wage moderation.

were simultaneously required for external reasons; indeed, that monetary policy could make a greater contribution to stabilizing the domestic business cycle by *reducing* interest rates to below the level in the leading partner countries—owing to the outflow of capital this induced—than by raising interest rates. Equally, it should turn out that a restrictive monetary policy did not cause significant growth and employment losses, and that the domestic business cycle was more heavily dependent on fiscal policy and other economic policy fields, including incomes policy, than on monetary policy.

What can be stated, in any case, is that the Federal Republic of Germany proved far more successful in achieving its economic policy aims during the period of fixed exchange rates than subsequently; not only in terms of economic growth and full employment, but also in terms of price stability (see Table 1).[4] This poses the question as to what extent the relatively favourable outcome of economic policy until 1969 and the relatively poor results achieved in the past 25 years are due, as suggested by Mundell's theory, to the policy mix. If this were so, the higher degree of price stability in the period of fixed exchange rates would have to be traced back, in the main, to a relatively low rate of global inflation and an incomes policy more conducive to monetary stability; the higher rate of economic growth and the lower unemployment primarily to fiscal policy; and external trends, i.e. the persistent current account and balance of payments surpluses, primarily to monetary policy.

This study will show that during the period of fixed exchange rates—except in phases of extreme cyclical overheating—the parties to collective bargaining exercised wage and price discipline and thus met their responsibility for ensuring price stability. To a great extent, the economic policy task of cyclical stabilization was performed by fiscal policy, which, to this extent, bore its responsibility for growth and employment in accordance with Mundell's theory. Monetary policy, for its part, was only able to play a supporting role in the early years, in which the D-mark was not convertible. After that, it was largely powerless in terms of stabilizing the domestic

---

[4] This was true not only of Germany, but also, to a greater or lesser extent, of the other OECD countries. Cf. Lindlar, 1997. In the period 1973–97 German economic growth amounted to just 2.1 per cent p.a., and productivity growth (per employee) to 1.9 per cent p.a. Since 1973 the unemployment rate has, on balance, risen steadily, to reach around 11 per cent in 1997, i.e. the same level as that at which in 1950, the Federal Republic embarked on the 'economic miracle'.1970 marked a watershed in the inflationary trend. For the entire period 1970–97 the average increase in the cost of living amounted to 3.5 per cent p.a. This figure was nearly double the annual average from 1952 to 1969, and this despite the fact that price and unit labour cost trends in the Federal Republic were successfully 'de-coupled' from the international 'inflationary train' by the trend appreciation of the D-mark during the period of flexible exchange rates. Cf. Lindlar and Holtfrerich, 1997, p. 233.

economy.[5] When the Central Bank Council raised interest rates in order to dampen down demand, it repeatedly had to learn the lesson summarized by Mundell as follows: a surplus country under inflationary pressure should relax the monetary conditions and raise taxes (or cut government spending).[6] However, it appears to have forgotten this lesson each time the next boom came along.

It was serendipitous for economic development in the Federal Republic prior to 1970 that the growth of the money stock and of liquidity was always generous owing to the 'open external-economic flank'. Against the background of relative wage discipline by the parties to collective bargaining, this meant that what contemporary observers called the 'Mengenkonjunktur' (lit: 'quantity' as against 'price' business cycle, i.e. rising output and employment instead of prices) was able to unfold unhindered. It is no coincidence that this occurred, against the background of almost complete price stability, between 1952 and 1955, when fiscal policy was making its maximum contribution to monetary stability, in the shape of hoarding repeated budget surpluses in the 'Juliusturm'.

To summarize: the division of tasks between the three most important policy areas was broadly in agreement with the lessons drawn from Mundell's theory during the period of fixed exchange rates. Monetary and economic policy was correspondingly effective.

2. A summary of economic and monetary trends

Tables 1–3 and Figures 1–4 on pages 310–17 present some of the most important data portraying economic and monetary trends in the Federal Republic.

---

[5] It is for this reason that the Bank deutscher Länder/Bundesbank always turned to those responsible for fiscal policy in search of support when steps were needed to apply the stabilization policy brakes.

[6] Cf. Mundell, 1962, p. 70.

TABLE 1: Economi

	Cost of living (rate of change in %)	Unemployment rate (in %)	Real economic growth (in %)	Investment as a share of output (in %)	Labour productivity per working hour (rate of growth in %)	Gross hourly wages (rate of growth in %)	Unit labour costs for entire economy (rate of growth in %)
1950		11.0		18.9			
1951	7.7	10.4	10.9	18.9	6.8	14.9	8.8
1952	2.1	9.5	9.0	19.4	3.6	7.8	0.9
1953	−1.8	8.4	7.9	20.6	4.2	4.8	0.6
1954	0.2	7.6	7.5	21.5	5.4	2.6	0.6
1955	1.6	5.6	12.1	23.5	6.5	6.8	0.3
1956	2.5	4.4	6.9	23.7	3.7	9.9	3.1
1957	2.0	3.7	5.7	22.5	6.9	8.7	2.7
1958	2.2	3.7	3.5	22.7	4.0	6.8	4.0
1959	1.0	2.6	7.4	24.0	7.9	5.4	−1.0
1960	1.4	1.3	9.0	24.3	8.2	9.3	2.1
1961	2.3	0.8	5.6	25.2	4.9	10.3	6.9
1962	3.0	0.7	4.0	25.8	5.9	11.5	4.5
1963	3.0	0.8	3.4	25.6	5.6	7.5	3.4
1964	2.3	0.8	6.8	26.6	7.7	8.4	1.8
1965	3.4	0.7	5.7	26.2	4.5	9.8	4.3
1966	3.5	0.7	2.8	25.5	3.3	6.6	4.1
1967	1.4	2.1	−0.2	23.1	5.8	3.2	0.2
1968	1.5	1.5	6.3	22.4	5.8	4.4	0.8
1969	2.8	0.9	7.8	23.2	6.8	9.0	3.6
1970	3.7	0.7	6.0	25.5	3.1	13.9	11.6

Sources: Deutsche Bundesbank; Council of Economic Experts and Federal Statistical Office.

trends, 1950–70

| Budget deficit/surplus | | | | Government debt at end of year | | | |
| Central government | | Total public sector | | Central government | | Total public sector | |
in DM billion	as % of GDP	in DM billion	as % of GDP	in DM billion	as % of GDP	in DM billion	as % of GDP
−1.0	−1.0	−0.5	−0.5	7.3	7.1	20.6	20.0
0.0	0.0	+1.5	+1.2	8.2	6.5	22.4	17.7
−0.5	−0.3	+1.0	+0.7	8.9	6.2	24.0	16.6
+1.5	+1.0	+3.0	+1.9	17.0	11.0	33.9	21.8
+0.5	+0.3	+2.0	+1.2	20.1	12.0	38.7	23.2
+2.0	+1.0	+3.0	+1.6	20.8	10.9	41.0	21.5
+1.5	+0.7	+3.0	+1.4	20.6	9.8	42.0	19.9
−2.0	−0.9	−0.5	−0.2	22.9	10.0	43.9	19.1
−1.5	−0.6	−2.0	−0.8	23.4	9.5	46.5	18.9
−3.0	−1.1	−1.5	−0.6	25.1	9.3	49.6	18.4
−1.0	−0.3	+3.0	+1.0	26.8	8.9	52.7	17.4
+1.1	+0.3	+2.1	+0.6	25.9	7.8	57.1	17.2
−1.2	−0.3	+0.2	+0.1	27.2	7.6	60.4	16.7
−2.7	−0.7	−4.0	−1.0	30.1	7.9	67.1	17.5
−1.0	−0.2	−5.2	−1.2	31.3	7.5	73.8	17.6
−2.0	−0.4	−8.8	−1.9	33.0	7.2	83.7	18.2
−2.4	−0.5	−7.5	−1.5	35.6	7.3	93.0	19.1
−8.5	−1.7	−15.9	−3.2	43.5	8.8	108.2	21.9
−4.4	−0.8	−9.3	−1.7	47.2	8.9	117.1	22.0
+0.8	+0.1	+1.3	+0.2	45.4	7.6	117.9	19.8
−1.4	−0.2	−3.9	−0.6	47.3	7.0	125.9	18.6

TABLE 2: Monetary trends, 1949–70

	Central bank money stock growth rate (in %)	Money stock M3 growth rate (in %)	Money market rate (in %)	Capital market rate (in %)	Bank loans to non-banks (rate of growth in %)	Free liquid reserves of the banks (in DM bn)
1949	16.5		3.24		95.2	0.3
1950	8.7	23.2	4.31	6.22	54.1	0.3
1951	15.4	21.3	6.01	6.39	25.9	1.3
1952	16.0	20.4	5.11	5.94	25.7	4.1
1953	10.3	19.3	3.57	6.11	24.5	5.1
1954	6.9	14.9	2.89	6.37	24.6	5.3
1955	10.1	12.1	3.16	6.10	19.5	5.7
1956	6.5	11.4	4.71	6.30	12.9	8.5
1957	10.8	16.1	3.96	7.10	10.8	14.2
1958	9.2	13.6	3.08	6.50	12.4	16.1
1959	7.8	16.1	2.70	5.80	18.6	17.4
1960	7.5	10.9	4.56	6.30	23.3	11.5
1961	11.6	14.8	2.93	5.90	15.2	14.7
1962	7.8	10.4	2.66	6.00	12.6	17.2
1963	8.1	9.9	3.00	6.10	12.3	17.4
1964	8.4	9.4	3.29	6.20	13.1	18.0
1965	9.0	10.6	4.10	6.80	12.8	15.6
1966	5.5	8.3	5.34	7.80	9.1	13.7
1967	6.7	12.0	3.35	7.00	10.3	24.9
1968	9.5	11.8	2.59	6.70	12.4	34.3
1969	9.4	9.4	4.81	7.00	14.8	31.0
1970	6.8	9.1	8.65	8.20	10.7	20.5

Central bank money stock:

Notes: Calculated from year's end to year's end. Because the Bundesbank is unable to provide data on the central bank money stock for the period 1948–59, the rate of growth of currency in circulation is used as a proxy in the period 1949–60. This can be justified, because the minimum reserve deposits, which are to be incorporated into the analysis, constitute merely a fraction of currency in circulation and would have to be incorporated at constant reserve ratios, which limits the variability of this factor. For this reason, the impact of this factor on the growth rate is in any case minimal compared with currency in circulation.

Sources: 1949–60: Deutsche Bundesbank, 1988, p. 20; 1961 and subsequent years: Bundesbank figures.

Money stock of M3:

Notes: Calculated from year's end to year's end.

Sources: Deutsche Bundesbank, 1988, p. 16. Between 1950 and 1954 this statistic was supplemented by savings deposits at statutory notice—not included in the original figures—by classifying two thirds of total savings deposits as savings deposits at statutory notice. This is approximately equal to the proportion of total savings deposits held as savings deposits at statutory notice during the second half of the 1950s. Data on total savings deposits are given in Bank deutscher Länder, 1955, p. 16.

Money market rate:

Notes: Day-to-day money rate, average annual values.

Source: Deutsche Bundesbank, 1988, p. 207.

Capital market rate:

Notes: Yield on fixed-interest securities outstanding, average annual values.

Sources: 1950–1954: Morawietz, 1994, p. 334. 1955 and subsequent years: Deutsche Bundebank, 1988, p. 207.

Bank loans to non-banks:

Source: Deutsche Bundesbank, 1988, p. 44.

Free liquid reserves:

Notes: 1949–57: at year's end; 1958 and subsequent years: annual average values.

Source: Data provided by the Bundesbank.

TABLE 3: External economic trends, 1949–70

	Current account balance in DM million	Capital account balance in DM million		External assets/liabilities in DM billion[a]				
				Bank deutscher Länder/Bundesbank			Credit institutions	
		Long-term	Short-term	Assets	of which: gold	Liabilities	Assets	Liabilities
1949	−262	49	0	0.85		0.55	0.05	
1950	−323	488	149	1.08		1.82	0.38	
1951	2,485	−79	−464	2.00	0.12	0.65	0.40	0.57
1952	2,726	−357	363	4.97	0.59	0.38	0.21	0.82
1953	4,148	−378	−320	8.37	1.37	0.05	0.25	1.45
1954	4,015	−438	−268	11.50	2.63	0.17	0.38	1.63
1955	2,676	−271	−369	13.29	3.86	0.14	0.54	1.92
1956	4,986	−365	203	18.32	6.23	0.19	0.74	3.02
1957	6,538	−390	−1,265	24.06	10.60	0.72	1.40	3.61
1958	6,628	−1,437	−1,292	27.03	10.96	0.39	2.05	3.47
1959	4,824	−3,629	−2,769	25.20	10.93	0.45	5.06	4.11
1960	5,612	−81	2,353	33.34	12.29	0.62	4.41	5.39
1961	4,033	−4,053	−956	32.01	14.43	0.75	7.32	6.67
1962	−686	−183	−414	30.96	14.49	0.61	8.88	6.80
1963	1,956	1,806	−1,186	33.53	15.14	0.46	10.36	7.69
1964	1,586	−894	−431	34.28	16.73	0.78	12.48	8.50
1965	−5,036	1,137	2,405	32.89	17.37	0.71	14.48	8.99
1966	1,712	−342	343	34.70	16.91	0.62	16.23	9.03
1967	11,428	−2,930	−8,918	35.09	16.65	1.17	24.01	10.37
1968	13,187	−11,201	5,076	41.93	17.88	1.44	34.96	16.24
1969	8,835	−23,040	4,361	28.05	14.70	1.46	49.56	23.15
1970	4,784	−934	17,647	51.73	14.34	3.55	52.79	33.45

[a] Figures at year's end. *Source:* Deutsche Bundesbank, 1988, pp. 15, 17, 26.

Note: In both the capital and current account balances a minus sign (−) denotes a deficit.   *Source:* Deutsche Bundesbank, 1988, p. 254f.

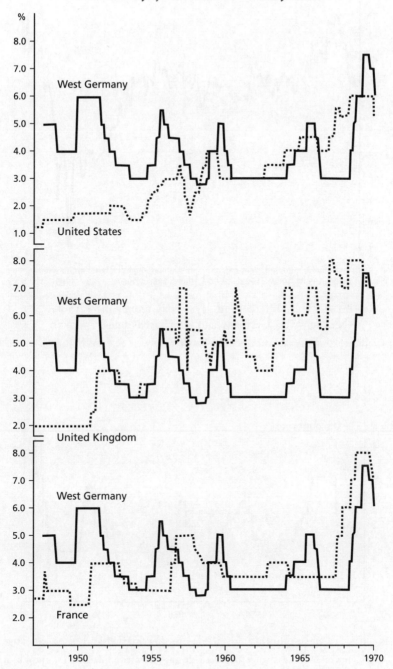

FIGURE I: International comparison of discount rates (end-of-month levels)

Source: Calculations by the Deutsche Bundesbank based on various sources (Federal Reserve Bulletin, Banque de France, Bank for International Settlements).

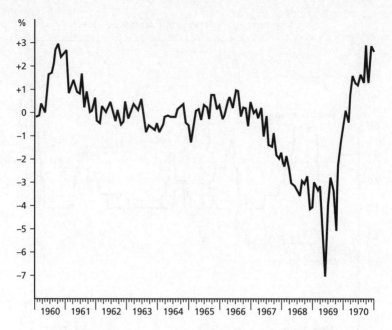

FIGURE 2: Difference in day-to-day money market rates
between West Germany and the United States, 1960–70

Note: + indicates that the rate is higher in West Germany.   *Source*: Deutsche Bundesbank.

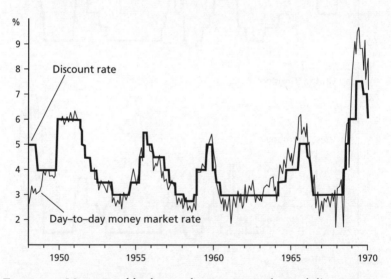

FIGURE 3: Mean monthly day-to-day money market and discount rates

Notes: Discount rate: if the change occurred during the second half of the month, it was ascribed to the following month. Day-to-day money market rate: 1949–59: arithmetic mean of the lowest and highest rates during the month; 1960–70: monthly average.

Source: Discount rate: Deutsche Bundesbank, 1988, p. 200. Day-to-day money market rate: up to December 1954: Bank deutscher Länder, 1955, p. 227; January 1955 to November 1959: various issues of the Monthly Reports of the Bank deutscher Länder/Bundesbank. From January 1960: Bundesbank figures.

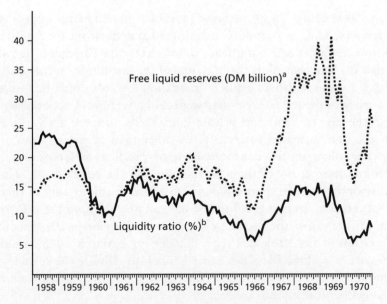

FIGURE 4: Free liquid reserves and liquidity ratio

[a] Domestic money market paper, money market assets abroad, unused rediscount quotas, excess balances (central bank balances less required minimum reserves) less Lombard loans by the Bundesbank.

[b] Free liquid reserves of credit institutions as % of their deposit volume (sight, time, and savings deposits—other than assets with a maturity of 4 years and more—held by non-banks and foreign credit institutions).

Source: Deutsche Bundesbank.

3. The institutions, goals, and instruments of monetary policy

The specific nature of the monetary policy role played by the Bundesbank, or any central bank, is to be seen not in the extent of its power or in its sole responsibility. The ability of a central bank, even when it is completely independent of the government, to control the monetary growth of an economy is restricted. Thus Otmar Emminger's remark in 1970 about the 'supplementary monetary government(s)' was apposite.[7] In the domestic arena, other political institutions and social groups act alongside the central bank, and in other countries, in addition to these, the respective central banks. The impact of decisions taken by one or more of these institutions on monetary policy can be greater than that of the Bundesbank. This is

---

[7] '*monetäre Nebenregierung(en)*'; cf. Emminger, 1970, p. 1072 and 1986a, pp. 174, 466. At the time he was referring to the inflow of foreign currency from abroad, which meant that the Bundesbank had lost control over the volume of money and credit in Germany.

certainly true of the 'supplementary monetary governments' opposing the Bundesbank, taken as a whole. On the other hand, the scope for the Bundesbank to exert an effective influence on monetary developments lies in the fact that the Bundesbank is the only one of the institutions mentioned that takes its decisions with an explicit orientation towards domestic monetary goals, whereas the monetary policy impact of government action usually— and in the case of firms and private households virtually always—results from decisions oriented towards goals other than monetary ones. Their monetary policy impacts constitute mere by-products and, moreover, may cancel one another out without intervention by the central bank. Thus in the case of these institutions the *divide* arises automatically out of their divergent interests, so that the Bundesbank can play the, *and the rule*, role.

The law, or rather the decree by the Allied occupying powers that led to the creation of the Bank deutscher Länder on 1 March 1948, stipulated as the core task of the Bank deutscher Länder 'to stabilize the currency and the monetary and credit system'. Other economic policy goals were mentioned neither directly nor indirectly.

Responsibility for the two classical functions of a central bank had been transferred to the Bank deutscher Länder, namely that of acting as the guardian of the currency and as the lender of last resort to financial institutions. In the Bundesbank Act (*Bundesbankgesetz*), the latter function was no longer mentioned. Under section 3 the Bundesbank received the additional duty of arranging 'for the execution of domestic and international payments', but its main task was here restricted to that of 'guardian of the currency': it was to 'regulate the amount of money in circulation and of credit supplied to the economy with the aim of safeguarding the currency'. Yet in the concluding report of the Parliamentary Committee on Money and Credit, issued on 28 June 1957, with which the Committee presented the finished draft legislation to the Bundestag, it was explicitly stated with respect to section 3 that, in addition to the Bundesbank, 'the Federal Government and parliament, and also others, such as the social partners' were responsible 'indeed primarily so' for safeguarding the currency.[8]

---

[8] In the reasons with which the Federal Government presented the draft legislation of the Bundesbank Act to the Bundestag in Oct. 1956, it had been stated with regard to section 3 that, while the stability of domestic purchasing power was of 'prime importance', other goals (external stability of the currency, full employment and steady economic growth) were also important targets for the Bundesbank. 'This will sometimes make it necessary, paying due regard to all circumstances, to find the optimum compromise for the "common interest" or the "well-being of the country"'. At the same time, it was argued, the government and other institutions bore responsibility for the realization of economic policy goals, including the safeguarding of the currency. 'For this reason good cooperation between all the responsible bodies, including the central bank, is no less important than its . . . independence from other institutions.'

Although its independence from instructions from the Federal Government was assured in section 12, the Bundesbank was simultaneously required, 'without prejudice to the performance of its duties', to 'support the general economic policy of the Federal Cabinet'.[9] In the 'Stability and Growth Act' of 8 June 1967 this requirement of the Bundesbank to support the government was concretized further. There it is stated in section 13, subsection 3 that all federal corporations under public law, of which the Bundesbank is one, should 'take account, within the framework of their tasks, of the goals set out in section 1'. Section 1 requires that economic and fiscal policy measures be 'taken in such a way that, within the framework of the market order, they contribute simultaneously to the stability of the price level, a high level of employment and external equilibrium at a steady and appropriate rate of economic growth'.[10]

In the context of fixed exchange rates, there are, in principle, three intermediate targets (or points of departure) for monetary policy. First, the money stock, all the various aggregates from M1 to M3 extended, or even just the monetary base, i.e. the stock of central bank money excluding the deposits held by public and private non-banks with the central bank; secondly, the free liquid reserves; and, thirdly, interest rates and the interest rate structure for loans of various types and maturities. The latter point of departure was seen by the Bundesbank as being closely linked with the influence it exerted on the volume and structure of the free liquid reserves.

The intermediate target of the monetary and credit policy of the Bank deutscher Länder in the reconstruction phase of the Federal Republic—the period between the currency reform in 1948 and the realization of full employment in the boom phase of 1955 to 1957—was, alongside its efforts to keep interest rates as low as possible because of their importance for investment and thus for economic growth and employment, primarily the accumulation of foreign currency reserves by means of export surpluses, in order to ensure that the—initially weak—D-mark became a strong currency. Until 1958 the Bank deutscher Länder, in evaluating the liquidity position of the commercial banks, focused exclusively on their *current* stocks of central bank money (primary liquidity, particularly the excess reserves). Until that year, it did not pay any attention to their *potential* central bank money (secondary liquidity) and thus the free liquid reserves.

In contrast to the approach adopted by today's so familiar monetarist perspective, the Bank deutscher Länder also considered the growth of the 'volume of money' (*Geldvolumen*); this it defined as the currency in circulation outside the banking system and the bank deposits that can be

---

[9] Bundesbank Act, 26 July 1957.
[10] *Gesetz zur Förderung des Stabilität und des Wachstums der Wirtschaft*, 8 June 1967.

withdrawn within 30 days (= sight deposits) of non-banks.[11] On the prevailing definition, the 'volume of money' grew in 1953, for example, by almost 13 per cent, which the Bank deutscher Länder did not perceive as a threat to price stability. It is characteristic of the view of monetary policy prevailing at the time that not only were time deposits of over 30 days and savings deposits not counted as part of the 'volume of money', but that they were thought to have a contractive influence on the money stock and thus on total monetary demand.[12] The impact was only on real economic growth (1953: +8.3 per cent; 1954: +7.7 per cent) and employment, while the cost of living fell by almost 2 per cent in 1953 and remained constant in 1954.

Between 1958 and the start of the 1970s, the central intermediate target for the Bundesbank's monetary policy was control of the so-called 'free liquid reserves' of the banks.[13] This was based on the view that the central bank cannot directly control the volume of bank deposit money, and thus the money stock, but rather the volume of the free liquid reserves of the banks and thus their scope for credit creation. By this means, it would be possible to exert an indirect influence on the economy's total monetary demand. During this period the west German central bank controlled a variable that incorporated, alongside the excess reserves of the banks, as the 'free part' of their *currently* available central bank money, the assets that they could convert at any time into central bank money from the central bank, i.e. *potential* central bank money. This was because experience had shown that the banks were keen to minimize their holdings of central bank money—above and beyond the minimum reserves—as they did not generate any interest income.[14]

---

[11] Including the public sector, which constitutes the difference between the definition of the 'volume of money' then in use and today's definition of M1. Cf. Bank deutscher Länder, Geschäftsbericht 1953, p. 14 and Issing, 1995, p. 9.

[12] Given that this 'increase in the volume of longer term borrowed funds held by the financial institutions', amounting to DM 10.5 billion in 1953, was about as high as the 'credit granted by the entire banking system' (DM 10.45 billion), it was considered that the rapid rate of credit creation, with its expansionary effect on the 'volume of money', had been almost completely offset. All that remained, therefore, was the expansionary effect of the inflow of foreign exchange (DM 3.5 billion) on the increase in the 'volume of money' (DM 3.3 billion). If the growth of the money stock had been calculated according to the current definition of M3, the central bank would have had to record a rate of growth of almost 20 per cent; the same applied in earlier years too (see Table 2).

[13] Emminger, 1968, p. 28, spoke in March 1968 of 10 years of experience with the 'liquidity policy of the central bank'. No direct confirmation that the policy actually started in 1958 can be found in the Minutes of Central Bank Council meetings.

[14] This is the reason why the Bundesbank concluded, in 1965, that the excess reserves 'were almost consistently insignificant from 1949 until the present day'. Deutsche Bundesbank, 1965, p. 30. During the period of fixed exchange rates the Bundesbank calculated free liquid reserves as follows: excess reserves, i.e. the central bank deposits of the banks (their

The scope for autonomous credit creation and thus the creation of money by the banks was determined by their 'liquidity ratio', i.e. their stock of free liquid reserves as a percentage of their deposit volume (see Figure 4). The difficulty here lay in the fact that the extent of the banks' free liquid reserves was influenced not only by the monetary policy pursued by the central bank, but also by market factors, namely changes in cash balances, the net deposits held by the public sector with the Bundesbank, public money market borrowing from the banking system, and Germany's net foreign currency position against the rest of the world.[15]

From the end of the 1950s up to the end of the system of fixed exchange rates at the start of the 1970s, foreign money market deposits, i.e. the foreign exchange stocks held by the financial institutions, constituted the market factor exerting the strongest influence on the free liquid reserves, and the one at whose mercy the Bundesbank often found itself in its efforts to control the free liquid reserves because of its obligation to intervene in order to maintain the D-mark exchange rate. The Bundesbank was far more readily able to offset the influences of changes in cash balances, on the other hand, which were closely correlated with changes in gross wage and salary income resulting from the rise in employment and, above all, wage growth,[16] and the two other market factors, because they could be forecast more easily or action could be better coordinated with the actors involved.

During the period from 1948 to 1970, the arsenal of central bank policy instruments was enlarged three times by the government. In 1948 the Bank deutscher Länder received, on the basis of legislation by the western Allies, an initial endowment of instruments in connection with the currency reform; for the first time in German history, these included minimum reserve and open market policy instruments. The next step was taken with the passing of the Bundesbank Act in 1957 and brought with it an extension of the scope for open market and deposit policy instruments. The third extension of the range of instruments at the disposal of the central bank occurred in the wake of the Stability and Growth Act of 1967, in the form of laws that gave the Bundesbank new ammunition to defend the economy against the threat posed to monetary stability by the inflow of capital from abroad (100 per cent minimum reserve ratios for foreign deposits, cash deposits).[17]

---

actual reserves) minus the minimum reserve requirement, unused refinancing facilities, that is rediscounting quotas and Lombard facilities, domestic money market paper owned by the banks to the extent that these were incorporated into the Bundesbank's market regulation, and foreign money market deposits owned by the banks.

[15] Deutsche Bundesbank, 1971*b*, p. 20.

[16] Since the mid-1960s this correlation has been strongly influenced by the move towards paying wages and salaries by bank transfer rather than cash payments.

[17] Cf. Stern *et al.*, 1972, p. 203.

4. Monetary and credit policy 1948–70

Of the banks' purely domestic sources of central bank money, the most important during the period under consideration was rediscount credit against bills of exchange.[18] By contrast Lombard credits played an entirely subordinate role.[19] For this reason, and because the Lombard rate was consistently—with a few exceptions towards the end of the period under consideration—one percentage point above the discount rate, little mention will be made in the following of changes in the Lombard rate.

The changes in the rediscount quotas introduced on 1 May 1952 will also be largely ignored, because they were scarcely taken up.[20] In contrast to the post-Bretton Woods era, they were, to quote a term mentioned to me by the Bundesbank official currently responsible for this area, a '*Luftnummer*' (freely translated: 'thin air').[21]

Alongside the interest-rate-policy instrument of the discount rate, it was largely the liquidity-policy instruments—the minimum reserves, open market operations, and swap transactions[22]—that were most important. By means of these instruments, the Bundesbank was able to tie up the banks' excess reserves and free liquid reserves. Consequently, attention will focus in the following on the deployment of these instruments.

Of the instruments oriented towards the external position, the most powerful, the exchange-rate instrument, was not available to the Bank deutscher Länder/Bundesbank during the period of fixed exchange rates. This was the responsibility of the Federal Government. Even so, substantial

---

[18] Of the total volume of central bank credits to domestic banks, they accounted for 88 per cent at the end of 1948, 82 per cent in 1958 and 86 per cent in 1968. Deutsche Bundesbank, 1988, p. 26.

[19] Securities repurchase transactions were not performed until 1980.

[20] Only in 1952 and at the end of the two following years, were they taken up to any significant extent, and even then the take-up rate was only between just under 40 per cent and rather more than 50 per cent. Not until the Bretton Woods system began to break up, under the impact of the foreign exchange turbulence of 1969 and 1970, did its importance increase once more, reaching a provisional record high at the end of Jan. 1970, at 77 per cent. These figures have been calculated from monthly time series data provided by the Bundesbank.

[21] While changes were in some cases relevant to individual banks operating at the upper limit of their quotas, they were of no significance for financial institutions as a whole.

[22] In its swap transaction the Bundesbank sold financial institution US dollars as a spot transaction and simultaneously agreed to buy them back at a later date (simultaneous forward counter-transaction). Usually the forward exchange rate was below the spot rate. In such cases the Bundesbank received payment (= 'deport') for fixing the exchange rate. If it was seeking to promote the export of money, it refrained from charging a deport in this way and conducted swap transactions at equal spot and forward rates or even offered a higher forward than spot rate (= 'report'). Cf. Deutsche Bundesbank, 1971*b*, pp. 57f.

importance will be attached to this instrument in the following discussion because the D-mark exchange rate played a strategic role in the overall currency and external economic policy of the Federal Republic, and the question of a D-mark revaluation was repeatedly a central issue of debate on monetary policy in the light of the persistent balance-of-payments surpluses posted by West Germany between 1951 and 1970.

Consideration will also be given to the developments that prompted the Central Bank Council to react with monetary policy decisions: were its restrictive measures a reaction to external deficits, domestic price increases, excessive wage growth, an inadequately restrictive fiscal policy or excessive free liquid reserves held by the banks? Were the motives for the decisions to relax policy external or domestic in origin, e.g. raising economic growth or the employment level, avoiding a deflationary price trend, promoting the capital market or helping the financial institutions out of liquidity difficulties (function of lender of last resort)? In the case of the last point, it will be important to answer the old question of whether the changes in discount rates imposed by the central bank followed the trends on the money market, which are strongly influenced by external developments, or whether they were able to determine money market trends.

The overall monetary policy strategy of the Bundesbank will also be examined. The question of whether it was politic to control the 'free liquid reserves' as an intermediate monetary policy target, or whether the banks' creation of money and credit was largely independent of the volume of their free liquid reserves will be investigated with the help of the 'liquidity ratio'.

a) The 'weak D-mark' period: 1948–51

The western occupying powers had ensured, in accordance with American wishes, that the Bank deutscher Länder, founded in preparation for the currency reform, could perform its functions as an independent institution, i.e. independent of the governments of the federal states, but at the same time all the important monetary policy decisions were subject to the approval of the Allied Bank Commission (ABC). The Commission was entitled to issue instructions to the Bank deutscher Länder and the Central Bank Council.[23]

In the case of differences of opinion regarding monetary policy, it tended to be the ABC that gave ground. Wilhelm Vocke, the President of the Board of Directors, maintained constant contact with the ABC—which had been

---

[23] Under article II of the Bank deutscher Länder Law of 1 Mar. 1948.

set up in the same building as the Bank deutscher Länder (in the Taunus-anlage 4–6)—and was largely in agreement with its approach. The President of the Central Bank Council, Karl Bernard, was more inclined to risk a confrontation from time to time. Vocke, with his staff at the Board, which prepared all the important monetary policy decisions, could have had the more influential position within the Central Bank Council. Yet he was not always able to get his way there.[24] This was due primarily to the fact that Vocke shared the opinion of the ABC that, in times of peace, credit policy should be oriented towards market conformity, rather than interventionism, and that a policy of high interest rates was a suitable response to a threat to monetary stability, whereas the presidents of the Land Central Banks gener-ally tended to favour lower discount rates with a view to production and employment considerations.[25]

With its very first monetary policy decision, taken on 15–16 June 1948, i.e. prior to the currency reform, the Central Bank Council departed from the expectations and views of the Allied side in a very characteristic way. Although they all pursued, in accordance with the then predominant Keynesian views, a policy of 'easy money' in their own countries—for instance at the time the discount rate of the Federal Reserve Bank of New York was just 1.25 per cent (see Figure 1)—the Allies had proposed to the German side a high discount rate of around 8 per cent. Yet the Central Bank Council decided—by 9 votes to 6—on a rate of 5 per cent, which, as was the case with later discount rates, was also valid for rediscounting treasury bills and as the interest rate for cash advances to government and the bizonal authority.

Also at the meeting on 15–16 June 1948, the Central Bank Council decided to send a circular letter to the Land Central Banks containing guidelines for the provision of credit. In the introduction it was stated, in a sentence of fundamental importance for the monetary policy course pursued in the subsequent period of economic reconstruction: 'the success of the currency reform will depend centrally on whether the financial institutions are in a position to direct credits to where they will be put to the best eco-nomic use, i.e. where they serve to maintain goods turnover and produc-tion.' The minimum reserve ratios which financial institutions were obliged

[24] Vocke was outvoted on a large number of decisions by the Central Bank Council, par-ticularly on rediscount policy.

[25] Vocke's reputation among the Allied banking specialists was correspondingly good, as is revealed by the following observation by a Bank of England expert on the German central bank scene: 'in practice, the President of the Board of Management (Vocke) does all the work and takes all the decisions, while the President of the Board of Directors [Bernard] does not cut so much ice.' (BoE Archives OV 34/92: Rootham, Note, 5 April 1950) This view was, as events in subsequent years were to show, incorrect.

to deposit interest-free with their Land Central Banks were set at 10 per cent for sight deposits and 5 per cent for time and savings deposits.[26]

Those responsible for the currency reform of 20 June 1948 were uncertain as to how large the monetary 'cloak' for the west German economy should be tailored in order to avoid—if too small—a deflation, with its negative effects on production and employment, and—if too large—inflation and thus once again undermining confidence in the new currency.[27] They therefore proceeded with great caution. The demand by private households for goods and services and the extent to which firms would put up their hoarded supplies of goods for sale could not be determined precisely. On top of this came the uncertainty surrounding the budget position following the currency reform that had involved tax cuts. It was unclear whether government would be able to adhere to the ban on running a budget deficit.[28]

Prior to the Second World War, the stock of money in the German economy, as defined by M3, had amounted to at least two-thirds of GNP. Now, against the background of an estimated GNP of DM 45 billion, a money stock of initially less than 10 per cent was to be provided by the end of July 1948 in the form of the initial endowment of private households, the public sector and enterprises, and the freeing of just half of the converted outstanding Reichsmark deposits (i.e. 5 per cent).[29] Even so, price trends were sharply inflationary, all the more so when, in September, the second *per capita* endowment was paid out, with a volume of almost DM 1 billion. Between June and October 1948 the cost of living rose by around 14 per cent,

[26] At that time, and in the entire subsequent Bank deutscher Länder period, the Central Bank Council took separate decisions (discount 1 per cent, Lombard 2 per cent) on the discount and Lombard rates that were to apply for business transactions between the Land Central Banks and the Bank deutscher Länder, which, in the final analysis, was responsible for making central bank money available. In addition, the Land Central Banks were obliged to hold minimum reserves with the Bank deutscher Länder. However, given that all these rates, which existed until the creation of the Bundesbank, owing to the two-stage nature of the German central bank system, were *de facto* only of importance with regard to the division of profits between the Land Central Banks and the Bank deutscher Länder, these decisions will be ignored in the following.

[27] This uncertainty was also prevalent within the Bank deutscher Länder, as is revealed by an 18-page exposé by the head of the Economics and Statistics Department, Eduard Wolf, issued on 14 Oct. 1948 and to which, on the very next day, a four-page postscript was added following the arrival of new statistical data (HA BBk B 3351 and 3402 [Wolf's files]).

[28] Although section 28 of the *Umstellungsgesetz zur Währungsreform* (Conversion law relating to currency reform) had imposed a ban on government deficits (cf. Harmening and Duden, 1949, p. 39), government had at its disposal deposits in the central bank system totalling DM 2.4 billion from the statutory provision of an initial monetary endowment. It remained to be seen how much of its deposits in the central bank system it would bring into circulation.

[29] Bank deutscher Länder, Geschäftsbericht 1948–9, p. 4.

and primary goods prices even faster.[30] This led to the decision by the military governments (*Viertes Gesetz zur Neuordnung des Geldwesens*—Fourth law on the reordering of the monetary system) of 4 October 1949 not to free the frozen half of the bank deposits converted into D-mark in full: instead, just 2/10 were unfrozen completely, 1/10 for creating medium- to long-term deposits, while the remaining 7/10 were written off entirely.[31] Overall, including the resources unfrozen in October, a money stock (defined in terms of M3) of around DM 13 billion had been created by statutory means.[32] On top of this, came the new creation of credit and thus money by the banks in the wake of the currency reform. At the end of October 1948, short-term bank loans to non-banks amounted to DM 3.8 billion, compared with DM 1.3 billion at the end of July.[33]

When the sharp rise in prices in the autumn of 1948 indicated the need for monetary policy action, the Central Bank Council initially took a wait-and-see attitude.[34] Instead of initiating measures to raise interest rates or minimum reserve requirements, it insisted on the Land Central Banks adhering particularly stringently to the guidelines for credit creation adopted in mid-June, i.e. by reinforcing selective control on lending. At the Central Bank Council meeting held on 2 and 3 November it was decided to rediscount bank bills for acceptance credit only if they served to finance foreign-trade transactions or administratively ordered storage ('import and storage agency bills').[35] On 16 November 1948, too, the Central Bank Council

[30] For the monthly data see Wallich, 1955, p. 72. This was largely because the government brought its central bank deposits quickly into circulation in July, Aug. and Sept. due to the need to finance spending and owing to a 'flood' of consumer purchasing, financed not only out of current income, but also out of consumers' converted savings accounts.

[31] Cf. Stucken, 1964, p. 204.

[32] Cf. Deutsche Bundesbank, 1976, p. 25.

[33] Cf. Bank deutscher Länder, Geschäftsbericht 1948–9, p. 5. A significant contribution to this sharp expansion was made by the expiry of the ban on credits via overdrafts—traditionally the predominant mode of credit provision in the credit business of German banks—on 8 Aug. 1948. Until that date, namely, section 32 of the *Drittes Gesetz zur Neuordnung des Geldwesens* (Third law on the reordering of the monetary system) had, in spite of protests by the Central Bank Council, forbidden banks from giving credits, except rediscount credits and loans to government. Cf. Harmening and Duden, 1949, pp. 40, 331. On the opposition of the Central Bank Council to the ban on overdrafts, see the Minutes of the 11th Central Bank Council meeting held on 24 June 1948 (HA BBk B 330/Drs. 142). The subsequent expansion of credit by the commercial banks was made possible primarily by the fact that they had received the central bank deposits from the initial endowment given to the public sector and were therefore highly liquid even without the credit and money created by the Bank deutscher Länder.

[34] Cf. the Minutes of the 19th and 20th Central Bank Council meetings held on 5 and 19 Oct. 1948 (HA BBk B 330/Drs. 142).

[35] The aim of this was to force the banks into the Lombard, which was one percentage point higher. Cf. Emmer, 1955, p. 56.

decided to tighten direct credit controls beyond the already practised credit guidelines only to the extent that the Land Central Banks were to exert pressure on the banks, and not, if at all possible, to expand their credit volume beyond the level as of 31 October 1948. Exceptions, in particular, credits to promote exports, were permitted.[36] With effect from 1 December 1948 the minimum reserve ratio for sight deposits was increased from 10 to 15 per cent, although only for financial institutions located in cities where a Land Central Bank was also based (*Bankplätze*, 'bank cities').

Yet an increase in the discount rate—which its proponents considered necessary, primarily for psychological reasons or in order to 'send a signal'— was voted down, against the wishes of the two presidents, by 7 votes to 6 on 2 November and indeed by 8 votes to 5 on 3 November, despite the fact that the speaker of the ABC, L. Ingrams, had urgently counselled this step, both by letter and by a personal appearance before the Central Bank Council.[37] Again with 7 votes to 6, this time—at the behest of the ABC—in a secret ballot, an increase in the discount rate was rejected once more on 16 November. This was despite the fact that the British and American members of the ABC, and German politicians, in particular Ludwig Erhard, had indicated their approval of the increase at a meeting convened expressly for this purpose with the two central bank presidents at the behest of the ABC, and after General Lucius Clay had, on 14 November, summoned Bernard to make clear the Americans' desire for a clear signal in favour of monetary restriction in the form of a rise in the discount rate.[38] At its meetings on 30 November/1 December and on 10 December 1948, the Central Bank Council again rejected a rise in the discount rate (the proposal was for an increase of 3 per cent), in each case by 7 votes to 6.

The opponents of an increase put forward three arguments: (1) Priority should be given to promoting production by providing an adequate amount of credit; (2) a rise in the discount rate raises the cost of production and thus serves to fuel inflation further; (3) an increase cannot slow the expansion of credit as effectively as direct credit controls by tightening the credit guidelines. In this third point the opponents were correct, to the extent that

[36] Promoting exports was from the very outset a particular aim of the western Allies, as this was the only way to render their aid programmes superfluous and for the economy of western Europe to be successfully reconstructed.

[37] In calling for a high discount rate, the ABC considered it necessary to inspire confidence in the stability of the new currency and to signal the determination of the Bank deutscher Länder to defend the new currency with the classical instruments of stability policy.

[38] It was at that time still unclear whether or not the ABC would impose a higher discount rate. This probably did not occur for the sole reason that the French ABC representative was opposed to it, a fact of which the members of the Central Bank Council had been made aware prior to their decision on 16 Nov.

the banks were swimming in liquidity and were not at all dependent on re-financing loans by the central bank.[39] On top of this came the fact that the day-to-day money rate, by means of which they could refinance themselves on the money market, remained far below the discount rate until the end of 1949 (see Figure 3).[40]

On the other hand, given the substantial excess reserves, it must be queried why the Central Bank Council did not decide to raise the minimum reserve requirement much earlier than actually occurred (1 December) and up to the statutory ceiling of 20 per cent. This would have tied up the excess reserves and helped render its discount policy more effective. In this respect it did not make full use of its scope for curbing the inflationary expansion of credit by the banks in the second half of 1948.

In its Annual Report, the Bank deutscher Länder commented as follows on the hesitant approach of the Central Bank Council to mopping up bank liquidity: that approach was unsuitable 'because, for those branches of the economy that, owing to the continued imposition of price controls, are un-able to, or can only just, finance themselves, borrowing constitutes the sole source of finance, whereas the productive development of the economy must not be choked off under any circumstances'.[41] The only sensible measure was to impose credit controls in as highly selective a way as possible. Here it is evident for the first time that the Central Bank Council, had put pro-duction considerations before those of monetary stability as it was to do later on numerous occasions.

At the end of 1948, though, the inflationary trend came to an end, the pace of credit growth declined and prices began to fall. The other side of this coin, however, was that unemployment, which since the currency re-form had risen from around 450,000 (an unemployment rate of 3.2 per cent) to not more than 800,000 at the end of 1948, began to increase significantly: to 1.3 million in the summer and autumn of 1949, accelerating to almost 2 million in February 1950, an unemployment rate of around 13 per cent.[42]

---

[39] Immediately after the currency reform their excess reserves amounted to around 50 per cent of the minimum reserve requirement (cf. Emmer, 1955, p. 55), and in Jan. 1949 still to as much as 35 per cent. In Jan. 1950 the excess reserves still represented 10 per cent. Not until the last quarter of 1950, following the outbreak of the foreign exchange crisis (see below), did they fall to the subsequently normal values of 3–4 per cent (all figures from the Bundes-bank). An increase in the discount rate would only have given the banks grounds for increasing their credit rates, because the interest rate regulations would have led to automatic adjust-ments. It would not, on the other hand, have restricted the banks' scope for granting credit.

[40] On the central importance of the overnight market for monetary policy see Bockelmann, 1996, pp. 53ff. For a detailed discussion of the money market see Brehmer, 1964.

[41] Bank deutscher Länder, Geschäftsbericht 1948–9, p. 6.

[42] This was largely due to the influx of refugees from eastern Germany and helped ensure that wage growth, following the expiry of the wage freeze on 3 Nov. 1948, remained moder-

It was not the decisions taken on credit policy that led to the turn-around,[43] but rather external and fiscal policy trends, together with a change in the consumer behaviour of private households. On the external front, towards the end of 1948 prices began to fall on a number of primary-goods markets, largely because of the onset of recession in the USA, which helped to stabilize prices. As far as fiscal policy was concerned, whereas in the first few months following the currency reform government had had to rely on its initial endowment in accounts held within the central bank system to cover its deficits, from the end of 1948 tax receipts flowed so generously that from the winter of 1948–9 it was able to park budget surpluses with the central bank and thus withdraw central bank money from circulation.[44] On top of this, came the fact that support under the Marshall Plan began to flow: because of the link to the Counterpart Funds, i.e. the requirement that German recipients of Marshall Plan aid had to deposit a corresponding sum in D-marks with the central bank, this exerted a contractive monetary policy effect.[45] A final important factor is that private households increasingly began to save, dampening the growth of consumer demand.[46] For all these reasons it was possible for the expansion of bank credits to be maintained without this forcing up prices.

The credit control measures—which in the form implemented by the Land Central Banks had in any case scarcely retarded the expansion of bank lending—were abolished on 22 March 1949. Not until May, though, did the Central Bank Council further relax the policy stance: abolishing the

ate. Although industrial output grew by almost 25 per cent in 1949, this was modest compared with the growth of around 50 per cent during the second half of 1948 alone. cf. Ritschl, 1985, pp. 164f. Wallich, 1955, p. 77, termed this 'a period of relative stagnation'. Even so, the rise meant that imports of primary goods increased so rapidly that West Germany's export surplus in merchandise trade moved into deficit in the first half of 1949; the deficit was widest in Dec. 1949. For these figures cf. Bank deutscher Länder, Geschäftsbericht 1948–9, pp. 2f.

[43] Wallich's sibylline comment on this question is as follows: 'the role played in this by a restrictive credit policy is a matter of personal judgement.' Wallich, 1955, p. 76.

[44] The central bank deposits of the German public sector rose from DM 1.8 billion at the end of 1948 to DM 3.3 billion at the end of 1949. Cf. Bank deutscher Länder, 1955, p. 26.

[45] Cf. Emmer, 1955, p. 58. The sum deposited rose sharply from DM 7.7 million to DM 1,028 million from the end of November to the end of December 1949. Although it then fell to around half of this value by the end of Jan. 1950, it subsequently rose once more, and from May 1950 remained at over DM 1 billion for two years. Cf. Bank deutscher Länder, 1955, p. 26. The deposits of Allied institutions in the central bank system had a similar effect: as German funds for the costs of occupation were gradually spent, they rose from around DM 0.5 billion at the end of Nov. 1949 to around DM 1.1 billion a month later; they remained at approximately this level for the next two years. Cf. Bank deutscher Länder, 1955, p. 26.

[46] Monthly data on changes in savings and time deposits, albeit containing a number of discrepancies, can be found in Bank deutscher Länder, 1955, p. 109 and in Wallich, 1955, pp. 73, 79.

restrictions on acceptance credits and cutting the minimum reserve ratios for sight deposits to 12 per cent in cities with a Land Central Bank and to 9 per cent for those without on 1 June 1949. On 24 May, when Erhard attended the Central Bank Council meeting and insisted on the need to 'give the economy a psychological boost', a cut in the discount rate of 0.5 per cent was adopted (by 10 votes to 2 with one abstention).[47] This was followed on 12 July by a further cut in the discount rate to 4 per cent (unanimous vote). In both decisions the desire to stimulate the capital market in the run-up to long-term bond issues was an important factor.[48] As of 1 September, there was a further relaxation of the minimum reserve requirement to 10 per cent in cities with a Land Central Bank and to 8 per cent in those without. In addition, the reserve rate for time and savings deposits was also changed for the first time, declining from 5 to 4 per cent. The unanimous decision to take these steps was justified with reference to the fact that, in mid-August, the excess reserves of the banks had fallen to just 7.1 per cent of their required reserve; given the current state of the economy, it was argued, increased tension on the money market and a withdrawal of liquidity from the commercial banks was undesirable.[49]

In this way, the Central Bank Council itself contributed to the subsequent relatively high level of excess reserves which, by and large, meant that its discount policy was irrelevant to bank liquidity. The day-to-day money rate remained substantially below the discount rate, which, despite the cuts in rates, still did not exert an expansionary impact on bank liquidity (see Figure 3). Thus it was primarily the easing of the minimum reserve conditions that enabled the banks to expand their short-term lending to private households and firms from DM 5.2 to DM 11.0 billion between March 1949 and the start of the Korean War in June 1950. In spite of this, prices continued to decline until, on the eve of the Korean War, they regained the level prevailing immediately after the currency reform. There can be no doubt that the Central Bank Council would have sacrificed significant growth and employment opportunities at that time had it pursued a potential-oriented monetary targeting strategy along contemporary lines.

In the last quarter of 1948 and the first four months of 1949, the banks had also received central bank money by virtue of the fact that foreign exchange from commercial export surpluses could be deposited with the

---

[47] Minutes of the 35th Central Bank Council meeting held on 24 May 1949 (HA BBk B 330/Drs. 142).

[48] Cf. the Minutes of the 35th and 36th Central Bank Council meetings held on 24 May and 12 July 1949 (HA BBk B 330/Drs. 142).

[49] Cf. the Minutes of the 41st Central Bank Council meeting held on 30–1 Aug. 1949 (HA BBk B 330/Drs. 142).

Bank deutscher Länder.[50] This source of liquidity dried up in the subsequent period, however, notably once the Federal Republic, immediately after its establishment, took part in the liberalization programme for inner-European trade initiated by the OEEC and the ECA (Economic Cooperation Administration, i.e. the Marshall Plan administration), established a liberalization rate of 50 per cent, and thus dismantled trade barriers faster than other European countries. The financing of import surpluses now deprived the commercial banks of liquid funds. For the first time, those banks were obliged to resort to the central bank to a massive extent. Whereas up until the middle of that year the volume of their central bank deposits and their refinancing liabilities had fluctuated, more or less in balance, between DM 1.2 and 1.6 billion, their refinancing volume had risen to almost DM 4 billion by November 1949. It remained approximately at this level until September 1950, while the central bank deposits of the banks declined at times to under DM 1 billion.[51] For the first time, the Bank deutscher Länder had the commercial banks 'under control'. Despite the high level of unemployment in the winter of 1949–50, it decided not to implement a further cut in the discount rate. To quote Wallich's succinct summary: 'its overall policy was under the influence of the priority of monetary stability and balance of payments equilibrium over full employment'.[52] It had, though, in August 1949 for the first time declared its willingness to finance a small job-creation programme initiated by the military governors and the economics and finance administrations, focused on support for investment and exports, with a volume of a modest DM 300 million; this was explicitly in anticipation of revenues expected to be realized soon after.[53] The Bank deutscher Länder rejected the growing criticism in 1949 that it was pursuing a deflationary policy by reference to the fact that both central bank and commercial bank credits had continued to expand.[54]

The unwillingness of the Central Bank Council to cut the discount rate further was also linked to the international turbulence resulting from the devaluation of the pound sterling by 30.5 per cent on 19 September 1949. Whereas other countries, for example the Scandinavian countries, also devalued by this rate, the D-mark was only devalued by 20.6 per cent,

---

[50] Cf. Wallich, 1955, pp. 73, 79.

[51] Cf. Bank deutscher Länder, Geschäftsbericht 1948–9, p. 8 and Geschäftsbericht 1950, p. 3.

[52] Wallich, 1955, p. 82.

[53] Cf. the Minutes of the 41st Central Bank Council meeting held on 30–1 Aug. 1949 (HA BBk B 330/Drs. 142). See also Giersch *et al.*, 1992, p. 58.

[54] Cf. Bank deutscher Länder, Geschäftsbericht 1948–9, p. 8. Wallich deals extensively with the various concerns about deflation raised not least by the occupying powers. Cf. Wallich, 1955, pp. 77–84.

implying a *de facto* revaluation against the other European countries. The Federal Government and the Bank deutscher Länder decided to adopt the lower rate primarily with the aim of avoiding domestic inflation.[55] And indeed, the imports from countries whose currency had been devalued to a greater extent served to exacerbate the decline in German prices. For the first time, the Central Bank Council found itself confronted by a conflict of goals—external versus internal equilibrium—but one that was precisely the reverse of the constellation that was to become typical of German monetary policy after 1950. In terms of the domestic economy, the monetary reins needed to be relaxed—the Bank deutscher Länder itself took this view —particularly when industrial output declined in the winter of 1949–50. But this was blocked by the external deficit. Initially, the Bank deutscher Länder wrote 'exports must be expanded by all possible means' as the economy was still too highly oriented towards the domestic market. The aim must be to regain balance of payments equilibrium 'without autarkic methods'.[56] This was entirely in accordance with Allied expectations and the line taken by the Federal Government, which, in a Memorandum of 15 December 1949 to the OEEC on economic development in West Germany, had declared: 'German economic policy will concentrate on stimulating exports'.[57]

Yet the Allies were not satisfied with such declarations: they wanted to see action. The Allied High Commission (AHC) issued a severe condemnation of the entire economic—and thus also monetary—policy of the Federal Republic in its answering letter of 7 February 1950 sent not only to the Federal Government but also to the Bank deutscher Länder.[58] It was only under this pressure that the Federal Government and the Bank deutscher

---

[55] Cf. the cabinet meeting with Bernard and Vocke on 21 Sept. 1949, in: Bundesarchiv, 1982, vol. 1, pp. 74ff. and the transcript, pp. 285ff. It was also argued that the Federal Republic should not be considered part of the sterling area. Abs considered the competitiveness of German exports not to be endangered only if the devaluation rate was at least 25 per cent.

[56] Bank deutscher Länder, Geschäftsbericht 1948–9, pp. 10, 13.

[57] Taken from the Allied High Commission's statement on this question of 7 Feb. 1950 (HA BBk B 330/2025 [Korrespondenz Vocke]). Both the memorandum and the government's response were also printed in the Neue Zürcher Zeitung on 20 Feb. and 6 Mar. 1950 respectively. On the historical background cf. Hagemann, 1984, pp. 90ff. The Economist published a summary of this 'memorandum war' on 11 Mar. 1950 under the title 'Economic Dogmatism in Germany'. Cf. Giersch *et al.*, 1992, pp. 59f.

[58] The High Commissioners did not share the Germans' bleak prognoses, and in particular criticized the lethargy of economic policy makers in the face of an unemployment rate that had risen to 13 per cent: the German side viewed this rise as 'structural' and was therefore prepared to accept it without taking counter-measures. The Commissioners called for demand-stimulation programmes and expansionary credit-policy measures from domestic sources, and decisively rejected the objection raised by the Federal Government that such measures could only be financed without risk by increasing Marshall Plan aid.

Länder proved willing to consider an additional stabilization programme in order to counter unemployment with a volume of DM 950 million (around 1 per cent of GNP). It was discussed on 8 February 1950, in the cabinet committee on the economy and was to be financed through lending by the Bank deutscher Länder, primarily in the form of temporary refinancing commitments in anticipation of future revenue.[59]

The implementation of the job-creation programmes made only sluggish progress. At the end of June 1950, the Bank deutscher Länder had been required to provide less than DM 300 million for all the job-creation programmes implemented until that point.[60] When, in May 1950, during cabinet discussions on an expansion of the job-creation programmes, the presidents of the Land Central Banks still proved unwilling to offer the Federal Government a loan of DM 1 billion to finance public and to subsidize certain private forms of investment, as requested by Erhard, the ABC suggested to the Federal Government that it would be appropriate to raise the money stock by unfreezing DM 3.5 billion from the 'shadow quota' (*Schattenquote*)[61] exclusively for the purpose of capital investment in order to stimulate the economy and to bring to an end the slightly deflationary price trend. By releasing funds from this shadow quota, it would be possible to increase the money stock even against the will of the Bank deutscher Länder. The Allies, after all, preferred genuine credit creation by the Bank deutscher Länder, i.e. a permanent increase in the money stock, to temporary start-up financing.[62] This threat did not fail to make an impression: while the Bank deutscher Länder still refused to grant the loan to

[59] This involved large-scale and long-term export orders, investment by the Federal Post Office, the Federal Railways and other transport institutions, by agriculture, industrial and private enterprises, and shipbuilding. In addition, a house-building programme with a volume of DM 2.6 billion was initiated. In the final analysis this was to be financed with Marshall Plan aid, but it was to receive initial financing by means of a rediscount commitment by the Bank deutscher Länder. Alongside five ministers (finance, economy, displaced persons, Marshall Plan, and labour), for the first time Adenauer himself attended the subsequent Central Bank Council meeting, held, at his behest, in Bonn on 1 Mar. 1950. Minutes of the 52nd, 53rd, and 54th Central Bank Council meetings held on 9–10 Feb., 22–3 Feb., and 1 Mar. 1950 (HA BBk B 330/Drs. 142).

[60] Bank deutscher Länder, Geschäftsbericht 1950, p. 27, Table 6, with detailed figures on the claims made on the Bank deutscher Länder each quarter. Hentschel, 1989, p. 715, note 2, gives an incorrect, lower, value.

[61] The *Schattenquote* was the still open claim arising out of section 2 of the Conversion Act, which had envisaged a general conversion of outstanding deposits in the ratio of 10:1 (in the event the conversion rate was actually 10:0.65), but which in addition had left open an additional claim of a maximum of DM 1 for RM 10 of outstanding deposits. The conversion of the 'shadow quota' along these lines took place by means of the *Altsparergesetz* of 14 July 1953.

[62] Cf. the cabinet meeting of 24 Feb. 1950, in: Bundesarchiv, 1984, vol. 2, pp. 226f.

the government—Vocke voiced his opposition to unfreezing any funds from the shadow quota in his answering letter to the chairman of the ABC, D. H. Macdonald—it declared its willingness to expand the scope for bank credit creation by the figure of DM 1 billion requested by Erhard, in order, 'to raise production and to reduce unemployment'.[63] Yet this would have been precisely the effect of unfreezing a corresponding sum from the shadow quota for the purpose of capital investment.

As early as the second quarter of 1950, the economy got up steam again. The renewed growth of employment and output was due primarily to rising exports and a revival of activity in the investment-goods industry.[64] In June 1950 unemployment was almost 450,000 lower than at its peak in February. The conflict between external and internal equilibrium evaporated prior to the outbreak of the Korean War on 25 June 1950.

The 'explosive expansion of the domestic market'[65] following the outbreak of the Korean War effectively rendered the job-creation programmes superfluous. Yet it was precisely during the second half of 1950 and the first quarter of 1951 that the Bank deutscher Länder credit for this purpose was used most intensively (up to a net figure of around DM 850 million). There was an explosive upturn in the total monetary demand. The propensity to save, which had earlier increased, collapsed. Rising prices on global markets and fear on the part of the population about the impact of the war on the young currency led, against the background of a sharp rise in the velocity of circulation of money, to a flight into fixed assets, and thus a sharp rise in domestic demand.[66] Via the transmission mechanisms of the collapse of saving activity, panic buying and a general flight into fixed assets, the Korean War, together with the impact of the tax cuts approved in April 1950 and the job-creation programmes, brought about an upturn on the typically

[63] The proposal was set out in a Memorandum of the ABC of 4 May 1950 and passed on to the Bank deutscher Länder by D. H. Macdonald, the British representative on the ABC in a letter of 16 May 1950 (HA BBk B 330/2033, Korrespondenz Vocke, vol. Ma). Vocke's reply of 5 June 1950 is also to be found there. Hentschel, 1996, p. 117, describes the entire process.

[64] Cf. Emmer, 1955, p. 60.

[65] Bank deutscher Länder, Geschäftsbericht 1950, p. 48.

[66] This was exacerbated to a significant extent by the decision taken in Apr. 1950 to cut income tax by an average of 17 per cent, backdated to 1 Jan. 1950. Excessive tax payments already made, however, were not reimbursed until after the start of the war. Because the government failed to reduce public spending, the budget moved into deficit and thus no longer exerted a contractive effect on the central bank money stock and bank liquidity, but rather an expansionary impact on total monetary demand. For further details on all the factors mentioned, cf. Bank deutscher Länder, Geschäftsbericht 1950, pp. 6ff. Peter Temin, 1995, who has recently argued that in fact no Korea boom occurred in West Germany during the first year of the war, is right only to the extent that this boom was not export-induced, as can be seen by merely glancing at the changes in the current account.

Keynesian pattern, initially driven by domestic demand.[67] In the second half of 1950 industrial output rose by 20 per cent, following a 6-month stagnation from November 1949 to April 1950 (with a 10 per cent contraction at the start of the winter).[68] To this extent a 'Korea boom' did indeed occur.[69]

During the first three months of the war, the inflationary impact of these factors did not make itself felt to any significant extent in the cost of living.[70] Not until the first half of 1951 was the inflationary trend reflected in the cost of living to the full extent, only to subsequently subside once more. In June 1951, namely, the cost of living was 10.6 per cent higher than in December 1950.[71] The inflationary trend did manifest itself immediately after the outbreak of war, however, in the domestic prices of home-produced and imported basic goods and on world markets. In July 1950 they were already 2.5 per cent higher than in June, in September 10 per cent, in December 17 per cent and in March 1951 as much as 27 per cent higher.[72] Subsequently, however, the inflationary trend subsided once more. These developments show that the Central Bank Council should have adopted a restrictive stance in the second half of 1950 for domestic economic reasons alone. Yet it was external economic reasons that were given for the change of course in credit policy.

The first restrictive measure was adopted by the Central Bank Council in September 1950 at the behest of Economics Minister Erhard.[73] The minimum reserve ratios were increased as of 1 October: for sight deposits from 10 to 15 per cent in 'the bank cities' and from 8 to 12 per cent elsewhere; for time deposits from 4 to 8 per cent; the minimum reserve ratios for

---

[67] These were also the reasons given by the Bank deutscher Länder back in 1950 for the 'Korea boom'. Cf. Bank deutscher Länder, Geschäftsbericht 1950, p. 6f.

[68] Cf. Statistisches Bundesamt, 1952, p. 209.

[69] The Keynesian interpretation of Giersch *et al.*, 1992, p. 62, is proved correct, whereas Abelshauser's hypothesis ('For the first time the west German economy experienced a growth push from the external position') has been falsified by Temin, 1995. Cf. Abelshauser, 1983, p. 68.

[70] Indeed, between June and Aug. it fell by 2 per cent, remaining constant in Sept. Not until Oct. 1950 did it gradually begin to rise, reaching around 2 per cent above the Aug./Sept. level in Dec., i.e. regaining the level of June 1950. Cf. Statistisches Bundesamt, 1952, p. 404.

[71] Between June and Dec. 1950 hourly wages rose by 7.5 per cent, and in the following six months by around 11.5 per cent, i.e. in the first year of the Korean War by around 20 per cent. Cf. Statistisches Bundesamt, 1952, p. 412.

[72] Cf. Bank deutscher Länder, Geschäftsbericht 1950, p. 3.

[73] On 23 Sept. 1950 Erhard wrote to Adenauer: '. . . I have managed, as it were illegally [because of the independence of the central bank of the German government; C.-L. H.], to ensure that, at its last meeting, the Central Bank Council raised the minimum reserve substantially'. The letter is printed in: Ludwig-Erhard-Stiftung, 1986, p. 191. Erhard expressed a similar view in a letter to Schäffer on 6 Dec. 1950; cf. Ludwig-Erhard-Stiftung, 1986, p. 240.

savings deposits were left unchanged in order to promote the formation of savings capital. Once again, the far greater potential scope for action—up to a maximum rate of 20 per cent—was not utilized.

The external position became increasingly precarious in the autumn of 1950. This was in the context of the official founding of the European Payments Union (EPU) on 19 September 1950, once the US Congress had approved the agreed dollar support as start-up capital for the EPU, applying retrospectively to 1 July.[74] In accordance with the agreement, West Germany liberalized the duties on its EPU imports to an official figure of 60 per cent—*de facto* to 77 per cent—in the last quarter of 1950.[75] As a pioneer in the trend towards trade liberalization, West Germany moved rapidly towards ever-greater balance of trade deficits within the EPU area and thus, given scarce foreign currency reserves, towards a major balance of payments crisis. This was all the more serious as 'dollar support' in 1950, at a total of just under US $500 million, amounted to less than half the previous year's figure.[76] The deficit position *vis-à-vis* the EPU resulted also from a substantial shift in the composition of the countries of origin of German imports—specifically, from the USA to the EPU countries—whereas the restructuring of German exports was precisely in the reverse direction.[77] Thus West Germany's 'dollar gap' steadily gave way to a shortage of EPU currencies.[78]

The Bank deutscher Länder Board of Directors wanted—as did Erhard—

[74] Cf. Bank deutscher Länder, Geschäftsbericht 1950, p. 53; Kaplan and Schleiminger, 1989, p. 87.

[75] Cf. Bank deutscher Länder, Geschäftsbericht 1950, p. 52.

[76] Cf. Bank deutscher Länder, Geschäftsbericht 1950, pp. 46, 51.

[77] Cf. Bank deutscher Länder, Geschäftsbericht 1950, p. 49. At the same time a significant normalization of the composition of export goods took place. Manufactured goods increased as a share of exports from slightly more than 50 per cent in 1949 to 65 per cent in 1950, thus moving towards the pre-war figure of 78 per cent. Cf. Bank deutscher Länder, Geschäftsbericht 1950, p. 48.

[78] This was intentional, however. As early as 2 Aug. 1950 Erhard had emphasized in a letter to Vocke that the most important aspect of the Korean crisis was to provide manufacturing industries with sufficient primary goods 'in order to ensure that no shortages occur in this area'. Ludwig-Erhard-Stiftung, 1986, p. 183. For the Bank deutscher Länder the following consideration came on top of this. Given that it was only interested in acquiring gold and convertible dollars, and not inconvertible European currencies, in order to bolster its currency reserves, it made sense to make as much use as possible of European drawing rights in order to be able to import the inputs urgently needed to rebuild the export sector. This enabled it to obtain a favourable starting point in international competition for scarce dollars. For this reason the Bank deutscher Länder argued in favour of Germany playing a pioneering role in reducing trade barriers against EPU countries, consciously taking the risk of the balance of payments moving into the red. Cf. Dickhaus, 1996, p. 79f. The calculation that in the longer term this would strengthen Germany's export base and its international currency position was entirely confirmed by subsequent developments.

to overcome the disequilibrium on the external position not by reversing the trend towards liberalization—i.e. imposing administrative restrictions on imports, but rather in the short run by market-based measures to dampen import demand and in the longer run by boosting exports. On 7 October 1950 the Bank deutscher Länder declared all the import licences granted until then to be invalid unless they were confirmed in the following week by contracts. At its meeting on 13 October 1950 the Central Bank Council, in agreement with the Federal Government, decided to re-introduce the cash deposit requirement of 50 per cent of the foreign currencies applied for when making an application for import licenses as of 16 October 1950; this amounted to a restriction on imports, but one in accordance with market principles.[79] At the same time the rediscountability of bank bills, which were normally used to finance imports, was limited to the level reached on 12 October 1950. In order to stimulate exports over the longer term, the Bank deutscher Länder and the Federal Government, alongside various export-promoting measures, pinned their hopes on a general squeeze on credit and a restrictive fiscal policy. The boom in domestic demand, particularly that for consumer goods, was to be dampened down and thus the economy forced to intensify its export activities.

The pressure for a restrictive fiscal policy came from the Bank deutscher Länder Board of Directors and from the Central Bank Council, particularly, in the latter case, from the opponents of a more sharply restrictive credit policy. They argued that it was not possible to counter a foreign trade deficit solely by credit policy means 'otherwise we will run the risk of depressing economic activity as a whole'.[80]

Vocke and the Bank deutscher Länder Board of Directors, on the other hand, also wanted to raise the discount rate substantially. During the decisive meeting held on 26 October 1950, with Konrad Adenauer—at whose behest the Central Bank Council met, as an exception, in the Federal Chancellery (at that time in the König Museum) in Bonn—and other federal ministers (Ludwig Erhard, Fritz Schäffer, Wilhelm Niklas for Food and Agriculture),

---

[79] This requirement had been in force in 1949, but had been suspended on 16 Feb. 1950. Cf. Kühne, 1984, pp. 62, 104f. The cash deposit rate was reduced to 25 per cent on 23 Dec. 1950, and as of 15 Jan. 1951 to as low as 5 per cent for imports with long delivery periods and subsidized imports. Cf. Ludwig-Erhard-Stiftung, 1986, p. 390.

[80] Cf. the transcript of the 70th Central Bank Council meeting held on 4–5 Oct. 1950, quoted in: Dickhaus, 1996, p. 90. Otto Pfleiderer remained of this view even after the rise in the discount rate. Cf. the transcript of the 76th Central Bank Council meeting held on 24 Nov. 1950 (HA BBk B 330/34). Dickhaus, 1996, p. 92. Some were worried that the German banking system was unstable and that tightening the restrictions on credit raised the threat of a banking crisis similar to that of 1931. Cf. Dickhaus, 1996, p. 91. It was not until the foreign-exchange crisis began to approach a new peak in the winter of 1951 that their concerns were to make an impact.

the Central Bank Council found itself confronted by a government camp in which opinions on the monetary policy measures proposed by Vocke and supported by Bernard were just as divided as in the Central Bank Council itself.[81] In the event the Central Bank Council raised the discount rate from 4 to 6 per cent against the opposition of Adenauer and Schäffer.

After the Central Bank Council had become aware of the fact that the banks were evading the freezing of the volume of bank bills by resorting to the refinancing of normal bills, it decided, on 2 November 1950, to reduce the refinancing volume of the banks (discount and Lombard) by 10 per cent by 31 January 1951. At the same time, it was stipulated that bank bills used to finance exports were no longer to be regarded as part of the volume of frozen bank bills.[82] However, because the reduction in the refinancing volume was performed by the Land Central Banks, and these made very generous use of the scope for allowing exceptions, this measure failed to achieve its aim.

From that point on, the Bank deutscher Länder emphasized the 'import dependence' of the German economy, particularly from the EPU area. The Bank deutscher Länder was no longer interested in imposing administrative restrictions on imports, not least because imports contributed to dampening down the inflation associated with the Korea boom. The Bank deutscher Länder Board of Directors also pinned its hopes on the special credit (*Sonderkredit*), the conditions attached to which were supposed to help the Board to push through its policy strategy against the recalcitrant Central Bank Council. This policy strategy aimed, by means of a restrictive monetary policy and a greater degree of price stability in Germany than abroad, to force the German economy into exports and thus simultaneously to strengthen the D-mark and to promote economic growth and employment.[83] This strategy was supported by the additional export-promotion measures implemented by the Federal Government at the behest of the OEEC (increase in the volume of Hermes export guarantees and the export credits at special conditions provided by the Kreditanstalt für Wiederaufbau

[81] The Bank deutscher Länder received support for the discount-rate hike of two whole percentage points—as an alternative to restrictive trade measures and as a means of achieving balance of payments equilibrium—from Economics Minister Erhard, whose political career depended on the success of his market-economic approach, not least in terms of the external position. Schäffer, the Minister of Finance, on the other hand, saw high interest rates as an additional burden on the federal budget to the extent that it would make it more expensive for government to borrow and service its debts. Chancellor Adenauer, who had sought the advice of the private banker Robert Pferdmenges in advance, was worried—with a view to the election hopes of the governing parties—about the still high level of unemployment, and viewed high interest rates as damaging to domestic economic activity.

[82] Cf. Bank deutscher Länder, Geschäftsbericht 1950, p. 96.

[83] Cf. Dickhaus, 1996, pp. 93, 96. More will be said on this in the following section.

(Reconstruction Loan Corporation), priority allocation of raw materials to exporters, tax allowances, etc.) and, as of 1 January 1951, by the Bank deutscher Länder in that export drafts were purchased not at the German discount rate but at the consistently lower discount rate of the target country.[84] The export orientation of German monetary policy was to prove very successful in the subsequent years.

In November 1950 the first EPU special credit provided to any country was granted to West Germany. It amounted to DM 120 million and was subject to certain conditions.[85] In February 1951 the foreign exchange crisis moved towards a second peak, in the wake of the military intervention in the war by the People's Republic of China at the end of November 1950. When the situation called for additional counter-measures, the Central Bank Council opted significantly to raise neither the discount rate further—the step favoured by Vocke in particular—nor the minimum reserve ratios.[86] Instead, by means of direct credit control, the banks were obliged to reduce their short-term credit volume by DM 1 billion by May 1951, with the concrete implementation of this policy being entrusted to the Land Central Banks, which were issued precise sums to be returned. Yet this was only finally decided after the Federal Government, following a recommendation made by the Central Bank Council in mid-February 1951, had opted to suspend import liberalization *vis-à-vis* the EPU area.[87]

[84] Cf. the memorandum of the Federal Government to the OEEC of 27 Nov. 1950 and the OEEC's survey of the 'implementation of German programmes to overcome the balance of payments difficulties *vis-à-vis* the European Payments Union' of 19 May 1951, printed in: Ludwig-Erhard-Stiftung, 1986, especially pp. 224, 394.

[85] The conditions were as follows: stringent maintenance of the restrictive credit measures already agreed and those envisaged by the Bank deutscher Länder, in order to create an 'organic' equilibrium between the demand for goods and the limited supply of imports; tax measures, in particular to dampen down consumer demand (increase in turnover tax, reduction of tax allowances) and to balance the budget, and the avoidance of deficit-financed policies of any sort; export promotion by means of tax and credit-policy measures, if necessary by means of privileged allocation of primary goods; improved control of movements of foreign currency, and measures to prevent purely speculative applications for import licences; establishing realistic interest rates in order to promote capital formation; rejection of D-mark devaluation. Cf. Emminger, 1986*a*, pp. 52f.

[86] Prior to the rejection by the Central Bank Council at its meeting held on 28 Feb./1 Mar. 1951 of the proposal to raise the discount rate to 10 per cent, the federal cabinet had, on a majority vote, spoken out against the rise in the discount rate at a special meeting held on 27 Feb., and decided to make public its opposition should such a rise be implemented. Cf. excerpt from the Minutes of the cabinet meeting quoted in: Ludwig-Erhard-Stiftung, 1986, p. 281.

[87] Cf. Emminger, 1986*a*, pp. 54, 57 and Vocke's letter to Adenauer of 26 Feb. 1951, in which he announced restrictions on credit and 'a short-term but drastic rise in the discount rate'. Ludwig-Erhard-Stiftung, 1986, pp. 275ff. Given the fact that, at this time, the cost of living was also rising dramatically, the proponents of a liberal market-oriented policy appeared to have failed. In the following week, Erhard's political career was on a knife-edge. Not only

Once the EPU special credit had been almost completely exhausted—at more than DM 91 million in February 1951—John McCloy expressed in a letter to Chancellor Adenauer on 6 March 1951 his mistrust of Erhard's liberal economic policy and demanded interventionist steering measures and the setting of supply priorities, just as the USA itself had done with the Defence Production Act of 8 September 1950 and the imposition of a state of emergency in December 1950. 'If, however, measures are not taken in the proposed direction, there is little prospect that the United States government can be persuaded to maintain dollar aid and to assist the west German government in acquiring vital raw materials.'[88] He warned that the Bank deutscher Länder should reinforce the foreign exchange control measures that it had initiated 'but not fully implemented' and argued in favour of a renewed increase in the cash deposits required of importers when applying for import licences, which had been reduced on 23 December 1950 from 50 per cent to 25 per cent. The catalogue of measures that, in his view, needed to be introduced included: 'rigorous implementation of the necessary restrictions on credit and a more stringent selection of the credits granted in order to ensure that they benefit needed investment and production'.[89]

In view of the increasingly acute foreign exchange crisis in Germany in February 1951, other European countries, too, gained the impression that the crisis had been due to the failure to rigorously implement restrictive measures, and that this in turn was to be traced back to the federalist structure of the west German central bank system. On 22 March 1950, after the preparatory work on the Bundesbank Act had already begun,[90] the EPU Board of Directors repeated its warning that the authority of the central bank in West Germany was in urgent need of strengthening.[91] This criticism was raised not least against the background of the experience gained by Vocke that all the restrictive measures he proposed were either rejected, delayed, or actually undermined by the Land Central Bank presidents.[92]

---

did the opposition attack him sharply, Adenauer, too, distanced himself from him, writing on 19 Mar. 1951: 'you personally bear a large proportion of the blame for the current situation in the economic sphere.' Ludwig-Erhard-Stiftung, 1986, pp. 301ff. (Minutes of a parliamentary debate on economic policy in the Korean crisis) and p. 341 (Adenauer's letter to Erhard).

[88] HA BBk B 330/3131. Also printed in Ludwig-Erhard-Stiftung, 1986, pp. 284ff. and in Abelshauser, 1982, pp. 734ff.

[89] In his answering letter to McCloy of 27 Mar. 1951, Adenauer expressed his complete willingness to cooperate and promised to reinforce various administrative control measures in order to promote exports important for armaments, particularly in connection with the new 'law on maintaining competitiveness' (*Wirtschaftssicherungsgesetz*). The letter is printed in Ludwig-Erhard-Stiftung, 1986, pp. 347ff. and in Abelshauser, 1982, pp. 739ff.

[90] On the genesis of the Bundesbank Act see Hentschel, 1988, pp. 3ff., 79ff.

[91] Kaplan and Schleiminger, 1989, p. 110.

[92] Cf. Dickhaus, 1996, p. 92.

The west German balance of payments position improved so quickly that as early as mid-1951 the Bank deutscher Länder could announce the end of the foreign-exchange crisis. On 20 September 1951 the Federal Government abolished the cash deposit requirement on imports. Whereas in February 1951 West Germany had not only fully utilized its normal EPU quota of DM 320 million but also the greater part of the special credit of DM 120 million, from March the export surpluses *vis-à-vis* the EPU area were sufficient to repay the special credit in full as early as May 1951, five months before it was due, and by the end of the year to pay off all Germany's debts to the EPU. For 1951 as a whole the trade balance ended up virtually in equilibrium, and a surplus was earned on the current account.[93] At the end of the year short-term bank loans to firms and private households were once again around DM 2 billion above the previous year's level,[94] and this despite the fact that the Central Bank Council had retained the higher discount and minimum reserve ratios until the end of May 1952, and since the autumn of 1951 the Bank deutscher Länder had undertaken a substantial volume of restrictive open market operations for the first time.[95]

b) Monetary and fiscal policy mercantilism: 1951–6

Based on the plans made during the Second World War, after 1945 the American government did its utmost to bring about a liberal global economic order within a cooperative, rather than—as in the interwar period—a nationalistic-antagonistic international environment. In Germany, too, in the light of experience of the National Socialist planned economy and autarky, which had culminated in war, and the complete devaluation of the currency, an autonomous market-economic conception had developed, particularly associated with the Freiburg 'ordo-liberal' school. In it, the state was accorded a strong role in setting the legal framework, the rules for

[93] In Jan. 1952 the Federal Government once again liberalized 57 per cent of EPU imports, and three months later raised this quota further to 76 per cent, putting it higher than the official degree of liberalization before the outbreak of the foreign-exchange crisis. Cf. Bank deutscher Länder, Geschäftsbericht 1951, pp. 54f. Cf. also Kaplan and Schleiminger, 1989, p. 113; Emminger, 1986*b*, pp. 26f.; Dickhaus, 1996, pp. 99ff. By the end of May 1951, 83 per cent of the credit restriction of DM 1 billion ordered by the Central Bank Council had been completed; the process was officially ended in Oct. In any case, the restriction was undermined by the banks, who expanded their medium- and long-term lending to a more than proportional extent. Cf. Dürr, 1966, pp. 139ff. and Geiger and Ross, 1991, pp. 146ff.

[94] Bank deutscher Länder, Geschäftsbericht 1951, pp. 20f.

[95] Cf. Wallich, 1955, p. 95 and Bank deutscher Länder, Geschäftsbericht 1952, p. 14; Emmer, 1955, pp. 66f.

competition, and the social order, but was otherwise to refrain from intervening in markets with administrative measures.[96] Imbued with this spirit,
the liberalization of domestic and foreign markets was the central maxim of
economic policy under Erhard following the currency reform.

This was also a central concern of Bank deutscher Länder policy. Vocke
expressed this to Volkmar Muthesius in the following terms:

all this here isn't in fact a 'proper economy' yet, and what he meant by that was
the, at that time—that is about the year 1950—, much more far-reaching and
profound cramping of economic life by state intervention under a planned and
command economy than at present [1956]. As one of the few, Wilhelm Vocke was
constantly aware of the disturbing effects of any form of regimentation of monetary
policy . . . This insight into the causal relationships between the command and
planned economy, on the one hand, and disturbances in the monetary system, on
the other, lies behind Vocke's claim that the command economy and inflation are
merely two aspects of the same thing.[97]

Initially, the west German foreign-exchange crisis of 1950–1 constituted
a setback to Erhard's move towards liberalization; at home, in connection
with currency reform, in particular the far-reaching liberalization of prices
and the abolition of most of the rationing measures, and, in terms of foreign
trade, following the first European liberalization agreement signed in October 1948, its extension in the autumn of 1949 and in particular following
the creation of the EPU on 1 July 1950. German government again began
to deploy mercantilist policies in order to promote exports and to block
competition from imports.[98]

However, given that the long-term policy pursued was that of liberalization, a mercantilist policy of generating export surpluses and the vital initial
need to strengthen west German foreign currency reserves had to use means

---

[96] Cf. Nicholls, 1994.

[97] V. Muthesius, Wilhelm Vocke, in: Vocke, 1956, p. 14.

[98] The 'Law on tax measures to promote exports' of June 1951 introduced tax allowances
(on income and corporation tax) for exports of manufactured goods, exempted external bills
from the tax on drafts and bills of exchange (Wechselsteuer) and transport insurance for foreign
trade from insurance tax, and provided for a reimbursement of turnover tax on exports, most
favourably for manufactured goods. West Germany's first customs tariff law, which came into
force on 1 Oct. 1951, was highly protectionist, albeit in covert form. The ad valorem customs
duties increased progressively as the manufacturing component rose: i.e. imports of primary
goods were usually not subject to duty, intermediate goods faced moderate customs duties of
10–20 per cent, whereas manufactured products faced the highest rates, mostly 20–35 per
cent. Cf. Hölscher, 1990, p. 38. In each case the effective tariff rate of protection was much
higher than the nominal one. These rates were, however, steadily reduced within the framework of GATT and later of the European Economic Community, in some cases unilaterally,
as a way of dampening down domestic inflation. This was evident from the outset of Erhard's
approach to competition and foreign-trade policy. Cf. Erhard, 1953 and Buchheim, 1990.

other than traditional foreign-trade mercantilism or protectionism. The solution to this dilemma lay in monetary and fiscal policy mercantilism. This was contingent on a system of fixed exchange rates without a self-regulating gold standard, i.e. one with a scope for an autonomous currency policy. The Bretton Woods system met this condition precisely. It enabled a country to gain a price-stability advantage without changing the exchange rate, thus making domestic products more competitive *vis-à-vis* foreign goods.

In retrospect, the fact that this strategy was successfully practised during the 1950s is evident not only from the substantial current account surpluses posted by West Germany between 1952 and the D-mark appreciation of 1961 and the fact that, against the background of a stable D-mark exchange-rate, price increases in the FRG (as measured by the GNP deflator) were, at an annual average of 3.4 per cent between 1950 and 1958, considerably lower than those in the rest of the OEEC (5.5 per cent p.a.).[99] In addition, it was documented in the Annual Report of the Deutsche Sparkassen- und Giroverband of 1959, published during the appreciation debate of 1960, with the demand that the 'monetary protectionism' of the Federal Republic be dropped in order to ensure domestic monetary stability.[100]

Of even greater significance is the fact that this approach had been conceived and planned by the Bank deutscher Länder, and in particular by Vocke, as a long-term strategy for monetary policy. In 1950 Alec K. Cairncross, in his capacity as EPU adviser, was to speak of 'Vocke's well-known deflationary inclinations'.[101]

First signs of the export orientation of monetary policy emerged in 1949. Even at this early stage, the Central Bank Council had been prepared, in the interest of promoting exports, to depart from the orthodox central bank rule that credits were only to be granted over the short term, and to make medium- and long-term loans available for this purpose. Considerations of international competitiveness played an important role in the choice of depreciation rate in September 1949.[102] Above and beyond this, the aim was to ensure that overall monetary policy was relatively restrictive. At the

---

[99] Giersch *et al.*, 1992, p. 109.

[100] Jahresbericht des Deutschen Sparkassen- und Giroverbandes für 1959, p. 12.

[101] Alec K. Cairncross, Bericht über die im Auftrag der EPU unternommene Deutschlandreise vom 28. Oktober bis 3. November 1950, dated from 9 Nov. 1950, printed in: Ludwig-Erhard-Stiftung, 1986, p. 208. Initially, however, Vocke was in favour of an exchange-rate adjustment, rather than deflation of the domestic economy. As early as 17 Aug. 1948, that is shortly after the currency reform, he criticized, with a view to the international competitiveness of the west German economy, the Allies for having set the D-mark exchange rate too high (at DM 1 = 30 cents) and stated his view to the Central Bank Council that an adjustment to '20 cents or lower' would soon be necessary. Dickhaus, 1996, p. 74.

[102] Cf. Dickhaus, 1996, pp. 75f., and on the previous sentence, p. 70.

Central Bank Council meeting of 26–7 October 1949 Vocke argued in favour of 'keeping domestic affairs tight in order to strengthen exports'.[103] The president of the Central Bank Council, Bernard, held the same conviction.[104] The majority on the Central Bank Council, however, did not accept this line of argument. It still pursued a would-be entirely domestically oriented course and in 1949 cut both the discount rate and the minimum reserve ratios. Even so, the west German discount rate, at 4 per cent, remained far higher than the rates in the Allied countries (see Figure 1). To this extent German monetary policy was more restrictive than that in other countries, even in this period.

A marked change occurred in the overall attitude of the Central Bank Council following the outbreak of the Korean War at the end of June 1950. Vocke and Bernard realized that this was their chance to implement their planned strategy, namely to promote exports by dampening domestic demand by means of a restrictive monetary policy.[105] In 1951 and indeed until 29 May 1952, the Central Bank Council not only kept the discount rate at the high level of 6 per cent, but also stuck to its credit-reduction decision of February 1951 until October that year, despite the fact that the Marshall Plan authority, the ECA (Jean Cattier),[106] and the Bundesverband des privaten Bankgewerbes, under its President, Pferdmenges, had called for a relaxation of the credit restrictions as early as the first half of 1951, following the swift resolution of the foreign exchange crisis. The central reason given for this position was, alongside the ever-present necessity of stabilizing wages and prices, that the restrictions on credit were to keep domestic demand at a low level in order to create a pressure to export, forcing industry on to foreign markets.[107] On 17 May 1951, in the wake of the inflation of

---

[103] Quoted in Dickhaus, 1996, pp. 70, 114.

[104] Otto Burkhardt, the President of the Landeszentralbank von Schleswig-Holstein, also supported this line at the Central Bank Council meeting on 27–8 Nov. 1949, stating that 'precisely the liberalization of foreign trade requires exerting pressure on domestic prices', quoted from Dickhaus, 1996, p. 71.

[105] Cf. Dickhaus, 1996, p. 93. At about this time, the foundation of the EPU was seen by the Bank deutscher Länder as 'a great opportunity for German exporters'. Dickhaus, 1996, pp. 85f. Earlier, Wallich, too, had identified this as the monetary policy strategy. Cf. Wallich, 1955, p. 80. Erhard fully supported this approach, writing to Vocke on 2 Aug. 1950 that 'a great opportunity for the future of German exports arises out of the current situation. If, namely, we are able through internal discipline to maintain the price level to a greater extent than other countries, our export strength will increase in the longer term and our currency will become denser (*dichter*) and more healthy, both internally and with respect to the dollar.' Ludwig-Erhard-Stiftung, 1986, p. 183.

[106] Cf. Emminger, 1986b and Ludwig-Erhard-Stiftung, 1986, pp. 418ff.

[107] Cf. Dickhaus, 1996, pp. 104f. and Ludwig-Erhard-Stiftung, 1986, p. 409 (Vocke's answering letter to the Bundesverband des privaten Bankgewerbes of 30 June 1951).

the first year of the Korean War, Vocke explained this stance to an interested audience of experts as follows:

of course, the high rates of inflation have been a cause of great concern to us, but, if you compare these with the foreign price levels and with the rates of inflation in other countries, you will see, with satisfaction, that we have consistently remained below them. And that is our chance, that is decisive, for our currency and especially for our exports. Raising exports is vital for us, and this in turn depends on maintaining a relatively low price and wage level. . . . As I have said, keeping the price level below that in other countries is the focal point of our efforts at the central bank, and it is a success of those efforts. That should be borne in mind by those who say to us: your restrictive measures are too tight, are no longer necessary.[108]

One year later, in the Bank deutscher Länder Annual Report for 1951 it was noted that 'in future, monetary and government stabilization policy will continue to have to take the greatest conceivable account of the external position'. 'In addition it is vital that west German gold and foreign currency reserves . . . are expanded.'[109]

As early as 1955, one observer (Wallich) noted on several occasions that west German monetary policy was hesitant in deploying domestic expansionary measures, in order to create a 'capacity reserve' for exports.[110] In 1990 Hajo Riese expressed his view that the Federal Republic had followed a 'mercantilist instinct', and that the strategy of the Bank deutscher Länder/Bundesbank was directed, in the final analysis, not towards price stabilization as such, but rather, to put it most graphically, towards 'combining the strength of the Deutsche Mark with its under-valuation'.[111] He considered it to be a 'myth' that a specific fear of inflation on the part of the German population was a predominant motive in achieving a relatively high degree of price stability in the Federal Republic.[112] Back in 1955

[108] Speech to the First Credit-policy Conference of the Zeitschrift für das gesamte Kreditwesen, a specialist publication, on 17 May 1951, published in: Vocke, 1956, p. 56. Of course, the fact that Vocke was later to prove one of the most determined opponents of any move to revalue the D-mark fits into this picture of monetary policy mercantilism.

[109] Bank deutscher Länder, Geschäftsbericht 1951, p. 19.

[110] Data on the degree of capacity utilization of the capital stock and the labour force can be found in Giersch *et al.*, 1992, pp. 10f.

[111] Riese, 1990, pp. 11, 13. A similar view can be found in Hölscher, 1994, p. 47. He talks about 'protectionism with the help of the under-valued Deutsche Mark' as a 'strategy', albeit only since the currency crisis of 1950–1.

[112] The popular view of the specifically German fear of inflation is given considerable room in Kennedy, 1991, pp. 6ff. Goodman, on the other hand, claims that the comparatively high degree of price stability in the Federal Republic has not been the result of an inflationary fear, and a social consensus based on it, but rather of a specific institutional structure, i.e. primarily of the independence of the central bank. Cf. Goodman, 1992, pp. 58, 100.

Robert Emmer concluded from his study of the monetary policy pursued by the Bank deutscher Länder that it had far from fully utilized its range of instruments in order to ensure price stability. Rather, it had always also pursued output-related and foreign-trade-policy goals. In cases of conflicting goals it had, he argued, accorded support to foreign trade priority over maintaining price stability and boosting output.[113]

Fiscal policy, too, had made decisive contributions to this mercantilist strategy particularly after the Korea crisis. It did this in the form both of special tax concessions (Export Promotion Act of 1951) and of guarantees for export credits (Hermes guarantees) and in macroeconomic terms by repeatedly posting budget surpluses (called 'Juliusturm'), which helped to dampen down domestic demand. On top of this came the enormous contribution made by the public sector to the macroeconomic savings-to-income ratio: 44 per cent between 1948 and 1960.[114] A similar effect was achieved by the generous support for private saving.[115] Following the outbreak of the German foreign exchange crisis in the wake of the foundation of the EPU, the EPU special credit was subjected to a package of conditions which amounted to the pursuit of a restrictive monetary and fiscal policy in order to dampen down domestic demand, and credit and tax-policy measures in order to promote exports. When the foreign exchange crisis peaked in February 1951, the AHC, in a memorandum to the Federal Government on 7 February 1950, demanded, among other things, that German economic policy be focused not merely verbally but effectively, 'on stimulating exports'.[116] Subsequently, the Allies would be unable to rid themselves of the

[113] Cf. Emmer, 1955, especially p. 69.

[114] Cf. Stolper and Roskamp, 1979, p. 388.

[115] As early as 1948, German pressure had ensured the inclusion of tax concessions on savings in section 10 of the income tax law. Until the end of 1954, up to 15 per cent of income could be set off against tax as special expenditure if it was transferred to savings accounts from which money could not be withdrawn for three years. Cf. Jahresbericht des Deutschen Sparkassen- und Giroverbandes für 1954, p. 9. As of 1 Jan. 1955, absolute ceilings were imposed on the amount of savings that was deductible from tax, and the periods during which the money was frozen were extended. From 1959 onwards savings no longer qualified for tax allowances, but were promoted by means of government grants. The substantial support for savings, especially up to 1955, served to dampen down domestic demand. In the USA, by contrast, precisely the reverse policy was pursued out of a typically Keynesian fear of the demand-reducing impact of savings: beginning in 1945, consumption was promoted by enabling the costs of interest payments on consumer loans to be deducted from income tax.

[116] HA BBk B 330/2025 (Korrespondenz Vocke). This can also be seen in the light of the fact that the ABC (together with Vocke) had in 1948–9 pushed for the Bank deutscher Länder to pursue a more restrictive interest-rate policy than was actually realized by the Central Bank Council. This would have enabled domestic demand to be curtailed more sharply and the incentives to export strengthened even at this early stage.

spirits they had conjured up in making this demand. Not only Vocke and
Bernard, but also the majority on the Central Bank Council, had recognized
the value of this strategy of monetary and fiscal policy mercantilism, and
pursued it, particularly after the Korean crisis, not merely successfully but
to excess.

Following this discussion of the *strategic* aspects, let us now turn to a
portrayal of the *tactical* monetary policy decisions taken in the 'economic
miracle' period after the Korea boom. In 1952 the overall economic situation eased. The current account remained in surplus and the terms of trade
improved owing to the sharp decline in import prices. Initially, however,
unemployment remained high at around 10 per cent at the turn of the year
1951–2, and around the same figure a year later. Investment rose as a share
of output, though, and economic growth remained extremely high in 1952,
at 9 per cent (see Table 1). In view of the high level of unemployment, calls
were made for measures to expand domestic demand, particularly by the
trade unions and circles close to the SPD.[117] These were directed not least
to the Bank deutscher Länder, which from the autumn of 1951 effectively
tightened its restrictive stance by means of extended open market operations
in those securities that it had purchased to finance job-creation programmes
and other government projects in 1949 and 1950; by this means it had tied
up DM 1.1 billion of bank liquidity by June 1952.[118] On the other hand,
this only partly offset the liquidity inflows to the banks from the sale to the
Bank deutscher Länder of foreign currency earned by virtue of the export
surpluses.

On 30 April 1952 the Central Bank Council took a first step towards a
relaxation of credit policy to the extent that, as of 1 May, the until then
uniform minimum reserve ratios were replaced by staggered rates for banks
in different locations and for different types of deposit. This implied a cut
in rates for smaller banks. Further marked cuts in minimum reserve ratios
were introduced on 1 September 1952 and 1 February 1953. On 28 May
1952 the Central Bank Council supported by 9 votes to 4 a proposal by
Bernard to cut the discount rate by one to 5 per cent. Prior to that, it had
been observed that credit creation by the banks was on the decline and was
being exceeded by the formation of monetary capital, and it was argued that
rising export surpluses had increased the liquidity of the money market.[119]

[117] Cf. Wallich, 1955, p. 93.
[118] Wallich took the view, though, that the sales on the open market were not intended to
have a restrictive impact, but were merely to get rid of unwanted central bank assets. Cf.
Wallich, 1955, p. 93.
[119] Further steps towards relaxation were postponed at the following meeting of the
Central Bank Council, with a view to the debt negotiations in London, in order to avoid
giving the impression that Germany's ability to pay was particularly great.

Between 20 August 1952 and 10 June 1953 the Central Bank Council cut the discount rate in three steps of half a point to 3.5 per cent. The last step was taken against the background of a major rise in liquidity on the money market owing to the current account surpluses, and despite the fact that it occurred in precisely the same month as the second tax reform after the currency reform had come into force, which reduced income tax by an average of 15 per cent and thus boosted domestic demand in the already booming economy.[120] In other words, the relaxation of monetary policy was motivated by external economic considerations. In the case of the last interest-rate cut, it was pointed out that the rate was still high in comparison with other countries (see Figure 1).

On 16 December 1953 the Central Bank Council agreed to a further step on the road to currency convertibility: the conversion of the blocked D-mark accounts for foreigners into 'liberalized capital deposits' ('libka Mark'), which came into effect as of mid-September 1954.[121] In view of Germany's pronounced surplus vis-à-vis the EPU, on 31 March 1954 the Central Bank Council unanimously recommended making all the stand-by loans from the credit agreement of the summer of 1952—totalling DM 317 million—available for re-payment.

On 19 May 1954 the Central Bank Council voted by 9 votes (including those of the two presidents) to 2 for a further cut in the discount rate of half a point to 3 per cent; this was justified exclusively in terms of the external currency position. Given that the Bank of England had just cut its rates to 3 per cent, it was argued that inactivity on the part of the Bank deutscher Länder would lead to a pronounced interest-rate differential vis-à-vis the rest of the world. By contrast, 'the economy was currently not in need of specific stimulatory assistance from the central bank'.[122] This, after all, would be provided by the imminent third reform of income tax, the 'Great' Tax Reform, which came into force on 16 September 1954; this reduced the top rate of tax from 74 to 55 per cent.[123]

At almost all the Central Bank Council meetings between 1951 and the peak of accumulated budget surpluses ('Juliusturm') at around DM 7.5 billion in September 1956,[124] it was registered with approval that the Federal Government was posting budget surpluses which had to be deposited

---

[120] Cf. Ehrlicher, 1994, p. 220.

[121] Cf. Kühne, 1984, p. 412.

[122] Minutes of the 169th Central Bank Council meeting held on 19 May 1954 (HA BBk B 330/Drs. 142).

[123] Cf. Ehrlicher, 1994, pp. 220f. Prior to currency reform the top rate (the highest marginal rate) had been over 100 per cent and the highest average rate 94 per cent.

[124] Cf. Emminger, 1986a, p. 78.

with the central bank system and which served to counteract the trend towards increasing liquidity arising out of the current account surpluses, without any action by the central bank.[125] Also positively received was the consistent and substantial rise in savings deposits, which, because it eased the minimum reserve obligations on the banks, was the very opposite of liquidity-reducing: this was because it was argued that, by virtue of its nature as a means of forming monetary capital, it enabled the banks to expand their short-term credit creation—at the time also rising sharply—without endangering price stability.

An additional argument for the cuts in the discount rate came from the capital market. The Central Bank Council wanted the capital market not only to be undistorted by interest-rate ties and tax allowances, but also one that could ensure an ample supply of capital at moderate interest rates. It took the view that low short-term money market rates and thus also low rates of interest on savings deposits would make private holders of monetary assets more interested in acquiring capital market securities; this, it believed, would reduce the rate of interest on the capital market and keep it down following the expiry of the second Capital Market Promotion Act on 1 January 1955.[126] This reflected the fact—as had been the case earlier with the hesitancy to raise the discount rate—that the decisions of the Central Bank Council were taken with a view not only to the goal of greater price stability than in other countries, but also to that of raising output.

As early as April 1955, when the Bank deutscher Länder published its Annual Report for 1954, it noted that a marked change had taken place in the inflationary climate during 1954.[127] In contrast to the previous year, certain prices went up during the second half of the year 'under the influence of a sharp rise in demand, and partly because of the upturn in various prices on world markets and because wage increases gradually began to make themselves felt'. Consequently, the Bank deutscher Länder, together with the Federal Government, followed economic trends with particular attention 'in order to counter any exacerbation of the situation with the means at its

---

[125] The motive behind this policy was not that of stabilization, however. Central government merely wanted to build up surpluses with a view to armaments spending in the future, particularly after the treaty establishing the European Defence Community (EDC) had been signed by the six Member States of the European Coal and Steel Community on 27 May 1952. It was serendipitous for economic stability in the Federal Republic that ratification of the treaty was protracted, and finally failed in 1954, because of the failure to gain the support of the French parliament. As a consequence, the actual military spending occurred only very much later than planned.

[126] On the impact of the capital market promotion acts and the development of the capital market see Borchardt, 1971, p. 165ff.

[127] Bank deutscher Länder, Geschäftsbericht 1955, p. 3.

disposal'. Moreover, in the summer of 1955 full employment, according to the prevailing definition, was reached, with unemployment running at under 5 per cent.[128] Consequently, wage growth, which had been declining since 1951, increased once more in 1955 (see Table 1).

Shortly afterwards, it was decided that things had gone far enough: the credit-policy reins were tightened in various ways, with the exclusive aim of cooling down the overheating economy, i.e. for purely domestic economic reasons: the external position was still characterized by export surpluses and the inflow of foreign currency. The Bank deutscher Länder made it clear that there could be no talk of restrictive measures for external reasons.[129] Therefore, the central bank was keen to continue with the abolition of the still existing restrictions on foreign currency and 'warmly' welcomed the fact that the Federal Government intended in addition to raise imports by reducing customs duties and taking other steps to facilitate imports. These external economic measures were oriented exclusively towards influencing the current account, i.e. reducing the current account surpluses. Clearly, the Bank did not initially realize that the abolition of foreign exchange restrictions, i.e. the move towards full D-mark convertibility, would not only stimulate goods imports, but would also open up a new source of foreign exchange inflows, namely via the capital account. For, as a de facto already convertible currency, and at that a relatively stable one, backed up by large currency reserves, the D-mark constituted an incentive for foreign capital to invest on the German money and capital market. This trend increasingly became evident in the following years, initiating the debates on the appreciation of the D-mark.[130]

The change to a restrictive credit policy stance began during May 1955, with large-scale sales on the open market. Because, back in 1954, the Bank deutscher Länder had run out of the stock of money market paper required for this purpose, it reached agreement in May 1955 with the Federal Minister of Finance that the minister would make money market paper available to it for DM 2 billion of the 3 per cent equalization claims of

---

[128] In an academic report on full employment commissioned by the United Nations in 1955 experts considered the state of full employment to have been achieved when unemployment among those looking for work had fallen to around 5 per cent. Cf. the paper entitled 'Währungsstabilität in der vollbeschäftigten Wirtschaft' presented by Heinrich Irmler, Vice-President of the Landeszentralbank von Niedersachsen, at the specialist conference of the Deutscher Raiffeisenverband e.V. in Lochmühle near Ahrweiler on 5 Nov. 1956, p. 6, in the original version of the text. Excerpts were published in: Bank deutscher Länder, Auszüge aus Presseartikeln, no. 139 of 21 Dec. 1956, pp. 2ff. As is well known, in the UK the full employment goal set by Lord Beveridge was defined more ambitiously, at 3 per cent.

[129] Cf. Bank deutscher Länder, Geschäftsbericht 1955, p. 1.

[130] For further details on this see Carstens, 1963 and Kaufmann, 1969.

the Bank deutscher Länder from currency conversion. In the first week of July 1955, the 'mobilization paper' sold reached a provisional high of DM 1.5 billion.[131] However, in view of the far higher inflows of liquidity from the export surpluses, which in 1955 still amounted to DM 2.7 billion (compared with DM 4.0 billion in 1954) on the current account despite a 27 per cent increase in goods imports, the open market operations were far from sufficient to dampen down demand. This remained true even allowing for the surpluses posted by German government, which were neutralized as deposits in the central bank system. Faced with money market rates that had risen above the discount rate owing to the open market operations and other withdrawals of liquidity (see Figure 3), the commercial banks once again increasingly resorted to their refinancing facilities with the central bank, which in previous years had been largely unnecessary.

For this reason, on 3 August 1955 the Central Bank Council decided to supplement its flexible and 'unobtrusive' open market policy by other, more 'visible' measures. In order to enforce 'moderation' and to prevent 'a continued expansion of the economic boom and full employment drifting into dangerous channels',[132] the discount rate was raised by half a point to 3.5 per cent and bank liquidity was cut by DM 0.5 billion by means of an increase of one percentage point in the minimum reserve ratios. At its meeting on 12 October 1955 the Central Bank Council decided to introduce an additional measure to dampen demand; it was decided that so-called 'construction bills' (*Bauwechsel*), which were used as an intermediary form of construction finance, but were not trade bills in the narrow sense, would no longer be re-financed.

As of the autumn of 1955, the Federal Government recognized that it could not leave stability policy to the Bank deutscher Länder alone. The *de facto* convertibility of the currency had, after all, served to blunt the latter's weapons. Erhard issued two government declarations to parliament on the responsibility of central government for steering the economy (on 19 October 1955 and 22 June 1956). From the autumn of 1955 the Federal Minister of Finance, Schäffer, expressed a similar viewpoint in the 'General Preliminary Remarks on the Budgetary Plans of the Federal Government'.[133]

In spite of the restrictive monetary measures, the credit demand of the

---

[131] Of this, however, only just over DM 0.5 billion amounted to a withdrawal of bank liquidity, because almost DM 0.3 billion of the new mobilization paper consisted of central government treasury notes that had already been in circulation and more than DM 0.6 billion was purchased by government agencies and paid for by equalization claims.

[132] Bank deutscher Länder, Geschäftsbericht 1955, p. 17.

[133] Cf. Dreißig, 1976, p. 738.

economy, which was expanding at the record rate of 12 per cent, remained brisk. In 1955 the volume of bank credit rose by 23 per cent, in spite of twofold pressure on bank liquidity from the persistent budget surpluses posted by German government and the strong growth of currency in circulation, owing primarily to the sharp rise in mass incomes.[134] This caused interest rates on the money market to rise significantly above the discount rate (3.5 per cent).[135] The relatively low discount rate was practically an invitation to the banks to exploit the scope for raising debt from the central bank system. During the first half of the year, they had reduced their refinancing liabilities to the central bank system by almost DM 1 billion, but in the second half of the year they expanded them by DM 2.3 billion. The degree of utilization of the discount quotas set by the Bank deutscher Länder reached a maximum of 45 per cent at the turn of 1955–6, and the figure declined slightly in the following months only because the Bank deutscher Länder increased the volume of quotas. Clearly, the net foreign exchange purchases of the Bank deutscher Länder, amounting to DM 2.2 billion in 1955, were insufficient for the banks to provide the liquidity necessary for them to expand their lending.

Vocke and the Central Bank Council were aware of all this. At the Central Bank Council meeting held on 12 October 1955, Vocke expressed his view that, given the tense situation on the money market, 'our discount rate is too low'. Yet, he argued, falling share prices and the rise in yields on the bond market are doing 'part of the Bank deutscher Länder's work for it'. He counselled, though, and did so again at a later meeting on 23 November, that the rise in the discount rate should be postponed. The Damocles sword of such a step in the future was, in his view, at least as effective as an actual rise in the discount rate. He added that it was an urgent wish of the government 'that we should do nothing at the present time, and should give precedence to the government with its [stabilization] programme'.[136]

Although the Bank deutscher Länder did not change the most important refinancing interest rate, the discount rate, between 3 August 1955 and 7 March 1956, the costs to the banks of obtaining liquidity on the money

[134] The latter resulted from a combination of a substantial rise in employment and significant wage increases.

[135] During late 1955, the day-to-day money rate was between 0.25 and 0.75 points, the rate for three-month money as much as 2.5 percentage points above the discount rate. Thus the money market rates were also markedly in excess of the selling rates for money market paper, which had been raised in a number of steps beginning in Aug. For this reason, from about July 1955 the open market policy of the Bank deutscher Länder was no longer able to exert a restrictive effect.

[136] Transcript of the 203rd Central Bank Council meeting on 12 Oct. 1955 (HA BBk B 330/88).

market had risen significantly. In view of the economic boom, the Central Bank Council considered this desirable. Yet it was in no way sufficient to prevent the banks from expanding their lending by 23 per cent in 1955. In fact the substantial margin between the discount rate and the money market rates was the source of excellent results for the banks in that year. Owing to the regulations governing interest rates on bank deposits, such rates, which were traditionally oriented towards the discount rate, remained low. Although the regulations also specified maximum rates of interest for lending, the banks enjoyed greater scope here to adjust rates to those prevailing on the money market.[137] Thus the banks benefited from an extremely marked widening of their interest-rate margins.[138]

Once again the Central Bank Council failed to utilize the possibilities open to it for slowing the expansion of bank lending and cooling down the—as it itself admitted—overheated economy. Its scope lay, in particular, in preventing the rise of refinancing credit by DM 2.3 billion in the second half of 1955 by imposing more sharply restrictive measures. The fact that, given the *de facto* convertibility of the D-mark (the 'open flank' of the external economy), the increased inflow of liquidity from abroad would probably have undermined such restrictions is another problem that the Central Bank Council failed to consider.

In the Central Bank Council, the inadequacy of the discount-rate hike of 3 August 1955 was repeatedly discussed in various ways. Eduard Wolf reported, at almost all meetings from the start of the autumn of 1955, that the discount rate was below the rates of interest on the money market, and that the Bank deutscher Länder had consequently lost touch with the money market. In the Central Bank Council meeting held on 11 January 1956, during the course of which some members proposed a rise in the discount rate, Wolf stated his view 'that for many years the economy has been subjected to an extraordinary withdrawal of purchasing power and liquidity by virtue of a contractive fiscal policy', that 'the proper task of credit policy is being performed not by credit policy itself but by fiscal policy on the basis of very different considerations' and that the central bank would be 'forced into a supportive position external to its own tasks and goals by being forced to meet the imperative [*sic*] need for financing initiated by the movement of public finance; in this way central bank lending is seemingly expanding despite the fundamentally restrictive stance taken by the central bank, which

---

[137] Dürr points out that the interest rates charged for lending were regularly cut to a lesser extent than the discount rate. Cf. Dürr, 1966, pp. 245, 248.

[138] In the case of the Deutsche Bank group, for instance, this contributed to an explosion of net profits from DM 8.8 (1953) and 9.5 million (1954) to DM 15.7 (1955) and 25.3 million (1956). Cf. Holtfrerich, 1995, p. 567.

has already led to erroneous interpretations of the effectiveness of central bank policy'.[139]

At the following Central Bank Council meeting on 25–6 January 1956, the proposal to raise the discount rate failed to win majority approval (5 votes to 6). Supporters of the proposal argued 'that the prevailing discount rate, in the light of the current situation on the money market, was no longer 'in accordance with the times' and 'in line with market trends'; revision was needed if the central bank was not to manoeuvre itself into the position of being the cheapest and most convenient money-procurement office. Credit that was scarce but cheap was a principle that must inevitably come into conflict with the market economy, the longer it prevailed the more serious the conflict.' The opponents of a rise in the discount rate, who, besides Bernard, surprisingly also included Vocke, argued, amongst other things, that such a step would 'be welcomed by certain banks in whose interest it would be, but would not be understood by the business community as a whole'.[140] The President of the Federation of German Industries (BDI), Fritz Berg, had, after all, in a public speech given in December 1955, criticized the Bank deutscher Länder for having 'struck a massive blow at the good business climate'[141] with the restrictive credit policies pursued since the August of 1955. This is the most graphic illustration of the extent to which Central Bank Council decisions on interest rates during that period took account of production-related aspects and interests, even to the extent of subordinating the recognized needs of proper monetary policy. Although there was no corresponding danger, it remained tied to its function of lender of last resort.

It appears that a shift in the balance occurred in February 1956. On 1 February Bernard sent a written invitation to the ministers of economics and finance to attend the next Central Bank Council meeting on 15 February, as the problem of raising bank interest rates had become acute. On the morning of the 15th, however, the ministers were unable to attend owing to restrictions on rail travel because of the icy conditions; for that reason the Central Bank Council declined to take the decision, and both ministers

---

[139] Minutes of the 210th Central Bank Council meeting held on 11 Jan. 1956 (HA BBk B 330/Drs. 142). In the last quarter of 1955, there had repeatedly been press criticism of the inadequately restrictive policy pursued by the Bank deutscher Länder.

[140] Minutes of the 211th Central Bank Council meeting held on 25–6 Jan. 1956 (HA BBk B 330/Drs. 142). On Vocke's vote: Transcript (HA BBk B 330/91).

[141] The Central Bank Council reacted to this with a special 2-page press statement in which it rejected Berg's allegations. Transcript of the 209th meeting of the Central Bank Council on 21 Dec. 1955 (HA BBk B 330/90). At the Central Bank Council meeting on 23 Nov. 1955 there had already been talk of the members of the Central Bank Council coming under persistent fire 'from business and its functionaries'. Transcript of the 206th Central Bank Council meeting on 23 Nov. 1955 (HA BBk B 330/89).

were invited to the next meeting of the Central Bank Council on 22 February 1956. That morning Schäffer rang up Bernard and formally requested that, in view of the absence of Erhard, who was on an official visit to England, the decision be postponed by a further week.[142] Accordingly, Bernard ensured that the matter was finally decided by the Central Bank Council on 7 March 1956: the decision was taken to raise the discount rate by one point to 4.5 per cent. Yet even this interest-rate hike meant that the Bank deutscher Länder was merely lagging behind the rise in interest rates on the money market, which continued to increase significantly owing to the persistent liquidity tensions during the winter months. Even after the discount-rate increase of 7 March, short-term interest rates were up to 0.75 percentage points higher than the discount rate. Accordingly, the re-financing liabilities of the banks *vis-à-vis* the central bank system peaked at almost DM 5.5 million in March 1956, a further rise of almost DM 1 billion on the end of 1955. Subsequently, the tense situation on the money market eased, however. The rise in the day-to-day money rate came to an end. In April it declined to a level equal to the discount rate (4.5 per cent).

How are the pronounced tensions during the first quarter and the subsequent relaxation to be explained? The increase in currency in circulation continued in 1956 for the same reasons as those mentioned above for the previous year, withdrawing liquidity totalling DM 1.2 billion from the commercial banks in 1956. Moreover, additional open market operations by the Bank deutscher Länder served to withdraw DM 1.1 million of liquidity from the banks during the first 11 months of 1956. During the first quarter of the year, the withdrawal of liquidity resulting from the budget surpluses had also been substantial, but this factor became steadily less important during the remainder of the year. Indeed, as the 'Juliusturm' began to be reduced—to the extent that the funds were not used to purchase armaments abroad—central government actually raised bank liquidity towards the end of the year.

However, the crucial factor in the shift in money market relations following the first quarter was the foreign exchange surpluses which the Bank deutscher Länder was forced to acquire. On this, the Bank deutscher Länder noted: 'whereas, during the first quarter of 1956, the rise in government central bank deposits had withdrawn considerably more resources from the banks than they were receiving from foreign exchange transactions with the Bank deutscher Länder, in the two following quarters the foreign exchange surpluses quickly gained the upper hand'.[143] In 1956 the banks gained

---

[142] The entire process is described in the Minutes of the 214th Central Bank Council meeting held on 7 Mar. 1956 (HA BBk B 330/Drs. 142).

[143] Bank deutscher Länder, Geschäftsbericht 1956, p. 44.

liquidity totalling DM 5.9 billion from this source, compared with just DM 2.2 billion in 1955. In both years this was almost exclusively a result of the surpluses on the current account, not the capital account. This was not to change until 1957.

In the phase of relaxation on the money market, the peak of economic overheating driven by domestic demand impulses had already passed, as evidenced by signs of a weakening of domestic investment. In the second quarter of 1956 the growth of foreign demand had taken on the role of the economic 'locomotive', against which domestic credit policy was of course totally powerless under a system of fixed exchange rates. Indeed, all restrictive measures could achieve at best was to reduce German demand for imports, thus expanding the unwanted foreign-exchange surpluses as a source of bank liquidity. They were thus inevitably self-defeating and therefore inconsistent with the target.

It was precisely in this situation that the Central Bank Council took its greatest step towards restricting lending. On 18 May 1956 it decided to raise the discount rate further by one point to 5.5 per cent. In order to dampen down the boom in exports (plus 28 per cent in the second quarter of 1956 compared with 12 months earlier), foreign bills, cheques, D-mark advances from foreign nationals and export drafts were purchased by the Bank deutscher Länder only at the general discount rate and not, as previously, at the lower discount rate of the partner country.

The consequence of these on-going restrictive measures was that the banks no longer had a financial incentive in arbitrage between the central bank rate and the money market rate. Almost as a mirror image of the rise in refinancing liabilities of the financial institution with the central bank system in the second half of 1955 and the first quarter of 1956, from around DM 2 to 5 billion, these liabilities declined once more to DM 2 billion between May 1956 and March 1957. Together with the above-mentioned withdrawal of liquidity owing to open market operations, the Bank deutscher Länder was thus able to neutralize to a great extent the impact of the foreign-exchange surpluses on domestic liquidity.

The sharply restrictive measures imposed on 18 May 1956 had been expressly welcomed by Erhard and Schäffer. Their prime concern was price stability, and they were worried about the economy overheating. They saw the credit policy decisions as part of their own government's stabilization programme. In April a Stabilization Policy Council (*Konjunkturrat*) had been set up on Erhard's initiative—and behind Adenauer's back—alongside the economic policy cabinet to coordinate monetary policy with fiscal and general economic policy. It consisted of Erhard, Schäffer, and Vocke. This in turn instituted the important 'Heads of Department Committee' (*Abteilungsleiterausschuß*). Initially, this met roughly once a month and performed the real work of coordination, not least regarding the above-mentioned stabilization programme.[144] This was based on the recognition that external economic trends had narrowed the domestic economic scope for central bank action, and that a greater share of stabilization policy was to be performed by fiscal policy.[145]

However, the credit restriction measures pushed through by Vocke in the Central Bank Council with the support of the ministers present, Erhard and Schäffer, met with stiff opposition, not only from the president of the BDI, Berg, but also from Adenauer, who was worried about the prospect of falling economic growth—which, by the way, did not materialize—in election year 1957 and the withdrawal of election campaign support by German industry. The matter reached a head on 23 May 1956, when Adenauer, at the annual general meeting of the BDI in Cologne, in agreement with Berg, distanced himself from the restrictive policies pursued by the Bank deutscher Länder with the following remark: 'a heavy blow has been struck at the German economy, and it is the little ones who will suffer most'.[146]

The decisions taken by the Central Bank Council strengthened Adenauer in his conviction that he must at all costs get rid of Vocke as president of the central bank. The statutory preparations, being implemented at an increasing pace, for converting the Bank deutscher Länder into the Deutsche Bundesbank offered an opportunity for this. In addition, he urgently wanted to move the central bank from Frankfurt to Cologne to bring it closer to the seat of government. During a discussion of the draft legislation for the Bundesbank Act in the cabinet meeting of 11 June 1956, he expressed his view that 'in choosing the location [of the Bundesbank] it should be borne in mind that the activity of the bank should be guided by the correct spirit. The current location of the Bank means that the Bank deutscher Länder leads a very separate life. The federal central bank should be susceptible to the political atmosphere as it, more than most other institutions, had to take this into account.'[147]

[144] Cf. Koerfer, 1987, pp. 110ff. and Hentschel, 1996, pp. 255f.; Berger, 1997, pp. 220ff. The minutes of the meeting are stored in the Bundesarchiv in Koblenz, B 102/1296 to 1298. The Bank deutscher Länder was initially represented there by Wolf, the Ministry of Finance by Oeftering and the Ministry of Economics by Müller-Armack.

[145] Usually it was in this Committee, too, that the Central Bank Council's plans for monetary-policy decisions were put up for discussion, while the central bank was able to raise its demands of fiscal policy unobtrusively. The Stabilization Policy Council existed until the Stability and Growth Act came into force on 8 June 1967, when other bodies took on these functions. The discount-rate hike of 18 May was also preliminarily discussed at the Heads of Department Committee.

[146] Quoted from: Koerfer, 1987, p. 117.

[147] Bundesarchiv, 1997, vol. 9, p. 19. The volume also contains (pp. 102ff.: cabinet meeting

On 19 October 1955, i.e. just over two months after the first rise in the discount rate, Erhard announced in a government declaration a contractive stabilization programme. It largely took the form of appeals to the parties to collective bargaining for wage and price moderation and to the various tiers of German government to reduce public sector construction orders. Large-scale tax cuts that had been planned were postponed. On 8 December 1955 and on 20 January 1956 the Bundestag passed two 'stabilization policy customs regulations' (*konjunkturpolitische Zollverordnungen*).[148] In June 1956 the government, with the agreement of the Bank deutscher Länder, took steps in the same direction with a more comprehensive second stabilization programme. The cuts in customs duties introduced by the first programme were extended until December 1957. A third 'stabilization policy customs regulation' reduced import duties on a large number of manufactured goods.[149] On 19 June 1956 the government decided to extend the trade liberalization *vis-à-vis* the dollar area that it had embarked on at the start of 1954.[150]

In 1956 the perverse effect of the restrictive measures aimed at dampening domestic demand manifested themselves in all clarity. For the first time the Bank deutscher Länder spoke of the external position developing 'against all the rules'.[151] Normally, the persistent economic boom in West Germany —in spite of the restrictive measures—should have led to a decline in export surpluses in 1956, as had occurred in the previous year. Yet the opposite

on 24 Aug. with Bernard and Vocke) further discussions on the location of the Bundesbank. The Bank deutscher Länder presidents were keen to ensure that the seat of the central bank remained in Frankfurt am Main. On the other hand, they were unable to receive support for their call, also raised at that meeting, for the social insurance institutions to be included in the obligation to deposit liquid resources with the Bundesbank.

[148] The rates of customs duty on inputs for the agricultural and construction sectors were cut by 50 per cent up to June 1956. Temporary cuts in duty were also imposed on foodstuffs and unsophisticated investment goods. Cf. Berger, 1997, pp. 112ff.

[149] Particularly from the consumer-goods sector, permanently by more than 25 per cent; as early as March 1955 duty rates on more than 700 customs positions had been cut, including for stabilization policy reasons, by 10–35 per cent.

[150] The promotion of imports through tax concessions also envisaged by the stabilization programme, on the other hand, was not implemented until July 1957. The government also took action with respect to the domestic economy. In June 1956 10 per cent of all its funds for capital spending were frozen and the provision of investment guarantees for private firms was suspended. While Bonn proved unable to restrict the degressive depreciation allowances for private-sector investment, as the Central Bank Council had suggested, it did significantly increase the incentives for saving in order to restrain consumer demand. The bundle of contractive measures enacted by the government had, however, to be set against the expansionary impact of the reduction in the income tax burden by virtue of the law of 5 Oct. 1956. Cf. Berger, 1997, pp. 116ff.

[151] Bank deutscher Länder, Geschäftsbericht 1956, p. 7.

occurred. As the cause of this 'rule-breaking', the Bank deutscher Länder ruled out both its own restrictive credit policy and price trends at home and abroad, which, it argued, had scarcely differed during the phase of accelerating export growth from the autumn of 1955 to mid-1956. Rather, it saw the explosive growth of exports primarily as a result of an investment boom —comparable to that which had occurred in Germany—among Germany's leading trading partners. Owing to their limited scope for supplying such goods, these countries' demand for investment goods had been directed towards the German economy, which had an elastic supply because of its traditional strength in that sector. 'Thus, the exports of scarcely any other country were as favourably influenced by cyclical trends as German exports.'[152]

Immediately after the announcement of the second restrictive stabilization programme by the Federal Government, on 27 June 1956 the Central Bank Council detected, on the one hand, initial signs of a relaxation, particularly in the basic-goods and investment-goods sectors, and, on the other, higher bank liquidity resulting from an influx of foreign currency. This impression was confirmed two weeks later. Industrial firms were attempting to place fund issues with interest rate coupons of 8 per cent on the capital market, because at times this rate was lower than that for short-term bank loans.

On 22 August, members of the Board of Directors reported to the Central Bank Council on further developments in the same direction and on a marked stabilization of price trends and bank lending. The rate of expansion in the construction sector was now also on the decline. Only the rise in mass income and thus the growth of consumer demand remained unabated. Despite substantial wage increases, the volume of savings deposits had declined since July. When this overall impression was confirmed again two weeks later, and, moreover, it was noted that the day-to-day money rate had fallen below the discount rate, it was decided to reduce the discount rate by half a point to 5 per cent; this had been proposed by Bernard, although Vocke voted against, with reference to the still undiminished rise in wages and consumer spending. The above-mentioned domestic economic factors played the main role in this decision, but at the same time it was explicitly stated that one aim was to reduce the interest-rate differential *vis-à-vis* the rest of the world, and to counter the disturbances caused by the resulting international monetary flows and the international criticism that could be expected of German interest-rate policy.[153] In addition, it was believed that by cutting

---

[152] Bank deutscher Länder, Geschäftsbericht 1956, p. 8.
[153] Cf. the Minutes of the 226th Central Bank Council meeting held on 5–6 Sept. 1956, p. 7 (HA BBk B 330/Drs. 142) and the transcript (HA BBk B 330/96).

the discount rate the propensity to save would, via a psychological causal mechanism, be bolstered and capital market rates brought down.

On 8 January 1957 Eduard Wolf took part in a meeting of the heads of department of the Stabilization Policy Council at the Ministry of Economics at the initiative and under the chairmanship of the head of the *Grundsatzabteilung* ('fundamentals department'), Alfred Müller-Armack. The latter had called the meeting in order to prevent the Bank deutscher Länder from cutting the discount rate. The boom in consumer spending had not yet subsided and the signs of relaxation were, it was argued, merely temporary in nature, all the more so as an increase in armaments spending had to be expected. Wolf, the capital market department of the Federal Ministry of Economics, and Erhard, who attended most of the meeting in person, took a different view, all the more so as they claimed that savings activity had increased once more at the end of the year. This was reported to the Central Bank Council meeting held on 9–10 January 1957 by Wolf. The Central Bank Council accepted his view that symptoms of market relaxation had been observed at least since the early autumn of 1956, and voted by 8 votes to 3 to cut the discount rate by half a point to 4.5 per cent;[154] the decision came after hearing the opinion of the ministers of economics and finance, who raised no objections, although Vocke was opposed. In the subsequent period the money market received a substantial volume of additional liquidity from the marked current account surpluses. The Bank deutscher Länder repeatedly cut the selling rate for money market paper and attempted to absorb bank liquidity by means of open market operations.

In the following months increasingly stiff opposition developed abroad to what was still seen as the Bank deutscher Länder's high interest rate policy. When, on 10 July 1957, the Central Bank Council again discussed in detail further cuts in the discount rate that had been proposed by some members, it was already under pressure from the OEEC council and the German member of the EPU Board of Directors, Hans Karl von Mangoldt.[155] The Bank deutscher Länder was not acting 'in accordance with the system', because 'we are not allowing the inflow of foreign currency to make its effects in terms of falling interest rates and rising prices'. Although the west German balance of payments was in surplus, the Bank deutscher Länder was pursuing a restrictive credit policy.

At this meeting Pfleiderer—who, according to Helmut Schlesinger, was

---

[154] By reducing the period of the purchase of export drafts it also further reduced the extent to which exports were promoted by central bank credits; in Feb. it also cut its funding of the Ausfuhrkredit AG (AKA).

[155] Transcript of the 249th meeting of the Central Bank Council on 10 July 1957 (HA BBk B 330/104). Cf. also Kaplan and Schleiminger, 1989, p. 260.

'very important for the Central Bank Council' and 'the only Land Central Bank president who was intellectually a match for Eduard Wolf'[156]—made the remarkable point that the balance of payments surpluses were the 'No. 1 problem'. Yet, along with others, he thought it doubtful that the speculative inflow of capital from the change in the terms of payment and other sources could be slowed by cutting the discount rate. Wolf posited that it was not the absolute level of German interest rates but the interest-rate differential *vis-à-vis* the rest of the world that was decisive, and this gap had narrowed in recent months following rises in foreign interest rates. Pfleiderer noted that the way in which German foreign currency reserves had been invested had contributed to the comparatively low interest rates abroad, particularly in the USA. This was because the influx of dollars was not, he argued, effectively withdrawn from the USA but was held as deposits with American banks or as US treasury bills, of which West Germany was the most important foreign purchaser. He considered this to be correct in terms of maximizing yield, but not in terms of monetary policy. For with these short-term capital exports, namely investing the gold earned from the current account surpluses with EPU countries in the USA, the Federal Republic was helping to ensure that American interest rates remained low and the interest-rate differential to the FRG remained considerable. He proposed holding a greater proportion of currency reserves as gold. In this he enjoyed the broad support of Vocke. It was probably as a result of this discussion that in the course of 1957 the gold reserves held by the west German central bank rose from DM 6.2 to DM 10.6 billion, i.e. by 71 per cent.[157] And in fact US money market rates remained higher than those in Germany during 1957, a fact that assisted in rendering the problems of the external position less acute.

Pfleiderer's comments during this meeting are noteworthy for another reason. In the face of the prevailing external position he called for a 'switch in the credit-policy instruments deployed, as we have, on balance, done in our most recent credit-policy decisions. We have, after all, if we look at our decisions as a whole, to a certain degree switched [from interest-rate policy] to liquidity policy.'[158] By this he was referring to the fact that, while the Bank deutscher Länder had cut the discount rate twice since September 1956, it had further tightened its stance as regards liquidity-policy measures. Open market policy was the most important: at the end of 1956 just DM 1.4 billion worth of mobilization paper had been sold on the market; by the

---

[156] In an interview conducted by the author with Helmut Schlesinger on 3 Mar. 1997.

[157] Cf. Deutsche Bundesbank, 1988, p. 26.

[158] Transcript of the 249th meeting of the Central Bank Council on 10 July 1957 (HA Bbk B 330/104).

end of October 1957 it was DM 5.6 million, i.e. a liquidity withdrawal of DM 4.2 billion within the space of 10 months.[159] On 10 April 1957 the Central Bank Council had decided to raise, as of 1 May 1957, the minimum reserve ratios for domestic deposits to 9–13 per cent and those for foreign liabilities to as much as 20 per cent (at the time, the maximum rate permissible) as a means of siphoning off bank liquidity. Indeed, as of 1 September 1957 foreign deposits, which—to the extent that they were convertible —had been subjected to an interest ban since 1948 (which remained in force until the spring of 1959) were subjected to the higher maximum rate of 30 per cent permissible under the Bundesbank Act of 30 July 1957.[160] Under the Bundesbank Act the federal states were obliged for the first time to deposit all their liquid funds with the Bundesbank, so that even deposit policy exercised a contractive effect on liquidity that countered the expansionary effects of the reduction of the 'Juliusturm' initiated by the 'Pie Committee' of the Bundestag. There was no further cut in the discount rate yet.[161]

c) Monetary policy on the horns of a dilemma: 1956–61

Since 1951 the successful stabilization policy pursued by monetary and fiscal-policy makers and the social partners led, by virtue of virtual price stability in Germany and high rates of inflation abroad, to substantial surpluses on the balance of trade and the services account; these surpluses— excluding trade with the GDR—peaked in 1957, at just under 3.7 per cent of GNP (see Table 3). Together with the net capital inflows, which also began in 1951, and which in 1957, following explosive growth in that year, accounted for 0.7 per cent of GNP, the resulting inflow of foreign currency swelled the foreign currency reserves of the Bank deutscher Länder from DM 0.7 billion at the end of 1950 to DM 17.6 billion at the end of 1957. This represented 7.6 per cent of GNP, 55 per cent of German imports, and 102 per cent of currency in circulation. By the end of 1957 the Bank deutscher Länder's overall foreign assets amounted to as much as 10.4 per cent of output, 75.4 per cent of imports, and 139 per cent of currency in

---

[159] Cf. Deutsche Bundesbank, Geschäftsbericht 1957, pp. 41f. The following figures are also to be found in this Geschäftsbericht. See also Berger, 1997, p. 69.

[160] Cf. Deutsche Bundesbank, 1988, p. 190.

[161] On 24 July 1957 the Central Bank Council considered taking such a step, but finally decided against after carefully—and very readably—weighing up the arguments. At the start of the debate Wolf reported that he had participated in a Heads of Department meeting at the Stabilization Policy Council, where there was considerable sympathy for the idea of a cut in the discount rate. Cf. the Minutes of the 250th Central Bank Council meeting held on 24 July 1957 (HA BBk B 330/Drs. 142).

circulation. The 'Vocke era' was also characterized by the fact that holdings of gold as a proportion of foreign exchange reserves rose from less than 10 per cent at the end of 1951 to more than 60 per cent at the end of 1957. In the 'Blessing era', which began at the start of 1958, a figure of around 50 per cent was maintained.[162]

The other side of the coin of this persistent trade surplus was that the German economy withdrew foreign currency from the other EPU countries during the period of the 'dollar gap', thus weakening their ability to build up the necessary cushion of foreign exchange reserves in order to realize the plans to make the European currencies convertible. Although West Germany, like the other EPU countries, posted a trade deficit with the USA, it far more than compensated for this by its surplus with the EPU, whereas in the case of the other EPU countries, particularly France and the UK, EPU deficits came on top of the dollar deficits. In other words, they had to cope with a 'D-mark gap' on top of their 'dollar gap'. And at the same time, by rapidly raising gold holdings as a proportion of its foreign exchange reserves, the Bank deutscher Länder began to weaken the gold backing and thus the role of the US dollar as the leading currency in the global monetary system,[163] a problem that was to become more acute in subsequent years and to manifest itself openly in the 1960s.

Following the imposition of credit restrictions by the Central Bank Council on 3 August 1955, it was expected that West Germany, as the surplus country, would make a greater policy contribution to achieving equilibrium in the balance of payments position of the European deficit countries, either by adjusting German price trends to the higher average rates of inflation prevailing in the EPU, or by revaluing the D-mark. Even then, the EPU Board of Directors criticized this interest-rate policy decision. Following the further hikes in the discount rate, bringing it to 5.5 per cent, in July 1956 it complained about 'the extreme domestic orientation of German policies and its neglect of external considerations'.[164] In the subsequent year,

---

[162] All figures calculated on the basis of Deutsche Bundesbank, 1988, pp. 5, 20, 26, 255. For the proportion of overall Bank deutscher Länder foreign assets consisting of gold, see Table 3. The 'gilding' of currency reserves during the Vocke era was primarily a success of the 'hardening' of the EPU, in the sense that a growing proportion of the bilateral deficits had to be paid in gold or dollars at the discretion of the debtor: initially, following the foundation of the EPU in July 1950, the proportion had been just 25 per cent, from 1954 50 per cent, but from 1955 it was 75 per cent. Given that during this period the price of gold on the London exchange was slightly below the official dollar parity, non-credited German surpluses were usually paid in gold rather than dollars. Cf. Emminger, 1986a, pp. 95f.

[163] Between 1950 and 1957, the gold backing of currency in circulation in the USA fell from 84 to 74 per cent. Cf. U.S. Bureau of the Census, 1975, pp. 993, 995.

[164] Report by the German EPU Director, von Mangoldt, quoted in Kaplan and Schleiminger, 1989, p. 253.

too, during which the Bank deutscher Länder had relaxed its interest-rate policy, but had acted restrictively in terms of liquidity policy—in particular through its open market policy and the rise in the minimum reserve ratios on 1 May—foreign criticism remained sharp. At the meeting of the ministerial representative committee of the OEEC held on 17–18 June 1957, German economic and stabilization policy was sharply attacked from all sides against the background of Germany's massive surpluses, completely isolating the country.[165]

As always in such cases, businessmen and foreign-exchange dealers had been the first to react. They put their money on an appreciation of the D-mark, by placing speculative funds in D-mark deposits with German banks, despite the fact that since 1948 they had been prohibited from paying interest on such deposits, and involving corresponding changes by the business community in the terms of payment, i.e. the time limits for payment for import and export transactions.[166]

Policy makers at the Bank deutscher Länder/Bundesbank had always seen their statutory task of safeguarding the currency in a double sense, namely to defend the external parities of the D-mark within the framework of the Bretton Woods system, and at the same time to ensure domestic price stability. In doing so, they interpreted their mandate in such a way that, in case of goal conflict, ensuring domestic economic stability, especially price stability, was to enjoy priority over a monetary policy oriented towards equilibrium in the balance of payments. After making its position clear in the spring of 1957,[167] in the spring of 1960 the Bundesbank stated its view as follows:

Faced with a choice between such regard to the external position and the requirements of maintaining the internal value of money, there could, however, be no doubt on the part of the Bank that priority should be accorded to the latter, because defending price stability is of fundamental importance for economic development as a whole, and because the disturbances that may arise out of a renewed increase in the inflow of foreign currency to the commercial banks can be more easily kept

---

[165] By threatening to declare the D-mark a 'scarce currency' within the EPU and to discriminate against German exports, the other countries called on Germany to make a contribution to regaining external equilibrium itself and to grant a special credit to the EPU in favour of France, which was undergoing a currency crisis. Emminger reported to the Central Bank Council on 26 June 1957 that, in addition, a number of countries had recommended 'faster expansion of domestic German demand accompanied by measures to push down prices (sweeping cuts in customs duties or currency revaluation), others a substantial export of private and public capital or massive repayment of foreign debt. Minutes of the 248th Central Bank Council meeting held on 26 June 1957 (HA BBk B 330/Drs. 142).

[166] Cf. Kaplan and Schleiminger, 1989, p. 255.

[167] Cf. Bank deutscher Länder, Geschäftsbericht 1956, p. 8.

in check and overcome than the consequences of drifting on to the dangerous path of higher inflation.[168]

Yet Germany's balance of payments surpluses served not only to put other countries with a trade deficit under deflationary adjustment pressure for as long as they refrained from devaluing their domestic currencies, it also led automatically to an inflationary adjustment pressure in the FRG due to the Bank deutscher Länder/Bundesbank's obligation to intervene in defence of the D-mark parity. Thus the debate in Germany about appreciation of the D-mark was not about a shift in monetary-policy priority from ensuring domestic price stability to generating a balanced external position. Proponents of a revaluation of the D-mark considered such a shift necessary in order to fend off the danger of 'imported inflation'. The debate was about whether the instrument of D-mark appreciation or other instruments should be deployed in defence of price stability in Germany and whether the situation was such—namely a 'fundamental disequilibrium'—that a change in parity was permissible under the statutes of the International Monetary Fund.

The Bank deutscher Länder/Bundesbank, in particular Vocke and Blessing, opposed each and every proposal for revaluation, and believed that external equilibrium could be regained primarily by means of capital exports. In 1958 a public controversy broke out with L. Albert Hahn on this issue. The latter propounded the 'boomerang hypothesis': he claimed that, contrary to the view taken by the central bank, longer term capital exports would not offset the current account surpluses but would increase the demand for German exports and so feed back into the surplus on the German current account for as long as the D-mark was undervalued.[169] In 1960 he spoke of the 'horns of a dilemma' in which the Bundesbank found itself, between the goals of exchange-rate and price stabilization.[170]

As late as March 1955, in the context of prolonging the EPU agreement and preparing the transition to convertibility of the European currencies, both the Federal Government and the Bank deutscher Länder had rejected the UK's proposal to allow greater exchange-rate flexibility by widening the intervention bands around the central rate from ±1 per cent to ±3 per cent.[171]

---

[168] Deutsche Bundesbank, Geschäftsbericht 1959, p. 3.

[169] Cf. Hahn, 1960, pp. 137ff. Hahn's views were discussed in detail at the 31st Central Bank Council meeting held on 18–19 Sept. 1958; see the relevant Minutes (HA BBk B 330/ Drs. 142) and Kaufmann, 1969, p. 195.

[170] Hahn, 1963, p. 206.

[171] Cf. Kaufmann, 1969, p. 193 and Kaplan and Schleiminger, 1989, pp. 218ff. The matter was discussed at the 189th meeting of the Central Bank Council on 16 Mar. 1955; the view taken by the Bank deutscher Länder that the proposition should be rejected was upheld. Cf. the confidential Supplementary Minutes of the 189th Central Bank Council meeting (HA BBk, Nachlaß Emminger, N–2/243).

At that time some members of the Central Bank Council went so far as to state that, in the case of a devaluation of the pound sterling in connection with the widening of the band width, they wanted to peg the D-mark to the pound, i.e. also to devalue. On 3 July of the following year, Erhard proposed—with a view to the next Council of Ministers meeting of the OEEC on 17–19 July 1956—in a letter to the then British chancellor of the exchequer, Harold Macmillan, a multilateral redefinition of exchange-rate parities at a conference to be called by Macmillan. Stable currencies were to retain their parities, while deficit countries were to devalue. This made more sense, he argued, than the theoretical alternative of countries with stable price levels revaluing. In an interview with the Financial Times on 11 July 1956 Erhard added that he was also prepared to agree to widening the intervention bands around the central rates to ±5 per cent if the deficit countries did not wish to lower the value of their parities. At the time Macmillan rejected Erhard's proposals on behalf of the British government because a devaluation of the pound sterling had come to be seen as a threat to the existence of the sterling area.[172]

What had happened in the intervening period that in German government circles a *de facto* appreciation of the D-mark was no longer rejected? Erhard, who, in view of the strength of Germany's export industry, saw the comprehensive reduction of foreign trade quotas and a swift transition to convertibility of all the European currencies as being in the German national interest, had argued in favour of the idea of floating exchange rates, the associated devaluation of the French franc and the pound sterling, and the *de facto* appreciation of the D-mark, as early as 1952.[173] Yet he had met with opposition on this, not only from international organizations—the European Payments Union and the International Monetary Fund (IMF)—but also from the Bank deutscher Länder and especially from Vocke. More important was the fact that Erhard could not force his will on the federal Cabinet responsible for this question. Adenauer, under the influence of his economic and monetary policy advisers, Robert Pferdmenges and Hermann Josef Abs, and BDI President Fritz Berg were, along with Vocke, resolutely opposed to the proposal of *de facto* appreciation.[174]

---

[172] Cf. Kaplan and Schleiminger, 1989, pp. 257f. and Hentschel, 1996, p. 277; Kaufmann, 1969, p. 193.

[173] As early as the end of 1952, Erhard had proposed allowing the EPU currencies to fluctuate within a band of ±5 per cent around the parity in order to win the partner countries over to the idea of convertibility. This was rejected by the Bank deutscher Länder. Cf. the Minutes of the 135th Central Bank Council meeting held on 17–18 Dec. 1952 (HA BBk B 330/Drs. 142) and Hentschel, 1996, pp. 192, 276.

[174] On the influence exerted by the two bankers and by the industrialist, Fritz Berg, cf. Koerfer, 1987, especially pp. 85f.

The Economic Advisory Council at the Federal Ministry of Economics, which, along with Erhard, in principle preferred liberal market economic solutions to state intervention, took the view that the current account surpluses were structural, and in its report of 3 June 1956 it spoke of a fundamental disequilibrium and the necessity of adjusting exchange rates. With this, and with a subsequent more detailed report on the external position (30 April 1957), it lent the Minister of Economics its full backing on the question of currency appreciation.[175] However, it also took the view that a unilateral rise in the D-mark parity was not the best solution, because the current account position with the dollar area was not in surplus, but rather in deficit. Moreover, the large number of debtor countries was matched on the other hand by a small number of creditor countries; for this reason the Council argued that the required differentiation in correcting exchange-rate relations could only be achieved by differential depreciation. Vocke, too, was not opposed to other currencies depreciating: it was up to the 'sick' currencies to undergo the operation of depreciation; there was no need to operate on a 'healthy' currency.[176] At the same time, because the Council recognized the inflationary dangers of pegging one's currency to currencies suffering from inflation and to unrealistic parities, it took the view, in contrast to Vocke, that a unilateral D-mark appreciation might after all be necessary in order to ensure domestic price stability.[177]

Within the Board of Directors and from 1958 on the Central Bank Council, Emminger was the odd man out as regards Bank deutscher Länder/Bundesbank opposition to currency appreciation. As early as June 1956, at the annual general meeting of the Ifo Institute in Munich, he spoke of the fact that the Federal Republic would 'import the inflation of other countries with its export and foreign exchange surpluses'. He thus coined the later generally accepted phrase 'imported inflation', much to the displeasure of Vocke. At that point he had still not spoken openly of D-mark appreciation as a counter-measure, but only of promoting capital exports, early debt repayment, reducing export-promotion measures, etc.[178]

---

[175] Cf. Wissenschaftlicher Beirat, 1973, pp. 296ff., 333ff.

[176] Cf. Kaufmann, 1969, p. 196, Emminger, 1986a, p. 86.

[177] Cf. Wissenschaftlicher Beirat, 1973, p. 343.

[178] Cf. Emminger, 1986a, p. 79 and the article in the Süddeutsche Zeitung about the speech (edition of 7 June 1956 under the title 'Wir importieren die Inflation des Auslandes'—'We are importing inflation from abroad'). Heinrich Irmler, at the time still Vice-President of the Landeszentralbank von Niedersachsen, was the first from the top floor of the central bank system to bring the topic of D-mark revaluation to public attention, in a lecture at a conference held by the Deutscher Raiffeisenverband on 5 Nov. 1956. Irmler identified 'a genuine dilemma'. If domestic demand were dampened down and the price level stabilized by means of a restrictive credit policy, this led, he argued, to the danger that the surpluses on the trade

368 VII. Monetary Policy under Fixed Exchange Rates (1948–70)

In a confidential memorandum entitled 'Germany's Surplus Position and Exchange-rate Policy' of 10 November 1956, Emminger clearly addressed the goal conflict between internal and external monetary stability, and voiced his opinion that appreciation of the D-mark was bound to occur sooner or later if domestic price stability was to be maintained. In order to limit the damage, he argued that the exchange-rate adjustment should be effected as quickly as possible. He proposed that the band-width of the dollar exchange rate should be provisionally widened from ±1 per cent to ±6–8 per cent and simultaneously that the D-mark exchange rate should be shifted towards the upper limit of this band.[179]

Only after Emminger had threatened to discuss the memorandum on the Central Bank Council was Vocke willing to put the paper up for discussion at a 'secret meeting' of the Board of Directors held on 12 December 1956. Emminger remained completely isolated on the Board. Although he recognized that a general realignment of parities would be particularly desirable for the deficit countries, he insisted that a unilateral appreciation of the D-mark might prove necessary in order to defend domestic price stability.[180]

The Central Bank Council did not budge one inch on the question of appreciation. On 10 July 1957 it issued a press statement to the effect that the rumours going around about an appreciation of the D-mark were baseless and that it was in agreement on this matter with the Minister of Economics.[181] As the outcome of a cabinet meeting held on 19 and 20 August 1957 on this question, at which both central bank presidents participated,

balance and the balance of payments would increase further, rather than decline. The original manuscript, with the title 'Währungsstabilität in der vollbeschäftigten Wirtschaft' (Monetary stability in fully employed economy) can be found in HA BBk, press archive. Excerpts were published in Deutsche Bundesbank, Auszüge aus Presseartikeln, no. 139, 21 Dec. 1956, pp. 2ff., significantly without the discussion of revaluation. All that remains there (on p. 4) is the passage in which it is stated that, out of the analysis of the situation, 'it is a logical conclusion that in fact the European countries in deficit should re-examine their exchange parities and might have to devalue. The inclination to do so is, however, not particularly great, at least at present.' The description of this dilemma appears in a similar form in: Landeszentralbank von Niedersachsen, 1957, pp. 8f. There it is stated: 'The restrictive policy would then [when foreign demand takes the place of the subdued domestic demand; C.-L. H.] counteract its own impact. On the other hand, it had to be considered that the only alternative to raising the cost of and restricting credit would have been to alter the international exchange rate of the Deutsche Mark.'

[179] HA BBk, N2–1243.
[180] Cf. Emminger, 1986a, pp. 79ff. In Sept. 1957 Emminger went public on the exchange-rate question for the first time, propounding in an essay his view that in theory floating exchange rates, as practised by Canada and Peru, which had been tolerated by the IMF, were possible under IMF statutes. Cf. Emminger, 1957, pp. 732ff.
[181] Cf. the Minutes of the 249th Central Bank Council meeting held on 10 July 1957 (HA BBk B 330/Drs. 142).

the Federal Government stated that 'in the light of all the economic factors, there is no need for a change in the relationship between the D-mark and the US dollar. All the rumours about plans for an appreciation of the D-mark are baseless. The Federal Government and the Bundesbank will continue to safeguard the stability of the German currency, which is held in such high esteem at home and abroad.'[182] This served to quieten down speculation about D-mark revaluation.

This also owed something to an internationally coordinated intervention. The French central bank raised its discount rate. The UK raised its base rates from 5 to 7 per cent, and, together with the German delegation, made an official statement at the August 1957 meeting of the IMF that there was no chance of a change in parities.[183] On 18 September the Central Bank Council cut the discount rate by half a point to 4 per cent on a unanimous vote. Its aim thereby was to promote 'the expansion of the domestic economy at the expense of exports, that is, without lasting effects for internal stability'.[184] However, one may conclude from the word 'lasting' (*nachhaltig*) that the Central Bank Council had, to a certain extent at least, opted to accept the adjustment inflation that was already getting under way.

Moreover, in the course of 1958 the external economic situation eased, to the extent that the USA was hit by recession. On top of this came the fact that France, the European country facing the most serious problems with trade deficits, took steps to reduce the demand for German exports: in August 1957 it introduced measures to ration foreign currency[185] and the French franc was *de facto* devalued by 17 per cent[186] (taxes on imports and export subsidies), followed by a genuine depreciation of 15 per cent in December 1958.

All the various half-point cuts in the discount rate—on 5 September 1956, 10 January and 18 September 1957, and on 16 January and 26 June 1958—and the final reduction by a quarter of a point on 8–9 January 1959, to the post-war record low of just 2.75 per cent, were to a great extent motivated by external economic considerations. In each case, the arguments of those who voted against, on the other hand, related to the domestic economy. For example, at the Central Bank Council meeting on 26 June 1958 it was argued that a wave of discount-rate cuts had occurred in other countries, a

---

[182] Cf. the Minutes of the 3rd Central Bank Council meeting held on 21–2 Aug. 1957 and the 249th Central Bank Council meeting held on 10 July 1957 (HA BBk B 330/Drs. 142 and 143).

[183] Cf. Kaplan and Schleiminger, 1989, pp. 262f.

[184] Cf. the Minutes of the 5th Central Bank Council meeting held on 18 Sept. 1957 (HA BBk B 330/Drs. 142).

[185] Cf. Kaplan and Schleiminger, 1989, pp. 263, 276.

[186] Cf. Emminger, 1986a, p. 88.

trend to which Germany must respond.[187] This motive manifested itself even more clearly at the Central Bank Council meeting held on 8–9 January 1959: following the 'transition to full convertibility [at the end of 1958], a further cut in the level of German interest rates is vital'.[188] Besides this, the view that cuts in short-term interest rates would increase the capacity of the capital market was also an important consideration; and, indeed, as interest rates fell, the capital market experienced its first bloom during the period 1957 to 1959. Yet it was also claimed that interest-rate cuts were appropriate to the domestic economic situation. In 1958 economic growth had fallen to just 3.5 per cent. In 1958 unemployment failed to decline (at 3.7 per cent), for the first time during the 1950s (see Table 1).

In 1959 and 1960 the next wave of buoyant economic activity rolled up. The rate of growth increased by more than 7.4 per cent to 9.0 per cent, the unemployment rate fell by more than 2.6 per cent to 1.3 per cent: over-full-employment had been achieved. Although wage growth remained moderate in 1959, at 5.4 per cent, collective wage bargainers did react to the tight labour market situation in 1960—typically, in the latter phase of the boom—with wage increases in excess of 9 per cent (see Table 1).

From the summer of 1959 the Central Bank Council became extremely worried about the overheating economy, and recognized the threat of inflation. As it was aware of the limited effectiveness of monetary policy restriction—the 'open flank' of the external economic position—it called on the Federal Government to pursue an anticyclical fiscal policy before itself raising interest rates. On 6 August 1959 Blessing and Vice-President Heinrich Troeger wrote a letter to Erhard, with copies sent to the Chancellor and the Minister of Finance, in which they identified the construction sector as being at the centre of the boom and called on the government to pursue an anticyclical public sector construction policy, including spreading public support for subsidized housing over a longer period. This, they argued, would avoid having to apply the brakes on credit, which would 'call into question the placing of government bonds', and would enable the 'quantity boom' (*Mengenkonjunktur*) to continue.[189]

Shortly afterwards the monetary authorities attempted once more to counter the inflationary threat, signs of which had already emerged, with measures oriented towards the domestic economy. Alongside other restrictive measures, e.g. promoting exports of money through swap transactions,

[187] Cf. the Minutes of the 26th Central Bank Council meeting held on 26 June 1958 (HA BBk B 330/Drs. 142).

[188] Minutes of the 38th Central Bank Council meeting held on 8–9 Jan. 1959 (HA BBk B 330/Drs. 142).

[189] HA BBk N–2/243.

the Central Bank Council raised the discount rate on 3 September 1959 from 2.75 per cent to 3 per cent, on 22 October to 4 per cent and on 2 June 1960 to 5 per cent. It noted that this created an incentive for interest-rate-induced capital imports, which came on top of those again speculating on an appreciation of the D-mark. It sought to counter this by imposing a ban on interest to keep out foreign money; this required the approval of the Federal Government, which was given. This amounted to a reversal of the trend towards economic liberalization and a renewed discrimination against international capital movements, which, upon the official transition to convertibility at the end of 1958, had only just been liberalized. In addition to its decision to raise interest rates, the Central Bank Council took steps on 2 June to dampen down bank liquidity: in particular, a rise in minimum reserve ratios on domestic and foreign deposits, although without fully utilizing its statutory scope (now 30 per cent). It also adopted a more active open market policy, within the framework of which the social security funds purchased a large volume of mobilization paper, and by freezing the 'Blessing billion'.[190]

One of the reasons for the failure of the 'credit-policy broadside'[191] of 2 June 1960 was the relaxation of the—until then restrictive—American credit policy initiated a week later (see Figures 1 and 2). The Bundesbank described this as a 'tragic coincidence'[192] that had practically pushed its restrictive credit policy 'out of the saddle'.[193]

At the behest of the Central Bank Council, Blessing wrote a letter to Adenauer (with copies sent to Ludwig Erhard and Franz Etzel) on 1 September 1960.[194] It was no longer possible, he wrote, effectively to counter inflation by credit-policy means alone. Instead it was not only necessary to reduce public spending to the absolute minimum, the surplus liquidity in the economy needed to be siphoned off by raising taxes and social insurance contributions. This would enable development aid to be increased which would alleviate the problem of foreign exchange surpluses.[195] A fiscal-policy

[190] This involved a voluntary commitment by the banks to retain in their possession DM 1 billion worth of mobilization paper, initially for two years, rather than being able, as was normal practice, to return them to the Bundesbank at any time in return for central bank money. This agreement served to restrict the free liquid reserves of the banks. In return, the Bundesbank refrained from imposing a further possible increase in minimum reserve ratios. Cf. Schmölders, 1968, p. 263.

[191] Emminger, 1986a, pp. 109f.

[192] Deutsche Bundesbank, Geschäftsbericht 1960, p. 5.

[193] Emminger, 1968, p. 14.

[194] Cf. HA BBk N–2/244.

[195] These had declined slightly, not on a cyclical pattern due to the boom, but merely because of a sharp rise in transfers and capital exports. Indeed, the surplus on the balance of trade had widened (see Table 3).

contribution to monetary stabilization by all tiers of German government of the order of DM 2 to 3 billion (GDP in 1960: DM 303 billion) was mentioned. The alternative was either adjustment inflation, or a fiscal pseudo-appreciation or an actual revaluation of the D-mark.

Back in December 1959 Emminger had put the issue of revaluation back on the Bundesbank's agenda. In his heavily revised paper of 20 January 1960, he expounded his view that this time it was not the deficits of European countries, but rather the balance of payments deficit of the USA that was the counterpart of Germany's surplus position. Given that this 'sick man' was unable to adjust its exchange rate, the problem was different from that in 1956–7. He argued in favour of a 7.7 per cent appreciation of the D-mark, i.e. from DM 4.20 to DM 3.90 per dollar.[196]

On 10 November 1960 the Bundesbank abandoned its orientation towards the domestic economy, which had once again failed, deciding on a cut of a full percentage point in the base rates; on 19 January 1961 this was followed by a further half-point reduction to 3.5 per cent.[197]

In February 1961 Bundesbank preparations for a further relaxation of the monetary stance led to conflict with the Federal Government. In confidential preliminary discussions both Erhard and the Minister of Finance Franz Etzel made their objections clear, and raised the prospect of an official veto. In contrast to previous cases, in this conflict it was the government representatives who played the part of the resolute defenders of domestic price stability; in the case of Erhard, albeit with the intention of underpinning the policy of domestic monetary stability with revaluation of the D-mark. Yet the Bundesbank was still determined to prevent precisely that. At heart, it had indicated with its discount-rate cuts that, contrary to the priorities it had always emphasized in public, defending the external stability of the currency had now moved into the foreground, whereas it had resigned and capitulated with respect to internal stability. It was clearly willing to accept the alternative to appreciation of the D-mark, i.e. adjustment inflation, and thus threw in its hand with Per Jacobsson, the head of the IMF, who had been arguing in favour of this strategy since 1956.

Erhard recognized, just as the central bank had in its earlier official pronouncements, that politicians and the population at large considered domestic price stability to be more important than retaining D-mark parities. He went on to the offensive, and on 20 February 1961 made the following

---

[196] Cf. HA BBk N–2/244. Cf. also Emminger, 1986*a*, pp. 106f.

[197] Erhard and Müller-Armack, his *Staatssekretär*, voiced reservations (albeit unofficially) about the first step, in particular its timing and magnitude, probably because this served to ease the external pressure for the D-mark revaluation they favoured. Government opposition to the second step was articulated more clearly, although once again without lodging an official veto, which would have served to suspend the decision for two weeks.

sharply worded declaration in a speech to the CDU parliamentary party: 'we have the Bundesbank, or Herr Blessing, to thank for these surpluses and the fact that we must pay a lot and that prices continue to rise'. Erhard criticized the relaxation of monetary policy initiated in November 1960 and wanted, in particular, to prevent the reduction in minimum reserve ratios planned for March. At a special meeting held on 25 February 1961 the Central Bank Council opted to take this step in any case, although the cut was moderate. It took the view that the Bank had to offset the withdrawal of bank liquidity observed at the time owing to the substantial capital exports (see Table 3), not least by means of a more active open market policy. During the discussion members of the Central Bank Council, in particular the Vice-President of the Bundesbank, Troeger, reacted vehemently to criticism from the Federal Government with a counter-critique:

the government, which desired full employment, has achieved full employment and is maintaining full employment, must pursue an active and conscious stabilization policy. It pursued this actively—the economic miracle; it must also pursue it negatively, if this is required by the economic situation. The fact that it is not doing so, that is our real dilemma [and not the appreciation question]. . . . Monetary policy is part and parcel of economic policy.[198]

After Blessing had received a number of disapproving phone calls from circles close to the governing CDU in the wake of Erhard's critique, he complained to Emminger: 'now they want to make me personally responsible, both for all price rises to come and for payments to the Americans and the rest of the world. By this means, the government is trying to save its own neck. I am not going to put up with it any longer. I am going to see the old man [Adenauer] and tell him I'm resigning.' Emminger, who, of his colleagues on the Board of Directors, had for some time had Irmler and, since 1960, also Wolf on his side on the question of revaluation,[199] answered: 'I do not approve the methods used by those in Bonn. But substantively I remain in favour of revaluation, primarily because otherwise the Bundesbank will be forced into a completely false position and will lose even more of its prestige. It is an impossible situation when the government is in favour of stability, whereas the central bank seemingly is not. We must get out of this position at all costs.'[200]

At a meeting held on 18 October 1960 to discuss the balance of payments surpluses and the question of revaluation, Adenauer made his position clear to his ministers Erhard, Etzel, and Heinrich von Brentano, and to

[198] Transcript of the special Central Bank Council meeting held on 25 Feb. 1961 (HA BBk B 330/175 l).

[199] Cf. Emminger, 1986a, p. 108.

[200] For all three quotes and the entire affair see Emminger, 1986a, pp. 122f.

Bundesbank President Blessing: 'I don't want to hear any more about appreciation until the general election [September 1961].' After that there was no basis for an objective debate on the Pros (Erhard) and Cons (Blessing) of currency appreciation. 'There was complete agreement that there can be no question of a revaluation'[201] was the pithy comment in the communiqué, whereby Erhard's agreement can only be understood as a contribution to mollifying the foreign exchange markets. Instead, assurances were given regarding the development aid favoured by the American government and efforts towards an anticyclical—i.e. restrictive—fiscal policy and a stability-promoting contribution by industry.

Just one day later, Erhard told the New York Herald Tribune that he was still in favour of an appreciation of the D-mark. Adenauer, under the influence of his advisers Abs and Pferdmenges from the banking sector and BDI President Berg, was particularly impressed by the following arguments against appreciation: first, even an exchange-rate adjustment upwards would cause concern among the German population, who, having experienced two currency reforms, were particularly sensitive about monetary stability. He felt that he could not afford this, as he wished to recommend his government for the next parliamentary election as a guarantor of stability. Secondly, currency appreciation would be interpreted as a hostile German act by western neighbouring countries. Thirdly, in the event of a deterioration in the global economic climate, German industry would not be able to bear the burdens resulting from currency appreciation.[202]

And indeed, in November 1960 the BDI proposed a 5-point programme as a contribution to price stabilization without appreciation: (1) an appeal to its members for price discipline; (2) a binding declaration of intent for industrial companies to purchase development-aid bills to the value of DM 1 billion (later DM 1.5 billion); (3) support for capital exports; (4) freezing part of investment capital with the Bundesbank; and (5) a gentlemen's agreement between the government and the construction industry concerning the postponement of construction projects that were not absolutely necessary. After an (alleged) promise by Adenauer to Fritz Berg that, in return, the D-mark would not be revalued was not honoured—by virtue of a cabinet decision on 3 March 1961, the D-mark was revalued by 5 per cent—Berg suspended the payments of DM 100,000 that German industry transferred every month to the CDU.[203]

---

[201] Both quotes and the entire affair are given in Emminger, 1986a, p. 118. That Blessing had considered revaluation necessary in a discussion with the Minister of Finance on 12 Sept. 1960, as Hentschel, 1996, p. 369, recently claimed to have discovered, must be a misperception on the part of the minister (Heinrich Krone) indicated by Hentschel as his source.

[202] Cf. 'Erhard For Revaluation of Currency', in: New York Herald Tribune, 20 Oct. 1960.

[203] On this section cf. Kaufmann, 1969, pp. 199ff.

In the run-up to the general election in November 1961, however, the CDU no longer had to dispense with financial election support from German industry. The choice of such a low revaluation rate in place of the rate of at least 10 per cent, preferably 15 per cent, considered necessary by the research department of the IMF,[204] went a long way towards taking account of industrial interests, and in no way led to anything like the catastrophe Berg had earlier repeatedly prophesied. It had, namely, been Adenauer himself who had blocked more far-reaching proposals that would not have been to the taste of industry, and who had chaired the decisive meeting on 28 February 1961 to prepare the cabinet decision. Adenauer's clever adviser Pferdmenges had paved the way for this with his reappraisal of the situation: he was no longer opposed to a revaluation. The most stubborn opponents of currency appreciation, Abs and Berg, had, significantly, not been invited. Erhard had wanted to propose a revaluation of 7.7 per cent, i.e. from DM 4.20 to DM 3.90 per dollar, in line with Emminger's suggestion of December 1959. Adenauer responded: 'why so complicated? It is much easier to do one's sums at DM 4.00 to the dollar, and we would be showing consideration to those affected.' Adenauer also abruptly dispensed with the idea of widening intervention bands instead of changing parities, according to Blessing's portrayal of the events, with the remark: 'then no one will know where he is. . . . After all firms must have a basis for their decisions.'[205]

One day earlier Blessing had rejected as 'rubbish' an alternative proposal to revaluation, namely, negative foreign-exchange rationing in order to deter short-term foreign money. At that point, Blessing, too, was no longer able to deny the necessity of currency revaluation: 'with a heavy heart and reluctantly, I concur'.[206] Following the official cabinet decision taken on 3 March 1961, that afternoon even the Central Bank Council explicitly approved the revaluation on a majority vote, although it was in fact merely obliged to record that the Federal Government had consulted the Bundesbank as required by law. In any case, the Central Bank Council had exhausted its scope for preventing the decision in favour of revaluation, and was clearly concerned about damage to the Bundesbank's reputation, the threat of which indeed existed, as the Minister of Economics Erhard had convincingly portrayed revaluation in public as a necessary measure for achieving economic stability.[207]

[204] Cf. James, 1996, pp. 113ff.
[205] Both quotes: Emminger, 1986a, pp. 124f.
[206] Quoted from Emminger, 1986a, p. 124.
[207] Blessing and virtually the entire Central Bank Council had, like Vocke before them, stubbornly opposed D-mark revaluation for years. In a joint press conference with Erhard immediately after revaluation, Blessing justified the year-long opposition of the Bank deutscher Länder/Bundesbank as follows: 'for a central bank—please understand this—the exchange-rate parity is sacrosanct and can only be changed once all the other means have not

d) Monetary policy without massive external pressure: 1961–7

The 5 per cent revaluation of the D-mark in March 1961 was seen by many, both in Germany and abroad, as inadequate. As a result, the foreign-exchange markets initially remained nervous. At the international level, however, energetic attempts were being made to calm the markets down. The governors of the leading central banks declared at their routine meeting at the Bank for International Settlements in Basle on 12 March 1961 'that further changes in exchange rates are under no circumstances to be expected'.[208] They reached agreement on short-term swap facilities with the help of which currencies coming under pressure were to be defended in future.[209]

At approximately that time, speculation on a further revaluation of the D-mark ended. This was partly because the Bundesbank relaxed its restrictive policy further. The purchasing rates for money market paper in the context of open market policy came down.[210] Finally, on 3 May 1961, it was decided to reduce the discount rate to just 3 per cent. Already, in February, March, and April 1961, the minimum reserve ratios on domestic deposits had been reduced. By contrast, as of 1 May 1961, the maximum permissible minimum reserve ratios were applied not only to the *increase* in foreign deposits—as had been the case since the start of 1960—but also to the *stock*. The banks were allowed, however, to subtract their stocks of bank deposits and money market investments abroad from the stock of foreign liabilities subject to the minimum reserve requirement (the so-called 'offsetting privilege'). Between May 1961 and June 1962 the Bundesbank undertook swap transactions at an unprecedented level.[211] This encouraged the holding of foreign exchange by the commercial banks rather than by the Bundesbank itself. The aim of this was again to block the inflow of liquidity from abroad,

---

brought success.' Blessing, 1966, p. 30; also printed in: Deutsche Bundesbank, Monatsbericht, Mar. 1961. As late as 17–18 Oct. 1960 at the Bundesbank Directorate and immediately prior to a decisive meeting with Adenauer on the question of revaluation on 18 Oct. 1960, and once again at the Central Bank Council meeting on 25 Feb. 1961, Blessing had threatened to resign if the D-mark were revalued. On 20 Feb. Erhard countered this by also threatening the parliamentary CDU that he would resign if the currency were *not* revalued. Cf. Emminger, 1986a, pp. 117f., 123 and James, 1996, p. 114. It was between these two poles that, on 28 Feb., Adenauer mediated the compromise of a 'weak' revaluation.

[208] Emminger, 1986a, p. 129.

[209] The exchange rate of the pound sterling was defended by means of this new stand-by mechanism until July 1961, with purchases totalling US $910 million, much of it from the Bundesbank. At the end of July the IMF moved to rescue the pound by offering medium-term drawing rights totalling US $2 billion.

[210] Cf. Deutsche Bundesbank, Geschäftsbericht 1960, pp. 47f.

[211] Cf. Müller, 1969, p. 13.

which was still substantial owing to the lower money market rates in the USA (see Figure 2). At the very least, it can be said that all these monetary-policy measures were justified in external economic terms.

In the second half of 1961 the capital account (short- and long-term) moved sharply into deficit. Indeed, following the surplus of DM 2.3 billion in 1960, it closed 1961 with a deficit of DM 5 billion, although this was partly because of the policy of repaying post-war debts before they were due. This, alongside an increase in the deficit on transfer account, also reflected a massive increase in German development aid, to a total volume of DM 4 billion.[212] In view of the easing of the external economic position, as of 1 February 1962 the minimum reserve ratios on foreign deposits were more than halved compared with their maximum level, bringing them below the rates on domestic deposits.

In 1962 the interest-rate differential *vis-à-vis* the USA was practically non-existent (see Figure 2). The current account also normalized from mid-1961. The surplus of DM 5.6 billion in 1960 was reduced to DM 4.0 billion in 1961, and in 1962 a slight deficit was actually recorded (minus DM 0.7 billion) (see Table 3). Substantial surpluses were not posted again until 1967. Indeed, during the cyclical upturn of 1965 Germany actually posted a deficit of DM 5.0 billion, indicating the absence of any 'tension between domestic monetary stability and balance of payments equilibrium' or of any conflict between 'external and internal equilibrium', phrases used by Blessing in June 1958 and January 1961, respectively, i.e. prior to the revaluation of the D-mark.[213] Of course, this was not merely a result of the modest 5 per cent revaluation, which, according to calculations by IMF experts, meant that German exports were 10 per cent lower than they would have been in the absence of revaluation;[214] it also reflected the fact that the revaluation had come so late that adjustment inflation, the alternative to revaluation, had already made its effects felt in the years 1960 to 1962, with annual wage growth of around 10 per cent and above, whereas in other industrialized countries, particularly the USA, wage cost trends had been far less stormy during these three years. Unit labour costs in West Germany rose by a total

---

[212] In Feb. 1961 the new US administration under President Kennedy had called on the German government—in the light of a 1960 balance of payments surplus of around DM 8 billion (currency account)—to participate in fair burden sharing. To this extent Emminger was correct to see the surpluses that preceded revaluation of the D-mark as the 'mid-wife of a systematic development aid policy' by the Federal Republic. Cf. Emminger, 1986a, p. 114.

[213] Speech given to the Deutscher Sparkassentag on 20 June 1958 in Cologne, published in: Blessing, 1960, p. 149. Speech given on 23 Jan. 1961 in Milan, published in: Blessing, 1966, p. 20. Here he also spoke about the Janus-faced nature of credit policy—'one face looks inward, the other outward' (p. 26) and the 'problem of internal equilibrium versus external equilibrium' (pp. 28f.).

[214] Cf. Emminger, 1986a, p. 133.

of 14 per cent, compared with just 8.6 per cent in the UK and minus 2 per cent in the USA.[215] This was also reflected in price trends. The rise in the cost of living accelerated continuously from less than 1 per cent in 1959 to around 3 per cent in 1962 and remained more or less at that level until 1966 (see Table 1).

When, at the end of 1963 and the start of 1964, speculative capital inflows once more began to disturb the external equilibrium, the minimum reserve ratios on foreign deposits were again raised to the maximum of 30 per cent (as of 1 April 1964), at which level they remained for almost three years. In order to regain the state of 'all quiet on the external front', fiscal and administrative measures were deployed to control international capital transactions. In 1963 the US administration announced an *Interest Equalization Tax*, which came into force retrospectively in 1964. In 1965 'voluntary' controls on capital exports from the USA were added; in 1968 they were made compulsory. Conversely, the German government announced the coupon tax law (*Kuponsteuergesetz*) in March 1964, which came into effect on 27 March 1965, with the aim of discouraging capital imports. It imposed a tax of 25 per cent on capital yields for fixed-interest securities issued by German institutions and held by non-residents.

The Bundesbank tolerated creeping inflation without imposing serious restrictions on the domestic economy over a period of several years. Blessing gave the following explanation for this in April 1962: 'if we want to have the advantages of integration, i.e. substantial foreign trade, the free flow of money and capital, and, resulting from this, a high standard of living, we must, so to speak, accept the disadvantages of integration, i.e. our behaviour must conform to the balance of payments. . . . National monetary policy can successfully counter creeping inflation only if the leading foreign partners also pursue a correspondingly restrictive monetary policy.'[216] At the time he conceded that the problem of monetary stability had not been satisfactorily solved. 'But I am not without hope that the problem can be mastered and that creeping inflation need not be our fate. . . . We, the central bank, are standing at arms.'

It stayed standing in this position for a number of years. The discount rate remained unchanged at 3 per cent until the start of 1965. This meant that financial institutions could refinance themselves at the Bundesbank at a real interest rate of zero, or close to zero. A similar situation had only occurred during the first year following the outbreak of the Korean War, when the discount rate—which had actually been raised substantially—implied a

---

[215] Cf. Emminger, 1986a, p. 165.
[216] Speech to a conference held by the Friedrich-Naumann Foundation in Bad Kreuznach on 6 Apr. 1962; published in: Blessing, 1966, pp. 101f. For the following quote cf. pp. 105f.

negative real interest rate on rediscount credits. In both cases, at least until February 1964, the day-to-day money rate was almost consistently below the discount rate (see Figure 3) so that it was cheaper for the financial institutions to refinance themselves on the private money market than at the central bank. This changed in the economic boom of 1964–5, to which pre-election gifts by the government, in particular in the form of tax cuts and higher social spending, made a substantial contribution in 1965. As the central bank began to apply the brakes, central government put its foot on the accelerator in pro-cyclical fashion. The central government budget deficit rose from DM 1 to DM 2 billion, and the overall public sector deficit from 1.2 to 1.9 per cent of GDP (see Table 1). It was the first cyclical upturn since that immediately following the currency reform that was driven not primarily by exports, but rather by domestic demand. It was this that caused the current account to move into deficit during the second half of 1964 and led to the above-mentioned deficit of DM 5 billion in 1965. The resulting foreign-exchange losses served to reduce bank liquidity substantially.

From March 1964 the day-to-day money rate was consistently above the discount rate despite the fact that the latter was raised to 3.5 per cent on 21 January 1965 and to 4 per cent on 12 August 1965 (see Figure 3). Rising base rates had been required for domestic economic reasons for some time, but were now, given the current account deficit, also in line with external economic requirements. However, even the higher discount rate implied zero or negative real discount rates, for in December 1965 the inflation rate was running at 4.2 per cent (year-on-year figure). During this phase it made sense for the banks to refinance themselves at the Bundesbank rather than on the private money market. Accordingly, the volume of Bundesbank refinancing rose—from DM 1.9 billion at the end of 1963—by DM 2 billion in 1964, DM 1.6 billion in 1965 and DM 2.6 billion in the first half of 1966.[217]

The Bundesbank was particularly concerned about wage growth, which was twice the rate of productivity growth (see Table 1), and the rise in the cost of living, which, at a year-on-year figure of 4.5 per cent in April 1966, had reached its highest level since the Korean War. On top of this came the further rise in the central government budget deficit, although the deficits of the other public sector budgets narrowed slightly. On 27 May 1966 the Central Bank Council decided unanimously on a further increase in the discount rate to 5 per cent.[218] Although this meant an end to the quasi-

[217] Cf. Deutsche Bundesbank, Geschäftsbericht 1964, p. 44; Geschäftsbericht 1965, p. 51 and Geschäftsbericht 1966, p. 40.
[218] Indeed, a proposal for a two-point increase was put up for discussion at this meeting of the Central Bank Council (HA Bbk B 330/431).

subsidization of the banks in the form of zero real interest rates for rediscount credits, the Central Bank Council had still not fully utilized its scope for raising the discount rate so as to moderate the demand for refinancing credits, as the day-to-day money rate remained above this level until the end of the year (see Figure 3). Yet the rise in the discount rate had once again placed the Bundesbank in a dilemma. It certainly managed to curb the momentum of the domestic economic boom, all the more so given that the capital market rate rose more or less in parallel to the discount-rate hikes, namely from 6.2 per cent in 1964 to 6.8 per cent in 1965 and 7.8 per cent in 1966.[219] Inflation, too, weakened sharply in the second half of 1966. Yet in the end this trend led to the mini-recession of 1967, the first time that the west German economy experienced a negative rate of economic growth.

The last of the above-mentioned increases in the discount rate led to renewed conflict with Bonn. Criticism of the high interest rate policy came not only from the Federal Government, but also from the spokesmen of the SPD opposition on economic policy, Karl Schiller and Herbert Ehrenberg, and the organizations representing the business community and the press, which normally supported the Bundesbank.[220] A few weeks prior to the fall of Chancellor Erhard in November 1966, the Federal Government publicly demanded that the Bundesbank end its restrictive stance.[221] Blessing was subsequently to concede that in 1966 he had attempted 'to put things in order with an element of brute force'.[222] Rumours went around that Blessing had brought about Erhard's fall.[223] Kurt Georg Kiesinger, the new Chancellor of the Grand Coalition, too, immediately—in his inaugural address to parliament—demanded a rapid end to the credit restrictions. However, in view of the fact that the new government still had to put its finances in order, and that wage growth was still not commensurate with monetary stability, the Central Bank Council did not allow itself to be impressed by this at its next meeting on 15 December 1966, nor by the presence of the new Minister of Economics, Schiller, and his call for a cut in interest rates. Although it sent out a signal in the form of a small cut in minimum reserve ratios that came into effect on 1 December 1966, it was not until 5 January 1967 that it took the first cautious step on interest rates, cutting the discount rate by half a percentage point (15 votes to 3 with 2 abstentions). It was argued that confidence in the Bundesbank must not be endangered and that it must therefore proceed with caution. A further relaxation would only be

---

[219] Cf. Deutsche Bundesbank, 1988, p. 207. Running yield on domestic fixed-interest securities; annual average figures.
[220] Cf. Caesar, 1981, p. 189.
[221] Cf. Holtfrerich, 1988, p. 146.
[222] Cf. Brawand, 1971, p. 56.
[223] Cf. Wildenmann, 1969, p. 14.

advisable once progress had been made on the questions of the budgets and wage growth, and once interest rates abroad had likewise fallen, as otherwise there would be an outflow of liquidity. These were the main arguments with which a more far-reaching cut of one point in the discount rate was voted down.[224] The relaxation of the policy stance continued in the following months, bringing the discount rate back to 3 per cent on 11 May and reducing the minimum reserve ratios on domestic and foreign deposits to a record low on 1 September. From August 1967 the Bundesbank maintained its policy of reducing interest rates by means of purchases on the open market.

At the start of the relaxation policy, the Federal Government took the fiscal-policy steps called for by the Bundesbank, among other things in the form of a budgetary stabilization law pushed quickly through parliament in December 1966. Schiller, who wanted to trigger a 'tailor-made upturn' by means of the government's demand-stimulation programmes of January and July 1967, publicly criticized this slow approach in April 1967 and opposed, albeit unsuccessfully, the re-appointment of Blessing as Bundesbank President, who faced re-election in 1967.[225]

This was partly because, in the spring of 1967, the Bundesbank initially rejected Schiller's plan for a second demand-stimulation programme to fight the recession, whereby this time it received support from employers, and was attacked by the trade unions. In the event, however, it was willing to provide moderate support, as it had done for the first programme, by boosting bank liquidity, among other things by incorporating medium-term fixed-rate notes with a maximum period to maturity of 18 months into the regulation of the money market.[226] Conflict also arose at this point in time over the final stages in the preparation of the Stability and Growth Act of 8 June 1967: the Federal Government wanted to make new credit-policy instruments available to the Bundesbank, but wanted a say in their deployment in return ('two-key principle'). In view of this the Bundesbank declined to accept the instrument of a 'credit ceiling' offered to it.[227]

In the course of 1967 the west German current account moved sharply into the black (see Table 3). The influx of foreign currency filled up the liquidity reserves of the banks in lasting fashion in the form of holdings of foreign currency (see Tables 2 and 3), effectively removing them from

---

[224] Cf. the Minutes of the 230th Central Bank Council meeting held on 5 Jan. 1967 (HA BBk B 330/Drs. 142).

[225] Cf. Holtfrerich, 1988, p. 146.

[226] Cf. Oberhauser, 1976, pp. 627f. and Deutsche Bundesbank, Geschäftsbericht 1967, p. 50.

[227] Cf. Stern *et al.*, 1972, p. 370. More generally on the Stability and Growth Act, cf. Abelshauser, 1987, pp. 163ff.

Bundesbank control. On the other hand, the surplus on the current account was completely offset by capital exports in 1967. In the main, this was due to the low level of interest rates in Germany and rising rates in the USA and the UK (which devalued the pound sterling by 14.3 per cent in November).[228]

Yet this dampening of domestic economic activity led to a massive shift on the current account, which swung around from a deficit of DM 5 billion in 1965 to a surplus of DM 1.7 billion in 1966 as a whole. And this surplus was merely the forerunner of surpluses of DM 11.4 billion in 1967 and DM 13.2 billion in 1968 (see Table 3). In the second half of 1966 alone this implied inflows of liquid funds to the banks totalling DM 3.6 billion.[229] About half of this figure was used to reduce their refinancing obligations to the Bundesbank, and the remainder to bolster their free liquid reserves, which in the course of the economic boom had contracted from DM 20 billion in January 1964 to DM 17 billion one year later, DM 15 billion in January 1966 and to as little as DM 11 billion in June of that year. Consequently, the liquidity ratio, i.e. free liquid reserves as a proportion of bank deposits, experienced an even sharper decline. It fell from 13.9 per cent in January 1964 to 10.6 per cent one year later, to 8.3 per cent in January 1966 and finally to a low of 5.8 per cent in June 1966. By January 1968 the free liquid reserves had once again risen to DM 33 billion and the liquidity ratio to 14.9 per cent (see Figure 4).[230] The banks had accumulated this liquidity mainly in the form of short-term bank deposits and money market assets abroad, which were subsidized by the Bundesbank in the form of concessions regarding the minimum reserve requirements ('offsetting privilege') and the form correspondingly taken by the swap rates in order to neutralize liquidity inflows. The decisive factor behind the substantial export of money, however, was the sharp relaxation of Bundesbank monetary policy in response to the 1967 recession, while at the same time interest rates were rising in the USA and the UK (see Figures 1 and 2).[231] This expansionary monetary-policy phase, too, was in line with the requirements of both internal monetary stability and the balance of payments.

To summarize, as early as the mid-1960s it was clear that the policy of controlling the banks' free liquid reserves had failed: despite the substantial dampening of the free liquid reserves, between the start of 1964 and the first half of 1966 the banks expanded lending (and thus also money) at annual growth rates of 13–14 per cent virtually without any restraint (see

---

[228] Cf. Emminger, 1986a, p. 137.
[229] Cf. Deutsche Bundesbank, Geschäftsbericht 1966, p. 37.
[230] Cf. also Deutsche Bundesbank, Geschäftsbericht 1966, p. 41.
[231] Cf. Deutsche Bundesbank, Geschäftsbericht 1967, pp. 49f.

Table 2).[232] The monetary policy concept had proved to be, as Schlesinger put it, a '*Milchmädchenrechnung*' (lit. a milk-maid's calculation; a naive miscalculation).[233]

Nor could it be claimed that, during this period, the Bundesbank had effectively and at the right time deployed its most important interest-rate instrument, the discount rate, in order to ensure domestic stability, i.e. to fight creeping inflation and to dampen down the economic boom, although it certainly had considerable scope for such action. When, in the spring of 1964, the banks began to demand a substantial volume of refinancing credits from the Bundesbank as the economy started to boom, it refrained from deploying this, its central interest-rate-policy instrument. It also permitted the banks to obtain DM 2.2 billion of central bank money in 1964 and DM 1.9 billion in 1965 by returning open market paper to the Bundesbank.[234] Sharply restrictive measures were applied only to inflows of liquidity from abroad (minimum reserve ratios at the maximum permissible level, swap policy); otherwise it relied on the liquidity-reducing impact of the coupon tax law. As far as the domestic economy was concerned, the Bundesbank limited itself to the traditional role of a central bank, namely that of lender of last resort for domestic financial institutions. In doing so, it was prepared to accept a certain degree of adjustment inflation. Along with the Federal Government, it rejected the idea of establishing an external economic buttress for a stability policy oriented towards the domestic economy, as called for by the Council of Economic Experts in its first Annual Report for 1964/5, with its proposal for a transition to floating exchange rates.[235] Although it was never explicitly formulated as such—least of all by Blessing, whose policy, however, showed this to be his view—annual inflation at a rate of 3 per cent was considered to be better than a 3 per cent p.a. revaluation of the D-mark, with all the consequences for German exporters

[232] Cf. also Deutsche Bundesbank, Geschäftsbericht 1966, pp. 46f. Narr-Lindner, 1984, also comes to the conclusion that monetary policy failed during this period, as does Kohler, 1979, also for the periods of restriction in 1959–60 and 1969–71.

[233] Interview given to the author on 3 Mar. 1997. As early as 1968, Emminger had noted that the experience of Bundesbank liquidity policy since 1958 had shown 'that sometimes an extraordinarily long braking-distance is necessary before the central bank's liquidity policy affects credit provision, currency in circulation and finally total effective demand in the economy. There is no direct relationship between central bank liquidity policy, on the one hand, and currency in circulation and total effective demand, on the other. Rather, the two are connected by a highly elastic rubber band.' Emminger, 1968, p. 28.

[234] Cf. Deutsche Bundesbank, Geschäftsbericht 1964, p. 44 and Deutsche Bundesbank, Geschäftsbericht 1965, p. 51.

[235] Cf. Sachverständigenrat, Jahresgutachten 1964/5, pp. 132ff. For the rejection of the proposal by the government, see pp. 146ff. Emminger, too, distanced himself from this proposal. Cf. Emminger, 1986*b*, pp. 75ff.

forecast by the IMF experts for the 1961 revaluation. The centrality of the goal of price stability had been called into question.

e) An attempt to resolve the dilemma: 1968–70

The situation changed in 1968. The current account surplus increased further against the background of price stability at home and inflationary trends abroad (USA: 4.1 per cent, budget deficits owing to the Vietnam War; UK: 4.9 per cent following the 14.3 per cent devaluation of the pound in November 1967; France: 4.6 per cent, exploding wages following the student unrest of May 1968 and the subsequent general strike; Japan: 5.5 per cent). Although the export of longer term capital also increased sharply, the position on the short-term capital account reversed on the previous year with a swing of DM 14 billion, recording a marked surplus. This involved an inflow of speculative funds, largely from France.

On top of this came the weakness of the dollar, the anchor currency of the Bretton Woods system. Its gold backing had become so thin that as early as 30 March 1967, following American threats of a partial troop withdrawal, Blessing assured the chairman of the Federal Reserve Board in a letter that in future the Bundesbank did not intend to exchange dollars for gold at the US Treasury. This was the precise reverse of the policy urged by Pfleiderer in 1957, and consistently pursued by Vocke. In 1968 the Bundesbank even declared its willingness to purchase 500 million dollars-worth of medium-term US Treasury bonds ('Roosa Bonds') to help ease American balance of payments problems.[236] The thin gold backing on which the international monetary system hung became even more apparent when, under the pressure of speculative demand for gold, in mid-March 1968 intervention by the western central banks on the London gold market was suspended and from then on the free gold price rose via the parity between gold and the dollar. This was the beginning of the end of the Bretton Woods system.

This time, the Central Bank Council initially refrained from deploying the minimum reserve ratio as an instrument to prevent an inflow of liquidity from abroad. Instead, in the first week of September 1968, as the foreign-currency 'wave' once again rolled towards the Federal Republic, the Bundesbank called on the Federal Government to revalue the D-mark in order to buttress its stability policy on the external front. Prior to this, not only Emminger and Irmler, but also Blessing had argued on the Central Bank

---

[236] Cf. James, 1996, p. 192. In 1971 Blessing admitted being 'personally guilty' of contributing by this means to the inflationary trend in Germany and the world. Cf. Brawand, 1971, p. 61.

Council for a D-mark revaluation and had managed to convince the majority of this necessity. Although the Council of Economic Experts, in a confidential special report, had also recommended the same measure, Schiller rejected the idea as 'an absurdity'.[237] Even a coordinated change in the exchange rates of the weak French franc and the strong D-mark, involving a devaluation and revaluation respectively of around 5 per cent could not overcome the opposition of Schiller and the Finance Minister, Franz Josef Strauß: the plan had been agreed in mid-November 1968 between the two central bank governors following a renewed wave of speculation. (In the first 20 days of November alone, the Bundesbank was forced to purchase DM 8.6 billion of foreign currency; this despite exporting DM 3.5 billion in the form of swap transactions.) The following monetary conference of the so-called Group of 10, held in Bonn on 20 November 1968, was confronted with the decision by the west German government to undertake merely a 'pseudo-revaluation': a special duty on exports and a tax allowance on imports, each of 4 per cent, were introduced. As had been the case at the time of the revaluation of 1961, this measure was inadequate, and not only in purely quantitative terms. For it affected only the trade balance and not, as in a normal revaluation, the entire current and capital accounts. The foreign ministers of finance and central bank governors were dismayed. Blessing had left the conference in anger 'because he didn't want to listen to the complaints of his foreign colleagues any longer'.[238] Emminger, who took his place, considered the meeting to be 'the most unpleasant monetary conference I ever attended'.[239] On television, Kiesinger declared that 'as long as I am head of this government as Chancellor, there will be no revaluation of the D-mark'.[240] He was subsequently unable to abandon his position until the end of his period in office—his party lost the general election at the end of September 1969—although he himself actually favoured revaluation.

On the day after the monetary conference, the Bundesbank, at the request of the Central Bank Council, distanced itself in a communication to the Chancellor and the two ministers responsible, as was subsequently leaked, from the official claim made by the government that the pseudo-revaluation had been decided 'in close agreement with the Bundesbank'. The Central Bank Council considered the pseudo-revaluation to be 'a pseudo-solution that, while it points in the right direction, does not appear suited to the task of lastingly calming the current unrest on the foreign exchange

[237] Cf. Emminger, 1986*a*, p. 141.
[238] Baring, 1982, p. 143.
[239] Emminger, 1986*a*, p. 146.
[240] Quoted in Emminger, 1986*a*, p. 143.

markets'.[241] Through their spokesmen, Helmut Schmidt and Rainer Barzel, the heads of the parliamentary SPD and CDU/CSU attacked the Central Bank Council for having 'stabbed its own government in the back' and for having 'left it in the lurch' respectively.[242] In the wake of this, calls were made for restrictions on the statutory independence of the Bundesbank.[243]

In France, de Gaulle accordingly rejected devaluation of the franc. Although the Group of 10 had promised him an extraordinarily large standby loan of 2 billion dollars, he ordered a rigorous policy of currency rationing, import quotas and export subsidies. Finally, however, at the start of August 1969, the French franc was indeed devalued by 11.1 per cent.

On the day after the currency conference, the minimum reserve ratio on the growth of the banks' foreign deposits was set at 100 per cent as of 1 December 1968 in order to prevent an inflow of money from abroad.[244] On 20 February 1969 the Central Bank Council decided, on a majority vote, to urge the government to replace the pseudo-revaluation by a genuine D-mark revaluation of more than 4 per cent. It was well aware of the fact that otherwise any restrictive domestic measure—and, in view of the booming economy, such measures were urgently needed—would be undermined by virtue of the external position.[245] Yet conversely, it was also argued on the Central Bank Council during this phase that a low rate of interest, by promoting capital exports, would in the current context have a more restrictive impact than a high rate of interest. In other words, the Bundesbank could only exert a restrictive effect on the banks' liquidity position by means of a 'perverse' deployment of its interest-rate policy. Thus the central bank had clearly recognized the necessity of underpinning, on the external front, by means of currency appreciation, attempts to dampen down the domestic economy by raising the cost of credit.

In March 1969 the Cabinet did nothing more than introduce fiscal-policy restrictions and steps to liberalize imports, namely freeze DM 1.8 billion of central government spending, utilize some of the additional tax revenue to repay foreign debts, and increase the existing import quotas.[246] After this,

[241] Minutes of the 277th Central Bank Council meeting held on 21 Nov. 1968 (HA BBk B 330/Drs. 142).

[242] Quoted in Emminger, 1986a, p. 147. On this 'tragi-comedy in three acts' see also Roeper, 1978, pp. 161ff.

[243] Cf. Caesar, 1981, p. 190.

[244] This was possible only because the ratios on the stock of foreign deposits were still low, and thus on average the maximum rates specified under the Bundesbank Act were not exceeded. Following the amendment of the Bundesbank Act on 22 July 1969, a 100 per cent minimum reserve on the growth of foreign deposits was possible without this affecting the existing maximum ratios.

[245] Cf. Emminger, 1986a, p. 150.

[246] Cf. Roeper, 1978, p. 164.

it was repeatedly pointed out on the Central Bank Council that abandoning the goals of 'external equilibrium' and 'price stability' in favour of maintaining the exchange-rate parity could not be reconciled with the Stability and Growth Act. It was argued that it was necessary to overcome the fundamental external economic disequilibrium in order to ensure domestic stability by means of either fiscal or monetary measures.

In March, Schiller was converted from Saul to Paul, and himself called for revaluation because he had recognized the inadequacy of the pseudo-revaluation.[247] He asked Emminger, an old friend of Kiesinger's, to win the Chancellor over to the idea of revaluation. The two duly met, but without the desired result. In any case, Strauß remained in the camp of those opposed to revaluation. He wanted to counter internal disequilibrium with restrictive fiscal-policy measures, and external disequilibrium by bringing forward foreign debt repayments.[248] Schiller, on the other hand, saw a threat to 'social symmetry', because, in view of the explosion of corporate profits, not least from exports, and the moderate collective agreements binding for a period of two to three years, a social 'bomb' was ticking; this duly exploded in September 1969, in the form of wild-cat strikes.

Yet no revaluation occurred until after the general election of 28 September. Instead, the revaluation question became election issue No. 1, and thus a question of party politics. The SPD and FDP, with the support of almost all economists and a broad section of public opinion, together with the Bundesbank as a silent ally, argued in favour of D-mark revaluation as a means of defending domestic monetary stability. With the backing of the usual interest groups, in particular the BDI, the CDU/CSU defended the stability of the exchange-rate parity. Even Karl Klasen and Wilhelm Vocke declared themselves publicly against revaluation.[249] The voters decided against an absolute majority for the Christian Democrats, their election goal, and thus ushered in the first social-democrat/liberal coalition government.

On 16 April 1969 the Central Bank Council had started to introduce restrictive interest-rate-policy measures. In the presence of Strauß and other opponents of revaluation, who raised no objections, the Council pushed up the discount rate from 3 to 4 per cent; the external economic scope for this appeared to have been provided by rising base rates in the USA and other countries. At the start of May, however, a new wave of speculation hit the D-mark. In the light of this, the Central Bank Council meeting held on

---

[247] This is confirmed by both Baring, 1982, p. 143 and Emminger, 1986a, p. 151.
[248] Cf. Baring, 1982, pp. 143f.
[249] Klasen and Franz Heinrich Ulrich (both members of the Board of Deutsche Bank) in a letter to the Börsenzeitung, 15 May 1969, and Vocke, Wilhelm: Richtige Paritäten—eine Utopie (Correct parities—utopia), in: Handelsblatt, 9–10 May 1969.

8 May 1969 again called on Schiller, the Minister of Economics, who was in any case open to the idea, to bring about a revaluation. The Minister of Finance, Strauß, let it be known to the Central Bank Council that he was opposed only to a unilateral D-mark revaluation, not to a multilateral adjustment of parities. Discussions also took place at that time on the Central Bank Council on closing the foreign exchange markets. On 1 June and 1 August the minimum reserve ratios on both domestic and foreign deposits were increased. Further discount-rate hikes were announced by the Central Bank Council on 19 June (to 5 per cent) and on 10 September 1969 (to 6 per cent) in order to force the Federal Government to revalue the currency.[250] That this occurred so shortly before the election date on 28 September— this was what was so unusual—was, given the prevailing external and internal economic dilemma, virtually a political decision by the Central Bank Council against the CDU/CSU.

To a far greater extent than the rise in interest rates, two other events led to the next major currency crisis: the resignation of de Gaulle on 27 April 1969 and a speech given by Strauß in Munich on 28 April 1969, in which he announced that if the currency were to be revalued it would have to be by at least 8 per cent. And besides, he was, he stated, opposed only to D-mark revaluation in isolation, not to a multilateral correction of exchange rates. In other countries, particularly in the English press, this was played up as a recognition of the necessity of revaluation.[251] Between 28 April and 9 May 1969 the Bundesbank faced an influx of DM 17 billion worth of foreign currency, the greatest wave of speculation against the D-mark exchange-rate up to that time. Schiller and Blessing again argued in favour of revaluation. At its meeting on 8 May the Central Bank Council voted unanimously in favour of this. Following preliminary discussions in a small group (with Blessing, Emminger, and Irmler), the Cabinet decided on 9 May, in the presence of Blessing, not to revalue the D-mark, 'finally, unequivocally and eternally' as the government spokesman, Conrad Ahlers (SPD), put it, to the great amusement of the attendant journalists.[252]

Instead of revaluation, the Federal Government merely introduced the following measures: the premature repayment of foreign debts, the consol-

---

[250] Cf. Baring, 1982, p. 145. To this extent it can be claimed that the Bundesbank contributed to the fall of the Kiesinger government, which had pinned its colours to non-revaluation. Cf. Emminger, 1986a, p. 168ff.

[251] Cf. Emminger, 1986a, pp. 153f. Excerpts from the speech were published by the Ministry of Finance in: Finanznachrichten, no. 97, 29 Apr. 1969.

[252] Cf. Baring, 1982, p. 145 and Emminger, 1986a, p. 156. Once again, this policy was in accordance with the wishes of BDI-President Berg and Abs. Of Germany's leading business managers, the President of the DIHT, Wolff von Amerongen, was one of the few who favoured D-mark revaluation.

idation of central government debts and the imposition of an anticyclical reserve (*Konjunkturausgleichsrücklage*), which, in accordance with the Stability and Growth Act, was to be frozen at the Bundesbank and later repaid. In fact, together with the Cabinet decision of 9 May, this initially served to calm speculation to some extent, and foreign capital was withdrawn from Germany once more. Shortly before the general election, however, a renewed wave of speculation set in. Three days before the election the government submitted to Bundesbank pressure and closed the official foreign-exchange markets. They were re-opened on the day after the election, but the government temporarily freed the Bundesbank from its obligation to intervene with respect to the dollar.[253] In the following weeks the value of the dollar fell to DM 3.70. Shortly after the new government under Brandt/Scheel took office, the D-mark parity was raised by 9.3 per cent from DM 4.00 to DM 3.66 per dollar. At the same time the measures taken under the pseudo-appreciation were reversed. This marked the return of the D-mark to the fixed-exchange-rate system of Bretton Woods.[254]

In the subsequent weeks more than DM 20 billion of speculative foreign capital left the country. This put a heavy strain on the Bundesbank's foreign-exchange reserves. For the first time in the entire post-war period, it was forced to draw on its IMF quota. This outflow of foreign capital also squeezed bank liquidity and induced the Central Bank Council to take a number of measures to bolster liquidity, including cuts in the minimum reserve requirements. With a view to the persistent price and wage inflation, however, interest-rate policy initially remained restrictive. Following the wild-cat strikes, the demand-pull inflation had given way to a wage-push inflation that was to continue in subsequent years. Emminger saw this, almost certainly correctly, as a consequence of the substantial delay in revaluing the currency.[255]

Because of the distinct narrowing of the current account surpluses in 1969 and 1970 and the fact that the capital account ran a record deficit in 1969, the external economic position once more offered the Bundesbank scope for a dear-money policy. On 4 December the Central Bank Council, in an unusual step, raised only the Lombard rate to 9 per cent. On 8 March 1970 the base rates were raised to a then unprecedented level in the history of the D-mark: the discount rate stood at 7.5 per cent and the Lombard rate at 9.5 per cent.

[253] The IMF agreed to this. Only the European Commission was opposed, out of concern about the Common Market and the Common Agricultural Policy. It would have preferred adjustment inflation. Cf. Emminger, 1986*a*, p. 162.

[254] This time neither the Netherlands nor any other country allowed its currency to revalue alongside the D-mark.

[255] Cf. Emminger, 1986*a*, p. 166.

Owing to the high German interest rates, in 1970 the deficit on the long-term capital account narrowed sharply from more than DM 23 billion in the previous year to less than DM 1 billion (see Table 3). The US Federal Reserve switched from a high to a low-interest-rate policy for domestic economic reasons, reducing the yield on the money market (for 3-month treasury bills) from 8 per cent in January 1970 to as low as 3 per cent in March 1971. Consequently, the American banks reduced their considerable volume of foreign debt on the Eurodollar market (by DM 13 billion in 1970) and thus flooded Europe with liquidity. The greater part of this flowed into the Federal Republic as short-term capital: in 1970 the short-term capital account ran a surplus of almost DM 18 billion (see Table 3). In 1970 the Bundesbank's foreign assets virtually doubled, despite the fact that the Central Bank Council began to cut interest rates in the second half of the year. Although it was able to reduce the free liquid reserves of the banks —primarily by raising the minimum reserve requirements—by one-third (see Table 2)—indeed, from May 1969 to May 1970 by more than one half, from DM 19 to 41 billion—bank lending continued to expand strongly, at a rate of more than 10 per cent. In particular, the monetary authorities proved unable to rein in wage growth; at around 14 per cent, the rise in gross hourly wages in 1970 almost reached the rate experienced during the Korea boom of 1951, while the rise in unit labour costs, at 11.6 per cent, was an all-time record (see Table 1). In spite of this, the adjustment inflation was not high enough to spoil the poker game of international investors betting on D-mark appreciation. The next international currency crisis, in 1971, was thus inevitable.

Neither central government nor the other areas of the German public sector made a fiscal-policy contribution to economic stabilization. In 1970 government budgets slid from small surpluses the previous year into a slight deficit (see Table 1). This was despite the fact that rapid economic growth, together with inflation, now running at more than 3 per cent, had led to a more than proportional rise in tax revenue. Fiscal policy was prevented from contributing to monetary stabilization by substantial wage rises in the public sector and the expansionary social policy pursued by the social-democrat/ liberal coalition. In the form of a non-repayable 'business cycle surcharge' on top of income tax (*Konjunkturzuschlag*) deposited with the Bundesbank, the Federal Government, in line with its responsibility under the Stability and Growth Act, made a completely inadequate attempt to dampen the booming economy, amounting to only DM 2.2 billion.[256]

[256] Cf. Deutsche Bundesbank, 1988, p. 28.

5. Conclusion

Between 1951 and 1970 it was not the west German central bank that was the most important source of bank liquidity and monetary growth, but rather what Otmar Emminger called the '*Ersatz-Notenbank*', the 'substitute central bank', i.e. the inflow of foreign exchange from abroad. Between the end of 1950 and the end of 1970 the central bank money stock rose, albeit with substantial fluctuations, from DM 11.4 billion to DM 67.8 billion, i.e. by DM 56.4 billion. Of this, DM 50.6 billion, i.e. around 90 per cent, came about by virtue of the increase in foreign currency reserves and other foreign assets of the Bank deutscher Länder/Bundesbank.[257]

In the face of this influx of foreign exchange—in the 1950s primarily from the current account and from the latter part of the 1950s, given *de facto* and later official convertibility of the D-mark, also from the capital account—the traditional measures of stability policy deployed by the central bank from 1955—increases in the discount rate and minimum reserve ratios or sales on the open market—were inadequate to prevent creeping inflation. Any liquidity tied up, any growth of the money stock or liquidity prevented by these measures was far more than offset by the 'substitute central bank'. If, back in the second half of the 1950s, the Bank deutscher Länder/Bundesbank had not only imposed higher minimum reserve requirements on foreign deposits (as of 1 May 1957) in order to stem the inflow of foreign currency, but had also deployed swap transactions on a massive scale, rather than merely deploying the traditional instruments of a domestically oriented restrictive monetary policy (as in 1955–6 and 1959–60), it would have tackled the problem of monetary stability at its roots. It could have done more for price stability in the second half of the 1950s and subsequently than it actually achieved if it had geared its policy to balance of payments equilibrium instead of pursuing a monetary policy that was, on the surface, oriented towards the domestic economy, but which was always doomed to failure under the pressure exerted by the balance of payments.[258] From 1955 it repeatedly found itself on the 'horns of a dilemma' owing to the structurally inappropriate orientation of the monetary-policy instruments deployed towards the domestic economy. The most effective measure would have been a timely and appropriate revaluation of the D-mark. Yet this in-

[257] Calculated on the basis of Deutsche Bundesbank, 1988, pp. 20, 28f. Central bank money stock = currency in circulation + deposits of domestic financial institutions, domestic firms and private individuals with the Bundesbank (including the 'cash deposit' 1950).

[258] As early as 1969, Müller, 1969, p. 80, concluded from his study that, given fixed exchange rates, 'central bank policy can effectively control the direction and volume of capital transactions'. He also mentioned convertibility as a precondition for this, however.

strument was not at the disposal of the central bank. The fact that the Central Bank Council did not want to employ it at times—in 1956–7 unanimously and in 1959–61 the majority—is symptomatic of the inappropriate orientation of its instrument deployment towards the domestic symptoms of overheating, rather than towards their external economic causes.

Even in the Vocke era, when the Bank deutscher Länder, until the advent of *de facto* convertibility of the D-mark in 1955, still enjoyed scope for monetary-policy action with a primarily domestic economic impact, the Bank deutscher Länder did not achieve its policy aim of establishing an international 'stability advantage', and the associated international competitive advantages, primarily by virtue of a restrictive monetary policy in defence of domestic monetary stability. Although German interest-rate policy appeared restrictive in domestic terms compared with that in other countries, particularly the USA, relative to the dynamism of west German economic growth monetary policy was not restrictive, except during the foreign exchange crisis of 1950–1. After all, the economic actors that made the decisive contributions to achieving relative price stability in the Federal Republic during the 1950s were not the members of the Central Bank Council, but rather firms which ensured rapid productivity growth, the parties to collective wage agreements (who initially kept west German unit labour cost trends below those of Germany's main competitors under the system of fixed exchange rates[259]) and the Federal Government, which, by accumulating budget surpluses in the 'Juliusturm' to a maximum of DM 7.5 million in September 1956, tied up more liquidity than the Bank deutscher Länder managed from the end of 1950 to the end of 1956 by raising the minimum reserve requirements by DM 2.5 billion and by net purchases of securities on the open market (DM 0.9 billion).[260]

Thus Vocke's pride in the Bank deutscher Länder's gold holdings was just as naive as that of the classical mercantilists. The Central Bank Council claimed to have movements in the price level under control. In reality it was virtually helpless in the face of the growth of the money stock. Its greatest contribution to the 'economic miracle' was that it did not consider this monetary growth to be a problem for the maintenance of price stability, but rather, in accordance with its orientation towards real output, to be a lubricant for the economic boom, at least for as long as collective pay bargainers did not react with a corresponding increase in unit labour costs.[261]

[259] Cf. Lindlar and Holtfrerich, 1997, p. 235.

[260] The total increase in the minimum reserve requirement and the open market sales of the Bank deutscher Länder/Bundesbank were calculated on the basis of the Monthly Reports of the Bank deutscher Länder/Bundesbank for 1958.

[261] This was equivalent to the view propounded by Flassbeck, 1990, p. 30: 'a necessary

From the start of *de facto* convertibility in 1955, restrictive monetary-policy measures impinged primarily on the external position, in the form of an increase in west Germany's current and capital account surpluses; this, in turn, exerted an expansionary effect on the volume of domestic money and liquidity. This is why the contribution to monetary stability made by the 'Juliusturm' until 1956 could not be replaced by the imposition of strict credit restrictions in that year, and it was in 1956 that creeping inflation set in (see Table 1).

A slight change of regime occurred during the Blessing era, to the extent that the increase in the central bank money stock was no longer fed solely by foreign exchange surpluses. Between the end of 1958 and the end of 1969, the central bank money stock rose by DM 27.9 billion, whereas there was scarcely any increase in the currency reserves and other foreign assets of the Bundesbank. This meant that domestic financial institutions and firms exported money and capital to an extent almost equal to that of the foreign exchange surpluses of this period, i.e. invested a corresponding proportion of their resources in foreign assets (for the financial institutions, see Table 3). The Central Bank Council supported this trend, in general terms through a low discount rate of 3 per cent, which it maintained, for example, from May 1961 to January 1965 (whereby it was forced to accept a moderate adjustment inflation), and, more specifically, through foreign-currency swap transactions with financial institutions.[262] This effort must be considered far more important in monetary-policy terms than anything else that the Central Bank Council might have achieved with its other instruments in terms of exerting an influence on the growth of domestic credit and money creation by the banks.

The restrictive policy of 1969–70, in the course of which the discount rate was increased in a number of steps from 3 per cent on 20 March 1969 to 6 per cent on 10 September 1969,[263] was only seemingly a case of falling

condition for employment growth is . . . an expansion of monetary demand that exceeds the growth of nominal wages.'; cf. also Flassbeck, 1988.

[262] At the end of Nov. 1968 and in mid-June 1970, the Bundesbank also undertook so-called 'outright' forward exchange transactions in US dollars on the foreign exchange market. It is characteristic of the lack of attention the Central Bank Council paid to instruments other than the standard tools of central bank policy that it was not the Central Bank Council itself that set the rates for swap transactions; this was left to the Bundesbank Directorate.

[263] This was followed by a further discount-rate hike to a record level of 7.5 per cent on 8 Mar. 1970. However, in this case the Central Bank Council acted not only with a view to the very sharp rise in domestic prices then under way, but also out of concern for the external position. Following the revaluation, after all, almost DM 20 billion worth of speculative funds had flowed out of the Federal Republic once more. The 'basic balance', too, the sum of the current account and the long-term capital account, had been seriously in the red during the first half of 1970. Cf. Deutsche Bundesbank, Geschäftsbericht 1970, p. 87.

back into old ways, and a reflection of the still existent structurally inappropriate orientation of the instruments deployed by the Bundesbank. This is due to a fundamental difference from the, in policy terms, similar course steered in 1955–6 and 1959–60: this time, the Central Bank Council had earlier argued in favour of deploying instead the most effective instrument to regain external economic equilibrium, namely D-mark revaluation at an early stage. By its restrictive policy—this time fully aware of its inappropriateness—the Central Bank Council intended to exacerbate the external economic crisis, in order to force the Federal Government to revalue the currency.

When Karl Klasen assumed the post of Bundesbank President in January 1970, he interpreted the Bundesbank's task of 'safeguarding the currency' differently from all his successors since then. He accorded economic growth equal priority to monetary stability. He recalled that not only inflation, but also unemployment had been 'a trauma' for the German people.[264] His preference for the term 'autonomous' over 'independent' to describe the status of the Bundesbank can be taken as indicating that he wished to pursue stability policy in cooperation and coordination with the Federal Government and its fiscal and other economic policies.

The key conclusion of my contribution is as follows. During the period of fixed exchange rates, the predominant policy mix, against the background of relatively moderate wage growth, consisted of an interaction between monetary and fiscal policy that, given a stability-oriented, contractive fiscal policy, especially until 1956, permitted a relatively expansionary monetary policy fed by foreign exchange surpluses, without endangering or missing by too great a margin the goal of price stability.[265] Even increases in the discount rate had an expansionary effect, because they generated balance of payments surpluses. Owing to the 'open external economic flank', after 1955 the Central Bank Council for long periods lacked the scope for pursuing a monetary policy able to effectively counter symptoms of domestic overheating. Even when and where it had such scope, it did not fully utilize it: for example, in boom phases it frequently held the discount rate below the day-to-day money rate (see Figure 3) and thus softened the restrictive impact of high day-to-day money rates. With respect to the minimum reserve ratios on domestic deposits, too, it never fully utilized the statutory maximum of 20 or 30 per cent; indeed, it remained substantially below this limit throughout the entire period.[266] Such behaviour implies that the Bundesbank was focusing on its function as lender of last resort.

[264] Cf. Marsh, 1992, p. 64.
[265] Dürr, 1966, pp. 160ff., comes to a similar conclusion.
[266] Cf. Deutsche Bundesbank, 1988, pp. 186f.

Instead, during this period fiscal policy assumed responsibility not only for promoting growth and employment, but also for ensuring price stability at times in which the macroeconomic equilibrium was threatened. Conversely, in taking its decisions on monetary policy the Bank deutscher Länder/Bundesbank had a view not only of ensuring price stability, but also of output-related goals. Thus the various institutional actors and instruments of economic policy assisted each other and cooperated.[267]

In the early 1970s a fundamental change occurred in the division of tasks between the institutions responsible for fiscal and for monetary policy. On the one hand, it was observed 'that the Federal Government did not wish to have its fiscal-policy scope restricted by virtue of an orientation towards monetary stability, and left the task of achieving price stability to the Bundesbank alone.'[268] On the other hand, following the breakdown of the Bretton Woods system, the Bundesbank enjoyed far greater scope for an autonomous monetary policy, having been freed from its obligations to intervene in defence of a fixed parity between the D-mark and the dollar. From that point on, the Bundesbank concentrated on fighting inflation, with its policy of monetary targeting.[269]

[267] Of course, this cooperation was not always without friction. As late as 1971–2 most actors within the Bundesbank considered coordination between the various economic policy institutions as a necessary condition for a successful stabilization policy, while the chances of a policy of monetary targeting, although under discussion, were still viewed with scepticism. In July 1971 the Bundesbank propounded the following view in its Monthly Report, on the question of cooperation with fiscal policy and other policy areas in the fight against inflation: 'the experience of the last 20 years has also shown, though, that credit-policy measures, together with an economic and fiscal policy pulling in the same direction, can, in the final analysis, dampen down these excesses and regain a better equilibrium in the economy, at least if it is not prevented from doing so by external economic influences.' Deutsche Bundesbank, 1971*a*, p. 19. In 1972, against the background of the then high rate of inflation, Heinrich Irmler stated his view that fiscal policy had the special task of playing its part in the fight against inflation, by working towards substantial budget surpluses that are then to be neutralized. Cf. Irmler, 1972, pp. 160f. In justifying this view he pointed not only to the limitations on the Bundesbank in fighting inflation owing to external ties and developments, but also the Bundesbank's concern to avoid abrupt changes in interest-rate trends. If quantitative fluctuations in the supply of money can only be avoided at the price of abrupt changes in interest rates, the Bundesbank would be expected to prefer a degree of interest-rate continuity.

[268] Woll and Vogl, 1976, p. 145. Cf. also Marsh, 1992, p. 37: 'the shift towards a [Bundesbank] policy giving unambiguous priority to maximizing price stability came only towards the end of the Bretton Woods system, when the commitment to steady exchange rates was necessarily downgraded.'

[269] This had been recommended by the Council of Economic Experts in its Annual Report for 1974/5, paras 364ff. Monetary policy should, to a considerable extent, free fiscal policy from responsibility for anticyclical policy. And indeed, since then, those responsible for fiscal policy have largely withdrawn from this field and have moved on to an expansionary course— one characterized by persistent budget deficits—that has continued until the present day. This is clearly revealed by the fact that, between 1950 and the first half of the 1970s, total

Since the end of the system of fixed exchange rates, the Central Bank Council has no longer hesitated to allow interest rates to rise rapidly, an option that had previously not been available to it for external economic reasons, in order to keep to its monetary target. Its new monetary policy strategy caused it to neglect what it itself had previously recognized as expedient in terms of real output and had actively practised, and what the leading commentators of the Bundesbank Act formulated as follows as late as 1973:

restrictions on liquidity and interest-rate hikes have a bad name in terms of preventing precisely those forms of investment that enable rapid productivity growth and thus help to prevent inflation. To the extent that monetary measures are considered suitable at all in such a case [namely, given full employment, maintaining the growth of aggregate demand within the limit set by productivity growth in order to avoid inflation; C.-L. H.], it has been widely recommended that the formation of savings capital be stimulated rather than the formation of real capital hindered.[270]

With a view to Mundell's theory, as described in the introduction, it can be concluded that, until the dissolution of the system of fixed exchange rates, the Bank deutscher Länder/Bundesbank was repeatedly forced under the pressure of foreign exchange surpluses to orient monetary policy entirely towards maintaining external equilibrium, whereas fiscal policy and collective pay bargaining, in accordance with Mundell's theory, made decisive contributions to domestic economic equilibrium (price stability, full employment, and economic growth). This was a central pillar of the relatively successful economic policy pursued until 1970.[271]

---

government debt in the Federal Republic, expressed as a percentage of GDP, revealed no trend towards expansion, remaining consistently slightly below 20 per cent (see Table 1), whereas this figure has increased more than threefold since then. Comparable time-series data for other industrialized countries reveal broadly similar structural breaks at more or less the same time. It can be concluded from this that there was an international cause behind this phenomenon: this cause was the breaking of the Bretton Woods system. That this structural discontinuity is able to explain on a global scale the more aggressive incomes policy pursued by trade unions in the 1970s has been shown by Holtfrerich, 1982.

[270] Spindler *et al.*, 1973, p. 21.

[271] During the last 25 years the reverse distribution of roles called for by floating exchange rates has been recognized neither by monetary, nor by fiscal and incomes policy. The, on average, higher rates of inflation, lower rates of growth and still rising unemployment rates can be seen as the outcome of this 'new' but incorrect 'assignment' of economic policy tasks since 1974. Cf. Kloten *et al.*, 1985, pp. 392, 395; and Kloten *et al.*, 1980, pp. 77ff. A further cause resides in the absence of intensive cooperation between those institutions responsible for monetary and fiscal policy and pay determination. Symptomatic of this in Germany is the fact that the 'economic cabinet', which used to come together almost once a month to discuss policy with the Bundesbank presidents, has, since 1970, met only once a year to discuss the government's Annual Report on the economy (information from the Federal Chancellery).

6. Sources and bibliography

Unpublished sources

Bank of England Archive (BoE)
Bundesarchiv Koblenz and Berlin
Historisches Archiv der Deutschen Bundesbank (HA BBk)

Bibliography

Abelshauser, Werner (1982): Ansätze 'korporativer Marktwirtschaft' in der Korea-Krise der frühen fünfziger Jahre, in: Vierteljahrshefte für Zeitgeschichte 30, pp. 715–56
Abelshauser, Werner (1983): Wirtschaftsgeschichte der Bundesrepublik Deutschland (1945–1980), Frankfurt a.M.
Abelshauser, Werner (1987): Die Langen Fünfziger Jahre. Wirtschaft und Gesellschaft der Bundesrepublik Deutschland 1949–1966, Düsseldorf
Bank deutscher Länder (1955): Statistisches Handbuch der Bank deutscher Länder 1948–1954, Frankfurt a.M.
Bank deutscher Länder (various): Auszüge aus Presseartikeln
Bank deutscher Länder (various years): Geschäftsberichte, Frankfurt a.M.
Baring, Arnulf (1982): Machtwechsel. Die Ära Brandt-Scheel, Frankfurt a.M.
Berger, Helge (1997): Konjunkturpolitik im Wirtschaftswunder. Handlungsspielräume und Verhaltensmuster von Bundesbank und Regierung in den 1950er Jahren, Tübingen
Blessing, Karl (1960): Die Verteidigung des Geldwertes, Frankfurt a.M.
Blessing, Karl (1966): Im Kampf um gutes Geld, Frankfurt a.M.
Bockelmann, Horst (1996): ³Die Deutsche Bundesbank, Frankfurt a.M.
Borchardt, Knut (1971): Realkredit- und Pfandbriefmarkt im Wandel von 100 Jahren, in: 100 Jahre Rheinische Hypothekenbank, Frankfurt a.M., pp. 105–96
Brawand, Leo (1971): Wohin steuert die deutsche Wirtschaft? Munich
Brehmer, Ekhard (1964): ²Struktur und Funktionsweise des Geldmarktes der Bundesrepublik Deutschland seit 1948, Tübingen
Buchheim, Christoph (1990): Die Wiedereingliederung Westdeutschlands in die Weltwirtschaft 1945–1958, Munich
Bundesarchiv (1982, 1984, 1997) (ed.): Die Kabinettsprotokolle der Bundesregierung, vols. 1, 2, and 9, Boppard am Rhein
Caesar, Rolf (1981): Der Handlungsspielraum von Notenbanken. Theoretische Analyse und internationaler Vergleich, Baden-Baden
Carstens, Reimer (1963): Die Aufwertungsdebatte, Tübingen
Deutsche Bundesbank (1961): Änderung des Wechselkurses der DM, in: Monatsbericht 13, 3, pp. 3–5
Deutsche Bundesbank (1965): Methodische Erläuterungen zur Analyse der Bankenliquidität, in: Monatsbericht 17, 4, pp. 29–37
Deutsche Bundesbank (1971a): Längerfristige Entwicklung des Geldvolumens, in: Monatsbericht 23, 7, pp. 11–28
Deutsche Bundesbank (1971b): Die währungspolitischen Institutionen und Instrumente in der Bundesrepublik Deutschland, Frankfurt a.M.
Deutsche Bundesbank (1976): Deutsches Geld- und Bankwesen in Zahlen 1876–1975, Frankfurt a.M.
Deutsche Bundesbank (1988): 40 Jahre Deutsche Mark. Monetäre Statistiken 1948–1987, Frankfurt a.M.

Deutsche Bundesbank (various): Auszüge aus Presseartikeln

Deutsche Bundesbank (various years): Geschäftsberichte, Frankfurt a.M.

Deutsche Bundesbank (various): Monatsberichte

Deutscher Sparkassen- und Giroverband (various years): Jahresberichte

Dickhaus, Monika (1996): Die Bundesbank im westeuropäischen Wiederaufbau. Die internationale Währungspolitik der Bundesrepublik Deutschland 1948 bis 1958, Munich

Dreißig, Wilhelmine (1976): Zur Entwicklung der öffentlichen Finanzwirtschaft seit dem Jahre 1950, in: Deutsche Bundesbank (ed.): Währung und Wirtschaft in Deutschland 1876–1975, Frankfurt a.M., pp. 691–744

Dürr, Ernst (1966): Wirkungsanalyse der monetären Konjunkturpolitik, Frankfurt a.M.

Ehrlicher, Werner (1994): Finanzpolitik seit 1945, in: Schremmer, Eckart (ed.): Steuern, Abgaben und Dienste vom Mittelalter bis zur Gegenwart, Stuttgart, pp. 213–47

Emmer, Robert E. (1955): West German Monetary Policy, 1948–54, in: Journal of Political Economy 63, pp. 52–69

Emminger, Otmar (1957): Internationaler Währungsfonds und Wechselkurspolitik, in: Zeitschrift für das gesamte Kreditwesen 10, pp. 732–6

Emminger, Otmar (1968): Zwanzig Jahre deutsche Geldpolitik. Rückblick und Ausblick, Stuttgart

Emminger, Otmar (1970): Zahlungsbilanz- und währungspolitische Probleme des internationalen Kapitalverkehrs, in: Zeitschrift für das gesamte Kreditwesen 23, pp. 1067–73

Emminger, Otmar (1986a): D-Mark, Dollar, Währungskrisen. Erinnerungen eines ehemaligen Bundesbankpräsidenten, Stuttgart

Emminger, Otmar (1986b): Ordnungs- und währungspolitische Probleme der Korea-Krise, in: Carstens, Karl et al.: Die Korea-Krise als ordnungspolitische Herausforderung der deutschen Wirtschaftspolitik. Texte und Dokumente, Stuttgart

Erhard, Ludwig (1953): Deutschlands Rückkehr zum Weltmarkt, Düsseldorf

Flassbeck, Heiner (1988): Preise, Zins und Wechselkurs. Zur Theorie der offenen Volkswirtschaft bei flexiblen Wechselkursen, Tübingen

Flassbeck, Heiner (1990): Geldwertstabilität in Raum und Zeit. Skizzen zu einem Zwei-Phasen-Konzept wirtschaftlicher Entwicklung in der Bundesrepublik Deutschland (und der Welt), in: Riese, Hajo/Spahn, Heinz-Peter (eds.): Geldpolitik und ökonomische Entwicklung. Ein Symposion, Regensburg, pp. 24–32

Geiger, Till/Ross, Duncan M. (1991): Banks, Institutional Constraints and the Limits of Central Banking: Monetary Policy in Britain and West Germany, 1950–52, in: Jones, Geoffrey (ed.): Banks and Money: International and Comparative Finance in History, Ilford, pp. 138–156

Gesetz über die Deutsche Bundesbank vom 26. Juli 1957, in: Bundesgesetzblatt 1957, part I, pp. 745–6 (Bundesbank Act)

Gesetz zur Förderung der Stabilität und des Wachstums der Wirtschaft vom 8. Juni 1967, in: Bundesgesetzblatt 1967, part I, pp. 582ff. (Stability and Growth Act)

Giersch, Herbert/Paqué, Karl-Heinz/Schmieding, Holger (1992): The Fading Miracle. Four Decades of Market Economy in Germany, Cambridge

Goodman, John B. (1992): Monetary Sovereignty. The Politics of Central Banking in Western Europe, Ithaca

Hagemann, Walter (1984): Von der Ordnungs- zur Konjunkturpolitik. Zur Funktionsentwicklung staatlicher Wirtschaftspolitik in Westdeutschland von 1948–1967, Essen

Hahn, L. Albert: Kapitalausfuhr (1960): Illusion und Wirklichkeit, in: Die Zeit vom 15. Juni 1958; reproduced in: Hahn, L. Albert (1960): Geld und Kredit. Währungspolitische und konjunkturtheoretische Betrachtungen, Frankfurt a.M., pp. 137–47

Hahn, L. Albert (1963): Über monetäre Integration, in: Hahn, L. Albert: Fünfzig Jahre zwischen Inflation und Deflation, Tübingen, pp. 200–18

Harmening, Rudolf/Duden, Konrad (1949): Die Währungsgesetze. Handausgabe mit ausführlicher Erläuterung der Umstellungsvorschriften, Munich

Hentschel, Volker (1988): Die Entstehung des Bundesbankgesetzes 1949–1957. Politische Kontroversen und Konflikte, in: Bankhistorisches Archiv 14, pp. 3–31, 79–115

Hentschel, Volker (1989): Die Europäische Zahlungsunion und die deutschen Devisenkrisen 1950/51, in: Vierteljahrshefte für Zeitgeschichte 37, pp. 715–58

Hentschel, Volker (1996): Ludwig Erhard. Ein Politikerleben, Munich

Hölscher, Jens (1990): Krisenmanagement und Wirtschaftswunder. Die Überwindung der Zahlungskrise 1950/51, in: Riese, Hajo/Spahn, Heinz-Peter (eds.): Geldpolitik und ökonomische Entwicklung. Ein Symposion, Regensburg, pp. 33–43

Hölscher, Jens (1994): Entwicklungsmodell Westdeutschland. Aspekte der Akkumulation in der Geldwirtschaft, Berlin

Holtfrerich, Carl-Ludwig (1982): Wechselkurssystem und Phillips-Kurve, in: Kredit und Kapital 15, pp. 65–89

Holtfrerich, Carl-Ludwig (1988): Relations between Monetary Authorities and Governmental Institutions. The Case of Germany from the 19th Century to the Present, in: Toniolo, Gianni (ed.): Central Banks' Independence in Historical Perspective, Berlin/New York, pp. 105–59

Holtfrerich, Carl-Ludwig (1995): Die Deutsche Bank vom Zweiten Weltkrieg über die Besatzungsherrschaft zur Rekonstruktion 1945–1957, in: Gall, Lothar *et al.*: Die Deutsche Bank 1870–1995, Munich, pp. 409–578

Irmler, Heinrich (1972): The Deutsche Bundesbank's Concept of Monetary Theory and Monetary Policy, in: Brunner, Karl (ed.): Proceedings of the First Konstanzer Seminar on Monetary Theory and Monetary Policy, Supplement 1 of Kredit und Kapital, Berlin, pp. 137–164

Issing, Otmar (1995): [10]Einführung in die Geldtheorie, Munich

James, Harold (1996): International Monetary Cooperation since Bretton Woods, Washington D.C.

Kaplan, Jacob J./Schleiminger, Günther (1989): The European Payments Union. Financial Diplomacy in the 1950s, Oxford

Kaufmann, Hugo M. (1969): A Debate over Germany's Revaluation 1961. A Chapter in Political Economy, in: Weltwirtschaftliches Archiv 103, pp. 181–212

Kennedy, Ellen (1991): The Bundesbank. Germany's Central Bank in the International Monetary System, London

Kloten, Norbert *et al.* (1980): Zur Entwicklung des Geldwertes in Deutschland. Fakten und Bestimmungsgründe, Tübingen

Kloten, Norbert/Ketterer, Karl-Heinz/Vollmer, Rainer (1985): West Germany's Stabilization Performance, in: Lindberg, Leon N./Maier, Charles S. (eds.): The Politics of Inflation and Economic Stagnation, Washington D.C., pp. 353–402

Koerfer, Daniel (1987): Kampf ums Kanzleramt. Erhard und Adenauer, Stuttgart

Kohler, Reinhard (1979): Grenzen der Bundesbankpolitik. Wirkungsanalysen restriktiver Zentralbankpolitik 1959–1974, Berlin

Kühne, Rudolf (1984): Die Regelungen für den Außenwirtschaftsverkehr unter der Geltung der besatzungsrechtlichen Devisenbewirtschaftungsgesetze, Frankfurt a.M. (printed as manuscript; Bibliothek der Deutschen Bundesbank)

Landeszentralbank von Niedersachsen (1957): Geschäftsbericht für das Geschäftsjahr 1956, Hannover

Lindlar, Ludger (1997): Das mißverstandene Wirtschaftswunder. Westdeutschland und die westeuropäische Nachkriegsprosperität, Tübingen

Lindlar, Ludger/Holtfrerich, Carl-Ludwig (1997): Geography, Exchange rates, Trade Structures: Germany's Export Performance since the 1950s, in: European Review of Economic History 1, pp. 217–46

Ludwig-Erhard-Stiftung (1986) (ed.): Die Korea-Krise als ordnungspolitische Herausforderung der deutschen Wirtschaftspolitik. Texte und Dokumente, Stuttgart

Marsh, David (1992): Die Bundesbank. Geschäfte mit der Macht, Munich

Morawietz, Markus (1994): Rentabilität und Risiko deutscher Aktien- und Rentenanlagen seit 1870: unter Berücksichtigung von Geldentwertung und steuerlichen Einflüssen, Wiesbaden

Müller, Heinz (1969): Die Politik der deutschen Zentralbank 1948–1967. Eine Analyse der Ziele und Mittel, Tübingen

Mundell, Robert A. (1960): The Monetary Dynamics of International Adjustment under Fixed and Flexible Exchange Rates, in: Quarterly Journal of Economics 74, pp. 227–57

Mundell, Robert A. (1962): The Appropriate Use of Monetary and Fiscal Policy for Internal and External Stability, in: IMF Staff Papers 9, pp. 70–9

Mundell, Robert A. (1963): Capital Mobility and Stabilization Policy under Fixed and Flexible Exchange Rates, in: Canadian Journal of Economics and Political Science 29, pp. 475–85

Narr-Lindner, Gudrun (1984): Grenzen monetärer Steuerung. Die Restriktionspolitik der Bundesbank 1964–1974, Frankfurt a.M.

Nicholls, Anthony James (1994): Freedom with Responsibility. The Social Market Economy in Germany, 1918–1963, Oxford

Oberhauser, Alois (1976): Geld- und Kreditpolitik bei weitgehender Vollbeschäftigung und mäßigem Preisanstieg (1958–1968), in: Deutsche Bundesbank (ed.): Währung und Wirtschaft in Deutschland 1876–1975, Frankfurt a.M., pp. 609–42

Riese, Hajo (1990): Das Forschungsprojekt 'Geldpolitik als Grundlage der ökonomischen Entwicklung der Bundesrepublik Deutschland', in: Riese, Hajo/Spahn, Heinz-Peter (eds.): Geldpolitik und ökonomische Entwicklung. Ein Symposion, Regensburg, pp. 2–17

Ritschl, Albrecht (1985): Die Währungsreform von 1948 und der Wiederaufstieg der westdeutschen Industrie, in: Vierteljahrshefte für Zeitgeschichte 33, pp. 136–65

Roeper, Hans (1978): Die D-Mark. Vom Besatzungskind zum Weltstar, Frankfurt a.M.

Sachverständigenrat zur Begutachtung der gesamtwirtschaftlichen Entwicklung (various years): Jahresgutachten, Stuttgart

Schmölders, Günter (1968): [2]Geldpolitik, Tübingen

Spindler, Joachim von/Becker, Willy/Starke, O.-Ernst (1973): [4]Die Deutsche Bundesbank. Grundzüge des Notenbankwesens und Kommentar zum Gesetz über die Deutsche Bundesbank, Stuttgart et al.

Statistisches Bundesamt (1952): Statistisches Jahrbuch für die Bundesrepublik Deutschland, Stuttgart

Stern, Klaus/Münch, Paul/Hansmeyer, Karl-Heinrich (1972): [2]Gesetz zur Förderung der Stabilität und des Wachstums der Wirtschaft, Stuttgart

Stolper, Wolfgang F./Roskamp, Karl W. (1979): Planning a Free Economy: Germany 1945–1960, in: Zeitschrift für die gesamte Staatswissenschaft 135, pp. 374–404

Stucken, Rudolf (1964): [3]Deutsche Geld- und Kreditpolitik 1914 bis 1963, Tübingen

Swoboda, Alexander K. (1973): Monetary Policy under Fixed Exchange Rates. Effectiveness, the Speed of Adjustment and Proper Use, in: Economica 40, pp. 136–54

Temin, Peter (1995): The 'Korea boom' in West Germany. Fact or Fiction?, in: Economic History Review 48, pp. 737–53

U.S. Bureau of the Census (1975): Historical Statistics of the United States. Colonial Times to 1970, Washington D.C.

Vocke, Wilhelm (1956): [2]Gesundes Geld. Gesammelte Reden und Aufsätze zur Währungspolitik, Frankfurt a.M.

Vocke, Wilhelm (1973): Memoiren, Stuttgart

Wallich, Henry C. (1955): Triebkräfte des deutschen Wiederaufstiegs, Frankfurt a.M.

Wildenmann, Rudolf (1969): Die Rolle des Bundesverfassungsgerichts und der Deutschen Bundesbank in der politischen Willensbildung. Ein Beitrag zur Demokratietheorie, Stuttgart

Wissenschaftlicher Beirat beim Bundesministerium für Wirtschaft (1973): Sammelband der Gutachten von 1948 bis 1972, ed. Bundesministerium für Wirtschaft, Göttingen

Woll, Artur/Vogl, Gerald (1976): Geldpolitik, Stuttgart

VIII. A New Approach to Monetary Policy (1971–8)

By Jürgen von Hagen

1. Introduction

In the 1970s a new monetary policy era began in Germany. After a quarter century during which the D-mark had been tied to the US dollar and the Bundesbank had virtually lost control of the money supply, in March 1973 the Bundesbank was relieved of its obligation to intervene on the foreign exchange markets with respect to the dollar. While this did not mean complete freedom from exchange-rate constraints, the strongest and most immediate external pressure had been removed. New paths opened up for monetary policy.

Before it was able to develop new concepts and strategies, the Bundesbank first had to establish its position, not least within Germany itself, as the leading body responsible for monetary policy. In retrospect, it is all too easy for the observer to conclude that the Bundesbank used its newly won freedom to establish a new regime of monetary control, symbolized by the announcement of monetary targets. Yet did the Bundesbank really pin its colours to the mast of price stability and a rules-based monetary policy, rather than succumbing to the temptation of short-term fine-tuning of aggregate demand on the Keynesian model?

Closer analysis reveals that this picture is too simple. During the 1970s the policy of monetary targeting was in many respects an experiment, and was certainly not unanimously accepted by policy makers. The first announcement of a monetary target constituted an attempt to depart from a stringent stability policy in a 'moderate' fashion. In the following years monetary policy can scarcely be said to have followed a medium-term orientation. In the final analysis one is forced to the conclusion that the survival of monetary targeting was due primarily to the fear that, if the Bundesbank had refrained from announcing a monetary target shortly before the start of the new European Monetary System (EMS), this would have created the impression that the Bundesbank had abandoned its stability-oriented stance. Is it the case then that the Bundesbank stumbled into the path that was subsequently to prove the right one, rather than consciously taking it?

This article describes developments during the years 1971 to 1978. The fact that the Bundesbank made available to the author a comprehensive range of sources means that monetary policy can be portrayed as the outcome of the decisions taken by the Bundesbank's Central Bank Council. On the one hand, this paints a subjective picture, for we do not allow other economic policy actors much space to state their case. On the other hand, and in accordance with the intentions of this book, an impression is given of the convictions and the doubts that played their part in the formulation of monetary policy during this period. Taking Niehans' view that monetary policy is, in the final analysis, a man-made 'art',[1] an understanding of the motives behind the decisions taken is necessary for an understanding of any monetary policy epoch. This analysis reveals that neither of the two metaphors—the conscious decision to take the new path, nor the stumbling into it—does justice to actual developments.

The portrayal of the period 1971–8 that follows is divided into three phases. The inflationary disequilibrium of the years 1971 and 1972 marks the point of departure. The subsequent phase, until 1974, marks a period of monetary policy emancipation and monetary stabilization. The years 1975 to 1978, finally, constitute a development phase towards a new concept of a policy of monetary stabilization. This article closes with the start of the EMS.

2. Powerless in the face of disequilibrium: German monetary policy at the start of the 1970s

a) The German economy in disequilibrium

At the start of the 1970s the Federal Republic of Germany found itself in a state of economic disequilibrium. Social conflict over income distribution created inflationary impulses, while the freedom of monetary policy action was tightly circumscribed by the exchange-rate system and the limited opportunities for the central bank to act.

Figure 1 shows the broad economic trends during this phase.[2] The stabilization at a high rate of growth in 1970 and 1971 was followed by a renewed upturn in 1972. Inflation, which reached 8 per cent in 1970 and 1971, eased

---

[1] Cf. Niehans, 1978, p. 336.
[2] Growth and inflation are measured in terms of the rates of growth of real GDP and of the GDP deflator.

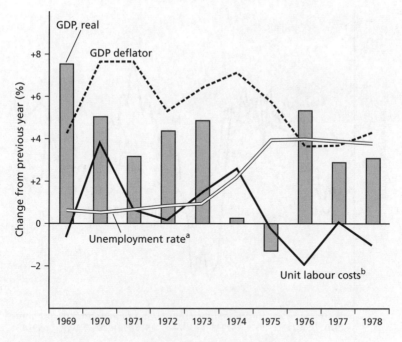

FIGURE 1: Economic indicators

[a] Unemployed as % of total labour force (employed and unemployed).
[b] Labour costs per unit of nominal GDP.

to 5 per cent in 1972, only to rise again to 7 per cent by 1974. All this was against the background of full employment. The Council of Economic Experts described the labour market in 1970 as 'swept clean'.[3]

High wage demands reflected the desire of the trade unions to shift the distribution of national income in favour of workers.[4] This is evident from the 'unit labour costs' curve in Figure 1, i.e. wage growth minus productivity growth. The collective bargaining strategy pursued by the trade unions was supported by the full-employment guarantee given by the government under Willy Brandt.[5] In 1971, in particular, wage growth constituted an important cause of inflation.[6] In the expectation of being able to pass on higher wages in the form of higher prices, employers put up little resistance to the trade unions' pay demands.[7]

---

[3] Cf. Sachverständigenrat, Jahresgutachten 1970/1, p. 15.

[4] Cf. Deutscher Gewerkschaftsbund, 1970.

[5] Cf. Sachverständigenrat, Jahresgutachten 1970/1, paras. 48ff.; Jahresgutachten 1971/2, paras. 64ff.

[6] Cf. Deutsche Bundesbank, Geschäftsbericht 1970, p. 8 and Deutsche Bundesbank, Geschäftsbericht 1971, p. 13.

[7] Cf. Sachverständigenrat, Jahresgutachten 1971/2, para. 64.

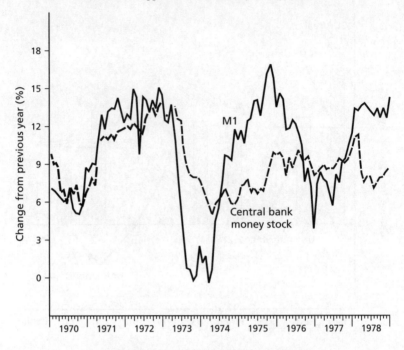

FIGURE 2: Growth of the money stock

Source: Deutsche Bundesbank.

The second source of conflict over income distribution arose from the government's growing claim on national income, a consequence of a large number of reforms and of an explicit target of the SPD-led government to increase public spending as a share of output. In 1969 and 1970 public revenue and spending represented around 40 per cent of GDP. In succeeding years spending rose persistently as a share of output, crossing the 50 per cent mark for the first time in 1975. The expansionary fiscal policy was in marked contrast to the necessity of a neutral or contractionary fiscal policy stance in order to bring inflation down.[8]

Monetary policy, too, failed to respond to the inflationary disequilibrium. From the second half of 1970, monetary growth—measured in terms of M1 or the central bank money stock—was very strong (Figure 2).[9] At the same

[8] The cyclical impulse is calculated as the difference between the actual and the cyclically neutral budgetary position, in each case with respect to GDP.

[9] M1 consists of currency in circulation plus the sight deposits of domestic non-banks held with domestic credit institutions. The central bank money stock consists of currency in circulation plus the sight, time, and savings deposits of domestic non-banks, the latter weighted with their respective minimum reserve ratios (as of Jan. 1974).

time bank lending to domestic non-banks was also expanding. Both factors contributed to rising inflation. The inappropriate rate of monetary expansion was an expression of the fact, acknowledged by the Central Bank Council of the Bundesbank, that to a large extent the Bundesbank had lost control of the money supply.

b) The Bundesbank's monetary concept

The difficulties facing monetary policy during this period and the subsequent developments can be better understood if we first consider, in broad terms, the monetary policy concept adopted by the Bundesbank. This concept can be summarized in the form of a series of principles.

1. The Bundesbank's monetary analysis focuses on the *change* in the stock of money; to this extent it is a flow analysis and not, as is otherwise typical of macroeconomics, an analysis of stock or asset figures.[10]

2. Within the framework of the monetary analysis the change in the stock of money is interpreted as the residual value of a series of fundamental market developments:

Change in the money stock =
  lending by domestic banks to domestic non-banks
+ change in the Bundesbank's foreign exchange reserves
  and the banks' net external assets
− change in the monetary capital of domestic non-banks
  held with domestic credit institutions
− central bank deposits of domestic public authorities
− other factors

As in the monetarist—and in contrast to the Keynesian—model of the money supply, it is the domestic credit market that is the focus of the monetary analysis.

3. An increase in the net external assets of the banks and the foreign exchange reserves of the Bundesbank leads to an expansion of the money stock unless they are absorbed by the formation of monetary capital, i.e. other bank liabilities, or are offset on the other side of the balance by increased bank lending.

4. The demand by the banks for central bank money is determined by the reserve requirement. Given, however, that the reserve requirement refers to deposits already created, the demand for central bank money at any point

---

[10] Cf. Brunner, 1973.

in time is exogenous, so that a variation in the monetary base does not affect the money supply. Herein lies the second difference from the monetarist analysis of the money supply.

c) The monetary policy dilemma

In this concept the Bundesbank has two indirect means of money stock control at its disposal.[11] Within the framework of its *interest-rate policy*—that is the setting of central bank rates—the Bundesbank influences market interest rates and thus, due to its interest rate elasticity, the *demand for credit*. Within the framework of its *liquidity policy* it influences the stock of free liquid reserves held by the banks, i.e. excess reserves held by the banks with the central bank and bank assets that they can convert at any time into central bank money.[12] Liquidity policy was based on the view that banks would attempt to maintain a broadly stable relationship between their free liquid reserves and domestic deposits, i.e. a stable liquidity ratio. Thus the creation (reduction) of free liquid reserves would, after a time-lag, lead to an expansion (decline) in the *supply of credit*.

By the start of the 1970s the idea of a stable liquidity ratio proved no longer appropriate.[13] The rapid expansion of the supply of credit and money in 1971 and 1972 occurred against the background of a relatively low and declining liquidity ratio. The Bundesbank recognized that the reason for this instability lay in the development of alternative means for banks to obtain liquidity owing to the establishment of effective money markets both at home and abroad.[14]

Within the framework of this concept the Bundesbank was to some extent able to use its interest-rate and liquidity policies to pursue different goals.[15]

---

[11] Cf., for instance, Deutsche Bundesbank, Geschäftsbericht 1970, pp. 19ff.; Deutsche Bundesbank, Geschäftsbericht 1972, pp. 26ff.

[12] Under the conditions prevailing in the early 1970s these were foreign exchange deposits held by the banks and unutilized rediscount quotas, money market paper issued by the Bundesbank with a guarantee of immediate repurchase at any time, and free Lombard facilities. Cf. Deutsche Bundesbank, 1973, pp. 47f.

[13] Cf. Deutsche Bundesbank, Geschäftsbericht 1970, pp. 21f.

[14] Cf. Deutsche Bundesbank, Geschäftsbericht 1973, p. 3. The Council of Economic Experts mentions as an additional source of the instability the change in the liquidity principles of the Federal Banking Supervisory Office in 1969 (cf. Sachverständigenrat, Jahresgutachten 1973/4, para. 172).

[15] This is exemplified by the decision by the Central Bank Council taken in Mar. 1971 to cut the rediscount quotas available to the banks—which would tend to push interest rates upwards—at the same time as cutting the discount rate: the latter aimed to reduce the interest-rate differential *vis-à-vis* the dollar, whereas the former was to reduce the liquidity of the

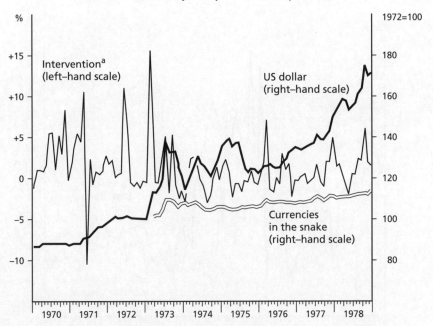

FIGURE 3: External value of the D-mark and intervention by the Bundesbank

ᵃ Monthly changes in the net foreign assets of the Bundesbank in relation to the monetary base.

Source: Deutsche Bundesbank, own calculations.

This division was only possible, however, as long as the inflow of foreign currency attracted by a positive international interest-rate differential was not in opposition to a tight liquidity policy. Herein lay the dilemma of German monetary policy in 1971 and 1972. The strong growth of credit and the money stock required a perceptibly restrictive policy, whereas the expansionary course adopted by the USA at the start of 1970 called for interest-rate cuts.[16] Figure 4 shows the rapid fall in German money market rates in the wake of US interest rates at the start of the 1970s. Cuts in the discount and the Lombard rates were made in conjunction with restrictive

banking sector and underpin the Bundesbank independent stability-oriented stance. Cf. Deutsche Bundesbank, Geschäftsbericht 1971, p. 17. In their empirical studies Willms and Neumann came to the conclusion that in the 1960s the Bundesbank was able to follow an independent domestically oriented course despite the pegged exchange rate; cf. Willms, 1971 and Neumann, 1977. On the other hand Alexander and Loef showed empirically that the Bundesbank's ability to control the money base was incomplete, particularly during periods of external disequilibrium; cf. Alexander and Loef, 1974.

[16] Cf. Deutsche Bundesbank, Geschäftsbericht 1970, pp. 14f.

FIGURE 4: Interest-rate movements

ᵃ Difference between maximum and minimum day-to-day money market rates in each month

Source: Deutsche Bundesbank, own calculations.

liquidity policy measures, although these were insufficient to limit the growth of the money stock to the required extent.[17] In the spring of 1971 the upward pressure on the currency was further increased by speculative capital inflows. Figure 3 illustrates the dimensions of the intervention—measured in terms of monthly changes in the net external assets of the Bundesbank in relation to the monetary base—required to counter the pressure for currency appreciation.

Thus the dilemma lay in the impossibility of reconciling internal and external goals of monetary policy. The Bundesbank spoke of the 'monetary policy triangle' (*währungspolitisches Dreieck*), consisting of the need for a restrictive monetary policy in terms of the domestic economy, the fixed exchange rate, and the liberalization of international capital movements.[18]

In the face of this problem, monetary policy was confronted with two

[17] Cf. Schlesinger, 1978.
[18] Cf. Deutsche Bundesbank, Geschäftsbericht 1970, p. 22.

pressing questions: first, how to achieve a satisfactory bulwark against the inflationary pressure from abroad, and secondly, what alternative the Bundesbank should adopt to the—clearly no longer practical—control of the liquidity ratio as a means of money stock control. The answers to these questions dominated developments in the years 1973 and 1974.

3. Emancipation of monetary policy

a) A bulwark against imported inflation

In principle security against imported inflation could be achieved in two ways: by 'unpegging' the currency or by restricting the free convertibility of the D-mark. In the early 1970s opinion on this issue was divided on the Central Bank Council. President Karl Klasen was in favour of maintaining fixed exchange rates and argued, not least with a view to the opportunities for German export industries, for restrictions on capital movements, although this gave rise to the impression[19] that exchange-rate policy was on the road to *dirigisme*.[20]

At the start of May 1971 the leading German economic research institutes and the Council of Economic Experts recommended abandoning the fixed exchange rate to the US dollar, the Council of Economic Experts pointing out the problems of allocative distortions associated with capital controls.[21] Karl Schiller, the Federal Minister of Economics, doubted the effectiveness of administrative controls[22] and publicly expressed support for floating the exchange rate.[23] After Schiller, in May 1971, had ordered the closing of the foreign exchange market, under pressure from the Central Bank Council, the latter argued against allowing the exchange rate to float: such a step was, it explained, in contradiction to the agreement that had just been reached to form a European Monetary Union. The problem with the dollar should be solved in cooperation with the European partners, and these preferred

---

[19] Cf., for example, Hagelstein, 1972.

[20] This view was also expressed by Klasen in his speech to the Hamburger Übersee-Club; cf. Klasen, 1971.

[21] Letter by the Council of Economic Experts of 6 May 1971 to the Federal Minister of Economics; published in: Sachverständigenrat, Jahresgutachten 1971/2, Appendix IV.

[22] This is manifested by numerous statements made by Schiller collated by Kannengießer and Barbier; cf. Kannengießer and Barbier, 1972.

[23] Kannengießer, 1972.

capital controls.[24] Floating the exchange rate would lead to an appreciation of the D-mark, and such an appreciation would prove less substantial and therefore less damaging to German exports within the framework of an action plan coordinated with Germany's EC partners.

Despite this, the government decided to allow the DM/US$ exchange rate to float as of 9 May. Initially the Bundesbank utilized the scope for action this offered to impose restrictive monetary policy measures. As early as that autumn, however, it became evident that the fight against inflation did not enjoy top priority. As the signs of an economic slow-down grew, the Central Bank Council cut the discount rate and minimum reserve ratios on 13 October in order to stimulate domestic demand and prevent an excessively pronounced appreciation of the D-mark.[25]

In the run-up to the return to a fixed exchange rate at the end of 1971 discussions within the Central Bank Council focused primarily on two measures to establish a bulwark against imported inflation: a requirement on foreigners to obtain approval for the acquisition of fixed-interest DM securities and an obligation on those taking out a foreign loan to deposit a certain percentage of its value interest-free with the Bundesbank, the so-called *Bardepot* ('cash deposit'). Only after the Smithsonian Agreement of December 1971 was Schiller willing to propose to the Federal Government a cash deposit ruling along the lines envisaged by the Bundesbank.[26] It was introduced for the first time on 1 March 1972 at a rate of 40 per cent.

The conflict between Schiller and the Bundesbank became more acute when, in the spring of 1972, the Bundesbank again demanded the introduction of an obligation to seek approval for the acquisition of fixed-interest DM securities. This was one of the factors leading to Schiller's resignation in June 1972, although it was more of an initiating than a causal one. On 29 June the government introduced the desired obligation for approval together with a tightening of the rules on the cash deposit obligation.[27] Schiller's successor as Minister of Finance, Helmut Schmidt, was more receptive to the Bundesbank's desires for administrative controls.[28] Yet in pushing for administrative controls the Bundesbank was manoeuvring itself into a difficult position, as under prevailing law it was the Federal Government that

[24] Cf. Sachverständigenrat, Jahresgutachten 1971/2, para. 237.

[25] In his speech of November 1971 Klasen emphasized that while a 'brake' must be applied to economic activity, this must not occur too one-sidedly; cf. Klasen, 1971.

[26] Schiller made this willingness conditional on a simultaneous cut in the discount rate.

[27] The Council of Economic Experts reacted immediately by pointing out in all clarity the allocative problems involved. Cf. the Sondergutachten vom 3. Juli 1972, published in: Sachverständigenrat, Jahresgutachten 1972/3, Appendix IV.

[28] Börsenzeitung, 22 Sept. 1972.

had the power to deploy such controls, which would have given it greater influence on monetary policy. While the Central Bank Council demanded of the government the formal responsibility for deploying the controls, Schmidt responded by calling for that responsibility to be divided between the Ministry of Finance and the Bundesbank.

The ineffectiveness of administrative controls became clearly apparent in the course of 1972, however.[29] From June the Bundesbank—with the express agreement of the Minister of Finance—cautiously adopted a more restrictive stance. The hikes in the discount rate, in each case of half a point, at short intervals (on 9 October, 3 November, 1 December, 12 January) reflected the aim of cautiously testing the strength of the bulwark against imported inflation. At the start of 1973 the dollar once again came under speculative attack, forcing the Bundesbank to intervene very heavily (Figure 3). In early February the Bundesbank Directorate recommended that the government close the foreign exchange markets. Instead the government tightened the controls on capital movements in order to permit a *European* solution.[30] The reaction by the Central Bank Council bears witness to the dramatic change in its attitude to controls: a large majority was in favour of temporarily suspending support for the dollar and at the same time declared that tighter controls were neither practicable nor likely to prove successful.[31]

Yet the position of the Minister of Finance had also changed compared with that in the spring of 1971. Schmidt emphasized the importance of exchange-rate policy for foreign policy:[32] politically, a crisis in the relationship with France would have resulted if Germany had 'gone it alone'. Conversely, there was optimism that France and the United Kingdom could be persuaded to back a European solution. Schmidt foresaw that the scope for an independent national monetary policy would come up against limits on the way to an economic and monetary union in Europe. The

[29] The Council of Economic Experts set out in detail how banks and firms were swiftly able to find ways to circumvent the controls; cf. Sachverständigenrat, Jahresgutachten 1972/3, paras. 224ff.; see also Schlesinger, 1978.

[30] Specifically this consisted of a reduction in the allowance not subject to the cash deposit obligation, an increase in the cash deposit ratio to a maximum of 100 per cent, and the imposition of the need for prior administrative approval for foreigners seeking to acquire equity and for Germans seeking to borrow abroad. Cf. Deutsche Bundesbank, Geschäftsbericht 1972, pp. 16ff.

[31] Emminger reports that Bundesbank President Klasen was unable to participate in the meetings held in Feb. and at the start of Mar. owing to illness. He claims that Klasen remained strictly opposed to floating the currency, however. Cf. Emminger, 1986, pp. 231f.

[32] In his later criticisms of the Bundesbank, Schmidt was to underline this basic principle: exchange-rate policy, he argued, was always a part of foreign policy and should not be left to a central bank alone. Cf. Schmidt, 1990a, b.

Federal Government warned the Bundesbank against blocking European integration.[33]

On 1 March 1973 the dollar crisis reached its peak. During the morning the Bundesbank was forced to purchase dollars on an unprecedented scale. In coordination with European partner countries, the foreign exchange markets were closed on 2 March 1973. When the markets reopened on 19 March, the D-mark was no longer tied to the dollar.

This did not mean that the Bundesbank was entirely free from external constraints. The European 'snake', set up in 1972 as a preliminary step towards the planned economic and monetary union was still in existence. Yet the obligation to intervene in the European exchange-rate system did not pose nearly as a great a threat to the Bundesbank's autonomy as the fixed exchange rate to the dollar.[34] Until 1976 the external position did not pose any serious problems in monetary policy terms.[35] By the end of 1974 the Federal Government had removed almost all of the controls imposed on capital movements.

b) Regaining money stock control

Once the obligation to intervene in support of the dollar had ended, the question of how best to regain control over the domestic money stock could be addressed. On this point, too, opinions within the Central Bank Council varied. A number of members preferred administrative controls to market-based approaches. In the course of 1972 the Bundesbank argued in favour of a new minimum reserve requirement based on the growth of bank credit.[36] The proposal for a *credit ceiling* was even more radical, as it would have allowed the Bundesbank to set the banks quantitative limits on the

[33] Shortly before, Schmidt had declared in a newspaper interview that Germany did not wish to depart from the general pace of inflation in the European Community. Cf. 'Schmidt: Inflation erträglicher als Aufwertungsdruck', in: Frankfurter Allgemeine Zeitung, 27 Jan. 1973.

[34] On the forms of regulation within the 'snake', cf. Deutsche Bundesbank, Geschäftsbericht 1971, pp. 52f.

[35] The lack of problems from the external position is evident from the relationship between the growth of foreign currency reserves and the growth of central bank money. Whereas between 1967 and 1973 the growth of foreign currency reserves exceeded that of central bank money by a factor of three, between the spring of 1971 and the end of 1977 the foreign currency purchased by the Bundesbank represented just half of the growth of central bank money.

[36] Its aim in doing so was to strengthen the link between credit and the minimum reserve requirement; cf. Deutsche Bundesbank, Geschäftsbericht 1972, p. 28. In the case of a passive minimum reserve the link between a new granting of credit and a higher minimum reserve is only indirect, as the deposits created by virtue of the credit being granted do not necessarily remain with the lending bank.

amount of credit created.[37] This would have marked a step down the path
to government administration of credit along the lines of the French model
of an *encadrement de credit*. In its Annual Report 1972/3 the Council of
Economic Experts issued urgent warnings about the dangers of such *dirigisme*.[38] The Minister of Finance, Helmut Schmidt, though, voiced sympathy for the Bundesbank's views.[39]

The Bundesbank's proposals for an amendment of the Bundesbank Act
passed on to the Federal Government contained both provisions. Both were
incorporated into the Ministry of Finance's White Paper. The 'credit ceiling',
however, was to be subject to a 'two-keys ruling', that is it could be introduced only jointly by the Bundesbank and the Minister of Finance. The implicit undermining of the autonomy of the Bundesbank and the unfortunate
consequences of such a provision for subsequent negotiations on the
harmonization of instruments between the central banks of the EC countries
diminished the attractiveness of this instrument.

In mid-January 1973 the Central Bank Council put up for discussion
three fundamental approaches to money stock control: credit ceilings, requiring a given liquidity ratio, and the direct control of the central bank
money stock. The requirement for a given liquidity ratio was dropped with
reference to the instability of the demand for free liquid reserves. Preparatory discussion papers pointed out that controlling the supply of central
bank money implied the abolition of all automatic mechanisms that forced
the Bundesbank to issue central bank money at the behest of others. The
Bundesbank was, it was argued, very much in a position to control the
central bank money stock with sufficient accuracy. In the future the Bundesbank, given a greater degree of freedom from external constraints, should
conceive of its policy as one of controlling the central bank money stock.
Reservations were expressed within the Council as to whether the Bundesbank had the instruments at its disposal required to do this. The summary
of the discussion makes it clear that at this point in time the majority of the
members of the Central Bank Council were already leaning towards stricter
control of the central bank money stock.[40]

Once intervention on the foreign exchange markets came to an end in
March, a new situation arose. Given that it could no longer be directly
converted into central bank money, foreign currency was no longer to be
considered a component of free liquid reserves. Owing to previous credit

[37] Cf. Deutsche Bundesbank, Geschäftsbericht 1972, p. 28.
[38] Cf. Sachverständigenrat, Jahresgutachten 1972/3, paras. 397ff.
[39] Cf. Börsenzeitung, 22 Sept. 1972.
[40] In subsequent meetings of the Central Bank Council reference was frequently made to
the agreement reached at the start of January to exert more stringent control over the money
stock.

policy measures, the free liquid reserves of the banks fell to practically zero.[41] Thus the Bundesbank acquired direct control over the supply of central bank money. To all intents and purposes the decision to control the supply of central bank money had already been taken.

The Bank immediately took advantage of its newly acquired freedoms in order to push through its restrictive stance and to ensure that no new free liquid reserves were created. Even when, in March, the day-to-day money rate in Frankfurt shot up periodically to 40 per cent, the Central Bank Council opted not to relax its stance (Figure 4). In mid-April the Council took the view that the banks should be forced to reduce their lending by means of a restrictive monetary policy stance. The Federal Government shared this view and passed on its opinion that, given the new freedom from external constraints, the Bundesbank should do its utmost to reverse the inflationary trend.

On 4 May the Bundesbank raised the discount rate to 6 per cent. In mid-May one member of the Directorate argued for a renewed increase, because it seemed that the prevailing opinion among banks was still that the Bundesbank would meet any additional demand for central bank money caused by increased lending. At the end of May this proposal received support, justified by the argument that the banks' confidence in the automatic recourse to central bank money ought to be broken forever. Together with the rise in the discount rate, on 30 May the Central Bank Council decided to suspend the Lombard loan facility in favour of the 'special Lombard facility', the volume of which the Bundesbank could better control.[42]

The desired reduction in the rate of monetary expansion began to emerge as early as mid-1973 (Figure 2). To this extent the new policy of 'money stock control with zero free liquid reserves' soon proved successful. On the other hand, it led not only to a high level of interest rates on the money market, but also to greater volatility of short-term rates (Figure 4). From 2.4 per cent in February the overnight money rate rose to an average of 11 per cent in March and to almost 15 per cent in April; in May it fell to 7.4 per cent, only to rise to almost 16 per cent in July. At the same time, the inter-bank spread in overnight interest rates rose in March to 13, in April to 28 and in August to as many as 33 percentage points. Such turbulence swiftly led to criticism of the Bundesbank that it was causing confusion and putting the fate of the entire banking system at risk.[43]

[41] Cf. Deutsche Bundesbank, Geschäftsbericht 1973, p. 3.

[42] Internally, the fact that in the spring of 1973 the Bundesbank gave the banks no significant scope to acquire central bank money was later considered to have constituted a visible change in policy and as a necessary condition for the effectiveness of a restrictive policy.

[43] See, for instance, 'Die Bundesbank spielt mit dem Feuer', in: Handelsblatt, 27 July 1973.

The new policy had to face two difficulties. If the Bundesbank wanted to control the central bank money stock directly, but at the same time avoid sharp fluctuations in interest rates, it had either to make liquidity available quickly and in the right quantities, or be able to forecast more or less accurately the economy's need for central bank money. The former required open market operations of a larger volume than the Bundesbank considered appropriate, while the latter proved difficult in practice, as the demand for central bank money can change quickly and substantially.

The second problem lay in the possible contradiction between a direct control of the monetary base and the required reserve policy: if the Bundesbank wanted a direct control of the monetary base, it had to accept in principle that the banking sector as a whole, and thus individual banks, might not be able to meet their minimum reserve requirements.[44] Some members of the Central Bank Council were of the opinion that the central bank could not reasonably impose a reserve requirement on the banks without ensuring that it was at least in principle possible to meet it. One of the preparatory discussion papers pointed out that high money market rates could in no way be seen simply as an appropriate punishment for bad liquidity planning on the part of an individual bank. On the other hand, an unconditional willingness to meet the banks' reserve demand would undermine monetary control.

A compromise between the minimum reserve system and an active control of the money stock was possible, however, if the Bundesbank refrained from short-term monetary control, and instead concentrated on the medium and longer term development of the central bank money stock. As early as June, one discussion paper pointed out that the real goal—forcing the banks on to a growth path of central bank money determined by the Bundesbank —was essentially long-term in nature and was not prejudiced by acceptance of seasonal and short-term fluctuations in the central bank money stock. Moreover, control over the medium-term growth path could also be exerted via a price variable, i.e. the interest rate conditions set by the Bundesbank. To use the phrase adopted by the Bundesbank, control of the central bank money stock thus became 'indirect control via the interest-rate lever' (*indirekte Kontrolle über den Zinshebel*).

Consequently, in the years that followed, the money market rate of interest, as an overall measure of the interest rate conditions set by the Bundesbank, increasingly became the decisive guideline variable for Bundesbank policy.[45] The central preconditions for the new concept were the all but

[44] Cf. Dudler, 1983, p. 44.
[45] Cf., for example, Deutsche Bundesbank, 1982, pp. 21ff. Von Hagen later described this procedure as 'controlling the supply price for central bank money' (*Steuerung des Angebotspreises für Zentralbankgeld*); cf. von Hagen, 1986.

complete absence of external constraints and the fact that the Bundesbank did not pursue a separate interest-rate target.

Some members of the Central Bank Council termed the new policy in June 1973 'control of the monetary base' (*Steuerung der Geldbasis*); similarly the 1973 Annual Report spoke of the 'direct control of the central bank money stock' (*unmittelbare Kontrolle der Zentralbankgeldmenge*).[46] Yet in the Bundesbank this view met with opposition for three reasons. First, because it suggested that the Bundesbank could control the central bank money stock directly, which, given the reserve requirement, was considered incorrect; second, because the claim to be controlling the monetary base led on to the difficult question of the appropriate monetary base target; third, there was a school of thought, inside and outside the Bundesbank, that believed that monetary policy should be oriented towards a medium-term target for the *money stock*, i.e. a non-bank aggregate, in order to achieve price stability over the longer term.[47] At the end of 1972 the EC Council of Ministers had adopted this latter approach, recommending that the central banks of the Member States should gear monetary policy towards a target rate of growth of the money stock.

Yet this proposal raised the question of the correct concept of the money stock. None of the traditional aggregates appeared particularly well suited to money stock control. At the end of 1973 a discussion paper presented to the Central Bank Council argued that, fundamentally, only an aggregate that attached different weightings to deposits of different degrees of liquidity, could be accepted as the money stock to be targeted. Aggregates consisting of simple sums of different components of the money stock, in contrast, would provide a distorted picture of monetary growth during periods of rising or falling interest rates. If, however, it were assumed that the different minimum reserve ratios reflected differences in the degrees of liquidity, the stocks of the various deposits weighted with their minimum reserve ratios could be aggregated to a new money stock aggregate: the *central bank money stock*, the new Bundesbank monetary aggregate, was born.[48] The fact that the assumption regarding the correlation between the degrees of liquidity and the minimum reserve ratios was hardly justified was accepted, just as was the fact that the very high weight accorded to currency

[46] Cf. Deutsche Bundesbank, Geschäftsbericht 1973, p. 4. This was in line with the interpretation made by the Council of Economic Experts; cf. Sachverständigenrat, Jahresgutachten 1973/4, paras. 170, 292.
[47] Cf. Friedman, 1968.
[48] It seems that the new aggregate had already been used for the purposes of analysis in the Economics Department of the Bundesbank. Internally there was talk at the start of the 1970s of the 'fictitious' central bank money stock, in which the effects of changes in reserve ratios were excluded.

in circulation could lead to problems. Given the negligibly small excess reserves of the banks, the new aggregate was almost identical to the monetary base and remained so as long as the required reserve ratios did not change markedly.[49] What was clever about the proposal was that controlling the central bank money stock was acceptable both to those members of the Central Bank Council who considered control of the monetary base desirable and to those who thought that such direct quantitative control of the base was impossible and who preferred to control a monetary aggregate. In any case, control of the central bank money stock was in accordance with the Bundesbank's policy of 'monetary control with zero free liquid reserves' pursued by the Bundesbank since March 1973.[50]

c) Experiences with open market policy

The new approach to monetary control required instruments that provided sufficient flexibility to allow for fluctuations in the demand for central bank money without calling into question medium-term control over the supply of money. The Bundesbank's traditional instruments were not suited to this purpose as they allowed the banks to take the initiative to too great an extent and because even frequent changes in the discount and Lombard rates would not have generated sufficient flexibility.

In the course of the public debate on a reform of the range of instruments, it was proposed, largely by commentators outside the Bundesbank itself, that monetary control should be primarily achieved by open market operations, as in the Anglo-Saxon countries.[51] This proposal was opposed by the Bundesbank itself, however. A number of presidents of the state central banks were worried that such operations, by virtue of their tendency towards spatial centralization, would strengthen the Bundesbank Directorate *vis-à-*

---

[49] Cf. Dudler, 1983. Neumann pointed out that the central bank money stock calculated at constant reserve ratios exaggerates fluctuations in the monetary base when the prevailing reserve ratios are lower than the assumed figures; cf. Neumann, 1975.

[50] As a result of this proposed interpretation, the new central bank money stock could be considered simultaneously as the monetary base (central bank money) and as a non-bank aggregate (money stock). This ambiguity was revealed when the Bundesbank presented its new aggregate to the public simultaneously as a monetary target (and thus as a non-bank aggregate) and as a monetary indicator (i.e. as monetary base); cf. Deutsche Bundesbank, Geschäftsbericht 1975. It led to criticism of the Bundesbank that its target variable did not meet any of the standard definitions of the money stock or the monetary base. Cf. Neumann, 1975 and Caesar, 1976.

[51] Cf., in particular, Deutsches Institut für Wirtschaftsforschung, 1973, pp. 206ff. and Sachverständigenrat, Jahresgutachten 1972/3, paras. 400ff., Jahresgutachten 1974/5, paras. 384ff.

vis the Central Bank Council, and called for corresponding corrections to the decision making procedures within the Bundesbank. Yet concerns were also expressed by the Directorate, as open market operations, given the narrowness of the capital market, could initiate substantial fluctuations in interest rates and thus make it more difficult to impose a restrictive policy.

In spite of these concerns, from March 1974 the Bundesbank began to make substantial purchases in the open market in order to prevent interest rates from rising in the face of growing public borrowing, although without aiming at artificially holding down the market rate of interest for an extended period. A number of motives were cited in justification of this: worries that the Federal Government might undermine the effect of high capital market rates by subsidising interest rates, doubts about the effectiveness of a high capital market rate for dampening aggregate demand, and concerns that high interest rates could push up costs and therefore also prices. The more active open market policy also aimed to make it easier for the government to refrain from resorting to central bank advances, the extraordinary growth of which since the start of 1974 was increasingly perceived as disturbing monetary policy. Holdings of government securities by the Bundesbank, which at the end of 1972 and 1973 had amounted to just DM 20 million and DM 4 million respectively, increased by a factor of 48 to December 1974.

In the first few days of July 1975 the Bundesbank purchased bonds to the value of DM 200 million; in July its securities portfolio expanded by a factor of nine. In mid-August a recommendation was issued to the Central Bank Council to avoid an increase in interest rates on the bond market at all costs. In view of the precarious state of the economy, the Federal Government recommended steps to prevent a rise in interest rates in order to avoid endangering the effectiveness of its programme of demand stimulation. In spite of warnings that, at artificially low interest rates, the Federal Government would no longer be able to gain access to the capital market, the interventionist policy stance was maintained.

By the late summer of 1975 the Bundesbank had expanded its portfolio of securities to a record figure of DM 3.9 billion. Given the widening yield differential with non-supported paper, however, the Federal Government found it extremely difficult to raise additional funds in the bond market. Finally, in October the policy of active open market operations was abandoned. The lesson learned was that, in the end, it was not possible to avoid a rise in capital market interest rates.

Although the end of active open market policy had a less substantial impact on interest rates than had been feared,[52] the experiment had shown

[52] Cf. Deutsche Bundesbank, Geschäftsbericht 1976, p. 18.

that, not least owing to the supposed interest-rate effects, it was very difficult for the Bundesbank to withstand the internal and external pressure to ensure favourable interest-rate conditions for the government. Therefore in subsequent years the Bundesbank, in developing its range of instruments, focused on the different variants of commercial bank refinancing, including open market operations with repurchase agreements, which were certain not to give rise to interest rate effects.[53]

4. Monetary stabilization policy

a) Monetary policy, fiscal policy, and macroeconomic stabilization

In the 1950s and 1960s stabilization policy in Germany had been primarily the responsibility of monetary policy. The Bundesbank had utilized its limited scope for action to pursue a rigorous policy of price stability. This stability policy orientation failed for the first time in the recession of 1966. The political reaction came in the form of the Stability and Growth Act, which provided fiscal policy with new and flexible instruments with which to influence the business cycle. The economic upturn in the years after 1967 appeared to confirm fiscal policy's claim to leadership in the management of aggregate demand, a role consistent with the American model of the 1960s and the intellectual climate, which Karl Schiller, the Minister of Economics, characterized in his famous statement: 'the business cycle is our will and not our fate!' (*Konjunktur ist unser Wille, nicht unser Schicksal!*).

Given that fiscal policy was subject to external constraints to a far lesser extent than monetary policy, the fight against the high rates of inflation at the start of the 1970s had to be based on a dampening of macroeconomic demand steered by fiscal policy.[54] The Minister of Finance, Alex Möller, who recognized this necessity, argued for cuts in public spending, but resigned in May 1971 having failed to receive cabinet backing for this approach. The fact that his successor, Schiller, also failed in this regard revealed the inability of the government to cope with the disequilibrium that had resulted from excessive demand and conflict over income distribution. It also clearly manifested the political asymmetry of fiscal demand management:

---

[53] Cf. Neumann and von Hagen, 1993, pp. 316ff.
[54] Cf. Deutsche Bundesbank, Geschäftsbericht 1971, p. 25.

the government found it easier to raise public spending in periods of inadequate demand than to cut public spending in times of excess demand.

The way out of this political dilemma lay in calling on monetary policy to shoulder part of the burden on fiscal policy. Accordingly, in its declaration of 18 January 1973 the government officially accorded monetary policy the prime role in stabilization policy. The Council of Economic Experts, too, in its 1972/3 Annual Report, called on monetary policy to assume greater responsibility for ensuring price stability.[55] This division of responsibilities did not meet with the undivided approval of the Central Bank Council. A number of members thought that, given the distributional conflict between employers' federations and unions, a more adequate incomes policy was required. Others were worried that the other economic policy decision makers could avoid shouldering responsibility if the Bundesbank were to assume more of the same. By pursuing a restrictive policy, they argued, the Bundesbank would be too likely to come into conflict with the economic policy pursued by the government. In spite of this, the Bundesbank, having regained control over the money stock, inevitably had to play a more active role in terms of stabilization policy, precisely because fiscal policy, in its view, was doing too little in this regard.

In its Annual Report for 1973 the Bundesbank declared the fight against inflation—in line with the economic policy goals set by the Federal Government—to be the principal goal of monetary policy.[56] The signs of a weakening of economic growth that emerged during 1973 and the oil price crisis that began that autumn were the occasion for a new division of tasks between monetary and fiscal policy. In its Annual Report of 1974 the Bundesbank declared that monetary policy was now primarily responsible for price stability, whereas the government's prime task was that of overcoming structural economic weaknesses.[57] In the summer of 1974 the government argued that despite stagnant output and rising unemployment the Bundesbank ought to maintain its tight-money stance: should the situation on the labour market become critical, the government planned to introduce employment policy measures.

---

[55] Cf. Sachverständigenrat, Jahresgutachten 1972/3, paras. 329ff. The Council of Economic Experts spoke of a failure by the government in the conflict between demand management and the provision of public goods. In his minority-view report, however, Claus Köhler rejected the implicit weakening of fiscal policy and pointed out that until 1966 it had been precisely the lack of an active fiscal policy in Germany that had been regretted.

[56] Cf. Deutsche Bundesbank, Geschäftsbericht 1973, p. 45.

[57] The Council of Economic Experts described the division of tasks even more clearly: while monetary policy was to look after price stability and maintain its restrictive course during 1974, fiscal policy was entrusted with the task of ensuring an adequate level of employment.

b) Economic developments 1974–8

While the focus of economic policy during the first half of the decade was on fighting an inflation fuelled by wage pressure and excessive demand, the situation changed following the oil-price shock in 1973. Attention increasingly also turned towards unemployment. Figure 1 shows how the German economy went into recession under the joint impact of monetary restriction and the oil crisis.[58] Unemployment rose, staying at a level of around 4 per cent from 1975 on.[59] 1976 saw a strong recovery of the German economy, but growth flattened out again in 1977 and 1978, with annual rates of real GDP growth of just under 3 per cent.

Not until about a year after the start of the recession did it become apparent that the trend towards rising inflation had been broken and that Germany had managed to decouple itself from the inflationary momentum of the other industrialized countries.[60] Following a shift in monetary policy to a more expansionary stance in 1975, however, inflation rose slightly in 1977 and once again strongly in 1978.

At the end of 1976 the D-mark began to appreciate once more, particularly against the dollar (Figure 3), a trend that was increasingly seen as posing a threat to German exports. From 1976 the Bundesbank sought to counter this threat by means of renewed substantial intervention in the foreign exchange markets; in 1976 this was largely within the context of the 'snake', in 1977 and 1978 primarily in support of the dollar.[61]

Given that the Federal Government was attempting to offset the employment effects of the oil crisis by means of additional public spending programmes, German fiscal policy remained expansionary. The gap between expenditure and revenue widened, so that government debt as a share of output rose sharply. Thus in the period 1974–6 monetary policy was very much under the shadow of rising government debt.

c) Monetary targeting

Soon after the declining rates of inflation had shown the first success of the new monetary control strategy, two rather different questions moved into

---

[58] The contribution to the recession made by monetary policy was analysed by Neumann, 1981.

[59] Cf. Deutsche Bundesbank, Geschäftsbericht 1973, pp. 34f.

[60] Cf. Deutsche Bundesbank, Geschäftsbericht 1974, pp. 16f.

[61] Cf. Pohl, 1988.

the focus of attention: the issue of the longer term monetary policy concept and the question of how monetary policy should respond to the ever more apparent weakness of economic growth.

Steadying monetary policy

Some members of the Central Bank Council emphasized that the Bundesbank should pursue a more consistent monetary policy course, one oriented primarily towards the goal of price stability. As early as January 1973 one member argued that monetary policy should be conducted in a steadier fashion, within the framework of a general rule agreed on in conjunction with the government. At the same time Helmut Schlesinger called for monetary policy to be oriented more towards medium-term economic trends.[62]

In 1974 the Council of Economic Experts criticized the fact that, in its view, the monetary restriction had hit the economy ill-prepared; the high wage demands and the employment losses of 1974 reflected incorrect expectations on the part of wage setters.[63] In order to avoid such errors, in the autumn of 1974 the Council proposed that the Bundesbank should announce a target for the growth of the money stock as a guide to the parties involved in wage bargaining. This proposal was taken up by the Federal Government, which intended to make a growth target for the central bank money stock part of its economic policy programme for 1975.

The idea of a medium-term growth target clearly fitted in with the concept of controlling the central bank money stock and was thus not new to the Bundesbank.[64] There were elements of this idea in the Annual Report for 1973, where it was stated that: 'as in 1973, in 1974 the Bundesbank will seek to control the central bank money stock in such a way that the volume of money and credit can expand to an extent compatible with the stability-oriented growth of the economy.'[65]

The first monetary target

In mid-1974 there were growing calls for a relaxation of monetary policy in order to bolster employment and growth. These calls were echoed by the leading German economic research institutes and the Council of Economic

---

[62] Cf. Mainert, 1974.
[63] Cf. Sachverständigenrat, Jahresgutachten 1974/5, paras. 131, 139f., 310.
[64] Cf. Bockelmann, 1989.
[65] Deutsche Bundesbank, Geschäftsbericht 1973, p. 45.

Experts.[66] Within the Bundesbank, too, the general feeling was that the policy stance should be relaxed.[67] The problem was to undertake the relaxation in such a way that neither the parties to collective wage bargaining nor the general public would gain the impression that the Bundesbank was departing from its stability-oriented course, thus fuelling renewed inflation expectations.

Announcing a monetary target was the way out of this dilemma as it offered an opportunity of signalling to the public both a policy relaxation and the intention of not allowing monetary growth to get out of control again. The Central Bank Council also took the view that, in the case of a persistent recession, reference to the monetary target would make it easier to withstand political pressure for more rapid monetary growth. Last but not least, a monetary target was in accordance with the wishes of those calling for a steadier, more rules-based policy. The decisive point was that setting a monetary target was opportune for a number of reasons and thus received majority support.

The specific choice of the target—8 per cent—underlines this coincidence of views. Given that in 1974 the central bank money stock had expanded by 6 per cent, announcing a target of 8 per cent for 1975 appeared a plausible way of indicating a more relaxed stance. Two further considerations offered support for the proposal of 8 per cent. First, the forecasts for real growth and inflation amounted to 2 and 6 per cent, respectively, for 1975. Thus a target of 8 per cent constituted a neutral policy oriented towards the expected growth of nominal output. Secondly, the rate of growth of potential output was put at 3 per cent and the 'unavoidable' rate of inflation at 5 per cent. Thus the target was also in accordance with a potential-oriented monetary policy. Thus members of the Central Bank Council with very different views on the correct monetary policy orientation were able to agree on a target rate of 8 per cent.

There was initially some reservation about publishing the target. A number of members were of the opinion that the flexibility of monetary policy ought not to be restricted by artificial barriers. Others expressed doubts whether the money stock could be controlled precisely enough. It was also questioned whether the relationship between nominal output and the money stock could be quantified with sufficient accuracy. The compromise was made possible by the proposal that on publication it was to be noted that *in the short term* there was *no close* correlation between movements in output and growth of the money stock, and that the target of 8 per cent

[66] Cf. Sachverständigenrat, Jahresgutachten 1974/5, para. 246.
[67] Cf. 'Bundesbank will Geldschleusen nicht bedingungslos öffnen', in: Handelsblatt, 31 Dec. 1974. On Klasen's position, see Steves, 1974.

seemed reasonable in terms of price stability *only from the current perspective*, so that the Bundesbank retained scope for policy action.[68]

'Limited steadiness' versus 'consistency with the situation'

While the convergence of the different views on the issue of the target rate facilitated the decision at the end of 1974 to adopt monetary targets, it did not remove the conflict over the underlying orientation of monetary policy. Sooner or later the Central Bank Council had to face up to a choice between a strategy of 'limited steadiness' (*eingeschränkte Verstetigung*), i.e. targeting monetary growth to the medium-term economic trend, and a policy 'consistent with the situation' (*situationsgerecht*), which in addition took account of cyclical fluctuations.[69]

In the 1970s the Bundesbank was unable to make a conscious decision in favour of the first alternative. This is evident from the derivation of the monetary target, which, in addition to the trend growth of output, also took account of the expected annual change in capacity utilization and in the velocity of circulation. It is also evident from the fact that the Bundesbank regularly embedded its monetary target in the macroeconomic target projections of the Federal Government. As early as 1975 the Bundesbank stated in its Annual Report: 'the relaxation of monetary policy manifested by the monetary target is to stimulate demand and create the scope for higher real growth'.[70] Otmar Emminger spoke in an interview given at the start of 1975 of 'relaxation measures by the Bundesbank to stimulate economic activity'.[71] In the 1976 Report we find: 'the Bundesbank and the Federal Government are aiming at . . . a real growth rate of 5 per cent'.[72] Finally, the 1977 Report defines 'strong economic growth and a further check on inflation'[73] as the

---

[68] Significantly, the Council subsequently discussed the possibility of a cut in interest rates. In view of the uncertainty surrounding the point in time at which an interest-rate cut would be appropriate, the proposal was accepted of waiting until the government's stabilization programme had passed parliament. The interest-rate cut duly occurred on 19 Dec. 1974 at the same time that the government's demand stimulation programme received parliamentary approval. Cf. 'Senkung des Diskontsatzes in der Bundesrepublik', in: Neue Zürcher Zeitung, 20 Dec. 1974.

[69] One discussion paper added to these two alternatives a third, the—in practice largely irrelevant—policy of radical steadying along the pattern of Friedman's longer term monetary rule. The paper pointed out that even in setting the target for 1976 the 'limited steadiness' would have led to a different target from the 'consistent' policy.

[70] Deutsche Bundesbank, Geschäftsbericht 1975, pp. 6f.

[71] '"Im Sommer die Tendenzwende"—Interview mit Bundesbank-Vize Otmar Emminger', in: Wirtschaftswoche, 21 Feb. 1975.

[72] Deutsche Bundesbank, Geschäftsbericht 1976, p. 23.

[73] Deutsche Bundesbank, Geschäftsbericht 1977, p. 33.

policy goal. Whereas the 1974 Report defined reducing inflation as the prime goal of monetary policy,[74] once initial successes had been achieved in this battle, the stability orientation and the strategy of steady monetary policy gave way once more to older ideas about steering real economic growth.

Initial experiences with monetary targets

In the first few months of 1975 the growth of the central bank money stock was in line with the announced target, although it weakened during the spring. As early as April, some members of the Central Bank Council called for a further cut in central bank rates in view of the weakness of economic growth, but this met with doubts about the success of such a short-term fine-tuning of economic activity. The opponents of such a step pointed out that, given the existence of a monetary target, monetary policy should not be oriented towards monthly economic data, but rather towards longer term considerations. Even so, the Bundesbank cut the Lombard rate at the end of April and the Lombard and the discount rates on 22 May. Six months after the first monetary target had been announced, the discount rate had fallen by two percentage points and the Lombard rate by three points.

From mid-1975 the Bundesbank permitted the banks to substantially expand their free liquid reserves. Past experience had shown that this would inevitably weaken control over the central bank money stock. In mid-August and again in mid-September the discount and Lombard rates were cut once more. At the end of October it was reported to the Central Bank Council that the growth of the central bank money stock had accelerated to an annual rate of 10 per cent. The Central Bank Council rejected a call for a further cut in base rates in order to counter the high rate of unemployment. In the *target month*, December 1975, the growth of the central bank money stock on an annual basis was around 10 per cent. Thus the first year closed with a marked overshooting of the target.

The discussion that took place at the end of the year within the Central Bank Council on the experience with the first monetary target painted a mixed, but overall positive picture. It was felt that the monetary target had been generally well received by the public and had been understood as a general orientation. In the course of the year it had been shown that the growth of the central bank money stock was subject to sharp fluctuations which could not be precisely controlled. The Bundesbank was right, it was argued, to have retained the target, although the estimated real growth of 2 per cent had not been achieved, because a downward correction of the target would have implied a procyclical monetary policy. Against this background

---

[74] Cf. Deutsche Bundesbank, Geschäftsbericht 1974, p. 1.

it was proposed that a monetary target be set for 1976 as well. However, in order to be less at the mercy of short-term fluctuations, the target should be formulated as a rate of growth of the average monetary stock in 1976 compared with the average in 1975.

In mid-December the Council adopted an average target of 8 per cent, following the government's expression of its positive attitude towards money stock control. It was to be emphasized on publication that this target represented a four-quarter target of just 5.5 per cent and thus a significant slow-down of monetary expansion.

d) Predominance of counter-cyclical policy— end of the monetary targeting strategy?

In view of the improvement in the real economy at the start of 1976 the Bundesbank was, in principle, able to concentrate once again on the monetary target and the inflation rate. To this extent 1976 was the first genuine litmus test for the monetary targeting strategy. From the outset it was apparent that the desired attenuation of monetary growth was not occurring. In mid-February the Central Bank Council rejected calls for a cut in interest rates in support of the still precarious state of the real economy, claiming that such a step would make it more difficult to meet the monetary target. While this decision suggested the binding nature of the target, subsequent developments lead one to suppose the opposite. As early as the start of April there were signs that, in view of growing free liquid reserves, there was a danger that the target would be missed. The overwhelming majority of the Central Bank Council shared this view, but, in deference to the weak state of the real economy, it did not implement counter measures until the start of May.

In a renewed discussion of the principles of monetary policy, some members of the Central Bank Council again called for more steadiness of monetary policy. To this it was objected that one could not simply ignore the short-term effects of monetary policy measures. It was precisely the flexibility of monetary policy that constituted its great advantage over other economic policy instruments. The monetary target was not, it was argued, immutable, but could be adjusted in response to changes in the business cycle.

Not until the autumn, once the cyclical depression during the summer months had been overcome, concern about economic growth had dissipated, and simultaneously signs of increasing conflict over pay levels had emerged, was there a growing willingness within the Council to counter the—in terms of the target—excessive monetary expansion. While by then it was too late to meet the target for the year as a whole, by limiting the magnitude of the overshoot the aim was to minimize the loss of credibility on the part of the Bundesbank and to signal to wage setters that it intended to stick un-swervingly to its stability orientation.

At the end of 1976 a discussion paper presented to the Central Bank Council drew attention to the fact that the strong orientation of monetary policy to actual economic growth was calling into question the rationale of monetary targeting. In spite of this the majority on the Council spoke out in favour of a continuation of the policy of monetary targeting as this had been positively received by public opinion at home and abroad. Contro-versy remained, however, on the actual meaning of a policy of monetary targeting. The view held by some members that the monetary target had exerted a salutary disciplinary effect and had become an internal yardstick for policy action was called into question by others. The desire of some that the Bundesbank should stick more closely to the target stood in contrast to the wish of others that the target should be subject to an internal 'margin' within which cyclical economic development could be steered. The Federal Government expressed its interest in a maintenance of the policy of monetary targeting, arguing that this served to steady monetary policy and take it out of day-to-day politics and that it strengthened the independence of the central bank. In mid-December the Central Bank Council agreed on an average target of 8 per cent for 1977, which, with a four-quarter target figure of 6–7 per cent, once again required a slowing of monetary expansion.

In the course of 1977, however, attention was once again focused on the state of the real economy. Once it became apparent that the government was likely to miss its growth target, the Bundesbank felt no longer able to impose the monetary restriction it had originally envisaged.[75] Not until the autumn were voices increasingly raised in the Central Bank Council drawing atten-tion to the danger of a loss of credibility resulting from renewed failure to meet the target. The criticism was made that in 1977 monetary policy had degenerated into a mere interest-rate policy in which the monetary target no longer had a role to play. The strong monetary expansion had created an inflationary potential that would confront monetary policy with problems as early as the coming year.

In connection with the discussion of the monetary target for 1978, the debate on the principles of monetary policy revived in the Central Bank Council. A discussion paper pointed out that the experimental stage that had begun in 1975 could not be continued indefinitely. The central bank

[75] The Bundesbank justified the target overshooting with reference to external influences and distortions in the central bank money stock; cf. Deutsche Bundesbank, Geschäftsbericht 1977, pp. 1f., 20ff.

had to address the question of whether it really took the target seriously. The paper found fault with the average target, which, it argued, had too little binding power, since the chances of reaching such a target were already predetermined by the base effect of the previous year and in the second half of the year success was almost completely predetermined by the policy pursued in the first few months. The orientation towards the government's growth forecast was also criticized, as it suggested a synchronic relationship between the money stock and nominal output, in contradiction to the claim that monetary policy effects were felt after a substantial time-lag. In addition, the growth forecasts had proved highly inaccurate. The paper closed by recommending that the time horizon of the target be extended beyond one year.

Yet opposing views were also presented in the course of the debate. The calendar year was, it was argued, suitable for influencing other annual decisions, such as wage bargaining and budget decisions. The orientation towards the government's growth target signalled to the public that the government supported the policy of monetary targeting. Finally, in order to ensure a greater scope for monetary policy action during the course of a year, the Central Bank Council could adopt an average target with a margin of one percentage point combined with a four-quarter target for the fourth quarter with a corridor of between two and three percentage points.

At the start of December one member of the Directorate voiced strong opposition to the policy of monetary targeting. Looking retrospectively at 1977, an improved *interest-rate policy*, involving earlier cuts in rates, would, he argued, have improved the state of the real economy, eased the external position, and perhaps even enabled the Bundesbank to control the monetary expansion more effectively by blocking the inflow of foreign currency. He doubted that the Bundesbank could evade political pressure and strengthen its independence by tying itself to objective data. Last but not least, he regarded as unacceptable to narrow the functions of the Central Bank Council to that of merely setting the monetary target. The Bundesbank should not give up the option of taking monetary policy action by virtue of having set a target. Another member lent support to the view that under no circumstances should the Bundesbank allow itself to become the slave of a mere number.

In spite of this controversy the Central Bank Council again announced a monetary target in mid-December. By and large it followed the proposal of setting an average target of 8 per cent coupled with a four-quarter target with a corridor of 5–7 per cent. As had been the case with the first monetary target, the announcement of the target in December 1977 was due in the final analysis to the desire on the part of the Central Bank Council to ensure that a monetary policy relaxation for real economic and external reasons was not interpreted by the public as a departure from the Bundesbank's stability-oriented course. Refraining from setting a target while at the same time cutting base rates would all too easily have created the impression that the Bundesbank had abandoned its steady monetary course.[76]

As early as the spring of 1978 it became apparent that the central bank money stock was expanding too rapidly. At the start of June 1978 the revision of the monetary target was adopted as an explicit point on the agenda for the Central Bank Council meeting. In the event, the Council preferred a public justification of its failure to meet the target—with reference to the distorting influence of currency in circulation on the measurement of money growth and the substantial inflow of foreign currency—over the alternatives of a revision of the target corridor upwards and of a temporary suspension of the monetary targeting policy.[77]

The Council emphasized that the decision on whether a failure to hit the target was to be tolerated had to be taken against the background of real economic trends. If the economy was to pick up and signs were to re-emerge of rising inflation, a tighter limit would have to be set on the extent to which the target could be overshot.

This scenario duly came to pass in the autumn and winter of 1978. In December it was reported to the Central Bank Council that there was scarcely any sector of the economy showing no sign of recovery. Once the period of weak economic growth had been overcome and inflation seemed set to rise once more, price trends, and with them the monetary target, once again gained importance in the deliberations of the Central Bank Council.

e) The European Monetary System: saviour of monetary targeting

1978 was again very much under the shadow of external developments. On the one hand, the loss of international confidence in the US dollar led to a significant appreciation of the D-mark (Figure 3). Within the Bundesbank this development was viewed with concern as it would inevitably cause problems for Germany's export industries. On the other hand, following

---

[76] The Bundesbank emphasized in its 1977 Annual Report that the failure to meet the target in 1977 should not be interpreted as a departure from the stability-oriented policy. The renewed announcement of a monetary target for 1978 showed that the base line remained unchanged; short-term deviations from this line for real economic and external reasons were to be expected even within the framework of a policy of monetary targeting. Cf. Deutsche Bundesbank, Geschäftsbericht 1977, pp. 20ff.

[77] Cf. Deutsche Bundesbank, 1978a, pp. 5f. In the previous Monthly Report, the Bundesbank had spoken of inexplicable changes in currency in circulation that had distorted the central bank money stock; cf. Deutsche Bundesbank, 1978b, pp. 17f.

the adjustment of the central rates within the snake in the autumn of 1977, signs were emerging of an imminent reform of the system. More comprehensive regulations involving mutual support by the central banks and an increased symmetry within the snake—i.e. the weakening of the predominant position of the D-mark as the hardest currency in the system—were discussed, primarily against the background of an extension of the snake to incorporate the United Kingdom and to facilitate the re-entry of Italy and France. On the one hand, the Bundesbank welcomed prospects of an enlarged snake, as a larger currency area eased the pressure on the D-mark from speculative capital inflows from the dollar area. On the other hand, it was worried that a larger currency association could decide to adopt a common policy *vis-à-vis* the dollar which in the final analysis would have meant even greater intervention by the Bundesbank to support the dollar.

In June 1978 the Central Bank Council discussed various reform options for the snake. The reforms included the creation of a fund for exchange-rate policy cooperation, the definition of the central rates on the basis of the European Unit of Account—the precursor of the ECU—and coordinated action with respect to the dollar. To this extent the initiative for the creation of the European Monetary System (EMS) taken by Chancellor Helmut Schmidt and the French President Giscard d'Estaing at the EC Summit held in Bremen at the start of July did not come completely as a surprise.

It is not possible within the limited space of this article to review all the events that succeeded this summit meeting. Yet the creation of the EMS is important in our context because it exerted a strong influence on the Central Bank Council, not least regarding the issue of monetary targeting. This became evident when, in December, the proposal to set a monetary target for 1979 was discussed. A number of members were firmly of the opinion that it was high time to abandon a policy with which the Bundesbank, given the repeated overshooting of annual targets, had long exposed itself to ridicule. Neither within nor outside the Bundesbank had the monetary target been taken seriously as a benchmark, they argued.

In the opinion of other members, there were two prime reasons for retaining a monetary target. First, it was already clear that inflation was picking up once more, and a monetary target would make it easier to impose a more restrictive monetary policy stance. It was true that little attention had been paid to the target in the past years, but this was because the Bundesbank had in any case pursued an expansionary course; this would change in 1979.

Secondly, many members emphasized the damaging signals that would be sent by a visible departure from the policy of monetary targeting at the start of the new EMS: this would give the public the impression that the Bundesbank was giving up its efforts to maintain price stability in the face of the new external constraints. This would fuel inflationary expectations, they argued. In fact one member of the Directorate who in 1977 had sharply criticized the concept of monetary targeting proposed the view that refraining from setting a target for 1979 would create an undesirable impression on public opinion. The same member also drew attention to the favourable reputation of the monetary targeting policy abroad. It was also offered for consideration that, precisely because of the imminent establishment of the EMS, it was necessary to retain the practice of setting monetary targets to convince the partners within the system and the public at large that a European exchange-rate system could be reconciled with a rigorous stability orientation. In the event a substantial majority on the Central Bank Council voted to announce a monetary target for 1979. At the same time the publication of the target was intended to emphasize the experimental nature of this policy to a greater extent than in the past and to moderate expectations that the target would be met.

One may speculate about what would have happened had the EMS not been established at that time. There is considerable evidence for the view that the Bundesbank would have abandoned its practice of announcing monetary targets at the end of 1978. This would have been all the more likely if the cyclical upturn had taken longer to materialize. On the other hand it would be over-simplistic to claim that the Bundesbank had only maintained its policy of monetary targeting because of the EMS. There were other, good reasons for doing so. Yet there is a certain historical irony in the fact that the introduction of new external constraints, which inevitably reduced the autonomy of the monetary authority, strengthened the hand of the proponents of monetary targeting on the Central Bank Council.

f) The policy of monetary targeting: an interpretation

The standard textbook description of monetary policy classifies the strategy of monetary targeting under the Tinbergian paradigm of an optimizing economic policy according to which economic policy decision makers deploy their instruments so as to maximize a goal function containing the target variables price stability, employment, and growth. In this paradigm monetary targeting represents a two-stage solution of an economic policy problem: the first stage consists of the calculation of the monetary target on the basis of the final goals, the second stage involves directing all instruments to the derived goal of controlling the money stock in accordance with the target value. The strategy of monetary targeting itself is justified with reference to the predominant sources of economic disturbances.[78]

---

[78] Cf. Brunner and Meltzer, 1967; Friedman, 1979; von Hagen, 1986; Poole, 1970.

As a description of the monetary targeting strategy pursued by the Bundesbank in the 1970s this portrayal misses the mark in (at least) two important dimensions. The two-stage nature of the decisions—which would have implied during the course of the year that monetary policy considerations focus on achieving the monetary target—is not evident from the discussions in the Central Bank Council. Equally, the Council in no way resisted the temptation to direct individual monetary policy measures to short-term employment-related goals, instead of initially, as the two-stage model requires, expressing the implications of current real economic trends in adjustments to the monetary target. Rather, the target served as a restriction that was observed more or less closely in decision making.

Notwithstanding the above, the Bundesbank sought to signal its firm stability orientation by adopting the monetary targeting approach. It is not possible to determine conclusively the extent to which this proved successful. Certainly, the decisive stabilization policy of the years 1973 and 1974 and the—in international standards—decidedly low rates of inflation in Germany during the 1970s served to reduce inflationary expectations. Whether the monetary target had an expectations-related effect on top of this is uncertain. What can be concluded is that, given the lack of internal ties between monetary policy and the monetary target, grave doubts were held within the Bundesbank itself as to whether the target was really able to perform its signalling function.

Secondly, the idea of an 'optimizing' Central Bank Council as a *positive* paradigm is inappropriate, at least in this period. The optimization of a goal function implies that decision makers weigh up individual goals against one another, so that the deployment of their instruments reflects compromises between conflicting goals. In this case, signs of a gradual overshooting of the monetary target, even if this was accorded only a small weighting in the goal function, should lead to a gradual departure from the previous stance of monetary policy. Further, a marked change in the goal attainment to be expected in one dimension, with unchanged conditions in other dimensions, should mean that the instruments deployed are shifted markedly in favour of the first single goal. The experience of the years 1975–8 shows that the Central Bank Council did not act in that way.

The decisions taken by the Central Bank Council can be understood more readily in an alternative paradigm. Put briefly, the paradigm is that a change in the monetary policy instruments occurs only when there are sufficient grounds for the change. The discussions in the Central Bank Council consistently reflected efforts to check out various 'motivational fields' for monetary policy to see whether a change in the current stance was called for. In the period considered here these fields regularly included the development of the real economy, international trends, developments in the money and capital markets and price trends. Changes in the monetary policy instruments occurred when the current developments in a sufficient number of these 'motivational fields' pointed in the same direction. The *convergence of the views* on the monetary target for 1975 discussed earlier provides a clear example of this. If there are sufficient grounds for a change in central bank rates, then—and again this is in contrast to the idea of an optimizing monetary policy—the magnitude of the change is predetermined: it amounts to either 50 or 100 basis points.

Observation of the decision making processes in the Central Bank Council reveals that the relative importance of the various determining spheres can change markedly over time. Whereas at the start of the 1970s price trends were a very important field, their importance diminished in the mid-1970s, giving way to employment considerations. As one member of the Directorate once emphatically stated, acute problems repeatedly forced their way in front of the, in principle, generally accepted need for stringent medium-term control of monetary expansion. Thus the danger of excessive monetary expansion was accorded a lower weighting once the inflation rate had declined and at the same time the importance of other spheres of economic policy rose.

In this context the monetary target constitutes an additional 'motivational field' that implicitly reinforced the importance of price trends as a sphere. Its nature as an intermediate target, however, as Schlesinger once emphasized, meant that the weight of this field depended on the importance of the inflation rate as a 'motivational field' itself. Yet this does not mean that the monetary target was redundant. Its importance in the decision making process was that it concretized the goal of price stability and, above all, projected it into a short-term time frame. The uncertainty surrounding the impact of current decisions on changes in the price level, and the relatively long time horizon of monetary policy measures compared with cyclical fluctuations, meant that monetary policy was prone to neglect the goal of price stability in its day-to-day action. The monetary target was helpful because the implications of current decisions for monetary growth could be seen more clearly and more quickly.

Seen from this perspective, it is also readily understood why the EMS became the saviour of monetary targeting. For the Bundesbank, incorporation into a new exchange-rate system implied the danger of a renewed loss of monetary control and thus, at the end of the day, a new inflationary threat. Therefore the new external restriction inevitably led to an increase in the importance of the goal of price stability as a 'motivational field' for monetary policy measures, not least because the Bundesbank was best able to withstand political pressure from government—which was responsible for the exchange-rate system—by reference to the goal of price stability. The increased importance of this field in the decisions by the Central Bank Council served to strengthen the monetary target, all the more so given that intervention in support of weaker partner currencies is reflected most rapidly in monetary trends, so that the latter serve as a yardstick for the compatibility of the exchange-rate system with the goal of price stability. Seen in this way, the EMS probably not only gave the impetus for the retention of the monetary targets, but also for the refinement of this policy in the direction of a more rigorous orientation towards medium-term potential growth, that is to a policy of 'limited steadiness' as pursued by the Bundesbank in the 1980s.

5. Bibliography

Alexander, Volbert/Loef, Hans-Edi (1974): Kontrolle der Geldbasis und ihrer Komponenten —Eine empirische Analyse für die BRD, in: Kredit und Kapital 7, pp. 508–41

Bleile, Georg (1975): Die neue Geldpolitik der Deutschen Bundesbank, in: Zeitschrift für das gesamte Kreditwesen 28, pp. 22–5

Bockelmann, Horst (1976): Streitfragen zur Kontrolle der Geldschöpfung durch die Notenbank. Paper read before the Committee for monetary theory and monetary policy of the Verein für Socialpolitik, Frankfurt a.M. 10 May

Bockelmann, Horst (1984): Orientierungspunkte der Geldpolitik, in: Kredit und Kapital 17, pp. 64–83

Bockelmann, Horst (1989): Haupt- und Nebensachen—der Kurswechsel in der Geldpolitik der Bundesbank 1973/74, in: Bub, Norbert/Duwendag, Dieter/Richter, Rudolf (eds.): Geldwertstabilität und Wirtschaftsstabilität. Festschrift für Helmut Schlesinger, Frankfurt a.M., pp. 191–202

Brunner, Karl (1973): A diagrammatic exposition of the money supply process, in: Schweizerische Zeitschrift für Nationalökonomie und Statistik 109, pp. 481–553

Brunner, Karl/Meltzer, Allan H. (1967): The meaning of monetary indicators, in: Horwich, George (ed.): Monetary process and policy, Homewood, pp. 187–207

Caesar, Rolf (1976): Die Rolle der Mindestreserve im Rahmen der Geldbasiskonzeption der Deutschen Bundesbank, in: Jahrbücher für Nationalökonomie und Statistik 191, pp. 229–50

Deutsche Bundesbank (1973): Neuabgrenzung der freien Liquiditätsreserven der Banken, in: Monatsbericht 25, 6, pp. 47–8

Deutsche Bundesbank (1978a): Neue geldpolitische Maßnahmen, in: Monatsbericht 30, 7, pp. 5–6

Deutsche Bundesbank (1978b): Die Wirtschaftslage im Frühjahr 1978, in: Monatsbericht 30, 6, pp. 13–46

Deutsche Bundesbank (1982): Zentralbankgeldbedarf der Banken und liquiditätspolitische Maßnahmen der Bundesbank, in: Monatsbericht 34, 4, pp. 21–6

Deutsche Bundesbank (various): Monatsberichte

Deutsche Bundesbank (various years): Geschäftsberichte, Frankfurt a.M.

Deutscher Gewerkschaftsbund (1970): Die wirtschaftlichen und sozialen Entwicklungsmöglichkeiten in der Bundesrepublik Deutschland, duplicated manuscript, Düsseldorf 7 October

Deutsches Institut für Wirtschaftsforschung (1973): Bundesbankgesetz und aktuelle Geld-politik, in: Wochenbericht 40, 23, pp. 201–08

Dudler, Hermann-Josef (1983): Instrumente und quantitative Hilfsmittel der kurzfristigen Geldmengenkontrolle, in: Ehrlicher, Werner/Richter, Rudolf (eds.): Geld- und Währungs-ordnung, Schriften des Vereins für Socialpolitik, N.F. vol. 138, Berlin, pp. 39–84

Emminger, Otmar (1986): D-Mark, Dollar, Währungskrisen. Erinnerungen eines ehemaligen Bundesbankpräsidenten, Stuttgart

Friedman, Benjamin M. (1979): Targets, instruments, and indicators of monetary policy, in: Brunner, Karl/Neumann, Manfred J.M. (eds.): Inflation, unemployment and monetary control, Supplement 5 of Kredit und Kapital, Berlin, pp. 248–87

Friedman, Milton (1968): The Role of Monetary Policy, in: American Economic Review 58, pp. 1–17

Geiger, Helmut (1988): Das Verhältnis von Refinanzierungs- und Offenmarktpolitik, in: Ehrlicher, Werner/Simmert, Diethard B. (eds.): Wandlungen des geldpolitischen Instru-mentariums der Deutschen Bundesbank, Supplement 10 of Kredit und Kapital, Berlin, pp. 129–42

Hagelstein, Bert (1972): Was Karl Schiller nicht unterschrieb, in: Handelsblatt, 3 July

Hagen, Jürgen von (1986): Strategien kurzfristiger Geldmengensteuerung, Hamburg

Irmler, Heinrich (1974): Ausführungen von Dr. Heinrich Irmler, in: Deutsche Bundesbank: Auszüge aus Presseartikeln, no. 75, pp. 1–5

Kannengießer, Walter (1972): Der ungeliebte Professor geht, in: Frankfurter Allgemeine Zeitung, 7 July

Kannengießer, Walter/Barbier, Hans D. (1972): Karl Schiller über Karl Schiller und seine Politik, in: Frankfurter Allgemeine Zeitung, 7 July

Klasen, Karl (1971): Aktuelle Probleme der Währungspolitik, in: Deutsche Bundesbank: Auszüge aus Presseartikeln, no. 89, pp. 1–8

Mainert, Alf (1974): Zentralbankgeldsteuerung—die neue Kreditpolitik der Bundesbank. Summary of a lecture held for the Bundesbank's internal training scheme, unpublished manuscript, November

Nemitz, Kurt (1980): Aspekte der Geldmarktsteuerung, in: Kredit und Kapital 13, pp. 323–37

Neumann, Manfred J. M. (1975): Konstrukte der Zentralbankgeldmenge, in: Kredit und Kapital 8, pp. 317–45

Neumann, Manfred J. M. (1977): A Theoretical and Empirical Analysis of the German Money Supply Process, in: Frowen, Stephen F./Courakis, Anthony S./Miller, Marcus H. (eds.): Monetary Policy and Economic Activity in West Germany, Stuttgart, pp. 73–124

Neumann, Manfred J. M. (1981): Der Beitrag der Geldpolitik zur konjunkturellen Entwick-lung in der Bundesrepublik Deutschland, in: Kyklos 34, pp. 405–31

Neumann, Manfred J. M./Hagen, Jürgen von (1993): Germany, in: Fratianni, Michele/Salvatore, Dominick (eds.): Monetary Policy in Developed Economies, Westport, CT/London, pp. 299–334

Niehans, Jürg (1978): The Theory of Money, Baltimore

Pohl, Reinhard (1988): Die außenwirtschaftliche Komponente der Geldversorgung, in: Ehrlicher, Werner/Simmert, Diethard B. (eds.): Wandlungen des geldpolitischen Instru-mentariums der Deutschen Bundesbank, Supplement 10 of Kredit und Kapital, Berlin, pp. 177–215

Poole, William (1970): Optimal choice of monetary policy instruments in a simple stochastic macro model, in: Quarterly Journal of Economics 84, pp. 197–216

Sachverständigenrat zur Begutachtung der gesamtwirtschaftlichen Lage (various years): Jahresgutachten, Stuttgart

Schiller, Karl (1972): Regierungsmotto 'Nach uns die Sintflut', in: Der Arbeitgeber 24, p. 560

Schillers Rücktritt—Addition von Ursachen (1972), in: ifo Schnelldienst 53, 22

Schlesinger, Helmut (1973): Die Geldpolitik als Mittel der Inflationsbekämpfung, in: Deutsche Bundesbank: Auszüge aus Presseartikeln, no. 54, pp. 1, 4–8

Schlesinger, Helmut (1978): Die Geldpolitik der Deutschen Bundesbank 1967–1977, in: Kredit und Kapital 11, pp. 3–29

Schlesinger, Helmut (1988): Das Konzept der Deutschen Bundesbank, in: Ehrlicher, Werner/ Simmert, Diethard B. (eds.): Wandlungen des geldpolitischen Instrumentariums der Deutschen Bundesbank, Supplement 10 of Kredit und Kapital, Berlin, pp. 3–20

Schmidt, Helmut (1990a): Die Bürokraten ausgetrickst, in: Die Zeit, 24 August

Schmidt, Helmut (1990b): Kampf gegen die Nationalisten, in: Die Zeit, 31 August

Simmert, Diethart B./Zweig, Gerhard (1980): Instrumente auf dem Prüfstand, in: Wirtschaftsdienst 60, pp. 226–30

Steves, Kurt (1974): Bonner Wünsche an die Notenbank, in: Die Welt, 11 October

Willms, Manfred (1971): Controlling Money in an Open Economy: The German Case, in: Federal Reserve Bank of St. Louis Review 53, 4, pp. 10–27

IX. Monetary Policy under Conditions of Increasing Integration (1979–96)

By Ernst Baltensperger

1. Introduction

During the period 1979–96 the Bundesbank had to meet a series of difficult challenges. It repeatedly faced sharp criticism both at home and abroad, and its policy was the subject of intense debate. Yet overall—in terms of its degree of goal attainment and the international reputation earned by the Bundesbank—this policy can undoubtedly be seen as an unequivocal success, at least compared to that pursued by the overwhelming majority of other central banks during the same period. This is manifested not least in the fact that under the terms of the Maastricht Treaty the Bundesbank served as a model for the establishment of a European central bank. It is therefore an interesting task to present and evaluate this policy, which, following the collapse of the Bretton Woods system of fixed exchange rates, first had to be defined in the early 1970s and then had to be gradually tested and developed.

The period 1979–96 has in common with the period 1971–8 that monetary policy, in contrast to the situation under the Bretton Woods system, could be conducted within a regime of, in principle, 'floating' exchange rates, giving the Bundesbank the scope for national control of the money stock. At an early stage the Bundesbank decided to make full use of this scope and to place it at the service of the goal of price stability (stability of the internal value of money). From the outset it did this by pursuing a policy of medium-term-oriented control of the money stock, and from 1975 within the framework of a strategy of announcing annual monetary targets, a strategy to which it has remained faithful to this day, even though over the years this policy has repeatedly been discussed and occasionally called into question both at home and abroad, and even within the decision making bodies of the Bundesbank itself.

In contrast to the previous period, from 1971 to 1978, however, by 1979 potential-oriented monetary targeting strategy had in principle already been established within the Bundesbank and had, provisionally at least, proved its worth, whereas in the former period the focus had been on developing and testing the concept. In an additional contrast to the previous period, in 1979 the European Monetary System (EMS) came into effect, a system of international agreements that meant for the monetary authorities in the Member States, and thus for the Bundesbank, new restrictions and intervention obligations. Yet the Bundesbank proved able successfully to maintain its stability-oriented monetary targeting strategy within such an exchange-rate system, this in the context of the increasing integration of European and global financial markets. Thus the Bundesbank has *de facto*, without this having been envisaged in the design of the system, become the dominant central bank and the D-mark the anchor currency in the EMS. At the same time the period also provides graphic illustration of the prime importance of the independence of the central bank from government. Only under such institutional conditions—and against the background of a keen awareness of the importance of price stability among the population—namely, was the Bundesbank able successfully to withstand the at times massive pressure from foreign and domestic political forces, and to stick to the stability-oriented policy it considered correct. At the same time the period also illustrates in all clarity that in an inflationary international environment there exists over the medium and longer term an irresolvable conflict between the aims of price stability (stability of the internal value of money) and nominal exchange-rate stability (external stability of the value of money).

The period considered here also saw, besides the development of the EMS, a number of decisive international economic events, such as the second oil-price shock at the end of the 1970s, the international debt crisis of the early and mid-1980s, the huge fluctuations in the exchange rate of the US dollar throughout the 1980s brought about by the monetary and fiscal policies pursued by the USA, and the collapse of share prices in the autumn of 1987. All these events generated thorny adjustment and decision making problems for the monetary authorities in Germany and elsewhere. A challenge of a very special sort that confronted the Bundesbank with extraordinary—in this case specifically German—problems in the final third of the period under consideration was German monetary union within the framework of German reunification in 1990. Also of fundamental importance are, of course, the plans for the creation of European Monetary Union that have become increasingly concrete since the start of the 1990s.

The observation period saw a constant development of the Bundesbank's monetary policy instruments, both as the result of a learning process from the accumulated experiences with these instruments and as an adjustment to changed conditions in the central bank's operating environment, in particular to the liberalization, internationalization, and intensification of competition in the banking and finance sector. More specifically, of central importance was the development of instruments suitable for a more flexible steering of the money market by means of open market policy measures and, linked to this, the gradual reduction in the importance of discount and Lombard rate policy, and the restructuring (and declining importance) of minimum reserve policy that occurred during the period.

The presentation of Bundesbank policy in this article is divided, inevitably rather arbitrarily, into six phases, each of which is characterized by a change in the monetary policy stance and the monetary policy environment: 1979–81 ('Monetary restriction'), 1982–5 ('Relaxation and normalization of monetary policy'), 1986–9 ('Monetary growth in excess of targets and slow return to restriction'), 1990–1 ('German monetary union'), 1992–4 ('The Bundesbank at the centre of international critique: gradual relaxation and monetary growth way above target'), and 1995–6 ('Normalization of monetary growth and continued interest-rate cuts').

For each of these phases a brief summary of monetary and exchange-rate policy activities by the Bundesbank, including the events occurring in its environment and the most important areas of conflict within monetary policy, the targets set by the Bundesbank and their attainment, the public debate on these matters, and an evaluation is given. Controversial issues of general interest and developments of special importance are discussed where appropriate. In conclusion, in a number of additional sections a summary is given of the most important lessons that can be learnt from an observation of German monetary policy during the last two decades. These refer among other things to the appropriateness and feasibility of a strategy of monetary targets, the operationalization of such a policy and the instrumentation required to this end, together with an overall evaluation of Bundesbank policy during the period considered and of the social and institutional context in which it occurred.

2. Monetary restriction: 1979–81

a) Point of departure and economic environment

The economic situation that presented itself to the Bundesbank at the start of our period, in 1979, was, seen at the time, rather comfortable. In 1978 real German GDP had grown by 3 per cent and grew in 1979 at a rate of 4.2 per cent, accompanied by high levels of capacity utilization, employment growth, and falling unemployment (unemployment rate: 3.3 per cent), and strong investment. The situation was less positive, on the other hand, in terms of inflation and monetary growth. Signs of an acceleration in the rate of inflation had emerged during the course of the previous year, and on annual average figures inflation reached 4.1 per cent in 1979, rising further from 1979 to 1981. This—not particularly surprising—trend arose against the background of the sharp increases in the price of oil from 1978 (second oil crisis) and strong monetary growth in the previous years. In 1978, in particular, the actual growth of central bank money of more than 11 per cent was far in excess of the target of 8 per cent originally set by the Bundesbank, not least due to the then prevailing strong orientation of monetary policy towards exchange rates. In international comparative terms, on the other hand, in particular compared with the USA, but also with leading European partner countries such as France, the UK, and Italy, German inflation remained moderate; indeed, the price stability differential *vis-à-vis* these countries widened further.

The massive increase in import prices, especially energy prices, also brought about a turnaround in Germany's current account position, with the Federal Republic posting a current account deficit for the first time in many years in 1979. The growing inflationary pressure and the shift in the current account induced the Bundesbank to fundamentally change its policy stance, leading to a sharply restrictive monetary policy until the end of 1981. The very robust state of the economy in the first year (1979) meant that this was initially relatively unproblematic. The maintenance of the restrictive stance in 1980 and 1981, however, was increasingly under the shadow of declining growth rates and a cyclical downturn. This was a consequence both of the global stabilization crisis which was then taking hold and the restrictive monetary policy pursued by the Bundesbank. In 1980 German GDP managed to grow by 1.0 per cent in real terms, with employment falling from the third quarter and rising unemployment; in 1981 real GDP stagnated and the unemployment rate rose to 4.8 per cent. In 1980 the current account deficit widened enormously on the previous year to DM 24 billion (although in volume terms exports remained relatively strong). From 1980 onwards another important development for the Federal Republic was the onset of a weakening of the D-mark. In 1979 the D-mark was still strong internationally, but it experienced marked depreciation beginning in 1980, particularly against the US dollar, but also within the EMS. Only in the course of 1981 did these processes in Germany's external position begin to be reversed, partly due to the policies implemented.

During this phase the current account position and the exchange rate became important additional target criteria for the Bundesbank, and as the economy increasingly cooled down they came more and more into conflict with the goal of smoothing out and stimulating the business cycle. This in turn gave rise to debate on this issue both within the Bundesbank itself and in the media. On the other hand, the monetary policy orientation towards Germany's external position was not in conflict with the aim of price stability during this phase. Given that inflation rose to 5.4 per cent in 1980 and 6.3 per cent in 1981 (annual average figures), this called for a restrictive monetary policy, just as did the need to strengthen the D-mark. It was not until towards the end of 1981 that all these processes began to turn around, enabling the Bundesbank to move over to a somewhat more relaxed stance.

During this period Bundesbank policy gave price stability and the external target criteria clear priority over stabilizing growth, based on the correct realization that stability of the real economy is not viable in the longer term without monetary stability. Rather less clear, on the other hand, is the extent to which it was the internal or the external value of money that was the predominant target for the Bundesbank. On the one hand it repeatedly emphasized the supreme importance of price stability and the fight against inflation, incorporating this view in internal decisions by the Central Bank Council. On the other hand, it equally frequently, if not more often, justified its restrictive policy in this period with reference to external 'adjustment requirements' and stability considerations. This ambivalence was also frequently expressed in the discussions in the Central Bank Council. In the final analysis, though, it is idle speculation to debate this point, given that in the prevailing situation there was no real conflict between the two target criteria.

Throughout the period 1979–81 government fiscal policy was clearly expansionary and gradually created a need for fiscal consolidation. Thus it offered the Bundesbank little support, indeed fiscal trends rendered its task more difficult.[1]

The EMS began quietly in March 1979, but subsequently faced tensions and the need to adjust central rates from as early as September 1979. Even in the first year of its existence it was evident that the Bundesbank would only be able to pursue an independent monetary policy in the face of the intervention obligations implied by the EMS in cases of international differentials in inflation rates for as long as the willingness to ease pressure by adjusting central exchange rate parities remained. The phase of relative D-mark weakness, which manifested itself within the EMS particularly in 1980, initially served to reduce tensions within the system, however. Not until 1981 did major shifts in central parities occur once more, this time with appreciation of the D-mark.

---

[1] The same was true to an even greater extent of the fiscal policy stance of the USA at the time.

b) The monetary policy of the Bundesbank in detail

Monetary targets and monetary growth

The will of the Bundesbank to pursue a monetary policy strictly oriented towards price stability manifested itself in a marked reduction in the targets for monetary growth during the period 1979–81 compared with the previous years. The methodological approach to the setting of monetary targets remained in principle unchanged on the previous years (and indeed over the entire subsequent period to the present day). The point of departure was an estimation of the growth of potential output; on top of this came a (depending on the situation prevailing at the time) rate of inflation considered 'unavoidable' and thus acceptable in the short term[2] (and later a correction for the secular change in the velocity of circulation and, in some years, a correction for negative developments that had occurred in previous periods). The monetary aggregate used as the target, central bank money, also initially remained unchanged. What was new in 1979, however, was the choice of a four-quarter target (from the fourth quarter of the previous year to the fourth quarter of the current year, instead of an annual average target) and the setting of a target corridor (rather than a single target figure), the breadth of which reflected the uncertainties facing the monetary authorities in setting the target. The corridor was to enable the Bundesbank, depending on cyclical trends on the one hand and exchange-rate developments on the other, to head for the upper or lower limit, a practice to which the Bundesbank has remained faithful to this day. The target was announced (and has been since) in the December of the previous year for the subsequent period. It has also become standard practice to review the targets in mid-year.

By markedly reducing the monetary target straight away in 1979, the Bundesbank intended to send out a clear signal on price stability. The following years saw successive further reductions in the target corridor: the target rates of growth for central bank money announced by the Bundesbank were 6–9 per cent for 1979, 5–8 per cent for 1980 and 4–7 per cent for 1981. The actual rates of growth were around 6 per cent in 1979, 5 per cent in 1980 and 4 per cent in 1981 (Figure 1). Thus in all three years the actual trend was along the lower limit of the announced corridor. This reflected the Bundesbank's concern with a persistently high rate of inflation and the weakness of the D-mark and in the current account position characterizing much of this period, and initially also the still strong growth of the

---

[2] Once price stability had been regained in the mid-1980s this was replaced by the concept of a 'normative' rate of inflation.

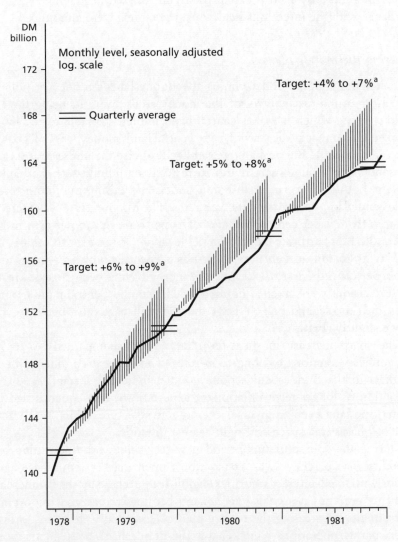

FIGURE I: Monetary targets and actual monetary
growth, 1979–81* (target and movement to date)

* Central bank money stock: currency in circulation (excluding the banks' holdings of
domestic notes and coins) plus the required reserves on domestic liabilities other than bank
debt securities subject to minimum reserves (calculated at constant reserve ratios, base: January
1974).

[a] Between the fourth quarter of the previous year and the fourth quarter of the current
year.

Source: Deutsche Bundesbank.

domestic economy. To this extent the trend realized in practice was in accordance with the intentions held when the targets were announced.

Steering the money market

The steering concept underpinning the Bundesbank's monetary policy is based on an indirect control of the money stock by influencing the conditions under which it makes central bank money available to the money market. Given that at the start of 1979 central bank money was still growing at a rapid rate, the Bundesbank was obliged to raise the interest rates under its control by a huge margin and to restrict the liquidity of the banking system, both by lowering rediscount quotas and raising minimum reserve ratios and also by increasing its base rates. The discount rate was increased in steps from 3 per cent at the start of 1979 to reach 7.5 per cent in May 1980, the Lombard rate from its initial level of 3.5 per cent to 9.5 per cent in May 1980, and in February 1981—as a 'special Lombard'—to as much as 12 per cent, the normal Lombard window having been closed. Most of these decisions were taken after intense debate in the Central Bank Council. Not until the second half of 1981 did the high base rates begin to come down slightly (Figure 2).

The sharp increase in short-term rates was accompanied by far less pronounced reactions by long-term rates. This vote of confidence by the markets in the Bundesbank's policy (which reflected a stabilization and reduction of longer-term inflationary expectations) consequently led to a flatter, and later even an inverse, interest-rate structure, which is characteristic of phases of a successful fight against inflation.

During the course of this period new techniques for fine-tuning bank liquidity via currency swap transactions, open market repurchase agreements with fixed-interest securities eligible for purchase by the Bundesbank, and later currency repurchase agreements became increasingly important as instruments for steering the money market. Essentially these are forms of open market operations which enable the Bundesbank to steer the money market far more flexibly than is possible using the traditional instruments of discount and Lombard rate policy or minimum reserve policy. In particular the Bundesbank saw the advantage of being able to take the initiative itself as regards maturity period and rates. The Bundesbank was seeking to reduce the central importance of the Lombard credit in this phase and to replace it with the new, more flexible instruments. As the use of these instruments increased, the day rate steered by them increasingly became the central interest rate targeted. Changes in the official base rates—the discount and Lombard rates—increasingly assumed a function that was primarily to send signals to the markets.

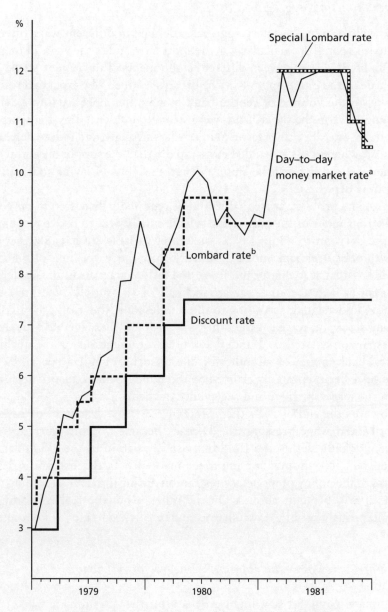

FIGURE 2: Base rates and the money market rate, 1979–81

[a] Monthly averages.
[b] Special Lombard rate from 20 February 1981 to 6 May 1982.
Source: Deutsche Bundesbank.

Other monetary aggregates

As is well known, monetary aggregates defined in different ways often fail
to move in parallel, particularly in the short term and in the wake of interest-
rate-induced shifts between different components of the money stock. This
was true of the phase 1979–81. The broadly defined M3 expanded roughly
parallel to the volume of central bank money; the more narrowly defined
M1 and M2, on the other hand, were strongly influenced by the sharp rise
in interest rates. For this reason M1 grew less strongly, and indeed negatively
in 1981, whereas M2 expanded more rapidly than the supply of central bank
money (reflecting portfolio shifts away from sight and savings deposits and
into time deposits).

In 1981 a problem arose that would be repeatedly discussed in the course
of the remainder of the period and which, finally, was to prove responsible
for the decision to adopt M3 as the target variable from 1988: the weak
growth of central bank money—in fact below the lower limit of the target
corridor—that was due primarily to the virtual stagnation of the demand
for cash (which accounts for around half of the supply of central bank
money) understated, according to the Bundesbank, the 'real' growth of the
money stock, or, to put it the other way around, it exaggerated the degree
of restriction exerted by Bundesbank policy. Limitations on the quality of
central bank money as an indicator due to such or similar 'special factors'
have since been repeatedly claimed by the Bundesbank to justify departures
from the target corridor and acceptance of them.

Towards the end of 1981 there were increasingly clear signs of an easing
of price and wage pressure; the D-mark became a strong currency once
more, not only within the EMS but also in relation to the US dollar, and
the current account position improved markedly. To this extent the desired
effects of the policy of monetary restriction during the three preceding years
were clearly brought about.[3] On the other hand, the real economy was
simultaneously cooling down sharply and threatened to move into recession.

c) Controversy over the appropriate degree of restriction

The phase 1979–81 saw intense debate on the question of whether the
monetary policy stance adopted was appropriate to the situation, or whether
it was excessively restrictive. In 1979 approval of the stance taken was

---

[3] The movements of capital market interest rates, inflation rates, and the external value of
the D-mark during the 1979–96 period considered in this article are presented in Figures 13
and 14.

relatively widespread, at least in Germany itself, and criticism of Germany's high interest rate policy came largely from abroad and in particular from the USA:[4] it was alleged that Germany had started an 'interest-rate war' which detracted attention from the domestic problems of US economic policy and was completely unjustified in economic terms. Yet as the real economic situation increasingly worsened in 1980 and 1981, criticism of the 'excessively restrictive stance' taken by the Bundesbank intensified, not least within Germany itself.

This is typical of phases characterized by the fight against inflation and monetary restriction and has been repeatedly experienced during similar phases and in other countries. There were two main thrusts to the debate. On the one hand there was a highly pragmatic discussion on the appropriate degree of restriction to be adopted by the central bank. This was linked closely to the weight attached to the various goals of central bank policy. Depending on whether stabilizing the domestic price level, the exchange rate or smoothing out the business cycle was considered most important as a goal of central bank policy, different commentators arrived at different recommendations.

On the other hand, there was also a debate that sought to analyse and evaluate monetary policy from a theoretical and fundamental perspective. Were the policies pursued being implemented in a stable fashion, or were they characterized by excessive instability? Was day-to-day policy in accordance with the claim that it was oriented towards medium-term potential output? Questions such as these led to debates on alternative monetary policy conceptions and strategies and their relationship to the reality of economic policy, and posed questions, for instance, as to the 'correct' monetary target aggregate, the advisability of using target corridors (rather than single-figure targets) and of multi-annual targets, or as to the appropriate instruments to be used in pursuit of monetary targets. The debate on these issues will now be briefly described and discussed.

Orientation of monetary policy to the external position

One of the central debates throughout the 1979–81 phase concerned the question of the weight attached to external economic factors in implementing monetary policy. Particularly in the years of current account and currency weakness—1980 and 1981—the debate took on a, for Germany, rather untypical form. During this phase, the criticism that the Bundesbank was oriented too closely towards the external position came primarily from

---

[4] With Henry Reuss, the influential chairman of the banking committee of the US House of Representatives, as its main exponent.

the camp of those emphasizing demand management as the prime target of monetary policy and who consequently denounced the Bundesbank's high-interest policy, which during this phase was primarily oriented towards external adjustment and bolstering the D-mark, as excessively restrictive and damaging to economic growth; in most cases they played down the inflationary threat posed by a policy of lower interest rates and faster monetary growth.[5] In 1980 and even more so in 1981, the criticism to which the Bundesbank was exposed from this quarter was extremely harsh, culminating in public reprimands by the then Chancellor Helmut Schmidt. What is striking is that these debates were conducted primarily in terms of a conflict between an external orientation (towards the exchange rate or the balance of payments) and an internal orientation in the sense of stabilizing the business cycle and the labour market. What was not taken sufficiently into account was the Bundesbank's declared priority target, that of internal price stability. Retrospectively, it appears that the demands made at the time for a significantly less restrictive policy were ill-justified given that the inflation rate in Germany remained persistently high until well into 1981, with no signs of success in the fight against inflation emerging until the start of 1982. To a certain extent, though, the Bundesbank itself contributed to this alignment of the debate in that all too frequently it sought to justify its policies with purely external arguments (strengthening the D-mark, balancing the current account).

The general reproach that Bundesbank policy in the period 1979–81 was too restrictive is certainly unjustified. In terms of its main aim, the fight against inflation, the Bundesbank's policy was at the end of the day very successful. If the recommendations made by the above-mentioned critics had been followed, this success would not have been achieved, or would have taken far longer. Given the central goal of price stability and the situation prevailing at the start of 1979, a clearly restrictive policy stance was unavoidable. Consequently, the correct view is that the Bundesbank, to the extent that it was at all responsible for the subsequent economic downturn, was so not because of its high-interest policy between 1979 and 1981, but because of its all too expansionary and excessively exchange-rate-oriented monetary policy in 1977–8, the knock-on effects of which then had to be corrected. In this respect, the Bundesbank exhibited a tendency to portray

---

[5] One of the most vehement critics of this school was Rüdiger Pohl of the University of Hagen (cf., for instance, Pohl, 1981), but some of the German economic research institutes were also critical. Ironically, Pohl and others expressing harsh criticism of the external orientation of the Bundesbank in the 1979–81 phase shifted ground in later phases characterized by opposite conditions on the foreign exchange market (a strong D-mark), and became unreserved proponents of an external orientation and the Bundesbank's supposed 'international responsibility' (see especially section 5).

the rising prices in the years 1980 and 1981 primarily as an exogenous occurrence resulting from the increase in oil and import prices and the weakening of the D-mark, which then had to be dealt with. The partial responsibility of the Bundesbank's own monetary policy in the years 1977–8 for this development cannot be overlooked, however.

A more highly differentiated critique came from those who supported Bundesbank policy in prioritizing the target of price stability. They called for a monetary policy more unequivocally oriented towards this goal, one with greater continuity and less regard for exchange-rate considerations.[6] Could, for example, a multi-annual target announcement at the start of 1979 have reduced inflationary expectations more quickly, thus making the adjustment process to lower rates of inflation proceed with less friction? Perhaps. But in retrospect it must be recognized that in fact the Bundesbank pursued a decidedly continuous monetary policy during the 1979–81 phase, and that it clearly proved successful, as evinced for instance by its influence on German long-term interest rates, in rapidly stabilizing and then reducing inflationary expectations. Would the recessionary phase in 1981–2 have been milder if the Bundesbank had relaxed its stance more quickly in 1981? Perhaps. It would be difficult to prove this assertion, however, as the recession was not restricted to Germany and, moreover, was neither particularly long nor deep.

What the 1979–81 period, together with the preceding phase (1977–8), clearly shows, however, is the risk to the Bundesbank's other goals that emerges if monetary policy is oriented towards the exchange rate. This does not mean that such risks should never be taken, but merely that one must be conscious of them.

Monetary target and monetary target variable

In Germany, and at the time worldwide, the concept of a monetary policy based on money stock control and on the announcement of monetary targets was widely endorsed. Yet it was never entirely uncontroversial, even in the 1979–81 period, neither among the general public nor in the Bundesbank's Central Bank Council. Thus even in this phase certain critics posed the question whether monetary targets made any sense at all 'in such uncertain times'. Having said that, no broadly based critique was developed on this basis during the 1979–81 phase.

The issue of the appropriate monetary target variables, on the other hand,

---

[6] Criticism of this type came from, among others, the Institut für Weltwirtschaft, Kiel (cf., for example, Trapp, 1979), Manfred J. M. Neumann of the University of Bonn (cf., for example, Neumann, 1982) and the Shadow European Economic Policy Committee, 1979.

was highly controversial. In particular, the monetary aggregate M1 was put forward as an alternative intermediate target and indicator variable in opposition to central bank money as favoured by the Bundesbank. This point was made most forcefully by the Institut für Weltwirtschaft, Kiel. The critique emanating from Kiel of the excessively restrictive stance adopted by Bundesbank policy and that of other opponents following a similar line of argument was closely linked to the choice of this indicator. Given that in high-interest phases the narrowly defined M1 typically lags behind more broadly defined aggregates (such as M3 or central bank money) owing to interest-rate-induced shifts from sight to time deposits, observation of M1 created the impression of a far higher degree of restriction than on the basis of central bank money. This shows that, in certain situations, each and every conception of the money stock has its disadvantages as a monetary policy indicator. In the medium and longer term, however, these differences largely disappear. The central idea behind a monetary targeting policy is that, by imposing rigorous constraint on monetary growth, a corresponding limitation on secular price level trends and thus a nominal anchoring of the price system can be assured. In principle, this is equally possible with various definitions of the money stock.

Target corridor

The decision by the Bundesbank to adopt a corridor for its target variable resulted in some criticism. The idea behind this corridor was that the central bank required a degree of scope with which to allow for developments that were unknown or could not be precisely foreseen at the time the targets were announced; such developments could occur on the foreign exchange and financial markets, or could involve real economic or price trends. In this conception, the announcement of the monetary target has the function of providing economic agents with information on the monetary policy intentions of the central bank, and therefore influences and anchors their expectations. For the central bank, this at the same time implies a binding commitment and an obligation to justify any failure to meet the target. The corridor grants the central bank the necessary—in view of the myriad uncertainties pertaining to monetary policy—flexibility in performing this task. In particular, the aim was to enable adjustments to monetary policy to be made within certain limits without this automatically being construed as missing the target. Under this concept, the width of the corridor was meant to reflect the factors of uncertainty prevailing at the time the target was set. Against this background, the Bundesbank initially selected a band width of three percentage points; later it reduced this to two percentage points.

This concept stands and falls by the width of the corridor selected and the conviction with which the central bank is able to justify the course of monetary growth within (or where applicable outside) the corridor. On its introduction in 1979 and in the following years, the idea of a corridor of three percentage points was criticized by various observers as making it more difficult for market agents to formulate their expectations and as a potential relapse into discretionary monetary policy.[7] When announcing the targets, the Bundesbank has sought from the outset to explain under which conditions (in particular, exchange rate and real economic trends) it would attempt to follow a path in the upper or lower region of the target corridor. And during the 1979–81 period it stuck to this very well. To this extent its approach is not essentially different from that of announcing conditional single-figure targets.[8] From today's perspective, against the background of 20 years of practical and academic debate and experience with monetary targets, the idea of announcing conditional targets, either in the form of single-figure targets or a corridor, appears unproblematic and well-established, as long as it is used sensibly, given the myriad uncertainties in the central bank's environment (cf. section 8).

d) New forms of steering the money market

The Bundesbank took an important step in the development of its range of instruments for steering the money market during the 1979–81 period. The introduction of open market policy instruments, particularly in the form of 'securities' repurchase agreements (open market transactions with a repurchase agreement), and the parallel decline in the importance of discount and Lombard policy marked the start of a process that, in the course of the 1980s, was finally to lead to the unambiguous replacement of the latter by open market instruments as the predominant means of provision and supply of central bank money. In 1980 securities repurchase agreements accounted for a share of 6 per cent of the creation of central bank money; by 1989 this figure was to rise to 60 per cent and in the 1990s to over 70 per cent.

The lowest refinancing rate offered by the Bundesbank is the discount rate; its low level implies a subsidy in the granting of discount credit. Thus the banks clearly have an interest in making use of such credits. The Bundesbank itself was keen to keep unused rediscounting quotas—which from

---

[7] Cf., for example, Neumann, 1979.

[8] The strategy followed by the Schweizerische Nationalbank, for example.

its point of view constituted potential central bank money not directly under its control—small by adjusting the quotas accordingly. For this reason, discount policy is not suitable as an active instrument for fine-tuning the money market. Moreover, due to the inherent element of subsidization, discount policy can frequently not be reconciled with the principle of competitive neutrality. The Lombard loan (i.e. a loan by the Bundesbank against security) traditionally has the function of meeting situations of peak demand on the money market. The interest rate for Lombard loans, which according to the original conception are available without quantitative limitations, is therefore always higher than the discount rate. In the restrictive phase 1979–80, during which the Lombard rate was adjusted to the tighter monetary environment only with time-lags and incompletely, falling below the day-to-day money market rate, the banks acquired Lombard loans in large quantities which, contrary to the original intention, threatened to become the normal means of bank financing. For this reason, the Bundesbank decided to introduce quantitative limits on Lombard loans as well, and in 1981 to actually close the Lombard window altogether for a while, and to introduce a special Lombard at a far higher rate. Because the precise conditions and the availability of this special Lombard were originally left open, this led initially to harsh criticism from the banks, and the claim that the Bundesbank was unsettling and damaging the functioning of the money market.

It was in order to complement these restrictions on the traditional refinancing channels, and against the background of the Bundesbank's reluctance to raise the discount and the Lombard rate even further, that the above-mentioned open market policy instruments were introduced, a policy variant that until then had been of negligible importance in German monetary policy (cf. section 9).

3. Relaxation and normalization of monetary policy: 1982–5

a) General trends and the monetary policy environment

If the phase from 1979 to 1981 was characterized by a sharply restrictive monetary policy with the aim of forcing down inflation, the following years, 1982–5, can be regarded as a phase of monetary relaxation and normalization, in the course of which the efforts begun in the previous years to regain price stability finally bore fruit. At the start of that phase inflation was still high—the annual average rate for 1982 was 5.3 per cent—but it fell steadily to 3.4 per cent in 1983, 2.3 per cent in 1984 and 2.2 per cent in 1985 (all figures annual averages). In line with this, capital market interest rates fell from their peak of 11.3 per cent in September 1981 to under 6 per cent at the start of 1986. The inverse interest-rate structure of the previous years normalized at a lower level.

1982 also saw the start of a turnaround in the German current account and in conditions on the foreign exchange markets. For the first time for many years the German current account ended 1982 in surplus once more, due to the decline in energy prices, the renewed appreciation of the D-mark, and the weakening of the domestic economy. This surplus was to increase dramatically in the subsequent years. On the foreign exchange markets the D-mark strengthened once more, at least against the European currencies. Initially, though, the US dollar remained strong and overvalued, and the foreign exchange and international financial markets were under the impact of at times substantial fluctuations and the international debt crisis.

Moreover, in the course of 1982 the German economy suffered, parallel to a marked weakening in global economic activity, a further cyclical set-back, which, as the Bundesbank itself admitted, came as something of a surprise. Real GDP contracted by 0.9 per cent in 1982, employment fell, and the unemployment rate rose to 6.7 per cent. Under these circumstances the Bundesbank oriented its monetary policy rather more towards bolstering economic recovery, cutting interest rates repeatedly in 1982 and at the start of 1983 and adopting other measures to expand liquidity. The decline in the rate of inflation and in inflationary expectations, together with a new set of external conditions, enabled it to take this approach without endangering the progress made in achieving price stability and meeting the monetary target. Indeed, cuts in Bundesbank interest rates parallel to a decline in inflation and falling capital market interest rates were, on the contrary, rational and uncontroversial in terms of price stability.

After three years of weak growth and recession, the recovery began in 1983, more or less simultaneously with other industrialized countries. Growth of real GDP was positive once more in 1983 at a rate of 1.8 per cent, although the labour market situation remained problematic and the unemployment rate rose to 8.1 per cent. In the course of 1984 and 1985 the upturn that had started in 1983 continued and accelerated, embedded in very strong growth of the world economy and reinforced by corresponding demand impulses from abroad. Real GDP growth amounted to 2.8 per cent in 1984 and 2.0 per cent in 1985, and was thus close to the estimated medium-term growth of potential output. After a time-lag, the labour market also benefited from this trend in the form of rising employment, although for structural reasons the unemployment rate remained at a high level in excess of 8 per cent.

Bundesbank monetary policy remained oriented towards maintaining the progress achieved in stabilizing the value of money, and it proved able to realize this aim throughout 1983 and 1984, apart from a few transitory disturbances, under more or less unchanged money market conditions and with monetary growth on target. In the course of 1985 the Bundesbank was able to cut its base rates in line with market interest rate trends as inflation rates and long-term interest rates stabilized at a low level.

From the start of 1982 to the end of 1985 the EMS was overshadowed by frequent tensions and the repeated need to adjust central rates. Changes in parities occurred several times during 1982 and 1983 and, following a somewhat quieter phase, again in the summer of 1985 and in April 1986. Yet, given the repeated willingness on the part of Member States to adjust exchange rate parities, at no time did the intervention obligations within the framework of the EMS diminish in decisive, not merely temporary, fashion the ability of the Bundesbank to control the German money stock.

German fiscal policy in the period 1982–5 was characterized by the initiation and implementation of a long-term consolidation programme, in the course of which it proved possible to limit spending growth and budget deficits significantly. Thus, in contrast to the previous period, fiscal policy did not pose serious problems for monetary policy during this phase, quite unlike the prevailing situation in the USA, which at the time was characterized by exploding budget deficits and the lack of political will to correct this disequilibrium.

b) The monetary policy of the Bundesbank in detail

Monetary targets and monetary trends

For 1982 and 1983 the Bundesbank set itself an unchanged target corridor, compared with the previous year, of 4–7 per cent growth of central bank money. For 1984 it reduced the upper limit of the corridor by one percentage point and moved over to the slightly narrower band width of 4–6 per cent. Finally, for 1985 it reduced the target corridor to 3–5 per cent in the light of the progress achieved in stabilizing the value of money. The actual rates of growth of central bank money were 6 per cent in 1982, 7 per cent in 1983, 5 per cent in 1984 and 5 per cent in 1985 (figures rounded). Thus the monetary target was met in all four years during this phase (Figure 3). In terms of such data, monetary policy during this period can certainly be considered to have been steady and confidence-building.

The formal mechanism used to derive the targets remained in principle unchanged on the previous years. For 1982 and 1983 the Bundesbank

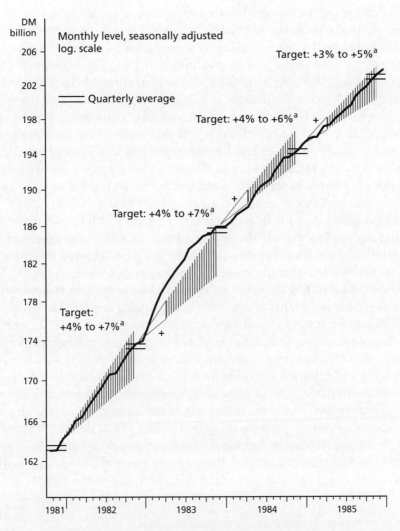

FIGURE 3: Monetary targets and actual monetary
growth, 1982–5* (target and ongoing movement)

* Central bank money stock: currency in circulation (excluding the banks' holdings of
domestic notes and coins) plus the required reserves on domestic liabilities other than bank
debt securities subject to minimum reserves (calculated at constant reserve ratios, base: January
1974).

+ The target corridor was not shaded up to March until 1984 (and retroactively in 1983)
because the central bank money stock is usually subject to major random fluctuations around
the turn of the year.

ᵃ Between the fourth quarter of the previous year and the fourth quarter of the current
year.

Source: Deutsche Bundesbank.

assumed growth of potential output of around 2 per cent; on top of this came an 'unavoidable rate of inflation' of 3.5 per cent, i.e. consciously chosen as being below the rate prevailing at the time the targets were announced. The targets were announced as conditional targets. The three-percentage-point width of the target corridor was supposed to reflect the factors of uncertainty, which were thought to be relatively high at the time the targets were announced. The weak state of the economy induced the Bundesbank, in accordance with the intentions it had previously announced in the case of such a development, to aim for the upper half of the target corridor in both 1982 and 1983. In 1983 central bank money expanded above the target corridor for virtually the entire year, but by the end of the year the upper limit of the corridor was reached more or less exactly.

The narrowing of the target corridor to a band width of two percentage points for 1984 reflected the Bundesbank's view that the degree of uncertainty had declined in the wake of the progress achieved in stabilizing prices and the fact that the money stock had grown along the upper limit of the corridor during the pervious year. The lowering of the target corridor as a whole for 1985 reflected the success in bringing down the inflation rate. The Bundesbank took this to represent the continuation of an in principle unchanged monetary policy, one oriented towards maintaining the progress achieved in stabilizing price trends. It is interesting that, in justifying the target for 1985, for the first time no explicit mention was made of the idea of an 'unavoidable' rate of inflation, at which some observers had taken offence and which had given rise to misunderstanding. Implicitly, however, an analogous rise in prices was again assumed when deriving the target, simply by expressing the estimated growth of potential output in nominal terms.[9] Actual growth of central bank money was in the lower and medium area of the target corridor in 1984 and in the upper half in 1985.

Money market steering measures and further development of open market policy instruments

At the start of 1982 the Bundesbank cautiously maintained the policy of slow relaxation it had adopted towards the end of the previous year. In the first months of the year the special Lombard rate was cut in two steps from 10.5 per cent to 9.5 per cent; finally, in May, it was abolished and replaced by the standard Lombard at an initial rate of 9 per cent. These interest-rate

---

[9] In the course of time the interpretation of this component of the monetary target was to change into that of a (low) 'normative' rate of inflation, i.e. that increase in prices that, given the statistical imprecision in measuring inflation and the improvements in the quality of goods and services on offer, appears compatible with price stability.

cuts were complemented by a 'feeling-one's-way' fine-tuning of bank liquidity oriented towards D-mark trends by means of open market operations with repurchase agreements in such a way that it could be quickly reversed. In mid-1982 the temporary weakness of the D-mark led to a hiatus in the interest-rate cuts. In the second half of the year the Bundesbank permanently expanded liquidity by means of 'coarse-tuning' measures (increase in rediscounting quotas, cuts in minimum reserves) and further cuts in base rates (to 5 and 6 per cent). Thus the easing of tensions on the money market continued, with interest rates falling markedly during the second half of the year; the day-to-day money market rate fell from 12 per cent at the start of the year to around 6 per cent by year's end (cf. Figure 4).

The Bundesbank maintained this policy at the start of 1983, cutting base rates in March to 4 and 5 per cent. From April, though, excessive liquidity, a temporary overshooting of the monetary target, and a weaker D-mark induced the Bundesbank to take modest counter-action, and in September to raise the Lombard rate once more to 5.5 per cent, enabling the monetary target for 1983 to be just met.

During 1984 the overall liquidity stance remained broadly unchanged and monetary growth proceeded according to plan. The rise in the discount rate in mid-year, coupled with an expansion of the rediscount facilities, was intended merely to bring the discount rate into line with the Lombard and money market rates and exerted little influence on market rates.

In the autumn of 1984 the Bundesbank took an important decision, one which served as a pointer to the future: greater use was to be made of the instrument of revolving securities repurchase agreements in supplying the banking system with central bank money. The implementation of this decision in February 1985 brought about a decisive development in the technique of money market steering through open market policy instruments, marking the transition to a more flexible form of steering. The Bundesbank wanted to return the Lombard loan, which during the preceding years of restrictive monetary policy had increasingly been used by the banks as a permanent and quantitatively important source of refinancing, to its original purpose, namely temporary refinancing in exceptional cases. At the same time it was keen to loosen the close ties between the day-to-day money market rate and the Lombard rate, thus gaining scope, within certain margins, to exert a more flexible influence on the short-term money market rate via the conditions set by the Bundesbank for open market operations. The Lombard rate was not suited to such fine-tuning as it could not be changed on a daily basis by small amounts. Moreover, compared with changes in base rates, it seemed likely that with open market operations there would be less danger of small, short-term changes being interpreted each time as fundamental shifts in the monetary policy stance. In order to realize this

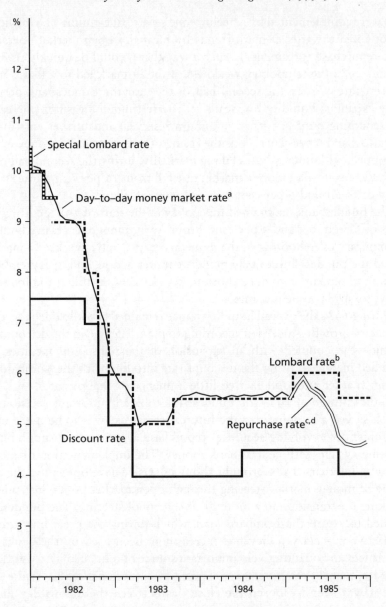

FIGURE 4: Base rates, repurchase rate, and money market rate, 1982–5

[a] Monthly averages.

[b] Special Lombard rate from 20 Feb. 1981 to 6 May 1982

[c] Monthly average rate of interest for securities repurchase transactions with maturities of one month, uniform allotment rate (fixed-rate tender) or marginal allotment rate (variable-rate tender).

[d] Not available until 1985.

Source: Deutsche Bundesbank.

planned change in the way it deployed its steering instruments, the Bundesbank offered repurchase agreements at rates slightly below the Lombard
rate. So as to avoid creating the impression that this implied a general relaxation of monetary policy, the Lombard rate was simultaneously raised from
5.5 to 6 per cent, accompanied by a generous supply of securities repurchase
agreements (in place of the 'long-term Lombard'). With these changes the
repurchase (or 'repo') rate, the rate applying for such repurchase agreements,[10] increasingly became the decisive orientation point for other money
market rates. Since then the day-to-day money market rate, in particular,
has followed the repurchase rate very closely. At the start of 1985 the banks
were initially rather disconcerted by the innovations in the Bundesbank's
steering techniques and complained of a loss of 'signal quality' and pre-
dictability in money market conditions. Yet this was first and foremost a
problem of getting accustomed to the changed situation.

From the spring of 1985 the Bundesbank reduced the repurchase rate in
small steps, thus bringing down the level of money market rates. In August
1985, finally, it adjusted the discount and Lombard rates to these developments, cutting them to 4 and 5.5 per cent respectively.

Movement of other monetary aggregates

Whereas during the previous high-interest phase (1980–1) the narrowly
defined monetary aggregate M1 had grown significantly less rapidly than
central bank money due to interest-rate-induced shifts out of sight and
savings deposits into time deposits, during the 1983–5 phase this process
reversed as interest rates fell: in 1983 M1 expanded by 8 per cent, in 1984
and 1985 by just over 5 per cent. The deviations from the rates of growth
of central bank money remained, however, comparatively modest, despite
in some cases substantial fluctuations within the course of a year, so that
from this quarter the quality of central bank money as an indicator was not
fundamentally called into question. M3 also grew, as usual, more or less
parallel to central bank money.

Even so, in 1983 the Bundesbank recognized that the quality of central
bank money as an intermediate target and a monetary policy indicator
appeared to have been reduced in certain phases due to temporary 'special
developments', in particular an unusually strong growth of currency in circulation at the start of 1983. Yet because this influence—which had emerged
in 1981 and was to make itself felt again in successive years—was only

---

[10] Set either as a fixed rate (in the case of a volume tender) or as an allotment rate (in the
case of a variable-rate tender).

temporary in nature, the Bundesbank, for the time being, did not feel that consequences had to be taken.

c) Public debate on monetary policy

The debate on the degree of restriction exerted by monetary policy continued in the 1982–5 period and remained controversial. Although in some cases this involved fierce criticism of the Bundesbank, overall, such criticism was more moderate than during the high-interest phase of 1980–1 and, all in all, Bundesbank policy enjoyed broad public support. The policy relaxation ushered in at the end of 1981 and beginning of 1982 was widely welcomed. Whereas, for some observers, the easing of the policy stance proceeded too slowly and hesitantly, others were concerned that the Bundesbank, given the renewed strength of the D-mark and the German balance of payments, could succumb to the temptation of returning to an old-school, anticyclical monetary policy that sought to manage aggregate demand. Indeed, the fact that the Bundesbank had all too frequently justified its restrictive stance in the 1980–1 phase with reference to external 'constraints', was now, given the reversal of the external constellation, being used by the critics in favour of monetary expansion to demand an uncompromising orientation of monetary policy towards bolstering economic growth and the labour market.[11] In some cases this critique was linked to a complete rejection of the strategy of monetary targets, and a call for their replacement by interest-rate targets or combined interest and monetary targets, in others to the view that the monetary target chosen was unjustifiably low, owing, among other things, to an excessively pessimistic estimate of potential output growth. Credit must be given to the Bundesbank for withstanding such criticism. The reproach that its policy was not giving the process of real economic recovery sufficient room and was thus responsible for weak growth, recession and rising unemployment (not to mention a renewed global economic crisis) could be rebuffed with relative composure by reference to the prevailing economic and labour market trends in other countries: it was indeed the case that the cyclical setback in Germany was neither more serious nor longer-lasting, and the labour market situation was if anything more favourable than that in countries such as France, the UK, or Italy,

[11] Rüdiger Pohl and the trade unions, in particular, unceasingly addressed such warnings to the Bundesbank (cf., for example, Pohl, 1982), and they were joined by political personalities such as Karl Schiller, the former SPD Minister of Economics and ex-Chancellor Helmut Schmidt. Cf. also Deutsches Institut für Wirtschaftsforschung, 1984, 1985.

which in this phase had adopted a less disciplined and more inflationary monetary policy. Comparison with the real economic consequences of the rather unsteady monetary policy pursued in the USA during this period is also rather flattering to the Bundesbank.

Conversely, the fears expressed during this phase that the Bundesbank, now that its external 'constraints' had been removed, would underestimate the inflationary threat and would return to an interventionist and expansionary policy also proved unfounded. Although during 1983 the money stock temporarily grew too rapidly, exceeding the target corridor and leading to sharp criticism from stability-conscious observers who feared a 'repeat of the mistakes made in 1978',[12] the Bundesbank was well aware of these dangers at an early stage—as is shown by the debates in the Central Bank Council—and reacted before the end of 1983 by tightening its stance. Although the Council of Economic Experts criticized these correction measures in the autumn of 1983 as being too limited, it should be noted that monetary policy did indeed return to a stability-oriented course and remained on it in succeeding years. Seen retrospectively, the policy pursued by the Bundesbank between 1982 and 1985 was very successful, much more so than would be supposed when looking back at the often highly controversial and turbulent debate of those years. All in all, in the phase 1982–5 the Bundesbank showed a steady hand, successfully completing the restrictive policy it had initiated in 1979 in response to the negative trends experienced between 1975 and 1978, this despite frequent assaults from various quarters. This is deserving of great praise.

Of course it is correct that it would have been better and would presumably have led to fewer real economic disturbances if the Bundesbank had maintained a more consistent policy across the entire period from 1975 to 1985, i.e. a policy characterized by less expansion between 1975 and 1979 and less restriction between 1979 and 1982. Yet it must be recognized that the negative trends occurred in the period from 1975 to 1978 and particularly in 1978. To the extent that the reproach of lack of constancy can be made, it should be targeted at this phase, not at the corrective phase 1978–81 made necessary by it, and certainly not at the consolidation phase between 1982 and 1985. And even then it is important to bear in mind that in the 1970s the Bundesbank had had only limited experience with the new policy of money stock control and that any central bank faces extremely difficult problems in coping with currency appreciation such as experienced by the Federal Republic of Germany in 1978.

---

[12] Cf., among others, Sachverständigenrat, Jahresgutachten 1983/4 or Rheinisch-Westfälisches Institut für Wirtschaftsforschung, 1983.

d) Reorientation of monetary policy?

The fact that by 1985 one could look back on 10 years of experience with monetary targets provided some observers and the Bundesbank itself[13] with an opportunity for a critical evaluation of that experience and a rethink through the fundamentals of monetary policy strategy. One of the central questions frequently asked in this context was whether the policies of the Bundesbank in the preceding 10 years had really been in accordance with its declared concept of a monetary policy oriented towards the medium-term growth of potential output. One aspect of this issue that was raised referred to the consistency of monetary policy and the call for a binding commitment on central bank policy for a period of more than one year in the form of multi-annual monetary targets. This tended to be linked to a rejection of (excessively broad) target corridors and of 'reservations' by the central bank regarding the monetary target. Behind all this stood the well-known monetarist position that the central bank ought to inform the public about its monetary policy intentions for at least the medium term in advance in as precise and reliable a form as possible, and that it should ensure a credible anchoring for price stability and corresponding inflationary expectations by choosing a rate of monetary expansion oriented to the real trend of economic growth and consistent with price stability. Critics such as Manfred J. M. Neumann or Jürgen Pfister considered that 1985, in view of the fact that price stability had been more or less achieved, would be a good year as a point of departure for a reorientation of monetary policy in this sense, that is for the transition to a genuine, medium-term-oriented policy of stabilization.[14] Clearly, there would no longer be place in such a policy for the idea of an 'unavoidable' rate of inflation (indeed, this was a child of the period of disinflation and had already been discarded by the Bundesbank for 1985).

The difficulties involved with multi-annual targets—and emphasized by the Bundesbank in its defence of the decision to retain conditional one-year targets with a corridor—lie in the fact that lasting changes may occur in the relationships between the money stock and goods prices (e.g. the velocity of circulation or the growth of potential output), that were unpredictable at the time the targets were set. This calls for flexibility on the part of monetary policy, particularly over extended periods of time, if a 'consistent' policy is not to lead to undesirable effects. Unconditional targets over longer periods and strict adherence to them would, it is true, be more favourable

---

[13] In its Annual Report for 1984; see also Schlesinger, 1985.
[14] Cf. Neumann, 1985 and Pfister, 1985.

in terms of binding commitment and credibility, but there is a trade-off between commitment and the ability to adjust to changed trends. Thus to an even greater extent than annual targets, multi-annual targets can really only ever be conditional targets. The experiences since 1985 have exposed the need for such flexibility even more clearly, and this necessity has increasingly been built into even monetarist concepts for monetary policy. An important question in this context is, however, whether it is possible to have such flexibility in the form of rule-bound mechanisms and thus to tie together flexibility and binding commitment.[15] Unlimited flexibility without a sufficient degree of rule-adherence clearly also brings with it the danger of inducing undesirable developments. In subsequent years the Bundesbank did not quite manage to avoid this danger completely, although it performed better than most other central banks. It must be doubted whether there is a significant difference in terms of impact and credibility between conditional multi-annual targets and annual targets with a clear commitment by the central bank to price stability. In both cases what is of central importance is a solid and credible anchoring of the will to achieve price stability. This, in turn, can only be achieved through corresponding policy action over a long period of time, and is conditional on central bank independence from government.

4. Monetary growth in excess of targets and slow return to restriction: 1986–9

a) General trends and the monetary policy environment

Throughout the entire period from 1986 to 1989, the economic upturn that had begun in 1983 continued without interruption in the Federal Republic of Germany, embedded in a growth phase of a comparable order of magnitude that encompassed the industrialized countries as a whole. But in 1986 and 1987 this was not yet apparent to many observers and to the Bundesbank itself. Thus concessions to the perceived risks to continued economic expansion continued to play a significant role. The average rate of real growth in Germany between 1983 and 1989 amounted to more than 2.5 per cent, peaking in 1988 at 3.7 per cent. Employment expanded and there was a trend towards lower unemployment, although the unemployment rate remained, for structural reasons, at a relatively high level compared to earlier

[15] Cf., for instance, the proposal made by McCallum, 1988 or Meltzer, 1987.

years of over 7 per cent. In 1988–9 capacity utilization was high and signs emerged that the economy was overheating. The global economy as a whole also grew strongly; only in the USA and the UK did economic growth begin to decline slowly in 1989. Initially inflation remained moderate in both Germany and the world economy. Indeed in 1986 the German rate of inflation was actually slightly negative (–0.2 per cent) under the influence of declining oil and import prices; in 1987–8 prices remained virtually stable. Yet given rapid growth of the money stock, strong domestic and foreign demand, contracting capacity reserves, and a deteriorating international inflationary climate, inflationary trends began to make themselves felt in Germany, too; in 1989 the rate of inflation rose to 2.8 per cent, compared with an average figure for the industrialized countries of 4.3 per cent.

The decline in inflation led in 1986–7 to a fall in international and German interest rates and a comparatively steep interest-rate structure. Substantial capital inflows and upward pressure on the D-mark prompted the Bundesbank to tolerate a high rate of monetary growth: in view of the strong D-mark and falling energy prices, there appeared to be little immediate risk of inflation. The stock market crash of autumn 1987, which induced central banks in most countries to provide the system with more than sufficient liquidity, initially reinforced this trend towards a more relaxed monetary policy stance. Not until it became evident, in the course of 1988, that the stock market crash, contrary to initial fears, remained practically without any impact on the global economic growth process, and concern about inflation increased was monetary policy tightened once more and did interest rates begin to rise. The Bundesbank, too, became increasingly concerned about the excessive stock of money caused by repeated overshooting of the monetary targets and changed course. Thus in monetary policy terms 1989 was 'placed at the service of preventive control of inflation', and saw a drastic tightening of the policy stance, with base rates rising to their highest level since 1982 and an inverse interest-rate structure from November 1989.

The years 1986–9 were characterized by a marked increase in current account imbalances. During this phase the German current account surplus grew to previously unheard of heights; this frequently served as a source of international criticism and led to calls for Germany to take steps to stimulate its economy. At the same time the US current account position moved deeply into the red. The foreign exchange and financial markets were characterized by turbulence and sharp volatility; the general trends were towards a stronger D-mark and weaker US dollar in 1986–7, a reversal of these tendencies in 1988 and the start of 1989, followed by a renewed reversal in the second half of 1989.

Also characteristic of this period was a strong trend towards calls for intensified international cooperation in exchange-rate and fiscal policy and the almost ritualized assertion of the will to such cooperation at international summit meetings and in international agreements (e.g. the Louvre Accord 1987). By and large, however, little more than lip-service was paid to these aims and the measures implemented to intervene on the foreign exchange markets had little lasting impact. For the Federal Republic, this trend towards cooperation was frequently linked to American demands that Germany pursue a more (or an even more) expansionary monetary policy.

In 1986–7 the EMS was characterized by at times severe tensions and realignments. In 1988–9, on the other hand, the situation remained largely calm. The fiscal situation in the Federal Republic of Germany, in terms of the size of the budget deficit, improved up until 1989 due to the strong, cyclically induced growth of fiscal revenues; spending growth was also strong, however. New and major challenges emerged at the end of the 1986–9 period, challenges which were to make their mark on German monetary and exchange-rate policy, and indeed policy in general, in the coming years: monetary union between the two former German states on the one hand and the increasingly concrete plans to intensify the integration of capital markets and establish European Monetary Union on the other.

b) The monetary policy of the Bundesbank in detail

Monetary targets and actual monetary trends

The most striking characteristic of the 1986–9 period was the significant and repeated overshooting of the monetary targets set by the Bundesbank in the first three years of this phase. Besides this, the transition from central bank money to M3 as the target variable in 1988 constituted an important watershed in the monetary policy of the Bundesbank.

The target corridor set by the Bundesbank for 1986 was 3.5–5.5 per cent. This marked a rise of half a percentage point on the previous year's target and reflected the assumption that the growth of potential output would be correspondingly more pronounced. Thus the monetary sphere was to permit strong real economic growth. In actual fact the money stock grew by almost 8 per cent, well above the target corridor. The trajectory of monetary growth was above the target corridor throughout the year (Figure 5). Following a temporary decline the rate of expansion rose again sharply in the second half of the year, attaining monthly values of up to 8.1 per cent. Besides central bank money, all the other monetary aggregates experienced comparable rates of growth. It was primarily external motives (restraining the appreciation of the D-mark in the face of strong capital imports), together with reservations about the resilience of economic growth, that induced the

Bundesbank to tolerate monetary expansion of this order of magnitude in 1986. The danger of inflation associated with this trend appeared slight in view of the upward pressure on the currency, the fall in energy prices and the virtually stable price level at the time. At the same time, the Bundesbank knew from its experience in the years 1978 and 1979 that while the correlation between the money stock and the price level can be dislocated for a time by the effects of currency appreciation and falling import prices, in the longer run it will reassert itself. Consequently, it was concerned about the monetary overhang that had arisen by the start of 1987.

The target corridor for 1987 was therefore set at 3–6 per cent, i.e. with the same central rate, but with a slightly broader corridor in response to the increased uncertainty. Given that the Bundesbank was still worried about the prospects for continued economic growth it initially envisaged monetary growth in the upper half of the corridor. Yet in the event monetary growth was once again way above the target corridor, again largely due to the importance attached to external target criteria, and in the autumn as a reaction to the stock exchange crash of October 1987. Overall, effective monetary growth again amounted to 8 per cent. As in earlier years it was decided that at the then prevailing low interest-rate level the growth of the money stock had been overstated by the rate of expansion of central bank money due to the central importance of currency in circulation in this aggregate. And indeed, M3 had expanded at the somewhat lower rate of 6.4 per cent. In the light of such considerations the Bundesbank adopted a target for M3, rather than central bank money, for 1988; this preference over central bank money (and over even narrower aggregates such as M1) has been maintained since. The Bundesbank calculated the target corridor—set for M3 for the first time and, exceptionally, not announced until January 1988—on the basis of real growth of potential output of 2 per cent, a normative inflation rate of 2 per cent and a supplement of 0.5 per cent to allow for the slightly higher growth of M3 over the longer term average compared with nominal productive potential. Retaining the band width of three percentage points, it arrived at a corridor of 3–6 per cent, exactly the same as in the previous year. While the target for 1988 was also exceeded, with actual monetary growth of just under 7 per cent, the extent to which the target was missed was less pronounced than in the previous years. In the first half of the year monetary expansion remained very strong; subsequently, though, the tightening of the policy stance implemented in the course of the year had a dampening effect. Towards the end of 1988 there was a sharp increase in the demand for cash due to uncertainty surrounding the possible introduction of a withholding tax on interest income. All the other monetary aggregates expanded faster than M3 in 1988.

The failure to meet the monetary targets in three successive years and the

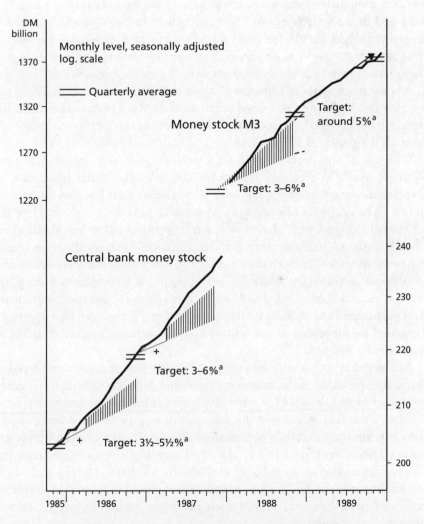

FIGURE 5: Monetary targets and actual monetary
growth, 1986–9* (target and ongoing movement)

* Until 1988, central bank money stock: currency in circulation (excluding banks' holdings of domestic notes and coins) plus the required reserves on domestic liabilities other than bank debt securities subject to minimum reserves (calculated at constant reserve ratios, base: January 1974). From 1988, M3: average of five bank-week return days; end-of month levels included with a weight of 50%.

+ The target corridor was not shaded until March because the central bank money stock is usually subject to major fluctuations around the turn of the year.

ᵃ Between the fourth quarter of the previous year and the fourth quarter of the current year.

Source: Deutsche Bundesbank.

associated inflationary threat was a source of consternation to the Bundesbank and induced it, as we have seen, to tighten its policy stance markedly.
Its growth target for M3 for 1989 was given for the first—and so far only—
time since 1978 without an explicit corridor as 'around 5 per cent'. Again
the calculation was based on real growth of potential output of 2–2.5 per
cent, a normative rate of inflation of 2 per cent and a supplement of 0.5 per
cent for the declining velocity of circulation of M3. On the other hand the
Bundesbank declined to impose a reduction for the monetary overhang built
up over the previous years.

With actual monetary growth of 5 per cent, the 1989 target was met.
Without doubt the central reason for this was the sharp tightening of
German monetary policy, in line with that of other west European countries
in this phase. A further factor was that plans to introduce a withholding tax
on interest income were abandoned, which contributed to a normalization
of cash balances and monetary growth. Euro deposits, on the other hand,
experienced strong growth, which induced the Bundesbank to define and
to observe increasingly closely a correspondingly extended monetary aggregate 'extended M3': equal to M3 plus Euro deposits and short-term bank
debt securities held by non-banks in the Federal Republic. This aggregate
expanded by more than 8 per cent in 1989, significantly faster than M3 as
traditionally defined.

At the end of 1989 and the start of 1990 the Bundesbank considered in
detail the question of the monetary overhang built up over the preceding
years and of its relevance for monetary policy. Did this monetary overhang
reflect a sustained increase in the demand for money or did it amount to a
merely temporary and thus potentially inflationary shift in liquidity preferences? The correct view to be taken of Euro-deposits and their liquidity
characteristics also remained unclear to the Bundesbank. Despite such difficulties, however, its faith in a monetary policy based on monetary targeting
remained unshaken, and indeed such problems would also apply to any
other policy concept.

*Money market steering measures and
additions to the range of instruments*

At the start of 1986 the Bundesbank adjusted its base rates, in response to
international trends, by cutting the repurchase and discount rates; the
Lombard rate remained unchanged until the start of 1987. This interest rate
level was subsequently maintained more or less unchanged despite strong
growth of the money stock. At the turn of the year 1986–7, strong liquidity
inflows together with upward pressure on the D-mark induced the Bundesbank to withdraw a total of DM 12 billion from circulation by lowering

rediscount quotas and raising minimum reserve ratios. In somewhat contra-dictory fashion, the discount, Lombard and repurchase rates were simul-taneously cut by half a point; this was intended as a signal that the measures to siphon off purchasing power were not intended as a tightening of the monetary policy stance. By the start of 1987 this left the repurchase rate at around 3.8 per cent (Figure 6).

In the course of 1987 turbulence on the financial markets and upward pressure on the D-mark led the Bundesbank to make repeated cuts in short-term interest rates. With the help of simultaneous increases in US rates, the foreign-exchange markets initially calmed down (stabilization of the DM–$ exchange rate in line with the Louvre Accord of February 1987). Temporary market rigidity in the wake of restrictive measures by the US Federal Reserve led in the autumn to the repurchase rate being dragged up for a short time by rising market rates. This trend came to a swift end, however, due to the stock market crash of October 1987. Along with most other central banks, the Bundesbank reacted swiftly with resolute measures to en-sure an adequate supply of liquidity and with renewed interest-rate cuts: the repurchase rate was brought down to 3.25 per cent, the Lombard rate cut to 4.5 per cent and the discount rate to an all-time low of 2.5 per cent.

At the end of 1987 and the start of 1988, tensions within the EMS and the commitment entered into under the Louvre Accord to bolster the weak dollar forced the Bundesbank to intervene heavily on the foreign-exchange markets and subsequently to siphon off the additional bank liquidity so created by reducing the outstanding stock of securities repurchase agree-ments (which reached its lowest level for three years). In order to avoid en-dangering its policy of flexible money market steering by means of this instrument, the Bundesbank decided in February 1988 on a permanent cut in rediscount quotas and their replacement by repurchase transactions.

In the first half of 1988 base rates remained practically unchanged at a low level. From mid-1988 the repurchase rate and the base rates were then gradually increased, initially in the form of a reversal of the relaxation meas-ures adopted in the autumn of 1987, and later as a change of policy stance in the real sense. As a result the repurchase rate was raised in numerous steps from 3.25 per cent in mid-1988 to reach 7.3 per cent at the end of 1989, the highest level since 1982. This marked a response by the Bundes-bank to growing fears of inflation. To many observers, however, these staged interest-rate hikes initially came as a surprise. In order to counter excessive fears about rising interest rates, during this phase the Bundesbank temporar-ily moved over to tenders at fixed interest rates in its repurchase transactions, allocating transaction at a price slightly below the market rate of interest, before subsequently returning to the variable-rate tender that it considered 'closer' to the market.

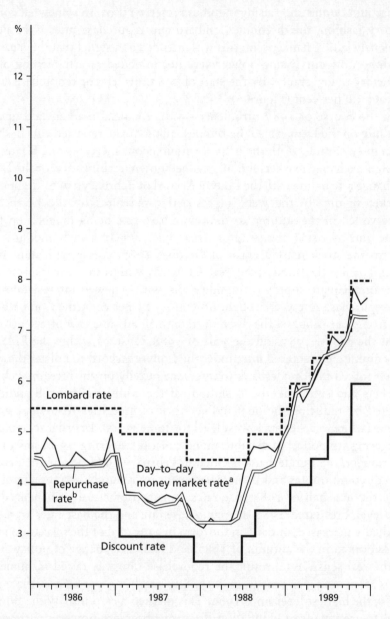

FIGURE 6: Base rates, repurchase rate, and money market rate, 1986–9

[a] Monthly averages.

[b] Monthly average rate of interest for securities repurchase transactions with maturities of one month; uniform allotment rate (fixed-rate tender) or marginal allotment rate (variable-rate tender).

Source: Deutsche Bundesbank.

In the second half of 1988 the Bundesbank sold large amounts of foreign currency in support of the D-mark and significantly expanded the outstanding stock of repurchase agreements, the importance of which increased once more. In its auction procedure the Bundesbank moved over to the 'American' allocation system (allocation at individual rather than uniform offering rates, in place of the 'Dutch' method previously used). This made the link between the repurchase rate and the money market rates even closer.

An additional important change in the range of central bank instruments during this period concerned the minimum reserve requirement. In May 1986 a cut in minimum reserve requirements decided back in December 1985 came into force. This measure was not linked to any monetary policy intentions, but rather, in accordance with demands raised by the banks, aimed to strengthen the international competitiveness of German financial institutes and marked the start of a process in the course of which over the next few years the regulations on minimum reserves were to change profoundly, although without in principle calling into question the minimum reserve requirement as an instrument of central bank policy. In order to ensure that the cut in the minimum reserve requirement was not taken as indicating a relaxation of monetary policy, it was accompanied by a cut in rediscount quotas of a comparable order of magnitude.

c) Was monetary growth above the target corridor justified?

Public debate of Bundesbank monetary policy between 1986 and 1989 focused on the failure to meet the monetary targets in the three years 1986 to 1988 and the resultant 'monetary overhang'. Did this overhang pose a threat to the Bundesbank's goal of price stability and should it therefore have led to a swift change of course? Or did it not constitute such a danger and was therefore justified? In this phase the conflict between those who considered price stability to be unequivocally the prime aim of monetary policy and those for whom steering aggregate demand and external targets were (at least) equally important centred on this question. The arguments put forward by the latter group[16] ranged between a general rejection of a monetary policy oriented towards monetary targets and the claim that special factors had led to a shift in the economy's liquidity preferences, and relied in large measure on the fact that inflation actually remained very low between 1986 and 1988. In the face of the, in their view, still precarious situation facing the real economy, these observers distinctly opposed any

---

[16] The main figure among which was again Pohl, who had become a member of the Council of Economic Experts. Cf., for example, Pohl, 1987.

tightening of the policy stance; indeed, in 1986 and 1987, they were still calling for a further relaxation of policy. What is remarkable is that critics of this school suddenly came up with strong arguments in favour of a monetary policy orientation towards the external position, whereas they had rejected this between 1979 and 1981.

This approach was frequently supported by similar arguments propounded by international—and in particular American—politicians and the media. At times this led to absurd demands being made on the Bundesbank; in August 1986 and autumn 1987, for instance, the then US Treasury Secretary, James Baker, diagnosed an infringement of the Louvre Accord and criticized the Bundesbank, despite the overshooting of its monetary targets, for an allegedly 'deflationary' policy. What was being called for, in effect, was for the Bundesbank to adopt the inflationary monetary policy then being pursued by the USA. The years following 1985 constitute a classical case study of the situation in which a central bank can find itself after a phase of disinflation has been successfully completed; the fact that price stability has been achieved, for the moment, means that public opinion is unresponsive to warnings of the risk of inflation in the future.

On the other hand, stability-conscious economists emphasized the time-lags involved in the causal relationship between the money stock and prices and warned of the danger of inflation in the future.[17] On this view, the price stability achieved represented the fruit of the restrictive policies pursued in the previous periods, and, correspondingly, monetary growth in excess of the target corridor would be reflected in price trends in the future.

This debate was also repeatedly conducted within the Central Bank Council of the Bundesbank. Actual Bundesbank policy was initially oriented more towards the view focusing on real economic trends and the external position, although not to the extent desired by many of its proponents. On the other hand, the Bundesbank remained very much aware of the risks involved in doing so, as the internal discussions within the Central Bank Council showed. In the course of 1988, and even more so in 1989, the realization of the need to initiate a change of direction clearly gained the upper hand.

Of course it is impossible—as is always the case with retrospective analysis—to determine exactly what effects an earlier shift to a more restrictive (and in this sense more constant) policy would have had. What is certain is that, by virtue of creating less of a monetary overhang, it would have meant lower rates of inflation—and, ideally, ensured price stability—in the years after 1988, and the sharp change of course in 1989 and succeeding

---

[17] Cf., for instance, the Annual Reports of the Council of Economic Experts in 1986 and 1988 (with a minority vote by Pohl) and Neumann, 1986 or Herz and Starbatty, 1989.

years would have been unnecessary. In view of the robust nature of the global growth process up until 1989, it can well be argued *ex post* that negative effects on the real economy and the labour market would probably have been minor and indeed that the effect might well have helped stabilize the business cycle. On the other hand, a more restrictive policy would have met with tough (or tougher) resistance at the international level, both from the USA and Germany's EMS partners. It is against this background that the acceptance of excessive monetary growth in terms of the monetary targets is most readily comprehensible. Moreover, it must be acknowledged in favour of both the Bundesbank and other observers that in 1986 and 1987 considerable uncertainty prevailed on the subsequent course of the economy, whereas this uncertainty has been resolved for the retrospective observer. Furthermore, it must be emphasized that German monetary policy would undoubtedly have found it easier to pursue a stable and consistent policy in these years if it had been able to embed this in a less volatile international environment, particularly with respect to the USA. No central bank, not even the Bundesbank, can detach itself completely from its environment.[18]

d) Change of monetary target variable

As mentioned above, from 1988 the Bundesbank shifted from central bank money to M3 as its target and indicator variable. M3 contains the same components, but the weighting is different. According to the Bundesbank's definition, central bank money encompasses cash balances plus the minimum reserve holdings by the banks on sight, time and savings deposits, calculated at the reserve rates prevailing in January 1974. The monetary aggregate M3, on the other hand, covers banks deposits in their totality. It is therefore far less susceptible to the influence of changes in cash balances. Originally the main advantages of central bank money were considered to be the early availability of the statistics and the Bundesbank's direct influence on and responsibility for this variable.[19]

The background to the Bundesbank's decision to adopt M3 was the 'overstatement' of monetary trends by central bank money in 1987 (as had occurred in earlier years and has happened since). Its heavy dependence on cash balances was considered to be problematic. Given the low level of

[18] The Bundesbank's reaction to the stock market crash in the autumn of 1987 was widely perceived as having been correct.

[19] These arguments led the Council of Economic Experts to prefer central bank money long after 1988.

interest rates at the time, and partly as a consequence of expectations of D-mark appreciation, cash balances rose sharply, so that by the end of 1987 currency in circulation accounted for 52 per cent of central bank money. By contrast, at that time cash in circulation represented just around 10 per cent of M3. The Bundesbank took the view that the advantages of central bank money were comparatively insignificant compared with the argument that it was too heavily dependent on fluctuations in cash balances.

The transition to M3 is defensible and warranted. Seen over the long term, the choice of indicator is relatively unimportant; the advantages and disadvantages lie primarily in the different characteristics if the two variables are used as a short-term indicator. Of course the change of variable changed nothing with regard to the central problem of excessive monetary expansion.

5. German monetary union: 1990–1

a) General trends and the monetary policy environment

The most prominent event for Germany in the years 1990 and 1991 was economic and political reunification of the Federal Republic and the GDR under the State Treaty signed on 1 July 1990. For German monetary policy, this event marked a watershed without precedent in its entire postwar history since 1948. The D-mark became the sole legal tender throughout the unified Germany; complete responsibility for monetary policy was transferred to the Bundesbank. This extension of the D-mark currency area to the federal states of the former GDR—introduced virtually overnight by political forces in the face of initial scepticism on the part of the Bundesbank—constituted a challenge of a very extraordinary kind for the central bank.

The global economic context during these years was characterized by a marked weakening of economic growth, initially in North America, the UK, and Sweden, increasingly followed by Continental Europe, but not by Japan. As a result of the impact of German reunification, Germany was for some time able to detach itself from this trend: real GDP in western Germany grew very rapidly, at 5.7 per cent in 1990 and 5.0 per cent in 1991, with rising employment and declining unemployment, although accompanied by accelerating inflation (1990: 2.7 per cent, 1991: 3.6 per cent). Not until the second half of 1991 did the cyclical downswing begin to make itself felt in Germany, too.

The situation was very different in eastern Germany, of course. The difficult process of restructuring the new Länder and integrating them into the market economic system, together with the loss of their traditional eastern European markets, innumerable barriers to investment, and demands for rapid wage growth led to a wave of mass redundancies and contracting output. Only in 1991 did the first signs of a slight improvement emerge.

German fiscal policy was highly expansionary in this phase, marked by strong spending growth, massive transfers to eastern Germany and a sharp increase in the budget deficit and government debt, whereby the initial fiscal situation had, it is true, been relatively favourable. In order to mitigate this trend, a number of contractive measures were taken in 1991 (introduction of a 'solidarity supplement' on income tax, rise in indirect taxes).

Rapid economic growth in Germany against the background of the cyclical downswing in the world economy and the resulting increase in imports and decline in exports led to a turnaround in Germany's current account position; in 1990 the surplus shrank markedly, and by 1991 had been converted into a substantial deficit. The D-mark remained stable within the EMS in 1990, strengthening against the dollar, but weakened slightly at the start of 1991 (strong dollar in the wake of the Gulf War), and stabilizing once more from the summer of 1991.

The international divergence in business cycle trends led to sharp differences between the monetary policy pursued by different countries. The USA, Canada, and the UK, followed subsequently by some continental European countries, moved over to a relaxed policy stance in the wake of the cyclical weakening of economic growth, whereas Germany (and Japan) retained a restrictive policy. As a result of this divergence in monetary policy trends, corresponding changes in international interest rates emerged. The interest-rate differential between the USA and Germany was reversed, and became very considerable, particularly at the short end. Within the EMS interest rates came steadily into line. In Germany the interest-rate structure became increasingly inverse in 1991.

Within the European Community, the desire to cooperate and achieve convergence, continuing the process towards a European monetary union, was repeatedly emphasized. The first stage of European Economic and Monetary Union came into effect on 1 July 1990 and the plans became more concrete still with the Maastricht Treaty of December 1991. The UK joined the EMS in 1990 and Italy dispensed with the extended band width for the lira. The idea of moving towards a *de facto* monetary union gained ground in political circles and on the financial markets, largely under the impression —which was subsequently to prove premature—that parity adjustments for political reasons would in future become increasingly difficult to realize. The Bundesbank sought to counter this trend, issuing warnings about prematurely dispensing with parity adjustments, but at the time such warnings were in vain.

At the end of 1991 the danger of a cyclical downswing emerged in Germany against the background of still considerable inflationary pressure, rapid wage growth, and very substantial fiscal deficits, but on the other hand the slow onset of an expansionary trend in eastern Germany.

b) The monetary policy of the Bundesbank in detail

Extension of the currency area and 'jump' in the money stock level

From a technical point of view the introduction of the D-mark in eastern Germany on 1 July 1990 and the incorporation of east German banks into the policies of the Bundesbank proved relatively unproblematic. The central difficulty facing the Bundesbank was the enlargement of its currency area and how to evaluate the implications of this enlargement for an adequate provision of liquidity. At the time reliable information was not available on the demand for money on the part of the east German economy and population and on the liquidity preferences of east German banks. Thus the Bundesbank initially oriented its on-going policies towards the line pursued to date for the west German Länder and based on a money stock calculation for the year 1990 that was restricted to western Germany, while attempting in a 'supplementary calculation' to take account of the enlargement of the currency area to cover the former GDR.

As a consequence of monetary union and the conversion rate between east and west German currencies set out in the State Treaty, at the start of July 1990 D-mark monetary stocks (as defined in M3) were created representing about 15 per cent of west German M3: i.e. there was a one-off 'jump' in the money stock level. The east German economy's longer term demand for money was very difficult to estimate but was expected to be lower. Given the fact that in the GDR liquid assets had been held practically exclusively in the form of money, it was expected that during the period following incorporation into the economic system of the Federal Republic a significant volume of such deposits would be converted into deposit forms bearing a higher rate of interest and not included in M3. On top of this, the east German banks initially held greater surplus reserves than were expected to be maintained in the longer term. Thus for this reason it could be expected that the inflated cash balances of the east German economy resulting from monetary conversion would to a certain degree automatically contract. And indeed, adjustment processes of this type did take place, particularly after the end of 1990. The additional requirement for money by the east German economy over the longer term was estimated at the start of 1991 at roughly 10 per cent of the west German level. Thus there remained a 'monetary overhang' of around 5 per cent.

For 1991 the Bundesbank then moved over to a money stock calculation and corresponding target for Germany as a whole. It is quite clear that the degree of uncertainty involved was far in excess of the usual order of magnitude.

Monetary growth, monetary target, and money market steering

The first issue that had to be addressed was whether, given the uncertainties due to reunification, it was at all prudent to stick to the policy of monetary targeting. The Bundesbank opted to retain its tried and tested policy. In setting the monetary target for 1990 it emphasized in its deliberations—which were restricted to western Germany—the continuity of its policy, deciding to follow with little change the targets set the previous year and justifying them in the same way. Returning to an explicit corridor, it set a target for M3 growth of 4–6 per cent.

Actual monetary growth in 1990 was initially moderate and for the year as a whole was on target, M3 expanding by just under 6 per cent. Growth of 'extended M3', on the other hand, was faster, reaching almost 8 per cent. The formation of monetary capital was also substantial. Up until the summer M3 growth proceeded along the lower limit of the corridor; subsequently the rate of growth increased and the money stock headed towards the upper limit (Figure 7). The Bundesbank achieved this trajectory of monetary growth against the background of largely unchanged conditions on the money market. The discount rate remained constant throughout the year at 6 per cent, the repurchase rate rose slightly during the course of the year, reaching around 8.5 per cent at year's end, and the Lombard rate was also adjusted from 8 to 8.5 per cent in November (Figure 8).

The monetary target for 1991 was left unchanged at 4–6 per cent, although it now applied to M3 for Germany as a whole and allowed, in terms of the initial level, for the 'jump' in the money stock due to reunification. Given the likelihood of a monetary overhang resulting from currency conversion and the associated risk of inflation, monetary growth was to proceed along the lower limit of the corridor.

An acceleration in the growth of the west German money stock at the end of 1990 induced the Bundesbank to raise its interest rates once more at the start of 1991: in February the Lombard rate was increased to 9 per cent and the discount rate to 6.5 per cent, while the repurchase rate initially remained at around 8.5 per cent. Further interest-rate hikes followed in August and December. By the end of 1991 the two base rates had reached

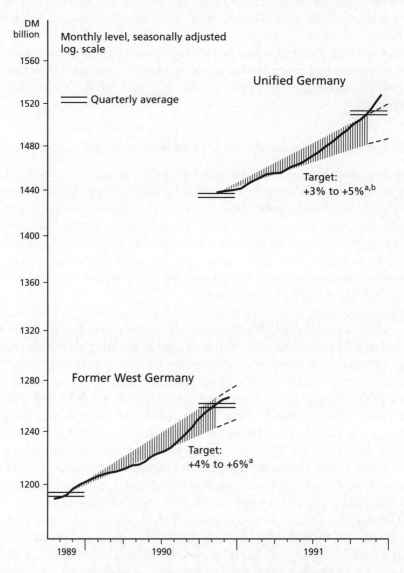

FIGURE 7: Monetary targets and actual monetary
growth, 1990–1* (target and ongoing movement)

* M3: average of five bank-week return days; end-of-month levels included with a weight
of 50%.

ᵃ Between the fourth quarter of the previous year and the fourth quarter of the current
year.

ᵇ In line with the revision of the monetary target in July 1991.

Source: Deutsche Bundesbank.

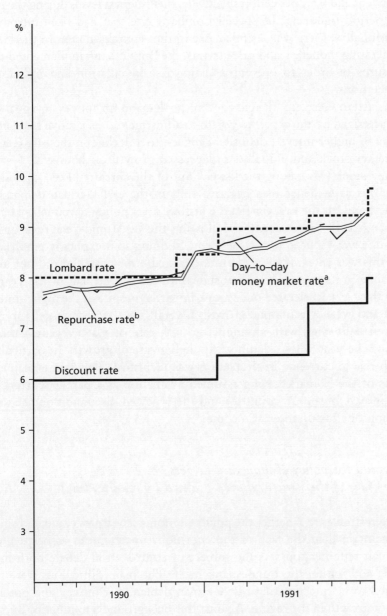

FIGURE 8: Base rates, repurchase rate, and money market rate, 1990–1

[a] Monthly averages.

[b] Monthly average rate of interest for securities repurchase transactions with maturities of one month, uniform allotment rate (fixed-rate tender) or marginal allotment rate (variable-rate tender).

Source: Deutsche Bundesbank.

8 per cent and 9.75 per cent respectively, their highest levels during the post-war period (ignoring the special Lombard rate that had been introduced occasionally); there was a similar rise in the repurchase rate. In the face of accelerating monetary and price trends, the Bundesbank implemented these measures in order to prevent a lasting rise in inflation and inflationary expectations.

In eastern Germany the changes in the demand for money in 1991 were characterized by the expected portfolio adjustments, i.e. a move from liquid forms to higher-interest deposits. This led to a decline in the east German monetary stock and, initially, to depressed growth of the overall German money stock (M3) along the lower limit of the corridor. The Bundesbank took this as evidence of a negative shift in the east German demand for money, and for the first time in the history of its policy of monetary targets it changed the target corridor following the usual mid-year revision; the corridor was reduced to 3–5 per cent. In doing so it explicitly emphasized that this was an expression of an unchanged basic goal, and did not imply a change in its monetary policy stance. In the second half of the year the growth of M3 accelerated once more, however, in spite of the higher interest rates and weaker economic growth. Overall the (revised) target for 1991 was virtually met, with an annual growth rate of 5.2 per cent, although closing the year with a significantly higher rate of growth. In particular, a sharp rise in currency in circulation was identified. This was explained in terms of the D-mark having assumed a function as a parallel currency in certain east European countries and the renewed discussion on the intro-duction of a tax on interest income.

c) Should the policy of monetary targets be retained in the face of the structural break caused by reunification?

The question as to whether the policy of monetary targets could and should be maintained in the face of the enormous uncertainties associated with German reunification was the subject of controversial debate both in the media and within the Bundesbank itself. The main difficulties were con-sidered to lie in estimating east German demand for money and potential output growth in the region. Against this background a number of Bundes-bank critics called for a more pragmatic monetary policy, steering 'on sight', without an explicit monetary target for the transition and for a limited subsequent adjustment period. The arguments for maintaining the tried and tested practice of annual monetary targets, which, after detailed discussion held sway on the Bundesbank Central Bank Council, on the other hand, were based largely on the idea that the continuity of the Bundesbank's monetary policy line needed to be demonstrated and a signal sent to domestic and foreign agents of the continued emphasis on price stability. The Bundesbank was well aware of the above-mentioned difficulties in deriving an appropriate monetary target, and indeed this led in 1991 to the first case of a redefinition of the target corridor following the mid-year revision. Refraining from announcing a monetary target would have brought with it the danger that the markets could have interpreted it as an abandonment of the stability-oriented policy practised until then or at least as a weakening of the will to implement such a policy. Also relevant was the awareness that the economic weight of eastern Germany as a whole was relatively minor, so that the risk of serious undesirable repercussions was limited. In retrospect it can be concluded that the monetary target did not play its role as a stability signal at all badly in those years, all the more so given the Bundesbank's willingness to make an appropriate adjustment in mid-1991 on the basis of new information.[20]

d) Public debate and international criticism

Overall, the policy pursued by the Bundesbank in 1990 was fairly well received, with domestic opinion reacting favourably even to the interest-rate hikes of November 1990 and the monetary target for 1991. In November the situation on the money market, where the day-to-day money market rate rose above the Lombard rate, was the subject of some debate with widespread perplexity on the Bundesbank's steering of the money market. The resultant sharp increase in Lombard loans led in turn to discussion within the Central Bank Council on a flexibilization of the Lombard rate, i.e. an automatic link between this rate and the money market rate. In the event it was decided not to go down this road, but the Lombard rate was raised to 8.5 per cent.

Growing concern about inflation, together with a highly expansionary fiscal policy and a rapid increase in government debt, moved the Bundesbank to raise interest rates further in 1991, the first hike occurring in February. This initiated a wave of sharp foreign criticism of the Bundesbank's high-interest policy, both from the USA and the rest of Europe. Slogans such as 'D-mark egoism' and a 'blow to monetary union' were bandied around. Calls were raised for the D-mark, with its specific problems emanating from reunification, to be decoupled from the EMS. This was soon followed by expressions of displeasure from German politicians, including

---

[20] On the stability of the monetary correlations in the period after 1990 see von Hagen, 1993 and Issing and Tödter, 1995.

Chancellor Helmut Kohl. Yet the Bundesbank remained unruffled by such criticism and correctly underlined the fact that its stability policy was not only in the interests of Germany. As an anchor for the EMS and the guarantor of its stability and viability, that policy was in the European and indeed international interest. Equally correctly, the Bundesbank also pointed to the responsibility—which at the time was not being adequately met—of fiscal policy and collective wage bargainers. Once again, the history of this period is a superb illustrative lesson in precisely what the independence of the central bank means in practice and just how indispensable this is for ensuring the implementation of a monetary policy oriented towards price stability.

The acceleration of inflation in the course of 1991 (to 4.9 per cent in July for western Germany) also led increasingly to criticism of the excessively expansionary monetary policy of the previous years and to calls for a more restrictive stance,[21] whereas others warned against applying the brakes too hard.[22] As we have seen, the Bundesbank opted to reduce its monetary target in mid-year and to raise interest rates further.

6. The Bundesbank at the centre of international censure: gradual relaxation and monetary growth way above the target: 1992–4

a) General trends and the monetary policy environment

In Germany the period 1992–4 continued to be overshadowed by the task of coping with reunification with the former GDR. In an international context the Federal Republic still found itself in an exceptional position. Whereas the global economy began to overcome its sluggish growth, albeit only very gradually, recovering significantly by 1994, most evidently in the English-speaking countries, in 1992 Germany experienced the end of the growth phase that had been maintained since 1983 and had been prolonged by the unification-induced boom. This asynchronic cyclical pattern also manifested itself in monetary and exchange rate policy and led, particularly in 1992, to massive tensions between Germany and its partner countries in North America and Europe, and to an unprecedented wave of criticism of the Bundesbank from abroad. As far as the relationship to the EMS countries was concerned, this conflict was reinforced by the lack of willingness—that had manifested itself in previous years, too—to adjust exchange-rate par-

[21] See for example Neumann, 1991.
[22] See for example Sievert, 1991 and Pohl, 1991.

ities: the EMS was considered as a sort of 'monetary-union-in-waiting'. The collapse of these illusions about fixed exchange rates led to extraordinary turbulence on the foreign-exchange markets and almost led to the demise of the EMS. In Germany the situation for the monetary authorities was exacerbated by the imposition of an unsustainable fiscal burden (this also occurred in many other countries) and very high wage demands (partly a cyclical phenomenon and partly owing to fears of inflation).

Economic growth in the industrialized countries as a whole was slightly faster in 1992—with annual GDP growth of 1.6 per cent—than it had been in 1991, but remained modest. Thus in many countries, both in north America and in Europe, monetary policy was seeking to adopt a more relaxed stance and was oriented towards stimulating the economy. The German economy was slowly running out of steam, but overall German GDP growth amounted to 2.2 per cent (1.8 per cent in western and 7.8 per cent in eastern Germany), with a more or less stable employment situation in the western half of the country and significant upward pressure on wages and prices. The employment situation in eastern Germany continued to deteriorate, however, in the face of the very rapid adjustment of east German to west German wage levels and the collapse of the region's traditional export markets in eastern Europe. In 1992 west German inflation reached 4.0 per cent, while east German prices were rising at a rate of 13.5 per cent. Thus the Bundesbank was forced to implement a policy restriction to some degree if it was not completely to lose sight of the goal of price stability. In spite of this the Bundesbank permitted very strong growth of the money stock and from the autumn of 1992 began a policy of cutting its base rates in numerous small steps. Capital market rates eased, declining from a peak of 9.2 per cent in October 1990 to 6.5 per cent in March 1993. The interest-rate structure remained inverse during 1992, but became slightly positive again in 1993.

The global economic upturn continued in 1993, initially at a moderate pace, against the background of a still tense fiscal situation, but declining inflation and interest rates in many countries. Economic growth was fastest in the USA, which experienced signs of overheating and, at the start of 1994, a change in the monetary policy stance was initiated accompanied by a trend towards a renewed increase in interest rates which soon began to affect European capital markets.

In Germany, by contrast, a serious cyclical downturn set in at the end of 1992. In 1993 German GDP contracted by 1.1 per cent (in western Germany by 1.9 per cent), accompanied by strong wage growth and moderate foreign demand. The west German unemployment rate rose to 7.3 per cent, the inflation rate simultaneously declined to 4.5 per cent, helped by falling import prices. Eastern Germany, on the other hand, recorded impressive real growth (8.9 per cent), although the labour market situation remained desolate and labour costs rose sharply. At the start of 1994 prospects improved considerably as the global economic climate brightened and wage settlements were more moderate. In 1994 Germany achieved unexpectedly rapid growth of real GDP of almost 3 per cent (2.2 per cent in western, 9.9 per cent in eastern Germany), although unemployment continued to rise for structural reasons. Inflation subsided to just under 3 per cent.

In the course of 1993 German monetary policy increasingly moved over to a more relaxed stance and a policy of interest-rate cuts, despite the still high current rate of inflation, in view of the economic downturn and signs that its relatively stringent policies in earlier years were yielding results. This approach was maintained in 1994 with very rapid overall monetary growth.

Germany's fiscal situation was characterized during the entire period by rapid increases in public spending and, in spite of higher tax and contribution rates, huge budget deficits. The external position was marked by current account deficits; the D-mark was strong and the US dollar generally weak.

The turbulence within the EMS in the autumn of 1992 forced the Bundesbank, because of its obligation to maintain parities, to purchase record amounts of foreign currency. After an extended period in which the financial markets had fallen for the illusion of a quasi monetary union, they suddenly rediscovered their—in objective terms perfectly justified—doubts about the scope for maintaining fixed exchange-rate parities. In the wake of the turbulence of that autumn, the D-mark was realigned (and appreciated) within the EMS for the first time since 1987. The pound sterling and the Italian lira left the EMS. Even so, enormous tensions and upheaval returned to the foreign exchange markets during 1993, accompanied by very large-scale intervention and renewed realignments. Finally, in August 1993 these developments led to intervention band widths being extended to ±15 per cent, and almost to the collapse of the entire system. Subsequently the EMS remained volatile, but this did not cause any further serious dislocations.

b) The monetary policy of the Bundesbank in detail

Monetary targets and actual monetary trends

Monetary trends in the period 1992-4 were characterized by strong monetary growth and severe overshooting of the targets, particularly in 1992. For 1992 the Bundesbank had set a target for M3 of 3.5-5.5 per cent. The slight increase of half a percentage point on the previous year reflected a compromise within the Central Bank Council between those members who, concerned about economic growth and with reference to 'special factors' influencing M3, wanted to raise the corridor by one percentage point and those who would have preferred to retain the previous year's target. The normative rate of inflation was left unchanged at 2 per cent; in view of the far higher prevailing rate of inflation, this reflected an ambitious aim in terms of price stability. At the end of 1991 M3 was already expanding rapidly and the rate of growth remained very high throughout 1992, up until the summer at a trend rate of around 8.5 per cent and in the autumn, exacerbated by the turbulence within the EMS, at a current rate of at times more than 10 per cent. In the event M3 growth of more than 9 per cent was recorded for the year as a whole, the greatest margin by which the monetary target had been exceeded since their introduction almost 20 years earlier (Figure 9).

The reasons behind the Bundesbank's willingness to accept such strong monetary expansion were the efforts not to impose unnecessary restriction on the—still favourable—development of the real economy and, more importantly, the great attention paid to exchange-rate developments and the international context. One additional factor contributing to strong M3 growth towards the end of 1992 was the planned introduction of a tax on interest income as of the start of 1993, which was reflected during this period in large-scale shifts out of domestic financial assets into cash balances and abroad. Moreover, the prevailing inverse interest-rate structure and the uncertainty about interest rate movements in the future induced investors to place funds in short-term time deposits, i.e. 'long-term funds' were temporarily invested in fixed-term deposits. Having said this, it is clear that, whatever the importance of such special factors—the impact of which is after all usually only short-term—the very rapid growth of the money stock could not primarily be attributed to such trends. All the other monetary aggregates grew even faster than M3 during 1992. The danger that this might create an inflationary potential could not therefore be overlooked.

Against this background the Bundesbank set its M3 target corridor for 1993 at 4.5–6.5 per cent. It assumed potential output growth of 3 per cent, a normative inflation rate of 2 per cent and a supplement of 1 per cent for the decline in the velocity of circulation of M3. Of itself this would have suggested a target corridor of 5–7 per cent. Yet the difficulty of setting the corridor was exacerbated by the substantial overshooting in the previous year and the above-mentioned 'special factors' whose medium-term import-ance was almost impossible to evaluate. Consequently, the Bundesbank al-lowed for the generous provision of liquidity at the start of the year by setting the corridor slightly lower. In the face of the prevailing inflation rate, which was running at 5 per cent, this target was to demonstrate the Bundes-bank's intention to maintain a stability policy oriented towards medium-term control of the money stock.

The first few months of 1993 were marked by a decline in currency in

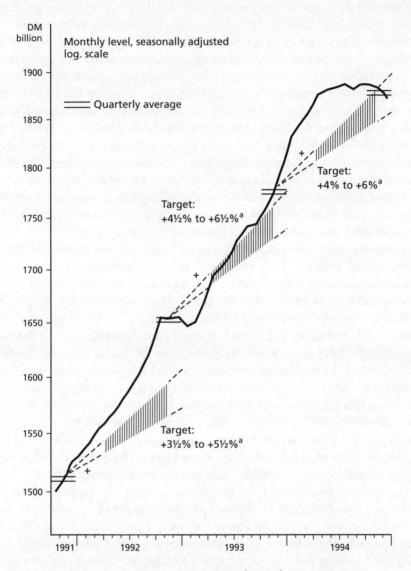

FIGURE 9: Monetary targets and actual monetary
growth, 1992–4* (target and ongoing movement)

* M3: average of five bank-week return days; end-of-month levels included with a weight
of 50%.

+ The target corridor was not shaded until March because M3 is usually subject to major
random fluctuations around the turn of the year.

ᵃ Between the fourth quarter of the previous year and the fourth quarter of the current
year.

Source: Deutsche Bundesbank.

circulation (as the special movements of the end of 1992 came to an end) and a corresponding normalization of M3 growth. For the year as a whole M3 growth remained more moderate than in the previous year at a rate of just over 7 per cent, but it was still high and the trend was uneven across the course of the year. 'Extended M3' also grew strongly.

For 1994 the Bundesbank reduced the target corridor slightly compared to the previous year to 4–6 per cent. The cut of half a percentage point reflected a corresponding decline in estimated real potential output growth; the other elements of the target derivation calculation remained unchanged. Initially the problem of meeting the target was exacerbated by the monetary overhang inherited from the two previous years. Moreover, the rate of monetary growth accelerated very sharply at the end of 1993 and beginning of 1994, partly owing to renewed debate on a tax on interest income, but also owing to the now prevailing global upturn in interest rates and the associated expectations of further rises in interest rates: investors were correspondingly reluctant to invest in long-term assets, and this led to a corresponding increase in time deposits. The Bundesbank assumed that these factors would automatically be rectified at some point and maintained its policy stance more or less unaltered. And indeed, in the latter part of 1994 a corresponding correction took place, supported by declining short-term interest rates and the widening of the interest-rate differential compared with long-term investments. By the end of the year M3 growth was slightly under 6 per cent, so that the target was hit for the first time for several years, although with a high level of liquidity in the economy (high initial level) and marked by a decline in time deposits (owing to interest-rate trends) but high rates of growth for all the other components of M3.

Money market steering

In the first half of 1992 the Bundesbank's interest rate policy remained restrictive with a view to rising inflation and in fact, in the face of stiff international opposition, was tightened further slightly. The discount and Lombard rates remained unchanged at 8 and 9.5 per cent respectively, while repurchase and money market rates rose slightly. In July, following the revision of the monetary target, the discount rate was raised to 8.75 per cent due to the excessively rapid growth of the money stock and the associated threat of inflation; repurchase and Lombard rates remained constant, however. At the same time the Bundesbank declared that it would not tighten its stance further and that the excessive growth of the money stock above the target corridor up to that point would be tolerated. A new situation arose in the autumn with the serious turbulence within the EMS. On the one hand, the EMS crisis and the obligation to intervene in order to maintain currency parities led to record inflows of foreign currency from purchases in support of other currencies, and these forced the Bundesbank to siphon off a corresponding volume of liquidity through repurchase transactions and sales of treasury bills, while, on the other hand, the Bundesbank was under immense international pressure to cut its interest rates. At the same time the appreciation of the D-mark served to dampen down inflation. Consequently, the Bundesbank—without intending a fundamental change in its policy stance —felt able to begin making cautious interest-rate cuts: on 15 September 1992 the discount and Lombard rates were reduced to 8.25 and 9.5 per cent respectively and the repurchase rate was gradually lowered (Figure 10).

As monetary expansion normalized at the start of 1993, partially in response to the previous excesses, and in addition signs emerged of improvements in the areas of fiscal policy and collective wage bargaining and of further inflation-dampening effects of the strong D-mark, the Bundesbank took the opportunity to make further, and in total very marked, cuts in its base rates and the repurchase rate, beginning in February 1993. In the course of the year the discount rate was reduced from 8.25 to 5.75 per cent, the Lombard rate from 9.5 to 6.75 per cent, with parallel reductions in the repurchase rate. Given that inflation subsided only very gradually and monetary growth remained strong, the Bundesbank implemented this process in the form of numerous, cautious and small-scale steps. In its weekly open market operations, it preferred the variable-rate tender procedure in phases in which interest rates were declining in order to determine the maximum scope for interest-rate cuts; in phases in which it did not intend to cut rates, on the other hand, it adopted the fixed-rate tender approach. The intention behind this was to implement the process of interest-rate reduction as quickly as was consistent with the process of price stabilization initiated by its earlier restrictive measures, but no faster than that. It explicitly rejected, on the other hand, a policy of forced interest-rate cuts motivated by cyclical or exchange-rate considerations. On the other hand, it allowed itself a relatively extended adjustment period and considerable scope in accepting overshooting of the monetary targets with a view to concerns about the state of the economy, exchange rate stability and the relations with European and American partner countries.

The renewed crisis within the EMS in July 1993 considerably exacerbated the Bundesbank's difficulties in steering the money market and again forced it to purchase very large amounts of foreign currency to stabilize exchange-rate parities and to compensate this with open market operations to limit the rise in the money stock. Thus the expansion of the band widths in the EMS to ±15 per cent was a necessary condition for the Bundesbank to regain its autonomy with respect to monetary control. Germany's partner countries, too, acquired correspondingly greater degrees of freedom by this

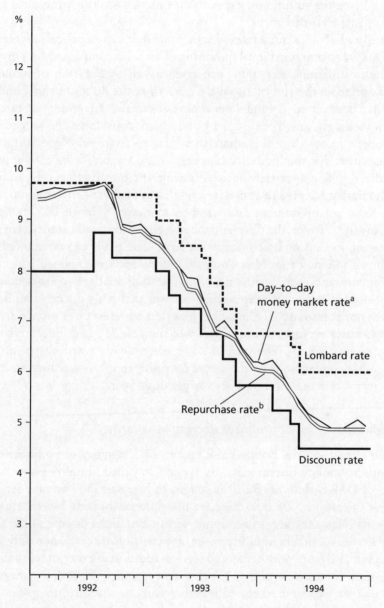

FIGURE 10: Base rates, repurchase rate, and money market rate, 1992–4

[a] Monthly averages.

[b] Monthly average rate of interest for securities repurchase transactions with maturities of one month (from October 1992, of two weeks); uniform allotment rate (fixed-rate tender) or marginal allotment rate (variable-rate tender).

Source: Deutsche Bundesbank.

means. From the autumn onwards, money market steering proceeded without any major disturbances.

The Bundesbank's more relaxed stance manifested by a process of interest-rate cuts was maintained until the spring of 1994, accompanied by a gradual decline in inflation rates, but once again by an acceleration of monetary expansion from the end of 1993. By May 1994 the discount and Lombard rates had been cut to 4.5 and 6 per cent respectively, the repurchase rate was correspondingly low. Because the Bundesbank considered the acceleration of monetary growth in this phase to be due to temporary 'special factors' and assumed that the 'liquidity blockage' would diminish in time, it maintained the policy approach initiated during the previous year. In addition the Bundesbank aimed to stimulate a move out of short-term and into long-term forms of investment and dampen monetary growth by attempting consciously to widen the differential between the long- and short-term rates of interest, by cutting base rates, as we have seen, while capital market rates continued to rise. From May 1994 the Bundesbank maintained its interest rates at constant levels against the background of relatively calm conditions on the money market; the repurchase rate was at about 5 per cent. Monetary growth normalized due to the higher long-term interest rates and the steeper interest-rate structure, and by the end of the year M3 had indeed returned to the target corridor. The start of 1995 subsequently saw a sharp contraction of M3, undershooting the target corridor, and thus a reduction of the monetary overhang built up over the previous years.

Modification of money market steering instruments

In February 1993 the Bundesbank undertook a significant modification of its liquidity policy instruments. By issuing so-called liquidity paper to the value of DM 25 billion (*Bulis*) it sought to broaden the basis for its open market operations. *De jure* these are non-interest-bearing federal treasury notes; *de facto* they are, in economic terms, Bundesbank emissions. These papers were to enable liquidity to be siphoned off directly, not only from banks but also from non-banks and were in addition, by way of repurchases, to be used to create liquidity. Yet this instrument never really managed to hold its own on the market and was therefore discontinued in 1994.

Associated with this innovation was a comprehensive redesign of the regulations on minimum reserve requirements, implemented in two stages in March 1993 and March 1994 and linked to a substantial cut in minimum reserve ratios. This was in accordance with German banks' long-held interest in improving their international competitiveness, and aimed to reduce the incentive to circumvent the minimum reserve requirements. The minimum reserve ratios for savings and time deposits were reduced in March 1993 to

2 per cent and those for sight deposits in March 1994 to 5 per cent. This served to reduce substantially the minimum reserves the banking system was obliged to hold. Despite this change in the regulations the Bundesbank continued to view the minimum reserve requirement as an essential policy instrument (creation of a stable demand by the banks for central bank money, role of a liquidity buffer on the money market).

c) Missed targets and 'special factors'

During the years 1992–4 criticism of the Bundesbank once again came from both sides of the spectrum of opinion. Some thought the Bundesbank's monetary policy was too expansionary,[23] others declared the Bundesbank's orientation towards the money stock to be incorrect and saw this as the reason for an unnecessary hardening of monetary policy, as the rapid growth of currency in circulation in the previous period did not, they argued, constitute an inflationary risk.[24]

In view of the failure to meet the monetary targets, in some cases by a wide margin, one of the central questions in the public debate in the years 1992–4 was whether this could be explained and justified with reference to 'special factors', and should therefore be tolerated, or whether, by contrast, this reflected a lack of constancy and resilience on the part of monetary policy and thus indicated the need for corrective action. At least in part this debate was associated, usually implicitly, with the question of the qualities of the monetary aggregate M3 as a monetary policy indicator.

The Bundesbank has repeatedly and emphatically pointed to various special factors to explain monetary trends deviating from its original target. Among others, these included most importantly the effects of German reunification, the impact of changes in taxation, the influence of EMS turbulence and effects associated with the inverse structure of interest rates. Yet it considered these factors to be essentially transitory influences that would sooner or later be offset by counter-trends and thus did not fundamentally change the long-term relationship between the money stock and prices. Against this background the Bundesbank was correct to consider in each case how a monetary overhang, once it had been built up, could be reduced and to be concerned about the inflationary consequences of such an overhang. This was in contrast to the position held by other observers who held that the temporary character of such special factors meant that the problem would resolve itself without counteraction by the monetary authorities. On

[23] Cf., for example, Scheide, 1994 and Neumann, 1993.
[24] Cf., for example, Deutsches Institut für Wirtschaftsforschung, 1992.

the other hand the Bundesbank addressed this task with a great deal of caution and restraint, with due regard to the real economy, the exchange rate and EMS partners. Specifically, it carried along the significant monetary overhang created in 1992 into 1994. To this extent it took a relatively high risk of the monetary overhang being absorbed by price increases.

It is therefore clear that the strong growth of the money stock in the phase 1992 to 1994 cannot simply be put down to the often-cited special factors. Equally, their role, especially in 1992 (and indeed in 1991) cannot merely be negated. In the final analysis however, the rapid growth of the money stock and the fact that targets were missed was due primarily to the existence of alternative goals and the regard paid to other interests: exchange-rate stability, supporting economic growth, international relations and sensibilities, and internal political pressure.

On the basis of such considerations, in the autumn of 1984, the Council of Economic Experts proposed a reduction of 2.5 percentage points from the monetary target as normally calculated in order to compensate for the overhang brought forward from 1992. Although the Bundesbank did not follow this recommendation, actual monetary growth in 1995 proved fairly consistent with this proposal.

Monetary growth between 1992 and 1994 certainly was not exemplary in terms of its constancy. Of course one can ask whether a more even trajectory for monetary growth, such as called for by the Council of Economic Experts, for example, would have led to greater instability in the real economy than actually occurred in reality. On the other hand, the lessons of this period, especially in 1994, show that it can be misleading to attach excessive importance to extrapolations of short-term developments, e.g. monthly changes at the start of the year. The Bundesbank's expectations that monetary trends would normalize during 1994 proved largely justified and a swift tightening of the monetary stance would have been inappropriate. At the same time, however, the period 1992–4 once again clearly shows that the Bundesbank pays substantial attention to secondary targets—i.e. besides the monetary and price trends, in particular those of smoothing out interest-rate movements and the business cycle and more generally of avoiding excessively abrupt changes—and that it is not completely immune to public and political pressure.

What is very clear is that the views of those who in the previous years had played down the risk of inflation and had demanded more substantial and swifter cuts in interest rates, proved unjustified, because as it was overall German inflation rates rose to values touching 5.1 per cent. If monetary growth in 1992 and 1993 had been even stronger, the reverse and normalization in the second half of 1994 and in 1995 would not have occurred so distinctly.

7. Normalization of monetary growth and continued interest-rate cuts: 1995–6

a) General trends and the monetary policy environment

The global economic environment in 1995–6 remained characterized by substantial international differences between cyclical trends. The US economy, following a short 'calming-down period' in 1995, continued its strong upturn, which had been maintained over many years, in 1996, with both labour market and price trends favourable. In Europe, on the other hand, the upswing became bogged down scarcely had it begun, with a parlous labour market situation and sluggish growth. Inflation rates declined throughout the OECD countries, reaching a very low level in historical terms.

Germany, too, experienced a weakening of the growth dynamics in 1995–6 compared with the previous year, with unexpectedly moderate growth of real GDP: 1.9 per cent in 1995 and an even lower figure of 1.4 per cent in 1996. Labour market trends remained unfavourable. Inflation, on the other hand, stabilized at a low level (1995: 1.8 per cent, 1996: 1.5 per cent). The weakening of growth was caused partially by at times significant upward pressure on the D-mark (against the US dollar, but also against some of the European currencies, in particular the lira), a corresponding decline in foreign demand, and rapid wage growth at the start of 1995. German fiscal policy remained tense, marked by high levels of public spending and the burden of transfer payments, budget deficits, and a pronounced need for consolidation.

On the capital markets a marked fall in interest rates began, and the interest-rate structure normalized. Much of Europe experienced, in anticipation of future participation in European Monetary Union by the countries in question, a relatively pronounced international harmonization of long-term interest rates. Exchange rate trends within the EMS remained comparatively calm.

b) The monetary policy of the Bundesbank in detail

Monetary target and monetary growth

For 1995 the Bundesbank had set itself an M3 target of 4–6 per cent. Derivation of this target corridor had been hampered by serious difficulties and uncertainties. The Bundesbank assumed a growth of 2.75 per cent for potential output, a medium-term normative inflation rate of 2 per cent and a supplement of 1 per cent for the decline in the velocity of circulation of M3. However, it imposed a reduction from the resultant figure of 5.75 per cent with a view to the excessive growth of the money stock in the previous years, setting a target of 5 per cent (±1 per cent). Given that the money stock was growing very slowly and indeed declined at the end of 1994 and the start of 1995, thus ensuring a correspondingly lower point of departure for the target zone for 1995, the Bundesbank considered this target consistent with a complete reduction of the monetary overhang built up over the preceding years.

At the start of 1995 the Bundesbank was concerned, if anything, about excessive monetary growth during the year. Actual monetary trends were in fact highly uneven and, overall, turned out to be precisely the opposite of this concern (Figure 11). At the start of the year the contraction of the money stock that had begun at the end of 1994 initially continued and indeed intensified. Up until the summer the money stock then grew moderately, with substantial formation of monetary capital; monetary expansion was somewhat faster in the second half of the year. For 1995 as a whole, M3 growth amounted to just 2.1 per cent, i.e. it was below the target corridor. The growth of short-term time deposits was particularly weak. Sight deposits expanded relatively strongly, as did savings deposits. M1 grew at a rate of 6.3 per cent. In view of the relatively generous initial liquidity situation (monetary overhang from the previous years) and the substitution of bank deposits by the new money market funds, which led to a downward shift in the demand-for-money function, the extent of which had not been foreseen when the target was set, the Bundesbank took the view that the economy had in fact been provided with sufficient liquidity despite the undershooting of the M3 target. It assumed that over a period of several years the rates of growth of both M3 and M1 would increasingly approximate to the 'target area'. Thus it saw no justification for compensating for the undershooting in 1995 by raising the target corridor for 1996.

For 1996 the target corridor for M3 was set at 4–7 per cent on the basis of assumed potential output growth of 2.5 per cent, a normative rate of inflation of 2 per cent and a supplement for the declining velocity of circulation of 1 per cent. In view of the instability of short-term monetary trends experienced recently, the corridor was widened to three percentage points. Both the Council of Economic Experts and the six leading economic research institutes in their joint report had proposed that the middle of the corridor set for 1995 should be taken as a point of departure for the 1996 monetary target instead of actual (average) level of M3 in the fourth quarter of 1995, the practice usually adopted by the Bundesbank; this would have

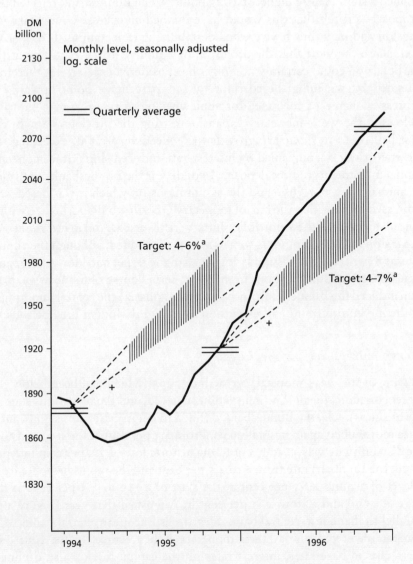

FIGURE 11: Monetary targets and actual monetary
growth, 1995–6* (target and ongoing movement)

* M3: average of five bank-week return days; end-of-month levels included with a weight of 50%.

+ The target corridor was not shaded until March because M3 is usually subject to major random fluctuations around the turn of the year.

ᵃ Between the fourth quarter of the previous year and the fourth quarter of the current year.

Source: Deutsche Bundesbank.

implied a significantly higher starting point.[25] The Bundesbank rejected this proposal as it felt that this would have implied an excessive monetary expansion and may thus have created destabilizing expectations. It did, however, share the view that the provision of liquidity in the economy at the start of 1996 could certainly no longer be considered excessive. It therefore intended by widening the corridor by one percentage point upwards to express a degree of tolerance for somewhat more rapid growth in 1996 following the weak monetary expansion during the previous year. In the first half of 1996 monetary growth was indeed very rapid, exceeding the target corridor, accompanied by interest-rate-induced shifts from monetary capital investments to time deposits. In mid-year the Bundesbank confirmed its annual target for 1996 and the assumptions on which it was based, and expressed its view that the rate of monetary growth would normalize within the current year as these portfolio shifts were reversed. And in fact monetary expansion in the autumn was somewhat more subdued, although the annual rate, at 8 per cent, was distinctly higher than the target corridor. At the same time the repeated fluctuations in the short-term course of monetary expansion induced the Bundesbank once again to emphasize the central importance of the medium-term rate of expansion over slightly longer time periods.

Money market steering measures

In view of the weak monetary growth in 1995 (which had been below the target corridor), the decline in inflation achieved, and the precarious state of the business cycle, the Bundesbank decided to cut its base rates significantly once more, albeit again in small steps. From 4.5 per cent at the start of 1995, the discount rate was steadily cut to the historic low of 2.5 per cent in April 1996, the Lombard rate from 6 to 4.5 per cent and the repurchase rate from a level of around 4.85 per cent at the start of 1985 to 3.3 per cent at the start of 1996 and as low as 3 per cent in August of that year (Figure 12). Parallel to that cut in central bank rates, other European central banks took comparable steps to relax their monetary policy stance. In the course of these cuts in base rates, interest rates on the capital market also declined, although not quite to the same extent as the fall in short-term rates; thus the interest-rate structure became decidedly steep. German interest rates remained at the lower end of the international range, against the background of a trend towards greater harmonization.

In the summer of 1995 the Bundesbank decided to continue with its reform of the regulations governing minimum reserve requirements begun in 1993. The minimum reserve ratios for sight deposits were cut further

[25] Sachverständigenrat, Jahresgutachten 1995/6.

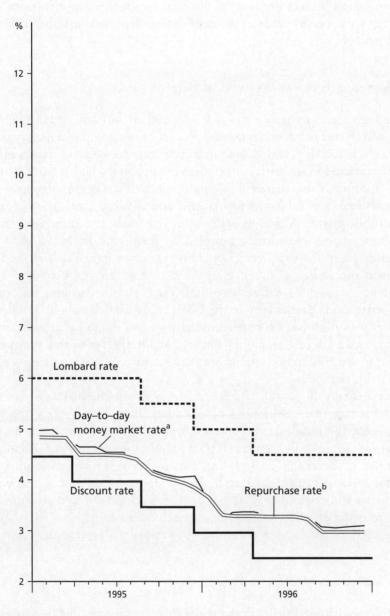

FIGURE 12: Base rates, repurchase rate, and money market rate, 1995–6

[a] Monthly averages.

[b] Monthly average rate of interest for securities repurchase transactions with maturities of two weeks, uniform allotment rate (fixed-rate tender) or marginal allotment rate (variable-rate tender).

Source: Deutsche Bundesbank.

(from 5 per cent to 2 per cent) as was that for savings deposits (from 2 per cent to 1.5 per cent), whereas the rate for time deposits remained unchanged at 2 per cent.

c) Monetary policy in the public debate

Although monetary policy was characterized in 1995 and 1996 by significant overall cuts in interest rates, the process of relaxing the monetary policy stance was too slow and lacking in forcefulness for some of the traditional domestic and foreign critics of Bundesbank policies, who felt that the stance was 'too tough' and 'harmful to employment'. Thus in this phase, too, the Bundesbank was subjected to frequent and in some cases harsh criticism from this quarter. Although each cut in rates won broad recognition and applause, it was immediately followed by further demands and soon by a resumption of the usual criticism. This was often linked to a rather naive faith in the ability of monetary policy to steer the real economy and a tendency to play down the risks of inflation.[26] Another striking feature was the renaissance, particularly in the USA, of the view that 'a little inflation' is useful as a lubricant for structural change and economic growth, a view that is based entirely on money illusion, and in the 1960s and 1970s made a major contribution to establishing the fateful inflationary process of the following decades.

Increasingly during this phase, criticism of the Bundesbank took the form of a fundamental questioning of the advisability of monetary targeting. However, the Bundesbank benefited from the clear support for its basic position expressed by the central political advisory organs, in particular the Council of Economic Experts and also many of Germany's leading economic research institutes. Overall, the Bundesbank exhibited a great deal of resilience and continuity in its policy in 1995 and 1996 and an impressive will to maintain price stability in a national and international environment characterized by sluggish economic growth and widespread nervousness.

d) Monetary targets for 1997–8

At the end of 1996 the Bundesbank decided, for the first time since adopting the policy of setting monetary targets, to extend its target horizon to two years. For both 1997 and 1998 a target growth rate of around 5 per cent

---

[26] In 1995 the proponents of this view showed a propensity to gear policy towards monetary aggregates, in view of the slow actual rates of monetary expansion, whereas they quickly abandoned this stance in 1996 as monetary growth strengthened.

was set. For 1997 the target was rendered more precise by setting a target corridor of 3.5–6.5 per cent. A corresponding step for 1998 was promised for the end of 1997. As in previous years, the target corridor was based on the assumption of a real growth of potential output of 2 per cent, a normative rate of inflation of 1.5–2 per cent and a secular decline in the velocity of circulation of M3 of 1 per cent. The Bundesbank declined to make a deduction for the overshooting of the 1996 target, given the only slight risk of rising inflation and the belief that M3 had exaggerated the extent to which liquidity relevant to spending had expanded (strong growth of the 'asset-components' of M3). At the same time the slightly lower target corridor compared with the previous year aimed to underline the Bundesbank's objective of maintaining stable prices.

The decision to set a two-year target reflected, on the one hand, the short-term volatility of M3 trends repeatedly identified in the previous years and thus a renewed emphasis on the medium-term nature of Bundesbank monetary policy. Yet in equal measure the decision was also due to the imminent 'interim period' in the run-up to European Monetary Union at the start of 1999. By giving a clear signal of stability and continuity for the entire remaining period of autonomous Bundesbank policy, the degree of uncertainty on the markets regarding monetary policy was to be limited as far as possible. At the same time the other European central banks and the future European Central Bank were to be ensured a clear benchmark for their own policies. In this sense the transition to a two-year target was to be understood as a conscious continuation of the policy pursued to date and in no way as a fundamental change of strategy. In particular, favourable initial conditions were to be created in order to offer monetary policy in the future monetary union the best possible chances of a successful start.

8. The Bundesbank's monetary policy strategy: do monetary targets make sense?

For more than 20 years now the Bundesbank has based its policy on steering the money stock in accordance with the growth of potential output. How convincing is this as a monetary policy strategy?

a) A policy of monetary stabilization with discretionary elements

The Bundesbank's own view of its policy approach is that it is trying to steer a middle course between the two extremes of a strictly rule-bound and a completely discretionary policy. This middle path can be termed a 'strategy of monetary stabilization with discretionary elements'.[27] It is self-evident that such a middle path can always be criticized from either side. Thus from one side the Bundesbank has again and again been criticized for its 'dogmatic monetarism', whereas it has not infrequently also been reproached for falling back into an old-style, purely discretionary policy.

The Bundesbank has sought to conform to the idea of stable monetary growth by:

- clearly specifying price stability as its prime policy aim;
- regularly (once a year) announcing its policy stance, in each case with reference to the policies and developments of the previous years and explaining the principles underlying the course announced;
- indicating the conditions under which it intends to deviate in a certain way from the course announced;
- deploying its instruments in as constant a fashion as possible, avoiding abrupt changes and course alterations, and in general basing its behaviour on a medium-term orientation.

The declared aims of these efforts to maintain a 'regular' and consistent policy are to provide information on the future course of monetary policy to economic actors as reliably and credibly as possible, to minimize uncertainties emanating from the monetary sphere and thus to facilitate and stabilize the formation of expectations and planning for the future by households and firms. Tying policy to rules and commitments helps to avoid the problems of time inconsistency and of lack of credibility, forces the central bank to justify itself in the case of undesirable developments and thus makes it easier for the market to discipline monetary policy.[28]

The discretionary elements of Bundesbank policy, on the other hand, find expression in the fact that its targets are (almost) always expressed as a corridor, sometimes one of considerable width, and are formulated together with certain conditions and reservations that in principle enable the Bundesbank to deviate from its announced middle course. The Bundesbank considers this indispensable in order to be able to react to changes in the relevant monetary interrelationships and the monetary policy environment that cannot be foreseen when the targets are set. As far as the definition of the corridor is concerned, it is also relevant that the central bank cannot steer its target variables exactly and in the short term, but only indirectly and over the medium-term.

---

[27] Issing, 1996, p. 286. For a general presentation of the monetary targeting policy pursued by the Bundesbank see Issing, 1992 or König, 1996.

[28] Cf., among others, Barro and Gordon, 1983 and Blackburn and Christensen, 1989.

In terms of these basic principles the Bundesbank does not differ fundamentally from the majority of other central banks. These basic principles, which are in accordance with a widely held view of monetary policy in modern academic discourse, are reasonable and easily defensible, but they tell us very little about the actual implementation of monetary policy in practice. The Bundesbank does differ—favourably—from most other central banks to the extent that it has attempted during the last 20 years to ensure that price stability is the prime goal of central bank policy and that it has laid comparatively great emphasis on the aspect of the constancy and continuity of its policy. In the final analysis, this difference is a very important one.

In addition the Bundesbank differs from the majority of other central banks in that for over 20 years now it has used a money stock variable in order to pre-announce and to explain its policy stance. It thus deploys a two-stage or intermediate target strategy in line with a long tradition in both the theory and practice of monetary policy. The uncertainty surrounding the short-term empirical relationships between the instruments and the final goals of monetary policy, including the time-lags involved, together with the comparative stability and reliability of long-term monetary relationships constitute the traditional justification for such an intermediate target strategy. A variable is selected as an intermediate target the course of which can be steered in the short term by the central bank to an adequate extent and which in the medium and long term and longer is tied reliably and rigidly to the final goal of central bank policy.

The choice of a monetary aggregate as intermediate goal and indicator of monetary policy is based on a basic conception of monetary relationships oriented towards the quantity theory of money, such as is consistent with a broad range of the macroeconomic and monetary policy models in use today, and not merely with a narrow monetarist conception. Not only this, it is also founded on many years of evidence of the medium-term relationship between monetary and price developments. In the form of price stability, the Bundesbank's prime policy goal was always the stability of that variable which, in the longer term, monetary policy, and only monetary policy, can reliably control. Equally, the Bundesbank has always been aware that it makes little sense to pursue real economic goals through monetary policy. Monetary policy can only influence real variables, if at all, in the short term. In the longer term the real effects of an expansionary monetary policy peter out; all that remains are their inflationary consequences.

Objections to this monetary policy strategy can be put forward on two levels: first at a fundamental level, secondly at the level of concrete implementation and practice. The Bundesbank has frequently been subjected to both forms of criticism.

b) Fundamental objections and alternatives

Frequently encountered is the criticism raised by those who prefer other variables to a monetary aggregate, especially interest rates and exchange rates, as the indicator for and intermediate objective of monetary policy. Interest-rate variables are usually propounded as the intermediary goal of monetary policy by those who consider that demand management is the primary task of monetary policy. Yet at a fundamental level, a policy of interest-rate steering aiming to influence the level of economic activity must be objected to on the grounds that it can at best achieve real effects only in the short term. For this reason monetary policy should concentrate on steering the price level, for this is the only task it can reliably be expected to perform. Yet it is precisely in this regard that the central weakness of a policy of interest-rate steering lies, as, in contrast to monetary targeting, it does not involve a clear anchoring of the price level. Although in principle, and for given initial conditions, an interest-rate policy can be formulated corresponding to each monetary target, and vice versa, an interest-rate policy is frequently far more complex and difficult to implement, as a reduction in long-term interest rates as a rule initially requires an increase in short-term rates (and vice versa): this is not readily appreciated by and explainable to politicians and the public at large. More importantly, interest rates, in particular long-term rates, are heavily dependent on expectations and other influences. They are thus difficult to interpret as a monetary policy indicator and difficult to control as a target variable. These objections apply all the more to real interest rates and interest-rate structure. There is no clear interrelationship between these variables and the price level.

In the case of a country that pegs its currency to that of another, stability-conscious nation, importing its price stability from the latter, a (nominal) exchange-rate target may well constitute an appropriate form in which to conduct monetary policy.[29] Such a tie must, however, be established in a completely fixed and credible form and implies complete abandonment of a country's monetary policy autonomy. It is therefore not a viable policy for a country that wishes to determine the quality of its currency itself or whose currency, as is the case with the D-mark, performs an anchor function within a system of exchange-rate parities. An exchange-rate policy is of course indirectly a money stock policy anyway, only in this case it is the money stock policy of the country to whose currency monetary policy has been tied. The real exchange rate is a completely inappropriate target vari-

---

[29] Cf., for example, Giavazzi and Pagano, 1988.

able for monetary policy; as in the case of interest rate targets, there is no way to ensure that the price level is anchored.

Nowadays, however, the central arguments against orienting monetary policy towards monetary targeting are based less on a fundamental preference for alternative intermediate target variables, but rather on the view that, given the development of modern financial markets and their internationalization, it is becoming increasingly difficult to steer and to interpret money stock aggregates. Frequently, reference is made to other countries, such as the USA or the UK, in which the monetary interrelationships have become clouded due to innovations in and refinement of the financial markets and their instruments, and which have therefore abandoned attempts at money stock control. With respect to Germany attention has been drawn in this context to the failure to meet monetary targets in recent years and the instability experienced in monetary trends. This leads to recommendations for a policy that relies, in place of the money stock, on a range of indicator variables and on direct inflation targets (inflation targeting[30]). If inflation targeting is taken to mean a strategy in which the central bank automatically reacts to deviations of the actual or the expected inflation rate from a target rate, it is clearly extremely tricky to dose the medicine correctly, given the long transmission mechanisms of monetary policy and the difficulties in making accurate forecasts for inflation. If, on the other hand, inflation targeting is conceived of as a single-stage monetary policy strategy, in which the central bank, taking account of all the information available, gears all the instruments at its disposal directly towards the final goal of controlling inflation, it represents a largely unspecified, open form of monetary policy ('looking at everything'), which can encompass monetary targeting as well as many other things.

Of course it can be maintained that the theoretically 'optimal' monetary policy takes all the relevant information into account and that therefore a monetary policy reaction function based on a single observable variable, the money stock, can only ever be second-best. If, however, this variable (the money stock) is the decisive variable for the medium and longer term changes in the target variables (the price level), and if, moreover, it is advisable to be cautious about reacting to all the different short-term disturbances resulting from uncertainty and time-lags and for reasons of credibility, this strategy may even so constitute a practical approach, and may even represent the best strategy realizable.

Optimal in theoretical terms would be a monetary policy in accordance

---

[30] On the strategy of direct inflation targets cf., among others, King, 1996 or Fischer and Zurlinden, 1994.

with a conditional rule that combines flexible reactions to short-term disturbances with a credible commitment to medium-term price stability. In practical terms, though, there is always a conflict between short-term flexibility and the credibility of a long-term commitment to a monetary rule. It is extremely difficult to distinguish a strategy of 'looking at everything' from a purely discretionary policy, with all the problems that such an approach poses. A policy based on the money stock does mean refraining from utilizing certain information, but has the advantage of tying policy reliably to its medium and longer-term goals, and thus subjects monetary policy to greater discipline, not least by making it more transparent and calling it to book to justify undesirable developments. In practice the differences are never as pronounced as they are in the text books. The Bundesbank, and indeed any central bank that has ever used monetary targets, takes into account other information besides the money stock that appears relevant to the changes in its target variables. The only question pertains to the weight accorded to such factors.

Of course it is the case that intermediate targets such as the money stock can only be effective as instruments of discipline to the extent that their realization is consistent with the final goal set and the preferences of the population in this regard; consequently, credible targeting of the final goals could also perform this disciplining function.[31] If central banks can really credibly anchor a price stability target, for example in the sense that its prestige is clearly and visibly linked to this goal, this may be sufficient. Yet precisely in order to anchor this commitment, it may well be helpful to set a monetary target and exploit the long-term correlation between money stock and price level.

For as long as the important monetary interrelationships between the money stock, nominal income, and the price level remain observable and stable over the medium and longer term, as appears, on the basis of the available empirical evidence, to have been the case in Germany,[32] it would not make sense to fail to exploit this by retaining the strategy, which has proved its worth for two decades, of medium-term money stock control. Specifically, what can be exploited is the fact that monetary trends foreshadow price trends. Abandoning this strategy could easily be interpreted as a negative signal—an abandonment of the policy of price stability as such

---

[31] Cf., among others, King, 1996.

[32] Cf. Deutsche Bundesbank, 1992, pp. 20ff.; Deutsche Bundesbank, 1995, pp. 19ff. and Deutsche Bundesbank, 1996, pp. 21ff.; cf. also Möller and Jarchow, 1996. Those who diagnose a collapse in the established monetary correlations for Germany frequently confuse the influence of temporary, for example interest-rate-induced, structural shifts, which practical monetary policy has always had to take account of, and the longer term stability of monetary correlations, which is the only relevant factor.

—and lead to serious loss of credibility. Thus the policy pursued by the Bundesbank—at least its basic principles and under the conditions that have prevailed until now—is well justified and convincing, whereas the arguments in favour of its abandonment are ill-founded. Of course there is no guarantee that conditions will remain the same in future, thus ensuring that this view remains valid.

Conversely, inflation targeting has been used by those countries whose record in fighting inflation has been second-rate. In many cases the transition to direct inflation targeting has been used to signal a change of regime and as a method by which the aim of price stability can be better anchored. It is evident that this argument for a shift in strategy to direct inflation targeting is of no importance in the case of Germany.

c) Objections to the form of implementation

Yet even acceptance in principle of a monetary policy strategy oriented towards money stock control leaves open numerous questions relating to the way in which such policy is implemented. The Bundesbank has repeatedly had to face up to criticism based on such questions. Central issues in the debate at this level have been the choice of monetary aggregate focused on by the Bundesbank as indicator and intermediary target for its policy, the use of a target corridor (instead of a single-figure target), the naming of additional conditions when targets are determined and the scope for discretionary action this creates, and the use of annual rather than multi-annual targets.

As we have seen, since 1988 M3 has played the key role as the indicator and intermediate target variable, whereas previously the Bundesbank had used central bank money. The reasons for the transition to M3 were portrayed in section 4, and need not be reconsidered here. The use of M3 itself, however, has repeatedly been called into question, particularly in recent years.

Like central bank money, M3 contains assets (time and savings deposits) whose function is to a large extent that of a store of value rather than a direct means of payment. Their inclusion is based on the view that these forms of financial investment also have a liquidity component and thus serve as substitutes for deposit forms whose character is indeed that of a means of payment. A view based on the traditional ideas of monetary theory, on the other hand, places greater emphasis on the character of money as a means of payment, and thus prefers to concentrate on those aggregates which express this most clearly, namely the two variables, currency in circulation and sight deposits, that are brought together in the aggregate M1.

In response, the Bundesbank has characterized as a disadvantage of M1 (and M2) its heavy dependence on interest rates and the far greater extent to which it is influenced by portfolio shifts between time and other deposits, compared with M3. Yet the Bundesbank's central argument in favour of M3 is an empirical one: on longer-term averages the correlation between M3, macroeconomic activity, and price trends has proved particularly close and stable for Germany.

On the other hand, for some time now, particularly in recent years, the Bundesbank has been forced to admit that the development and internationalization of the money and financial markets has made it increasingly difficult to interpret appropriately and also to steer short-term fluctuations in M3. In recent years the Bundesbank has been forced more and more often to point to various 'special factors' in order to explain short-term deflections in monetary trends, and thus to be able to argue that they are 'tolerable', i.e. not decisive for the creation of an inflationary or deflationary potential: 'At times the frequent occurrence of disturbing influences has marred the compass function of M3 on a short-term perspective. The result is that the advantages of money stock control are now more evident from the medium-term perspective.'[33]

Here the asset-components of M3 play a particularly important role. The growing importance of Euro deposits and the admission of money market fund certificates as a close substitute for time deposits has served to exacerbate such distortions. For this reason the Bundesbank has paid increasing attention to a correspondingly wider aggregate ('extended M3'). Yet this is even further away from the direct control of the Bundesbank, and the degree to which such deposits are substitutes for means of payment is unclear. In the light of these considerations it can be asked whether it would not be sensible increasingly to rely on a narrower aggregate, rather than to extend M3 further.

The greater susceptibility of M3 to short-term disturbances has induced the Bundesbank to lay increasing stress on the medium-term orientation of its policy. This is a sensible response and is a move in the direction of a longer term target perspective, e.g. in the form of multi-annual rather than annual targets, frequently propounded by monetarist-oriented critics. Until recently the Bundesbank has rejected this with the argument that it would lead to adverse trends if the underlying monetary correlations were to change permanently. Longer term target-setting is indeed subject to this danger if the targets are formulated unconditionally. The objection does not apply, however, if conditions and corrections for negative trends, for example if the trend velocity of circulation were to change, are admitted. Of course, in the case of conditional multi-annual targets with the possibility of correction, too, monetary policy credibility depends in the final analysis

---

[33] Deutsche Bundesbank, Geschäftsbericht 1995, p. 84.

on the ability of the central bank to explain and justify convincingly deviations from and corrections to the targets.[34]

The use of conditionally formulated targets and (relatively broad) target corridors has been repeatedly criticized from a monetarist perspective with reference to the discretionary room for manoeuvre they offer the Bundesbank. A well-known problem linked to the use of target corridors is that the full exploitation of the corridor permits an unforeseen growth trend in that it shifts the point of departure for the corridor during the subsequent period ('base drift'). A multi-annual target would be a more stringent target in this respect.

The choice of the 'correct' monetary aggregate in implementing a monetary targeting policy, together with the questions of corridors and additional conditions when targets are set are among the most frequently discussed aspects of monetary policy, in Germany as elsewhere. And indeed such questions are not without their importance. On the other hand, their role must be seen in the correct proportions. Over the long term all the monetary aggregates move more or less in parallel, in some cases at slightly different, but explainable, trend rates. What is central to monetary policy is to anchor the trend movement of one monetary aggregate, and thus price trends, credibly. In principle this is possible irrespective of the choice of monetary strategy.

At an even more fundamental level it can be concluded that while the monetary policy strategy deployed by the central bank is clearly important, what is decisive in the final analysis is the will to maintain price stability underpinning the use of such strategies. This in turn must be based on an awareness of the advantages of price stability and the costs of inflation and monetary instability that is firmly embedded in popular and political consciousness. This is the fertile soil on which monetary strategies consistent with price stability and the willingness to implement them grow. Monetary targets are both instruments to implement this will and its expression.

9. The instruments deployed by the Bundesbank

The Bundesbank controls the money stock indirectly by influencing the conditions of demand and supply on the market for central bank money. The overall money stock and the interest-rate conditions are determined by

---

[34] The practice of the Schweizerische Nationalbank since 1990 offers an example of the use of multi-annual monetary targets, and also of the difficulties that can be associated with such a policy.

the supply of central bank money provided by the central bank, the demand for central bank money by banks and non-banks, and the interaction between conditions on the money market with those on the other financial and on goods markets. The central bank can influence money market conditions either by steering the quantity of central bank money it makes available (in which case it must accept the resulting money market interest rate and its fluctuations) or by steering the money market rate of interest (in which case it must adjust the quantity of central bank money it makes available to the demand materializing at the interest rate chosen). From the very outset the Bundesbank opted for the latter method, i.e. for indirect control of the money stock, including that of central bank money, via a steering of money market interest rates.[35] The main instruments at the disposal of the Bundesbank to this end are open market operations, refinancing policy (discount and Lombard policy) and minimum reserve policy.

There have been major changes in the form taken by the various instruments and in their deployment and relative importance. This was due, on the one hand, to the experience gained over the years with the various instruments and, on the other, and more importantly, to the developments on the financial markets and their institutions (financial innovations, liberalization, globalization, and increasing international competitive pressure). The central thrust of these changes was the rise of open market operations from a comparatively unimportant monetary policy instrument to the Bundesbank's predominant means of providing central bank money. This was matched by the relative decline in the importance of discount and Lombard policy and of minimum reserve policy.[36]

a) Open market operations

The various instruments of central bank policy each have specific advantages and disadvantages. The main advantage of open market operations, that which is largely responsible for its rise to prominence as the most important instrument of monetary policy in practice—not only in Germany but also in other countries—is its flexibility and reversibility, and the fact that the initiative behind open market operations lies entirely with the central bank. Because open market operations by the Bundesbank primarily take the form of securities repurchase agreements following a tender procedure, they can be realized under virtually competition-neutral conditions, that is without

[35] An example of direct steering of the quantity of central bank money is the Schweizerische Nationalbank. For a comparison of the different steering procedures cf. von Hagen, 1988.
[36] On developments in and the deployment of the various instruments, cf. Issing, 1994 and Deutsche Bundesbank, 1994, pp. 61ff.

distorting and discriminatory effects with regard to parts of the financial and economic system; this is also an important aspect of this instrument.

The step towards greater use of open market policy instruments in 1979–80 was accompanied by a discussion of the 'noiseless' character of this instrument. This was perceived as an advantage over the traditional instruments of refinancing and minimum reserve policies, which were frequently criticized for being 'too noisy'. In the first instance, this meant that such instruments exerted a relatively massive influence on expectations. They were seen as 'coarse-tuning instruments' with a strong signalling function, and not particularly suitable for short-term 'fine-tuning'.

While it is certainly the case that refinancing policy and minimum reserve policy are less well suited to fine-tuning than open market operations, for the above-mentioned reasons (flexibility and reversibility), the argument regarding the different 'noise level' or the greater 'signalling effect' is less convincing. For as soon as open market operations advance to become an important, if not the most important, instrument of central bank policy, the markets will closely observe and speculatively interpret their actual and supposed future use just as they do for other instruments. This hypothesis has been clearly confirmed by the trend in Germany.

b) Refinancing policy

Whereas in the 1970s and the first half of the 1980s discount and Lombard policy was heavily utilized, from the mid-1980s the volume of refinancing loans remained more or less limited to the level achieved at that point, with refinancing facilities virtually fully exploited. Refinancing policy proved ill-adapted to fine-tuning the money market, as the Bundesbank has no direct influence on the degree to which outstanding rediscount quotas are utilized and, moreover, it tends to be unwilling to alter refinancing rates and quotas too frequently. The latter problem could, in principle, be solved by introducing an automatic mechanism in the form of a fixed link between refinancing rates and market rates, as used by the Swiss and Canadian central banks, for instance. Yet frequently this runs counter to the desire of the central bank to keep its base rates as a discretionary policy instrument, in particular to set signals, but also to underline its own power. Thus, proposals for a flexibilization of the Lombard rate have been put up for debate and discussed in the Central Bank Council, but in the event they have always been rejected. An additional problem with refinancing policy is that it is difficult to retain competitive neutrality when allocating quotas.

Lombard policy, which according to its underlying idea serves primarily to bridge over short-term bottlenecks in banks' liquidity, has always been of less quantitative importance, even though, as described in the preceding sections, it has at times been used for purposes other than its original aim, thus temporarily inflating its importance. There can be doubt, though, as to whether it remains a necessary and indispensable instrument of Bundesbank policy, enabling as it does the central bank to perform its function of lender of last resort.

c) *Minimum reserve policy*

As far as minimum reserve policy is concerned, it was always considered an advantage that minimum reserves ensured a closer relationship between bank reserves and the overall money stock and that the banks were unable to circumvent the direct restrictive effect of an increase in minimum reserve requirement. The weight of these arguments fell sharply, however, with the internationalization of capital markets and the resultant increase in the scope for international substitution, and in particular with the rise and growth of the Euromarkets, which are not subject to minimum reserve obligations. The scope for circumvention that has emerged as a result of these developments has decisively reduced the effectiveness of the minimum reserve requirement as an instrument. The comparatively heavy burden of minimum reserve requirements on German banks has increasingly been seen as a competitive disadvantage for the German banking and finance sector. Over the years, correspondingly frequent calls were made by the banks to abolish the minimum reserve requirement. For these reasons, but only after overcoming substantial initial scepticism and internal reluctance, the Bundesbank repeatedly cut minimum reserve ratios between 1985 and 1996; since then they have remained at a very modest level. Even so, the Bundesbank has repeatedly emphasized that it intends to retain the minimum reserve instrument as an important complement to open market operations. Thus the cuts in rates are to be seen as a measure to enable this instrument to be retained over the long term at a level consistent with the competitiveness of German banks. The main arguments put forward by the Bundesbank for its retention —and also for its desirability for a future European Central Bank—are that the obligation to hold a minimum reserve implies a guarantee of a stable basic demand from the banking system for central bank money, fulfils a buffer function on the money market and thus helps to smooth out changes in money market interest rates. On the other hand, the minimum reserve policy is no longer deployed by the Bundesbank to actively steer money market conditions via changes in the minimum reserve requirement and the associated provision or withdrawal of central bank money.

Yet the issue of the underlying importance and necessity of the minimum reserve policy is a controversial one in both academic and policy-related discourse. It can validly be claimed that an adequate degree of monetary control can be achieved even without minimum reserves. Yet at the low minimum reserve ratios currently prevailing in Germany such discussions are largely academic. The maintenance of a minimum reserve obligation by the Bundesbank can be justified as a security measure.

The discussion on the admission of money market funds was also conducted largely in the light of minimum reserve consideration. Initially the Bundesbank attempted to prevent their introduction because of the associated narrowing of the base for the minimum reserve requirement. Their introduction in 1993—once the Bundesbank had abandoned its opposition, while remaining sceptical—further accelerated the weakening of the minimum reserve requirement as a policy instrument described above.

The Bundesbank sought to compensate for each decline in the importance of the minimum reserve by reinforcing its open market instruments. Generally speaking, the intensification of the trend towards internationalization and international competitive pressure served to raise the relative importance of those instruments whose effect is neutral in competitive terms, that is in particular open market policy in all its forms, while weakening and reducing the relative importance of those operating through regulations and restrictions on behaviour, the prime example being the minimum reserve requirement.

Overall it can be concluded that, during the past 20 years, the Bundesbank has established and maintained a well-functioning range of appropriate instruments which have undoubtedly enabled it to implement its policies in an efficient and goal-oriented fashion.

10. The Bundesbank as role model?

The Bundesbank is justifiably seen as a highly successful, if not the most successful central bank of the past two decades. With regard to European Monetary Union it has taken on the function of 'role model' for the European Central Bank set out in the Maastricht Treaty on the pattern of the Bundesbank. In the light of this let us conclude by considering the relationship between the strategic goals and the day-to-day policies of the Bundesbank, the degree of goal attainment and the way it has dealt with conflicts between various goals of monetary policy. This section closes with a consideration of the importance of the independence of the Bundesbank for its policy success.

a) Strategy, current policy, and conflicting goals

Has the Bundesbank always remained faithful to its concept of a stabilizing medium-term-oriented monetary targeting policy? Or was this concept mere 'window-dressing', a theoretical trimming for a still largely pragmatic and discretionary policy? Opponents of the strategy of monetary targets sometimes propounded this latter argument, in order to express that the Bundesbank did not in fact need this cognitive 'straight-jacket' for its policy and could retain its course while removing the constraint.[37] On the other hand, monetarist-oriented proponents of money stock control have frequently criticized the Bundesbank for failing to implement its official strategy as rigorously as necessary and in its day-to-day policy making for falling back into old-style discretionary behaviour.[38] In this case the critique has been linked to a call to retain the strategy, but to ensure that the practical, day-to-day conduct of monetary policy is more closely oriented to it.

Of course over the last 20 years there have repeatedly been situations in which, in terms of a strict text-book view of its strategy, current Bundesbank policy must be said to have deviated from strategy. Indeed, it is scarcely conceivable that this could be any different in practical monetary policy terms, as policy must be realized in a concrete environment of day-to-day politics with all its constraints and the influences of interest groups of various types. It is therefore subject to a wide variety of interferences which cannot always be resisted, even in an optimum institutional context, not least in order to avoid endangering this context and its own independence in the political process.

Consequently, the relevant yardstick for evaluating the day-to-day policy of the Bundesbank—and any other central bank—should be not so much the 'pure', text-book formulation for its underlying strategy, but rather the central idea behind and the basic orientation of the policy required by this strategy. If this perspective is taken, the Bundesbank must be given good marks in any comparison of its current policy with the underlying strategy, at least compared with most other central banks. For a period of more than 20 years it has remained faithful to the basic orientation of its strategy to a comparatively high degree, and has always found its way back to the strategy despite numerous difficulties and transitory confusion. It has proved that it has a steady hand and has not been prone, unlike many other central banks,

---

[37] Cf., for example, Bofinger, 1994, who termed the setting of monetary targets by the Bundesbank a ritual.

[38] Cf., among others, Neumann, 1982, 1985.

to hectic shifts in strategy. The comparative success of its policy is due in no small measure to the relative continuity of that policy.

The fact that, despite this, opinions on the current policy of the Bundesbank have at times diverged widely, is primarily due—as emphasized in the more detailed presentations of sections 2–7—to the different weightings attached to the various goals of monetary policy. The Bundesbank has consistently declared its adherence to price stability as its prime goal, while at the same time mentioning other target criteria, in particular smooth cyclical trends, stable financial and exchange-rate markets, and external equilibrium, as being aspects relevant to its policy. It has also repeatedly emphasized that it cannot conduct its policy in a vacuum and, in particular, must take account of the decisions taken by fiscal policy makers and collective wage bargainers.

And indeed, many situations have arisen in which such influences and deference can be identified. Particularly strong, besides the ever-present concern with the state of the business cycle, was the *influence of external developments*, a trend that was especially pronounced in the phase 1979–81 in the face of currency weakness and the current account deficit, but also later in the context of a reverse external constellation. External considerations have frequently induced the Bundesbank to move to a policy of influencing exchange and interest rates, which brought it into conflict with its monetary targets and the underlying aim of price stability. Its position in this regard was further complicated by the frequent and in some cases massive interventions on the foreign exchange markets it was forced to make by virtue of its obligations under the EMS. These were most extreme in 1992 and 1993, but were also relevant in earlier years.

With regard to its policy orientation towards the external position, the Bundesbank must be credited with the fact that it has always seen this primarily as a means of avoiding abrupt changes and instabilities, and that it has always been aware that in an inflationary environment it is impossible at the end of the day to achieve price and exchange rate stability simultaneously. In case of doubt it has always opted for price stability, perhaps not quite as rigorously in every case as would be desirable in terms of the goal of monetary stability, but certainly in international comparative terms with great clarity and conviction. For this it is deserving of great praise.[39]

Similar considerations apply to the *regard paid to the business cycle*. Given

---

[39] There were, however, particularly in the phase 1979–81 important voices in the Central Bank Council and in the Directorate itself who saw the monetary target primarily as an instrument of stabilizing the external position, i.e. as a temporarily useful means of averting the threat of a crisis of confidence in the D-mark, while remaining highly sceptical of the strategy of monetary targets. Yet in the final analysis these voices were insufficient to carry the day.

the extent of the criticism to which the Bundesbank has been exposed from German observers oriented towards demand stimulation and from the international media and politicians, one is forced to attest it an extremely high degree of resilience, even if from the point of view of observers oriented towards price stability it too frequently took into account the exchange rate and interest rates. In the period under consideration here, this form of criticism, accompanied by corresponding attempts to exert pressure, arose for the first time in all its ferocity in 1980 and 1981, reappearing in 1986–8 and in the period following German reunification, 1991–3.

In addition the Bundesbank, along with any other central bank, has also had to take account of *fiscal policy*. At times this called on it to confront difficult situations. Especially in the years since 1990 it has enjoyed very little support from this quarter due to the budget deficits resulting largely from German reunification. If public spending lays claim to economic resources and public borrowing rises, there is always the latent danger that monetary policy will come under pressure to permit the money stock to expand 'in compensation', and thus to reduce the cost of financing and counter the threat of stiffening interest rates. It is extremely difficult, but at the same time extremely important, to maintain a course oriented towards monetary stability under such conditions, as submission by monetary policy to fiscal policy, nourishing fiscal expansion by monetary expansion, could exert fateful incentive effects on fiscal policy and in the longer run lead to its *de facto* predominance over monetary policy.[40] Of central significance in this regard is the institutional independence of the central bank from the government. This has been of great assistance in helping the Bundesbank withstand such dangers.

One factor to which attention is frequently drawn, particularly in the German discussion, is the *importance of the wage determination process* for monetary policy and the dependence of monetary policy on it. It is indeed the case that rapid wage growth, given its effects on the labour market and employment, can confront the central bank with a difficult decision, namely either to accommodate cost increases monetarily and thus allow prices to rise in line with costs, or not to do so and instead accept in the short run cuts in the level of employment. This is a classical monetary policy dilemma. Yet this analysis is by itself superficial. The collective bargaining system is not exogenous with reference to monetary policy. Rather, wage demands are made with a view to expected price trends. A monetary policy that is strictly oriented towards price stability and is announced and anticipated accordingly is the best way of retaining the collective bargaining system within a framework consistent with price stability. The Bundesbank has always been

[40] On coordination between monetary and fiscal policy see Sargent and Wallace, 1993.

acutely aware of this, and it is not least here that the advantage of a policy of pre-announcing credible monetary targets lies. This advantage can be exploited by the monetary authorities both in periods of actively reducing inflation, as the Bundesbank was forced to do in 1979–81 or after 1990, and in phases in which its aim was to restrain inflation at a low level and to prevent inflationary expectations from gaining ground, as in the mid-1980s.

b) To what extent has the Bundesbank met its targets?

Just how successful has Bundesbank policy been since 1979, measured in terms of its degree of goal attainment? This question needs to be addressed given the not infrequent failure to meet the monetary targets, particularly in recent years. Again it is clear that this evaluation can be made with respect to an ideal scenario without any errors, or in comparison to the performance of other central banks.

In determining the degree of goal attainment a distinction must be made between deciding this question on the basis of the final goals of monetary policy or against the announced intermediate target for monetary growth. In terms of the monetary targets set, the degree of goal attainment by the Bundesbank is, in statistical terms, not bad, but not particularly good: of the 18 targets set between 1979 and 1996 the Bundesbank hit eleven and missed seven (1986, 1987, 1988, 1992, 1993, 1995, and 1996), in some cases by a long mark. Measured in terms of the central final goal, however, the degree of goal attainment, while also not perfect, was strikingly good, at least in international comparison, and this without decisive disadvantages in terms of the development of the real economy. Both the German inflation rate itself and the fluctuations in this rate over time have been relatively low.[41]

One is tempted to argue that what is decisive for the credibility of the central bank is the degree of goal attainment with respect to the final goal, and that provided this is sufficiently high, the fact that intermediate targets have been missed is of minor importance. This is an overly simplistic view, however, and in the final analysis places a question mark over the rationale for intermediate monetary targets at all. What is decisive for the credibility of the central bank when it misses its targets, whether these are intermediate targets or final goals, is that it is able to explain and justify this in a suitably

---

[41] It is probably not least for this reason that the financial markets in Germany have been characterized to a far lesser extent than in the USA and other countries by innovations and structural discontinuities and, in their wake, by instability and changes in the basic monetary relations. This in turn has enabled the monetary targeting strategy to be maintained there until the present day.

clear fashion and that it is able convincingly to signal a return to a course compatible with price stability, or that it can show why a deviation from a given monetary target does not contradict the final goal of price stability. This is all the easier the less often it has failed to achieve its final goal. It is in this sense that the final goal is indeed central. In this respect, i.e. in justifying its policy, the Bundesbank has been all in all very successful, even in periods posing great challenges, particularly in the years since German reunification in 1990.

c) The independence of the Bundesbank

What has been the significance of the Bundesbank's independence for its actual policies? The Bundesbank is widely considered to be one of the most independent central banks in the world. It is entitled to this reputation, and this with regard to all the various dimensions of independence (degree to which it is subject to instructions from government, degree to which the instruments of monetary policy are at its sole disposal, degree to which its leading figures are independent). At the same time it is clear that in a democratic state the independence of the central bank can only ever be relative. In particular, it can be granted by parliament, but it can also be withdrawn by parliament. Independence keeps the central bank out of day-to-day politics, but conversely implies clear responsibilities towards government and the population as a whole, and presupposes that the tasks of the central bank are clearly set out in advance.

There are solid theoretical arguments and a convincing body of empirical evidence for the view that there is a clear correlation between the independence of the central bank and monetary stability (price stability).[42] Conversely there is no evidence that this, in terms of long-term averages, is achieved at the cost of below-average real economic development or an increased instability of real economic variables.

German monetary policy since 1979 offers frequent illustration of the practical importance of central bank independence. There can be little doubt that a central bank that was more heavily dependent on the government would at various phases during this period not have been able to guarantee the stability-oriented policy maintained by the Bundesbank, and that the resultant policy, for instance in the years 1980–1, 1986–7 or 1991–3, would have been more expansionary and associated with higher inflation. Government representatives have usually—not least in discussions in the Central

---

[42] Cf., for instance, Cukierman, 1992 and Alesina and Summers, 1993.

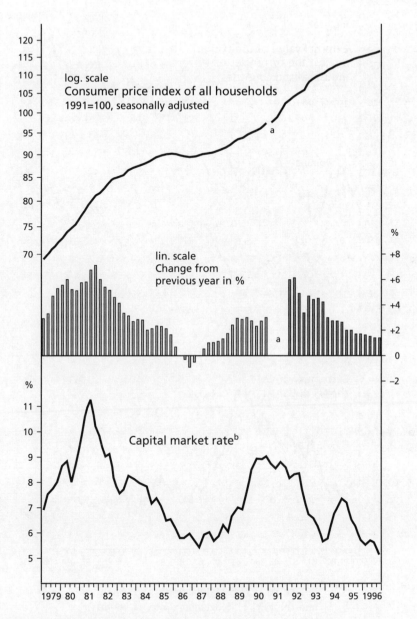

FIGURE 13: Quarterly price movements and capital market rates, 1979–96

[a] From 1991, unified Germany.
[b] Yield on domestic bonds outstanding.

Source: Deutsche Bundesbank.

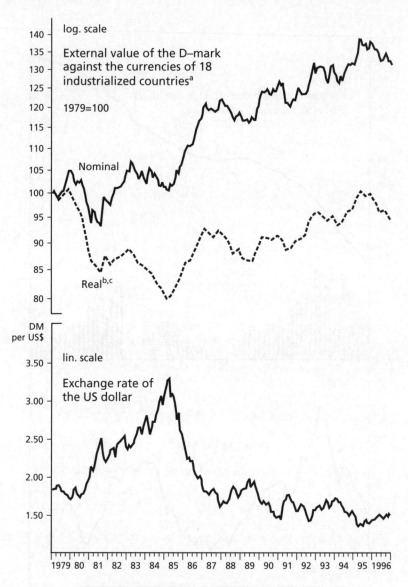

FIGURE 14: External value of the D-mark
and the DM/US$ exchange rate, 1979–96

[a] Weighted external value.

[b] External value adjusted for the differences in national price movements (as measured by the prices of total turnover).

[c] Quarterly.

Source: Deutsche Bundesbank.

Bank Council—argued for a more expansionary policy and thus played down the inflationary risks associated with such an approach. Similarly they tended to be more prepared to submit to attempts from abroad to pressure the monetary authorities to pursue a more expansionary monetary policy.

The independence of the central bank is a crucial instrument for establishing credibility and ensuring a policy of price and monetary stability. It is therefore vital that this independence is maintained and is instituted for the European Central Bank as stipulated in the Maastricht Treaty. On the other hand, independence must not be viewed in absolute terms. Independence will not automatically create credibility, both because independence can be granted and also withdrawn by political bodies, and because it can be interpreted and exercised in different ways, depending on the prevailing 'stability culture' and inflationary mentality. Even a central bank whose independence is guaranteed by the constitution must earn credibility over the longer term. Measures compromising this credibility can therefore prove very costly. Independence is not a sufficient, but it is an essential prerequisite if the Bundesbank—or its European successor institution—is to continue to play its exemplary monetary policy role.

11. Sources and bibliography

Unpublished sources

Bank of England Archive (BoE)
Bundesarchiv Koblenz
Historisches Archiv der Deutschen Bundesbank (HA BBk)
Ludwig-Erhard-Stiftung

Bibliography

Alesina, Alberto/Summers, Lawrence (1993): Central Bank Independence and Macroeconomic Performance: Some Comparative Evidence, in: Journal of Money, Credit and Banking 25, pp. 151–62

Barro, Robert/Gordon, David (1983): Rules, Discretion and Reputation in a Model of Monetary Policy, in: Journal of Monetary Economics 12, pp. 101–21

Blackburn, Keith/Christensen, Michael (1989): Monetary Policy and Policy Credibility: Theories and Evidence, in: Journal of Economic Literature 27, pp. 1–45

Bofinger, Peter (1994): Real Target behind Bundesbank Ritual, in: Financial Times, 22 December

Cukierman, Alexander (1992): Central Bank Strategy, Credibility and Independence: Theory and Evidence, Cambridge, Mass.

Deutsche Bundesbank (1992): Zum Zusammenhang zwischen Geldmengen- und Preisentwicklung in der Bundesrepublik Deutschland, in: Monatsbericht 44, 1, pp. 20–9

Deutsche Bundesbank (1994): Die Geldmengensteuerung der Deutschen Bundesbank, in: Monatsbericht 46, 5, pp. 61–75

Deutsche Bundesbank (1995): Überprüfung des Geldmengenziels und Neuordnung der Mindestreserve, in: Monatsbericht 47, 7, pp. 19–37

Deutsche Bundesbank (1996): Geldmengenziel 1996 und Senkung der Notenbankzinsen, in: Monatsbericht 48, 1, pp. 21–30

Deutsche Bundesbank (1979–96): Geschäftsberichte, Frankfurt a.M.

Deutsche Bundesbank (1979–96): Monatsberichte

Deutsches Institut für Wirtschaftsforschung (1984): Muß der deutsche Zins im Schlepptau Amerikas bleiben?, in: Wochenbericht 51, 13, pp. 149–56

Deutsches Institut für Wirtschaftsforschung (1985): Geldpolitik nicht wachstumsgerecht: Hoher Realzins hemmt Investitionen, in: Wochenbericht 52, 33, pp. 374–81

Deutsches Institut für Wirtschaftsforschung (1992): Verfehlte Geldpolitik, in: Wochenbericht 59, 31/32, pp. 385–9

Fischer, Andreas/Zurlinden, Mathias (1994): Geldpolitik mit formellen Inflationszielen: Eine Übersicht, in: Geld, Währung und Konjunktur 12, 1, pp. 65–76

Giavazzi, Francesco/Pagano, Marco (1988): The Advantage of Tying One's Hand: EMS Discipline and Central Bank Credibility, in: European Economic Review 32, pp. 1055–77

Hagen, Jürgen von (1988): Alternative Operating Regimes for Money Stock Control in West Germany: An Empirical Evaluation, in: Weltwirtschaftliches Archiv 124, pp. 89–107

Hagen, Jürgen von (1993): Monetary Union, Money Demand, and Money Supply: A Review of the German Monetary Union, in: European Economic Review 37, pp. 803–27

Herz, Bernhard/Starbatty, Joachim (1989): Viel Worte, wenig handfeste Taten, in: Rheinischer Merkur, 30 June

Issing, Otmar (1992): Theoretische und empirische Grundlagen der Geldmengenpolitik der Deutschen Bundesbank, in: Wirtschaftsdienst 72, pp. 537–48

Issing, Otmar (1994): Experience Gained with Monetary Policy Instruments in Germany, in: Monetary Policy Instruments: National Experiences and European Perspectives, 17. Symposium zur Bankgeschichte, 10. Juni 1994, Frankfurt a.M., pp. 47–58

Issing, Otmar (1996): [6]Einführung in die Geldpolitik, Munich

Issing, Otmar/Tödter, Karl-Heinz (1995): Geldmenge und Preise im vereinigten Deutschland, in: Duwendag, Dieter (ed.): Neuere Entwicklungen in der Geldtheorie und Währungs- politik, Schriften des Vereins für Socialpolitik, N.F. vol. 235, Berlin, pp. 97–123

King, Mervyn (1996): Direct Inflation Targets, in: Deutsche Bundesbank (ed.): Monetary Policy Strategies in Europe, Munich, pp. 45–75

König, Reiner (1996): The Bundesbank's Experience of Monetary Targeting, in: Deutsche Bundesbank (ed.): Monetary Policy Strategies in Europe, Munich, pp. 107–40

McCallum, Bennett (1988): The Case for Rules in the Conduct of Monetary Policy: A Concrete Example, in: Giersch, Herbert (ed.): Macro und Micro Policies for More Growth and Employment, Tübingen, pp. 26–44

Meltzer, Allan (1987): Limits of Short-Run Stabilization Policy, in: Economic Inquiry 25, pp. 1–14

Möller, Herbert/Jarchow, Hans-Joachim (1996): Zur Umlaufsgeschwindigkeit von M3, in: Jahrbücher für Nationalökonomie und Statistik 215, pp. 308–27

Neumann, Manfred J. M. (1979): Beteuerungen haben sich abgenutzt (interview), in: Wirt- schaftswoche 33, 25, pp. 60–4

Neumann, Manfred J. M. (1982): Quo vadis, Geldmengenpolitik?, in: Sparkasse 99, 3, pp. 73–5

Neumann, Manfred J. M. (1985): Auf dem Weg zu einer Realtrendorientierung der Geldpolitik, in: Sparkasse 102, 3, pp. 88–91

Neumann, Manfred J. M. (1986): Für mehr Stabilität: Rauf!, in: Wirtschaftswoche 40, 33, pp. 63–4

Neumann, Manfred J. M. (1991): Die Bundesbank sollte sich nicht beirren lassen, in: Wirtschaftsdienst 71, 9, pp. 439–42

Neumann, Manfred J. M. (1993): Deutsche Geldpolitik: Anker oder Stimulanz für Europa?, in: Wirtschaftsdienst 73, pp. 175–80

Pfister, Jürgen (1985): Geänderte Prioritäten in der Geldpolitik, in: Sparkasse 102, 7, pp. 254–9

Pohl, Rüdiger (1981): Bundesbank im Schlepptau des Auslands? Eine geldpolitische Analyse, in: BfG Wirtschaftsblätter 29, 7, pp. 1–5

Pohl, Rüdiger (1982): Die Geldpolitik der Deutschen Bundesbank im Lichte steigender Arbeitslosigkeit, in: WSI-Mitteilungen 35, pp. 15–22

Pohl, Rüdiger (1987): Brauchen wir eine neue geldpolitische Konzeption?, in: Wirtschaftsdienst 67, 7, pp. 339–45

Pohl, Rüdiger (1991): Ist die Geldpolitik zu restriktiv?, in: Wirtschaftsdienst 71, 9, pp. 435–8

Rheinisch-Westfälisches Institut für Wirtschaftsforschung (1983): Senkung von Diskont- und Lombardsatz trotz überschießender Geldausweitung—Wiederholung alter Fehler? Konjunkturbrief 2

Sachverständigenrat zur Begutachtung der gesamtwirtschaftlichen Entwicklung (various years): Jahresgutachten

Sargent, Thomas/Wallace, Neil (1993): Some Unpleasant Monetarist Arithmetic, in: Sargent, Thomas: ²Rational Expectations and Inflation, New York, pp. 173–210

Scheide, Joachim (1994): Geldpolitik mit hohem Risiko, in: Börsen-Zeitung, 20 May

Schlesinger, Helmut (1985): Zehn Jahre Geldpolitik mit einem Geldmengenziel, in: Gebauer, Wolfgang (ed.): Öffentliche Finanzen und monetäre Ökonomie, Frankfurt a.M., pp. 123–48

Shadow European Economic Policy Committee (1979): Europe Enters the Eighties, in: Banca Nazionale del Lavoro Quarterly Review 129, pp. 117–32

Sievert, Olaf (1991): Beim Bremsen sollte die Bundesbank nicht übertreiben, in: Frankfurter Allgemeine Zeitung, 13 August

Trapp, Peter (1979): Die Geldpolitik der Bundesbank auf einem umstrittenen Kurs, in: Handelsblatt, 11 September

X. German Monetary Policy as Reflected in the Academic Debate

By Rudolf Richter

This article deals with the academic debate on monetary policy during the past 50 years, especially that in (West) Germany. It seeks to make a contribution to unravelling the history of the theory, or better the dogma, of central bank policy. Theoreticians, in contrast to historians, love to generalize and speculate; accordingly, the article covers more the broad lines of debate, rather than entering into the details, and I have not hesitated to indulge in supposition.

The last 50 years, 1948–98, began with a variant of the international gold-exchange standard and ended with the start of an international paper standard. The break occurred at around the middle, between 1971 and 1973.[1] The pace of this change becomes evident if one looks back a further 50 years, to the start of this century, the heyday of the international gold standard. Paper money was then considered to be suitable only for use in emergencies, and not at all for international exchange.[2] Only a few, abstract-thinking economists considered an international paper standard possible and desirable, among them Knut Wicksell, the founder of the modern theory of money.[3] He was the leading money theorist of the first third of this century. John Maynard Keynes, initially completely under the influence of Wicksell,[4] did not take his place until 1936, with the publication of his revolutionary *General Theory*. Keynes' ideas dominated the theory of money and monetary policy in the second third of this century and beyond, at least until the collapse of the Bretton Woods system in 1973. Somewhat less than the last third of the century has been heavily influenced by the ideas of Milton

---

[1] On 15 Aug. 1971 the USA suspended the redeemability of the dollar in gold; the suspension was intended to be temporary, but was to prove permanent. On 19 Mar. 1973 the D-mark was definitively allowed to float against the US dollar and the currencies that did not participate in block floating.

[2] Cf. Wieser, 1927, p. 684.

[3] Cf. Wicksell, 1898, p. 179.

[4] See Keynes, 1924, 1930.

Friedman, and the monetarist counter-revolution he initiated. It is these three names—Wicksell, Keynes, and Friedman—that characterize contemporary thinking on the theory of money and monetary policy. Besides them, the theory of money has received important stimuli over the last 50 or 70 years from a number of other economists, including John R. Hicks, James Tobin, and Robert E. Lucas, stimuli that have not been without impact on economic policy, and were honoured with Nobel prizes. Achievements in the German-speaking countries have been more modest; the number of theoreticians and policy makers in the monetary field that have achieved international recognition is rather limited.

The presentation is divided into four phases, defined, inevitably arbitrarily, by a mixture of real-economic and theoretical-historical developments. The historical economic points of division selected are the revaluation of the D-mark in 1961, the collapse of the Bretton Woods system in 1973, and the end of the US policy of 'benign neglect' with respect to the dollar exchange rate in 1985. They more or less equate with the turning points between the phases in the history of West German theorization on money.

1. 1948–60: the economic miracle and Keynesian seductions

This period was one of reorientation and revitalization, not only in economic terms, but also in terms of economic theory. Outside Germany, in the western world, began the heyday of Keynesianism. Inside the Federal Republic the new school of thought seeped through only gradually; it was given a mixed reception by older economists and was welcomed, initially hesitantly, but then with growing enthusiasm, by their younger colleagues.

a) The international debate, 1948–60

The international debate of these years was dominated by the ideas of J. M. Keynes, ideas that were to retain their predominance until well into the 1960s. As with all theories of money, this debate is a melody over the underlying chords of the *quantity theory of money*. The quantity theory was recognized as fundamental, but Keynes argued that its conclusions applied only in the long run, and 'in the long run we are all dead'.[5] What it does not explain is the process by which the economy adjusts to a change in the money stock. This critique had already been made by Wicksell, who ex-

[5] Keynes, 1924, p. 80.

plained the effect of an increase in the money stock on prices by his *theory of interest spread.*[6]

Yet Wicksell did not consider the investment side of money in his theory. This is what Keynes did in his *General Theory*, another focus of which was the problem of expectations and disequilibrium, also neglected by Wicksell. In Keynes' theory, cash balances are held not only for transaction purposes, but also as assets, a new thought that was important for the theoretical conclusions drawn by Keynes: the interest rate on money is determined not only by the supply of money, but also by the liquidity preference. Additional money can disappear in the 'liquidity trap', rather than reducing interest rates and stimulating investment. Consequently, Keynes doubted the prospects for a successful monetary employment policy.[7]

The influence of Keynesianism on monetary economists in the 1950s is reflected in the American Patman Report (1952) and the British Radcliffe Report (1959). In both reports the majority of the economics experts questioned argued in favour of according priority to the goal of employment over that of price stability. In addition, the Radcliffe Report took up Keynes' liquidity preference theory by considering the money stock as being only part of the *liquidity structure* of the economy: 'it is the whole liquidity position that is relevant to spending decisions in the economy'.[8]

The majority of economists, particularly the younger ones, were convinced at the time that they were in a position to control the economic process, by means of a scientifically founded policy, more effectively than they had been before. Major cyclical fluctuations and high unemployment, not to mention long-term unemployment, were held to be things of the past.

b) The German discussion—basic themes and examples

At a time of high unemployment and scarce foreign exchange, it is not surprising that the problems of employment and the balance of payments were the central topics of the monetary-policy debate. The base lines and examples considered below are restricted to these two central themes.

The debate on the goals of central bank policy

Keynesian views predominated in this area, both among members of the Economic Advisory Council, which at the time included most of the

---

[6] Cf. Wicksell, 1898, p. VI.
[7] Cf. Keynes, 1936, p. 164.
[8] Radcliffe Report, 1959, section 389.

better-known economics professors, and among non-members of that Council. There was little support for the classical counter-position; their most prominent representative was Friedrich A. Lutz, who at the time was not a member of the Economic Advisory Council. A special role was played by supporters of Silvio Gesell.

(1) In 1949 the Economic Advisory Council of the American and British occupational zone of Germany (*Verwaltung für Wirtschaft*) argued against tying policy to a monetary rule and in favour of allowing central bank management scope for discretion. Moreover, the central bank should not orient its policy towards a single goal—such as price stability—but rather towards an 'overall analysis of the economic situation'.[9] The 'acceptance of temporary budget deficits' was seen as justified if they were used to finance public investment projects.[10] Keynesian influence, a mode of thought along the lines of the IS-LM diagram, is so strong that it cannot be overlooked, even though its report was the product of a commission whose composition was highly heterogeneous (22 professors, of whom 17 of economics,[11] three of law[12] and two social scientists[13]).

The Economic Advisory Council was well aware of the fact that the prevailing problem of unemployment could not be resolved without creating new jobs, i.e. not without an increase in investment activity. The scope for a 'monetary capital formation policy' was discussed, once again very much along Keynesian lines: initially, investment does not raise the output of consumer goods, while on the other hand nominal incomes rise immediately. In order to avoid inflation, saving must therefore be promoted 'by all means'. Saving, in turn, means the 'destruction of active money'.[14] In order to prevent the employment-promoting effects of primary investment from being offset by saving, new investment impulses must be provided at the same time and to the same extent as the volume of saving. For this reason, it is not considered contradictory to pursue simultaneously a policy of public investment financed by an increase in the money stock and a policy of promoting saving.[15]

This is a way of thinking characteristic of 'hydraulic Keynesianism', as Alan Coddington was later to deprecatingly term it.[16] The economy is

---

[9] Cf. Wissenschaftlicher Beirat, 1950, p. 66.
[10] Cf. Wissenschaftlicher Beirat, 1950, p. 68.
[11] Von Beckerath, W. Hoffmann, Koch, Kromphardt, Lampe, Liefmann-Keil, Miksch, Möller, Müller-Armack, Peter, Preiser, Rittershausen, Sauermann, Schiller, Veit, Weisser, Wessels.
[12] Böhm, Hallstein, Raiser.
[13] Von der Gablentz, von Nell-Breuning.
[14] See Preiser, 1950, p. 251.
[15] Cf. Wissenschaftlicher Beirat, 1953, p. 29.
[16] Cf. Coddington, 1976.

seen as a circular monetary flow, with leakages and external inflows. There are no markets and no steering through prices, wages, or interest rates. It must be said, though, that German central bank and fiscal policy successfully pursued this policy and was to be given 'good marks' for its performance.[17]

In the consultations prior to the passing of the Bundesbank Act, the Economic Advisory Council again argued against basing central bank policy on a strict monetary rule. Yet it would not be politic to include no guidelines at all concerning monetary policy in the law. It toed the Keynesian line completely, as expressed in the Council's report of 3 June and 8 July 1956, in which full employment was given priority over price stability, and it was underlined that '(for) a change in the money stock to have a positive effect on the business cycle . . . cooperation between the central bank and the government (is) necessary'.[18]

(2) The classical counter-position was unwaveringly propagated by *Friedrich A. Lutz*.[19] Unemployment, he argued, is minimum-wage unemployment, a reduction in which requires a fall in real wages. This can be achieved by an inflationary monetary policy, provided workers do not insist on maintaining their real wage level. If they do so, an increase in overall demand merely leads to inflation and not to additional employment.[20] Lutz predicted the then unknown phenomenon of stagflation and argued against a monetary employment policy.

(3) The supporters of *Silvio Gesell*, among them Otto Lautenbach, presented a *Begehren zur Sicherung der Deutschen Mark* (Petition for the safeguarding of the Deutsche Mark).[21] They called for the central bank to be assigned—to put it in modern terms—a concrete, statutory inflation target, more precisely one of zero per cent. In this way the hoarding of money in consequence of deflationary expectations and the associated sharp decline in employment could be avoided. In his critique, Wilhelm Krelle argued that the central bank should not be given a single target, but rather a bundle of targets including, alongside the inflation rate, saving, investment, employment, and the exchange rate.[22]

(4) *Wolfgang Stützel* doubted whether the central bank was at all in a position to stabilize a price index through control of the money stock.[23] In

[17] Cf., for instance, Stolper and Roskamp, 1979; Wallich, 1955 or Häuser, 1959.
[18] Wissenschaftlicher Beirat, 1957, p. 42.
[19] See Lutz, 1951.
[20] Cf. Lutz, 1951, p. 255.
[21] Cf. Gesellschaft für wirtschaftswissenschaftliche und soziologische Forschung, 1951.
[22] Cf. Gesellschaft für wirtschaftswissenschaftliche und soziologische Forschung, 1951, pp. 24f.
[23] Cf. Stützel, 1960.

his view, monetary policy could not be performed via the money stock, but only via the *liquidity effect*.[24] Besides, given fixed exchange rates, domestic price trends are determined by the rest of the world because of the 'direct price effect'.[25]

The idea of the *liquidity effect* stemmed from Keynes and was also mentioned in the Radcliffe Report. It was not the money stock in whatever form, but the liquidity structure that influenced interest-rate and price trends. Apart from Stützel, other prominent German proponents of this liquidity-based line of argument were Otto Veit and Claus Köhler.[26]

The concept of the *'direct price effect'* (in the context of fixed exchange rates) was an idea pronounced by Stützel: the application of the law of one price to the international economy, a linkage that—as Samuelson was later to show[27]—had been perceived neither by David Hume nor by subsequent theorization of the automatic gold-flow mechanism. The Bank deutscher Länder,[28] for instance, argued entirely on the Hume model, i.e. without taking account of the direct price effect. It is not that surplus foreign exchange are the 'bacilli'[29] of inflation; rather the direct price effect is the vehicle with which 'we import creeping global inflation into the Federal Republic'.[30] Given fixed exchange rates, balance of payments surpluses are the consequence of a restrictive monetary policy, and not the cause of domestic price rises; prices are dragged up by the direct price effect.[31] With this insight, Stützel anticipated the *monetary approach to the determination of the balance of payments*, developed anew and propagated 10 years later by Robert Mundell, Harry Johnson and their followers.[32]

The debate on the convertibility of the D-mark

The central issue in the debate on full convertibility of the D-mark was the answer to the problem of the 'magic triangle', the trick of simultaneously achieving price stability, full employment and balance of payments equilib-

---

[24] Cf. Stützel, 1960a, pp. 19ff.

[25] Cf. Stützel, 1960, p. 29.

[26] See Veit, 1957 and Köhler, 1970a.

[27] Cf. Samuelson, 1980.

[28] In the Annual Report for 1953 it is stated that the central bank had 'consciously allowed, in so some cases even promoted' the liquefying effect of the inflow of foreign exchange, in order to 'follow the rules of the classical gold standard'. Bank deutscher Länder, Geschäftsbericht 1953, p. 16.

[29] Cf. Stützel, 1960, p. 4.

[30] Stützel, 1960a, p. 30.

[31] Cf. Stützel, 1961, p. 27.

[32] See Mundell, 1968 and Johnson, 1972b.

rium with full convertibility. The two extreme conditions under which the trick (possibly) succeeds are:

- fixed exchange rates together with international cooperation between the industrialized nations in the area of stability policy;
- 'floating' exchange rates.

Opinion in Germany was predominantly for fixed exchange rates—the Economic Advisory Council, the Bank deutscher Länder/Bundesbank and economists such as Herbert Giersch, Hans Möller, and Wolfgang Stützel, for example. The proponents of 'floating' exchange rates represented the outsiders and included L. Albert Hahn, Friedrich A. Lutz, and the supporters of Silvio Gesell.

Let us consider some examples of the positions taken in the debate:

(1) The Economic Advisory Council at the Ministry of Economics argued for retention of the system of fixed exchange rates, even after achieving full convertibility, because: 'a foreign trade system organized on market principles, in particular, must be able to rely on stable exchange rates.'[33]

It did not envisage precisely fixed exchange rates, but rather rates that would be allowed to fluctuate within a relatively narrow band.[34] The need for coordinating employment policy with Germany's trading partners was underlined.[35] Changes in exchange-rate parities should not be precluded in principle, but should remain the exception.

(2) *Herbert Giersch* and *Hans Möller* argued against freely floating exchange rates. They were worried about sharp fluctuations in exchange rates and incorrect evaluations of investment possibilities. Floating exchange rates would also remove the compulsion arising from the balance of payments position to fight inflation from the outset. The advantage that floating exchange rates would isolate healthy countries from inflation-ridden countries was, they argued, overshadowed by the danger of a corrosion by inflationary countries of the international division of labour, with all the political consequences that entailed. For this reason no attempt should be made to isolate inflation by means of floating exchange rates; rather, the genesis and diffusion of inflationary pressure should be prevented by international cooperation on economic policy.[36]

(3) *Hans Möller* once again argued in favour of retaining the system of fixed exchange rates even after achieving full convertibility. He saw this as a way of promoting international cooperation.[37] Offsetting inflows of foreign

[33] Wissenschaftlicher Beirat, 1953, p. 93.
[34] Wissenschaftlicher Beirat, 1953, p. 94.
[35] Wissenschaftlicher Beirat, 1953, p. 95.
[36] Cf. Giersch and Möller, 1952.
[37] Cf. Möller, 1957, p. 502.

exchange could be avoided if fiscal policy, rather than monetary policy, were used to fight inflation (e.g. by antedating tax payments).[38] Clearly the additional tax revenue would have to be hoarded by the state. Möller was thinking here—similarly to Häuser[39]—along Keynesian lines: export surpluses do not exert an inflationary effect if the corresponding income surplus is saved. No consideration is given to the change in interest rates. Yet in fact interest rates would be expected to rise in this case and, as with a restrictive monetary policy, this would attract foreign currency.

(4) *Wolfgang Stützel* argued in favour of a system of *absolutely* fixed exchange rates,[40] for a 'gold currency without gold',[41] because it was only in such a system that no government could afford 'to completely ignore monetary issues and to borrow without limit in domestic currency'.[42]

However, Stützel offered no clear solution to the problem that, for n countries, there are only $n-1$ exchange rates as a target variable for monetary policy. In other words, one of the countries needs a target variable other than the exchange rate. This must be a real variable (such as the price of gold) or a nominal variable that is linked sufficiently closely to a real variable (for example the money stock).[43]

(5) *Friedrich A. Lutz* was the proponent of floating exchange rates, with the clearest arguments of any economist in the German-speaking countries during this epoch.[44] He claimed that it was perfectly possible to introduce floating exchange rates on moving to full convertibility, provided several countries took this step simultaneously.[45]

In response to the argument that floating exchange rates could initiate a wage-price spiral, Lutz argued that higher wage demands could only be realized by the trade unions if the central bank made the necessary resources available. And if it were claimed that it did not have the power to refuse to do so 'it must also be said that it does not have the power to refuse to finance wage increases that (under fixed exchange rates) can be demanded for many other reasons'. Looking at it this way, the trade unions would be determining monetary policy in either case.[46]

The opinion in the Bank deutscher Länder/Deutsche Bundesbank

Based on its Annual Reports for the years 1948–60, in which the Bank deutscher Länder/Bundesbank set out and justified its policy, the following brief conclusions can be drawn.

[38] Cf. Möller, 1957, p. 588.

[39] See Häuser, 1959, p. 169.

[40] See Stützel, 1960, *a*.

[41] Stützel, 1960*a*, p. 101.

[42] Stützel, 1960, p. 10.

[43] Cf. Richter, 1990, pp. 180ff.

[44] Cf. Lutz, 1951, 1954, 1955, 1959.

[45] Cf. Lutz, 1954, p. 128.

[46] Cf. Lutz, 1955, pp. 24f.

In accordance with contemporary conventional wisdom, the Bundesbank oriented policy not towards a single target variable, but towards a bundle of goals, including, besides the magic triangle,[47] such variables as bank liquidity, savings, investment activity, productivity growth, cyclical trends, and fiscal policy. It is difficult to tell whether the maintenance of purchasing power was always given priority. The reasons given for inflation were, amongst others, wage increases[48] and 'imported inflation' in the sense used by David Hume.[49]

It was noted with regret that convertibility of the D-mark served to restrict the autonomy of national credit policy,[50] but nevertheless the Bundesbank wanted to stick to fixed exchange rates.[51]

Bundesbank efforts to stabilize business fluctuations featured consistently.[52] The possibility, indeed the necessity, of an anticyclical monetary policy was accepted by those responsible for the policies of the West German central bank, as it was by the majority of contemporary monetary economists, both in Germany and abroad.

2. 1961–72: Keynesianism, the exchange-rate debate, and the start of the monetarist counter-revolution

The period between 1961 and 1972 was characterized by the growing impact of Keynesian theory on German economic policy—which reached its peak with the Stability and Growth Act of 1967 and the associated change in the Constitution—the exchange-rate debate and the start of the monetarist counter-revolution. Within the international debate, 'hydraulic' Keynesianism—i.e. economic thinking in terms of circular flows, without markets and price steering—was replaced by the neoclassical synthesis. Markets, particularly financial markets, began to play a role in the macro- and not just the microeconomic discussion. The field of monetary macro-economics developed. Econometric models were expanded to incorporate money and financial markets. The theory of optimal control, illustrated

---

[47] Cf. Deutsche Bundesbank, Geschäftsbericht 1958, p. 1.
[48] Cf. Deutsche Bundesbank, Geschäftsbericht 1959, p. 2 and Geschäftsbericht 1960, p. 2.
[49] Cf. Deutsche Bundesbank, Geschäftsbericht 1953, p. 16 and Geschäftsbericht 1954, p. 21.
[50] Cf. Deutsche Bundesbank, Geschäftsbericht 1959, p. 3.
[51] Cf. Deutsche Bundesbank, Geschäftsbericht 1959, p. 4.
[52] Cf. Deutsche Bundesbank, Geschäftsbericht 1953, p. 1; Geschäftsbericht 1955, p. 1; Geschäftsbericht 1957, p. 1 and Geschäftsbericht 1959, p. 1.

graphically by space travel, was taken over by economics. It was the heyday of the theory of quantitative economic policy.

The task in West Germany was seen to be that of perfecting what had been achieved. Belief in the scope for fine-tuning had increased, as had the conviction that external disturbances could be filtered out by means of floating exchange rates. Meanwhile, the monetarist counter-revolution, led by Milton Friedman, began to take form. It dominated debate in the leading international journals, and towards the end of the 1960s began to infiltrate into West Germany. The first German monetarists appeared on the scene, and the monetary policy of the Bundesbank came under fire. A lively discussion commenced.

a) The international debate, 1961–72

At the start of the 1960s Keynesianism was still unchallenged as the predominant macroeconomic theory, albeit in the modified form of the neoclassical synthesis developed by Hicks, Patinkin, Tobin, Gurley, and Shaw.[53] This synthesis was elaborated further by subsequent contributions by Patinkin, Tobin and the comprehensive, revised second edition of Patinkin's *Money, Interest and Prices,* published in 1965.[54]

The neoclassical synthesis enables the banking system and financial intermediaries to be embedded in the overall macroeconomic system and thus the *liquidity approach to the theory of money* to be addressed in a more satisfactory way. The theory of the creation of money appears in a new light. Tobin, for example, attacks the prevailing view that the commercial banks can create money as they see fit.[55] He argued that the banks could expand their deposit volume only if they are able to place a corresponding volume of loans on the market; their scope for so doing is not unlimited, however.

Tobin's argument is not without its effects on the then prevailing justification for minimum reserves: what is decisive for controlling the commercial banks is not the existence of minimum reserves, but rather the provision of 'unborrowed reserves' by the central bank.[56]

The liquidity theory propounded by the Keynesians was subjected to intense criticism by Friedman. What was important, he argued, was control of the money supply, as in the short term there was a close correlation between the money stock and employment, but one that could not be

[53] See Hicks, 1946; Patinkin, 1956; Tobin, 1958; Gurely and Shaw, 1960. The term 'neoclassical synthesis' was coined by Samuelson, 1966, pp. 1111, 1271, 1543.
[54] See Patinkin, 1961 and Tobin, 1967.
[55] Cf. Tobin, 1967.
[56] Cf. Tobin, 1967, p. 9.

used for employment policy, because changes in the money stock affected national income only after a time-lag, the duration of which was difficult to predict.[57] Thus a monetary employment policy would have a destabilizing rather than a stabilizing effect.[58] Consequently, the central bank ought to refrain from pursuing a short-term employment policy, and should restrict its activities to bringing about steady growth of the money stock. In order to ensure that this occurred, it ought to be obliged to allow the money stock to grow at a fixed rate.[59]

Also belonging to this period are the two famous conclusions drawn by Friedman, namely that, in the longer term, an inflationary policy can keep neither unemployment nor interest rates at a low level.[60]

The first proposition relates to the concept of the Philips Curve trade-off, which cannot function in the longer term because, in the final analysis, employment is determined by real wages, not by nominal wages. The second argument is based on the experience that the nominal interest rate rises by the expected inflation rate (Fisher relation).

The crucial debate on 'fixed versus floating exchange rates' had been opened by Milton Friedman back in 1950, with his critique of the Bretton Woods system.[61] In Germany the same view was propounded somewhat later, but with equal vehemence, by Egon Sohmen.[62] In response to the objection that floating exchange rates would be unstable, Friedman and, later, Sohmen and Johnson argued—incorrectly—that fluctuations in rates would be prevented by profitable speculation.[63]

Stützel and Charles P. Kindleberger can be taken as representatives of the opposing view.[64]

Sohmen and Mundell distinguished themselves with a Keynesian variant of the theory of floating exchange rates that played an important role in the exchange-rate debate of the 1960s in Germany.[65] According to this theory, a monetary stabilization policy is not only conceivable under conditions of floating exchange rates, it is also more effective than under fixed rates. The reason behind this is that, under floating rates, the Keynes-effect is supplemented by an export-surplus effect.[66] However, the Mundell–Sohmen model

---

[57] Cf. Friedman, 1956 and Friedman and Schwartz, 1963.
[58] Cf. Friedman, 1958 and Friedman and Meiselmann, 1963.
[59] Cf. Friedman, 1960, p. 100.
[60] Cf. Friedman, 1968.
[61] See Friedman, 1953.
[62] See Sohmen, 1969.
[63] Cf. Friedman, 1953, p. 158; Sohmen, 1961/1969 and Johnson, 1972a.
[64] Cf. Stützel, 1960 and Kindleberger, 1981.
[65] Cf. Sohmen, 1967 and Mundell, 1961.
[66] Cf. Sohmen, 1967, p. 521.

did not consider exchange-rate expectations, restricting the degree to which their results could be generalized.

b) The German discussion—basic themes and examples

Here too, the main topics of debate were determined by the prevailing economic policy problems: foreign exchange surpluses and speculative capital movements, concern about imported inflation, and the desire to maintain consistent and appropriate economic growth. Thus the debate on monetary policy concentrated on the For and Against of floating exchange rates and on an anticyclical growth policy. Among academic economists, a broad front in favour of floating exchange rates developed in the course of the exchange-rate debate. In May 1969 almost 100 economics professors signed a 'protest resolution' against the decision by the Federal Government not to revalue the D-mark,[67] in October of the same year, 51 economics professors lent their support to a public declaration written by Giersch and Sohmen in favour of greater flexibilization of the D-mark exchange rate.[68] Keynesianism won the day in the stability and growth debate.

The intellectual preparatory work was soon followed by deeds: in external economic terms, the provisional liberalization of the D-mark/US dollar exchange rate between 10 May and 17 December 1971, and permanent liberalization on 19 March 1973; in domestic economic terms, the institution in 1963 of the Council of Economic Experts, which was entrusted with the task of reporting on macroeconomic trends, and, in June 1967, the implementation of the Stability and Growth Act, together with the associated amendment to article 109, 4 of the German Constitution. This new institutional framework was intended to help achieve, simultaneously and 'within the framework of the market economic order', four economic policy goals: stable prices, a high level of employment, external economic equilibrium, and steady growth at an appropriate rate. This, together with the call for floating exchange rates, marked the zenith of the neoclassical synthesis—a bringing-together of the theories of Walras, Wicksell, Hicks, and Keynes. This was the prevailing ('new') teaching of its time, as presented in German textbook fashion by Giersch, or by Richter, Schlieper, and Friedmann.[69] The Phillips Curve trade-off formed part of this school of thought. This fact

---

[67] The declaration was in opposition to the 'non-revaluation decision by the cabinet, which was justified not in economic terms, but by tactical electoral considerations'. 'Die Mai-Revolte der Professoren', in: Der Volkswirt, no. 21, 23 May 1969, pp. 29f.

[68] Für freie Wechselkurse, 1969.

[69] See Giersch, 1977 and Richter et al. 1973.

was summed up in real-world politics by Helmut Schmidt, the then Federal Minister of Economics and Finance, in his famous saying: 'it seems to me that the German people—to put it simplistically—can live with 5 per cent inflation better than with 5 per cent unemployment.'[70]

Safeguarding the currency under fixed or floating exchange rates: the exchange-rate debate in Germany in the 1960s

This was a controversial debate at both the theoretical and practical-political levels. The main protagonists were, on the one hand, Egon Sohmen, and on the other, Wolfgang Stützel, who argued unswervingly for fixed exchange rates. Sohmen had managed to convince Herbert Giersch, who began to argue in favour of floating exchange rates as a member of the Council of Economic Experts. The background to the conflict involved concern about rising rates of creeping inflation, which in the 1960–3 period was running at double the rate experienced between 1952 and 1959 (2.8 per cent compared with 1.26 per cent).

(1) The Council of Economic Experts, with Herbert Giersch as its *spiritus rector*,[71] stated in its first Annual Report its view that international price linkages were the main source of inflation.[72] Consequently, the Council argued for a move to floating exchange rates, with reference to a report by Friedrich A. Lutz and Egon Sohmen. Among other things, the report repeated the above-mentioned Sohmen–Mundell hypothesis of the greater effectiveness of monetary policy under floating exchange rates.

The Council of Economic Experts stuck to this view until the Annual Report of 1969/70, although it did also describe other possible solutions to the problem of importing inflation, including Stützel's idea of a 'hardened currency standard' (*gehärteter Devisenstandard*)[73]—and argued, as did Stützel or Köhler, for absolutely fixed exchange rates within the EEC countries in the form of a European currency union.[74]

(2) The Economic Advisory Council at the Federal Ministry of Economics, whose membership composition was far broader than that of the

[70] Cf. 'An höheren Steuern kommen wir nicht vorbei'. SZ interview with Helmut Schmidt, in: Süddeutsche Zeitung, 28 July 1972.

[71] Initially the composition of the Council of Economic Experts was as follows: W. Bauer (chairman), P. Binder, H. Giersch, H. Koch, F. W. Meyer. The last-mentioned was replaced in February 1966 by W. Stützel, who, however, left the Council in September 1968 because of a fundamental, substantive difference of opinion with the other members. Giersch withdrew in 1970. Naturally, the composition of the Council in each year was not without influence on the content of the respective Annual Reports.

[72] Cf. Sachverständigenrat, Jahresgutachten 1964/5, p. 90.

[73] Cf. Sachverständigenrat, Jahresgutachten 1966/7, p. 147.

[74] Cf. Sachverständigenrat, Jahresgutachten 1971/2, p. 101.

Council of Economic Experts,[75] dealt with the 'continuous price increases of our time' in its report on 29 January 1966 without even mentioning international price linkages.[76] It considered changes in national price levels to be the result of changes in real supply and monetary demand[77]—a Keynesian idea. A restrictive monetary policy with the aim of stabilizing the price level would lead to unemployment and was thus contrary to the employment goal. The Economic Advisory Council thus felt unable to recommend it. Instead it proposed competition, growth, and structural policy measures in order to counter long-term inflationary trends.[78]

In its report on 25 November 1967, the Economic Advisory Council argued in favour of fixed exchange rates.[79] Here, too, the concept and idea of international price linkages were studiously avoided.

(3) *Wolfgang Stützel* continued to argue in favour of absolutely fixed exchange rates and full convertibility.[80] The system of (absolutely) fixed exchange rates combined with full convertibility served as the 'task-master of governments'.[81] Floating exchange rates, he claimed, helped to accelerate creeping inflation and obstructed world trade—fears that did not prove justified in practice. What Stützel did appreciate, however, was that exchange rates cannot be equated with goods prices, but should rather be considered to be, as he put it, *Bestandshaltepreise* (stock-holding prices), i.e. analogous to prices of assets that must be seen in the light of their expected resale price.[82] In this respect, too, Stützel was years ahead of theoretical developments, in this case of the portfolio approach to the determination of exchange rates, as later formalized by William Branson.[83] The same is true of his explanation of national balance of payments deficits, which he interpreted—as economists such as Ronald McKinnon and Wallace Oates were later to do[84]—as the result of individual saving behaviour.[85]

Monetary stabilization policy in the world of the neoclassical synthesis

The central hypothesis of the monetary stabilization policy of the neoclassical synthesis—the 'new' Keynesianism of the 1960s—was still the

[75] In 1965 it was composed of 21 economists, including among them overt supporters (Giersch, Lutz) and opponents (Möller, Veit) of floating exchange rates.

[76] Cf. Wissenschaftlicher Beirat, 1973.
[77] Cf. Wissenschaftlicher Beirat, 1973, p. 483.
[78] Cf. Wissenschaftlicher Beirat, 1973, p. 485.
[79] Cf. Wissenschaftlicher Beirat, 1973, pp. 509ff.
[80] Cf. Stützel, 1969.
[81] Stützel, 1973, p. 95.
[82] Cf. Stützel, 1973, p. 159.
[83] See Branson, 1977.
[84] See McKinnon and Oates, 1966.
[85] See Stützel, 1953.

Wicksell–Keynes effect, as illustrated in the textbooks by the IS-LM diagram. New aspects included the integration of the financial markets, in particular the markets for financial intermediaries, and the extension of the theory of the supply of money (the theory of the money creation multiplier, the origins of which went back to the 1920s). Empirical studies, rather than theoretical speculation, played an important role here. A (small) number of such studies are to be found in the German literature of this period.

(1) What is decisive for the effectiveness of a monetary stabilization policy in the world of the IS-LM diagram is the elasticity of the demand for money with respect to the interest rate. Of the few empirical studies into this question, those by König, Roskamp and Laumas and by Westphal deserve mention.[86] They determined interest-rate elasticities that differed significantly from zero, even if the values were rather low. This implies, at least, that a monetary stabilization policy would have a weak effect, irrespective of the 'open flank' of the balance of payments. As far as the 'open flank' was concerned, the problem consisted of offsetting capital movements. On this question we find nothing more than expressions of opinion during the 1960s in Germany. Empirical studies were not conducted until very much later (for example by Neumann).[87] According to his results, during the 1960s around 50 per cent of a monetary restriction was offset by capital inflows from abroad. Richter and Teigen obtained rather different results, namely no offsetting effect during the period 1960.1–1966.6 and almost perfect offsetting during the period 1966.7–1972.12.[88]

(2) German literature on economic theory in this period focused largely on coming to terms with the debate in the English-speaking world on the integration of the money market into macroeconomic models. Stützel's 'Saldenmechanik' (lit.: balance mechanics) and the Bundesbank's macroeconomic financing calculations served as models here.[89] The Keynesian liquidity theory of money was the predominant paradigm. Monetary policy studies focused on bank liquidity, the free liquid reserves, and the liquidity ratio. Monetary policy consisted of restricting liquidity, and thus raising the price of borrowing and vice versa. It was in such terms that the Council of Economic Experts continually discussed the Bundesbank's monetary policy.[90] Characteristic of the Keynesian mode of thinking at this time was also the concept of a 'potentialorientierte Kreditpolitik' (potential-oriented credit policy) developed by Köhler.[91]

Opinions remained divided on the question of the priority of price

---

[86] See König, 1968; Roskamp and Laumas, 1970 and Westphal, 1970.
[87] See Neumann, 1978b.
[88] Cf. Richter and Teigen, 1982a.
[89] Cf. Köhler, 1962, 1970a; Jarchow, 1970; Richter, 1967, 1968; Jarchow et al., 1970.
[90] Cf., for instance, Sachverständigenrat, Jahresgutachten 1970/1, pp. 40ff.
[91] Cf. Köhler, 1971.

stability. The Council of Economic Experts, for instance, emphasized in its Annual Report 1970/1 that: 'attaching great importance to price stability does not mean giving it priority.'[92]

The advent of the monetarists

The penetration of monetarist ideas towards the end of the 1960s brought the scholarly debate on German monetary policy to life. The Bundesbank came under fire. The tidy checklists and fancy models of the neoclassical synthesis were all shaken up, the self-assurance of its proponents began to show cracks. What had seemed impossible began to materialize, albeit slowly at first: economists took leave of the hope that the Wicksell–Keynes effects could be utilized to maintain a high level of employment. An unforeseen change of consciousness was initiated, one without which the confidence of so many of today's economic experts in the feasibility of the planned European Monetary Union, while EU Member States retain responsibility for fiscal policy, would be inconceivable.

The monetarist counter-revolution was brought to Germany by Karl Brunner, not least by the series of conferences initiated by him in 1970 under the title *Konstanzer Seminar für Geldtheorie and Geldpolitik*. The early German monetarists, who were initially made light of and not taken seriously, included Hans G. Monissen, Manfred J. M. Neumann, Jürgen Siebke, and Manfred Willms.[93]

Monissen criticized Köhler's argument that the quantity theory took a one-sided view of the role of money and neglected the importance of credit.[94]

Neumann focused his attention on the central monetary-policy topic in the Brunner–Meltzer line[95] of monetarist thought, the so-called intermediate targets and indicators of monetary policy.[96] He argued that the Bundesbank oriented its policy evaluation towards bank liquidity, whereas it was the extended monetary base that was the correct yardstick for German monetary policy.[97] He called on the Bundesbank to abandon the liquidity indicator, together with the 'intellectually inadequate' liquidity concept; shortly afterwards, it did just that.

One of the targets of Neumann's attacks was the position taken by *Köhler*, who criticized the teachings of Milton Friedman and defended the liquidity

[92] Sachverständigenrat, Jahresgutachten 1970/1, para. 217, p. 69. The Council consisted at the time of W. Bauer, Cl. Köhler, N. Kloten, and O. Sievert.
[93] See Monissen, 1971, 1973; Neumann, 1971, 1972; Siebke and Willms, 1970.
[94] Cf. Köhler, 1970a, pp. 200ff. and Monissen, 1973, p. 149.
[95] Cf. Brunner and Meltzer, 1967.
[96] Cf. Neumann, 1971, 1972.
[97] Cf. Neumann, 1972, p. 170.

theory of monetary policy.[98] Köhler's concept of a potential-oriented credit policy was included in the Annual Reports of the Council of Economic Experts, of which Köhler was a member, for 1971/2 and 1972/3, but the Council also mentioned the money stock as the 'target variable and indicator of monetary control', a line it was subsequently to adopt whole-heartedly.[99]

The Economic Advisory Council at the Ministry of Economics continued to reject subjecting the central bank to binding rules, and thus also to the 'Friedman rule'.[100] It did state, however, that: 'the question of the areas in which discretionary decisions can and should be subject to a binding rule is to be decided on a case-by-case basis.'[101]

The opinion in the Bundesbank 1961–72

Unlike the situation in the previous period, the targets of Bundesbank policy were now precisely specified, namely price stability, a high level of employment, and external economic equilibrium. The ranking did not remain invariant; sometimes external economic equilibrium is in first place.[102] It was emphasized that the Bundesbank was to seek to meet several targets at once.[103] There was again talk of 'imported inflation', once more in the sense used by David Hume and not by Wolfgang Stützel.[104] There was no change in the rejection of floating exchange rates.[105] What was decisive for the balance of payments problems, it was argued, was not the nature of the international currency system, but the exchange-rate policy pursued in the leading countries.[106]

Stabilization of the business cycle remained one of the Bundesbank's aims.[107] On several occasions it was stated that coordination between monetary and fiscal policy was desirable,[108] or the fact that monetary policy required the active support of fiscal policy was underlined.[109]

All in all, the Bundesbank's position, as revealed in its Annual Reports,

[98] Cf. Köhler, 1970b.
[99] Cf. Sachverständigenrat, Jahresgutachten 1972/3, para. 397.
[100] Cf. Wissenschaftlicher Beirat, 1973, pp. 597ff.
[101] Wissenschaftlicher Beirat, 1973, p. 617.
[102] Cf. Deutsche Bundesbank, Geschäftsbericht 1968, p. 23.
[103] Cf. Deutsche Bundesbank, Geschäftsbericht 1966, p. 1.
[104] Cf. Deutsche Bundesbank, Geschäftsbericht 1962, pp. 4f. and Deutsche Bundesbank, 1968, p. 15.
[105] Cf. Deutsche Bundesbank, Geschäftsbericht 1962, p. 19.
[106] Cf. Deutsche Bundesbank, Geschäftsbericht 1964, p. 41.
[107] Cf. Deutsche Bundesbank, Geschäftsbericht 1961, pp. 12ff.; Geschäftsbericht 1965, p. 14; Geschäftsbericht 1970, p. 1.
[108] Cf. Deutsche Bundesbank, Geschäftsbericht 1964, p. 22; Geschäftsbericht 1967, p. 19.
[109] Cf. Deutsche Bundesbank, Geschäftsbericht 1969, p. 29; Geschäftsbericht 1972, p. 25.

was very close to the then prevailing neoclassical synthesis. The Bundesbank was clearly convinced of the Wicksell–Keynes effect exerted by interest-rate policy.

3. 1973–84: monetarism under scrutiny: a new monetary policy, managed floating

19 March 1973 was a memorable day in the long history of money. On that day the international paper standard took its first perceptible steps,[110] an institutional arrangement that, as late as the start of this century, experts such as Friedrich von Wieser had considered impossible. Yet the change came unexpectedly, by way of the collapse of the Bretton Woods system that many favoured. A new orientation was required for monetary policy, and the teachings of Milton Friedman won the day. The Bundesbank adopted a pragmatically tinged monetarism.

Alongside the older line of monetarist thought initiated by Friedman, a new, more abstract school, initiated by Robert Lucas, developed which brought in the hypothesis of rational expectations. Tobin (1980) was later to term these two schools 'Monetarism Mark I' and 'Monetarism Mark II'; for the latter he introduced the now generally accepted term 'new classical macroeconomics'.[111] Characteristic of both approaches is their clear message, which essentially consisted of the economic-policy teachings of classical economics—modernized and supplemented with stochastic shocks—that just 10 years earlier the majority of the profession had held to have been dead, and buried by Keynes. Although the new school of thought agreed that money is not neutral, its non-neutrality cannot be used to steer the business cycle. Moreover, the 'long term' with which changes in the money stock allegedly affect prices is short enough to be experienced by those initiating an inflationary policy. Indeed, according to the theory of rational expectations, a systematic monetary policy will be completely anticipated and allowed for by economic actors: it immediately affects prices and thus remains ineffective. Only unpredictable changes in the money stock have (short-term) employment effects.

In the 1970s, Keynesianism in the Federal Republic of Germany was swept away by monetarism just as quickly as it had established itself 10

---

[110] The gold exchange standard ended, as already mentioned, *de facto* on 15 August 1971 with the suspension of the redeemability of the US dollar in gold, although its organizational shell persisted until 19 March 1973.

[111] Cf. Tobin, 1980.

years earlier. The turnaround was facilitated by rising inflation in the Western world and disappointment about the political abuse of fine-tuning, as envisaged in the Stability and Growth Act. Yet in their turn the proponents of floating exchange rates were also to be disappointed. The promised stability of exchange rates failed to materialize, and, contrary to what had been expected, central banks—other than the Federal Reserve Bank—intervened to a previously unheard-of extent.[112]

a) The international debate—a brief sketch

Initially the hypotheses put forward by Friedman made little ground against the sophisticated models of the proponents of the neoclassical synthesis, a multitude of first-rate theoreticians and econometricians, who were initially able to defend their positions (e.g. Tobin or Klein). It was not until the arrival of Robert Lucas, a theoretician of equal calibre, and his rational expectations hypothesis that the decisive blow against the Keynesians was struck.[113]

Two central arguments put forward by Lucas drove the Keynesians into a corner:

1. *the policy-ineffectiveness hypothesis*,[114] the claim that a systematic monetary policy is ineffective,[115] and
2. *the econometric policy evaluation critique*,[116] according to which the econometric structural parameters are not independent of economic-policy interventions, which meant that the expensive econometric models currently in use were not suitable for policy simulation, let alone for optimum control of the economy. The result of this was that, 'after Lucas', econometrics was not the same as before.

The Keynesians found themselves in a difficult position following Lucas' critique. Hicks talked of the *Crisis in Keynesian Economics*.[117] Tobin, one of the leading Keynesian theoreticians, admitted that the lack of adequate micro-foundations for (Keynesian) macroeconomics had led to false prognoses.[118] What was clear was that the Keynesians had lost their role as

[112] Cf. Jurgensen, 1984.
[113] Cf. Lucas, 1972.
[114] Cf. Lucas, 1973.
[115] Cf. Sargent and Wallace, 1975 and Barro, 1976. For a readable summary cf. Maddock and Carter, 1982, p. 50. A comprehensive synopsis of the theory and econometrics of the Phillips Curve trade-off is provided by Santomero and Seater, 1978.
[116] Cf. Lucas, 1976.
[117] Hicks, 1974.
[118] Cf. Tobin, 1980.

protagonists in the debate on monetary and fiscal policy. They put all their energy into rear-guard actions, in particular against the rational expectations hypothesis, which they finally, in a slightly different and weaker form, managed to incorporate into their models. It became a type of economic sport to show that a systematic monetary policy could be used to raise employment or growth even if the rational expectations hypothesis applied. Even the policy of monetary targeting was accepted, although a 'modified activist monetary policy' was proposed—in which the initiative remained with the central bank—in place of a strict monetary rule.[119]

The most prominent book on money written in this period was penned by Jürg Niehans.[120] It was written in the tradition of Hicks and Patinkin, that is in the style of the neoclassical synthesis. Niehans stressed, however, at the end of his book that central bank policy will remain an art, whatever progress is made by monetary theory.[121]

b) The debate in Germany—basic themes and examples

The academic debate on monetary policy during this period was dominated by the monetarist counter-revolution. The idea of fine-tuning embodied in the Stability and Growth Act that had just been passed was rejected by a growing number of economists. The relationships between the money stock and economic activity, argued the Council of Economic Experts, for instance, had not been determined with sufficient conviction. Consequently, the central bank should refrain from attempting to control the economy by monetary means and should pursue a monetary policy that was neutral in terms of the business cycle.[122] To this end it ought to expand the monetary base at a rate equal to the growth of potential output plus a rate of inflation considered unavoidable. Apart from the addition of the 'unavoidable rate of inflation', that was straight from the mouth of Milton Friedman. On this view, monetary policy now had only one goal: the stability of the price level!

The first great topic of debate in this phase was, accordingly, monetary targeting. The German Keynesians went on the defensive, but remained faithful to the concept of liquidity policy that had been the basis of the Radcliffe Report.

The second major topic for discussion was the managed floating pursued by the leading central banks. The idea of absolutely fixed exchange rates, at

---

[119] Cf. Fischer, 1980, p. 232.
[120] Cf. Niehans, 1978.
[121] Cf. Niehans, 1978, p. 294.
[122] Cf. Sachverständigenrat, Jahresgutachten 1974/5, p. 155.

least within the EEC countries, was raised. The European Monetary System was set up, although with a different aim, namely to counter the trend towards the D-mark becoming the leading European currency,[123] which nevertheless occurred.

Monetary targeting versus liquidity policy

Following the collapse of the gold exchange standard, the Bundesbank was finally in a position to pursue the goal of internal stability of the D-mark without consideration of the external value of the exchange rate and the balance of payments. In doing so, it had to base its policy on a real anchor, either directly (as in the case of a target inflation rate) or indirectly (as with a monetary target under the assumption of a stable demand-for-money function). Friedman recommended the latter, arguing that it was easier for the monetary authorities to control a monetary aggregate than the direct price target. What is important to realize is that indirect real anchoring via nominal national income, the liquidity quota, the short-term interest rates, the interest-rate structure, the real rate of interest, etc. is no less problematic, or even more problematic, than anchoring by means of the money stock.

The two leading matadors in the German debate on the question of monetary targeting versus liquidity policy in this period were Manfred J. M. Neumann and Rüdiger Pohl. What were their arguments, and what were the views of the Council of Economic Experts and the Economic Advisory Council on this subject?

(1) *Manfred J. M. Neumann* in a slightly milder form, the doctrines of Milton Friedman, including the hypothesis of the *dominance of monetary impulses*, which was the reason why monetary policy ought to move from its cyclical orientation to a *trend orientation*, underpinned by a corresponding binding monetary rule.[124] Neumann did depart from Friedman, however, in recommending that the '*monetary rule* should be subject to an *emergency exit clause*'.[125]

The monetary target should be achieved by 'expanding *open market operations* to make them the dominant instrument of monetary policy, and their application as a *quantitative policy*'.[126] It was also necessary to 'change to formulating the *monetary target for several years in advance*'.[127]

A quantitatively oriented monetary policy implies that 'the market should

---

[123] Cf. Sachverständigenrat, Jahresgutachten 1978/9, p. 153.

[124] Cf. Neumann, 1974, pp. 69f.

[125] Neumann, 1974, p. 70.

[126] Neumann, 1974, p. 70 (author's italics).

[127] Neumann, 1977, p. 258 (author's italics).

be left to determine the *level of interest rates* and also the exchange rates' if the central bank wanted to avoid undermining its own policy.[128]

Neumann—and the *Europäische Schatten-Wirtschaftskomitee* (Shadow European Economic Policy Committee) he had established—criticized the Bundesbank for its *anticyclical orientation towards monetary expansion*.[129]

On the *stability of the demand-for-money function*, Neumann wrote: 'there is little evidence . . . of a lasting change in cash-balance behaviour.'[130] He criticized the frequent failure to meet the announced monetary targets. The problem of *credibility* was at bottom very simple: 'monetary targets, once announced, must be met'.[131]

(2) *Rüdiger Pohl* took the Keynesian line in the manner of the neoclassical synthesis, as found in the Radcliffe Report. Along with Köhler,[132] Pohl considered *bank liquidity* to be the central determining factor behind monetary activities.[133] This is the mechanism by which the credit volume of the banks is controlled.[134] The aim of monetary policy should be to steer the credit volume of the banks, and not the volume of money.

The following comments are to be made on that: both aims are equally good for determining the purchasing power of money under the paper standard, provided the demand functions for money and for bank loans are stable. As far as the supply side is concerned, the liquidity concept, which is linked to bank liquidity, must assume a stable *credit-creation function*, whereas monetarist theory, where it is linked to a monetary-base concept, must assume a stable *money-creation function*. Representatives of the monetary-base concept, such as Brunner and Meltzer, made this latter assumption.[135] German proponents of the liquidity concept were silent on this issue. In his calculation of the maximum possible volume of credit, Köhler explicitly left open the question as to 'whether the banks will seek to fully exploit the scope for credit creation offered to them'.[136]

In contrast to the monetarists (J. M. Neumann among them), Pohl underlined the necessity of a monetary employment policy. Quite in the tradition of Keynes, he argued for a demand-oriented employment policy[137] and for the monetary stance to be relaxed in order to stimulate the economy.[138]

---

[128] Neumann, 1977, p. 259 (author's italics).
[129] Cf. Neumann, 1978*a*.
[130] Neumann, 1979*a*, p. 23.
[131] Neumann, 1985, p. 88.
[132] Cf. Köhler, 1970*a*.
[133] Cf. Pohl, 1975, p. 10.
[134] Cf. Pohl, 1973*b*, p. 106 and 1973*a*, p. 33.
[135] Cf. Brunner and Meltzer, 1964.
[136] Köhler, 1977, p. 128.
[137] Cf. Pohl, 1977, p. 9 and 1982*a*, p. 16.
[138] Cf. Pohl, 1980*b*, p. 2 and 1983*a*, p. 2.

Besides Pohl and Köhler, the work of Duwendag, Kath, Oberhauser, and Simmert is noteworthy among that conducted by German liquidity theorists.[139] They all expressed scepticism concerning the use of the money stock as an intermediate target, and called for monetary policy to be based on bank liquidity.

(3) The concept of the *liquidity base*, the sum of the volume of central bank money and free liquid reserves, constitutes a compromise between the monetary base and bank liquidity as an intermediate target.[140] The money multiplier can be applied to the liquidity base in analogous fashion.[141] By this means, a money-supply function can be determined that allows for liquidity behaviour. In this form, the arguments put forward by the German liquidity theorists, led by Claus Köhler, Rüdiger Pohl, and Alois Oberhauser, could be integrated into the monetarist approach.

(4) The Council of Economic Experts, of which Claus Köhler was a member between 1970 and 1973, adopted his concept of the '*rechnerisches Kreditmaximum*' (arithmetic credit maximum).[142] This led to criticism of the Council by Neumann and Brunner.[143] From its 1972/3 Annual Report on, however, the majority on the Council argued in favour of a monetarist monetary policy. The liquidity position is only to be found in minority votes.[144]

The Council of Economic Experts argued in favour of announcing the monetary-policy stance for several years in advance, while at the same time considering it inadvisable to issue an exact target variable.[145] In line with the monetarist position, it advocated a quantitative open market policy.[146]

(5) The Economic Advisory Council also recommended a steady, quantitatively oriented monetary policy in this period, although initially still with a Keynesian touch.[147] Later, in its report of February 1981, the Economic Advisory Council adopted the line taken by the Council of Economic Experts, and recommended that monetary policy be unequivocally oriented towards the internal value of the D-mark. The exchange rate determined, on this basis, on the foreign exchange markets should 'in principle be

[139] Cf. Duwendag, 1976; Kath, 1979; Oberhauser, 1976, 1977, 1980; Simmert, 1976.

[140] More precisely: currency in circulation + minimum reserves of the banks + free liquid reserves of the banks. Cf. Fautz, 1975; Pohl, 1978; Richter *et al.*, 1978.

[141] The liquidity quotient merely has to be added to the minimum reserve ratio. Cf. Richter and Teigen, 1982*a*.

[142] Cf. Sachverständigenrat, Jahresgutachten 1972/3, paras. 141–7.

[143] Cf. Brunner and Neumann, 1972.

[144] Cf. Sachverständigenrat, Jahresgutachten 1973/4, paras. 382–93 (Köhler), Jahresgutachten 1982/3, para. 150 (Krupp), and Jahresgutachten 1985/6, para. 419.

[145] Cf. Sachverständigenrat, Jahresgutachten 1974/5, para. 316 and Jahresgutachten 1985/6, para. 235.

[146] Sachverständigenrat, Jahresgutachten 1985/6, paras. 383ff.

[147] Cf. Wissenschaftlicher Beirat, 1977, pp. 633f.; 1978, p. 853.

accepted'.[148] Similarly, the Economic Advisory Council expressed (in January 1983) its scepticism of the effectiveness of a discretionary monetary employment policy. The contribution to be made by monetary policy to employment was, rather, to ensure the stability of monetary policy itself.[149]

Central bank intervention on the foreign-exchange markets: managed floating 1973–84

The fluctuations in the D-mark/US dollar exchange rate after March 1973 ran counter to the assurances given by the proponents of foating exchange rates that they would remain stable. Initially the D-mark was seriously overvalued, a situation that lasted for more than seven years, peaking on 3 January 1980 at a rate of 1.7062 DM/US $. This was followed by a five-year rise in the value of the dollar, far beyond purchasing power parity, to hit a maximum of 3.4690 DM/US $ on 26 February 1985. Whatever the reasons behind this development, the fears expressed by Stützel and other opponents of floating exchange rates seemed to have been confirmed. Stützel had possibly been thinking in terms of speculative bubbles. At that time neither he, nor Friedman and Sohmen had an appropriate theory at their disposal. Such a theory was only developed after recognition of the rational expectations hypothesis.[150]

Sohmen had dealt with examples of destabilizing speculation during the interwar period.[151] He considered the chaotic circumstances of the period to have been responsible for the destructive speculation. In addition, he took the view that the monetary authority and the government had, if required, sufficient monetary and fiscal policy instruments at their disposal to enable them to induce private speculators to adopt the line they favoured. The fear that 'destabilizing speculation' could ever dominate events was, he argued, based on the assumption that the central bank had completely abandoned control over monetary policy.[152] Thus, in contrast to Friedman, Sohmen was already thinking in terms of a sort of managed floating, although only as an emergency measure.

Whatever the reasons, the fact was that, following the liberalization of the dollar exchange rate, central banks intervened frequently and heavily in the foreign exchange markets and, as Jurgensen emphasized, frequently gave priority to exchange-rate considerations over domestic economic goals.[153]

---

[148] Cf. Wissenschaftlicher Beirat, 1983, p. 1093.
[149] Cf. Wissenschaftlicher Beirat, 1983, pp. 1218f.
[150] Cf. Azariadis, 1981 and Blanchard and Watson, 1982.
[151] Cf. Sohmen, 1973, pp. 73ff.
[152] Cf. Sohmen, 1973, p. 76.
[153] Cf. Jurgensen, 1984, p. 83.

The Bundesbank was no exception in this respect.[154] Given that it was the exchange rate of the dollar that was regularly the target of intervention on the foreign exchange markets, McKinnon was later to speak of the 'Floating-Rate Dollar Standard, 1973–1984'.[155] There was no lack of critical commentaries—from various quarters and with various motivations—on Bundesbank intervention in the foreign exchange markets. Let us consider some examples.

(1) Dyed-in-the-wool *monetarists* such as Milton Friedman considered the interventions by the Bundesbank to be a 'waste of tax-payer money.... The "people of the market economy" should also leave the dollar to the market'.[156] Manfred J. M. Neumann criticized the excessive monetary expansion in 1978 as being a consequence of the Bundesbank's policy of intervening in the foreign exchange markets.[157]

(2) *Keynesians*, in principle well disposed towards government intervention, saw intervention by the Bundesbank as an unwelcome competitor of a monetary employment policy. Rüdiger Pohl, for instance, stated his view that 'the secondary target of external equilibrium has already almost displaced the primary targets, or at least the target of full employment. The weightings must be brought back into line.'[158] The trend towards a weaker D-mark against the dollar (after 1980) continued, despite the efforts of the Bundesbank.[159] 'The hope that a system of floating exchange rates could effectively protect Germany against inflationary impulses from abroad has proved illusory.'[160]

(3) The Council of Economic Experts repeatedly turned its attention to the intervention by the Bundesbank on the foreign exchange markets. In its 1978/9 report, it openly expressed its disappointment over the way the system of floating exchange rates had developed: '(it has not been possible) to form more or less stable medium, let alone long-term, expectations regarding even the most important exchange-rate parities in the world'.[161]

The sustained depreciation of the dollar confronted the Council with a 'riddle':[162] it could not be explained by reference either to the current account, or to interest-rate or inflation differentials, or to purchasing power parity. The Council studiously avoided mentioning the possibility of a

---

[154] Cf. Neumann, 1984.
[155] McKinnon, 1993, p. 29.
[156] Friedman, 1977.
[157] Cf. Neumann, 1979a, p. 21.
[158] Pohl, 1980a, p. 1.
[159] Cf. Pohl, 1981.
[160] Pohl, 1982b, p. 386.
[161] Sachverständigenrat, Jahresgutachten 1978/9, para. 337.
[162] Sachverständigenrat, Jahresgutachten 1983/4, para. 189.

speculative bubble. In the following year it wrote that the disorientation (of the markets) could, at bottom, be traced back to the fact 'that economic policy has not offered the orientation it could, in principle, have given'.[163] Policy itself is volatile. This cannot be changed by central bank intervention on the foreign exchange markets or a short-term interest-rate policy oriented towards the exchange rate.[164]

The opinion in the Bundesbank 1973–84

Whereas in the academic sphere the arguments for a monetary employment policy had become a minority opinion, the Bundesbank's Annual Reports repeatedly make mention of a monetary-policy orientation towards the level of economic activity in Germany.[165]

On introducing the monetary target, the Bundesbank wrote that it was not in a position to control the central bank money stock in the very short term precisely in accordance with the target fixed for the longer term.[166] It rejected the proposal of announcing a monetary target for several years in advance with the argument that it would then be unable to take account of unpredictable and serious shocks (such as oil-price increases).[167]

Particularly instructive in this context are the views of Helmut Schlesinger. He emphasized that the monetary policy pursued in the past few years had always been a compromise between the strategy of an anticyclical monetary policy and that of a medium-term orientation.[168] The Bundesbank was moderately anticyclical, but at heart took a long-term view. It was true, though, that, compared with earlier years, 'it had undoubtedly become less sensitive to short-term cyclical fluctuations in economic activity, . . . on the other hand, the Bundesbank cannot and does not intend to dispense from the very outset with any scope for monetary policy to exert moderate countervailing influence'.[169] Schlesinger reported that the Bundesbank used the central bank money stock as an intermediate target, and not as an instrument variable, in controlling monetary expansion.[170] Moreover, while the Bundesbank was independent of other branches in economic policy, its success in pursuing its aims 'is called into question if all those involved in

---

[163] Sachverständigenrat, Jahresgutachten 1984/5, para. 365.
[164] Cf. Sachverständigenrat, Jahresgutachten 1984/5, para. 366.
[165] Cf. Deutsche Bundesbank, Geschäftsbericht 1975, p. 1; Geschäftsbericht 1977, p. 1; Geschäftsbericht 1982, p. 1.
[166] Cf. Deutsche Bundesbank, Geschäftsbericht 1975, p. 12.
[167] Cf. Deutsche Bundesbank, Geschäftsbericht 1984, p. 40.
[168] Cf. Schlesinger, 1980, p. 37.
[169] Schlesinger, 1980, pp. 38f.
[170] Cf. Schlesinger, 1980, p. 64.

the economic process fail to adjust their claims on potential economic output in conformity with the target'.[171] In other words, the independence of the central bank is a necessary, but not a sufficient condition, for a stable currency. This view was expressed even more tersely by Irmler: 'the central bank alone cannot . . . entirely safeguard the currency.'[172]

4. 1985–96: monetarism goes, institutional economics comes—in small steps

In this period the expansionary force of the ideas initiated by Friedman and Lucas declined: the monetarist movement came to an end. The Keynesians recovered and regrouped under the banner of New Keynesian Economics (NKE), under which young theoreticians held their own against Monetarism Mark II (New Classical Economics—NCE) by providing a microeconomic foundation for Keynesian hypotheses. They failed to achieve a come-back in economic-policy terms, however.

Yet within both schools of thought, New Keynesian Economics and New Classical Economics, there lurked a third force, a growth with roots in both classical and anti-classical traditions: modern institutional economics. Its formal analytical elements were based on informational economics, an element of classical theory that, back in the early 1970s, had set revolutionary new accents with the hypotheses of 'efficient markets' and 'rational expectations formation', and that now, enriched by game theory, was used to address the problem of asymmetric information. The problem of opportunistic behaviour by politicians ('dynamic inconsistency') was considered, adding a new facet to the rules-versus-discretion debate. Concepts such as reputation or brand-name capital could now be encountered in contributions to the theory of monetary policy. The idea of contracts, in particular the principal–agent approach in its various forms, was increasingly applied to the theory of money lending and financial intermediaries, and also to the theory of monetary policy. And, just as 10 years earlier monetarist terminology had—seemingly overnight—left its mark on economists' jargon, institutional-economic terms—such as transaction costs, sunk costs, costly state verification, credibility problems, agency, incentive compatibility, adverse selection, free-rider problem, etc.—began to appear in the literature on monetary theory.[173] Besides this, concepts derived from other

---

[171] Schlesinger, 1980, p. 64.
[172] Irmler, 1982, p. 65.
[173] Cf. a standard text on monetary economics, such as Mishkin, 1995.

schools of thought, such as political economy, public choice and constitutional economics, were taken up and shed a new light on aspects of the national and international 'monetary constitution'.

Yet the 'revolution' of institutional economics came only in small steps. The public's attention was still gripped by the dispute between monetarists and Keynesians and for a long time failed to notice the change. There was no Big Bang, as had been the case with the monetarist counter-revolution, no simple eight or five theses, no monetarist or Keynesian certainties any more. What occurred, rather, was a slow change in the mode of thinking, in the perspective taken on economic problems, the understanding of classical tenets and Keynesian objections. Not surprisingly, there was soon talk of a pragmatic synthesis—or eclectic mixture—of the teachings of monetarists and Keynesians.

a) The international debate

Monetarism began to lose momentum as an offensive force. The Federal Reserve abandoned monetary targeting. Direct 'inflation targeting', a concept rejected by Friedman, came into fashion.[174] By contrast, the Keynesians stirred themselves once more, with Gregory Mankiw playing a leading role.[175] Mankiw and Romer brought out a two-volume collection of essays by representatives of New Keynesian Macroeconomics (NKM)[176] in which rational expectations and time inconsistency are integrated into the micro-level basis of Keynesian assumptions. The basic aim is to show that even under the conditions of the rational expectations hypothesis (REH) a systematic monetary policy can exert an impact on the real economy.[177]

The successors to the old Keynesians were a modest bunch. They were happy to have fought off the attacks launched by Lucas and to have returned to a state 'similar to that of the 1960s'.[178] Yet no attempt was made to take a step forward down the Keynesian path, to develop a new theoretical model comparable to that developed by Lucas. All that was achieved was to restore the Keynesian position: there was no sense of a new challenge, no assumption of intellectual leadership, and no new economic policy.

---

[174] Cf. Friedman, 1960, pp. 87f. Currently (1996) the central banks of New Zealand, Canada, the UK, Sweden, Finland, Australia, and Spain set explicit inflation targets. On this issue cf. McCallum, 1996.

[175] Cf., for instance, Mankiw, 1990.

[176] Cf. Mankiw and Romer, 1991.

[177] Cf. Mankiw and Romer, 1991, p. 2.

[178] Cf. Mankiw and Romer, 1991, p. 15.

This was not true of Monetarism Mark II, the New Classical Macro-economics (NCM), however, which was developed into a consistent theory. The importance of the problem of information was recognized and prop-agated, an important precursor of modern institutional economics. The mechanistic way of thinking was abandoned, according to which the brakes need to be applied to the inflationary process in the same way as to a car travelling at top speed: slowly, so that the passengers are not, so to speak, sent flying through the windscreen.[179] The problem of the reputation of political management was taken up. As a consequence of these new insights, a radical new way of thinking about economic policy measures was required, argued Lucas, namely in terms of dynamic games in which rules play an important role.[180] Thus it was that the game-theoretic approach of modern institutional economics suddenly and substantively forced its way into mon-etary macroeconomics. The idea of a non-cooperative game between those setting nominal wages and the central bank, introduced by Kydland and Prescott, had an electrifying effect, not least on the elaboration of the theory of the political business cycle initiated by Nordhaus, with work by Alesina and Rogoff and Sibert.[181]

In the monetary macroeconomics of open economies, the Keynesian school of thought remained predominant, with Dornbusch as its leading spokesman.[182] Empirical support was provided by, amongst others, Frankel, Obstfeld, and Rogoff.[183] The extreme volatility of floating exchange rates compared with inflation differentials remained a topic of debate.[184] There was a revival of the discussion of 'fixed versus floating exchange rates'. The argument propounded earlier in Germany by Stützel that fixed exchange rates exert a disciplinary effect on central banks was taken up in a somewhat diluted form by McKinnon.[185] He argued that central banks should defend the exchange rates of the three most important currencies—US dollar, yen and D-mark—within a narrow band and should aim for a predetermined global monetary target.

Non-cooperative games situations and reputation problems, against the background of Keynesian assumptions about prevailing conditions, were applied to questions of international (economic) policy coordination in

[179] Cf. Sargent, 1986, Chap. 3.
[180] Cf. Lucas, 1987, p. 18.
[181] Cf. Kydland and Prescott, 1977; Nordhaus, 1975; Alesina, 1987; Rogoff and Sibert, 1988. For an overview see Nordhaus, 1989; Persson and Tabellini, 1990, chap. 5; Gärtner, 1994.
[182] Cf. Dornbusch, 1976.
[183] Cf. Frankel, 1979, 1982; Obstfeld, 1982, 1985, 1986; Rogoff, 1980, 1984.
[184] Cf. Obstfeld and Rogoff, 1996, p. 608, Fig. 9.2.
[185] Cf. McKinnon, 1974, 1984, 1988.

general.[186] For instance, the concept of international regimes,[187] as explored by political scientists, was a field of application of Williamson's transactions-cost and reputation-games theories.[188]

The infiltration of the theory of monetary policy by institutional economics was revealed at an early stage in the debate on the old topic of *rules versus discretion*. In a world with uncertain expectations, tight formal rules backed by the force of law are impractical. The credibility of promises made by a monetary authority becomes a problem. In the relevant theoretical models, central bank management is threatened by a 'loss of reputation', a purely subjective variable, at the hands of the users of money.[189] This is a variant of the institutional economic concept of self-enforcement. However, the threat of imposing a loss of utility on central bank management, a handful of civil servants—as opposed to a financial loss, as in the case of the owner of a firm—is not sufficiently credible to be seriously regarded as an instrument of currency defence. Thus the independence of the central bank alone does not offer security against opportunistic behaviour by central bank management.[190]

In the debate on monetary macroeconomics we once again find a trend towards a synthesis or at least an eclectic mixing of 'opposing' methods.[191] In the debate on monetary policy issues, Blanchard and Fischer, however, once again applied the Keynesian fixed-price model—the model behind the IS-LM diagram—in which money, by assumption, has a significant influence on the level of output.[192]

b) The debate in Germany—basic themes and examples

As in previous years, the debate on German monetary policy in this period was dominated by the economic problems prevailing at the time—to the extent that they were considered relevant to monetary policy: the high level of unemployment, in the face of which, according to the new conventional wisdom, monetary policy is powerless; the Bundesbank's policy of monet-

---

[186] Cf., among others, Hamada, 1979 and Currie and Levine, 1985. A great body of literature is being developed in this field. See, for example, Canzoneri and Gray, 1985; Rogoff, 1987; Giavazzi and Pagano, 1988. A summary is provided in Dornbusch and Giovannini, 1990, pp. 1270f.

[187] Cf. Keohane, 1984.

[188] An overview is provided by Alt *et al.*, 1988.

[189] Cf. Barro and Gordon, 1983, p. 108.

[190] Cf. Richter, 1996.

[191] Cf., for example, Fischer, 1988.

[192] Cf. Blanchard and Fischer, 1989, p. 530.

ary targeting, with its frequent and at times dramatic over- and undershooting of targets; and the exchange-rate policy pursued by the Bundesbank in the face of the 'diplomatically' initiated depreciation of the US dollar and its stabilization at a low level. New problems included the internationalization or globalization of the economy, which, reinforced by the opening of the Iron Curtain, began to dominate the theoretical debate on monetary matters in Germany. Topics are the coordination of central bank intervention on the foreign exchange markets by the G-7 countries, and—a topic that is not considered here—monetary union between the two Germanys in 1990 and preparations for a monetary union between the EEC countries. All three topics have something to do with agreements or treaties, perhaps the most important of which were the Plaza Agreement (1985), the Louvre Accord (1987), and the Maastricht Treaty (1991). Thinking in terms of such agreements became popular. In coping with these issues, all that economists could to was supplement their established macro way of thinking by the methods of the new political and institutional economics. This occurred slowly and in small steps.

Pro and contra monetary targeting by the Bundesbank

No new arguments were brought forward in the debate pro and contra monetary targeting by the Bundesbank. The frequent failure to hit the monetary target confirmed opponents in their critique of the target selected by the Bundesbank and defenders in their critique of the monetary policy pursued by the Bundesbank. Opponents and defenders came from the same camps as before: adherents of the liquidity concept—followers of Wolfgang Stützel (such as Peter Bofinger and Wolfram Engels) or of Claus Köhler (Rüdiger Pohl)—and supporters of monetarism—disciples or 'grandchildren' of Karl Brunner (Manfred J. M. Neumann, Jürgen von Hagen). The Council of Economic Experts stuck to monetary targeting and repeated its call for a rigorous stabilization policy by announcing the course of monetary expansion several years in advance.[193] The Economic Advisory Council, on the other hand, was silent on this issue.

Rüdiger Pohl remained the leading critic of Bundesbank policy. He argued that the monetary target was an 'empty ritual', by which the Bundesbank implied to the public a binding commitment that it in fact failed to honour because, from the very outset, it reserved the right to deviate from the target in the face of unexpected events.[194] Pohl has unswervingly propagated the view set out in the Radcliffe Report, according to which the central bank

---

[193] Cf. Sachverständigenrat, Jahresgutachten 1985/6, para. 235.
[194] Cf. Pohl, 1987a, p. 345.

must pay attention to a range of target variables, including the money stock, interest rates, bank liquidity, and the credit volume.[195] Moreover, he has remained in favour of the view that monetary policy carries a share of the responsibility for the level of employment.[196] A Phillips Curve relationship exists in the short run, provided 'monetary expansion (is not taken) as an occasion for higher wage demands'.[197] Finally, Pohl had repeatedly emphasized that, in spite of floating exchange rates, external disequilibrium remains an important factor for German monetary policy.[198]

Peter Bofinger and *Wolfram Engels* also criticized the Bundesbank's failure to meet its monetary targets.[199] The purpose of the monetary targets, they argued, was to provide the public with an idea of the action the central bank could be expected to take, which was impossible if the Bundesbank failed to meet its targets. This called into question the credibility of the Bundesbank.

Manfred J. M. Neumann, indefatigable defender of the Bundesbank's policy of monetary targeting, also emphasized the necessity of maintaining the credibility of monetary policy, and was, in this respect, likewise critical of Bundesbank policy.[200] However, he later claimed to have discovered, in the course of an econometric study, that in the short term the Bundesbank oriented policy not towards deviations from the monetary target, but rather towards excessive inflation, appreciation of the D-mark and shocks to the demand for money; this fact was known to market actors, and they took account of it in reaching their decisions. For this reason, and owing to the repeatedly evinced independence of the Bundesbank, the German central bank had, Neumann argued, retained its credibility despite repeated failures to meet the monetary targets.[201]

The Council of Economic Experts, on the other hand, took the view that the Bundesbank 'cannot be obliged rigorously to implement a monetary target'.[202] This was impossible given the uncertainty about the future.

It can be said in elaboration of this that the Bundesbank can, however, promise the markets that it will stick to a plausible decision making principle. This idea was put forward by David Kreps, who interpreted the principle, together with the way in which it was communicated, as the 'cor-

---

[195] Cf. Pohl, 1987*a*, p. 344, and minority vote on the Council of Economic Experts, Jahresgutachten 1987/8, p. 173.
[196] Cf. Pohl, 1987*c*.
[197] Pohl, 1987*c*, p. 175.
[198] Cf. Pohl, 1983*b*, 1994; Pohl and Kißmer, 1990.
[199] Cf. Bofinger, 1994 and Engels, 1992.
[200] Cf. Neumann, 1985.
[201] Cf. Neumann, 1996, p. 199.
[202] Cf. Sachverständigenrat, Jahresgutachten 1987/8, p. 174.

porate culture'.[203] In the case of the Bundesbank, the expression 'stability culture' has become generally accepted.[204]

It is evident from what has been said that a monetary target need not be merely an 'empty ritual' simply because it is not always met. Targets, subject to reservations, can therefore serve as a useful guide to the public. It must be possible to monitor adherence to the target and the markets must be convinced of the effectiveness of the principle (the monetary target) with respect to the final goal of monetary stabilization. At the same time, it is equally clear that an 'exception must remain the exception'.[205] As far as the credibility of the promise of monetary stability is concerned, important factors alongside the independence of the central bank are the efforts made by the government in this regard and the credibility of the threat of its non-reelection by money users.

Coordination of central bank intervention on the foreign-exchange markets

The sharp medium-term fluctuations in the D-mark/US dollar exchange rate between January 1980 and December 1987 provided a new source of criticism of the system of floating exchange rates. Calls were made for co-ordinated intervention by the central banks on the foreign-exchange markets.

The Council of Economic Experts warned that such calls were leading down the wrong path.[206] Marked fluctuations in real exchange rates, it argued, were the result of differences between and the volatility of national monetary and fiscal policies.[207] An effective system of floating exchange rates, however, had as a pre-condition a consistent and credible stability policy. Steps needed to be taken to ensure that this pre-condition was satisfied.

Yet the Council of Economic Experts omitted to mention the fact that a country can derive a temporary advantage, to the detriment of its trading partners, from currency depreciation. Thus the floating exchange rate is not least a strategic variable of the central banks. This means that a country that refrains thus from intervening on the foreign-exchange markets—such as the USA between 1973 and 1984—does so at the price of incurring a strategic disadvantage. In such a case the other central banks may tacitly agree on allowing their currencies to depreciate against that of the inactive country. While this did not occur, or at least the Bundesbank was not involved

[203] Cf. Kreps, 1990.
[204] Cf. Richter, 1994, p. 82.
[205] Sachverständigenrat, Jahresgutachten 1995/6, para. 235.
[206] Cf. Sachverständigenrat, Jahresgutachten 1986/7, paras. 254ff.
[207] Cf. Sachverständigenrat, Jahresgutachten 1986/7, para. 257.

in such collusion, it is sufficient that the markets believe it has occurred for self-reinforcing speculation against the currency of the inactive country to be initiated. Whatever the reason for the massive revaluation of the US dollar between 1980 and 1985, a policy of 'benign neglect' of the exchange rate by the central bank cannot be pursued indefinitely in the face of such a development, even if it appears that, as occurred, the rate starts to decline once more. Thus it was that on 22 September 1985 the USA, together with the two main surplus countries, Japan and Germany, and with the UK and France (the Group of Five), agreed, under the so-called Plaza Agreement, to work together more closely in order to bring about a managed depreciation of the dollar. The 'managed' depreciation of the dollar continued for a further two years. Subsequently, in order to stop the decline, the Group of Five, plus Canada and Italy, met at the Louvre on 22 February 1987 and agreed in the so-called Louvre Accord, 'to cooperate closely to foster stability of exchange rates around current levels'.[208]

The concept of 'hegemonic cooperation' can be drawn upon in order to explain this development,[209] with the USA playing the role of hegemonist.[210] Both reputation and hegemonic means of exerting pressure were important. For dyed-in-the-wool monetarists, however, who are convinced of the relevance of the rational expectations hypothesis, this consideration is incomprehensible. They take the view that what is to be expected in the long run is also to be expected in the short run, owing to the REH. According to this view, the central banks seek from the outset to stabilize the decisive—according to the monetary approach of exchange-rate theory—variable, i.e. the rate of growth of the national money stock. Thus, given floating exchange rates, monetary policy is a purely national affair. It is in this sense that the public declaration issued by eight German professors, led by Manfred J. M. Neumann, on 7 January 1988 needs to be understood. They called on the monetary authorities not to sacrifice the monetary target to the exchange-rate goal.[211] The Council of Economic Experts also rejected any idea of an exchange-rate orientation and called for greater efforts to steady the growth of the money stock by introducing a multi-annual monetary target.[212]

Rüdiger Pohl, who is opposed to monetary targets and, incidentally,

---

[208] International Monetary Fund, 1988, p. 58.

[209] Cf. Keohane, 1984, p. 49 and Snidal, 1985.

[210] Cf. Richter, 1989.

[211] Cf. Neumann, 1988. Other signatories included Herbert Giersch, Otmar Issing, Hans K. Schneider, Jürgen Siebke, Roland Vaubel, Manfred Willms, Artur Woll.

[212] See Sachverständigenrat, Jahresgutachten 1985/6, paras. 234–44; Jahresgutachten 1986/7, paras. 257–9; Jahresgutachten 1989/90, para. 134; Jahresgutachten 1995/6, paras. 422–5.

supports fixed exchange rates, has taken a very different view. According to him, international cooperation in monetary and exchange-rate policy is a decisive factor. Consequently Pohl has no objection to the Bundesbank temporarily pursuing an exchange-rate orientation.[213]

The opinion in the Bundesbank 1985–96

A number of factors were made responsible for the (in some cases substantial) overshooting of the monetary targets, initially external economic influences, subsequently turbulences in the wake of monetary union between the two Germanys. The monetary target was largely defended with reference to Kreps' 'focal principle', namely, the fact that the binding commitment on the part of the central bank can be monitored (given the transparent nature of the pre-announced monetary targets) helps to reinforce the stability-oriented expectations of the public.[214] In addition, quite in accordance with Friedman's claims, reference was made to the long-term stability of the basic monetary relationships in Germany, trends that held even after German unification.[215]

The Bundesbank repeatedly pointed to its external economic adjustment constraints,[216] which caused it problems even after the Louvre Accord. This, it claimed, restricted its scope for action.[217]

Monetary anticyclical policy has remained on the agenda. The Bundesbank continues to pay attention to the overall business climate, for instance to the consequences of the (sharp) depreciation of the US dollar[218] or the deep recession in West Germany, which has left 'deep marks on output and employment'.[219]

5. Conclusion

Like sport, the academic world is very much a nationalistic affair. This is true not least of the theory of monetary policy. Germany is not among the

---

[213] Cf. Pohl, 1987*b*, p. 72.

[214] Cf. Deutsche Bundesbank, Geschäftsbericht 1995, p. 86.

[215] Cf. Deutsche Bundesbank, Geschäftsbericht 1995, p. 85.

[216] Cf. Deutsche Bundesbank, Geschäftsbericht 1986, p. 3; Geschäftsbericht 1987, p. 1; Geschäftsbericht 1989, p. 41.

[217] Cf. Deutsche Bundesbank, Geschäftsbericht 1992, p. 8; Geschäftsbericht 1993, pp. 46, 93.

[218] Cf. Deutsche Bundesbank, Geschäftsbericht 1986, p. 1.

[219] Deutsche Bundesbank, Geschäftsbericht 1993, p. 1.

winners in this 'event'; they come from Sweden (Knut Wicksell), England (John Maynard Keynes and John R. Hicks) and the USA (Milton Friedman and Robert E. Lucas). Of the German economists mentioned in this article, Wolfgang Stützel has been most prominent in terms of generating original ideas on monetary policy, ideas, however, that neither he nor anyone else in Germany sought to bring into the international debate. Keynesianism (in the 1950s/1960s) and monetarism, that in numerous variants have dominated monetary policy over the past 50 years, are American imports. They have dominated the debate on German monetary policy. Practical central bank policy with its (later so-called) interest rate lever of monetary control, is based to this very day on the interest-spread theory of the Swede Knut Wicksell. Alongside this, the quantity theory of money remains in force. In this respect the comment made by Wicksell on the quantity theory in the preface to *Interest and Prices* remains true today: 'in reality there is no second theory that could be given the name of a thought-out and coherent theory of money'.[220]

As far as actual practice is concerned, Germany undoubtedly, by virtue of the monetary policy it has pursued over the past 50 years, holds a position within the leading group of the world's central banks; the average annual rate of inflation has been just under 3 per cent. Yet even after the exchange rate of the dollar was allowed to float, the 'external adjustment constraint'[221] remains a problem for Bundesbank policy. Given the strategic games situations that repeatedly occur in the exchange-rate policy of large industrialized nations, actors can scarcely avoid playing the game of exchange-rate-diplomatic chess, and central banks and governments repeatedly find themselves encroaching on each other's territory.

Yet, academic thinking along the lines of the quantity theory or monetary macroeconomics is an insufficient basis for the game of exchange-rate diplomacy. Cognitive elements of modern institutional economics, in particular contractual economics and political economy, must also be incorporated. These considerations are located in an area, in which German economics once played a leading role, initially in the form of the younger *historische Schule* (historical school), with Gustav Schmoller as its leading figure, and later in the form of the 'ordo-liberal' theory of Walter Eucken and Franz Böhm. It is regrettable that, in spite of this tradition, the institutional economic debate on international monetary policy has remained so narrow. The international paper standard is, in contrast to the gold standard, scarcely conceivable without negotiated international cooperation. In strategic games situations such as are encountered by the paper-standard central banks in

---

[220] Wicksell, 1898, p. III.
[221] Deutsche Bundesbank, Geschäftsbericht 1986, p. 1.

their exchange-rate policy, actors who wait for the invisible hand to take effect usually suffer strategic disadvantages: it is better to negotiate. International agreements—which after all can stop well short of monetary union —may also help to keep the peace. One is struck by the contemporary relevance of the sentence with which Knut Wicksell, 15 years before the outbreak of the First World War, concluded *Interest and Prices*:

'The fact that the implementation of the international paper standard . . . necessarily requires international agreements of a long-term and more or less incisive nature is, for me at least, one reason more to favour it. In each new step towards cooperation between peoples for economic or scientific purposes, I gladly welcome a new guarantee for the maintenance and strengthening of that good upon which, in the final analysis, the fortuitous achievement of all other material and immaterial goods depends —international peace.'[222]

6. Postscript

As was shown, the Bundesbank followed—partly immediately, partly with a time-lag—the most active thoughts of the time. In the 1950s it conducted its policy, in accordance with the dominant opinion, with reference to a large series of targets (some eight or nine), without clearly indicating that the maintenance of the purchasing power of money was its primary goal, and it primarily favoured fixed exchange rates. In the 1960s the Bundesbank reduced the number of its targets to three—the then fashionable 'magic triangle'—but continued to favour fixed exchange rates in spite of a widespread change of opinion among German economists. In the 1970s and early 1980s the Bundesbank changed over to a pragmatically coloured monetarism, following a self-imposed money supply target, though it still observed the old three targets of the magic triangle and apparently did not always give stable prices priority. Furthermore, it continued, as Helmut Schlesinger put it diplomatically, not to 'renounce from the very outset any possibility of a moderately anticyclical counteracting stance of monetary policy'.[223] In the final period, the years since 1985, the Bundesbank continued its 'enlightened' monetarist policy by sticking to the money supply target, in spite of so many missed hits, and it continued to pay attention not only to the purchasing power of the D-mark but also to the German business situation, and to foreign exchange market developments.

[222] Wicksell, 1898, p. 179.
[223] Cf. Schlesinger, 1980, p. 38.

With the monetary policy opinions (or fashions) of our profession changing so radically and frequently during the last 50 years—a development not without influence on the Bundesbank—what was the secret of the Bundesbank's success in maintaining one of the lowest inflation rates in the world?

Two answers will be suggested. First, the Bundesbank was alert to the most active thoughts of the time, though with a sense of compromise: it never became dogmatic. Assuming that macroeconomic fashions are caused by genuine problems of their time, one may argue that their filtering by conservative (i.e., 'time-consistent'), pragmatically oriented central bankers may have resulted in an opportune monetary policy. Second, not only the supply of but also the demand for money matters, i.e. the wishes and beliefs of the money users. The German public of the last 50 years, and thus German voters, after having lost their savings twice within 25 years, definitely wanted a stable currency. No Bonn government in its right mind would have dared to stage an inflationary fiscal policy and to put the Bundesbank under pressure. Thus, German public opinion, not only the independence of the German central bank, contributed to the Bundesbank's success. In fact, in a democratic state with a paper currency, public opinion—the voters' desire for sound money—is a *conditio sine qua non* of stable money.[224] This seems to have been forgotten, or is being played down, by the proponents of the European Monetary Union, who appear to be convinced that the independence of a supranational European Central Bank will be a sufficient guarantee of a stable euro.

7. Bibliography

Alesina, Alberto (1987): Macroeconomic Policy in a Two-Party System as a Repeated Game, in: Quarterly Journal of Economics 102, pp. 651–78

Alt, James E./Calvert, Randall L./Humes, Brian D. (1988): Reputation and Hegemonic Stability: A Game Theoretic Analysis, in: American Political Science Review 82, pp. 445–66

Azariadis, Costa (1981): Self-Fulfilling Prophecies, in: Journal of Economic Theory 25, pp. 380–96

Barro, Robert J. (1976): Rational Expectations and the Role of Monetary Policy, in: Journal of Monetary Economics 2, pp. 1–32

Barro, Robert J./Gordon, David B. (1983): Rules, Discretion and Reputation in a Model of Monetary Policy, Cambridge, Mass.

Blanchard, Olivier J./Fischer, Stanley (1989): Lectures on Macroeconomics, Cambridge, Mass./London

---

[224] Cf. Richter, 1996.

Blanchard, Olivier J./Watson, Mark (1982): Bubbles, Rational Expectations and Financial Markets, in: Wachtel, Paul (ed.): Crises in the Economic and Financial Structure, Lexington, Mass.

Bofinger, Peter (1994): Die Bundesbank jagt ein Phantom, in: Frankfurter Allgemeine Zeitung, 15 May

Branson, William H. (1977): Asset Markets and Relative Prices in Exchange Rate Determination, Stockholm

Brunner, Karl/Meltzer, Allan H. (1964): Some Further Investigations of Demand and Supply Functions for Money, in: Journal of Finance 19, pp. 240–83

Brunner, Karl/Meltzer, Allan H. (1967): The Meaning of Monetary Indicators, in: George Horwich (ed.): Monetary Process and Policy: A Symposium, Homewood, Ill.

Brunner, Karl/Neumann, Manfred J. M. (1972): Monetäre Aspekte des Jahresgutachtens 1971/72 des Sachverständigenrats, in: Weltwirtschaftliches Archiv 108, pp. 257–85

Canzoneri, Mathew B./Gray, Joanna (1985): Monetary Policy Games and the Consequences of Non-Cooperative Behavior, in: International Economic Review 26, pp. 617–25

Coddington, Alan: Keynesian Economics (1976): The Search for First Principles, in: Journal of Economic Literature 14, pp. 1258–73

Currie, David/Levine, Paul (1985): Macroeconomic Policy Design in an Interdependent World, in: Buiter, Willem H./Marston, Richard (eds.): International Economic Policy Coordination, Cambridge, pp. 228–68

Deutsche Bundesbank (1968): Das Ausmaß der Geldentwertung seit 1950 und die weitere Entwicklung des Geldwertes. Expert Opinion of the Bundesbank dated 21 July 1965. Filed at the request of the Federal Fiscal Court, in: Monatsbericht 20, 3, pp. 3–19

Deutsche Bundesbank (various years): Geschäftsberichte, Frankfurt a.M.

Dornbusch, Rudiger (1976): Expectations and Exchange Rate Dynamics, in: Journal of Political Economy 84, pp. 1161–76

Dornbusch, Rudiger/Giovannini, Alberto (1990): Monetary Policy in the Open Economy, in: Friedman, Benjamin M./Hahn, Frank H. (eds.): Handbook of Monetary Economics, vol. 2, Amsterdam, pp. 1230–1303

Duwendag, Dieter (1976): Die neue Geldpolitik der Deutschen Bundesbank: Interpretationen und kritische Anmerkungen, in: Konjunkturpolitik, Zeitschrift für Angewandte Konjunkturforschung 22, pp. 265–306

Engels, Wolfram (1992): Alte Leier, in: Wirtschaftswoche 46, 45, p. 198

Eucken, Walter (1952): Grundsätze der Wirtschaftspolitik, Tübingen

Fama, Eugene F. (1980): Banking in the Theory of Finance, in: Journal of Monetary Economics 6, pp. 39–58

Fautz, Wolfgang M. (1975): Geldbasis und Liquiditätsbasis. Alternative analytische Rahmen für die Untersuchung von Geld- und Kreditprozessen in der Bundesrepublik Deutschland, in: Kredit und Kapital 8, pp. 145–269

Fischer, Stanley (1980): On Activist Monetary Policy with Rational Expectations, in: Fischer, Stanley (ed.): Rational Expectations and Economic Policy, Chicago, pp. 211–47

Fischer, Stanley (1988): Recent Developments in Macroeconomics, in: Economic Journal 98, pp. 294–339

Frankel, Jeffrey A. (1979): On the Mark: A Theory of Floating Exchange Rates Based on Real Interest Differentials, in: American Economic Review 69, pp. 610–22

Frankel, Jeffrey A. (1982): In Search of the Exchange Risk Premium: A Six-Currency Test Assuming Mean-Variance Optimization, in: Journal of International Money and Finance 1, pp. 255–74

Friedman, Milton (1953): The Case for Flexible Exchange Rates, in: Friedman, Milton: Essays in Positive Economics, Chicago, pp. 157–203

Friedman, Milton (1956): The Quantity Theory of Money—A Restatement, in: Friedman, Milton (ed.): Studies in the Quantity Theory of Money, Chicago, pp. 3–21

Friedman, Milton (1958): The Supply of Money and Changes in Prices and Output, in: The Relationship of Prices to Economic Stability and Growth, Compendium of Papers, Submitted by Panalists Appearing Before the Joint Economic Committee, U.S. Government Printing Office, Washington D.C., pp. 249–50

Friedman, Milton (1960): A Program for Monetary Stability, New York

Friedman, Milton (1968): The Role of Monetary Policy, in: American Economic Review 58, pp. 1–17

Friedman, Milton (1977): Das Stützen des Dollars verschwendet Steuergelder, in: Welt am Sonntag, 11 December

Friedman, Milton/Meiselmann, David (1963): The Relative Stability of Monetary Velocity and the Investment Multiplier in the United States, 1897–1958, in: Brown, Edgar C. *et al.*: Stabilization Policies. A Series of Research Studies Prepared for the Commission on Money and Credit, Engelwood-Cliffs, pp. 165–268

Friedman, Milton/Schwartz, Anna J. (1963): A Monetary History of the United States 1867–1960, Princeton

Für freie Wechselkurse (1969), in: Zeitschrift für das gesamte Kreditwesen 22, 18, p. 1030

Gärtner, Manfred (1994): Democracy, Elections, and Macroeconomic Policy: Two Decades of Progress, in: European Journal of Political Economy 10, pp. 85–109

Gesellschaft für wirtschaftswissenschaftliche und soziologische Forschung (1951) (ed.): Das Begehren zur Sicherung der Deutschen Mark im Lichte wissenschaftlicher Kritik, Heidelberg-Ziegelhausen

Giavazzi, Francesco/Pagano, Marco (1988): The Advantage of Tying One's Hands: EMS Discipline and Central Bank Credibility, in: European Economic Review 32, pp. 1055–74

Giersch, Herbert (1977): Konjunktur- und Wachstumspolitik in der offenen Wirtschaft, Wiesbaden

Giersch, Herbert/Möller, Hans (1952): Zum Problem der Konvertierbarkeit, Paris

Gurley, John G./Shaw, Edward S. (1960): Money in a Theory of Finance, Washington D.C.

Hamada, Koichi (1979): Macroeconomic Strategy and Coordination under Alternative Exchange Rates, in: Dornbusch, Rudiger/Frenkel, Jacob A. (eds.): International Economic Policy, Baltimore, MD, pp. 292–324

Hankel, Wilhelm (1970): Reformen des internationalen Währungssystems—Warum, wohin?, Lecture to the Friedrich-Ebert-Foundation. Bundesministerium für Wirtschaft, Bad Godesberg

Häuser, Karl (1959): Das Inflationselement in den Exportüberschüssen der Bundesrepublik Deutschland, in: Weltwirtschaftliches Archiv 83, pp. 166–88

Hicks, John R. (1946): Value and Capital. An Inquiry into Some Fundamental Principles of Economic Theory, Oxford

Hicks, John R. (1974): The Crisis in Keynesian Economics, Oxford

International Monetary Fund (1988): World Economic Outlook. A Survey by the Staff of the International Monetary Fund, Washington D.C.

Irmler, Heinrich (1982): Geldpolitk aus der Sicht der Deutschen Bundesbank—historisch und theoretisch, in: Starbatty, Joachim (ed.): Geldordnung und Geldpolitik in einer freiheitlichen Gesellschaft, Tübingen, pp. 58–72

Jarchow, Hans-Joachim (1970): Der Bankkredit in einer Theorie der 'Portfolio Selection', in: Weltwirtschaftliches Archiv 104, pp. 189–210

Jarchow, Hans-Joachim/Rühmann, Peter/Engel, Günther (1970): Geldmenge, Zinssatz, Bankenverhalten und Zentralbankpolitik, in: Weltwirtschaftliches Archiv 105, pp. 304–33

Johnson, Harry G. (1972a): The Case for Flexible Exchange Rates, in: The Federal Reserve

Bank of St. Louis Review 51 (1969) 6, pp. 12–24; reprinted in: Johnson, Harry G.: Further Essays in Monetary Economics, London, pp. 198–228

Johnson, Harry G. (1972b): The Monetary Approach to Balance-of-Payments Theory, in: Johnson, Harry G.: Further Essays in Monetary Economics, London, pp. 229–49

Jurgensen, Philipp (1984): Bericht der Arbeitstagung über Interventionen an den Devisenmärkten, in: Ehrlicher, Werner/Richter, Rudolf (eds.): Devisenmarktinterventionen der Zentralbanken, Schriften des Vereins für Socialpolitik, N.F. vol. 139, pp. 83–113

Kath, Dietmar (1979): Das Geldmengenziel der Deutschen Bundesbank, Diskussionsbeiträge des Fachbereichs Wirtschaftswissenschaft, no. 7, Gesamthochschule Duisburg

Keohane, Robert O. (1984): After Hegemony. Cooperation and Discord in the World Political Economy, Princeton

Keynes, John M. (1924): A Tract on Monetary Reform, London

Keynes, John M. (1930): A Treatise on Money, vol. 1, The Pure Theory of Money, London

Keynes, John M. (1936): The General Theory of Employment, Interest and Money, London

Kindleberger, Charles P. (1981): The Case for Fixed Exchange Rates, 1969, in: The International Adjustment Mechanism. Proceedings of the Monetary Conference Melvin Village, New Hampshire, October 8–10, 1969, Boston, pp. 93–108. Reprinted in: Kindleberger, Charles P. (1981): International Money. A Collection of Essays, London, pp. 169–82

Köhler, Claus (1962): Der Geldkreislauf. Geldtheoretische Thesen im Spiegel der Empirie, Berlin

Köhler, Claus (1970a): Geldwirtschaft, vol. 1: Geldversorgung und Kreditpolitik, Berlin

Köhler, Claus (1970b): Thesen und Gegenthesen. Bemerkungen zu Milton Friedmans monetärem Konzept des 'New Liberalism', in: Weltwirtschaftliches Archiv 105, pp. 31–47

Köhler, Claus (1971): Potentialorientierte Kreditpolitik, Berlin

Köhler, Claus (1977): Geldwirtschaft. vol. 1: Geldversorgung und Kreditpolitik, 2nd, revised edition, Berlin

König, Heinz (1968): Einkommenskreislaufgeschwindigkeit des Geldes und Zinsveränderungen: Eine ökonometrische Studie über die Geldnachfrage in der BRD, in: Zeitschrift für die gesamte Staatswissenschaft 124, pp. 70–90

Kreps, David M. (1990): Corporate Culture and Economic Theory, in: Alt, James E./Shepsle, Kenneth A. (eds.): Perspectives on Positive Political Economy, Cambridge, pp. 90–143

Kydland, Finn E./Prescott, Edward C. (1977): Rules rather than Discretion: The Inconsistency of Optimal Plans, in: Journal of Political Economy 85, pp. 473–91

Lucas, Robert E., Jr. (1972): Expectations and the Neutrality of Money, in: Journal of Economic Theory 4, pp. 103–24

Lucas, Robert E., Jr. (1973): Some International Evidence on Output-Inflation Tradeoffs, in: American Economic Review 63, pp. 326–34

Lucas, Robert E., Jr. (1976): Econometric Policy Evaluation: A Critique, in: Brunner, Karl/Meltzer, Allan H. (eds.): The Phillips Curve and Labor Markets, Carnegie-Rochester Conference Series on Public Policy 1, pp. 19–46

Lucas, Robert E., Jr. (1987): Model of Business Cycles, Oxford

Lutz, Friedrich A. (1951): Trugschluß als 'Dollarknappheit', in: Zeitschrift für das gesamte Kreditwesen 4, 19, pp. 462–5

Lutz, Friedrich A. (1954): Das Problem der Konvertibilität europäischer Währungen, in: ORDO, Jahrbuch für die Ordnung der Wirtschaft 6, pp. 79–131

Lutz, Friedrich A. (1955): Rezept Kursflexibilität, in: Zeitschrift für das gesamte Kreditwesen 8, 1, pp. 23–5

Lutz, Friedrich A. (1959): Gefahren und Vorteile einer leichten Inflation, in: Das Problem der Geldwertstabilität. Report on the economic part of the 20th Meeting of the Federation of German Economic Research Institutes in Bad Godesberg on 21 June 1957, Berlin, pp. 10–21

McCallum, Bennett T. (1996): Inflation Targeting in Canada, New Zealand, Sweden, the United Kingdom, and in General, Bank of Japan (ed.): IMES Discussion Paper 96–E–21, Tokyo

McKinnon, Ronald I. (1974): A New Tripartite Monetary Agreement or a Limping Dollar Standard. Essays in International Finance 106, Princeton

McKinnon, Ronald I. (1984): An International Standard for Monetary Stabilization, Policy Analyses in International Economics 8, Washington D.C.

McKinnon, Ronald I. (1988): Monetary and Exchange Rate Policies for International Financial Stability: A Proposal, in: Economic Perspectives 2, pp. 83–104

McKinnon, Ronald I. (1993): The Rules of the Game: International Money in Historical Perspective, in: Journal of Economic Literature 31, pp. 1–44

McKinnon, Ronald I./Oates, Wallace E. (1966): The Implications of International Economic Integration for Monetary, Fiscal and Exchange Rate Policy, Princeton Studies in International Finance 16, Princeton

Maddock, Rodney/Carter, Michael (1982): A Child's Guide to Rational Expectations, in: Journal of Economic Literature 20, pp. 39–51

Mankiw, N. Gregory (1990): A Quick Refresher Course in Macroeconomics, in: Journal of Economic Literature 28, pp. 1646–60

Mankiw, N. Gregory/Romer, David (1991): New Keynesian Economics, vol. 2, Cambridge, Mass./London

Mishkin, Frederic S. (1995): The Economics of Money, Banking, and Financial Markets, New York

Möller, Hans (1957): Probleme der Geld- und Kreditpolitik bei Währungskonvertierbarkeit, in: Beckerath, Erwin von (ed.): Wirtschaftsfragen der freien Welt, Frankfurt a.M., pp. 579–92

Monissen, Hans G. (1971): Analyse der Keynesianischen Liquiditätspräferenzfunktion, in: Kredit und Kapital 4, pp. 27–56

Monissen, Hans G. (1973): Geldversorgung und Kreditpolitik: Kritische Anmerkungen zur monetären Konzeption von Claus Köhler, in: Kredit und Kapital 6, pp. 134–56

Mundell, Robert A. (1961): A Theory of Optimum Currency Areas, in: American Economic Review 51, pp. 657–65

Mundell, Robert A. (1968): International Economics, New York

Neumann, Manfred J. M. (1971): Zwischenziele und Indikatoren der Geldpolitik, in: Kredit und Kapital 4, pp. 398–420

Neumann, Manfred J. M. (1972): Bank Liquidity and the Extended Monetary Base as Indicator of German Monetary Policy, in: Brunner, K. (ed.): Proceedings of the First Konstanzer Seminar on Monetary Theory and Monetary Policy 1970, Kredit und Kapital 5, pp. 165–217

Neumann, Manfred J. M. (1974): Stabilisierungspolitik stabilisieren, in: Wirtschaftswoche 28, 25, pp. 69–74

Neumann, Manfred J. M. (1977): Längerfristige Orientierung der Geldmengenkontrolle, in: Sparkasse 34, 8, pp. 258–60

Neumann, Manfred J. M. (1978a): Gegen antizyklische Finanz- und Geldpolitik, in: Frankfurter Allgemeine Zeitung, 6 June

Neumann, Manfred J. M. (1978b): Konterkarrierende Kapitalbewegungen, eine Überprüfung der deutschen Evidenz, in: Kredit und Kapital 11, pp. 348–424

Neumann, Manfred J. M. (1979a): Geldpolitik in der Fehlentwicklung, in: Wirtschaftsdienst 59, 1, pp. 19–24

Neumann, Manfred J. M. (1979b): Beteuerungen haben sich abgenutzt, in: Wirtschaftswoche 33, 25, pp. 60–4

Neumann, Manfred J. M. (1982): Quo vadis, Geldmengenpolitik?, in: Sparkasse 99, 3, pp. 73–5

Neumann, Manfred J. M. (1984): Auf der Suche nach der Interventionsfunktion der

Deutschen Bundesbank, in: Ehrlicher, Werner/Richter, Rudolf (ed.): Devisenmarktinterventionen der Zentralbanken, Schriften des Vereins für Socialpolitik, N.F. vol. 139, Berlin, pp. 9–38

Neumann, Manfred J. M. (1985): Auf dem Weg zu einer Realtrendorientierung der Geldpolitik, in: Sparkasse 102, 3, pp. 88–91

Neumann, Manfred J. M. (1988): Geldmengenziele nicht zur Disposition stellen, press release, Bonn

Neumann, Manfred J. M. (1996): Monetary Targeting in Germany, Bank of Japan, Institute for Monetary and Economic Studies, Discussion Paper Series 96–E–15, Tokyo

Niehans, Jürg (1978): The Theory of Money, Baltimore/London

Niehans, Jürg (1984): International Monetary Economics, Oxford

Nordhaus, William D. (1975): The Political Business Cycle, in: Review of Economic Studies 42, pp. 169–90

Nordhaus, William D. (1989): Alternative Approaches to the Political Business Cycle, in: Brookings Papers on Economic Activity 2, pp. 1–68

Oberhauser, Alois (1976): Geld- und Kreditpolitik bei weitgehender Vollbeschäftigung und mäßigem Preisanstieg (1958–68), in: Deutsche Bundesbank (ed.): Währung und Wirtschaft in Deutschland 1876–1975, Frankfurt a.M., pp. 609–42

Oberhauser, Alois (1977): Liquiditätstheorie des Geldes als Gegenkonzept zum Monetarismus, in: Kredit und Kapital 10, pp. 207–32

Oberhauser, Alois (1980): Die deutsche Geldpolitik zwischen 1968 und 1978, Part 3, Geld- und Währungspolitik I + II, Fernuniversität-Gesamthochschule Hagen, Hagen

Obstfeld, Maurice (1982): Aggregate Spending and the Terms of Trade: Is there a Laursen-Metzler Effect?, in: Quarterly Journal of Economics 97, pp. 251–70

Obstfeld, Maurice (1985): Floating Exchange-rates: Experience and Prospects, in: Brookings Papers on Economic Activity 2, pp. 369–464

Obstfeld, Maurice (1986): Capital Mobility in the World Economy: Theory and Measurement, in: The National Bureau Method, International Capital Mobility and Other Essays, Carnegie-Rochester Conference Series on Public Policy 24, pp. 55–104

Obstfeld, Maurice/Rogoff, Kenneth (1996): Foundations of International Macroeconomics, Cambridge, Mass.

Patinkin, Don (1956): Money, Interest, and Prices. An Integration of Monetary and Value Theory, Evanston, Ill.

Patinkin, Don (1961): Financial Intermediaries and the Logical Structure of Monetary Theory. A Review Article, in: American Economic Review 51, pp. 95–116

Patinkin, Don (1965): Money, Interest and Prices. An Integration of Monetary and Value Theory, New York

Patman Report (1952): Monetary Policy and the Management of the Public Debt. Their Role in Achieving Price Stability and High-Level Employment, Part 1, U.S. Government Printing Office, Washington

Persson, Torsten/Tabellini, Guido (1990): Macroeconomic Policy, Credibility and Politics, Chur/London

Pohl, Reinhard (1978): Hat sich die neue geldpolitische Strategie der Deutschen Bundesbank bewährt?, in: Vierteljahrshefte zur Wirtschaftsforschung 1, pp. 5–21

Pohl, Rüdiger (1973*a*): Grundzüge einer liquiditätstheoretischen Konzeption für die Zentralbankpolitik, in: Köhler, Claus (ed.): Geldpolitik—kontrovers, Cologne, pp. 21–39

Pohl, Rüdiger (1973*b*): Geldbasis versus Liquiditätssaldo. Ein Vergleich zweier geldpolitischer Konzepte, in: Köhler, Claus (ed.): Geldpolitik—kontrovers, Cologne, pp. 94–108

Pohl, Rüdiger (1975): Geld- und Kreditpolitik: Warten auf den Umschwung. Geldstromanalyse für das 1. Quartal 1975, in: WSI-Mitteilungen 28, pp. 283–93

Pohl, Rüdiger (1977): Gegen die Unterbeschäftigungsmentalität. Geldpolitische Analyse für das Frühjahr 1977, n.p.

Pohl, Rüdiger (1980a): Geldpolitik auf falschem Gleis. Konjunkturpolitische Analyse für den Winter 1980/81, Fernuniversität Hagen, Lehrgebiet Geld, Kredit, Währung, Hagen

Pohl, Rüdiger (1980b): Die Stunde der Geldpolitik. Konjunkturpolitische Analyse für den Sommer 1980, Fernuniversität Hagen, Lehrgebiet Geld, Kredit, Währung, Hagen

Pohl, Rüdiger (1981): Bundesbank im Schlepptau des Auslands? Eine geldpolitische Analyse, in: BfG Wirtschaftsblätter 29, 7, pp. 1–5

Pohl, Rüdiger (1982a): Die Geldpolitik der Deutschen Bundesbank im Lichte steigender Arbeitslosigkeit, in: WSI-Mitteilungen 35, pp. 15–22

Pohl, Rüdiger (1982b): Zur Bedeutung des internationalen Inflationsverbundes für die Preisniveauentwicklung in der Bundesrepublik Deutschland, in: Ehrlicher, Werner/Simmert, Diethard B. (Hrsg): Geld- und Währungspolitik in der Bundesrepublik Deutschland, Berlin, pp. 358–99

Pohl, Rüdiger (1983a): Die Geldpolitik ist noch nicht ausgereizt. Geldpolitische Analyse für den Winter 1982/83, Fernuniversität Hagen, Lehrgebiet Geld, Kredit, Währung, Hagen

Pohl, Rüdiger (1983b): Konditionierte Zinssenkung. Geldpolitische Analyse für den Winter 1993/94, Berlin

Pohl, Rüdiger (1987a): Brauchen wir eine neue geldpolitische Konzeption?, in: Wirtschaftsdienst 67, 7, pp. 339–45

Pohl, Rüdiger (1987b): Geldpolitik in der Dollarfalle. Geldpolitische Analyse für den Sommer 1987, Berlin

Pohl, Rüdiger (1987c): Flexible Orientierung der Geldpolitik, in: Vierteljahrshefte zur Wirtschaftsforschung 3, pp. 175–6

Pohl, Rüdiger (1994): Die Geldpolitik der Bundesbank unter veränderten weltwirtschaftlichen Rahmenbedingungen, in: Jens, Uwe (ed.): Langfristige Strukturprobleme der deutschen Wirtschaft, Baden-Baden, pp. 15–27

Pohl, Rüdiger/Kißmer, Friedrich (1990): Die Bedeutung externer Ungleichgewichte für die deutsche Geld- und Währungspolitik zwischen 1973 und 1988, in: Riese, Hajo/Spahn, Heinz-Peter (eds.): Geldpolitik und ökonomische Entwicklung. Ein Symposion, Regensburg, pp. 61–80

Preiser, Erich (1950): Geldschöpfen oder Sparen?, in: Jahrbücher für Nationalökonomie und Statistik 162, pp. 321–35

Radcliffe Report (1959): Committee on the Working of the Monetary System. Report, London

Richter, Rudolf (1967): Die Rolle der Banken in makroökonomischen Modellen. Ein Beitrag zur Einbeziehung der Finanzierungsrechnung in die makroökonomische Theorie, in: Jahrbücher für Nationalökonomie und Statistik 180, pp. 441–62

Richter, Rudolf (1968): The Banking System within Macro-Economic Theory, in: The German Economic Review 6, pp. 273–93

Richter, Rudolf (1989): The Louvre Accord from the Viewpoint of the New Institutional Economics, in: Journal of Institutional and Theoretical Economics 145, pp. 704–19

Richter, Rudolf (1990): Geldtheorie. Vorlesungen auf der Grundlage der allgemeinen Gleichgewichtstheorie und der Institutionenökonomik, Berlin

Richter, Rudolf (1994): Institutionen ökonomisch analysiert, Tübingen

Richter, Rudolf (1996): Theorie der Notenbankverfassung aus der Sicht der Neuen Institutionenökonomik, in: Bofinger, Peter/Ketterer, Karl-Heinz (eds.): Neuere Entwicklungen in der Geldtheorie und Geldpolitik, Festschrift für Norbert Kloten, Tübingen, pp. 119–36

Richter, Rudolf/Teigen, Ronald L. (1982a): Commercial Bank Behavior and Monetary Policy in an Open Economy, West Germany 1960–1980, in: Journal of Monetary Economics 10, pp. 383–405

Richter, Rudolf/Teigen, Ronald L. (1982b): Devisenreserven und Geldvolumina. Eine beschreibende Analyse für die Bundesrepublik Deutschland 1960–1980, manuscript, Universität des Saarlandes, Saarbrücken

Richter, Rudolf/Schlieper, Ulrich/Friedmann, Willy (1973): Makroökonomik. Eine Einführung, Berlin

Richter, Rudolf/McMahon, Patrick/Regier, Hans-Jürgen (1978): Determinants of Free Liquid Reserves in the Federal Republic of Germany 1960–1972, in: Zeitschrift für die gesamte Staatswissenschaft 134, pp. 686–702

Richter, Rudolf/Schlieper, Ulrich/Friedmann, Willy (1981): Makroökonomik. Eine Einführung, 4th, revised and enlarged edition, Berlin

Rogoff, Kenneth (1980): Tests of the Martingale Model for Foreign Exchange Futures Markets, in: Essays on Expectations and Exchange Rate Volatility, Ph.D. dissertation, MIT, Cambridge, Mass.

Rogoff, Kenneth (1984): On the Effects of Sterilized Intervention: An Analysis of Weekly Data, in: Journal of Monetary Economics 14, pp. 133–50

Rogoff, Kenneth (1987): Reputational Constraints on Monetary Policy, in: Carnegie-Rochester Conference Series on Public Policy 26, pp. 141–81

Rogoff, Kenneth/Sibert, Anne (1988): Elections and Macroeconomic Policy Cycles, in: Review of Economic Studies 55, pp. 1–16

Roskamp, Karl W./Laumas, Gurcharan S. (1970): The Demand for Monetary Assets in the West German Economy: Evidence from Short-Run Data, in: Zeitschrift für die gesamte Staatswissenschaft 126, pp. 468–83

Sachverständigenrat zur Begutachtung der gesamtwirtschaftlichen Entwicklung (various years), Jahresgutachten, Stuttgart

Samuelson, Paul A. (1966): The Collected Scientific Papers of Paul A. Samuelson, vol. 2, Cambridge, Mass.

Samuelson, Paul A. (1980): A Corrected Version of Hume's Equilibrating Mechanism for International Trade, in: Chipman, John S./Kindleberger, Charles P. (eds.): Flexible Exchange Rates and the Balance of Payments, Amsterdam, pp. 141–58

Santomero, Anthony M./Seater, John J. (1978): The Inflation-Unemployment Trade-off: A Critique of the Literature, in: Journal of Economic Literature 16, pp. 499–544

Sargent, Thomas J. (1986): Rational Expectations and Inflation, New York

Sargent, Thomas J./Wallace, Neil (1975): Rational Expectations, the Optimal Monetary Instrument, and the Optimal Money Supply Rule, in: Journal of Political Economy 83, pp. 241–54

Schlesinger, Helmut (1980): Die geldpolitische Konzeption der Deutschen Bundesbank, Part 2, focusing on monetary policy I + II, Fernuniversität-Gesamthochschule, Hagen

Siebke, Jürgen/Willms, Manfred (1970): Das Geldangebot in der Bundesrepublik Deutschland, in: Zeitschrift für die gesamte Staatswissenschaft 126, pp. 55–74

Simmert, Diethard B. (1976): Plädoyer für mehr Geld, in: Wirtschaftswoche 30, 49, p. 66

Simons, Henry C. (1936): Rules Versus Authorities in Monetary Policy, in: Journal of Political Economy 44, pp. 1–30

Snidal, Duncan (1985): The Limits of Hegemonic Stability Theory, in: International Organization 39, pp. 579–614

Sohmen, Egon (1961, 1969): Flexible Exchange Rates, 1st and 2nd (revised) edition, Chicago/London

Sohmen, Egon (1967): Fiscal and Monetary Policies under Alternative Exchange-Rate Systems, in: Quarterly Journal of Economics 81, pp. 515–23

Sohmen, Egon (1973): Wechselkurs und Währungsordnung, Tübingen

Stein, Jerome L. (1976): Inside the Monetarist Black Box, in: Stein, Jerome L. (ed.): Monetarism, Amsterdam, pp. 183–232

Stolper, Wolfgang F./Roskamp, Karl W. (1979): Planning a Free Economy: Germany 1945–1960, in: Zeitschrift für die gesamte Staatswissenschaft 135, pp. 374–404

Stützel, Wolfgang (1953): Leistungsbilanzen, Zahlungsbilanzen—Konvertibilität, in: Berliner Bank (ed.): Mitteilungen für den Außenhandel (1953) 61, pp. 5–8 (slightly revised reprint in: Stützel, 1973)

Stützel, Wolfgang (1960): Währungspolitik und Wirtschaftsverfassung, Supplement to the Mitteilungen der Industrie- und Handelskammer, Dortmund, October

Stützel, Wolfgang (1960a): Ist die schleichende Inflation durch monetäre Maßnahmen zu beeinflussen?, in: Inwieweit ist die schleichende Inflation durch monetäre Maßnahmen zu bekämpfen? Report on the economic part of the 23rd Meeting of the Federation of German Economic Research Institutes in Bad Godesberg on 15 and 16 June 1960 (Discussion Contributions), Berlin

Stützel, Wolfgang (1961): Das sogenannte Dilemma der deutschen Währungspolitik: Lehrjahre im Neuland einer voll konvertiblen Währung, in: Der Deutsche Volks- und Betriebswirt 7, 2, pp. 22–7

Stützel, Wolfgang (1969): Währungskurse = Zahlungsversprechen. Wechselkursmanipulationen sind keine Alternative zu wirtschaftlicher Disziplin, in: Die Presse, 1–2 February, p. 5

Stützel, Wolfgang (1973): Währung in weltoffener Wirtschaft. Lehrstücke der Währungspolitik—unter der Herausforderung des Tages, Frankfurt a.M.

Tobin, James (1958): Liquidity Preference as Behavior Towards Risk, in: Review of Economic Studies 25, pp. 65–86

Tobin, James (1967): Commercial Banks as Creators of 'Money', in: Hester, Donald D./Tobin, James (eds.): Financial Markets and Economic Activity, New York/London, pp. 1–11

Tobin, James (1969): Monetary Semanticy, in: Brunner, Karl (ed.): Targets and Indicators of Monetary Policy, San Francisco, pp. 165–74

Tobin, James (1980): Asset Accumulation and Economic Activity. Reflections on Contemporary Macroeconomic Theory, Chicago

Veit, Otto (1957): Liquiditätspolitik statt reiner Diskontpolitik, in: Veit, Otto: Die veränderte Währungspolitik und ihre Folgen, Frankfurt a.M., pp. 51–8

Wallich, Henry C. (1955): Mainsprings of German Revival, New Haven

Westphal, Uwe (1970): Theoretische und empirische Untersuchungen zur Geldnachfrage und zum Geldangebot, Kieler Studien no. 110, Tübingen

Whitman, Marina v. N. (1975): Global Monetarism and the Monetary Approach to the Balance of Payments, in: Brookings Papers on Economic Activity 3, pp. 419–536

Wicksell, Knut (1898): Geldzins und Güterpreise. Eine Studie über die den Tauschwert des Geldes bestimmenden Ursachen, Jena

Wieser, Friedrich von (1927): Geld, in: Elster, Ludwig/Weber, Adolf/Wieser, Friedrich von (eds.): Handwörterbuch der Staatswissenschaften, vol. 4, Jena, pp. 681–717

Willms, Manfred (1970): Das Rezept der Geldmengentheoretiker, in: Der Volkswirt 24, 23, pp. 48–9

Willms, Manfred (1971): Controlling Money in an Open Economy: The German Case, in: Review of the Federal Reserve Bank of St. Louis 53, 4, pp. 19–27

Wissenschaftlicher Beirat bei der Verwaltung für Wirtschaft des Vereinigten Wirtschaftsgebietes (1950): Gutachten 1948 bis Mai 1950, ed. Bundeswirtschaftsministerium, Göttingen

Wissenschaftlicher Beirat beim Bundesministerium für Wirtschaft (1953): Gutachten vom Juni 1950 bis November 1952, ed. Bundeswirtschaftsministerium, vol. 2, Göttingen

Wissenschaftlicher Beirat beim Bundesministerium für Wirtschaft (1957): Gutachten vom Januar 1955 bis Dezember 1956, ed. Bundeswirtschaftsministerium, vol. 4, Göttingen

Wissenschaftlicher Beirat beim Bundesministerium für Wirtschaft (1973): Sammelband der Gutachten von 1948 bis 1972, ed. Bundeswirtschaftsministerium, Göttingen

Wissenschaftlicher Beirat beim Bundesministerium für Wirtschaft (1977): Gutachten vom März 1973 bis November 1975, ed. Bundesministerium für Wirtschaft, vol. 8, Göttingen

Wissenschaftlicher Beirat beim Bundesministerium für Wirtschaft (1978): Gutachten vom November 1976 bis November 1977, ed. Bundesministerium für Wirtschaft, vol. 9, Göttingen

Wissenschaftlicher Beirat beim Bundesministerium für Wirtschaft (1983): Gutachten vom Januar 1981 bis Juni 1983, ed. Bundesministerium für Wirtschaft, vol. 11, Göttingen

Wissenschaftlicher Beirat beim Bundesministerium für Wirtschaft (1989): Europäische Währungsunion, Gutachten, Studien-Reihe 61, ed. Bundesminister für Wirtschaft, Bonn

Wissenschaftlicher Beirat beim Bundesministerium für Wirtschaft (1990): Gutachten vom Juni 1987 bis März 1990, ed. Bundesministerium für Wirtschaft, vol. 13, Göttingen

Wissenschaftlicher Beirat beim Bundesministerium für Wirtschaft (1994): Ordnungspolitische Orientierung für die Europäische Union, Gutachten, BMWi Dokumentation no. 356, ed. Bundesminister für Wirtschaft, Bonn

Part Four

ASPECTS OF MONETARY POLICY
IN THE TWO GERMANYS

XI. The Central Bank and Money in the GDR

By H. Jörg Thieme

1. Introduction

Providing a description of the origins and development of the monetary system in the GDR is at once interesting and difficult. Interesting, because following German reunification it ought to be possible to analyse the monetary side of administrative socialism, to review the interplay between socialist ideology and the pragmatic approach to monetary relations under a system of central economic planning over a period of more than 40 years. Interesting also because Western research into the GDR was long dominated by the view—a view shared by the theorists of socialism and the official policy of the GDR—that 'money doesn't matter in socialism'. On the other hand, it is difficult, given the limited space available, to explain in detail the vast range of monetary reforms, administrative reshuffles and reorganizations, and their economic consequences. This is not helped by the lack of empirical material available for the monetary sector, which was deemed secret in the GDR; a reading of internal Staatsbank documents, which is possible today, actually reveals less than one might hope, because the theoretical stance and political objectives in the GDR clearly affected the structure, quantity, and quality of the data.

This essay begins by roughly outlining the restructuring of the entire banking system in the post-war period and the currency reform of 1948 (Section 2). It goes on to define the significance of money and credit in the context of central economic planning, to ascertain the role of the central bank in the planning process, and to describe its monetary targets and instruments (Section 3). Finally, it analyses certain problems which derive from a target-oriented approach to controlling the money stock within a socialist system and the consequences of this (Section 4).

My thanks go to my research assistant, Christof Welker, for his valuable preparatory work and his patience during the discussion of the contents.

2. Origins and development of the monetary system after 1945

a) The restructuring of the banking system

The rebuilding of the monetary sector in the Soviet occupation zone following the end of the War can be divided into two phases. In the first phase
(1945–8), the existing structures of a largely private-sector, two-tier banking
system were destroyed. In accordance with communist doctrine, the banks
were generally nationalized, although many of the institutions were initially
only provisional. In the second phase (from 1948), the banking system, in
conjunction with the monetary reform, was increasingly centralized; it was
headed by a central bank with wide-ranging powers. Gradually, the monetary system was integrated into the central planning of the overall economy
(a Soviet-style centrally administered economy); from 1951, the banking
sector, headed by the central bank, was an effective instrument of central
planning, guidance, and control of macroeconomic processes.

Nationalization and reconstruction (1945–8)

When the War ended in May 1945 and the Soviet occupation zone was
created in one part of Germany, the policy framework for the establishment
of a Soviet-style centrally administered economy was prepared and put into
place. The Soviet Military Administration in Germany nationalized all the
most important sectors of industry and all the banks. As early as April 1945
(i.e. even before the end of the War), the banks in the areas occupied by
Soviet troops were forced to close, and all bank deposits, securities, and
contents of safety deposit boxes were confiscated.[1]

The restructuring of the banking system was initially intended to ensure
the availability of money and credit for reconstruction. In order to rephase
time periods of deposits and to shift the risk spread, existing cash holdings
were to be concentrated in the banking sector.[2] At the same time—initially
without a currency reform—the pent-up inflation which had built up owing
to the war economy of the National Socialists was to be tackled. Monetary
and other assets of the 'capitalist class' and assets obtained from involvement
in the National Socialist regime were to be expropriated during this process
of restructuring and nationalized as 'people's property'.

[1] Cf. Befehl des Chefs der Besatzung, 1956, p. 115.
[2] Cf. the relevant legislation: Chef der Besatzung der Stadt Berlin, 1956, pp. 115–18.

To start with, the banking system was reorganized at Länder level. The newly founded provincial and Länder banks were public-law institutions of the respective Länder governments and acted as all-purpose banks. They were responsible for providing loans to industry and commerce and to municipal companies; they also held the corresponding deposits. They were responsible for non-cash payments and the cash transactions of the budgets of the various Länder. They had no powers to issue banknotes.

The newly formed savings banks took on the banking business of the general public and issued short-term and long-term loans for housing. In November 1945, agricultural loan cooperatives were reopened for the farming sector, and cooperative banks were reopened for crafts and trades in January 1946.[3] Whilst these used the infrastructure inherited from their predecessors, they were not legal successors to the previous savings banks and loan cooperatives. Twenty-five private banks were also initially allowed to reopen under specific conditions, but were nationalized in the period up to 1952. All the banks had the restrictive mandate to cut the surplus of Reichsmarks and to nationalize remaining private property: all deposits and assets from the time before 9 May 1945 were blocked and later, after having been tested for 'lawful acquisition', were mainly liquidated during the currency reform and allocated to the various Länder governments. There was no redress for the former owners, since by law the newly established banks were not the legal successors of the former banks. All outstanding loans were called in immediately, also being credited to the accounts of the Länder governments. Small savers and those unable to work (with funds of up to RM 3,000) were given RM 300 and RM 400 respectively. These measures were supplemented by a price freeze on agricultural and industrial goods, the continued payment of wages and salaries at the post-war level, and food rationing based on ration cards.[4] The rates of income and corporation tax distinguished between private and state-owned companies; the peak rate for state-owned companies was 65 per cent; private firms had to pay up to 95 per cent.

In this transitional phase, because there was no centralized credit planning until 1951, the reopened commercial banks based the way they granted credit on the traditional criteria of viability and liquidity for commercial loans. The impact of these measures on inflation was inadequate. It is impossible to ascertain exactly how many Reichsmarks were actually removed from the economy. The level of the blocked private assets is estimated at

---

[3] Cf. Befehl des Obersten Chefs, 1956, pp. 122ff. and Befehl Nr. 14, 1956, p. 125.

[4] The official version of GDR documents assessed this measure as a contribution 'towards an effective curbing of inflation and towards a safeguarding of the fundamental rights of the workers'. Kohlmey, 1956, p. 25.

approximately RM 37 billion. Loans totalling about RM 2.3 billion from the period before 9 May 1945 were called in, but approximately RM 1.87 billion of this was paid out again to small savers. There were also substantial stocks of hoarded cash which were returned to the banks and could thus be used for deposit money creation. Finally, and illogically, the occupying power itself put new cash totalling around RM 12 billion into circulation.[5] This money came from confiscated cash holdings at the banks, Reichsmark reserves from the Reichsbank, and from newly printed scrip money (known as occupation tokens). As a consequence, the stock of cash in the Soviet occupation zone rose sharply until the currency reform in 1948, when a total of RM 28.05 billion was submitted for exchange.

Because of the scarcity of goods, which was supposed to be regulated via ration cards at fixed prices, monetary demand evolved on black markets, where the prices reflected the actual potential for inflation. This was also recognized by the relevant authorities, but was interpreted as 'sabotage by black marketeers and speculators, particularly people from the overthrown classes, of the card-based supply to the population',[6] and legislation was enforced to stop it.

In preparation for the currency reform for the whole of Germany and for the centralization of the banking system, five Emissions- und Girobanken were established at Länder level in February 1947. They were in charge of the money stock and payments in each of the Länder; the banks and savings banks refinanced themselves from them. At the same time, they were given responsibility for the bank transactions of the Länder budgets, but had no powers to issue banknotes. The existing provincial and Länder banks were reorganized as Landeskreditbanken; they granted credit to the many newly established state-owned companies. Finally, mention should be made of the Garantie- und Kreditbank AG, which settled all reparations payments and business involving Soviet-owned firms (the so-called Soviet AGs, or Soviet joint-stock companies). It ceased operation in 1956.

Centralization of the banking system and establishment of a central bank (after 1948)

On 21 May 1948, the Deutsche Emissions- und Girobank was placed in charge of this new banking system. Its remit was to coordinate and supervise the activities of the Länder Emissions- und Girobanken and to settle payments between the Länder of the Soviet occupation zone. Following the

[5] Cf. Abeken, 1955, p. 9.
[6] Dewey, 1956, p. 8.

currency reform (of 24 June 1948), it was renamed 'Deutsche Notenbank' on 20 July 1948. It was empowered to issue banknotes and had a nominal capital of DM 100 million.[7] It henceforth performed the functions of the state's own bank and the bankers' bank. It was gradually given all monetary responsibilities and was made directly accountable to the top political decision makers; in March 1950, the Länder Emissions- und Girobanken and the Landeskreditbanken were integrated into the Deutsche Notenbank. It dealt with all short-term loans and was thus not only the sole 'commercial bank', but also the financial and clearing centre of the entire economy and the supreme authority in control of centrally planned monetary and non-monetary processes ('control by the mark').

In order to improve the role played by the banking sector in the fulfilment of the plan and in checking that 'socialist credit principles' were being strictly applied, two additional central institutions were established: the Deutsche Investitionsbank, with responsibilities for all long-term loans, in October 1948, and the Deutsche Bauernbank, as the bank in charge of the agricultural loan cooperatives, in 1950. Finally, Deutsche Handelsbank AG was founded in 1956; it was responsible for all transactions with other countries and was replaced in 1966 by Deutsche Außenhandelsbank AG (with the state as the main shareholder). In the single-tier banking system, these special-purpose banks were departments of the Deutsche Notenbank, and were subject to its instructions and supervision.

A comprehensive reform of the banking system on 1 January 1968 aimed to replace this single-tier set-up by a two-tier banking system. The Deutsche Notenbank was renamed 'Staatsbank der DDR' and until July 1974 was responsible only for doing the work of a central bank, i.e. safeguarding a money stock in line with the plan.[8] Depending on the sector, traditional banking business was transferred to the Industrie- und Handelsbank (for industry and commerce, formerly the Investitionsbank), the Bank für Landwirtschaft und Nahrungsgüterwirtschaft (for farming and the food industry, formerly the Landwirtschaftsbank), the savings banks (for individual savers), the Bank für Handwerk und Gewerbe (for crafts and trades) and Deutsche Außenhandelsbank AG.[9] When issuing loans, they were to base their decisions on the likely yields of the projects to be funded, and also had scope to set interest rates. However, the discretionary powers of the commercial banks were substantially reined in as early as 1971, and the two-tier banking system was completely abolished in July 1974.

[7] Cf. Bilanzen der Deutschen Notenbank (Bundesarchiv NG, 3188).

[8] The tasks, instruments, and development of the mandate of the Staatsbank and how it was integrated into central planning are described below. Cf. Frenzel, 1989, pp. 69ff.

[9] Cf. Mülhaupt and Fox, 1971, pp. 14ff.

b) The currency reform of 1948

Political background, policy framework, and implementation

Three years after the end of the War—particularly in the Western part of Germany—reconstruction was so well advanced that a functioning and stable monetary system needed to be created to ensure the continuation of efficient economic activity and economic growth. All non-radical attempts to curb the potential for inflation inherited from the war economy had failed; the Reichsmark had ceased to function as money.[10] The prices of goods were fixed by the state, and numerous black markets were springing up on which scarce goods, foreign currency (US dollars), and gold were exchanged. In both the West and the East, the monetary system needed a radical currency reform.

In the run-up to the currency reform, the victorious powers attempted to introduce a common monetary policy for all four occupation zones. However, the respective political conceptions of how to design a new economic and social system for the whole of Germany were so divergent that all attempts at a single currency reform failed. They would have meant the loss of influence and control in Germany either for the Soviet Union or for the western Allies. On 20 March 1948, the Soviet Union blocked the monetary negotiations in the Allied Control Council, and the western Allies then took advantage of this to launch a separate monetary reform; the Americans had actually already decided to go for a separate reform.[11] There were signs of the approaching division of Germany and the beginning of the Cold War in Europe, even if the currency reform in the West of Germany was not the actual cause.[12]

The currency reform was implemented in the Western zones on 21 June 1948.[13] The administration in the Soviet occupation zone was forced to respond for economic, political, and psychological reasons; in fact, a separate currency reform with 'socialist objectives' had already been prepared. Following the currency reform in West Germany, there was a risk of an influx of stocks of old Reichsmark notes (which had been valid in all four zones), which would merely have added to the existing surplus of Reichsmark

---

[10] Payment was often rendered in scarce goods, such as cigarettes. Economic activity was regressing to the level of a barter economy.

[11] Cf. Buchheim, 1988, pp. 210f.

[12] Cf. Möller, 1976, p. 441.

[13] This measure was viewed in the Soviet zone as a 'decisive step along the road towards an economic division of Germany by the imperialist domestic and foreign powers and towards the preparation of a basis for West German aggression', Kohlmey, 1956, p. 27.

TABLE 1: First cash exchange of 24–8 June 1948 (in million)

	Existing money	Coupon marks	Exchange rate
Private households	1,364.3	1,364.3	1:1
	5,300.9	530.1	10:1
Total private households	6,665.2	1,894.4	3.5:1
Companies/organizations	580.0	58.0	10:1
Members of Soviet army	97.1	97.1	1:1
Blocked accounts	208.4	20.8	10:1
Total non-banks	7,550.7	2,070.4	3.65:1
Cash holdings of banks	20,500.0	2,050.0	10:1
Total banknotes	28,050.7	4,120.4	6.8:1

Source: Währungsreform in der Sowjetischen Besatzungszone 1948, p. 1 (Archiv der Kredit-anstalt für Wiederaufbau, Berlin office).

currency in the Soviet zone. If the structure of the overall economic plan was to be safeguarded, it was vital to bring the money stock in the Soviet zone into line with the production potential. And, as in West Germany, a restructuring of the currency situation was important for psychological reasons. The 'new money' was to be a symbol of the new economic stability under socialism, and was intended to alleviate uncertainty among the general public.

The currency reform in the Soviet occupation zone (24–8 June 1948) was intended both to create the monetary conditions for the central planning of economic processes *and* to change the property ownership system.[14] In addition to its economic function, the currency reform therefore particularly pursued social policy objectives. The printing of the new notes had been prepared, but the work was not finished in time. For this reason, the old banknotes initially had coupons stuck on to them and remained in use (Table 1), until they were exchanged at a 1:1 rate for new banknotes desig-nated 'Deutsche Mark der Deutschen Notenbank' (DM) between 25 and 28 July 1948.[15] Within those four days, the population had to deliver the old paper money to the banks, each individual receiving DM 70 for RM 70.

[14] Cf. SMAD-Befehl Nr. 111/1948, 1956, pp. 193ff.
[15] Cf. SMAD-Befehl Nr. 124/1948, 1956, p. 242 and Roeper, 1978, pp. 31ff. The name of the currency was to change twice more: in 1964 into 'Mark der Deutschen Notenbank' and in 1974 into 'Mark der DDR'.

TABLE 2: Result of the cash exchange of
25–8 July 1948* (in million DM)

Private households	1,908.7
Companies/organizations	427.1
Total non-banks	2,335.8
Cash holdings of banks	1,761.3
Total banknotes issued	4,097.1
Coins issued	
50 pfennig coins	48.2
5 and 10 pfennig coins	23.0
1 pfennig coins	2.0
Total coins exchanged	73.2
Reconciling items	−1.0
Total initial supply	4,169.3

* Conversion of coupon marks into D-marks
at 1:1

Source: Währungsreform in der Sowjetischen
Besatzungszone 1948, p. 1f. (Archiv der Kreditanstalt für Wiederaufbau, Berlin office).

TABLE 3: Results of the deposit money exchange (in million)

	RM on 23 June 1948	DM	Conversion
Total current and other deposits	15,410	7,872	2:1
of which:	6,907	690	10:1
Preferential exchange	8,503	7,182	1.2:1
Total savings deposits	4,653	1,138	4.1:1
of which:	491	491	1:1
	2,313	462	5:1
	1,609	161	10:1
initially blocked	240	24	10:1
Total deposit money exchanged	20,063	9,010	2.2:1

Source: Währungsreform in der Sowjetischen Besatzungszone 1948, p. 2 (Archiv der Kreditanstalt für Wiederaufbau, Berlin office).

The coins remained valid in line with their nominal value and were replaced from October 1948 (Table 2).

The exchange rates diverged greatly so as to take account of political and economic considerations (Table 3).[16] Assets acquired by state-owned companies since 8 May 1945 were exchanged at 1:1, private companies were given a rate of only 10:1 for the same assets. For private savings accrued since 8 May 1945, each individual was permitted to exchange the first RM 100 at 1:1, up to RM 1,000 at 5:1 and above RM 1,000 at 10:1. All debts were kept at their old nominal value with the exception of debts owed to private individuals: these were devalued at 10:1.[17]

This also applied to all debts entered into before 9 May 1945. There were no such problems for state-owned companies. The debts they had inherited from their predecessor companies were cancelled in full. All the reconciling items deriving from the revaluations during the currency reform in the banks were credited to current accounts held for them at the central bank; this was the equivalent of creating primary money. The revaluation losses were thereby centralized at the Deutsche Notenbank; in return, it received treasury notes from the relevant Länder which the Länder settled from called-in debt and confiscated assets. On 30 September 1949, the accounts of the Deutsche Notenbank recorded treasury notes from the Länder totalling DM 26.664 billion, and these were paid off in the period up to 1954.[18] These Länder treasury notes were the equivalent of the equalization claims in West Germany. For statutorily required cancellations of inherited debt, the Deutsche Notenbank was credited with debt register claims. At the time of German monetary union in 1990, claims still existed on the state budget at the level of the initial supply of banknotes and coins (M 4.169 billion).

It is worth noting the exchange of assets from the time before 9 May 1945, as depicted in Table 4: all funds of more than RM 3,000 were tested for 'lawful acquisition' before they were exchanged. Enrichment during the Third Reich, money from speculative transactions, and illegal income, and income from black market dealings were regarded as unlawful.[19] Political interpretations of the criteria meant that many of these assets were confiscated. Where it was established that the funds had been lawfully acquired, the funds of individuals and private companies were devalued at 10:1 and transformed into a 'redemption bond for existing assets', which earned 3

---

[16] Cf. Rittmann, 1986, pp. 360ff.

[17] Agriculture was an exception. In order to promote its recovery, debts from loans issued between 1945 and 1948 were devalued at 5:1.

[18] Cf. Abeken, 1955, p. 55.

[19] Cf. SMAD-Befehl Nr. 111/1948, 1956, pp. 197f.

TABLE 4: Revaluation of funds acquired before 9 May 1945*
(in million)

	Existing funds in RM	DM
Citizens resident in the Soviet zone	26,030	2,603
Citizens resident outside the Soviet zone	2,200	220
Total revalued funds	28,230	2,823

* Conversion at 10:1.

Source: Währungsreform in der Sowjetischen Besatzungszone 1948, p. 3 (Archiv der Kreditanstalt für Wiederaufbau, Berlin office).

per cent interest from 1 January 1949 and was redeemed in the period up to 1972. The total amount of blocked funds was estimated at RM 37 billion, and in return DM 2.823 billion was entered as claims on the debt register. The bonds of citizens resident outside the Soviet occupation zone remained blocked; their redemption was settled during the process of German reunification, in an ordinance dated 27 June 1990.

As a result, no private individuals or companies were able to dispose directly of their sharply depreciated assets, whereas state-owned companies could immediately dispose of such deposits. The cash balances of the banks, companies, and organizations were also revalued at 10:1.

The assets of public authorities, in contrast, were treated like those of state-owned companies: all funds were revalued at 1:1 up to any amount, and tax arrears were also retained at a full nominal value, but advance tax payments were converted at 10:1. Flows like wages, prices, pensions, levies, grants, etc. remained unchanged.[20]

Political and economic effects of the currency reform

The economists in the GDR all took a positive view of the effects of the currency reform although—as officially confirmed—there continued to be an excess money stock and thus a potential for inflation even after it had taken place. This was due to uncertainties about the precise level of the existing stock of Reichsmarks and the production potential.[21] Rising production and productivity would of course have quickly absorbed the excess money

[20] Cf. Sprenger, 1991, pp. 246ff.
[21] Cf. Ehlert et al., 1985, pp. 318f.

stock. The political objectives of the currency reform, i.e. to remove assets from the 'capitalist class' and from those who had 'profited from the War', to nationalize the means of production, and to foster the establishment of state-owned companies, were deemed to have been achieved.

It is indeed the case that the concept of 'unlawful origin' of assets was interpreted very broadly, resulting in relatively arbitrary expropriations without the precise origins of each individual asset having been investigated. The conversion rates further weakened the private companies and substantially restricted their ability to function, so that they were able to participate in the process of economic recovery only to a very limited extent. The conversion of funds lawfully acquired before 9 May 1945 into a mandatory loan caused a considerable capital deficiency in private companies, which was exacerbated by the exchange rates. It is hard to tell whether and to what extent the change in currency in East Germany did actually cut the excess money stock, as intended, because there is a lack of empirical data on the macroeconomic indicators needed for this—such as the production potential. Similarly, the movements of black market prices is not much use as an indicator of inflation, since they tend, rather, to reflect the scarcity only of certain goods, and no systematic figures for defined periods are available. The best approach is to draw a comparison with the West German currency reform: after that took place, there was no significant potential for inflation or imbalance on the goods markets. The initial supply of cash and deposit money, the population figures, and the national income statistics (1950) are the best yardsticks for comparison.

The rough comparison given in Table 5 of initial per-capita monetary provision and the relationship between the money stock and national income in East and West indicates the potential for inflation with which the GDR started out after its currency reform.

TABLE 5: Comparison of the initial supply of money in East and West

	Soviet zone (DM-Ost)	Western zones (DM-West)
Cash and deposit money (million)[a]	11,400	13,200
Cash and deposit money *per capita*	600	275
Notes and coins in circulation *per capita*	178	132
Cash and deposit money as % of national income[b]	39.2	13.8

[a] Excluding cash holdings of the banks.
[b] National income/net national product at market prices.

Source: Kreditanstalt für Wiederaufbau, Berlin office, Appendix to materials, p. 3.

The main cause of this was the instrumentalization of the currency reform for social policy purposes: it was utilized thoroughly to nationalize private assets; there was a clear preference for state-owned companies, state banks, and public sector budgets over the private sector (conversion of cash holdings, differentiation of conversion rates, relief from inherited debt, etc.). All the rules and regulations governing the currency reform were interpreted in terms of the 'class struggle' and aimed at a 'revolutionary' socialist reshaping of society. Economic factors were disregarded; as a result, it was not possible to create adequate monetary conditions for the establishment of administrative central planning without potential inflation. The excess money stock which existed from the start was exacerbated by the fact that non-monetary growth remained sluggish after the currency reform. The political decision makers were aware of this potential for inflation. They treated symptoms by maintaining the ration card system at prices fixed by the state and relentlessly fighting the black markets. The consequence of this was that the potential for inflation found expression not in higher price levels, but in an increase in undesired cash holdings, queues, etc.

The official statements on the currency reform repeatedly emphasized the economic rationale behind this economic policy measure, and claimed that it had taken account of the interrelationships that exist according to the quantity theory of money between the growth of the money stock and production potential (in the socialist interpretation: the law of monetary circulation). However, none of the documents contains specific statements of objectives or even operationalizations. The official reports take the form of ex-post descriptions of the situation without any evaluation or analysis of errors.[22] This leads to the impression that the currency reform was clearly politically motivated and planned, and that the vast number of *ad hoc* decisions were justified ideologically—the consequence being that economists from the same theoretical school could not criticize them either. Note must also be taken of the dominant influence of the Soviet occupying power, which had to authorize all decisions.

Overall, the reconstruction of the monetary sector in East Germany and, in particular, the currency reform cannot be interpreted as a rational process of economic policy decisions with systematic objectives, choices of instruments, and checks on efficiency; nor is this to be expected in the economic and political circumstances. The currency reform was designed and imple-

---

[22] Cf. here the overall account protocols of the currency reform/cash exchange (Bundesarchiv Koblenz and Berlin, NG, 3176) and the correspondence with the Soviet Military Administration in Germany, instructions and reports on the first and second currency conversions, deficits, and reconciling items, special cases, destruction of old banknotes, blocked accounts, and very old assets (Bundesarchiv Koblenz and Berlin, NG, 822).

mented in the way it was because of the concentration of power in the hands of a few people who based their actions on a political interpretation of Marxist economic theory, coupled with the dominant supervision by the Soviet Military Administration.

3. Money and credit in the GDR

a) The role of money in the socialist planned economy

For a long time, both GDR literature and Western research were dominated by the view that money played no more than a passive role under socialism because of the primacy of non-monetary central planning. Here, passivity means that the use of money has no effect on the economic planning of the decision makers, i.e. use of money affects neither real nor nominal variables. The political leadership (and its bureaucracy) decides on the use and production of scarce resources and goods within a system of central planning which fully encompasses all subordinate economic agents and works on the basis of balances on the plan's non-monetary accounts. The use of money facilitates planning when prices are fixed by the state and enables better monitoring of the fulfilment of the plan: money therefore functions only as an instrument of clearing and control.

This stance was based on historical dogma, i.e. the view of Karl Marx that money is specific to the capitalist approach to production, and must become insignificant once the anarchy of the market economy is overcome.[23] However, it was soon argued in the GDR that the relationship between goods and money would only wither away entirely in the final stage of communist society, and that money would have to be tolerated during the transitional phase of socialism. First, this was due to the impossibility of detailed non-monetary central planning and accounting—the system had been derived from a theory of central economic planning which used very restrictive model assumptions.[24] In practice, aggregate variables were frequently subject to central planning and accounting, and this requires the use of money as a unit of account. Secondly, it was noted in the GDR in the 1950s that rudimentary market relations continued to exist in the transitional phase and that cash in particular would have to function as a medium of exchange and payment. Thirdly, the function of money as an incentive was repeatedly

[23] Cf. Marx, 1885/1989, vol. 2, pp. 35ff., 119ff.
[24] Cf. Hensel, 1959, pp. 170ff.

emphasized. Savings or payments of wages or bonuses in a monetary form were to create incentives which were needed because of a residual bourgeois mentality. However, the use of money and the law of monetary circulation could be applied 'deliberately' and exploited to achieve socialist objectives.[25]

To this extent, money came to be regarded as having various functions in the GDR. All deposit money transactions continued to be viewed as passive, because they were fully integrated into central planning and it was assumed that there was no scope for decision making by individual economic agents in the socialist sector of the economy (i.e. the state-owned companies and state organizations). In contrast, it was admitted that cash in circulation could indeed influence real and nominal variables in the economic process, because scope did exist for commercial decisions in the private sector; it was believed that exploiting these in the interest of the individual economic agent could create disproportions. This view, which also had its advocates in Western literature,[26] resulted in a strict separation between the circulation of cash and the circulation of deposit money. The upshot was that all the policy measures regarding the money stock in the GDR were initially focused on controlling the notes and coins in circulation: the stocks of cash were to be controlled in such a way that—taking into account the estimated velocity of cash—they could develop in parallel to the centrally planned stock of consumer goods for the population, thus avoiding discrepancies between the stock of consumer money and the stock of goods.[27] Fear of uncontrolled amounts of cash then caused the political leadership of the GDR to formulate legislation to curb the holding of cash in the private sector and to undertake a surprise reform of cash in 1957: in this 'minor' currency reform on 13 October 1957, each GDR citizen was only permitted to exchange DM 300 into newly printed cash. The remainder of the old cash was credited to accounts at the Deutsche Notenbank.[28] Another significant concept in this

[25] Cf. Dewey, 1956, p. 8.
[26] Cf. Grossman, 1968, pp. 4ff.; Haffner, 1987, pp. 203ff.; Nove, 1980, pp. 297ff.
[27] Cf. Kohlmey and Dewey, 1956, pp. 16ff. In the 1960s, however, the stock of notes and coins in circulation was (in the face of resistance from the Staatsbank) deliberately increased by more than the growth in production, because the GDR leaders of the time took the Stalinist view that purchasing power (in the form of the money stock) must advance faster than output (the goods stock) in order to achieve positive effects in real terms and avoid the cyclical crises suffered by capitalism. In addition, the wage stock was increased disproportionately, presumably in order to motivate the labour force. This ran counter to the internal logic of central planning.
[28] A total of DM 267.5 million was destroyed by this currency reform: DM 263.4 million was not submitted for exchange, and investigations rendered DM 4.1 million of the credited amounts valueless. The then leadership of the GDR deliberately disseminated the false information that DM 600 million had been destroyed. Cf. Deutsche Finanzwirtschaft, 1957, p. 321.

context was that cash has to be backed by gold, because Marx had made the value of money dependent on its gold content. For this reason, a fictitious gold equivalent of 0.399902 grams of fine gold for the Ostmark was stipulated by law in the GDR between 1949–50 and 1971.[29] In the early 1970s, the official view that the value of money depends on a gold content existing purely on paper was finally abandoned.

At the same time, a process of monetary rethinking commenced in the GDR: shaken by the difficult problems of economic development in the 1960s, which—as in other socialist countries—were largely due to the inefficiencies of administrative central planning, economic reforms intended largely to decentralize economic decision making powers were promulgated and implemented for a time (1963: 'New economic system of planning and control' [NÖSPL]; 1968: 'Economic system of socialism' [ÖSS]). As a result, monetary policy attached significance not only to cash transactions in the private sector but also to deposit money transactions in the socialist sector; the money stock aggregates regarded as being of economic relevance were redefined to include deposit money.[30] This discussion in the GDR was certainly also influenced by the few new approaches to monetary theory in Western analyses drawing comparisons between the systems, which rejected the argument that money in socialism was passive and that discrete circulations of money existed.[31]

According to this neo-quantity theory of money, money always performed various functions in socialist planned economies. In addition to its undisputed function as a means of accounting, money (cash and deposit money) also acted in the GDR as a means of payment which cut transaction costs and thus brought positive welfare effects. Finally, money competed as a store of value with other types of assets (scarce consumer durables, Western currency, real estate, insurance savings, savings deposits), particularly, but not only, in the private sector. As in market economies, positive welfare effects are the yardstick for the use of money in socialist planned economies. To the extent that the economic agents in the private and socialist sectors of the economy were able to create scope for decision making within the system of administrative planning and to use this in the interest of the individual agent,[32] the active role of the various functions of money became relevant, and controlling the monetary aggregates became a policy issue for the GDR's monetary authorities.

---

[29] Cf. Ökonomisches Lexikon, 1967, p. 1046.
[30] Cf. Ehlert *et al.*, 1985, p. 89.
[31] Cf. Grossman, 1983; Podolski, 1973; Thieme, 1977–8.
[32] Cf. Hartwig, 1987, pp. 18ff.

b) Monetary planning and the central economic plan

How the system worked

The functions of money in administrative socialism, central monetary planning, and the monetary policies of the Staatsbank in the GDR can only be understood when seen against the background of the all-embracing central planning of the non-monetary economic process.[33] The GDR's State Planning Commission produced commodity-based accounts of input, output, and use; these formed the basis for all economically relevant decisions about the use of available resources (non-monetary and human capital), their regeneration over time (investment) and external economic supplementation (exports/imports). Since it was impossible to undertake complete non-monetary planning for objective reasons (an inconceivable number of inter-linkages) and the time involved (one-year or two-year economic plans), the detailed planning focused on strategically important sectors of the economy; the number of these central accounts varied, depending on the state of the economic reforms. Aggregated figures were used for planning and accounting in the other sectors; the subordinate planning institutions in the planning hierarchy (ministries, associations of state-owned companies, district economic councils, state-owned companies, etc.) broke these aggregate figures down into planning targets, and the fulfilment of these targets was monitored.

Under the system of central economic planning which was practised —with occasional modifications—until 1989, as roughly sketched out here, the task of monetary planning was to determine in advance the monetary aggregates needed for the planned non-monetary transactions.[34] The approach taken was to use the law of monetary circulation: the planned non-monetary variables were converted into monetary units using the prices fixed by the state, and the quantity of money required was derived from this, taking into account the velocity of money forecast.

This method was based on a comprehensive system of financial accounts: the state budget plan, the balance of money earned and spent by the socialist sector of the economy, the balance of money earned and spent by the population (including the remaining private companies), the balance of cash received and disbursed by all state institutions, banks and companies, the credit position, the financial position of the state, and the balance of payments. The planned figures were subsequently checked against the actual figures and helped to monitor fulfilment of the plan.

[33] Cf. Hensel, 1959, for the structure and logic of macroeconomic non-monetary planning.
[34] For more details cf. Gutmann, 1954, pp. 13ff. and Hartwig, 1987, pp. 44ff.

TABLE 6: Budget plans of the GDR for 1975 and 1988 (in billion DM)

	Expenditures			Revenues	
	1975	1988		1975	1988
cience/technology	1.5	3.3	State-owned companies	78.0	180.2
ıvestment	3.4	10.4	Socialist cooperatives/		
ıbsidies	14.2	66.5	private craftsmen	5.0	10.3
ulture/social affairs	39.7	72.2	Wage tax/social insurance	10.7	18.3
oreign trade and payments		37.8	Foreign trade and payments		20.7
lousing	4.3	16.0	Culture/social affairs	12.7	22.4
efence/security	9.6	21.6	Other	8.3	17.8
ther	41.5	41.7			
otal	114.2	269.5	Total	114.7	269.7

urce: Höfner, Ernst/Kaminsky, Horst: Einschätzung zur Stabilität der Währung der DDR, appendix -7 (Archiv der Kreditanstalt für Wiederaufbau, Berlin office, GVS B11–291/89 Berlin [East] 1989).

Domestic economy

Because of the all-embracing role played by the state in administrative socialism, the state budget plan was of key significance for the system of accounts. The main source of revenue was the levies from the socialist sector of the economy (transfer of net profits, product-based levies, levies for the production and trade fund, and contributions to social funds); the main expenditure items were investment, price subsidies, defence, the government apparatus, and cultural and social work. The budget plan, for which the actual figures from two selected years are presented in Table 6, also formed part of the comprehensive financial position of the state.[35]

The account plan for the socialist sector of the economy consisted of the aggregated balance of monetary income and expenditure. These figures were disaggregated to produce the monetary plans for the individual companies. They detailed planned revenues, expenditures, borrowings, debt repayments, and the planned transfers of profits to the state budget and to corporate funds. The formation and expenditure of the financial assets were listed separately, with planned borrowing—because of its effect on the money stock—being particularly significant.

[35] Cf. Gurtz and Kaltofen, 1982.

TABLE 7: Structure of the credit account of the Staatsbank der DDR
(in billion Mark, position at end of year)

	1970	1989		1970	1989
Credits			Deposits/gold assets		
to companies	82.7	270.4	of companies	18.8	48.3
to housing and social			of housing and social		
organizations	22.6	108.5	organizations	3.9	12.3
to the population	0.9	2.9	Savings and insurance		
			assets of the population	59.1	174.4
			Cash in circulation	7.4	17.0
Other credits	6.1	39.6	Other assets	20.3	54.3
to foreign countries	3.2	47.1	Foreign debts	6.0	162.2
Total	115.5	468.5	Total	115.5	468.5

Source: Staatsbank der DDR, Kennziffern zur Entwicklung des Geld- und Kreditvolumens
(Archiv der Kreditanstalt für Wiederaufbau, Berlin office).

The balance between the stock of consumer money and the stock of goods
was planned via the account of money earned and spent by the population.
On the basis of given prices, forecast savings levels and planned availability
of consumer goods, it was possible to determine the level of nominal incomes needed for a periodical market clearance.

Because of the special significance attached to notes and coins in circulation, the Staatsbank produced an annual cash turnover account intended to
monitor cash stocks. It was based on the planned cash turnovers of the banks
and the reported cash requirements of the socialist sector of the economy.
All companies, banks and organizations had to transfer cash holdings to the
Staatsbank.

These accounts covered periodical flows; they were supplemented by the
macroeconomic credit account, which contrasted all credits with deposits
and cash holdings on a certain day, including the external positions in Ostmarks (Table 7). This inventory account is important in terms of money
stock theory, because it reveals the macroeconomic volume of cash and
deposit money issued. For this reason, the credit account was subject to the
approval of the Council of Ministers of the GDR. The plan was based on
the draft plans from the ministries, the applications of the banks for credit,
and annual estimates of the cash requirement, taking account of the forecast
velocity. The authorities responsible for undertaking the planning were
the Staatsbank, the State Planning Commission, and the Finance Ministry.

The credit account was broken down to derive the lines of credit for the banks.

These accounts—supplemented by the account for the insurance system —were collated horizontally to form the financial position of the state, the aim being to ascertain the aggregate of all flows and stocks of finance and to bring them into line with the non-monetary plans.[36] The target of achieving revenue surpluses each year in the state budget plan (successfully until the mid-1980s!) led to a rising burden of levies on the socialist sector of the economy, with companies increasingly financing themselves from loans; some traditional government activities were also separated out of the state budget, transferred to other institutions and financed by credit (house-building companies took over responsibility for building state facilities).

Foreign economy

Since domestic and external economic relations were kept strictly separate, all external economic transactions were covered separately in two balances of payments.

An account was drawn up of the planned income and expenditure of foreign currencies from export and import transactions on the basis of centrally planned foreign trade transactions. The development of credit flows between the GDR and other countries was recorded in the external credit inventory account. A further inventory account listed the foreign currency reserves and claims and obligations regarding other countries. All three subordinate accounts of the current account were divided into groups of countries: COMECON countries, OECD countries, OPEC countries, Latin American countries, West Germany, and developing countries with which bilateral relations were maintained.

All these external sub-accounts were then netted out: the foreign currencies were converted into 'valuta' marks on the basis of fixed exchange rates (termed 'basic' rates) set by the state. The 'valuta' mark was merely an internal, fictitious unit of account in the GDR to create comparability between different currency units. The internal balance of payments denominated in Ostmarks was then produced by converting the export revenues recorded in 'valuta' marks at exchange rates set specifically for different countries and goods (i.e. using various exchange coefficients (*Richtungskoeffizienten*) to correct the basic rates). In this way, a wide range of exchange rates specific to different countries and goods and varying over time existed; they remained a well-guarded state secret, because they revealed the actual competitiveness of GDR products on the world market.

[36] Cf. Frenzel, 1989, p. 83.

c) Functions of the Staatsbank and the banking system

Structure and political integration

The GDR's banking system was—except during a short period (1968–74)—organized as a single tier. The Staatsbank was the central issuing bank and the central loan, cash, and clearing institution for the whole economy. It was at all times a key agency of the Council of Ministers and had to provide the monetary conditions appropriate to the central plans adopted. The President of the Staatsbank had a seat and a vote on the Council of Ministers. The Staatsbank was directly accountable to the Council of Ministers and had to obey its resolutions: 'the Staatsbank of the German Democratic Republic . . . is the central organ of the Council of Ministers for implementing in its entirety the monetary and credit policy adopted by the Party and the Government.'[37] The President and Vice-President were appointed by the Chairman of the Council of Ministers. They in turn nominated directors and branch managers.

The Staatsbank was at no time independent in its decision making; it acted as an agent for the central planning administration and only enjoyed very limited scope to take decisions and impose monetary sanctions if the plans were not being fulfilled. Greater autonomy—in the sense of independence—would not have been compatible with the system, because that would have endangered the central planning and thus the foundations of the economic and political system.

Until 1967, the Staatsbank functioned both as a central and as a commercial bank. However, between 1945 and 1967, the Minister of Finance was directly responsible for a few banks (Deutsche Investitionsbank, Deutsche Bauernbank, savings banks, Bank für Handwerk und Gewerbe, Postal Giro and Savings Offices, and the Postsparkasse and the Reichsbahnsparkasse, i.e. the savings banks of the post office and railways). This meant that, *de facto*, the ministry was able to conduct a separate credit policy of its own, bypassing the central bank and without any need for approval from the central bank: this further heightened the dependence of the central bank on the political decision makers up to 1967.

Between 1968 and 1974, the two general economic reforms mentioned above (NÖSPL; ÖSS) ended the direct control of the finance minister over the central bank and also introduced a sort of two-tier banking system. The central bank was renamed 'Staatsbank' and its functions were restricted to the traditional ones of a central bank. This led directly to conflicts between

[37] Gesetz über die Staatsbank, section 1.

central monetary planning and the actual developments controlled decentrally (on the credit market), which presented a threat to the entire system, and the political decision makers reacted by considerably restricting the discretionary powers of commercial banks as early as 1971. In July 1974, the whole two-tier banking system was abolished. The attempt to establish a decentralized economic system (a 'socialist market economy') failed, not least because of the monetary side. All the central bank and commercial bank functions were concentrated back in the Staatsbank (Figure 1).

The other banks were allocated specific tasks for certain sectors of the economy and were answerable to the Staatsbank; the President of the Staatsbank had authority to instruct and supervise them. They basically acted as branches of the Staatsbank. The Staatsbank set the principles and conditions for payments, clearing, and credit. The lack of competition in the way the responsibilities were distributed was intended to increase the efficiency of monetary control: the savings banks were responsible for the population; farms held their accounts at the Bank für Landwirtschaft und Nahrungsgüterwirtschaft; and cooperative banks for crafts and trades were responsible for the craft firms. Together with its branches, the Staatsbank accounted for most of the business in the banking sector; it was responsible for industry, the construction sector, trade, and transport.

Tasks in the domestic economy

By law, the Staatsbank was charged with 'actively influencing the continuous growth of the economy, the increase in labour productivity, and the preservation of the stability of the currency'.[38] In order to fulfil this mandate, the Staatsbank had to assume three functions (in addition to issuing notes and coins): clearing, financing, and supervising/sanctioning.

The bank was able to fulfil its clearing function, because all companies had to keep their money stocks in accounts and to transfer payments via the banking system. Cash was only allowed to be used for wage payments of up to M 200 to private individuals. Loans from one company to another were prohibited; there were no credit markets. As cashless payments (transfers and cheques) also became more common in the private sector, the clearing function became increasingly important in this sector as well.

The financing function consisted of issuing loans for operating resources and investments to the socialist and private business sectors, to housebuilding companies, and—to a limited extent—to consumers; the figures stipulated in the plan for the credit account were 'issuing directives'. Increasing company losses, bottlenecks in supply and liquidity, and rising

---

[38] Gesetz über die Staatsbank, section 1.

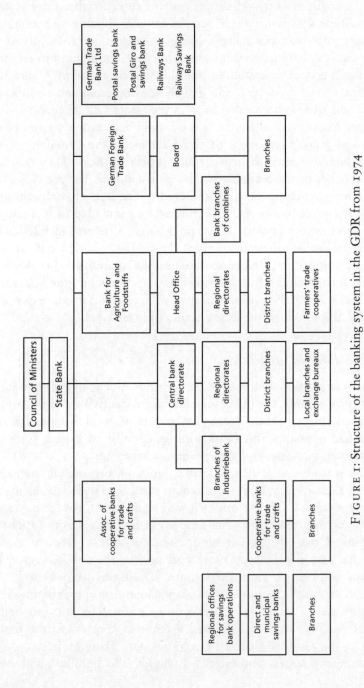

FIGURE 1: Structure of the banking system in the GDR from 1974

Source: Bundesministerium für innerdeutsche Beziehungen, 1985, p. 147.

transfers of earnings to the state budget kept increasing the proportion of credit in the total volume of financing, making it more and more difficult for the Staatsbank to fulfil its financing function in a way that would maintain stability.

The Staatsbank's supervision and sanction function referred to planning and the implementation of the plan ('control via the mark'). Supervision of planning was intended to ensure at an early stage that resources were used efficiently. Reports on monetary stability were intended to ensure that the planning process did not endanger the stability of the money in circulation —if necessary via a veto on non-viable investment projects. The Staatsbank was therefore a member of all the important decision making bodies, where its role was to uphold its stability-oriented mandate.

As the plan was implemented, the Staatsbank maintained detailed supervision of the repayment of debts and the formation and expenditure of corporate funds (supervision of the money and wage stocks). The Staatsbank visited the companies to analyse them, advised them on how to improve efficiency (capacity utilization, inventories, etc.), tackled violations of the plan, and monitored the reports made by the companies in order to ensure that no discretionary scope for action which did not conform with the plan would develop in the companies.[39]

If violations of the plan were detected, the Staatsbank had a range of instruments to impose sanctions. If credit agreements were breached, it could call in the debt from the company; if repayment was late, it could retrospectively raise the basic interest rate (5 per cent) to up to 12 per cent (up to 18 per cent between 1967 and 1974). Cuts in the basic rate to as little as 1.8 per cent were possible if the quality of production was particularly good, and increases in the rate to 8 per cent could be imposed if the output was of bad quality or late: this was intended to boost the efficiency of production. The bank could also tighten operational supervision, cut bonus funds, and appoint supervisory bodies to monitor the work of companies.

Despite the many instruments at its disposal, the Staatsbank's actual influence remained very limited. The main reason was its total dependence on the political decision makers. It had no influence on decisions to close loss-making companies; that was politically undesirable in view of the aim of full employment. It is true that the state budget then subsidized these companies, but in doing so it shifted more and more of the responsibility for this into the credit system, thereby causing the Staatsbank indirectly to finance the state budget by creating money. Similarly, the punitive interest rates were not an effective sanction mechanism, because they did not represent a tough

[39] Cf. Pütsch, 1978, pp. 138ff.

budget restriction. At the end of the day, the Staatsbank had to provide the monetary back-up to make all the political decisions work, and this considerably increased the potential for conflict between the Finance Ministry and the Board of the Staatsbank.

The system of international payments

The monopoly on external economic relations in the GDR consisted of monopolies on foreign trade and on foreign payments. As in the domestic economy, central institutions planned all non-monetary foreign trade deals; special foreign trade companies managed the trade in goods.[40] The Deutsche Außenhandelsbank and the Deutsche Handelsbank, both of which acted entirely in line with instructions from the Staatsbank, were responsible for settling all international payments. The Ostmark was not convertible; imports and exports of it were prohibited. Transactions with other countries were based on world market prices recalculated as domestic prices; the conversion coefficients were adjusted to meet the needs of the various plans. Losses arising from discrepancies between the planned and actual prices were covered by the state budget, profits had to be transferred to it. The price differences deriving from all foreign trade were accumulated on an account set up specifically for this purpose.

On behalf of the Staatsbank, the Deutsche Außenhandelsbank bought and sold the foreign currency needed for foreign trade, and processed international credit relationships (mostly on the basis of bilateral agreements on foreign trade) and international payments. The foreign trade companies had to sell their foreign currency (revenue from exports) to it or buy that currency from it (to purchase imports). There were multiple exchange rates for individual countries and categories of goods; these were deliberately used to direct foreign trade. Responsibility for setting the exchange rates rested with the President of the Staatsbank. The Deutsche Handelsbank was exclusively responsible for the financial management of transit trade.

Foreign trade between the socialist member countries of COMECON was mainly settled in transferable roubles. This currency existed only in the form of deposit money obtained by drawing tranches (in accordance with fixed country quotas) from the International Bank for Economic Cooperation based in Moscow. The transferable rouble was fixed at a set rate against the Western currencies. Because the socialist countries' national currencies were not convertible, they were supposed to negotiate the transaction prices with their partners and pay them in transferable roubles. Strictly speaking, the transferable rouble only acted as a means of clearing and not as a means

---

[40] Cf. Buck, 1980, pp. 144ff.

of barter or a store of value, because no uniform prices for goods were used in trade between the socialist countries.[41]

d) Money supply and monetary targets

The production of money in accounting terms

In the GDR's single-tier banking system, the Staatsbank had the exclusive right to issue credit/set maximum credit levels and to issue currency. Both credit and currency were central bank money: there was no separate right for commercial banks to create deposit money themselves. In this way—unlike the situation in market economies—there was only one form of money stock. This rendered monetary instruments like refinancing policy, open-market policy, or minimum reserve policy superfluous: money was created when the Staatsbank issued credit and was destroyed when the loans were repaid to the Staatsbank. With the exception of the currency reserves, the Staatsbank's credit account comprised the total extent and structure of the macroeconomic money stock.

On the asset side of the credit account there were the elements of money supply creation: credits to the socialist and private sector, to the housing sector, and to social organizations and institutions, to private individuals and, from 1974, to investment projects which were regarded as state projects and were to be repaid from the state budget. The central bank thus indirectly financed the state budget. Central bank money was also created by exchanging currency reserves held by the foreign trade companies. However, this item comprised the entire net foreign position of the GDR, including assets in transferable roubles, which strictly speaking did not assume any monetary function. In addition, there were the foreign currency stocks held by private individuals, which really functioned as money because they were either sold to the Staatsbank or used to buy goods in state Intershops or on black markets. An influx (or outflow) of foreign currency thus always implied an increase (or drop) in the money stock.

The liability side of the credit account comprised the monetary holdings of various types: private cash holdings, the deposits of private individuals, of the socialist and private business worlds, of the public budgets, of the house-building companies, and of social organizations and institutions. In addition, the balance of accumulated budget surpluses had to be included on both sides of the account. They siphoned-off liquidity from the economy, served only to safeguard the liquidity of the public budgets, and thus did

[41] Cf. Clement, 1990, pp. 191ff.

not function as a means of payment. There were also various other items
on both sides of the balance sheet.[42]

Definitions of the money stock

As in market economies, the money stock can be defined either from the
origin side or from the expenditure side. On the expenditure side, the amount
of money available for transaction purposes, as a currency purely for domestic use, consisted of the cash holdings of private individuals, the current
account and savings account deposits of the private individuals (which did
earn interest and thus also acted as a store of value but could be withdrawn
at any time and were thus comparable to current accounts at banks in market
economies), and the deposits of companies, the house-building sector, and
the state budget, adjusted for the accumulated budget surpluses.

This definition is similar to the traditional M1 money stock measure and
is used in section 4 for an empirical analysis. In addition to cash held in the
GDR, the foreign currency (especially D-mark) held by private individuals
should also be included; however, as the amount of this cannot be determined statistically and it accounted for a small proportion of the total money
stock, it is disregarded. A broad money stock measure, roughly comparable
to M3, would have to include the entire expenditure side of the balance
sheet, i.e. also those deposits held by private individuals which acted solely
as stores of value. The definition of the money stock derived from M1 is
narrower than that officially used in the GDR, which corresponded to the
entire balance on the credit account on one day, i.e. including all stores of
value and not adjusted for the state budget item. Also, the net foreign position was excluded, but this does not make sense, because when the GDR
was a net debtor—as it was from 1964—foreign currency loans from the
Deutsche Außenhandelsbank were sold for Ostmarks to the foreign trade
companies to secure the planned imports of goods. As a result, the money
stock fell in line with the net debt position. To this extent, the definition of
the money stock in the GDR did not reflect the monetary stimuli correctly.

Targets and indicators of monetary policy

In the restrictive model of a system of central non-monetary and monetary
planning, there would be no place for a specific central bank monetary

---

[42] The other items included the initial provision of cash from the 1948 currency reform
and claims against the state budget deriving from this time, funds of the state insurance
companies, other assets and liabilities of the banks, and payments going through the clearing
process.

policy. In practice, however, such a policy was necessary in the socialist planned economies, because imperfections in non-monetary planning and price-setting created uncertainties for monetary planning. These uncertainties were exacerbated by the scope for decision making in the state-owned companies and the private sector; this scope was used in order to raise revenue for individual economic agents even if it meant that the macroeconomic planning targets were not fulfilled. This made it impossible for the Staatsbank to determine the precise money stock required in advance, resulting in mismanagement of the monetary aggregates. In order to arrive at the desired 'unity of monetary and non-monetary planning', an intermediate monetary target was needed—one closely related to the targets of monetary policy, capable of being guided by the monetary authorities, and quickly and precisely measured. Although the interrelationships were not explicitly dealt with in GDR literature on monetary theory, they can be derived from it and demonstrated by it.[43]

The prime target of monetary policy in the GDR was the stability of money in circulation,[44] which consisted of three components: a stable development of money income in the population, monetary stability in the sense of a stable price level, and a constant long-term velocity of money, i.e. a stable relationship between money supply and national income. The stability of the development of money income was to be achieved by the state setting wages in line with productivity trends and by administrative price-setting. The fulfilment of the two objectives was the responsibility not of the Staatsbank but of the political leadership, which set retail prices in particular according to social criteria.

The Staatsbank was therefore solely in charge of managing the money stock in order to prevent a superabundance or deficiency of currency and deposit money in the economy. Even a socialist planned economy with a single-tier banking system adhered to the principle that the supply of money corresponds to the demand for money. The decision makers in the GDR assumed that price inflation could be adequately prevented by having prices fixed by the state and aimed at a constant long-term velocity of money in order to create a stable relationship between money supply and national income. This led to a need for an intermediate monetary target, similar to the objective of a potential-oriented monetary policy in Western market economies: the money stock should grow at the same rate as real national income.

This was also stated in the official GDR literature: 'for monetary policy,

---

[43] Cf. Thieme, 1982, pp. 192f. and Hartwig, 1987, pp. 65ff. and Hartwig and Thieme, 1985, pp. 175ff.
[44] Cf. Ehlert *et al.*, 1985, pp. 36ff.

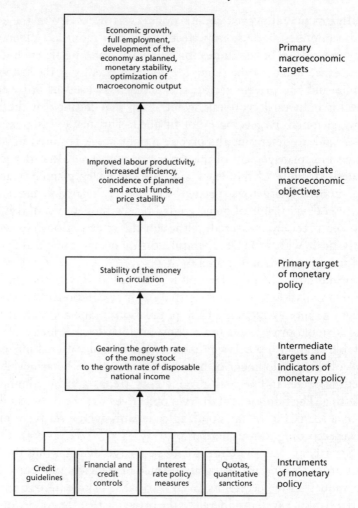

FIGURE 2: Interrelationship between targets
and tools of monetary policy of the GDR

this implies a need to couple the growth in the money stock to the development of disposable national income.'[45] The relevant income variable was
national income, adjusted for the balance of foreign trade and the reconciling
items resulting from the price conversions undertaken for foreign trade; it
was described as the 'domestically used' or 'disposable' national income.

The instruments of monetary policy needed for this were based on the
planning of currency and deposit money in circulation and control of the

---

[45] Schmidt and Waldhelm, 1984, p. 438.

volume of credit. The provision of credit to socialist companies accounted for the bulk of the volume of credit. Logically, the Staatsbank and its widespread network of branches concentrated on controlling this; to do so, it had recourse to interest-rate tools, legal criteria on issuing credit, company checks, and credit quotas (cf. section 3c). The currency in circulation was influenced by differentiated interest rates for sight deposits and savings-oriented insurance policies.

Figure 2 summarizes the relationships between objectives, intermediate targets and instruments of monetary policy in the GDR, showing clearly that monetary policy was always strictly subordinate to the macroeconomic objectives and political functions.

4. Effects and functional problems of monetary control in the GDR

a) Control of the money supply and inflation

Measurement problems and empirical findings

In formal terms, the policy basis for an efficient control of the money supply and thus of the inflation rate did exist in the GDR. There was a consistent interrelationship between objectives and tools and a centralized apparatus for monetary control which had an exclusive right to produce money.

In reality, the Staatsbank evidently found it far more difficult to achieve potential-oriented growth in the money stock.

As Figure 3 shows, a distinction can be made between three phases of monetary policy in the GDR: until 1970, the growth rate of the money stock was dramatically greater than that of real disposable national income, and a substantial potential for inflation from cash holdings was created. In the early years of this phase, the monetary surplus from the currency reform continued to make itself felt.[46] From 1971, the Staatsbank in the GDR—especially in comparison with other socialist countries—did reasonably well at conducting a stability-oriented policy; it came closest to achieving its objectives between 1971 and 1980; in the run-up to 1989, the stability-oriented approach of the preceding years softened again to some extent. The first phase in particular saw abrupt cyclical fluctuations in the money supply.

---

[46] As already mentioned (footnote 27), the GDR leadership's deliberately expansionary monetary policy in the 1960s exacerbated this problem.

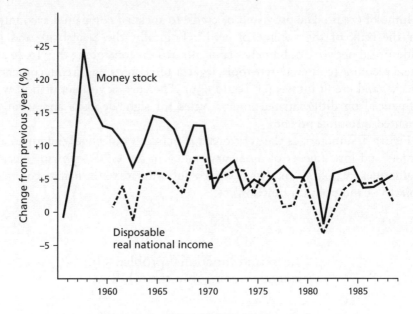

FIGURE 3: Growth of the money stock
and the disposable real national income of the GDR*

* For the definition of the money stock, see section 3(d).

Source: Staatsbank der DDR, Kennziffern zur Entwicklung des Geld- und Kreditvolumens (Archiv der Kreditanstalt für Wiederaufbau, Berlin office), author's own calculations.

The lack of free prices makes it difficult to measure monetary imbalances. The state-administered prices were not influenced by the growth in the money stock; further, they were also an instrument of economic and social policy and thus totally distorted. The officially recorded price indices are therefore useless. Because the transmission of monetary stimuli was interrupted by government-fixed prices, any inadequacies in the growth of the money stock initially only influenced the cash holdings of the economic agents and their behaviour (inflation in cash holdings or 'pent-up' inflation). The nominal money holdings were devalued not by rising prices in the official sector but by the increasing impossibility of obtaining goods at all (rationing of goods at fixed prices). This meant that the potential inflation deriving from the cash holdings could only—if at all—be alleviated to the extent that the administered price level rose or transactions were possible on black markets at free prices. Because of strict controls, the inflation in cash holdings was extremely persistent. To arrive at a precise indicator of the potential for inflation, it is necessary to measure the unplanned (involuntary) change in the cash-holdings coefficient. Because this is impossible, the

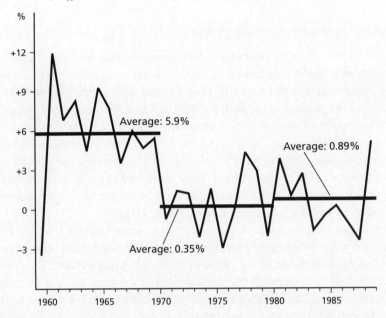

FIGURE 4: Growth rates of the cash-holding coefficient of the GDR*

* cf. Footnote 48.

Source: Staatsbank der DDR, Kennziffern zur Entwicklung des Geld- und Kreditvolumens (Archiv der Kreditanstalt für Wiederaufbau, Berlin office), author's own calculations.

intermediate monetary target can only be used to provide approximate indications of the planned development of cash holdings. If the intention is to keep the velocity of money stable, the growth rate of the cash-holdings coefficient would have to be equivalent to zero in the long term.[47] Figure 4[48] confirms that in the first period of very expansionary monetary policy, the cash-holdings coefficient recorded a continuous and very sharp rise.

After the early 1970s, the growth rate of the cash-holdings coefficient diminished substantially. The systematic interrelationship between the development of the money stock and cash-holdings coefficient confirms its usefulness as an indicator of inflation. Taking this yardstick, the Staatsbank did relatively well at avoiding a substantial potential for inflation from the 1970s.

[47] Cf. Hartwig and Thieme, 1979, p. 108.
[48] The reader is reminded that the money stock aggregate used here also comprises money in its function as a store of value (private savings deposits which could be used as a medium of exchange at any time).

Causes of monetary mismanagement

A vital factor affecting monetary developments was the way money was created when credit was issued. If the temporary monetary imbalances are to be explained, it is necessary to take a closer look at the pattern of credit demand in the private sector and, particularly, in the state-owned companies.

As in market economies, the companies were able to achieve their own individual objectives by optimizing their operations. The main aims were to maximize the income of the employees and to increase the power, security, and respect of the management under the socialist social system.[49] Under the prevailing system, these aims could only be achieved if the management succeeded in fulfilling or exceeding planning targets.

The incentive structures in place (bonus systems) meant that the risk of failure to fulfil the planning targets had to be avoided. Such risks resulted from the imperfections of the administrative planning system: shortages of materials, faulty input products, machinery down-times, and sudden changes in directives were the norm, and endangered companies' ability to fulfil the plan. To protect themselves against this, companies took advantage of the fact that they had more information than the planning authorities. When the plan was being drawn up, they fought for low output targets and the highest possible input figures, because this would create leeway for coping with potential bottlenecks.[50] The consequence was an excessive need for finance. The better the companies were at realizing their own interests in the planning and banking system by providing distorted valuations, listing fictitious projects, etc., the greater was the demand pull for credit, which increased the money stock without any corresponding rise in real output. The payment of such non-performance bonuses meant that this effect also impinged on the private sector. The asymmetrical distribution of information between companies and planning authorities thus implied a permanent danger of a demand pull for credit which put any stability-oriented monetary policy at risk.[51] The cause of this lay not in the actions of the Staatsbank, but in the system itself.

The private sector's direct influence on the macroeconomic demand for credit was limited. Consumer credit accounted for a small proportion of the overall volume of credit; it was tied to the purchase of durable consumer goods (e.g. cars), and the repayment was regulated in detail. Even so, the purchases and cash holdings of the private sector did have an indirect influ-

---

[49] Cf. Leipold, 1988, pp. 238ff.; Kuczynski, 1978, pp. 229ff.

[50] It was possible to observe how companies in the GDR tended very much to hoard materials, which also enabled them to barter scarce resources amongst themselves.

[51] Cf. Hartwig and Thieme, 1987, p. 227.

ence on corporate credit demand: if, because the wrong quality or quantity had been planned, the goods on offer did not meet with private-sector demand, the companies had to tolerate a rise in current inventories and take up additional credit in order to meet their payment obligations. Consumer restraint and increased private-sector cash holdings obstructed the planned return of the money to the corporate and banking sector. As a result, the money could not be destroyed as planned within the intended period.

In order to counter these demand-side credit factors and to be able to control the volume of credit and thus the nominal money stock so that the target would be attained, the supply side of credit would have had to make use of efficient instruments to alter the price and ration the quantity. However, the Staatsbank's interest-rate instruments were at best blunt: interest-rate sanctions were intended to reduce company profits and thus the level of the bonus funds. In many cases, companies were able to allege that they had made improvements in the quality of the goods, permitting them to raise prices and thus to pass on the additional costs deriving from interest rates to the consumers (hidden price inflation). Furthermore, it was not the profits, but the net output or labour productivity figures which determined the level of the bonus funds. It is likely that corporate credit demand even reacted abnormally to increased interest rates, because companies with a weak financial base had already anticipated the costs of future interest-rate sanctions in their credit demand. At best, therefore, interest-rate rises had no effect; in many cases, they led to a rise in credit demand.

The second way to control the volume of credit was for the Staatsbank to ration the quantity, which it did in isolated cases. However, this always resulted in an institutional conflict, because such measures meant that the whole planning process had to be revised, entailing a great deal of administration and conflicts of interest between the various authorities. A more fundamental reason why the quantitative sanction failed was a fundamental defect in the system: because of the macroeconomic objective of full employment, companies could not go bankrupt. The banks were forced either directly or indirectly, to bail out loss-making companies.[52] The companies either received non-planned credits at higher interest rates, which resulted in the interest-rate-averse demand effect described above, or the state budget subsidized them directly. Since the state budget was unable to cope with this in the long term, government tasks which ought really to have been funded from taxes were increasingly shifted to the credit sector from the mid-1980s, and thus funded by an increase in the money stock. The volume of government work financed each year from the credit system stood at M 1.9 billion in 1986 and had risen to M 11.7 billion by 1989. In total, the

[52] Cf. Thieme, 1990, pp. 85ff.

state budget owed the banking system M 12 billion in 1970, M 43 billion in 1980 and no less than M 123 billion in 1988, including M 42 billion in loans for residential construction. Following the eighth party congress of the SED from 15–19 June 1971, social policy and house-building policy particularly contributed to the increasing credit-based funding of the state budget.[53] In addition, the amount of levies imposed on companies was increased, and this in turn resulted in increased borrowing by companies. The proportion of loan-funded investment by companies rose from 5 per cent (1965) to 40.3 per cent (1980) and 60 per cent (1989). The loss-making companies were directly or indirectly bailed out by the banks. This leads to interesting conclusions regarding the GDR's credit market.

The macroeconomic credit demand function comprised the demand for credit from the private sector and that from the state-owned business sector; demand for credit from the private sector was so small that it can be disregarded. Demand for credit from state-owned companies generally depended on the interest rate for credit, the real national income, the amount they needed to offset unforeseeable deficiencies in the plan, and the cash holdings of private individuals. It can be assumed that there is a positive relationship between all of these variables, including the interest rate, and the level of demand for credit, i.e. any increase in one of the variables, also resulted in a rise in demand for credit from state-owned companies. Because the companies had better information than the planning authorities, they could also ensure that their desire for credit would be fulfilled at any time.

As a result, the supply of money and credit was—as in market economies —determined endogenously: the companies particularly (as they could not go bankrupt) had a massive influence on the level of borrowing and thus on the money supply. The institutions responsible for monetary policy only had limited control over the supply of credit and money under this system.

This is confirmed empirically for the GDR, at least over certain periods. However, the monetary authorities were increasingly successful from the 1970s onwards at controlling corporate demand for credit, and the 1971–80 period was particularly stability-oriented. In comparison with the policies of other central banks in socialist planned economies, the monetary policy of the Staatsbank in the GDR was a great success.

The effects of monetary stimuli

If monetary imbalances are of relevance in a socialist planned economy, it

---

[53] Cf. Höfner, Ernst/Kaminsky, Horst, Einschätzung zur Stabilität der Währung der DDR, pp. 23f. (Archiv der Kreditanstalt für Wiederaufbau, Berlin office, GVS B11–291/89, Berlin [East] 1989).

is necessary to investigate how economic agents react to them, with any non-monetary effects being of particular interest. In the case of the GDR, certain systemic peculiarities need to be noted when undertaking this type of transmission analysis: because the scope for decision making was limited, because the number of relevant assets was limited, and because the GDR economy was an almost entirely closed system for economic agents, quantitative reactions were restricted. Nevertheless, once it has been put into context, the theory of wealth developed for market economies is an appropriate means of explaining the reactions, because even in the GDR the assets had different yield rates and portfolio switching involved transaction costs. Given that prices of goods and factors were fixed by the state, rationing and black markets were of vital significance. In the GDR, as in other socialist planned economies, the short-term and long-term effects of monetary stimuli were affected by the formation and anticipation of expectations.[54]

In the GDR's closed socialist planned economy, in which the state's planning agencies determined all macroeconomic variables (especially the price level and the nominal wage), with the exception of the actual labour supply, there was officially full employment, which the state ensured via its centrally planned demand for labour. The 'socialist unemployment' which was to be observed at all times in the GDR can be explained as follows: those supplying labour set the actual amount of labour they supplied in line with the real wage and were able independently to vary the quality or intensity of their labour input (e.g. leisure on the job), and this influenced output via the production function. The actual supply of labour therefore equalled the planned ceiling of full employment minus the 'social employment', which was determined by the person supplying the labour and which, in economic terms, would have failed to materialize. This depended on the real wage, although it was uncertain, in view of the rigid prices, whether it would be possible to spend an increased nominal income on goods at all. Often, increased nominal income was not matched by a rise in output in line with demand, which caused a rise in cash holdings and a rationing of demand on the consumer goods market. Those supplying labour therefore built expected changes in the price level and cash holdings into their calculations.

This realistically assumes that, in view of the autoregressive expectations assumed here,[55] the people supplying labour in the GDR only temporarily laboured under the illusion that every additional unit of income in the form of money actually represented a realizable claim on the national product.

Where there was an expansionary monetary stimulus without a nominal

---

[54] Cf. Thieme, 1987, pp. 300ff. for more details of this model.
[55] This is realistic inasmuch as economic information in the GDR was not available, or available only at very high cost.

wage increase, the rate of social employment initially remained unaltered, because expectations were not immediately adjusted. Once (after some time) the expectations had been adjusted to the rise in nominal and—at a constant price level—real cash holdings, those supplying labour reduced their real supply of labour; the rate of social employment rose. In consequence, macroeconomic output fell. This means that real effects of monetary stimuli can be derived from the variable actual qualitative supply of labour determined by those supplying labour, and that these effects are of empirical relevance.

Where black markets existed, our investigation must be widened: scarce goods and services (e.g. of craftsmen) were traded in the GDR's second economy; these had been produced in the official sector or on the black market itself and were bartered for other goods and services or for Western currency, and in the consumer goods sector even for Ostmarks.[56] It can plausibly be assumed that those supplying labour expanded the availability of labour in the second economy at least partially at the expense of the supply of labour in the official sector, or by substituting leisure time. In many cases, additional input factors (in the form of materials, machinery, or intermediate products) were removed from the official sector. The effects on macroeconomic output depend on the different levels of labour productivity in the two sectors. It is clear that productivity in the private sector was higher than that in the state sector; however, the removal of material and labour may also have caused a disproportionately steep drop in productivity in the official sector, which more than offset the positive effects of the second economy. It should also be remembered that monetary surpluses expressed themselves in the form of price inflation in the second economy.

Quantitative rationing and the inflation in cash holdings also had long-term adverse effects on growth, because scarce input factors needed to be used in the formation and anticipation of expectations in order to avoid the consequences of inflation.[57]

The omnipresent quantitative rationing meant that inflation of cash holdings caused queues. The costs arising from waiting (e.g. shopping during working hours) had a negative impact on the input of labour in companies. Rationing and high transaction costs incurred in the purchase of a specific good created incentives to buy those consumer goods which might be useful in barter exchanges. The scarcity of goods was exacerbated by the hoarding of scarce goods for barter. This distorted the basis of information about consumer requirements, leading to misallocations in subsequent planning periods. Quantitative rationing thus limited the functions of money; barter-

---

[56] Cf. Sell and Thieme, 1980, pp. 127ff., for the significance of Western currencies in the GDR.
[57] Cf. Cassel, 1987, p. 277.

ing of goods and services dramatically increased the transaction costs. In addition to the 'commodity money' created, Western currency was also used as a means of payment, because it could be used to purchase scarce goods in the Intershops. Finally, rationing was also overcome by exploiting personal connections (buying goods 'off the back of a lorry') and by corruption, which also caused considerable costs to society and reduced overall prosperity. These activities created the network of black markets, on which the demand for production factors on the part of state-owned companies frequently competed with a demand for the same factors on the black market.

The interpersonal distribution of income and wealth was also influenced by quantitative rationing and the inflation of cash holdings: anyone unable to get round the rationing in some way, or without recourse to black markets, had to bear the costs of inflation of cash holdings, which reduced his real income. Similarly, those whose income was not brought into line with the rate of inflation of cash holdings (e.g. those on welfare and pensioners) also suffered because they had less funding with which to offset the consequences of inflation.

b) Foreign trade, foreign debt, and currency reserves

In the GDR, the most important objective of economic policy was to achieve equilibrium on the balance of payments, which was understood to mean a long-term constancy of foreign currency reserves, as achieved when the value of imported and exported goods was equal and the credit position was zero. As with other sectors of the economy in the GDR, all external activity was centrally directed; the planned external revenue and expenditure was documented in the Finance Ministry.

The procedures of central planning and control for external transactions were extremely complex: the (internal) balance of payments was deemed to be in equilibrium when the positive and negative differences between the planned and actual prices in foreign trade cancelled out and the values of imports and exports as calculated in Ostmarks were equal. To achieve this, the central planning administration used various instruments of foreign trade policy and monetary policy, such as export subsidies, preferential and foreign-currency loans for foreign trade companies, and the so-called exchange coefficients (*Richtungskoeffizienten*), which were used to convert world market prices into internal (Mark) prices for specific companies, and which led to a wide variety of fictitious exchange rates. Deficits on foreign trade which arose out of differences between the planned and the actual prices or quantities had to be financed from the state budget.

The development of the GDR's foreign debt needs to be broken down

TABLE 8: International competitiveness of the GDR

Year	Foreign currency yield[a]	Exchange rate against the US$[b]	Exchange rate against the DM[b]
1970	0.537	7.56	1.80
1975	0.519	5.50	2.20
1980	0.454	4.75	2.50
1985	0.338	7.80	2.60
1987	0.255	9.20	4.00
1988	0.246	8.14	4.40

[a] 'Valuta' marks earned from exports per Ostmark.

[b] Commercial exchange rate in trade with non-socialist economies including the exchange coefficients ('Richtungskoeffizienten') (in Mark der DDR).

Sources: Höfner, Ernst/Kaminsky, Horst: Einschätzung zur Stabilität der Währung der DDR, appendix 4 (Archiv der Kreditanstalt für Wiederaufbau, Berlin office, GVS B11–291/89, Berlin [East] 1989); List of the Staatsbank, appendix 4 (Archiv der Kreditanstalt für Wiederaufbau, Berlin office, GVS b5–1374/88, Berlin [East] 1988).

by region and period. There were no deficit problems with other socialist countries, because GDR products were very competitive. Deficits arose only in the early 1970s, especially in trade with the Soviet Union; between 1975 and 1988, because of rising oil prices, the GDR earned surpluses in trade with other COMECON countries.[58]

Because of the increasingly obvious deficiencies in innovation and growth in the GDR as compared with Western market economies from the mid-1960s, policy on foreign trade and payments was reoriented: a (limited) uptake of hard-currency loans was intended to close the gap in technology that had arisen. Domestic output was oriented more to Western markets in order to boost exports and to enable the loans to be served. Cooperation between companies and the barter of goods and services (not involving foreign currency) were intended to prevent balance-of-payments deficits.[59] As Table 8 shows, the international competitiveness of the GDR recorded a continuous decline.

[58] From 1988, the GDR began having foreign trade difficulties with the Soviet Union. Cf. Höfner, Ernst/Kaminsky, Horst, Einschätzung zur Stabilität der Währung der DDR, pp. 14f. (Archiv der Kreditanstalt für Wiederaufbau, Berlin office, GVS B11–291/89, Berlin [East] 1989).

[59] Cf. Buck, 1980, pp. 153f.

Net borrowing in hard currencies from Western industrial countries rose until 1983 because the level of dependence on imports grew and GDR goods became less competitive on the world markets. The state budget absorbed the foreign trade deficits of companies, causing the level of internal debt to rise. Between 1985 and 1988 alone, the claims of foreign trade companies on the state budget rose from M 24.5 billion to M 65 billion.[60]

Paradoxically, the GDR administration actually made the weak growth even worse because hard-currency loans were not used much—if at all—to purchase capital goods. They were spent on imports of consumer goods or hoarded: the Commercial Coordination Section (KOKO) headed by Alexander Schalck-Golodkowski, which was in charge of acquiring foreign currency, had hoarded almost US $10 billion by 1989,[61] which was invested abroad to earn interest. These foreign currency reserves originated in loans and were intended to document the international solvency and credit-worthiness of the GDR (putting 'liquidity ahead of profitability'). It seems likely that only Schalck-Golodkowski and Günter Mittag were aware of these high currency reserves, and not the *Politbüro*, which assumed there was a far higher net external debt (of approximately US $21 billion). In fact, the net external debt amounted to about US $14 billion in 1989, so the GDR certainly did not come to grief in a 'debt trap'.[62] The GDR was without doubt solvent in 1989. However, the international competitiveness of the GDR's economy had deteriorated dramatically, which would have caused financial problems in servicing the debt in the longer term.

5. Monetary experiments in socialism: conclusions

The history of the mark in the GDR is interesting and instructive in various ways.

First, the numerous institutional reforms show that supplying money under a system of central planning and controlling in a socialist society is certainly not without problems. Indeed, the nationalized ownership of the means of production, the decentralized availability of information, the scope for decision making that exists in the planning process, and, finally, the fact

---

[60] Cf. Höfner, Ernst/Kaminsky, Horst, Einschätzung zur Stabilität der Währung der DDR, Appendix 4 p. 1 (Archiv der Kreditanstalt für Wiederaufbau, Berlin office, GVS B11–291/89, Berlin [East] 1989).

[61] In 1982, GDR assets held in Western banks amounted to only between US $1 and 2 billion, but had reached approximately US $6 billion by 1985. Cf. Volze, 1996, p. 703.

[62] Cf. Volze, 1996, p. 701, and estimates of the Bundesbank which arrived at similar conclusions as early as 1990. Cf. Deutsche Bundesbank, 1990, p. 26.

that state-owned companies cannot go bankrupt all combine to produce a system in which the conditions determining the central bank's ability to impose strict controls on the money stock are unfavourable.

Secondly, the analysis shows clearly that one key problem facing the central bank as it controlled the money stock in the GDR—as in other countries with central planning—was that of supplying the economy with monetary holdings in a way which would preserve stability *and* at the same time of directing capital into productive uses in the (single-tier) banking system. Because of the lack of efficient capital markets, this dual function continually created conflicts of interest which were resolved politically. To this extent, the central bank, which was dependent on political decisions (especially on the financing of the budget deficit, which had been rising in the GDR from the mid-1980s) had no independent responsibility of its own to bring to bear on monetary processes.

Thirdly, a comparison with other socialist countries shows that, in the circumstances, the central bank of the GDR did relatively well at controlling the supply of money to the GDR economy—particularly from the 1970s onwards—in a stability-oriented manner, and thus at avoiding serious cycles of inflation of cash holdings or prices. This indicates that the Staatsbank actually had a very strong position in the GDR's power structure. As the lack of innovation and growth, and especially the quality of the capital stock in the GDR at the end of the 1980s prove, it was not possible to ensure an efficient allocation of capital in the long term in the single-tier banking system. This, together with the distortions and mismanagement in the non-monetary sector of the economy, which were inherent in the system itself, is the reason for the economic failure of the socialist experiment in the GDR.

6. Key events in monetary policy

28 April 1945   Order to close the banks in the Soviet occupation zone.

23 July 1945   Order to block funds from the time before 9 May 1945 and to establish provincial and Länder banks and savings banks. In the ensuing months, reopening of state banks for individual sectors of the economy.

21 May 1948   Establishment of the Deutsche Emissions- und Giro-bank as a predecessor of the Deutsche Notenbank.

24–8 June 1948   Currency reform in the Soviet zone. Initially, the Reichsbank banknotes had coupons stuck onto them before they were exchanged for new banknotes from 25–8 July.

20 July 1948	Deutsche Emissions- und Girobank renamed Deutsche Notenbank and given the right to issue notes and coins.
13 October 1957	Exchange of cash in the so-called 'minor currency reform'.
1 December 1967	Dissolution of the Deutsche Notenbank and founding of the Staatsbank der DDR. Establishment of a two-tier banking system giving scope to the commercial banks. Role of the Staatsbank restricted to that of a central bank.
1 July 1974	End of the two-tier banking system with the reintegration of the Industrie- und Handelsbank into the Staatsbank. Currency renamed 'Mark der DDR'.
1 July 1990	Monetary union with the Federal Republic of Germany ends the monetary independence of the GDR.

7. Sources and bibliography

Unpublished sources

Archiv der Kreditanstalt für Wiederaufbau, Berlin office
Bundesarchiv Koblenz and Berlin

Bibliography

Abeken, Gerhard (1955): Das Geld- und Bankwesen in der sowjetischen Besatzungszone und im Sowjetsektor Berlins 1945 bis 1954, Bonn

Befehl des Chefs der Besatzung der Stadt Berlin betr. Bankenschließung from 28 April 1945, no. 1 (in extracts) in: Kohlmey, Gunther/Dewey, Charles (1956) (eds.): Bankensystem und Geldumlauf in der Deutschen Demokratischen Republik 1945–1955, Gesetzessammlung und Einführung, Berlin (East), p. 115*

Befehl des Obersten Chefs der Sowjetischen Militär-Administration—des Obersten Befehlshabers der Gruppe der sowjetischen Okkupations-Armeen in Deutschland no. 146 from 20 November 1945, in: Kohlmey, Gunther/Dewey, Charles (1956) (eds.): Bankensystem und Geldumlauf in der Deutschen Demokratischen Republik 1945–1955, Gesetzessammlung und Einführung, Berlin (East), pp. 122–4

Befehl Nr. 14 from 15 January 1946. Betrifft: Wiedereröffnung der Gewerbe-Handwerker-Banken (gew. Volksbank) in der von den Sowjets besetzten Zone Deutschlands, in: Kohlmey, Gunther/Dewey, Charles (1956) (eds.): Bankensystem und Geldumlauf in der Deutschen Demokratischen Republik 1945–1955, Gesetzessammlung und Einführung, Berlin (East), p. 125

Buchheim, Christoph (1988): Die Währungsreform 1948 in Westdeutschland, in: Vierteljahrshefte für Zeitgeschichte 36, pp. 184–231

Buck, Hansjörg (1980): Stabilisierung der Außenwirtschaftsbeziehungen von administrativ-sozialistischen Wirtschaftssystemen durch Zahlungsbilanz- und Finanzpolitik, in: Schüller,

Alfred/Wagner, Ulrich (eds.): Außenwirtschaftspolitik und Stabilisierung von Wirtschaftssystemen, Stuttgart, pp. 143–94

Bundesministerium für innerdeutsche Beziehungen (1985) (ed.): ³DDR Handbuch, Cologne

Cassel, Dieter (1987): Inflation und Inflationswirkungen in sozialistischen Planwirtschaften, in: Thieme, H. Jörg (ed.): ²Geldtheorie. Entwicklung, Stand und systemvergleichende Anwendung, Baden-Baden, pp. 263–94

Chef der Besatzung der Stadt Berlin: Order no. 01 dated 23 July 1945. Neuorganisierung der deutschen Finanz- und Kreditorgane, in: Kohlmey, Gunther/Dewey, Charles (1956) (eds.): Bankensystem und Geldumlauf in der Deutschen Demokratischen Republik 1945–1955, Gesetzessammlung und Einführung, Berlin (East), pp. 115–18

Clement, Hermann (1990): Funktionsprobleme der gemeinsamen Währung des RGW, in: Wagener, Hans-Jürgen (ed.): Monetäre Steuerung und ihre Probleme in unterschiedlichen Wirtschaftssystemen, Berlin, pp. 187–212

Deutsche Bundesbank (1990): Die Währungsunion mit der Deutschen Demokratischen Republik, in: Monatsbericht 42, 7, pp. 14–29

Deutsche Finanzwirtschaft 11 (1957) 2, p. 321

Dewey, Charles (1956): Die Planung und Regulierung des Geldumlaufs in der Deutschen Demokratischen Republik, Berlin (East)

Ehlert, Willi/Hunstock, Diethelm/Tannert, Karlheinz (1985) (eds.): Geld und Kredit in der Deutschen Demokratischen Republik, Berlin (East)

Frenzel, Paul (1989): Die rote Mark: Perestroika für die DDR, Herford

Gesetz über die Staatsbank der Deutschen Demokratischen Republik from 19 December 1974, in: Gesetzblatt der Deutschen Demokratischen Republik, part 1, no. 62, Berlin (East) 1974, pp. 580–2

Grossman, Gene (1968) (ed.): Money and Plan, Berkeley

Grossman, Gene (1983): A Note on Soviet Inflation, in: Joint Economic Commitee, Congress of the United States (ed.): Soviet Economy in the 1980's: Problems and Prospects, Washington D.C., pp. 267–86

Gurtz, Johannes/Kaltofen, Gotthold (1982): Der Staatshaushalt der DDR, Berlin (East)

Gutmann, Gernot (1954): Theorie und Praxis der monetären Planung in der Zentralverwaltungswirtschaft, Stuttgart

Haffner, Friedrich (1987): Monetäre Zentralplanung und Volkswirtschaftsplanung, in: Thieme, H. Jörg (ed.): ²Geldtheorie. Entwicklung, Stand und systemvergleichende Anwendung, Baden-Baden, pp. 194–216

Hartwig, Karl-Hans (1987): Monetäre Steuerungsprobleme in sozialistischen Planwirtschaften, Stuttgart

Hartwig, Karl-Hans/Thieme, H. Jörg (1979): Schwankungen von Geldmenge, Umlaufgeschwindigkeit und Inflationsrate: Diagnose und Meßprobleme in unterschiedlichen Wirtschaftssystemen, in: Thieme, H. Jörg (ed.): Gesamtwirtschaftliche Instabilitäten im Systemvergleich, Stuttgart, pp. 97–115

Hartwig, Karl-Hans/Thieme, H. Jörg (1985): Monetary Goals and Indicators in Centrally Planned Economies: The Example of the German Democratic Republic, in: Jahrbuch der Wirtschaft Osteuropas 11, pp. 173–86

Hartwig, Karl-Hans/Thieme, H. Jörg (1987): Determinanten des Geld- und Kreditangebotes in sozialistischen Planwirtschaften, in: Thieme, H. Jörg (ed.): ²Geldtheorie. Entwicklung, Stand und systemvergleichende Anwendung, Baden-Baden, pp. 217–39

Henning, Friedrich-Wilhelm (1993): ⁸Das industrialisierte Deutschland 1914 bis 1992, Paderborn et al.

Hensel, Karl Paul (1959): ²Einführung in die Theorie der Zentralverwaltungswirtschaft, Stuttgart

Kohlmey, Gunther (1956): Das Geldsystem der Deutschen Demokratischen Republik, Berlin (East)

Kohlmey, Gunther/Dewey, Charles (1956) (eds.): Bankensystem und Geldumlauf in der DDR, 1945 bis 1955, Gesetzessammlung und Einführung, Berlin (East)

Kreditanstalt für Wiederaufbau, Berlin office (1996): Appendix to materials 'Mit der D-Mark zur Wirtschafts-, Währungs- und Sozialunion und zur Deutschen Einheit', Berlin

Kuczynski, Waldemar (1978): The State Enterprise under Socialism, in: Soviet Studies 30, pp. 313–53

Leipold, Helmut (1988): 5Wirtschafts- und Gesellschaftssysteme im Vergleich, Stuttgart

Marx, Karl (1885/1989): Das Kapital, vol. 2, 29th edition, Berlin (East)

Möller, Hans (1976): Die westdeutsche Währungsreform, in: Deutsche Bundesbank (ed.): Währung und Wirtschaft in Deutschland 1876–1975, Frankfurt a.M., pp. 433–83

Mülhaupt, Ludwig/Fox, Ursula (1971): Das Bankwesen der Deutschen Demokratischen Republik, Wiesbaden

Nove, Alec (1980): Das sowjetische Wirtschaftssystem, Baden-Baden

Ökonomisches Lexikon (1967), 2 vols., Berlin (East)

Podolski, Tadeusz (1973): Socialist Banking and Monetary Control, Cambridge

Pütsch, Manfred (1978): Die Staatsbank der Deutschen Demokratischen Republik, Frankfurt a.M.

Rittmann, Herbert (1986): Deutsche Geldgeschichte seit 1914, Munich

Roeper, Hans (1978): Die D-Mark. Vom Besatzungskind zum Weltstar, Frankfurt a.M.

Schmidt, Hans/Waldhelm, Jürgen (1984): Die aktive Rolle des Geldes bei der planmäßigen Ausnutzung der ökonomischen Gesetze des Sozialismus für die effektive und proportionale Gestaltung der intensiv erweiterten Produktion, in: Wirtschaftswissenschaft 32, pp. 437–43

Sell, Erwin/Thieme, H. Jörg (1980): Nebenwährungen bei zentraler Planung des Wirtschaftsprozesses, in: Schüller, Alfred/Wagner, Ulrich (eds.): Außenwirtschaftspolitik und Stabilisierung von Wirtschaftssystemen, Stuttgart, pp. 127–41

SMAD-Befehl Nr. 111/1948 über die Durchführung der Währungsreform in der sowjetischen Besatzungszone Deutschlands, in: Kohlmey, Gunther/Dewey, Charles (1956) (eds.): Bankensystem und Geldumlauf in der Deutschen Demokratischen Republik 1945–1955, Gesetzessammlung und Einführung, Berlin (East), pp. 193–200

SMAD-Befehl Nr. 124/1948 über den Geldumtausch, in: Kohlmey, Gunther/Dewey, Charles (1956) (eds.): Bankensystem und Geldumlauf in der Deutschen Demokratischen Republik 1945–1955, Gesetzessammlung und Einführung, Berlin (East), pp. 242–3

Sprenger, Bernd (1991): Das Geld der Deutschen: Geldgeschichte von den Anfängen bis zur Gegenwart, Paderborn et al.

Thieme, H. Jörg (1977–8): Inflation in westlichen Marktwirtschaften und östlichen Planwirtschaften, in: List Forum 9, pp. 290–309

Thieme, H. Jörg (1982): Geldpolitik im Wirtschaftssystem der DDR, in: Gutmann, Gernot (ed.): Basisbereiche der Wirtschaftspolitik in der DDR, Asperg, pp. 187–212

Thieme, H. Jörg (1987): Produktions- und Beschäftigungswirkungen monetärer Impulse in sozialistischen Planwirtschaften, in: Thieme, H. Jörg (ed.): 2Geldtheorie. Entwicklung, Stand und systemvergleichende Anwendung, Baden-Baden, pp. 295–318

Thieme, H. Jörg (1990): Geldangebotssteuerung bei unterschiedlichen Unternehmens- und Marktverfassungen, in: Wagener, Hans-Jürgen (ed.): Monetäre Steuerung und ihre Probleme in unterschiedlichen Wirtschaftssystemen, Berlin, pp. 77–98

Volze, Armin (1996): Ein großer Bluff? Die Westverschuldung der DDR, in: Deutschland-Archiv 29, pp. 701–13

XII. The Role of the Bundesbank in Intra-German Payments

By Jochen Plassmann

1. Introduction

'Intra-German payments' means payments between the Federal Republic of Germany and the German Democratic Republic (GDR), which operated both legally and technically on a very different basis from payments with other countries. The legal basis for intra-German payments was formed by the Allied foreign exchange control laws, which remained in force until the GDR acceded to the Federal Republic in 1990.

Commercial payments took place through the clearing system of intra-German trade used to settle payment of strictly bilateral deliveries of goods and services in both directions. The agreement of an interest-free overdraft facility (known as the 'swing') ensured that payments could be settled relatively smoothly even if their timing did not always coincide. One characteristic of this 'tied' system of payments was that each side could only use the credited units of account for purchases in the other state.

However, in addition to the 'tied' system of payments, a continuously increasing volume of 'free' payments developed with the GDR in the course of time; this was operated via 'free' accounts, i.e. in free (non-tied) D-marks through accounts held by the GDR at West German banks. These 'free accounts' were used both for merchanting trade with the GDR and for substantial government payments, e.g. for the upgrading of the *autobahn* on the transit routes to West Berlin and for the payment of the annual lump-sum transit fee. In theory, it would have made sense and fitted in with the system to make the government payments in units of account as well, not least in order thereby to create a reserve of units of account for intra-German trade. However, this was strictly rejected by the GDR, which was interested in acquiring unfettered foreign currency income with which to serve the loans it had taken up on the Euromarket. Just how significant the non-tied D-mark income was for the GDR can be seen from the fact that the surplus of such D-mark payments amounted to about DM 2 billion a year for the GDR from the late 1970s until 1989, i.e. the GDR had access to a high level of foreign currency income each year in the form of non-tied payments from the Federal Republic, and such revenue was far more important for it than the two billion D-mark loans which it received in 1983 and 1984, and which attracted so much attention.

The system of commercial intra-German payments was not the only one to operate according to special rules: there was also a separate system governing non-commercial payments. Treaties with the GDR were concluded on only two aspects: the transfer of maintenance payments and, to a limited extent, the transfer of blocked private accounts. In addition to this, however, there were a large number of unilateral non-commercial payments to the GDR which were primarily permitted on humanitarian grounds. These particularly included payments to the 'Genex-Geschenkdienst', which totalled DM 3.5 billion by 1989. The Genex-Geschenkdienst ('Genex present service') was an institution established by the GDR in 1962 via which goods which were either unavailable in the GDR, or for which there was a long waiting list, especially private cars, could be ordered for immediate delivery to the recipient—the payment being made in *Valuta*, i.e. freely convertible foreign currency.

There was another peculiarity in the system of non-commercial payments with the GDR: in each state, foreign exchange regulations generally blocked all funds owned by people resident on the other side. Whilst the GDR basically maintained the system of blocked accounts in order to stop foreign currency leaving the state, the priority of the Federal Republic was to protect the inhabitants of the GDR from the requirement contained in the GDR Foreign Exchange Act that they offer and hand over to the state any funds held in the West.

The Bundesbank played a key role in intra-German payments. As the authority responsible for foreign exchange, it was in charge of operating and authorizing payments, and, as the clearing bank, it was in charge of implementing the agreements on clearing concluded with the GDR. Whilst the technical implementation of the clearing transactions was purely a banking matter, the Bundesbank's activities as the foreign exchange authority must primarily be seen in the light of government policy on relations between the two German states.

2. Interzonal payments following the division of Germany into occupation zones

When the War ended in May 1945 and Germany was divided into four zones of occupation, commercial transactions between the zones virtually came to a standstill. The Potsdam Declaration of 2 August 1945 stated that

'Germany shall be treated as a single economic unit', and there were plans for common policies on commerce, currency, transportation, and communications. In line with this decision, commercial transactions started moving again between the occupation zones, first between the US and the British zones (subsequently the 'Bizone') and later also with the French zone. Since there was little change in the economic system in the western occupied zones, it was possible for payments there to be settled via the existing banks. In contrast, most of the existing banks in the Soviet occupied zone were closed down, industry was nationalized, and trade in goods with the Western zones of occupation was permitted only very gradually, with the Soviet model of strictly monitored barter trade becoming the method used.[1]

The first agreement between the Bizone and the Soviet zone on reciprocal trade in goods was concluded in Minden on 18 January 1947; it provided for the settlement of payments via accounts of the East Berlin Stadtkontor (a municipal bank) at the Land Central Banks in Hanover, Frankfurt am Main, and Karlsruhe. This agreement marks the beginning of intra-German trade. However, the Soviet blockade of Berlin put a halt to interzonal trade as early as 1948. It was not until the so-called Jessup–Malik Agreement of the Four Powers of 4 May 1949, which led to the end of the Berlin blockade, that the conditions were created for a recommencement of interzonal trade.[2]

The recommencement of interzonal trade was agreed in the Frankfurt Agreement of 8 October 1949. It contained all the major principles subsequently included in the Berlin Agreement of 20 September 1951, which remained in force until 1990. The Frankfurt Agreement was concluded between the currency areas of the *Deutsche Mark (DM-West)* and the currency areas of the *Deutsche Mark* of the Deutsche Notenbank (*DM-Ost*), since the Federal Government refused to recognize the GDR under international law. In order to make it clear that the agreement covered both Berlin (West) and East Berlin, both sides were referred to not as the 'currency area' (in the singular) but as the 'currency areas'. The need to stipulate an exchange rate between the Western and the Eastern Mark was avoided by stating that all payments were to be made via clearing accounts at the two central banks denominated in units of account. It was left to each side to decide how to convert the units of account into the respective currencies; whilst on the West German side the rate of 1 unit of account = DM 1 was retained until the end of the clearing system on 30 June 1990, the secret 'exchange coefficient' (*Richtungskoeffizient*) was altered several times by the East

---

[1] Cf. Kühne, 1974, pp. 4ff.

[2] The link made in the Jessup–Malik Agreement between free access to West Berlin and unimpeded interzonal trade was a significant factor behind the smooth operation of intra-German trade in the following years.

German side over the years, ending in an exchange rate of 1 unit of account = 4.40 Mark der DDR (*Ostmark*; M), although the fiction of a 1:1 rate was maintained for the outside world.[3] The Frankfurt Agreement and the subsequent Berlin Agreement both contained an inter-bank agreement between the central banks in the West and the East (the Bank deutscher Länder and the Deutsche Notenbank), stipulating the details of the clearing system.

3. System of payments under the Allied foreign exchange control laws; responsibility and role of the Bank deutscher Länder and the Land Central Banks

As far as West Germany was concerned, the particular relationship between the two German states meant that commerce and payments between the Federal Republic of Germany and Berlin (West) on the one hand and the German Democratic Republic and Berlin (East) on the other were not categorized as foreign trade and payments, but were instead *sui-generis* trade which, until the accession of the GDR to the Federal Republic of Germany in 1990, was governed by the foreign exchange control laws adopted by the Allies in their respective zones of occupation after the end of the War.[4] Under these foreign exchange control laws, all of which contained the same provisions, all transactions in intra-German trade and payments were prohibited unless they were expressly authorized.

Article III figure 15 letter c of Military Government Law no. 60 transferred much of the responsibility for carrying out the Allied foreign exchange control laws to the Bank deutscher Länder, which was established on 1 March 1948. The bank had already been given responsibility for issuing licences by General Licence no. 8 of the Military Government.

When, in 1957, in accordance with section 1 of the Bundesbank Act, the Bank deutscher Länder was merged with the Land Central Banks and the Berliner Zentralbank to become the Deutsche Bundesbank, article III figure 15 letter c of Military Government Law no. 60 was the only provision of the law to remain in force, so that the powers granted to the Bank deutscher

---

[3] In effect, the introduction of the 'exchange coefficient' devalued the Ostmark, although the leaders of the GDR did not wish to admit this to the outside world. The rate in force in 1990 was a very good reflection of the productivity gap between the Federal Republic and the GDR. It would therefore have made sense to take this rate as the basis of intra-German monetary union: it was certainly more realistic than the rate chosen by those responsible in western Germany.

[4] Cf. Military Government Law no. 53 for the US and British zones; Ordinance no. 235 for the French zone; Kommandatura Decree no. 500 for Berlin.

Länder were transferred to the Bundesbank. Similarly, the powers originally granted to the Berliner Zentralbank were transferred to the Bundesbank.

In addition to the responsibilities for governing the system and issuing licences, the Bank deutscher Länder (and later the Bundesbank and the Land Central Banks) was also granted a right to obtain information and carry out audits under foreign exchange control laws in accordance with article III of Military Government Law no. 53 in conjunction with article 2 paragraphs 1 and 2 of Law no. 33 of the Allied High Commission. To meet this responsibility, the Bundesbank issued guidelines on the surveillance of intra-German trade and audits of banks, in order to enforce the foreign exchange control laws.

4. Clearing transactions and the 'swing' under the Berlin Agreement and the inter-bank agreements between the Deutsche Bundesbank and the Staatsbank der DDR

The Frankfurt Agreement was replaced in 1951 by the Berlin Agreement and, in the version dated 16 August 1960, this formed the treaty basis for intra-German trade until mid-1990. Details of technical payment arrangements were regulated by an agreement concluded between the Bank deutscher Länder and the Deutsche Notenbank, according to which all payments had to be settled via clearing accounts held centrally by the Deutsche Bundesbank and the Staatsbank der DDR.[5]

The swing system already adopted under the Frankfurt Agreement was continued under the Berlin Agreement of 1951 and the maximum swing set initially at 30 million units of account. The Frankfurt Agreement had given permission for the Federal Government's cash account to be debited when the swing was used, but this was never done: instead, the swing was provided by the Bundesbank alone from 1951 on.

The Bundesbank used section 3 of the Bundesbank Act as the legal basis for the provision of the swing: that states that the Bundesbank shall ensure the due execution by banks of payments within the country. It was assumed that settlement of the centralized payments in accordance with the Berlin Agreement was only possible if the two central banks allowed each other

---

[5] In the 1950s and 1960s, up to 8 clearing accounts existed, but the number decreased in the 1970s to two: sub-account 1/2 for trade in goods and sub-account 3 for trade in services. In addition to sub-accounts 1/2 and 3, the Bundesbank operated another account under the Berlin Agreement for the Staatsbank der DDR, Special Account S, for special payments outside the clearing system.

overdraft facilities on the clearing accounts, on the understanding that this was a technical overdraft facility which 'swung' in both directions. Problems therefore always arose when the swing became more like a permanent loan, since in this case section 3 of the Bundesbank Act no longer provided a secure legal basis. When the swing was extended in 1975–6, this concern was dealt with as follows: the Bundesbank made the provision of the swing dependent on the willingness of the Federal Government to provide the funds necessary to finance the swing in instalments at the request of the Bundesbank. However, the Bundesbank never took advantage of this possibility, which was agreed in an exchange of letters with the Federal Ministry of Economics. Since the average swing utilized by the GDR in the 1980s decreased substantially and, in 1988 and 1989, the Bundesbank itself actually took advantage of the swing, the question of the legal basis of the swing ceased to play a role. In those years, the question of credit-worthiness was a priority for the GDR, and the fact that it made little use of the swing was deliberately intended as an indication of credit standing, even if this brought economic disadvantages for the GDR. The *Politbüro* had issued a call putting 'liquidity ahead of profitability'.

The swing was increased several times over the years. In 1968, the Federal Government concluded an agreement with the GDR, to run until 1975, under which the level of the swing was made dependent on the volume of intra-German trade and set at 25 per cent of the previous year's purchases from the GDR. It was also agreed that there should be no annual settlement of accounts. This 'dynamic' swing system was intended to boost the amount of goods purchased from the GDR, i.e. when the GDR increased its deliveries to the Federal Republic, it was rewarded with a higher swing. At the time, the West German side assumed that by the time the swing agreement expired in 1975, the GDR would be in a position to achieve a balanced trade in goods between the two sides without an increased swing. These expectations were not fulfilled, so that the 25 per cent arrangement was extended, subject to the condition that the swing would not exceed 850 million units of account. In 1982, this arrangement was replaced by an agreement under which the swing was gradually reduced to 600 million units of account in the period up to 1985. The last swing agreement of 5 July 1985 again provided for a ceiling of 850 million units of account for the 1986–90 period.

The swing arrangements granted to the GDR were always the focus of great public attention, because the swing was regarded as a political instrument. When it was extended in 1976, for example, attention centred on the agreement by the GDR in return to reduce some of the recent increases in the minimum amounts to be exchanged by West Germans visiting the GDR. In 1982 and 1986, the GDR agreed in return to provide injections of convertible currency enabling the transfer of blocked funds from the GDR to West German recipients. The swing played a major role in financing intra-German trade until the 1970s. Subsequently, trade credits, provided both with and without Federal guarantees, formed the main source of finance. These were supplemented from the 1970s by tied loans for deliveries of capital goods to the GDR, which were also settled via clearing accounts and required Bundesbank authorization under foreign exchange control rules. As a result, the cumulative credit balance with regard to the GDR, i.e. the net debts of the GDR arising from intra-German trade, amounted to about 3.5 billion units of account at the end of 1985; trade credits accounted for about 2 billion, tied loans for 1.3 billion and the swing for only 192 million units of account. Despite this, the swing system remained of great significance for the GDR in subsequent years. Even when little use was made of it, the swing had an important role as a liquidity reserve and for the assessment of the credit standing of the GDR by West German and foreign banks. The availability of the swing particularly served to cement the 'umbrella theory', according to which the Federal Republic would bail out the GDR if it encountered difficulties in meeting its payments.[6]

5. Provision of tied and untied loans to the GDR; GDR debt owed to the Federal Republic

Until mid-1983, the Bundesbank only authorized loans to the GDR when they served to finance transactions in intra-German trade or merchanting transactions by West German transit traders with the GDR. All loans for other purposes or untied financial loans were rejected without exception until that time. In agreement with the Federal Government, this restrictive approach to authorization was justified by the argument that the GDR was only capable of taking up a limited amount of debt from the Federal Republic and that the GDR's remaining capacity to take up debt should be utilized to finance intra-German trade—since this trade was particularly significant in terms of intra-German policy (it helped to hold the country together; it recognized the special relationship between the two states). On these

---

[6] It should be noted that, in addition to the swing, the Bundesbank had provided another method of funding intra-German trade in the form of the Gesellschaft zur Finanzierung von Industrieanlagen (Gefi—Industrial Plant Financing Company) with rediscount facilities under 'Gefi Ceiling II' (amounting latterly to DM 200 million) which could be used on a revolving basis. Cf. Table 1 for developments in intra-German trade and the swing from 1970 to 1989.

grounds, the Bundesbank also rejected all refinancing transactions by German banks to cover loans extended to the GDR by foreign banks (indirect loans to the GDR). The principle that only loans which served the financing of intra-German trade should be authorized was expanded in mid-1983 and 1984, when the two untied billion-mark loans to the GDR were authorized; these loans were guaranteed by the Federal Government and authorized at its request when the GDR's debt position on the Euromarket deteriorated as a result of the crisis in Poland. The Federal guarantees for these loans were justified by the Federal Government on grounds of intra-German policy, as the GDR made humanitarian concessions in return, particularly the removal of automatic firing installations on the intra-German border and improved rules governing intra-German travel. It was also argued that the guarantees did not involve any risk, since if the GDR had failed to keep up with its payments, the Federal Government would have been able to withhold corresponding amounts from the lump-sum transit fees. At the time, it was asked whether intra-German policy could generally provide an objective basis for authorizations under the Allied foreign exchange control laws, as these laws did not expressly mention any specific objective. At the time, the Bundesbank answered this question in the affirmative and regarded intra-German policy as an objective criterion for authorizations, not least because parliament had decided that the Allied foreign exchange control laws should remain in place for intra-German transactions precisely for reasons of intra-German policy.[7] These authorization principles remained unchanged until 1990. Loans to the GDR were authorized only if they benefited intra-German trade or were justified by intra-German policy in other ways. It should also be said that attention was paid to the level of GDR debt owed to the Federal Republic and that the loans were granted for normal commercial periods.

The bilateral debt of the GDR always remained within reasonable limits when measured against factors like the debt-service ratio—not least owing to the Bundesbank's policy on authorization. Consequently, it was possible for the financing of intra-German trade to run fairly smoothly, even at the time when the GDR was facing a critical debt situation on the Euromarket. The reason why intra-German trade did not suffer from the GDR's debt position on the Euromarket in 1982–4, but actually benefited from the situation, was that the bilateral debt in units of account was small in comparison with West German purchases from the GDR, and the clearing transactions represented a separate system which was fenced-off from the GDR's debts to the West in freely convertible currency. At the time, the Bundesbank and the Federal Ministry of Economics shared the view that any moratorium by

---

[7] Cf. section 47(1) the Foreign Trade and Payments Act and the related legislation.

the GDR on the Euromarket could not be applied to the clearing system because any inclusion of the intra-German clearing system in a moratorium would effectively revoke the Berlin Agreement and thus end the special status of intra-German trade.

6. Non-commercial payments with the GDR

a) Legal basis for the Bundesbank's policy on authorization

Whereas agreements were concluded very early on with the GDR for the commercial field, non-commercial payments remained largely ungoverned by such agreements, with the exception of two agreements reached on certain aspects in 1974: the GDR was not interested in adopting any relevant rules. This meant that the Bundesbank generally had to regulate the non-commercial field on its own, and its policy on authorizations was sometimes vigorously attacked by the GDR and its lawyers. In one case involving administrative law being brought against the Bundesbank, it was stated: 'as a foreign exchange authority under Military Government Law no. 53, the Deutsche Bundesbank is claiming a power to issue decrees on intra-German commerce, and is thus laying claim to legislative powers.' The conclusion was drawn that: 'the Bundesbank, as an *ersatz* legislator, is a relict of occupation law and a striking violation of the constitution. Its communications (General Licences) are therefore null and void.'

How justified were these accusations? The impression is correct that the Bundesbank played a key role in intra-German payments which extended far beyond the mandate usually given to a central bank. Under the Foreign Trade and Payments Act, the Bundesbank only has a restricted and secondary responsibility for capital transactions, but Allied law gave it very far-reaching and primary powers of governance and authorization in intra-German transactions, and it used these powers to issue General Licences, individual and block licences, and communications on the settlement of payments with the GDR. To this extent, the statement that the Bundesbank was an *ersatz* legislator was not actually wrong. It is also correct that the military authorities had left it to the discretion of the Bundesbank to decide what arrangements it made and whether to issue licences or not. The Allied foreign exchange control laws did not impose any rules or restrictions, but merely created a general prohibition and empowered the Bundesbank to make rules and issue licences. The transfer of such far-reaching powers to an executive organ was not really possible under the Basic Law, but was tolerated by the Federal Constitutional Court for a transitional period on the grounds that the legislation had been inherited from the occupation. Over the years, the possibility of replacing the occupation law by Federal legislation was reviewed several times, but always postponed in the light of the Berlin problem.

b) The Bundesbank's approach to authorization and its underlying objective

Non-commercial payments with the GDR were subject to the principle that assets of GDR residents located in the Federal Republic were frozen under foreign exchange control rules. In principle, therefore, banks were only allowed to hold blocked accounts and blocked security deposits for GDR residents. Disposal of the assets was permitted only under the rules of the General Licence or on issuance of an individual licence. On the one hand the purpose of this arrangement was to create rules with the GDR on a basis of reciprocity, and the Basic Treaty of 1972 did provide for this. If the assets had been unilaterally released on the West German side, there would have been no chance of a solution on a basis of reciprocity. Agreements on a basis of reciprocity did create problems for the GDR to the extent that GDR residents were scarcely willing to transfer D-marks into the GDR to be disbursed in Ostmarks, whereas a transfer in the other direction, from the GDR, was an attractive proposition for citizens of the Federal Republic. On the other hand the block was intended to protect GDR residents from the requirement contained in the GDR law on foreign currency that assets in such currencies be offered and handed over to the state. The 1973 judgement of the Federal Constitutional Court regarding the Basic Treaty ruled that whenever GDR residents came under the area protected by the state system of the Federal Republic, they had a right to protection from the state; this also applied to assets held at West German banks. The protection thus aimed to protect GDR residents from interference by their own foreign exchange authorities. The GDR made repeated attempts to gain access to these foreign currency accounts. One such attempt was the so-called 'information and transfer campaign' by the Industrie- und Handelsbank der DDR: the Bundesbank succeeded in blocking it.

The Industrie- und Handelsbank der DDR was hived off from the GDR's Deutsche Notenbank in 1968. In 1970–1, it attempted to gain powers of disposal over D-mark accounts of GDR citizens held in West German banks. The account holders in the GDR had to sign declarations of assignment and conferments of authority over their accounts in the West in return for advance payments in Ostmarks, although they could have no interest in doing so, since the D-mark was much in demand in the GDR. The conferments of authority entitled a West Berlin lawyer to demand information, access to savings books, the re-allocation of the accounts and the transfer of the assets. The campaign aimed to deprive the account holders of the power of disposal of their assets and to make the foreign currency available to the GDR. Once the nature of the campaign was understood, the Bundesbank declared that information and disposal on the basis of these conferments of authority represented an impermissible transaction intended to circumvent the law and thus stopped the information from being given and the transfers from being made. After the end of the GDR, it became apparent that this campaign had been a centrally directed attempt by the GDR to obtain foreign currency owned by its citizens, and that the campaign had been run by the Ministry for State Security and the Commercial Coordination Section directed by Alexander Schalk-Golodkowski.

c) *Non-commercial payments not covered by government agreements*

The Bundesbank unilaterally permitted a large number of payments to be made, primarily on humanitarian grounds. These included payments (e.g. voluntary support payments to GDR residents) via sub-account 3, which was actually intended for the settlement of payments for commercial services, payments via 'free' accounts or the GDR's Genex-Geschenkdienst (present service). More than DM 3.5 billion was transferred via the Genex-Geschenkdienst alone to the GDR between 1962 and the end of 1989 with permission from the Bundesbank. The Genex-Geschenkdienst was very attractive because it could be used to order goods which were in short supply in the GDR, especially private cars, cheaply and for immediate delivery in return for payment in D-marks; the Bundesbank also permitted payments by GDR residents to the Genex-Geschenkdienst for 'presents' to themselves; these payments were deducted from the blocked accounts they held in the Federal Republic. However, the transfer of blocked assets was restricted to certain quotas, in order to prevent all the blocked funds from moving into the GDR via the Genex-Geschenkdienst: that would in turn have weakened the West German negotiating position, which aimed to achieve the release of the blocked funds of West German citizens held by the Staatsbank der DDR. In addition to these transfer payments, the Bundesbank authorized a great deal of payments referring to West Germany; these included transactions in real estate and securities by GDR residents, and the result was that those transactions were not really subject to any restrictions on investing their assets in the Federal Republic.

d) Agreements of 25 April 1974 with the GDR
on blocked funds and maintenance payments

It was not until 1974 that the first two agreements were concluded with the GDR on non-commercial payments; these governed the transfer of blocked funds and the transfer of maintenance payments. Previous attempts by the Bundesbank to agree rules with the Staatsbank der DDR had always been rejected by the Staatsbank. The conclusion of these agreements was based on the Supplementary Protocol re article 7 of the Basic Treaty with the GDR, according to which the Federal Republic of Germany and the GDR would enter into negotiations towards arrangements for non-commercial payments and clearing transactions in the interest of those affected. The agreements signed on 24 April 1974 each consisted of an inter-ministerial agreement between the Finance Ministries and an agreement on implementation between the two central banks. Under the agreement on blocked funds, each GDR resident could in principle transfer DM 1,000 a month at a rate of 1:1, whilst the Bundesbank on the West German side could only permit pensioners, people on social welfare, and orphaned minors to transfer money, and that only up to DM 600 per quarter. The reason for this unequal treatment was that it had been possible to conclude the agreement on blocked funds only on the basis of a balance between West–East and East–West payments, and that considerably fewer applications for transfers were made from the GDR than from West Germany. The reason why GDR residents made so little use of the agreement was partly the unfavourable exchange rate of 1:1, but also the fact that the alternatives, i.e. cash withdrawals, purchases in the Intershop and orders of goods via Genex, were much more attractive. It might have seemed obvious to set a different exchange rate, which might have led to a more balanced flow of payments, or to have part of the money paid out in D-marks, but the GDR was unable to accept this in the negotiations: for reasons of political prestige, it insisted on the 1:1 rate and could not countenance any disbursements in D-marks.

Despite the restriction imposed on the transfer entitlement on the West German side, the Bundesbank was faced in 1975–6 with an ever-increasing queue of West German transfer applications which could not be processed owing to a lack of offsetting funds. As a result, the Bundesbank had to stop accepting transfer applications from West Germans for more than two years from May 1976. The situation only improved when, in connection with the agreement on the construction of the Berlin-Hamburg *autobahn*, the GDR agreed to provide DM 50 million a year in quarterly instalments from 1979 to 1982 for the processing of West German transfer applications. As a result of agreements regarding the swing, the GDR then provided DM 60 million a year until 1985 as a contribution towards the transfer of blocked funds. This contribution was raised to DM 70 million a year for the 1986–90 period. Also, the GDR made a one-off payment of DM 60 million at the beginning of 1990 to cover the deficit that had accrued, so that it finally contributed more than DM 770 million towards the transfer of blocked funds. Thanks to these injections of currency, which represented a genuine loss of convertible currency for the GDR, citizens of the Federal Republic who were entitled to receive the transfers obtained blocked funds at a 1:1 rate totalling more than M 830 million out of blocked funds amounting to an undisclosed total; in the same period, i.e. from the entry into force of the agreement until mid-1990, only DM 62 million out of a total stock of approximately DM 3 billion was transferred to GDR residents.

The agreement on maintenance payments created rules for the transfer of such payments and replaced the limited volume of clearing transactions which had previously been possible via the youth welfare office. Under the agreement, maintenance payments to meet eligible family obligations and certain compensation payments could be made at a 1:1 rate via special clearing accounts at the Bundesbank and the Staatsbank der DDR. Unlike the agreement on blocked funds, this agreement did not include the principle that transfers should be balanced; instead, the accounts were balanced via Special Account S. From the time when the agreement entered into force until mid-1990, maintenance payments totalling DM 177 million were transferred to GDR residents and maintenance payments totalling DM 104 million were transferred to citizens of the Federal Republic.

e) Travel payments

Travel by citizens of the Federal Republic to the GDR represented an important source of foreign currency for the GDR. In net terms, the GDR earned well over DM 1 billion a year in foreign currency from travel (Table 2), i.e. the politically and ideologically undesirable influx of visitors was of extremely great importance for the GDR as a source of foreign currency.

It was not until 1985–6 that it was possible to reach agreement with the Staatsbank der DDR on the use of credit cards, travellers' cheques, and Eurocheques during trips to the GDR. The payments were settled centrally via a D-mark account held at the Bundesbank for the GDR's Deutsche Außenhandelsbank.

After the Berlin Wall came down, a common fund of up to DM 3 billion was set up to help visitors from the GDR obtain means of payment; from 1 January 1990, they were able to obtain DM 200 a year in return for Ostmarks: DM 100 was exchanged at the rate of 1:1 and the other DM 100 at

1:5. Almost DM 2.2 billion of the fund was used, 75 per cent of it being provided by the Federal Republic and the other 25 per cent by the GDR. The introduction of the D-mark in the GDR on 1 July 1990 rendered the fund obsolete.

7. Payments with the GDR in untied D-marks via 'free' accounts and foreign accounts authorized under foreign exchange rules; concealed transfers to purchase the freedom of prisoners

Besides the clearing transactions under the Berlin Agreement, the clearing transactions under the agreements on blocked funds and maintenance payments and the payments from blocked accounts, the Bundesbank also permitted certain payment transactions with the GDR in untied D-marks. The payments were settled via freely accessible accounts authorized by the Bundesbank, known as the 'free' accounts; they were held at West German banks, primarily on behalf of banks and foreign trade companies in the GDR. These accounts were originally used only for the settlement of payments by the GDR with other countries via West German banks. From the 1970s, however, the accounts were also used for a substantial volume of payments from the Federal Republic to the GDR and vice versa. The transactions which were permitted in untied D-marks included merchanting trade with the GDR, which amounted to several billion D-marks a year and produced substantial surpluses for the GDR from 1982. Also, transactions with third countries based on cooperation with the GDR were settled in untied D-marks, as long as the goods were shipped directly abroad (and did not form part of intra-German trade). Further, substantial intergovernmental payments were made to the GDR in untied D-marks via free accounts; these included the annual lump-sum transit fee of DM 525 million and payments towards transport projects in the GDR, such as the construction of the Berlin-Hamburg *autobahn* for DM 1.2 billion. In the other direction, the GDR paid grants totalling DM 770 million towards the transfer of blocked funds to eligible West Germans via the free accounts. Also, currency transactions by West German banks with the GDR were conducted via free accounts; the Bundesbank permitted any bank to engage in cash dealings without restriction and in dealings in futures up to a certain level of liability for the GDR. Unlike the income from units of account, which had to be used for purchases in intra-German trade, the GDR was able to dispose freely of the money accruing to it on free accounts. However, it was not allowed to become overdrawn on the free accounts.

The surplus of payments in free D-marks accruing to the GDR amounted to approximately DM 2 billion a year in the 1980s, i.e. the GDR obtained a considerable influx of foreign currency each year from untied payments with the Federal Republic, which it was able to use for trade with Western countries or to service its debts in foreign currencies.

The Federal Government's payments, totalling DM 3.4 billion, to purchase the liberty of prisoners were not made via free accounts. Instead, the freedom was bought with the permission of the Bundesbank via 'church transactions B'.[8] The payments were made to the Diakonisches Werk, which primarily supplied raw materials to the GDR, as it also did via 'church transactions A'. Basically, it was a concealed transfer, since economically there was no difference between the GDR's receiving raw materials and thus saving foreign currency or first obtaining foreign currency and then procuring the raw materials required. The purchase of liberty for prisoners was primarily included in the church transactions with the intention of avoiding or at least hiding the shame of direct payments for the release of prisoners (trafficking in human beings).

8. Political and legal background to the role played by the Bundesbank in intra-German trade and payments

The significance of intra-German trade for the Federal Republic was that it held the two German states together and secured free access to West Berlin. The Bundesbank safeguarded the special status of intra-German trade under foreign currency legislation and, by providing the swing, made a not inconsiderable contribution towards the functioning of trade between the two Germanys. It used foreign currency rules to manage the provision of credit to the GDR in such a way that the GDR's debt to the Federal Republic always remained within reasonable limits; as a result, the clearing system was not put at risk and the Federal Republic was never exposed to blackmail attempts by the GDR, as could have been the case via threats to default if the bilateral debt had been greater. On the other hand, the economic significance of intra-German trade for the Federal Republic was outweighed by the political role. In terms of overall foreign trade, the proportion of intra-German trade always remained below 2 per cent, but its importance for the small and medium-sized companies involved, which accounted for about 80 per cent of it, should not be underestimated.

---

[8] In addition to 'church transactions B' (the 'B' stood for Bundesregierung, or Federal Government), via which the Diakonisches Werk der evangelischen Kirche Deutschlands implemented the transfer of goods for the negotiated purchases of liberty on behalf of the Federal Government, there were also 'church transactions A and C'. These were for payments made by the two main churches to support their sister churches in the GDR.

For the GDR, on the other hand, the economic significance of intra-German trade took priority over the political function. This can be seen simply from the fact that intra-German trade accounted for more than 10 per cent of the GDR's foreign trade and that it helped to fill gaps: production failures and deficiencies in central planning could be quickly and smoothly offset via intra-German trade. Also, the exemption from tariffs and levies brought the GDR considerable economic advantages.

The Bundesbank's restrictive approach to authorizing loans to the GDR helped the Federal Government to use Federal guarantees to obtain political concessions from the GDR in return for the two billion-mark loans. Once again, the emphasis was on political considerations when these two loans and the guarantees were authorized. The accusation made by the former citizens' movement in the GDR that the Federal Government had delayed the collapse of the GDR by several years by granting the loans is hard to justify. Quite apart from the fact that the Soviet Union would not have given up the GDR in 1981–2, even a moratorium on payments by the GDR would not have signified its collapse. The GDR did not use the loans to settle mature debts or to finance investment in improving its economic efficiency. Instead, it kept the equivalent value as assets in Western banks. It was more important for it to be able to record higher assets in the statistics of the Bank for International Settlements as a demonstration of its solvency than to invest in its obsolete manufacturing plant. The assets of the GDR as recorded by the Bank for International Settlements rose from about US $2 billion at the end of 1982 to almost US $10 billion in 1989. Similarly, the net debt owed by the GDR to the West only rose slightly over the same period, to approximately US $13 billion. If the loans had not been made, and the GDR had become insolvent, and this shock had resulted in economic and political reforms in the GDR, history might even have taken a different course as was roughly the case in Hungary for example. After all, the GDR regime was brought to its knees not by its external debts but internally by the changed political situation in the Soviet Union and the lack of prospects in the GDR, which led to the exodus of people, to the formation of a political opposition and finally to the mass protests.

It is true that the Bundesbank was given primary responsibility for intra-German trade and payments and virtually unlimited discretion, but in fulfilling its mandate it did coordinate its actions with the Federal Government and basically supported the political objectives of the Federal Government regarding relations between the two Germanys. When it issued General Licences, it was practically issuing decrees, which is why it was accused of being an *ersatz* legislator. With hindsight, the system of intra-German trade and payments, which was frequently mocked as a fossilized relic, proved its value: the political objectives pursued via the system were achieved.

TABLE 1: Development of intra-German trade and the swing
(in million DM/units of account)

Year	Deliveries to the GDR[a]	Purchases from the GDR[a]	Utilization of swing at year end by GDR	Ceiling on swing
1970	2,484	2,064	424	440
1971	2,652	2,584	429	440
1972	2,960	2,395	581	585
1973	2,938	2,688	613	620
1974	3,662	3,256	620	660
1975	4,028	3,391	756	790
1976	4,470	3,938	718	850
1977	4,663	4,071	660	850
1978	4,754	4,066	795	850
1979	5,093	4,792	798	850
1980	5,875	5,855	814	850
1981	6,129	6,350	583	850
1982	7,080	6,988	491	850
1983	7,681	7,562	481	770
1984	7,251	8,241	273	690
1985	8,585	8,158	192	600
1986	7,837	7,344	194	850
1987	7,366	7,119	233	850
1988	6,838	7,333	−124[b]	850
1989	7,702	7,768	−97[b]	850

[a] Deliveries and purchases comprise both goods and services.
[b] (–): Credit balance of the Staatsbank der DDR at the Bundesbank.

Source: Deutsche Bundesbank, Dept. IZ 1, Tabellen zum Innerdeutschen Zahlungsverkehr, No. IV/1989.

TABLE 2: Payments in freely convertible currency. Payments by the Federa▪

Year	Payments by the Federal Republic to the GDR								Private
	Government agencies				Commercial companies				Private
	Federal Govern-ment	Federal Post Office	Berlin Senate	Total 1+2+3	For goods ship-ments	For mer-chanting trade	For other services	Total 5+6+7	Durin travel
	1	2	3	4	5	6	7	8	9
1980	915	11	22	948	80	419	66	565	1,24▪
1981	1,042	12	25	1,079	78	723	50	852	1,29▪
1982	999	17	25	1,042	105	1,922	28	2,055	1,34▪
1983	741	38	25	803	96	2,022	38	2,156	1,40▪
1984	706	20	29	755	93	2,893	170	3,155	1,42▪
1985	593	38	29	659	106	1,816	103	2,025	1,40▪
1986	682	32	27	741	88	1,182	38	1,307	1,30▪
1987	644	20	25	688	85	898	30	1,013	1,33▪
1988	613	23	99	735	76	796	47	919	1,40▪
1989	591	23	33	646	74	1,006	74	1,155	1,35▪

Note: Differences in totals due to rounding.

Source: Deutsche Bundesbank, Dept. IZ 1, Tabellen zum Innerdeutschen Zahlungsverkehr, nos. I/198▪ und IV/1989.

...Republic to the GDR and payments by the GDR to the Federal Republic (DM million)

itizens		Total payments by the Federal Republic 4+8+11	Payments by the GDR to the Federal Republic				Surplus of payments by the Federal Republic over payments by the GDR	
			Mer-chanting trade[b]	Pay-ments from Account S	Other payments	Total payments by the GDR 13+14+15	excluding mer-chanting trade 18+13−6	including mer-chanting trade 12−16
Other payments[a]	Total 9+10							
10	11	12	13	14	15	16	17	18
94	1,435	2,947	821	12	262	1,096	2,254	1,852
85	1,482	3,412	775	19	280	1,074	2,391	2,338
96	1,540	4,637	511	66	274	851	2,374	3,786
22	1,629	4,588	1,616	73	288	1,977	2,206	2,611
14	1,637	5,548	1,652	66	270	1,987	2,320	3,560
09	1,612	4,296	1,110	45	272	1,427	2,163	2,869
19	1,526	3,574	695	48	334	1,078	2,011	2,497
17	1,554	3,256	750	46	338	1,134	1,973	2,121
19	1,625	3,279	801	46	340	1,187	2,096	2,092
47	1,606	3,407	1,082	43	496	1,622	1,861	1,785

[a] Mainly payments to the Genex-Geschenkdienst.
[b] Transactions by merchanting traders in the Federal Republic and by merchanting traders in the GDR (from 1984).

9. Bibliography

Bopp, Helmut (1983): Wirtschaftsverkehr mit der DDR, Baden-Baden

Deutsche Bundesbank (various years): Innerdeutscher Zahlungs- und Wirtschaftsverkehr, Tabellenheft der Abteilung IZ 1, published by Deutsche Bundesbank, Frankfurt a.M.

Deutsche Bundesbank (1989): Merkblatt über den innerdeutschen Wirtschafts- und Zahlungsverkehr, Zusammenstellung der wichtigsten gesetzlichen Bestimmungen und Verordnungen zur Regelung des innerdeutschen Wirtschafts- und Zahlungsverkehrs sowie der Allgemeinen Genehmigungen der Deutschen Bundesbank und der dazu gegebenen Erläuterungen, published by Deutsche Bundesbank, Frankfurt a.M.

Deutsche Bundesbank (1990a): Die Bilanz des Zahlungsverkehrs der Bundesrepublik Deutschland mit der Deutschen Demokratischen Republik, in: Monatsbericht 42, 1, pp. 13–22

Deutsche Bundesbank (1990b): Die Währungsunion mit der Deutschen Demokratischen Republik, in: Monatsbericht 42, 7, pp. 14–29

Haendcke-Hoppe, Maria (1989): Die Wirtschaftsbeziehungen zwischen beiden deutschen Staaten; in: 40 Jahre innerdeutsche Beziehungen, Schriftenreihe der Gesellschaft für Deutschlandforschung, vol. 29, Jahrbuch, Berlin, pp. 119–39

Kühne, Rudolf (n.d. [1974]): Der interzonale Zahlungsverkehr innerhalb Deutschlands in den Jahren 1945 bis 1973, published by Deutsche Bundesbank, Frankfurt a.M.

Volze, Armin (1996): Ein großer Bluff? Die Westverschuldung der DDR, in: Deutschland-Archiv 29, p. 701–13

XIII. German Monetary Union

By Manfred E. Streit

1. Introduction

The monetary union of 1 July 1990 is a prominent feature of an unprecedented event in German history: the Germans in the GDR revolted peacefully and successfully to overthrow a totalitarian regime. The introduction of the D-mark into eastern Germany initiated a shock therapy for a socialist economic system which, even in the view of the GDR's planning commission, was on the verge of collapse. German Economic, Monetary, and Social Union (GEMSU) transferred not only the monetary system but also the other elements of the west German economic constitution to eastern Germany. That represented a radical institutional break with the socialist past, without parallel in any of the other countries in transition.

This analysis divides into the following sections: first, it shows why, despite the frequent attempts to draw comparisons between the currency reform of 1948 and the currency union of 1990, there are fundamental differences between the two events (Section 2). This demonstrates why the lessons learnt in the post-war period were of limited value when it came to formulating economic policy for GEMSU. It goes on to argue why the GDR's monetary system did not permit a smooth organizational and institutional transfer to the west German system (Section 3). Section 4 analyses the currency conversion, and Section 5 describes how the monetary transformation actually took place in eastern Germany and the solutions arrived at in the course of that process. The final section evaluates the solutions found.

My particular thanks go to Dr Uwe Mummert for his support. He bore the main burden of the necessary research, drafted preliminary versions and was constantly engaged in debate with me. I would also like to thank my other staff members and the doctoral students of the Institute's 'Institutional Economics and Economic Policy' department for checking the paper and providing valuable advice.

2. The currency reform of 1948: a historical parallel?

Both before and after monetary union, historical parallels were sought so that advantage could be taken of previous experience. The limitations of such an approach soon became apparent.

GEMSU was not a currency reform in the sense of a restructuring of an economy's monetary system, as occurred in Germany in 1923–4 after a period of hyper-inflation. Nor did it involve the accession of a region to the area of validity of a currency and the economic constitution of another country with a similar economic system, as happened to the Saarland in 1959. Even the comparison with the currency reform of 1948 will show that the situation in 1990 was fundamentally different.

If a comparison is to be drawn, the relevant factors are not only the initial monetary and real economic conditions: since economic and social union took place at the same time as monetary union, there would also have to be parallels with the abrupt transformation of the system which occurred in 1990. Whenever a system is transformed, there is a radical reform of the institutions[1] which form the parameters in which commerce and society operate. These institutions exert a major influence on monetary and real economic developments. It follows that the initial institutional situation must also be included in the comparison.

a) Initial monetary conditions

In 1948, the monetary situation was characterized by a substantial excess stock of money, high debts on the part of the banks, and a rejection of the Reichsmark by the population. The excess money stock and the banks' debts were the consequence of the 'silent' financing of armaments by the National Socialist government.[2] This financing occurred under an economic system which had certain features of a centrally administered economy. These were,

---

[1] Institutions represent restrictions on human behaviour in repeated interactions. In analysing any group, one finds generally recognized rules which are backed by an enforcement mechanism. The relevant enforcement mechanism is a commonly used criterion for drawing distinctions. Such behavioural rules, the enforcement of which relies on the state's monopoly on force, are termed external institutions. Internal institutions, on the other hand, are behavioural rules based on private sanction mechanisms; they include conventions, customs, and moral standards. Cf. e.g. Kiwit and Voigt, 1995, and Lachmann, 1963, who makes a similar distinction between 'internal' and 'external' institutions.

[2] Cf. e.g. Stolper et al., 1966, pp. 188ff. or Abelshauser, 1983, p. 46, for the technical details.

particularly, that the factors of production were increasingly being allocated by the state, that consumer goods were rationed, that salaries and wages were fixed, and that price controls were in force. The monetary sector was also characterized by restrictions on corporate finance, restrictions on money holdings for individuals, and controls on foreign currency. The inflationary consequences of the growing monetary surplus were repressed by price controls and rationing.

After the end of the War, the system of price controls and rationing used by the German government was largely retained. The Reichsmark itself remained legal tender. This meant that, at the time of the monetary reform, twelve years of repressed inflation had to be tackled. The excess money stock in the form of cash and deposit money was estimated at 90 per cent of the monetary holdings.[3] Added to this was the overindebtedness of the banks, because the deposits were offset by worthless claims on the Reich. The monetary reform removed both the excess money stock and the excess debt: once all the conversions had taken place, the money stock (as defined in M3) actually recorded for exchange was reduced to one-fifteenth of its nominal value, apart from a *per capita* allowance of 60 Marks. The worthless claims of the banks on the Reich were cancelled. In compensation for residual debts, the banks were granted claims on the Länder and later on the Federal Government.[4]

In the period between the end of the War and the currency reform, the significance of black market activities kept growing. Rising fears of undisguised inflation or a currency reform caused confidence in the Reichsmark to dwindle. Fewer and fewer goods made their way into the legal economy. Instead, they were hoarded, either so that people had sufficient assets for barter, or out of fear that inflation would result in monetary assets losing their value. It is estimated that, by the end, only half of output was traded on legal markets.[5] As a result, the Reichsmark had increasingly ceased to function as a medium of exchange and a store of value. The 'cigarette currency' was symbolic of the growing rejection of the official means of payment.

At first glance, the monetary situation in 1990 does reveal certain parallels with the position in 1948. As had been the case when the National Socialists managed the economy, an excess money stock also formed in the GDR's centrally administered economy. Once again, the cause was on-going finan-

---

[3] Cf. Colm *et al.*, 1955, pp. 221f. and Reichsbankleitstelle, Hauptverwaltung der Reichsbank für die britische Zone: Wie kann eine Währungsreform auf Drei-Zonen-Basis durchgeführt werden? Hamburg 11 Dec. 1947 (HA BBk B 330/4584).

[4] For more details cf. Stolper *et al.*, 1966, pp. 242ff.

[5] Cf. Wolf, 1947, pp. 229ff.

642 *XIII. German Monetary Union*

cing with money created by the state. It also happened 'silently', albeit in a different fashion. The intention was to demonstrate the superiority of the socialist system over the capitalist economies, which tended to incur budget deficits. The budget deficit in the GDR was disguised by making companies hand over increasing amounts of money to the state. Their corresponding need to refinance themselves was met by loans from the Staatsbank or its subordinate banks. Credit was not used as an allocative instrument imposing hard restrictions on the companies. The priority was on the objectives of material planning (Section 3a). The principle was that 'nothing ever fails because of money'.[6] The Staatsbank der DDR provided its own indications of a growing excess money stock. According to its calculations, the volume of money and credit rose considerably faster after 1975 than the national income generated.

Unlike the situation in 1948, the 'silent' deficit financing in the GDR did not lead to worthless claims and thus excessive debts on the part of the banks. As state executive agencies, they had a different function in the socialist system anyway (Section 3a). This also meant that the 'debts' registered for the companies had to be interpreted appropriately (Section 3b); this was not achieved by the chosen 'inherited debt' solution to the problem (section 5).

In the GDR, as in the Third Reich, prices were fixed by the state and so the excess money stock could not express itself in undisguised inflation. However, inflation was not repressed as rigorously as it had been by the National Socialist regime. Only the prices of basic consumer goods were kept stable, whereas the prices of more luxurious goods were increased sharply. This is also reflected in a study by the GDR's Finance Ministry and the Staatsbank.[7] Even so, there was still an excess money stock. Calculations by the Finance Ministry and the Staatsbank der DDR put it at about 15 per cent of monetary holdings.[8] Even if the reliability of official GDR statistics is seriously in doubt, the excess money stock in 1990 must have been far smaller than in 1948.

---

[6] Authors' collective, 1990, p. 21.

[7] In a study dated 27 Nov. 1989, the price rises in industry, the construction sector, and agriculture together were given as 56.9 per cent against 1975. For consumer goods and services, the increase in the price level was given as 16.5 per cent over the same period. Cf. Einschätzung zur Stabilität der Währung der DDR, submitted by: Minister für Finanzen und Preise, Präsident der Staatsbank der DDR, Berlin 27 Nov. 1989 (Bundesarchiv Koblenz and Berlin, DN1 VS13/90 vol. 6). In contrast, the GDR's annual statistical records document that the Mark's purchasing power remained fairly stable. This stability was achieved by manipulating the basket of goods, which contained too many basic consumer goods (whose prices were kept stable) and too few luxury goods (whose prices were rising).

[8] Cf. Einschätzung zur Stabilität der Währung der DDR, submitted by: Minister für Finanzen und Preise, Präsident der Staatsbank der DDR, Berlin 15 Dec. 1989 (Bundesarchiv Koblenz and Berlin, DN1 VS13/90 vol. 5).

Nor was there any rejection of the Mark in the GDR as had happened with the Reichsmark. However, long before monetary union, the D-mark had already become a sort of second currency, granting access to goods which were otherwise unobtainable.[9] Its circulation was tolerated. In fact, since it was accepted as payment in Intershops, the state even turned it into a source of foreign currency revenue. Also, as in other socialist systems, it was impossible to realize monetary income satisfactorily, and so a black economy evolved, supplemented by barter. However, after the Berlin Wall came down, confidence in the Mark der DDR (Ostmark; M) dwindled rapidly. This was boosted by an oversimplification that became widely believed in East Germany. The D-mark was increasingly viewed as an instrument with which to solve the GDR's economic problems.[10] People tended to ignore the extent of the transformation needed. Political statements during the 1990 election campaign even fostered this misapprehension.[11]

The conclusions to be drawn at this stage are that, despite certain parallels, the monetary situation in 1990 differed from that of 1948, inasmuch as it was easier to tackle the purely monetary challenge. It is true that there were substantial gaps in the information available about the monetary position in the GDR. But when it came to assessing the monetary risk involved, it had to be borne in mind that, in terms of Germany as a whole, this was only a partial monetary reform for one economic area, whose population and national product were smaller than those of the state of North Rhine-Westphalia. Also, as in 1948, it was possible to rely on an established central bank organization to manage the project.

b) Initial conditions of the real economy

Making a reliable estimate of the real economic situation of the GDR at the end of 1989, and even in the period prior to monetary union, was certainly no easy task. There were suspicions that the east German infrastructure and production plant were in a bad state, but the true extent of the deterioration was greatly underestimated in the West. In October 1989, a working group

[9] The amount of D-marks in circulation in the GDR was estimated at up to DM 4 billion. Cf. Rüden, 1991, pp. 82f.

[10] Cf. Willgerodt, 1991, p. 174.

[11] This, and the use of terms like 'Wende' (i.e. turnaround) (used by Egon Krenz, who had resigned as Chairman of the State Council of the GDR) and 'Aufschwung Ost' (i.e. Upswing East) (used by the west German Government) to signify the radical break with the socialist past, meant that people in both eastern and western Germany underestimated the harsh real economic measures that would be needed to cope with the legacy of socialist economic mismanagement.

led by the Chairman of the State Planning Commission, Gerhard Schürer, produced a secret study for the Council of Ministers of the GDR: this study reveals that in 1988 the capital stock was eroded by between 52 and 67 per cent in the various sectors.[12] Assuming that this study is realistic, the following must also be borne in mind when assessing its economic significance: a failure to reinvest generally means a drop in productivity owing to ageing production plant; also, production to meet planning targets is likely to signify a specificity of capital stock which at best will only happen to coincide with the needs of the market in an international division of labour. If the estimate of the GDR's productive capacity under altered conditions was based on assumptions of what we now know to have been an unrealistically high capital stock, this is not simply because the data of the GDR had been manipulated. The miscalculation by policy makers, experts, and the public in West Germany was partly due to a false reading of the actually existent 'socialist' economy.[13] People had known for decades about the serious immanent dysfunctioning of socialist systems, but neither the politicians nor many economists paid sufficient heed to this knowledge. Furthermore, analyses and policy proposals did not always take adequate account of the fundamental differences between the systems.

In contrast, the situation in 1948 was easier to grasp, and no one could fail to see the destruction and dismantling resulting from the War and its aftermath. However, the industrial plant left in 1945, and even the amount left behind after the dismantling, was still greater than it had been before the War. It can therefore be assumed that the ongoing investment up to 1945 had produced an industrial capital stock with a relatively favourable age structure, and that the dismantling up to 1948 had only had a limited impact.[14] Most importantly, the specificity of the capital stock had only been influenced by twelve years of varying intensities of centralized intervention by the state, aimed at self-sufficiency, and by 15 years of price controls. This contrasted with the GDR in 1989, which was suffering from a total of 56

[12] The individual figures according to the study: 53.8 per cent for industry; 67 per cent for the construction industry; 52.1 per cent in the transport sector and 61.3 per cent in agriculture, forestry, and food. Cf. Schürer, 1995, p. 17.

[13] The statistical material produced by the Deutsches Institut für Wirtschaftsforschung (DIW) is symptomatic of a distorted understanding of the realities—and this material actually formed an important source of data for the Federal Government as it negotiated the Unification Treaty with representatives of the GDR. Cf. Bundesministerium für innerdeutsche Beziehungen, 1987, Part B. Neither was any doubt cast on the accuracy of the official data from the GDR nor was any account taken of the lack of comparability between valuations made in the planned and market economies. But even an analysis of the physical data actually available gives clear indications of the dire state of the GDR's economy. Cf. Lippe, 1996.

[14] Cf. e.g. Krengel, 1958, for details of the capital stock.

years of government interference, general isolation from the world market after 1948, and the consequences of the failure to reinvest.

The initial condition of the real economy in 1990 was thus fundamentally different from that of 1948. Following the currency reform of 1948, and following investment to overcome the damage caused by war and dismantling, the remaining, high-quality capital stock was relatively quickly used to boost output.[15] In contrast, the comparatively high production level in the GDR in 1990 relied on an extensive use of capital stock and natural resources and could not be maintained. Most of the capital stock was inappropriate for manufacturing under world-market conditions, and the demand from other COMECON countries that had been guaranteed by the position in the COMECON system disappeared once they started reforming their own economies.

c) *Initial institutional conditions*

In institutional terms, it might seem natural to draw a parallel between monetary union in 1990 and the 1948 currency reform, because both also involved a change of system. However, a closer look reveals far-reaching differences. Despite the introduction of government intervention, the economic system in the Third Reich from 1933 to 1945 remained basically unchanged. The intervention was really only superimposed on the market-oriented institutions of the Weimar Republic. The intervention did imply a selective restriction on the freedom of private-sector agents in the form of government instructions. But, *de jure*, they remained independent owners under existing private law. The same applied to many companies. Within the limitations imposed by the government intervention, their owners were still able to act at their own discretion.[16]

After the War, the Allies initially kept the intervention system in place. The system was not changed until the currency reform. In terms of the initial institutional situation, the main task was to remove the superimposed system of economic planning. The same applied to the monetary system. However, there were also some institutional reforms. First, section 28 of the Conversion Law prohibited public sector deficit financing, although the Allies could permit exceptions to the ban. Also, it was established in law that the Bank deutscher Länder was independent of political instructions. Both of these measures were institutional responses to the political misuse of the banking system which had engendered a potential for inflation. They

---

[15] Cf. e.g. Stolper *et al.*, 1966, pp. 255f.
[16] Cf. Waltmann, 1994, p. 140; Schmieding, 1990, p. 157.

were also intended to boost confidence in the new currency, the *Deutsche Mark*.[17] With their constitution for the central bank, the Allies set a precedent which was later to become a key feature of the economic system of the Federal Republic of Germany.

Whereas the banking system and institutions in the Western zones were restored and improved, the banking system in the Soviet zone was totally transformed following the establishment of the GDR. The credit reform of 1949 placed the commercial banks under the control of the newly established Deutsche Notenbank (renamed Staatsbank der DDR in 1968) and charged them with implementing the state's economic plans (Section 3a). As a consequence, the monetary system of the GDR, as part of the socialist economic system, had to be replaced in its entirety in 1990 if it was to fit into a market-oriented economic system. Monetary union did this by replacing it with the west German system.

In 1948, therefore, the Federal Republic (as it was to become) only had to withdraw the state from the commercial sector, whereas a break with the existing institutions was unavoidable in the GDR in 1990. The situation was made worse by the fact that almost the whole of the GDR economy was owned by the state. In comparison, as already mentioned, the ownership of most property had been left untouched by the National Socialist regime.[18] Once the regulations had been revoked, property rights regained their original function and provided the incentives needed for the market to work.[19] The relatively small amount of expropriations and relating claims for restitution and the uncertainties about ownership rights did not have any serious consequences after 1948.[20] In contrast, the return of property and unresolved ownership disputes after the 1990 monetary union became much debated sources of uncertainty which hampered economic development.

The institutional situation in 1990 was thus very different from that of 1948. Then, it had merely been necessary in western Germany to reactivate a market economy that had been temporarily and only partially suspended. In 1990 in eastern Germany, in contrast, an entirely new market economy had to be institutionalized. Of course, the conceptual basis for this policy was considerably simplified by transferring the west German system of institutions. But a number of problems of transition remained. For example, it could not necessarily be assumed that the rules governing behaviour between the economic actors which had developed over the preceding four

---

[17] Cf. Möller, 1991, pp. 222f.

[18] This statement is not intended to trivialize the significance of the expropriations related to the discrimination and persecution of sections of the population by the Nazi regime.

[19] Cf. Watrin, 1990, pp. 42f.

[20] Cf. Möller, 1991, pp. 231ff.

decades (internal institutions) would fit into the new parameters set by the state. External institutions need to be supported by corresponding attitudes and values if they are to orient people's actions as smoothly as possible. This would suggest that, if the newly found scope for economic decision making was to be used profitably, the new institutional conditions would necessitate adjustment at many levels. This is another major difference from the 1948 currency reform. It stems from the fact that in 1948 there was still much in place on which to base the rules and underlying values of a private-sector society that are needed for a market system to function. That cannot simply be assumed for the 1990 transition.

Given the contemporary institutional conditions set by the state, it was necessary to take account of the specific characteristics of the monetary system as designed for a centrally planned economy, in order to achieve a smooth and low-cost monetary transformation.

3. The monetary system to be transformed by monetary union

The GDR's monetary system shared all the characteristics of a monetary system typical of centrally planned economies. It therefore differed fundamentally from the Federal Republic's market system. Not all politicians or, to an even greater extent, the public, were sufficiently aware of this. It is clear that many similarities in the use of technical terms contributed to this. In order to understand the problems relating to the transformation of the GDR's monetary system, it is useful to sketch out the typical features of the existing system against the background of monetary union.[21]

a) Money and credit as instruments of economic planning

The 'control via the Mark'

The GDR's monetary system was—like all socialist economic and social systems—dominated by the state's intention of planning the material (non-monetary) economy. Unlike its position in market economies, the monetary system was not a constituent functional element of the economic system, but the expression of a stop-gap solution. This was because none of the socialist systems was able to collate all non-monetary economic processes in a complex society with a division of labour and to subject them to planning

---

[21] A comprehensive analysis of the GDR's monetary system is contained in H. Jörg Thieme's essay in this publication.

calculations based on purely non-monetary variables.[22] In consequence, this meant that material planning had to be supplemented by a monetary side. However, the money was unable to fulfil its allocative functions as a medium of exchange in a system with free price formation, because the system of central planning was retained. This coexistence of material planning and the supplementary monetary side resulted in functional distortions in all planned economies.

Since the ability to plan the material economy was limited, the central planning authorities had to restrict themselves to categories of goods which were considered to be a political priority or a bottleneck and introduce fixed prices for the purposes of their calculations and for rewarding labour.[23] At the same time, there was a division between the spheres of production and consumption. In the sphere of production, the principle of central material planning was maintained, but in the sphere of consumption, the private individual had discretionary powers. However, the scope of these powers was restricted to a choice between goods and services provided by the state. There was nothing like the independence of consumer choice that exists in a market system.

The separation between the spheres of production and consumption was matched by different possibilities of disposing of money. In the sphere of production, money was subordinated to the needs of central planning. Its role was to stimulate and control performance and thus ensure that output adhered to the plan. The financial relationships were used correspondingly to control the companies.

In order to ensure that the Mark could be used to control the companies, there were specific rules on the use of money and credit and a banking system tailored to these tasks.[24] The Staatsbank undertook the supervision of the companies via a network of branches and special-purpose banks.[25] The companies were only allowed to undertake financial transactions in the form

[22] This practically confirms what Mises, 1920, and subsequently in particular Hayek, 1935, 1945, treated analytically whilst highlighting the problem of information.

[23] In the case of the GDR, millions of types of goods contrasted with approximately 5,000 accounts balancing planned output and demand quantities. Via a hierarchical system of responsibility and confirmation of the plans by higher-ranking bodies, the Council of Ministers was responsible for approximately 300 accounts, the State Planning Commission for about 500, the ministries and equivalent central state agencies for about 1,000 and the combines and local and regional authorities for some 3,000. Cf. Leipold, 1988, pp. 204ff. for this and for the process of planning and accounting.

[24] Cf. Mummert, 1995, pp. 72ff. for the following remarks.

[25] In the GDR, this hierarchical banking system consisted of the Staatsbank der DDR, 15 district offices, and 180 local branches, plus another 41 branches of the Industriebank. This organizational structure also corresponded to the various planning levels. Cf. Pleyer and Tömp, 1980, p. 2.

of book money and thus had to go through the banking system. The companies were therefore not permitted to hold cash or enter into independent credit relations with other companies. They were also prohibited from disposing freely of their financial resources. The principle that a company's finance should be earned by the company itself in theory meant that companies financed themselves, but because the companies were required to transfer any 'earned' funds to the state, they were not able to finance a significant amount of investment using their own funds. There were also statutory requirements governing the financing of 'current assets', which included raw materials, auxiliary materials, and operating resources, etc., stipulating that they be partly funded by credit. The companies were thus forced to finance themselves on credit, the aim being to ensure that the banks could check that they were fulfilling the plan. The loans were not an expression of independent decisions taken at company level, nor were they based on private savings made available to the companies in the form of loans by intermediaries.

However, in the reality of the socialist system, the limitations of 'controlling via the Mark' soon became apparent. The contradictions within the system were too great. The method of control by credit was ill-suited to resolving the ever-present principal–agent problem. Not least, failures of planning and allocation were reflected in 'soft' plans, and their inevitable consequence was 'soft' loans.

With regard to private individuals and private businesses, a perfect forecast of income positions would have been needed in order to avoid monetary disruption. Since this was not possible, restrictions were also imposed on the independence of monetary transactions at the level of consumption. There were only limited opportunities for private agents to borrow money, and the loans issued were strictly tied to specific purposes. Despite this, considerable uncertainties remained in the planning process. They particularly resulted from the fact that, with all its deficiencies, material planning did not make it possible to link output and compensation in a way which would ensure stability.

Two interim findings should suffice to underpin these remarks. First, the monetary system proved unable to fulfil its allocative function. The system had all the problems of a stop-gap solution—which is how the combination of material planning and a supplementary monetary system has to be viewed. There are compelling reasons why no financial discipline in the strict sense was possible in planned economies like that of the GDR. And where it could have been used as a sanctioning instrument, it was generally sacrificed to the needs of fulfilling the material plan. The tendency towards monetary oversupply was—as Eucken[26] rightly supposed—immanent in the

[26] Cf. Eucken, 1990, p. 117.

system.[27] Secondly, the organization of the credit system and credit relationships reflected all the inadequacies of the state's attempts to plan. There was thus a fundamental incompatibility with market-oriented credit systems and credit relationships.

The quality of the money

Money and credit thus had unavoidable deficiencies as instruments for implementing centralized material planning. If one takes the general functions of money as a yardstick for assessing cash and deposit money in the GDR, one is at risk of misjudging the situation. The misjudgement arises when the structure of the monetary system, which is dominated by the attempts to plan the material economy, is neglected. The planning system does not simply require that the state own the means of production. It also necessitates the clearest possible separation between the levels of production and consumption. This separation means that there can be no interdependency of prices. The prices themselves served as a means of settlement at the production level and as a means of rationing at the consumption level. Goods were 'handed over' to private individuals in return for the payment of fixed prices. The related indirect exchange did not permit the establishment of any markets worth the name, as there was no opportunity for market-oriented reactions on the supply side. Such reactions would have disrupted planning and the implementation of the plan. They were in any case impossible, because the companies could not dispose of the means of production independently. The formation of savings by private individuals was also decoupled from the non-monetary economic system. Any linkage would have required the integration of the decision not to consume and of the interest paid into a functioning system of intertemporal allocation. It proved impossible, however, to find anything even remotely resembling a convincing planning device to replace functioning capital markets. It would also have had to serve as a replacement for entrepreneurial behaviour on those markets and in the companies.

A functional assessment of the money in the purses and on the accounts of private individuals comes to the following conclusions: even for private individuals, money fulfilled the characteristic functions it has in market economies only superficially and to a limited extent. The Mark did appear to be an appropriate unit of account, medium of exchange, and store of value, at least for private individuals. However, this finding has to be seen in the light of fixed prices, chronic shortages of goods, and restrictions on convert-

[27] One material consequence should at least be considered: the insufficient discipline caused unplanned non-monetary structures to arise and continue.

ibility. For the business sector as a whole, the functions of money—despite all the niceties of detailed planning and incentives—were reduced to those of a unit of account. Because the state tried to plan the material economy centrally and thus separated the levels of production and consumption, money was unable to create any interdependence between decisions of allocation. It was impossible to make systematic use of money's ability to cut information costs and transaction costs. Money was thus not an instrument for determining value.

This assessment of the quality of money in planned economies in general, and in the GDR in particular, is not new; nor are the reasons behind it. None the less, there was insufficient awareness, both before and after monetary union, of the point made almost 70 years earlier by Ludwig von Mises.[28] In prevailing economic theory, the discussion of a socialist accounting system which would be comparable to the market economy has continued to neglect this finding, even in the very recent past.[29] That has been due to inappropriate assumptions about the information needed for planning, to a lack of reflection about the institutions of a planned economy, and to the definition of the planning problem as a simple maximization under constraints. Money played virtually no role here. These theoretical misjudgements meant that the policy makers were often confronted with ideas which failed to take account of the nature and scale of the transition problem.[30] However, in the case of GEMSU, there are also political and economic reasons why the politicians preferred not to explain the implications that the collapse of the socialist system would have for the population in eastern and western Germany.[31]

b) Implications for the monetary transition

The attempt to plan the material economy centrally thus stopped money being an instrument of valuation, which, in market economies, helps to create an interdependence between all decisions on allocation. This had serious implications for the project of monetary transition: the values of real assets stated in the accounts and the monetary stocks and flows in the GDR were of no meaningfulness for the currency conversion. Any conversion of the

---

[28] His main point, which is convincingly argued, is that it is *a priori* impossible to determine value in terms of money in a socialist system. Cf. Mises, 1920, p. 90.

[29] Stiglitz, 1994, is a striking example. Cf. e.g. Streit, 1995, pp. 16ff., regarding the deficiencies of prevailing economic theory which are of relevance here.

[30] Cf. e.g. Streit and Mummert, 1996, for the disappearance of deficiencies in institution theory now taking place.

[31] Cf. Streit and Mummert, 1996, pp. 24ff.

Ostmark into D-marks would have to be arbitrary. Previous exchange rates
for the Ostmark could not serve as reliable indicators (Section 4). That would
have required a link between them and the economic processes in the GDR.
The supply of Ostmarks was insufficient to create a genuine market, and
there was no corresponding demand for foreign currency. A revaluation of
the stocks and flows of the GDR could not begin until after monetary union,
as eastern Germany became integrated into western Germany's market system and into the world economy.[32]

When the assets and liabilities of the GDR were revalued, insufficient
account was taken of the peculiarities of the monetary system being transformed. For example, it should have been borne in mind that there was no
separation between the state, the banking system, and the corporate sector
in the GDR. As stated above, all borrowings and lendings, apart from those
involving private individuals, were monetary reactions of the state planned
economy. Loans by the banks to companies and to the state were transactions between different state organizations. They should therefore have been
offset against each other when a statement of the GDR's assets and liabilities
as needed for the currency conversion was produced.[33]

If the GDR's asset and liability statement had been consolidated accordingly, the asset side would have comprised the value of all land, buildings,
plant and equipment, and receivables from abroad and private individuals.
The liability side would have consisted of cash holdings and deposits of
individuals and the foreign debts, and then the net assets, if any, would have
been registered as a surplus. Inevitably, the value of the assets under the new
market conditions was unknown. In consequence, the financial assets of private individuals would in principle then have had to be blocked and declared
to be claims on the revenue from the sale of state-owned companies and
land after deduction of the net foreign debt of the GDR.

If this approach had been deemed politically unacceptable, there would
have been an alternative solution: taking the conversion rates agreed in the
Treaty as a basis, the net financial assets of private individuals on 30 June 1990
amounted to DM 119.2 billion, according to the accounts of the Staatsbank.[34]

[32] This was a unique case in terms of transition policy. All the other countries in transition
attempted the revaluation via adjustment inflation. The intention was to absorb the inflationary push via a programme of stabilization. Cf. e.g. Streit and Mummert, 1996. The
Bundesbank's mandate to pursue a policy of stability prohibited such a transition strategy,
quite apart from the fact that in pan-German terms it was only a transformation of part of
the economy via integration into the area of validity of the D-mark.

[33] This view is also reflected in a study by the International Monetary Fund, cf. Lipschitz,
1990, p. 4, and was primarily advocated in Germany by Willgerodt, 1990, pp. 319ff.

[34] That was DM 7,000 per head, and equal to roughly four-fifths of the savings formed
by private individuals in West Germany within one year (1989).

The net foreign liabilities of the GDR amounted to about DM 15 billion. Taking this alternative solution, it would have been necessary to fund a total of DM 134.2 billion (net financial assets of private individuals plus net foreign debt of the GDR), i.e. in view of the unknown value of the non-monetary assets of the GDR, the Federal Government would have had to provide a state guarantee in the form of equalization claims for the converted net financial assets of private individuals in the GDR and to shoulder the net foreign liabilities. Neither of these approaches was adopted. Instead, the existing debt of the state-owned and cooperative business sectors and of the municipalities was brought forward into the market economy. The GDR's financial system was therefore converted in a manner which failed to take account of the institutional nature of the system.

The recognition of the existing credits and debts was also extremely dubious in terms of property law.[35] The words of one economist can be taken to express this view, which is now also shared by a number of legal experts: 'credit, interest-rate and capital markets are . . . the market economy's competing mechanisms, and alternatives to the socialist planning and steering of investment. Such allocative systems, which would undermine the planning system, were impossible in the former GDR and in all other COMECON countries. For this very reason, it is impossible to equate or place equivalent value on loans in planned economies and loans in market economies. In socialist economies, credit existed and functioned only as an accounting item necessary for the realization of the plan. It was not a legal title of ownership or asset in the market sense, and was therefore not protected by law! Or even worthy of such protection. However, with the currency conversion of 1 July 1990, these loans, which were insubstantial in terms of real assets, acquired a new quality in terms of constitutional law.'[36]

[35] This view was strengthened with the debate about a relevant ruling by the local court in Magdeburg dated 4 Nov. 1992, about the divergent opinion of the District Court in Magdeburg, the confirmation thereof by the Federal Court of Justice and the ensuing complaint of unconstitutionality. The District Court had recognized the connection between the obligation of GDR state firms to hand over funds to the state extensively and the resulting need for credits in order to finance the dictated projects and production, and had ruled in favour of offsetting 'by netting, as it were' (cf. Scholz, 1994, p. 304). In the substantiation of its ruling dated 8 Apr. 1997, the Federal Constitutional Court likewise came to the conclusion that, in terms of its prerequisites, its functions, and the consequences of liability, lending in the GDR differed markedly from lending in a market economy. Even so, the complaint of unconstitutionality was rejected since, from the point of view of constitutional law, the legislative processes that gave rise to the procedures adopted were unobjectionable. Moreover, the legislator, in the Court's view, must be allowed particular latitude since he could not fall back on historical precedents; however, there was, at the same time, an urgent need to take action (Bundesverfassungsgericht, 1997, pp. 47ff.). For the legal debate, cf. Matthiessen, 1994 and Schachtschneider, 1996, and the literature listed there.

[36] Hankel, 1992, pp. 32f.

Political decisions resulted in monetary relics deriving from the centrally planned economy being transferred to the market economy. The extent to which these decisions were shaped by unrelated and inappropriate considerations must remain open. However, public choice analysis provides evidence that the way the conversion was handled must have been welcomed, in particular with respect to the Federal budget (Section 6b). The approach adopted considerably reduced the initial level of equalization claims, claims which would inevitably result in government borrowing. The openly registered 'costs of unification' fell correspondingly.

4. Monetary union as part of a shock therapy

The actual conversion of the GDR's monetary system was preceded by a process of analysis, the prime focus of which was not initially on establishing a monetary union. The main policy issue was how to transform an east German economic system on the verge of collapse. An expeditious monetary union was primarily placed on the political agenda by the east German population, partly by people moving across to the West (exit) and partly by demonstrations (voice).

a) Conditions for a monetary union

For the Bundesbank, the transfer of the Federal Republic's monetary constitution to the GDR was an indispensable precondition for monetary union. Responsibility for monetary policy should remain exclusively in its hands after monetary union. It therefore demanded that the State Treaty with the GDR should ensure that, when monetary union took place, the Bundesbank Act and the instructions issued by the Bundesbank would apply in the GDR just as in the Federal Republic. The west German Banking Act should also apply in the GDR, and foreign banks should be free to establish themselves there. All rules governing fixed interest rates and currency restrictions should be lifted until monetary union, and the possibility of public sector agencies in the GDR taking up loans should be restricted. The Bundesbank also demanded that it be allowed to open its own office in Berlin and a further 15 or so branches in the GDR.

The Bundesbank's conditions coincided with the intentions of the Federal Government. In addition to the necessary agreements on currency and monetary policy, the latter wanted the clearest possible rules for the future economic system in force in the GDR.[37] The official offer to the GDR for negotiations on a monetary union itself emphasized that 'simultaneously . . . the necessary legal preconditions for the introduction of a social market economy must be put in place by the GDR'.[38] It was thus clear right from the start that a monetary union would entail a radical change in the economic system.

The de Maizière government had no objections of principle to the introduction of the social market economy in the GDR. However, it did initially object to a full transfer of responsibility for monetary policy to the Bundesbank, and the consequent loss of sovereignty over economic policy. In the view of the GDR, the Staatsbank should retain these powers even after a monetary union, or should at least have an executive role of its own. The GDR delegation only gave way on this point after an ultimatum from the west German head of delegation, Hans Tietmeyer.[39]

The State Treaty of 18 May 1990 basically implemented the west German side's ideas on transforming the institutions. GEMSU marked the end of the centrally planned economy in the GDR. It was replaced by the market economy institutions of the Federal Republic. Article 1 para. 3 of the State Treaty on GEMSU officially stipulated that the social market economy was the economic system common to both contracting parties. This was the first time that this economic system had been given a quasi-constitutional status in Germany.[40]

b) Economics and politics of the monetary conversion

Dubious grounds for the setting of the conversion rate

As stated above (Section 3b), there were no convincing economic indicators by which to determine an objectively justified conversion rate. The system of central planning of the domestic economy had necessarily isolated it from economic relations with other countries, quite apart from the fact that it was impossible to establish any convincing interdependency between all prices.[41]

---

[37] Cf. Tietmeyer, 1994, pp. 65f.

[38] Kohl, 1990, p. 194.

[39] Cf. Tietmeyer, 1994, pp. 77, 87. At the time, Tietmeyer was a member of the Directorate of the Bundesbank. At Chancellor Kohl's request, he was released from those responsibilities to act as the head of delegation.

[40] Cf. Willgerodt, 1990, p. 311.

[41] This was also admitted by the economists of the Humboldt University when they—albeit misleadingly—said: 'a precise determination of the exchange rate based on real economic relations will remain ineffective if the GDR fails to gradually align its prices to international price structures.' Authors' collective, 1990, p. 59.

The different exchange rates in existence were thus of dubious usefulness: The GDR's official exchange rate of M 1 to DM 1 existed for the sake of its political image and for the compulsory exchange of money by visitors to the GDR. It is true that market rates for the Ostmark had formed in the Federal Republic. But there must be a question mark over their significance, since they resulted from very specific transactions on largely isolated markets.

It was just as impossible to determine an exchange rate on the basis of the theory of purchasing power parity. Even if the logical force behind the theory itself is not in doubt, such an approach was inappropriate[42] because the preconditions for establishing purchasing power parity patently did not exist. The GDR had no competitive markets integrated into world trade and there were no homogeneous baskets of goods which could be compared. The composition of the basket of goods in the GDR had been set by the state, the quality of the east German products contained in it was generally lower than in West Germany, the prices were fixed by the state and some of them kept stable, and many consumer durables were either unavailable or only obtainable after long periods of waiting.

There was thus no convincing way to establish the 'correct' exchange rate between the two currencies. But it was important to pay attention to economic considerations regarding the impact of a conversion rate on different monetary and social objectives.

Monetary and economic policy aspects of the conversion

It was becoming clear that monetary and economic policy would have to perform a delicate balancing act, and the approach adopted was to use several conversion rates for the Ostmark rather than one. The Bundesbank defined the task to be resolved in the State Treaty as follows: 'in the preparations for the Treaty, it was basically necessary to strike a delicate balance between important economic, social, and political criteria. Equal weight had to be given to keeping the inflationary risk of the currency conversion as small as possible, to trying to safeguard the competitiveness of GDR companies as far as possible, to limiting the burden on the budget, and to making the conversion socially acceptable for the populations of both the GDR and the Federal Republic.'[43]

The task of keeping the risk of inflation as low as possible was a matter for the Bundesbank. In accordance with its statutory mandate, and in the

---

[42] Calculations of this type are to be found in Sinn and Sinn, 1991, p. 37, which also provides a review of comparable approaches. A critical stance on this is taken by e.g. Bofinger, 1990 and Neumann, 1992.

[43] Deutsche Bundesbank, 1990b, p. 15.

light of its approach to implementing monetary policy, its primary task had to be to supply the GDR with an initial stock of money which fitted in with its potential-oriented monetary targeting policy for the whole of Germany. From this perspective, the critical parameter was the exchange rate for those GDR stock variables which would affect the money stock. This necessitated estimates of how much the production potential in the whole of Germany would grow as a result of the accession of the GDR, of the velocity of circulation of money in eastern Germany after conversion, and of the money stock of the GDR.

There was great uncertainty about all the variables needed to determine a conversion rate that would be geared to monetary stability. This was particularly true of the level of output in the GDR to be expected under the new market system. The Bundesbank based its calculations on estimates of the gross national product of the GDR by the Deutsches Institut für Wirtschaftsforschung, which had come up with a figure of approximately DM 230 billion for 1988. That was equal to 9.5 per cent of the gross national product of the Federal Republic. By taking this figure as a guideline, the Bundesbank *de facto* assumed that the estimate was correct. However, it was only regarded as a rough indication, 'since the level of potential company closures (was) unknown'.[44]

There was also uncertainty about the velocity of money in the GDR and how it would develop after monetary union. Non-cash payments were relatively underdeveloped and there was a lack of trade credits between companies, suggesting that the velocity of money would initially be lower than in west Germany. There were conflicting assumptions with regard to the cash holdings of private individuals. On the one hand, a shopping spree was expected. On the other, it could be argued that the upheaval resulting from GEMSU would make people more cautious. In view of such imponderables, the Bundesbank decided to assume a velocity of money in line with that in West Germany.[45]

Finally, it was necessary to determine the GDR's money stock. For this, the Bundesbank had to rely on figures from the Staatsbank, and there were question marks over their reliability, too. At the same time, it was necessary to interpret correctly the system of financial interrelationships between the agencies of the GDR and to put them into West German categories. There were certainly some misinterpretations: the Staatsbank regarded the GDR's foreign trade companies as banks. Consequently, the bank deposits of these companies were not listed in the consolidated accounts of the banking system. As they were viewed as inter-bank loans, they were not included in

---

[44] Deutsche Bundesbank, 1990*b*, p. 20.
[45] Cf. Bofinger and Kloten, 1997, p. 6.

the money stock aggregates, either. However, the foreign trade companies ceased to be regarded as banks when monetary union took place, and so their claims became sight deposits held at the former GDR banks and thus affected the money stock. It is therefore estimated—depending on the source—that, when monetary union took place, the money stock grew by DM 20 to 30 billion more than expected.[46] Such a misinterpretation would obviously not have occurred if a thorough consolidation of the credit situation in the GDR had been undertaken.

A further question was: which monetary aggregate should be used to determine the conversion rate in order to dampen any impact on the money stock? Should calculations be based on M1 or M3? As explained in H. Jörg Thieme's article, the GDR's monetary system was fundamentally different from that of a market economy. There were thus considerable differences in the variety of financial investment opportunities. In particular, the periods for which money was invested were generally shorter in the GDR. The possible forms of financial investment were thus considerably more liquid than in West Germany. This meant that the relationship between M1 and M3 was different from that in the Federal Republic. There, in 1990, M1 was about 36 per cent of M3, but it was about 60 per cent of M3 in the GDR. As a result, the conversion rates needed to ensure stability varied widely, depending on whether M1 or M3 was taken.[47] In line with its previous monetary targeting policy, the Bundesbank decided to take M3 as a basis for its approach to the exchange rate for the stock variables affecting the money stock.

When the money stock was being determined, it was also unknown how it had developed under the Modrow government and how it would continue to develop once that government had been replaced by the de Maizière government until monetary union.

The Bundesbank was therefore confronted with some major imponderables when it developed its ideas on a stability-oriented conversion rate for the stock variables of the GDR which were of relevance to the money stock. However, the risk posed by miscalculations was limited, since it was likely that, even after monetary union, economic activity in West Germany would still be of much greater relative importance, and would thus determine whether the pan-German money stock would develop in a stability-oriented fashion.[48]

---

[46] Cf. Deutsche Bundesbank, 1990c, pp. 6f.; Sinn and Sinn, 1991, pp. 52f.

[47] Cf. Bofinger, 1990, pp. 27f.

[48] Even though the actual conversion rate was higher than the Bundesbank had intended, the money stock of the GDR still accounted for only about 13 per cent of the pan-German money stock.

The criterion that the competitiveness of GDR companies should be safe-guarded as far as possible involved both stocks and flows. The stocks referred to the debts owed by east German companies to the banks of the GDR. Because no consolidation of the credit situation to take account of the nature of the system of central planning in the GDR took place (Section 3b), the conversion rate affected the competitiveness of east German companies. It determined the level of their debts and the related burden of interest payments and redemption. Furthermore, the levels of corporate debt affected their chances of privatization.[49] This initially led to the question of whether, in order to increase the competitiveness of companies, a different conversion rate should be taken for the relevant assets on the accounts of the Staatsbank (and thus also for its claims on companies) than the rate which, for reasons of stability, seemed appropriate for those liabilities which were of relevance to the money stock. The assessment of this was rendered more difficult by the fact that, for the conversion to be 'socially acceptable', the GDR population at least expected a general conversion of savings deposits at the rate of 1:1.[50] If applied to all the relevant balance sheet items on both the asset and liability sides, such a conversion rate would not have coincided with the aims of stability or competitiveness.

If an attempt had been made at least to take account of competitiveness when converting the debt allocated to companies, by taking a rate of, say, 2:1, and converting the other savings deposits at 1:1, the criterion of limiting the burden on the budget would have had to be disregarded. Such an asymmetrical conversion of the asset and liability sides of the Staatsbank's balance sheet would have resulted in a substantial gap in the accounts of the banks of the GDR. To close it, equalization claims on the state totalling up to DM 100 billion would have had to be granted. And these claims would have had to bear interest at a level enabling the banks to pay market interest rates on the savings deposits. The resulting additional government borrowing would have had to be shouldered by the Federal budget in the medium term.

The conversion of the stock variables thus created a virtually insoluble conflict between the objectives of providing the GDR with an initial supply of D-marks in a stability-oriented manner, of attempting to safeguard the competitiveness of east German companies, of the acceptability of the exchange rate, particularly for east German savers, and of limiting the burden

[49] Cf. Bofinger, 1990, p. 30.
[50] Right from the start, the Chancellor was also thinking of a limited exchange at a 1:1 rate. 'The 1:1 formula would naturally be of immense political and psychological importance: it would signal to the people in the GDR that it was a question of solidarity between equals—and not a patronising gesture by the rich to the poor cousin.' Kohl, 1996, p. 262.

on the Federal budget. The Bundesbank tried to cut through this Gordian knot by initially advocating a symmetrical conversion of all relevant stock variables in a 2:1 ratio. In the light of 'special social aspects', M 2,000 per inhabitant would be excluded from this, and exchanged at 1:1.[51]

The competitiveness of east German companies was affected not only by the conversion of the debt allocated to them but also by the conversion of flows. The conversion rate for the obligations of companies under ongoing contracts determined the initial level of wages and labour costs. The Bundesbank wanted to ensure that 'there would be an appropriate relationship between the wages now to be paid in D-marks and the macroeconomic performance of the GDR, so as not to endanger the competitiveness of GDR companies right from the outset'.[52] This necessitated information not only on labour productivity but also on how much the companies could earn in a market environment. It proved very difficult even to evaluate productivity, quite apart from the second component of performance. The Bundesbank estimated that productivity averaged between 33 and 40 per cent of that of west German companies. It therefore concluded that, from the point of view of competition, gross wages in the GDR should amount to only one-third of west German levels after monetary union.

However, there was an additional objective to be borne in mind when establishing the conversion rate for wages and salaries. A major reason why the offer of a monetary union had been made was the substantial level of migration from East to West Germany. If wages were converted at too low a rate, it was feared that the migration would continue. For this reason, it was necessary to ensure that the wages did not fall below the level of social welfare (which had to be set anew for the GDR). The same applied to the determination of pensions; in converting these, social policy objectives had priority.

With a view to competitiveness, the aim of the Bundesbank was to have a wage differential between western and eastern Germany which took into account the different productivity levels. This wage level for eastern Germany could then have formed a basis for further market-oriented adjustments, and for a greater spread in the excessively uniform wage structure in eastern Germany.[53] The Bundesbank advocated that compensation be paid in Ostmarks prior to conversion, in order to offset the loss of real income expected when the worst price distortions, and particularly the massive subsidies for major consumer goods, were abolished prior to conversion. Converting the wage level reached in this way at a rate of 1:1 was regarded

[51] Cf. Deutsche Bundesbank, 1990*a*, p. 2.
[52] Deutsche Bundesbank, 1990*b*, p. 15.
[53] Cf. Deutsche Bundesbank, 1990*a*, p. 3.

by the Bundesbank as a serious weakening of the competitiveness of east German companies. For this reason, it recommended a conversion at 2:1. If wages were converted at 1:1 and the distortions in the price structure were not removed until later, causing sharp price rises, it feared a price-wage spiral endangering the stability of the D-mark. At least two elements of this assessment by the Bundesbank must have raised difficulties. First, there were only a few, very rough indications of how to determine the level of compensation payments. In planned economies, it is just as impossible to determine realistic price structures, and the resulting changes in the baskets of goods, as it is to work out purchasing power parities. Secondly, it is doubtful whether following the recommendations of the Bundesbank would have resulted in less pressure to adjust real wages.

Political decisions and safeguarding the value of money

The proposal made by the Bundesbank described above (generally 2:1, except for M 2000 savings per inhabitant), which had been coordinated with the Federal Ministry of Finance, met with virtually no positive response in the political debate.

People in the GDR had other ideas. Following the parliamentary elections and the ensuing coalition negotiations, the de Maizière government presented a proposal in mid-April according to which money holdings would generally be converted at a 1:1 rate and the debts of GDR companies largely cancelled. Wages and salaries should be converted at a 1:1 rate. The GDR's negotiators reduced their demands in the course of the negotiations. On 30 April, the east German side signalled its acceptance of a conversion of stocks at 2:1, but only on condition that further basic amounts in addition to the first M 2,000, i.e. basic amounts between M 4,000 and M 6,000, according to age group, were also exchanged at 1:1. However, as far as the conversion of current payments was concerned, the GDR representatives continued to insist on a 1:1 rate. They did recognize the problems that such a rate would present for the competitiveness of GDR companies, but believed that these should be alleviated by specific trade-policy measures in the form of import quotas and tariffs. Just how this was to be achieved within GEMSU is impossible to ascertain.

In west Germany, the Bundesbank's recommendation of a general conversion rate of 2:1 also failed to meet with a positive response, either in the ruling coalition or among the opposition. Most politicians preferred conversion at a 1:1 rate. This particularly applied to the conversion of flows. As the head of the Federal Republic's delegation, Hans Tietmeyer, said: the Federal Ministry of Finance, the Federal Ministry of Economics, and the Federal Chancellery all had 'great understanding for the position of the

Bundesbank', but any conversion rate apart from 1:1 was regarded as unrealistic 'in view of the political resistance in the GDR and the public statements by important coalition and opposition politicians in Bonn'.[54] On 1 May, the west German coalition therefore gave the go-ahead for the compromise proposal. The 'Gordian knot' described above 'was finally cut through with the sword of a political decision, probably not quite at the right place'.[55]

A consequence of this decision was that monetary union expanded the money stock in a way which did not correspond to the Bundesbank's non-inflationary intention. However, it has to be remembered that the initial supply of D-marks provided in the course of monetary union was actually of less significance than was realized at the time.[56] This was also true of the consequences of failure by the Bundesbank to estimate the money stock correctly. If the money stock had expanded too much, the consequence at most could have been a one-off increase in the price level. It would not have caused inflation in the sense of price increases over a prolonged period. Furthermore, it should not be forgotten that the expansion in the money stock would only be able to engender a relatively small increase in the price level. The actual rise in the money stock amounted to 14.7 per cent of the west German money stock. Compared with the increase of 9.5 per cent initially aimed at by the Bundesbank, therefore, the pan-German money stock was thus 5.2 percentage points too high after monetary union. This was coupled with an overvaluation of the production potential of the GDR. Current estimates say it was only 7 per cent of the west German potential.[57] This implies that the expansion in the money stock exceeded the potential-oriented level by 7.7 percentage points. Even including the above-mentioned failure to encompass the deposits of foreign trade companies, the error in the expansion of the money stock was at most 10 per cent. The impact on the money stock was therefore not small, but was not large enough to engender a dramatic rise in the price level.

In view of the spending pattern of private individuals after monetary union, it was widely expected that the excess money stock would be absorbed by price increases. Straight after the opening of the borders in November 1989, the residents of the GDR had withdrawn a considerable proportion of their savings to obtain consumer goods from the Federal

---

[54] Tietmeyer, 1994, p. 78.

[55] The then Vice-President of the Bundesbank, Helmut Schlesinger, 1990, p. 21.

[56] This was, however, very hard to assess before monetary union. The HWWA calculated that M1 would increase by about 28 per cent and M3 by about 14 per cent on the day of monetary union. Cf. Hesse, 1991, p. 8.

[57] Cf. Thieme, 1994, p. 149.

Republic.[58] This trend was expected to continue after monetary union.[59] At the same time, there was already a high level of capacity utilization in West Germany. Furthermore, it was feared that the increase in demand would coincide with a decline in the goods available from east German companies, since these would suffer from competition with western competitors and some of the supply would therefore disappear.

However, even if the money stock had been assessed correctly, monetary policy might still have unintentionally made possible a rise in the price level over several periods. For example, there were uncertainties about how the east German production potential would develop and what the velocity of money would be, not only before, but also after, monetary union. In general, the quality of the statistical data needed for a stability-oriented monetary policy remained poor for quite some time after monetary union. This even led to recommendations that the Bundesbank should suspend its potential-oriented monetary policy for a time and instead 'feel its way' in expanding the money stock.[60]

However, the Bundesbank continued to base its policy on the trend in nominal production potential.[61] As it lacked sufficient information about developments in eastern Germany after monetary union, this simply implied a continuation of the trend as estimated for West Germany prior to monetary union.[62] West Germany was retained as the statistical basis for assessing the development of the price level and the velocity of money. Although the Bundesbank estimated that there had been an excessive expansion in the money stock as a consequence of politically determined exchange rates, it exercised restraint on undertaking corrections. However, there was no urgent need for action anyway. Despite the excess supply of money, the pan-German money stock only recorded a very small expansion until well into 1991. This is mainly because east German individuals and companies increasingly transformed their savings deposits at statutory notice into longer term financial investments (with maturities of more than four years).[63] As

[58] Cf. Schrettl, 1991, p. 4.

[59] There were also divergent opinions, suggesting that the increased unemployment resulting from monetary union would cause people to save more as a precautionary measure. Cf. e.g. Burda, 1990.

[60] Cf. Pohl and Thiemer, 1990, pp. 89f. and Sherman, 1990.

[61] Cf. Deutsche Bundesbank, 1991, p. 14.

[62] The Bundesbank believed its policy basis was left unaffected by the changes owing to monetary union simply in view of their relative significance: 'the difference in size between the Federal Republic and the GDR [about 10:1 in terms of national product; M. E. S.] itself suggests that the familiar structural relations will return to the Federal Republic in the longer term despite the inclusion of the GDR in the currency area of the D-mark.' Deutsche Bundesbank, 1990*b*, p. 20.

[63] Cf. e.g. Bofinger and Kloten, 1997, pp. 9ff.

a consequence, the ratio of the eastern German to the western German M3 money stock had fallen from 14.7 per cent to 11.5 per cent by mid-1991.[64]

The interim conclusion to be drawn from this is that the choice of the conversion rates for the Ostmark was based on a political decision. Priority was given to social acceptability and to reducing the burden on the Federal budget, rather than to monetary stability and the competitiveness of east German companies. Despite this, the Bundesbank was not presented with any serious problems in ensuring monetary stability because the risk pertaining to non-potential-oriented increases in the money stock was limited. Also, in terms of the money stock, both demand and the way private individuals disposed of their financial assets in the GDR after monetary union tended to foster stability.

5. The monetary transition

Once the modalities of conversion had been agreed politically,[65] the Bundesbank was responsible for managing the technical details of the conversion and—in line with article 10 para. 3 of the State Treaty—for discharging its mandate to ensure stability, as defined in the Bundesbank Act, in east Germany as well, once monetary union had taken place.[66] If it was to be able to fulfil its mandate to ensure stability, another task remained to be done. This lay outside the competence of the Bundesbank and was of considerable significance for economic policy. The GDR's banking system had so far experienced some half-hearted restructuring; it needed to be 'fully developed into a competition-based financial sector'.[67] Moreover, the inherited debt resulting from the inadequate way the credit situation in the planned economy had been dealt with (Section 3b) needed to be processed.

---

[64] Cf. Deutsche Bundesbank, 1991, p. 15.

[65] The general conversion rate for assets and liabilities was 2 Ostmarks to 1 D-mark. Notwithstanding this, there was a preferential conversion rate of 1 Ostmark to 1 D-mark for: up to 2,000 Marks for persons born after 1 July 1976; up to 4,000 Marks for persons born between 2 July 1931 and 1 July 1976; up to 6,000 Marks for persons born before 2 July 1931. Assets of persons resident outside the GDR which accrued before 31 Dec. 1989 were converted at a rate of 2:1, assets accrued subsequently at a rate of 3:1.

[66] Article 10 para. 2 of the State Treaty stipulated that a stable monetary value was aimed at in both areas covered by the treaty. That is not only a clearer mandate in terms of substance than the one given in section 3 of the Bundesbank Act: it also permits less scope for any commitment to other objectives where these are incompatible with the goal of stability. Cf. Willgerodt, 1990, pp. 311ff.

[67] Deutsche Bundesbank, 1990b, p. 17.

a) Implementation of monetary union

Currency conversion

The conversion to the D-mark and the provision of cash involved a considerable amount of organizational and logistical preparation.[68] Since the GDR did not agree to an unrestricted transfer of responsibility for monetary policy to the Bundesbank until 4 May 1990, the latter had a period of only just under eight weeks in which to prepare monetary union in the GDR. It was also unable to start work on establishing its temporary administrative office in Berlin and the 15 regional branches until May. The branches were supported by the central banks of the west German Länder in terms of both staff and materials. The Land Central Banks also supplied the notes and coins.[69]

Establishment of means for refinancing

In the GDR's system of monetary planning, the attempts to 'control via the Mark' meant that the banks had no independent powers of refinancing themselves. They thus had virtually no assets at the beginning of monetary union which they could have used to refinance themselves. The State Treaty on GEMSU therefore had to include special arrangements regarding the refinancing of the east German banks.[70] The last such arrangements expired at the end of 1992.

Conversion of the banks' balance sheets

The balance sheets of the GDR's banks, like the corporate accounts, were to be transformed in line with the modalities set out in the State Treaty.[71] The differences between the conversion of the banks' assets and liabilities created gaps in the balance sheets. These gaps were closed by so-called equalization items in the accounts. The GDR government had itself already set up an equalization fund to act as debtor or creditor for the banks' balancing items resulting from the currency conversion.[72] Monetary union meant that the west German rules on the equity capitalization of banks now also

---

[68] For a detailed presentation cf. Kreditanstalt für Wiederaufbau, 1996, pp. 156ff. and Deutsche Bundesbank, 1990d.

[69] Cf. Tietmeyer, 1994, p. 88.

[70] Cf. Deutsche Bundesbank, 1989.

[71] Cf. articles 7 and 8 of Appendix 1 of the Treaty on GEMSU, Bundesgesetzblatt of 25 June 1990 II, p. 518.

[72] This arrangement also applied to the GDR's foreign trade companies, because these maintained commercial credit relations; cf. Kreditanstalt für Wiederaufbau, 1996, p. 181.

applied in the GDR: the banks' equity must amount to at least 4 per cent of the balance sheet total, or one-thirteenth of the volume of credit.[73] If the equity of the former GDR banks was insufficient for this, the gap was also to be closed by the granting of equalization claims.

However, no equalization claims were issued prior to German unification. The relevant provisions were included in the State Treaty via the 'Deutsche Mark Balance Sheet Act'. The debtor of the equalization claims was now a west German fund entitled 'Currency Conversion Equalization Fund' (*Ausgleichsfonds Währungsumstellung*).[74] After German reunification, balance-sheet equalization claims assumed an additional role: they were used not only to close gaps in balance sheets resulting from the asymmetrical conversion, or as a substitute for equity capital, but also to cover losses incurred by the banks from bad debts.

Interest was subsequently paid on the equalization claims from 1 July 1990. The agreements concluded in the State Treaty (Appendix 1, article 8, section 4) set the interest rate in line with the terms on the inter-bank market in Frankfurt (three-month FIBOR). The redemption of the equalization claims began on 1 July 1995, and is to take 40 years. The equalization claims were financed from the 'Currency Conversion Equalization Fund', a public-law agency, whose funds were initially administered by the Staatsbank Berlin (formerly Staatsbank der DDR). When the Staatsbank was closed at the end of 1994, the management of the equalization fund was taken over by the Kreditanstalt für Wiederaufbau (Reconstruction Loan Corporation).

The final allocation of equalization claims is not to occur until after the conversion calculations and the opening D-mark balance sheets of the eastern German banks have been audited by the Federal Banking Supervisory Office. The relevant audit was originally to have been completed by 31 December 1994. However, equalization claims were provisionally allocated even before that. They can be transformed into marketable bearer bonds and thus traded on the capital market or used for refinancing from the Bundesbank. At the end of 1994, the value of the provisional equalization claims issued in advance amounted to about DM 76 billion, of which DM 64 billion were securitized as bearer bonds. In contrast, the equalization liabilities only amounted to DM 1.3 billion. This meant that the equalization fund produced a claim on the Federal Republic of Germany totalling about DM 75 billion at the end of 1994.[75] So far it has proved impossible to finally allocate all the equalization claims, since not all the opening D-mark balance sheets have been confirmed to date. For example, certain transactions inherited

---

[73] Principle I (Grundsatz I) of the Federal Banking Supervisory Office in the version dated 19 Dec. 1985.

[74] Cf. Welcker, 1991, p. 198.

[75] Cf. Kreditanstalt für Wiederaufbau, 1996, pp. 180ff.

from the GDR have yet to be finally processed, and some assets have yet to be fully determined. This means that it is still impossible to ascertain the final amount of equalization claims to be granted. It is currently estimated that the volume of equalization claims will eventually amount to about DM 95 billion (written in December 1996).

In line with the Unification Treaty, a credit-processing fund (*Kreditabwicklungsfonds*) was established when the GDR acceded to the territory of the Federal Republic. This fund was a special Federal budget entrusted with bringing together the GDR budget deficit, the debts from the allocation of equalization claims, the obligations of the Federal Government from its liability as guarantor of the Staatsbank Berlin, and the costs of settling the claims and liabilities incurred by taking over the GDR's state responsibilities with regard to other countries and the Federal Republic. At the same time, the credit-processing fund paid interest on the securities issued to the banks by the equalization fund. The credit-processing fund was hired off from the Federal budget. The original intention was to offset the losses from the processing of credit with the anticipated revenues earned by the Treuhand agency (Treuhandanstalt) from selling the former companies of the GDR. These revenues failed to accrue. Instead, the Treuhand agency ended its privatization work with a deficit totalling DM 256 billion.[76] On 1 January 1995 this deficit, together with the debt relief for the housing sector of the former GDR, amounting to about DM 30 billion, the 'Currency Conversion Equalization Fund', which is expected to amount to approximately DM 95 billion, and the GDR budget deficit of DM 28 billion, were combined to form the 'Redemption Fund for Inherited Liabilities' (*Erblastentilgungsfonds*). This fund is likewise a special Federal fund. In total, therefore, the burden is expected to be about DM 400 billion. The 'Redemption Fund for Inherited Liabilities', which will contain this debt, will be redeemed by payments from the Federal budget and potential Bundesbank profits.[77]

b) Transformation of the banking system

Institutional transformation

The first steps towards transforming institutions took place in the GDR even before 1 July 1990. On 1 April, the 'Act Amending the Act of 1974 on the Staatsbank der DDR', which had been adopted by parliament on 8

---

[76] Cf. Kreditanstalt für Wiederaufbau, 1996, p. 179.

[77] The fund receives the following transfers from the Federal budget each year: transfers to the value of 7.5 per cent of the liabilities of the 'Redemption Fund for Inherited Liabilities' and transfers from the profits made by the Bundesbank which exceed DM 7 billion. Cf. Kreditanstalt für Wiederaufbau, 1996, p. 188.

March 1990, i.e. under the Modrow government, entered into force. The central bank and commercial bank functions of the Staatsbank were separated in the organizational structure. However, there were initially no changes in the ownership structure of the commercial banks. At the same time, the east German banks were permitted to enter into all types of banking business. It should be noted that this did not by any means fully liberalize the GDR's banking system. As before, foreign—i.e. also west German—banks were not permitted to establish themselves there. Foreign banks only had the right to open offices, but were not allowed to lend money.[78]

When the State Treaty on GEMSU entered into force on 1 July 1990, the monetary constitution of the Federal Republic was transferred to the GDR. The institutional changes also affected the economic constitution of the GDR. General freedom of contract and establishment and freedom to choose one's occupation and place of work were introduced, as was the key economic legislation of the Federal Republic. The rules of the GDR were adapted or conflicting rules of the GDR were declared null and void (without being listed in detail). The general adjustment of the legislation took on a more specific form in Appendices to the State Treaty. The Appendices stipulated the legislation to be adopted, revoked or amended or to take effect prior to the entry into force of the Treaty as well as rules which were due to be introduced in the GDR at a later stage. The final institutional transformation took place when the GDR acceded to the territory of the Federal Republic of Germany on 3 October 1990.

Restructuring of the banking system

As a consequence of the institutional changes on 1 April 1990, the Staatsbank transferred its 'commercial banking functions' to the newly established Deutsche Kreditbank AG (DKB) and the Berliner Stadtbank AG (Figure 1). This transfer meant that most of the debts owed to it by industrial companies and the housing sector were transferred to the DKB. In other words, the reorganization of the banking system initially involved nothing but the creation of new state banks.[79]

The DKB set up two joint ventures on 1 June 1990 with Deutsche Bank and Dresdner Bank: Deutsche Bank-Kreditbank AG and Dresdner Bank-Kreditbank AG. Both joint ventures took over the branches and staff of the Staatsbank der DDR and the relationships with companies inherited from the planned economy. The DKB also contracted out to them the processing

---

[78] Cf. Gaddum, 1991, p. 192.

[79] Dennig, 1991, p. 128, points out that a Verkehrsbank, a Postbank, and a Reise- und Touristenbank were also established on 1 Apr. 1990. These were also wholly state-owned.

of its inherited loans. At the end of 1990 and in early 1991, the DKB sold its shares in the joint-venture banks to the respective partner bank. Shortly afterwards, they were integrated into the parent companies.

As of 1 July 1990, the Staatsbank der DDR became the Staatsbank Berlin, a public-law corporation. It was charged with managing the contracts of the Staatsbank der DDR with respect to third parties and with supporting the currency conversion in conjunction with the Bundesbank on the basis of the State Treaty. When the GDR acceded in October 1990, the Federal Republic of Germany became the guarantor of the bank. It was now charged with administering and settling the claims and liabilities inherited from the GDR with regard to other countries and with administering the 'Currency Conversion Equalization Fund'. When the Treuhand agency concluded its privatization work at the end of 1994, the Staatsbank Berlin was merged into the Kreditanstalt für Wiederaufbau. The other banks of the GDR were comprehensively reorganized in the period following monetary union. The result is summarized in Figure 1.[80]

The banking system in eastern Germany was consolidated in the period up to the end of 1992.[81] In terms of the population, there were now about half as many bank branch offices as in the west of Germany. Only a few new banks were established.[82] No former GDR banks were acquired by foreign banks.

Processing of the inherited debt

The inadequate treatment of the credit situation inherited from the planned economy was exacerbated by developments prior to monetary union: rather than being consolidated when a two-tier banking system was established in the GDR on 1 April 1990, the debts owed to the Staatsbank by state-owned firms were almost all transferred to the DKB.[83] When the GDR acceded, the DKB was transferred to the Federal Government's Treuhand agency, which thus became both the owner of the former state-owned companies and the DKB's main debtor.

---

[80] For further details cf. Kreditanstalt für Wiederaufbau, 1996 and Gawel, 1994.

[81] By Sept. 1992, the number of savings banks and credit cooperatives had fallen, owing mainly to mergers, to about 450, with about 4,500 branches. West German banks also established 1,300 branches.

[82] Cf. Deutsche Bundesbank, 1992, pp. 17f.

[83] Following monetary union, the DKB was the main creditor of the former GDR companies, at DM 87 billion. It was followed by the Genossenschaftsbank Berlin, at about DM 8 billion, the Berliner Stadtbank AG, at about DM 4.5 billion, and other banks with smaller shares of the remaining legacy of debt, totalling DM 2.5 billion. Cf. Cloes, 1991, p. 659. There were also state loans to the housing sector totalling some DM 40 billion.

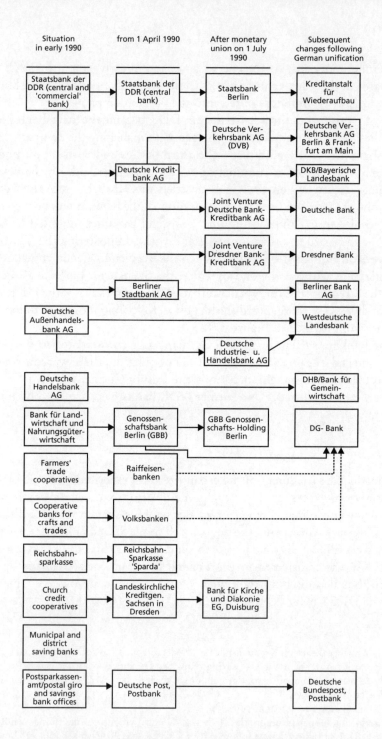

FIGURE 1: Restructuring of the banking system

Source: Kreditanstalt für Wiederaufbau, 1996, p. 337. Additions and amendments by the author.

The DKB's assets mainly comprised inherited loans to what were now Treuhand companies and state lending to the housing sector. Its liabilities consisted of obligations to the Staatsbank Berlin. At the time of monetary union, the Staatsbank's claims on the DKB were mainly offset by deposits of savings banks and cooperative banks. Following monetary union, however, a substantial amount of these deposits were withdrawn.[84] The outflow of liquidity in the third quarter of 1990 alone amounted to about DM 25 billion, or roughly one-quarter of the claims on the DKB which needed to be refinanced.

The consequence of this development was a substantial outflow of funds from the Staatsbank Berlin. As the bank was unable to call its claims on the DKB and, initially, the Berliner Stadtbank AG and the Genossenschaftsbank Berlin at short-notice, the gaps that arose were likewise closed by borrowing on the capital market.[85] By the end of 1991, the amount borrowed on the capital market already totalled DM 97.4 billion.[86] A large proportion of this sum took the form of floaters, i.e. a form of short-term bond bearing interest at the money market rate. Given the inverse interest-rate structure prevailing at the time, this was the most expensive form of financing.[87] In addition, financing via the Staatsbank Berlin caused additional costs, as the bank charged the DKB a margin for its financial operations. Moreover, the Staatsbank failed to benefit from the relatively better conditions for government bonds on the capital market. If the DKB had refinanced itself via the Treuhand agency, it could have benefited from preferential conditions, assuming that the Treuhand agency's credit line had been increased. The muddled system of refinancing caused by the way the inherited loans were treated thus

---

[84] A leading cause of this development was the temporary increase in withdrawals by the public of their savings in order to satisfy long-cherished consumer wishes, to acquire securities bearing higher interest rates, and to invest the money in other banks. But the savings banks and cooperative banks were also increasingly eager to withdraw their deposits from the Staatsbank in order to exploit more attractive investment outlets. On top of this, there were organizational changes in the savings banks and the Volks- und Raiffeisenbanken, for whom—in place of the Staatsbank—the Deutsche Girozentrale and the DG-Bank assumed the role of liquidity holder.

[85] Prior to this, a standstill agreement had been concluded with the savings banks in the third quarter of 1990, in order to give the Staatsbank a breathing space.

[86] Cf. Kadow, Günter: Die Staatsbank wickelte die DDR-Altschulden ab, in: Börsenzeitung, 27 May 1993, p. 20.

[87] For example, in Nov. 1991, bonds from the Staatsbank and the Federal Government each totalling about DM 4 billion were placed on the market almost simultaneously. The Staatsbank offered a bond with a variable interest rate, the Federal Government 4-year treasury notes. The interest rate for the bonds issued by the Staatsbank was about 9.3 per cent; the rate for the Federal bonds 8.84 per cent. At the end of 1992, the volume of syndicated bonds and loans was about DM 74.5 billion; cf. Kadow, DDR-Altschulden, p. 20. In total, then, the difference in interest rates results in about DM 372 million in unnecessarily paid interest.

resulted in additional, avoidable, financing costs. Even this brief analysis of the muddled way the inherited debt was refinanced is enough to demonstrate the validity of a judgement reached after a special investigation by the Federal Court of Auditors: that it would have been cheaper to consolidate the inherited loans back at the Staatsbank as quickly as possible after monetary union.[88]

The failure to consolidate the credit relations caused even more avoidable costs, since the Treuhand agency, or rather its companies, had to service their inherited debts. The Treuhand agency also had to refinance itself to do so. The then President of the Treuhand agency, Birgit Breuel, confirmed that the costs of refinancing were not low when she made a statement regarding a different matter to the Bundestag's committee of inquiry into the Treuhand agency: 'and then there are the inherited loans: we have about DM 80 billion of the DM 100 billion or so in inherited loans: that means interest payments of about DM 27 billion. That's DM 107 billion. Quite an interesting figure, which people tend to overlook when they talk up our mountain of debt. And then there are other expenses. Once again, they consist to a large extent of interest payments, because we have financed ourselves on the capital market and paid interest on that, too.'[89]

Further costs were caused by the fact that the claims relating to inherited GDR debt were administered not by the creditor banks (still in the public sector) but under contract by private banks. These costs would not have arisen either if there had been an immediate consolidation. But above all, the Court of Auditors criticizes overcharging for this service. It also found sufficient evidence that, when the shares and business of GDR banks were sold to west German banks, claims arising from inherited GDR debt were sold below value.[90] When the purchase price was set, no account was taken of the fact that the debt was secured by equalization claims on the Federal

---

[88] The report on the special investigation was widely covered in the press, even being quoted directly. Reference is made here to these press articles, although the report itself is drawn on as well. The Federal Ministry of Finance had classified the report as 'confidential' because of 'confidential commercial data'. This classification is dubious. After the report was presented, Bundestag member Otto Schily stated that it was not right for the Federal Government to evade public accountability by claiming a duty of confidentiality. Bundestag member Friedhelm Julius Beucher suspected that there was a deliberate cover-up, because of the explosive nature of the Court of Auditors' accusations; cf. 'Bonn weist Rechnungshof-Vorwürfe zurück', in: Frankfurter Allgemeine Zeitung, 10 Nov. 1995.

[89] Deutscher Bundestag, 1994, p. 252.

[90] In the case of two sales, the assessment by the Court of Auditors was expressly confirmed by the Treuhand agency. This also applies to the doubts expressed by the Court of Auditors, as is whether the sales negotiations took place in an orderly fashion in which each side's interests were properly represented. Cf. Bundesrechnungshof, 1995, p. 31.

Government.[91] When the value of apparently dubious inherited debt was adjusted, the banks were issued with equalization claims at the appropriate level. The Court of Auditors therefore criticizes the fact that the banks lacked incentives to enforce claims on parties owing inherited debt.

The approach adopted thus gave rise to considerable costs. The rather restrained judgement of the Court of Auditors was this: 'it therefore cannot be ruled out that the final cost to the Federal Government would have been lower if it had directly taken over the inherited debt.'[92] The following point is also important: if the inherited debt had been dealt with in a manner which took due account of the way the planning system had produced it, the entire problem, including the expensive favours done to certain banks, could have been avoided.

On top of this, the failure to consolidate the debts in a manner consistent with the old GDR system created an unnecessary barrier to the transition process in the east of Germany: the inherited debt influenced the fate of individual companies even before potential privatization, because the assessment of the viability of each Treuhand company included its burden of inherited debt (which had been the result of arbitrary planning).[93] Also, the way the inherited debt was dealt with varied widely from one Treuhand company to another. All purchasers could demand that the Treuhand agency should assure responsibility for the debt prior to the sale, or could pass the debt on to the Treuhand agency by reducing the purchase price correspondingly. However, large companies in particular were remitted their debt, even after the sale had taken place. This resulted in a subsequent unequal treatment of the purchasers of Treuhand agency assets. The discrimination against the former agricultural cooperatives was particularly great. Unlike the Treuhand companies, they were unable to pass the inherited debt on the Treuhand agency, as there was no change in ownership. As a result, monetary union saddled them by law with debt on the incurrence of which they

[91] Furthermore, once the equalization claims were converted into bearer bonds, they could be used for repos with the Bundesbank. This produced substantial interest-rate advantages for the banks. In other words, the equalization claims did affect the results. This should also have been borne in mind when setting the purchase price. Cf. Bundesrechnungshof, 1995, p. 27.

[92] Bundesrechnungshof, 1995, p. 27. This criticism is even more forceful given the fact that, contrary to the statements made for the report by the Federal Ministry of Finance, the inherited debt of municipalities is now also being included in the 'Redemption Fund for Inherited Liabilities'.

[93] This had to be admitted by a representative of the Bundesanstalt für Vereinigungsbedingte Sonderaufgaben, the successor to the Treuhand agency, in oral proceedings before the Federal Constitutional Court in Naumburg/Saale on 28 Jan. 1997, particularly regarding the assessment of the potential viability of agricultural cooperatives.

had had virtually no influence in the GDR and which still represents a considerable financial burden on them today.[94]

6. Concluding assessment

German monetary union was a major element of an unprecedented shock therapy. At the same time as the D-mark became the legal tender of East Germany, the socialist economic and social system was transformed by the transfer of the west German institutional framework.[95]

a) Responsibilities of the Bundesbank

Basically, in the context of the monetary transformation of the former GDR, the Bundesbank was responsible for converting the currency as politically prescribed and for extending its policies to safeguard monetary value to the eastern part of Germany. It ensured a smooth currency conversion in both organizational and technical terms, although the deadlines it had to meet were extremely tight. The risks of inflation from the currency conversion were also kept in check. The Bundesbank was therefore able to fulfil its mandate to safeguard the value of money. This did not always meet with a positive reaction in Germany or abroad—because of related changes in interest rates—but serves as proof of its genuine independence. With regard to the political prescriptions for the currency conversion, priority was given —against the bank's advice—to social acceptability and to limiting the burden on the Federal budget, rather than to the competitiveness of GDR companies.

When the inherited debt was converted, the Bundesbank's advice to do so at the rate of 2:1 was taken. However, it would be difficult to justify this advice in the terms of the diagnosis of the prevailing situation within the GDR. For example, the Bundesbank emphasized that the banks in the GDR were 'part of a centralized system of allocation, limitation, and clearing on behalf of central economic planning with specific mandates for each organisation' and that domestic 'banking business' was mainly performed by the

[94] For details cf. e.g. Mummert, Uwe: Der Bund sollte die Altschulden der Landwirtschaft streichen, in: Handelsblatt, 28 Jan. 1997.

[95] It has not been possible to engage in a more detailed discussion of the steps towards monetary transformation in terms of institutional theory or to provide a deeper analysis of the actions of those involved from the point of view of political economy. For that, cf. Streit and Mummert, 1996, pp. 19ff.

Staatsbank.[96] Given this diagnosis, it is hard to avoid conclusions about the need to consolidate credit relationships. It is even less compatible with the view, which was still being maintained recently, that debt forgiveness for individual cases would be better than general debt forgiveness.[97] The reference to the fact that the assets were also allocated arbitrarily by planning authorities cannot justify a policy of a discretionary allocation of debt oriented along the same lines. That would imply responding to the arbitrary nature of economic planning with fresh arbitrary acts, in order to create 'comparable starting conditions'[98] in terms of competition. In fact, it is not necessary 'to level the playing field' in that way; after all, when companies are sold, any differences in (net) assets between companies which are of market relevance are already reflected in the bids made.

Any advice not based on a thorough consolidation of the credit situation was inevitably going to present problems. It meant that inherited loans unexpectedly needed to be regarded as assets/liabilities in market terms. When setting the conversion rate, they therefore needed to be examined to ascertain their ability to retain value—something they could not have, given how they were created. It also meant that an objectively impossible link had to be created. Monetary quantities from a system in which valuations worthy of the name were *a priori* impossible had to be transformed into those of a market system.[99]

b) Responsibilities of the political decision makers

The politicians were responsible for deciding on the modalities of conversion and setting the restructuring of the east German banking system in motion. This included decisions on how to deal with the credit positions deriving from the planned economy.

The conversion rates were set in line with political considerations. Apart

---

[96] Deutsche Bundesbank, 1990*b*, p. 17.

[97] Cf. Deutsche Bundesbank, 1996, p. 51.

[98] Deutsche Bundesbank, 1996, p. 51.

[99] When they produced their recommendation in spring 1990 (cf. Arbeitsgemeinschaft Deutscher Wirtschaftswissenschaftlicher Forschungsinstitute, 1990), the economic research institutes similarly failed to question the situation which would be created by a failure to deal with the credit situation in a manner that took the previous system into account. This was also true of subsequent proposals in the same direction. After all, the failure itself produced a certain situation and gave rise to market-based interpretations which no longer permitted any analysis which might have corresponded to the way the debts were created, and the role they played in the GDR system. When, in autumn 1990, the DIW pointed to the state as the originator of corporate debt, and again called for a cancellation of debt, it was therefore already too late. Cf. e.g. Pohl, 1990, p. 508.

from that, the conversion was dominated by the rather unconvincing treatment of the credit situation created by central planning. As planned and market economy variables were unjustifiably equated, people were given the impression that the deposits of private individuals were directly offset by the money owed by companies to banks. This made the muddled system of refinancing virtually inevitable. It did a substantial amount of damage to Federal assets. If the credit relationships had been dealt with in a manner appropriate to the system, taking the second option discussed above (Section 3b), it would merely have been necessary to set a conversion rate for the financial assets of private individuals in the GDR. The equalization claims needed to fund the financial assets would then have been clearly defined. The transparency of this approach and the related political debate about the 'costs of unification' during the 1990 election campaign may have acted as a deterrent. However, the costs resulting from the inherited-debt approach have to be borne by the taxpayer.

The way the banking system was reorganized following monetary union is also less than convincing. First, there is the unrefuted criticism made by the Court of Auditors that sales were made below value at the expense of the Federal budget, and that services were contracted out at too high a cost (Section 5b). Also, the reorganization did not always conform to the principles of the west German economic system. A major segment of the GDR's banking system was simply transferred from one state owner to another (Figure 1). This is true irrespective of the variety of forms resulting from the involvement of the Federal Government, the Länder, the municipalities, and state-controlled companies in the banking sector of the Federal Republic. Deutsche Bank and Dresdner Bank gained substantial advantages over potential competitors from the joint ventures as they built up their network of branches, not least because there was a great shortage of real estate suitable for banks at that time. The related effect of a temporary restriction on market access is of overall significance in terms of economic policy because it resulted from the fact that the two big banks enjoyed special treatment from the DKB. Finally, it is striking that hardly any foreign banks were involved, not even in cases where there was more time to organize the sale of former GDR banks. No particular efforts to gain new competitors appear to have been undertaken. And it is impossible to tell how great the impact of general barriers to market access was, given Germany's rigid banking market.

Overall, therefore, expensive mistakes were made by those responsible for policy in the course of monetary union. In mitigation, it can be said that a lot of decisions had to be taken in a very short time against a background of very limited information. It can also be said that the central basis for action—the State Treaty—was the result of a process of difficult political negotiations, and inevitably took due account of public sensitivities, particularly in eastern Germany.

Finally, as indicated, the advice proffered by academics was not free from misinterpretations of the system that GEMSU was supposed to transform. The same probably applies to a range of legal repercussions, which failed to take account of how central planning worked and of the fact that the whole economic order of the GDR, i.e. the foundation of monetary stocks and flows, had disappeared. To this extent, the statement that the general basis for transactions had disappeared is probably correct.[100] On the other hand, there were also some well-founded academic findings and recommendations which took the peculiarities of the GDR system into account.[101] And even before monetary union took place, there was no lack of warnings—including some from the Bundesbank—about potential mistakes in economic policy and wage agreements after monetary union.

None of this in any way lessens the significance of GEMSU for German unification. However, the political decisions criticized here reflect both misinterpretations of the GDR's planning system and opportunistic obfuscation. It would be interesting to compare them with the analytical and political stance that Ludwig Erhard took regarding potential monetary union. After the uprising in east Germany in 1953, hopes were briefly awakened that the Soviet Union would give reunification a chance after the failure of the Ulbricht regime. Erhard said that if this were to happen, east Germany should be included in the west German monetary system, and wrote the following: 'in view of the totally distorted command economy and the economic terror in the Soviet zone, it is utterly impossible to make any predictions about the real purchasing power of the Ostmark. This process [i.e. of monetary restructuring; M. E. S.] will then inevitably and ruthlessly reveal everything about the economic situation in the Soviet zone, and there can be no doubt that the result will be worrying, perhaps even devastating. In other words, we must anticipate a sharp gap in performance between East and West, and there are bound to be serious repercussions on the social situation of the population. Even so, we must have the courage to urge clarity and truth, because only then can the cure begin and take effect.'[102]

---

[100] Cf. Matthiessen, 1994, p. 156. Similarly cf. Schachtschneider, 1996, pp. 167ff.

[101] For example, there is a whole range of literature comparing the economic systems. The official reports on the state of the nation in divided Germany had also contained accurate depictions of the GDR's monetary system for decades.

[102] Erhard, 1962, p. 227.

7. Sources and bibliography

Unpublished sources

Bundesarchiv Koblenz and Berlin
Historisches Archiv der Deutschen Bundesbank (HA BBk)

Bibliography

Abelshauser, Werner (1983): Wirtschaftsgeschichte der Bundesrepublik Deutschland 1945–1980, Frankfurt a.M.
Arbeitsgemeinschaft Deutscher Wirtschaftswissenschaftlicher Forschungsinstitute (1990): Die Lage der Weltwirtschaft und der westdeutschen Wirtschaft im Frühjahr 1990, in: Wochenbericht 57, 15, pp. 183–9
Authors' collective (1990): Geld, Kredit, Finanzen aus neuer Sicht, Berlin
Bofinger, Peter (1990): The German Monetary Unification (GMU). Converting Marks into D-Marks, in: Federal Reserve Bank of St. Louis Review 7/8, pp. 17–36
Bofinger, Peter/Kloten, Norbert (1997): The German Currency Union of 1990—A Critical Assessment. The Impact on German Monetary Policy, in: Frowen, Stephen F./Hölscher, Jens (eds.): The German Currency Union of 1990, a critical assessment, Basingstoke *et al.*, pp. 203–21
Bundesministerium für innerdeutsche Beziehungen (1987) (ed.): Materialien zum Bericht zur Lage der Nation im geteilten Deutschland, Bonn
Bundesrechnungshof (1995): Bericht über die Abwicklung von Altkrediten der ehemaligen DDR und die Übernahme von Geschäften ehemaliger DDR-Kreditinstitute durch andere Geschäftsbanken gem. §88 Abs. 2 BHO, Frankfurt a.M., 27 September
Bundesverfassungsgericht (1997): Leitsatz zum Urteil des Ersten Senats vom 8. April 1997 (1 BvR 48/94)
Burda, Michael C. (1990): The Consequences of German Economic and Monetary Union, Center for Economic Policy Research, Discussion Paper no. 449, London
Cloes, Roger (1991): Altschulden belasten Treuhand mehr als nötig, in: Die Bank 12, 657–660
Colm, Gerhard/Dodge, Joseph M./Goldsmith, Raymond W. (1955): A Plan for the Liquidation of War Finance and the Financial Rehabilitation of Germany, 20 May 1946, offprint in: Zeitschrift für die gesamte Staatswissenschaft 111, pp. 204–84
Dennig, Ulrike (1991): Die Finanzstruktur in den neuen Bundesländern, in: Wirtschaftsdienst 71, pp. 125–31
Deutsche Bundesbank (1989): ⁵Die Deutsche Bundesbank. Geldpolitische Aufgaben und Instrumente, Sonderdrucke der Deutschen Bundesbank no. 7, Frankfurt a.M.
Deutsche Bundesbank (1990a): Press release on the Resolution of the Central Bank Council, Frankfurt a.M., 2 April
Deutsche Bundesbank (1990b): Die Währungsunion mit der Deutschen Demokratischen Republik, in: Monatsbericht 42, 7, pp. 14–29
Deutsche Bundesbank (1990c): Kurzberichte: Monetäre Entwicklung, in: Monatsbericht 42, 10, pp. 5–9
Deutsche Bundesbank (1990d): Technische und organisatorische Aspekte der Währungsunion mit der Deutschen Demokratischen Republik, in: Monatsbericht 42, 10, pp. 25–32
Deutsche Bundesbank (1991): Überprüfung des Geldmengenziels 1991, in: Monatsbericht 43, 7, pp. 14–17
Deutsche Bundesbank (1992): Abschlußbericht der Vorläufigen Verwaltungsstelle, Berlin

Deutsche Bundesbank (1996): Funktion und Bedeutung der Ausgleichsforderungen für die ostdeutschen Banken und Unternehmen, in: Monatsbericht 48, 3, pp. 35–53

Deutscher Bundestag (1994): Beschlußempfehlung und Bericht des 2. Untersuchungs-ausschusses 'Treuhandanstalt' nach Artikel 44 des Grundgesetzes, Deutscher Bundestag, 12. Wahlperiode, Drucksache 12/8484, Bonn 31 August

Erhard, Ludwig (1962): Wirtschaftliche Probleme der deutschen Wiedervereinigung, in: Erhard, Ludwig: Deutsche Wirtschaftspolitik, Düsseldorf/Vienna/Frankfurt a.M., pp. 224–36

Eucken, Walter (1990): Grundsätze der Wirtschaftspolitik, 6th revised edition, Tübingen

Gaddum, Johann W. (1991): Die Markt- und Wettbewerbssituation des Bankensektors in den neuen Bundesländern, in: Gröner, Helmut/Kantzenbach, Erhard/Mayer, Otto G.: Wirt-schaftspolitische Probleme der Integration der ehemaligen DDR in die Bundesrepublik, Berlin, pp. 191–9

Gawel, Erik (1994): Die deutsch-deutsche Währungsunion. Verlauf und geldpolitische Kon-sequenzen, Baden-Baden

Hankel, Wilhelm (1992): DDR-Altschuldenregelung. Bilanz- oder Budgetunwahrheit?, in: Deutsche Zeitschrift für Wirtschaftsrecht 2, pp. 32–5

Hayek, Friedrich A. (1935): The Nature and History of the Problem, in Hayek, Friedrich A. (ed.): Collective Economic Planning, London, pp. 1–40

Hayek, Friedrich A. (1945): The Use of Knowledge in Society, in: American Economic Review 35, pp. 519–30

Hesse, Helmut (1991): Zweifache Währungsunion. Probleme und Aussichten, Kieler Vorträge, N.F. 118, Institut für Weltwirtschaft an der Universität Kiel, Kiel

Kiwit, Daniel/Voigt, Stefan (1995): Überlegungen zum institutionellen Wandel unter Berück-sichtigung des Verhältnisses interner und externer Institutionen, in: ORDO 46, pp. 117–48

Kohl, Helmut (1990): Signal der Hoffnung und Ermutigung für die Menschen in der DDR, in: Presse- und Informationsamt der Bundesregierung: Bulletin no. 25 of 15 February, pp. 193–5

Kohl, Helmut (1996): Ich wollte Deutschlands Einheit, Berlin

Kreditanstalt für Wiederaufbau (1996): Mit der D-Mark zur Währungs-, Wirtschafts- und Sozialunion und zur deutschen Einheit. Eine Dokumentation, Berlin

Krengel, Rolf (1958): Anlagevermögen, Produktion und Beschäftigung der Industrie im Gebiet der Bundesrepublik von 1924 bis 1965, Berlin

Lachmann, Ludwig M. (1963): Wirtschaftsordnung und wirtschaftliche Institutionen, in: ORDO 14, pp. 63–77

Leipold, Helmut (1988): ⁵Wirtschafts- und Gesellschaftssysteme im Vergleich: Grundzüge einer Theorie der Wirtschaftssysteme, Stuttgart

Lippe, Peter von der (1996): Die politische Rolle der amtlichen Statistik in der ehemaligen DDR, in: Jahrbücher für Nationalökonomie und Statistik 215, pp. 641–74

Lipschitz, Leslie (1990): Introduction and Overview, in: Lipschitz, Leslie/McDonald, Donogh (eds.): German Unification. Economic Issues, Washington, pp. 1–16

Matthiessen, Holger (1994): Die DDR-Staatsbankkredite als Rechtsproblem der deutschen Einheit, Baden-Baden

Mises, Ludwig von (1920): Die Wirtschaftsrechnung im sozialistischen Gemeinwesen, in: Archiv für Sozialwissenschaften 47, pp. 86–121

Möller, Hans (1991): Ordnungspolitische Aspekte der westdeutschen Währungs- und Wirtschaftsreform von 1948 mit vergleichenden Hinweisen auf die Währungsstabilisierung von 1923 in der Weimarer Republik und auf die Einführung der DM in der DDR am 1. Juli 1990, in: Wagener, Hans-Jürgen (ed.): Anpassung durch Wandel. Evolution und Trans-formation von Wirtschaftssystemen, Berlin, pp. 209–37

Mummert, Uwe (1995): Informelle Institutionen in ökonomischen Transformationsprozes-sen, Baden-Baden

Neumann, Manfred J. M. (1992): German unification. Economic problems and consequences, in: Carnegie-Rochester Conference Series on Public Policy 36, pp. 163–210

Pleyer, Klemens/Tömp, Jürgen (1980): Grundzüge des Bankrechts in der DDR, in: Recht in Ost und West, Zeitschrift für Rechtsvergleichung und innerdeutsche Rechtsprobleme 24, 1, pp. 1–8

Pohl, Reinhard (1990): Alt-Schulden der DDR-Betriebe: Streichung unumgänglich, in: Wochenbericht 57, 36, pp. 503–09

Pohl, Rüdiger/Thiemer, Andreas (1990): Realwirtschaftliche Voraussetzungen und monetäre Implikationen einer gesamtdeutschen Währungsunion, in: RWI-Mitteilungen 41, 1/2, pp. 83–92

Rüden, Bodo von (1991): Die Rolle der D-Mark in der DDR. Von der Nebenwährung zur Währungsunion, Baden-Baden

Schachtschneider, Karl-Albrecht unter Mitarbeit von Olaf Gast (1996): Sozialistische Schulden nach der Revolution. Kritik der Altschuldenproblematik. Ein Beitrag zur Lehre von Recht und Unrecht, Berlin

Schlesinger, Helmut (1990): Die währungspolitischen Weichenstellungen in Deutschland und Europa, in: Siebke, Jürgen (ed.): Monetäre Konfliktfelder der Weltwirtschaft, Berlin, pp. 17–32

Schmieding, Holger (1990): Der Übergang zur Marktwirtschaft: Gemeinsamkeiten und Unterschiede zwischen Westdeutschland 1948 und Mittel- und Osteuropa heute, in: Die Weltwirtschaft 1, pp. 149–60

Scholz, Rupert (1994): Anmerkung zum Urteil des BGH vom 22. Oktober 1993, in: Juristen Zeitung, pp. 304–05

Schrettl, Wolfram (1991): Economic and Monetary Integration of the two Germanies, in: Economic Systems 15, pp. 1–17

Schürer, Gerhard (1995): Analyse der ökonomischen Lage der DDR mit Schlußfolgerungen, GVS b5-1155/89 vom 27. Oktober 1989, offprint in: Schürer, Gerhard (1995): Enthüllungen zum Staatsbankrott der DDR, in: Orientierungen zur Wirtschafts- und Gesellschaftspolitik 64, pp. 15–23

Sherman, Heidemarie C. (1990): Geldpolitik vor neuen Aufgaben, in: Wirtschaftskonjunktur 42, pp. R1–R4

Sinn, Gerlinde/Sinn, Hans-Werner (1991): Kaltstart, Tübingen

Stiglitz, Joseph E. (1994): Whither Socialism? Cambridge, Mass./London

Stolper, Gustav, continued by Häuser, Karl/Borchardt, Knut (1966): Deutsche Wirtschaft seit 1870, 2nd expanded edition, Tübingen 1966

Streit, Manfred E. (1995): Wohlfahrtsökonomik, Wirtschaftsordnung und Wettbewerb, in Streit, Manfred E.: Freiburger Beiträge zur Ordnungsökonomik, Tübingen, pp. 3–28

Streit, Manfred E./Mummert, Uwe (1996): Grundprobleme der Systemtransformation aus institutionenökonomischer Perspektive, Max-Planck-Institut zur Erforschung von Wirtschaftssystemen, Diskussionsbeitrag 09/96, Jena

Thieme, H. Jörg (1994): Währungsunion in Deutschland: Konsequenzen für die Geldpolitik, in: Gutmann, Gernot/Wagner, Ulrich (eds.): Ökonomische Erfolge und Mißerfolge der deutschen Vereinigung. Eine Zwischenbilanz, Stuttgart/Jena, pp. 131–58

Tietmeyer, Hans (1994): Erinnerungen an die Vertragsverhandlungen, in: Waigel, Theo/Schell, Manfred: Tage, die Deutschland und die Welt veränderten. Vom Mauerfall zum Kaukasus. Die deutsche Währungsunion, Munich, pp. 57–117

Waltmann, Frank (1994): Wirtschaftssysteme. Ökonomische Grundstrukturen des National-sozialismus und der DDR im Vergleich, in: Kühnhardt, Ludger et al. (eds.): Die doppelte deutsche Diktaturerfahrung. Drittes Reich und DDR—ein historisch-politikwissenschaft-licher Vergleich, Frankfurt a.M., pp. 125–39

Watrin, Christian (1990): Der schwierige Weg von der sozialistischen Planwirtschaft zur marktwirtschaftlichen Ordnung, in: Schulenburg, J.-Matthias Graf v.d./Sinn, Hans-Werner (eds.): Theorie der Wirtschaftspolitik. Festschrift zum 75. Geburtstag von Hans Möller, Tübingen, pp. 26–46

Welcker, Johannes (1991): Anmerkungen zur Entwicklung des Bankwesens in den fünf neuen Bundesländern, in: Sparkasse 108, 5, pp. 198–203

Willgerodt, Hans (1990): Probleme der deutsch-deutschen Wirtschafts- und Währungsunion, in: Zeitschrift für Wirtschaftspolitik 39, pp. 311–23

Willgerodt, Hans (1991): German Economic Integration in a European Perspective, in: ORDO 42, pp. 171–87

Wolf, Eduard (1947): Geld- und Finanzprobleme der deutschen Nachkriegswirtschaft, in: Deutsches Institut für Wirtschaftsforschung: Die deutsche Wirtschaft zwei Jahre nach dem Zusammenbruch. Tatsachen und Probleme, Berlin, pp. 195–262

Part Five

THE INTERNATIONAL SCENE

XIV. The International Role of the Deutsche Mark

By Jacob A. Frenkel and Morris Goldstein

1. Introduction

In 1948, when the D-mark was created as part of Germany's monetary reform, its international role was negligible. Starting essentially from scratch after the war, it had none of the characteristics that one typically associates with an international currency, and thus presented no competition for the dominant reserve currencies of the day (the US dollar and the pound sterling). Along with other European currencies, it did not become convertible (even for current account transactions) until the late 1950s. The International Monetary Fund's (IMF) Annual Report first mentions the D-mark as a reserve currency only in 1972.

The D-mark's international position is quite different today—nearly fifty years after its inception. On most measures, the D-mark emerges as the second most important international currency in the world. It has long since established itself as the *de facto* anchor of the European Monetary System (EMS), and the institution which controls its issue and protects its external value—the Bundesbank—has become the model for the European System of Central Banks in a forthcoming European Economic and Monetary Union (EMU). Moreover, the institutional framework that has been so instrumental in the strategic management of the D-mark has had a major impact on official thinking and practice much beyond Europe—particularly as regards the merits of an independent central bank and of a goal for monetary policy that gives primacy toward the long-run pursuit of price stability.

In this article, we discuss and assess the evolving international role of the D-mark. In Section 2, we provide a capsule summary of the factors that have been proposed in the literature as influencing a currency's international use. Section 3 then analyses how the D-mark presently fares on each of the dimensions of an international currency—relative to other leading international currencies and, data permitting, to outcomes in earlier periods. In

We are grateful to C. Fred Bergsten and Randy Henning for helpful comments on an earlier draft, to Robert McCauley (of the Bank for International Settlements) for sharing his data with us, and to Neal Luna for exceptional research assistance.

Section 4, we go beyond the traditional yardsticks of international currency status to highlight issues on which management of the D-mark by the Bundesbank has heavily influenced practice and thinking in other countries. Finally, Section 5 offers some brief concluding remarks.

2. Factors affecting international currency use

The explanation for why some currencies are subject to much wider international use than others is a multi-faceted one. Not only does money serve several functions—as a medium of exchange, a unit of account, and a store of value—but also the international use of a currency spans both the official and private sectors. What's more, the process is affected both by market-driven forces and by official attitudes regarding the benefits and costs of serving as an international currency. Finally, politics as well as economics enters into the picture.

By now, there is an extensive literature on the determinants of international currency use.[1] Our reading of that literature suggests that the following seven factors, taken together, tell the story: (1) confidence in the value of the currency over the long term; (2) openness, depth, breadth, and dynamism of the country's financial markets; (3) economic size and political muscle; (4) structure of the country's foreign trade, its choice of exchange arrangements, and the nature of its debt payments; (5) optimal portfolio considerations; (6) the advantages of incumbency, cum network effects among the functions of money; and (7) official attitudes, policies, and practices to promote/discourage international use. We discuss each of these factors in turn.

a) Confidence in long-term value

The more confident economic agents are about the prospect of a currency maintaining its purchasing power, the better placed that currency is to fulfil the three functions of money on an international scale. As such, the literature has quite appropriately emphasized the mean rate of inflation and its vari-

[1] See Ben-Bassat, 1980; Bergsten, 1975, 1977; Black, 1989; Deutsche Bundesbank, 1995b, 1997; Dooley et al., 1989; Dornbusch, 1988; Eichengreen, 1997; Eichengreen and Frankel, 1996; Emminger, 1977; Frankel, 1995; Frenkel, 1983; Frenkel and Goldstein, 1991; Garber, 1996; Grassman, 1973; Hale, 1995a, b; Heller and Knight, 1978; Kenen, 1983; Krugman, 1980, 1984; McCauley, 1997; McMahon, 1982; Oppers, 1996; Page, 1977, 1985; Rieke, 1982; Sasaki, 1995; Tavlas, 1991; Tavlas and Ozeki, 1992.

ability (over time periods of a decade or longer) as a key indicator of suitability for international currency use.[2] The external value of the currency, that is, the long-term behaviour of the nominal exchange rate, has sometimes also been employed directly as a measure of confidence—usually as regards holdings of currency. Because relative purchasing-power-parity (corrected for productivity bias) holds tolerably well for nominal exchange rates among the major currencies over long time-periods, the internal and external measures of confidence often yield similar qualitative conclusions.[3]

Beyond that, other factors that either might presage a secular depreciation of the currency or that might invite a speculative attack have been identified as influencing confidence. On the former count, a large net international debtor position—and to a lesser extent, a large current account deficit—have been regarded as increasing both the incentives for, and the likelihood of, a depreciation.[4] Echoing the Triffin dilemma, a high and/or rising ratio of liquid short-term (government) liabilities to short-term liquid assets (particularly international reserves) is typically interpreted as a threat to confidence. Finally, at least one analyst has argued that a relatively large foreign-trade sector is a handicap to reserve-currency status, since it is often associated with powerful special interest groups which want to encourage currency depreciation to bolster trade competitiveness.[5]

b) Open, deep, broad, and dynamic financial markets

Market participants want to be able to execute financial transactions free of restrictions, at low transactions cost, with access to a broad array of financial instruments, and with counterparties who are both credit-worthy and knowledgeable about their specific needs. Financial centres that can offer that menu of financial services will enhance the international use of their currencies. Moreover, financial institutions operating in those centres will be placed to serve as bankers to the rest of the world.

While restrictions/taxes on capital inflows/outflows have traditionally been singled out as the main financial impediment to international currency use, most recent analyses—carried out in the wake of financial liberalization and spreading capital account convertibility—adopt a broader view of 'openness'. More specifically, a lack of openness has increasingly referred to limitations on financial activities and products and to explicit and implicit

---

[2] See Kenen, 1983 and Tavlas, 1991.
[3] See Obstfeld, 1995, for one such empirical application.
[4] See Eichengreen and Frankel, 1996 and Frankel, 1995.
[5] See Hale, 1995a.

barriers to the 'contestability' of domestic financial markets (including, for example, a less receptive official attitude to financial innovation by foreign-owned firms operating in the domestic market). In a similar spirit, transactions costs are seen as dependent not only on explicit taxes (e.g. stamp duties, withholding taxes, turnover taxes, costs arising from reserve requirements for banks, etc.), bond and stock issuance procedures, and brokerage commissions, but also on the quality of the supporting infrastructure (e.g. payment and settlement systems, custodial services, reserve-management services provided by the home central bank to others). Particularly important for the breadth and depth of financial markets is the availability of a highly liquid treasury bill market (since central banks prefer to hold their reserves in this form), of good hedging facilities, and of an active, generalized repo market. Big, well-capitalized banks that can recycle savings internationally and that offer a broad range of customized financial services are likewise seen as a boon to wider currency use.

c) Economic size and political muscle

Economic size, typically captured by the country's share of global real output and of global trade flows, matters for international currency use on at least three grounds: large countries have a larger natural 'constituency' for the home currency than smaller ones (particularly in view of the significant 'home bias' in portfolios of investors);[6] larger size gives the country greater negotiating power in the currency composition of trade flows (i.e. it makes it easier for that country's exporters and importers to shift currency risk to the other party); and large size makes the country less vulnerable to one of the potential costs of being a reserve currency, namely, the risk that domestic monetary policy will be overwhelmed by foreigners wishing to acquire or dump domestic currency-denominated assets in large numbers. It has frequently been observed that the three largest economies in the world are also the ones whose currencies have the widest international use, that the United States and the United Kingdom had unchallenged roles as the leading international currencies during periods when they accounted for at least 25 per cent of global output, and that the gradual decline in the US share of world output over the past 25 years has tracked (better than most other indicators) the gradual decline in the reserve-currency role of the dollar.

Political factors enter the picture in two ways. Some observers argue that a key currency must provide a safe depository for foreign funds and that such safety cannot be assured without national military and political

---

[6] See Goldstein and Mussa, 1994, for a discussion of 'home bias' in international portfolios.

strength.[7] In this connection, it is noted that the dominance of the pound sterling and the dollar coincided with the periods during which the United Kingdom and the United States served as the most impregnable bastions of national security. A broader interpretation of this view is that it is easier to assert economic leadership when the country's political/military leadership on the world stage is acknowledged. A second argument is that political considerations will often impinge on countries' reserve-management practices, cushioning what might otherwise be sharper changes in key-currency status. The prime example is the series of support operations for the pound sterling in the two decades after the Second World War (to deal with the problems of blocked sterling balances and large UK current account deficits); in a similar vein, one might argue that the political influence of the United States acted in the late 1960s to limit substitution away from the dollar and to delay the onset of floating.

d) Structure of foreign trade, choice of exchange arrangements, and currency-denomination of debt payments

There are basically two ways of modelling countries' holding of foreign exchange reserves: the mean–variance approach (see below), under which the composition of reserves is treated as another optimal portfolio problem (that is, finding reserve positions that yield the highest rate of return for a given level of risk); and the transactions approach, under which the currency composition of the authorities' exchange market activities dominate the decision (that is, the preferred currency composition is the one that minimizes transactions costs associated with conducting foreign trade, undertaking exchange market intervention, and making debt payments).

In empirical analysis of individual countries' holdings of reserve currencies (based on confidential data submitted to the IMF), researchers have favoured the transactions approach. The main conclusion of those studies is that countries will hold a high share of currency x in their reserves if they peg their exchange rate to currency x, if they have a lot of bilateral trade with country x, and if a high share of their debt payments is denominated in currency x.[8] While bilateral trade patterns and the currency peg are relevant for reserve holdings of both industrial and developing countries, the

---

[7] See, for example, Bergsten, 1975. A counter-argument is that the need to compete as a military power can weaken a country's economic performance. In this regard, some experts made the case that the need to compete militarily with the Soviet Union weakened the ability of the United States to compete economically with the Japanese and the Germans; see Makin and Grassi, 1989.

[8] See Dooley *et al.*, 1989 and Heller and Knight, 1978.

currency denomination of debt payments seems to matter mainly for developing countries.

In addition to affecting reserve holdings, the composition of foreign trade also influences the currencies in which foreign trade is invoiced. Here too, the empirical literature has established a number of robust patterns. The following three merit explicit mention: trade in primary products is typically invoiced in US dollars (and to a lesser extent in pound sterling and IMF Special Drawing Rights); trade between industrial and developing countries is typically denominated in either the currency of the industrial country or the US dollar; and trade in differentiated manufacturing products is likely to be invoiced in the currency of the exporter.[9] This implies that the international use of non-dollar reserve currencies is likely to be increasing, *ceteris paribus*, when their trade with developing countries is on the rise, when the share of primary products in their foreign trade is falling, and when their manufactured exports are growing robustly.

e) Optimal portfolio considerations

Much of the early empirical work on the composition of international reserve holdings (both as between gold and reserve currencies, and among reserve currencies) adopted a portfolio approach.[10] Application of that approach has diminished over time, reflecting a combination of conceptual and data problems: the theory applies to the distribution of wealth among net holdings of particular assets, whereas foreign exchange data cover only gross holdings; the theory also should encompass all financial assets and liabilities —not just reserve holdings; and the mean–variance optimization ought to be done for a single country, whereas the applications of the approach (not having access to confidential IMF individual-country data) have used data on country groups.[11]

If there has been any pattern in the results of these portfolio exercises, it has been that the share of non-dollar key currencies in the reserves of industrial countries was lower over the 1976–85 period than suggested by optimal mean–variance considerations; there was also a suggestion that industrial countries may have been farther away from their optimal reserve portfolios than developing countries.[12]

---

[9] See Grassman, 1973; Page, 1977, 1985; Magee and Rao, 1980; Tavlas, 1991.
[10] See Kouri and Braga de Macedo, 1978; Ben-Bassat, 1980; Healy, 1981; Dornbusch, 1988.
[11] See Dooley *et al.*, 1989.
[12] See Dooley *et al.*, 1989.

f) Advantages of incumbency, and network effects among the functions of money

One popular definition of an international currency is 'one that people use [internationally] because everyone else is doing it'.[13] Implicit in this definition are several significant economic concepts. The theory of 'vehicle' currencies suggests that a vehicle currency will emerge whenever indirect exchange costs through the vehicle are lower than direct exchange costs between two non-vehicle currencies.[14] Moreover, there is strong empirical evidence that transactions costs in foreign exchange markets (bid–ask spreads) are inversely related to the volume of such transactions;[15] put in other words, economies of scale operate to increase the incentives to centralize transactions in one currency. The wider the use of a given currency, the higher the probability of an individual buyer/seller finding a matching currency transaction, thereby lowering search costs; likewise, widespread use increases familiarity with that currency.[16]

Economies of scale in international currency use are likely to be reinforced by economies of scope across the different functions of money. For example, if the bulk of private international financial transactions are denominated in dollars, then countries will be more likely to intervene in foreign exchange markets and to hold their international reserves in dollars. Similarly, if the dollar is the main vehicle currency in international trade, then countries will have a greater incentive to peg their exchange rates to the dollar. And on and on.

The implication of this line of argument is that once a currency becomes the leading international currency, there will be forces at work making it easier to retain that status; by the same token, there will be inertia to switching away from that currency—even if the properties that propelled it to that prominence are becoming less evident over time.[17] This does not mean, of course, that such switches will not take place—only that the incumbent has an advantage that will lead to a rather low elasticity of substitution below some threshold change in the variables determining international currency use.[18]

---

[13] Frankel, 1995, p. 9.

[14] See Black, 1989; Chrystal, 1984; Krugman, 1980.

[15] See Black, 1989.

[16] See Tavlas, 1991.

[17] In this connection, an analogy is often drawn with the standard keyboard. Although it is clearly possible to design a new keyboard that would be more efficient than the existing one, the widespread use of the standard one, along with the costs of switching to a new design, makes such substitution unlikely.

[18] Another implication is that there can be multiple stable equilibria.

g) Official attitudes, policies, practices to promote or discourage international currency use

It follows from the preceding discussion that a country cannot establish its currency as an international one if there is no genuine international demand for it. That being said, this does not preclude two other possibilities, namely, that the country can discourage foreigners from using its currency, and alternatively, that, at least at the margin, the country can encourage international use.

Which of these two attitudes a country adopts should depend on its evaluation of the benefits and costs of serving as an international currency. On the positive side of the ledger, a country might see at least four advantages. First, to the extent that foreigners wish to hold its currency abroad in non-interest-bearing form (that is, as banknotes), it will be earning seignorage; as discussed in Section 3, for several international currencies, enough of the outstanding currency in circulation is held abroad (as an alternative to the unstable domestic currency) to make a far from trivial contribution to seignorage earnings. Second, even when its liabilities are held abroad in interest-bearing form, international currency status may contribute to a lower interest rate than would otherwise be the case; more generally, international currency status can make it easier for a country to finance balance-of-payments deficits. Third, by serving as a vehicle currency in foreign trade, currency risk can be shifted to traders in other countries. And fourth, because international currency use is typically linked with being an international financial centre, home-country financial institutions are apt to capture more of the world's business.

Given these potential benefits, why have some countries (including Germany and Japan) been ambivalent about, or opposed to, having their currencies subjected to growing international use? The main reason seems to be unpredictability and loss of control.[19] More specifically, there is a concern that once foreigners have already acquired, or believe they can acquire, a significant amount of the country's liquid liabilities, a change in the risk-return outlook may provoke either a large-scale capital inflow or a run on the currency, with adverse implications for monetary policy control and for broader policy objectives.[20] Although, with open capital markets, pressure could also come from the actions of domestic residents, information about,

---

[19] See Henning, 1994.

[20] To the extent that international currency use makes it easier to finance balance-of-payments deficits, some countries may feel that this will reduce adjustment incentives—storing up trouble over the longer term.

and leverage on, domestic residents are viewed as greater than those on foreign holders.

In cases when a country does wish to discourage international use of its currency, it can prohibit foreign institutions from engaging in certain activities in the domestic financial market, it can put implicit or explicit taxes on foreign capital inflows, it can limit issuance of those financial instruments that foreigners wish to hold, and it can limit the international activities of its own residents. None of these options is without cost and some of them are not likely to be fully effective. Nevertheless, these costs have to be weighed against the expected benefits/costs of the alternative. Symmetrically, countries wishing to promote international currency use can liberalize their foreign exchange and financial regulations, offer financial instruments that appeal to non-residents, and provide financial infrastructure services on attractive terms (relative to the competition).

3. The D-mark as an international currency

In this section, we apply the characteristics and criteria outlined above to evaluate the current international status of the D-mark. In so doing, we highlight certain features of Germany's economic performance that underlie the D-mark's relative attractiveness as an international currency (e.g. inflation performance and economic size), as well as standard indicators of international currency use (that is, the D-mark's role as a store of value, as a unit of account, and as a means of payment in the official and private sectors).

a) Relative inflation performance

Table 1 compares 23 industrial countries in terms of the mean inflation rate over the period 1950–95. For that period as a whole, Germany achieved the lowest mean inflation rate (less than 2.9 per cent, in terms of the consumer price index). The other two major reserve currencies, the dollar and the yen, emerge in fifth and eighth places, respectively.[21] In each of the four decades from 1950 to 1990, Germany never ranked lower than fourth in the inflation league tables; thus far in the 1990s, however, Germany has

---

[21] Japan's anti-inflationary track record over the post-war period comes out better if one looks at wholesale price inflation rather than consumer price inflation; see, for example, Goldstein and Isard, 1992.

TABLE 1: Industrial countries, ranked by mean

1950–9		1960–9		1970–9	
Country	$\overline{\Delta P}$	Country	$\overline{\Delta P}$	Country	$\overline{\Delta P}$
Portugal	0.68	Greece	1.95	*Germany*	4.89
Germany	1.13	Luxembourg	2.17	Switzerland	4.98
Switzerland	1.14	USA	2.33	Austria	6.10
USA	1.82	*Germany*	2.39	Luxembourg	6.50
Belgium	1.84	Australia	2.46	Netherlands	7.06
Luxembourg	2.07	Canada	2.53	USA	7.10
Canada	2.41	Belgium	2.66	Belgium	7.13
Italy	3.02	Switzerland	3.12	Canada	7.38
Japan	3.04	New Zealand	3.21	Norway	8.37
UK	3.51	Austria	3.34	Sweden	8.57
Netherlands	3.81	Norway	3.49	France	8.90
Denmark	3.81	UK	3.53	Japan	9.09
Ireland	3.86	Italy	3.62	Denmark	9.29
Sweden	4.42	Sweden	3.77	Australia	9.83
New Zealand	5.00	France	3.87	Finland	10.41
Norway	5.57	Ireland	4.00	New Zealand	11.46
Finland	6.14	Portugal	4.02	Greece	12.31
France	6.17	Netherlands	4.12	Italy	12.33
Spain	6.25	Finland	5.05	UK	12.63
Greece	6.50	Denmark	5.34	Ireland	12.75
Australia	6.51	Japan	5.35	Spain	14.39
Austria	6.77	Spain	5.75	Portugal	17.14
Iceland	8.07	Iceland	10.82	Iceland	29.55

Source: IMF, International Financial Statistics, CD-ROM (September 1996).

slipped to 12th place (albeit with a mean inflation rate still less than 3.2 per cent).

The United States did very well in holding down inflation in the 1950s and 1960s, saw its anti-inflationary reputation slip badly in the 1970s, and then improved its inflation performance in the 1980s and 1990s (with the mean inflation rate dropping from over 7 per cent in the 1970s to about 3.5 per cent in the 1990s); nevertheless, its ordinal ranking among industrial countries has deteriorated over the past three decades.

Over the past 15 years, Japan has registered the lowest mean inflation rate among the industrial countries. Its third-place finish among the three major inflation rate of consumer prices ($\overline{\Delta P}$), 1950–95

1980–9		1990–5		Total (1950–95)	
Country	$\overline{\Delta P}$	Country	$\overline{\Delta P}$	Country	$\overline{\Delta P}$
Japan	2.53	Japan	1.66	*Germany*	2.87
Netherlands	2.87	Denmark	2.08	Switzerland	3.18
Germany	2.90	France	2.42	Luxembourg	3.75
Switzerland	3.27	Belgium	2.61	Belgium	3.94
Austria	3.84	Ireland	2.64	USA	4.11
Luxembourg	4.72	Norway	2.67	Netherlands	4.24
Belgium	4.90	Canada	2.68	Canada	4.44
USA	5.55	Netherlands	2.70	Japan	4.57
Canada	6.51	New Zealand	2.75	Austria	4.78
Denmark	6.91	Finland	2.83	Denmark	5.78
Finland	7.32	Luxembourg	2.95	Norway	5.95
France	7.38	*Germany*	3.17	France	6.04
UK	7.43	Austria	3.24	Sweden	6.05
Sweden	7.94	Australia	3.30	Australia	6.35
Norway	8.34	USA	3.50	UK	6.47
Australia	8.41	Switzerland	3.55	Finland	6.66
Ireland	9.34	UK	4.42	Ireland	6.86
Spain	10.25	Sweden	5.24	New Zealand	7.22
Italy	11.20	Italy	5.27	Italy	7.25
New Zealand	11.86	Spain	5.42	Spain	8.67
Portugal	17.64	Iceland	5.59	Portugal	9.66
Greece	19.49	Portugal	8.25	Greece	10.71
Iceland	39.16	Greece	15.06	Iceland	19.77

currencies for the 1950–95 period as a whole reflects primarily its relatively weak anti-inflationary record during the first three decades. Among the minor reserve currencies, the only close competitor to Germany on holding down inflation is Switzerland, which prior to the 1990s, was consistently among the lowest inflation countries—a track record that landed it in second place among all industrial countries over the last 45 years.

Clearly, to the extent that stability of internal purchasing power counts for international currency use, the D-mark and the Swiss franc have gained a leg up on the competition from their countries' sustained low-inflation performance; Japan has, however, given the yen very strong anti-inflationary credibility over the past 15 years, and the United States has made significant strides in erasing the memory of earlier inflationary excesses.[22]

b) Behaviour of nominal, bilateral exchange rates

Figure 1 provides a snapshot of how the exchange rate of the D-mark has evolved *vis-à-vis* the US dollar and the Japanese yen over the 1950–96 period. Taking the period as a whole, the dollar has depreciated by 65 per cent *vis-à-vis* the D-mark, corresponding with an appreciation of the D-mark against the dollar of 180 per cent. The yen, by contrast, has appreciated against the D-mark by 30 per cent, corresponding with a depreciation of the D-mark against the yen of 20 per cent. The appreciation against the dollar has been fairly relentless, with a large reversal occurring only during the 1980–5 Reagan years. In contrast, the D-mark's movement against the yen can be split into two distinct subperiods: a thirty-year period of mounting appreciation running up to 1980, and then a twenty-year episode of depreciation since then, with the largest decline taking place over the 1993–(mid-)1995 years.

For many purposes, it makes sense to look at real rather than nominal exchange rates, or at effective rather than bilateral exchange rates, or at interest rates together with changes in nominal exchange rates rather than at nominal exchange rates alone.[23] Nevertheless, to the extent that confidence in an international currency is buoyed, *ceteris paribus*, by a secular appreciation in its nominal exchange rate *vis-à-vis* other international currencies, Figure 1 suggests that the D-mark has witnessed a large, long-term increase in its value against the dollar, while experiencing (at least over the past two decades), a moderate fall in value against the yen.

c) Net creditor/debtor position

Among the major industrial countries, Germany currently has the second largest net external asset position; only Japan is a larger net creditor. In

---

[22] In terms of the variability of inflation rates, Germany has registered the second-best performance among all industrial countries for the 1950–95 period—just marginally below that of Switzerland. The United States winds up in sixth place on inflation variability, and Japan 14th.

[23] If one looks at the behaviour of nominal and real effective exchange rates since the advent of generalized floating (i.e. early 1973), one again finds that the D-mark has shown less appreciation than the Japanese yen, but more than that for the US dollar; see Mussa *et al.*, 1994.

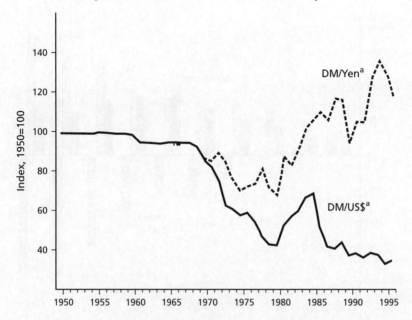

FIGURE 1: DM/US$ and DM/yen nominal exchange rates, 1950–95

[a] A downward (upward) movement in the curve denotes an appreciation (depreciation) of the D-mark.

Source: International Monetary Fund, International Financial Statistics, Sept. 1996.

contrast, after several decades of being the world's largest net creditor, the United States shifted in the early 1980s into a net debtor position, and is now by far the world's largest net debtor. Figure 2 shows the evolution of net external asset positions for the key-currency countries (in billions of US dollars). Table 2 provides a longer and more detailed picture of how Germany's foreign assets and liabilities have grown over the entire 1949–95 period.

Reference to the third column of Table 2 confirms that Germany has been a net international creditor since the late 1950s, with the size of that net creditor position peaking at over DM 520 billion in 1990; since then, however, and reflecting the effects of unification, five years of current account deficits (cum asset price changes) have cut that net asset position roughly in half (by the end of 1995).[24] Relative to GDP, Germany's net asset position (at the end of 1994) was about half the size of Japan's.

[24] It has been estimated that roughly 60 per cent of the decline in Germany's net external asset position between end-1991 and mid-1995 reflected deficits on current account transactions; see Deutsche Bundesbank, 1996.

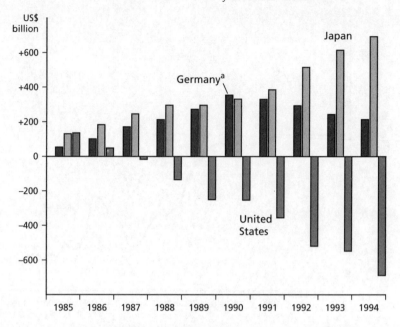

FIGURE 2: Net external assets of major industrial countries* (end-of-year level)

* The data are not fully comparable owing to different valuation methods.

a From end-1990 Germany as now territorially defined.

Source: Deutsche Bundesbank, Monatsbericht, January 1996, p. 33.

TABLE 2: Germany's foreign assets and liabilities (DM billion; end-of-period)

Year	Assets		Liabilities		Net assets
	All currencies	of which: DM	All currencies	of which: DM	
1950	3.9		8.6		−4.7
1955	21.4		24.0		−2.6
1960	63.4		40.1		23.3
1965	91.1		65.5		25.6
1970	186.2		126.9		59.3
1975	322.3	137.8	266.5	173.0	95.8
1980	502.7	241.6	438.9	339.6	63.8
1985	841.3	394.7	711.4	583.4	129.9
1990	1,644.4	802.0	1,122.2	918.0	522.2
1995	2,381.6	1,164.6	2,136.2	1,661.1	245.4

Source: Deutsche Bundesbank.

From 1946 to 1981, the United States built up a large net international creditor position, experiencing current account deficits in only seven of those 36 years. From 1982 on, however, the United States has run current account deficits for 15 straight years, and has transformed its position into the world's largest debtor (with a net liability position exceeding US $680 billion at the end of 1994).[25] This deteriorating net external position produced the United States' first-ever deficit on net investment income in 1994.

As illustrated in Figure 2, Japan has seen its net credit position grow (both absolutely and relative to GDP) under the influence of sustained current account surpluses (there have been only two years in the past twenty in which the current account was in deficit)—and this despite frequent large losses on assets denominated in foreign currency (linked, in turn, to sharp appreciations of the yen *vis-à-vis* these currencies).

To the extent that a strong net external asset position increases confidence in the long-term value of an international currency, the yen and the D-mark hold an advantage over the US dollar.

d) Economic size

Table 3 and Figure 3 provide a snapshot of relative economic size for each of the major reserve currencies—the former concentrating on real output shares, and the latter on foreign trade shares.

It is preferable to make real output comparisons using purchasing-power-parity exchange rates (rather than market exchange rates). On this basis, Table 3 reports that the German economy (in 1995) was slightly larger (22 per cent) than one-fifth the size of the US economy, and about 60 per cent the size of the Japanese economy. German output is about 30 per cent greater than that of France, and 40 per cent greater than that of the United Kingdom.

In 1950, the German economy was roughly 13 per cent as large as the US economy, about two-thirds as large as the economy of the United Kingdom, roughly the same size as that of France, and about one-third larger than the economy of Japan. Sticking just to those five major reserve-currency countries, the next 45 years witnessed a fall in the US share from roughly 65 per cent of the total to just over 50 per cent. Simultaneously, the UK share fell sharply (from 13 to 8 per cent), the Japanese share mushroomed (from 6 to 19 per cent), Germany's share rose moderately (from 8.5 to 11.5 per cent), and France's share increased marginally (from 8.5 to 9 per cent).

---

[25] The USA's net liability position has grown further since then, reflecting current account deficits of US $148 billion in 1995 and US $165 billion in 1996.

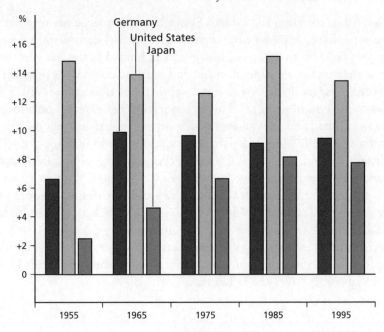

FIGURE 3: Share of world trade*

* Share of world trade defined as a country's exports plus imports in relation to global exports plus imports.

Source: International Monetary Fund, International Financial Statistics, Sept. 1996.

TABLE 3: Real GDP as share of US GDP (PPP weighted, 1985 prices)

Country	1950	1960	1970	1980	1990	1995
Germany	13.20	20.83	22.21	21.51	19.57	22.11
Japan	9.50	16.16	29.99	34.96	39.85	37.37
France	13.30	15.55	18.72	18.49	17.10	17.04
UK	20.02	19.48	16.41	16.43	16.31	15.73
US	100.00	100.00	100.00	100.00	100.00	100.00

Source: International Monetary Fund estimates.

Reviewing trends in terms of world output, the main conclusions would be as follows: with the exception of Japan, all the major reserve-currency countries have seen their share of world output decline over the past 30 years, as the share of developing countries has risen significantly; there has been a steady decline in the US share of world output (from 27 per cent to 21 per cent, using purchasing power parity [PPP] weights); Germany's output share has also declined appreciably, although the advent of unification (not surprisingly) provided a temporary halt to that decline; Japan's output share has risen sharply; the United Kingdom's output share has fallen sharply; and France has also experienced a fall in its output share—but a more modest fall (in percentage terms) than Germany.

Turning to Figure 3, Germany is currently the second largest trading nation (behind the United States but ahead of Japan), with a share of global trade (exports plus imports) in the neighbourhood of 10 per cent (in 1995). Over the past 40 years, Germany has also managed to increase its share of global trade, at the same time that the United States has suffered a decline in its trade share and Japan has registered a tripling of its share.

As argued in Section 2, greater economic size enhances international use of a country's currency. On this count, the D-mark operates at a considerable disadvantage relative to the US dollar—and at a smaller disadvantage (taking output and trade shares together) relative to the Japanese yen. On the other hand, its size gives it an advantage over the other (non-G-3) reserve currencies.

e) Open, deep, and broad financial markets and official attitudes/practices toward international currency use

German financial markets have long since become 'open'—in the sense that a wide range of domestic and foreign financial institutions can move capital in and out of the country. Participation by foreign residents in German financial markets and by German residents in foreign financial markets has been on a strong upward trend, especially over the past dozen years. Unlike several other reserve-currency countries (Japan, the United States, and France), Germany has avoided episodes of serious banking-sector difficulties. The last 25 years have seen a progressive liberalization and modernization of Germany's financial markets—a process that has accelerated during the 1990s (*Finanzplatz* Frankfurt) under the impetus of increasing European financial integration and enhanced competition among European financial centres in a prospective EMU. There has likewise been a gradual but steady softening in the Bundesbank's previous aversion to wider international use of the D-mark. Recently, there is also evidence of convergence in regulatory and market practices as between countries characterized by the German-type, bank-oriented model of financial structure and those that fit more the Anglo-Saxon, securitized mould.[26] And Frankfurt won the EU competition

[26] In this connection, Dziobek and Garrett, 1996, note that regulatory barriers to universal banking in the United States are eroding (e.g. interstate regulations have been liberalized,

to host the European Monetary Institute and a future European Central Bank.

Still, there is a broad consensus among analysts that while the gap may be narrowing, the financial markets of Germany and Japan have put international use of their currencies at a disadvantage relative to the US dollar and the pound sterling.[27] Size, liquidity, transparency, market integrity, receptivity to financial innovation, and availability of investment banking skills all favour New York and London over Frankfurt and Tokyo. In addition, Germany faces strong financial competition within continental Europe from France (which modernized its financial sector earlier on), and its room for manoeuvre on taxes and financial regulations has in the past sometimes been sharply constrained by arbitrage flows to Luxembourg. Finally, while giving greater weight to considerations of competitiveness with other European financial centres than in the previous three decades, German monetary authorities remain cautious about approving regulations or market practices that would weaken their monetary control and limit their ability to keep inflation in check.

A Deutsche Bundesbank study made in 1992 gives a chronology of deregulation and liberalization in Germany's financial markets over the period 1949–89. As reported by Montgomery, the process of deregulation and modernization of Germany's financial markets has continued—and probably accelerated—during the 1990s, as indicated, inter alia, by the following measures: the establishment of a financial futures and options exchange (the DTB); the development of a commercial paper market; a significant lowering of reserve requirements on sight, savings, and time deposits; exemption of reserve requirements on securities repurchase agreements; repeal of taxes on securities transfers and on new issues of securities, along with a lifting of approval procedures for the issue of D-mark fixed-income securities; easier access by foreign banks and non-banks to the D-mark bond market (including the authority for German subsidiaries and branches of foreign banks to act as lead managers for such bond issues); the passage of the Second Financial Market Promotion Act (which, among other things, ended the prohibition on money-market mutual funds, founded the Federal Securities Supervisory Office, made insider trading an offence, and increased disclos-

'super regional' banks are on the ascent, and the repeal of the Glass–Steagall Act has been happening in small increments); simultaneously, German universal banks are acquiring foreign investment firms to build up their securities market expertise, the Deutsche Bank recently adopted US accounting rules, and Frankfurt has implemented a whole set of market-friendly reforms to increase its attractiveness as a European financial centre.

[27] See, for example, Eichengreen and Frankel, 1996; Frankel, 1995; Häusler, 1994, Japan Center for International Finance, 1995; Montgomery, 1995; Oppers, 1996; Sasaki, 1995; Tavlas, 1991.

ure requirements for securities positions); adoption by a few German corporations of international accounting standards; and a series of measures to increase ownership and liquidity of German equity markets (including the historic privatization of Deutsche Telekom, the restructuring and centralization of regional stock exchanges, a widening in the ranges of permissible assets for German investment and money-market funds, the facilitation of security borrowing and lending operations, and reductions in the minimum par values of German shares). Indicators of foreign participation in German financial markets (e.g. foreign holdings of German money-market paper, bonds, and shares), as well as of German participation in foreign financial markets, likewise point to a sharply rising trend over the past decade or so.[28]

Table 4, taken from Sasaki, compares the size of capital markets—both in absolute figures and relative to GDP—for Germany, Japan, and the United States (in 1994).[29] The dominant observation is the large size of the US market relative to Japan—and even more so, relative to Germany; even after accounting for differences in GDP, the US market emerges as very large relative to those of Germany and Japan. The differences are particularly pronounced at the short end of the yield curve and for instruments (treasury bills) that are the main vehicles for countries' holdings of international reserves (because of their liquidity and very low credit risk). These figures also reinforce the conclusions of Goldstein and Mussa, drawn from interviews with a wide range of market participants in the G-7 countries, that the US government securities market is the most liquid government bond market by a wide margin; the next tier would include the bench-mark issues of Japanese government bonds, the bench-mark D-mark bonds, and French OAT issues.[30]

Table 5, drawn from Montgomery, compares stock market turnover and capitalization (as a ratio to GDP) for each of the G-7 countries (in 1994).[31] Germany emerges in fifth place on turnover and in sixth place on capitalization; the United Kingdom and the United States top the list. Here too, the implication is that liquidity in German securities markets has been lower than in some other major reserve-currency countries. The fact that a significant portion of financial transactions for D-mark-denominated assets takes place in London and Luxembourg (e.g. the futures contract on the 10-year Bund is more heavily traded on LIFFE in London than it is on the DTB in

[28] See Montgomery, 1995; Deutsche Bundesbank, 1996, 1997. For example, foreign investors held D-mark assets totalling DM 1,439 billion at the end of 1995, compared with DM 771 billion at the end of 1990, and DM 268 billion at the beginning of the 1980s; see Deutsche Bundesbank, 1997.
[29] Sasaki, 1995.
[30] Goldstein and Mussa, 1994.
[31] Montgomery, 1995.

TABLE 4: Size of capital markets in Germany, the USA, and Japan in 1994

Short-term capital markets	Billions US$	Per cent GDP	Medium- and long-term capital markets	Billions US$	Per cent GDP
Germany					
Total	323.1	16.8	Total	1,852.4	96.3
Call money	298.9	15.5	Federal bonds	419.8	21.8
Promissory notes	10.9	0.6	Other public bonds	337.5	17.6
Treasury bonds	13.2	0.7	Local government bonds	386.8	20.1
			Mortgage bonds	121.1	6.3
			Other bank bonds	374.9	198.5
			Corporation bonds	1.9	0.1
			Foreign bonds	210.3	10.9
USA					
Total	2,314.9	34.4	Total	8,427.6	125.2
Repo	536.9	8.0	Treasury bonds	3,126.0	46.5
Commercial paper	412.4	6.1	Federal agency bonds	2,149.3	31.9
Certificates of deposit	601.9	8.9	Munis	955.8	14.2
Bankers acceptances	29.8	0.4	Corporation bonds	2,196.5	32.6
Treasury bonds	733.8	10.9	Foreign bonds	220.4	3.3
Japan					
Total	1,041.1	22.1	Total	4,227.3	91.9
Call money	428.6	9.1	Japanese government		
Promissory notes	82.8	1.8	bonds	2,021.4	42.9
Certificates of deposit	185.3	3.9	Local government bonds	294.2	6.2
Commercial paper	99.0	2.1	Government		
Treasury bonds	113.3	2.4	guaranteed bonds	199.9	4.2
Foreign bonds	15.0	0.3	Bank debentures	770.0	16.3
Gensaki	117.0	2.5	Corporation bonds	422.1	9.0
			Foreign bonds	80.5	1.7

Source: Sasaki, 1995.

TABLE 5: Stock market turnover and
capitalization, 1994* (percentage of GDP)

Country	Turnover	Capitalization
Germany	25.10	25.45
USA	53.32	76.47
Japan	24.43	73.18
United Kingdom	90.71	115.41
France	46.29	34.13
Italy	11.58	15.54
Canada	29.32	58.40

* Turnover and capitalization are for listed domestic
company shares.

Source: Montgomery, 1995.

Frankfurt) and that two of Germany's largest banks have recently moved
their investment-banking operations to London, also testify to the competitive pressures experienced by Germany's financial markets.

Analyses of why Frankfurt and Tokyo have been at a disadvantage relative
to New York and London point to a number of factors.[32] In Germany's
case, the height and coverage of reserve requirements, the interest withholding tax, the business capitalization tax, the limited role of private pension
systems, the slower progress on disclosure requirements for securities and
on penalties for insider trading, a lower availability of trained professionals
with investment banking and/or derivative-trading expertise, and certain
inflexibilities in the labour market (e.g. constraints on overtime and weekend
work), have each played a role. Turning to Japan, the inhibiting factors most
often cited by analysts and market participants are the limited supply of
government treasury bills, the transfer tax on government securities, the
withholding tax on interest income, inadequate transparency in administrative processes, unequal terms of competition with domestic financial firms,
relatively high issuing costs in the Samurai bond market, outdated settlement procedures for government securities, relatively slow approval procedures for new financial instruments (particularly for derivative products),
and the reluctance of the Bank of Japan to extend banking services to foreign

---

[32] Here too, there are strong advantages of incumbency. Because London and New York
have long histories of being financial centres, they benefit from the economies of scale and
scope associated with concentrating financial business in a single location.

central banks (at concessional prices matching those charged by the Federal Reserve Bank of New York).[33]

Official attitudes toward the costs/benefits of being an international reserve currency have also affected the outcome.[34] It is not that the German authorities have not seen benefits associated with becoming a more important financial centre (especially in recent years), or that they were not aware of the external demand for D-mark assets associated with Germany's growing reputation for financial stability. It is, rather, that they have consistently been concerned that wider international use of the D-mark—along with the capital market and regulatory policies that would encourage such use—could well carry too high a price in terms of the higher priority to implement effectively domestic stabilization—particularly when the central bank has to restrict the amount of credit on anti-inflation grounds.[35]

In the late 1960s and early 1970s, this concern was stoked by massive capital inflows, associated with the absence of monetary policy coordination via fixed exchange rates—inflows too large to be combated for long by sterilization operations alone.[36] The same kind of problem reemerged during the Exchange Rate Mechanism (ERM) crises of 1992–3—but this time within Europe (rather than between Europe and the United States).[37] In between,

[33] See Garber, 1996; Japan Center for International Finance, 1995; Sasaki, 1995 and Tavlas and Ozeki, 1992.

[34] In Japan, the concern with wider international use of the yen seems to have centered on the effect of abrupt shifts in currency preferences on the volatility of the exchange rate and on the position of exporters, as well as on the dislocation costs for the domestic financial industry of large-scale deregulation. In the United States, real debate about the costs/benefits of being a reserve currency has been infrequent; one round took place during late 1960s and early 1970s (i.e. around the collapse of Bretton Woods, the creation of the special drawing rights (SDR), and meetings of the Committee of Twenty), and another in the late 1970s (i.e. when the dollar rescue package had to be assembled and when there was a live discussion of a 'substitution account' in the IMF); see Solomon, 1977 and James, 1996.

[35] As Tietmeyer has put it, 'The Bundesbank has always paid attention to preventing reforms of the financial markets from rocking the foundations of monetary policy.' Tietmeyer, 1994, p. 410.

[36] See Emminger, 1977 and Rieke, 1982. As noted by Tavlas, 1991, controls on capital outflows were relaxed during the 1950s, whereas various policies were utilized throughout the 1970s to discourage capital inflows, including higher minimum reserve requirements on deposits owed to non-residents, and a 'gentlemen's agreement' between the Bundesbank and German banks that only German banks could lead-manage D-mark-denominated bond issues. The more fundamental response to capital inflows in the early 1970s was of course the move to a floating exchange rate. Issing, 1994, shows that over the 1950–73 period, changes in external assets were the dominant source of changes in central bank money; this was not the case thereafter. The last capital import restrictions were removed at the beginning of the 1980s; see Freedman, 1996.

[37] See Tietmeyer, 1994 and Goldstein et al., 1993. In response to the ERM crisis, the Bundesbank made it clear that it would not accept an obligation to provide 'unlimited intervention' within the ERM; in addition, the bands around ERM parities were widened substantially.

there were concerns that the growth of D-mark-denominated assets in the Euro-markets (together with the lesser sensitivity of foreign banks to German policy objectives) could act as a significant offset to domestic credit tightening, that the growth of short-term assets not subject to reserve requirements would diminish the tax base and render the demand for money less predictable, that an increased supply of short-term government securities could make it more difficult to implement tight monetary policy (since it would increase the government's own borrowing costs), and that easy approval for new, high-risk financial instruments and activities could eventually involve the monetary authorities in large-scale bail-outs (that, too, could conflict with the need to focus monetary policy on price stability).[38] Wider international use of the D-mark was thus always regarded as something that should emerge as a by-product of financial stability—and not as a competing objective. Interestingly enough, one doesn't see this same tension between internal stabilization and international use of the currency in either the United States or the United Kingdom.

Thus far, we have looked only at the extent to which the D-mark possesses various desirable characteristics of an international currency. We turn next to various indicators of international currency use.

f) Currency composition of official holdings of international reserves

Despite being one of the most closely watched indicators of international currency use, estimates of the currency composition of official reserve holdings are subject to relatively wide margins of error for at least three reasons: not all countries/holders report regularly the currency composition of their reserves to the IMF (including Taiwan, which has the second largest holdings of international reserves in the world);[39] with the explosive growth of derivatives, a central bank can quickly alter its currency position (without that change appearing in the official on-balance-sheet figures);[40] and the figures are sensitive both to whether currency holdings are evaluated at current or constant exchange rates, and to whether dollar holdings of EMS countries (against which ECUs were issued in 1979) are included in the dollar component or not.[41] In addition, it cannot be assumed (at least over short time

[38] See Deutsche Bundesbank, 1990; Henning, 1994; Häusler, 1994; Issing, 1994, 1995.
[39] Frankel, 1995 and Oppers, 1996, report the reserve holdings of Taiwan, Province of China, as in the neighbourhood of US $93 billion.
[40] See Garber, 1996, on this point.
[41] See Oppers, 1996. If one goes beyond foreign-exchange reserves to consider international reserves more broadly, there is the additional problem that the United States still values its gold reserves at the old official price (rather than the market price); this leads to a significant under-statement of its true reserves.

TABLE 6: Currency composition of official holdings of international reserves, 1980–95

Currency	1979	1980	1981	1982	1983	1984	1985	1986	1987	1988	1989	1990	1991	1992	1993	1994	1995
(a) Eichengreen and Frankel, 1996 and International Monetary Fund, Annual Report[a]																	
D-mark	10.9	12.5	11.5	10.8	9.5	10.3	12.2	11.2	11.3	12.4	15.5	15.4	13.8	12.0	12.7	12.9	12.5
US dollar	59.2	52.9	56.2	55.6	55.4	55.2	49.8	48.0	47.3	47.4	45.0	44.4	44.8	49.0	50.4	50.4	51.4
Yen	3.0	3.5	3.5	3.6	4.0	4.7	6.4	6.1	5.9	6.1	6.3	7.2	7.7	7.0	7.1	7.4	6.5
Pound sterling	1.7	2.5	1.9	2.1	2.1	2.5	2.6	2.0	1.9	2.2	2.2	2.8	3.0	2.9	2.8	3.1	3.1
French franc	1.2	1.4	1.3	1.2	0.8	0.9	1.0	0.6	0.7	0.9	1.2	2.1	2.4	2.1	2.0	1.9	1.7
ECU	12.5	15.7	13.9	12.5	13.0	10.4	10.3	10.6	12.0	10.0	9.1	8.5	8.8	8.9	7.5	7.0	6.0
SDR	4.8	3.9	5.3	5.9	4.5	4.5	5.0	5.1	4.3	3.9	3.6	3.3	3.2	2.0	2.0	2.0	2.2
(b) Oppers, 1996[b] *Shares at current exchange rates*																	
D-mark		14.8	12.8	12.2	11.7	12.5	15.0	14.5	14.5	15.6	18.9	18.7	16.7	14.5	15.5	15.5	
US dollar		69.4	70.8	69.9	70.0	69.1	63.9	65.9	66.1	63.3	58.9	56.0	58.2	62.7	63.3	63.1	
Yen		4.3	4.3	4.6	4.9	5.7	8.0	7.8	7.5	7.6	7.7	8.8	9.3	8.5	8.7	8.5	
Pound sterling		2.9	2.1	2.3	2.5	2.9	3.0	2.5	2.4	2.7	2.7	3.4	3.6	3.4	3.4	3.8	
French franc		1.7	1.3	1.0	0.8	0.8	0.9	0.8	0.8	1.0	1.4	2.4	2.9	2.5	2.2	2.0	
Swiss franc		3.2	2.6	2.6	2.3	2.0	2.3	2.0	1.9	1.9	1.5	1.4	1.3	1.2	1.3	1.1	
Dutch guilder		1.3	1.1	1.1	0.8	0.7	1.0	1.1	1.2	1.1	1.1	1.1	1.1	0.6	0.6	0.5	

D-mark	17.2	16.5	16.0	17.0	19.7	19.7	16.4	14.5	17.0	19.4	17.7	16.1	14.6	16.6	15.5
US dollar	63.8	62.4	59.8	57.9	53.6	52.6	59.7	64.9	60.3	55.3	55.0	57.3	60.6	61.0	63.1
Yen	8.1	8.3	9.3	9.4	11.2	13.2	11.3	9.1	9.1	10.4	11.6	11.5	10.2	9.4	8.5
Pound sterling	1.7	1.5	1.9	2.2	3.0	2.7	2.4	2.0	2.2	2.5	2.7	3.0	3.4	3.4	3.8
French franc	1.3	1.2	1.1	1.0	1.1	1.0	0.9	0.8	1.1	1.5	2.2	2.7	2.5	2.4	2.0
Swiss franc	3.9	3.2	3.4	3.2	3.1	3.0	2.3	1.9	2.1	1.7	1.4	1.3	1.3	1.4	1.1
Dutch guilder	1.5	1.3	1.4	1.1	1.1	1.3	1.3	1.3	1.2	1.1	1.0	1.0	0.6	0.7	0.5
Unspecified	2.4	5.6	7.2	8.2	7.3	6.5	5.7	5.6	7.1	8.1	8.3	6.9	6.7	5.0	5.5
(c) Bank for International Settlements estimates[c]															
D-mark	14.1	13.4	12.9	13.6	15.6	15.9	16.3	16.5	19.1	19.0	16.9	15.0	15.6	15.9	16.1
US dollar	69.6	68.7	69.6	68.3	63.4	64.6	63.7	62.6	58.4	54.8	56.2	60.9	61.4	60.7	61.4
Yen	4.5	4.9	5.7	6.1	8.1	8.2	8.2	8.1	8.0	8.9	9.3	8.6	8.5	8.8	7.6

[a] In per cent of end-of-year, total foreign exchange reserves, including SDRs.
[b] In per cent of end-of-year, total foreign exchange reserves, excluding SDRs. The US dollar portion of ECUs was added to the US dollar portion.
[c] In per cent of reserves.

periods) that actual holdings of a particular reserve currency are equal to desired holdings (since large holders typically record large increases in their holdings of weak currencies just after they have intervened to support the value of these currencies).

With these caveats in mind, Table 6 presents estimates of the currency composition of official reserve holdings drawn from three recent studies: Eichengreen and Frankel, Oppers, and the Bank for International Settlements (BIS).[42] The Eichengreen–Frankel study uses foreign exchange reserves including SDRs in the denominator, excludes dollar balances against ECU reserves, and values reserves at current exchange rates. Oppers considers only foreign exchange reserves (excluding SDRs) and adds dollar balances held against ECU reserves back into dollar-reserve totals; in addition, Oppers presents currency shares under both current and constant (end-1994) exchange rates. The BIS figures include Taiwan and dollar balances held against ECU reserves, use current exchange rates, and also present figures for 1995.

On the basis of the estimates shown in Table 6, along with partial figures on reserve holdings for earlier time periods, the following five conclusions seem evident. First, by all measures, the US dollar remains the dominant reserve currency, accounting for between one-half to two-thirds of total foreign exchange holdings. Second, by all measures, the D-mark and the Japanese yen emerge as the second and third leading reserve currencies, respectively, with the D-mark's share roughly double that of the yen and about one-fourth that of the dollar; the next currencies/official reserve assets in line are the ECU, the pound sterling, the SDR, the French franc, and the Swiss franc. Third, over the past 25 years, the dollar's share of reserves has declined gradually but significantly, with most of the decline occurring in the 1970s; both the D-mark and the yen, starting from very low levels, have gradually but significantly increased their shares over this period. Fourth, over the past fifteen years, the dollar's share shows a modest decline—with much (one-half to three-quarters) of the erosion of that share in the 1980s being reversed in the 1990s;[43] over this same period, the D-mark's share registers a small increase, while the share of the yen rises appreciably (although the yen's share declines in the 1990s). Fifth, the changing shares of

[42] Cf. Eichengreen and Frankel, 1996; Oppers, 1996; Bank for International Settlements, 1996.

[43] Explanations for why the dollar's share in official reserve holdings has risen in the 1990s stress two factors. First, developing countries which have registered the largest increase in reserves are those that have both aligned their currencies with the dollar and hold relatively high shares of dollars in their reserves; see Bank for International Settlements, 1996. Second, the weakness of the dollar in the 1990s has induced large-scale intervention in support of the dollar by other industrial countries, and this intervention has resulted in an accumulation of dollars in their reserves; see Frankel, 1995. Presumably, these two factors have been more than enough to offset dollar sales by some Asian developing countries that have reportedly acted to diversify away from the dollar in their reserve holdings.

three major reserve currencies in reserves over the past 25 years follows in an approximate way their changing shares of world and OECD real output over this period.

g) *Private holdings of reserve currencies abroad*

In countries where the domestic currency serves as a very poor and volatile store of value, residents often take refuge in one of the major reserve currencies for purposes of hedging and transacting.

Establishing the amount of reserve currencies held abroad is a tricky business because it cannot be observed directly. For example, while the proportion of currency circulating outside the German banking system is known, the split between domestic non-banks and currency held abroad is not. As such, a variety of methods has been employed to arrive at estimates of currency circulating abroad—either drawing inferences from time periods/countries where foreign demand for the currency can be assumed to be much lower, or utilizing econometric estimates of currency demand functions.[44] For example, a first hint that the US dollar and the D-mark have been subject to increasing demand abroad comes from a comparison of the time behaviour of currency holdings as a percentage of private consumption or of GDP. Because of financial innovations (e.g. the increasing use of cashless payments), one would expect currency holdings per unit of consumption/GDP to be declining over time. This is in fact what one observes, say, in France and the United Kingdom. In contrast, this ratio has been increasing in Germany and the United States since the second half of the1970s;[45] in addition, the increase is restricted (at least in Germany) to large denomination banknotes (DM 500 and 1,000).

Three main conclusions have emerged from studies of currency held abroad. First, the dollar and the D-mark are the two leading reserve currencies used for cash transactions abroad, with the amount of dollars circulating abroad probably about three times as large as that of D-marks.[46] Second, the share of currency outstanding that is circulating abroad appears to be 'large'—on the order of 30–40 per cent for the D-mark, and 50–70 per cent for the dollar.[47] Third, at least in the case of the dollar, the net flow of currency held abroad shows a rising trend over the past 15 years.[48]

[44] See Deutsche Bundesbank, 1995*a* and Porter and Judson, 1995.
[45] See Deutsche Bundesbank, 1995*a*.
[46] See Eichengreen and Frankel, 1996. The other two countries for which *per capita* currency holdings are relatively high are Japan and Switzerland—but we are not aware of estimates of the amount of their currencies held abroad.
[47] See Deutsche Bundesbank, 1995*a* and Oppers, 1996.
[48] See Porter and Judson, 1995.

h) Currency share of international assets

The greater the confidence that market participants have in a reserve currency, the more likely they are, *ceteris paribus*, to denominate financial contracts in that currency. As such, analysts have often looked to the currency denomination of eurocurrency deposits, external bond issues, external bank loans, and long-term debt of developing countries as indicators of international currency use.

In most cases, such international assets are examined separately. However, McCauley at the BIS has recently put together a time series (for the 1980–95 period) that combines international bonds, cross-border bank liabilities to non-banks, eurocurrency liabilities to non-banks (from 1984), and euronotes (from 1989); in addition, he has calculated the shares of each of the three leading currencies in this 'international assets' aggregate.[49] The results are presented in five-year intervals in Table 7. At the end of 1995, the dollar's share in such international assets was about 38 per cent (much below its share in international reserve holdings); the shares for the D-mark and Japanese yen were 15.5 and 12 per cent, respectively. As for trends, it is noteworthy that the dollar's share, after rising in the first half of the 1980s, has fallen rather steadily and significantly since then.[50] In contrast, the share of the yen has been on a consistent upward climb over the past 15 years (with the 1995 share approximately four times higher than the 1980 share). As for the D-mark, its share shows no evidence of a clear trend—hovering in the 12–15 per cent range for most of this period.

If one looks beneath the international assets measure to its main components, several conclusions are evident from other studies.[51] For eurocurrency deposits, the dollar's share has fallen from roughly three-quarters in the early 1980s to slightly less than one-half in the mid-1990s; the D-mark and the yen are again in second and third place, respectively (with 1994 shares of about 17 and 5 per cent, respectively). On the side of external bank loans, the dollar's dominance is most pronounced, with a share above 80 per cent—pretty much where it was at the beginning of the 1980s; year-to-year fluctuations in the shares of the D-mark and yen are marked but do not alter the conclusion that their shares are typically much below those for other international assets. Finally, the dollar is least dominant for external bond issues,

[49] McCauley, 1997.

[50] The BIS notes that the fall in the dollar's share of this international-asset construct over the 1980–95 period is tracked pretty closely by the decline in the United States' share of G-10 countries' output over the same period.

[51] See Eichengreen and Frankel, 1996; Oppers, 1996; Tavlas, 1991 and International Monetary Fund, 1996.

TABLE 7: International assets*

	1980	1985	1990	1995
Currency (in billions of US dollars)				
D-mark	72.9	87.7	365.0	713.9
US dollar	280.4	671.8	1,344.5	1,743.8
Yen	15.8	54.7	232.3	568.8
G–10 (Europe only)	118.4	178.2	838.7	1,565.1
All assets	492.4	1,058.0	2,986.9	4,600.1
Currency shares (per cent)				
D-mark	14.8	8.3	12.2	15.5
US dollar	56.9	63.5	45.0	37.9
Yen	3.2	5.2	7.8	12.4

* International assets includes international bonds, cross-border bank liabilities to non-banks, eurocurrency liabilities to domestic non-banks (from 1984), and euronotes (from 1989).

Source: Bank for International Settlements estimates.

with an average 1990s share in the neighbourhood of 30–40 per cent; this is also an asset category where the share of the yen usually exceeds that of the D-mark—an outcome that reflects the yen's growing role in the long-term debt of developing countries (particularly those in East Asia).[52] Like its behaviour for the international assets aggregate, the D-mark's share in these individual asset categories displays no strong trend over the past 15 years.

i) Trading in foreign exchange markets

The global foreign exchange market is the largest financial market in the world, with average daily turnover (in April 1995) estimated to be of the order of US $1.2 trillion. Table 8 presents a summary of the currency composition of the global, over-the-counter, foreign exchange market, drawn from the BIS' last three triennial surveys. In 1995, the dollar was involved

[52] See Eichengreen and Frankel, 1996 and Sasaki, 1995. It is noteworthy that there was a marked shift in the currency composition of developing country bond issues in 1995 away from the dollar and toward the yen and the D-mark; more specifically, the yen's share of new bond issues rose to 26 per cent (versus 13 per cent in 1994), and the D-mark's share to 10 per cent (versus 3 per cent in 1994); see International Monetary Fund, 1996, for a discussion of the factors behind this shift.

TABLE 8: Global, gross foreign-exchange-market
turnover* (in per cent)

Position	1989	1992	1995
Currency composition			
D-mark	27	40	37
US dollar	90	82	83
Yen	27	23	24
Pound sterling	15	14	10
French franc	2	4	8
Swiss franc	10	9	7
Other currencies	29	28	31
All currencies	200	200	200
Geographic composition			
Germany		5	5
USA	16	16	16
Japan	15	11	10
UK	26	27	30
France	3	3	4
Switzerland	8	6	5
Singapore	8	7	7
Hong Kong	7	6	6

* For currency composition, at least one side of a transaction denominated in the above currencies was counted, and since each transaction involves two currencies, the total is 200 per cent by definition. The geographic location for turnover was determined by where the transactions were entered into, not the location where the transaction was ultimately booked or managed.

Source: International Monetary Fund, 1996.

in 83 per cent of all transactions[53]—about the same as in 1992, but down somewhat from the 90 per cent level of 1989.[54] The D-mark and the Japanese yen again show up in second and third place, accounting (in 1995) for

[53] As noted in Table 8, since each currency transaction involves two currencies, the total is 200 per cent by definition.

[54] Because foreign exchange trading tends to be implemented via vehicle currencies, there is a (transactions-cost) incentive for official exchange-market intervention likewise to be carried out via vehicle currencies. Unfortunately, data on the currency composition of exchange-market intervention are limited, both as regards coverage and timing. Tavlas, 1991, reports that the dollar's share of official exchange-market intervention within the EMS fell from roughly 70 per cent in 1979-82 to about 25 per cent in 1986-7; over the same period, the D-mark's share in EMS intervention rose from 24 to 59 per cent.

37 and 24 per cent of trades, respectively; the D-mark's share is up significantly from its 1989 level, while the yen's share has fallen slightly. Among EMS currencies, the French franc and several minor currencies have gained ground relative to the pound sterling and the Swiss franc (and probably relative to the D-mark as well); turnover in emerging market currencies is apparently also on the rise.[55]

As regards geographical concentration, Table 8 documents that London continues to be the dominant trading centre—taking 30 per cent of trades in 1995, up from the 26–27 per cent shares recorded in the two previous surveys. New York and Tokyo are next in line, with 16 and 10 per cent, respectively, of the market. Frankfurt emerges in seventh place (in both 1992 and 1995), accounting for approximately 5 per cent of foreign exchange trades.

j) Currency pegs

In choosing among alternative exchange arrangements, some countries have chosen to peg their exchange rates to one of the major reserve currencies—either because such a peg is seen as a superior nominal anchor for monetary policy than the available alternatives, or because the variability of exchange rates under a floating regime is viewed as damaging to resource allocation and foreign trade performance. Others have concluded that the costs of fixed or heavily managed exchange rates exceed the benefits.

In reviewing the evolution of exchange arrangements for IMF member countries over the 1980–96 period, three features stand out. First, among those countries that peg to a single currency, the US dollar continues to be dominant, accounting in 1996 for approximately 30 per cent of all currency pegs (including basket pegs).[56] Second, and contrary to other indicators of international currency use, the French franc shows up in second place, while the D-mark and the yen are not represented at all. Given the leading role that interest-rate policy in Germany plays for interest rate-policy throughout Europe, and given the constraint that ERM exchange-rate obligations place on monetary policy, the *de facto* link of the D-mark to other European currencies is much greater than the *de jure* one; similarly, the yen's influence on exchange-rate and monetary policies in other Asian countries is greater than the pegging figures suggest.[57] Nevertheless, the absence of official pegs

[55] See International Monetary Fund, 1996.
[56] Frankel and Wei, 1994, report that among East Asian countries which chose a basket peg the US dollar typically carries a higher weight in the basket than the yen.
[57] See Frankel, 1995 and Sasaki, 1995. Three of the more popular answers for why Asian

to the D-mark and the yen remains striking. Third, over the past 15 years, both dollar pegging and single currency pegs overall have become distinctly less popular, while floating exchange arrangements (of one kind or another) have become much more so. Whereas dollar peggers represented 41 per cent of all peggers in 1980, the corresponding percentage in 1996 was 31 per cent; more dramatically, while approximately one-quarter of IMF member countries chose floating exchange arrangements in 1980, that share had risen to more than one-half in 1996.

k) Currency invoicing in international trade

Data on the currency invoicing and payment of international trade are not as complete or as current as for some other indicators of international currency use. Still, Tables 9 and 10 permit us to draw three key conclusions about global patterns of currency use and about Germany's currency-invoicing practices in particular.

To begin with, the US dollar again emerges as the chief unit of account and means of payment, with slightly less than half (48 per cent) of world exports denominated in dollars in 1992. Table 9 also documents that the D-mark falls comfortably into second place (at 15 per cent)—well ahead of the French franc, the pound sterling, and the Japanese yen (each with shares in the 5–6 per cent range),[58] and that only the dollar and the D-mark have currency invoicing shares that are much above their shares in world trade.

Second, looking at trends over the 1980–92 period, the data point to a significant decline in the dollar's share—from about 56 per cent (of world exports) in 1980 to 48 per cent in 1992; almost all of that decline occurs during the 1980–87 period, and, according to Thygesen et al., it is linked with a fall in the value of exports from OPEC countries (which are almost exclusively denominated in dollars).[59] Over the same dozen years, the D-mark's share rises slightly from under 14 to over 15 per cent, the yen's share more than doubles from a very low base, and the shares of the pound sterling and the French franc stay more or less constant. Tavlas has argued that the increase in Germany's share would be larger, but for the falling proportion

countries chose not to peg to the yen are that their trade patterns are diversified enough to make basket pegging more attractive, that these countries have been able to control inflation without resort to an exchange-rate-based nominal anchor, and that the trend appreciation of the yen would unduly compromise their competitiveness.

[58] Based on earlier data analysed in Tavlas, 1991, it would be expected that the ordinal ranking of countries by invoicing shares in world imports would be similar to the export rankings.

[59] Cf. Thygesen et al., 1995.

TABLE 9: Currency share in the denomination of international trade* (in per cent)

Currency	1980		1992	
	Currency share of world exports	Ratio of currency share to a country's weight in world trade	Currency share of world exports	Ratio of currency share to a country's weight in world trade
D-mark	13.6	1.4	15.3	1.4
US dollar	56.1	4.5	47.6	3.6
Yen	2.1	0.3	4.8	0.6
Pound sterling	6.5	1.1	5.7	1.0
French franc	6.2	0.9	6.3	1.0
Italian lira	2.2	0.5	3.4	0.7
Dutch guilder	2.6	0.7	2.8	0.8

* The world trade shares account for the influence of country size in world trade. For example, for the US dollar, the ratio is defined as: (share of world exports denominated in dollars)/(share of USA in world trade).

Source: Thygesen *et al.*, 1995.

of Germany's trade conducted with developing countries (since such trade is typically invoiced in the currency of the industrial country).[60]

Third, as shown in Table 10, about three-quarters of Germany's exports and about one-half of its imports are denominated in the national currency; in addition, the use of the national currency to denominate trade has been falling over time for exports but rising for imports. Data put together by Thygesen *et al.* for seven industrial countries (including Germany) confirms that these patterns in the currency-invoicing of Germany's foreign trade are more widespread: that is, use of the national currency is typically higher for exports than imports, and it has been falling over time for exports while rising for imports.[61] The Thygesen data also reveal that among the seven industrial countries (the USA, Germany, Japan, France, the UK, Italy, and the Netherlands), Germany's use of the national currency to denominate exports and imports is second only to the United States. Although Japan's currency-invoicing practices are over time converging toward those of other industrial countries, it is still an outlier: (in 1992) slightly more of its exports were denominated in dollars than in yen, and four times as many in the case of its exports.

[60] Tavlas, 1991.
[61] Japan, however, is an exception to these trends; see Thygesen *et al.*, 1995.

TABLE 10: D-Mark share of German
foreign trade* (in per cent)

Year	Exports	Imports
1980	82.5	43.0
1985	79.5	47.8
1990	77.0	54.3
1991	77.5	55.4
1992	77.3	55.9
1993	74.3	54.1
1994	76.7	53.2
1995	74.8	n.a.

* Import shares were calculated on the basis
of import payments; from July 1990, the import data also include the imports of the new
Länder.

Source: Deutsche Bundesbank estimates.

Table 11 presents an overview of the preceding discussion by portraying
an ordinal ranking of the three key reserve currencies according to thirteen
characteristics and indicators of international currency use; since we exclude
other reserve currencies from the comparison, the range of rankings goes
only from one (highest) to three (lowest).

Taken as a group, these characteristics/indicators provide strong evidence
that the US dollar remains by far the leading international currency. On
most counts, the dollar is less dominant now than it was 50, 30, or even 15
years ago, although there are definite signs of a rebound during the 1990s—
at least for several key indicators.

As documented in Table 11, the D-mark has a solid claim to being regarded as the second leading reserve and investment currency. In that lofty
position, it has received a major boost from its superior inflation performance and has also been aided by its net international creditor position. The
size of the German economy gives the D-mark an advantage relative to most
reserve currency countries—but acts as a disadvantage relative to the dollar
and (for the last 20 years or so) to the yen as well. The D-mark is used
significantly more than the yen in holdings of foreign exchange reserves, in
private currency holdings abroad, in the currency invoicing of international
trade, and as a unit of account for international assets. Like the yen, the
major hurdles to the D-mark having attained greater international currency
use are the incumbency advantages of the dollar, the lower breadth, depth,

TABLE 11: Characteristics and indicators of international currency use*

Characteristic/indicator	Germany	USA	Japan
(1) Advantages of incumbency	2	1	3
(2) Control of inflation	1	2	2
(3) Behaviour of nominal, bilateral exchange rate	2	3	1
(4) International net creditor/debtor position	2	3	1
(5) Economic size			
(a) Real output (PPP weights)	3	1	2
(b) Foreign trade (exports plus imports)	2	1	3
(6) Financial markets (openness, breadth, depth, dynamism)	2	1	2
(7) Official attitudes toward international currency use	2	1	2
(8) Share of official holdings of international reserves	2	1	3
(9) Share of international assets (bonds, cross-border and euro-currency liabilities of banks, euronotes)	2	1	3
(10) Private holdings of currency abroad	2	1	3
(11) Trading in foreign exchange markets	2	1	3
(12) Exchange arrangements, currency pegs	2	1	2
(13) Invoice currency in international trade	2	1	3

* 1, 2, 3 = Ordinal ranking of the three major currencies; 1 (3) denotes highest (lowest) international currency use or most (least) of characteristic that promotes international currency use. Ranking excludes other reserve currencies.

and dynamism of its financial sector, and official concerns that a greater international currency role might conflict with higher policy priorities.

4. Other dimensions of the international role of the D-mark (and the Bundesbank)

Traditional indicators of international currency use, helpful as they are, do not convey the full measure of the D-mark's international role. The other dimensions of the D-mark's influence abroad are best appreciated if one recognizes that the influence of a currency cannot be divorced from the institution that manages that currency; indeed, section 3 of the Bundesbank Act of 1957 directs the Bundesbank to 'regulate the amount of currency and credit in circulation with the aim of safeguarding the currency'.[62] Adopting that broader perspective, there are at least three key international influences that merit explicit mention.

First, the D-mark and the monetary policy of the Bundesbank have served since the early 1980s as the *de facto* nominal anchor for the countries participating in the Exchange Rate Mechanism (ERM) of the EMS. The gradual hardening of exchange rate commitments within the ERM became the mechanism by which previously high-inflation members chose to discipline their own monetary policies, and it was to the Bundesbank and its anti-inflationary credibility that these countries turned for monetary policy leadership. Even today, it is still commonplace for other European countries to gauge how far they have progressed on monetary stability by examining market interest rates on their own government securities relative to those on German, Deutsche mark denominated issues. Even more striking, there is little doubt that the Bundesbank has been the 'model' for the European Central Bank.[63] The D-mark's role in the EMS is the focus of another article in this volume.

Second, and going beyond Europe, no other central bank has been more influential in advancing the case for central bank independence. In documenting and analysing the growing trend toward greater independence for central banks around the world, Debelle and Fischer cite three foundations for this new orthodoxy: the success of the Bundesbank and the German economy over the past forty years; the theoretical academic literature on the inflationary bias of discretionary policy making; and the empirical academic literature on central bank independence.[64] Interestingly enough, the Bundesbank has repeatedly expressed its reservations about the practicality and desirability of a rule-based monetary policy regime,[65] while championing the case for shielding monetary policy from political influence.

While there are many alternative definitions and measures of central bank independence, the German central bank is typically ranked as the most politically independent when cross-country comparisons are made (by political independence, we mean the central bank's ability to pursue low inflation without political interference).[66]

[62] The Bundesbank is also required to support the general economic policy of the Federal Government—but only in so far as this does not prejudice its ability to carry out its main function; see Issing, 1993.
[63] 'The Bundesbank model was the guiding principle behind the pertinent provisions of the Maastricht Treaty, in particular those concerning the independence of the future European Central Bank System'. Issing, 1993, p. 9.
[64] Debelle and Fischer, 1995.
[65] See, for example, Issing, 1993, 1995.
[66] Eijffinger and De Haan, 1996, distinguish between personnel independence, financial

The existing literature on empirical links between central bank independence and economic performance has recently been admirably surveyed by Eijffinger and De Haan.[67] Three of their main conclusions are worth noting: (1) there is an inverse relation over long time periods (a decade or more) between central bank independence, on the one hand, and the level and variability of inflation rates, on the other;[68] (2) central bank independence does not appear to be significantly related to economic growth, or to the variability of growth, or to unemployment;[69] and (3), somewhat surprisingly, there is little indication that the most independent central banks suffer lower output costs during recessions than less independent ones (indeed, the evidence points to Germany, and, to a lesser extent, the United States, having higher 'sacrifice ratios'—that is, output losses per unit reduction in the inflation rate—than other industrial countries with less independent central banks).[70] In short, central bank independence seems to be related to improved economic performance (lower inflation with no apparent growth costs) but there is a mystery as to why central bank credibility shows up more in asset markets than in labour markets.

The third area of international influence relates to the goals of monetary policy. During the past decade, more and more countries have accepted the proposition that long-run price stability should be regarded as the primary goal of a central bank. The factors contributing to this second new orthodoxy have recently been analysed by Fischer.[71] He emphasizes that inflation has come to be recognized as costly (both economically and socially), that a long-run (but not a short-run) trade-off between inflation and unemployment has been found to be inconsistent with the econometric evidence, that

independence, and policy independence; within policy independence, they further discriminate between goal independence and instrument independence; see also Grilli *et al.*, 1993 and Cukierman, 1992.

[67] Eijffinger and De Haan, 1996.

[68] This inverse relationship between central bank independence and inflation holds for both industrial and developing countries. Eijffinger and De Haan, 1996, argue, however, that while legal independence is a good proxy for autonomy in the case of industrial countries, one should turn to proxies like the turnover rate of the central bank governorship or the political vulnerability of the central bank when performing tests for developing countries.

[69] Because central bank independence is negatively related to inflation, but seemingly has no significant negative effect on economic growth (at least in industrial countries), several analysts have characterized it as a 'free lunch'.

[70] See Ball, 1994 and Debelle and Fischer, 1995. While the explanation for inter-country differences in sacrifice ratios is not yet in hand, Debelle and Fischer, 1995, argue that industrial countries face a real trade-off between the length and depth of recessions and the variability of inflation, that this trade-off is not best left to a central bank that is isolated from political pressures, and that the Bundesbank should be held to greater accountability for its actions. Adenauer, 1993, contains an earlier criticism of Bundesbank independence.

[71] Fischer, 1996.

double-digit inflation rates have similarly been shown to be bad for economic growth, that the long-run pursuit of price stability (where price stability is interpreted as an inflation rate of say, 1–3 per cent) has shown itself
in most cases to permit sufficient leeway for counter-cyclical policy, and
that an explicit numerical inflation target, together with a transparent framework for making monetary policy decisions, makes it difficult for the potential inflationary consequences of monetary expansion to be overlooked.

It is doubtful that any central bank has done more to promote acceptance
of this view about the primacy of price stability than the Bundesbank. Its
constitutional marching orders have been framed in that way. Underlying
its monetary targets (since 1975) has been an explicitly stated goal for inflation. While it has often overshot both its monetary and its inflation
targets, the fact remains that over the past 45 years Germany has turned in
the best inflation performance in the world.[72] As discussed in Section 3,
when other elements of the institutional policy regime (e.g. the exchange
rate regime, supervision of financial institutions, liberalization measures that
would promote the D-mark's international role) have been seen as threatening the Bundesbank's ability to carry out its low-inflation mandate, the
choice has consistently been made in favour of the latter. And when the time
came to frame the statutes for a future European Central Bank, the German
authorities were insistent that while full employment and growth should be
explicitly mentioned, it needed to be clear that these goals should be pursued
only to the extent that they did not conflict with the primary goal of price
stability.

Two caveats should be noted. First, the primacy of its low inflation goal
notwithstanding, there is strong evidence that the performance of the real
economy has also influenced the monetary policy decisions of the Bundesbank. Although it may not have been described as such in official statements,
the record shows that the Bundesbank has frequently resorted to counter-
cyclical monetary easing to reduce the frequency and severity of recessions.
As shown in a recent empirical study by Clarida and Gertler, the Bundesbank, for the most part, has adjusted short-term interest rates according
to a modified 'Taylor rule' (in which short-term real interest rates are raised
as either anticipated inflation or real output rise relative to target). In fact,
Clarida and Gertler see a strong parallel between the conduct of Bundesbank
policy in the post-Bretton Woods era and how the US Federal Reserve has
operated since 1987.[73]

---

[72] According to figures provided in Clarida and Gertler, 1996 and Goldman Sachs, 1996,
the Bundesbank missed its monetary and inflation targets/goals in about half the years over
the 1975–96 period.
[73] Clarida and Gertler, 1996.

Second, not *all* of the policy views that have accompanied the management of the D-mark over the past few decades have been endorsed by others —either within Europe or more broadly. In this connection, more than a few G-10 countries remain to be convinced of, *inter alia*: the desirability/ sustainability of monetary aggregates as the key intermediate target for monetary policy in the face of significant financial innovation; the need for minimum reserve requirements to assure an adequately stable demand for central bank money; and the wisdom of placing primary responsibility for bank supervision outside the central bank.[74] In addition, the German authorities have during certain periods been sharply criticized—both within Europe and across the Atlantic—for (allegedly) imparting a 'deflationary bias' to European growth (by not reducing interest rates more rapidly in the face of slow growth/rising output gaps), for not pressing harder for a revaluation of the D-mark in the wake of German unification, and for not being more receptive to proposals for international coordination of macroeconomic policies.[75]

5. Concluding remarks

We have endeavoured in this article to bring together the factors that in the space of 50 years have propelled the D-mark from a new currency to the second most important reserve and investment currency in the world. Before concluding, it is perhaps appropriate to offer three brief remarks on some implications of our previous analysis for the D-mark's likely successor, namely the euro.

First, in several respects, the factors that drive international currency use are favourable to the euro developing over time into a serious rival to the dollar. If all fifteen EU countries eventually qualify for EMU and adopt the euro as their currency, the resulting currency area will have a combined GDP (in purchasing-power-parity terms) that is almost the same as that of the United States. The statutes and mandate of the European Central Bank, along with the entry conditions and stability pact for EMU, also provide some protection against macroeconomic policies that would erode confidence in the long-term value of the new currency. If monetary stability

[74] See Freedman, 1996 and Eijffinger and De Haan, 1996.
[75] See Bergsten and Henning, 1996, for a discussion of differences in policy views among the G-7 countries. On the specific issue of D-mark revaluation after German unification, it is often argued that Germany repeatedly proposed such a revaluation—only to have it blocked by some of its ERM partners, who were unwilling to accept devaluation of their own currencies.

can be maintained, there is a natural constituency in eastern Europe that might wish to peg to the euro. And if Europe can create an integrated, large, liquid, fixed-income financial market—including a large, liquid treasury-bill market—it could greatly reduce one of the main shortcomings that has previously limited the inroads it has been able to make on the dominant position of the US dollar. Moreover, as we have argued above, there are network effects across the different functions of money—so that increased euro activity in one dimension will increase activity in other dimensions.

Second, and operating in the opposite direction, it is easy to underestimate the influence of incumbency and inertia on the evolution of reserve currencies over the short-to-medium run; likewise, it is easy to overestimate the impact of moderate portfolio shifts (by the official sector) and of improvements in the liquidity of financial markets on major currency exchange rates.

Several recent calculations are instructive. Eichengreen and Frankel have examined the historical relationship between economic size and the currency composition of official reserve holdings.[76] In one exercise, they consider a scenario where the D-mark/euro currency area and the yen currency area each have the same (PPP-weighted) real GDP as the United States, and where the three currency areas together account for one-half of world GDP (so that each accounts for one-sixth of the total). They estimate that the shares of the D-mark and the yen in official reserves would then increase markedly (to roughly 28 and 16 per cent, respectively)—but nowhere near enough to approach the dollar's share (which would remain in the neighbourhood of 60 per cent). In a more recent econometric exercise[77] that links currency reserve shares to shares of global GDP and global exports, as well as to historical inheritance (proxied by the lagged reserve share), Eichengreen finds that the influence of historical inertia is much greater for the dollar than for either the D-mark or the yen. He also argues that most of the increase in the euro's reserve share relative to the present reserve share of the D-mark will likely occur at the expense of EU currencies and minor reserve currencies—not at the expense of the dollar.

Scenarios that depend on large exchange rate changes to motivate large changes in international currency use should also be subject to caveats and quantitative realities. In this respect, McCauley and White have argued persuasively that improvements in the liquidity of European fixed-income markets would not only increase the demand for debt denominated in euros but would also increase the supply—thereby blunting the exchange rate impacts.[78] Moreover, McCauley notes that existing stocks of government debt

---

[76] Eichengreen and Frankel, 1996.
[77] Eichengreen, 1997.
[78] Cf. McCauley, 1997; McCauley and White, 1997.

are so large that moderate portfolio shifts (by the official sector) between the dollar and the euro would be unlikely to generate large changes in exchange rates. By his estimates, the existing stock of government debt for the G-10 countries is about US $10 trillion. Using a simple portfolio model where the dollar and the euro are imperfect substitutes, where all portfolio rebalancing is accommodated via exchange rate changes (that is, interest rates do not respond), and where existing stocks of government debt denominated in dollars and euros are each US $3 trillion, he concludes that the dollar would have to fall by only a few per cent to restore portfolio balance in response to a portfolio supply shift of say, US $30 billion from dollars into euros.

The lesson to be drawn from these quantitative exercises is that in the absence of a severe and prolonged deterioration in the performance of the US economy, it is difficult to envisage very large shifts in international currency use taking place over relatively short periods of time.[79]

Finally, potential does not equal performance. As the Bundesbank itself has argued on many occasions, credibility for monetary policy cannot be borrowed; it has to be earned. The European Central Bank will begin with no track record. If the euro is to be 'as good as the D-mark,' and if the euro is to become a strong rival to the dollar based on a reputation for monetary stability, it clearly has a tough act to follow.

6. Bibliography

Adenauer, Konrad (1993): Address to the Federal Association of German Industry, Cologne, 23 May (cited in Issing, Otmar [1993]: Unabhängigkeit der Notenbank und Geldwertstabilität, Stuttgart)

Ball, Laurence (1994): What Determines the Sacrifice Ratio? in: Mankiw, N. Gregory (ed.): Monetary Policy, Chicago 1994, pp. 155–82

Bank for International Settlements (1996): 66th Annual Report, Basle

Ben-Bassat, Avraham (1980): The Optimal Composition of Foreign Exchange Reserves, in: Journal of International Economics 10, pp. 285–95

Bergsten, C. Fred (1975): The Dilemmas of the Dollar, New York

Bergsten, C. Fred (1997): The Impact of the Euro on Exchange Rates and International Policy Coordination, in: Masson, Paul R./Krueger, Thomas H./Turtelboom, Bart G. (eds.): EMU and the International Monetary System, International Monetary Fund, Washington D.C., pp. 17–48

Bergsten, C. Fred/Henning, Randall (1996): Global Economic Leadership and the Group of Seven, Institute for International Economics, Washington

---

[79] Indeed, Eichengreen, 1997, finds that the short-run effect of changes in US economic size on the dollar's reserve share is approximately one-tenth as large as the long-run effect.

Black, Stanley (1989): Transactions Costs and Vehicle Currencies, IMF Working Paper no. 89, Washington

Chrystal, Alec (1984): On the Theory of International Money, in: Black, J./Dorrance, G. (eds.): Problems of International Finance: Papers on the Seventh Annual Conference of the International Economics Study Group, New York, pp. 77–92

Clarida, Richard/Gertler, Mark (1996): How the Bundesbank Conducts Monetary Policy, NBER Working Paper no. 5581, Cambridge

Cooper, Richard N. (1992): Will An EC Currency Harm Outsiders?, in: Orbis 36, 4, pp. 517–31

Cukierman, Alex (1992): Central Bank Strategy, Credibility, and Independence, Cambridge

Debelle, Guy/Fischer, Stanley (1995): How Independent Should a Central Bank Be?, in: Fuhrer, Jeffrey (ed.): Goals, Guidelines, and Constraints Facing Monetary Policymakers, Federal Reserve Bank of Boston, Boston, pp. 195–221

Deutsche Bundesbank (1990): Die längerfristige Entwicklung der Weltwährungsreserven, in: Monatsbericht 42, 1, pp. 34–55

Deutsche Bundesbank (1991): Zur Bedeutung der D-Mark als Fakturierungswährung im Außenhandel, in: Monatsbericht 43, 11, pp. 40–4

Deutsche Bundesbank (1992): Finanzplatz Deutschland—Rahmenbedingungen und neuere Entwicklungen, in: Monatsbericht 44, 3, pp. 23–31

Deutsche Bundesbank (1995a): Der D-Mark-Bargeldumlauf im Ausland, in: Monatsbericht 47, 7, pp. 65–71

Deutsche Bundesbank (1995b): Gesamtwirtschaftliche Bestimmungsgründe der Entwicklung des realen Außenwerts der D-Mark, in: Monatsbericht 47, 8, pp. 17–37

Deutsche Bundesbank (1996): Neuere Entwicklungen des deutschen Netto-Auslands-vermögens und der Kapitalerträge, in: Monatsbericht 48, 1, pp. 29–51

Deutsche Bundesbank (1997): Die Rolle der D-Mark als internationale Anlage- und Reserve-währung, in: Monatsbericht 49, 4, pp. 17–30

Dooley, Michael/Lizondo, J. Saul/Mathieson, Donald J. (1989): The Currency Composition of Foreign Exchange Reserves, in: Staff Papers, International Monetary Fund 36, pp. 385–434

Dornbusch, Rudiger (1988): Exchange Risk and the Macroeconomics of Exchange Rate Determination, in: Dornbusch, Rudiger: Exchange Rate and Inflation, Cambridge, pp. 125–51

Dziobek, Claudia/Garrett, John (1996): Convergence of Financial Systems and Regulatory Policy Challenges in Europe and the United States, American Institute for Contemporary German Studies, Working Paper no. 19, Washington

Eichengreen, Barry (1997): 'Comments' on Bergsten: Impact of the Euro, in: Masson, Paul R./Krueger, Thomas H./Turtelboom, Bart G. (eds.): EMU and the International Monetary System, International Monetary Fund, Washington D.C., pp. 49–57

Eichengreen, Barry/Frankel, Jeffrey A. (1996): The SDR, Reserve Currencies, and the Future of the International Monetary System, in: Mussa, Michael L./Boughton, James M./Isard, Peter (eds.): The Future of the SDR in Light of Changes in the International Financial System, International Monetary Fund, Washington D.C., pp. 337–77

Eijffinger, Sylvester/De Haan, Jakob (1996): The Political Economy of Central Bank Independence, Special Papers in International Economics 19, Princeton University

Emminger, Otmar (1977): The D-Mark in the Conflict Between Internal and External Equilibrium, 1948–1975, Essays in International Finance no. 122, International Finance Section, Princeton University, Princeton June

Fischer, Stanley (1996): Why Are Central Banks Pursuing Long-Run Price Stability?, in: Federal Reserve Bank of Kansas City: Achieving Price Stability, Jackson Hole, pp. 7–34

Frankel, Jeffrey A. (1995): Still the Lingua Franca: The Exaggerated Death of the Dollar, in: Foreign Affairs 74, 4, pp. 9–16

Frankel, Jeffrey/Wei, Shang-Jin (1994): Yen Bloc or Dollar Bloc? Exchange Rate Policies of the East Asian Economies, in: Ito, Takatoshi/Krueger, Anne O. (eds.): Macroeconomic Linkage: Savings, Exchange Rates, and Capital Flows, Chicago, pp. 295–333

Freedman, Charles (1996): What Operating Procedures Should Be Adopted to Maintain Price Stability: Practical Issues, in: Federal Reserve Bank of Kansas City: Achieving Price Stability, Jackson Hole, pp. 241–86

Frenkel, Jacob (1983): International Liquidity and Monetary Control, in: Furstenberg, George von (ed.): International Money and Credit: The Policy Roles, International Monetary Fund, Washington D.C., pp. 65–109

Frenkel, Jacob/Goldstein, Morris (1991): Macroeconomic Implications of Currency Zones, in: Federal Reserve Bank of Kansas City: Policy Implications of Trade and Currency Zones, Kansas City, pp. 157–212

Garber, Peter M. (1996): The Use of the Yen as a Reserve Currency, Economics Department, Brown University, unpublished manuscript, February

Goldman Sachs (1996): One More M3 Target, German Weekly Analyst, Issue no. 44, Frankfurt a.M., 22 November, pp. 1–6

Goldstein, Morris/Isard, Peter (1992): Mechanisms for Promoting Global Monetary Stability, in: Goldstein, Morris et al.: Policy issues in the evolving International Monetary System, IMF Occasional Paper no. 96, Washington D.C., pp. 1–36

Goldstein, Morris/Mussa, Michael (1994): The Integration of World Capital Markets, in: Federal Reserve Bank of Kansas City, Changing Capital Markets: Implications for Monetary Policy, Kansas City, pp. 245–314

Goldstein, Morris et al. (1993): Exchange Rate Management and International Capital Flows. IMF International Capital Markets Report, Part I, Washington: IMF World Economic and Financial Surveys, April

Grassman, Sven (1973): A Fundamental Symmetry in International Payments Patterns, in: Journal of International Economics 3, pp. 105–16

Grilli, Vittorio/Masciandaro, Donato/Tabellini, Guido (1993): Political and Monetary Institutions and Public Financial Policies in the Industrial Countries, in: Economic Policy 13, pp. 341–92

Group of Thirty (1982): Reserve Currencies in Transition, New York

Hale, David (1995a): Is the Dollar Losing Its Reserve Currency Status? Special Report, Kemper Financial Services, Chicago 16 March

Hale, David (1995b): A Yen for Change: Why the Yen as a Reserve Currency is not Farfetched, in: International Economy 9, pp. 10–13

Häusler, Gerd (1994): The Competitive Position of Germany as a Financial Centre, in: Central Banking 5, pp. 44–55

Healy, James (1981): A Simple Regression Technique for the Optimal Diversification of Foreign Exchange Reserves, unpublished manuscript, International Monetary Fund, Washington

Heller, Robert/Knight, Malcolm (1978): Reserve Currency Preferences of Central Banks. Essays in International Finance no. 131, International Finance Section, Princeton University, Princeton December

Henning, Randall (1994): Currencies and Policies in the United States, Germany, and Japan, Washington: Institute for International Economics, September

International Monetary Fund (various years): Annual Report, Washington

International Monetary Fund (1996): International Capital Markets: Developments, Prospects, and Key Policy Issues, Washington D.C.

Issing, Otmar (1993): Unabhängigkeit der Notenbank und Geldwertstabilität, Stuttgart

Issing, Otmar (1994): Experience Gained with Monetary Policy Instruments in Germany, in: Monetary Policy Instruments: National Experiences and European Perspectives, Frankfurt a.M., pp. 42–58

Issing, Otmar (1995): Stability of Monetary Policy—Stability of the Monetary System: Experience with Monetary Targeting in Germany, Paper presented to Symposium of the Swiss National Bank in Gerzensee, March 17, printed in: Deutsche Bundesbank: Auszüge aus Presseartikeln no. 22, pp. 4–9

James, Harold (1996): International Monetary Cooperation Since Bretton Woods, New York

Japan Center for International Finance (1995): Opinions and Strategies of Foreign Financial Institutions Regarding the Tokyo Money and Capital Markets, Tokyo

Kenen, Peter B. (1983): The Role of the Dollar as an International Currency. Group of Thirty Occasional Paper no. 13, New York

Kouri, Pentti/Braga de Macedo, Jorge (1978): Exchange Rates and the International Adjustment Process, in: Brookings Papers on Economic Activity 1, pp. 111–50

Krugman, Paul (1980): Vehicle Currencies and the Structure of International Exchange, in: Journal of Money, Credit, and Banking 12, pp. 513–26

Krugman, Paul (1984): The International Role of the Dollar: Theory and Prospect, in: Bilson, J./Marston R. (eds.): Exchange Rate Theory and Practice, Chicago

Leaky, Michael P. (1996): The Dollar as an Official Reserve Currency Under EMU, in: Open Economies Review 7, pp. 371–90

McCauley, Robert (1997): The Euro and the Dollar. BIS Working Paper, Basle

McCauley, Robert/White, William (1997): The Euro and European Financial Markets, in: Masson, Paul R./Krueger, Thomas H./Turtelboom, Bart G. (eds.): EMU and the International Monetary System, International Monetary Fund, Washington D.C., pp. 324–88

McMahon, Christopher (1982): The United Kingdom's Experience in Winding Down the Reserve Role of Sterling, in: Group of Thirty: Reserve Currencies in Transition, New York, pp. 42–9

Magee, Stephen/Rao, Ramesh (1980): Vehicle and Nonvehicle Currencies in International Trade, in: American Economic Review 70, pp. 368–73

Makin, John/Grassi, Anneliese (1989): Introduction, in: Makin, John/Hellmann, Donald (eds.): Sharing World Leadership: A New Era for America and Japan? Washington D.C., pp. XIX–XXIII

Marris, Stephen (1995): Deficits and the Dollar: The World Economy at Risk, Washington

Masson, Paul R./Turtelboom, Bart (1997): Transmission of Shocks Under EMU, The Demand for Reserves, and Policy Coordination, International Monetary Fund, January

Montgomery, John (1995): Germany: Selected Background Issues, IMF Staff Country Report no. 95/101, International Monetary Fund, Washington

Mussa, Michael et al. (1994): Improving the International Monetary System, IMF Occasional Paper no. 116, International Monetary Fund, Washington

Neumann, Manfred J. M. (1986): Internationalization of German Banking and Finance, in: Internationalization of Banking: Analysis and Prospects, Korea Federation of Banks, Seoul, pp. 67–144

Obstfeld, Maurice (1995): International Currency Experience: New Lessons and Lessons Relearned, in: Brookings Papers on Economic Activity 1, pp. 119–220

Oppers, S. Erik (1996): Trends in the International Use of the U.S. Dollar, International Monetary Fund, Washington, unpublished manuscript

Organization for Economic Co-operation and Development (1995): Economic Outlook 58, December

Page, S. A. B. (1977): Currency of Invoicing in Merchandise Trade, in: National Institute Economic Review 81, pp. 77–81

Page, S. A. B. (1985): The Choices of Invoicing Currency in Merchandise Trade, in: National Institute Economic Review 85, pp. 60–72

Porter, Richard/Judson, Ruth (1995): The Location of U.S. Currency: How Much is Abroad, Board of Governors of the Federal Reserve System, unpublished manuscript, Washington

Rieke, Wolfgang (1982): The Development of the D-Mark as a Reserve Currency, in: Group of Thirty: Reserve Currencies in Transition, New York, pp. 16–23

Sasaki, Fumiyuki (1995): Promoting the Yen's Internationalization, in: Nomura Research Institute Quarterly 4, 4, pp. 20–39

Solomon, Robert (1977): The International Monetary System, 1945–76: An Insider's View, New York

Tavlas, George (1991): International Use of Currencies: The Case of the D-Mark. Essays in International Finance no. 181, International Finance Section, Princeton University, Princeton

Tavlas, George/Ozeki, Yazuru (1992): The Internationalization of Currencies: An Appraisal of the Japanese Yen, IMF Occasional Paper no. 90, International Monetary Fund, Washington

Thygesen, Niels *et al.* (1995): International Currency Competition and the Future Role of the Single European Currency. Towards a Tripolar Regime? London/The Hague/Boston, pp. 67–95

Tietmeyer, Hans (1994): Overview, in: Federal Reserve Bank of Kansas City (ed.): Changing Capital Markets: Implications for Monetary Policy, Kansas City, pp. 405–16

XV. The Bundesbank and the Process of European Monetary Integration

By Peter Bernholz

1. The economic background

Since the collapse of the gold exchange standard during the Great Depression in the 1930s, the international monetary system has been governed by the discretionary manipulation of paper currencies by central banks. The Bretton Woods system conceived after the Second World War implied a return to a watered-down version of the gold exchange standard, since it reserved the convertibility of US dollars into gold at fixed parities only for monetary authorities. As it held the bulk of the world's gold reserves, however, the United States was not forced to adhere to the rules of a gold exchange standard. President Nixon abandoned limited gold convertibility in 1971 as soon as the decline of gold reserves started causing problems for the domestically oriented US monetary policy of the time. It follows that the Bretton Woods era was also characterized by the interaction of discretionary national monetary systems, particularly as revaluations and devaluations were expressly envisaged in the statutes of the International Monetary Fund.

For discretionary monetary systems, there are three options for regulating international monetary relations: fixed or 'floating' exchange rates between currencies, or a single currency encompassing several countries. All three options involve a range of problems. A *system of fixed exchange rates* provides little scope for an independent monetary policy. For example, if one country pursues a more expansionary monetary policy than others, its price

This essay is based in large part on documents in the Archives of the Deutsche Bundesbank made available to the author. The thirty-year waiting period means that exact sources cannot be provided from 1968 onwards, and in such cases, reference is merely made to the Historisches Archiv der Deutschen Bundesbank. To enable an examination at a later date, one copy of this essay citing all sources has been deposited in the Historisches Archiv der Deutschen Bundesbank, and a further copy has been retained by the author. I wish to express my thanks to Messrs. Gunter Baer, Andrew Crockett, Leonhard Gleske, Helmut Schlesinger, Hans Tietmeyer and Jean-Claude Trichet for the interviews they gave, and to Carsten Detken of Swiss Bank Corporation for data for Figures 3b and 4.

level will start to rise at a faster rate than that of its partners. The balance of payments deteriorates and currency reserves are lost. If the situation becomes critical, market players will use the fear of a devaluation to start selling the currency, not only to speculate, but also to hedge receivables denominated in it. This in turn only exacerbates the situation, forcing either a shift in monetary policy or a devaluation.

Under a fixed-exchange-rate system with n participants, only $n-1$ exchange rates can be set freely. It follows from this that only $n-1$ countries must intervene to maintain the parities. Over time, the nth country will become the reserve currency country. As long as its financial markets are sufficiently broadly based, this will be the country which adopts the least expansionary monetary policy, because its currency is the most scarce. This country will thus control monetary expansion and inflation in all other countries which stick to the fixed exchange rate and do not devalue. However, this may result in tension for both economic and political reasons.

Under a system of floating exchange rates, rates are not only extremely volatile, but will also overshoot in the medium term.[1] If a country follows a more expansionary monetary policy,[2] its currency will suffer from sustained undervaluation.[3] This boosts exports and puts a brake on imports, which is unwelcome to the other countries because their own competitive positions will deteriorate. On the other hand, an undervalued currency increases the price of imported goods, often resented in the country concerned.

A single currency linking several countries would escape the problems associated with fixed or floating exchange rates. However, it would also eliminate the ability to compensate for undesirable wage and price trends by changing the exchange rates. This would be especially crucial if wage and price levels are rigid, and if inadequately integrated credit and capital markets prevent a compensation through interregional financial flows. These problems are discussed in the literature under the heading of 'Optimum Currency Areas'.[4] Other problems concern the loss of national monetary sovereignty and the organizations and rules which determine the common monetary policy.

The European Economic Community (EEC), and later the European Community (EC) and the European Union (EU) have had to face up to these problems since the Treaty of Rome was signed in 1957. The difficulties posed by fixed and floating exchange rate systems have resulted in repeated calls for a European Monetary System (EMS), and finally European Monet-

---

[1] Cf. Bernholz, 1982.
[2] Cf. Dornbusch, 1976.
[3] Cf. Bernholz et al., 1985.
[4] Cf. Kawai, 1992.

ary Union (EMU), with the problems posed by a single currency presenting one of the major obstacles to its implementation.

2. The principal actors and their interests

At a European level, the actors involved in monetary integration are the Heads of State or Government meeting within the Council (Council), the Council of Ministers of Economic and Financial Affairs (Ecofin), the Monetary Committee (MC) and the Committee of the Governors of EU central banks (Governors' Committee, GC). The MC was established by article 105(2) of the Treaty establishing the European Economic Community (EEC Treaty), and its statutes were adopted by the Council of Ministers on 25 February 1958. Its membership comprises two representatives of each country—one nominated by the government and one by the central bank—plus two from the Commission. Its primary function is to advise Ecofin and prepare monetary matters for Ecofin meetings. It promotes the coordination of monetary policy and monitors the monetary and fiscal policy of the Member States and the Community. It can deliver opinions to Ecofin and the Commission on its own initiative.

The GC was initially set up by the central banks as an informal body on the basis of article 105(1) of the EEC Treaty, which expects them to cooperate in the coordination of economic policy.[5] The 'Committee of the Governors of the central banks of the Member States of the European Economic Community' was formally established by a Council decision on 13 April 1964. Its members are the governors of the national central banks or their deputies. A member of the Commission is invited to attend its meetings.

At the national level, the actors are the heads of state or government, the ministers of economic, financial, and foreign affairs, and the central banks. In Germany, the latter also includes the Central Bank Council, which is responsible for decisions on monetary policy. The Federal Ministry of Economics was responsible for German monetary policy until 1972, when this task was transferred to the Federal Ministry of Finance. The different rules regulating the responsibility of government and central banks in the Member States are important. Whereas the central banks in most countries were essentially subordinated to the finance ministries during the period reviewed, the Bundesbank Act gives the Deutsche Bundesbank a large degree of independence. This has led to misunderstandings, since other governments

[5] Cf. letter from the President of the Deutsche Bundesbank Karl Blessing to the Federal Minister of Economics Ludwig Erhard, 14 Jan. 1958 (HA BBk N-2/K72).

have frequently not understood that the German government cannot influence Bundesbank policy as it pleases.

The specific interests of the actors were, and are, necessarily dissimilar. Together with their foreign ministers, the heads of state or government are motivated by general domestic and foreign policy issues. Following the disaster of the Second World War, the guiding principle of French and German statesmen in particular, but also of their Italian, Dutch, Belgian, and Luxembourg colleagues, was to create institutions in (western) Europe which would prevent any return to European power politics. This caused Jean Monnet and Robert Schuman to propose the establishment of the European Coal and Steel Community in 1950, a suggestion which was seized on by Konrad Adenauer for precisely the same reasons. In addition to the expected economic benefits, the same motive led to the EEC Treaty of 1957, and eventually to the Maastricht Treaty. Statements by German Chancellors to the Central Bank Council explicitly emphasize this aspect. It can also be a matter of personal interest to the politicians concerned to ensure that their name goes down in history as a key contributor to the process of European unification.

Former German Chancellor Helmut Schmidt recently underlined the motive of safeguarding peace again: 'The progress made in European integration . . . corresponds to Germany's vital, long-term strategic interest in ensuring peace if our country wishes to avoid a third anti-German coalition. All Chancellors from Adenauer to Kohl have been guided by this insight. . . . Compared with this essential goal, all the nit-picking about the technical details of monetary union . . . is of secondary importance.'[6]

Heads of state and government also have to pay attention to domestic policy matters because they are focused on getting re-elected. For this reason alone, the insular position of the UK means that Westminster, for example, pursues different objectives from the French government. However, both the French and the Germans are also forced to make domestic policy concessions to voters and pressure groups such as the farming lobby.

The goals of economics and finance ministries are more heavily influenced by economic and fiscal policy considerations. Because the ministers and the parties they represent want to be re-elected, they too must pay heed to pressure groups and the electorate, and are interested in expanding the power and authority of their ministries.

The European Council and Ecofin reflect the interests of their members. Where these diverge, the result will be compromise or no decision at all. This is frequently concealed by empty phrases.

---

[6] Schmidt, Helmut: Deutsches Störfeuer gegen Europa, in: Die Zeit, 29 Sept. 1995, p. 1.

Like the European Parliament, the European Commission is interested in adding to its powers by enlarging the jurisdiction and sphere of influence of the Community. This may lead to conflict with the Council and Ecofin, as the latter in particular will often resist any attempt to restrict national sovereignty.

The interests of the central banks are determined by the degree of independence from government they enjoy and by any statutory goals imposed on them. In countries where the central bank has to act on the instructions of the finance minister, or where the careers of the central bankers depend on their political masters, goals whose success increases the re-election chances of ministers and their parties will be given greater weight by the central bank. In addition to price stability, these goals also include employment and growth targets.

Central banks often try to influence the state of the economy. A more expansionary monetary policy at the right time before elections will stimulate economic activity and employment, but price increases will only emerge once the elections are over. On the assumption that voters have short memories, inflation can then be curbed by a tighter monetary policy.

Finance ministers will also try to have the central bank finance part of their budget deficit. They prefer low interest rates to keep service on public sector debt low, while a degree of inflation cuts its value in real terms.

As a consequence, dependent central banks will pursue a more expansionary monetary policy than their independent counterparts, and these countries will have a higher rate of inflation. This prediction is confirmed by empirical research.[7]

This contrasts with the special position of the Deutsche Bundesbank, whose independence is guaranteed by the Bundesbank Act, in which price stability is laid down as its prime objective. Although it is required to support the economic policy of the government of the day, this requirement is subordinated to its prime objective. The national bank of The Netherlands (DNB) is one of the other central banks obliged to pursue similar objectives.

With the GC consisting of the governors of the national central banks, it was inevitable that there would be differences of opinion among its members. Regular compromises were therefore necessary to reach a common position. However, even the heads of dependent central banks would like to be more independent, and could try to use the GC to further this aim.

Apart from the two Commission members, the MC consists of an equal number of nominees from the governments and the central banks. The

[7] Eijffinger and De Haan, 1996.

interests of governments and the Commission are therefore reflected to a stronger degree in this body than in the GC.

The range of interests represented means that occasional conflicts are more or less unavoidable. Two examples illustrate this. At the end of 1962, the Commission presented an action programme which included a proposal on the formal institution of a Council of the Central Bank Governors of the EEC (GC). This met with considerable resistance from the Federal Ministry of Economics, which noted that such a committee 'would raise particular problems in Germany because the relationship between the central bank and the government in the Federal Republic is far less 'integrated' than in countries with a more 'progressive' regime. In many cases, the German government only learned of the Bundesbank's decisions from the press, and was therefore hardly interested in letting the Bundesbank cooperate even less with the government under the guise of a new committee. Rolf Gocht advanced the opinion that cooperation between the central banks should only happen under the aegis of the EEC Council of Ministers.'[8]

This conflict was only resolved after several meetings between representatives of various ministries and the Bundesbank, and an exchange of correspondence between Bundesbank President Karl Blessing and *Staatssekretär* Ludger Westrick, once Blessing had undertaken to submit regular reports on the meetings of the GC to the Minister of Economics.[9]

Another conflict emerged between the Federal Chancellor and the Bundesbank during preparations for the implementation of the European Monetary System (EMS), which came into force in March 1979. In this case, the initiative had been taken by French President Valéry Giscard d'Estaing and German Chancellor Helmut Schmidt, partly on the basis of the foreign policy aspects already described. They decided that the negotiations should initially be conducted secretly by their experts Bernard Clappier, President of the Banque de France, and Horst Schulmann, *Ministerialdirektor* (Director-General) of the Federal Chancellery. The Bundesbank and the responsible ministries were excluded from these talks because, according to Giscard d'Estaing: 'the Bundesbank President, Otmar Emminger, is unsympathetic to this plan. He does not want to be forced to sell Deutschmarks to support the weak currencies, because this could encourage inflationary trends in Germany.'[10]

---

[8] Cf. memo by Schleiminger relating to the inter-departmental meeting on proposals by the EEC Commission on monetary and fiscal cooperation in the EEC, 17 July 1963, Frankfurt am Main (HA BBk B 330/1841).

[9] Cf. letter from the President of the Deutsche Bundesbank Blessing to Westrick, Staatssekretär in the Federal Ministry of Economics, 23 Sept. 1963 (HA BBk B 330/1841).

[10] Giscard d'Estaing, 1991, pp. 124f.; cf. Emminger, 1986, pp. 357f. and also Schmidt, 1987.

That the Bundesbank was excluded is confirmed by a letter from its President to the Chancellor in June 1978, in which he asks for a meeting[11] before 4 July. He noted that because he was informed only about the outline of the arrangements, it would be difficult to comment on the plans and intentions without a more thorough knowledge of the details.

3. European monetary integration— initial situation and approaches

The 1957 EEC Treaty contains no more than the rudiments of a common monetary policy. According to article 104, each Member State is required to 'ensure the equilibrium of its overall balance of payments ... while taking care to ensure a high level of employment and a stable level of prices'. To achieve these objectives, article 105 provides for cooperation between the central banks and the establishment of a Monetary Committee (MC) to facilitate the coordination of monetary policy.

Together with articles 67 to 81, article 106 calls for the liberalization of payments and capital movements. The Commission is required to make proposals for the coordination and liberalization of foreign exchange policy to the Council, which then issues appropriate directives. However, protective measures are allowed in the case of disturbances in the functioning of the capital market in any Member State. It should be noted in this context that free currency convertibility had not been completely restored when the EEC Treaty was signed, and that there were still various restrictions on payments and capital movements.[12] The non-resident convertibility of the European currencies was only implemented at the end of 1958 by the European Monetary Agreement (EMA).

Article 107 of the EEC Treaty makes changes in exchange rates a matter of common concern. Article 108 sets out the procedure to be followed if a Member State has balance of payments difficulties. In such cases, the Commission investigates the situation and recommends suitable measures. If the measures instituted prove to be insufficient, a qualified majority of the Council can grant mutual assistance. This may include a concerted approach to international organizations, reductions in customs duties, increased quotas, and limited credits with the agreement of the countries concerned. In the event of a sudden balance of payments crisis, article 109

[11] Cf. Emminger, 1986, p. 358.
[12] Cf. Section 8a of this essay.

allows immediate protective measures to be instituted. The Commission and the other Member States must then be informed without delay. After receiving an opinion from the Commission and consulting the MC, the Council can amend, suspend, or abolish the protective measures by a qualified majority.

Given the goal of economic union, the monetary policy provisions of the EEC Treaty outlined above were regarded as insufficient from the outset. Critical voices were heard during the ratification debates in the Bundestag and the Bundesrat in 1957. Bundestag member Fritz Hellwig (CDU/CSU parliamentary group) commented: 'the main shortcoming is that there still isn't any binding basis in the treaties for developing a common monetary policy'.[13]

The Committee on Long-Term Economic Policy, Financial Affairs and Investment made a similar report to the European Parliament in December 1958 (Rapporteur Ph. C. M. van Campen [Netherlands]): 'the economic unity of Europe must be established in all areas. Monetary policy is one of the most important areas. . . . Various parties have stated that the inadequate monetary policy provisions are one of the most serious flaws in the Treaty.'[14]

This criticism soon produced initiatives to fill the gaps. There were four main efforts, each of which was preceded by proposals from committees, politicians, central banks, academics, or associations. The first of these was a Commission action programme for Stage Two which was announced on 29 October 1962. The second was launched by a memorandum from the Commission to the Council on the coordination of economic and monetary policy (12 February 1969) under the aegis of its Vice-President Raymond Barre, and culminated in the Werner Report. The third initiative emerged in 1978 at the instigation of Giscard d'Estaing and Helmut Schmidt and resulted in the EMS. Finally, the fourth move was based on a suggestion by German Foreign Minister Hans-Dietrich Genscher and resulted in the 1992 Maastricht Treaty.

The ultimate goal of a single European currency and a European central

---

[13] Minutes of the 200th Session of the Bundestag on 21 March 1957 (Statement by the Federal Government), p. 11365, cited in: Vermerk von Kühnel betreffend die Einheitliche Währungspolitik im Gemeinsamen Markt—Kritik im Bundestag und im Bundesrat an den einschlägigen Bestimmungen des EWG-Vertrages, 27 Mar. 1958, Frankfurt am Main (HA BBk N–2/68).

[14] Bericht des Ausschusses für langfristige Wirtschaftspolitik, für Fragen der Finanzen und Investitionen des Europäischen Parlaments über Fragen der langfristigen Wirtschaftspolitik, der Finanzen und Investitionen anläßlich der Ersten Gesamtberichte der Europäischen Atomgemeinschaft vom Dezember 1958, Berichterstatter Philippus C. M. van Campen, Kapitel V: Die Währungspolitik, Abschnitt a) Die Währungsstabilität, Unterabschnitt 36 (HA BBk B 330/1841).

bank played a role from the very outset. The report on the coordination of monetary policy published on 7 April 1962 by the Economic and Financial Committee of the European Parliament (EP) (Rapporteur Ph. C. M. van Campen) concerned itself with this idea. The EP supported this concept in a resolution passed on 17 October 1962.[15] Finally, the Commission's action programme for Stage Two of the EEC Treaty was submitted to the Council of Ministers on 29 October 1962. This proposed that monetary union should be the goal of Stage Three of the EEC, from 1966 to 1969.[16]

It should be noted that it was the Commission and leading politicians who generally promoted the further development of economic and monetary integration. There were scarcely any initiatives in this direction from central banks or economics and finance ministers. The Deutsche Bundesbank evidently made no move at all to promote monetary integration, but other central banks were not quite as restrained. In his capacity as President of the GC, for example, the Governor of the Belgian central bank put forward a proposal 'Towards a greater convergence of foreign exchange policies within the Community' (3 April 1978), and the Belgian President of the MC presented his thoughts on 'Rapprocher les monnaies Européennes' on 22 March 1978.

Considering the divergent interests of the actors outlined above, this was no surprise. The Commission and the EP were concerned with extending European authority, and thus their own. Like the foreign ministers, the heads of state and government, and in particular the German and the French ones, were motivated by the now familiar domestic and foreign policy interests. The economics and finance ministers, on the other hand, were not particularly happy with any moves to limit their own powers, except for those tasks which were generally vote-losers.[17] This was compounded in Germany by concerns about the effects it could have on *Ordnungspolitik*, as there were fears that the EEC would lean heavily towards intervening in the markets.

The Bundesbank's stance is also understandable. It is obliged by the Bun-

---

[15] Cf. Generalsekretariat der Räte der Europäischen Gemeinschaften, Vom Europäischen Parlament am 17. Oktober 1962 angenommene Entschließung über die Koordinierung der Währungspolitik im Rahmen der EWG, 1396/62 (ASS 463), 19 Oct. 1962 (HA BBk B 330/1840).

[16] Cf. Das Aktionsprogramm für die 2. EWG-Stufe, wording of the chapter: Die Währungspolitik des Memorandums der EWG-Kommission zum Aktionsprogramm der Gemeinschaft für die zweite Stufe, das am 29. Oktober 1962 dem Ministerrat und dem Europäischen Parlament übergeben wurde, in: Vereinigte Wirtschaftsdienste, Europa, Frankfurt am Main, no. 225 of 31. Oct. 1962, cited in: Deutsche Bundesbank, Auszüge aus Presseartikeln no. 86, 16 Nov. 1962, pp. 7–10.

[17] Cf. Vaubel, 1991a.

desbank Act to maintain monetary stability. But in view of the more relaxed monetary policy stance in most other Member States and the dependent status of their central banks, would not any assignment of responsibilities to European institutions, let alone a monetary union, lead to less stability-oriented monetary policy? If this were so, the Bundesbank would have to present counter-proposals preventing any substantial limitation of its powers. If the current political climate meant that the prospects for this looked poor, its goal would have to be to influence the organization of the new European central bank in such a way that the greatest possible degree of monetary stability would be ensured.

Of course, it is also possible to put another interpretation on the Bundesbank's motives. No organization willingly relinquishes its powers or contributes to its own demise. This applies equally to monetary authorities. For example, once the International Monetary Fund's original duties[18] had disappeared in 1973, it secured its continued existence by creating new tasks for itself. The Bank for International Settlements did the same after the Second World War. Former German Chancellor Helmut Schmidt believes that this motive is the driving force behind the behaviour of the Deutsche Bundesbank: 'in reality, the gentlemen of the Bundesbank, whom freely floating exchange rates have now made more powerful than at any time before 1993, have a simple motive for rejecting monetary union: they don't want to become a mere branch office under the thumb of a central bank which is even *more* independent than they are today.'[19]

In fact it is difficult to separate these two motives, as they both result in largely identical behaviour. The impression gained from statements made in closed-door sessions of the Central Bank Council and from interviews, however, is that foreign policy aspects were by no means ignored. The obvious deduction from this is that safeguarding the value of money was the prime factor driving the Bundesbank's behaviour.

But why were other central banks' policies rather more active? There are three main reasons. First, they were not independent. Secondly, the Bundesbank's monetary policy soon gained it a leading role in the European system of fixed exchange rates, something which was not always appreciated elsewhere. Thirdly, the other central banks were interested in obtaining large balance of payments credits and in influencing the system. Because this was also an objective of their finance ministers, such objectives inevitably carried more weight at dependent central banks.

[18] Cf. Vaubel, 1991*b*.
[19] Schmidt, Helmut: Der zweite Anlauf, die letzte Chance, in: Die Zeit, 5 Apr. 1996, p. 4.

4. The period until the collapse of the Bretton Woods system

a) Background and problems

During the first 15 years of its existence,[20] all EEC Member States were members of the Bretton Woods system. They were linked by pegged exchange rates, although the dollar parities and thus the middle rates among them could be changed. At 3 per cent (instead of 1.5 per cent), the bands between the EEC currencies, within which the exchange rates could move freely around the middle rate through currency arbitrage, were twice those of their bands against the dollar. Free (non-resident) convertibility was finally introduced by the European Monetary Agreement, which replaced the European Payments Union (EPU),[21] although there were still various exchange controls between the EEC countries, particularly as regards capital movements.

In this initial situation, the EEC countries were faced with the following tasks: (1) The elimination of the remaining exchange controls and the introduction of the free movement of capital; (2) The prevention of revaluations and devaluations, as these affected the terms of trade for exports and imports (to do this, the national balances of payments had either to be maintained in equilibrium or financed); (3) The narrowing of the bands between the EEC currencies. After the introduction of the Common Agricultural Policy, stable exchange rates became even more important, since any change resulted in a corresponding adjustment of the agricultural prices fixed by the EEC in the countries concerned.

The Bundesbank was aware of these problems and responsibilities right from the beginning, as evidenced by two position papers from Directorate member Otmar Emminger: 'Monetary policy problems in the Common Market' (July 1957) and 'Monetary aspects of the Common Market' (29 May 1958). In the latter, he noted that: 'free trade, services and capital movements are the cornerstone, indeed the raison d'être, of the Common Market. . . . The irreversible liberalization of trade and payments cannot be achieved without a healthy monetary policy'.[22] He rejected not only financing facilities to solve balance of payments problems, but also floating exchange rates. The first of these (envisaged in article 108 of the EEC Treaty)

---

[20] Cf. also Cezanne and Möller, 1979.
[21] Cf. Kaplan and Schleiminger, 1989.
[22] Taken from: Monetäre Aspekte des Gemeinsamen Marktes by Otmar Emminger, 29 May 1958, p. 1 (HA BBk B 330/1840); cf. also Währungspolitische Probleme des Gemeinsamen Marktes by Otmar Emminger, July 1957 (HA BBk B 330/1840).

could only be regarded as a short-term, non-automatic bridging facility. Otherwise, there would be a temptation to ignore external solvency, which would infect the entire Community with inflation. Floating exchange rates led to a lack of monetary and fiscal discipline and swings between under- and overvaluation. These would inevitably distort trade relations. They would also tend to restrict the freedom of capital movements, and probably of movements of goods and services as well. The politically motivated tendency to delay any necessary realignments was not confined to fixed-exchange-rate systems.

He remarked that it was difficult to coordinate economic and monetary policy, and that compromises should never be allowed to undermine the strength of all the EEC currencies. The Community's monetary problem could only be solved if all Member State monetary policies were non-inflationary and tailored to balance of payments needs. But this in itself was not enough. 'The key factors affecting the proper degree of equilibrium will be *wage growth*, *fiscal policy* and *monetary and credit policy*, and coordination must be focused on these areas.'[23] It should start by correcting unrealistic (fixed) exchange rates. This was achieved in part by the devaluation of the French franc on 27 December 1958. Emminger then addressed the issue of monetary union,[24] which he regarded as quite out of the question at the time. It could 'only be the culmination of a process of complete integration once a common supreme political and fiscal authority has been instituted'.[25]

These comments not only illustrate the problems from the viewpoint of the Deutsche Bundesbank, but also disclose its objectives very clearly. The degree to which these have been pursued so closely up to the present is quite remarkable.

b) Developments up to 1964

Monetary developments in the EEC started[26] with the creation of the MC, whose statutes were adopted by the Council on 18 March 1958, and of the (still informal) GC. The establishment of the MC was occasioned by a French memorandum. The German response was positive. In particular, it drew attention to the importance of having a harmonized business cycle policy

[23] Monetäre Aspekte des Gemeinsamen Marktes by Otmar Emminger, 29 May 1958, p. 18 (HA BBk B 330/1840).
[24] Monetäre Aspekte des Gemeinsamen Marktes by Otmar Emminger, 29 May 1958, pp. 24f. (HA BBk B 330/1840).
[25] Monetäre Aspekte des Gemeinsamen Marktes by Otmar Emminger, 29 May 1958, p. 25 (HA BBk B 330/1840).
[26] Cf. Section 8a of this essay.

because different national business cycles generally affected the balance of payments. It appears that this view was shared by other countries, as the Council decided on 9 March 1960 to institute a 'Short-term Economic Policy Committee', with the task of coordinating such policy.

The Bundesbank wanted to be represented on the MC because it was responsible for monitoring the monetary situation and making recommendations. The records do not tell whether its efforts were successful, as the French memorandum spoke only of individuals 'who are directly responsible for monetary policy in their country'.[27] In a memo on the EEC's MC dated 27 July 1957, Emminger reported on the meeting of an *ad hoc* group in Paris on 16–17 July 1957, noting that the right of the central banks to be represented on the MC had been anchored in article 5.2 of the draft statutes, the result of a hard-won compromise.

The transition to Stage Two of the EEC started on 1 January 1962. This was followed shortly thereafter by the 'van Campen Report' to the EP (7 April 1962). Chapter V dealt in detail with monetary policy, resulting in an EP resolution on 17 October 1962 calling for the implementation of a common monetary policy through a stepwise federalization of the central banks under a new central authority.[28]

The Commission responded to this initiative by submitting a programme for Stage Two of the EEC Treaty, covering all aspects of economic policy, to the Council of Ministers and the Parliament on 29 October 1962. It made the following proposals for *monetary policy*:

1. Fixed exchange rates at the latest by the end of the transitional period, scheduled for 1962–5 (Stage Two). This should be preceded by consultations on changes to the discount rate, to minimum reserves, rediscount credits, central bank lending to the state, and to exchange rates.
2. The system of consultations should evolve into one of recommendations.
3. A common stance on all key decisions in respect of non-EEC countries, including on IMF drawing facilities, relations with reserve currency countries, and reforms to the international monetary system.
4. The maximum amounts of mutual assistance to be granted under articles 108 and 109 of the EEC Treaty should be defined as a ratio of gold and currency reserves.

[27] Sekretariat der Regierungskonferenz für den Gemeinsamen Markt und Euratom, Arbeitsgruppe für den Gemeinsamen Markt, Französisches Memorandum betreffend die Einsetzung eines Währungsausschusses, p. 6, 15 Oct. 1956, Brussels (HA BBk N–2/K 68).
[28] Cf. Generalsekretariat der Räte der Europäischen Gemeinschaften, Vom Europäischen Parlament am 17. Oktober 1962 angenommene Entschließung über die Koordinierung der Währungspolitik im Rahmen der EWG, 1396/62 (ASS 463), 19 Oct. 1962, Brussels (HA BBk B 330/1840).

5. Capital movements should then be liberalized further.
6. Looking forward to Stage Three, the establishment of a monetary union was envisaged after 1965 by an amendment to the EEC Treaty.
7. The MC (and a deputies' committee) should become an official body of the EEC.
8. A joint body should be set up to deal with matters for which finance and/or economics ministers and central bank governors were responsible. Its meetings would be prepared by the MC.
9. The coordination of wage and fiscal policy was recommended in support of monetary policy.[29]

Owing to the particular interests of the Bundesbank, the Federal Ministry of Economics, and the Federal Ministry of Finance, these proposals met with little enthusiasm. At its meeting on 25 October 1962, the Central Bank Council agreed with Emminger that technical and legal reasons ruled out consultations preceding each and every decision on monetary policy. Strengthening cooperation in the Monetary and Governors Committees would suffice, but the corresponding coordination of budgetary and fiscal policy would also have to be ensured.[30]

In a 'Statement on the Action Programme of the Commission of the EEC for Stage Two' on 16 November 1962, the Federal Ministry of Economics (Department E) also expressed its view that the elimination of fluctuation bands, the idea of monetary union, and a European reserve currency were all premature. This was on top of reservations concerning questions of economic regime related to centralized decision making in Brussels and state (framework) planning. The Ministry rejected the idea of fixing budget volumes and mutual assistance levels (article 108 EEC Treaty).

These viewpoints were confirmed in various inter-departmental meetings. For example, Günther Schleiminger from the Bundesbank rejected any notion of mutual assistance obligations at a meeting on 16 November 1962. He said that prior consultations could only be considered for the broad course of monetary policy, and that monetary policy could not be coordinated in isolation from fiscal policy. The request from the German Foreign Office not to deliver exclusively negative opinions is worth noting. The

---

[29] Cf. Das Aktionsprogramm für die 2. EWG-Stufe, wording of the chapter: Die Währungspolitik des Memorandums der EWG-Kommission zum Aktionsprogramm der Gemeinschaft für die zweite Stufe, das am 29. Oktober 1962 dem Ministerrat und dem Europäischen Parlament übergeben wurde, in: Vereinigte Wirtschaftsdienste, Europa, Frankfurt am Main, no. 225, 31 Oct. 1962, cited in: Deutsche Bundesbank, Auszüge aus Presseartikeln no. 86, 16 Nov. 1962, pp. 7–10.
[30] Cf. the Minutes of the 128th Central Bank Council meeting held on 25 Oct. 1962, p. 10 (HA BBk B 330/194).

Bundesbank emphasized that consultations were all that were possible as regards the question of a common monetary policy stance in respect of non-EEC countries.

These reservations were incorporated into the German opinion. As objections were also received from other countries, the Commission submitted a draft Council resolution on cooperation in the field of monetary relations on 19 July 1963[31] which took account of many of these misgivings. The result of this first major attempt at European monetary integration was rather modest. In addition to resolutions by the Council to set up EEC committees on budgetary policy and Medium-Term Economic Policy, it passed the following resolutions on monetary policy on 8 May 1964:[32]

1. The GC was formally established as an EEC committee.
2. Consultations in the MC were to be held on all key decisions or statements by Member States concerning international monetary relations. The Member States could only take decisions after these consultations *unless this was impossible under the circumstances, and in particular owing to the timetable for instituting the planned measures* (author's italics).

At the same time, the Council declared that, in accordance with article 107 of the EEC Treaty, consultations between the Member States—to include the Commission as well—should be held before any change in exchange rate parities. The procedures for this were to be defined in an opinion by the MC, which was subsequently submitted on 12 December 1964. It specified that the procedure must be secret, and that the consultations should be held in the MC, which was to be convened by the Chairman at short notice.

Secrecy and the need to meet quickly are vital because of the speed of foreign exchange markets and their immediate reaction to information. For this reason, the Bundesbank had also argued that prior consultation as set out in (2) was, under certain circumstances, technically impossible. But because of these restrictions prior consultations repeatedly proved to be impossible in the event of monetary crises.

Despite a range of initiatives, some private, during the ensuing years, no further progress was made concerning monetary integration. The '1964 Initiative' which Commission President Walter Hallstein presented to the President of the Council on 1 October 1964 deserves mention. It adopted the monetary policy items in the October 1962 action programme. There was also a European initiative by the German government. The draft

[31] Cf. Kommission der Europäischen Wirtschaftsgemeinschaft, Die Währungs- und Finanzpolitische Zusammenarbeit in der Europäischen Wirtschaftsgemeinschaft (Mitteilung der Kommission an den Rat), I/Korn (63) 216, 19 June 1963, Brussels (HA BBk B 330/1841).
[32] Cf. Europäische Wirtschaftsgemeinschaft, 1964.

initiative, prepared by representatives from the foreign, economics, and finance ministries, proposed more objective rules for monetary policy, the pooling of foreign exchange reserves, and joint decisions on their composition.[33] Both initiatives were rejected at a meeting of the Central Bank Council on 15 October 1964,[34] and Emminger was directed to present the Bundesbank's stance to the government and the ministries.

The position of the Central Bank Council was put forward during talks at the Federal Ministry of Economics. It was argued that the pooling of foreign exchange reserves could lead to automatic granting of credit, and that rigid rules for monetary policy were simply impossible to draft.[35] At the said meeting, Emminger concluded by stating 'that neither the law nor its conscience permits the Central Bank Council to relinquish its share of responsibility for monetary stability'.[36]

It is interesting to note that the German Foreign Office prevented the Bundesbank from receiving a copy of the German European initiative, which was intended to be presented to the Council of Ministers on 10–11 November 1964.[37] Was this because the German Foreign Office was afraid that the Bundesbank's resistance would be successful?

c) Developments 1964–73

The monetary integration of the EC (which was created on 1 July 1967 by merging the three existing communities) received a new impetus from proposals by Luxembourg's Prime Minister Pierre Werner at the end of 1968 and a Commission memorandum to the Council (the 'Barre Memorandum') on 12 February 1969. In addition to improving the consultation procedure, better statistical data, and an agreed procedure on international monetary

[33] Cf. the extract from the Federal Government's Draft European Initiative, Appendix 2 to the letter from Bundesbank Directorate member Otmar Emminger to the members of the Central Bank Council, 9 Oct. 1964 (HA BBk B 330/435).

[34] Cf. the Minutes of the 177th Central Bank Council meeting held on 15 Oct. 1964 (HA BBk B 330/435).

[35] Cf. memo from Schleiminger relating to the talks in the Ministry of Economics on 21 Oct. 1964 on monetary policy proposals in the Federal Government's European Initiative of 26 Oct. 1964, Frankfurt am Main (HA BBk B 330/5696) and memo from Ungerer and Jennemann relating to the EEC of 9 Nov. 1964 (HA BBk B 330/5696).

[36] Cf. the Minutes of the 17th Central Bank Council meeting held on 15 Oct. 1964, p. 7 (HA BBk B 330/5696).

[37] Cf. Vermerk von Schleiminger betreffend die Besprechung im Wirtschaftsministerium vom 21. Oktober 1964 über die währungspolitischen Vorschläge im Rahmen der Europa-Initiative der Bundesregierung vom 26. Oktober 1964, Frankfurt am Main, p. 2 (HA BBk B 330/5696).

policy cooperation, it addressed the concept of a standard unit of account, more concrete arrangements for mutual assistance, the creation of a common fund, the elimination of the fluctuation bands, parity changes by mutual agreement only, and the definitive, final pegging of exchange rates. The background to these initiatives was the problems caused to the Common Agricultural Policy by parity changes.[38]

Initial discussions in the GC and MC, at the central banks and ministries, were lively. In particular, they focused on the financing facilities for balance of payments problems, the reduction and elimination of fluctuation margins, and the creation of a European fund. The Bundesbank and the GC dealt with detailed technical problems and the opportunities for, and consequences of, narrowing the fluctuation bands.[39] For the first time, the Central Bank Council held that a concession on the financing facility could be justified.[40] Subsequently it gradually abandoned its resistance to automatic, very short-term EC credits, a probable consequence of the monetary crises between 1968 and 1970. These showed that more or less automatic short-term swap credits could not be avoided in a crisis. Following the devaluation of the franc on 10 August 1969, for example, France was granted a limited swap credit of US $400 million, with Belgium receiving US $100 million for 3 months. The Bundesbank also expected that if an EC mechanism were to be instituted, lending would be spread over several countries and short-term credits could be repaid quickly after a monetary crisis, because speculative money flows would be reversed. At the same time, however, the Chairman notified the Central Bank Council of the Directorate's intention of spelling out to the Federal Government in great detail the total extent of its financial support.[41]

The volume of this financial support was so important to the Bundesbank because any drawing of D-mark credits by a foreign central bank for interventions on the foreign exchange market leads to D-marks being sold, for instance against US dollars or French francs. This increases the monetary base and makes control of the money supply more difficult. Unless it is compensated, for instance by open market operations, there is a risk of inflation.

The monetary crises from 1968 to 1970 highlighted the fact that the Bretton Woods fixed-exchange-rate system would either collapse or have to be modified.[42] The EC countries soon agreed (Ecofin) in Venice, 29–30 May

---

[38] Cf. Section 4a of this essay.
[39] Cf. Historisches Archiv der Deutschen Bundesbank.
[40] Cf. Historisches Archiv der Deutschen Bundesbank.
[41] Cf. Historisches Archiv der Deutschen Bundesbank.
[42] Cf. Historisches Archiv der Deutschen Bundesbank.

1970)[43] that fixed parities should be maintained if the Bretton Woods bands were widened, or if there was a move towards floating exchange rates.

The Council meeting of the heads of government and state of the EC in The Hague on 1–2 December 1969 finally decided to implement Economic and Monetary Union (EMU) in several stages, and to complete the transition to European Monetary Union by 1978. An *ad hoc* committee headed by Luxembourg's Prime Minister Pierre Werner was asked to prepare a report. This was presented to the Council and the Commission on 8 October 1970 as a phased plan for EMU by the end of the 1970s ('Werner Report').[44] It summarized proposals from various countries into a compromise. On the basis of this report, the Commission then presented the Council of Ministers with three drafts for the stepwise introduction of EMU—which often differed substantially from the report—by strengthening cooperation between national central banks and coordinating short-term economic policy.

Differences of opinion had already arisen during the preparatory work. In early 1969, Belgium and France had insisted in the MC that the bands should be narrowed soon, while The Netherlands and Germany wanted to delay this until Stage Three of EMU, once progress had been made in harmonizing economic and monetary development.[45] There was another standoff in the GC on the subject of creating a reserve fund, which was intended to be developed into a sort of common central bank. Belgium and France wanted to move to such a reserve fund at an early date, but Germany and The Netherlands supported its establishment in Stage Three. The President of the Bundesbank described the Franco-Belgian plan as extremely dangerous.[46] The differences in opinion on this matter in the Werner Committee led even in May 1970 to a letter from the Belgian Prime Minister to the German Chancellor, who subsequently asked the Federal Minister of Economics (in a letter dated 27 May 1970) to investigate the possibility of a compromise.

The Bundesbank and the Federal Ministry of Economics also had reservations about extending automatic loans in a monetary crisis, but these were calmed by specifying ceilings.

The Commission drafts diverging from the Werner report generated serious reservations at the Bundesbank and the Federal Ministry of Economics, reflected in the German opinion submitted to the Council meeting

[43] Cf. Historisches Archiv der Deutschen Bundesbank.

[44] Cf. Bericht an Rat und Kommission über die stufenweise Verwirklichung der Wirtschafts- und Währungsunion in der Gemeinschaft (Werner-Bericht), Brussels 8 Oct. 1970, printed in: Hellmann, 1972, pp. 134–59.

[45] Cf. Historisches Archiv der Deutschen Bundesbank.

[46] Cf. Historisches Archiv der Deutschen Bundesbank.

on 23 November 1970. One point of criticism was that the goal of political union had been completely sidelined, and that no parallel progress in economic and monetary policy was guaranteed. It rejected the idea of directives by the Council of Ministers (Ecofin) on monetary policy. These would jeopardize the statutory independence of the Bundesbank. It also rejected the procedure whereby monetary policy measures diverging from these directives could only be instituted after obligatory consultation with the other central banks. In the opinion of the Central Bank Council, the GC—which supposedly was intended as a preliminary stage on the road to the final goal of a Federal Reserve Board—should be responsible for deciding guidelines independently of the Council of Ministers. Greater consultation and the coordination of monetary and lending policy during Stage One should not affect the statutory provisions covering the Bundesbank.[47] The German Minister of Economics told the Central Bank Council[48] that economic and monetary policy coordination had to be completely parallel, and that no institutional changes incompatible with the Bundesbank Act could be allowed in the first stage. In the government's view, the independence of the Bundesbank should be maintained until the final stage, if at all possible. The government intended proposing the autonomous Bundesbank as the model for the European central bank.

Although France now appeared to be interested not only in a quick conclusion to the negotiations on monetary union, but also in acquiring the ability to influence German monetary policy and gaining easier access to balance of payments aid, it rejected the idea of relinquishing sovereign rights to European institutions in Stages Two and Three.[49] Owing to this position (which was probably shared by other Member States), the German reservations, and the monetary crisis of 1971–3 leading up to the collapse of the Bretton Woods system, the outcome of this second attempt at EMU was again modest.

What were the concrete results? On 9 February 1970, the central banks agreed to introduce a short-term monetary support mechanism (three months, prolongation by a further three months possible) with total automatic quotas of 1,362.5 million EMUA (see below). The quota volumes were limited and tied to conditions. On 6 March 1971, the GC decided to narrow the bands around bilateral EC currency parities from 1 June 1971. Because of a monetary crisis, however, this decision was not implemented until 24 April 1972, with a ±2.25 per cent band. At the GC meeting on 10 April 1972, the EC central banks also agreed on the rules for the new

---

[47] Cf. Historisches Archiv der Deutschen Bundesbank.
[48] Cf. Historisches Archiv der Deutschen Bundesbank.
[49] Cf. Historisches Archiv der Deutschen Bundesbank.

intervention system and for settlements. The first six months would be an experimental phase. At the request of Germany—and based on an earlier French proposal—they agreed that no partner country could hold more than 10 per cent of another country's quota in its currency reserves without the consent of the central bank concerned. In doing so, the Bundesbank wanted to prevent the D-mark from becoming a reserve currency in the EC. The EC candidates UK, Ireland, Denmark, and Norway signalled their interest in this scheme, as did some other countries.

Other results were the introduction of the medium-term mutual assistance scheme allowed under article 108 of the EEC Treaty (with maximum quotas and conditions) by a Council decision of 22 March 1971, very short-term (one month) unlimited assistance by the central banks on 10 April 1972 and the establishment by Ecofin of the European Monetary Cooperation Fund (EMCF) on 12 September 1972. The EMCF was responsible for settlements, accounting, and processing very short-term and short-term credits. It was managed by the central bank governors, and was operated by the Bank for International Settlements (BIS) in Basle as their agent. Finally, the European Monetary Unit of Account was created on 3 April 1973 (1 EMUA = 0.88867088 g fine gold, corresponding to the value of the dollar up to 1971).

5. The EEC's Exchange Rate Mechanism

The Exchange Rate Mechanism (ERM), often referred to as the 'snake' in the 'tunnel', was set up by the Basle Agreement on 24 April 1972.[50] The tunnel was the wider dollar band against which the EEC currencies moved. Inside the tunnel, the snake of the EEC currencies moved against each other within a narrower band. After the end of the Bretton Woods system and the abandonment of fixed parities against the dollar, it was simply referred to as the (currency) snake.

The new ERM soon faced serious problems, initially as a consequence of the collapse of the Bretton Woods system.[51] On 23 June 1972, the UK switched to floating exchange rates following a monetary crisis. Italy left the ERM on 13 February 1973 for the same reason. The resulting monetary crisis also affected Germany and other countries. Following a 3 per cent revaluation of the D-mark, the EC Council of Ministers decided on 19 March 1973 to float dollar rates and keep the ERM (but without the UK, Italy,

[50] Cf. for this section also Thygesen, 1979.
[51] Cf. Section 8b of this essay.

TABLE 1: Inflation, 1971–8 (rise in cost of living indices in %)

ountry	D	I	Ne	S	No	UK	Dk	B	F
flation	42.14	149.57	69.38	84.51	81.14	145.96	96.57	75.15	89.47
omparison ith Germany	—	107.43	27.24	42.37	39.00	103.82	54.43	33.01	47.33

y: D = Germany, I = Italy, Ne = The Netherlands, S = Sweden, No = Norway, UK = United Kingdom, k = Denmark, B = Belgium, F = France.

urce: Deutsche Bundesbank calculations based on OECD data.

and Ireland). Sweden and Norway joined the ERM as associated non-members. The fate of the snake can be deduced from the record of the EEC exchange rate arrangement, 1972–8 (see Section 8b). Of major consequence was France's departure in early 1974 owing to a monetary crisis. It rejoined in 1975, but left again for good in 1976. This left only a 'mini-snake' in which the D-mark played the role of a reserve currency. The high-flown plans to develop the system towards European EMU[52] had failed.

What were the roots of this unsatisfactory course of events? It is clear that they were no different from those which led to the collapse of the Bretton Woods system. In discretionary monetary systems, governments and central banks were not willing to subordinate their domestic policy goals to a monetary policy tailored to meet their balance of payments needs, or to gear their monetary policy to that of the country with the dominant currency. The members and associate members of the snake also failed to meet these conditions (Table 1), particularly as their inflation rates were 27.24–107.43 per cent higher than in Germany across the entire 1972–8 period. It is no surprise that those countries with the highest inflation rates—Italy and the UK—left the ERM at the start. Luxembourg and Ireland are not included in Table 1 because the former did not have its own currency and the Irish punt was pegged to sterling.

Could the ERM have been saved by changing the parities more often? This would have been difficult. First, such changes cannot be too frequent or too large, or massive speculative and hedging purchases on the foreign exchange market would jeopardize the system. For example, currency unrest forced the Bundesbank to intervene to the tune of around DM 8 billion

[52] Cf. Entschließung des Rates und der Vertreter der Regierungen der Mitgliedstaaten vom 21. März 1972 betreffend die Anwendung der Entschließung vom 22. März 1971 über die stufenweise Verwirklichung der Wirtschafts- und Währungsunion in der Gemeinschaft (Balser Abkommen), reproduced in: Krägenau and Wetter, 1993, pp. 108f.

between the end of July and 15 October 1976,[53] which seriously compromised its anti-inflationary monetary policy. But if inflation differentials are wide, larger, more frequent parity realignments are necessary.

Secondly, governments are reluctant to change parities,[54] and, once agreed, such changes are often too little and too late. The government are afraid that devaluations will cost them political prestige and/or higher inflation.[55] But they are cautious about revaluations as well, as they harm the competitive position of their exporters and industries competing with imports. It should not be forgotten that markets react quickly to information, while the political process, with lengthy preparations by civil servants, governments, and international bodies, is slow and cumbersome. Monetary policy decisions are consequently often taken too late in response to market pressure. This also applies to exogenous shocks, such as the 1973–4 oil-price shock. Their effect on the balance of payments may differ from country to country.

If countries in a fixed-exchange-rate system delay parity changes, currencies with higher inflation rates tend to revalue in real terms. Figure 1 shows that this was the case for the Belgian, Danish, and Dutch currencies against the D-mark. In contrast, floating exchange rates, given a higher inflation rate, made the pound sterling and the lira undervalued. The same happened to the French franc after it left the snake. The associated members of the snake experienced similar fates.

It has to be stressed, however, that the strains could have been reduced, and France's departure prevented, if German monetary policy had been more expansionary. German politicians were confronted by tensions between their European policy aims and their anti-inflationary policies. This had been recognized even before the snake was set up, and had been brought to the Chancellor's attention in various memos as early as 1969.[56] But the Bundesbank was not willing to engage in a more expansionary policy, a position which generally received the support of the German government. The only alternative was to try to persuade the other countries to adopt a more stability-oriented policy.

But various other EC Member States—and the Commission itself—were following a different course. In addition to ultimately fruitless plans to revive efforts towards EMU (the Fourcade proposal in December 1974, the Marjolin Report in March 1975, the Tindemanns Report in December 1975, the Duisenberg proposal in 1976, the Ortoli and Jenkins proposals in September 1977 and the Commission's own proposal in November 1977), yet

---

[53] Cf. Historisches Archiv der Deutschen Bundesbank.
[54] Cf. Historisches Archiv der Deutschen Bundesbank.
[55] Cf. Historisches Archiv der Deutschen Bundesbank.
[56] Cf. Historisches Archiv der Deutschen Bundesbank.

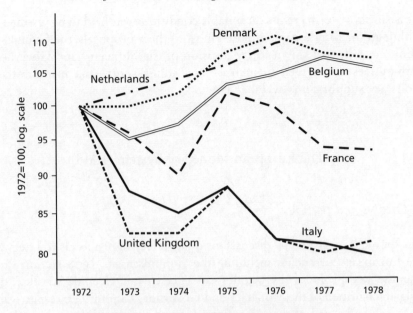

FIGURE 1: Real D-mark exchange rates
in the European Exchange Rate Mechanism*

* Various parity changes in 1973, 1976, 1977, and 1978. France was not a member between 21 January 1974 and 10 July 1975, or after 15 March 1976. The United Kingdom and Italy were not members.

Source: Deutsche Bundesbank.

further proposals were discussed. These aimed at increasing the short-term support quotas, extending the term of very short-term support (and eliminating interest on it), transferring some of the national reserves to the EMCF and expanding its powers (including giving it the right to extend loans), redefining the EMUA as a basket of currencies, and establishing an EC target zone for the dollar. Most of them were presented or supported by France.[57] Although calls for a target zone and for converting the EMUA into a basket of currencies were rejected, as was the French demand for 'symmetrical' intervention, the GC decided on 10 December 1974 to start intervening secretly against the dollar on a trial basis to prevent any difference over the previous day's official rate from exceeding 1 per cent.

In 1973, the Commission had already proposed a sixfold increase in the quotas for short-term monetary support and extending the term from 6 to 12 months. Only a small minority on the MC supported these plans and the proposal to communitize the reserves. On the other hand, a limited in-

[57] Cf. Historisches Archiv der Deutschen Bundesbank.

crease in short-term credits on suitable conditions was held to be justified.[58] Although the Bundesbank opposed most of these proposals, the Council of Ministers followed the majority decision of the Monetary and Governors Committees and agreed to increase and adjust short- and medium-term monetary support in November 1977.[59]

6. The European Monetary System (EMS)

a) Origins and features

The first half of 1978 saw discussions on a variety of proposals to integrate the European currencies, including the Commission's '1978 Action Programme' and proposals by Jacques van Ypersele and Cecil de Strycker, the Belgian chairmen of the Monetary and Governors Committees respectively, in March and April of that year. From around June on, information about the Giscard d'Estaing/Schmidt initiative and the secret talks between Clappier and Schulmann to work out the details started seeping through. Giscard and Schmidt tried to exclude the ministries and the Bundesbank, so as to prevent any resistance at too early a stage. The draft was only distributed on the evening prior to the meeting of the heads of state and government in Bremen on 6–7 July 1978. After Schulmann had outlined the plan to him on the phone, however, the President of the Bundesbank asked the Chancellor for a meeting before 4 July. According to Emminger,[60] complete information was provided thereafter. After the Bremen Summit, the Chancellor notified the Bundesbank of the results by telex on 8 July.

What were the motives of these two politicians, what was the reaction in other countries, and how did the ministries and the Bundesbank respond? What were the original details of the plans and how were they changed? And what was the result of the hectic flurry of activity in the ministries, the Council of Ministers, the Council of the Heads of State or Government, the Bundesbank, the MC, and the GC in the second half of 1978?

The lesson that Giscard had drawn from the snake was that a European exchange rate system, something he believed vital for the survival of the EC, would only function if the burden was shared equally between the strong and the weak currencies. If an exchange rate had reached the intervention

---

[58] Cf. Historisches Archiv der Deutschen Bundesbank.
[59] Cf. Historisches Archiv der Deutschen Bundesbank.
[60] Cf. Emminger, 1986, p. 358.

point, both central banks had to intervene in concert.[61] Such a system would likewise have satisfied the French inclination towards a more expansionary monetary policy. Giscard also believed that the Germans, and in particular Bundesbank President Emminger, would follow their selfish national anti-inflationary policy in all monetary issues.[62]

Helmut Schmidt based his concept on the foreign policy considerations described above in Section 1. Faced with German partition, tension along the Iron Curtain, the precarious situation of West Berlin, and the weight of the country's Nazi past, (West) Germany needed the support of the EC and NATO for its foreign policy to be successful. In his memoirs,[63] Schmidt also mentions that he aspired to establish a fixed-exchange-rate system for the EC; he wanted to put pressure on those governments with extreme monetary and fiscal policies to achieve convergence and create a European currency as a counterweight to the dollar and the yen. This is confirmed by the documents available. In his statement to the Central Bank Council,[64] the Chancellor emphasized that his prime consideration was to rescue the Common Market. He also highlighted the impact on Germany's international position and the country's ties with the dollar.

Otmar Emminger is probably also right when he claims that: 'when France left for the second time in 1976, it was clear that it would be most unlikely to rejoin the "snake" a third time. There was a distinct feeling that something else would have to be created.'[65]

Schmidt tried to include the UK in the plans from the outset—especially for political reasons—but was rebuffed. Although the UK continued to take part in the negotiations, it remained outside the EMS for the time being.

What then were the key points under discussion when the decisions were being formulated in the second half of 1978 and early in 1979? These started with the extension of the terms for very short-term and short-term monetary support, and an increase in the quotas for short- and medium-term support and the rallonges of the short-term support. For the very short-term financing facility, the majority favoured an extra 30 days, with Belgium even calling for an extension of up to one year. This was opposed by The Netherlands and Germany. For the short-term support mechanism, France wanted the term to be extended from three to six years, with a similar prolongation of the one-off extension.[66] The French and the Commission

[61] Cf. Giscard d'Estaing, 1991, pp. 124f.
[62] Cf. Giscard d'Estaing, 1991, pp. 122–5.
[63] Cf. Helmut Schmidt, 1987.
[64] Cf. Historisches Archiv der Deutschen Bundesbank.
[65] Emminger, 1986, p. 357.
[66] Cf. Historisches Archiv der Deutschen Bundesbank.

supported a proposal to almost quadruple aggregate medium- and short-term monetary support, while an alternative plan put forward by the Federal Ministry of Finance—in contrast to the Bundesbank, which did not see any need for enlargement—called for an increase of around 34 per cent. The British and the Italians even went as far as demanding the free availability of the EMUA reserves (the name ECU was subsequently agreed) acquired at the EMCF against deposits of national currency.[67] Unlike the Bundesbank, the Federal Ministry of Finance also assumed at first that such reserves could be used to open additional credit lines.[68]

In line with the intentions of Giscard and Schmidt, a number of new elements were introduced into the discussions. These included the recalculation of a European monetary unit of account defined as a basket of currencies (later the ECU, which replaced the EMUA on a one-to-one basis), symmetrical intervention if there was a risk of fluctuation margins being exceeded, and the transfer of national reserves to the EMCF, which would assume responsibility for short- and medium-term support. Finally, common intervention against the dollar was envisaged.

The French, British, and Italians supported the idea of a basket-based currency, and intervention if a currency hit the floor or ceiling value of the bands around the exchange rates set against this currency basket. In contrast, The Netherlands and Germany supported the bilateral fixing of all cross rates between the currencies. These would then be used to calculate the unit of the basket of currencies once the individual currencies had been weighted.[69] The Bundesbank was afraid that adopting a basket-only solution—something which the German Chancellor initially supported—would create an inflation community because the value of the basket currency would change reflecting the average of national inflation rates. It also expected this solution to cause excessive intervention obligations against the dollar, something which could jeopardize its monetary autonomy.[70] In the event, the Bundesbank's position was adopted for the German negotiation team.

Faced with these more far-reaching proposals and partial support for them by the Chancellor and the Federal Ministry of Finance, the Bundesbank found itself in a weaker position than usual. However, it did have the unconditional support of the Federal Ministry of Economics and its minister, Otto Graf Lambsdorff.[71] It also sought support by talking to various interest groups, including trade unions, and to experts in the CDU/CSU

[67] Cf. Historisches Archiv der Deutschen Bundesbank.
[68] Cf. Historisches Archiv der Deutschen Bundesbank.
[69] Cf. Historisches Archiv der Deutschen Bundesbank.
[70] Cf. Historisches Archiv der Deutschen Bundesbank.
[71] Cf. interview by the author with Hans Tietmeyer on 9 July 1995.

parliamentary group.[72] A meeting between the Bundesbank Directorate and representatives of the banking industry was held at the Chancellor's office on 13 September, with the representatives of the banks and the Minister of Economics supporting the Bundesbank's position. The Bundesbank President emphasized that exchange rate realignments should be quick and discreet, that the foreign exchange buying obligation, the credit facilities and the intervention requirement must be limited, and that the basket system should not be the reference model for intervention. Central bank autonomy should not be abandoned. The Chancellor agreed to these five points,[73] which had already been stated by the Bundesbank President during a cabinet meeting.[74]

Unlike relations with the Federal Ministry of Economics, conflict arose between the Bundesbank and the Federal Ministry of Finance. In addition to differing positions on extending monetary support, the Federal Ministry of Finance was inclined to support the limited extension of very short-term support. For political reasons, it opposed the option to leave the EMS supported by the Bundesbank in case an extreme level of intervention threatened to undermine its anti-inflationary monetary policy.[75] A compromise was eventually reached on all points.

What was the outcome of these protracted national and international negotiations? At the Franco-German talks on 14–15 September in Aachen, a compromise was agreed on the issue of setting the intervention points, using the parity grid. However, the question of whether the ECU would be used as the indicator for intervention within the fluctuation band (intramarginal intervention) was left open. With the UK now isolated, Ecofin then decided to formulate the central rates (parities) in ECUs. A Belgian compromise proposal formed the basis for intramarginal intervention.[76] The agreement which was then concluded between the central banks therefore contained a divergence indicator, which stipulated that if a currency diverged from the ECU central rate by 75 per cent of the maximum permitted divergence, it was presumed that measures (e.g. intramarginal intervention) would be taken to prevent exchange rate tensions.

The very short-term financing facility was extended by half a month. Settlement was principally in the currency of the creditor in the EMCF. The remainder (not more than 50 per cent) could be settled in full or in part in ECUs. The other conditions remained unchanged.

---

[72] Cf. Historisches Archiv der Deutschen Bundesbank.
[73] Cf. Historisches Archiv der Deutschen Bundesbank.
[74] Cf. Historisches Archiv der Deutschen Bundesbank.
[75] Cf. Historisches Archiv der Deutschen Bundesbank.
[76] Cf. Historisches Archiv der Deutschen Bundesbank.

Short-term monetary support was increased to ECU 14 billion, and medium-term support to ECU 11 billion. This saw maximum German financing obligations rise from a previous ECU 5.0 and 1.2 billion to ECU 12.3 and 3.1 billion. Non-members of the EMS, such as the UK, were barred from receiving support. The central banks expressed their willingness to transfer 20 per cent of their reserves to the EMCF in exchange for ECUs. But as some countries and the Bundesbank had legal objections to transferring their reserves without any contractual arrangements under article 236 of the EEC Treaty, these remained the property of the central banks, which assigned them to the EMCF using revolving 3-month swaps. They would be transferred for good once a contractual arrangement had been agreed by the end of the transitional period. This period would see no change to the EMCF, which would continue to be administered by the BIS. All accounts were kept in ECUs. This meant that currency losses or gains could arise if a currency was revalued or devalued.

The agreements came into force at a meeting of Ecofin and the GC in Washington on 13 March 1979, following a delay of almost three months due to French insistence on changes to the agricultural compensation scheme. The most important arrangements were in turn spelled out in an accord between the central banks, with the Council resolving the increase in medium-term support. The 2.25 per cent band remained, but it could be extended in exceptional cases to ±6 per cent, which Italy promptly adopted. The entry rates for the snake currencies were their existing parities, and the market rates on 12 March 1979 applied to the other currencies (with a 0.5 per cent discount for the lira). The value of the ECU was defined using these parities once Ecofin had fixed the weighting of the currencies in the basket. 1 ECU was set at 1 EMUA.

The Bundesbank was able to achieve its most important objectives, albeit with concessions on the term of the very short-term financing facility and the volume of short-term monetary support. It regarded the adoption of the parity grid and the fixing of the bands around these parities as an important success.[77] Even more important to the Bundesbank was the commitment by the Chancellor and the government to agree to the suspension of the Bundesbank's intervention requirement if its stability-oriented monetary policy was threatened.[78] Minister of Finance Hans Matthöfer took advantage of this only a few months later when, in September 1979, he

[77] Cf. interview by the author with Hans Tietmeyer on 9 July 1995 and with Leonhard Gleske on 9 June 1996.
[78] Cf. Historisches Archiv der Deutschen Bundesbank and Statement by Minister of Economics Graf Lambsdorff to the Bundestag on 6 Dec. 1978, Verhandlungen des Bundestags, vol. 108, Plenarprotokolle 8/119–8/133, p. 9503; cf. Emminger, 1986.

threatened to suspend intervention if exchange rates in the EMS were not realigned.[79]

b) Further plans for the EMS

The plans to extend the EMS in a second stage met with failure. The first idea to be dropped was the reorganization of the EMCF as a European Fund with functions similar to that of a central bank and the definitive transfer of foreign exchange reserves. A majority on the GC held the view that such far-reaching changes would have to be based on an amendment to the EEC Treaty, subject to Council ratification under article 236. In early 1980, the Bundesbank also emphasized that the functions of a European Fund should not be extended over those of the EMCF before rates of inflation had converged.[80] Conditions for the development of the EMCF into a European central bank had already been announced at that early stage. These proved to be similar to those formulated later for European Monetary Union (EMU).[81]

In November 1980, the German Minister of Finance stated that the Federal Government would not be following up plans for the further institutional development of the EMS for the time being.[82] However, he also emphasized in March 1982 that the Bundesbank would have to be willing to transfer foreign exchange reserves to a European Fund and accept restrictions on national authority if the EMS evolved into a zone of stability.[83]

Subsequent discussions focused on increasing the acceptance limit for the 50 per cent settlement in ECUs, the use of the very short-term financing facility for automatic, capped *intramarginal* intervention, the private use of ECUs, and a common intervention policy against the dollar. In March 1982, the Bundesbank rejected these proposals without an amendment to the EEC Treaty.[84]

These proposals emanated from the Commission. They were supported by France and Italy and re-emerged in 1987. France also demanded more symmetrical intervention (including in French francs), and the Commission proposed setting common targets instead of the stability standards specified by the Germans. There were also calls for the coordination of intramarginal

---

[79] Cf. interview with Hans Tietmeyer on 9 July 1995; cf. also Historisches Archiv der Deutschen Bundesbank.
[80] Cf. Historisches Archiv der Deutschen Bundesbank.
[81] Cf. Historisches Archiv der Deutschen Bundesbank.
[82] Cf. Historisches Archiv der Deutschen Bundesbank.
[83] Cf. Historisches Archiv der Deutschen Bundesbank.
[84] Cf. Historisches Archiv der Deutschen Bundesbank.

intervention, i.e. the participation of several central banks, and the extension of very short-term monetary support.[85]

After prolonged hesitation, the Central Bank Council decided on 16 June 1987 to allow the private use of ECUs in Germany.[86] The positive development of the EMS, the low level of utilization of short and medium-term monetary support, the rapid settlement of balances and French criticism of German policies that year also prompted the Bundesbank to signal its willingness to raise the 50 per cent ECU acceptance limit for settlements, and to use the very short-term financing facility limited by a ceiling for intramarginal intervention as well.[87] The GC reached an agreement to this effect in September 1987, although the requirement for the creditor country to consent to intramarginal monetary support remained intact. The Ecofin directive of 24 June 1988 on the full liberalization of capital movements by mid-1990 should also be mentioned (with transitional arrangements for Spain, Portugal, Greece, and Ireland). Another important step was the inclusion of article 102a in the EEC Treaty by the Single European Act (SEA), which came into force on 1 July 1987 to complete the single European market. This requires an amendment to the EEC Treaty under article 236 for any institutional changes to promote the further development of economic and monetary policy.

c) The development of the EMS

EMS development was positive[88] and resulted until 1992 in a zone of relative exchange rate stability and declining inflation rates. However, it is doubtful if the EMS had anything to do with this latter trend, as it also occurred in non-member states (Table 2). Nevertheless, Denmark, Belgium, The Netherlands, and Austria, which had always been full or associate members of the snake and the EMS, recorded the lowest inflation rates.[89] The D-mark emerged as the key currency in the system. The countries with the highest inflation rates (Table 3) were those with the shortest membership in the EMS.[90] Greece was never a member, Spain and Portugal joined only in 1989 and 1992, and the UK was only briefly in the EMS from 1990 to 1992. Italy left in 1992.

---

[85] Cf. Historisches Archiv der Deutschen Bundesbank.
[86] Cf. Historisches Archiv der Deutschen Bundesbank.
[87] Cf. Historisches Archiv der Deutschen Bundesbank.
[88] Cf. also Gros and Thygesen, 1988 and Fratianni and von Hagen, 1990.
[89] Cf. also Giovannini, 1992 and the bibliography cited there.
[90] Cf. Section 8c of this essay.

TABLE 2: Average annual rates of inflation, 1963–95 (change in cost of living indices)

	1963–7	1968–72	1973–7	1978–82	1983–7	1988–92	1993–5	1963–95
Australia	2.65	4.27	13.07	9.63	7.65	5.22	2.80	6.63
Austria	3.50	4.27	7.64	5.15	3.05	3.03	2.95	4.29
Belgium	3.48	4.00	9.75	6.25	4.33	2.66	2.19	4.79
Canada	2.72	3.92	8.91	10.29	4.54	4.17	1.41	5.32
Denmark	5.77	6.24	10.81	10.75	5.13	3.26	1.79	6.47
France	3.21	5.52	10.35	11.71	5.70	3.06	1.83	6.10
Germany	2.81	3.47	5.58	4.75	1.57	3.10	3.00	3.49
Ireland	4.14	7.57	16.09	15.21	6.27	3.15	2.09	8.01
Italy	4.83	3.89	16.17	16.40	8.98	5.84	4.56	8.80
Japan	5.63	5.69	12.73	4.65	1.37	2.19	0.63	4.88
Netherlands	4.47	6.02	8.61	5.48	1.53	2.12	2.45	4.47
New Zealand	3.46	6.58	12.98	14.87	11.51	4.33	2.26	8.25
Norway	4.08	6.04	9.38	9.70	7.24	4.21	2.07	6.32
Portugal	4.24	6.58	21.40	21.09	18.78	11.18	5.27	12.88
Spain	8.32	5.68	17.15	16.01	9.24	6.04	4.65	9.79
Sweden	4.36	5.01	9.64	10.28	6.52	7.05	3.32	6.77
Switzerland	3.74	4.35	5.60	4.14	2.30	4.04	1.99	3.84
UK	3.35	6.59	16.30	11.96	4.64	6.33	2.49	7.58
USA	1.91	4.65	7.71	9.76	3.32	4.30	2.78	5.01
Arithmetic mean	4.04	5.28	11.57	10.43	5.98	4.49	2.66	6.51

Source: Deutsche Bundesbank calculations based on OECD data.

TABLE 3: Inflation, 1978–94 (percentage rise in cost of living indices)

Country	D	B	F	I	Ne	S	P
Inflation	65.67	92.39	153.94	323.00	58.47	207.12	850.35
Country	UK	Dk	Fi	Irl	Au	E	Gr
Inflation	188.64	135.81	155.53	210.39	78.66	300.33	1388.14

Key: D = Germany (West Germany only), B = Belgium, F = France, I = Italy, Ne = The Netherlands, S = Sweden, P = Portugal, UK = United Kingdom, Dk = Denmark, Fi = Finland, Irl = Ireland, Au = Austria, E = Spain, Gr = Greece.
Source: Deutsche Bundesbank calculations based on OECD data.

There are three distinct phases of the EMS. The first was from 1979 to 1983, the second until around 1990, and the third thereafter. The first phase was marked by a relatively expansionary monetary policy in various countries and sometimes substantial parity changes (see Table 4). Proof of the expansionary monetary policy are the high average inflation rates (Table 2) for Italy (16.40 per cent), Ireland (15.21 per cent), Denmark (10.75 per cent), and France (11.71 per cent) in 1978–82. Only the inflation rates of Belgium and The Netherlands approached those in Germany. This caused tensions which also had a political impact. In April 1981, for example, the French prime minister wrote to the German chancellor, expressing a wish for a cut in German money market rates, which had been increased on 19 February. Whether this was connected with the upcoming French presidential elections is a matter of interpretation. The Bundesbank Directorate opposed this request and expressed its hope that the Bundesbank and the government would again share a common view on monetary policy.[91] Prior to this, the heads of state and government, meeting in Breda on 4–5 April 1981, had called on the MC[92] to examine the possibility of concerted interest-rate cuts. However, the Bundesbank stuck to its policy, and tensions within the EMS were only relieved by parity alignments. A key role in this was played by French monetary policy, which still remained expansionary under President François Mitterand's first government.

The second stage of the EMS started with a fundamental shift in French policy in March 1983. This phase was marked by a more stable monetary policy and falling inflation rates (see Table 2 for 1983–7 and 1988–92). The result was fewer and smaller parity changes (see Table 4), with the exception of the 8 per cent devaluation of the Irish punt in 1986. There was no change in parities in 1984, or between 1988 and 1992.

The shift in French policy occurred during the changeover to the second socialist administration under President Mitterand. During the German coalition talks in March 1983, French Finance Minister Jacques Delors approached German Minister of Finance Gerhard Stoltenberg and Chancellor Kohl (using Michel Camdessus as his intermediary) with a request to support his planned switch to a policy of stability by a joint approach to changing the parities. A few days later, Stoltenberg, accompanied by his personal assistant Horst Köhler, and Hans Tietmeyer from the Bundesbank, flew to Paris, where this question was discussed with Jacques Delors and his inner circle. Delors emphasized that the parity change was indispensable on domestic policy grounds, particularly because of massive resistance in his own party, where there was a strong faction which wanted to leave the

---

[91] Cf. Historisches Archiv der Deutschen Bundesbank.
[92] Cf. Historisches Archiv der Deutschen Bundesbank.

TABLE 4: Revaluations/devaluations in the EMS (in % compared with all other participating currencies)

Date[a]	DM	BFR/LFR	DKR	FF	IR£	HFL	LIT	£	DR	PTA	ESC
1979											
24 September	+2.0		−2.86					(+3.07)	—[b]	—[b]	—[b]
30 November			−4.76						—[b]	—[b]	—[b]
1981											
23 March							−6.00	(+22.73)	—[b]	—[b]	—[b]
5 October	+5.50			−3.00		+5.50	−3.00	(−9.89)	—[b]	—[b]	—[b]
1982											
22 February								(+8.27)	—[b]	—[b]	—[b]
14 June	+4.25	−8.50	−3.00	−5.75		+4.25	−2.75		—[b]	—[b]	—[b]
1983											
21 March	+5.50	+1.50	+2.50	−2.50	−3.50	+3.50	−2.50	(−10.90)	—[b]	—[b]	—[b]
18 May								(+8.58)	—[b]	—[b]	—[b]
1985											
22 July	+2.00	+2.00	+2.00	+2.00	+2.00	+2.00	−6.00	(+7.47)	(−11.54)	—[b]	—[b]
1986											
7 April	+3.00	+1.00	+1.00	−3.00		+3.00		(−13.31)	(−26.95)	—[b]	—[b]
4 August					−8.00			(−8.40)	(−2.29)	—[b]	—[b]

TABLE 4: (cont.)

Date[a]	DM	BFR/LFR	DKR	FF	IR£	HFL	LIT	£	DR	PTA	ESC
1987											
12 January	+3.00	+2.00				+3.00		(−7.75)	(−8.71)	—[b]	—[b]
1990											
8 January							−3.68	(−0.68)	(−20.31)		
8 October								+5.13[c]	(−7.95)		
1992											
14 September	+3.50	+3.50	+3.50	+3.50	+3.50	+3.50	−3.50[d]	—[d]	(−16.08)	+3.50	+3.50
17 September										−5.00	
23 November							(−6.50)	(−17.12)	(−4.57)	−6.00	−6.00
1993											
1 February					−10.00		(−6.68)	(−1.19)	(−2.79)		
14 May								(+2.58)	(−2.13)	−8.00	−6.50

[a] Date on which devaluation/revaluation took effect.
[b] Currency was not a component of the ECU basket at this date.
[c] Participation in the ERM: pound sterling from 8 October 1990, Escudo from 6 April 1992.
[d] Membership in the ERM suspended from 17 September 1992.

Key: BFR/LFR = Belgian/Luxembourg Franc, DKR = Danish Krone, FF = French Franc, IR£ = Irish Punt, HFL = Netherlands Guilder, LIT = Italian Lira, £ = pound sterling, DR = Greek Drachma, PTA = Spanish Peseta, ESC = Portuguese Escudo.

Note: Values in brackets = notional values as the currency was not a member of the ERM.

Source: Deutsche Bundesbank.

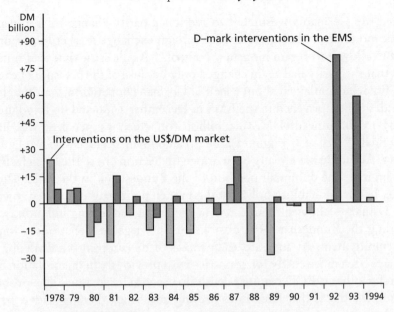

FIGURE 2: Federal Reserve and Bundesbank interventions
on the US$/DM market, and D-mark intervention in the EMS*

* Provision of central bank money (+); absorption of central bank money (–).

Source: Deutsche Bundesbank.

EMS and introduce an import tax. A stabilization policy was therefore in
France's and Europe's best interests. It was touch and go whether he could
push this policy through.[93] A joint Franco-German request was then made,
and the D-mark was revalued by 5.5 per cent on 21 March 1983, accompanied by a 2.5 per cent devaluation of the franc (see Table 4). A unilateral
revaluation of the D-mark was rejected.[94] France then adopted an anti-
inflationary stance, and other formerly less stability-oriented EMS members
followed its example.

Inflation and interest rates in the EMS converged during this second phase
(Table 2). This was probably one of the prime factors behind the Spanish
(1989) and British (1990) decisions to join the system. Norway (1990),
Sweden (1991), and Finland (1991) tied their currencies to the ECU. Austria
stuck to a fixed rate between the schilling and the D-mark.

But these years were not without tensions, either. In 1987, the Bundesbank

[93] Interview by the author with Hans Tietmeyer on 9 July 1995; cf. also Historisches
Archiv der Deutschen Bundesbank.
[94] Cf. Historisches Archiv der Deutschen Bundesbank.

asked the German government to request a parity change to stop central bank money from being created by foreign exchange market intervention, and to allow it to regain monetary control.[95] At the same time as it pointed out that the parity had again changed only because of the pressure of events, the French complained about a lack of German cooperation,[96] although the Bundesbank intervened in the EMS in December 1986 and up to 9 January 1987 to the tune of DM 36.1 billion (of which 55 per cent was intra-marginal)[97] (see also Figure 2). The realignment occurred on 12 January 1987. Attention has already been drawn (in Section 6b) to the French efforts to eliminate the dominant position of the Bundesbank in the EMS. On the other hand, the stability policy of the French politicians—oriented towards the D-mark—allowed them to claim the credit for cutting inflation, while holding the Bundesbank responsible for any negative deflationary impact on employment. At any rate, the process of deflation in the EMS appears to have been more costly for countries with previously higher inflation rates than for other OECD countries with floating exchange rates. The probable reason for this is that fixed rates prevent any shock therapy with a strong revaluation in real terms, and that the necessarily gradualist approach can only achieve a slower drop in inflation expectations.[98] The complaints by France and other countries about German policies are therefore understandable.

The main events affecting the third phase of the EMS after 1990 have been German unification, the preparations for EMU, and the 1992–3 EMS crisis. With the exception of a minor devaluation of the lira at the start of 1990, there have been no parity changes since 1987 (see Table 4), although the real exchange rate of the peseta and the escudo rose sharply up to 1991, and that of the pound sterling and the lira less so (Figure 3a). It is therefore not surprising that various members of the Central Bank Council opposed the efforts of the Commission and Ecofin to make realignments a taboo subject.[99]

The situation became increasingly precarious, first because freedom of capital movements had been largely realized by 1990, and secondly because German monetary policy had come under increasing strain owing to the expansionary fiscal policy resulting from German monetary union and unification in 1990. In principle, this should have demanded at least a temporary revaluation of the D-mark. Instead, the Bundesbank tried to master

[95] Cf. Historisches Archiv der Deutschen Bundesbank.
[96] Cf. Historisches Archiv der Deutschen Bundesbank.
[97] Cf. Historisches Archiv der Deutschen Bundesbank.
[98] Cf. de Grauwe, 1990.
[99] Cf. Historisches Archiv der Deutschen Deutsche Bundesbank.

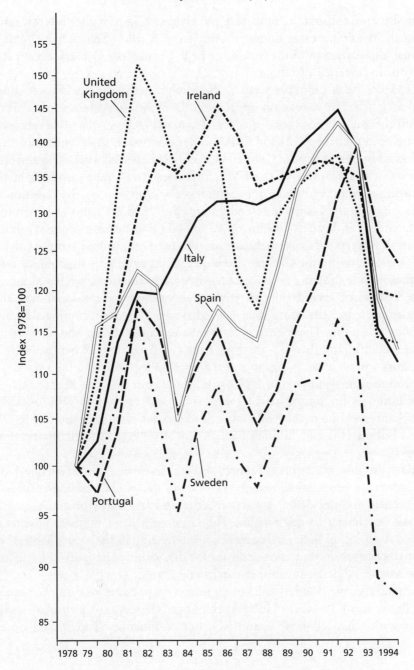

FIGURE 3a: Real D-mark exchange rates in the EMS, 1978–94*

* Consumer price index in the country in question, converted to D-mark and divided by the German consumer price index.

Source: Deutsche Bundesbank.

the situation through its monetary policy, resulting in higher interest rates. Finally, the dollar came under pressure from April to September 1992. As usual, this caused tensions within the EMS because the D-mark became the favourite currency of refuge.[100]

Despite these ominous factors, the foreign exchange markets remained calm at first. There was no appreciable D-mark intervention in the EMS until the end of the second quarter of 1992 (Figure 2). The markets were convinced that the plans for EMU, under discussion since 1988 and then adopted by the European Council in Maastricht on 7 February 1992, would lead to the transition of the EMS currencies to a single currency at the existing parities. However, this confidence was shaken by the rejection of the Treaty in the Danish referendum on 2 July, and the announcement of a referendum in France. Intramarginal intervention became necessary, but a Danish interest-rate hike helped calm the markets, at least temporarily.[101] However, a rise in the German discount rate on 17 July 1992, coupled with opinion polls showing an uncertain outcome of the French referendum on 20 September, served only to strengthen unease.[102] The dollar was also under pressure. Investors then started unwinding their sterling, lira and peseta positions. These currencies weakened appreciably, and speculators started betting on their devaluation. From 28 August to 16 September, obligatory intervention in support of the lira totalled DM 29.2 billion, on top of intramarginal support of DM 9.5 billion. From 11 to 16 September, the same figures for pound sterling were 33.1 and 5.2 billion DM. Total D-mark intervention in the EMS in the third quarter of 1992 amounted to DM 87.2 billion, DM 5.67 billion of which was offset in the fourth quarter (Figure 2).

Despite this, the British, French, and Italian finance ministers rejected a Bundesbank proposal to realign the lira and the pound sterling parities in particular, and decided at a secret meeting in Paris-Bercy on 26 August to make no change to the parities. The German finance minister adopted a neutral position.[103] At an informal Ecofin meeting in Bath on 5 September, parity changes did not even come up for discussion. The British, Irish, and Italians demanded a cut in German interest rates.

In the end, the Bundesbank saw its monetary policy at risk. At the request of Bundesbank President Helmut Schlesinger, there was a meeting in Frankfurt with Chancellor Kohl and Minister of Finance Theo Waigel on 11

---

[100] Interview by the author with Helmut Schlesinger on 10 Apr. 1995; cf. also Historisches Archiv der Deutschen Bundesbank.
[101] Cf. Historisches Archiv der Deutschen Bundesbank.
[102] Interview by the author with Andrew Crockett on 20 Apr. 1995.
[103] Letter from Tietmeyer to the author, 11 Oct. 1996.

September, at which—following initial hesitation by Kohl because of his fear of damaging repercussions for the Maastricht Treaty—they agreed on an attempt to achieve a realignment after seeing the cost of intervention. *Staatssekretär* Köhler and Bundesbank Vice-President Tietmeyer proceeded first to Paris to talk to the French finance minister and to GC Chairman Jean-Claude Trichet, and then to Rome, where they met the Italian finance minister and Carlo Azeglio Ciampi, the Governor of the Banca d'Italia. They encountered considerable resistance at first. The French did not want any decision before their referendum, and the Italians were opposed to a devaluation. In the end, the French abandoned their opposition to an Italian initiative, and the Italians said that they would request a devaluation.[104]

Contrary to German expectations, however, the Italians did not make a formal request to institute realignment negotiations. Jean-Claude Trichet did not convene the GC, but tried to reach a solution by phone and fax.[105] On 13 September the lira was devalued by 3.5 per cent and all other EMS currencies were revalued by the same amount. The Bundesbank cut its interest rates as promised. But these steps did nothing to calm the markets. Together with the lira, the pound sterling in particular was now under pressure, leading to substantial intervention by the Bank of England and the Bundesbank. The situation was exacerbated by an interview which Schlesinger gave to the Wall Street Journal and the German Handelsblatt financial newspaper, in which he stated that the problems had not been conclusively resolved, and that a more wide-ranging realignment would have been better. He also said that the pound sterling could not move into a similar plight to that of the lira.[106] The Handelsblatt sent the press agencies a summary on the Tuesday evening in which the positive remarks on the pound had been omitted. On the evening of 15 September, the agency report burst into a meeting between Chancellor of the Exchequer Norman Lamont and Bank of England Governor Robert Leigh-Pemberton to discuss the defence of the pound the next day. It made depressing reading: 'And I said, when this message came as to what Schlesinger was supposed to have said, *That's it, the game's up.*'[107]

A statement by the Bundesbank late that evening, at the request of the Governor of the Bank of England, that the interview had not been authorized was too weak to be of any help. The next day, *Black Wednesday*, the

---

[104] Cf. interview by the author with Hans Tietmeyer on 9 July 1995 and with Helmut Schlesinger on 10 Apr. 1995; cf. also Historisches Archiv der Deutschen Bundesbank.

[105] Cf. interview by the author with Hans Tietmeyer on 9 July 1995 and letter from Tietmeyer to the author, 11 Oct. 1996.

[106] Cf. Benkhoff, Werner: Zinssenkung war Angebot der Deutschen Bundesbank, in: Handelsblatt, 17 Sept. 1996.

[107] Interview by the author with Andrew Crockett on 20 Apr. 1995.

UK (following massive reserve losses amounting to more than US $10 billion on a single day) and Italy announced to the MC that they were quitting the EMS. The peseta was devalued by 5 per cent. But this was not the end of the unrest. Further devaluations of the peseta and the escudo followed on 23 November 1992 (by 6 per cent), and by 8 and 6.5 per cent on 14 May 1993 (see Table 4). The Irish punt was devalued by 10 per cent on 1 February 1993.

From the end of June 1993, the French and Belgian francs, the Danish krone, the peseta, and the escudo all weakened, and the Banque de France was forced to increase intramarginal interventions.[108] It in turn needed to be supported, and the Bundesbank also intervened massively (Figure 2). This despite the fact that, thanks to 10 years of stability-oriented policy, the franc was certainly not overvalued (Figure 3b) and was able to continue holding its value afterwards (in June 1992, 100 francs were quoted at DM 29.705, on 24 August 1996 at DM 29.26). A likely reason for this was the Bundesbank's reluctance to cut interest rates because inflation rates were still high, at around 4 per cent.

Following lengthy and difficult bilateral negotiations and talks in the MC from 30 July onwards, the finance ministers and central bank governors agreed to widen the bands to ±15 per cent from 2 August 1993, with The Netherlands staying at ±2.25 per cent against the D-mark. The claim that this spelled the end of the EMS as a system of fixed exchange rates is rejected by central bankers;[109] as the parities continued to be the reference point for monetary policy, speculators could be scared off and there had been a *de facto* return to the old fluctuation band. Finland and Italy rejoined the EMS at the end of 1996.

The events of 1992–3 had a negative political fallout for the Federal Republic of Germany[110] and damaged the reputation of the Bundesbank. The Danes, Belgians, French, and British accused it of being overly obsessed with inflation and of damaging the EMS and the planned monetary union. Helmut Schmidt even talks of Waigel's and Tietmeyer's collaboration in the *de facto* destruction of the successfully functioning EMS.[111] However, this is not true because Tietmeyer in particular had pleaded forcefully for a general parity realignment. It is also unclear whether the British had been contacted—officially or unofficially—before Black Wednesday on 12–13

[108] Cf. Historisches Archiv der Deutschen Bundesbank.

[109] Cf. interview by the author with Andrew Crockett on 20 Apr. 1995, with Helmut Schlesinger on 10 Apr. 1995, with Hans Tietmeyer on 9 July 1995 and with Jean-Claude Trichet on 9 Dec. 1996.

[110] Cf. Historisches Archiv der Deutschen Bundesbank.

[111] Cf. Schmidt, Helmut: Der zweite Anlauf, die letzte Chance; in: Die Zeit, 5 Apr. 1996, p. 4.

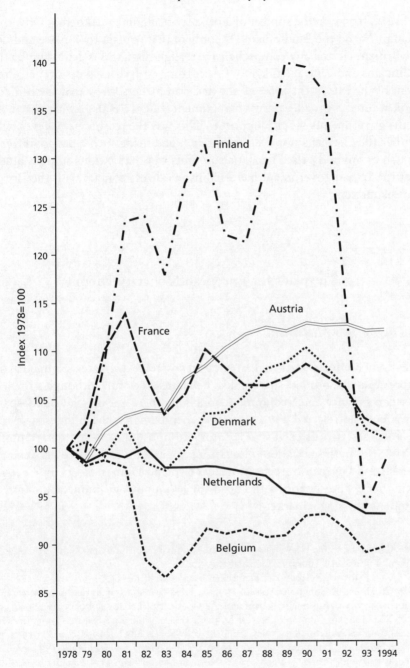

FIGURE 3b: Real D-mark exchange rates in the EMS, 1978–94

* Consumer price index in the country in question, converted to D-mark and divided by the German consumer price index.

Source: Deutsche Bundesbank.

February 1992 on the subject of a broader realignment. Whereas Governor Ciampi[112] and the Bundesbank[113] confirm that contact took place and that the British rejected any comprehensive realignment, this is denied by British politicians and central bankers.[114] According to Jean-Claude Trichet, President of the MC at the time, all the decision makers knew that the Bundesbank wanted a broader parity realignment, but were also aware that none of the governments would support it. This was the reason, he believes, why neither the Germans nor even the French had made such a proposal to the British or anybody else. Trichet also points out that various sources hinted that the Italian government had established direct contact with the British on this matter.[115]

7. The plans for European Monetary Union[116]

a) The road to Maastricht

The French efforts (with Italian support) to achieve greater symmetry and 'more equitable burden-sharing' had been unsuccessful. Although a Franco-German Finance and Economic Council had been set up (the Bundesbank President had rejected any *non-voting* membership), the Bundesbank successfully asserted its exclusive statutory responsibility for monetary policy in 1988.[117] In this situation, discussions apparently took place between the French and German Foreign Ministers (Roland Dumas and Hans-Dietrich Genscher), who identified the need for economic and monetary union to complete the single market.[118]

[112] Cf. 'Monday Interview: Enduring symbol of stability', interview with Carlo Azeglio Ciampi, in: Financial Times, 12 Oct. 1992, p. 30.
[113] Cf. Historisches Archiv der Deutschen Bundesbank.
[114] Cf. House of Commons, Session 1992–3, Treasury and Civil Service Committee, First Report: The 1992 Autumn Statement and the Conduct of Economic Policy, London 1992, pp. X-XV; House of Commons, Session 1992–3, Treasury and Civil Service Committee: The Future Conduct of Economic Policy, Minutes of Evidence, 28 Oct. 1992, London 1992, pp. 29–33; House of Commons, Official Report: Parliamentary Debates (Hansard), vol. 212, London 1992, pp. 100–07 (24 Sept. 1992: Norman Lamont), pp. 313f. (20 Oct. 1992: John Major).
[115] Cf. interview by the author with Jean-Claude Trichet on 9 Dec. 1996.
[116] Cf. for this section Kenen, 1995.
[117] Cf. Historisches Archiv der Deutschen Bundesbank.
[118] Cf. interview by the author with Hans Tietmeyer on 9 July 1995.

Genscher seized the initiative with his 'Memorandum on the Creation of a European Monetary Area and a European Central Bank' of 26 February 1988. Although it was originally intended for internal discussion in the FDP, it was forwarded to the Bundesbank the same day. In this document, he postulated the need for a European monetary area with a central bank to complement the single market. He insisted that a European Central Bank should be functionally, personally, and financially independent of national and EC institutions, and that it should be forbidden to finance public expenditure. He argued that the central bank's priority must be monetary stability, and that the core elements of the Bundesbank Act should be applied. Countries which were not yet willing to join could become members later. For its implementation, Genscher proposed that the European Council in Hanover on 27–8 June 1988 should establish a body to work out the principles.

The timing of this initiative had been well chosen. The EMS appeared to be working well. France had committed itself to a policy of stability which had been copied by other countries. The proposal made allowance for the misgivings of France and other Member States about the dominance of a Bundesbank motivated solely by the goal of price stability in line with German needs.[119] Finally, the new article 102a of the EEC Treaty stipulated that institutional changes in the field of monetary policy could only be made by amending the Treaty.

Finance Minister Stoltenberg's response to the proposal was not particularly enthusiastic. He emphasized that capital movements in particular had to be fully liberalized,[120] and that talk of more far-reaching proposals was premature. However, a future European Central Bank would have to be independent and organized along federal lines.[121] Despite this, the European Council in Hanover on 27–8 June 1988, under the presidency of the German Chancellor, appointed a study group under the President of the EC Commission, Jacques Delors,[122] which presented its 'Report on Economic and Monetary Union in the EC' in April 1989. The Delors Committee Report was accepted by the Council for further negotiations on 26/27 June. Delors had already pointed out that 'the institution which administers this (European) currency would have to have the same degree of autonomy as the Bundesbank—or this institution will not exist'.[123] He introduced this

---

[119] Cf. Historisches Archiv der Deutschen Bundesbank.
[120] Interview by the author with Hans Tietmeyer on 9 July 1995.
[121] Cf. Historisches Archiv der Deutschen Bundesbank.
[122] Cf. for what follows Gros and Thygesen, 1988.
[123] Cf. 'Den Zeitplan einhalten', interview with Delors, in: Die Wirtschaftswoche, 24 Mar. 1988, pp. 31–4.

as an objective[124] to the Committee, which correspondingly proposed an independent, federal European System of Central Banks (ESCB) comprising the national central banks. As its executive bodies, it proposed an ESCB Governing Council and an Executive Board. The Governing Council would consist of the governors of the national central banks and the Executive Board, and there should be an adequate term of office for its members. The ESCB Governing Council would have to report every year to the European Parliament and the European Council. The system should be committed to the goal of price stability from the start of Stage Three. It should be responsible for monetary policy, exchange rate management, management of the currency reserves and a functioning payment system. It should be prohibited from lending to the public sector. Monetary union (Stage Three) would occur when irreversible convertibility of the currencies had been achieved together with the elimination of the fluctuation bands, plus the irrevocable fixing of exchange rates combined with the full liberalization of capital movements.

Other proposals by the Delors Committee included the need to amend the EEC Treaty; parallel coordination of economic and monetary policy; the need for a binding framework for national fiscal policy, together with greater mobility of the production factors and price flexibility. This latter was needed because, in a monetary union, the unequal impact of shocks in the Member States could no longer be offset by exchange rate changes. A common regional and structural policy was also necessary. The doubling of the Structural Fund by 1993, which had already been agreed, might be insufficient.

The Report concluded that the final phase of EMU should be implemented over two stages without any timetable decided by the Council. The first stage should start on 1 July 1990 with the full liberalization of capital movements. All Member States should join the EMS and the central banks should be given greater autonomy. The status of the GC should be upgraded, and its job would be to make proposals on the coordination of monetary and exchange rate policy. However, majority votes would be non-binding. Some countries supported the transfer of these functions to a European Reserve Fund (ERF).

Stage Two would see the establishment of the ESCB, which would absorb the EMCF and the GC. It would gradually assume responsibility for some monetary policy decisions. For example, it would establish monetary policy guidelines for the Community and establish an operational framework for monetary policy. As in Stage One, exchange rate realignments would still be possible.

---

[124] Cf. interview by the author with Gunter Baer on 29 May 1995.

The plans for EMU received a boost in 1990 from German unification. France, Germany, and other countries too were now even more eager to integrate the Federal Republic into Europe.[125]

The Central Bank Council's initial response to the plans for monetary union in 1988 was cautious,[126] although it had already made known some of its demands, such as autonomy, a federal structure, and price stability as the prime objective of any European central bank. It should not be allowed to finance government deficits. There was also the question of which countries were willing and able to participate in monetary union. Even the issue of the seat of the central bank was addressed by Bundesbank President Karl Otto Pöhl at a press conference following the Central Bank Council session on 5 May 1988. *Staatssekretär* Tietmeyer confirmed that the government and the Bundesbank were largely at one on this question.

The Bundesbank's stance is expressed in a letter by its President to the Chancellor on 1 June 1988. He stated that EMU would take a long time, and required the common formulation of economic and financial policy. Exchange rate realignment options should most certainly be retained prior to EMU, otherwise the stronger countries would have to transfer resources; this could cause political problems. The single market did not need a single currency, and a parallel European currency was undesirable on stability policy grounds. Above all, the liberalization of capital movements had to be completed. This was followed by the requirements for any move towards EMU mentioned above. The GC should be entrusted with the corresponding studies. However, this request was not met in full in Hanover as the Delors Committee contained three independent experts and the President of the Commission (as its chairman) in addition to the central bank governors.

The key points of the Delors Report corresponded to the Bundesbank's objectives. However, in a letter to the Chancellor in June 1989, shortly before the Madrid Conference, the Bundesbank pointed out that expanding the powers of the GC in Stage One was questionable unless there was a binding political commitment to EMU. Before negotiations started, the priorities should be the full liberalization of capital movements, the convergence of underlying economic and fiscal conditions, and the participation of all Member States in the EMS. Creating a European central bank system with responsibility for monetary policy in Stage Two would require an amendment to the Bundesbank Act; this was unlikely to find widespread support in the Federal Republic of Germany.

However, the Bundesbank realized that monetary union was probably

[125] Cf. interview by the author with Hans Tietmeyer on 9 July 1995; cf. also Historisches Archiv der Deutschen Bundesbank.
[126] Cf. Historisches Archiv der Deutschen Bundesbank.

inevitable for political reasons, as many countries were not willing to accept its domination in the longer term. Its aim would therefore have to be to eliminate the weaknesses in the Delors Report, particularly as regards Stage Two.[127] During the subsequent negotiations, the Bundesbank accordingly supported the idea of keeping the GC independent of Ecofin during Stage One, contrary to the wishes of the British in particular, and opposed any arrangements which would restrict the rights of the Central Bank Council under the Bundesbank Act. Parallel policies in the run-up to EMU must be ensured.[128] The finance minister accepted most of these demands and underscored the importance of the Bundesbank's support for the open domestic public debate.[129]

The Bundesbank opposed the gradual transfer of monetary policy powers to the ESCB in Stage Two. It argued that this would lead to overlapping responsibilities and would therefore jeopardize price stability. Hence the ESCB should only be established once it was known which countries were willing to peg their exchange rates for good and operate a common monetary policy, and when.[130] The German government indicated its support for this position early in 1991.[131] A Dutch compromise proposal for a European Monetary Institute instead of the ESCB during Stage Two then solved this problem.

Another of the Bundesbank's worries was how to fix and change parities with outside countries if external exchange rates with them were fixed, an issue on which it sought the participation of the ESCB.[132]

b) The main provisions of the Maastricht Treaty on European Monetary Union (EMU)

The Bundesbank saw most of its goals realized in the Maastricht Treaty, which was signed on 7 February 1992 and submitted to the national parliaments for ratification. However, it had not been able to prevent a fixed timetable for the start of Stages Two and Three. It had been able to win improvements in the way possible parities to non-members had to be determined. However, despite the basket fixing, the ECU would carry an exchange rate risk until the start of Stage Three. The Bundesbank viewed

---

[127] Cf. also Wissenschaftlicher Beirat beim Bundesministerium für Wirtschaft, 1990.
[128] Cf. Historisches Archiv der Deutschen Bundesbank.
[129] Cf. Historisches Archiv der Deutschen Bundesbank.
[130] Cf. Historisches Archiv der Deutschen Bundesbank.
[131] Cf. Historisches Archiv der Deutschen Bundesbank.
[132] Cf. Historisches Archiv der Deutschen Bundesbank.

the agreements on political union as unsatisfactory, and believed that further problems could arise from the burdens imposed by the Cohesion Fund.[133] The Minister of Finance, on the other hand, said that he was not convinced of the need for a political European federal structure for monetary union,[134] and that any reworking of the agreements was out of the question. He also thanked the Central Bank Council for its support and cooperation.

As far as the Statute of the ECB was concerned, the Treaty adopted the proposal of the GC, under the chairmanship of Bundesbank President Pöhl, almost unchanged. It stipulates the freedom of the ECB from any outside instructions (article 107) and lays down price stability as its primary objective. Its subsidiary task is to support the general economic policies of the Community (article 105). The ESCB comprises the ECB and the national central banks (article 106). It is quite possible that the decision to retain the national central banks was partly motivated by a desire to maintain existing positions and jobs, besides the important aspects of monetary policy management and decentralization. This at least seems to have been the case in the Delors Committee.[135]

The ECB has the exclusive right to authorize the issue of banknotes and coins (article 105a). After consulting the ECB, and with the object of price stability, the Council can conclude agreements on external exchange rates (with non-Community currencies). In the case of floating exchange rates, it can adopt 'general orientations' for exchange rate policy in relation to non-Community currencies (article 109).

The Governing Council of the ECB comprises up to six members of the Executive Board plus the governors of the national central banks. The term of office of the Executive Board is eight years and is not renewable (article 109a). The term of office of the governors is at least five years (Protocol on the Statute of the ESCB and the ECB, article 14.2). The central banks are not permitted to take instructions from other bodies as regards their tasks in the ECB (Protocol article 7). The ECB Governing Council formulates monetary policy, adopts guidelines and takes decisions; the Executive Board implements them and prepares meetings of the Governing Council (Protocol, article 12). Article 14.2 has been criticized because a term of office for central bank governors of less than eight years with an option for renewal jeopardizes the independence of members of the ECB Governing Council.

The ESCB starts operating at the beginning of Stage Three. Until then, the central banks remain responsible for monetary policy. For the second

---

[133] Cf. Historisches Archiv der Deutschen Bundesbank and Deutsche Bundesbank, 1992, p. 54.

[134] Cf. Historisches Archiv der Deutschen Bundesbank.

[135] Interview by the author with Gunter Baer on 25 May 1995.

stage, which started on schedule on 1 January 1994, an independent European Monetary Institute (EMI) was established (article 109f). Its task is to strengthen cooperation between the central banks and the coordination of their monetary policies with the aim of ensuring price stability, and to monitor the functioning of the EMS. It is also entrusted with the technical preparations for Stage Three, in particular as regards the instruments and procedures for monetary policy, with promoting the efficiency of cross-border payments, and with preparing European banknotes. The GC and the EMCF have been merged with the EMI, whose Council consists of a President and the governors of the national central banks.

The 'convergence criteria' and the transition to the third stage are governed by article 109j of the EEC Treaty and the Protocols on the Excessive Deficit Procedure and the Convergence Criteria referred to in article 109j. The Council is required to decide by a qualified majority no later than 31 December 1996 whether a majority of Member States meet these criteria, whether it is appropriate to enter the third stage and when it should start. If no date has been set by the end of 1997, Stage Three will start on 1 January 1999. Before 1 July 1998, the Council will decide which Member States fulfil the conditions. A derogation applies to the other Member States; if they meet the criteria at a later date, the derogation can be lifted by a qualified majority of the Council.

The Treaty contains four convergence criteria:

1. The achievement of a high degree of price stability: according to article 1 of the Protocol, the average rate of inflation in the year prior to the examination may not exceed the average inflation rate of the three best-performing Member States in terms of price stability by more than 1.5 per cent.
2. The sustainability of the government financial position: the deficit may not exceed 3 per cent and the ratio of government debt to GDP may not exceed 60 per cent (article 1). These figures are based on a Dutch proposal. Under article 104c(2), they are not binding if the deficit ratio has declined substantially and continuously and reached a level close to the reference value, or if it is only exceptional and temporary; and if the ratio of government debt to GDP is diminishing sufficiently and approaching the reference value at a satisfactory pace.

    The fiscal policy regulations also apply after the transition to Stage Three. Violations can be punished with (admittedly weak) sanctions.
3. Observance of the EMS fluctuation bands for two years without a devaluation. What is unclear is whether the 'normal' band can also be interpreted as the ±15 per cent applying since 1993.
4. The durability of convergence achieved by a Member State and its partici-

pation in the EMS. The first of these criteria is achieved if, in the year before the examination, the average long-term interest rate of the country does not exceed the average interest rates of the three Member States with the lowest interest rates by more than 2 per cent (Protocol, article 4). Finally, the UK and Denmark are not obliged to participate in Stage Three.[136]

c) Further developments and prospects

As we have seen, the negative first referendum in Denmark, coupled with uncertainty about the outcome of the French referendum on the Maastricht Treaty, triggered the EMS crisis in 1992. The French eventually voted in favour of the Treaty by a narrow margin, as did the Danes in a second referendum, once the exemption referred to above had been granted. German opposition was also substantial. Starting in May 1992, a majority of economics professors publicly criticized the Treaty and its Protocols.[137] Although banks and industry are generally positive towards EMU, opinion polls were still showing that this was not the case among the majority of the population at large in 1996. The situation in Denmark, the UK, Austria, Finland, and Sweden is similar.

On 12 October 1993, the Federal Constitutional Court dismissed a complaint of unconstitutionality against the Law of 28 December 1992 on the Treaty on European Union. However, the court also ruled that the timing of the third stage of EMU 'should be regarded as a target rather than any legally enforceable date'. The German Bundestag may 'implement its intent to allow the future monetary system to commence only if strict stability criteria are met, as set out in article 23(3) of the Basic Law'.[138] This can be interpreted in such a way that the Federal Republic of Germany has some sort of right of withdrawal from the Treaty towards the start of Stage Three if the convergence and stability criteria are not met.[139]

The Central Bank Council was by no means enthusiastic about the implementation of monetary union, although the viewpoints of the members varied widely, as was the case during the talks to prepare the Maastricht Treaty. The Bundesbank sees itself as the guardian of the stability of any

[136] Cf. Protokoll, 1994, pp. 77, 79.
[137] Cf. 'Maastricht II/Colloquium an der Universität Hohenheim, Wirtschaftsprofessoren gegen Währungsunion' in: Handelsblatt, 6 Nov. 1995, p. 8.
[138] Urteil des Bundesverfassungsgerichts, 12 Oct. 1993, in: Europäische Grundrechte-Zeitschrift, year 20, no. 17, 18 Oct. 1993, p. 442.
[139] Interview by the author with Andrew Crocket on 20 Apr. 1995.

future European currency, and gives priority to the application of the criteria over compliance with the timetable.[140] The Bundesbank President draws attention to the need for greater political unity as a basis for monetary union, something which Giscard d'Estaing (in a 'Manifesto for a Federal Europe'[141]) and Commission President Jacques Santer[142] had already deemed necessary. Another problem was that not all Member States could participate in monetary union immediately. How would Europe cope with this?[143]

Other members of the Directorate raised additional problems. What would happen if flawed collective bargaining agreements increased unemployment in particular countries? Could the ECB withstand the political pressure? Was the labour market sufficiently flexible to react to exogenous shocks once parity realignments had been abolished? The (political) pressure for an additional social union, for equalization by financial transfers[144] and wage convergence would cut this flexibility still further and increase unemployment if the ECB backed down. There were also doubts whether the provision in the Maastricht Treaty prohibiting support for a Member State threatened with bankruptcy would be observed in practice. But if this was the case, it would be easier to finance deficits using the emerging single capital market. The provisions underpinning sound public finances were inadequate, and as the date drew near, the convergence criteria would be increasingly challenged.[145]

There are equally plausible arguments to counter these undoubtedly serious reservations. The Scandinavian Monetary Union and (apart from the temporary suspension of convertibility by Italy) the Latin Currency Union functioned for many decades until 1914 without political union. The main problems associated with the latter were because it was a bimetallic system, a scheme which was then more or less abandoned. Of course, the situation of a monetary system with discretionary paper money is different, but the Maastricht Treaty meets almost all the conditions to make it as stable as the D-mark. Floating or adjustable exchange rate systems are also faced with a number of problems. For example, different monetary policies and external shocks can result in over- and undervaluations, with a negative impact on employment, inflation and growth. If the EMU participants do not rescue countries threatened with bankruptcy, as envisaged in the Treaty, the capital markets will soon assert their control function through greater interest

[140] Cf. Tietmeyer, 1996, pp. 421–30.
[141] Cf. Giscard d'Estaing, 1995.
[142] Cf. 'Kein Europa à la carte', interview with Jaques Santer, in: Industrie, 25 Jan. 1995, pp. 10–12.
[143] Cf. Historisches Archiv der Deutschen Bundesbank.
[144] Cf. Historisches Archiv der Deutschen Bundesbank.
[145] Cf. Issing, 1995, pp. 1–7.

differentials or by refusing credit. This would be better than the current practice of cutting government debt by creating inflation. There were several 'healthy state bankruptcies' under Philip II of Spain without affecting the stability of the currency—a global currency of the day.

But back to developments in contemporary Europe. The EMI started operating at the beginning of 1994. Following lengthy discussions, agreement was reached on 29 October 1993 that the EMI—and the successor ECB—would be located in Frankfurt. It started work at once on the technical problems of the transition to Stage Three, on the kind of monetary policy and its instruments, on simplifications to the payment system in Stage Three, and the introduction of cash transactions.[146] In early 1994, the Commission set up a study group charged with submitting a report by 31 October 1994 on the transition to the single currency. The result was the Commission's Green Paper. On the basis of this work, the Heads of State or Government, meeting in Madrid on 16 December 1995, agreed on a scenario for the introduction of a single currency—now named the euro—at the start of Stage Three of EMU on 1 January 1999. The proposal by the German Minister of Finance for a fiscal stability pact during the period after the establishment of EMU was accepted at the Dublin Summit on 13 December 1996 and put into more concrete terms at the Ecofin meeting in Nordwijk on 6 April 1997. Under this scheme, countries whose budget deficit is greater than 3 per cent of GDP after EMU will have to pay a deposit. If the situation does not improve within three years, the deposit is forfeited and paid as a penalty to the 'sound' EMU participants. The sanction consists of a fixed amount of 0.2 per cent of GDP plus a variable component of up to 0.5 per cent of GDP, depending on the level of the deficit overshoot. The fixed amount lapses from the second year onwards. However, a budget deficit exceeding 3 per cent of GDP is permitted if the latter decreases by more than 2 per cent. If it drops by between 0.75 and 2 per cent, the Council will decide whether or not an excessive deficit exists. An accelerated ten-month examination procedure was also agreed.

An EMS II with fixed parities to the euro and wider fluctuation margins was also planned for the countries unable to participate in EMU in 1999. This idea had the strong backing of France and Ireland, which were afraid of competition from undervalued currencies. EMS membership is voluntary, but is also a condition for participating in EMU because of the exchange rate criteria. The parities are fixed against the euro with an eye to future participation in EMU. Together with the participating countries, the ECB is also obliged to intervene in the currency market to maintain the exchange rate within the fluctuation band, but only as long as this does not jeopardize

---

[146] Cf. Europäisches Währungsinstitut, 1995.

the goal of price stability. All participants can demand negotiations on parity realignments, and the bands can be narrowed.

The designs for euro banknotes selected by the EMI were presented in 1997.

Three phases are planned for the transition to Stage Three of EMU. (On Phase A see below.) All inter-bank transactions will be conducted in euros in Phase B, although the conversion of book money will be left to the markets. The ESCB will exclusively use the euro in all money market and foreign exchange operations, and accounts at the ESCB will be converted to euros. The ECU will be converted to euros at the ratio of 1:1. Government debt issues maturing after the year 2001 must be denominated in euros.

In Phase C, euro notes and coins will be introduced on 1 January, and national notes and coins will cease being legal tender on 1 July, 2002. The bulk of the switch by the public and private sectors, as well as by households (e.g. accounting systems, vending machines), to the euro will occur then. Phase A (from around early 1998) will be used to harmonize national legislation, establish the ECB and the ESCB, start producing euro notes and coins, and prepare for currency conversion in the financial and banking sectors.

The Bundesbank argued strongly for an intermediate monetary target. In talks at the EMI on the instruments of monetary policy, it supported discount and minimum reserve policies in addition to open market operations and Lombard facilities.[147]

Preparatory work at the EMI has now reached an advanced stage. One of the potential strategies it suggests for the ECB is to define a money supply or direct inflation target. In practice, there could also be mixed forms combining elements of both targets.

The most important instrument proposed by the EMI is an open market policy of four types of operation with different maturities. The option to impose minimum reserve requirements is also being prepared. The ESCB should also be able to conduct foreign exchange intervention. Work is under way to enable the ECB to compile statistical aggregates, and the EMI is collaborating with the central banks to develop a cross-border payment system.[148]

What other developments can be expected? Will EMU actually happen, and if so, when? Will it be successful? Opinions differ strongly. At the moment, the economic situation does not favour the fiscal convergence criteria, although the inflation and long-term interest rate criteria are satisfied by

---

[147] 'Dr. Tietmeyer discusses the role and instruments of monetary policy', in: BIS Review 189, Basle, 17 Oct. 1994, pp. 1–13, cf. also Historisches Archiv der Deutschen Bundesbank.
[148] Europäisches Währungsinstitut, 1997.

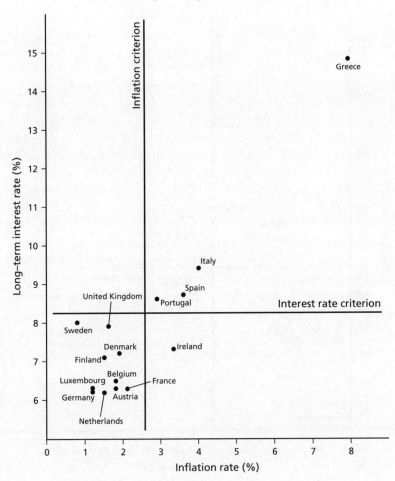

FIGURE 4: Inflation rates and long-term interest
rates in the European Union in 1996* (annual averages)

* Inflation criterion 2.57%, interest rate criterion 8.23%.

Source: Europäisches Währungsinstitut, Jahresbericht 1996, p. 59; inflation rates for the
United Kingdom and Ireland, inflation criterion and interest rate criterion: our own calculations.

most Member States (Figure 4). France and Germany might not be able to
meet the fiscal criteria in 1997 (Figure 5). Opinion is unanimous, however,
that there can be no EMU without France and Germany. What options are
open to the politicians if this happens? The only alternatives are to postpone
EMU or to interpret the criteria more generously. This could be justified,
for example, by defining the 3 per cent deficit ratio and the 60 per cent (of
GDP) bench-mark for government debt as the average over an economic

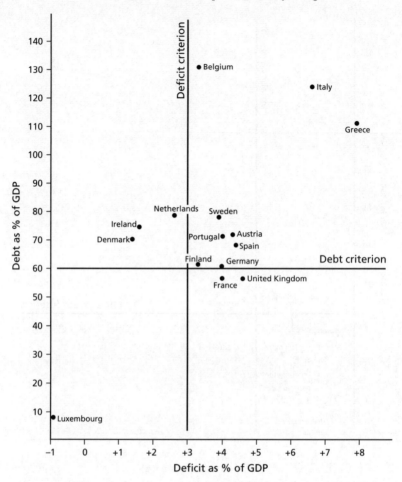

FIGURE 5: Deficits and public sector debt in the European Union in 1996*
* Estimated; public sector deficit and debt criteria 3% and 60% of GDP.
Source: Europäisches Währungsinstitut, 1996, p. 59.

cycle. But how would the Bundestag or the Federal Constitutional Court react to that?

Coupled with the high level of unemployment, the sceptical attitude of the public in the relatively stable countries could also cause political problems. Will the opposition parties be able to resist an opportunity to exploit the anti-EMU mood in Germany, or support a more expansionary monetary policy in France to reduce unemployment? Chancellor Kohl and Foreign Minister Klaus Kinkel have already warned the SPD against pandering to popular opinion in the debate on Germany's European policy.[149] And together with the current Chancellor's 'party colleagues Tietmeyer (and) Stoiber', former Chancellor Helmut Schmidt branded his own fellow SPD members Schröder (and) Spöri as 'strategic pygmies in just the same sense.[150]

In any event, the decision will have to be a political one, although the German principle of separation of powers means that the Bundesbank will continue to be responsible for working towards the stability of the new currency.

8. Summary of the major facets and features of monetary integration in Europe

a) Record of the beginnings of integration, 1955–68

5 August 1955	European Monetary Agreement signed.
25 March 1957	Treaties on the Establishment of the European Economic Community and of the European Atomic Energy Community (EURATOM) signed in Rome.
1 January 1958	EEC and EURATOM Treaties come into force.
18 March 1958	Council Resolution on the Statute of the Monetary Committee.
27 December 1958	Announcement of the convertibility of all major European currencies, European Monetary Agreement (EMA) comes into force. European Payments Union (EPU) dissolved.
9 March 1960	Council Resolution on the Coordination of the Conjunctural Policy of the Member States (establishment of the Short-term Economic Policy Committee).
1 January 1962	Start of the transition to Stage Two of the EEC.
7 April 1962	Report by the Economic and Financial Committee of the European Parliament on Monetary Coordination in the EEC ('van Campen Report').
29 October 1962	Memorandum from the Commission of the EEC on the Community's Action Programme for Stage Two.

[149] 'Kohl gegen den Währungspopulismus der SPD, Scharping fordert Ergänzung des Maastricht-Vertrages', in: Neue Zürcher Zeitung, 9 Nov. 1995, p. 1.
[150] Schmidt, Helmut: Der zweite Anlauf, die letzte Chance, in: Die Zeit, 5 Apr. 1996, p. 4.

19 June 1963	Communication from the Commission to the Council on 'Monetary and Fiscal Cooperation in the European Economic Community'.
13 April 1964	Formal establishment of the 'Committee of the Governors of the central banks of the Member States of the EEC'.
15 April 1964	Council Resolution on the Establishment of a Committee for Medium-Term Economic Policy.
8 May 1964	Council Resolution on Cooperation between the responsible administration departments of the Member States in the field of budgetary policy (Budget Committee).

b) Record of the EEC exchange rate arrangement, 1972–8

24 April 1972	The Basle Agreement gives rise to the 'snake' in the 'tunnel' in accordance with a Council Decision of 21 March 1972 and a resolution by the national central banks of 10 April 1972. Participants: Belgium, Federal Republic of Germany, France, Italy, Luxembourg, Netherlands.
1 May 1972	The UK and Denmark join.
23 May 1972	Norway becomes an associate member.
23 June 1972	The UK and Denmark leave.
11 October 1972	Denmark rejoins.
13 February 1973	Italy leaves.
19 March 1973	Switch to block-floating; the Council of Ministers decides to release the central banks of the EC from their obligation to intervene in US dollars. The tunnel disappears, but the snake remains; Sweden becomes an associate member; D-mark revalues by 3%.
3 April 1973	Regulation on the Establishment of a European Monetary Cooperation Fund is approved by the Council in Luxembourg on the basis of article 235. It comes into force on 6 April 1973.
29 June 1973	D-mark revalues by 5.5%.
17 September 1973	Netherlands guilder revalues by 5%.
16 November 1973	Norwegian krone revalues by 5%.
21 January 1974	France leaves.
10 July 1975	France returns.
15 March 1976	France leaves again; Special Agreement by the Bene-

	lux States of August 1971 to narrow the band to 1.5% is suspended. The fluctuation margin is now 2.25%.
18 October 1976	D-mark revalues by 2%; Danish krone devalues by 4%, Norwegian krone and Swedish krona devalue by 1%.
4 April 1977	Swedish krona devalues by 6%, Danish and Norwegian krone devalue by 3%.
29 August 1977	Sweden leaves. Danish and Norwegian krone devalue by 5%.
13 February 1978	Norwegian krone devalues by 8%.
16 October 1978	D-mark revalues by 4%. Belgian franc and Netherlands guilder devalue by 2%.

c) Record of accessions to, and withdrawals from, the EMS

19 June 1989	Spain joins the ERM. The fluctuation margin for the Spanish peseta is set at ±6% during a transitional period.
8 October 1990	The UK joins the ERM. The fluctuation margin for pound sterling is set at ±6% during a transitional period.
6 April 1992	Portugal joins the ERM. The fluctuation margin for the escudo is set at ±6% during a transitional period.
8 September 1992	Finland abandons the unilateral pegging of the finnmark to the European Currency Unit (ECU).
17 September 1992	Sustained currency unrest in the EMS sees the UK and Italy suspending the participation of their currencies in the ERM until further notice.
19 November 1992	Sweden abandons the unilateral pegging of the Swedish krona to the ECU.
10 December 1992	Norway abandons the unilateral pegging of the Norwegian krone to the ECU.
2 August 1993	As a temporary measure, the finance ministers and central bank governors decide to widen the fluctuation margins for obligatory intervention by participants in the ERM to ±15% of the unchanged bilateral central rates effective 2 August (instead of ±2.25% and ±6% for Spain and Portugal). The existing ±2.25% band is only retained between The Netherlands and Germany (based on a bilateral agreement).

9 January 1995   Austria joins the ERM with a fluctuation margin of ±15%.

14 October 1996   Finland joins the ERM.

25 November 1996   Italy rejoins the ERM.

9. Sources and bibliography

Unpublished sources

Historisches Archiv der Deutschen Bundesbank (HA BBk)

Bibliography

Bericht an Rat und Kommission über die stufenweise Verwirklichung der Wirtschafts- und Währungsunion in der Gemeinschaft (Werner-Bericht), Brussels 8 October 1970, reproduced in: Hellmann, Rainer (1972): Europäische Wirtschafts- und Währungsunion. Eine Dokumentation, Baden-Baden, pp. 134–59

Bernholz, Peter (1982): Flexible Exchange Rates in Historical Perspective. Princeton Studies in International Finance 49, Princeton University

Bernholz, Peter/Gärtner, Manfred/Heri, Erwin (1985): Historical Experiences with Flexible Exchange Rates, in: Journal of International Economics 19, pp. 21–45

Cezanne, Wolfgang/Möller, Hans (1979): Die Europäische Union als Währungsunion? Baden-Baden

Deutsche Bundesbank (1992): Die Beschlüsse von Maastricht zur europäischen Wirtschafts- und Währungsunion, in: Monatsbericht 44, 2, pp. 45–54

Deutsche Bundesbank (various): Auszüge aus Presseartikeln

Deutscher Bundestag (various) (ed.): Verhandlungen des Bundestages, Plenarprotokolle

Dornbusch, Rudiger (1976): Expectations and Exchange Rate Dynamics, in: Journal of Political Economy 84, pp. 1161–76

Eijffinger, Sylvester C. W./De Haan, Jakob (1996): The Political Economy of Central-Bank Independence. Special Papers in International Economics 19, Princeton University

Emminger, Otmar (1986): D-Mark, Dollar, Währungskrisen. Erinnerungen eines ehemaligen Bundesbankpräsidenten, Stuttgart

Europäisches Währungsinstitut (1995): Der Übergang zur Einheitlichen Währung, Frankfurt a.M. November

Europäisches Währungsinstitut (1996): Jahresbericht 1996

Europäisches Währungsinstitut (1997): Die Einheitliche Geldpolitik in Stufe 3. Festlegung des Handlungsrahmens, Frankfurt a.M.

Europäische Wirtschaftsgemeinschaft (1964): Informationen—Der Rat, Amtsblatt der Europäischen Gemeinschaften, 7. Jahrgang no. 77

Fratianni, Michele/Hagen, Jürgen von (1990): The European Monetary System Ten Years After, in: Carnegie-Rochester Conference Series on Public Policy 32, pp. 173–242

Giovannini, Alberto (1992): European Monetary System, in: The New Palgrave Dictionary of Money and Finance, vol. 1, London, pp. 800–05

Giscard d'Estaing, Valéry (1991): Macht und Leben. Frankfurt a.M.

Giscard d'Estaing, Valéry (1995): Manifeste pour une nouvelle Europe fédérative, abgedruckt in: Le Figaro, 11 January

Grauwe, Paul de (1990): The Cost of Disinflation and the European Monetary System, in: Open Economies Review 1, pp. 147–73

Gros, Daniel/Thygesen, Niels (1988): The EMS: Achievements, Current Issues and Directions for the Future, in: CEPS (Centre for European Policy Studies), Paper no. 35, Brussels

Gros, Daniel/Thygesen, Niels (1992): European Monetary Integration: From EMS to EMU, London

Hellmann, Rainer (1972): Europäische Wirtschafts- und Währungsunion. Eine Dokumentation, Baden-Baden

House of Commons (1992a): Session 1992–93, Treasury and Civil Service Committee, First Report: The 1992 Autumn Statement and the Conduct of Economic Policy, London, pp. X–XV

House of Commons (1992b): Session 1992–93, Treasury and Civil Service Committee: The Future Conduct of Economic Policy, Minutes of Evidence, 28 October 1992, London

House of Commons (1992c): Official Report: Parliamentary debates. Hansard, vol. 212, London, pp. 100–07 (24 September 1992: Norman Lamont), pp. 313–14 (20 October 1992: John Major)

Issing, Otmar (1995): Europa: Politische Union durch gemeinsames Geld? Lecture on being awarded the Prize of the Informedia Foundation in Frankfurt on 3 July 1995, cited according to: Deutsche Bundesbank: Auszüge aus Presseartikeln, no. 50, pp. 1–7

Kaplan, Jacob J./Schleiminger, Günther (1989): The European Payments Union: Financial Diplomacy in the 1950s, Oxford

Kawai, Masahiro (1992): Optimum Currency Areas, in: The New Palgrave Dictionary of Money and Finance, vol. 3, London, pp. 78–81

Kenen, Peter B. (1995): Economic and Monetary Union in Europe. Moving beyond Maastricht, Cambridge

Krägenau, Henry/Wetter, Wolfgang (1993): Europäische Wirtschafts- und Währungsunion, Vom Werner-Plan zum Vertrag von Maastricht, Analysen und Dokumentation, Baden-Baden, pp. 108–09

Protokoll betreffend Dänemark und Protokoll über einige Bestimmungen betreffend das Vereinigte Königreich Großbritannien und Nordirland des Vertrags über die Europäische Union vom 7. Februar 1992, reproduced in: Europäische Union, Europäische Gemeinschaft (1994): Die Vertragstexte von Maastricht mit den deutschen Begleittexten, Presse- und Informationsamt der Bundesregierung, Bonn

Schmidt, Helmut (1987): Menschen und Mächte, Berlin

Schmidt, Helmut (1990): Wir schaffen ein Europäisches Währungssystem, from: Die Deutschen und ihre Nachbarn, Berlin 1990; excerpt in: Die Zeit, 31 August

Thygesen, Niels (1979): The Emerging European Monetary System: Precursors, First Stages, Policy Options, in: Bulletin de la Banque Nationale de Belgique 54, 1 (4), pp. 87–125

Tietmeyer, Hans (1996): Erfahrungen und Perspektiven für die WU in Europa, Lecture to the northern discussion group of the Friedrich Ebert Foundation in Hamburg on 30 January 1995, in: Tietmeyer, Hans: Währungsstabilität für Europa. Beiträge, Reden und Dokumente zur europäischen Währungsintegration aus vier Jahrzehnten, ed. Zentralbankrat der Deutschen Bundesbank, Baden-Baden, pp. 421–30

Vaubel, Roland (1991a): A Public Choice View of International Organization, in: Vaubel, Roland/Willett, Thomas D. (eds.): The Political Economy of International Organizations, Boulder, pp. 27–45

Vaubel, Roland (1991b): The Political Economy of the International Monetary Fund: A Public Choice Analysis, in: Vaubel, Roland/Willett, Thomas D. (eds.): The Political Economy of International Organizations, Boulder, pp. 204–244

Wissenschaftlicher Beirat beim Bundesministerium für Wirtschaft (1990): Gutachten vom 20./21. Januar 1989: Europäische Währungsordnung, in: Gutachten vom Juni 1987 bis März 1990, ed. Bundesministerium für Wirtschaft, vol. 13, Göttingen, pp. 1473–80

ANNEX

Abbreviations

ABC	Allied Bank Commission
AG	Aktiengesellschaft
AHC	Allied High Commission
AKA	Ausfuhrkredit AG
a.M.	am Main
AWG	Außenwirtschaftsgesetz (Foreign Trade and Payments Act)
BAKred	Bundesaufsichtsamt für das Kreditwesen (Federal Banking Supervisory Office)
BDI	Bundesverband der deutschen Industrie (Federation of German Industries)
BdL	Bank deutscher Länder
BGBl	Bundesgesetzblatt (Federal Law Gazette)
BIS	Bank for International Settlements
BminG	Bundesministergesetz (Act on Federal Ministers)
BMWi	Bundeswirtschaftsministerium
BoE	Bank of England
BRRG	Beamtenrechtsrahmengesetz (Civil Service Framework Act)
BVerfGE	Entscheidungen des Bundesverfassungsgerichts (Rulings of the Federal Constitutional Court)
BVerwG	Bundesverwaltungsgericht (Federal Administrative Court)
BVerwGE	Entscheidungen des Bundesverwaltungsgerichts (Rulings of the Federal Administrative Court)
CD	Certificate of Deposit
CDG Plan	Colm–Dodge–Goldsmith Plan
CDU	Christlich-Demokratische Union Deutschlands
Chap.	Chapter
CIS	Confederation of Independent States
COMECON	Council for Mutual Economic Assistance
CSU	Christlich Soziale Union Bayern e.V.
DAFOX	Deutscher Aktienindex für Forschungszwecke
DANAT bank	Darmstädter und Nationalbank
DDR	Deutsche Demokratische Republic (GDR)
DIHT	Deutscher Industrie- und Handelstag
DIW	Deutsches Institut für Wirtschaftsforschung
DKB	Deutsche Kreditbank AG
DM	Deutsche Mark/Deutsche Mark der Deutschen Notenbank (GDR)
D-mark	Deutsche Mark
DTB	Deutsche Terminbörse (financial futures and options exchange)
EC	European Community
ECA	Economic Cooperation Administration (Marshall Plan administration)
ECB	European Central Bank
Ecofin	Council of Ministers of Economic and Financial Affairs
ECT	EC Treaty

ECU	European Currency Unit
ed./eds.	editor/editors
EDC	European Defence Community
EEC	European Economic Community
e.g.	for example
EMA	European Monetary Agreement
EMCF	European Monetary Cooperation Fund
EMI	European Monetary Institute
EMS	European Monetary System
EMU	European Monetary Union
EMUA	European Monetary Unit of Account
EP	European Parliament
EPU	European Payments Union
ERF	European Reserve Fund
ERM	Exchange Rate Mechanism
ESCB	European System of Central Banks
et al.	et alii
etc.	et cetera
EU	European Union
EURATOM	European Atomic Energy Commission
f./ff.	following
FDP	Freie Demokratische Partei
FIBOR	Frankfurt Interbank Offered Rate
fol.	folder
FRBNY	Federal Reserve Bank of New York
FRF	French francs
FRG	Federal Republic of Germany
GAB	General Arrangements to Borrow
GATT	General Agreement on Tariffs and Trade
GC	Governors' Committee
GDP	gross domestic product
GDR	German Democratic Republic
Gefi	Gesellschaft zur Finanzierung von Industrieanlagen
GEMSU	German Economic, Monetary, and Social Union
GeschOBReg	Geschäftsordnung der Bundesregierung (Standing Orders of the Federal Government)
GG	Grundgesetz (Basic Law)
GM	Gold Marks
GNP	gross national product
HA BBk	Historisches Archiv der Deutschen Bundesbank
HGrG	Haushaltsgrundsätzegesetz (Act on Budgetary Principles)
HWWA	Institut für Wirtschaftsforschung, Hamburg (previously: Hamburgisches Weltwirtschafts-Archiv)
i.e.	id est
IfZ	Institut für Zeitgeschichte, Munich
IMF	International Monetary Fund
JCS	Joint Chiefs of Staff
kg	kilogram
KOKO	Abteilung für Kommerzielle Koordinierung (Department for Commercial Coordination)
KWG	Gesetz über das Kreditwesen
LIFFE	London and International Financial Futures Exchange

LSE	London School of Economics
LZB	Landeszentralbank (Land Central Bank)
M	Mark/Mark der DDR
MAE	Ministère des Affaires Etrangères
MC	Monetary Committee
Mefo	Metallurgische Forschungsgesellschaft (Metallurgical Research Company)
NA	National Archives, Washington
NAFTA	North American Free Trade Agreement
NATO	North Atlantic Treaty Organization
NCE	New Classical Economics
NCM	New Classical Macroeconomics
n.d.	no date
NKE	New Keynesian Economics
NKM	New Keynesian Macroeconomics
no./nos.	number/numbers
NÖSPL	Neues ökonomisches System der Planung und Leitung (New economic system of planning and control)
NS	Nationalsozialismus/nationalsozialistisch
NSDAP	Nationalsozialistische Deutsche Arbeiterpartei
OECD	Organization for Economic Cooperation and Development
OEEC	Organization for European Economic Cooperation
Oficomex	Office for External Trade of the Military Government
OMGUS	Office of Military Government for Germany, United States
OPEC	Organization of Petroleum Exporting Countries
ÖSS	Ökonomisches System des Sozialismus (Economic system of socialism)
p./pp.	page/pages
p.a.	per annum
para./paras.	paragraph/paragraphs
PPP	purchasing power parity
RBG	Reichsbankgesetz (1875 Reichsbank Act)
REH	Rational Expectations Hypothesis
RGBI	Reichsgesetzblatt
RGZ	Entscheidungen des Reichsgerichts in Zivilsachen
RM	Reichsmark
RVO	Reichsversicherungsordnung (Reich Insurance Code)
SDR	special drawing rights
SEA	Single European Act
SED	Sozialistische Einheitspartei Deutschlands
SHAEF	Supreme Headquarters Allied Expeditionary Forces
SMAD	Sowjetische Militäradministration in Deutschland (Soviet Military Administration in Germany)
SMH	Bankhaus Schröder, Münchmeyer, Hengst Co
SNB	Schweizerische Nationalbank
SPD	Sozialdemokratische Partei Deutschlands
SS	Schutzstaffel
StGB	Strafgesetzbuch (Criminal Code)
StWG	Stabilitäts- und Wachstumsgesetz (Stability and Growth Act)
SWIFT	Society for Worldwide Interbank Financial Telecommunication
TEU	Treaty on European Union (Maastricht Treaty)
USSR	Union of Socialist Soviet Republics
vol./vols	volume/volumes

VWG	Vereinigtes Wirtschaftsgebiet
VwGO	Verwaltungsgerichtsordnung (Rules of Procedure of the Administrative Courts)
VwVfG	Verwaltungsverfahrengesetz (Administrative Procedure Act)
ZBR	Zentralbankrat (Central Bank Council)

Tables and Figures

Figures are set in italics

Index of Names

Index of Institutions

Subject Index

The Authors

Ernst Baltensperger, born in 1942, has been Professor of Economics at the University of Bern since 1984. He studied economics at the University of Zurich (Lic. oec. publ.) and at Johns Hopkins University, Baltimore, USA (Ph.D.). 1968–79 Professor of Economics at Ohio State University, USA. 1979–82 Professor at the University of Heidelberg, 1982–4 at the University of St. Gallen. Guest fellowships and professorships at the Swiss National Bank and numerous American and European universities. 1984–96 editor of the Schweizerische Zeitschrift für Volkswirtschaft und Statistik. Associate Editor of the Journal of Money, Credit, and Banking (1976–93), of the Journal of Banking and Finance (since 1987), and the Open Economies Review (since 1997). President of the Eidg. Kommission für Konjunkturfragen (Swiss Business-Cycle Commission) between 1988 and 1994.

Publications include: Alternative Approaches to the Theory of the Banking Firm, in: Journal of Monetary Economics 6 (1980), pp. 1–37; (together with H. Milde) Theorie des Bankverhaltens. Studies in Contemporary Economics, Berlin/Heidelberg 1987; (together with T. Jordan) Die Schweiz und die Bestrebungen zur Bildung einer Europäischen Währungsunion, Bern 1993.

Peter Bernholz, born in 1929, is emeritus Professor of Economics, specializing in monetary and international economics; most recently (1971–97) he was Professor and head of the economics department at the University of Basle. He studied economics at the universities of Marburg and Munich, graduating in 1953; doctorate in 1955 (Dr. rer. pol.); 1956–62 research assistant in Frankfurt and Munich; habilitation in 1962. 1963/4 Rockefeller Fellow at the universities of Harvard and Stanford, 1964–6 lecturer at the University of Frankfurt, 1966–71 Professor at the Technical University Berlin. Guest professorships in the USA at the Massachusetts Institute of Technology, Virginia Polytechnic Institute, at Stanford University, George Mason University, and the University of California, Los Angeles. Corresponding member of the Bavarian Academy of Science. President of the European Public Choice Society 1974–80; member of the Scientific Advisory Council to the German Federal Ministry of Economics since 1974; 1988–90 member of the EC Macroeconomic Policy Group; since 1992 member of the Board of the Mont Pelerin Society.

Publications include: Außenpolitik und Internationale Wirtschaftsbeziehungen, Frankfurt a.M. 1966; Währungskrisen und Währungsordnung, Hamburg 1974; Institutional Requirements for Stable Money in an Integrated World Economy, in: The Cato Journal 10 (1990), pp. 485–501; (together with F. Breyer) Grundlagen der Politischen Oekonomie, Tübingen ³1993/4; Necessary and Sufficient Conditions to End Hyperinflations, in: Siklos, P. L. (ed.): Great Inflations of the 20th Century, Aldershot, UK/Brookfield, USA, 1995, pp. 257–87.

Christoph Buchheim, born in 1954, has been Professor of Economic and Social History at the University of Mannheim since 1991. He studied economics, modern history, and sinology in Munich and Oxford. 1982 doctoral thesis, 1989 habilitation in economic and social history, both at the University of Munich. 1979–85 research assistant in the department of economic history at the University of Munich, 1985–9 Fellow of the Institute of Contemporary History.

Publications include: Die Währungsreform 1948 in Westdeutschland, in: Vierteljahreshefte für Zeitgeschichte 36 (1988), pp. 189–231; Die Wiedereingliederung Westdeutschlands in die Weltwirtschaft 1945–1958, Munich 1990; Einführung in die Wirtschaftsgeschichte, Munich 1997.

Günter Franke, born in 1944, has been Professor of International Financial Management at the University of Constance since 1983. 1963–7 he studied business management at the University of Hamburg and Saarland University. Following a period as Visiting Associate Professor in the USA, habilitation in 1975 at Saarland University. 1978 President of the European Finance Association. Until 1983 Professor of Financial Economics at the University of Gießen. Since 1989 guest lecturer at the European Institute for Advanced Studies in Management, Brussels.

Publications include: Costless Signalling in Financial Markets, in: Journal of Finance 42 (1987), pp. 809–22; (together with H. Hax) Finanzwirtschaft des Unternehmens und Kapitalmarkt, Berlin ⁴1998; Transformation of Banks and Bank Services, in: Journal of Institutional and Theoretical Economics 154 (1998).

Jacob A. Frenkel, born in 1943, has been Governor of the Bank of Israel and Weisfeld Professor of the Economics of Peace and International Relations at the University of Tel Aviv since 1991. In 1965 he obtained a BA in economics and political science and in 1967 studied economics at the Hebrew University in Jerusalem, 1969/70 MA and Ph.D. at the University of Chicago. 1973–87 member and David Rockefeller Professor of International Economics of the economics faculty of the University of Chicago. 1987–91 economic adviser and research director at the IMF. Periodically editor of the Journal of Political Economy and chairman of the governors' council of the Inter-American Development Bank. Member of the G-30, Research Associate of the National Bureau of Economic Research, member of the Econometric Society, and honorary foreign member of the American Academy of Arts and Sciences.

Publications include: (together with G. Johnson) The Monetary Approach to the Balance of Payments, London 1976; (together with A. Rezin) Fiscal Policies and Growth, Cambridge, Mass. ³1996; (together with M. Goldstein) The International Monetary System: Key Analytical Issues, ²1996.

Morris Goldstein, born in 1944, has held the Dennis Weatherstone chair of International Finance at the Institute for International Economics in Washington DC since 1995. BA in economics at Rutgers College, doctorate in economics at New York University. For twenty-five years at the IMF, during the last eight years as deputy director of the research department; responsible for the work of the department in the area of systemic questions and the annual capital market emission of the IMF for North America, Europe, and Asia; co-author of the annual International Capital Markets Report of the IMF. In 1979 also Senior Technical Adviser to the US Treasury.

Publications include: (together with M. Kahn) Income and Price Effects in International Trade, in: Kenen, Peter (ed.): Handbook of International Economics, vol. 1, Amsterdam 1985, pp. 1041–1105; (together with D. Folkerts-Landau *et al.*) International Capital Markets, Part I, Exchange Rate Management and International Capital Flows, IMF World Economic and Financial Surveys, Washington DC, April 1993; The Case for an International Banking Standard, Washington DC, 1997.

Jürgen von Hagen, born in 1955, has been Professor of Economics at the University of Bonn and Director of Economic and Social Studies at the Centre for European Integration Research in Bonn since 1996. He studied economics in Dortmund and Bonn (1977–81) and was research assistant to Prof. Dr. Manfred J. M. Neumann at the Institute for International Economic Policy of the University of Bonn between 1981 and 1987. In 1985 doctoral thesis (Dr. rer. pol.). 1987–92 Assistant Professor and Associate Professor of Business Economics and Public Policy at the Indiana University School of Business, USA, and researcher at the Center for European and German Studies, University of California. 1992–6 Professor of Economics and managing director of the Institut für Aufbaustudien of the University of Mannheim. Research consultant to the IMF, Washington DC, and consultant to the European Commission, DG II, the Inter-American Development Bank, and the Federal Reserve Board. Editor of the Open Economies Review, the Journal of Finance and Economics, and European Transatlantic Studies.

Publications include: (together with B. Eichengreen) Federalism, Fiscal Restraints and EMU, in: American Economic Review 86 (1996), pp. 134–8; Monetary Policy and Institutions in the EMU, in: Swedish Economic Policy Review 4 (1997), pp. 51–116; Central Banking as a Political Principal Agent Problem, in: Economic Enquiry 35 (1997), pp. 378–94.

Carl-Ludwig Holtfrerich, born in 1942, has been Professor of Economics at the Free University Berlin since 1983. He graduated in economics in 1966 and received his doctorate (Dr. rer. pol.) in 1971 from the University of Münster, followed by three years in the foreign trade department of the BDI (German employers' federation). From 1974 assistant professor and in 1979 habilitation in the economics department of the FU Berlin, 1980–3 Professor of Economic and Social History at the University of Frankfurt a.M. Visiting teaching and research posts at Harvard University, Oxford University, and the Wilson Center, Washington DC.

Publications include: Die deutsche Inflation 1914–1923, Berlin/New York 1980; Interactions in the Word Economy. Perspectives from International Economic History, New York/London 1989; Economic and Strategic Issues in U.S. Foreign Policy, Berlin/New York 1989; Wirtschaft USA: Strukturen, Institutionen, Prozesse, Munich/Vienna 1991; (as co-author) Die Deutsche Bank 1870–1995, Munich 1995.

Otmar Issing, born in 1936, has been a member of the Board of the Bundesbank and of the Central Bank Council, from 1990 to May 1998, and an Honorary Professor at the University of Würzburg since 1991. Since June 1998 he has been a member of the Board of the European Central Bank and of the European Central Bank Council. He initially studied ancient philology, then economics at the University of Würzburg, with study periods in London and Paris (1954–60). 1962 doctoral thesis, 1965 habilitation, followed by teaching assignments at the Universities of Marburg and Erlangen-Nuremberg. 1973–90 Professor of Economics at the University of Würzburg, chair of Economics, Money, and International Economic Relations. Since 1980 member of the Scientific Advisory Council to the German Federal Ministry of Economics (currently suspended), 1988–90 member of the German Council of Economic Experts. Member of the Academy of Science and Literature in Mainz (since 1991) and of the Academia Scientiarum et Artium Europaea (since 1991).

Publications include: Einführung in die Geldtheorie, Munich [10]1995; Einführung in die Geldpolitik, Munich [6]1996.

Harold James, born in 1956, has been Professor of History at Princeton University since 1986. He studied history at Cambridge University between 1975 and 1978 and was subsequently a Fellow of Peterhouse College, Cambridge, UK, until 1986. Guest Professor at the Institut des Hautes Etudes Internationales, Geneva 1996.

Publications include: The Reichsbank and Public Finance in Germany 1924–1933, Frankfurt a.M. 1985; The German Slump. Politics and Economics 1924–1936, Oxford 1986; German Identity 1770–1990, London 1989; Vom Historikerstreit zum Historikerschweigen, Berlin 1993; International Monetary Cooperation since Bretton Woods, Washington/New York 1996; Rambouillet, 15. November 1975: Die Globalisierung der Wirtschaft, Munich 1997.

Wolfgang Kitterer, born in 1943, has been Professor of Wirtschaftliche Staatswissenschaften (approximating to 'public economics') at the University of Cologne since 1995. He studied economics at Saarland University, where he received his doctorate (Dr. rer. pol.) in 1975, followed by three years as a researcher at the Rheinisch-Westfälisches Institut für Wirtschaftsforschung in Essen. For four years head of the Institute of Applied Economic Research in Tübingen. Habilitation in Tübingen in 1983; 1984–95 Professor of Financial Economics at the University of Kiel.

Publications include: Rechtfertigung und Risiken einer Finanzierung der deutschen Einheit durch Staatsverschuldung, in: Hansmeyer, Karl-Heinrich (ed.): Finanzierungsprobleme der deutschen Einheit I, Schriften des Vereins für Socialpolitik, N.F. Vol. 229/I, Berlin 1993, pp. 39–76; Tax Versus Debt Finance of Public Investment: A Dynamic Simulation Analysis, in: Kredit und Kapital 27 (1994) 2, pp. 163–87; Intergenerative Belastungsrechnungen ('Generational Accounting')—Ein Maßstab für die Belastung zukünftiger Generationen?, in: Oberhauser, Alois (ed.): Finanzierungsprobleme der deutschen Einheit IV, Spezielle Finanzierungsaspekte im Zeitablauf, Schriften des Vereins für Socialpolitik, N.F. Vol. 229/IV, Berlin 1996, pp. 215–75.

Manfred J. M. Neumann, born in 1940, has been Professor of Allgemeine Staatswissenschaften (approximating to 'public policy'), especially economic policy, at the University of Bonn since 1981. He studied economics in Göttingen, Erlangen-Nuremberg, and Marburg between 1960 and 1964, gaining his doctorate from Marburg in 1966; 1967–9 economics department of the Bundesbank; 1969–73 research assistant at the University of Constance; 1973–81 Professor for Monetary Theory at the Free University Berlin. Responsible for the Constance Seminars on Monetary Theory and Monetary Policy and chairman of the Scientific Advisory Council to the German Federal Ministry of Economics.

Publications include: Monetary Policy and Uncertainty, Baden-Baden 1986; Implementing Monetary Policy in Germany, in: Board of Governors of the Federal Reserve System: Financial Sectors in Open Economies, Washington DC 1990, pp. 499–528; Monetary Reform, The New Palgrave Dictionary of Money and Finance, London 1992, Vol. 2, pp. 751–6; Seigniorage in Japan and Germany, in: Bank of Japan: Monetary and Economic Studies 14 (1996) 1, pp. 104–42.

Jochen Plassmann, born in 1936, is a Bundesbank Director. After a banking apprenticeship at Deutsche Bank in Cologne, he studied law in Munich, Freiburg i.Br., and Cologne. In 1962 first state law exams at the Oberlandesgericht (Higher Regional Court) in Cologne. 1964 doctorate (Dr. juris utriusque) from the University of Cologne, 1963–6 graduate trainee at the Bundesbank in Frankfurt a.M., 1966 examination for the higher banking service ('bank assessor'), 1966–72 section leader in the foreign department of the Bundesbank with varying responsibilities, 1973–90 active in the division of payments and trade between the GDR and the FRG, head of division since 1975.

The Authors835

Publications include: Genehmigungspraxis der Deutschen Bundesbank bei der Kreditgewährung an die DDR, in: Politik und Kultur 14 (1987) 1, pp. 51–60.

Rudolf Richter, born in 1926, is emeritus Professor of Economic Theory; most recently (1964–94) he was active at the University of Saarbrücken. Between 1946 and 1949 he studied business management in Frankfurt a.M., receiving a doctorate in economics in 1951, followed by a habilitation in economics in 1953. One-year Rockefeller Fellow in the USA (Columbia, University of Michigan, Harvard/MIT). Guest professorships at the universities of Minnesota and Michigan (1967/8, 1985, 1994). Visiting Fellow at the Hoover Institution, Stanford University (1986, 1990, 1995), 1961–4 Professor of Economic Theory in Kiel. 1978–94 editor of JITE, since 1995 co-editor.

Publications include: (together with U. Schlieper and W. Friedmann) Makroökonomik. Eine Einführung, Berlin/Heidelberg ⁴1981; Geldtheorie. Vorlesung auf der Grundlage der Allgemeinen Gleichgewichtstheorie und der Institutionenökonomik, Berlin ²1990; (together with E. G. Furubotn) Neue Institutionenökonomik. Eine Einführung und kritische Würdigung, Tübingen 1996.

Klaus Stern, born in 1932, has been Professor of Public Law, Administrative Law, and General Law at the University of Cologne since 1966. He studied law and economics in Erlangen, Innsbruck, and Munich. First and second state law exams in Munich in 1955 and 1960, doctoral thesis in 1956, habilitation in public law in Munich in 1961. 1962–6 professor at the Free University Berlin. Since 1976 judge at the Constitutional Court of the state of North-Rhine/Westphalia.

Publications include: Das Staatsrecht der Bundesrepublik Deutschland, vol. 1, Munich ²1984: Grundbegriffe und Grundlagen; vol. II, Munich 1980: Staatsorgane, Staatsfunktionen, Finanz- und Haushaltsverfassung; vol. III/1, Munich 1990; vol. III/2 Munich 1994: Allgemeine Lehren der Grundrechte; (together with K.-H. Hansmeyer und P. Münch) Kommentar zum Gesetz zur Förderung der Stabilität und des Wachstums der Wirtschaft, Stuttgart ²1972; Die staatsrechtliche Stellung des Bundesrechnungshofes und seine Bedeutung im System der Finanzkontrolle, in: Zavelberg, H. G. (ed.): Die Kontrolle der Staatsfinanzen, Berlin 1989, pp. 11–42; (together with B. Schmidt-Bleibtreu) Verträge und Rechtsakte zur Deutschen Einheit, vols. 1–3, Munich 1991; Der Staat des Grundgesetzes. Ausgewählte Schriften und Vorträge, Cologne 1992.

Manfred E. Streit, born in 1939, has been Director of the Institutional Economics and Economic Policy Department of the Max Planck Institute for Research into Economic Systems in Jena and Honorary Professor of Economics at the University of Jena since 1993. He studied economics and basic law at Saarland University from 1959 to 1963; 1963–6 academic assistant, leading to a doctorate (Dr. rer. pol.) in 1996; 1966–8 research assistant to the German Council of Economic Experts; 1968–71 lecturer in economics at the University of Reading, UK. 1971–90 Professor of Economics at the University of Mannheim; 1980–3 seconded to the European University Institute in Florence. 1990–3 Professor of economics at the University of Freiburg i.Br.

Publications include: Theorie der Wirtschaftspolitik, fourth revised edition, Düsseldorf 1991; Freiburger Beiträge zur Ordnungsökonomik, Tübingen 1995; Systemwettbewerb im europäischen Integrationsprozeß, in: Immenga, Ulrich/Möschel, Wernhard/Reuter, Dieter (eds): Festschrift für Ernst-Joachim Mestmäcker zum siebzigsten Geburtstag, Baden-Baden 1996, pp. 521–35.

H. Jörg Thieme, born in 1941, has been professor of economics at the University of Düsseldorf since 1990. He studied economics and law at the universities of Erlangen, Nuremberg, and Marburg, graduating in economics in 1964 and receiving a doctorate (Dr. rer. pol.) from the University of Magdeburg in 1968. 1969–72 research assistant at the University of Gießen. 1972–7 Professor of Economics at the University of Essen. 1977–90 Professor of Theoretical Economics at the Ruhr University of Bochum. 1990–2 Founding Deacon (1992–4 Vicedeacon) of the Economics Faculty of the Heinrich-Heine University in Düsseldorf. 1991–3 Chairman of the Committee for the Comparison of Economic Systems in the Verein für Socialpolitik. 1993–7 Chairman of the Board of the Academy of German Cooperatives.

Publications include: Geldtheorie. Entwicklung, Stand und systemvergleichende Anwendung, Baden-Baden ²1987; Soziale Marktwirtschaft. Ordnungskonzeption und wirtschaftspolitische Gestaltung, 2ⁿᵈ revised edition, Munich 1994 (translated into Chinese, Polish, Bulgarian and Korean); (together with J. Siebke) Geldpolitik. Zwanzig Jahre Geldmengensteuerung in Deutschland, Baden-Baden 1995.

Hans Tietmeyer, born in 1931, has been President of the Bundesbank since 1993 and Honorary Professor of Economics at the University of Halle-Wittenberg since 1996. Since June 1998 he has been a member of the European Central Bank Council. He studied in Münster, Bonn, and Cologne, graduating in economics from the University of Cologne in 1958. 1959–62 managing director of the Cusanuswerk student support programme. 1960 Dr. rer. pol. from the university of Cologne. 1962–82 German Federal Ministry of Economics. 1982–9 Secretary of State in the Federal Ministry of Finance. Since 1990 member of the Board of the Bundesbank, 1991–3 Vice-president of the Bundesbank. Since 1994 Chairman of the G-10 central bank governors. In the 1970s and 1980s Chairman of the EC Committee on Economic Policy, chairman of the OECD Working Party on Structural Adjustment Policy, and chairman of the EC Monetary Committee. Since 1990 part-time chairman of the Board of Trustees of the German Federal Environmental Foundation. Since 1995 member of the papal Academy of Social Sciences in Rome.